the
AMERICANA ANNUAL

1986

GROLIER

AN ENCYCLOPEDIA OF THE EVENTS OF 1985
YEARBOOK OF THE ENCYCLOPEDIA AMERICANA

This annual has been prepared as a yearbook for general encyclopedias. It is also published as *Encyclopedia Year Book.*

© GROLIER INCORPORATED 1986

Copyright in Canada © by Grolier Limited

Library of Congress Catalog Card Number: 23-10041

ISBN: 0-7172-0217-8

ISSN: 0196-0180

Printed and manufactured in the United States of America

Grolier Enterprises, Inc. offers a varied selection of both adult and children's book racks. For details on ordering, please write:

Grolier Enterprises, Inc.
Sherman Turnpike
Danbury, CT 06816
Attn: Premium Department

Contents

Feature Articles of the Year

The Alphabetical Section

Entries on the continents, major nations of the world, U.S. states, Canadian provinces, and chief cities will be found under their own alphabetical headings.

The Year in Review

By Peter Jennings, ABC News
Anchor and Senior Editor, "World News Tonight"

The year-end television news summary invariably provides a startling reminder of how powerful some of the year's images were: President Ronald Reagan and Soviet leader Mikhail Gorbachev shaking hands at their first summit meeting; the captain of a hijacked TWA jetliner looking out from his cockpit window on the tarmac at Beirut airport, calmly discussing the situation while a hijacker holds a gun to his head; a multinational rescue team picking through the ruins of a hospital in Mexico City, searching for—and finding—infants who had

survived a devastating earthquake; a young Colombian girl buried up to her neck in a sea of mud, which had resulted from a volcanic eruption; the bodies of 248 American soldiers laid out in a temporary morgue at Gander in Newfoundland, their chartered jet having crashed on takeoff as the soldiers were returning home from peacekeeping duties in the Middle East.

Not all the lasting images were sad: in London and Philadelphia, and around the world, the human spirit got a lift from the Live Aid Concert to raise money for the victims of famine in Africa; the U.S. space shuttle program moved along with nine successful flights; and the first sight of the ocean liner *Titanic* on the floor of the Atlantic was a rare glimpse into a mysterious and ill-starred past.

Though 1985 may not be remembered purely as "the year of terrorism," it became increasingly clear that international terrorists, particularly those with roots in the Middle East, had become a much deadlier force. At year-end, twin attacks on Israeli targets at Rome and Vienna airports confirmed a new and bloody tactic of indiscriminate killing.

Two hijackings in 1985 held much of the world in thrall. In June a TWA jetliner was hijacked to Beirut by Lebanese Shiite Muslims who demanded the release of Lebanese Shiite prisoners held in Israel. In October the Italian liner *Achille Lauro* was hijacked by Palestinians while cruising in the Mediterranean. The loss of life in each case was limited to a single passenger, but the degree of frustration felt by powerful governments was very high. There was widespread international approval when the United States struck back for the *Achille Lauro* incident, virtually hijacking the hijackers as they were being transported to freedom on an Egyptian plane.

It was the worst year in aviation history. Almost 2,000 persons died in accidents involving commerical aircraft. In August, in the worst airline crash ever, 520 persons died when a Japan Air Lines 747 crashed into a mountain outside Tokyo. In June more than 300 were killed when an Air India 747 plunged into the Irish Sea; a bomb was suspected.

During 1985, Americans became more accustomed to fellow citizens being arrested for spying for the Soviet Union. Among those facing trial were John Walker, a retired Navy warrant officer accused of running a spy ring that included other members of his family, and Richard Miller, the first FBI agent to be tried for espionage.

The Reagan administration and the CIA were particularly embarrassed by a high-level Soviet defector who may not have been a defector at all. There was much fanfare in September when Vitaly Yurchenko, a senior KGB officer, was reported to have defected and disclosed valuable information about Soviet espionage in the West. When he showed up at the Soviet Embassy in Washington in November insisting that he had been kidnaped and wanted to go home, there was considerable confusion in the intelligence community.

President Reagan began his second term in 1985. Surgery for cancer in July did not noticeably slow him down for long. The president's legislative priorities led to a mixture of success and stagnation. He told the nation at his second inaugural

that revising the country's tax code was his highest domestic priority. He managed to squeeze a modified tax reform bill through the House of Representatives, but 1986 loomed as a difficult year because many Senate leaders believed that reducing the federal budget deficit deserves more urgent attention. In December, Congress did pass a historic bill aimed at balancing the federal budget, but few politicians believed that it would stand unscathed for the next five years.

The overall U.S. economy grew at a slightly slower rate than had been predicted by the administration and many economists. The stock market became extremely bullish late in the year, with the Dow Jones finally going over 1,500 for the first time in history during December. But while investors were told that they could look forward to profitable days in the market, many American farmers faced very grim prospects. The governor of the Farm Credit System said that it would need many billions of dollars to stay solvent. Thousands of farmers faced foreclosure because they could not keep up with loan payments.

The year was studded with personalities. The body of the Nazi war criminal Josef Mengele, the "Angel of Death," was found in South America. The actor Rock Hudson died of AIDS. By the end of the year, the number of known AIDS cases had doubled to 16,000. Public fear of the disease reached epidemic proportions. Still no cure was in sight.

Heinrich Böll, the West German author, died, as did Yul Brynner, Sam Ervin, Marc Chagall, Henry Cabot Lodge, Orson Welles, Eugene Ormandy, and E.B. White.

The biggest gaffe of the year: Coca-Cola introduced a new taste. There was rebellion in the ranks of Coke drinkers, and the company changed its mind.

There was increasing pressure on President Ferdinand Marcos of the Philippines, the Sandinista government of Nicaragua, and the white minority government of South Africa. Civil unrest in South Africa never let up during the year. More than 1,000 persons died in acts of violence there. Most were nonwhites protesting the government's racial policies.

Americans marked the tenth anniversary of the end of the war in Vietnam. Veterans of that war finally began to feel as if they had come home.

In sports, Pete Rose of the Cincinnati Reds surpassed one of baseball's most coveted benchmarks, Ty Cobb's 4,191 career hits. He was a shining example of the best in the game during a year in which new drug scandals made headlines.

It was a year in which the press often made as much news as it reported. The former U.S. commander in Vietnam, Gen. William Westmoreland, sued CBS for libel; he later dropped the case. The former Israeli defense minister, Ariel Sharon, sued *Time* for libel and did not completely prevail either.

At year-end, a vast array of American newspapers chose Britain's princess of Wales, Lady Diana, as the personality of the year. She and her husband, Prince Charles, had barnstormed through Washington and Florida in November. Americans, who still sometimes hanker for a little royalty in their lives, were agog. And why not?

January

2   Meeting in Los Angeles, President Ronald Reagan and Japan's Prime Minister Yasuhiro Nakasone agree to a series of high-level talks on ways to open U.S. markets to Japanese goods.

Norway announces that a low-flying object believed to be a Soviet cruise missile crossed its territory and crashed somewhere in Finland on Dec. 28, 1984.

3   The 99th U.S. Congress convenes in Washington, DC.

8   At the end of two days of talks in Geneva, U.S. Secretary of State George P. Shultz and Soviet Foreign Minister Andrei Gromyko agree that the two nations would resume nuclear-arms negotiations on an unspecified date in the near future.

President Reagan announces that White House Chief of Staff James A. Baker 3d and Secretary of the Treasury Donald T. Regan would switch positions.

10   Daniel Ortega Saavedra is sworn in as president of Nicaragua.

President Reagan announces three more changes in his cabinet: Donald P. Hodel will be nominated as secretary of the interior; John S. Herrington would succeed Hodel as secretary of energy; and William J. Bennett will be named secretary of education.

12   France announces that it is sending 1,000 additional troops to its South Pacific territory of New Caledonia. The island government declares a state of emergency after an intensification of violence over the issue of independence.

13   A train derailment in eastern Ethiopia kills 392 persons.

14   The Israeli cabinet approves a plan to withdraw Israeli troops from Lebanon in three stages over six to nine months.

15   Brazil's electoral college elects Tancredo de Almeida Neves, 74, as the nation's first civilian president in 21 years.

17   Calm returns to the Caribbean island of Jamaica after three days of rioting set off by sharp increases in fuel prices.

Pete Souza, The White House

In a brief White House ceremony on Sunday, January 20, Ronald Reagan was formally sworn in for a second presidential term. Chief Justice Warren Burger administered the oath. On January 21, the Reagans attended nine inaugural balls.

Bill Fitz-Patrick, The White House

20 San Francisco quarterback Joe Montana leads the 49ers to a 38–16 victory over the Miami Dolphins in Super Bowl XIX.

21 In the Capitol Rotunda in Washington, Ronald Reagan and George Bush are sworn in publicly for a second presidential and vice-presidential term. Cold weather forces cancellation of the outdoor ceremonies, including the inaugural parade. In accordance with the Constitution, the president and vice-president took their oaths officially on January 20.

23 The Philippine government formally charges 26 men, including Chief of Staff Gen. Fabian C. Ver, in connection with the 1983 assassination of opposition leader Benigno S. Aquino, Jr.

24 A federal district court jury in Manhattan finds that *Time* magazine did not libel former Israeli Defense Minister Ariel Sharon in a 1983 article about the massacre of Palestinians at two West Beirut refugee camps in 1982.

26 Pope John Paul II arrives in Caracas, Venezuela, on the start of a 12-day visit to Latin America.

27 Carrying four astronauts, the space shuttle *Discovery* lands at Cape Canaveral, ending a three-day secret military mission.

30 Nine members of the Organization of Petroleum Exporting Countries (OPEC) agree to price cuts for the first time in the 25-year history of the cartel. Four other member nations dissent.

The U.S. Department of Commerce reports that the nation's trade deficit reached a record $123.3 billion in 1984.

February

1 Paul G. Kirk, Jr., is elected chairman of the Democratic National Committee.

4 President Reagan sends to Congress his federal budget for fiscal 1986. Revenues and expenditures are estimated at $793.7 billion and $973.7 billion, respectively.

The United States announces that New Zealand has "definitively turned down" a U.S. request for a port visit by a Navy destroyer because the U.S. government would not reveal whether the ship carried nuclear weapons.

THE PROPOSED U.S. BUDGET DOLLAR

fiscal year 1986

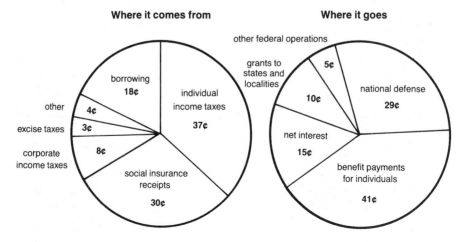

Where it comes from

borrowing 18¢
individual income taxes 37¢
other 4¢
excise taxes 3¢
corporate income taxes 8¢
social insurance receipts 30¢

Where it goes

other federal operations
grants to states and localities
5¢
10¢
national defense 29¢
net interest 15¢
benefit payments for individuals 41¢

U.S. Vice-President George Bush (extreme left) *and House Speaker Tip O'Neill listen as Britain's Prime Minister Margaret Thatcher tells a joint session of Congress that it is "our strength, not their [Soviet] goodwill, that brought the Soviet Union to the negotiating table in Geneva."*

5   The border between Spain and Gibraltar, which had been virtually closed since June 1969, is reopened.

8   Opposition leader Kim Dae Jung returns to South Korea after more than two years in exile in the United States.

    Gen. Vernon A. Walters, a 68-year-old longtime diplomat, is named to succeed Jeane J. Kirkpatrick as chief U.S. delegate to the United Nations.

12   In general elections in South Korea, the ruling Democratic Justice Party retains its majority in the National Assembly, but the New Democratic Party, formed by opposition leaders once banned by President Chun Doo Hwan, makes a strong showing.

14   Jeremy Levin, the Beirut bureau chief of Cable News Network kidnapped in Lebanon in March 1984, escapes to freedom.

17   Murray P. Haydon, a 58-year-old former autoworker, becomes the third person to receive a permanent artificial heart.

18   Gen. William C. Westmoreland, former commander of U.S. troops in Vietnam, ends his $120 million libel suit against CBS. The network says that it respects the general's "long and faithful service to his country" but stands by the fairness and accuracy of *The Uncounted Enemy: A Vietnam Deception,* the 1982 documentary that prompted Westmoreland's suit.

19   The U.S. Supreme Court rules that federal minimum wage and hour rules cover employees of publicly owned transit systems.

20   During a three-day visit to Washington, Britain's Prime Minister Margaret Thatcher addresses a joint session of Congress.

23   By a vote of 63–31, the U.S. Senate confirms Edwin Meese 3d as attorney general.

25   In elections for a new National Assembly in Pakistan, seven cabinet aides of President Zia ul-Haq are defeated.

27   The central banks of the United States and six European nations take successful action to check the rise of the U.S. dollar against other major currencies.

    At the end of a three-day burst of diplomatic activity, which included an exchange of envoys and the highest-level contacts in more than two years, Israel supports Egypt's call for peace talks with a joint delegation of Jordanians and Palestinians.

28   In Newry, Northern Ireland, Irish Republican Army terrorists fire mortar shells into a police base, killing at least nine persons and injuring dozens of others.

    Louisiana Gov. Edwin E. Edwards is indicted by a federal grand jury on conspiracy charges.

March

1   Twelve years of military rule come to an end in Uruguay, as a civilian, Julio Maria Sanguinetti is sworn in as president.

President Reagan announces that he will not ask Japan to extend its voluntary export quotas on cars.

3   Britain's coal miners call off their 12-month-old strike without a settlement.

5   U.S. undercover agents arrest Norman B. Saunders, the chief minister of the Turks and Caicos Islands, and two aides on charges of using the Atlantic island chain as a base for smuggling drugs to the United States.

President Reagan vetoes a farm credit bill that would have provided federal loan guarantees to farmers with debt problems. The president had announced the broadening of a separate program in early February.

11   Mikhail S. Gorbachev is named chairman of the Soviet Communist Party following the March 10 death of Konstantin Chernenko.

In the largest United Nations conference to date on drought and famine relief for Africa, representatives of more than 70 nations and scores of private aid groups meet in Geneva.

12   U.S. and Soviet negotiating teams meet in Geneva for the opening session of renewed arms limitation talks.

15   Ohio Gov. Richard Celeste orders 71 state-chartered banks and savings and loan institutions closed for three days to stop a multi-million-dollar run on deposits.

18   At the end of a two-day meeting in Quebec, Canada's Prime Minister Brian Mulroney and President Reagan sign agreements on defense, acid rain, trade, and fishing.

The American Broadcasting Companies agree to a buyout by Capital Cities Communications Inc. for some $3.5 billion.

19   After a week of fighting described as the heaviest in their four-year-old war, Iraqi forces appear to have repelled a major Iranian offensive.

Mikhail Gorbachev (far right), the newly chosen secretary-general of the Soviet Communist Party, leads the official delegation at the funeral of his predecessor, Konstantin U. Chernenko. Soviet leader for 13 months, Chernenko died of heart failure March 10.

AP/Wide World

20 During a two-day visit to Washington, Argentine President Raul Alfonsín addresses a joint session of Congress.

President Reagan names William Brock as U.S. secretary of labor. Brock would succeed Raymond J. Donovan who resigned after being ordered to stand trial on fraud and larceny charges.

21 In Uitenhage, South Africa, police fire into a crowd of blacks, killing 19. The blacks were marching to a service for three activists killed in a clash with police the week before.

The Israeli army attacks four Shiite Muslim villages in southern Lebanon, killing 21 persons described as "terrorists." Also killed are two members of a CBS News camera crew.

24 Arthur D. Nicholson, Jr., a 37-year-old U.S. Army major, is shot and killed by a Soviet guard during a reconnaissance mission in East Germany.

27 In New York City, Bernhard H. Goetz is indicted on charges of attempting to murder four youths on a subway in December 1984. Goetz has claimed self-defense in the controversial case.

28 The U.S. House of Representatives gives final approval to President Reagan's request for 21 additional MX missiles.

29 In a special session of the Greek Parliament, Christos Sartzetakis of the ruling Socialist Party is elected president.

Ending years of negotiations, Spain and Portugal both agree to terms for becoming members of the European Community.

31 The Christian Democratic Party of President José Napoleon Duarte wins national legislative elections in El Salvador.

April

1 The Villanova Wildcats upset the defending champion Georgetown Hoyas, 66–64, to win the NCAA men's basketball title.

6 Sudan's President Jaafar al-Nemery, who held power for nearly 16 years, is deposed in a coup led by his defense minister.

7 Soviet leader Mikhail Gorbachev announces a moratorium on the deployment of medium-range nuclear missiles. The United States, calling the gesture a "political ploy," rejects a freeze.

9 The government of Japan introduces measures to open the nation's markets to foreign goods. In a rare televised appeal, Prime Minister Yasuhiro Nakasone calls on the Japanese people to buy more foreign-made products.

Mayor Tom Bradley of Los Angeles is overwhelmingly elected to an unprecedented fourth term.

12 In the 16th flight of the U.S. space shuttle program, Sen. Jake Garn (R-UT) lifts off with six other crew members for a seven-day mission aboard *Discovery*.

13 Albania's President Ramiz Alia is chosen first secretary of the Albanian Workers' (communist) Party. Enver Hoxha, who died April 11, had led the party since 1944.

14 Britain's Prime Minister Margaret Thatcher ends a ten-day, seven-nation tour of Asia to promote trade relations.

18 According to the U.S. Commerce Department, the growth rate of real gross national product slowed to 1.3% for the first quarter of the year.

Ted Turner, the Atlanta broadcaster, announces a $5.41 billion plan to gain a controlling interest in CBS, Inc., and then merge the network with his own Turner Broadcasting System Inc.

Los Angeles Mayor Tom Bradley was reelected to an unprecedented fourth term on April 9. The 67-year-old Democrat captured more than 67% of the vote. He defeated City Councilman John Ferraro.

AP/Wide World

Richard Hoffman, Sygma

A 15-member military council, headed by former Defense Minister Gen. Abdel Rahman Suwar el Dahab (front row, center) governs in Sudan after President Jaafar al-Nemery was deposed April 6. A five-day general strike led to the coup.

21 Brazil's President-elect Tancredo Neves, whose illness kept him from taking office March 15, dies. Vice-President José Sarney, the acting president, automatically becomes president.

24 Representatives of 80 African and Asian countries meet in Bandung, Indonesia, to mark the 30th anniversary of the 1955 Asia-Africa Conference, which laid the groundwork for the Nonaligned Movement.

Jack C. Burcham, 62, the oldest human patient yet to receive a permanent artificial heart, dies ten days after the device was implanted.

Pope John Paul II names 28 new cardinals, including archbishops John J. O'Connor of New York and Bernard F. Law of Boston.

26 Meeting in Warsaw, leaders of the Warsaw Pact nations ratify a 20-year extension of the Soviet-led military assistance alliance. The original 30-year treaty was due to expire May 15.

30 Vietnam marks the tenth anniversary of the fall of Saigon, now called Ho Chi Minh City, to North Vietnamese communist forces.

May

1 Declaring Nicaraguan actions a threat to U.S. national security, President Reagan orders an embargo on trade with that country and bans Nicaraguan aircraft and ships from the United States.

Pro-Solidarity marchers in Poland counter government-sponsored May Day rallies with protests against price increases and other state policies.

2 Government leaders of the seven major industrial democracies come together in Bonn, West Germany, for the three-day 11th annual economic summit conference.

5 After weeks of controversy, President Reagan carries through on his planned visit to the German military cemetery at Bitburg, West Germany, which contains the graves of 49 Nazi Waffen SS troops. He then travels to the Bergen-Belsen Nazi concentration camp to honor the victims of the Holocaust.

6 The U.S. space shuttle *Challenger* and a seven-member crew complete a successful seven-day scientific mission.

8 On the eighth day of his ten-day European trip, President Reagan assails the Soviet Union in an address to the European Parliament in Strasbourg, France.

The nations of Western Europe and the United States mark the 40th anniversary of V-E day, when Nazi Germany formally surrendered to Allied forces in World War II.

11 After two days of bomb explosions in New Delhi and three northern Indian states, at least 80 people are dead and 150 others injured. Militant Sikh separatists are blamed.

12 Illinois Gov. James R. Thompson commutes the sentence of Gary Dotson for an alleged rape in 1977. Dotson's supposed victim, Cathleen Crowell Webb, declared in March that she had made up the story of the rape.

In the Netherlands, Pope John Paul II encounters hostile protests against Church policies.

14 U.S. Secretary of State George Shultz and Soviet Foreign Minister Andrei Gromyko hold six hours of talks in Vienna.

16 El Salvador's President José Napoleon Duarte meets in Washington with President Reagan and proposes the resumption of negotiations with Salvadoran leftist rebels.

20 Israel releases 1,150 Palestinians and other Arab prisoners in exchange for three Israeli soldiers taken during the 1982 invasion of Lebanon.

Nicaragua's President Daniel Ortega ends a three-week tour of Eastern and Western Europe. The first stop was Moscow in late April, at which time the Soviet leadership promised to give Nicaragua "assistance in resolving its urgent problems. . . ."

21 India's Prime Minister Rajiv Gandhi arrives in the Soviet Union on his first official state visit since taking office in 1984.

AP/Wide World

Cathleen Crowell Webb tells the Illinois Prisoner Review Board that she falsely accused Gary Dotson of rape in 1977.

In Philadelphia, May 13, at least 50 homes were destroyed by a fire that began after police dropped a bomb on the roof of a stronghold of the radical group MOVE. Some $5 million in damage resulted; 300 persons were left homeless.

Brad Bower, Picture Group

22   At the end of a two-day meeting in Brussels, the 14 defense ministers of NATO sign an agreement aimed at reducing the organization's reliance on nuclear weapons and improving conventional defenses.

25   A cyclone and tidal wave batter southeastern coastal Bangladesh, killing up to 10,000 people, leaving 250,000 or more homeless, and damaging vast areas of farmland.

26   Danny Sullivan wins the Indianapolis 500.

28   President Reagan announces his plan for simplifying the U.S. tax system. The plan would reduce the number of personal income-tax brackets to three.

29   Before the European Cup soccer championship at Heysel Stadium in Brussels, British fans charge a grandstand filled with Italian rooters, and rioting breaks out. Some 40 persons are killed and more than 200 others are injured.

30   The Edmonton Oilers win the National Hockey League's Stanley Cup for the second consecutive year.

31   King Hussein of Jordan ends three days of talks in Washington with President Reagan and other high-level U.S. officials.

June

Claus von Bülow listens to court proceedings during his highly publicized eight-week trial on two counts of attempted murder against his wealthy, socialite wife, Sonny. He was found innocent June 10.

AP/Wide World

1   The National Election Board of Peru declares Alan García Perez the nation's president-elect.

2   Prime Minister Andreas Papandreou and his Pan Hellenic Socialist Movement (PASOK) win Greece's parliamentary elections.

4   The U.S. Supreme Court rules, 6–3, that an Alabama law authorizing daily one-minute periods of silent meditation or prayer in public schools is unconstitutional.

9   The Los Angeles Lakers defeat the Boston Celtics to capture the National Basketball Association championship.

10   Israel completes the third and final phase of its military withdrawal from Lebanon, leaving behind advisers and observers in the southern security zone it had created.

President Reagan announces that the United States will continue to abide by the 1979 Strategic Arms Limitation Treaty (SALT II), which had never been ratified by the Senate.

In a retrial in Providence, RI, Claus von Bülow is acquitted on two charges of attempting to murder his wife, Martha (Sonny) von Bülow, in 1979 and 1980.

12   The U.S. House of Representatives votes $27 million in humanitarian aid to Nicaraguan contras (rebels); the Senate passed $38 million in nonmilitary aid June 6. (In an April vote, the House had rejected all forms of aid to the contras.)

13   During a four-day state visit, India's Prime Minister Rajiv Gandhi addresses a joint session of the U.S. Congress.

14   Shortly after takeoff from the Athens airport, two Lebanese Shiite Muslim gunmen hijack TWA flight 847 en route from Cairo to Rome. In exchange for the 153 passengers and crew on board, the hijackers demand the release by Israel of 766 mostly Shiite prisoners.

To curb inflation, Argentina's President Raul Alfonsín orders a wage and price freeze, the creation of a new currency, and a halt on government deficit spending. The measures come three days after an agreement with the International Monetary Fund on an economic austerity program for the country.

25 At the end of a four-day meeting in Geneva, the Organization of Petroleum Exporting Countries votes small price cuts to firm up the cartel's clout amid falling prices on the world market.

A spokesperson for Rock Hudson discloses in Paris that the actor is suffering from AIDS.

27 Uganda's President Milton Obote is ousted in a military coup.

29 The Soviet Union announces a unilateral moratorium on nuclear testing until Jan. 1, 1986.

August

1 The U.S. House and Senate approve a joint resolution on the fiscal 1986 federal budget, ending months of deadlock. After passage of the bill, Congress adjourns for its August recess.

6 At the Hiroshima Peace Memorial Park in Japan, some 55,000 people attend ceremonies marking the 40th anniversary of the atomic bombing of that city.

Guyana's President Forbes Burnham, who led the country since 1964, dies. Desmond Hoyte is sworn in as his successor.

The U.S. space shuttle *Challenger* ends an eight-day mission described as "superbly successful" despite the premature breakdown of a main engine shortly after takeoff.

7 Broadcaster Ted Turner announces that he is ending his takeover bid for CBS, Inc.

8 Pope John Paul II arrives in Lomé, Togo, on the first leg of a 12-day tour of Africa.

9 At least 52 persons are dead after three days of rioting in black townships around Durban, South Africa.

11 Six plant workers and 134 area residents are treated for injuries after a toxic gas leak at a Union Carbide pesticide plant in Institute, WV.

12 In the worst air disaster ever involving a single plane, a Japan Air Lines Boeing 747 crashes in the mountains northwest of Tokyo, killing 520 passengers and crew members.

Barling, "The Christian Science Monitor" © 1985 TCSPS

The Christian Science Monitor

Baseball fans had a scare and rock 'n' roll fans had a treat during the summer. Major league ballplayers went on strike August 6, but the walkout lasted only two days. Rocker Bruce Springsteen, meanwhile, sold out stadium concerts everywhere.

13 Political allies of the Philippines' President Ferdinand Marcos defeat an impeachment move in the National Assembly.

15 In the ongoing Iran-Iraq war, Baghdad claims to have launched its largest bombing attack yet against Iran's chief oil export terminal on Kharg Island, leaving it "demolished."

20 In the Punjab, India, moderate Sikh leader Harchand Singh Longowal is assassinated.

21 The U.S. State Department accuses the Soviets of using a dangerous chemical to track the movements of U.S. diplomats in Moscow.

25 In a widening spy scandal, a senior secretary in the office of West Germany's President Richard von Weizäcker is arrested on espionage charges. Two days earlier it was reported that Hans Joachim Triedge, Bonn's senior counterintelligence officer, had defected to East Germany.

27 Nigeria's head of government Maj. Gen. Mohammed Buhari is overthrown in a bloodless military coup.

U.S. Defense Secretary Caspar Weinberger announces that DIVAD, a mobile antiaircraft weapon being developed for the Army, is being canceled. It is the first time the Pentagon has scrapped a major weapons program during production.

September

1 During a seven-day flight by the space shuttle *Discovery,* the 20th mission of the U.S. shuttle program, astronauts perform a dramatic repair job on a dormant satellite.

2 A team of U.S. and French researchers is reported to have located the S.S. *Titanic,* lost in 1912.

4 In Chile, an antigovernment protest called by the banned Communist Party and the moderate opposition results in six deaths and 550 arrests in various cities.

8 Ivan Lendl defeats John McEnroe to win the men's singles title at the U.S. Open tennis tournament. Hana Mandlikova beat Martina Navratilova to take the women's crown the day before.

9 In a ten-hour battle, forces loyal to Thailand's Prime Minister Prem Tinsulanonda put down a military coup. Two U.S. television reporters are killed in the fighting.

10 Eleven Western European nations meeting in Luxembourg agree on limited economic, cultural, and military sanctions against South Africa for its apartheid policy. A day earlier, U.S. President Reagan reversed his position and ordered limited trade and financial sanctions against the Pretoria government.

Leftist rebels in Nicaragua kidnap the eldest daughter of President José Napoleón Duarte.

Norway's coalition government led by Conservative Prime Minister Kåre Willoch is narrowly returned to power.

11 Baseball star Pete Rose of the Cincinnati Reds gets the 4,192nd hit of his career, breaking Ty Cobb's all-time record.

12 Britain expels 25 Soviets after a recently defected Moscow intelligence agent exposed a major espionage network.

15 Sweden's Prime Minister Olof Palme wins a second consecutive three-year term, as his Social Democratic Party retains tenuous control of parliament in national elections.

16 In one of China's most extensive high-level leadership shuffles since Communist rule began, the Party announces the retirement of 10 of the 24 members of the Politburo.

The opening of the 1985–86 school year was marked by sometimes heated debate over whether children with AIDS should be in the classroom.

D. Fineman, Sygma

17 The UN General Assembly convenes its 40th annual session.

18 President Reagan announces that the Rev. Benjamin Weir, held hostage in Lebanon for 16 months, has been released and is back in the United States with his family.

Emergency rescue teams in Mexico City look for survivors of the September 19 earthquake and its aftershock.

19 A major earthquake rocks southwestern Mexico, devastating parts of Mexico City and three coastal states.

20 France's Defense Minister Charles Hernu resigns and the head of its intelligence agency is dismissed in a growing scandal over the July sinking in New Zealand of a Greenpeace antinuclear protest ship, the *Rainbow Warrior*.

Pierre Marc Johnson, who had served as Quebec's minister of justice, became head of the Parti Québécois and on October 3 was sworn in as provincial premier. His father, Daniel, also had been a Quebec premier.

23 President Reagan announces a plan to subsidize some exports in an effort to open foreign markets to U.S. goods; he also says the administration will put pressure on countries with "unfair" trading practices.

27 After pummeling the eastern Carolinas, Hurricane Gloria sweeps up the Atlantic Coast through New York and into New England.

Soviet Prime Minister Nikolai A. Tikhonov, 80, retires and is replaced by Nikolai I. Ryzhkov, 55.

In a meeting at the White House with Soviet Foreign Minister Eduard A. Shevardnadze, President Reagan welcomes a new arms proposal from Moscow calling for 50% cuts in the offensive nuclear arsenals of both superpowers.

28 Eric Arturo Delvalle is sworn in as the new president of Panama after the resignation of President Nicolas Ardito Barletta.

29 Pierre Marc Johnson, 39, a moderate, replaces René Lévesque as leader of the Parti Québécois. He will automatically become premier of Canada's largest province.

30 Jordan's King Hussein confers at the White House with President Reagan. After the meeting, Reagan says he believes direct Jordanian-Israeli peace talks could start before year's end.

October

1 Israeli planes bomb the headquarters of the Palestine Liberation Organization near Tunis, Tunisia, killing 72.

Adm. William Crowe, Jr., is sworn in as chairman of the U.S. Joint Chiefs of Staff, replacing Gen. John Vessey, Jr.

2 Soviet leader Mikhail S. Gorbachev arrives in France on an official four-day visit, his first to a Western nation since coming to power in March.

6 Portugal's Social Democratic Party, led by 46-year-old Anibal Cavaco Silva, wins parliamentary elections.

7 The United States declares that it will no longer comply automatically with the decisions of the International Court of Justice in The Hague.

The U.S. space shuttle *Atlantis* completes its first flight, a four-day secret mission for the Defense Department.

9 At least 150 persons are killed in Ponce, Puerto Rico, when heavy rains trigger a massive mudslide.

10 U.S. Navy fighter planes intercept an Egyptian jet carrying four Palestinian terrorists and force it to land in Sicily. The terrorists had hijacked the Italian cruise ship *Achille Lauro* on October 7 and surrendered in Egypt two days later in exchange for a promise of safe passage.

11 The International Physicians for the Prevention of Nuclear War is named the winner of the 1985 Nobel Peace Prize.

A ten-day celebration marking the 40th anniversary of the United Nations was held at New York City headquarters beginning October 14.

The World Bank and International Monetary Fund conclude joint annual meetings in Seoul, South Korea. The United States proposed a $29 billion plan to aid the world's debtor nations.

© A. Tannenbaum, Sygma

December

2 Gen. Fabian Ver of the Philippines, on leave as military chief of staff, and 25 codefendants are found not guilty in the 1983 slaying of opposition leader Benigno Aquino, Jr.

Soviet dissident Yelena Bonner, the wife of Andrei Sakharov, arrives in Rome at the start of a three-month trip to the West for medical treatment.

Robert Bourassa and his Liberal Party win provincial elections in Quebec, Canada.

3 The U.S. space shuttle *Atlantis* lands at Edwards Air Force Base in California after a successful seven-day mission.

4 U.S. President Reagan announces the resignation of Robert C. McFarlane as his national security adviser and names Vice Adm. John M. Poindexter to succeed him.

6 The United States and Great Britain sign an accord giving the latter a role in research on the Strategic Defense Initiative.

8 Meeting in Geneva, the Organization of the Petroleum Exporting Countries (OPEC) abandons its official price structure, to concentrate on capturing a "fair" share of the world market.

In Guatemala, Marco Vinicio Cerezo Arévalo of the Christian Democratic party wins runoff presidential elections.

12 A chartered DC-8 jetliner carrying 248 U.S. soldiers and eight crew members crashes after takeoff in Gander, Newfoundland. There are no survivors.

President Reagan signs into law the Gramm-Rudman bill, mandating a balanced federal budget by 1991.

In Guyana, Desmond Hoyte of the People's National Congress is sworn in as president after winning December 9 elections.

16 Paul Castellano, reputed head of the powerful Gambino organized crime family, is shot dead in New York City.

The Dow Jones industrial average closes at a record 1,553.10.

17 Meeting in New Delhi, India's Prime Minister Rajiv Gandhi and Pakistan's President Zia ul-Haq agree to a "step-by-step" approach to the normalization of relations.

18 A mistrial is declared in the fraud and conspiracy trial of Louisiana's Gov. Edwin W. Edwards.

20 Three gunmen surrender to French police at an airport in Nantes, one day after taking 32 hostages in a city courtroom. None of the hostages is hurt.

22 South African police arrest the antiapartheid activist Winnie Mandela after she defied a ban forbidding her to enter Soweto, the black township where she lives.

Three inmates who escaped from the Perry Correctional Institute in Greenville, NC, on December 19, along with the woman who commandeered a sight-seeing helicopter to pick them up from the prison yard, are captured by police in Georgia.

26 Warring militias in Lebanon report an agreement, mediated by Syria, to end ten years of civil war.

At least 140 pre-Columbian artifacts are found missing from the National Museum of Anthropology in Mexico City.

27 A total of 15 persons are killed in simultaneous attacks by Palestinian terrorists on El Al Israeli Airlines check-in counters at airports in Rome and Vienna.

30 Pakistan's President Zia declares an end to eight and a half years of martial law.

After a jury failed to reach a verdict, a federal district judge declared a mistrial in the case against Edwin W. Edwards. At a subsequent news conference, the Louisiana governor called the decision the "most important election" of his life and by "the greatest majority ever."

AP/Wide World

SOUTH AFRICA:1985
A Year of Confrontation, Violence, Unrest

By Patrick O'Meara and N. Brian Winchester

About the Authors. Patrick O'Meara and N. Brian Winchester are director and associate director, respectively, of the African Studies Program at Indiana University. A graduate of the University of Cape Town, South Africa, Dr. O'Meara coedited *Southern Africa: The Continuing Crisis* and other works. Dr. Winchester has written for various publications, including George De Lury's *World Encyclopedia of Political Systems and Parties*.

South Africa is in the midst of an internal crisis of unprecedented magnitude. In 1985, demonstrations against apartheid (an Afrikaans word meaning "apartness," the government policy of racial segregation) swept through black townships and gave rise to increasingly violent confrontations between protesters and security forces. The death toll since the current unrest began in late 1984 was near 1,000, and, after the government declared a state of emergency in July, there were more than 5,000 political arrests and detentions. Foreign condemnation, meanwhile, was more intense, broader in scope, and more sustained than ever before. To that extent, 1985 seemed to be a watershed year for South Africa.

A new constitution implemented in September 1984 by the government of President Pieter W. Botha had given limited political representation to the nation's so-called Coloured—racially mixed—and Asian peoples. But blacks, who make up approximately 70% of the population, continued to be denied rights, however. (Whites make up about 17% of the population; so-called Coloureds and others, 13%.) The result was an escalation of violent protest. Similarly, the emergency measures adopted in July 1985 had the opposite effect of what the government intended, actually inciting blacks to more violence.

Throughout the year, as in the past, black nonviolent opposition was met by white intransigence. This in turn led to black violence and officially sanctioned state violence in a

cycle of escalating confrontation. The politicization of funerals is illustrative of this violence born out of repression. Until they were banned in August, funerals had become the major vehicle for black political discontent because most other political gatherings by blacks had been prohibited. Africans by the thousands would gather before the funerals of victims of the violence to hear antiapartheid speeches and political songs and express their often violent opposition to the government and its policies. In response, the government set new conditions for the funerals of those who died from "unnatural" causes in areas under the state of emergency. Outdoor funerals were banned, and services could be held for only one deceased person at a time and could be carried out only by ordained ministers who were prohibited from criticizing the government, advocating any alternative form of government or boycotts, or condemning the state of emergency. In defiance of the government's restrictions, blacks continued to hold mass funeral rallies to protest government violence. One held in early December was attended by diplomats from 11 Western nations, an unmistakable sign of Western displeasure with South Africa's handling of the crisis.

Significantly, the 1985 violence was largely confined to the black townships, in only a few instances spilling over into white urban areas. Most of the intimidation, arrests, property damage, arson, injuries, and death occurred in these zones of violence, with the result that many whites complacently sense no immediate personal threat. The targets of black rage often were those who were seen to collaborate with the apartheid system—such as black policemen and urban councillors and suspected informers—some of whom were stoned or burned to death. The government's response to the intensity, scope, and duration of the upheaval in 1985 was a combination of repression and cosmetic reform that might have been effective 25 years earlier but now seemed only to ignite and fuel further black discontent.

Effective black power also was channeled in nonviolent ways through nationwide boycotts of white businesses and through the power of organized strikes. In 1985, black labor unions—including the recently formed 500,000-member Congress of South African Trade Unions (COSATU), the largest in South Africa's history, and the United Democratic Front (UDF), the country's largest nonparliamentary opposition movement with 600 affiliated organizations and at least 1.5 million members—began to play an increasingly important role in overall black political strategy for change.

Prominent among black leaders in 1985 were the Rev. Allan Boesak, one of the founders of the UDF, and Anglican Bishop Desmond Tutu of Johannesburg, the 1984 Nobel Peace laureate, both of whom have vigorously and publicly campaigned against apartheid but who have rejected violence as well. The single most prominent symbol of black resistance and political aspiration, both for blacks within South Africa and among opponents to apartheid around the world, was Nelson Mandela. The leader of the outlawed African National Conference (ANC), Mandela had been a political prisoner for

Desmond M. Tutu was enthroned as the first black Anglican bishop of Johannesburg, South Africa, in February 1985. Addressing the congregation, the 1984 Nobel Peace Prize winner offered to act as an intermediary between the nation's white minority government and its underground opponent, the African National Congress. Instead the bishop witnessed increased violence and confrontation in his homeland throughout the remainder of the year.

© Mark Peters, Black Star

© William Campbell, Sygma

AP/Wide World

On July 31 the South African government announced restrictions on funerals for black victims killed during unrest in black townships. Mass outdoor funerals, such as the one above, had become the principal means for blacks to express publicly their opposition to the government. Accompanied by her daughters, Winnie Mandela (left, center) arrives at Cape Town airport en route to visit her husband, Nelson Mandela, the imprisoned leader of the African National Congress. The year ended with Mrs. Mandela being arrested for ignoring a police banning order.

23 years, first in the infamous Robben Island prison and more recently at Pollsmoor prison near Cape Town. Even moderate black leaders insisted that any attempt to resolve South Africa's worsening crisis must involve Mandela, but the government refused to release him until he publicly rejects the use of violence. The ailing Mandela consistently demanded unconditional release, and the government's unwillingness to compromise was symptomatic of its unwillingness to yield on anything but cosmetic changes.

The State of Emergency. On July 21 the Pretoria government declared a state of emergency for the first time since 1960, when widespread violence and rioting followed the deaths of 69 blacks in a confrontation with police in Sharpeville. The 1985 state of emergency initially covered 36 magisterial districts, under which the police and army were given wide powers of detention without a warrant or trial, the right to search houses or buildings at any time, the right to impose curfews, and full indemnity from all legal claims arising from their actions "in the service of the state." The immediate detention of several hundred political, religious, labor, and educational leaders served only to incite greater violence.

Before a provincial congress of the ruling National Party in Durban, August 15, President Pieter W. Botha declared that he was "not prepared to lead white South Africa and other minority groups on a road to abdication and suicide." The speech was a disappointment to those who had hoped for change. During the year, the government did express willingness to review the laws limiting black mobility—including the carrying of a pass in white areas, photo left.

The declaration of the state of emergency was an indication that the violence was continuing to escalate and that the police were losing control of the African townships. There had been increasing pressures for reform both from within and from outside South Africa, and expectations were raised that President Botha would introduce necessary reforms in Durban on August 15, at the first of four scheduled speeches to the annual National Party Congresses. Instead, he offered only to negotiate with some blacks for limited political change and merely hinted that he might be willing to make more concessions later. The gist of his presentation was that he would not institute extensive reforms and that he was "not prepared to lead white South Africans and other racial minority groups on a road to abdication and suicide."

President Botha's equivocation over the matter of reform might be understood as fear of a conservative backlash from within his own party. In subsequent speeches, he remained intransigent to meaningful change, to the disappointment of those reform-minded white South Africans, especially in the business community, who were becoming increasingly alarmed at the effect that the unrest was having on the economy. In Botha's fourth and final address to the National Party Congress in Port Elizabeth in October, he elaborated on his suggested "reforms," but, as in his earlier speeches, these remained ambiguous and limited. He rejected outright the idea of one man, one vote in a unitary state because it would lead to "the dictatorship of the strongest black group." He proposed instead a common citizenship and a confederation of geographic and ethnic units with separate racial groups having responsibility for their "own affairs." On matters of "mutual concern," such as defense or foreign policy, structures would be created to permit discussion and negotiation with the proviso that one group would not dominate. Botha was thus attempting to find a formula that would ensure white domination while appearing to appease black political demands.

© Sygma

© Bisson, Sygma

In late August 1985 a crowd gathered at a Cape Town stadium in preparation for a march to the prison where Nelson Mandela is jailed. After protesters jeered at police and refused to disperse, a police commander gave the order to "clean up." The police charged the crowd with clubs and whips, right. In late 1984 a combined force of South African army troops and police encircled the township of Sebokeng, above, and then conducted house-to-house searches. The township had been the scene of several weeks of riots.

The value of South Africa's currency, the rand, fell dramatically during August, causing heavy trading at many foreign exchange departments. By month's end foreign banks had refused to extend deadlines for the repayment of South Africa's debt, the rand had dropped to its lowest level ever, and the government had closed temporarily the nation's stock and currency markets.

AP/Wide World

International Financial Pressures. By late August the international economic fallout from South Africa's worsening internal political crisis had become fully apparent. The rand fell to its lowest level ever (U.S.35¢), and as a result the government suspended trading on the stock and currency markets for several days. The government also reintroduced strict exchange control regulations to avoid a drain on its foreign-exchange resources and implemented a two-tier currency system with the introduction of a "financial rand" for foreigners investing in South Africa. The financial rand is quoted on currency markets at a lower rate than the commercial rand and cannot be transferred out of South Africa as dollars. On September 1 the South African government announced a freeze until December 31, subsequently extended to March 31, 1986, on the repayment of the principal on the country's short-term foreign debts of $10–$15 billion, of which $1.9 billion represented government borrowing. South Africa's available foreign-exchange reserves were approximately $2.5 billion, with an equal amount available from foreign-trade surpluses. International bankers responding to the ongoing political crisis in South Africa refused to lend new money or to renew loans, which, in turn, further hurt the already deteriorating rand. These moves were of considerable embarrassment to South Africa because of the harm they did to its credit rating and because it had taken considerable pride in its debt repayment record.

Right-Wing Reaction. In the first major test of strength after the government's announced intention to institute modest reforms, right-wing parties opposed to *any* reforms won one by-election and made substantial gains in three out of four others on October 30. Though the narrowness of the electoral margin in what had been safe seats might have been interpreted as a signal of white opposition to attempts at reform—even limited ones—the swing to the extreme right in no way threatened the ability of the National Party to govern; it continued to hold

123 out of 178 seats in the all-white parliament. Indeed, on the day following the election, President Botha insisted that the government would not move away from its program of reform.

While most Afrikaners continued to support the ruling National Party in 1985, right-wing factions over the past few years split off to form their own parties. The Conservative Party, with 18 seats in the white parliament, was led by Andries Treurnicht, a former cabinet minister. It has grown in strength and is opposed to any form of constitutional reform, in particular to majority rule. To the right is the Reconstituted (Herstigte) National Party (HNP), led by Jaap Marais, which won its first parliamentary seat in the October 30 by-election and, on the extreme right, the Afrikaner Resistance Movement (ARM) led by Eugene Terre' Blanche. The HNP and ARM are not just opposed to reform but openly advocate white supremacy. Though for the time being right-wing opposition remains divided, its combined political potential was a source of concern to Botha and his ruling National Party since the balance of power may be moving to the right.

Restrictions on the Press. Intensive foreign press coverage of events in South Africa in 1985 was seen by the government as biased and distorted, with an undue influence on decision makers and others abroad. As a result, in November, the government imposed severe restrictions, with accompanying stiff penalties for noncompliance, on foreign and domestic print and broadcast journalists covering or filming "any public disturbance, disorder, riot, public violence, strike, or boycott." Journalists were not allowed into areas of unrest without police permission. Notwithstanding these restrictions, oppression and violence as well as the opinions of black South African leaders continued to receive prominent foreign media coverage. The domestic press also came under greater scrutiny with legal action against the editor of *The Cape Times,* Anthony Heard, for publishing an extensive interview with Oliver Tambo, the first full statement by the exiled African National Congress (ANC) president to appear in the South African press in 25 years. The specific charge against Heard, who faced a possibility of three years' imprisonment, was for quoting a "banned" person, illegal under the Internal Security Act.

Unofficial Dialogue with the ANC. In September seven business leaders and newspaper editors held six hours of talks in Zambia with representatives of the African National Congress and Tambo. The business community had been growing increasingly concerned about black anger and the slow pace of reforms and decided to make direct contact with the ANC. The delegation was led by Gavin Relly, the chair of Anglo-American Corporation. President Botha saw the meeting as a "betrayal," and because of his condemnation some Afrikaans businessmen did not attend. Despite major disagreements between the ANC and the business leaders, particularly over the question of nationalization, the talks were of importance because ultimately, according to Relly, "there was considerable

unanimity of view about the importance of South Africa structuring a coherent and sensible society in the future.'' For Tambo the talks were important because they were a step in trying to find ways to end ''the violence of apartheid.''

Initial efforts by a few Dutch Reformed Church clergy and Afrikaans students from Stellenbosch University to meet with the ANC were thwarted by the government, but in December, students and representatives of different churches met with African nationalists in Harare, Zimbabwe.

External Pressures. Sporadic antiapartheid campaigns have been part of the European and American political scenes for more than 25 years. Numerous lobby groups, churches, and student organizations led the early antiapartheid demonstrations and campaigns against political and economic support for the Pretoria regime. The Sharpeville massacre in 1960 and the Soweto uprising in 1976 in particular triggered significant student, church, and community opposition, which ultimately contributed to South Africa's exclusion from international sports competitions, the passage of a number of strongly worded United Nations antiapartheid resolutions, and partial divestment actions by certain academic and religious institutions. In general, however, South Africa continued to be widely viewed by politicians and investors alike as politically stable and a good economic risk.

A wave of public protest against South Africa's apartheid system sprung up throughout the United States. Demonstrations at the nation's colleges, including one at the University of Berkeley, below, rekindled memories of the 1960s. Many marchers were demanding that state and local governments as well as universities sell their South African-related holdings.

Since it is a misdemeanor in the United States to protest within 500 ft (152 m) of an embassy, more than 3,000 demonstrators, including Rep. Patricia Schroeder (D-CO), right, were arrested outside South Africa's Embassy in Washington.

AP/Wide World

The duration, intensity, and scope of the current crisis, however, sets it apart from previous upheavals. Even the pro-government Afrikaans daily *Die Beeld* noted in August that South Africa had never before been so isolated.

The ambassadors to South Africa from more than a dozen nations, including the United States and member nations of the European Community (EC), were recalled to protest the July declaration of the state of emergency. In addition, the voluntary codes of conduct for U.S., Canadian, and EC businesses in South Africa were all strengthened. By year's end, in the United States alone, 14 states and the Virgin Islands as well as 41 cities had passed laws or binding regulations prohibiting or restricting the investment of public or pension funds in South Africa. An additional 20 states and numerous cities had similar legislation pending or under consideration. As a result of increasing political instability and serious questions about profitability in the long run, American banks began to reduce the number and size of loans to South Africa in 1985. In a little more than one year, almost 30 multinational corporations either left altogether or began to reduce their involvement. On the other hand, more than 300 U.S. corporations had combined investments estimated at $2.3 billion. The total U.S. investment, including bank loans and stock holdings, was calculated at close to $15 billion.

In response to these concerns and other pressures for official action against South Africa's policy of racial domination, the U.S. Congress in 1985 debated legislation that, if passed, would have prohibited most new bank loans, the sale of nuclear power equipment and technology, the export of comput-

ers to government agencies, and the sale of South African Krugerrand gold coins in the United States. The bill proposed stiff penalties for violations of sanctions and specified that if significant progress toward eliminating apartheid were not made within 12 months, the president would have to invoke far stricter measures. These would include withdrawing South Africa's most-favored-nation trading status, banning new commercial investment in South Africa, and prohibiting the further importation of South African products. On September 9, just before the Senate was to vote on compromise measures already overwhelmingly approved by the House of Representatives, President Ronald Reagan signed an executive order imposing his own limited version of sanctions. These fell short of what Congress wanted and failed to include automatic sanctions if South Africa did not make significant reforms.

The actions of South Africa's other main business partners were somewhat mixed: France took a surprisingly strong position in announcing an immediate ban on all new investment in South Africa, while Great Britain and West Germany publicly opposed such sanctions. Japan continued to maintain the fiction that it had prohibited direct investments in South Africa for many years, even though Japanese–South African trade approached $3 billion in 1985 and Japanese cars and other goods were produced in South Africa by local companies operating under Japanese licenses.

Significant action was also taken by other countries, such as Canada, which announced a ban on the sale of computers to South African security forces, restrictions on the importation of Krugerrands, and a strengthening of the voluntary code of conduct for Canadian companies operating in South Africa. In September, Canada's Minister of External Affairs Joe Clark threatened additional diplomatic and economic sanctions, including severing diplomatic relations and a voluntary ban on crude oil and gas sales if the policies of apartheid were not changed. In addition, the Canadian government allocated $1 million to assist the families of political prisoners and detainees.

The violence and arrests of 1985 further diminished what chances remain for nonviolent change in South Africa. The dramatic arrest in December of Winnie Mandela, wife of the imprisoned ANC leader, for attempting to return to her home in Soweto in defiance of a police banning order, underscored white opposition to compromise. Greater and greater black violence, including escalation of urban sabotage, such as the bombing of a shopping center near Durban in late December, alleged to have been carried out by the ANC, will almost surely lead to the government's increased reliance on the military to restore domestic peace. At the same time, more and more angry young blacks seem unwilling to commit themselves to a nonviolent solution. The government's reforms until now have sought to achieve the impossible—maintaining white power while attempting to appease black discontent. An enduring resolution must entail a willingness on the part of whites to negotiate an equitable share of power and an end to apartheid.

AP/Wide World

A ban against the import of South Africa's Krugerrand gold coins was part of President Reagan's sanction program. Other nations and organizations, including the Commonwealth, acted similarly.

THE AMERICAN FARMER
PAST, PRESENT, AND FUTURE

by Sen. Mark Andrews (R-ND)

It is 6:00 A.M. and, like generations before him, a farmer sits quietly down to breakfast in anticipation of a long, hard day of work. Working to help feed the world, the farmer sometimes finds things going smoothly and at other times faces the natural adversities that could destroy a whole year's work in one storm, one tornado, or one insect plague. A farmer knows this struggle, but it is more than a way to earn a living; it is a way of life. Maybe this farmer will be listening to the early morning market reports or maybe he is simply listening to the first newscasts of the day.

In listening to the morning news in 1985, he may well have heard a description of the catastrophe striking his own farm or that of a neighbor. For declining farm income and a tightening of farm credit were instrumental in leading to an unusually large number of farm foreclosures and focused national, as well as international, attention on the American farmer. It was

a tumultuous year for U.S. agriculture, and the country watched anxiously while crisis after crisis unfolded.

Diversity. American farmers have accepted and utilized the most advanced technology available to produce their goods. In the past 100 years, farming has seen more progress than during man's entire history. Yet the farmer knows that these changes cannot prevent a season without rain from bringing ruin. As efficiency has increased, the farm core has not changed. Ninety-seven percent of U.S. farms are owned by individuals or partnerships. A family—with the help of a hired hand or two—can, and does, still operate a farm on its own.

American agriculture contains amazing diversity in both the types of farms and the products raised on those farms. There are colossal differences between the large-scale diversified California operations and the Florida orange groves compared with the more family-oriented, Iowa-Nebraska corn and hog operations and the open wheat fields of the Dakotas and Kansas. This diversity is a source of both benefits and problems to U.S. agriculture. It makes it very difficult to develop a comprehensive and equitable agricultural policy and to find simple solutions to specific problems facing groups of farmers. That diversity, plus differences in philosophy among various farm groups, often pits one segment of the industry against another.

History. The policies of the federal government in the last 125 years have had a decided effect on American farming. The Homestead Act of 1862, offering 160 acres (65 ha) to settlers who agreed to reside on and work the land for a minimum of five years, had particular impact. Between 1868 and 1879, 70 million acres (28 million ha) of public land were distributed under this statute. It was the catalyst that brought the land into production, developed communities, built schools and roads, and created a tax base to support the new communities.

During the 1930s the New Deal programs for agricultural America helped bridge the gap in life-styles that existed between rural and urban America. The Rural Electrification Act of 1935 brought electricity to most farms by the 1940s—thus making the daily chores, from milking cows to washing clothes, easier and more manageable. But rural America needed more than electricity, and it also needed money. The need for agricultural credit was in part satisfied by the Farm Credit Act of 1933. Eventually, the Farm Credit Act gave birth to what has become the Farm Credit System, including the Production Credit Association, the Federal Land Banks, and the Bank for Co-ops.

Also during the New Deal, the Agricultural Adjustment Administration, the forerunner of the Agricultural Stabilization and Conservation Services (ASCS), was created. The ASCS is the agency responsible for administering many of the loans and price support programs currently offered by the federal government. These programs, implemented during Franklin Roosevelt's four administrations, have influenced rural life and farming in a profound and lasting way.

About the Author: A farmer from Mapleton, ND, U.S. Sen. Mark Andrews serves on the Senate's Committee on Agriculture, Nutrition, and Forestry. Prior to his election to the Senate in November 1980, Mr. Andrews was a member of the U.S. House of Representatives for some 17 years. A graduate of North Dakota State University with a degree in agriculture, Senator Andrews is a past president of the North Dakota Crop Improvement Association and a current member of the Republican National Farm Council.

Change. The 20th century has brought dynamic change to the United States. America has been transformed from a mostly rural society to an industrial giant fueled by an increasingly sophisticated information network. With these transformations, the population migrated in large numbers into the nation's urban areas. Thus, the number of people remaining on farms dwindled in proportion to the ever-increasing population of the cities.

In the 1930s there were approximately 6.5 million farms in the United States. Today that number is slightly more than 2 million. As the number of farms has shrunk, the number of people fed by each individual farmer has skyrocketed. The average farmer in 1985 fed 79 people, compared with 1940 when one farmer fed 10.7 people. This growth would have been impossible without creative and progressive ideas for new tilling techniques, the use of modern fertilizer and pesticides to ward off disease and insects, and appropriate conservation practices. Refining agricultural techniques to produce greater yields has brought parallel developments in the area of financial and marketing services.

Progress is dominated by technology. On a farm of the 1940s, a farmer might have had a 40-horsepower tractor capable of pulling a 12-foot cultivator that today has been replaced by a 150-horsepower tractor capable of pulling a 30-foot cultivator. Advancements in chemistry have changed agricultural production and expanded the farmer's scientific expertise. Today's farmer has to select among 20 or more different chemicals that are capable of controlling weeds, insects, and other pests that can reduce yields. He has to know which chemicals he can safely combine and which ones will be deadly to him or his crops.

There are approximately 932 million acres (377 million ha) of farmland in the United States today, with an average acreage of 416 acres (168 ha) per farm. The average farm varies on a state-by-state basis from the 80-acre (32-ha) farm in Rhode Island to the 300-acre (121-ha) farm in Minnesota to the 1,100-acre (445-ha) farm/ranch in North Dakota, to the 2,800-acre (1 134-ha) ranch in New Mexico. To a large degree, the size of the farm is determined by the minimum amount of land required to earn a living.

A wide range of crops are produced in each region of the country and within each state. According to the *1985 U.S.-State Agricultural Data* from the Economic Research Service of the U.S. Department of Agriculture (USDA), the five top cash commodities produced in the United States were: cattle/calves ($28.7 billion), dairy products ($18.8 billion), corn ($12.2 billion), soybeans ($12.0 billion), and wheat ($9.0 billion).

In the past, most of the agricultural produce grown in the United States was consumed domestically. However, since 1970, the American farmer has become a provider of food on a much larger scale, resulting in his greater dependence on the export market. Currently, 40% of U.S. commodities are exported. Again according to *U.S.-State Agricultural Data,* the five largest commodities exported were: corn ($7.0 billion), wheat and flour ($6.7 billion), soybeans ($5.7 billion), live-

James A. Sugar, Black Star

The American farmer has always been the backbone of the nation's agricultural system. Although the number of farms has decreased, the average size has risen substantially.

Number of Farms (millions)

Average Farm Size (acres)

5.648	213	3.963	297	2.949	374	2.428	429	2.+	416

1950 **1960** **1970** **1980** **1985**

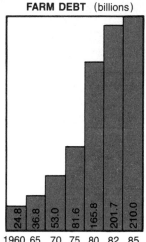

FARM DEBT (billions)

24.8	36.8	53.0	81.6	165.8	201.7	210.0

1960 65 70 75 80 82 85

stock and produce ($3.5 billion), and horticulture products ($2.6 billion). Another example of the diversity of American agriculture is farm cash income. According to the USDA, it has remained fairly level since 1980 at $35–40 billion. It peaked in 1980 at $40 billion and has tapered off since then to the lower end of an estimated $33–39 billion in 1985. Within this figure for farm income, there is a story of winners and losers. The cash income of crop farmers dropped by 20%, while livestock farm's cash income rose 6%. Among crop farms, the income from cash grains and cotton declined while the income from horticulture, fruit, and other crops rose. In livestock, poultry farms had higher cash incomes while the incomes from dairy and cattle, hogs, and sheep declined.

The total U.S. farm debt in 1985 was about $210 billion. This figure was down slightly from 1984 but up 27% from $165 billion in 1980. Increasing debt in the face of decreasing farm income indicates troubled times ahead for the U.S. agricultural sector. To make matters worse, the value of assets was declining. These assets are used as collateral when seeking loans for such expenses as seed, fertilizer, chemicals, and machinery. Since 1981, total farm assets have decreased about $59 billion to $1.031 trillion in 1984. That means that farmers will have increasing difficulty finding collateral to secure loans, and it will become increasingly difficult to find credit.

Between 1984 and 1985 the value of farmland in the United States declined as much as 25% in some areas and 12% overall. In parts of the Corn Belt and the central part of the nation, farmland values have fallen 40–50% since 1981. The overall farm debt/asset ratio rose from 20% to 22% from January 1984 to January 1985, due mostly to the decline in asset value.

The Situation in 1985. In 1985 the situation on the average farm was not quite so bright as many had hoped. As mentioned earlier, farm income was down, the asset base was

Mounting debts and discouraging prospects for the future are forcing a growing number of American farmers to sell their land and equipment. From 1981 to 1985, more than 20,000 U.S. farms were sold at auction.

Max Winter, Picture Group

President Reagan and General Secretary Gorbachev spent a total of five hours in private discussion at their Geneva summit. Reagan described his counterpart as "a good speaker and a good listener."

AP/Wide World

12 President Samuel K. Doe of Liberia announces that loyalist forces have foiled an attempted coup.

13 The volcano Nevado del Ruiz in Colombia erupts twice, causing floods and mudslides that kill up to 25,000.

15 Great Britain and Ireland sign a treaty giving the latter a formal consultative role in the governing of Northern Ireland. Unionists denounce the agreement.

20 Ending one of the bloodiest five-day periods in South Africa in more than a year, 13 persons are killed in clashes with police in the black township of Mamelodi, near Pretoria.

21 U.S. President Reagan and Soviet leader Gorbachev conclude their three-day summit in Geneva. No major breakthroughs were made, but both sides characterize the talks as promising.

Former U.S. counterintelligence analyst Jonathan Jay Pollard is arrested in Washington and charged with selling classified code information to Israel.

23 Retired CIA analyst Larry Wu-Tai Chin is arrested in Washington and accused of supplying classified documents to China.

Iran announces that Ayatollah Hussein Ali Montazeri has been formally designated as the eventual successor to Ayatollah Ruhollah Khomeini as the nation's religious leader.

24 Egyptian special forces storm an EgyptAir jetliner that had been hijacked two days before en route from Athens to Cairo and then forced to land in Malta. About 60 passengers are killed.

Pope John Paul II opens an extraordinary two-week Synod of Bishops to review the Second Vatican Council of 1962–65.

Voters in Honduras elect José Azcona Hoyo of the Liberal Party as president; the outcome is contested.

29 Left-wing Japanese extremists disrupt the morning rush hour in Tokyo and Osaka by knocking out 23 major commuter lines.

13   Belgium's governing coalition, led by Prime Minister Wilfried Martens, is returned to power in parliamentary elections.

15   Nicaragua's President Daniel Ortega declares a yearlong state of emergency in response to U.S. "aggression."

23   Morocco's King Hassan II announces a unilateral cease-fire in his country's war with Western Saharan rebels.

24   As part of the United Nations' 40th anniversary celebration, U.S. President Reagan addresses the General Assembly. More than 80 heads of government and other special envoys have or will have addressed the body during the ten-day observance.

Leftist rebels in El Salvador release the daughter of President José Napoleón Duarte, kidnapped one month earlier.

25   Argentina's President Raúl Alfonsín declares a 60-day state of siege following a series of bombings said to be linked to the political right and former military junta leaders.

27   The Kansas City Royals win baseball's World Series with an 11–0 victory in Game 7 over the St. Louis Cardinals.

28   Retired U.S. Navy warrant officer John Walker, Jr., pleads guilty to spying for the Soviet Union and receives a life sentence. As part of the plea bargain, his son, Michael Walker, receives a sentence of 25 years.

29   Liberia's military ruler Samuel K. Doe and his National Democratic Party are declared the winners of that country's first multiparty election, held on October 15.

AP/Wide World

Having escaped to the Soviet Embassy in Washington, KGB officer Vitaly Yurchenko claims that his reported defection during the summer was really a case of abduction by the CIA.

November

4   Vitaly Yurchenko, a Soviet intelligence officer who reportedly had defected to the West during the summer, announces at the Soviet Embassy in Washington that he had been kidnapped and drugged by U.S. agents. He claims to have escaped the CIA and says he will return to the Soviet Union. U.S. officials strongly deny his story.

5   Off-year elections are held across the United States.

Tanzania's President Julius K. Nyerere retires at age 63, turning over the office to Ali Hassan Mwinyi.

6   The U.S. space shuttle *Challenger* concludes a seven-day mission sponsored and run by West Germany.

Poland's General Secretary Wojciech Jaruzelski assumes the presidency and turns over the premiership to Zbigniew Messner.

7   In Bogotá, Colombia, government troops raid the Palace of Justice and free several hundred hostages taken by leftist M-19 guerrillas the day before. Among the 100 or more persons killed are the president of the Supreme Court.

Otis R. Bowen, a former governor of Indiana, is named to succeed Margaret Heckler as U.S. secretary of health and human services. Heckler resigned October 1.

8   The five-party government coalition of Italy's Prime Minister Bettino Craxi, which had collapsed October 17 over his handling of the *Achille Lauro* incident, wins a vote of confidence in the Senate. It had been confirmed by the Chamber of Deputies two days earlier.

9   Challenger Gary Kasparov of the Soviet Union defeats countryman Anatoly Karpov for the world chess championship.

Prince Charles of Great Britain and Diana, princess of Wales, arrive in Washington for a much-publicized three-day visit.

AP/Wide World

15 Pilots of United Airlines end a 29-day strike.

19 Thirteen persons, including four U.S. Marines and two U.S. civilians, are killed by leftist guerrillas in El Salvador.

21 In São Paulo, Brazil, forensic experts confirm that a skeleton exhumed two weeks before unquestionably is that of Dr. Josef Mengele, the fugitive Nazi criminal.

23 An Air India jetliner suddenly explodes and crashes into the Atlantic Ocean near Ireland, killing all 329 persons aboard. A bomb is suspected.

A bomb blast at Japan's New Tokyo International Airport in Narita kills two baggage handlers and four other workers.

24 Francesco Cossiga, 56, a Christian Democrat, is elected to a seven-year term as president of Italy, a largely ceremonial post. He succeeds Sandro Pertini, who retired.

The U.S. space shuttle *Discovery,* carrying a crew that includes a Saudi prince and a French pilot, ends a seven-day mission.

30 The remaining 39 Americans being held hostage by Lebanese Shiites in Beirut, Lebanon, are released, driven to Damascus, and flown to West Germany on their way home. Arrangements for the release were mediated by Syria.

From the hijacking to the release, the Lebanese hostage crisis got heavy TV coverage.

J. L. Atlan, Sygma

July

At the 18th annual convention of the National Organization for Women, held July 19–21 in New Orleans, Eleanor Smeal, above, defeated incumbent Judy Goldsmith to become president.

Four days after major abdominal surgery August 13, President Reagan enjoys a visit by Chief of Staff Regan (right) and Vice-President Bush at the Bethesda (MD) Navy Medical Center.

1 The Israeli cabinet declares a state of economic emergency and imposes a broad series of austerity measures to cut inflation.

2 Longtime Foreign Minister Andrei Gromyko is named president of the USSR. Eduard A. Shevardnadze becomes foreign minister.

3 Prime Minister Eugenia Charles of Dominica is sworn in for a second term. She won reelection July 1.

6 The Zimbabwe African National Union of President Robert Mugabe wins Zimbabwe's first national election since independence.

7 West Germany's Boris Becker, 17, becomes the youngest player ever to win the men's singles title at Wimbledon. Martina Navratilova won her sixth women's crown the day before.

10 The Soviet Union and China sign a $14 billion bilateral trade pact for 1986–90.

Navy Adm. William J. Crowe, Jr., is named to succeed Gen. John W. Vessey as chairman of the Joint Chiefs of Staff.

13 Live Aid, a rock music telethon staged in Philadelphia and London, raises an estimated $70 million for African famine victims.

15 A growth removed from the large intestine of President Reagan in surgery July 13 is found to be cancerous. The growth had been found during the removal of a benign polyp July 12.

More than 2,200 delegates from around the world gather in Nairobi, Kenya, for the 11-day UN Decade for Women Conference.

19 An earthen dam bursts in northern Italy, releasing a wall of mud and water that kills more than 200 persons.

James C. Miller III is named to succeed David A. Stockman as director of the Office of Management and Budget. Stockman's resignation was announced July 9.

20 South Africa's Prime Minister Pieter W. Botha declares a state of emergency, the first of its kind there in 25 years, to quell growing unrest in the nation's black townships.

Officials of the European Monetary Committee (EMC) devalue the Italian lira against the other EMC currencies. The lira had plunged on the Milan foreign currency exchange the day before.

23 President Reagan welcomes China's President Li Xiannin to the White House. U.S. and Chinese officials sign a long-delayed cooperation agreement on nuclear power.

24 India's Prime Minister Rajiv Gandhi and Sikh leader Harchand Singh Longowal sign an accord to ease tensions in the Punjab.

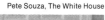

Al Stephenson, Picture Group

The American Agriculture Movement and other farm groups marched on Washington early in the year, calling for debt aid, stronger price supports, and other subsidies. Though some help was forthcoming, many farmers were dismayed at the administration position.

Dennis Brack, Black Star

eroding, and credit was becoming more difficult for farmers to obtain. In addition, much of the progress that had been made in improving the rural living conditions was at a standstill or receding. Part of the dilemma for the farmer in the mid-1980s was that, while the U.S. farmer received less, the price paid by importers increased dramatically because of the higher value of the dollar abroad. As interest rates and a growing federal deficit kited the American dollar, the international market made it difficult for farmers, and other producers, to make the return they had planned on. For example, in Rotterdam, the Netherlands, a major port for U.S. products entering Europe, one U.S. dollar brought 1.99 Dutch guilders in 1980, and in 1984 brought 3.21 guilders. This resulted in a 60% increase in the cost of U.S. agricultural commodities abroad; thus, the American farmer's ability to compete in the world market was severely impeded. Add to this situation the protectionist government policies of other nations and the farmers' need to sell three out of every five bushels of grain

Ben Weaver, Camera 5

FarmAid, a benefit concert held in Champaign, IL, on September 22, raised a reported $10 million in contributions. More than 50 country & western and rock 'n' roll acts performed in the 14-hour event.

produced to markets abroad and the result was disastrous for American farmers.

The Future. As we approach a new century, American agriculture is at a crossroad. It is apparent that the U.S. economy, and the farm agriculture sector in particular, must adapt to a new international environment that promises to be totally different from that of the past. Technology, macroeconomics, and integration of agricultural production into the international economic system will significantly affect the future of American agriculture. Technology will continue to have a substantial and growing impact on the production capabilities of the American farmer. The Congressional Office of Technology Assessment (OTA) estimates that there are approximately 150 emerging technologies that could revolutionize agriculture. The ability to control and increase the size of cattle for beef, control the sex of dairy calves and increase their milk production by 10% without increasing their food intake, and alter crops genetically in order to increase their resistance to disease and pests and to produce their own fertilizer are just three exciting possibilities.

The effect of macroeconomic policy on American agriculture also will alter the course of the farm economy. In the last few years the agricultural sector has become "one of the most credit-dependent, interest rate–sensitive sectors of our economy." Accordingly, it has become acutely sensitive to the Treasury's fiscal and monetary policies. Consequently, it is likely that farming will become increasingly affected by changes in monetary policy and real interest rates than by farm legislation and USDA policy. In the book *A Tough Row to Hoe: The 1985 Farm Bill and Beyond,* William Galston estimates that reducing the federal deficit to 2% of the gross national product (GNP) would mean a multibillion-dollar increase in annual farm income—anywhere from a 25–60% increase. This action could stabilize land values and decrease pressure on lending institutions. Without any positive change in fiscal and monetary policy, real interest rates will continue to jeopardize farm livelihood, as will the resulting tight money policies. This of course would translate into still thousands more leaving the farmlands.

Third, American agriculture must move toward a broader integration into the world economy. This can be done in two ways. We can either restrict production to avoid surpluses of overpriced commodities or else expand the export base.

These three elements molding the future of American agriculture are not dissimilar from those affecting other sectors of the economy. However, they seem to hold an inordinate amount of influence over agriculture and must be properly factored into our agricultural planning. If we plan judiciously and do not restrict the efficiency of the American farmer, we can continue to help feed the world. We must protect the farmer from careless fiscal policies and make certain that the door to international trading is kept wide open for our agricultural commodities markets. The family farm is still uniquely and truly an American institution supplying consumers with quality food and fiber at reasonable prices and giving the nation an opportunity to share its abundance with the world.

AP/Wide World

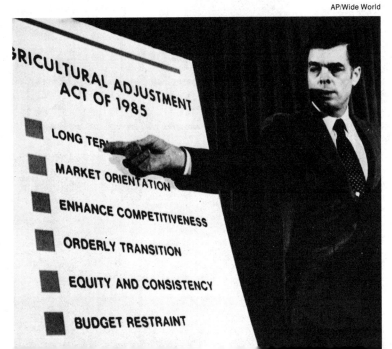

Secretary of Agriculture John Block unveiled the administration's farm bill February 22. The controversial, market-oriented program was designed to reduce the federal role in American agriculture. After extensive debate and modification in the House and Senate, President Reagan on December 23 signed an omnibus bill reauthorizing farm programs for fiscal 1986–90. The total cost was estimated at $170 billion.

CRIME
THE VICTIM'S RESPONSE

By Hubert Williams

On Dec. 22, 1984, Bernhard Hugo Goetz, a 37-year-old electronics engineer who had been badly beaten by muggers four years earlier, boarded a New York City subway train, carrying a concealed handgun. On the train, four teenagers approached him—threateningly, he said—and asked for $5. Goetz drew out his gun and fired five shots, hitting each of the youths. One of them was paralyzed below the waist.

What Goetz did was illegal, and he would face criminal charges for it. Nevertheless, in the weeks following the incident, large numbers of citizens expressed support for his act. Some said they were "sick and tired" of being helpless victims; others voiced frustration with the criminal justice system. For the public, journalists, and criminologists, the shooting and its aftermath raised complex questions about acceptable responses to danger, fear, frustration, and crime victimization. Was the groundswell of support for Goetz an indication that Americans are consumed by a fear of crime and convinced that the criminal justice system cannot deal effectively with offenders? Would the expressions of favor for Goetz swell into a tide of similar acts by other frightened citizens? What can be done about people who take the law into their own hands?

Reactions and Reasons. Several months after the incident, it appeared that Americans were in fact no more likely to take the law into their own hands than they had been before. Still not known, however, was the extent to which the initial public response to Goetz's act had signaled widespread fear of crime and frustration with the criminal justice system. For as criminologists, criminal justice practitioners, and law enforcement specialists have continued to consider these issues, it has been recognized that the support for Goetz may have had bases

About the Author: Hubert Williams is president of the Police Foundation, a Washington-based nonprofit organization for the study of police policies and practices. He assumed that post in mid-1985, after serving 11 years as director of the Newark, NJ, police force. He had been a member of that force for a total of 22 years.

In New York City and elsewhere, the fear of crime in recent years has given rise to such citizen patrol organizations as the Guardian Angels, identifiable by red berets.

Photo left: © Andy Levin, Black Star

© Charles Steiner, Picture Group

other than simple fear. For some people, at least, Goetz may have been just an example of a traditional type of American hero. To them he represented the lone actor who, by his wits or the use of violence, was able to prove himself more powerful than either the outlaws or the system. Praise for such solitary heroes may be loudest when they act in the name of a good, or at least popular, cause. Among those who have been so admired are presidents, astronauts, religious leaders, and others whose deeds could be considered noble. On the other hand, certain lone figures who have acted in the name of lawlessness—from Western gunfighters to 1920s bank robbers—became popular folk heroes.

When people applaud this kind of hero, they may, at some level, mean to support the idea of robbing big banks or shooting threatening youths on subways. It is at least as likely, however, they they are applauding someone who had the courage to do something daring for which they would lack the nerve. Certainly some percentage of Goetz's supporters were people who are simply afraid of crime. And perhaps some greater percentage shared a strong concern for the victims of crime. But the public reaction to Goetz indeed was a complex one, with a variety of bases in American history and culture.

Managing Fear. To the extent that public attitudes and reactions to crime are governed by fear, the law enforcement and criminal justice communities increasingly are seeking new understandings and methods of control.

The response to subway gunman Bernhard Goetz (center, page 47), who claimed self-defense in a December 1984 shooting, underscored public frustration with the criminal justice system. According to a Gallup poll, 46% of American adults keep a gun or other weapon to deal with a possible crime.

There is no research that indicates whether people would feel less afraid if they were, like Goetz, in a state of armed readiness against potential criminals. It is known, however, that fear of crime is related to several personal characteristics. Age, sex, and ethnic background appear to be related to the probability of an individual experiencing fear of crime, as are a number of social and other environmental factors. Since 1982 the Police Foundation, in cooperation with the National Institute of Justice and the police departments of Houston (TX) and Newark (NJ), has been conducting research on strat-

Defending Against Crime: *An Opinion Poll*

On February 28 and March 1, 1985, the Gallup Organization conducted a poll for Newsweek magazine on the Bernhard Goetz case, self-defense, and protection against crime. Telephone interviews were conducted with 1,009 randomly selected adults.

Among the more interesting results of the poll were that a clear majority of respondents approved of Goetz's action; more than two thirds believed that taking the law into one's own hands may be justified by circumstances; and nearly half did not have strong confidence in police protection from violent crimes. Nevertheless, 78% said that they thought the streets would be more dangerous if most people carried guns. (The margin of error is plus or minus 4 percentage points; some "Don't Know" responses are omitted.)

From what you know about the Goetz case so far, do you tend to approve or disapprove of Goetz shooting four youths on a New York subway?

Approve	57%
Disapprove	28%
Don't know	15%

Do you feel that taking the law into one's own hands, often called vigilantism, is justified by circumstances?

Always	3%
Sometimes	68%
Never	23%

If the situation arose, would you use deadly force against another person in self-defense?

Yes 78%   No 13%   Don't know 9%

If most people carried guns, do you think the streets would be safer or more dangerous?

Safer	11%
More dangerous	78%
No difference	3%
Don't know	8%

Which of the following steps do you take or have you taken to deal with crime?

Keep a gun or other weapon	46%
Try not to go out alone at night	54%
Avoid certain areas even during the day	43%
Carry a gun or other weapon	10%
Carry a defensive device such as Mace, a whistle, or alarm	17%

How much confidence do you have in the ability of the police to protect you from violent crime?

Great deal	15%
Quite a bit	37%
Not very much	39%
None at all	6%
Don't know	3%

Do you think the Goetz incident has made people more willing to physically resist criminals or not?

Yes 55%   No 24%   Don't know 21%

egies that the police might employ to reduce fears not directly tied to actual crimes. One important finding has been that the availability of the police for frequent, informal contact with citizens does reduce fear levels, perhaps because the citizens come to feel that the police do care about average, law-abiding people—even those who are not victims—and their problems.

At the same time, police and other criminal justice agencies also are becoming more concerned with the impact of actual victimization. In this case, follow-up telephone contact by the police with victims did not have the desired effect of

© Andrew Sacks, Black Star

© Rob Nelson, Picture Group

Without taking the law into one's own hands, say law enforcement officials, the ordinary citizen can combat crime in a variety of ways. Martial arts have become increasingly popular, both for self-defense and for their exercise value. For the home, an alarm system or a well-trained guard dog can provide effective protection.

© Rosanne Olson, Black Star

reducing fear levels, perhaps because the calls came too long after the crime. New programs being implemented by Houston and several other police departments are designed to involve the police much more quickly and directly in the identification and resolution of victim problems.

Research has shown that victims may suffer more from emotional upset than from physical harm or property loss. For example, persons whose homes have been robbed may have to relocate before they can lose the sense that their private space has been irreparably violated. The person who has been robbed may have lost money or valuable possessions, but he or she also may experience feelings of diminished dignity and personal efficacy. And of course, many victims experience heightened levels of fear.

Some victims may deal with such feelings by retreating—either by moving away from the crime scene or by withdrawing from public streets into locked homes. Others, rather than take flight, may fight to restore lost dignity and the sense of being able to take care of one's self. The possibility of the latter response may be the most important reason to consider carefully the behavior of Bernhard Goetz. To the extent that victims react with a combination of fear and anger that drives them to attempt retaliation, they may become a risk to the safety of citizens around them and may risk becoming felons themselves.

Other cases of the urge to retaliate describe the victim's relief when the retaliation is not actually carried out. Writing in *The New York Times,* a man told of his reaction to an attempted burglary of his home. After the incident, the man got his shotgun from the attic and used it to guard his family and property for two nights. The opportunity for retaliation never did present itself, and the gun was returned to the attic. The owner later was glad. In a similar case, a professor recounted having been beaten and robbed in his own neighborhood by a group of young males. Normally a nonviolent person, the professor spent several days walking the area with a pistol in his pocket, hoping the same group would approach him again. Months later, he expressed relief at not having encountered them and horror at the thought of what he might have done.

Assistance Programs. There are no reliable data on the frequency with which crime victims feel a real urge to retaliate, and there is no reason to believe that any significant number of those who actively seek retaliation or who adopt potentially lethal methods of self-protection actually become assailants. Still, the fact that some victims do react with deadly anger is an indication of the kinds of psychological needs that some victims may have. And indeed it is this very type of need to which new police victim assistance programs may be best able to respond.

In these programs, officers are trained not only to provide the victim with information about available victim services but also are trained to assess the psychological state of the person. If the officer determines that the victim is likely to suffer emo-

tional problems as a result of the crime, the officer may recommend either that the victim seek counseling or that a mental health agency have follow-up contact with the victim. If a psychological problem is not apparent, the officer at least can:

- listen attentively to the victim's story, allowing him or her to "talk through" the incident and any resulting feelings,
- indicate to the victim that the police understand the troubling nature of the incident,
- help the victim handle any immediate practical problems that may have resulted from the incident,
- assure the victim that he or she is not responsible for the incident,
- predict for the victim the kinds of emotional reactions that he or she might experience,
- explain the steps that will occur in the police's handling of the case,
- inform the victim of available victim services,
- provide information about ways to prevent similar incidents in the future,
- and leave the victim with the name and number of someone at the police department to contact for assistance or additional information about the case.

Across the United States, police departments are conducting an increasing number of community crime prevention and victims assistance programs.

© Robert A. Isaacs, Photo Researchers

While such contact by the police certainly cannot eliminate all of the trauma for the crime victim, research indicates that attention to the issues outlined above addresses many of the concerns common to crime victims. As the first institution with which a victim typically has contact after the crime, the police department—if officers are properly trained—is in the best position to help reduce post-victimization trauma.

This kind of involvement by police departments represents another in the growing number and variety of victim assistance programs sponsored by the criminal justice system. Some type of victim assistance program now can be found in all 50 states. According to the National Organization for Victim Assistance, 27 states help fund general victim and witness assistance programs in local communities; 49 states have funding for domestic violence programs; and 34 states fund services for sexual assault victims. In addition, 39 states and the Virgin Islands support victim compensation programs to help cover costs deriving from the crime. And although these figures represent a dramatic increase over the past decade in official attention to the needs of crime victims, fewer than 20% of all prosecutors' offices in the United States have units that provide assistance to victims and other prosecution witnesses. Moreover, since only about 10% of all suspected offenders ever are prosecuted, it is apparent that programs based at this level of the criminal justice system do not affect the great majority of victims.

While it will never be possible to spare all citizens from being victims of crime, the new approaches currently being tried may help reduce both the physical and psychological trauma of crime. In doing so, they may also help reduce the society's fear of crime and the urge to retaliate.

BACK PAIN
Risks, Causes, Cures

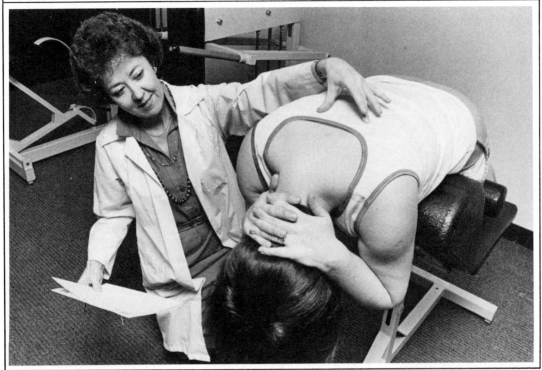

Brian Willer, "Maclean's"

By Dr. Augustus A. White III

Back pain is one of the most troublesome and complex medical problems in the United States today. At least three out of every five adults will have a significant complaint of back problems at some time in their lives. Back pain is second only to the common cold as a cause of time lost from work, representing more than $16 billion in costs. In some industries, as much as 5% of annual revenue may go to medical expenses, workmen's compensation, and other outlays for employees with low-back problems.

There is, however, a brighter side to the problem. Within three weeks of injury, 70% of people with back pain will have recovered; within three months, 90% will be well again. Moreover, with the help of some basic education and treatment, most back pain sufferers will survive the ordeal without any serious long-term consequences.

Who Gets Backaches—And How? Anyone is susceptible to a pain-inducing back injury, but some population groups have been shown to be at higher risk than others. The most likely sufferers are 25–50 years old. Men are slightly more prone to

About the Author: Dr. Augustus A. White III is professor of orthopedic surgery at Harvard Medical School and orthopedic surgeon-in-chief at Boston's Beth Israel Hospital. Dr. White is widely recognized for his work in spine research and has contributed numerous articles to professional journals. His books include *Your Aching Back—A Doctor's Guide to Relief* (1983). Dr. White wishes to acknowledge the assistance of Ms. Susan Adams in the preparation of this article.

have back pain than women, though pregnant women are particularly susceptible. Cigarette smokers, people who spend a great deal of time driving a motor vehicle, practical nurses, package and other material handlers—especially those involved in frequent bending, lifting, and twisting—and people with sedentary occupations are all prone to have backaches.

The causes of back pain are numerous and varied. Perhaps the best known is the displaced or herniated intervertebral disc. Located between the bones of the spinal column, intervertebral discs are similar in structure to a jelly doughnut. As a natural aging process, the nucleus tends to dry out and the exterior layers become more brittle and fragmented. One consequence of this change may be displacement of some part of the disc to a position in which it irritates other tissues and nerves, causing back and/or leg pain (sciatica). This is one of the most severe forms of back pain, whose treatment may involve surgical intervention.

Another common cause is arthritis, or inflammation of the spinal joints. The human spine includes a number of small joints, each about the size of a thumbnail, which are vulnerable to virtually any kind of arthritis. The most common types affecting the spine are degenerative (wear) arthritis and ankylosing spondylitis, a painful inflammatory condition that ultimately results in stiffening of the back.

Sports activities, an accidental fall, or vigorous lifting or jerking also may give rise to back pain. If excessive force is exerted on the spine, the result can be a small bone fracture or a rupture or strain of muscles and ligaments. The pain usually occurs immediately, but in some cases there is a delay of several hours or days.

Pregnancy is a frequent cause of back pain because of the increased body weight, the forward shift of the center of gravity, and some laxity of the ligaments resulting from hormonal changes. In women after menopause, an important cause of back pain is osteoporosis. In this condition, a loss of mineral content makes the bones in the spine much more vulnerable to fracture. Even minor physical stress, as from misstepping off a curb or lifting a baby, can cause a small fracture.

Finally, any discussion of the causes of backache must include the psychological component. It has been shown that stress, depression, financial problems, or even general dissatisfaction with work or home life can be a significant factor in the onset or perpetuation of back pain.

Prevention. Although accident and aging contribute heavily to the incidence of back injury, there are several things a person can do to shift the odds in his or her favor. These can be remembered as the three Es: education, exercise, and eating.

Basic knowledge and understanding are important in the prevention of any disease, especially back pain. Familiarity with the structure and the mechanics of the spine may help a person avoid injury or recover faster from it. Figure 1 is an anatomical picture of the human back, showing the upper (cervical), mid- (thoracic), and lower (lumbar) spine, as well as

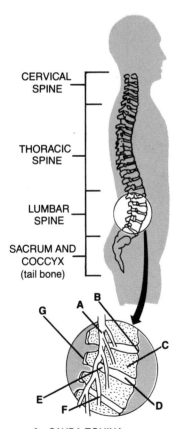

CERVICAL SPINE

THORACIC SPINE

LUMBAR SPINE

SACRUM AND COCCYX (tail bone)

A. CAUDA EQUINA
B. DISC (annulus fibrosus)
C. VERTEBRAL BODY
D. DISC (nucleus pulposus)
E. DISC (herniated)
F. SCIATIC NERVE ROOT
G. SPINOUS PROCESS

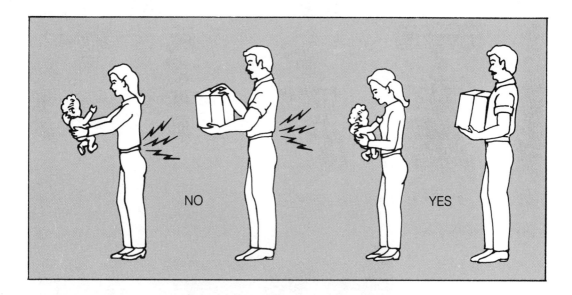

NO

YES

other basic structures. Included in the diagram are the intervertebrate discs discussed above. Figure 2 demonstrates some of the mechanical activities that are potentially damaging to the unconditioned spine. Lifting heavy loads too far away from the body or bending forward with the spine unsupported are perhaps the best ways to hurt one's back. Another key point in spine mechanics is illustrated by the tavern foot rail. Some enterprising innkeeper recognized that with prolonged standing it is much more comfortable and less taxing on the back to have one foot supported on a rail. This flexes the hip and relaxes an important psoas muscle that attaches to the front of the spine on one end and just below the hip joint on the other. Another simple rule is to avoid excessive twisting and arching, motions that put stress on the disc, posterior bone structures, and those thumbnail spine joints.

Next in the three Es comes exercise. Its value in back pain prophylaxis was evidenced by a study of Los Angeles firemen, which showed that those who were in good physical condition and not overweight were less likely to report absent from work because of back pain than were their poorly conditioned, overweight colleagues. This, naturally, also raises the importance of the third E—eating, or rather, eating in moderation. The more excess weight a person carries, the greater the stress on the spine. In a person who is overweight, the center of gravity is shifted forward by a protuberant abdomen, making the spine more susceptible to strain or injury. The rules for the final two Es, therefore, are easy: exercise more and eat less.

Nonsurgical Treatments. The treatments for back pain are as numerous and varied as the causes. Among the nonsurgical treatments, oral medication is usually the first. These may include aspirin and other anti-inflammatory drugs, steroids, pain killers, muscle relaxants, and mood-elevating drugs. Then there are a number of drugs that can be injected in various places. Steroids may be given intramuscularly, intrave-

The forces on the back depend on the weight of the object lifted, the weight of the upper body, muscle force, and arm lever. In the two "NO" diagrams, the people carrying the objects away from their bodies create long arm levers, requiring more muscle force. In the "YES" diagrams, the lever is shorter and the muscle—and back—forces are reduced.

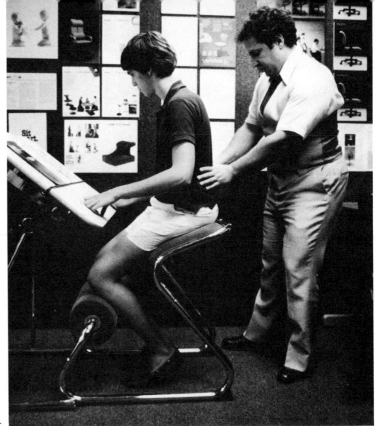

The pervasiveness of back pain has given rise to a multimillion dollar market for special chairs, pillows, massagers, and other aids. Among the hottest sellers is the Balans chair, actually a stool with a seat and padded knee rest. The sloped design takes pressure off the spine and forces the user to maintain proper posture.

Steve Liss, Gamma-Liaison

nously, or in the back itself. Local anesthetic agents may be directed to several regions of the spine. More recently, two enzymes—chymopapain and collagenase—have been developed for independent injection into the intervertebral disc.

There are also ways to change the stresses on the spine and relax its muscles. These include bed rest, the use of braces and corsets, spinal manipulation, spinal traction, exercise, weight loss, massage, and application of heat to the back muscles.

Another group of treatment modalities involves blocking or inhibiting the pain signals that come from the back and go to the brain. These include TENS (transcutaneous electrical nerve stimulation), acupuncture, cold-pack stimulation, facet joint denervation (destruction of nerves around back joints), and implantation of neurostimulators.

Finally, there are a number of cognitive and behavioral treatments that involve back pain schools, pain rehabilitation programs, biofeedback, and psychotherapy as well as specific behavior modification programs.

Because the causes of back pain are so varied and often so complex, it is difficult to prescribe any generalized self-management program. Certainly there is no reliable substitute for medical evaluation and treatment by a competent physician. In the case of minor back pain, however, the sufferer may be helped by a few easy self-care procedures: one to two weeks of bed rest with aspirin and an electrical heating pad; gradual return to normal activities; and the institution of a specific exercise program, such as swimming. For those who

improve only slowly, a corset may be used. For those who show no improvement after about two weeks, medical consultation should be sought.

Surgery. In only rare circumstances is surgery required to alleviate back pain. In very rare cases, a tumor or infection might demand surgical treatment. Another disorder that might require an operation is a very large herniated disc that has caused paralysis and/or loss of control of bladder function. Except for the previously described situations, surgery for back pain is almost always elective. That is, the patient has a choice. For a disc problem, surgery is appropriately considered when the patient has had six to eight weeks of nonoperative management, including one to two weeks of bed rest. In addition, there should be certain abnormalities on physical examination and some evidence of a disc problem visible on a CT (computerized tomography) scan or a myelogram (X ray taken with fluid in the spinal canal). With the proper indications and a qualified surgeon, the patient can expect an 80–95% chance of good results.

Spinal surgery may be appropriately considered for a number of other conditions. In some patients, long-standing back pain can be caused by scoliosis (curvature of the spine) or spondylolisthesis (abnormal displacement of the spine). These conditions may be helped by a broad category of back operation called spine fusions. In these procedures, bone is transplanted from elsewhere in the body (or from a donor) and implanted into the spine; solid bone eventually develops across one or more segments of the spine, eliminating motion and thereby relieving the pain. As in the case of any type of surgery, a patient who has any uncertainties about the procedure or feels at all pushed or rushed should seek a second opinion.

The Future. Advances in the treatment of back pain will depend in large measure on the extent and quality of basic research. There are several areas in which new, in-depth studies will be particularly helpful in understanding the causes and possible treatments of back disorders. Epidemiology is one such area. For example, population studies have already shown that people who smoke, lift a lot, or drive a lot are prone to disc problems. Future research into the role of psychological and emotional factors in back pain should prove valuable in designing prevention and treatment techniques. Anatomical and biomechanical research should provide new insights into just what spinal structures cause back pain under what conditions. Biomedical research will shed light on the role of nutrition and toxic substances in back pain. And clinical research will develop new and better surgical and nonsurgical treatment methods for the backache sufferer.

In short, there is a serious need for a great deal more research in the field of back pain. Private individuals, private foundations, government agencies, and the business community all have a vested interest in contributing to research on this widespread and complex problem.

Bo Brown, Rothco

"I'm having back trouble— can't get my boss off it."

EAST ASIA
—From World War to Economic Emergence

E. Jahn, Bruce Coleman

Hong Kong's Connaught Center is a fitting symbol of the development that has occurred not only in the colony but in East Asia generally.

About the Author: Ron Richardson is deputy business editor of the *Far Eastern Economic Review,* published in Hong Kong. As a member of the magazine's editorial staff since 1976, Mr. Richardson has witnessed firsthand the economic growth occurring in Taiwan, South Korea, and Hong Kong. He also has been a member of the staff of *The Guardian,* London, and has written numerous articles for the *Financial Times* of London and the London *Times.*

By Ron Richardson

Late in the summer of 1945, farmers were working the patchwork of fields along the coast of Pinang Island, off the northwest coast of the Malay Peninsula. For the first time in three and a half years Japanese occupation forces were not lurking nearby. Today those farms are lost under a sprawl of electronics factories. Similarly in 1945, the malodorous fishing port of Pohang in South Korea was celebrating the departure of the Japanese constabulary after 35 years of colonial occupation. Today the city is the site of one of the most modern steel plants in the world.

Japan itself, physically and psychologically shattered by defeat in a war of its own making and in shock over the deaths of at least 120,000 of its people fallen victim in man's first nuclear attacks, was just starting to realize that its government was to be in the hands of its conqueror, the United States. Today Japan has developed an industrial capability sufficient to surpass even the United States as an exporter of manufactured goods. It also is challenging many of the industries of its one-time ruler in the conqueror's home markets.

In the 40 years since the end of World War II, the area of East Asia, Japan's former wartime empire, has emerged as the world's fastest-growing economic region. Led by Japan, the only economy in the Far East with a significant manufacturing base before 1945, many of the non-Communist countries of East Asia have mounted a concerted drive for economic development based on production of goods intended primarily for export. Those nations that have made the effort—notably Japan itself, South Korea, Taiwan, Singapore, the colony of Hong Kong, Malaysia, Thailand, and to a lesser extent the Philippines and Indonesia—have been outstandingly successful. With economies geared especially toward trade, their annual rate of increase of exports since 1950 has averaged about 18%—half as much again as the growth of world trade in the same period. Propelled by the surge of development in East Asia, the share in global trade of the whole Asian region, stretching from Afghanistan to the Pacific island states, has grown from about 13% in 1950 to just more than 18% in the mid-1980s.

Japan's Economic Recovery—A Model. The model and catalyst for this remarkable economic performance has been Japan, which, based on statistics gathered by the International Monetary Fund (IMF), has achieved real (after allowing for inflation) economic growth of more than 900% since 1950. The total real value of output of Japan's economy in the mid-1980s is more than ten times what it was in 1950, when much of the reconstruction from the wartime devastation was complete. (By comparison, for the same period, the total real output of the United States has grown just more than four times and of the industrialized world as a whole about 3.5 times.)

The defeat suffered by Japan in the Pacific War was the turning point in the transformation of East Asia from a collection of colonies and languishing kingdoms into the rising industrial states of today. Japan emerged from the war with its industries wrecked by U.S. bombing. In the process of rebuilding, with the help of extensive U.S. aid, factories were modernized by the installation of the latest equipment. The occupation administration, headed by Gen. Douglas MacArthur and unfettered by domestic political constraints, was able to push through modernizing reforms that would have been impossible under normal circumstances in the face of vested interests.

Tenant farming was abolished, freeing millions of peasants from the land, and a strong civilian bureaucracy, fostered by MacArthur to block the reemergence of a military leadership, began the economic planning that chartered a course for Japan's industries for the decades ahead. The new, civilian leaders realized that the only way they could secure for their industries the vital raw materials that their nation had failed to win through military conquest was through imports. To pay for these imports, Japan had to produce products that the rest of the world needed. The extent to which Japan has achieved this goal has inspired other East Asian states to follow in its footsteps.

Japanese workers oversee production at a watch manufacturing plant. The efficiency and dedication of the Japanese work force, especially now in the high-tech industries, have become known worldwide and have contributed to the nation's economic miracle.

François Lochon, Gamma-Liaison

R. Ian Lloyd

Malaysian Industrial Development Authority

Silk products and computer chips are produced for export in Thailand and Malaysia, respectively. Thailand began emphasizing the processing of its agricultural products, including silk, in the 1960s. Malaysia has been developing an industrial base, including electronics, textiles, and autos for some 15 years.

Economic Strategy. Many of the states have copied Tokyo's formula of relying on strong central guidance from business with the aim of fostering industries that, drawing on such relative economic advantages as low labor costs, up-to-date plants, or superior know-how, could sell manufactured goods on the world market. Some nations, including Taiwan, South Korea, Thailand, and Malaysia, have adopted official multiyear economic-objective plans. Others, including Singapore and the Philippines, have relied on strong, informal government direction of business to achieve the desired goals. Only in Hong Kong has the government eschewed the role of pacesetter. Of course, central economic planning alone has not ensured success. Burma, the buffer between East and South Asia, has followed a socialist path with a notable lack of success, while Indonesia has experienced great difficulty in planning itself away from dependence on the exports of oil and gas.

Matsumoto, Sygma

The economic strategy that has set these countries apart from others also trying to achieve economic expansion is that they have consciously set out to produce manufactured goods that people in other countries want to buy. This, in turn, generates the income to pay for the import of products needed for economic development that they themselves cannot manufacture efficiently.. Most other countries have followed a path of import substitution—building factories to make goods to replace imported products. All too frequently, the latter plan leads to the establishment of uneconomic industries, which can survive only if competing imports are artificially impeded, and yields little or no export revenue.

Strong Influences. Beyond the strategy itself and the strong role taken by government, there are other factors common to most of the middle-income countries of East Asia that help account for their economic emergence. Most important is the

The city of Tokyo, Japan's capital, underwent extensive rebuilding following the air raids of World War II. Today it is a modern, Westernized city of more than 8 million people—a major industrial, financial, commercial, and cultural center of the area.

strong influence of Confucian ideals. The typical Confucian hierarchical social structure, in which great deference is paid to leadership and directions from social superiors are obeyed as a matter of course, is the norm in the region's five leading economic powers—Japan, South Korea, Taiwan, Singapore, and Hong Kong. Other states of the region, while having different social structures, all have large and commercially powerful Chinese—and hence Confucian-influenced—minorities. The Confucian ethic has made the societies, or important parts of them, willing to accept the coordination or regimentation that seems an integral part of their economic progress.

Another—unquantifiable—factor is the "siege mentality" that features prominently in the daily life of the region's top achievers. Put simply, there is a widespread feeling—often reinforced by political exhortation—that outside forces will overwhelm these states if they fail to push forward with the maximum effort. In Japan it has been the need to compensate for a dangerous lack of natural resources; in Hong Kong there is the need to overcome the pressures on space and resources caused by successive waves of refugees from China; in Singapore it is the politically reinforced feeling that the nation is an isolated Chinese enclave in a hostile Malay world; while in South Korea and Taiwan it has been the perceived threat of military attack by North Korea and China, respectively.

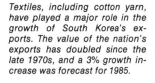

Textiles, including cotton yarn, have played a major role in the growth of South Korea's exports. The value of the nation's exports has doubled since the late 1970s, and a 3% growth increase was forecast for 1985.

Individual Performances. The mix of these ingredients in different states and the times at which they began to have an impact have varied. Japan began its economic climb during the postwar U.S. administration (1945–52) and reached top momentum during the 1960s when the economy almost trebled in size. South Korea, devastated by a war with North Korea (1950–53), was considered an international pauper until a military coup led by Gen. Park Chung Hee in 1961 imposed disciplined economic planning and curbed corruption. Until Park's assassination in October 1979, South Korea's gross national product (GNP) grew by an annual average of 9.7%. After a pause during the political uncertainty before the emergence of a new strongman, Gen. Chun Doo Hwan, growth resumed, and South Korea's exports in 1984, at $29.24 billion, were about 540 times greater than in 1962.

Hong Kong began its surge of economic growth in the late 1960s when its small labor force was rapidly expanding by an influx of refugees from the turmoil of the Cultural Revolution in neighboring China. Hong Kong had already possessed considerable resources of capital and entrepreneurial skill in long-established British trading companies and Chinese businessmen who left their homeland ahead of the Chinese Communists in 1949. The introduction of new workers set off a surge of growth that saw exports grow from about $1.5 billion in 1967 to $28.4 billion in 1984. While the government in Hong Kong has not played the role of pacesetter to growth as in the other newly industrialized Asian countries, it has fostered the development of both a highly flexible industrial structure and a massive banking and financial sector. This has enabled the economy to react rapidly to shifts in the world market and maintain its growth rate at an annual average of almost 9% a year since 1967.

Aircraft parts are manufactured at a plant in Bandung, Java, Indonesia. Since Java has more advanced transport and electric-power facilities than other parts of Indonesia, the island is the center for much of the nation's manufacturing enterprises.

R. Ian Lloyd

Singapore's electronic industry, a mainstay of the economy, now produces higher value goods, including computer peripherals and medical instruments. High productivity and low inflation combine to make Singapore's manufactured products competitive on the world scene.

Singapore's growth began simultaneously with its withdrawal from the Federation of Malaysia and full independence in August 1965. The former British colony—for a century a major naval base and entrepôt—followed a path mapped out by the government, under the strong leadership of Prime Minister Lee Kuan Yew, to make the city-state viable based on a well-educated and disciplined labor force. The strategy succeeded to the extent that the economy almost trebled in size (in real terms) in the first decade of independence and has more than doubled again since then. A trade boom, which began in the 1970s, took the exports of the nation of 2.5 million predominantly overseas Chinese to $24 billion in 1984, nearly the same as the total exports of China itself with a population more than 400 times as large.

Taiwan, the last member of East Asia's class of high achievers, began its economic climb with a mixed legacy. For the 51 years to 1945, the island had been a Japanese colony and had seen development in such areas as farming and transport. Little progress was made in the turbulent years between the return of the island to China after the Japanese surrender and the arrival from the mainland at the end of 1949 of the defeated remnants of the Chinese Nationalist government and the army of Gen. Chiang Kai-shek. But within a few years, and despite heavy military spending, Taiwan under its strict Nationalist leadership began an uninterrupted march of industrial growth. In fact, the GNP grew by about 1,350% between 1952 and 1984. During the same period, exports turned in average annual growth of more than 21% and reached $30.5 billion in 1984.

Other states in the region—notably Malaysia, Thailand, and the Philippines—have more recently begun to follow the path of Japan and the newly industrialized states. The former British colonies making up Malaysia, using income from rich commodity-producing industries to finance coordinated devel-

Taiwan's Visitor's Association

opment, have been the most successful. Since the early 1970s plants making products ranging from textiles and electronic goods to automobiles have been established, and many such goods have been intended for foreign markets. Neighboring Thailand, too, has adopted an industrial development strategy to wean itself from its traditional dependence on rural exports.

The Philippines—which is linked with Malaysia, Thailand, Singapore, Indonesia, and tiny Brunei in the regional economic grouping of the Association of Southeast Asian Nations (ASEAN)—was successful in the late 1970s and early 1980s in building up its light industry. Then a political crisis following the assassination of opposition leader Benigno Aquino in 1983 caused a massive flight of capital from the country, and the subsequent failure to meet foreign debt repayments sent the economy into a tailspin. Still, even today, with the country's problems far from resolved, electronic components have maintained their position as the top foreign-exchange earner ahead of the traditional sugar and copper.

Countries in other parts of the world have copied with varying success the export-oriented growth strategy of the East Asians. Some Latin American states recorded rapid advances before an international debt crisis overwhelmed their plans. Other nations, undoubtedly, still will try to imitate the Asian program. But a necessary ingredient for success is open and growing foreign markets to absorb the new industrial goods flowing in increasing volume and variety from Third World countries. The very success of the new industrial states has challenged entrenched, often inefficient, and usually politically sensitive industries in the developed countries. Such a challenge has provoked steadily increasing barriers to trade in mass-produced industrial goods. Unless international action successfully reverses this trend, the scope for other developing countries to travel the export-led path followed by East Asia since the end of World War II will be limited.

A crowded Taipei department store is indicative of Taiwan's robust economy. Although the store features primarily domestically made products, some imported items are sold.

Editor's Note: As the year drew to a close, it became clear that the new economic powers of East Asia had suffered a slowdown. Details of 1985 developments are discussed in the individual country articles in the alphabetical section, beginning on page 84.

Arthur Sirdofsky, Gamma-Liaison

THE AMERICAN MENU
1985-Style

About the Author: Mimi Sheraton is food critic for *Time* magazine and contributes articles on food, restaurants, and interior design for a variety of other publications. Previously she was food critic for *New York* magazine and *The New York Times*. Of several books, her latest (with the comedian Alan King) is *Is Salami and Eggs Better than Sex?* (1985). Says Ms. Sheraton: "What I like to do most is eat. I'm especially crazy about restaurants because there is always an element of excitement about a meal and the scene."

What are Americans eating in the mid-1980s? The simplest answer, judging by what we read and hear, is everything. Not all of the food all of the time, mind you, but just enough to pay lip service to every "in" concern for health, to fulfill the desire to be in fashion (what are "they" eating?), and to meet the practical limitations of time, availability, and income.

It is hard to believe that there has ever been more frenzy and more confusion about the choice of diet, and it is impossible to miss the irony of contrast: while much of the world is wondering where its next meal is coming from, most Americans are worrying about what to eat next.

Contradictions. Taking it from the top with the diet of the visible minority—the stylish and affluent for whom much of the food press writes—it would seem that contradiction is

everyone's favorite dish. Seldom in the history of fashion has so much importance been placed on thinness to the point of skinniness; seldom in the history of social fashion has it been so essential to be able to talk about food, to know and be seen in the latest hot restaurants, and to have discovered the richest, costliest imported chocolates (as much as $30 a pound), the creamiest, runniest ripening cheeses, and the shop that sells the freshest homemade pasta. To resolve those mutually exclusive activities—remaining thin while eating—much of fashionable society is afflicted with a sort of mass bulimia, the disease of gorging and disgorging. Only in this case the gorging at $50 or $60 a head for dinner is followed by extreme exercise such as jogging or by doing time in posh reducing spas where the cost of starving can run as high as $2,600 a week.

Equally contradictory are the voiced concerns about healthful eating. Ever since the U.S. Senate issued dietary guidelines in 1977 suggesting that the American diet was too high in fats, calories, sodium, and sugar and recommending instead diets based on vegetables, fruits, grains, fish, and chicken, there have been fits and starts in that direction. Answers on surveys indicate that the richest and best educated are interested in such changes and, as a result, restaurant menus are reflecting those shifts. Beef is rarely seen on standard menus, and poultry and veal ride high. Fish has become so much in demand that former trash varieties such as weakfish, blowfish, and dogfish are being renamed ocean trout, sea squab, and ocean cod. Heretofore unconsidered fish such as mako shark, mahimahi, orange roughy, and squid are tripling in price. Chicken seems the glamour meat of the decade, fulfilling as it does all of the low-calorie, low-fat requirements without actually being the fish so many people still hate.

Dan Wynn

Fashionable Foods: The contradictions of the American diet are evidenced by an obsession with sweets and a new demand for low-fat beef alternatives. Some chocolate lovers will spend $30 per pound for gourmet brands. Meanwhile, old standards and new varieties of fish are selling like hotcakes. Said one distributor: "We can't keep enough. . . . If it swims, it's edible."

Jeffry W. Myers, Freelance Photographers Guild

Never mind that the chicken we eat is often pumped with chemicals and that the fish comes from polluted waters so that there are frequent scares about mercury or PCB pollution. Similarly, produce markets are offering an undreamed of variety, and small boutique farms are growing tiny vegetables, fresh herbs, and tomatoes not much larger than teardrops (called Persianettes) to fill the demand. Salad bars in supermarkets and fast-food chains are increasing, as are stories of the sulfites used as preservatives to keep these precut salad ingredients from turning brown.

As middle-class Americans voice similar concerns, fast-food chains are adding salad bars, chicken, and fish items. Meanwhile, hamburgers are more popular than ever, and the way America eats chicken most frequently is fried in grease. Barbecued ribs are the rage across the country; whether of beef or pork, they are as fatty and as delectable as ever, and their basting sauces are high in both salt (sodium) and sugar.

Taste Trends. Foremost among the high-fashion trends is the rage for American food, whether it is dubbed new, down-home, regional, or momma cooking. Domestic products along with American recipes are the new exotica, and in such cities as New York, Chicago, and Los Angeles, the restaurant names we hear are Carolina, Texarkana, Memphis, American Café, American Harvest. A host of pseudo-diners are springing up as well—Debevic's in Chicago, Fog City in San Francisco, Cadillac in Los Angeles.

Italian food is replacing French as the status cuisine of the moment, and here, too, the buzzword is new—meaning wafer-thin pizzas with such improbable, non-Italian toppings as duck breast or lamb sausage with goat cheese and grilled lettuce, or

Vance Heflin, Black Star

For lunch on the run, salad bars and hot-food bins seem to be everywhere—on streetcorners, in variety stores, and even in supermarkets. Cheese has remained as popular as ever, and not just with crackers. The new dining exotica includes a variety of cheese toppings and sauces. Goat cheese is a favorite.

William Roman, Arete

Hungry Yuppies might supplement a frozen dinner with fancy hors d'oeuvres or a light side dish from an upscale deli.

shrimp and avocado with, God help us, yogurt. In much the same way, new pastas are proliferating, tossed with smoked salmon and dill or goat cheese (it's everywhere) and broccoli or even in some cases strawberries. Pasta, by the way, is another '80s glamour food, now that complex carbohydrates are considered more healthful than proteins. Runners stoke up on pasta before the big meet, as do high-toned society ladies who have theirs tossed with tiny vegetables and a glossing of cream.

Oriental foods fit the new health rules, based as they are on the quick stir-frying of vegetables, usually in no-cholesterol vegetable oil. Most can be flavored with hot chili peppers, another currently popular taste. Mexican food is also big for the same reason, although it is almost uniformly badly prepared. And whole-grain Greek pita bread, being natural round pockets, are the minimalist's favorite holder for sandwich fillings.

Peter Menzel, Stock Boston

Word gets out quickly about a good Italian restaurant. Pasta is one of the glamour foods of the 80s, and Italian is replacing French as the status cuisine of the moment. The tablecloths, anyway, haven't changed much.

Nobody's Home on the Range. Restaurant madness has swept the Yuppie population, and ambitious strivers scrape all of their funds together night after night to be seen—dressed to the nines in retro, punk, or thrift shop fashions—in the latest madhouse eatery. When they are not eating in restaurants and extolling the wonders of the fresh and the freshly prepared, they are heating up (microwaving, to be exact) gruesome little frozen dishes that approximate airline food in smell, texture, and taste. That category of foods is one of the hottest sellers in supermarkets mostly because, surveys indicate, the young and the hungry are too tired to cook their own dinners. "Too tired from what?" you might ask. Be ready for the answer: exercising. It's a wonder they do not stop running and start cooking. But their tolerance for these frozen foods explains why they so readily accept bad cooking in many of the huge, noisy, public-square type restaurants they frequent.

With it all, there are some positive trends, most especially the appreciation of our country's own cuisine and in the encouragement being given to young chefs proud of the trade they have selected. If premature hype does not render them unteachable, the culinary future looks bright.

One of the biggest changes since the mid-1970s is the move away from home cooking. Ten years ago cooking schools were packed, and the food processor was the altar of the kitchen. Now the quick and the instant is demanded, and along with eating out and buying frozen foods there is an increase of freshly prepared take-out foods from tony delicatessens and markets. In fact, retail food markets, feeling the competition of restaurants, are going into the prepared-food business with salad bars, cooked dishes, and grilled chickens.

Production of videocassettes of cooking lessons is booming, but given the current anti-cooking sentiments, one suspects they are being watched primarily as entertainment, the viewers munching popcorn (another nonfood of the weight-conscious young set of the 1980s) or digging into one of their mini-frozen dinners (300 or less calories for a main course) with the washed-out pasta, the gray chicken, and the water-logged baby carrots all neatly compartmented.

America's taste in food is becoming more sophisticated, we food writers like to tell ourselves, but the bottom line indicates our self-congratulations may be premature.

If all of this sounds like a helter-skelter mess, then I have reported accurately. It's hard to believe that 30 years ago, and still in some parts of the world, each generation ate what their parents ate with a sense of tradition, completeness, and unconfused self-identity, the need for which in human nutrition has not yet been determined.

Steve Liss, "Time" Magazine

Diversification: Burgers and fries still nourish a booming fast-foods business, but the word of the day in franchising is diversification. The major chains offer lighter sandwiches, chicken, salad bars, and sometimes an original restaurant design. Diversification of tastes in desserts is seen in the popularity of frozen yogurt, frozen tofu, and other ice-cream substitutes.

C. Johnson, Gamma-Liaison

Jane DiMenna

Toys of the 1980s

—Some Innovations but Many Old Favorites

By Pamela G. Hollie

About the Author: As a reporter for the Business Day section of *The New York Times,* Pamela G. Hollie keeps track of the latest developments and trends in many markets, including toys. A graduate of the Columbia University School of Journalism, Ms. Hollie wrote for *The Wall Street Journal* and *The Honolulu Advertiser* before joining the *Times* in 1977.

The toys of the 1980s, like the miniature swords of the 18th century or the hobbyhorses of the 19th century, are products of the technology, life-style, attitudes, superstitions, and emotions of their age.

At the beginning of the decade, it appeared that electronics had conquered toyland. In 1982, electronic trolls, monsters, and visitors from space invaded nearly 15 million American homes and became a $7 billion industry. But Americans soon tired of zapping electronic creatures. They turned instead to traditional toys, cuddly dolls, and board games, which were more in tune with the trend in the country toward basic American values and old-fashioned skills. Sales of games that tested the intellect and encouraged social interaction became popular again. Trivial Pursuit, a new question-and-answer board game that rewarded such areas of knowledge as science, sports, history, and the arts, was the best-selling adult game of 1984.

It seemed that the electronic toys created a backlash among parents who preferred that their children play with toys and games that encouraged creative activity or inspired friendship or leadership qualities. Failing that, a toy should at least be cute like the teddy bear. In 1984 stuffed bears came out of hibernation, and more than $200 million worth of furry friends were sold.

But the runaway best-sellers were homely, pudgy Cabbage Patch kids, which captured the hearts and pocketbooks of Americans of all ages. For a fee of about $25, a Cabbage Patch kid could be adopted from almost any toy store. They became

the marketing phenomenon of the decade and so popular that when stores ran short of them before Christmas 1983, parents rioted to get a chance to buy one. In 18 months, more than 20 million Cabbage Patch dolls were sold—enough dolls so that every child in America between the ages of three and eight could have one.

The toy industry, a $12 billion-a-year business, produces more than 150,000 different kinds of toys every year. Only about 3,000 are new toys. Like the automobile industry, the toy industry is under constant pressure to introduce new models and shapes to tempt the buying public. The most innovative of the new toys introduced in the 1980s were influenced by robotics. These toys looked like vehicles but could be transformed into robots.

A toy that is hot one year can easily fade into obscurity the next. The average life of a new toy is just four years. The chief reason for the short life of most toys is the tendency of the toy industry to oversaturate the market with look-alike toys. As soon as a toy becomes popular, dozens of copies, often cheaper than the original, are available in a matter of weeks. In 1981 the Ideal Toy Corporation sold 10 million Rubik's Cubes, a puzzle named for Ernö Rubik, the Hungarian who invented it in 1974 as a class aid at the Budapest Academy of Applied Arts. But copies flooded the market, and demand died out in 1983.

There are classics in the toy industry. They are chiefly toys that continue to suit young children generation after generation, like building blocks or push toys. New generations have continued to like Etch A Sketch and Silly Putty. And G.I. Joe, a male action character, has remained a popular toy despite times when warlike characters fell into disfavor. In 1985, when a wave of emotion swept the United States on the tenth anniversary of the end of the Vietnam war, G.I. Joe made a comeback as a "real American hero." Likewise, the Barbie doll has endured. In 1984, Barbie celebrated its 25th birthday. The following year, it was estimated that the Barbie doll population had exceeded the American population.

During the 1980s the toy industry was weakened by the collapse of the electronic-toy business. Many companies already were suffering from the effects of recessions and periods of high interest rates. When consumer sales dropped in 1982, toy stores were forced to cut prices to move inventories. As a result, profits of toy makers were squeezed severely despite efforts to reduce toy-production costs by contracting more and more manufacturing offshore in Hong Kong, Taiwan, and South Korea. In a weakened state, the industry went through a period of consolidation and acquisition. CBS Inc. purchased Ideal Toys, the maker of Erector Sets, Betsy Wetsy dolls, and Trouble board game. Quaker Oats Company, the diversified cereal company, bought Fisher-Price, a leader in children's preschool toys. General Mills, another food company, acquired Kenner Products and Parker Brothers, which made children's toys and board games. Hallmark Cards, Inc. bought Binney & Smith, which makes 1.8 million Crayola crayons each year.

Although tastes in toys vary through the years, some, including Etch A Sketch and Silly Putty, below, remain popular for decades. Etch A Sketch was introduced in 1960, and Silly Putty began amusing children a few years earlier.

The Ohio Art Co.

Binney & Smith Inc.

Current trends in toy marketing include an emphasis on collectibles—toy lines that come in series—and traditional favorites, such as dolls and other cuddly items. The new GoBots, below top, a robotic toy series, and the 26-year-old Barbie doll, right, were popular collectibles of 1985. Of the more than 150,000 different kinds of toys produced annually, some 3,000 are entirely new. In 1985, Fisher-Price presented the Bubble Mower, below, a child-size lawn mower that blows bubbles, as "something for the spring."

Jane DiMenna

Tonka Toys

Fisher-Price

Licensing and Collectibles. Also in the 1980s, it has appeared that larger, more diversified toy companies might be able to overcome more easily the dependence on the Christmas selling season, when toy companies do 60% of their business. For decades toy-industry executives talked about breaking the dependence on the Christmas selling season. The licensing of toy characters to nontoy companies for use on clothing, sheets, shoes, and hundreds of other consumer products seemed to provide a partial answer to the seasonal problems of the toy industry. Through licensing, toy makers were able to generate year-round sales. During the early years of the decade, licensing grew into a $40 million business. Marketers projected sales of $100 million by 1990.

Licensing also opened avenues for a new era of toy promotion. Toy characters became movie stars with contracts for endorsements and television specials. To give toys life and to lengthen playtime, stories were created for toy characters. With the stories came licensing opportunities for spin-off products. Nearly every successful toy of the 1980s was accompanied by what toy companies began to call prepackaged fantasies. Such fantasy worlds with good and bad characters, vehicles, and homes meant larger and larger toy lines. Toy families expanded and the licensing opportunities multiplied.

Toy companies saw an opportunity to build into the system elements that would make certain toys collectibles. The Cabbage Patch kids, already individualized by computer-directed selection of hair, skin, and eye color, also were marked so that possible collectors could tell what year they were produced. For those who wanted to adopt an extensive Cabbage Patch family, Coleco, the marketer of the dolls, produced siblings including twins and then tiny baby dolls called Preemies. There were also Cabbage Patch accessories like high chairs and strollers.

Sophisticated marketing soon led toy companies into the entertainment business. By the mid-1980s it was difficult to tell which came first, the entertainment or the toy. Promotional hype escalated to the point that the introduction of fantasy characters resembled the fanfare that surrounded emerging movie stars of the powerful Hollywood studios of the 1930s. In 1985, Mattel produced She-Ra, a female action character and a member of the growing Masters of the Universe family. At the same time, Mattel announced that She-Ra would be the star of a feature film. There would be a record. There would be a music video and a hardcover book as well as a 65-episode television series.

Television Promotion and Toy Safety. Many parents opposed the toy industry's hard sell. A group called Action for Children's Television was particularly vocal about the use of television programming to promote toys. Children, they said, could not distinguish between programming and commercials. In addition, they complained that there were already too many commercials on television. According to the Federal Trade Commission in 1980, the average child, age 2 to 11, saw 20,000

Andrew Popper

The Boston-based Action for Children's Television and others contend that some TV programs are nothing more than toy commercials. In April 1985 the Federal Communications Commission again rejected a motion to halt such programming.

commercials costing $600 million during a single year. The highest concentration came during the Christmas selling season in the fourth quarter. During that time, toy companies traditionally spent up to 90% of their advertising budgets.

During the 1980s the toy industry came under increasing pressure from parents to provide emotionally and physically safe toys. Toys that promoted deviant or aggressive behavior came under particular attack. In addition, parents and community groups held the toy industry accountable for advertising and toy descriptions that seemed inappropriate for children. Zartan the Enemy doll, which was described in 1984 as "an extreme paranoid schizophrenic," had to be repackaged so that the character would not be offensive to those people who suffer mental-health disorders.

Through the use of pediatricians, teachers, and child psychologists, the toy industry became more aware of the emotional power of toys. And toys were closely tested for safety, according to federal and voluntary toy testing requirements. Under stiffer standards, toy companies found that the chances of a new toy idea reaching the public decreased substantially. More than 90% of the new toy ideas in the 1980s never reached production.

New toy safety standards, however, eliminated hazardous toys, including bows and arrows, cap pistols, and missiles from toy store shelves. Concerned about the estimated 600,000 toy-related injuries each year, toy companies assumed much of the responsibility for child safety by adopting standards for toy-package labeling to restrict the use of certain toys to only children of specified ages.

Although toy marketing, testing, and advertising reached a new sophistication, in many respects, the toys of the 1980s have changed very little from toys of earlier decades. Most toys still reflect the adult notion that play should prepare children for an adult world. Through such role models as Ken and Barbie, G.I. Joe, or She-Ra, children were to learn friendship, courage, and strength. From the hug of a teddy bear, parents hoped that children would experience the tenderness and companionship that have made generations feel secure.

Fisher-Price

Since there is no federal legislation governing safety standards for all toys, the various companies establish their own safety tests and requirements.

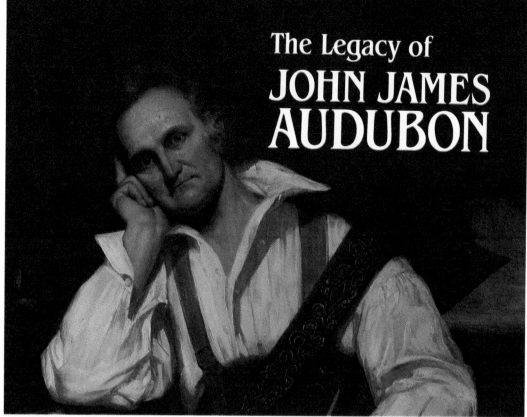

The Legacy of
JOHN JAMES AUDUBON

By Russell W. Peterson

If John James Audubon, the American painter and naturalist, could have been here in 1985 for his 200th birthday celebration, he no doubt would have been amazed at the strength and breadth of the conservation movement he unconsciously helped to spawn.

Audubon himself was no conservationist. The illegitimate son of a French sea captain, Audubon was born in Haiti on April 26, 1785. He developed an interest in drawing birds during his boyhood in France. At age 18 he was sent to America to make his fortune. After going bankrupt in 1819, however, Audubon began concentrating on his bird drawings. In the eyes of his in-laws, some of whom had been his partners and creditors in failed business ventures, John James wasn't good for much at all.

"He neglects his material interests," said one, "and is forever wasting his time hunting, drawing, and stuffing birds, and playing the fiddle. We fear he will never be fit for any practical purpose on the face of the Earth."

What Audubon did do exceedingly well was to roam the wilds of North America from Florida to Newfoundland, identifying, observing, collecting, and drawing the birds of that continent. Whether his subject was a bald eagle or ruby-throated hummingbird, Audubon painted it life-size. Most important, he was the first wildlife artist to portray birds as living, breathing creatures and to show them as dynamic components of a larger environment.

In so doing, Audubon made millions of Americans aware of birds and of the wonder and beauty of nature.

The American artist George P. A. Healy painted Audubon's portrait in London in 1838. Wrote Healy: "I painted him in a costume he wore when he went in search of his birds—a sort of Backwoodsman's dress."

About the Author: Russell W. Peterson was president of the National Audubon Society from 1979 to August 1985. He is a former governor of Delaware (1969–73) and former chairman of the U.S. Council on Environmental Quality (1973–76).

Audubon's four-volume classic, "The Birds of America," was published by the London engraver Robert Havell from 1827 to 1838. The original paintings were done in watercolor overlaid with pastel. Background settings and botanical accessories were rendered by assistants and apprentices, and fine detail was added by Havell in the engraving process. Of the 435 plates in "Birds of America," many included both male and female portraits. Among these were the Fork-tailed Petrel (above), the White-crowned Sparrow (below left), and the Blue Yellow-backed Warbler (below right).

The bald eagle (above) that Audubon used for his model was shot along the Mississippi River in 1820. In his portrait of the Yellow Shank (below), a South Carolina landscape was painted by assistant George Lehman.

People, Places, and Things

Maureen Lambray, Sygma

Names in the News: *Clara Hale, 79,* left, *who runs a home in New York City for children of heroin-addicted mothers, was singled out as "an American hero" in President Reagan's State of the Union address. Sharon Christa McAuliffe, below left, a 36-year-old high school teacher in Concord, NH, was selected from more than 11,000 applicants to be the "first private citizen passenger in the history of space flight"; she was scheduled to fly in a U.S. space shuttle mission in late January 1986. And Jacques Cousteau, below, whose 75th birthday was celebrated in June, sailed from France to New York aboard the "Alcyone," a sailing ship he helped develop that has a superefficient system of cylindrical aluminum "turbo sails."*

Al Tannenbaum, Sygma

Sygma

Kaku Kurita, Gamma-Liaison

© Harry Benson 1985

Special Sites: *Expo '85, above, a science and technology festival in Tsukuba, Japan, was held from March 17 through September 16. Following the theme of "Dwellings and Surroundings— Science and Technology for Man at Home," 28 Japanese corporations and 47 foreign countries set up exhibits to display their most futuristic developments. Organizers hoped that the spectacle would inject life into nearby Tsukuba Science City, a multibillion-dollar project intended to be the world's best-equipped scientific research and development complex. Below: In New York City's Central Park, Strawberry Fields, an "International Garden of Peace," was created by Yoko Ono in honor of her late husband, John Lennon. The opening ceremony was held on October 9, the birthdays of both Lennon, who would have been 45, and his son Sean, who turned 10. The Italian government contributed an elaborate round mosaic with the word "Imagine" (the name of Lennon's 1971 hit album and single) at the center of a sunburst.*

Saskia Grooms, NYC

Philip Amdal, "Time" Magazine

Americana: *Playful, colorful, and ingenious, the works of the Tennessee-born artist Red Grooms were the subject of a major retrospective that began at the Pennsylvania Academy of the Fine Arts in Philadelphia and moved on to several other cities. Twenty-nine years of his work included paintings, sculptures, 3-D cut-out tableaux ("sculpto-pictoramas"), cartoon animations, and live-action short films. "Local," above, a 1971 color lithograph, is typical of his style. Coca-Cola, meanwhile an American institution for 99 years, was the subject of a widespread consumer revolt. The makers announced in April that the formula for the famous soft drink would be changed. But when the new, sweeter, less fizzy version hit the shelves, a hue and cry arose from customers everywhere. As a result, the company announced in July that it would bring back the original recipe under the name Coca-Cola Classic. Old Coke stalwarts in Seattle, left, and elsewhere were jubilant.*

Harlem Highlights: *On 125th St. in Manhattan, the legendary Apollo Theatre,* right, *held a star-studded, six-hour gala show on May 4 to mark its 50th anniversary and official reopening. The launching pad for major black musicians from the age of vaudeville to rhythm & blues to rock 'n' roll, the Apollo had been closed since 1976. On hand for the gala were the likes of Diana Ross, Smokey Robinson, Sammy Davis, Jr., and dozens of others. And the Harlem Globetrotters, after 69 years of entertaining audiences with their basketball antics, entered a new era. The act wouldn't change much, but the cast of characters now would include a woman: 5'11", 26-year-old Lynette Woodard,* below. *In 1981, at the University of Kansas, Woodard had been voted the nation's top woman collegiate player. In 1984 she was the captain of the U.S. women's Olympic team.*

John Barr, Gamma-Liaison

Charles Steiner, Picture Group

The
Alphabetical Section

Photos Matsumoto (left) and Arthur Grace, Sygma

The major world powers in 1985 marked the 40th anniversary of the end of World War II and of the beginning of the nuclear age. U.S. President Ronald Reagan celebrated American–German reconciliation with a controversial May visit to a military cemetery at Bitburg, West Germany, *above.* At Peace Memorial Park in Hiroshima, Japan, *opposite page,* some 55,000 people commemorated the atomic bombing of that city in August 1945. Amid the year's solemn remembrances and ongoing dip-

lomatic wrangling over nuclear arms control, the 1985 Nobel Prize for Peace was awarded to the International Physicians for the Prevention of Nuclear War, a five-year-old group founded jointly by U.S. and Soviet doctors. The organization, said the Nobel Committee, has contributed to "an increase in the pressure of public opposition to the proliferation of atomic weapons and to a redefinition of priorities, with greater attention being paid to health and other humanitarian issues."

ACCIDENTS AND DISASTERS

AVIATION

Jan. 1—Twenty-nine persons are killed in a crash of an Eastern Airlines jet, southeast of La Paz, Bolivia.

Jan. 18—A Chinese airliner lands unsuccessfully at Jinan, China, killing 38 persons.

Jan. 19—A Cuban airliner crashes just after leaving Havana, killing 40 persons.

Jan. 21—A chartered airliner crashes just after takeoff from Reno, NV; 67 persons are killed.

Feb. 19—A Spanish airliner smashes into a mountain while approaching the airport at Bilbao, Spain, killing all 148 on board.

Feb. 22—An Air Mali passenger plane explodes outside Timbuktu, killing 50 persons.

March 28—A commercial airliner strikes a mountain in southern Colombia, killing 40 persons.

May 3—A Soviet airliner and a small military plane collide in midair in the western Ukraine, killing about 80 people.

June 23—An Air-India jetliner falls off the coast of Ireland, killing all 329 people on board.

July 24—A Colombian Air Force cargo plane, providing passenger service during a pilot strike, crashes near Leticia, Colombia, killing about 80 people.

Aug. 2—A U.S. Delta jetliner goes down in a thunderstorm near the Dallas-Fort Worth airport, killing 136.

Aug. 12—A Japan Air Lines 747 jetliner crashes into a mountain range northwest of Tokyo, killing 520.

Aug. 22—At Manchester Airport in northern England, a British charter jet catches fire, killing 54.

Sept. 6—In Milwaukee, a twin-engine jetliner fails on takeoff, killing all 31 persons on board.

Dec. 12—A chartered jetliner carrying American soldiers crashes on takeoff from Gander, Newfoundland, killing all 256 on board.

FIRES AND EXPLOSIONS

Jan. 9—Fire in an old people's home in Grandvilliers, France, kills 24.

Feb. 25—An explosion in a coal mine in Forbach, France, kills 22 men.

April 21—In the Bico region of Luzon Island in the southern Philippines, 44 persons are killed in a fire in a moviehouse complex.

April 26—Fire in a psychiatric hospital in Buenos Aires kills 79 persons; 247 others are injured.

May 11—In Bradford, England, fire in the spectator stand of a soccer match kills 54 persons.

May 17—An explosion in a Japanese coal mine kills 61 workers on the northern island of Hokkaido.

May 26—Explosions on two oil tankers docked at a refinery across from the Rock of Gibraltar kill at least 28.

June 25—A series of explosions in a fireworks plant near Hallett, OK, kills 21 persons.

July 12—In China's Guangdong province, a gas explosion in the Meitian coal mine kills 53 persons.

July 26 (reported)—In Taoyuan, Hunan province, China, an April explosion in a fireworks factory kills 82.

LAND AND SEA TRANSPORTATION

Jan. 12—In northeastern Peru a boat sinks in the Amazon River; 50 persons are missing and feared dead.

Jan. 13—In eastern Ethiopia a train derails and plunges into a ravine, killing 392 people according to government reports.

Feb. 12—Fire on an Indian passenger liner bound for Madras from Singapore kills 18; 16 are missing.

Feb. 23—Fire on a passenger train in eastern India kills at least 34, according to the Indian government.

March 27—A school bus plunges into a reservoir near Johannesburg, South Africa, killing 41 students.

May 27—A boat on the Chambal River near Morena, India, capsizes, drowning at least 74 passengers.

Aug. 3—In Flaujac-Gare, France, about 300 mi (483 km) south of Paris, two passenger trains collide, killing 35 and injuring up to 165.

Aug. 18—In northeastern China near the tourist island of Taiyang Island Park, a ferry capsizes, killing at least 110 people.

Aug. 31—Two trains collide near Argenton, France, killing 49 persons.

Sept. 1—In the Malakand region of Pakistan, a bus falls into a mountain ravine, killing 40 persons.

Sept. 11—Two trains collide near Viseu, Portugal, killing 54 persons; 64 others are missing.

Sept. 21—In Punjab Province, Pakistan, a school bus overturns, killing at least 30 children.

Oct. 5—On the Karnaphuli River near Chittagong, Bangladesh, a ferry hits a fishing trawler and breaks in half; as many as 100 people are missing.

Nov. 1—A fuel truck explodes in the village of Karnataka, India, killing 25 persons.

Nov. 15—A boat capsizes in the Chambal river in the Indian state of Uttar Pradesh; at least 60 people are feared drowned.

STORMS, FLOODS, AND EARTHQUAKES

Jan. 15—Near Vitória, Brazil, a rockslide caused by heavy rains kills at least 26 people.

Jan. 21—Subzero temperatures across the eastern United States have left at least 40 people dead in 15 states.

Jan. 28 (reported)—In the Brazilian states of Espírito Santo, Minas Gerais, and Rio de Janeiro, flooding caused by month-long rains has killed at least 122.

Jan. 30–Feb. 2—Cold, snow, and ice in the United States contribute to the deaths of 24 persons.

March 3—An earthquake in Chile in and around Santiago and in Valparaiso, San Antonio, Rancagua, and Viña del Mar kills at least 177 people.

March 30 (reported)—Across Bangladesh, storms from early season monsoons kill 750 people.

May 25—A cyclone hits the coastal islands of southeastern Bangladesh, killing perhaps as many as 10,000 people.

May 31—Tornadoes in Ontario, Canada, and in Ohio, Pennsylvania, and New York kill 90 persons.

July 1 (reported)—Flooding in five Philippine provinces and in Manila kills some 78 people.

Aug. 1—A thunderstorm with rain and hail causes floods in Cheyenne, WY, killing at least 12 people.

Aug. 6–7—Storms sweep Europe from the French Mediterranean to Denmark, killing at least 16 people.

Aug. 8 (reported)—Storms, floods, and typhoons in China have killed 527 people in the last two months.

Aug. 31–Sept. 2—Hurricane *Elena* hits the Gulf Coast of Florida and Mississippi, causing four deaths.

Sept. 19–20—Two earthquakes strike Mexico City and nearby Mexican states, killing at least 5,600 people.

Sept. 21 (reported)—Flooding in central India, particularly in the state of Uttar Pradesh, kills about 150 people.

Sept. 26–27—Hurricane *Gloria* sweeps up the U.S. eastern seaboard from North Carolina to New Jersey, New York, Connecticut, and New Hampshire, killing 3.

Oct. 7—North of Ponce, Puerto Rico, a mudslide buries Mameyes, a hillside shantytown, killing as many as 150.

Oct. 21—A landslide at a gold mine in Monkayo, southern Philippines, kills at least 30 people.

Oct. 28—Hurricane *Juan* hits Louisiana's Gulf Coast, killing seven persons; eight others are missing.

Nov. 5—A storm, the remnant of Hurricane *Juan*, that caused rivers to flood in Pennsylvania, West Virginia, and Virginia causes 35 deaths.

Nov. 8–11—Heavy snowstorms in the western United States and as far east as the Great Lakes region kill 13 persons, most of them in traffic accidents.

Nov. 19–23—Hurricane *Kate* sweeps up the Atlantic into the Gulf of Mexico, hitting Jamaica; Cuba; Key Largo, FL; and the Florida panhandle; 24 persons die.

MISCELLANEOUS

Feb. 7—An apartment building collapses in Castellaneta, Italy, killing 34 persons.

May 9—The roof of a public swimming pool in Uster, Switzerland, collapses, killing at least 13 people.

May 26—At a Mexican soccer match in Mexico City, ten persons are trampled to death as fans try to force their way into the sports stadium.

July 19—A dam collapses in the Dolonite Alps near Stava and Tesaro, Italy, killing at least 208.

Aug. 13—In Bombay, India, a crowded building in a slum area collapses, killing at least 52 people.

Oct. 15—In Dhaka, Bangladesh, the roof of an auditorium collapses, killing at least 50 students.

Nov. 13—In west-central Colombia, the *Nevado del Ruiz* volcano erupts, causing floods and mudslides; about 23,000 people are dead and missing.

ADVERTISING

In 1985 all three parts of the advertising industry—advertiser companies, ad agencies, and the media—were hit full force by the trend of corporate mergers and acquisitions that has characterized U.S. business in recent years.

Mergers and Acquisitions. The rash of major media acquisitions included the first-ever purchase of a national television network, with Capital Cities Communications' acquisition of ABC Inc.; Time Inc.'s first buy of an outside magazine, *Southern Living;* and Gannett Co.'s first purchase of major market newspapers, the *Des Moines Register* and *Detroit News.*

June was the month for ad-agency marriages. One of them, between D'Arcy Mac-Manus Masius Worldwide, the longtime agency for such products as Cadillac and Budweiser, and Benton & Bowles, the agency behind the well-known Mr. Whipple ad campaign for Procter & Gamble's Charmin bathroom tissue, was the largest ad-agency merger in history. It created a new entity, called D'Arcy Masius Benton & Bowles, which, with media billings of about $2.4 billion, became one of the world's ten largest ad agencies. Lorimar, best known as the producer of *Dallas* and other top-rated TV shows, was behind the other major June merger. A few years earlier Lorimar had bought its first agency, Kenyon & Eckhardt, which had devised the Chrysler Corp. ad campaign using Lee Iacocca. In 1985 it acquired Bozell & Jacobs, the agency for American Airlines, with plans to merge it with Kenyon & Eckhardt in January 1986. With an estimated $1.2 billion in media billings, Bozell, Jacobs, Kenyon & Eckhardt would be among the world's 15 largest agencies.

The number one spot among ad agencies worldwide also changed hands during 1985, though not because of a merger. The U.S.-based Young & Rubicam surpassed Dentsu, a Japanese agency.

Among advertiser companies, the leadership kept changing hands because of acquisitions of major consumer goods companies. In June, R.J. Reynolds Industries agreed to buy Nabisco Brands, making it the largest U.S. advertiser company. With combined annual ad expenditures of $1.01 billion, according to *Advertising Age,* it surpassed Procter & Gamble's $872 million. The ranking changed again in September, when Philip Morris Inc. announced the acquisition of General Foods Corp., creating an annual ad expenditure of $1.02 billion. But then Procter & Gamble moved back into the top position with its announced purchase of Richardson-Vicks, with combined annual ad spending of about $1.04 billion.

Cola Wars. While mergers and acquisitions will have a major effect on the advertising of many well-known brands in coming years, 1985 brought what was perhaps the biggest news affecting any major brand name product in recent history. The decision to introduce a reformulated Coca-Cola, announced in the spring, was met with such enormous resistance by consumers that the company had to bring back the old product just a few months later under the name Coca-Cola Classic. Rival Pepsi-Cola, which had been running aggressive comparative ads for some time, had an advertising field day poking fun at its rival's formula change and then Coke's reversal. One of Pepsi's ads from before the Coke formula change won the top prize at the International Advertising Film Festival in Cannes, France. In that commercial, a Pepsi-drinking archaeologist of the future finds a Coke bottle among some ruins and cannot figure out what this "relic of the past" is.

Firsts. Pepsi-Cola, which broke new ground in celebrity TV advertising in 1984 when it used pop singer Michael Jackson, took things a step further in 1985, when it included Geraldine Ferraro, the 1984 vice-presidential candidate, in a commercial for Diet Pepsi. Former President Richard Nixon also appeared for the first time as a commercial presenter in 1985, though it was only to plug the serialization of his new book in a Denver newspaper. And Beatles music was adapted for major U.S. advertising use for the first time, in commercials for Lincoln-Mercury.

There were also some firsts in special effects and electronic advertising. IBM France created a magazine ad that, with a built-in microchip, played Beethoven's *Für Elise* when the ad was opened to a certain page. Honeywell spent $1 million to develop a pop-up magazine ad showing a three-dimensional corporate headquarters. And in TV special effects new ground was broken with an ad for the Canned Food Information Council in which the motions of a real woman were analyzed and encoded by a computer and then transferred to a computer-generated robot image.

Ad Volume. The 1984 Olympic Games in Los Angeles made that year a hard one to follow in terms of ad volume gains. In addition, as 1985 progressed it looked as if the economy was slowing down. Original forecasts of a 9.7% increase in U.S. ad expenditures were revised downward at midyear to 9.1%, with the total expected to reach $95.9 billion.

Other. One 1985 development that will become more and more evident to TV viewers was agreement by all three broadcast networks to allow stand-alone, 15-second commercials—as opposed to the standard 30 seconds—in certain time slots. As for regulatory lobbying, the year ended somewhat differently from the way it began. Early in 1985 there were growing lobbies to ban beer and wine advertising on television and to forbid the use of celebrities in any alcohol ad. By midyear, however, both movements had lost momentum.

STEWART ALTER, *"Advertising Age"*

No end in sight for the fighting in Afghanistan: an Afghan rebel inspects a downed Soviet helicopter.

AFGHANISTAN

The sixth year of fighting between Soviet troops in Afghanistan and the rebel *mujahidin* (guerrillas) saw an increase in the intensity of combat and the number of casualties on both sides. Moscow stepped up its campaign to "Sovietize" Afghanistan through propaganda, education, and police terror, and the new Kremlin leadership gave signs of wanting a political solution to the conflict. Yet both sides were as determined as they were frustrated, and an end to the fighting was not in sight.

Military Developments. During 1985 the Soviet Union launched five major offensives to relieve besieged garrisons and to cut supply routes to the *mujahidin*. The Soviets relied largely on elite commando and paratroop units rather than on the Afghan army. This resulted in heavy casualties on both sides. The focal combat points were the besieged towns of Barikot and Khost close to the Pakistan border. The Soviets succeeded at high cost in temporarily breaking the sieges and resupplying the garrisons, but they could not close the supply routes.

Perhaps to prepare the Russian people for a long war and no longer able to hide the growing casualties, the Soviet media began to report the conflict in a somewhat different light: Russian soldiers were depicted in heroic battles as defenders of the motherland rather than as Afghan benefactors. Meanwhile, polls of Soviet travelers in the West revealed growing opposition to the war: only 55% of Communist Party members interviewed supported the war. And Western journalists interviewed a growing number of Soviet military defectors. In November a defecting Soviet soldier sought asylum in the U.S. Embassy in Kabul but, after conferring with the Soviet ambassador, chose to return home.

The Afghan resistance went on the attack with improved combat organization and air defenses. It successfully blunted the Soviet offensives and nearly captured the town of Khost, which it hoped to make the capital of a liberated zone. But it failed in that effort after it ran out of ammunition and the Soviets introduced a new and decisive weapon into the battle, the MI-28 Havoc armored helicopter. In Kabul, *mujahidin* rockets destroyed transport planes and repeatedly struck the Soviet Embassy. The most notable resistance success was a sabotage operation at the major Soviet air base in Shindand, which destroyed 20 MiG fighter planes, nearly one third of the Afghan air force.

The growing effectiveness of the resistance reflected an increase in outside military aid from Middle East countries and the U.S. Central Intelligence Agency (CIA). Bipartisan support in the U.S. Congress for the Afghan resistance gathered momentum. Covert aid was raised to $250 million, and by year's end more than ten bills to aid the Afghan rebels were making their way through Congress.

Political Developments. In Afghanistan the Soviets tightened information to the outside world and threatened severe punishment of Western journalists who enter the country illegally. The first American casualty was Charles Thornton of the *Arizona Republic,* killed while accompanying a *mujahidin* combat group. Moscow also stepped up its "Sovietization" campaign. High Afghan officials who defected to Pakistan described a totalitarian program of propaganda, secret police terror, revisions of school curricula, internal espionage, youth or-

ganizations, and training in the USSR for thousands of officials, army officers, and young people—all aimed at creating a new Afghan Marxist society. President Babrak Karmal convened a *Loya Jirgah* (Great Tribal Council) in Kabul, seeking to win the allegiance of tribal leaders with lavish entertainment, bribes, and exhortations to patriotism. The tribal leaders took his gifts and departed unconvinced.

The seven major resistance factions joined together to form the Islamic Unity of Afghan Mujahidin, which was supported by former Afghan King Zahir, exiled in Rome. Gulbuddin Hekmatyar, leader of the Hezb-i-Islami faction, was selected as the organization's first rotating chairman. In November he traveled to New York to claim, unsuccessfully, Afghanistan's seat in the United Nations.

The Kremlin, meanwhile, stepped up pressure on Pakistan. *Pravda* reported in March that Soviet leader Mikhail Gorbachev personally warned Pakistan's President Zia ul-Haq that military aid to the Afghan rebels was an unfriendly act. The article also claimed that Pakistan was harboring CIA bases and guerrilla training camps staffed by American instructors. The warnings by Moscow were underlined by increased air and artillery attacks across the Pakistan border.

Diplomatic Developments. U.S. President Ronald Reagan announced in January that "Afghanistan is a serious impediment to improvement of relations between the United States and the Soviet Union." In June the United States and the USSR held unproductive bilateral talks on Afghanistan at the assistant secretary of state level in Washington. At the same time in Geneva, the Pakistani and Afghan foreign ministers were holding the fourth round of proximity talks under UN auspices. The sticking point remained the Soviet refusal to agree to any troop withdrawal schedule and their precondition that all military aid to the Afghan freedom fighters cease. A fifth round of talks in August was equally unproductive, and a sixth round was scheduled for December. These negotiations coincided with increased cross-border attacks on Pakistan in which many Pakistanis were killed or wounded.

In 1985 three important reports on Soviet human-rights violations in Afghanistan were published. One, prepared for the UN Human Rights Commission by Austrian law professor Felix Ermacora, accused the USSR of following the prescription of 19th-century Prussian Gen. Karl von Clausewitz for defeating a peoples' war by creating an atmosphere of terror through atrocities and genocide. Another report, by the Helsinki Watch, concluded that "an entire country is dying." And Amnesty International reported that Soviet actions amounted to a new holocaust and compared world indifference to the Afghan massacre to the way in which reports of the Jewish holo-

---

AFGHANISTAN • Information Highlights

Official Name: Democratic Republic of Afghanistan.
Location: Central Asia.
Area: 249,999 sq mi (647 497 km²).
Population (mid-1985 est.): 14,700,000.
Chief Cities (March 1982): Kabul, the capital, 1,036,407; Kandahar, 191,345; Herat, 150,497.
Government: *Head of state,* Babrak Karmal, president (took power Dec. 1979). *Head of government,* Soltan Ali Keshtmand, prime minister (named June 1981). *Policy-making body—*57-member Revolution Council.
Monetary Unit: Afghani (50.6 afghanis equal U.S. $1, July 1985).
Foreign Trade (1984 U.S.$): *Imports,* $940,000,000; *exports,* $680,000,000.

---

caust were ignored during World War II. President Reagan, in a speech at the UN in October, cited Afghanistan as a major point of friction between the United States and the Soviet Union. He also raised the issue with General Secretary Gorbachev at their Geneva summit meeting in November. Both leaders agreed on the need for a political solution, but no new concrete plan emerged. Also in November, the UN General Assembly voted for the seventh time to demand the withdrawal of Soviet troops from Afghanistan.

Economic Developments. The Soviet Union, continuing its program to integrate the Afghan economy with its own, extended new rail and road links into Afghanistan. The Soviet economic aid program rose to $600 million in 1985, from $13 million before the Soviet invasion in December 1979. The new Soviet five-year plan (1986–1991) included, for the first time, costs of infrastructure projects in Afghanistan. The new Afghan five-year plan was tilted toward Soviet-Afghan integration by allocating only 10% of spending to agriculture but 27% to transportation and 38% to the development of mineral exports for the USSR. Deliberate Soviet destruction of the rural infrastructure accelerated the movement of rural dwellers either into exile as refugees or to Afghan cities where they could be more readily coerced, bribed, or controlled. This movement also deprives the freedom fighters of necessary food, shelter, resources, and popular backing.

In 1985 there was a worldwide movement to increase economic aid to the 3 million Afghan refugees in Pakistan and the beginning of an effort to help civilians in the liberated areas inside Afghanistan. The U.S. government joined other donors by contributing an additional $23 million in nonmilitary aid and approved legislation permitting the Agency for International Development (AID) to establish medical assistance programs, schools, and agricultural centers inside Afghanistan. A special section of the AID mission in Pakistan was set up for this purpose.

LEON B. POULLADA
University of Nebraska, Omaha

AFRICA

Much-needed rain came to most of sub-Saharan Africa, harvests were better, and even some food surpluses were realized. These improving conditions along with increased humanitarian food aid (*see* special report, page 90) eased the immediate crisis, and attention began to turn to longer term solutions of overall African problems in 1985. Coups occurred in a number of African states. In Sudan and Nigeria new military regimes already had implemented some reforms and appeared to be moving in a less repressive direction than their predecessors. A coup in Uganda seemed not to have improved that country's chronic instability or the human-rights violations that have plagued it for 15 years. There was a one-party election in Ivory Coast, a competitive multiparty election in Zimbabwe, and a nominally multiparty election in Liberia, though tainted by allegations of fraud. The year may be best remembered for the peaceful transfers of power in Sierra Leone and Tanzania in which presidents who had ruled for more than 20 years voluntarily relinquished power, and the intensification of violence and repression in South Africa.

Electoral Politics. In at least one important aspect, electoral politics closely resembled the electoral activity of 1984. There were nearly half a dozen elections in east, west, and southern Africa in both years. Most were elections that sought to generate popular support for regimes or to raise national political consciousness. Voters, however, did not have a meaningful choice since in most cases there was only one official party candidate. Nonetheless, in at least two of the 1985 elections, an event of far greater significance than the elections themselves took place. Two of Africa's elder statesmen, Julius Nyerere of Tanzania and Siaka Stevens of Sierra Leone, voluntarily relinquished power in favor of handpicked successors, Ali Hassan Mwinyi and Maj. Gen. Joseph Saidu Momoh, respectively. In the Ivory Coast, President Félix Houphouët-Boigny, 80, was reelected unopposed for a sixth term, and the office of vice-president was eliminated at the president's request. The chairman of the National Assembly would be empowered to run the Ivory Coast for an interim period. Nyerere will remain chair of Tanzania's sole political party until 1987.

The election in Liberia, billed as that country's first "one-man, one vote" election since independence, was marred by charges that illegal military voting centers were created at the last minute to enable soldiers and their families to vote more than once for Samuel Doe. The president of Liberia since April 1980, Doe crushed an attempted coup on November 12.

In June and July white and black Zimbabweans went to separate polls in an open and

© A. Brucelle, Sygma

President Julius Nyerere of Tanzania, who led his country since its independence in 1961, retired in November.

democratic election to vote for a new House of Assembly. On June 27, Ian Smith's Conservative Alliance of Zimbabwe (CAZ) won a decisive victory of 15 out of 20 seats in a separate election for Zimbabwe's 35,000 registered white voters. The Zimbabwe Independence group, a loose organization of former CAZ members, won four seats, and one seat was won by an independent. Prime Minister Robert Mugabe's response was that whites, by their vote for the Smith group, had rejected his policy of reconciliation. Then, in early July nearly 3 million Africans voted for 79 of the 80 seats in the House of Assembly, the death of one Zimbabwe African National Union Patriotic Front (ZANU-PF) candidate having caused a postponement in one constituency. The ruling ZANU-PF was returned to power with 63 seats, still short of the 70 needed to constitutionally bring about one-party rule by 1987. The Zimbabwe African People's Union (ZAPU) won all 15 seats in Matabeleland, opposition leader Joshua Nkomo's stronghold, and the Zimbabwe African National Union took one seat. Mugabe's continuing challenge is to find a way to bring disparate opposition elements together in a unified Zimbabwe.

Military Intervention. After years of attempting to deal with a worsening economic situation, an unresolved civil war between north and south, and the added burdens of drought-induced famine and more than 1 million refugees from neighboring Ethiopia, Chad, Uganda, and Zaire, the 15-year regime of President Jafaar al-Nemery was overthrown on April 6 in a bloodless coup d'état led by Sudan's Defense Minister Gen. Abdel Rahman Suwar el Dahab. Christian opposition to Nemery's announced intentions to impose Islamic law on Muslims and non-Muslims alike and pressures for economic reform from the International Monetary Fund (IMF) and other international donors also contributed to the immediate crisis, which provoked military intervention.

At the beginning of the year in an effort calculated to reduce public resentment, Nemery had lifted the state of emergency that he had imposed in 1984 to control the rebellion in the south, released political prisoners, and curtailed some of the harsher punishments imposed by Islamic law. His actions were a case of too little, too late. The takeover followed a week of riots and strikes, the immediate cause of which was an increase in food prices but also a clear reflection of general dissatisfaction with the Nemery regime. Gen. Suwar el Dahab and the other military officers who organized the coup formed a Transitional Military Council and promised open and fair elections within a year. Two immediate changes were the emergence of dozens of political parties ranging from Communist to Muslim fundamentalist and, in July, an indication of a shift away from an exclusive pro-Western commitment, with the signing of a Sudanese-Libyan agreement.

On July 4, a little more than a year since the military in Guinea had seized power after the death of President Sekou Touré, Col. Diarra Traoré led an attempted "palace" coup against President Lansana Conté. Traoré, who had been prime minister until December 1984 when he was demoted to minister of education, overestimated his support in the army and was unable to hold Radio Conakry for more than several hours before troops loyal to President Conté recaptured it. Traoré and a number of government and military leaders alleged to have been involved in the coup were arrested, and Traoré was said to have been executed. Ethnic rivalries were acknowledged to have been a key factor leading to the coup. Traoré and most of those involved were from Guinea's largest ethnic group, the Malinke, to which the late President Sekou Touré also belonged, while Conté and troops loyal to him represent other ethnic minorities.

Once again extreme ethnic hostilities in Uganda led one faction within the 20,000-strong military to stage a coup d'état. In July, after a month of in-fighting between the Lango and the Acholi, Milton Obote's civilian regime was toppled, the sixth Ugandan government to have fallen since independence in 1962. Milton Obote, a Lango, was alleged to have given preferential treatment in military promotions to his fellow Lango. Power was seized from Obote by Lt. Brig. Basilio Olara Okello. The new head of state, Lt. Gen. Tito Okello, now faced the difficult task of persuading one-time defense minister turned rebel Yoweri Museveni into joining his government instead of continuing to wage a guerrilla war as his National Resistance Army (NRA) had done against Obote for four years. Milton Obote, who was Idi Amin's predecessor and successor, had been unable to restore Uganda's shattered economy or to create a sense of national unity.

Citing misuse of power and continued economic mismanagement, the Nigerian military intervened in August for the sixth time since independence and for the second time within 20 months. The Army chief of staff and leader of the coup, Gen. Ibrahim Babangida, announced in a radio speech that the previous military regime had failed to curb the general deterioration in the standard of living, failed to reestablish public accountability, was unable to stop the rising crime rate, and refused to hear differing political opinions or to take into account the effects of its policies on civil liberties. Babangida moved quickly to reestablish freedom of the press and to release political prisoners and journalists detained by the previous regime. He also announced the creation of a committee to review human-rights conditions and the role of the Nigerian Security Organization, which had been used to silence public dissent. These reforms immediately won widespread support and approval throughout Nigeria. However, just as Maj. Gen. Mohammed Buhari's government was not able to blame all of Nigeria's troubles on the previous civilian regime of President Shehu Shagari, Babangida would have a limited amount of time to deal with a staggering foreign debt in the face of severely reduced oil revenues and the renegotiation of an IMF loan to avoid the fate of his predecessors.

Political Instability in South Africa. For South Africa the intensity and scope of violence during the year was greater than at any time in recent history. More than 700 blacks died, and thousands were arrested and detained during the state of emergency that at first covered 36 magisterial districts and later the city of Cape Town and 80 mi (129 km) surrounding it. This declaration was the first since the 1960 Sharpeville crisis in which the fatal shooting of 69 black South Africans by the police resulted in widespread rioting and unrest. These conditions were exacerbated by South Africa's most severe economic crisis since the 1930s. There was a growing feeling within South Africa and

(Continued on page 92)

Famine Relief

Harry Benson, Sygma

In a charity famine relief project dubbed USA for Africa, 46 top stars on January 28 recorded "We Are the World."

The rains finally returned to portions of famine-stricken sub-Saharan Africa in 1985, breaking a five-year drought that killed hundreds of thousands by starvation or disease brought on by malnutrition. But the crisis was far from over, as the underlying causes of recurrent famine on the continent had not been addressed. Long-term assistance would be needed to improve agricultural productivity in Africa, the only area of the world where population growth continues to outpace food production. Meanwhile, the need for emergency food aid persisted. Starvation continued in Ethiopia, where civil strife and an uncooperative government have prevented international relief agencies from reaching those in greatest need of food and medicine. Floods brought on by the rains themselves have isolated famine victims in other countries, such as Chad and the Sudan.

The year saw an unprecedented outpouring of official and private donations to Africa. Moved by television images of starving Ethiopian children, citizens of the United States and Western Europe flooded a wide range of private volunteer organizations, including Catholic Relief Services, CARE, and Oxfam, with money for food and medical supplies as well as trucks and other equipment needed to deliver

the aid to the famine victims. One of the most effective fund-raising efforts was undertaken by British and American rock musicians. USA (United Support of Artists) for Africa raised more than $50 million through sales of its "We Are the World" record and video. On July 13, 1985, another group, Band Aid Trust, and its U.S. subsidiary, Live Aid, raised another $70 million from televised concerts in Philadelphia and London. The private organizations often have worked in conjunction with such agencies of the United Nations as UNICEF (the children's fund) and the Office of the UN High Commissioner for Refugees (UNHCR) to provide food and medical aid to famine victims.

Citizens of the developed nations also pressed their governments to step up official aid to the affected countries. The United States, through the Agency for International Development (AID), committed more than $262 million in food relief to Ethiopia alone in fiscal 1985, part of a $1.8 billion allocation for famine relief throughout Africa.

Although exact figures are unavailable, international donors are thought to have sent 7.5 million metric tons in food aid to Africa in 1985, double the amount shipped in 1983. A large portion of it, however, never reached the famine victims themselves. According to AID Ad-

ministrator M. Peter McPherson, only about 40% of the almost 1.8 million metric tons of official U.S. food aid had been delivered by mid-June; the rest lay rotting in ports, often because of a lack of trucks and railroad transportation to the affected areas. UNICEF also reported that the famine victims in greatest need of relief were not receiving it because of unreliable and often inappropriate distribution.

Political concerns also have hampered relief efforts, especially in Ethiopia, where the Soviet-supported regime is accused by its opponents of using the famine as a weapon to quell civil unrest. The Ethiopian army is reported to have strafed convoys carrying food to the remote regions of Eritrea and Tigre, which are largely under rebel control, while the government has forcibly relocated the regions' inhabitants to areas under its control.

These and other man-made problems are cited by many relief workers as far more serious elements in sub-Saharan Africa's crisis than the drought itself. They point to the need for long-term development aid, including seed, fertilizers, and tools, aimed at improving agricultural productivity and helping the people to become self-sufficient and better prepared to survive the next drought. Many fear that the people now living in feeding centers will become overly dependent on food handouts if they are not soon returned to their land. But because years of overuse and erosion have depleted the soil in many areas, for many there is little to go home to. The World Bank has estimated that 14 African countries lack sufficient land to feed their growing populations if cultivated according to traditional, subsistence farming methods. Innovative techniques used to promote agricultural self-sufficiency in Asia and Latin America during the 1960s and 1970s —fast-growing varieties of rice, corn, and wheat, for example—are not applicable to much of Africa's hot, dry climate. Agricultural researchers only now are developing the drought-resistant strains of sorghum, millet, and other staple crops needed to increase food production there.

Long-term development efforts require a stable political climate and careful planning. Not all types of development aid are appropriate, as many African nations have discovered in recent years. Nigeria and other countries on the continent borrowed heavily in the 1970s to build huge industrial complexes in an effort to join the ranks of the developed nations. The world recession of 1981–82 left them without buyers for their traditional exports—minerals and other commodities—and without revenue to meet their loan repayments. The resulting debt crisis has further eroded their efforts to become self-sufficient.

Despite the need for appropriate long-term development aid, the need for emergency food relief continued as 1985 ended. The rains came too late in many regions to affect the year's harvest, and many farmers lacked seeds or were too weak from malnutrition and disease to sow them. Tens of millions of sub-Saharan Africans still were suffering, and relief workers feared that the attention of Americans and other donors would wane before the crisis is over. According to the United Nations, $1.7 billion in new commitments by donor countries was needed to alleviate the "unprecedented crisis" that persists in 20 African nations.

MARY H. COOPER

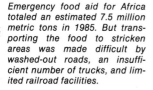
Emergency food aid for Africa totaled an estimated 7.5 million metric tons in 1985. But transporting the food to stricken areas was made difficult by washed-out roads, an insufficient number of trucks, and limited railroad facilities.

© Giansanti, Sygma

President Gnassingbe Eyadema of Togo welcomes Pope John Paul II during the latter's African tour in August.

predicted to increase by between 5.3% and 5.6% in 1985. An 18% further devaluation of the previously devalued currency also contributed to the recovery.

Until recently Zaire's economy was considered among the worst on the continent and the country was among the most indebted nations in Africa. In the period 1984–85, Zaire was forced to institute reforms insisted on by Western bankers in return for new loans. The IMF demanded a massive currency devaluation, an end to import and foreign-currency restrictions, and huge cuts in government spending. By late 1985, Zaire was showing tentative signs of recovery.

In contrast, Liberia, despite the largest amount of U.S. aid in its history, has barely been able to pay the debt service to its creditors, has been forced to reschedule loan repayments, and faces increasing unemployment and a decline in its per capita income. The United States was reluctant to maintain aid at its current levels as a result of President Samuel Doe's intimidation of potential opponents in the October election.

The African nations—excluding Nigeria, which is classified as an oil-exporting nation—owe the IMF $7.2 billion, or nearly one fifth of all IMF outstanding loans. Repayment would be a major preoccupation of most of these nations in the immediate future and beyond.

UN Decade for Women. The end of the United Nations Decade for Women was observed in July in Nairobi, Kenya, with a governmental conference attended by 2,200 delegates and a parallel forum for 14,000 delegates from nongovernmental organizations. The president of Kenya, Daniel arap Moi, and UN Secretary-General Javier Perez de Cuellar formally opened the conference. Key issues included wage differentials between women and men performing work of equal value, inequities in marriage agreements, the need for special remedial measures necessary to relieve the burden placed on women, and fair distribution of responsibilities between men and women. (*See also* WOMEN.)

Papal Visit. On August 8, Pope John Paul II began a 12-day journey to six sub-Saharan African countries—Togo, Ivory Coast, Cameroon, Central African Republic, Zaire, and Kenya. The pope also addressed a rally of young Muslims in Morocco on his first official visit to an Arab country. The trip to Africa was of particular importance because there are now more than 70 million Roman Catholics in Africa, nearly 15% of the continent's total population. Important themes in the pope's addresses included the repudiation of apartheid in South Africa and an emphasis on a church that is "fully Christian and fully African."

abroad that events in 1985 signaled the start of a process of profound change. The speed and direction of that change was uncertain. (*See* feature article, page 26.)

Economic Realities. Governments in Africa continued to experiment with policies to counteract their grim economic plight. In June, President Samora Machel of Mozambique introduced a program of economic reforms, including the sale of state businesses to private owners, a new private investment code, lower taxes, and the lifting of a number of import-export restrictions in an effort to attract foreign investors. The action was an apparent recognition of the ineffectiveness of some of his socialist policies, including the nationalization of industries. In a similar move, Tanzania's President Nyerere lifted the ban on private ownership of rental housing and the sale of a number of state farms to private entrepreneurs.

In order to secure the $1 billion in new loans necessary to improve its economic situation, Ghana has had to meet conditions imposed by the IMF, World Bank, and European Community (EC). As a result of strict reforms, the economy reportedly grew 7.6% in 1984 and was

PATRICK O'MEARA
N. BRIAN WINCHESTER
African Studies Program, Indiana University

AGRICULTURE

As world agriculture moved toward a situation of abundant food supplies, it became clearer that abundance is a mixed blessing. Some governments that had successfully encouraged agricultural growth were enjoying a more favorable balance of trade but were wrestling with expensive farm surpluses. Farmers and agribusiness, having met the challenge of increasing production, learned again that market abundance may mean low prices, and low prices over several years may bring hard times.

In the U.S. Midwest, bumper crops of corn and soybean could not stem the rising tide of farm and business bankruptcies and failed farm-credit institutions. Farmers and their friends organized protests and massive rallies to publicize their plight. The governor of Iowa announced a mortgage moratorium, by which credit agencies could not foreclose on farms. Neither Congress nor the president, however, could be persuaded to authorize a program of higher prices linked with strong production controls. Meanwhile, U.S. domestic prices for wheat, corn, and soybeans declined to the floors set by government "loan" prices, and meat producers took heavy losses because of low prices in late summer and early fall. (*See* feature article, page 36.)

A trend toward national self-sufficiency in agriculture was evidenced worldwide. Europe, long a major food importer, was fast approaching a change in status to that of net food exporter. Among the world's most populous nations, China met its domestic demands for corn, cotton, and soybeans, and India's 1985 wheat crop provided a surplus for export.

Agriculture also became more diversified within countries, as oilseed production expanded both in north temperate Canada and tropical Brazil. Europe and the United States, with homegrown sweeteners from corn and sugar beets, became less reliant on sugarcane from the tropics.

U.S. Trade. The U.S. share of world agricultural exports continued its four-year slide, although the nation still towered over all others in its exports of feed grain, wheat, soybeans, and cotton; U.S. rice exports also were large, second only to Thailand's. Hampered on the one hand by the high value of the dollar, U.S. exports were aided somewhat by an expanded Public Law 480 program, under which surpluses are donated or sold on concessional terms.

U.S. agricultural imports were expected to surpass the 1984 record, narrowing the still-positive balance of agricultural trade. About 65% of these imports were considered to be competitive with domestic products, and no immediate relief for U.S. producers was seen. Indeed, long-term prospects were for production surfeits due to emerging biotechnology.

For example, a new hormone—bovine somatotropin—whose release was expected soon may increase a dairy herd's milk production by as much as 30%. Meanwhile costly dairy control programs in the United States and the European Community were being overwhelmed by surpluses, and on both continents the number of dairy farmers was declining.

Western Europe. Western Europe's 1985 agricultural production was projected at slightly below that of the 1984 record. The EC, under its Common Agricultural Program (CAP), maintained price supports at levels well above U.S. and world prices for grains, dairy products, meat, and other products. In 1985 the EC was a major trade competitor, exporting wheat, corn, sugar, and dairy products, but at a high cost under the CAP budget. CAP deficits in 1985 resulted in frantic conferences among CAP members. Economists called for CAP reforms, but member governments remained responsive to the demands of various producer groups, postponing, for example, major reductions in agricultural prices. Spain and Portugal looked forward to joining the EC on Jan. 1, 1986.

Despite strong prices and high production, some European farmers faced debt crises similar to those of U.S. farmers because national governments—particularly those of West Germany, the Netherlands, and Denmark—had provided incentives for farmers to invest heavily in modern technology.

Canada, Australia, New Zealand. Wheat exporters, including Canada, suffered from a smaller world market. Canada's low volume of wheat exports, due in part to reduced supplies from a 1984 drought, depressed the shipping industry on the St. Lawrence Seaway.

However, large shipments of Canadian hogs were exported to the United States for slaughter, mainly because of favorable currency exchange rates, causing protests from both Canadian packinghouse workers and U.S. hog producers. Several Midwestern state governments embargoed Canadian hogs, and a U.S. federal agency imposed levies on them. Meanwhile, Canadian poultry production increased as more chicken was consumed in Canadian homes and fast-food outlets. Canada's government, jointly with provincial governments, proclaimed a new national stabilization program for red meat.

In Australia, dry weather resulted in reduced wheat production, but stocks were already large from two consecutive big crops. With rising input costs and smaller profits, some Australian farmers compensated by expanding crop acreage. New Zealand farmers also were increasing acreage of field crops.

Eastern Europe. Soviet farm production rose in 1985, including increased animal feed supplies and an improved wheat harvest. The USSR met its reduced wheat import needs by

purchasing from a number of countries, failing to meet the minimum purchase requirement under a 1983 U.S.-Soviet trade agreement. The improvement was due in large part to better crop conditions. Also, morale had improved within the agricultural sector, as Mikhail Gorbachev's coming to power raised expectations of management reforms. Plans for 1986 called for rapid expansion of acreage farmed under "improved technology."

In other Eastern European countries, production was down from high 1984 levels mainly because of dry weather. But agricultural imports also were reduced through restrictive import policies, apparently in an effort to improve deteriorating trade balances.

Asia. With few exceptions, Asian countries showed higher production, contributing to a new optimism that the world's increasing billions of people need not be short of food. China registered an 8% growth in wheat production and planted an even larger acreage for 1986. In addition to reducing wheat imports, China became a competitor of the United States in exporting feed grains to South Korea and Japan. In part because of competition from Asian exporters, U.S. exports to Japan—one of its largest agricultural markets—were expected to fall, along with U.S. exports to the Asian continent as a whole. Japanese farmers meanwhile diverted 500,000 ha (1.24 million acres) away from rice—a surplus crop—to wheat, barley, and forage.

Indonesia achieved status as a rice exporter in 1985. Malaysia achieved record highs in the production and export of palm oil. India was able to export half a million tons of wheat from its bumper crop. Even the Philippines, with a lagging agriculture, gained endorsement and funding from the International Monetary Fund for an economic recovery program.

Latin America. Per capita agricultural output increased by 2% in Latin America, partly because of improved weather, particularly in the Andean countries. Latin American agriculture became more diverse, with wheat production increasing in Chile, oilseeds in Argentina, and frozen orange juice in Brazil. Brazil, Argentina, Chile, and Mexico continued to rely on their agricultural exports to achieve a positive trade balance and to finance their debt payments. At the same time, food was needed for domestic populations, and governments operating under anti-inflationary fiscal policies were able to provide fewer incentives to farmers.

Reduced demand for sugarcane and the collapse of sugar prices devastated the economies of ten Central American and Caribbean countries, which were unsuccessful in seeking a larger share of the U.S. sugar market.

Africa. The famine-plagued Sahelian countries experienced good rains, which improved pasture conditions and crop prospects. More time was needed, however, for weakened nomadic animals to be rejuvenated and for seeds to be replenished and planted.

Good rainfall produced record grain harvests in Tunisia and Eastern Algeria. In sub-Saharan Africa, Kenya's and Southern Africa's agricultures recovered sharply from a 1984 drought, and Zimbabwe and Zambia harvested large corn crops. Nevertheless, the sub-Saharan region continued to face serious shortages of food. Prices were declining on several major African exports including coffee, cocoa, and tea.

Don F. Hadwiger
Iowa State University

Tass from Sovfoto

Improved crop conditions yielded a strong Soviet wheat harvest, and imports were reduced. The morale of the Soviet agricultural sector was boosted by the promise of reform under the new Gorbachev regime.

ALABAMA

Judicial and legislative news dominated Alabama headlines in 1985.

Federal Court Activity. Most national attention was directed toward Alabama with regard to the indictment and trial of eight black voting-rights activists who were charged with irregularities in connection with Democratic primaries and runoffs held in 1984. In trials held between July and October in Selma, Birmingham, and Tuscaloosa, most testimony focused on the accusation that the defendants were responsible for the unauthorized casting of numerous absentee ballots in predominantly black Perry, Sumter, Lowndes, and Greene counties. However, most of the defendants were acquitted of all or most of the charges brought against them. National black leaders, including the Rev. Jesse Jackson, charged that the federal prosecutions represented an effort by the administration of President Ronald Reagan to suppress black (and heavily Democratic) voter turnout in upcoming 1986 elections.

In other race-related litigation, the U.S. Supreme Court on April 16 threw out a state law denying the vote to persons convicted of crimes involving "moral turpitude" on grounds that the statute originally had been passed as another barrier to black political participation.

In June the U.S. Supreme Court ruled that Alabama's law setting aside daily moments of silence, with prayer as one stated option, was unconstitutional, despite a friend-of-the-court brief by Reagan administration attorneys. The High Court ruled that the Alabama legislature had an improper intent "to return prayer to the public schools."

Legislative Sessions. The legislature met in both regular and special sessions in 1985. Early in the year the legislature approved a bill limiting lawsuits against fellow employees and supervisors by workers hurt on the job. At the same time, workers' compensation benefits were boosted considerably. It was argued that the superseded legislation discouraged further industrial development in the state.

Also in special session, the legislature approved a plan by the administration of Gov. George C. Wallace for investing state oil and gas lease revenues, primarily for the benefit of the state's beleaguered general fund. State voters approved a trust fund in a May 14 referendum. Some local officials opposed the constitutional amendment because it did not provide for locally guaranteed shares in the additional revenues.

The regular session opened on February 5 and closed on May 20. Major legislation enacted included a record $2.17 billion education budget and a career ladder–merit pay plan for teachers. Also, the legislature raised the drinking age from 19 to 21. This action was necessary to prevent the loss of federal highway funds. The legislature declined to pass a law mandating the use of seat belts.

The legislature met again, in special session, in August and September. In these meetings a $310 million bond issue for education was approved. Emotionally argued but not approved was a bill requiring notification of parents before an abortion could be performed on a teenage girl.

Governor Wallace. The year marked the midpoint in Governor Wallace's fourth term in office. There was much speculation about whether he would seek a fifth in 1986. Early polls showed Wallace had more support among state voters than any other candidate, although not a majority. The governor was operated on in Denver on July 24 in an effort to relieve continuing pains related to the paralysis from which he has suffered since the 1972 attempt on his life. Early reports were that the operation was successful, and in the fall the governor and a party of business leaders went to Asia on an industry-hunting trip.

Tenn-Tom Waterway. The long-debated 234-mi (377-km) Tennessee-Tombigbee Waterway, a multibillion-dollar project involving extensive canal construction and river navigation improvement, was dedicated in early June. The waterway connects the Tennessee River on the north and the Tombigbee on the south to provide a major new outlet for water traffic to the Gulf of Mexico. Proponents believe it will considerably enhance the prospects for economic development in the Deep South. (*See also* ENGINEERING, CIVIL.)

Severe Weather. In January and February, 15 north Alabama counties were declared disaster areas due to damage inflicted by massive snow and ice storms. In early September additional millions in losses were suffered in coastal Alabama when Hurricane Elena struck that area.

WILLIAM H. STEWART
The University of Alabama

ALABAMA • Information Highlights

Area: 51,705 sq mi (133 915 km²).
Population (July 1, 1984 est.): 3,990,000.
Chief Cities (July 1, 1984 est.): Montgomery, the capital, 184,963; Birmingham, 279,813; Mobile, 204,923; Huntsville, 149,527.
Government (1985): *Chief Officers*—governor, George C. Wallace (D); lt. gov., Bill Baxley (D). *Legislature*—Senate, 35 members; House of Representatives, 105 members.
State Finances (fiscal year 1984): *Revenues,* $6,195,000,000; *expenditures,* $5,191,000,000.
Personal Income (1984): $39,869,000,000; per capita, $9,992.
Labor Force (June 1985): *Civilian labor force,* 1,797,800; *unemployed,* 165,100 (9.2% of total force).
Education: *Enrollment* (fall 1983)—public elementary schools, 510,814; public secondary, 211,087; colleges and universities, 171,381. *Public school expenditures* (1982–83), $1,486,520,630 ($2,177 per pupil).

An attempt by Alaska's Republican-controlled Senate to impeach Gov. William Sheffield, right, failed. The Democratic chief executive was charged with perjury before a grand jury.

AP/Wide World

ALASKA

In Alaska, 1985 was a highly charged political year, with some events occurring that attracted national attention. At the top of the list was the attempt by the Republican-controlled state Senate to impeach the incumbent Democratic governor, William Sheffield. The Alaska constitution requires that the motion for impeachment be made by the Senate, with the House of Representatives conducting the actual trial. The members of the Senate Rules Committee obtained the services of Sam Dash, former Senate counsel during the Watergate hearings, to assist them in their determinations. The governor was charged with perjury before a grand jury that was examining the awarding of a state contract to a group that included a strong Sheffield supporter. The hearings ended when it was determined that there was not sufficient evidence to demonstrate that perjury had in fact occurred. The political nature of the event was demonstrated by the subsequent appeals of Republican senators, all participants in the hearings, for restraint on the part of the governor when issues involving their districts were concerned.

Allegations of corruption were not limited to the upper levels of state government. One of the first acts of the new administration in the North Slope Borough (the jurisdiction in which the Prudhoe Bay and Kuparek oil fields are lo-

cated) was to commission an audit of borough finances. The audit suggested that a misuse of borough funds had occurred, involving not only other jurisdictions in Alaska, but also implicating firms from outside the state.

Economy. "Local hire" again became a major issue in Alaska, particularly in the interior regions of the state. A 1984 Supreme Court ruling *(James Francis v. the State of Alaska)* resulted in the overturning of requirements that contractors doing business with the state provide resident workers with employment preference over nonresidents. However, the continuing influx of nonresident workers into the Alaska labor force, plus a statewide unemployment rate that remained at least 2 full percentage points above the national rate, intensified efforts directed at local government regulation of contractor hiring policies. The issue was emphasized in several local elections in 1985 and promised to become more heated with seasonal increases in unemployment rates.

Projections of oil revenues generated from the North Slope oil fields continued to be low. However, a decision by the administration of President Ronald Reagan, clearing the way for non-North Slope-produced oil to be sold to Pacific Rim countries, brightened the economic picture somewhat for oil producers in the state.

ANCSA Report. Thomas Berger, the Canadian jurist commissioned by the Inuit Circumpolar Conference to evaluate the effects of the

Alaska Native Claims Settlement Act (ANCSA) on the Native people of Alaska, issued his final report on that project during 1985. Popularly known as the Berger Commission Report, the findings of this project were both expected and controversial. Chief among the conclusions reached by the commission was the assessment that most Native people have been adversely affected by ANCSA, with the most criticism reserved for the corporate structure mandated by the act. In brief, the corporate structure was seen to adversely affect traditional socio-political values, to attempt to wrongly impose economic values and methods of operation on a people, and to needlessly endanger an entire way of life—centered on subsistence activities—in order to accomplish non-Native established and defined goals. The report specifically endorsed Native self-government in order to continue the cultural patterns of subsistence as well as to maintain Native control of traditional village lands in Alaska.

As could be expected, opposition to the report centered around the corporate Native leadership in the state, as well as those non-Native residents of the state concerned with provisions in federal and state legislation requiring that a preference be given to subsistence hunters over sport hunters when management of wildlife resources is undertaken. Regulations adopted to manage the Game Units within the state for 1985 had placed severe restrictions on so-called urban hunters, while allowing rural residents normal access to moose and caribou.

Other. For the first time in its history, the Iditarod Sled Dog Race was won by a woman, Libby Riddles. Also, in a continuing effort to promote tourism as a basic industry in the state, an effort involving interests from the major urbanized areas was formed to advance Alaska as host for the 1992 Winter Olympics.

CARL E. SHEPRO, *University of Alaska*

ALBANIA

With the death of Enver Hoxha, Albania's aged (76) Stalinist dictator, of heart disease on April 11, 1985, observers wondered if the country might begin at last to moderate its dogmatic Marxist regime and abandon its self-imposed isolation from most of the world.

Hoxha's Regime. Hoxha (pronounced haw' dja) was the world's longest-ruling Communist leader. He was born in Gjinokaster, in southern Albania, on Oct. 16, 1908, the son of a Muslim cloth merchant, and educated in Albania and at the University of Montpellier in France. He was a founder of the Albanian Workers' (Communist) Party (AWP) in 1941 and a guerrilla leader against the occupying Italian and German forces in World War II. In 1944 the AWP set up a provisional postwar government, and Hoxha was elected the party's first secretary, a post he held, along with a changing variety of other top party and government offices in the People's Republic proclaimed in 1946, until his death.

Under Hoxha's harsh, puritanical rule, Albania became "the only truly Marxist and atheistic country"—and the poorest country in Europe (with an estimated per capita annual income of $820). His unswerving Marxist orthodoxy provoked a series of bitter splits between Albania and "revisionist" Communist

Ramiz Alia, 59, succeeded the late Enver Hoxha as first secretary of the Albanian Workers' Party on April 13.

SIPA/ Special Features

ALBANIA · Information Highlights

Official Name: People's Socialist Republic of Albania.
Location: Southern Europe, Balkan peninsula.
Area: 11,100 sq mi (28 748 km²).
Population (mid-1985 est.): 3,000,000.
Chief City: (1981 est.): Tiranë, the capital, 220,000.
Government: *Head of state,* Ramiz Alia, president of the Presidium (took office November 1982) and first secretary of the Albanian Workers' Party (April 1985). *Head of government,* Adil Çarçani (took office January 1982). *Legislature* (unicameral)—People's Assembly, 250 members.
Monetary Unit: Lek (7 leks equals U.S.$1, July 1985).
Gross National Product (1982 est. U.S.$): $2,580,-000,000.

regimes—with Yugoslavia in 1948, the Soviet Union in 1961, and China after 1976. Albania became an isolated, totally self-reliant, secretive fortress-state. Its borders were sealed to outsiders and foreign influences. Few Albanians were permitted to travel abroad, only about 100 to study abroad. An average of 3,000 foreign visitors were admitted annually. Believing that "the only religion an Albanian needs is Albania," Hoxha had all religious activities outlawed in 1967, with penalties for violations ranging from ten years' imprisonment to death. Opposition was dealt with quickly and drastically. Some 40,000 political prisoners were sent to labor camps. An attempted military coup was crushed in 1974.

The most serious threat to Hoxha occurred in 1981, when his long-time associate and premier since 1954, Mehmet Shehu, attempted unsuccessfully to overthrow him. Labeled a secret agent for several foreign powers, Shehu was said to have committed suicide. But in February 1985 the country's major newspaper, *Zeri i Popullit,* stated that he had been "liquidated."

Seven days of national mourning were declared for Hoxha; all foreign diplomats were barred from the funeral on April 15.

The New Leader. On April 13, the 11th Plenum of the AWP Central Committee elected Ramiz Alia to succeed Hoxha as first secretary. Alia, 59, had been a youthful partisan in World War II and a member of Hoxha's inner circle since the 1960s, holding a large number of party and government positions. He became Albania's head of state (chairman of the Presidium of the People's Assembly) in 1982 and had been handling many of Hoxha's day-to-day duties since 1984.

Foreign Relations. Although Alia vowed to remain loyal to Hoxha's policy of national isolation and ideological purity, there were early signs that modest changes could be expected, at least in Albania's foreign relations. Alia played host to a succession of high-level delegations from Italy, France, Great Britain, Japan, and the Third World. In 1984, Albania had agreed to establish diplomatic relations with Canada and Australia. On Jan. 9, 1985, a similar agreement with the Ivory Coast was announced. Negotiations continued between Albania and West Germany.

In 1984, Albania had enlarged its cultural and economic ties with Greece, Italy, Turkey, and Austria. In February-March 1985, it signed trade accords with Vietnam, Turkey, and the People's Republic of China. Albania's neighbors, Greece and Yugoslavia, received special attention. In January 1985, Albania signed an economic agreement with Greece envisioning sharp increases in mutual trade and cooperation in fishing and agricultural projects. On January 12 a second frontier crossing-point with Greece was opened at the Kakavia Pass. On March 8 the two signed a cultural exchange agreement. A continuing point of friction, however, was the sensitive status of the sizable ethnic Greek minority in southern Albania.

On January 11, Yugoslavia and Albania celebrated the completion of the railway from Shkodër, in northern Albania, to Hani i Hotit on the joint border. Yugoslavia pledged to continue the line to Titograd, thus connecting the small Albanian railway system to the European rail network. But polemics continued over alleged Yugoslav mistreatment of ethnic Albanians in the Autonomous Province of Kosovo.

JOSEPH F. ZACEK
State University of New York at Albany

ALBERTA

The year 1985 witnessed a reversal of provincial emigration and saw the arrival of two important visitors, Queen Mother Elizabeth, for the first time since 1939, and the Most Rev. Robert Runcie, archbishop of Canterbury.

Despite still-unsettled economic conditions, Albertans proved surprisingly generous in response to both local and international charitable appeals.

ALBERTA · Information Highlights

Area: 255,284 sq mi (661 188 km²).
Population (July 1985 est.): 2,350,400.
Chief Cities (1981 census): Edmonton, the capital, 532,246; Calgary, 592,743; Lethbridge, 54,072; Red Deer, 46,393; St. Albert, 31, 996.
Government (1985): *Chief Officers*—lt. gov., Helen Hunley; premier, Don Getty (Progressive Conservative). *Legislature*—Legislative Assembly, 79 members.
Provincial Finances (1984–85 fiscal year budget): *Revenues,* $9,756,000,000; *expenditures,* $10,-006,000,000.
Personal Income (average weekly earnings, July 1985): $449.80.
Labor Force (Sept. 1985, seasonally adjusted): *Employed workers,* 15 years of age and over, 1,252,000; *Unemployed,* 115,000 (9.2%).
Education (1985–86): *Enrollment*—elementary and secondary schools, 467,680 pupils; postsecondary (full-time, 1985–86)—universities, 42,000; community colleges, 25,170. (All monetary figures are in Canadian dollars.)

Government and Politics. The year opened with an increase in the provincial income tax, almost unnoticed, and appointment of Alberta's first woman lieutenant governor, Helen Hunley, a former minister of municipal affairs. Peter Lougheed resigned as premier and leader of the Progressive Conservative Party. His successor was Don Getty, a one-time cabinet colleague.

A by-election to fill the legislative vacancy caused by the death of Grant Notley, Alberta leader of the New Democratic Party, resulted in the choice of James Gurnett.

Agriculture. This was a disappointing year for both ranchers and farmers. In southern Alberta, both grain and hay crops were virtually wiped out by drought, aggravated by a plague of grasshoppers. In the central part of the province, yields were good, but the Peace River area suffered from lack of moisture for the third time in four years. Generally, weather in September delayed harvests and lowered grades. Conditions outside Canada adversely affected both prices and markets.

Business and Finance. Collapse of the Edmonton-based Canadian Commercial Bank and Calgary's Northland Bank followed recent failures of western mortgage and trust companies and difficulties in Alberta credit unions.

West Edmonton Mall, believed to be the world's largest shopping center, completed construction of its third phase, which consisted largely of recreational facilities. Construction employment in the province improved somewhat but still remained far below normal. Starts were up in single-family dwellings; otherwise the industry remained stagnant. Rental vacancies decreased significantly.

Expected benefits from deregulation of the Canadian oil and gas industry were largely offset by a decrease in world oil prices. Exports of natural gas to the United States were also lower than anticipated. Purchase of Gulf's Edmonton refinery and western retail outlets by federally owned Petro-Canada did not meet approval of the industry, oriented as it is to private ownership.

Labor. Despite low wage increases in both the public and private sectors—from zero to 2–3%—there was little labor unrest. One exception was a prolonged strike by public health nurses.

Literary and Performing Arts. September saw the opening of Calgary's C$80 million Center for the Performing Arts. The same month witnessed the publication of *The Canadian Encyclopedia* in Edmonton, acclaimed as the year's most important Canadian publication.

Education. For the first time, the Alberta government extended the power to grant degrees (other than theological) to a private institution, Camrose Lutheran College. Other such colleges were expected to seek the same privilege in the near future.

Canapress Photo Service

Don Getty (seated), 52, a former football player and provincial cabinet minister, became Alberta's 11th premier.

Professional Sport. For the second successive year the Edmonton Oilers won the Stanley Cup, emblematic of the championship of the National Hockey League.

JOHN W. CHALMERS
Concordia College, Edmonton

ALGERIA

Algeria continued to move toward closer ties with the West in 1985. President Chadli Benjedid made the first official visit to the United States by an Algerian head of state since the North African country gained independence in 1962. Growth in gross national product (GNP) increased to more than 6%, and the inflation rate fell below 4%. However, the demand for consumer goods, housing, and jobs outstripped their availability. The labor force was expanding rapidly, a source of growing pressure on the Chadli government.

Foreign Relations. Just before Chadli's visit to Washington in April, President Ronald Reagan lifted a long-standing ban on U.S. military sales to Algeria. The move opened the door for possible purchases of American weaponry to support Chadli's plan to modernize Algeria's

AP/Wide World

President Reagan officially welcomed Algeria's President Chadli Benjedid to the White House on April 17.

armed forces and to reduce dependency on the Soviet Union. The two leaders also signed a joint economic agreement to facilitate trade and the transfer of American technology to Algeria. Two months later, the Reagan administration announced the sale of up to one million metric tons of wheat to Algeria under an export subsidy program.

In June, Algerian officials enhanced their reputation for skillful diplomacy by successfully negotiating the release of 60 hostages, mostly Americans, being held by Islamic militants who had hijacked a plane in Athens. The U.S. government, recalling Algeria's role in gaining the release of Americans in the 1980–81 Iranian hostage crisis, had persuaded Chadli to allow the hijackers to land in Algiers.

The war in the Western Sahara continued to be the most contentious foreign policy issue. Chadli's support for the Polisario Front in its battle for control of the territory is a key factor in Algeria's relations with other countries. Chadli's visit to Dakar in mid-May was a major turning point in relations with Senegal. Differences between the former presidents of the two countries over the Western Sahara had strained relations for years. President Chadli later visited Tunisian President Habib Bourguiba to express Algerian solidarity in the crisis precipitated by Libya's expulsion of Tunisian workers.

ALGERIA • Information Highlights

Official Name: Democratic and Popular Republic of Algeria.
Location: North Africa.
Area: 919,487 sq mi (2 381 471 km²).
Population (mid-1985 est.): 22,200,000.
Chief Cities (Jan. 1, 1983): Algiers, the capital, 1,721,607; Oran, 663,504; Constantine, 448,578.
Government: *Head of state,* Chadli Benjedid, president (took office Feb. 1979). *Head of government,* Abdelhamid Brahimi, prime minister (appointed Jan. 22, 1984).
Monetary Unit: Dinar (4.956 dinars equal U.S.$1, Aug. 1985).
Gross Domestic Product (1984 U.S.$): $51,900,-000,000.
Economic Index (1984, Algiers): *Consumer Prices* (1970 = 100), all items, 312.2.
Foreign Trade (1984 U.S.$): *Imports,* $10,285,-000,000; *exports,* $12,795,000,000.

Politics. In September, Islamic fundamentalists resumed antigovernment activity for the first time in several years. A hitherto unknown group called the Islamic Jihad of Sheikh Sadeq el-Moundhiri claimed responsibility for an armed raid on a police school in Soumaa, a bomb explosion outside the Algerian embassy in Beirut, and other incidents. The group charged that the Chadli government encouraged violations of Islamic law and morality. In May the government had tried and released many of the fundamentalists who were detained in 1982 after demonstrations and clashes between Islamic groups and students.

Earlier in the year, government police cracked down on demonstrators in the Casbah, the old quarter of Algiers. The collapse of a neglected building set off the protest, which culminated in a demonstration against housing and water shortages and generally squalid living conditions in the quarter. In the past, Algeria's social calm rarely has been marred by incidents of social unrest.

Abdennour Ali Yahia, a well-known attorney and one of the government's harshest critics, was detained in July, along with other members of the Algerian Human Rights League. His arrest was connected with his leadership role in organizing the league, launched one month earlier to protest violations of human rights in Algeria.

The Economy. Increases in agricultural productivity and housing construction were among the top priorities of the 1985–89 development plan, which was delayed a few months due to uncertainty about oil and natural gas prices. Since nearly all of Algeria's limited arable land is already under cultivation, improved agricultural techniques are considered vital to progress toward the goal of food self-sufficiency. The plan also calls for higher profits to farmers and manufacturers and other incentives to stimulate production. In 1985 the producers of cereals and pulses received major increases, and the prices of basic foods went up.

Progress was made on trade agreements involving liquefied natural gas (LNG), part of Algeria's continuing effort to diversify the hydrocarbon industry and lessen its dependence on crude oil. A massive five-year countertrade agreement was signed, involving the exchange of Algerian LNG for Brazilian imports needed for rail, hydroelectric, and housing projects. Algeria also settled a long-standing LNG dispute with Spain, a prerequisite to the renewal of trade between the two countries, and signed a 20-year contract to supply LNG to Yugoslavia.

However, Distrigas Corp. of Boston canceled its contract to import LNG from Algeria. In addition, Algeria's four major European LNG clients were pushing to renegotiate their contracts to obtain more favorable terms.

PAULA M. HIRSCHOFF, *"Africa Report"*

ANTHROPOLOGY

The year 1985 was replete with significant anthropological activity and news.

Anthropoid Origins in Asia? New fossil jawbone fragments of Amphipithecus, a primate, first found in 1937, were reported to have been discovered by a Mandalay Arts and Sciences University field team in Burma's Pondaung Hills. The fragments are estimated to be 40 to 44 million years old. The additional bones together with the fragments found previously provide a nearly complete picture of the species' lower jaw including several teeth. The teeth and jaw show features associated with anthropoids rather than prosimians. Dr. Russell L. Ciochon of the Institute of Human Origins, Berkeley, CA, the team's senior investigator, said that the bones are representative of the most ancient species that are ancestral to monkeys, apes, and humans and "raise the possibility that the origin of Anthropoidea could have been in southern Asia."

60th Anniversary of the Taung Baby. The Taung Diamond Jubilee International Symposium was held at the University of the Witwatersrand, Johannesburg, and the University of Bophuthatswana, Mmabatho, Jan. 27 to Feb. 4, 1985. The Taung Diamond Jubilee was organized to celebrate 60 years since the first discovery by Raymond Dart of an australopithecine, prehuman, fossil now called *Australopithecus africanus* (the Taung baby). Philip Tobias, the successor to Dart in the department of anatomy at the University of the Witwatersrand, organized the symposium to provide an opportunity to examine the development of paleoanthropology from the early discoveries, through many controversies, to the modern science. Dart, now 92, was present at the symposium, and he and Tobias agreed that the continuing controversies were "a sign of an intellectually vigorous profession."

DNA and Human-Ape Relationships. A new technique of making DNA comparisons called DNA-DNA hybridization was developed by Charles Sibley and Jon Ahlquist of the department of biology at Yale University. After completing more than 20,000 DNA comparisons among the birds of the world, they began measuring genetic distances among the hominoids (*Homo sapiens,* chimpanzee, gorilla, orangutan, and gibbon). They reported that gibbons diverged from the hominoid line 18 to 22 million years ago, the orangutan, 13 to 16 million years ago, the gorilla, 8 to 10 million years ago, but humans and chimpanzees split only 6 to 8 million years ago. The method not only gives branching order but times. Sibley and Ahlquist believe that their method is inherently more powerful than other methods, including that of Allan Wilson and Vincent Sarich of the University of California, Berkeley, which depend on differences in protein structure.

Activist Anthropologists. Although field anthropologists have long provided assistance to the peoples they study, institutionally organized efforts have been stepped up in recent years. Two organizations, Cultural Survival, Inc., founded in 1972 and based in Cambridge, MA, and the London-based Survival International, have as their core a group of anthropologists dedicated to helping native cultures survive in the modern age, resist assaults on their ancestral land, and prevent the destruction of their often fragile environments.

In Namibia, for example, anthropologist Claire Ritchie is helping Ju/wa Bushmen resist plans by the South African government to resettle them in the west and turn their land into a nature reserve. And John Marshall of the !Kung-San Foundation has been assisting the Ju/wasi (which means "ourselves" or "the people") implement their plan of a mixed-crop, stock-farming economy.

In Nicaragua, Theodore Macdonald, the projects director of Cultural Survival, has been helping Miskito Indians resolve a land dispute with the Sandinista government. Among the other peoples in jeopardy by modern political and economic forces are the Zuni tribe of New Mexico, the Mouti Pygmies of Zaire, and the Yanomani Indians of Brazil and Venezuela.

According to Marcus Colchester of Survival International, there is much to be gained from preserving such cultures. "These peoples have a deep knowledge of their environment to contribute," he says, "and also a knowledge of what it is to be human."

Books. A number of books of more than specialized interest were published in 1985. *The View from Afar* by Claude Lévi-Strauss is a collection of essays that may be the last of his work in anthropology. Although the essays range widely through the author's interests, he also speaks of the end of his teaching days and the 50-year span of his academic career. The title seems to refer to Lévi-Strauss' penchant to view life in grand scale but then to examine behavior and ideas in minute detail. In the end, he refers his examination back to the patterns of the observed, perhaps to all of human life.

Marshall Sahlins, a professor of anthropology at the University of Chicago, published *Islands of History*. Brilliantly written, though not easy to read, it provides an education on historical anthropology, a growing developing theory. It also presents fascinating insights into Polynesian culture. Sahlins' point is that historical process is structural, shaped by culture, and cannot be understood without examining the behavior of real persons. Sahlins uses events in Polynesian history to develop his arguments. Among the topics discussed are the ways power and political succession are conceived and expressed in Polynesia.

HERMAN J. JAFFE
Brooklyn College, CUNY

ARCHAEOLOGY

While discoveries in the field contributed to archaeological study in 1985, some of the greatest contributions of the year came from the fruition of long-term systematic studies. Shipwrecks, well-preserved bodies, and "lost cities" dominated the field reports.

Eastern Hemisphere

Tools and Bones. By studying microscopic wear patterns on comparative sets of Inuit (Eskimo), experimental, and archaeological tools, scientists at Johns Hopkins University confirmed the presence of bone tools as early as the stone choppers and flakes at Olduvai Gorge in Tanzania 1.75 million years ago. Medium-size bone fragments were used to process some soft substance, like marrow, while heavier, longer bone pieces were used for tasks like digging or butchery.

Radiocarbon dating on a burial in the Grotta Paglicci in northwest Italy showed it to be ca. 23,000 years old and belonging to the Gravettian Industry, which hitherto had produced very few burials. A pubescent youth was equipped with flint tools and wore 36 hart deer canines, apparently attached to a cap.

Neolithic Studies. Recent archaeological and paleolinguistic evidence have combined to create a detailed picture of ancestral Polynesian culture. A marine-adapted technology emerged some time after 1500 B.C., based on bark cloth, stone and shell adzes, effective fish hooks, and outrigger oceanic canoes. Taro root, pigs, dogs, and fowl were the main domesticated foodstuffs, but protein derived mainly from fish. Coastal hamlets featured ceremonial platforms called *malae,* and tribes were headed by chiefs called *ariki.*

Archaeologists have clarified some of the enigmas of paleolinguistics for the early Indo-Europeans of western Eurasia ca. 3000 B.C. They concluded that the chief (*reg*) of these folk held a weakly developed office that accrued much responsibility but little wealth.

Archaeologists had long debated whether the Neolithic acceptance of Near Eastern domesticated plants and animals had spread by population movement or by acculturation of Mesolithic hunters. A recent joint archaeological-genetics study has explained the expansion of early European farming largely by population growth and local migratory activity.

Prehistoric Teeth. Stuck to the teeth of a late Bandkeramik skeleton near Lake Constance in West Germany was gum from birch bark. The material apparently had been used as a kind of chewing gum. It was also used for hafting projectile points and gluing together broken pottery.

On the island of Langeland, Denmark, a male cranium in the Funnel-Beaker megalithic chamber tomb (3200 B.C.) exhibited a neat round hole in a tooth that had dental caries. A dentist confirmed that drilling such a hole would have alleviated the abcess, and experiments verified that the hole was bored with a flint drill tip.

A Nabataean warrior found in a mass grave near Jerusalem also had dental problems ca. 200 B.C. In one abcessed tooth, a bronze wire had been inserted into the diseased root canal, exemplifying an early form of filling.

Bronze Age Shipwreck. At a depth of 330 ft (100 m) off the coast of Turkey, a sponge diver spotted some ancient debris that proved to be the oldest shipwreck ever found—3,400 years old. The 65-ft (20-m) Mycenaean vessel carried a cargo of copper ingots and tin, as well as gold objects, amphorae full of glass beads, an elephant tusk, and a hippopotamus tooth.

Near Eastern Civilization. The translation of cuneiform inscriptions on stone from Mesopotamia revealed a set of simple recipes from 1750 B.C. The foods were well-oiled and included a lot of onions but little salt. Eighteen kinds of cheese are described, along with pickled grasshoppers for snacks. Meanwhile, scholars from the University of Pennsylvania published the first volume of their dictionary of Sumerian, with numerous other volumes to appear in the future.

A recently concluded Israeli project that had spanned nearly two decades further revealed the Jerusalem established by King David and King Solomon ca. 1000 B.C. On a slope southeast of the present city, the site features a 59-ft (18-m) stepped support wall for the fortifications and a 33-ft (10-m) shaft that permitted women to go down to the Gihon Spring for water within the protection of the walls. Household pottery, Rhodian wine jugs, a cow bone flute, female fertility figurines, and a thronelike stone toilet seat were among the objects found.

Iron Age Faces. Knowledge of face tissue and cranial fragments excavated in 1977 from a tomb at Vergina, near Salonika, Greece, enabled English scientists to reconstruct the visage of the person buried there. On the basis of grave goods, archaeologists had already identified the person as Philip II of Macedonia, the father of Alexander the Great. That conclusion was confirmed on completion of the facial reconstruction, which revealed a telltale injury at the right eye.

Well-preserved Iron Age bog bodies are common in southern Scandinavia, but archaeologists reported the first complete bog body found in England, at Wimslow. The 2,500-year-old Celt had been garroted until his neck was broken.

Medieval Paris. While digging a new entrance to the famous Louvre museum, workers unearthed traces of Paris dating from the 12th century. These include stone house founda-

After a 16-year search, a U.S. team of bounty hunters and archaeologists discovered the Spanish galleon Atocha, which sank some 40 mi (64 km) west of Key West, FL, in 1622. The ship's treasure was reportedly worth up to $400 million.

Tucker, Gamma-Liaison

tions and the royal castle before construction of the Louvre. Pots, glass vessels, Ming Chinese porcelain, coins, and numerous dice were found. Many of the dice were loaded.

Western Hemisphere

Paleo-Indians. In two rock shelters at Tequendama, Colombia, archaeologists found evidence of human occupation superimposed on volcanic-infiltrated Pleistocene deposits. The earliest cultural material includes bifacial leaf-shaped tools, oval keeled scrapers, endscrapers and rectangular scrapers with retouched margins. The distinctive corner perforators are known from a few Paleo-Indian sites in North America.

New World Bodies. At the floor of a pond near Titusville, FL, preserved in peat, scientists discovered the bodies of about 50 Archaic Indians dating from ca. 5000 B.C. Two of the skulls contained largely intact brains, with the DNA still preserved.

Aridity plus embalming helped preserve the bodies of 7,000-year-old hunting and gathering Indians in Chile's northern desert near Arica. The Chincorro Culture dissected its dead with pelican beaks and applied embalming techniques more elaborate than those of the ancient Egyptians. The mat-wrapped bodies were buried collectively in sand graves.

In a shallow cave at Qilakitsog in west Greenland, the cold wind had freeze-dried eight Inuits, buried ca. 1475. A four-year-old boy had symptoms of Downs Syndrome, and the adult women had facial tattoos.

Canadian anthropologists tracking the ill-fated Franklin Expedition, which sought the Northwest Passage in 1848, found the well-preserved bodies of two expedition members.

Village Indians. Routine rescue archaeology in the Ozark Mountains of southern Missouri revealed the earliest known village of the Mississippi Culture, ca. A.D. 700, and produced the largest pre-Columbian settlements yet found in North America. The Missouri site exhibits shell-tempered pottery, maize gardens, and oval houses.

Lost Cities. The most celebrated archaeological event of the year was an expedition to a "lost city" located on the steep, cloud-covered eastern slope of the Andes in Peru. Called Gran Pajaten, the remote jungle site was inhabited by a previously unknown pre-Hispanic civilization that may date from A.D. 500. The ruins had been discovered and briefly examined in the early 1960s but then abandoned. The 1984–85 expedition reported a city of cylindrical, two-story stone buildings decorated with mosaics and other designs. Also found were burial towers, terraced fields, wood carvings, fabrics, pottery, and other items.

In the jungles of Honduras, a British team located a long-rumored "lost city" of the Payan tribe. The 1.5-sq-mi (3.8-km²) site is dominated by a large stone platform. Other finds included stone structures, decorated pottery and stones, and stone axes.

Historic Archaeology. The Spanish galleon *Atocha,* which sank in a storm off Key West, FL, in 1622 while en route to Spain with gold and other treasures, was found by private venture salvagers who conscientiously included professional archaeologists on the staff. The treasure includes jewelry, silver ingots, gold chains, and coins.

And archaeologists digging in the trash pit at a prepresidential homesite of Abraham Lincoln in Illinois found fine imported English China, cut glass crystal, and other evidence of the way of life and the tastes of the well-to-do in the 19th century.

RALPH M. ROWLETT
University of Missouri-Columbia

Peter Aaron, Esto

The new Humana Building, headquarters of the health-care organization in Louisville, KY, was one of the year's most discussed buildings. It was designed by Michael Graves.

ARCHITECTURE

While many leading architects and architectural critics might like to say that 1985 was the year in which the increasingly stripped-down and squared-off boxes of the International Style—the norm for commercial and, to a lesser extent, residential construction for the previous three decades—finally disappeared from credible building designers' palettes, what these leaders in the profession hoped for was far from true. It was true that many of the recently developed concepts that they espoused —such as the decorative Postmodern Style, building preservation, and fitting new construction in sympathetically with what was preserved—were well established. But what Heinrich Klotz, director of the Gwerman Museum of Architecture in Frankfurt, had observed in 1984—that the new style, despite its ornament and increased visual interest, was more of a revision of the International Style (or modernism) than a revolution—seemed more of a possible explanation. Noted critic Vincent

Scully, writing in *The New York Times* in 1985, took a similar view, saying that certain celebrated Postmodern projects could be seen, on closer inspection, to be little more than filling the developer's floor area and height limitations as allowed by local codes. Or, in other words, they were little more than the stripped-down economic box dressed up.

And leading architects did continue to work in the International Style, often molding it in creative ways that its formulators at the Bauhaus in 1920's Germany never envisioned any more than they envisioned its simplicity being molded into low cost. These leading architects remained among the recipients of awards in prestigious programs. They included Hans Hollein, the recipient of the 1985 Pritzker Prize for outstanding design, and the previous year's recipient of that prize, Richard Meier. They included the members of the Miami design firm Arquitectonica who imbue their basic geometric buildings with brilliant, sometimes clashing colors; and Renato Severino, whose buildings completed in 1985, as exemplified by the Mount Pleasant Corporate Center in New York, use modernism's rectangular windows and panels to form large overall patterns—or decoration.

Outstanding examples of Postmodern Style —which used historic, decorative models for its point of departure—announced for construction during 1985, included a 40-story office building in Chicago, said by its architects, Johnson and Burgee, to be designed in English Jacobean manner. (These architects had designed the premiere large-scale Postmodern building, the AT&T headquarters in New York.) And outstanding examples included the Escondido Civic Center, a large complex to be designed for that California town in the Mediterranean manner by associated architects Pacific Associates and Daniel and Mann, Johnson & Mendenhall, who won the right to do so in a national design competition.

New Buildings. Buildings completed during the year in the Postmodern Style include offices designed in the Tuscan manner for the American Academy of Pediatrics in Elk Grove, IL, by Hammond Beeby and Babka; and, possibly most noteworthy of all buildings completed during the year, The Humana Building housing offices for that health-care organization in Louisville, KY. It was designed by Michael Graves in a manner that might best be called a cross between a Roman temple and a space rocket. (Graves also designed one of the earliest Postmodern buildings, the Portland (OR) justice center, and was and had been one of the strongest advocates of the style in academic circles.)

More modest examples of the style included a library in Avon, CT, designed by architects Galliher Schoenhardt & Baier in almost literal Romanesque style. The most surprising Postmodern building of the year was a school addi-

tion in Middlebury, CT, that was also an outstanding example of fitting in. It was designed by architects Gwathmey Siegel & Associates who had gained a strong reputation for design in the International Style.

Divergent styles could have been cataloged as Hi-tech, as exemplified by an announced project for Chicago's O'Hare airport by Murphy/Jahn, Envirodyne Engineers and Schal Associates, associated architects and engineers; or as exemplified by an announced project for Houston's downtown convention center by a large consortium of designers, including Golemon & Rolfe Associates, Jon S. Chase, Molina & Associates, Haywood Jordan McCowan, and Moseley Associates.

Rehabilitation. The rehabilitation of existing structures, a process threatened by the proposed elimination of tax laws favorable to it, nonetheless continued at an increasing pace. It was due to the previous momentum of both the tax laws and a growing, entrenched appreciation by the general public for restored buildings. Examples included the remodeling of a 500,000 sq ft (46 450 m²) warehouse into a design center in Boston (by architects Earl Flansburgh & Associates); a major hotel remodeling, Morgans in New York by Andrée Putman; a mixed-use market and theater in Portland, OR (by SERA Architects); and the remodeling of a convent into housing for the elderly in Fall River, MA (by the Boston Architectural Team Inc.). One rehabilitation project announced during the year for Minneapolis also was an example of the growing popularity of mixed use —the incorporation of different functions, such as housing and offices, into the same buildings. Known as block 10 of the St. Anthony Falls Historic District, this project promised to make use of several 19th-century mills for housing, retail, and a hotel and was designed by joint venture architects Hayber Associates and Architectural Associates.

No better idea of the diversity of styles in which distinguished buildings had recently been built could be achieved than by seeing the winners of the American Institute of Architects annual award program (*see page 106*). The winners represented all of the concerns, directions, and styles—from restoration to fitting buildings into their contexts, from historic recall to the continued use of the International Style, to Hi-tech.

The year could be said to be one in which the public entered the architectural, or at least the architectural planning, field en masse. While many of the older cities had, many years before, attacked the problem of their disappearing special characters with landmark preservation laws meant to protect their older buildings, and other cities, such as New York, had tried to shift development from their concentrated cores through special zoning, San Francisco architects began to respond to a

PRESIDENTIAL AWARDS FOR DESIGN EXCELLENCE

In a Jan. 30, 1985, ceremony in the Indian Treaty Room of the Old Executive Office Building, President Reagan presented the first Presidential Awards for Design Excellence. Sponsored by the National Endowment for the Arts, the awards are intended to recognize merit in federal design. The first 13 winners were:

Seattle Foot, a plastic device that permits an amputee to run, developed by Dr. Ernest Burgess of Seattle's Prosthetics Research Foundation and sponsored by the Veterans Administration

Boston's Charles River flood control and navigation improvement and pollution abatement system, developed by the Army Corps of Engineers and C.E. Maguire Inc.

Graphic and Visual Communication System, a high-tech logo and graphic system, developed by the National Aeronautics and Space Administration

Unigrid Design Program, a coordinated pamphlet design, developed by the National Park Service

Linn Cove Viaduct, Blue Ridge Parkway, Asheville, NC, built by the National Park Service and the Federal Highway Administration

Historic Preservation Tax Incentives Program, sponsored by the National Park Service

Franklin Court, Philadelphia, a redesign of the original Benjamin Franklin house and print shop, developed by the National Park Service

Art-in-Architecture Program of the General Services Administration

Intercity Bridge, across the Columbia River connecting Pasco and Kennewick, WA

Transportation Symbol Signs, adapted by the American Institute of Graphic Arts for the U.S. Department of Transportation

The Gardens, San Mateo, CA, a 186-unit garden-apartment complex, subsidized by the Department of Housing and Urban Development

Scattered Infill Housing Project, Charleston, SC, public housing, sponsored by the Department of Housing and Urban Development

New Partnership for Restoring American Cities, St. Paul, MN, urban redevelopment, sponsored by the Department of Housing and Urban Development

Franklin Court

Independence National Historic Park

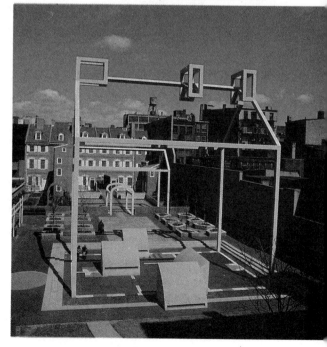

The Charles Shipman Payson Building, Portland, ME, designed by I.M. Pei & Associates, was honored by the American Institute of Architects. According to the jury, the art museum should serve as a "model for urban revitalization."

AMERICAN INSTITUTE OF ARCHITECTS

1985 Honor Award Winners

Commercial/Institutional Projects

Pike Place Market restoration, Seattle; G.R. Bartholick architect/planner; "one of the best mixed-use environments in the United States"

San Juan Capistrano Library, San Juan Capistrano, CA; Michael Graves; "a masterful transformation of the Spanish mission vernacular into a modern composition"

Middlebury Elementary School, Middlebury, CT; Tai Soo Kim/Hartford Design Group; "a marvelously cheery and refreshing learning environment"

The Atheneum, New Harmony, IN; Richard Meier & Partners; "a highly personal vision of an architectural ideal"

AB Volvo corporate headquarters, Göteborg, Sweden; Mitchell/Giurgola Architects; "an atmosphere of elegance and quality rare in corporate environments"

Charles Shipman Payson Building (Portland Museum of Art), Portland, ME; I.M. Pei & Partners; "a compelling building that enriches its community without overpowering it"

Weyerhaeuser Technology Center, Tacoma, WA; Skidmore, Owings & Merrill; "the building is not so much an object in its environment, as part of its environment"

Residential Projects

Pacific Townhouses, Santa Monica; Rebecca Binder and James Stafford; a "vision of postindustrial housing"

Church Court Condominiums, Boston; Graham Gund Associates; "a masterpiece of contextual design"

Tidewater House, Eastern Shore, MD; Hugh Newell Jacobsen; "a house that displays . . . skillful composition and detailing, and perfect compatibility with climate and site"

Roosevelt Solar Village, Roosevelt, NJ; Kelbaugh + Lee; "a model of low-income housing for the elderly"

Chilmark residence, Martha's Vineyard, MA; Robert A.M. Stern Architects; "a beautifully designed object that, through its fresh interpretation of the New England shingle-style coastal cottage, evokes a clear sense of place"

sweeping new zoning plan, enacted in 1984 under strong public pressure. The plan was to not only reduce the allowable bulk and height of all buildings but would sculpt their collective massing toward a central peak, a plan thought complementary to the city's surrounding hills.

Never before had a city gone so far as to determine an overall character for itself. It was an idea that seemed perfected for, if not by, the new wave of more human concerns in architectural design.

Charles Hoyt, *"Architectural Record"*

Camera Press London from Photo Trends

In Argentina nine former junta members were tried on such charges as human-rights violations, murder, and torture.

ARGENTINA

President Raúl Alfonsín gave the highest priority in 1985 to reorganizing the Argentine military establishment. An anti-inflation program drastically reduced inflation and facilitated debt renegotiations.

Military Issues. Alfonsín hoped to assure democratic rule by professionalizing the politicized armed forces and placing them under civilian control. Also, he was determined to reduce military spending by 50%. Responding in March to heightened criticism of Alfonsín's rule by military elements apparently challenging his political authority, the president retired 16 of the highest-ranking officers—ten generals, four rear admirals, and two air force brigadiers. In April, Alfonsín denounced a civilian-military coup attempt as part of a destabilization campaign of kidnappings, machine-gun attacks, and bombings. On the death in May of Raúl Borras, minister of defense, Alfonsín named another civilian, Roque Carranza, to the post.

A state of siege, declared by President Alfonsín on October 25 in response to months of right-wing terrorist activity, including dynamite explosions at public institutions, was lifted on December 9. Six military men and six civilians were ordered arrested for the bombings. Discontent within the armed forces had

been growing during a six-month trial on human-rights charges of members of military juntas serving between 1976 and 1982.

This unprecedented trial of nine military men ended on October 21. The former junta members were tried by a federal appeals court on charges of human-rights violations, murders, illegal denial of freedom, torture, robbery, illegal searches, and disappearances of more than 9,000 persons. The accused military personnel, in general, accepted responsibility for human-rights violations but claimed that they were not guilty of the charges since they were following instructions from a constitutionally elected government mired in a revolutionary war. The verdict came on December 9. Former president Jorge Videla and Adm. Emilio Massera received life sentences. Another former president, Roberto Viola, was given a 17-year term. Adm. Armando Lambruschini was sentenced to eight years, and air force Brig. Gen. Orlando Agosti to four-and-a-half years. Four officers were acquitted.

Gen. Leopoldo Galtieri, Adm. Jorge Anaya, Brig. Gen. Basilio Lami Dozo, and 13 other officers were formally charged with negligence and misconduct in Argentina's highest military court in August for their role in the Falkland (Malvinas) Islands conflict with Great Britain in 1982. A committee investigating those within the military forces who were re-

---

ARGENTINA • Information Highlights

Official Name: Argentine Republic.
Location: Southern South America.
Area: 1,068,297 sq mi (2 766 889 km²).
Population (mid-1985 est.): 30,600,000.
Chief Cities (1980 census): Buenos Aires, the capital, 2,908,001; Córdoba, 990,007; Rosario, 935,471.
Government: *Head of state and government,* Raúl Alfonsín, president (took office Dec. 10, 1983). *Legislature*—Senate and Chamber of Deputies.
Monetary Unit: Austral (0.8000 austral equals U.S.$1, Dec. 2, 1985).
Gross Domestic Product (1982 U.S.$): $69,326,-000,000.
Economic Indexes (1984): *Consumer Prices* (1980 = 100), all items, 17,604.5; food, 17,894.4. *Industrial Production* (1980 = 100), 94.
Foreign Trade (1984 U.S.$): *Imports,* $4,583,000,000; *exports,* $8,107,000,000.

---

sponsible for 1,000 Argentine wartime fatalities had recommended the death penalty for the top three commanders. The prosecutor requested only discharges and imprisonment for the officers. A verdict was expected by the end of the year.

Elections. Midterm elections were held for the first time in 20 years, on November 3. Some 6,000 posts at the federal, state, and local levels were filled. With 43% of the popular vote, Alfonsín's Radical Party strengthened its representation at all levels, gaining impressively in the provinces. The government saw the victory as an endorsement of its controversial economic austerity program and of its trial of former junta members.

Following the defeat of the main opposition party, the Peronists (with about 35% of the vote), Vicente L. Saadi, leader of the party's traditional wing, submitted his resignation. The defeat was attributed to a deepening split between traditionalists, who preferred the authoritarian style of leadership imprinted on the party by its founder, Juan Domingo Perón, and a dissident faction of "renovators," who favored a more democratic approach to partisan affairs. Contributing to the party division was the absence of day-to-day direction by former President Isabel Perón, widow of the founder, chosen by both factions as their leader. Mrs. Perón, residing in Madrid, resigned from her posts in February, after the divergent factions had held separate party conventions.

Economic Austerity. The economy went from bad to worse in January and February, causing the International Monetary Fund (IMF) to stall with a $16 billion refinancing package, on an outstanding foreign debt of $48 billion, and thus block the disbursement of either $4.2 billion in promised funding by private banks or a $1.4 billion IMF standby loan that had been negotiated in December 1984. President Alfonsín abruptly removed Economics Minister Bernardo Grinspun and central bank president Enrique García Vásquez on

February 19. Juan Sourrouille, head of planning, was elevated to the economy post and Alfredo Concepción went to the bank.

A severe austerity program to halt runaway inflation of over 1,000% annually was announced by the Alfonsín government on June 14. Called the Austral Plan, it prescribed wage and price freezes, a reduction of government deficits, a prohibition against printing unsupported money, and issuance of a new unit of currency called the austral. Five months after introduction of the plan, inflation had been reduced from 30% a month to about 2%. Among the initial consequences of the scheme were a shrinking of the economy by 3.5% in the second quarter, a 15% drop in production, and a decline of 30% in real wages.

Economic policies of the Alfonsín government heightened unrest within unionized sectors of the work force. Another general strike was called by the General Confederation of Labor (CGT) on May 23. Workers' unions and also commercial and banking employees demanded relief from oppressive economic and social schemes. An 11-hour "day of protest" organized by the CGT drew some 60,000 to downtown Buenos Aires on August 29, ten weeks after Alfonsín's economic austerity plan went into effect. The CGT blasted the plan's wage freeze and a rash of layoffs that it produced.

Foreign Relations. In January, Argentina accused Great Britain of aggression for having awarded offshore exploration and exploitation rights east of the British-held Falklands to a U.S.-owned oil and gas company. Argentina stated in February that, in addition to the sovereignty dispute, the issues involving the Falkland Islands were the lifting by Britain of a 150-mi (241-km) exclusion zone around the archipelago and resumption of commercial and diplomatic relations with London. Addressing the sovereignty theme during an appearance at the United Nations on March 21, President Alfonsín restated Argentina's refusal to enter into negotiations with Great Britain in which sovereignty of the Falklands was not on the agenda. Prime Minister Margaret Thatcher reiterated that sovereignty over the islands could not be discussed with Argentina because the Falklands were British.

The Falkland Islands exclusion zone would be maintained even if Argentina were to cease hostilities with Great Britain, according to the Thatcher government. By British estimates, Argentine military capabilities in 1985 surpassed those of 1982, when Argentina had briefly occupied the Falklands. Foreign Minister Dante Caputo denounced before the Organization of American States and also the United Nations the opening by Great Britain of a $420 million airport near Port Stanley in May. Caputo called it a strategic base and charged that the British would be introducing nuclear

devices into a nuclear free zone. Rejecting those contentions, Great Britain attempted, in July, to normalize commercial relations with Argentina by unilaterally lifting a three-year-old trade embargo. Argentina's response was to underscore the inseparability of normal relations and the sovereignty issue.

A treaty with Chile over maritime limits in the South Atlantic and possession of three small islands in the Beagle Channel—Lennox, Nueva, and Picton—was submitted to both houses of congress. The Chamber of Deputies approved the instrument in December 1984, and the Senate ratified it in February. The only negative votes came from the Peronist Party. Acting President Victor Martínez signed the pact into law on March 26. Bilateral talks with Chile were held in June on cooperation in the Antarctic region. The talks ranged from exchanges of scientific and navigational information to the exploitation of mineral resources.

President Alfonsín visited President Reagan at the White House on March 19 and addressed a joint session of Congress on the following day. In conversations with U.S. officials, Alfonsín stressed the need for U.S. economic aid to support the democratic trend in Argentina and among some of its neighbors. He underscored Argentine determination to honor its foreign debt. Argentina's head of state criticized U.S. involvement in Central America and urged a reduced U.S. military presence there.

LARRY L. PIPPIN, *University of the Pacific*

ARIZONA

Illegal immigration, nuclear power, the declining copper industry, and pollution were major issues in Arizona during 1985.

Sanctuary Movement. Illegal immigration, always a controversial topic in this state, became more so in 1985 as the Justice Department brought charges against 12 members of Sanctuary Movement. The movement, which comprises a small group of Christian activists, has ignored immigration laws in aiding persons fleeing political persecution in Central America to enter the United States. (*See also* special report, page 441.)

Nuclear Power. In May the first nuclear chain reaction occurred at the state's controversial Palo Verde Nuclear Plant. The $9.3 billion plant, under construction for 13 years and more than three years behind schedule, was way ahead in cost overruns and mechanical problems. When completed it will be the largest nuclear plant in the nation and one of the largest in the world.

Copper. Employment in the state's copper industry continued to fall precipitously as one operation after another closed down. The impact on the state economy over the year was reflected in an 11% drop in wages and benefits paid, and a 26% reduction in state revenues. Forecasts for the industry remained gloomy.

Pollution. Closely related to the economic woes of the copper industry was the continued operation of a large smelter in Douglas. This smelter, in the southeast corner of the state, and two others across the border in Mexico represent the largest uncontrolled source of pollution in the West. Regulatory moves were stymied by the Phelps Dodge Corporation's threat to close the operation unless its exemption from federal air pollution regulations was extended. Critics argued that the damage to public health and the environment, as a result of a "gray triangle" of wet and dry acid rain falling continuously in the region, required immediate regulatory action.

Dissatisfaction with the state legislature's reluctance to address the issue of groundwater pollution gave rise to a number of local groups seeking action. Continuing evidence of toxic chemicals in underground aquifers, which supply drinking water for a substantial segment of the state's growing population, was the cause for concern.

Indians. A dispute continued between Navajo and Hopi Indians over reservation lands in northeastern Arizona, with hundreds of Navajo resisting government attempts to move them off land awarded to the Hopi under a 1974 act of Congress. Mediation efforts by former Interior Secretary William P. Clark failed to resolve the dispute, and the outlook was dim for completing the relocation program by the July 1986 deadline.

Legislation. Among other 1985 decisions, the Arizona legislature approved a higher gasoline tax, increased penalties for crimes against children, and established a commission on the Arizona environment.

Education. Fifty-five percent of Arizona students scored above the national average in standardized tests in 1985.

JAMES W. CLARKE, *University of Arizona*

ARIZONA • Information Highlights

Area: 114,000 sq mi (295 260 km²).
Population (July 1, 1984 est.): 3,053,000.
Chief Cities (July 1, 1984 est.): Phoenix, the capital, 853,266; Tucson, 365,422; Mesa, 193,931; Tempe, 118,336; Glendale, 113,888.
Government (1985): *Chief Officers*—governor, Bruce E. Babbitt (D); secretary of state, Rose Mofford (D). *Legislature*—Senate, 30 members; House of Representatives, 60 members.
State Finances (fiscal year 1984): *Revenues*, $4,552,000,000; *expenditures*, $4,046,000,000.
Personal Income (1984): $36,151,000,000; per capita, $11,841.
Labor Force (June 1985): *Civilian labor force*, 1,443,600; *unemployed*, 98,300 (6.8% of total force).
Education: *Enrollment* (fall 1983)—public elementary schools, 350,961; public secondary, 152,267; colleges and universities, 213,437. *Public school expenditures* (1982–83), $1,208,045,927 ($2,524 per pupil).

ARKANSAS

State programs to stimulate economic development in Arkansas were hampered by unfavorable economic events such as a 10% raise in electric utility rates, a $52 million investment loss by Worthen Bank and Trust Company, closing of textile and clothing mills, cutbacks in paper mill and timber production, and the shutdown of all Reynolds Metals Company aluminum production mills in the state.

Legislature. The Arkansas General Assembly convened twice—for a 68-day regular biennial session and, three weeks later, for a five-day special session to correct errors of the regular session. The legislature mandated the investment of at least 5% of public employee retirement funds in Arkansas-related investments and overrode a veto of a four-cent-per-gallon increase in the gasoline tax. It restricted abortions after the 25th week of pregnancy, authorized parents to teach their children at home, and by a "ripper bill" replaced the existing three-member state claims commission with a five-member commission. The special session reduced tax credits, just authorized by the regular session, for donations to public and private colleges because of the potential state revenue loss. Responding to extensive criticism, it required home-school students to pass a test before reaching the age of nine. The state law permitting silent prayer in public schools was amended to allow only silent meditation.

The Governor. Third-term Gov. Bill Clinton strengthened his image as the chief proponent of the people's welfare and one of the state's most powerful politicians. He vigorously defended his teacher competency testing program before state and national audiences and successfully sponsored a legislative program to generate hundreds of millions of dollars for economic development. He also mediated Senate and House differences on the state budget bills and personally participated in efforts to persuade business firms to locate or buy in Arkansas, even leading a trade mission to Japan.

The Courts. The federal appellate court cast doubt on the death sentence in Arkansas by setting aside the state law requiring juries made up only of persons willing to impose the death sentence. It also ordered a third trial for James Dean Walker, twice convicted by the state for shooting a North Little Rock policeman in 1963. A municipal court gave the mayor of Alexander a 30-day jail sentence and a $200 fine for violating the Freedom of Information Act by withholding city financial records from a city alderman, but the prosecutor refused to handle the case on appeal.

Education. In March, Arkansas became the first state to test its teachers for competency. Ninety percent of the 28,000 teachers examined passed the test, required for teacher recertification, but the percent passing varied from 97% in Carrol County in northwest Arkansas to 65% in Lee County in the Mississippi River delta region.

Utilities. The Arkansas Public Service Commission, with the encouragement of Governor Clinton, approved a rate agreement with the Arkansas Power and Light Company (AP&L) after a year of heated public debate. The agreement stated that Arkansas ratepayers would be responsible for only 28.8% of AP&L's parent company's share of a $5.3 billion construction cost for the Grand Gulf nuclear power plant built in Mississippi, rather than the 36% share set by the Federal Energy Regulatory Board. A Little Rock attorney filed a taxpayer's suit in a state court challenging the settlement.

WILLIAM C. NOLAN
Southern Arkansas University

ARMS CONTROL

In the area of arms control between the United States and the Soviet Union, 1985 was a year during which many proposals were made but little of substance was agreed on. The year also was punctuated by charges and countercharges as to cheating on previous arms-control agreements and by disagreements over which nation was ahead in various categories of weapons.

Geneva Talks. Three times during 1985, U.S. and Soviet arms-control negotiators met in Geneva, Switzerland, to discuss areas of potentially mutual interest where agreement on arms limitations might be arranged. The U.S. team was headed by President Ronald Reagan's personal representative, Max Kampelman (*see* BIOGRAPHY), and the Soviet delegation was led by Viktor Karpov. The year's final arms-control meeting was adjourned in November with a promise by both delegations that talks would be continued in 1986.

Much of the discussion at the Geneva talks centered on the U.S. delegation's call for "deep cuts" in the nuclear arsenals of both nations, an approach that characterized previous Reagan administration proposals. For their part, the Soviets suggested a 50% reduction in nuclear arms. The fundamental problem was that the U.S. proposal referred only to strategic nuclear missiles, particularly those that would give either side a destabilizing first-strike advantage, while the Soviet reduction plan applied to all nuclear weapons, including U.S. tactical nuclear weapons stationed in and around the NATO countries of Western Europe.

In the fall, Soviet leader Mikhail S. Gorbachev proposed that the Soviet Union and the United States agree to a 12-month halt in the testing of nuclear weapons. In making the suggestion, Gorbachev reiterated the Soviet decision of August that it would conduct no further nuclear weapons testing in 1985. In reply, the United States noted that the Soviet's unilateral moratorium was meaningless because Moscow had already completed its test series for the year. And in response to the Soviet suggestion for a one-year ban on nuclear-weapons testing, Washington expressed concern over how a moratorium on small-weapons tests could be adequately verified for compliance. The leaders of Argentina, Mexico, Sweden, Tanzania, Greece, and India offered to assist in the verification of the test ban, but neither of the superpowers accepted the offer.

Cheating. In a restatement of previous allegations, the Reagan administration charged that the Soviet Union was violating provisions of the SALT (Strategic Arms Limitation Talks) II arms accord. As the year ended, a report was prepared for the president that set out the options for the United States should the Reagan-Gorbachev summit meeting fail to resolve the American complaints. Among the possible responses would be for the United States to terminate the 1979 agreement, which was never ratified by the Senate but whose terms have been followed by the Reagan government. Another option would be to breach the limit on submarine-launched ballistic missiles (SLBMs) in summer 1986 by adding a new Trident submarine to the Navy's fleet without retiring a Poseidon submarine. The Reagan-Gorbachev summit in November did not produce any substantive progress in arms control.

SDI/"Star Wars." President Reagan's proposal to conduct research on a Strategic Defense Initiative (SDI) system, called "Star Wars" by opponents, raised two basic questions for arms-control proponents. The first question was whether SDI should be included in arms-control talks between the two superpowers. Moscow repeatedly stated the importance of discussing SDI, but Washington insisted that it would not negotiate on the pro-

AP/Wide World

The United States was represented at the Geneva talks by (l-r) John Tower, Max Kampelman, and Maynard Glitman.

gram. Spokespersons for the Reagan administration bolstered their arguments for not negotiating away the SDI by maintaining that the Soviets actually were ahead of the United States in SDI-type development. Many arms controllers outside the government argued that SDI should be bargained away in return for substantive concessions on the part of the Soviet Union. Examples they suggested were sharp reductions in large Soviet intercontinental ballistic missiles (ICBMs) with apparent first-strike capability, or an agreement for on-site inspections within the Soviet Union to verify compliance with arms agreements on small and mobile weapons not easily counted by satellite.

The second major question regarding SDI was whether the testing of such a system would be a violation of the 1972 ABM (Antiballistic Missile) Treaty. Claiming that testing indeed would constitute a violation, opponents argued that development of SDI would launch an unrestricted arms competition in space. Such a race would prove financially burdensome, with neither nation gaining any more security than it already had. Spokespersons for the U.S. Department of Defense, on the other hand, argued that the full ABM Treaty permits testing of an SDI system and calls for limitations talks only before deployment.

See also MILITARY AFFAIRS.

ROBERT M. LAWRENCE
Colorado State University

Stuart Rome, Courtesy of the Albuquerque Museum

Fleur Hales, Field Museum of Natural History

ART

The growing public appetite for art in the United States was further evidenced in 1985 by the dozens of museums that moved into, or were planning, new, expanded, or renovated quarters. Meanwhile, important new exhibitions continued to be held around the world. Despite apparent improprieties at two major houses, auction sales expanded, and new price records were set. There was some controversy over publicly displayed sculptures. And several instances of vandalism, as well as natural deterioration, made art restoration and preservation an increasingly important activity.

Museum News. After the opening of the expanded Museum of Modern Art in spring 1984, New York City's three other major art museums announced expansion programs. The Whitney Museum of American Art plans a ten-story addition, designed by Michael Graves, that will more than double the museum's space; opponents of the project say that the original building, designed by Marcel Breuer, will be overwhelmed. The Guggenheim Museum will build an 11-story addition for gallery, storage, and office areas; the structure will be put up behind Frank Lloyd Wright's original building. Finally, the Metropolitan Museum of

Art is readying 90,000 sq ft (25 000 m²) of new space to house its growing collection of modern art; the Southwest Wing is expected to open in early 1987.

Two smaller museums opened in New York during the year. The Forbes Magazine Galleries on lower Fifth Avenue houses the private collection of the Forbes family, including more than 500 toy ships and 12,000 miniature soldiers, a fine collection of jewelry, objets d'art, and the fabled Fabergé Easter eggs made for the Russian imperial family. The new Isamu Noguchi Museum in Long Island City is devoted entirely to the works of that artist. Included is an outdoor sculpture garden that realizes Noguchi's dream of a self-created setting which is itself a work of art.

But New York was hardly the only place where new or expanded museums were sprouting up. Additions were to be unveiled at the Virginia Museum of Fine Arts in Richmond, the Hood Museum at Dartmouth College in Hanover, NH, and the Arnot Museum in Elmira, NY. In coming years there will be new or expanded facilities for the Los Angeles Museum of Contemporary Art, the Art Institute of Chicago, the Seattle Art Museum, the Getty Museum in Malibu, CA, the Museum of African Art in Washington, DC, and others.

In Europe, Paris celebrated the reopening of its Musée des Arts Décoratifs. Its once dingy rooms were refurbished to provide worthy settings for the museum's unique collection of furniture and accessories from the Middle Ages to the 20th century.

International Exhibitions. After stops in Paris, London, and Cologne, the treasures from the Basilica of San Marco in Venice were on view at New York's Metropolitan Museum. This treasury, perhaps the richest still extant, contains objects used in the liturgy and as reliquaries over the centuries. The items on display ranged from a 6th-century bishop's chair in alabaster to a 15th-century silver gilt pastoral staff. Also included were a variety of precious objects from the Late Classical, Fatimid, and Byzantine periods.

Another international exhibition, titled "The Age of Caravaggio," opened at the Met early in 1985 and subsequently was on view in Naples at the Museum of Capodimonte. Including the art of northern Italy in the 16th century, the show traced Caravaggio's beginnings as well as the work of his contemporaries.

Three other major international shows were devoted to modern painters. The Museum of Modern Art in New York was host to a slightly modified version of a retrospective, originally shown at the Grand Palais in Paris, of the work

of Henri Rousseau (1844–1910). Marking the centennial of his first public exhibition, the show includes 59 of Rousseau's most important works. Many of the paintings—in his "primitive" or "naive" style, with humans and animals arranged stiffly in the landscape—had never before been seen in the United States. The second retrospective featured Marc Chagall, the Russian-born painter who died in March 1985 (*see* special report, page 116). And the Guggenheim Museum in New York presented the last of its three exhibitions reviewing the career of the Russian artist Wassily Kandinsky (1866–1944). The 1985 show focused on work done in Paris between 1933 and his death; more than 200 items were shown.

Historical and Nonwestern Exhibitions. Some of the most important shows of the year introduced the art of other cultures to a wide audience. "Maya: Treasures of an Ancient Civilization" featured 275 artifacts of stone, pottery, jade, shell, gold, and other metals. The objects reflected 3,500 years of Mayan life, from ca. 2000 B.C. to the arrival of the Spaniards. The most comprehensive show of its kind, "Maya" was organized by the Albuquerque Museum in New Mexico but opened first at the Museum of Natural History in New York and was scheduled to go to Los Angeles, Dallas, Toronto, and Kansas City before ending in Albuquerque. The exhibition included museum pieces from Mexico, Guatemala, and Belize never before shown outside those countries.

At New York's Metropolitan Museum, "The Art of Pre-Columbian Gold: The Jan Mitchell Collection" attracted attention for the beauty and richness of the objects—masks, collars, knives, and other ornamental as well as utilitarian objects, all made of gold with exquisite craftsmanship.

Two major exhibits of African art were held in New York during the year. "The Art of Cameroon" at the American Museum of Natural History presented many works borrowed from the tribal kings of that African country, including ancestor figures, ceremonial masks, jewelry, and furniture from shrines still in use and not open to the public. And a show called "Sets, Series, and Ensembles" at the Center for African Art brought together groups of objects as they were actually constituted.

The Festival of India, which was enormously successful in England in 1982, was being repeated on an even larger scale in the United States in 1985–86, with dozens of cultural events portraying the artistic and cultural achievements of India. The series of events began in the summer of 1985 with an exhibition on Indian science at the Museum of Science and Industry in Chicago. It continued in September at the Metropolitan Museum with a vast show on Indian art, including paintings, sculpture, textiles, arms and armor, and jewels; a smaller show emphasizing terra-cotta sculpture

Oriassa State Museum, Bhubaneswar

Among the works shown in "The Sculpture of India" was an 11th-century image of the elephant-headed god Ganeśa.

opened at the Brooklyn Museum in November. The arts of the historic city of Fatehpur Sikri were featured at the Asia Society in New York in October. Not part of the Festival program but indicative of the interest in India was a show called "The Sculpture of India: 3000 B.C. to 1300 A.D.," held at the National Gallery from May to September.

An unusually large number of exhibitions of drawings, both by Old Masters and modern artists, also took place during the year. "Old Master Drawings from the Albertina" came to the National Gallery in Washington and the Pierpont Morgan Library in New York, showing some of the treasures of the collection of Duke Albert von Sachsen-Teschen, son-in-law of Maria Theresa. Begun in 1776 and still housed at Duke Albert's palace in Vienna, the collection now consists of more than 600,000 drawings and prints from the 15th century on. Among the ones on loan were works by such giants as Rembrandt, Dürer, Fra Bartolomeo, Poussin, and Rubens. In New York several of the Morgan Library's own Dürers were added.

"The Age of Caravaggio," one of the year's important international exhibitions, included "The Musicians," left, and other 16th-century masterpieces.

From the Museum of Fine Arts in Budapest a selection of 100 drawings collected by the Esterhazy family, patrons of the arts in the 18th century, traveled to the United States. Titled "Leonardo to Van Gogh," the show opened at the National Gallery and continued to Chicago and Los Angeles. It was the first time that many of these drawings—by such artists as Raphael, Dürer, Poussin, Watteau, and Cézanne —were shown outside Hungary.

The French Romantic painter Théodore Géricault (1791–1824) was the subject of an exhibition of more than 100 watercolors and drawings assembled at the École des Beaux Arts in Paris and shown at the Morgan Library and at museums in San Diego and Houston.

At the Drawing Center in Soho, New York's rapidly growing art neighborhood best known for its contemporary shows, "Drawings from Venice: Masterpieces from the Museo Correr" attracted crowds during the summer to view such masters as Guardi, Longhi, and Tiepolo. At the same time, the Met drew on its own holdings to show 170 Dutch drawings centered around Rembrandt. "The Drawings of Henri Matisse" at the Museum of Modern Art, including 150 works on paper of which about a third had never been on view before, spanned that artist's entire career, from about 1890 to 1952. "Frankenthaler: Works on Paper, 1949–84" and "Mark Rothko: Works on Paper" were seen at the Guggenheim before traveling to other cities.

Auction News. As in previous years, auction sales continued to expand and several price records were broken. But the sensational news concerned accusations of questionable practices at the two leading auction houses. At Christie's, Chairman David Bathurst resigned following disclosures that in 1981, while head of the New York branch, he falsely reported that three paintings had sold for a total of $5.6 million when in fact only one of the eight in the sale had fetched a bid above the reserve price. The auction house was fined $80,000, and the licenses of two of its top executives were suspended by the New York City Department of Consumer Affairs. Sotheby's, meanwhile, was accused of selling at auction a number of valuable books and manuscripts that had belonged to a rabbinical school in Berlin. The auction house claimed that it was dealing through an agent, while in fact it was dealing directly with the man who had smuggled the materials out of Nazi Germany but had no clear title to them. In a court-approved settlement, Sotheby's agreed to buy back some of the most valuable works so that they might go to Jewish institutions in New York and Jerusalem instead of to private owners.

Sotheby's again was the leading art auction house, with estimated 1984 sales of $642 million; Christie's recorded some $475 million in sales. Both figures represented an advance over the previous year. The most notable sale of the year was Andrea Mantegna's *Adoration of the Magi,* one of his few paintings still in private hands. The work was sold at Christie's in London to the Getty Museum in Malibu for $10.4 million, the most ever paid for a single painting. The sale of Florence J. Gould's Impressionist paintings at Sotheby's in New York brought the highest total for an art collection, $32.6 million; one of those paintings, Van Gogh's *Landscape with Rising Sun,* fetched $9.9 million; another, Toulouse-Lautrec's *The Lady Clown Cha U Kao,* sold for $5.28 million, a record for that artist. Observers noted, how-

ever, that only first-rate works were commanding such high prices and that there were many cases in which owners, perhaps misled by the publicity attending record-breaking sales, had set so high a reserve price that the work remained unsold.

Public Art. Since 1962 the U.S. federal government has allocated up to 0.5% of the cost of its building projects for public art, commissioning works for $7 million from about 200 artists in a program considered highly successful. In 1985, however, discontent with one of the works, "Tilted Arc," a sculpture by Richard Serra installed in 1981 at Federal Plaza in lower Manhattan, reached such a pitch that the General Services Administration (GSA) held a public hearing to decide whether it should be moved. Thousands of people working in the area, as well as some art critics, objected to the sculpture—a 120-ft (37-m) steel wall—both on aesthetic grounds and because it impedes free use of the plaza itself. In spite of numerous pleas in its defense by other art critics and artists, the administrator decided to have the work moved, saying "Public art has a public responsibility." He suggested that in the future community participation be sought during the process of selection of such federally funded public art. Another of Serra's sculptures, "Twain," consisting of eight panels of steel up to 10 ft (3 m) high and forming an irregular triangle 125 ft (38 m) on each side in downtown St. Louis, also incurred so much opposition that a bill to have it removed was being considered by the city aldermen.

Restoration and Preservation. Because of a variety of factors—vandalism, natural deterioration, pollution, and others—great works of art are being damaged at an accelerated rate. In response, museums have made art restoration and preservation an integral part of their activities, and a growing number of institutions are offering graduate degrees in that specialty.

Cases of outright vandalism in 1985 included the burning of a Rubens at the Kunsthaus in Zurich and the slashing of eight large contemporary paintings on the concourse of the mall at the State Capitol in Albany, NY. The more common form of destruction, however, comes from the natural deterioration of materials used in the works themselves. This may result from untried techniques used by the original artist, as in the case of Leonardo's *Last Supper,* which already needed to be restored 20 years after its completion. Restored and repainted many times since, that masterpiece has been the object of a painstaking effort to save every flake.

Damage to paintings is usually limited to surface dirt, and a careful cleaning can work miracles. Michelangelo's recently restored *Sistine Chapel* in Saint Peter's, for example, is now as colorful and bright as it was originally. But air pollution and mass tourism are creating new hazards for some of the world's great relics and monuments. The prehistoric caves at Lascaux, France, for example, have been closed for many years now. More recently the area inside the Parthenon was put off limits. And at Stonehenge, officials were forced to fence in the ancient stone monument to protect it from incidental or careless damage.

Heist. In one of the largest and most brazen art thefts of the century, five gunmen on October 27 entered the Marmottan Museum in Paris, held museum guards and visitors at gunpoint, and fled with nine major Impressionist paintings. Among them were *Impression, Sunrise* by Monet and *Bathers* by Renoir.

ISA RAGUSA, *Princeton University*

At an auction in London, the Getty Museum of Malibu, CA, paid $10.4 million for Mantegna's "Adoration of the Magi," a record for one painting.

chagall

(1887–1985)

UPI/Bettmann Newsphotos

Artist's Collection

On March 28, 1985, the world of modern art lost a master. Marc Chagall, 97, died at his home in France. During a career of some 75 years, the Russian-born artist worked in a variety of artistic media. His stained glass window "The Tribe of Joseph," above, is at the synagogue attached to the Hadassah Medical Center in Jerusalem. The window, completed in 1960, was based on the account of the 12 tribes given in Genesis. "I and the Village," right, Chagall's 1911 painting that is "both human and universal," now is exhibited at New York's Museum of Modern Art.

Entrancing, lyrical, lavish in color, and highly personal in style, the artistic creations of Marc Chagall earned him a place among the masters of the 20th century. As popular and prolific as any artist of his generation, Chagall channeled his magical, kaleidoscopic vision into a broad range of artistic media—paintings, murals, frescoes, stained glass, stage settings, lithographs, tapestries, and more. His imagery and style remained relatively unchanged through eight decades, but he was never part of any school or movement. Steeped in the folklore of his native small-town Russia and the homely mysticism of his family's Ha-

sidic tradition, Chagall's works are filled with brilliantly colored roosters and cows, milkmaids and fiddlers, angels, floral bouquets, and embracing lovers—all floating in air, upside-down, or otherwise freed from physical space. Having studied in Paris early in the century, Chagall borrowed various modernist techniques—such as cubism and abstraction —but only to serve his own imaginative vision.

In addition to hundreds of paintings, Chagall's best-known works include four huge murals at New York's Lincoln Center; a ceiling painting at the Paris Opéra; mosaics and tapestries at the Knesset (Parliament) in Jerusa-

The Museum of Modern Art, New York

lem; a museum of biblical works that bears his name in Nice, France; and stained glass windows at UN headquarters in New York, the French cathedrals of Metz and Rheims, and the Hadassah Hebrew University in Jerusalem.

Marc Chagall died on March 28, 1985, at his home in St. Paul de Vence, in the south of France. He was 97. At the time of his death, a major exhibition of his work was on display at the Royal Academy of Arts in London. From May 12 to July 7, the collection was shown at the Philadelphia Museum of Art. It was the first time in four decades that a Chagall retrospective had been mounted in the United States.

Fifty-two public and private collectors agreed to lend their Chagalls to the show, which brought together more than 200 of his works.

In the exhibition catalog, curator Susan Compton wrote of Chagall: ''There have been few artists this century who have combined such a sensuous enjoyment of the act of painting with such wide-ranging and thought-provoking subject matter. It is his genius at responding to the age-old comedies and tragedies woven by man into legends and myths which gives Chagall's work in every medium such depth of meaning, in addition to its appeal to the eye.''

ASIA

Asia observed two significant anniversaries in 1985: the 40th of the Bandung Conference (the first meeting of the leading nations of Asia and Africa) and the tenth of the Communist victory in Vietnam. The 1955 Bandung nations reassembled in Indonesia, while the Vietnamese celebrated their 1975 triumph.

Continuing Conflicts. Mainland Asia's two persisting wars, in Cambodia and Afghanistan, involved the presence of foreign Communist armies—those of Vietnam and the USSR, respectively. In its April victory anniversary, Vietnam signaled to the rest of Asia the extent of its military preparedness. Subsequently, Hanoi said that its troops would leave Cambodia by 1990. But few believed that they would be withdrawn, given the continued presence of 40,000 Vietnamese forces in neighboring Laos. Others doubted that they could be removed, given increased Chinese military assistance to anti-Hanoi resistance forces and new U.S. aid to the same side.

Vietnamese troops in Cambodia numbered more than 160,000, about the same size as the Soviet military presence in Afghanistan. But the 1985 Soviet offensive fell far short of breaking the back of the Afghan resistance.

The island nations of Sri Lanka and the Philippines experienced widening civil strife in the first half of the year. A midyear cease-fire and diplomatic talks in Bhutan encouraged hopes that Tamil Indian separatist terrorism (and majority Sinhalese counterviolence) would end in Sri Lanka. In the Philippines, however, more than 4,500 deaths and an increase in the number of Communist insurgents (to 12,500 combatants) indicated that the civil war was escalating.

Diplomacy. Attending Indonesia's Bandung commemoration was China's Foreign Minister Wu Xueqian. He was the highest Chinese official to visit the country since a break in diplomatic ties 20 years earlier following an abortive Communist coup attempt. The Indonesians subsequently told the Vietnamese that they would not resume relations with China—with which Hanoi still engaged in border clashes—until the United States recognized Vietnam. Jakarta also urged the Vietnamese to cooperate with Washington concerning recovery of the remains of American dead and missing in action (MIA). Hanoi agreed in October to joint search efforts with the Americans.

The United States, stepping up its diplomatic activity, hosted Chinese President Li Xiannian, Japan's Premier Yasuhiro Nakasone, and Indian Prime Minister Rajiv Gandhi. India interceded unsuccessfully with Moscow concerning American proposals for Soviet disengagement from Afghanistan.

Continuing Sino-Soviet talks to normalize strained relations made only limited progress, although the two governments signed a five-year trade pact. Mikhail Gorbachev's cool reception of Vietnam's visiting Le Duan reflected the USSR's high priority of Sino-Soviet normalization.

China also received foreign visitors, including Singapore's Premier Lee Kuan Yew. China's President Li Xiannian traveled to Thailand and Burma to discuss the USSR's increasingly active presence in Southeast Asia—as evidenced in its expanded Cam Ranh Bay naval base. Beijing (Peking) encouraged the rapprochement of North and South Korea—largely to counter Soviet influence in Pyongyang.

Internal Politics. Asia's two largest states, China and India, continued their efforts to stabilize their volatile political systems. India's Prime Minister Gandhi's government party, which overwhelmed the opposition in December 1984 national elections, won state elections in March—but by no means decisively. Gandhi's party lost elections in September, however, in troubled Punjab state.

China's aging Deng Xiaoping, rushing to complete a changing of the political guard before his retirement (or death), named new and younger members to the ruling Communist Party's Politburo. Ten out of 24 members were retired, and six new members were named.

Burma's 75-year-old General Ne Win also sought to ensure a proper succession to his long rule by having President (and General) San Yu named to the number two party post. Pakistani President Zia-ul Haq strengthened his hold on power by amendment of his nation's constitution, while Bangladesh's President H. M. Ershad extended his own appointment as army head.

Economy. The economic growth of non-Communist Asian countries continued, although less spectacularly than in previous years. (*See* feature article, page 56.) For the first time since the rapid expansion of their economies, increases in exports from South Korea, Taiwan, Singapore, and Hong Kong were lower than the general growth in international commerce. Even Japan, in the year's first quarter, experienced its slowest growth in a decade. But Japan's economy overtook the United States as the world's second-wealthiest nation in terms of overseas assets. Japan also gained on the United Kingdom, still the leader in this respect.

China, while continuing the break with rigid central planning, also slowed down the pace of economic liberalization that some thought may have gone "too fast, too far."

The overvaluation of the American dollar adversely influenced the U.S. trade balance with key Asian trading nations. Asian leaders and exporters were even more alarmed by protectionist pressures in Washington.

RICHARD BUTWELL
California State University, Dominguez Hills

The Comet Giacobini-Zinner was photographed in July from southern Arizona. In September, a U.S. spacecraft sailed through its tail in the first such encounter with a comet.

NASA

ASTRONOMY

Both in the United States and Australia, astronomers received go-aheads in 1985 to build the largest instruments ever constructed for observations at radio wavelengths. The American project, called the Very-Long-Baseline Array, will combine the signals from ten antennas 25 m (82 ft) in diameter scattered across the continental United States, Puerto Rico, and Hawaii. With an effective diameter of 8 000 km (5,000 mi), this instrument will permit the detection of extremely tiny and distant celestial sources. The Australia Telescope, as it is called, is much more compact; its eight antennas in New South Wales will have a maximum separation of only 320 km (200 mi).

Notwithstanding widespread opposition by optical astronomers, the Carnegie Institution of Washington on June 25 closed the famous 100-inch (254-cm) reflecting telescope at Mount Wilson Observatory in California. Other instruments at Mount Wilson, including two unique telescopes for studying the Sun, are scheduled to close in 1986, as Carnegie increases funding for its observatory at Las Campanas, Chile.

Comets. Despite predictions that the 1985–86 showing of Halley's Comet would be rather unspectacular, astronomers became excited when this famous visitor suddenly and surprisingly brightened in late 1985. As 1986 approached, it seemed that Halley's Comet would be bigger and brighter than indicated by even the most optimistic forecasts. In early November, expert observers saw the comet with only their unaided eyes, and in mid-November it was viewed throughout the world by persons using binoculars. The reappearance of Halley's Comet after 76 years sparked such interest among the public that some manufacturers of optical equipment and memorabilia could not keep up with consumer demand.

In 1985 a spacecraft launched by the European Space Agency and two launched by Japan joined a pair of Soviet probes scheduled to rendezvous with Halley's Comet in March 1986. But these spacecraft will not be the first to intercept a comet, for on Sept. 11, 1985, the United States' International Cometary Explorer (ICE) flew through the tail of Comet Giacobini-Zinner. Findings from that mission, in which the explorer passed within 7 850 km (4,880 mi) of the comet's nucleus, confirmed that comets are celestial "dirty snowballs." Water molecules were detected in abundance, but dust particles were 10–100 times fewer than had been thought. The latter observation was good news for the Halley probes, since frequent high-energy impacts by dust particles could destroy an approaching spacecraft.

Solar System. At a conference held in March, Soviet planetologists described to Western scientists the results from their Venera 15 and 16 probes. Using radar, these spacecraft mapped features as small as 1–2 km (0.6–1.2 mi) across on Venus' cloud-shrouded surface and measured their heights to an accuracy of 50 m (165 ft). During the eight-month mission in 1983–84, the Veneras found that the planet's skin had been molded by volcanic activity, crustal movement, meteoritic impact, and other processes not yet understood. The

Soviet scientists concluded that Venus' surface has evolved less rapidly than that of our planet and is 500 million to one billion years old. Geologically, this means that Venus is a more active body than Mars but less active than Earth.

The origin of chondrites, the most common kind of meteorite to strike the Earth, has remained a mystery. Thanks to a computer simulation, however, it now appears that these stony bodies may come from the asteroid belt. It was found that asteroids located some 400 million km (250 million mi) from the Sun and having a composition similar to the chondrites can be thrown abruptly Earthward by the gravitational influence of the planet Jupiter.

Recent analysis indicates that Neptune is encircled by a ring of particles. The planet thus joins its gas-giant neighbors (Jupiter, Saturn, and Uranus) in sporting such a feature. This discovery stems from observations made in July 1984, when Neptune passed close to a star whose light was dimmed briefly. The fading was interpreted as due to opaque matter 10–20 km (6–12 mi) wide and located some 76 000 km (47,000 mi) from the center of the planet.

Brown Dwarf Stars. In late 1984 it was announced that a star known as Van Biesbroeck 8 had a possible planetary companion. Further studies have shown that this curious object is actually a star that was just too small to ignite. Such so-called "brown dwarfs" are unable to maintain a sufficiently high temperature to convert hydrogen into heavier elements, the basic process by which stars shine. It now appears that VB-8B, as the companion is called, is about two billion years old and has roughly 5% the Sun's mass but only 0.002% its brightness.

Old X-ray Sources. Bright X-ray sources found near the center of our Milky Way galaxy are often caused by the interaction between two stars that revolve around each other. One component is a neutron star (a few tens of kilometers in diameter and so densely packed that a teaspoon of its material would weigh a billion tons); the other is an ordinary star like our Sun.

As these so-called "binary systems" evolve, the neutron star pulls matter away from its companion. At first this gas forms a disk around the neutron star, but then it crashes onto the latter's surface at 25% of the speed of light to produce the X rays. As the neutron star gains more and more mass, it must rotate faster and faster. Thus, the oldest binary X-ray sources should feature the most rapidly spinning neutron stars.

Discovering an old X-ray binary was not easy. Only after a decade of searching was the first one uncovered; GX5-1 in the constellation of Sagittarius was found to contain a neutron star rotating 100 times per second. The evidence, however, was indirect and required a good deal of analysis. GX5-1 did not exhibit regular pulses, as would be expected from a spinning neutron star. Rather, it featured trains of "quasi-periodic" pulses that required unscrambling. Astronomers concluded that the curious signals from GX5-1 are due to regular pulses from the neutron star, combined with those from short-lived clumps of matter spinning in its circumstellar disk.

Galaxies. The farther we look into space, the closer we come to seeing objects as they were at the time of creation. In 1985 two astronomers at Lick Observatory in California observed a galaxy that may be only a few percent younger than the universe itself. Interestingly, the intrinsic brightness of this object seems to be quite ordinary, like that of our own Milky Way galaxy. It appears to be undergoing only moderate evolution. Nevertheless, this detection of so young an object gives hope that a truly primeval galaxy—one that has not undergone extensive star formation—may be found.

Largely through recent observations at infrared wavelengths, a picture has emerged that many galaxies undergo relatively brief but widespread episodes of star formation sometime during their lives. When this happens, the infrared luminosity of such a "starburst" galaxy increases enormously. For example, Arp 220 in the constellation of Serpens emits 50 times as much energy in the infrared as our Milky Way galaxy does at all wavelengths combined. Often this luminosity is accompanied by maser emission (the radio equivalent of an optical laser) from the hydroxyl radical, a phenomenon also suggesting stellar birth.

For the most luminous infrared galaxies, up to 100 billion newborn stars would be needed to produce the observed emission. But what could trigger such a massive spawning? In the last year or two, a growing consensus has developed that collisions between galaxies are responsible. During such an event, the gases from both galaxies merge and become compressed, encouraging the formation of particularly dense pockets that later collapse gravitationally under their own weight to produce the new stars.

LEIF J. ROBINSON, *"Sky & Telescope"*

AUSTRALIA

For Prime Minister Robert J. Hawke's Labor government, in its second term and its third year in office, 1985 was a year when its central policy on industrial and taxation matters and foreign affairs came under test. Most commentators continued to shore up the Hawke image; however, the earlier euphoria continued to fade. By December, a leading newspaper commentator expressed the fear that "a foreign trade and debt emergency" might soon reach a crisis point and so confront the Hawke government with "a mortal threat."

A 4% rise in gross domestic product (GDP) was accompanied by rising inflation (about 8%), a record external deficit, and a weak dollar. The farm sector was under its severest price-cost strains since the 1930s. Banking underwent major change with the licensing of more than a dozen foreign banks. Plans to introduce a comprehensive "consumption tax" collapsed under the pressure of public (and especially union) opposition and were replaced by proposals to place more of the overall tax burden directly on business operations and profits and to introduce a capital gains tax.

The budget, presented in August, was designed to relieve pressure on real and financial resources by keeping a rein on growth in outlays; expenditure was set 8.4% higher (an increase in real terms of an estimated 1.3%) against receipts up 12.6%. Money-supply targeting was dropped due to distorting effects from deregulation and institutional change on all the monetary aggregates.

Much of the fire of business and associated groups concerned with the revived inflationary pressures was directed at the government's close cooperation with the Australian Council of Trade Unions (ACTU), particularly the "prices and incomes accord" that assured wage escalation tied to cost-of-living increases, and the government's compliance with ACTU dictum on taxation changes.

On foreign policy issues, especially cooperation with the United States, Hawke faced strong resistance from his own party's left. On some specific issues he was forced to soften his pro-U.S. stance.

Economic Course. The year's economic performance was marked by an early decline of 20% in the value of the Australian dollar, slightly higher inflation, and unemployment hovering around 8%. Strong domestic activity was heavily dependent on government outlays (with a trimmed federal deficit still running at almost A$5 billion a year). Building (70% of it in the public sector) showed a strong rise, then eased. Rural groups were disadvantaged by growing cost slowdowns in the export markets on which their viability depended.

Strong but spotty expansion of the overall economy boosted profitability in the corporate sector, setting in train a strong rise in the stock market, which reached record levels when it was further buoyed by takeover-merger moves.

Major areas of concern were the weakness of the Australian dollar, continued high levels of deficit spending, a hemorrhaging current account, and very high interest rates, combined with weakness in world commodity markets and a loss of international competitiveness. Planned tax changes were seen as "antibusiness" and "discriminating against the private sector."

Foreign Affairs and Defense. The major foreign policy issue concerned the maintenance of the Australia-U.S. (ANZUS) treaty link irrespective of New Zealand's move to ban all visits by nuclear ships. Relations between Canberra and Washington were strengthened in the dialogue over the New Zealand issue, with Australia endorsing U.S. views and at the same time seeking to maintain the ANZUS alliance, without renegotiation or reworking, in the event that New Zealand dropped out from the partnership.

The Labor Party's left wing continued to exert pressure on the U.S. alliance and uranium exporting but was consistently overwhelmed within caucus and in cabinet policy-making. Nevertheless a vocal minority expounding anti-American views continued to secure disproportionate prominence in the media. As a result of factional pressure, Hawke withdrew from any role in MX missile and Strategic Defense Initiative (SDI or "Star Wars") activities.

On South Africa, Hawke took a firm anti-apartheid stand. In October former Prime Minister Malcolm Fraser was appointed as Australia's representative on the Commonwealth six-member committee formed to promote dialogue between the South African government and the black population. The appointment met with a mixed reception.

The Political Round. Most 1985 political activity was aimed not at gaining immediate votes but at winning media attention and support.

To sharpen the image of the Liberals, John Howard, a former treasurer in the Fraser government, replaced Andrew Peacock, former foreign minister, as party leader. Howard was seen as a more clearly defined alternative to Labor than Peacock, who became the party's spokesman on foreign affairs.

Passing attention was given to rifts within the Labor Party on a variety of matters of substance. Most commentators considered that Labor had been successful in avoiding more

---

AUSTRALIA • Information Highlights

Official Name: Commonwealth of Australia.
Location: Southwestern Pacific Ocean.
Area: 2,967,895 sq mi (7 686 848 km²).
Population (mid-1985 est.): 15,800,000.
Chief Cities (June 30, 1983): Canberra, the capital, 255,900; Sydney, 3,332,600; Melbourne, 2,864,600; Brisbane, 1,138,400.
Government: *Head of state,* Elizabeth II, queen; represented by Sir Ninian Martin Stephen, governor-general (took office July 1982). *Head of government,* Robert Hawke, prime minister (took office March 11, 1983). *Legislature*—Parliament: Senate and House of Representatives.
Monetary Unit: Australian dollar (1.4633 A$ equal U.S.$1, Nov. 21, 1985).
Gross Domestic Product (1983 U.S.$): $144,100,000,000.
Economic Indexes (1984): *Consumer Prices* (1970 = 100), all items, 375.4; food, 370.4. *Industrial Production* (March 1985, 1980 = 100), 103.
Foreign Trade (1984 U.S.$): *Imports,* $23,424,000,000; *exports,* $23,986,000,000.

wounding outcomes to the divisive issues on which the left took its stand; these included Hawke's earlier undertaking on tests involving both the MX missile and the SDI. The left bowed, at least temporarily, to Hawke's plan for introducing an ID card to reduce tax and welfare cheating.

The rural crisis brought what the *Australian* saw as a "new and much-needed vitality" into rural politics through the creation of the National Farmers Federation as an organization concentrating on pressing the views of the farm sector to the government, at the same time bypassing the National Party, traditional voice of rural interests. Across the volatile rural consistency, the Liberal Party appeared to be outflanking the National Party. At the same time the Liberal Party appeared to be regaining support from organized business at Hawke's expense.

In the background, the power of unions was a potent issue, and it threatened to flare into even more active form. The government's moves in support of court fines and other measures imposed on intransigent unions that enjoyed the ACTU's backing brought the issue of union power to the forefront of attention when bans, secondary boycotts, and picket violence in isolated disputes led to public statements from the ACTU.

In a major union-government confrontation, the government of Queensland ordered the dismissal of 1,000 electricity workers who defied an Industrial Commission order not to strike over use of contract labor; in spite of serious blackouts the government refused to reinstate the workers, taking the view that unions too often got their way simply because no one stood up to them. In "leading the way in the fight against militant strike action," the government stood firm against sporadic moves by transport workers and others who attempted to disrupt business when the power workers were not taken back. The dispute showed a lack of union solidarity, however, and the Queensland government strengthened its determination to "push on with its plans to deregulate the state's labor market."

Changing Patterns. Australian society has become noticeably more polarized in recent years according to a consultant sociologist Phil Ruthven. He told a business seminar that Australia's traditional middle-class image was no longer valid. In 1969, Ruthven said, 70% of Australians were middle class compared with about 30% currently. Australia now was made up of "winners, losers, and survivors." Ruthven blamed "well-intentioned legislation" for the change. Multiple-income households had become extremely well-off; they were in a group of favored people now numbering 40% of the population. Due to inflation and other factors, more poor people than ever before had emerged and now numbered about 30%. Be-

tween these groups stood the survivors: middle-class people with jobs whose standard of living had declined steadily over 15 years.

A judicial ruling in a sex discrimination case upset the established principle that women should retire at 60 (against 65 for men). As a result, matters relating to pension entitlement ages came under active review. Sociologists pointed to various inequalities facing the elderly, including the matter of the eligibility age for pensions and means whereby the retirement income system can support a graying population. Since federal pensions were established in 1908, the proportion of the population eligible for the age pension has risen to the present level of 85% of Australia's "aged" population (women over 60, men over 65 years) receiving a part or full pension. A major report on the retirement income system was in preparation.

On October 26 the federal government handed over title to Ayers Rock, central Australia, to members of the Aboriginal community, whose representative accepted ownership of the rock (Uluru) from Governor-General Sir Ninian Stephen. The site was immediately leased back to the government as a tourist site. The move created widespread dispute on whether the transfer of ownership was justified and whether the rock had been given to the right people.

In midyear the 36-member National Aboriginal Conference, elected by Aboriginals throughout Australia, was disbanded and its activities came to an end after seven years during which it was said to have been in "endless conflict" in its efforts to secure greater Aboriginal rights to land.

A restructuring of the broadcast industry began after a television satellite, Aussat, launched by the U.S. space shuttle, made TV services possible in even the remotest areas. Three commercial TV services, as well as the government-funded Australian Broadcasting Corporation, were involved in Aussat. Viewers in isolated localities needed to buy a receiving dish for signals.

Victoria's National Gallery staged the most comprehensive exhibition ever assembled of the Impressionist-style paintings of the Heidelberg School that rose in Melbourne in the 1880s. Called "Golden Summers: Heidelberg and Beyond," the exhibition, which opened in October, featured important works by the central Heidelberg exponents—Tom Roberts, Sir Arthur Streeton, Charles Conder, and Frederick McCubbin—and others.

In Sydney, plans were approved for Australia's first monorail system, with six driverless trains operating a harborside circuit of the city. The promoters planned to have the system in operation by 1988. In Melbourne work began on a Gallery of Sport that will house the Sport Australia Hall of Fame.

R. M. YOUNGER, *Australian Author*

At Belvedere Castle, Vienna, May 15, U.S. Secretary of State Shultz and Soviet Foreign Minister Gromyko joined their counterparts from the Western European nations in marking the 30th anniversary of the Austrian State Treaty.

Haslinger Photo

AUSTRIA

The year 1985 marked the 40th anniversary of the establishment of the Second Republic and the 30th anniversary of the Austrian State Treaty. Moderate economic growth continued, but the wine industry was hurt by scandal.

Foreign Affairs. Amendments to the Austrian foreign trade law went into effect Jan. 1, 1985, providing for severe penalties for violation of the terms of licenses issued for the import of goods to Austria. The measures were designed to meet charges by Washington that advanced technological material from the United States was being reexported to Eastern bloc countries. The new laws also added various types of computer equipment to the list of goods requiring Austrian export permits.

On January 24, Italy released the last of its Nazi war criminals, Walter Reder, who had been convicted for a 1944 massacre in the village of Marzabotto, near Bologna. Austria had long requested clemency for the prisoner, said to be seriously ill. Reder was flown to Graz, where he was met by Defense Minister Friedhelm Frischenschlager and taken to a military hospital. This gave the appearance of an official reception and brought vigorous protests from the people of Marzabotto and Jewish leaders. Chancellor Fred Sinowatz announced that the minister had made a "serious political mistake" but stood by him when the opposition People's Party demanded Frischenschlager's resignation. The Freedom Party, to which the defense minister belonged, threatened to quit the coalition government if he was forced to resign. Frischenschlager publicly apologized, and the vote of no confidence was defeated.

Austria invited the foreign ministers of the four signatory powers of the State Treaty of 1955 (the United States, Soviet Union, Great Britain, and France) and of seven neighboring states to an anniversary celebration on May 15. A six-hour discussion between U.S. Secretary of State George Shultz and Soviet Foreign Minister Andrei A. Gromyko the day before drew much attention.

Economy. Austria's gross domestic product (GDP) was expected to grow at a rate of 2.5% for 1985, the same as for the previous year.

Late in April the agricultural ministry notified the West German state of Rhineland-Palatinate that adulterated Austrian wine had been discovered. The full scandal did not break until July 11, however, when West Germany announced the confiscation of thousands of bottles of imported Austrian wine that had been doctored with diethylene glycol, a chemical used in automobile antifreeze. This sweetened the wine and enabled sale at a higher price. The Austrian government did not issue its first public warning until July 22. Numerous arrests were made, and more than 4.7 million l (1.2 million gal) of wine, mostly from the Burgenland, were impounded. Other countries soon banned the sale of Austrian wines, the United States on July 25. The Austrian parliament later enacted strict wine-control legislation.

ERNST C. HELMREICH, *Professor of History Emeritus, Bowdoin College*

AUSTRIA • Information Highlights

Official Name: Republic of Austria.
Location: Central Europe.
Area: 33,369 sq mi (83 835 km²).
Population (mid-1985 est.): 7,500,000.
Chief Cities (1981 census): Vienna, the capital, 1,531,346; Graz, 243,166; Linz, 199,910; Salzburg, 139,426; Innsbruck, 117,287.
Government: *Head of State,* Rudolf Kirchschläger, president (took office July 1974). *Head of government,* Fred Sinowatz, chancellor (took office May 24, 1983). *Legislature*—Federal Assembly: Federal Council and National Council.
Monetary Unit: Schilling (18.64 schillings equal U.S. $1, Oct. 4, 1985).
Gross National Product (1983 U.S.$): $67,240,000,000.
Economic Indexes (1984): *Consumer Prices* (1970 = 100), all items, 226.0; food, 203.9. *Industrial Production* (1980 = 100), 104.
Foreign Trade (1984 U.S.$): *Imports,* $19,612,000,000; *exports,* $15,724,000,000.

The Yugo, left, a Yugoslavian import priced at around $4,000, helped give rise to a new U.S. market segment, the "mini-compact." Modernistic design was the trend among new domestic models, including the Mercury Sable, below left, and the Oldsmobile Toronado.

Yugo America, Inc.

Ford

Oldsmobile

AUTOMOBILES

The 100th birthday of successful operation of the world's first passenger car brought another precedent-setting milestone to the world's dominant automobile and truck-owning country. U.S. sales of new cars and trucks achieved an all-time record of 15.6 million cars and trucks in the 1985-model year ended Sept. 30, 1985, only three years after a severe recession slashed sales to merely 10.2 million in the 1982-model year.

It was in the autumn of 1885 that Karl Benz drove his gasoline-engine "Benzine" car, a three-wheel two-seater, through the streets of Mannheim, Germany. The "first car" had a bicycle-type belt-and-chain transmission, and Benz secured the world's first driver's license.

Now, 100 years later, more than 456 million cars and trucks operate on the world's highways, of which the United States has 163,861,169 or approximately 36%. The dramatic impact of the development of the automobile on the living standards and economies of the United States and virtually all other countries since 1885 was underscored by the 1985-model-year record in the United States, including a peak for imported cars.

While combined sales of cars and trucks in 1985 surpassed the previous 1978-model-year high by nearly 300,000 units, cars alone still fell short of their 1973 record of 11.9 million. Surging demand among Americans for light trucks and a new crop of compact vans pushed the vehicle total to record ground as overall truck sales reached nearly 4.6 million, exceeding the former high of 4.2 million set in 1978.

General Motors, long the number one automaker, collected 41% of U.S. vehicle sales in the 1985-model year. Ford Motor Co. accounted for 21%; Chrysler Corp., 11%; American Motors, 2%; and imports or import-sponsored domestic makes, 25%. The GM and Ford shares in the previous peak year of 1978 were far higher at 47.6% and 26.9%, respectively, indicating the escalation of U.S. sales of foreign-built cars and trucks through the early 1980s.

In fact, the import share was close to 30% in the final sales periods of 1985, reflecting the relaxation of Japanese export quotas on cars to the United States in April 1985, as well as rising sales of "captive" imports by GM and Chrysler. Demand for higher-priced European makes also remained strong through 1985, and "internationalization" of the U.S. industry was

marked by a steady rise in the number of actual or proposed U.S. assembly plants involving Japanese automakers acting unilaterally or in joint ventures with U.S. partners.

Seeking to lower development and production costs, each of the Big Three auto producers in the United States put into gear joint-venture projects with Japanese partners during the 1985-model year. GM's Chevrolet division sold more than 16,000 Nova subcompacts assembled with Japan's Toyota at a plant in Fremont, CA. Ford and Mazda began construction of a plant in Flat Rock, MI, and Chrysler teamed up with Mitsubishi for a facility to be erected in Bloomington-Normal, IL.

In addition, GM chose a small Tennessee town, Spring Hill, as the location for the 6,000-worker assembly-plant complex where the futuristic Saturn small car will be built. Governors of more than 30 states had sought the Saturn plant, with which GM hopes to equal the manufacturing efficiencies of the Japanese automakers.

Two domestic subcompacts led the 1985-model-year sales parade–Chevrolet's Cavalier with 422,927 retail deliveries and Ford's Escort with 410,978. Chevrolet also claimed the 1985-model-year lead over Ford in trucks, with 1,259,292 sales.

The domestic entries were joined in 1985 by Nissan's Sentra subcompact car, built at the Japanese producer's Smyrna, TN, plant along with compact Nissan trucks. Another Japanese automaker, Honda, steadily boosted production of Accord subcompact cars at its Marysville, OH, plant and announced plans for a substantial expansion in its domestic output.

The 1986 Models. Shifting tastes toward performance and modernistic design played a prominent role in late-1985 debuts of two restyled domestic car lines. From Ford, which had begun to veer away from the traditional boxy design look in the early 1980s, came the radically styled midsize family cars—Ford Taurus and Mercury Sable—priced at about $12,000.

GM checked in with three trendy-looking luxury coupes and a four-door sedan from three of its divisions—the Buick Riviera, Oldsmobile Toronado, and Cadillac Eldorado coupes and the Cadillac Seville sedan. The front-drive Taurus/Sable and $15,000–$18,000 GM luxury coupes represented a determined bid by the Detroit-headquartered automakers to regain sales seized by the "upscale" imports.

GM also introduced a more conventionally styled front-drive series of family sedans—the Buick LeSabre and Oldsmobile Delta 88—each replacing a rear-drive line as part of GM's ongoing program to downsize every series and convert it to front drive.

Chrysler Corp. planned to unveil two new sporty compacts in the spring of 1986, the Plymouth Sundance and Dodge Shadow, plus a new pickup truck named the Dakota. American Motors introduced the Jeep Comanche pickup truck, while Volkswagen United States entered the second year of domestic output of the Golf subcompact car at Westmoreland, PA.

The Imports. U.S. sales of imported cars rose 11.4% in the 1985-model year to a record 2,681,635 units, reflecting the stepped-up shipment of Japanese makes with the easing of quotas for the 1985–86 fiscal year.

However, strength among imports on the American market was shared between the Japanese and European makes. The top five import sellers continued to be from Japan—Toyota, Nissan, Honda, Mazda, and Subaru—but all European entries except those from France posted volume gains in 1985. Volkswagen's jump to sixth among the imports was one of the highest from 1984 at 33% as its imported Jetta notchback series outsold the domestic Golf hatchbacks.

Also on the rise was a new market segment, the "minicompacts" sized below the vast array of subcompacts. Chevrolet's imported Sprint, built by Japan's Suzuki, opened up the minicar field, and it was joined in late 1985 by the Yugo GV from Yugoslavia and Suzuki's own Samurai utility vehicle. Japan's ninth automaker, Daihatsu, was testing the Charade mini for a 1987 U.S. debut.

MAYNARD M. GORDON
Editor, "Motor News Analysis"

WORLD MOTOR VEHICLE DATA, 1984

Country	Passenger Car Production	Truck and Bus Production	Motor Vehicle Registrations
Argentina	137,206	30,117	4,900,000
Australia	340,000	35,000	8,172,200
Austria	5,629	5,370	2,616,654
Belgium	211,815	37,646	3,606,675
Brazil	538,444	326,322	11,584,119
Canada	1,021,536	807,747	14,311,000
Czechoslovakia	180,150	50,112	2,882,830
France	2,713,289	348,863	23,683,600
East Germany	190,000	41,000	3,660,003
West Germany	3,753,719*	255,298	26,362,592
Hungary	–	11,866	1,412,490
India	63,802	117,117	1,967,150
Italy	1,439,283	161,894	22,170,000
Japan	7,073,173	4,391,747	42,931,580
South Korea	158,503	106,858	785,316
Mexico	231,578	112,120	6,918,683
The Netherlands	108,598	13,617	5,118,000
Poland	276,700	55,080	3,910,881
Romania	100,000	60,000	410,000
Spain	1,176,893	131,876	10,318,114
Sweden	352,585	59,011	3,222,020
United Kingdom	908,906	224,825	18,308,563
United States	7,773,332	3,151,449	163,861,169†
USSR	1,330,000	879,400	19,020,513
Yugoslavia	235,994	36,404	3,032,265
Total	30,321,135	11,450,739	456,031,476‡

* Includes 284,437 micro-buses. † U.S. total includes 126,727,873 cars and 37,133,296 trucks and buses. U.S. total does not include Puerto Rico, which has 1,164,111 vehicles. ‡ World total includes 352,315,845 cars and 103,715,631 trucks and buses. Other countries with more than one million vehicle registrations are: China, 1,000,000; Denmark, 1,634,734; Finland, 1,597,956; Greece, 1,620,908; Indonesia, 1,744,073; Iran, 1,725,000; Malaysia, 1,262,532; New Zealand, 1,694,808; Nigeria, 1,180,000; Norway, 1,578,000; Portugal, 1,433,000; Saudi Arabia, 2,110,000; South Africa, 4,013,900; Switzerland, 2,717,310; Thailand, 1,125,000; Turkey, 1,316,286; and Venezuela, 2,755,000. Source: Motor Vehicle Manufacturers Association of the United States, Inc.

AP/Wide World

A woman in Dhaka casts her ballot in a national referendum held to indicate approval/disapproval of the regime.

BANGLADESH

Bangladesh in 1985 continued to suffer political and economic uncertainties.

Politics. National elections, originally slated for December 1984, were rescheduled for April 6, but party protests against martial law and strikes by students, doctors, lawyers, and engineers forced their cancellation. President H. M. Ershad reimposed martial law, banned political activities, closed the universities, and arrested top opposition leaders. On March 21, he held a nationwide referendum to register support for his regime. In May, nonparty elections to the 460 upazilla (subdistrict) councils were held, despite outbreaks of violence, with an estimated turnout of more than 40%. Following the elections, martial law restrictions were eased and the universities were reopened.

The major opposition parties continued to be divided into two major groupings: a rightist seven-party alliance led by the Bangladesh National Party (BNP) of Begum Khaleda Zia and a leftist 15-party group led by the Awami League of Sheikh Hasina Wajed. Both groups continued to press for a five-point program that included an end to martial law and restoration of civilian government.

In a further political maneuver, Ershad created a new five-party pro-government National Front. In addition to the Janadal, created in 1983 under similar government sponsorship, the front included the Muslim League, a BNP splinter faction led by Shah Azizur Rahman, and two other component units of the seven-party alliance.

Economy. Developments in the economy were mixed, with real gross domestic product (GDP) growing at 3%. Industrial output increased by more than 6%. Balance-of-payment and foreign-exchange reserves benefited from increased export earnings, but the balance-of-payments position came under considerable pressure, with a drawdown of more than $130 million in reserves during the first four months of fiscal year 1985.

Despite a governmental attempt to tighten monetary policy, inflation rose to 15%, the highest level since 1980–81. Worker remittances dropped by about 22% to $430 million, boosting the current account deficit to $1.5 billion. The taka continued to depreciate.

Winter food grain harvests rose 1.7% to a record 16 million tons, but spring crops were adversely affected by the weather. A major cyclone hit Bangladesh in May. In June, troops were called out in eastern and northern regions of the country to rescue 100,000 people marooned by monsoon floods. Despite the resultant damage to food output, the improved efficiency of the distribution system helped to avert famine conditions.

Foreign Relations. President Ershad toured several Asian countries to encourage foreign investment in Bangladesh.

Bangladesh played an active role in South Asian affairs. Relations with neighbors, especially India, improved. Indian Prime Minister Rajiv Gandhi and other heads of state visited Bangladesh following the May cyclone.

WILLIAM L. RICHTER
Kansas State University

BANGLADESH • Information Highlights

Official Name: People's Republic of Bangladesh.
Location: South Asia.
Area: 55,598 sq mi (143 998 km²).
Population (mid-1985 est.): 101,500,000.
Chief Cities (1981 census): Dhaka, the capital, 3,458,602; Chittagong, 1,388,476; Khulna, 623,184; Rajshahi, 171,600.
Government: *Head of state,* Hussain Mohammed Ershad, chief executive (assumed power March 24, 1982) and president (Dec. 1983). *Head of government,* Ataur Rahman Khan, prime minister (took office March 30, 1984).
Monetary Unit: Taka (28.0 taka equal U.S.$1, June 1985).
Gross National Product (fiscal 1983 U.S.$): $11,600,-000,000.
Economic Indexes: *Consumer Prices* (Dec. 1984, 1972 = 100), all items, 624.8; food, 620.1. *Industrial Production* (1983, 1980 = 100), 104.
Foreign Trade (fiscal 1984 U.S.$): *Imports,* $2,042,-000,000; *exports,* $934,000,000.

Nervous depositors wait to withdraw money from the Old Court Savings & Loan in Randallstown, MD, in May. A run on thrifts forced the governor to limit withdrawals to $1,000 at such institutions statewide. Two months earlier, Ohio S&Ls also were hit by a run.

AP/Wide World

BANKING

The year 1985 was a significant one for commercial banks and the other members of the U.S. financial services industry. Many of the developments had an adverse effect on the industry's image.

Run on Thrifts. Prime among the events that weakened public confidence in the banking system were the failures or near failures of several savings and loan associations (S&Ls) in Ohio and Maryland whose deposits were not insured by either the Federal Deposit Insurance Corporation (FDIC) or the Federal Savings and Loan Insurance Corporation (FSLIC). In Ohio the trouble originated with government securities dealers that misused S&L funds. The crisis was triggered by depositors fearfully withdrawing their savings from banks and S&Ls when it was learned that the private-insurance pools protecting deposits in nonfederally-insured institutions could be depleted by a major run. When in mid-March thrift customers throughout Ohio began lining up to withdraw their funds, Gov. Richard F. Celeste ordered the temporary closing of 70 such institutions. In mid-May, Maryland Gov. Harry R. Hughes ordered 102 privately insured S&Ls to limit withdrawals to $1,000. Though the runs were quickly halted in both states, they set off loud calls for reform of deposit protection in thrift institutions.

Failures. Fears for the soundness of the banking system also stemmed from the failure of a number of banks, about 100 out of 15,000, that faced difficulties because of loans to the agricultural sector (*see* feature article, page 36) and to the petroleum industry.

As in the 1930s, the preponderance of bank failures resulted from the deterioration of economic conditions in specific regions. Responses to the difficulties included pressure on the banks to become more lenient on repayment terms. In Iowa, in fact, the state imposed a moratorium on repayment of bank debt. Bankers contended that this would make them far less likely to make new loans to farmers unless the credit standing of the borrowers were far stronger than in the past.

Similarly in international lending, public officials of both the United States and other nations have counted on the banks to exercise leniency in reestablishing repayment terms. The banks have even been exhorted to make more loans to nations that have not met the repayment terms on loans already outstanding.

Banking Practices. As if these problems were not enough, U.S. banks have also come under attack for their policies in handling consumer business. Both consumer groups and legislators have complained about the high service charges that banks have been imposing and about the amount of time that many banks take before they let customers use funds from checks that have been deposited in their accounts.

The banks see justification in the rising service charges and the amount of time required before deposited sums are called "good" or collected funds. The service charges reflect the fact that the public no longer must sit with checking accounts that earn no interest or savings accounts whose yields have been limited by interest-rate ceilings. When banks were prevented by law from paying going rates for savings and checking account funds, they made

money on consumer deposits and could subsidize other services with the profits from the underpayment. Now that they must pay going rates for both checking and savings money, they can no longer continue this subsidization but rather must make each service pay its own way. The public, however, is used to free or cheap banking and does not readily accept the new pricing policies.

As for the delay of several days before a deposited check becomes collected funds, bankers claim that they need the time to ensure that the checks deposited are good. Most outside observers, however, feel that the banks have been taking advantage of the public. It was widely expected that both legislation and modification of banking practices would shorten the time between the deposit of a check and the availability of the funds to the depositor.

Electronic Banking. While banks have been under pressure to modify service charges and collection practices, the ground swell of interest in electronic funds transfer continues unabated. For bankers well recognize that electronic movement of money is far cheaper and quicker than handling paper transactions. Thus, banks have been adding more and more automatic teller machines (ATMs) and are looking at point-of-sale terminals (which allow a store customer to move money directly from his or her bank account directly to the store cashier). They also are working to increase public acceptance of banking in the home, as well as other means of replacing the paper check with electronic movement of funds.

While the check will not disappear, bankers feel that they will at least slow down the growth of paper transactions by the switch to electronic banking. One way of encouraging the transition would be to offer lower service charges for moving money electronically than for using a teller—just as the telephone company encouraged direct dialing of long-distance calls with attractive rate discounts for calls that do not involve an operator. Also with price incentives, bankers are looking to promote a switch from credit card purchasing, which gives the public time to pay its bills, to use of debit cards, in which the money moves immediately.

Also in the area of electronic banking, banks are further perfecting their ATM networks so that the holder of an automatic teller machine card can use it anywhere in a large region or even the whole country.

Expansion. While banks are trying to give the public broader geographical access to their accounts through ATM networks, they also are expanding their own territories—within individual states and at the interstate level as well.

The time has long past when a U.S. bank had to be confined to one state. As of mid-1985, 22 states allowed banks from other states to come inside their borders, provided there is reciprocity. And in a major 1985 U.S. Supreme Court decision *(Northeast Bancorp v. Board of Governors),* the justices held, 8–0, that so-called "regional banking compacts" do not violate federal law or the Constitution. Under such compacts, neighboring states band together and allow banks from within the region to cross state lines to serve customers. The *Northeast* case had to do with such an arrangement between Massachusetts and Connecticut —called The New England Compact—which authorized mergers between banks from those two states but excluded others. The suit had been filed by Citicorp of New York, which objected to the exclusion. Having lost the case in the Supreme Court, banks in New York and other similarly affected states hoped that Congress would provide a "trigger"—allow them to go nationwide in a specific number of years. In any event, further geographic expansion of banking territory was one of the main developments of 1985.

"Scrambled Finance." Finally, 1985 saw further efforts by U.S. banks to enter insurance, investment banking, and other diverse financial fields. Meanwhile, nonbanks, such as Sears Roebuck and Merrill Lynch, continued efforts to expand their banking powers. The so-called "nonbank banks"—organizations that evade banking laws by not offering some specific bank service, such as commercial loans—continued to flourish. Efforts in Congress to outlaw nonbank banks did not come to fruition.

With thrifts diversifying, banks trying to broaden their powers, and nonbank banks flourishing, 1985 saw a continuation of the era of "scrambled finance"—attempts by each type of organization to offer the services and compete for the business of the others. As nonbanks gain more banking powers, the Federal Reserve Board may have to worry about its weakened ability to control credit. The public, however, has benefited from the broader services and higher savings rates that this new competition has brought.

Canada. The condition of banking in Canada during 1985 was not dissimilar from that in the United States. The most noteworthy development was the failure of several banks— something not seen since the 1920s. As in the United States, the cause of the failures was problems with agricultural and petroleum loans. The government tried to bail out Edmonton's Canadian Commercial Bank, but $250 million could not save it. Also closing its doors was the Calgary-based Northland Bank. One result of the failures was to reinforce the dominance of five giant banks whose markets had been threatened by deregulation proposals similar to those that have been enacted in the United States.

Paul S. Nadler
Rutgers University

BELGIUM

Four issues dominated the year: installation of missiles, political responsibilities in the wake of a May soccer riot, economic difficulties, and October elections.

Missiles. In 1979 the North Atlantic Treaty Organization (NATO) voted to deploy nuclear-armed missiles in Western Europe to counter the deployment of Soviet SS-20 missiles. Belgium, however, had delayed receipt of 48 cruise missiles pending results of Soviet-U.S. disarmament talks. These talks broke off in December 1983. Urged not to rupture alliance solidarity, Prime Minister Wilfried Martens in March 1985 announced deployment of the first 16 missiles at Florennes air base south of Brussels.

Martens' coalition of Walloon and Flemish Christian Democrats and Liberal Reformers (conservatives) gained support on the issue from small conservative parties outside the coalition. Martens' government thereby survived a parliamentary vote, despite defections from the left wing of the Christian Democrats. Socialists, especially those from Flanders, opposed the deployment.

Riot. On May 29, 41 persons were killed and 260 injured in a riot at Heysel Stadium prior to the World Cup soccer championship match. A parliamentary investigating committee placed major blame on inebriated British fans, but it also criticized the Belgian police. Insufficient precautions were taken, the committee said, and when violence occurred, the police failed to respond promptly or effectively. Interior Minister Charles-Ferdinand Nothomb, whose office supervises the police, refused to accept political responsibility and was backed by Martens. This posture provoked the resignation of Justice Minister Jean Gol, leader of the French-speaking Liberals and, like Nothomb, a deputy premier. Five other Liberals followed suit, and

AP/Wide World

Prime Minister Wilfried Martens asks Parliament to support the deployment of nuclear cruise missiles in Belgium.

Martens tendered his resignation to King Baudouin. The king rejected the offer, thus avoiding a summer electoral campaign, and asked Martens to lead a caretaker regime. Elections scheduled for December were moved up to October 13.

Economy. The Martens coalition had pledged economic reform. Some progress was made, as the economy experienced real growth of 2% in 1984, a higher figure than anticipated. Exports and corporate profitability went up. Inflation fell to 6.4% at the end of 1984, and to 4–5% by the middle of 1985. Unemployment remained near 14% despite government job-creation programs. Although deficits fell, by January government debt exceeded 100% of the gross national product. A budget cut of 26.8 billion Belgian francs (about $432 million) therefore was announced in March. To combat unemployment, the caretaker government agreed on a new-jobs program and a $1.3 billion tax reduction.

Elections. Dissolution of the Chamber occurred in September, following a dispute over funding of Dutch- and French-speaking schools. The campaign focused on economic issues, as Socialists criticized Martens' program of reduced public spending coupled with tax incentives to private industry. Counter to predictions, the Christian Democrat–Liberal coalition gained 2 seats, for a total of 115 of the 212 in the Chamber. The Christian Democrats gained 8, to reach a total of 69, while the Socialists received 6, to hold 67. The Greens rep-

resentation grew from 4 to 9. Liberals lost 6 seats, the Flemish People's Union lost 5, and the Front of French-Speaking People lost 3. The Communists lost both their seats and therefore would not be represented in Parliament for the first time since World War II. The 49-year-old Martens quickly established the 33d government since 1944 on the pattern of his previous coalition.

Other. Pope John Paul II received a rousing welcome during his May visit. In June alleged members of Communist Combatant cells were arrested, yet the terrorist organization's attacks on NATO and industrial targets continued.

J. E. HELMREICH, *Allegheny College*

BIOCHEMISTRY

In 1984–85 biochemists further defined the role of oncogenes, elucidated the chemistry of the insulin receptor, and used gene-cloning techniques for a variety of purposes.

Oncogenes. Oncogenes are normal cellular genes that sometimes malfunction and cause cancer. Although their normal specific function has remained a mystery, several clues have begun to emerge. The latest hint came from studies with yeast cells by scientists at Cold Spring Harbor (NY) Laboratory who were investigating the biochemical role of *ras* oncogenes, implicated in several cancers. The *ras* genes are found not only in human and animal cells but also in yeast cells; the latter, in fact, contain two such genes. The yeast cells are able to survive with either one but not if they are deprived of both. When the yeast cells were genetically engineered so that the *ras* genes were replaced with corresponding human genes, the yeast cells were still viable. This meant that the human and yeast genes are closely related. Further studies found that the *ras* genes regulate yeast growth by controlling the production of cyclic AMP, a molecule known to have vital functions in almost all aspects of the cell's metabolism. Whether the *ras* genes function in a similar fashion in human and animal cells remains unknown.

Several researchers also succeeded in inserting hybrid oncogenes (genes fabricated by fusing segments from two different oncogenes) into mice. In one such attempt, the regulatory region of the *myc* oncogene was replaced with a similar segment taken from the mouse mammary tumor virus (MMTV). (The regulatory region acts as an "on-off" switch, controlled by a specific signal.) The idea behind this hybrid oncogene was to free *myc* of its dependence on the hormone PDGF (the normal activator) and to bring it under the control of lactogenic hormone (which stimulates milk production) and glucocorticoid, both of which activate MMTV. The hybrid gene was injected into fertilized mouse eggs, which were then implanted in foster mothers. The resulting progeny carried the hybrid gene in all of their cells, including eggs and sperms. When these mice were bred, the females showed a strong tendency to develop breast cancer during pregnancy. It was notable that the hybrid gene was expressed in mammary glands of lactating mice since the MMTV is activated by hormones in the mouse's breast. The experiment demonstrated that specific oncogenes can be targeted to specific tissues with the use of a proper regulatory segment. This provides a powerful tool for studying the biochemical role of oncogenes.

Insulin Receptor. One of the major goals of biochemists has been to define the chemical structure of the insulin receptor. Receptors are proteins located on cell surfaces to which insulin attaches as its first step in producing effects on the cell. By cloning the gene for the protein that gives rise to the human insulin receptor, scientists deduced the exact sequence of the 1,370 amino acids of the protein. This protein is ultimately cut by the cell into two subunits and joined with a duplicate pair to form each active receptor. This achievement should explain why some severe diabetics fail to respond to insulin and whether this is due to the malfunctioning receptors.

Research on the insulin receptor also revealed that it shares some similarities with the receptor for epidermal growth factor (EGF), believed to stimulate growth in skin cells. The interest in this similarity is heightened by the fact that one of the known oncogenes serves as a blueprint for part of the EGF receptor. Whether the gene for the insulin receptor is also oncogenic remains uncertain.

Other Achievements. And 1985 saw other spectacular discoveries. First, intact DNA was extracted from an Egyptian mummy believed to be 2,400 years old and was successfully cloned. Second, biochemists cloned the genes for two important proteins, factor VIIIC and von Willebrand factor, that go into the complex chemical cascade leading to the blood clot. The absence of either protein results in the two most common bleeding disorders, hemophilia and von Willebrand's disease. It is expected that in a few years these patients could be treated with the pure proteins rather than blood transfusions. Third, biochemists partially solved the mystery of how newly synthesized proteins find their way to specific compartments contained within plant and animal cells. The targeted proteins carry a specific sequence of amino acids—called the leader sequence—by which a specific compartment is recognized. So crucial are the leader sequences that when one was deliberately attached to a foreign protein it, too, ended up in a compartment recognized by that leader. This represents an important technique for genetic engineers.

PREM P. BATRA, *Wright State University*

BIOGRAPHY

A selection of profiles of persons prominent in the news during 1985 appears on pages 131–43. The affiliation of the contributor is listed on pages 591–94; biographies that do not include a contributor's name were prepared by the staff. Included are sketches of:

BAKER, James Addison, III

On Jan. 8, 1985, President Reagan announced what became known as the great job switch of his second term. Under the plan, White House Chief of Staff James A. Baker III and Secretary of the Treasury Donald T. Regan changed positions. In announcing the change, the president said that "upon confirmation . . . Jim Baker would become chief economic spokesman for my administration and would remain a designated member of the National Security Council." Baker's nomination was approved by the Senate by a 95–0 vote on January 29. The former Texas lawyer soon made clear that he was "happy as a clam" with his new position. As treasury secretary, he planned to make tax reform and reform of the international monetary system his top priorities.

Although not a member of the original Reagan team of conservative Californians, James Baker was the White House chief of staff throughout the first term. He not only was a member of the Baker-Deaver-Meese team but also masterminded the president's 1984 reelection campaign. In the process, he gained the reputation of being a workaholic and a compulsive manager. According to the president, he was "deeply involved in the planning and presentation of all the major initiatives" of the Reagan administration.

Background. James Addison Baker III was born in Houston, TX, on April 28, 1930. Following graduation from Princeton University in 1952, he spent two years in the Marine Corps. He then decided to follow in his father's and grandfather's footsteps and take up law. Baker obtained a law degree with honors from the University of Texas and was admitted to the Texas bar in 1957. Since a strict rule against nepotism prevented him from joining the family law firm, he began practicing with Andrews, Kurth, Campbell & Jones in Houston.

A nominal Democrat during his early years, Baker worked in the unsuccessful Senate campaign of his longtime friend, George Bush, in 1970. As a result of the experience, he became "absolutely, totally, pure Republican." In 1975–76 he was an undersecretary of commerce in the Ford administration, and in 1976 he played a key role in Ford's drive for a full presidential term. Following Ford's defeat, Baker returned to his Texas law position. In 1978 he lost in his only bid for elective office, the attorney generalship of Texas. The following year he was made chairman of George Bush's presidential election committee. Following Bush's withdrawal from the presidential race and his nomination as vice-president, Baker was a senior adviser for the Reagan-Bush committee and later a member of the transition team.

James Baker's first wife, Mary, died in 1970. They were the parents of four sons. In 1973 he married Susan Garrett, a mother of three children. Their own daughter, Mary Bonner Baker, was born in 1977.

BENNETT, William John

The appointment of William J. Bennett as the new U.S. secretary of education easily won congressional approval on Feb. 6, 1985. Bennett, chairman of the National Endowment for the Humanities since November 1981, had been named to the cabinet post by President Reagan on January 10. Such Rightist organizations as Moral Majority and the Heritage Foundation had favored the appointment, believing that Bennett would seek to reduce the federal role in education, aid Christian academies, and inspire conservative values generally.

Controversy resulted immediately following Bennett's first news conference as education secretary. He alienated liberals by backing President Reagan's budget cuts for college-student loans saying that students seeking such assistance ought first to divest themselves of stereos, cars, and beachside vacations. He criticized job-oriented colleges for neglecting the humanities.

Opposition surfaced at an April Senate subcommittee meeting to consider confirmation of two Bennett appointees. Sen. Lowell P. Weicker, Jr. (R-CT), the subcommittee's chairman, challenged Eileen Marie Gardner for the views she expressed in a report written for the Heritage Foundation, stating that federal spending for the handicapped shortchanged other education programs. The senator also questioned the appointment of Lawrence A. Uzzell, who favored eliminating most federal aid to education. Bennett defended them before Senator Weicker, the father of a handicapped son, but later accepted their resignations.

Conservatives generally supported Bennett for appointing "some extraordinary good conservatives" to Education Department positions and for backing President Reagan's tuition tax credits and vouchers for children to attend a school of their parents' choice. Congress has rejected those plans.

On July 2, Secretary Bennett criticized as "ridiculous" the U.S. Supreme Court's decision barring as unconstitutional public-school systems from conducting remedial and enrichment classes at parochial schools. He also announced a reorganization of the department's research function. Research work now would be directed by an assistant secretary for research and improvement. The National Institute of Education, the government's educational research agency since 1973, would cease to exist. It had been criticized by some for promoting liberal educational studies.

Background. William John Bennett was born on July 31, 1943, in Brooklyn, NY. He received a bachelor's degree from Williams College in 1965, a doctorate from the University of Texas in 1967, and a law degree from Harvard in 1971. He then served as assistant to the president of Boston University (1972–76), executive director of the National Humanities Center in Triangle Park, NC (1976–79), and its director and president (1979–81). Dr. Ben-

nett also has taught at North Carolina State University and the University of North Carolina.

The secretary returned temporarily to the classroom as the 1985 school year began. (See also EDUCATION.)

FRANKLIN PARKER

BROCK, William Emerson, III

The atmosphere changed at the U.S. Department of Labor on April 29, 1985, when William E. Brock III, 54, of Tennessee was sworn in as the 18th U.S. secretary of labor. Brock's predecessor at the Labor Department, Raymond J. Donovan of New Jersey, had resigned in March after a New York State judge refused to dismiss criminal charges against him. Donovan had been on a leave of absence from his Cabinet post since shortly after being indicted in September 1984 on charges of larceny and fraud in connection with a subway construction project, and activity at the Labor Department had virtually halted during Donovan's absence. Labor leaders, including AFL-CIO President Lane Kirkland, welcomed Brock's appointment. Kirkland noted that "while we have not always agreed, he has earned our respect," and that he looked forward to a "new and constructive relationship" with the department.

Business groups greeted Secretary Brock as one of their own. Edward Walsh of the U.S. Business and Industrial Council described him as "very clearly a pro-business conservative on just about everything."

Speaking at the National Press Club, the new secretary carved out three "settled issues," basic principles of labor-management relations that he considers immune from challenge. They are: collective bargaining, equal opportunity in the workplace, and freedom from "avoidable risks of health and safety" in the workplace.

Among his early acts as secretary, Brock picked Stephen I. Schlossberg, for 20 years general counsel for the United Automobile Workers, as deputy undersecretary for labor-management relations. He also opened a campaign for a subminimum wage for young people and postponed for 18 months any federal regulation of field sanitation for farm workers. Instead he called on the states to tackle that issue.

Background. William Emerson Brock III was born on Nov. 23, 1930, in Chattanooga, TN. After graduation from Washington and Lee University in 1953 and a three-year stint in the Navy, he became an executive with his fam-

ily's business, the Brock Candy Co. The new labor secretary came to Washington in 1963 as a Republican member of Congress from Chattanooga—the first Republican in 40 years to be elected from Tennessee's third district. In 1970 he was elected to the U.S. Senate, defeating Sen. Albert Gore, a liberal Democrat. After losing his Senate seat to James Sasser in 1976, he became chairman of the Republican National Committee. In the latter post, he worked to open the GOP to all Americans and move it toward majority status. In 1981, President Reagan appointed him U.S. trade representative with the rank of ambassador.

The future labor secretary married Laura Handly in 1957. They had three sons and a daughter. Mrs. Brock died of cancer as 1985 ended.

See also LABOR.

GORDON H. COLE

BUMBRY, Grace Ann

When George Gershwin's *Porgy and Bess* was staged by the Metropolitan Opera in New York in 1985, Grace Bumbry led the cast to critical acclaim in the starring role of Bess. It had taken *Porgy* 50 years to reach the Met stage; Bumbry, however, was already a regular.

The Met originally wanted to present Gershwin's three-and-a-half-hour opera in 1935 but lost its bid because the composer insisted on an all-black cast, then an impossibility. A truncated version was presented on Broadway instead and became well known. When the Met chose Bumbry for the lead in its restored, full-length 1985 version, she confessed to some initial misgivings, both for the opera's musical-theater image and for its uncomplimentary portrayal of blacks. After studying the music, however, she reported a complete turnaround: "It's just as important, just as difficult as a Strauss opera," she told *People* magazine.

Bumbry has ample experience to make that judgment. In her 25 years on the operatic stage, the mezzo-soprano has become famous for roles in operas ranging from Wagner's *Tannhäuser* to Bizet's *Carmen*.

Background. Grace Ann Bumbry was born in St. Louis, MO, on Jan. 4, 1937, the youngest child of a freight handler and a schoolteacher. Her first musical training came at home, where she was urged to study the piano and join the church choir. Later, a high school choir director encouraged her to study voice. She sang

William E. Brock III

Grace Bumbry

Photos, AP/Wide World

at numerous talent contests and won most, including a 1954 appearance on *Arthur Godfrey's Talent Scouts*.

Bumbry went on to study voice at Boston University and at Northwestern University, where she took classes given by the famous German opera singer Lotte Lehmann. She followed Lehmann to California and continued to study under her for the next three years; then, in 1959, she went to Europe to take advantage of the concert and opera opportunities there. Her operatic debut came in Paris in 1960, as Amneris in *Aïda,* and brought immediate acclaim.

The event that brought her to international attention, however, was the 1961 Wagner festival at Bayreuth, West Germany. Bumbry, the first black to take part in the festival, sang the role of Venus in *Tannhäuser* and brought down the house. Still largely unknown in the United States, she was invited by Jacqueline Kennedy to perform at the White House the following year. Concert and opera appearances in her home country followed.

Now one of the Met's leading stars, Bumbry has appeared at most of the world's major opera houses, including La Scala in Milan, Covent Garden in London, Teatro Colón in Buenos Aires, the Berlin Opera, and the Vienna Opera. She divides her time between an apartment in New York and a villa in Switzerland.

ELAINE PASCOE

COSBY, Bill

Comedian Bill Cosby had the television hit of the 1984–85 season with *The Cosby Show,* a new situation comedy that was consistently at or near the top of the ratings. Bucking current trends, the show avoids racial issues and quick one-liners in favor of in-depth—and funny—examinations of the daily family problems of a doctor (Cosby), his lawyer wife (Phylicia Ayers-Allen), and their five children. In many ways, it mirrors the star's own family life.

Off camera, Cosby exercises considerable creative control, often producing material that is developed by the show's writers. He has a reputation as a demanding, but fair, perfectionist on the set. Off it, he guards his personal life from the spotlight of publicity (he has been married to the former Camille Hanks for more than 20 years and like his television counterpart has five children).

Background. William Henry Cosby, Jr., was born on July 12, 1937, in the Germantown district of Philadelphia. A class clown who excelled in sports, he left school in the tenth grade and completed his high-school education while serving in the U.S. Navy. In 1961, after discharge from the Navy, he enrolled at Temple University on an athletic scholarship.

A career in professional football seemed likely; but, while still in college, Cosby began to perform comedy routines at several Philadelphia nightclubs. In 1962 he took a leave of absence from school to appear at the Gaslight Cafe in New York City. He soon withdrew from school altogether and began what turned out to be a meteoric rise on the nightclub circuit, playing in Chicago, Washington, Toronto, and Las Vegas in addition to New York. The appeal of his routines, which ignored race and drew heavily on childhood experiences, brought television appearances as well.

A major change in Cosby's career came in 1965, when he was signed for a dramatic role, as an undercover agent, in the television series *I Spy*. He was the first black to appear in such a role. He also starred in his own comedy show, *The Bill Cosby Show* (1969; 1972–73), and won a total of four Emmy Awards during the period.

At the height of his career, Cosby curtailed his schedule to earn a doctorate in education at the University of Massachusetts at Amherst (1972–77), saying that he intended to become a teacher. Although the Cosbys continue to spend much of their time in Amherst (at one of their five residences), Bill never truly left show business. His career has been marked by a total of 10 film roles, 22

AP/Wide World
Bill Cosby

comedy albums—8 of which won Grammy awards—commercials, and continued nightclub and television appearances.

He is the author of *The Wit and Wisdom of Fat Albert* and *Bill Cosby's Personal Guide to Power Tennis*.

ELAINE PASCOE

DeVRIES, William Castle

In an unprecedented and highly publicized series of operations beginning in 1982, Dr. William C. DeVries has pioneered the implantation of permanent artificial hearts in human patients. On Dec. 2, 1982, at the University of Utah Medical Center in Salt Lake City, DeVries replaced the diseased heart of 61-year-old retired dentist Barney B. Clark with a polyurethane-and-aluminum pump called the Jarvik-7; Clark survived 112 days on the device. Dr. DeVries performed a second implantation of the Jarvik-7 (named for its inventor, Dr. Robert K. Jarvik) on Nov. 25, 1984, at the Humana Heart Institute in Louisville, KY; the recipient was a 52-year-old former federal employee named William J. Schroeder, who recovered so well that he eventually left the hospital. And in 1985, Dr. DeVries repeated the procedure two more times at Humana: February 17 on 58-year-old retired autoworker Murray P. Haydon, and April 14 on 62-year-old retired railroad engineer Jack C. Burcham. Haydon responded well to the surgery and the artificial heart, but Burcham died after ten days.

Background. The son of a physician and a nurse, William Castle DeVries was born Dec. 19, 1943, in Brooklyn, NY. His father, serving with the U.S. Navy, was killed in action during World War II, and his mother took William to live in her home state of Utah. William was raised in Ogden as a Mormon. He attended the University of Utah on an athletic scholarship, receiving a B.S. in 1966. He continued on at the Utah College of Medicine, where he came under the wing of Dr. Willem Kolff, who had built the first successful kidney dialysis machine and helped develop the heart-lung machine. After obtaining his M.D. in 1970, DeVries did his internship in surgery at the Duke University Medical Center in North Carolina. He served as a resident there in cardiovascular and thoracic surgery from 1971 to 1979.

William C. DeVries

Photos, AP/Wide World

Robert J. Dole

Dr. DeVries returned to the University of Utah in 1979 to continue research on the artificial heart. He was appointed chairman of the division of cardiovascular and thoracic surgery and assistant professor of surgery, as well as chief of thoracic surgery at the Salt Lake VA Medical Center. As a principal of Symbion, Inc., an artificial heart research company founded by Drs. Kolff and Jarvik, DeVries became the first surgeon authorized by the U.S. Food and Drug Administration to perform the implant procedure. In late 1984, having performed the procedure once, the now renowned surgeon left Utah for the Humana Heart Institute in Kentucky, where he brought a substantial part of the artificial-heart program.

Dr. DeVries is the author of more than 50 articles for medical publications and has received numerous awards and honors. He is married to the former Ane Karen Olsen, and the couple has seven children. Dr. DeVries enjoys reading poetry, and he listens to classical or country music in the operating room.

See also MEDICINE AND HEALTH.

DOLE, Robert Joseph

During 35 years in politics, Kansas Republican Sen. Robert J. Dole has established himself as a forceful defender of conservative principles and a slashing critic of his Democratic opponents. Nevertheless, according to many observers, it was his pragmatism rather than any ideological purity that led the GOP caucus in November 1984 to elect him Senate majority leader in the 99th Congress, succeeding the retiring Sen. Howard Baker, Jr. (R-TN).

Since taking the oath of office on Jan. 3, 1985, Dole has played a strong, active role in controlling the Senate floor and as a party mediator. Trying to preserve as much of President Ronald Reagan's program as possible, Dole has focused particular attention on cutting the federal budget deficit. He was criticized in his home state for siding with the administration in opposing farm-credit legislation, and White House officials were pleased with his efforts on behalf of MX missile funding and aid to the Nicaraguan Contras. Ever the pragmatist, however, the 62-year-old Dole has differed from the Reagan line when necessary to build a workable Senate program. At midyear, for example, he indicated that the president's tax revision proposal would have to wait for Congress to complete its deficit-reduction work.

Background. Robert Joseph Dole was born in Russell, KS, on July 22, 1923. He was educated at the University of Kansas, where he got his bachelor's degree, and at Washburn Municipal University in Topeka, where he studied law. On completing law school, he enlisted in the U.S. Army and served as a platoon leader in Italy until he was severely wounded by a shell burst. Recovery took three years and left him with a withered and almost useless right arm. It also left him with a continued interest in programs to aid the handicapped.

Dole won his first campaign, for a seat in the Kansas legislature, in 1950. Two years later he was elected to the first of four two-year terms as Russell County attorney. He won a seat in the U.S. House of Representatives in 1960 and moved up to the Senate after the election of 1968.

His aggressiveness as a defender of the Nixon administration won him national attention and the gratitude of the president, who in 1971 recommended him for chairman of the Republican National Committee. In that post Dole was a loyal Nixon partisan. During the early stages of the Watergate scandal he sought to rebut attempts to link it to the White House, but his independence and outspokenness evidently offended some Nixon aides; after the 1972 elections he was asked to leave the chairmanship. This turned out to be a blessing in disguise since it removed Dole from direct connection with the White House during the most politically damaging phase of the Watergate scandal. Even so, Dole had to wage an uphill battle to retain his Senate seat in 1974.

In 1976, Senator Dole was President Gerald Ford's surprise choice as his vice-presidential running mate on the Republican ticket. It was evidently Dole's conservative record that was responsible for the selection. Ford needed someone to placate the conservative supporters of Ronald Reagan, whom he had just defeated for the GOP nomination. And he also wanted someone who could take the offensive against the Democratic ticket. The senator staged a tough campaign, but the Ford-Dole ticket was defeated on November 2.

Although unsuccessful in a bid to win the Republican presidential nomination in 1980, Dole was easily reelected to a third Senate term. And with the GOP taking over a majority in that body, Dole became chairman of the Senate Finance Committee.

During his years in Washington, Dole has earned a reputation for his biting, rapid-fire one-liners. He says he has no time for hobbies, but his wife says he is a "sun worshiper." In 1948, Dole married Phyllis Holden, a

physical therapist, who first met him at the hospital where he was recovering from his war wounds. The marriage ended in divorce in 1972, and in 1975 Dole married Mary Elizabeth Hanford, who serves as secretary of transportation in the Reagan administration. He has a daughter, Robin, by his first marriage.

See also UNITED STATES—Domestic Affairs.

ROBERT SHOGAN

FIELD, Sally

Portraying the resilient widow Edna Spalding proved a revelation for actress Sally Field. Field credits her character in the acclaimed film *Places in the Heart* (1984) with fostering a change within herself; namely, discovering "that people are meant to need one another." The actress indicated that the character, who was trying to rear two children and survive on a cotton farm in the depression era of the 1930s, made Field "ready to be involved."

For her performance in *Places in the Heart,* Field received the best actress Academy Award in March 1985, her second win in that category. She previously had won the Oscar in 1980 for her strong performance in *Norma Rae* (1979), a role that also had brought her the 1979 Cannes Film Festival best actress award.

Background. Sally Field was born in Pasadena, CA, on Nov. 6, 1946, the daughter of drugstore owner Richard Field and Margaret Field, a Paramount starlet. Her parents were divorced when she was four, and later her mother married actor and stuntman Jock Mahoney. Sally began performing at an early age and has said that there was never a time when she did not want to be an actress.

Television was Field's training ground. She initially was seen in the *Gidget* series (1965–66) and then as

Sally Field

AP/Wide World

Sister Bertrille in *The Flying Nun* (1967–69). Her last television series was the short-lived *Girl With Something Extra* (1973–74).

Besides her regular series, she appeared in various television drama-series episodes and was in several television movies. Her most notable made-for-television movie was the two-part *Sybil* (1976). In that film she played a woman with multiple personalities. Her performance in the title role won her an Emmy and brought about increased recognition of her acting talents.

Field made her motion-picture debut in *The Way West* (1967). She appeared in *Stay Hungry* (1976) and in a group of films with actor Burt Reynolds, including *Smokey and the Bandit* (1977), *The End* (1978), *Hooper* (1978), and *Smokey and the Bandit II* (1980). Other major films include *Absence of Malice* (1981), *Back Roads* (1981), *Kiss Me Goodbye* (1982), and *Murphy's Romance* (1985).

Seemingly indifferent to the glitter of Hollywood, Sally Field has been involved in the nuclear disarmament movement. An early first marriage that ended in divorce produced two much-loved sons. In late 1984 she married Alan Griesman.

See also MOTION PICTURES.

GORBACHEV, Mikhail Sergeyevich

Within hours of the death of Soviet party leader Konstantin Chernenko on March 10, 1985, a new general secretary of the Communist Party was elected—Mikhail S. Gorbachev. Not only was a much younger man (54) now in charge, but power had shifted finally from the old generation of Soviet politicians who had risen during the long dictatorship of Joseph Stalin to a new generation trained under Nikita Khrushchev and Leonid Brezhnev. Gorbachev had already impressed Westerners during a 1984 visit to Great Britain with his intelligence, personal charm, and self-deprecating humor. His fashionable and sophisticated wife, Raisa, had also made an impact on the media. Hopes were raised that the West could "do business" with the new generation of Soviet leaders, and in the Soviet Union itself a mood of optimism seemed to follow the news of Gorbachev's election to the top spot.

Background. Mikhail Sergeyevich Gorbachev was born on March 2, 1931, in the Stavropol region of southern Russia. His childhood and early teen years were a time of violent upheaval in the Soviet Union; he was ten when Nazi Germany invaded the USSR. In 1952, while a law student at Moscow University, Gorbachev joined the Communist Party. After graduation he returned to Stavropol, where he worked as a specialist on agricultural problems and began his climb through the party bureaucracy. He first served in the Komsomol, the Communist youth organization, rising by the early 1960s to head the Stavropol Regional Komsomol Committee. By 1970 he had risen to the position of Communist Party first secretary for the entire Stavropol region.

Gorbachev's achievements in Stavropol were recognized by the central party leaders, and in 1978 he was brought to Moscow as party secretary for agriculture. Despite several poor grain harvests, Gorbachev was named to the Politburo in 1980; at age 49 he was the youngest member of that policy-making body. Gorbachev developed close ties with then-KGB (secret service) chief Yuri Andropov, and his influence rose when Andropov became party leader in November 1982. He worked closely with Andropov, and speculation grew that the young agricultural specialist would succeed the ailing Kremlin leader. But when Andropov died in February 1984, the party turned to another member of the old generation, Chernenko, as general secretary. As Chernenko's health weakened, Gorbachev clearly emerged as the most likely successor. His trip to Britain in December 1984 was seen as the "coming out" of a major world leader. Even before Chernenko's death, Gorbachev was said to be directing the day-to-day affairs of the Soviet party and government.

Within months of his accession, Gorbachev consolidated his position by realigning the party leadership. In July, for example, Eduard A. Shevardnadze replaced Andrei A. Gromyko as foreign minister; Gromyko took over the ceremonial post as president of the USSR; and Grigory V. Romanov, widely regarded as a Gorbachev opponent, was removed from the Politburo. In another move, two months later, Nikolai I. Ryzhkov, who had been appointed by Gorbachev to the Politburo in April, succeeded Nikolai A. Tikhonov, 80, as premier.

To political leaders in the West and the Soviet bloc, he made it clear that he was determined to accelerate domestic economic development and maintain the Soviet Union's international position. (*See* USSR.)

RONALD GRIGOR SUNY

KAMPELMAN, Max M.

On Jan. 18, 1985, Max M. Kampelman, a Washington lawyer and diplomat, was named chairman of the U.S. delegation to the renewed arms-control talks with the Soviet Union in Geneva, Switzerland. Kampelman also was chosen to head the subgroup discussion on space weapons at the three-part Geneva negotiations, which opened in March. A conservative Democrat, Kampelman had been a senior adviser to the U.S. delegation to the United Nations (1966–67) and had served in the final months and early years of the Carter and Reagan administrations as co-chairman of the U.S. delegation to the Madrid Conference on Security and Cooperation in Europe. In the latter position, Kampelman earned a reputation for tough, pragmatic negotiating and a hardline attitude toward the Soviets.

In and out of government for years, Max Kampelman has also been one of the most prominent figures in the city of Washington, DC. He runs the Washington office of the New York–based law firm of Fried, Frank, Harris, Shriver & Kampelman, of which he has been a partner since 1956. In addition, he has been chairman of the city's public broadcasting station, WETA; a moderator of the long-running television show *Washington Week in Review;* chairman of Freedom House; vice-chairman of the Coalition for a Democratic Majority; honorary president of the Anti-Defamation League of the B'nai B'rith,

Max M. Kampelman

AP/Wide World

and an active figure in many other civic, educational, and cultural organizations and institutions.

Background. Born Nov. 7, 1920, in New York City, Kampelman earned a B.A. from New York University in 1940 and a law degree from the same school in 1945. An idealistic young man, he worked as an organizer for the International Ladies' Garment Workers' Union and declared himself a conscientious objector during World War II. After the war, Kampelman studied political science at the University of Minnesota, taking an M.A. in 1946 and a Ph.D. in 1951. A protégé of the late Hubert Humphrey, Kampelman first went to Washington in 1949 as the senator's legislative counsel, a position he held until 1955. It was during the Cold War of the 1950s that Kampelman gradually traded his pacifist ideals for a belief in peace through strength.

Though his experience and political conservatism have earned him a trusted role in the Reagan administration, Max Kampelman remains a committed Democrat. In fact, during the presidential campaign of 1984, he was a foreign policy adviser to Democratic candidate Walter F. Mondale. Kampelman lives in northwest Washington with his wife, the former Marjorie Buetow; they have five children.

See also ARMS CONTROL.

KENNEDY, William Joseph

In 1982, William Kennedy was working as a part-time lecturer at the State University in Albany, NY, and writing fiction in virtual anonymity. He had written three ambitious novels that had gotten little attention, and his fourth had just been turned down by a dozen publishers. *Ironweed,* that fourth novel, finally was published in 1983, and within the next year Kennedy had won a Pulitzer Prize, a National Book Critics Circle Award, and a $264,000 MacArthur Foundation Fellowship. Previously dismissed as a self-conscious writer of regional fiction, Kennedy now was recognized for his exuberant language, vital characters, and vivid evocation of New York State during the 1920s and 1930s.

Ironweed, evoking the depth and humanity still alive in an alcoholic bum, completed a trilogy set in and near Albany during Prohibition and the Depression. The first volume, *Legs* (1975), is a fictional life of the notorious bootlegger and gangster Jack "Legs" Diamond. The second work, *Billy Phelan's Greatest Game* (1978), is based on the 1933 kidnapping of the nephew of a powerful Albany politician.

Background. William Joseph Kennedy was born on Jan. 16, 1928, in north Albany, NY. His youth was spent in the colorful world of small-time local politicians, barrooms, and pool halls. After graduating from Siena College in 1949, Kennedy served two years in the U.S. Army and began a career in journalism. He was a reporter for the *Albany Times-Union* until 1956 and then moved to Puerto Rico, where he became managing editor of the *San Juan Star.* While in Puerto Rico, Kennedy also took a creative writing course with Saul Bellow. Returning to Albany in 1963, Kennedy wrote feature articles for the *Times-Union* and worked on his fiction on the side. His first novel, *The Ink Truck* (1969), was the story of an Albany newspaper strike, blending social criticism and almost surrealistic adventures. The book was barely noticed, but Kennedy left newspaper work to write full time. With the success of *Ironweed* more than a decade later, *The Ink Truck* was reissued, sales of his other books soared, and Kennedy was asked to write the screenplay for Francis Ford Coppola's feature film *The Cotton Club* (1983).

The themes and style of Kennedy's novels reflect the influence of Joyce, Beckett, and Faulkner as he mythologizes forgotten people whose experience reveals universal truths. In his lively essay collection *O Albany* (1983), Kennedy describes his native region "as various as the American psyche itself, of which it was truly a crucible."

JEROME STERN

LENDL, Ivan

Overdue or not, tennis star Ivan Lendl of Czechoslovakia finally was judged a champion in 1985. Since turning professional in 1979, Lendl had twice won the prestigious Volvo Grand Prix Masters (1982, 1983) and had taken home the winner's check from numerous lesser tournaments. He had led his country to a Davis Cup championship (1980), and at one point he had put together a string of 44 victories in match play. Then in 1984 he powered his way to his first Grand Slam championship, taking the French Open. Nevertheless, it was not until 1985 that the 6'2", 175-lb (1.88-m, 79-kg) right-hander earned the full respect of the tennis world. On the strength of some ten tournament victories, most notably the U.S. Open, Lendl was recognized as the year's top male player.

Having lost three straight U.S. Open finals entering the 1985 event, Lendl silenced criticisms that he could not win "the big one." Moody and volatile on the court, the determined 25-year-old came up against defending champion John McEnroe in the title match on September 8. Lendl never played better. With a drilling serve and a powerful forehand volley, he routed Mac in straight sets, 7–6, 6–3, 6–4.

Background. Ivan Lendl was born on March 7, 1960, in the northern Czechoslovakian city of Ostrava. His mother and father both were nationally ranked tennis players, and by age 4, Ivan was hitting balls against a wall. His parents later enrolled him at a local sports club, where the youngster had instruction from a veteran tennis coach. He played in his first tournament at age 8 and by his teens was participating regularly in national sports-club tournaments. In 1975, Lendl began entering major international junior tourneys, and within two years he was ranked as the top men's junior player in the world. After his first season as a professional, 1979, *Tennis* magazine named him rookie of the year.

Never a media darling, Lendl is protective of his private life. He makes his home in Greenwich, CT, where he keeps several German shepherd dogs and his collection of expensive cars. In addition to Czech and English, Lendl speaks Russian, German, and Slovak.

AP/Wide World

Franco Modigliani

School, the University of Chicago, the University of Illinois, Carnegie-Mellon University, and Northwestern University. In 1962 he joined MIT, where he remains institute professor.

Universally respected in the community of economists, Modigliani has a reputation for working well with colleagues and closely with students. A consummate academic, he has been described as slightly disheveled, prone to forgetfulness—and possessed of a quick, extraordinarily incisive mind.

MODIGLIANI, Franco

On Oct. 15, 1985, Professor Franco Modigliani of the Massachusetts Institute of Technology was named the winner of the Nobel Memorial Prize in Economic Science. The 67-year-old native of Italy, now a U.S. citizen, was cited for his "extremely important" work in the areas of household savings behavior and the functioning of financial markets. His analysis of savings, called the "life-cycle theory," published in 1954, holds that people generally save only for their retirement, not for their heirs; individuals tend to save the most during their peak earning years so as to ensure spending power throughout life. That analysis is said to be vital in determining the effects of various national pension programs. Modigliani's theory on financial markets, also formulated in the 1950s, holds that the real value of a company is not based on the size or structure of its debt but on investors' expectations of its future profitability. Said one member of the Nobel selection committee, "His work in the late '50s provided the basis for modern corporate finance."

Background. The son of a physician and a volunteer social service worker, Franco Modigliani was born in Rome, Italy, on June 18, 1918. He attended the University of Rome, earning a doctorate in jurisprudence in 1939, but on his own he had been studying economics. A Jew, Modigliani and his new wife, Serena, fled Mussolini's Italy and arrived in the United States in 1940. Settling in New York City, he attended the New School for Social Research, receiving a Ph.D. in social science in 1944. He began his teaching career at the New Jersey College for Women and subsequently served on the economics faculties at Bard College of Columbia University, the New

MONTANA, Joseph C.

In leading the San Francisco 49ers to their second Super Bowl championship in four years, Joe Montana in 1984–85 lent credence to the argument that he is the best quarterback in the National Football League (NFL). On his way to winning the game's Most Valuable Player award—also for the second time—the 5'9", 195-lb (1.75-m, 88-kg) Pennsylvania native passed for a record 331 yards, as the 49ers defeated the Miami Dolphins, 38–16, in Super Bowl XIX. In January 1982, Montana passed and ran the 49ers to a 26–21 victory over the Cincinnati Bengals in Super Bowl XVI. After his first six years as a professional, Montana was the top-rated passer in NFL history (based on a complex statistical ranking system). Through the 1984 season, he had completed 1,324 of 2,077 pass attempts (63.7%), for 15,609 yards.

Background. An only child, Joseph C. Montana was born on June 11, 1956, in Monongahela, PA. With the encouragement of his father, a finance company manager, Joe grew up playing football, basketball, and baseball. His boyhood idol was Joe Namath, the quarterback of the New York Jets who was himself a Pennsylvania native.

After starring in several sports at Ringgold High School in Monongahela, Montana was given a football scholarship to Notre Dame University. He sat out the 1976 season with a separated shoulder and entered his sophomore year as the team's third-string quarterback. He finally got a chance to play in the third game of the 1977 season, and he led the Fighting Irish to an exciting come-from-behind victory over rival Purdue. With Montana at the helm, Notre Dame went on to become the top-ranked team in the nation. Throughout his college

Photos, AP/Wide World

Joe Montana

Daniel Ortega

career, the coolly efficient quarterback displayed an uncanny ability to rally his team from the brink of defeat in the final minutes of a game—earning him the nickname "Comeback Kid." The most memorable example was the 1979 Cotton Bowl, in which the Irish were losing to Houston by 22 points late in the third quarter but won the game, 35–34, on a Montana pass in the closing seconds.

A third-round pick in the 1979 NFL draft, Montana made only brief appearances during his rookie year with the 49ers. Halfway into the 1980 season, however, with the team floundering, Coach Bill Walsh turned to the blond-haired, blue-eyed scrambler as his field general. Montana responded well and wound up leading the league in pass-completion percentage, with 64.5%. Only one year later, Montana and the 49ers were in their first Super Bowl.

ORTEGA SAAVEDRA, Daniel

When Nicaragua's Sandinista rebels captured Managua in July 1979 and drove President Anastasio Somoza Debayle into exile, they took over a country in ruins, the result of bitter civil war and widespread looting by departing Somoza followers. The new leadership—called the Government of National Reconstruction—was composed of a five-member junta, coordinated by Daniel Ortega Saavedra, a young leader of the Sandinista National Liberation (FSLN) guerrilla war against Somoza. In November 1984, after ruling the country for five difficult years, the junta held popular elections for the presidency and National Assembly. Ortega, 40, was elected president with 63% of the vote, and he was inaugurated Jan. 10, 1985.

Under military, economic, and diplomatic pressure from the U.S. administration of Ronald Reagan and with Nicaragua's economy in trouble, Ortega sought and received aid from the Soviet Union, Cuba, Mexico, and a host of other nations. After the Reagan administration announced an embargo on Nicaraguan trade in May 1985, President Ortega made his second trip to Moscow and other European capitals seeking—and obtaining—more financial assistance, as well as new markets for Nicaraguan goods formerly exported to the United States. Domestically, Ortega has promoted land redistribution to the peasants, cooperative labor and union movements, public health, and widespread education programs. He repeatedly has expressed his willingness to work with the United States but contends that he can make no concessions, nor expand the elements of de-

mocracy at home, while his nation remains under "siege."

Background. Born Nov. 11, 1945, in La Libertad, Nicaragua, Daniel Ortega Saavedra came from a struggling middle-class family long opposed to the Somoza dynasty. His father fought under Augusto César Sandino himself, after whom the Sandinistas are named. Daniel and his brothers served the revolution while still boys. One younger brother, Camilo, was reportedly killed in 1978; another younger brother, Humberto, now serves in the Sandinista government as minister of defense.

After finishing secondary school, Ortega enrolled at the Central American University in Managua to study law, but he dropped out after a few months to join the FSLN. Although he was much younger than most of the guerrilla leaders, he became head of the FSLN's urban resistance campaign. In 1967 he was captured by Somoza's Guardia Civil, and he remained in jail until a prisoner exchange in late 1974. Exiled to Cuba, he received training in guerrilla warfare and returned secretly to Nicaragua to rejoin the Front. Within the movement, Ortega led the largest of three factions—called the Terceristas, or Third Party—which was the most moderate and least ideological.

Daniel Ortega is a small, quiet, intense man always seen in tinted glasses. He neither drinks nor smokes, jogs regularly, and works 15 hours a day. Sandinistas and opponents alike respect his integrity.

THOMAS L. KARNES

PAPANDREOU, Andreas George

The year 1985 was one in which Greece's Prime Minister Andreas Papandreou reaffirmed the independent, highly individualistic, and often unpredictable style that has characterized his life in politics. In February the 66-year-old Socialist leader created new tensions with the United States—his foreign policy has often been labeled "anti-American"—by making a four-day visit to the Soviet Union, where he signed a series of accords. In March, Papandreou suddenly withdrew his support for Parliament's reelection of President Constantine Caramanlis, who withdrew from the race and resigned; the candidate of Papandreou's choice was elected. And in national elections June 2, the charismatic premier and his Pan Hellenic Socialist Movement (PASOK) won a clear victory over the New Democracy Party with 45.8% of the vote and 161 seats in the 300-member Parliament.

Background. Born Feb. 5, 1919, Andreas Papandreou is the son of George Papandreou, the late politi-

cian who represented the liberal wing of Greek politics and served several terms as prime minister. Andreas was arrested in 1939 by the Greek dictatorial regime for being a member of a Trotskyite student group, and he emigrated to the United States the following year. Papandreou continued his education there, earning a doctorate in economics from Harvard University. He became a U.S. citizen in 1944 and served in the U.S. Navy for two years. Later, after an academic career at Harvard, the University of Minnesota, and Northwestern, he was chairman of the department of economics at the University of California, Berkeley. Divorced from his first wife, he married Margaret Chant of Illinois in 1951. They have four children, all born in the United States.

In 1964, having returned to Greece and renounced his U.S. citizenship, Papandreou was elected as a deputy to the Greek Parliament and joined the cabinet of his father, who was then prime minister. But Andreas' name soon was linked with a shadowy left-wing army organization called Aspida, a connection he denied. The elder Papandreou's wish to control the defense ministry led to a break with King Constantine in 1965, and a severe government crisis resulted. When a military dictatorship took power in 1967, Andreas Papandreou was imprisoned. A hue and cry from many U.S. scholars helped secure his release, and he spent the next few years in exile, including a stay in Canada. With the overthrow of the dictatorship in 1974 and the establishment of a republic under the leadership of Prime Minister Caramanlis, Papandreou founded PASOK. In October 1981, by which time Caramanlis was serving as president, Papandreou and PASOK were swept into office with a smashing victory in parliamentary elections.

GEORGE J. MARCOPOULOS

PICKENS, Thomas Boone, Jr.

Perhaps the most consequential—and certainly the most controversial—figure in American business today, independent Texas oilman T. Boone Pickens has been a prime mover in the merger mania sweeping U.S. industry during the 1980s. In a series of bold corporate takeover initiatives, he has forced a major realignment of the nation's largest energy companies. As the founder, president, and chairman of the board of Mesa Petroleum, an independent oil and gas producer, Pickens has taken on such giants as Cities Service, Gulf Oil, and Phillips Pe-

troleum. His impact on the energy business has been likened to that of Jay Gould and Jim Fisk, who forced the consolidation of U.S. railroad lines in the late 1800s.

Like other "corporate raiders," Pickens launches his attacks by buying up a large percentage of a company's stock and offering to purchase other stockholders' shares at a higher price than the market value; the threat is to buy up 51% of the stock and take control of the company. Pickens, however, has never actually acquired a major corporation. Insisting that he is on the side of the small shareholder, Pickens' strategy is to scare management into buying back stocks at a higher, more realistic market price. The high-powered Texan claims that his takeover battles have earned $12 billion for 750,000 small investors and $800 million for Mesa and its partners. His fight for Cities Service, for example, forced that company to merge with Occidental Petroleum in 1982, earning Pickens' group $31.5 million. A similar effort in 1984 forced Gulf Oil, the nation's fifth-largest oil company, to sell out to Number 4 Chevron, yielding $760 million to Pickens' Mesa Partners II. In March 1985, his bid for 11th-ranked Phillips Petroleum resulted in an $89 million profit. But then in May, 12th-ranked Unocal Corp. gave Pickens his first major takeover defeat. In a complex settlement based on a court ruling, Pickens agreed to a "break even" deal; Mesa Partners II, however, was said to have incurred a loss of $100 million in expenses.

Background. Born May 22, 1928, in Holdenville, OK, Thomas Boone Pickens, Jr., grew up in the shadow of working oil wells. His father, a chronic gambler, bought and sold oil leases; his mother ran the town's gas-rationing program during World War II. When Thomas was in high school, the family moved to Amarillo, TX, where he now lives on a 14,000-acre (5 668 ha) ranch. Pickens attended Texas A&M University on a basketball scholarship but, after suffering a broken elbow, transferred to Oklahoma State in his sophomore year. After graduating with a degree in geology in 1951, he went to work for Phillips Petroleum, where his father was employed as a lease broker.

Four years later, Pickens left Phillips to explore for oil on his own. Securing $100,000 in loans, he formed his first company, Petroleum Exploration, in 1956. Combining a keen business sense, hard work (Pickens is an admitted "workaholic"), and enough oil and gas finds to attract investors, he gradually built up his assets and formed Mesa Petroleum in 1964. By the 1980s, he said, "it was cheaper to look for oil on the floor of the New York Stock Exchange than in the ground."

T. Boone Pickens

Vutch, Gamma-Liaison

REGAN, Donald Thomas

As Ronald Reagan prepared to begin his second term as president, the chief executive announced that Donald T. Regan would resign as secretary of the treasury and become chief of staff at the White House. In turn, the current chief of staff, James A. Baker III, would be nominated as treasury secretary. In announcing the change, President Reagan said that Regan, a former longtime Merrill Lynch official, was a "proven successful executive" with "broad domestic and international experience." The president also emphasized that the Regan-Baker job switch was entirely voluntary and that both men welcomed "an opportunity to assume new challenges." In his new post, Regan would remain a member of the president's Cabinet and be designated a member of the National Security Council.

The new chief of staff took over at the White House in early February and immediately began to put his own stamp on the post. Whereas the president formerly relied on the advice and counsel of the Baker-Deaver-Meese triumvirate, now there would be one principal White House adviser, a "totally one-man show." In an attempt to centralize the White House staff, Regan appointed a group of top assistants who would act as sort of corporate vice-presidents or sergeants.

Although Regan soon gained the reputation of being one of the "most powerful chiefs of staff" in modern

White House history, he was criticized by some for failing to map out an overall domestic strategy and for a lack of political acumen.

Background. Born in Cambridge, MA, on Dec. 21, 1918, Donald Thomas Regan was graduated from Harvard University in 1940. A member of the Marine Corps during World War II, he saw action in the Pacific campaign and rose to the rank of lieutenant colonel. After the war he joined an executive training program at Merrill Lynch and remained with the company until he took over at the treasury. The future presidential adviser was appointed executive vice-president of Merrill Lynch in 1964, president four years later, and chief executive officer in January 1971. During his tenure as the company's chairman of the board and chief executive officer (1973–80), Regan oversaw Merrill Lynch's "single-minded effort to diversify." As treasury secretary, Regan worked hard for enactment of the president's 1981 tax bill and became a complete disciple of supply-side economics.

On July 11, 1942, Donald Regan married Ann Gordon Buchanan. They are the parents of two daughters and two sons.

SARNEY, José

On April 21, 1985, José Sarney became the first civilian chief executive of Brazil in 21 years. His ascent to the presidency came on the death of President-elect Tancredo de Almeida Neves. The 75-year-old opponent of military rule died following seven operations, the first of which was performed on March 15, the day before Sarney was sworn in as vice-president and designated interim (acting) president.

President Sarney pledged direct elections in 1988; yet his detractors began discussing a possible direct presidential election sooner. (Neves and Sarney were chosen by an electoral college.) Aware of such machinations, the new Brazilian leader struck a conciliatory chord in his first major speech, promising a government of "harmony, change, work, morality, and austerity . . . [that] will be implacable against corruption." (*See also* BRAZIL.)

Background. José Sarney was born on April 30, 1930, in São Bento, a small town in the impoverished northeastern state of Maranhão. He was baptized José Riba-

José Sarney
Claudio Edinger, Gamma-Liaison

mar Ferreira da Costa, but at age 18 he changed his name to José de Sarney in honor of his father, Sarney Araujo Costa. President Sarney was one of 14 children whose father was a federal prosecutor of modest means. He now recalls that his father sold the future chief executive's typewriter to help finance his schooling at São Luis. Sarney earned his law degree at São Luis where he briefly worked as a journalist.

Politics soon captured the interests of the young lawyer-writer, who was elected a federal deputy in 1956. One year after the 1964 military takeover, he was elected governor of Maranhão. As the state's leader, he was considered a moderate, effective administrator, who belonged to a freer-thinking generation known as the "bossa nova" movement. He directed the construction of bridges, roads, and other public works, especially in remote areas of the state. Despite his popularity and accomplishments, the president, Gen. Ernesto Geisel, vetoed his reelection. Sarney was twice elected senator (1970 and 1978).

Indicative of the flux of Brazilian politics, Sarney has switched parties three times—most recently to leave the pro-military Democratic Social Party (PSD) to accept the number two spot, with Neves, on the ticket of the new Liberal Front Party. This perceived act of betrayal alienated many members of the PSD and the armed forces. For instance, on Inauguration Day the departing president, Gen. João Baptista Figueiredo, refused to participate in Sarney's swearing-in ceremony.

A novelist and poet, José Sarney married Marly Macicira in 1952. The couple have three children.

GEORGE W. GRAYSON

SEAVER, George Thomas

One of the most articulate, intelligent players in major league baseball, pitcher Tom Seaver is also an exceptional athlete whose skills remain sharp at an age when lesser men have been forced into retirement. Pitching for the Chicago White Sox in 1985, at age 40, he compiled a respectable 16–11 record and 3.17 earned run average (ERA). The highlight of the season came on August 4, when he became only the 17th pitcher to earn 300 career victories. Number 300 was a six-hit, 4–1 triumph over the New York Yankees at Yankee Stadium. Many of the 54,032 fans that afternoon proved fiercely partisan in support of "Tom Terrific," who had spent much of his career in New York with the Mets.

For the 6'1", 220-lb (1.85-m, 100-kg) California native, a certain Hall-of-Famer, win 300 was another notable milestone in a remarkable career. The intensely competitive right-hander captured the National League Rookie of the Year Award in 1967 with the Mets. He has won the Cy Young Award as the league's best pitcher three times (1969, 1973, 1975) and has led his league in strikeouts five times and in ERA and victories three times each. He holds or shares nearly a dozen records, including most years with at least 200 strikeouts (10), most strikeouts in a game (tie, 19), and most consecutive strikeouts in a game (10). By the end of the 1985 season, his 19th, Seaver's career record was 304–192, with a 2.81 ERA. His 3,537 strikeouts ranked him third on the all-time list.

Background. George Thomas Seaver was born in Fresno, CA, on Nov. 17, 1944. His father was a successful businessman and once a member of the U.S. Walker Cup golf team. Tom was an all-city star in both baseball and basketball at Fresno High School, from which he was graduated in 1962. After a short tour of duty with the active reserve of the U.S. Marines, Seaver attended Fresno City College and then the University of Southern California (USC). He was graduated from USC with a bachelor's degree in 1968, after he had begun his baseball career.

Signed by the Mets on April 3, 1966, Seaver won his first major league game by defeating the Chicago Cubs, 6–1, on April 20, 1967. He had perhaps his greatest year in 1969, when he went 25–7 and led the "Miracle Mets" to the world championship. Two of Seaver's greatest

games were his 19-strikeout performance against San Diego on April 22, 1970, and a no-hitter for the Cincinnati Reds against St. Louis on June 16, 1978.

Seaver became a Red on June 15, 1977, when the Mets traded him rather than meet his salary demands. New York reacquired him on Dec. 16, 1982, but lost him after the 1983 season, when the White Sox selected him in the free-agent compensation pool.

The youthful-looking pitcher is married to the former Nancy Lynn McIntyre. The Seavers have two daughters and make their home in Greenwich, CT. Tom enjoys playing bridge, solving crossword puzzles, traveling, and a variety of cultural pursuits.

DAN SCHLOSSBERG

SIMON, Marvin Neil

Neil Simon, often thought of as America's most prolific playwright, remained a formidable force on the entertainment scene in 1985. His plays *Biloxi Blues* (1985), *Brighton Beach Memoirs* (1983), and a revival of *The Odd Couple* (1965) were running concurrently on Broadway, and the newly released film *The Slugger's Wife* was appearing in many theaters. Simon's creative pace was not of recent origin. For more than two decades, he has produced numerous Broadway hits and, in fact, once had four Broadway plays running at the same time.

With the autobiographical *Biloxi Blues,* Simon broke new artistic ground, producing what some critics consider his best work. In the words of *New York Times* theater critic Frank Rich, Simon "lets his plot [in *Biloxi Blues*] develop from character rather than the other way around." Simon indicates that he has become more cinematic in his approach, calling for, in his recent plays, multiple sets in which to place the action rather than the single setting used in many earlier plays.

Background. Marvin Neil Simon was born in New York City on July 4, 1927. After serving in the U.S. Army Air Force (1945–46) and attending New York University (1946), he began writing theatrical sketches (along with his brother Danny) and writing for television. He wrote for two Phil Silvers series (NBC, 1948; CBS, 1958–59), the *Tallulah Bankhead Show* (NBC, 1951), the *Sid Caesar Show* (NBC, 1956–57), and the *Garry Moore Show* (CBS, 1959–60).

His first Broadway show was *Come Blow Your Horn* (1961), cowritten with his brother. This success was followed by a string of memorable plays, including *Barefoot in the Park* (1963), *The Star Spangled Girl* (1966), *Plaza Suite* (1968), *The Last of the Red Hot Lovers* (1969), *The Gingerbread Lady* (1970), *The Prisoner of Second Avenue* (1971), *The Sunshine Boys* (1972), *California Suite* (1976), *Chapter Two* (1977), *They're Playing Our Song* (1979), *I Ought To Be in Pictures* (1982), and his most recent works. He also wrote the book for the musicals *Little Me* (1962), *Sweet Charity* (1966), and *Promises, Promises* (1968).

Simon adapted many of his plays for the screen, as well. His original screenplays include *The Out-of-Towners* (1970), *The Heartbreak Kid* (1972), *Murder by Death* (1976), *The Goodbye Girl* (1977), *The Cheap Detective* (1978), and *Max Dugan Returns* (1983).

Many accolades have come Simon's way. He has won the theater's Tony award three times (1965, 1975, 1985) and has been nominated for Emmy awards and for the Oscar. Though he is highly successful, he admits to being driven insane by people only concerned with success, especially in the form of a play's critical notices.

Simon was widowed in 1973 after a 20-year marriage. That same year he married actress Marsha Mason; they later were divorced. He has two daughters by his first marriage.

SLANEY, Mary Decker

It was only another of many, many triumphs in the running career of 27-year-old Mary Decker Slaney, but it left her with a special sense of satisfaction and relief. On July 20, 1985, in a highly publicized 3,000-m race at the Crystal Palace in London, she defeated Zola Budd in a rematch of their controversial race in the 1984 Summer Olympics at Los Angeles. It was the first matchup between the two rivals since L.A., where Budd collided with Slaney and forced her to drop out of her first Olympic appearance and to miss her chance for a gold medal. Now in London, Slaney reeled off the second-best time at that distance in her career—8 minutes, 32.91 seconds —and won easily.

Later in the season, on September 7 in Rome, Slaney lowered her time in the 3,000 to an American record of

Neil Simon

Mary Decker Slaney

Photos, AP/Wide World

8:25.83. The crowning achievement of her remarkable outdoor campaign, however, came on August 21 in Zurich, where she set a new world record for the mile, with a time of 4:16.71. On her way to 14 straight victories during the season, she also set new American records in the 800 m (1:56.90), the 1,000 m (2:34.80), and the 5,000 m (15:06.53). These were added to three other American records she already held: in the 1,500 m (3:57.12), the 2,000 m (5:32.70), and the 10,000 m (31:35.20).

Background. Mary Teresa Decker was born on Aug. 4, 1958, in Bunnvale, NJ. She was the second of four children of John Decker, a tool-and-die maker and part-time pilot, and his wife, Jacqueline. In the late 1960s the family moved to California, settling in Garden Grove, a suburb of Los Angeles. At the age of 11, Decker, on a whim, entered a cross-country race sponsored by the local parks department for grade-school students. She won by "a long ways" and was smitten by the sport. With professional training, she gradually emerged as a national and then world track-and-field star.

After graduating from Orange High School in 1976, Decker enrolled at the University of Colorado on a track scholarship. She dropped out in 1978, however, to devote herself full-time to running. Slaney's career has been plagued by numerous injuries, and she has often competed in pain. Several times she was forced to undergo corrective surgery, but her dramatic comebacks always brought her to new heights. The 1982 season was an especially dazzling one for the tenacious, long-striding middle-distance star, as she set three world records, four American records, and four indoor records.

A lithe woman with blue eyes and brown hair, Slaney is 5'6" (1.68 m) tall and usually competes at 105 lbs (48 kg). Decker's first marriage was to marathon runner Rob Tabb in 1981; it ended in divorce in 1983. On Jan. 1, 1985, she married Richard Slaney, a British discus thrower who carried her from the stadium when she fell at the Los Angeles Olympics. Slaney designs and makes her own clothes, and her hobbies include oil painting, skiing, and bowling.

GEORGE DE GREGORIO

Bruce Springsteen

AP/Wide World

SPRINGSTEEN, Bruce

A decade after the release of *Born to Run,* the 1975 LP that catapulted him into rock 'n' roll superstardom, Bruce Springsteen was still rising to new heights of popularity and acclaim. His seventh album, *Born in the U.S.A.,* released in summer 1984, proved to be his most popular. More than a year after it hit the racks, *Born in the U.S.A.* was still on the Top 10 charts; at some 13 million copies worldwide, it was also the biggest seller in the history of Columbia Records—the label on which "The Boss" began recording in 1973. Touching on vintage Springsteen themes of backstreet alienation, broken dreams, lost jobs, lost love, shattered lives—and faith in hard times—*Born in the U.S.A.* elevated the elfin New Jersey native to the status of hero, symbol, and musical spokesman of the American working class.

As record stores were being cleaned out of his album, Springsteen was also drawing millions of fans on his Born in the U.S.A. Concert Tour. Launched in summer 1984, the concert series sold out stadiums across the United States and Europe into the fall of 1985. From Los Angeles to New York and Paris to Tokyo, ticket sales were faster and more frenzied than rock promoters could remember.

And those were not the only excitements for Springsteen in 1985. In February he won the Grammy award as best male rock vocalist for "Dancing in the Dark" (a song on *Born in the U.S.A.*). And in May he was married to model Julianne Phillips.

Background. Of Dutch and Italian descent, Springsteen was born on Sept. 23, 1949, in the working-class town of Freehold, NJ. Bruce attended a local parochial school, but he was an indifferent student and hard to discipline. At age 13, after seeing an Elvis Presley special on television, young Springsteen scraped together $18 and bought a second-hand guitar from a pawn shop. "From the beginning," he later said, "my guitar was something I could go to."

In addition to the guitar, Springsteen taught himself to play the harmonica and piano. While in high school he hooked up with local pickup bands, playing at neighborhood bars and music clubs. After a brief stint in community college, Bruce devoted himself full-time to playing and writing music. His big break came in 1972, when a friend introduced him to Mike Appel, a producer and manager at Columbia Records. Springsteen's first LP was *Greetings from Asbury Park* in 1973, followed by *The Wild, the Innocent and the E Street Shuffle* in 1974. With their musical energy and lyrical virtuosity, both albums won the attention of critics and began building Springsteen a devoted following. Neither one, however, had near the commercial success of *Born to Run,* which traced a desperate day in the life of a New Jersey–shore teenager. Subsequent Springsteen albums included *Darkness on the Edge of Town* (1978), *The River* (1980), and *Nebraska* (1982).

WALTERS, Vernon Anthony

As the new U.S. ambassador to the United Nations, Lt. Gen. Vernon A. ("Dick") Walters viewed his top priority as ending the diplomatic "lynching of the United States by resolution." He took over the UN job—with its Cabinet rank—on May 22, 1985, succeeding Jeane J. Kirkpatrick. Walters said he saw the post, which he took on at the age of 68, as the natural culmination of his long career in world affairs.

As an indication of his tactics, he promptly embarked on a trip to Europe to discuss with officials there a joint Western approach to issues on the UN agenda. "My strong suit is dealing with people," he said. "Convincing them to do things that the United States wants them to do, and dissuading them from things the United States does not want them to do."

In this effort, Walters had two advantages—a wide acquaintance with national leaders from all parts of the

Vernon Walters

Photos, AP/Wide World

Elie Wiesel

world and a command of seven foreign languages (French, Spanish, Italian, German, Portuguese, Dutch, and Russian). He had shown his grasp of linguistic nuance during a six-hour meeting with Fidel Castro in 1982. The Cuban president noted that they had both been educated by Jesuits, and Walters replied in Spanish with a deft pun: "Yes, but I remain *fidel* ('faithful')."

Background. Vernon Anthony Walters was born in New York City on Jan. 3, 1917, but spent most of his formative years in Britain and France. He enlisted as a U.S. Army private in 1941 and served during most of World War II as an aide to Gen. Mark Clark in Italy. He began his diplomatic career in 1945 as a military attaché in Brazil and later served as an aide and interpreter for W. Averell Harriman and Presidents Truman, Eisenhower, and Nixon. His mouth was cut by glass as he rode through a rock-throwing mob with Vice-President Nixon in Caracas, Venezuela, in 1958. Later, as a military attaché in Paris, Walters helped arrange the secret meetings at which Henry Kissinger initiated peace talks on Vietnam and the establishment of relations with China.

He served as deputy director of the Central Intelligence Agency (1972–76) and as a business consultant and lecturer (1977–81). Returning to government service in 1981, the lifelong bachelor became ambassador at large, logging an average of 10,000 mi (16 000 km) per week in visits to some 100 countries as President Reagan's personal troubleshooter.

Walters' memoirs, *Silent Missions,* were published in 1978.

MICHAEL J. BERLIN

WIESEL, Elie

A survivor of the Nazi concentration camps of Auschwitz and Buchenwald, the Romanian-born author and educator Elie Wiesel has devoted his life's work to bearing witness to the horrors of the Holocaust. In more than 20 books, as well as numerous articles, lectures, plays, and other writings, each relating to that pivotal experience, he has endeavored "to unite the language of humanity with the silence of the dead." In April 1985, Wiesel, the chairman of the U.S. President's Commission on the Holocaust, was awarded a Congressional Gold Medal of Achievement, the nation's highest civilian

honor, in a ceremony at the White House. Inscribed in the medal were the words "Author, Teacher, Witness"; in making the presentation, President Ronald Reagan called Wiesel "testimony that the human spirit endures and prevails." The slight, 56-year-old writer used the occasion to implore President Reagan not to go through with his planned visit to the German military cemetery at Bitburg, which contains the graves of 49 Nazi SS troops.

Background. The son of pious Hasidic parents, Shlomo and Sarah, Eliezer Wiesel was born on Sept. 30, 1928, in the town of Sighet, Transylvania. Largely at his mother's insistence, Elie studied the Jewish scriptures and the teachings of the Hasidic masters, as well as the secular classics. In spring 1944, Wiesel and his family were rounded up and sent to the Auschwitz concentration camp in Poland, where his parents and a sister were killed. The experience was to shape his life and career. "Never shall I forget that night, the first night in camp, which has turned my life into one long night," he tells in his first book, *Night* (1960). In 1945 he was sent to the Buchenwald concentration camp in Germany as a slave laborer.

After liberation in 1945, Wiesel lived in Paris, first as a student of philosophy at the Sorbonne and then as a journalist for Israeli, French, and U.S. newspapers. In 1956 he moved to the United States, obtaining his citizenship seven years later. In 1972 he was appointed Distinguished Professor of Judaic Studies at the City College of the City of New York, and since 1976 he has held the Andrew W. Mellon Chair in the Humanities at Boston College. In addition to *Night,* his best-known works included *Dawn* (1961), *The Jews of Silence* (1966), *A Beggar in Jerusalem* (1970), *The Oath* (1973), *A Jew Today* (1978), and *The Testament* (1980). His latest book, *The Fifth Son* (1984), won France's Grand Prize for Literature, one of Wiesel's numerous international distinctions. In the United States he has received more than 20 honorary degrees. In February 1985, some 70 members of the West German parliament proposed Elie Wiesel as a candidate for the 1985 Nobel Peace Prize. His work, they said, "has encouraged people around the world to reach a higher grade of moral sensitivity."

Wiesel lives in New York City with his wife, Marion, who translates most of his writings from French into English, and their son, Shlomo Elisha.

LIVIA E. BITTON-JACKSON

In La Paz in July, Indian women carry posters supporting the presidential candidacy of Victor Paz Estenssoro.

BOLIVIA

During 1985, Bolivia verged on economic, social, and political chaos. The gravity of the economic situation was evident early in the year, when it was disclosed that inflation in 1984 had been 2,177%, that the government deficit had been equivalent to 60% of the gross domestic product (GDP), that export earnings were only $700 million ($1 billion in 1980), and that the foreign debt reached $4.1 billion.

By August 1985 the inflation rate was running more than 14,000%, according to the government, the highest in the world. In June, overdue payments on the debt to international banks reached $927.8 million.

Organized labor reacted strongly against the economic situation, with two major general strikes and many other walkouts. In March the Central Obrera Boliviana (COB) went on strike, demanding a 400–500% wage increase and other concessions. After almost three weeks and mediation by the Catholic Church, President Hernán Siles Zuazo agreed to a 400% increase for some workers but only 15–60% for most.

In May the Siles government devalued the peso by 40% and decreed a 75% increase in bread prices. It also demanded that employers raise wages by 500% to offset the year's price increases. The month of June was highlighted by general strikes in the departments of Santa Cruz and Chuquisaca.

Bolivians voted in general elections on July 15. Former President Hugo Banzer Suárez won the popular vote, but no candidate gained a 50% majority. The runner-up was former President Victor Paz Estenssoro, whose National Revolutionary Movement earned a plurality in Congress. Because of the lack of a popular majority, Congress was left to decide the presidential result, and on August 5 it named Paz Estenssoro. When Banzer threatened to resist the decision by force, the presidents of Argentina, Uruguay, and Colombia went to La Paz and dissuaded him from doing so.

On August 29 the new president announced a "shock treatment" for the economy. The peso was floated, effectively bringing about a devaluation of 95%; trade restrictions were lifted; wages and salaries were frozen; state-subsidized stores were abolished; state tin mining and oil drilling firms were decentralized; the Bolivian Development Corporation was abolished; and prices for several basic commodities were increased substantially.

The austerity program provoked another general strike by the COB, which lasted more than three weeks. The government arrested a number of union leaders, and the church again intervened as mediator.

Much of Bolivia's economy and society continued to be dominated by the cocaine trade. In February the government's antinarcotics chief estimated that coca production would increase 13% during the year. In August the U.S. Congress passed a foreign aid bill that conditioned aid to Bolivia on recognizable success in combating the cocaine problem.

ROBERT J. ALEXANDER, *Rutgers University*

BOLIVIA • Information Highlights

Official Name: Republic of Bolivia.
Location: West-central South America.
Area: 424,163 sq mi (1 098 581 km²).
Population (mid-1985 est.): 6,200,000.
Chief Cities (1982 est.): Sucre, the legal capital, 79,941; La Paz, the actual capital, 881,404; Santa Cruz de la Sierra, 376,912; Cochabamba, 281,962.
Government: *Head of state and government,* Victor Paz Estenssoro, president (took office Aug. 6, 1985). *Legislature*—Congress: Senate and Chamber of Deputies.
Monetary Unit: Peso (1,500,000 pesos equal U.S.$1, September 1985).
Gross National Product (1983 U.S.$): $4,900,-000,000.
Economic Index (June 1985): *Consumer Prices* (La Paz, 1970 = 100), all items, 4,838,267; food, 5,780,387.
Foreign Trade (1984 U.S.$): *Imports,* $631,000,000; *exports,* $773,000,000.

BRAZIL

The death of President-elect Tancredo de Almeida Neves elevated José Sarney to the presidency at a time when Brazil, the Third World's most debt-ridden nation, faced herculean economic problems.

Government and Politics. On January 15, Brazil's electoral college by a vote of 480 to 180 selected Neves to become the country's first civilian president in 21 years. The 74-year-old former governor of Minas Gerais state was standard-bearer of the Brazilian Democratic Movement Party (PMDB) that had long urged a return to democracy. Key officers of the armed forces backed his opponent, Paulo Salim Maluf, the conservative head of the ruling, pro-military Democratic Social Party (PDS). Still, Neves had gained the trust of influential military men by pledging in late 1984 that his administration, in contrast to that of President Raul Alfonsín in neighboring Argentina, would forswear reprisals against officers for abuses of human rights committed during more than two decades of military control.

In a nationwide address following his election, Neves averred that his would be the "last indirect election"—a reference to the PMDB's commitment to choosing future chief executives by popular vote. He also praised President João Baptista Figueiredo and the army for not aborting the transition to civil rule and promised "real, effective, daring, and irreversible changes," including the drafting of a new constitution. With respect to the economy, Neves cited as his highest priority reducing inflation that had reached 223% in 1984. Additionally, he favored job creation, a more equitable distribution of wealth, the sale of smaller state companies to private businessmen, greater assistance to the impoverished northeast, and a larger role for unions and workers. Appealing personal qualities, combined with a popular program, earned Neves a wide spectrum of political support from Communists on the left to financiers on the right.

Unknown to all but his closest associates, Neves suffered from severe intestinal disorders —a fact that he hoped to keep secret until his inauguration lest the transition to democracy be threatened. Yet, so acute was his illness that he required surgery on the eve of his scheduled mid-March inauguration. Critics contend that this operation for diverticulitis was performed precipitately and without adequate preparation. In any case, Neves' condition deteriorated, and—despite a half-dozen subsequent operations involving Brazilian and U.S. physicians—he died on April 21.

This tragedy catapulted to the presidency José Sarney (see BIOGRAPHY), a man whose life epitomized the turbulent nature of Brazilian politics. Born into a humble family in 1930, Sarney entered politics soon after earning a law

AP/Wide World

Brazilians generally were saddened by the illness and death of their respected president-elect, Tancredo Neves.

degree. He won election first as a federal deputy (1956) and then as governor of his home state of Maranhão (1965). When the military barred his serving a second gubernatorial term, he was twice elected as a PDS federal senator (1970, 1978). Sarney left the Democratic Social Party—which he had headed until 1984—to join the Liberal Front Party that endorsed Neves. In return, Sarney was selected as the old politician's running mate under the banner of the Democratic Alliance Coalition. This perceived act of apostasy aroused the wrath of many of Sarney's former PDS colleagues, as well as members of the armed forces. Former

President Figueiredo, for example, refused to take part in the new president's swearing-in ceremony.

Aware of his precarious position, Sarney struck a conciliatory chord in his first speech to the nation. Specifically, he committed himself to implementing the program of Neves, whose life he extolled as "an exercise in dialogue and conciliation." Sarney added, "I will not permit the flame of hope awakened in Brazil to be extinguished."

To brighten that flame, Sarney backed legislation, passed by Congress on May 8, to restore direct presidential elections, universal suffrage, and elections for the mayors of state capitals. The legislation also assured Brasília representation in Congress for the first time. It removed, moreover, all restrictions on political parties—a change that allowed the Communists, banned since 1947, to register. The omnibus bill provided for the election in November 1986 of a Constituent Assembly that would both prepare a new constitution and fix the length of Sarney's term. Approval of the measure frustrated a move by left-wing legislators to commence direct elections as early as late 1985.

Electoral reform and personal popularity aside, Sarney has not been able to govern forcefully. Opposition to continued military governance and respect for Neves were the most important adhesives holding together the Democratic Alliance. Now that the generals have relinquished power and Neves is dead, foes of the dictatorship have begun fighting among themselves. Particularly bitter were intramural battles preceding the November 15 municipal elections that found cabinet members—supposedly allied in backing Sarney's programs—working against each other on the hustings. Also disquieting for the country's nascent democracy was the behavior of political parties. Bitter factionalism afflicted the five parties that existed when Figueiredo left office,

while 25 new parties sprang up with their objective being more to advance the careers of ambitious politicians than to promote ideas or programs. Skeptics such as playwright Dias Gomes have concluded that "the new system is the old system with a face-lift."

Economics. Brazil's generals dramatically modernized and expanded the nation's economy, now the world's tenth largest. The officers constructed factories, highways, railroads, hydroelectric facilities, and ports in what has been termed Brazil's "great leap forward." However, foreign loans, contracted when interest rates were low, financed much of this development. The result was that while the country now boasts infrastructure crucial to long-term economic progress to show for the military's prolific spending, it also staggers under a $103 billion foreign debt. Unlike many debtor states, Brazil exports enough goods and services to finance its external obligations. Indeed, an $11 billion trade surplus was estimated for 1985. But the government owes 70% of the external debt, while public firms earn only 20% to 25% of the nation's hard currency. Consequently, the government has had to buy dollars from the private sector to pay its import bill. Brasília has accomplished these purchases, made with cruzieros, by incurring ever larger budget deficits—a practice that assures a three-digit inflation rate and investor squeamishness about the future.

As an antidote to Brazil's ills, the International Monetary Fund (IMF) has urged reduced federal spending in exchange for new credits. Early in 1985, the IMF suspended disbursements on the remainder of a $4.2 billion loan package when the Brazilians failed to meet targets for braking inflation and controlling the money supply.

To win the favor of the IMF and other creditors, Sarney announced on July 4 a $6.5 billion austerity plan whereby he would halt spending on 18 key projects—in energy, mining, and steel—until these investments could be reviewed. Meanwhile, he would increase tax revenues by $2.9 billion through speedier collection procedures, while trimming official spending by $3.6 billion.

This action, which led to a resumption of negotiations with the IMF, appeared as a victory for Finance Minister Francisco Dornelles. Dornelles, who is Neves' nephew, is a firm proponent of fiscal austerity and strict monetary controls to reduce interest charges that had risen to 24% above the inflation rate of 220% for 1985. Yet, Dornelles' triumph was short-lived, for he resigned in August in a policy dispute with Planning Minister João Sayad and presidential adviser Paulo Luis Rosenberg. Both of these officials believe that Brazil can maintain a healthy growth rate of 5% or more and service its foreign debt without undertaking draconian belt-tightening steps that would

---

BRAZIL • Information Highlights

Official Name: Federative Republic of Brazil.
Location: Eastern South America.
Area: 3,286,525 sq mi (8 512 100 km^2).
Population (mid-1985 est.): 138,400,000.
Chief Cities (1980 census): Brasília, the capital, 1,176,908; São Paulo, 7,032,547; Rio de Janeiro, 5,090,700; Salvador, 1,491,642.
Government: *Head of state and government,* José Sarney, president (took office April 21, 1985). *Legislature*—National Congress: Senate and Chamber of Deputies.
Monetary Unit: Cruzeiro (8,870 cruzeiros equal U.S. $1, Nov. 18, 1985).
Gross National Product (1983 U.S.$): $211,000,-000,000.
Economic Indexes (1984): *Consumer Prices* (São Paulo 1972 = 100), all items, 31,450; food, 40,623. *Industrial Production* (September 1984, 1980 = 100), 85.
Foreign Trade (1984 U.S.$): *Imports,* $15,210,-000,000; *exports,* $27,005,000,000.

sharpen social unrest. This unrest has been evident in strikes launched by metalworkers, teachers, doctors, nurses, postal carriers, and transportation employees. Although promising to combat inflation, Dilson Domingos Funaro, Dornelles' successor, appeared to share the economic views of Sayad and Rosenberg.

In a September speech at the United Nations, Sarney set the confrontational tone of Latin American leaders concerning international debt. He warned that "exorbitant" repayment rates menaced his country's newly restored democracy. Brazil, he stated, would not "pay its foreign debt with recession, nor with unemployment, nor with hunger."

GEORGE W. GRAYSON
College of William & Mary

BRITISH COLUMBIA

The economy of British Columbia continued to experience slow growth during 1985. In June the unemployment rate was 14.8%, and one in seven British Columbians was dependent on welfare payments. Community food banks continued to provide supplementary food supplies to the jobless. The attraction of better job opportunities elsewhere resulted in a net outflow of population to other provinces. Despite the stimulus of public investment in Expo 86, the Coquihalla highway, the Vancouver-Lower Mainland's Advanced Light Rapid Transit System, and the Annacis bridge, construction employment remained more than 25% below 1982 levels. Final preparations for the C$1.5 billion Expo 86 were on schedule. The possibility of a $300–400 million deficit, however, continued to make this a controversial project.

Public Policy. The main theme of the provincial government's legislative program and budget for 1985 was "Partnership for Economic Renewal." Expenditure for 1985–86 was estimated at $9,056,000,000, up 3.5% from the previous year, and revenue at $8,166,000,000. The renewal program emphasized increased economic cooperation between the provincial and municipal governments and provided for special tax incentives, electricity rate discounts, and the establishment of Special Enterprise Zones. Such budgetary measures as the five-year freeze on water rental rates, small business employment tax credits, elimination or reduction of certain property taxes on machinery and equipment, and a tax credit venture capital assistance program were designed to help job creation. The total cost of the 1985 tax changes over the next three years was estimated at $955 million. A Critical Industries Commissioner was appointed to help secure the reopening or continuation of business enterprises in designated industries. A $300 million, five-year reforestation program under the federal-provincial Economic and Regional Development Agreement also was announced.

Access to the U.S. market for British Columbia's lumber products was threatened by protectionist measures before the U.S. Congress, and Premier William R. Bennett called for freer trade arrangements with the United States. The official dedication of the $2 billion Revelstoke Dam in August 1985 drew further attention to the province's energy surplus and the effort to obtain a hydroelectric power export contract in the California market.

Government. The members of the Legislative Assembly voted themselves higher pension benefits and increases in their expense allowances. The latter were later rolled back after their referral to the Compensation Stabilization Commissioner. The standing orders of the Legislative Assembly also received a major overhaul for the first time in more than 50 years.

The government's restraint policies created further strains within the education system. The Vancouver and Cowichan school boards persisted in their refusal to comply with the Ministry of Education's budget directives and were replaced by government-appointed one-man trustees. Concern over provincial university funding led to the resignation of the president of the University of British Columbia. Equally controversial were the new powers given to the Medical Services Commission over doctors' billing numbers. These enable the government to control the numbers and distribution of doctors within the province.

For most British Columbians, 1985 was the year of the hot dry summer. These conditions resulted in a severe outbreak of forest fires that endangered several communities and therefore heightened public awareness of the hazard. Some 3,600 forest fires consumed 590,000 acres (240 000 ha) of forest land and pushed fire-fighting expenditures to a record $120 million.

NORMAN J. RUFF, *University of Victoria*

BRITISH COLUMBIA · Information Highlights

Area: 366,255 sq mi (948 600 km²).
Population (July 1985 est.): 2,894,200.
Chief Cities (1981 census): Victoria, the capital, 64,379; Vancouver, 414,281; Prince George, 67,559; Kamloops, 64,048; Kelowna, 59,196.
Government (1985): *Chief Officers*—lt. gov., Robert G. Rogers; premier, William R. Bennett (Social Credit Party). *Legislature*—Legislative Assembly, 57 members.
Provincial Finances (1986 fiscal year budget): *Revenues*, $8,166,000,000; *expenditures*, $9,056,-000,000.
Personal Income (average weekly earnings, July 1985): $439.33.
Labor Force (September 1985, seasonally adjusted): *Employed workers*, 15 years of age and over, 1,235,000; *Unemployed*, 185,000 (13.0%).
Education (1985–86): *Enrollment*—elementary and secondary schools, 524,210 pupils; postsecondary (full-time, 1985–86)—universities, 35,720; community colleges, 21,750.
(All monetary figures are in Canadian dollars.)

Several thousand Turks demonstrated in Paris in late March to protest discrimination against Muslim Turks living in Bulgaria.

© Mohamed Lounes, Gamma-Liaison

BULGARIA

In 1985, Bulgaria was confronted with a wave of domestic violence and continuing criticism and censure from abroad.

Terrorism. In May the government announced that more than 30 people had died in a series of terrorist bombings that had begun about August 1984, apparently in connection with the 40th anniversary of the Communist takeover in Bulgaria. The explosions occurred in a wide variety of places (including Plovdiv, Varna, Burgas, Ruse, Shumen, and Targovishte), especially in train stations and airports, and were attributed primarily to the Bulgarian Socialist Party in Exile or rebellious members of the ethnic Turkish minority. On May 19 the Bulgarian National Assembly approved stiffer penalties (up to capital punishment) for the illegal possession and use of firearms and explosives and enlarged the powers of the police and border guards to search suspected terrorists.

Bulgaria's Ethnic Minorities. But even greater violence resulted from the government's intensified campaign, begun in 1983, to require all ethnic Turks in Bulgaria to take Slavic names, in an attempt to create "a single nationality state." The Turkish minority, estimated at 500,000 to 1 million, offered bloody resistance to troops and police sent in to enforce the policy, especially in ethnic Turkish strongholds in southern Bulgaria and the Dobrudja region. In August the government of Turkey asserted that at least 1,000 ethnic Turks had been killed. Several thousand more were imprisoned, Istanbul claimed, primarily in Belene, a camp on a Bulgarian island in the Danube. In response to the recall of the Turkish ambassador to Bulgaria and formal Turkish protests to the Bulgarian ambassador in Turkey in February-March, Bulgaria insisted that the assimilation of the ethnic Turks was "spontaneous and voluntary." It rejected a proposal to meet with Turkey to discuss the possible mass emigration of its ethnic Turks to Turkey. On March 21, some 40,000 Turks demonstrated in Istanbul, calling for censure and an economic boycott by Muslim countries against Bulgaria.

Bulgaria also exchanged recriminations with Yugoslavia over the status of one another's Macedonian minority—the Socialist Republic of Macedonia in Yugoslavia and the ethnic Macedonians in Bulgaria.

Foreign Relations. In February the United States and Bulgaria clashed over drug smuggling. U.S. Ambassador Melvyn Levitsky charged that Bulgaria was refusing to take action against known narcotics dealers and that KINTEX, the Bulgarian government-operated arms concern, was dealing in drugs. Bulgaria claimed that the United States had arbitrarily halted talks aimed at coordinating control of narcotics and drug traffic. But on May 17 the Bulgarian National Assembly approved heavier penalties for illegal dealings in drugs and arms.

Bulgaria also continued to draw bad publicity over its alleged role in the attempt to assassinate Pope John Paul II in 1981. The trial of five Turks and three Bulgarians accused of participating in the conspiracy began in Rome on May 27. Bulgaria continued to deny any role.

JOSEPH F. ZACEK
State University of New York at Albany

BULGARIA • Information Highlights

Official Name: People's Republic of Bulgaria.
Location: Southeastern Europe.
Area: 42,823 sq mi (110 912 km²).
Population (mid-1985 est.): 8,900,000.
Chief Cities (Dec. 31, 1982): Sofia, the capital, 1,082,315; Plovdiv, 367,195; Varna, 295,038.
Government: *Head of state,* Todor Zhivkov, chairman of the State Council and general secretary of the Communist Party (took office July 1971). *Head of government,* Georgi (Grisha) Filipov, chairman of the Council of Ministers (took office June 1981).
Monetary Unit: Lev (1.046 leva equal U.S.$1, July 1985).
Gross National Product (1983, 1981 U.S.$): $35,400,000,000.
Economic Index: *Industrial Production* (1983, 1980 = 100), 115.
Foreign Trade (1984 U.S.$): *Imports,* $12,668,000,000; *exports,* $12,829,000,000.

BURMA

President San Yu, the 67-year-old soldier who succeeded General Ne Win, 74, as head of state in 1981, consolidated his position as political heir apparent.

Politics. Reelected to Parliament in October together with other members of Burma's single party, the Burma Socialist Program Party (BSPP), San Yu had assumed the new post of BSPP vice chairman two months earlier. The return to the 489-seat assembly of other leaders of the government—Premier Maung Maung Kha, deputy premiers Tun Tin and Kyaw Htin, and Council of State Secretary Aye Ko—indicated that the aging and ailing Ne Win had settled on the succession team that would rule the country when he retired from politics. Kyaw Htin also served as defense minister and armed forces chief of staff.

Ne Win, however, was not yet ready to step down from power and was elected to an additional four-year term as party chairman by the 1,186 delegates to the fifth congress of the BSPP, which claimed a membership of 2.3 million.

A longtime party stalwart as well as professional soldier, San Yu had been secretary of the governing BSPP between 1964 and 1981 and secretary of the Council of State (cabinet) from 1974 to 1981. He also was named to the party executive committee at the August BSPP congress.

Insurgencies. The ethnic minority Karens and the Communists, the two most troublesome of Burma's several insurgent groups, pursued different strategies in 1985. The 4,000 Karen rebels, badly hurt by intensified operations against them by the army, blew up a train on the Rangoon-Mandalay line in July, killing 67 persons. The 12,000-man Communists, weakened by drastically reduced (if not halted) Chinese aid, were largely inactive and were forced to rely increasingly on opium production and sales (and possibly new Soviet arms help through neighboring Laos).

In the 12 months prior to March 1985, 1,870 insurgents and 566 soldiers were killed.

Economy. The drop in world market prices for Burmese exports, particularly rice, resulted in a fall in foreign-exchange reserves, which dipped to less than U.S. $50 million. The country's foreign debt, meanwhile, rose more than $200 million during the year to $3 billion. The debt-service ratio was slightly less than 45%. Rice declined 40% in price since 1981. Exports of the grain represented 53% of Burma's outgoing trade, with teak next at 27%.

Stepped-up operations against the Karens in eastern Burma increased the black market price, but did not stop the flow, of smuggled goods from Thailand.

Foreign Relations. Improved Burmese-Chinese relations were reflected in President

---

BURMA • Information Highlights
Official Name: Socialist Republic of the Union of Burma.
Location: Southeast Asia.
Area: 261,217 sq mi (676 552 km²).
Population (mid-1985 est.): 36,900,000.
Chief City: Rangoon, the capital.
Government: *Head of state,* U San Yu, president (took office Nov. 1981). *Head of government,* U. Maung Maung Kha, prime minister (took office March 1977). *Legislature* (unicameral)—People's Assembly.
Monetary Unit: Kyat (8.326 kyats equal U.S.$1, July 1985).
Gross Domestic Product (1982–83 est. U.S.$): $5,900,000,000.
Economic Index (Rangoon, July 1984): *Consumer Prices* (1970 = 100), all items, 322.9; food, 328.3.
Foreign Trade (1984 U.S.$): *Imports,* $239,000,000; *exports,* $310,000,000.

San Yu's 1984 visit to Beijing (Peking), Rangoon's reciprocal hosting of China's President Li Xiannian in March, and BSPP Chairman Ne Win's trip to the Chinese capital in May. The leaders discussed trade, Cambodia, and the Soviet role in the area.

The two countries also cooperated in the redemarcation of their common border.

RICHARD BUTWELL
California State University

BUSINESS AND CORPORATE AFFAIRS

"The economic blahs won't go away." This was a lead quotation in the Sept. 16, 1985, issue of *Fortune* magazine. The U.S. economy was in a state of suspense, no one quite sure whether it was going up or down. The Dow Jones Industrial average hit new highs, climbing to above 1,500, while the gross national product (GNP) was increasing at an annual rate of only about 2%, and the unemployment rate seemed to be stuck at around 7%. The economic pluses and minuses were not being shared very equally across the country. Some areas were experiencing an unemployment rate of more than 13%, while in other areas the rate was below 4%. Real trouble spots were in the steel, textile, and lumber industries. And certain other industries, even the "Silicon Valley" computer industry, were feeling some adverse economic impact.

Toward the end of 1985, many of the nation's business chiefs were extremely nervous about the economy and considered the enormous U.S. trade deficit the single biggest reason for the jitters. Ruben Mettler, chairman of TRW Inc., said, "When we compete with exports, business is weak; when we compete directly with imports, it is extremely difficult." There was an increasing call for protectionist measures by Congress, with the cry coming from many in the business community as well

as from members of labor unions that were being adversely affected by foreign goods. There was evidence of a scaling back of capital spending by many businesses.

A real economic depression was felt by many in agriculture. In spite of increases in various government programs to aid farmers, farm income continued to plummet and there were many farm foreclosures. (*See* feature article, page 36.)

Profits and Losses. Corporate profits continued on the skids through the year from the exceptionally good results for 1984. Corporate profit margins for 1984 ran at more than 5% of sales; in 1985 they dipped to only 4.4% of sales. The big question toward the end of the year was how soon sprightlier business would bring an end to the steady slide in profits.

Major losses during 1985 were incurred by such large companies as: Fluor Corporation, which, by taking a $410 million write-off in its natural resource operations, anticipated losses for 1985 to amount to $600 million; Union Carbide, which, following its 1984 disaster in Bhopal, India, was confronted with lawsuits totalling more than $100 billion, plus a third-quarter loss of $543 million; Commodore, which like many computer companies felt the impact of too many computers on the market and faced a fourth-quarter loss of $80 million; the Manville Corporation, which worked diligently to find a way to meet the burden of paying $2.5 billion in its many asbestos-related health claims; LTV Steel Company, which reported a loss of $472 million for just one quarter during 1985; and Wheeling-Pittsburgh Steel Corporation, which filed for court protection from creditors under Chapter 11 of the federal bankruptcy laws.

Savings and Loan Associations. Little in the business press received as much publicity as the failures of savings and loan associations (S&Ls) during 1985. When customers of Cincinnati's Home State Savings heard that their bank stood to lose $140 million or more as a major investor in ESM Government Securities,

which defaulted early in March, they began withdrawing money so fast that banking regulators closed the institution. That action led the governor to declare a bank "holiday," closing all 70 of the privately insured S&Ls in the state. Within a matter of days the thrifts were allowed to open for business as usual if they proved their solvency and applied for federal insurance. By the end of the year the furor had become history. (*See also* BANKING.)

Auto Industry. The 1985-model year was the most successful sales year in the history of the U.S. auto industry. Auto companies sold 15.6 million domestic and imported 1985 model cars and trucks during the year ending September 30, nearly 300,000 more than the previous record set in 1978. Some of the success was due to the discounting done at the end of the model year, but more was due to the low financing rates of 7% to 8% that also were being offered. In addition, more dealers were getting into the car-leasing business.

Other big auto news was the selection by General Motors of Spring Hill, TN, as the site for its large new Saturn auto assembly plant. This was followed by an announcement that Chrysler, in cooperation with Mitsubishi, would be building a large new auto assembly plant in Bloomington-Normal, IL. (*See also* AUTOMOBILES.)

Management Personnel. The year 1985 saw many significant changes among top corporate officials. John Sculley, who replaced founder Steven Jobs as chief executive officer of Apple Computer, announced Jobs' resignation in September. At Beatrice Companies, controversial Chairman James L. Dutt was ousted in August, but with a severance arrangement of $3.8 million; Donald P. Kelly was expected to be the company's new CEO. Sears, Roebuck named Edward A. Brennan as its new chief executive officer.

See also INDUSTRIAL PRODUCTION; RETAILING; STOCKS AND BONDS; UNITED STATES—The Economy.

STEWART M. LEE, *Geneva College*

AP/Wide World

Steven Jobs (right), *one of the founders of Apple Computer, resigned as chairman after a reported struggle with President John Sculley* (left) *and the board of directors. Sculley became CEO, and Jobs started a new venture in hardware and software for universities.*

Takeovers

Without a scorecard it was almost impossible to keep up with all the activity, to tell who was buyer and who was seller, who was sought and who was being secretly eyed by a suitor. It was a deadly game and the stakes grew increasingly large, and as they did the players grew more secretive. Big corporations sought smaller ones, and smaller ones went after the big. Raiders, backed by huge lines of credit, sought control of companies they considered underpriced. And in many instances executive employees sought to buy out shareholders of their company and make it private.

This was the market for businesses themselves, not just their products, and it was on such a monumental scale that billion-dollar deals became almost commonplace. In the first nine months of 1985 alone at least 38 such deals were completed, with the total amount approaching $100 billion. Ownership of more than 1,200 major companies had changed by September, and before the year was out the number would exceed the total of any other, both in transactions and dollar volume.

Even companies not directly involved in takeovers and buyouts were affected. Some restructured themselves to better control their shareholders. Others sold off unproductive assets, put cash to work, cut costs, and tried to raise the market value of their shares, the better to protect themselves from raiders.

Called by any of various names—mergers, acquisitions, takeovers, leveraged buyouts—the restructuring of American industry continued in 1985 at a pace perhaps swifter even than in 1984.

Major Acquisitions. Shell Oil became part of Royal Dutch-Shell for $5.7 billion. General Foods Corp. joined Philip Morris Inc. for $5.6 billion. General Motors, which a year earlier had bought Electronic Data Systems for $2.6 billion, won the bidding for Hughes Aircraft with an offer of $5.2 billion. Nabisco Brands, a food company whose labels were as old as most Americans, became part of R.J. Reynolds, once a tobacco company, for $4.9 billion. Allied Corp. took over Signal Companies for $4.5 billion to $4.9 billion, and Beatrice Companies, a food conglomerate, went late in the year to Kolberg Kravis, a private investment firm, for about $6 billion.

The pace never ceased. Before the year was out American Broadcasting Cos. was swallowed by smaller Capital Cities Communications for $3.5 billion, and R. H. Macy & Co., the giant retailing chain, was being readied for purchase by some of its executives in a leveraged buyout, the type of deal in which money is provided by loans on the company's assets. In December the General Electric Company agreed to acquire the RCA Corporation. The deal was valued at $6.28 billion.

Banks too were involved, not just in arranging financing but in buying other banks. Citicorp, the New York–based financial conglomerate, took over Great Western Financial Corp. Bank of America absorbed Oregon Bank, and Chase Manhattan merged with Continental Bank in Arizona.

But perhaps the most sought after of all were companies that owned popular retail brands, especially those with names so well and so long entrenched that marketing people considered them almost impervious to competition. Some even referred to them as franchises to make money. Better to buy the franchise, they said, than risk millions of dollars trying, and most likely failing, to come up with comparable products. In acquiring Richardson-Vicks, Procter & Gamble won title to NyQuil, the cold medicine; Vidal Sassoon shampoos; and Clearasil, a skin ointment. When Philip Morris bought General Foods it acquired Jell-O and Maxwell House coffee. When Greyhound, once a bus company, acquired Purex Cleaning Products, it won the Purex Bleach and Brillo Soap Pad labels.

The Causes. Other than the desire to obtain franchises, the reasons for mergers were as numerous as the companies involved. Some explanations, however, seemed to apply to many transactions. A less restrictive antitrust policy was often cited for some of the big deals. Observers maintained that companies saw a proverbial window of opportunity and, fearful it would be slammed, wasted little time in acquiring the company or products they wanted. The government's hands-off policy was defended and condemned. It was defended because, it was argued, it took big companies to compete with big foreign operators and thus reduce the balance of trade deficit; it was condemned for what some people thought was an oligopolistic concentration of market power.

Synergism, the notion that each of two companies would be more effective together than they were apart, was offered as an explanation for mergers, but critics wondered if this were so. Some acquired companies, the critics observed, often were sold off bit by bit, with only a nugget kept. Easy money—quickly available, although at a high cost—was credited by many with priming the deals. And without question, the fact that shares of a great many companies were priced below book

A cartoonist views the general rise in the number of corporate takeovers and, in particular, the attempt—eventually unsuccessful—by Atlanta broadcaster Ted Turner to acquire CBS.

"This Sort of Thing Could Give Capitalism a Bad Name"

© Tom Flannery, "The Baltimore Sun"

value had a great deal to do with spurring takeover activity.

The latter explanation did not suffice for many people. They maintained that in some instances pure greed was the motivator, especially for those individuals who were termed the corporate raiders, including T. Boone Pickens (*see* BIOGRAPHY), Irwin L. Jacobs, Carl Icahn, and others, who sometimes launched hostile, or at least unwelcome, assaults on corporate management, seeking to win away shareholders with bids above the existing market prices. But the raiders had vastly different views of themselves.

Pickens, for example, sent copies of his takeover philosophy to news people, contending that in seeking to oust poor corporate managements he was doing a favor for all shareholders, employees, and the corporate community in general. And Icahn, at a gathering of chief executive officers hosted by the Diebold Group and *Chief Executive* magazine, came forth with remarkable clarity if not diplomacy. "The biggest problem this country faces is mismanagement," he asserted. "You don't see the best men running companies today. It's due to what I call an anti-Darwinian theory: The survival of the unfittest. The guy who gets to the top in 80 to 85% of these big companies is a political guy. He's the guy who used to be the head of the fraternity in college. He's not a bad guy. . . . He's good to have a drink with. . . . Today he's a [chief executive officer] CEO who's there to play golf and sit on the board."

The Consequences. No matter, chief executives had a higher opinion of themselves and they fought back. While the raiders sometimes were accused of "greenmail," or attempting to be bought off at higher-than-market prices for their shares, some CEOs were accused of being all too willing to ruin the company by

borrowing heavily to buy up company stock and keep it from the hands of the intruders.

There were other consequences too, and throughout the year Congress and regulatory officials were concerned by some or all of them. It could hardly be ignored, for instance, that mere rumors of a company taking over another or of being taken over itself could serve to put a premium on stock prices that was unsupported by earnings. And most followers of the stock market could easily see that insiders, having knowledge of pending mergers, were buying and selling in advance of the public.

Less obvious, but probably more important, was still another consequence. Billions of dollars of equities were disappearing, to be replaced by debt. And in many instances, it was noted, the borrowed money came from abroad. Total debt of companies in the Standard & Poor's 400-stock index rose from 47.8% of equity, or book value, in 1979 to 58.5% of equity in 1984, and then continued to rise throughout 1985. Federal Reserve data added evidence, showing that in 1984, $77 billion in equity was lost in leveraged buyouts and other external transactions. And the pace picked up in 1985.

Still another consequence lay in the future. Much of the money used in buyouts, such as that being pursued by Macy's executives at year's end, was borrowed on assets of the company, the hope being that the company's earnings would then help retire the debt. But nobody knew the future, and therefore they had no hard evidence of their ability to repay the debt, especially if interest rates rose or the economy fell into a recession.

There were many questions being discussed about mergers, acquisitions, buyouts, and takeovers as the year ended. But perhaps none have more potentially dangerous consequences than the question of debt.

JOHN CUNNIFF

San Diego Mayor Roger Hedge-cock leaves the county proba-tion office October 9, after being convicted on 13 counts of per-jury and conspiracy to break election laws. In December he was sentenced to one year in the custody of a sheriff, three years probation, and a $1,000 fine. He also resigned from office.

AP/Wide World

CALIFORNIA

This year was one of steady if undramatic change in California. State finances were healthy, with an $867 million surplus. The National Aeronautics and Space Administration (NASA) prepared to launch space shuttles from Vandenberg Air Force Base in Santa Barbara County in 1986. Gov. George Deukmejian (R) began to plan for a reelection campaign in 1986, as did Sen. Alan Cranston (D). The governor and legislature, working together in gingerly fashion, approved new and expanded programs in welfare, prison expansion, automobile safety, child care, and toxic waste cleanup. And the state began operating its new lottery in October.

State Budget. A state budget of $35.2 billion was adopted by the legislature and the governor. More than 4,000 bills were introduced, of which 1,607 became law. Of 224 that were vetoed, none was overridden. Major legislation generally represented compromises between liberal legislative leaders and the conservative governor.

Public Welfare. Perhaps the policy that will have the greatest long-term importance was a new welfare rule requiring all able-bodied persons—except mothers with children under six years—to get work, take job training, or go to school, as a condition for receiving aid. A $20 million fund was created to provide full care for the state's 75,000 homeless mentally ill. Most of these people were in need as a result of the policy of the 1970s of releasing persons from state hospitals for local outpatient care.

Crime and Prisons. With more criminals being convicted and for longer terms, state prisons were seriously overcrowded. An emergency program for prison construction has seen projects fall behind schedule and become bogged down in labor and location disputes. By year's end, less than one half of the spaces scheduled for 20,000 additional inmates had been completed. Governor Deukmejian did sign 75 anticrime bills, including a $78.8 million

appropriation to continue the emergency program. A new prison in Los Angeles County was held up in the Assembly.

Seat Belts. California became the 17th state to require the use of seat belts in nearly all cars and trucks and is the first to require the manufacturers to equip all new cars with automatic restraints from 1989 onward.

Toxic Wastes. The legislature allocated funds from a $100 million bond issue to clean up toxic wastes that endanger water supplies or pose other public health hazards. An additional $22.5 million was voted from the general fund.

Education. In April, Joshua L. Smith was named chancellor of the state's troubled community college system. He brought with him an outstanding reputation from Manhattan Community College, New York. The California system was starting its fourth year of declining enrollments.

Rejected Reforms. A proposal backed by the governor that would have changed taxation of multinational firms in the state to their advantage was shunted aside by legislative leaders, who were angry at the governor's refusal to

---

CALIFORNIA • Information Highlights

Area: 158,706 sq mi (411 049 km²).
Population (July 1, 1984 est.): 25,622,000.
Chief Cities (July 1, 1984 est.): Sacramento, the capital, 304,131; Los Angeles, 3,096,721; San Diego, 960,452; San Francisco, 712,753; San Jose, 686,178; Long Beach, 378,752; Oakland, 351,898.
Government (1985): *Chief Officers*—governor, George Deukmejian (R); lt. gov., Leo McCarthy (D). *Legislature*—Senate, 40 members; Assembly, 80 members.
State Finances (fiscal year 1984): *Revenues,* $50,634,000,000; *expenditures,* $44,716,000,000.
Personal Income (1984): $371,202,000,000; per capita, $14,487.
Labor Force (June 1985): *Civilian labor force,* 12,762,700; *unemployed,* 963,800 (7.6% of total force).
Education: *Enrollment* (fall 1983)—public elementary schools, 2,813,524; public secondary, 1,275,493; colleges and universities, 1,730,847. *Public school expenditures* (1982–83), $11,050,-353,922 ($2,733 per pupil).

back strong sanctions against South Africa. The tax reform was intended to make the state more attractive for industrial investment.

Once again, the legislature failed to reorganize the state's outmoded workers' compensation system for persons injured on the job. The agency suffers from bureaucratic inefficiency and offers low benefit payments. Attempts at reform have been stymied by the inability of conflicting interest groups to compromise.

Lottery. The state lottery went into action on October 3, with ticket sales well beyond the official expectations. It had been opposed by many, including the governor, as a tax on the poor. In 1984 voters passed an initiative that was largely financed by lottery equipment manufacturers.

Politics. Mayor Tom Bradley of Los Angeles trumpeted a large reelection triumph as a basis for trying again to win the governorship over George Deukmejian. (*See* LOS ANGELES.) In 1986 three state supreme court justices, most prominently Chief Justice Rose E. Bird, would face the voters on retention in office for another term. Conservatives seeking to remove Bird are well financed. They argue that she has politicized the court and substituted personal views for law.

CHARLES R. ADRIAN
University of California, Riverside

CAMBODIA

The year 1985 was the seventh of Vietnam's occupation of Cambodia. The war continued between Vietnam's 160,000-man occupation force and about 50,000 Cambodian guerrillas who oppose them. The war has developed a seasonal pattern to which the people are forced to adjust as they struggle with man-made and natural disasters.

Military Developments. During the dry season, from December to May, while farmers plow their fields and plant their rice and other crops, the Vietnamese invariably try to wipe out the guerrillas and their bases on the border between Cambodia and Thailand. In the rainy season, from June to November, the pace of actual fighting slows, except for occasional guerrilla raids behind the Vietnamese lines in

Cambodia. In this half of the year, the focus is on political warfare as both sides try to strengthen their organizations and increase their international support.

In 1985 the Vietnamese achieved more success than usual in their dry season offensive, overrunning the major bases of the three main guerrilla groups. These groups comprised the followers of Prince Sihanouk and Son Sann (both non-Communist), and Pol Pot, the Communist leader who killed millions of his countrymen when he ruled Cambodia (1975–79). Nevertheless, most of the guerrilla forces managed to retreat into Thailand, where they regrouped and resumed their harassment of Vietnamese forces in Cambodia.

The Political Scene. The political struggle, which began in June as the dry season ended, was also more intense in 1985. Some observers believed that Vietnam's leaders were becoming more confident that their country could maintain itself against foreign threats. Hanoi might feel the time was right to begin seeking better relations with its neighbors.

In Phnom Penh the staunchly pro-Hanoi foreign minister, Hun Sen, became prime minister as well. He told journalists that the dry season offensive proved that Vietnam could not be pushed out of Cambodia by the guerrillas. After meeting with Hun Sen, Vietnam's foreign minister, Nguyen Co Thach, said the government in Phnom Penh would soon be able to sustain itself, and Vietnamese forces would withdraw from Cambodia by 1990.

The year 1985 also marked the tenth anniversary of the reunification of Vietnam, and it may have seemed to Vietnamese leaders a propitious time to settle old disputes—on terms favorable to Hanoi. For ten years, Vietnam had viewed China as its main enemy (and the main supporter of the Cambodian guerrillas). The price of a genuine truce with China might be a Vietnamese withdrawal from Cambodia.

For their part, the Cambodian guerrillas also showed some interest in testing Hanoi's aims. They announced that their most feared leader, Pol Pot, had resigned—perhaps in order to see how Vietnam would respond.

According to Western reporters who visited Cambodia during the year, many people seemed to prefer the Vietnamese occupation to the brutal rule of Pol Pot that came before. During Pol Pot's four-year revolution, hundreds of thousands—perhaps millions—of people were murdered because he considered them "class enemies." Now, more than 40% of the people who survive are children under 16 years old. Many are undernourished. Production of rice and fish, the staple foods, are down by half since 1970. The country was severely hit by drought and then floods in 1985, and food would probably have to be imported.

PETER A. POOLE
Author, "Eight Presidents and Indochina"

CAMBODIA · Information Highlights

Official Name: People's Republic of Cambodia or Coalition Government of Democratic Cambodia.
Location: Southeast Asia.
Area: 69,898 sq mi (181 035 km²).
Population (mid-1985 est.): 6,200,000.
Chief City (1983 est.): Phnom Penh, the capital, 600,000.
Government: *Head of state,* Heng Samrin (took office 1981). *Head of government,* Hun Sen, prime minister (took office Jan. 1985).
Monetary Unit: Riel (4 riels equal U.S.$1, 1984).

AP/Wide World

Prime Minister Brian Mulroney (left) held talks with President Ronald Reagan at Quebec City, March 17-18.

CANADA

In 1985, Canadians got used to a new government; proclaimed the equality provisions of their new Charter of Rights and Freedoms; worried about war, drought, acid rain, and taxes; experienced the nation's first bank failures in 62 years; and, for a few delirious autumn weeks, dreamed that a Canadian baseball team might make it to the World Series.

Conservatives. The 211 parliamentary seats that voters gave Brian Mulroney's Progressive Conservatives (PCs) in the September 1984 elections (out of 282) represented the widest Canadian political consensus since 1958. A central question, however, was whether it was also a mandate for conservatism in the style of U.S. President Ronald Reagan and British Prime Minister Margaret Thatcher. Business leaders, some academics, and many in Mulroney's caucus hoped so, and in 1985 some of their wishes certainly came true. New agree-

ments with Alberta and Newfoundland ended the previous regime's National Energy Program (NEP) and moved gas and oil prices toward world levels. Promises to restore separate service identities to Canada's unified armed forces led to three new sets of American-style uniforms. Deregulation began to take hold in Canada's vast transportation industry. Public-sector "downsizing" promised to cut 15,000 of 258,000 federal employees. And the Progressive Conservative government's first budget, presented to the House of Commons by Minister of Finance Michael Wilson on May 23, sought to cut corporate taxes, exempt capital gains, reduce the deficit, and increase consumer taxes. Also cut were the indexing features of Canada's federally funded old-age pensions and family allowances.

The business community and many Conservatives, however, were not appeased. Dreams of drastic change did not come true. An expected flood of business talent was deterred by low civil-service salaries; instead, existing bureaucrats were shuffled. Instead of more defense spending, military budgets were cut; Canada's navy celebrated its 75th anniversary as far from modernization as ever. Wilson's budget cut only C$1.1 billion from a $34.9 billion federal deficit, only a quarter as much as powerful business lobbies had demanded. While the NEP and the Foreign Investment Review Agency vanished as vestiges of economic nationalism, the publicly owned Petro-Canada acquired enough service stations and refineries to become Canada's biggest oil company. That deal, part of a complex acquisition of Gulf Canada by the Reichmann family, was hotly debated. So were huge government grants to save a Domtar Inc. paper mill in rural Quebec and an oil refinery in Montreal. This was all politics as usual.

Prime Minister Mulroney was determined to end the jinx of one- or two-term government that has pursued his party in the 20th century. His recipe was to make friends, avoid trouble, and develop the "Teflon coating" that seemed to protect his political idol, Ronald Reagan. Universal social programs, amounting to half the federal deficit, were proclaimed a "sacred trust." When angry old-age pensioners protested even the partial loss of their inflation protection, it took only five weeks before Mulroney forced his finance minister to back down. The prime minister's year-long insistence that he had nothing to do with unpopular or scandalous decisions strained media credulity, but Mulroney's popularity with voters apparently remained high. His wife, Mila, celebrated the first anniversary of the 1984 election victory by giving birth to the Mulroneys' fourth son.

Free Trade. The year saw an unexpected enthusiasm develop among Canadian opinion-leaders for an effort to negotiate a free-trade arrangement with the United States. For some

it was a natural response to the mood of protectionism in the U.S. Congress. The United States is Canada's largest trading partner, and being locked out of American markets was too frightening to contemplate. For Prime Minister Mulroney, who grew up in an American-owned company town (Baie Comeau, Quebec), it was a comfortable idea and one that gave his young government a sense of purpose. A "Free Trade" campaign was conveniently launched at the "Shamrock Summit," the carefully choreographed meeting of Mulroney and President Reagan in Quebec City, March 17–18.

Canadians might have marveled that a party which had campaigned from 1878 to 1963 on political and economic nationalism could reverse itself so easily. But the Progressive Conservatives reflected a new consensus among business leaders, most provincial premiers, and many academic economists. Alberta's Peter Lougheed rallied support for a free-trade agreement from all provincial premiers except Ontario's David Peterson, a Liberal. The Macdonald Royal Commission on the Economic Union and Development Prospects for Canada, created in 1982 by the Trudeau government, delighted the new government with a ringing endorsement of free trade as part of its remarkably conservative recipe for the nation's future. The commission dared Canadians to "venture into untried ways that will demand open-mindedness, courage, innovation, and determination." The few audible critics wondered whether panic, not audacity, would propel Canada's "leap in the dark." By early October, Mulroney could inform the American president that Canada was ready to deal, although he wanted low-key negotiations.

Political Battles. Having lost the 1984 election in part because of Brian Mulroney's skillful charges of gross patronage, the Liberals got political mileage out of disclosures that the new government was rewarding its own friends. Legal patronage went to firms employing sons of the minister of justice; a brother-in-law of the finance minister got a large advertising contract; and a college chum of the prime minister got a job in a major law firm by bringing in government business. The media caused the government trouble. Minister of Defence Robert Coates resigned in February after reports that he had visited a sleazy nightclub in West Germany; he was replaced by Mulroney's deputy, Erik Nielsen. Michael Wilson, the finance minister, also must have been tempted to resign when the prime minister forced him to revise his May budget and when Mulroney imposed a new deputy finance minister, Montreal labor lawyer Stanley Hartt, without prior consultation.

The autumn was no easier. Minister of Fisheries John Fraser stepped down in September after a Canadian Broadcasting Corporation (CBC) program disclosed a scandal over tuna

AP/Wide World

The government was hurt by a scandal surrounding Defence Minister Robert Coats. He resigned on February 12.

sales. Star-Kist, a subsidiary of the U.S.-based H. J. Heinz Co., Canada's largest seafood processor, had persuaded Fraser to let one million cans of rancid or decomposing tuna be put on sale; Thomas Edward Siddon became the new fisheries minister. And then on September 25, Minister of Communications Marcel Masse quit after the police began investigating charges that he had overspent on his 1984 election. However, Masse was subsequently exonerated of the charges, and he returned to the position.

Mulroney's 1984 victory had been helped by the fact that he had a friendly or neutral government in nine of the ten provinces. As usual, in 1985 the pendulum began to swing back. Newfoundland's Premier Brian Peckford won reelection in April, but the PCs suffered unexpected losses. In the Yukon, a territory the Conservatives promised to make a province, the New Democrats won a narrow victory over the ruling Conservatives in May. In Ontario the same month, a pact between the two opposition parties marked the end of 42 years of rule by the PCs; Premier Frank Miller was succeeded by the Liberal David Peterson. Familiar faces in federal-provincial battles of the 1970s—Ontario's Davis, Quebec's René Lévesque, and Alberta's Peter Lougheed—all retired, but the tradition of combat was only

CANADA • Information Highlights

Official Name: Canada.
Location: Northern North America.
Area: 3,851,791 sq mi (9 976 139 km²).
Population (mid-1985 est.): 25,400,000.
Chief Cities (1981 census): Ottawa, the capital, 295,163; Montreal, 980,354; Toronto, 599,217.
Government: *Head of state,* Elizabeth II, queen; represented by Jeanne Sauvé, governor-general (took office May 14, 1984). *Head of government,* M. Brian Mulroney, prime minister (took office Sept. 17, 1984). *Legislature*—Parliament: Senate and House of Commons.
Monetary Unit: Canadian dollar (1.3669 dollars equal U.S.$1, Oct. 30, 1985).
Gross National Product (second quarter 1985 C$): $449,300,000,000.
Economic Index: *Consumer Prices* (July 1985, 1981 = 100), all items, 127.6; food, 122.1.
Foreign Trade (1984 C$): *Imports,* $73,933,000,000; *exports,* $86,817,000,000.

temporarily muted. By year's end, even Conservative premiers were angry at Ottawa's efforts to shift costly programs to the relatively ill-financed provinces. Mulroney's basic 1984 promise, national harmony, was being tested.

Economy, Industry, Banking. If battles over patronage, rotten tuna, and federal-provincial finance would not change governments, the state of the economy might. In central Canada, the early-1980s recession was over, but national unemployment remained at more than 10%. Inflation, at only 4% for the year, further justified Mr. Mulroney's 1984 claim that "jobs, jobs, jobs" were the only issue that mattered. His government's policy, underlined in the May budget, relied on incentives for the private sector to expand employment. If there was progress, it was slow, local, and confined largely to minimum-wage service industries. (*See also* page 159.)

As Ontario and Quebec industries slowly recovered from recession, forestry, farming, and fishing remained in trouble. The worldwide and U.S. markets both were inhospitable. Nature turned nasty. Cold water off Newfoundland cut yields from the inshore fishery. The fourth year of prairie drought shriveled wheat and forced ranchers to slaughter their herds; early snowfalls completed the prairie crop disaster. Spruce budworms and acid rain threatened forest stands in central Canada. The plight of British Columbia's forest industry—the province's $23 billion mainstay—was cast in relief by the worst fires in years. Logging companies and their workers launched legal and political battles for the right to cut the province's last great timber preserves on the Queen Charlotte Islands, but environmental groups and native organizations fought back.

Canadian bankers had always taken pride that their institutions had survived the Depression of the 1930s without a single default. In March 1985 the new government tried to protect that record with a $250-million bailout of Edmonton's Canadian Commercial Bank. The gamble failed. Over the Labor Day weekend, the government was forced to step in and close the bank. Then, five weeks later, it did the same with the Calgary-based Northland Bank. Suddenly, all small banks looked risky, though fears were eased somewhat when the Quebec-based National Bank absorbed the shaky Mercantile Bank. Westerners blamed the Trudeau government's National Energy Policy for destroying a regional economy; insiders whispered of wild mismanagement and a sea of "nonperforming" loans that no responsible banker ever should have made. The collapses owed at least something to the custom of allowing chartered banks to pay for their own inspector-general, a practice that would be looked into by a Royal Commission under Justice Willard Estey of the Supreme Court of Canada. Meanwhile, the Mulroney government had to redeem its pledge to both insured and uninsured depositors by collecting close to $1.5 billion from taxpayers. It was a harsh blow to deficit cutters, and the bank failures also curbed the new government's plans for more free-wheeling financial institutions.

Equality. The equality provisions of Canada's Charter of Rights and Freedoms, contained in Section 15, finally took effect on April 17, 1985. Approved three years before, the provisions had been delayed by the enormous legal ramifications of banning discrimination on the basis of "race, national or ethnic origin, color, religion, sex, age or mental or physical disability." In practice, Ottawa and the provinces had done very little to adjust, trusting that citizens and courts would remember that these and other Charter rights were subject to "reasonable limits prescribed by law."

The ramifications of a young constitution for litigious Canadians kept judges and courts busier than ever. "It's a great time to be a lawyer," boasted a Toronto attorney. In 1985, Canada's courts sharply restricted breathalyzer tests, overturned laws against Sunday shopping (if the reason was religious), and questioned the right to censor obscene movies. Abortion, a hot issue in Canada, fostered suits for the rights of the unborn. Dr. Henry Morgenthaler, Canada's leading abortion-rights activist, was acquitted by a Toronto jury on abortion charges, a verdict overturned on appeal. After four earlier jury acquittals in predominantly Catholic Montreal, Morgenthaler faced a new judicial ordeal and the certainty that antichoice activists would keep up their crusade.

Other highly publicized trials saw a German-born Toronto publisher, Ernst Zundel, convicted under a little-used Criminal Code provision for spreading false news—specifically, that the Holocaust had not occurred. An Alberta public school teacher, Jim Keegstra, was convicted for teaching his students that Jewish conspirators controlled the world. Both

THE CANADIAN MINISTRY

M. Brian Mulroney, prime minister
George H. Hees, minister of veterans affairs
Duff Roblin, leader of the government in the senate
Joe Clark, secretary of state for external affairs
Flora MacDonald, minister of employment and immigration
Erik H. Nielsen, deputy prime minister and minister of defence
John C. Crosbie, minister of justice
Roch La Salle, minister of public works
Donald F. Mazankowski, minister of transport
Elmer MacKay, minister of revenue
Jake Epp, minister of national health and welfare
Thomas Edward Siddon, minister of fisheries and oceans
Sinclair Stevens, minister of regional industrial expansion
John Wise, minister of agriculture
Ramon J. Hnatyshyn, president of the queen's privy council for Canada and leader of the government in the house
David E. Crombie, minister of Indian affairs and northern development
Robert R. de Cotret, president of the Treasury Board
Perrin Beatty, solicitor general
Michael Wilson, minister of finance
Jack B. Murta, minister of state (tourism)
Harvie Andre, associate minister of defence
Otto J. Jelinek, minister of state (fitness and amateur sport and multiculturalism)
Frank Oberle, minister of state for science and technology
Charles J. Mayer, minister of state (Canadian Wheat Board)
William H. McKnight, minister of labour
Walter F. McLean, minister of state (immigration), status of women
Thomas M. McMillan, minister of environment
Patricia Carney, minister of energy, mines and resources
André Bissonnette, minister of state (small businesses)
Suzanne Blais-Grenier, minister of state (transport)
Benoit Bouchard, secretary of state
Andrée Champagne, minister of state (youth)
Michel Côté, minister of consumer and corporate affairs, Canada Post Corporation
James F. Kelleher, minister for international trade
Robert E. Layton, minister of state (mines)
Marcel Masse, minister of communications
Barbara J. McDougall, minister of state (finance)
Gerry S. Merrithew, minister of state (forestry)
Monique Vézina, minister of external relations
Stewart McInnes, minister of supply and services

cases were appealed while Canadians debated whether the accompanying publicity had been good or bad. The cause of a number of suspicious baby deaths at Toronto's Hospital for Sick Children remained uncertain after a yearlong Royal Commission investigation.

Further constitutional reform was on no one's agenda. René Lévesque's 22-point list of conditions to bring Quebec into the 1982 constitution fell flat. Provincial premiers and Indian leaders both frustrated Prime Minister Mulroney's effort to settle the aboriginal rights issue. British Columbia's Premier Bill Bennett summed up the differences by insisting on defining the concept before signing. On one question, the government ignored native protests: just before "Equality Day," Parliament repealed the long-standing provision that robbed Indian women, but not men, of their status if they married a non-Indian. That done, the Con-

servative government gave notice of a sweeping transfer of power to Indian band councils. Whether the funds necessary for native management of health, education, and housing would disappear in Ottawa's deficit cutting, as a leaked discussion paper had suggested, remained an unresolved question.

Foreign Affairs. Free trade, the Strategic Defense Initiative (SDI, also known as "Star Wars"), and sharing the $7 billion cost of renovating the continent's North Warning System were all aspects of the Mulroney government's desire to make friends with the Reagan White House. A parliamentary committee found most Canadians opposed SDI, and the government's compromise was to opt out officially but to allow Canadian firms to get what business they could. There was far more agreement about the need to rebuild an obsolete North Warning System. Canadians were more sensitive to the Arctic than Washington may have realized when it refused to seek permission for the U.S. Coast Guard vessel *Polar Sea* to use the disputed North West Passage. Canadian authorities discreetly reminded Washington that the U.S. determination to internationalize the Passage might also be welcome in Moscow. Minister of External Affairs Joe Clark pledged firm assertion of Canada's sovereignty over the Arctic, including construction of a $500 million icebreaker to match the *Polar Sea.*

With little of Pierre Elliott Trudeau's prestige or experience, Brian Mulroney was willing to make a modest, conciliatory debut in the international arena. NATO was promised 1,500 more Canadian military personnel (at the expense of units in Canada). Widespread Canadian criticisms of White House policy on Nicaragua were not pressed forcefully. And when Commonwealth leaders met in Nassau in October to demand mandatory sanctions against their former member, South Africa, Mulroney performed his prearranged role as mediator between the Afro-Asian majority and Britain's Margaret Thatcher.

Canada suffered its share of the worldwide epidemic of terrorism. In March, Armenian gunmen assaulted the Turkish embassy in Ottawa, killing a young Canadian security guard. The June crash of an Air-India jumbo jet off the coast of Ireland, believed to have been caused by a bomb explosion, killed all 329 persons aboard, including 279 Canadians. The same day at Japan's New Tokyo International Airport in Narita, a bomb exploded from inside luggage unloaded from a Canadian Airlines Boeing 747; two baggage handlers were killed. Both plane bombings were widely attributed to Indian Sikh extremists.

Diversions. Canadians, as usual, spent much of their spare time as sports spectators. However much Ontario and Quebec might be prospering in the post-recession period, the West could boast the Edmonton Oilers and

Number 99, Wayne Gretzky; Toronto's once-triumphant Maple Leafs ended the 1985 season as the worst team in the National Hockey League (NHL). Sporting pride rose when a Canadian team, culled from teams eliminated in the NHL play-offs, placed second in the world championships at Prague; it was Canada's best showing since 1962. In soccer, a game few Canadians even watched, the national team quietly qualified for the 1986 World Cup. And baseball, a sport Canadians had watched for years, zoomed in popularity when the Americans and Dominicans of the Toronto Blue Jays took their club to the verge of a World Series berth—only to lose to the Kansas City Royals in the seventh game of the American League Championship Series.

Beyond sports, there were few landmark cultural achievements. One was the publication of Mel Hurtig's massive three-volume *Canadian Encyclopedia.* Financing, as the preface gratefully noted, had been provided by the ill-fated Canadian Commercial Bank. Less conspicuous sources found money for the most expensive Canadian movie ever made, *Joshua Then and Now,* produced by Ted Kotcheff from a novel by Mordecai Richler.

See also articles on individual provinces and territories.

DESMOND MORTON
Erindale College, University of Toronto

The Economy

In 1985 the Canadian economy continued to spin upward. Seasonally adjusted monthly employment figures during the first two quarters, with the exceptions of the months of January and June, showed a consistent gain ranging from 0.8% in April to 0.2% in August. Consequently, the average jobless rate during the second quarter dropped to 10.6% from 11.1% recorded for the first quarter. The confidence of consumers and business firms in the economy grew rapidly. This was reflected by a significant upturn in the growth of various sectors such as retail trade, residential construction, and foreign trade.

Retail Trade. In August, seasonally adjusted retail sales reached an all-time monthly high of $10.8 billion, a rise of 12.5% from the same month a year earlier. In August, as compared with July 1985, the sales of new cars, household furnishings, and appliances shot up 3.5%, 2%, and 4.1% respectively. If consumer confidence in the economy was maintained during the final months of the year, retail sales for 1985 could top $130 billion, well above the 1984 total of $116 billion.

Housing. Similarly, in the construction sector a dramatic increase in housing starts from a postrecession low annual rate of 122,000 units in December 1984 to 184,000 in September 1985

further stimulated the level of economic activity. Though a downward drift in mortgage rates, robust employment, and income growth now were on the wane, a flare-up in resale home prices, plus a decline in apartment vacancy rates to 1.9% in the first half of 1985 from 2.7% a year earlier, suggested that the demand for new houses would be sufficient to keep housing starts near the September level through year's end.

Foreign Trade. Again a strong upturn in foreign purchases of energy and agricultural and energy products jolted the Canadian trade figures for September 1985 by contributing exports worth $10.7 billion and creating a trade surplus of $1.8 billion for the month. Although September's trade figures closed the second quarter with a flourish, the balance of trade for the July-September period fell significantly short of performance in the first half of 1985.

Overall. The economy on the whole, however, grew as is evident from lean inventories and a stronger level of new orders for the manufacturing sector. In fact, all industry output—real gross domestic product (GNP)—increased by 0.3% between July and August. That rise comes on the top of July's 1.8% advance and June's 1.4% pace. The overall growth for the entire year was expected to exceed 4%.

The expectation, however, was that strong growth would not last. By year's end the elements responsible for causing growth in 1985 were expected to weaken, creating the prospect of slower growth in 1986. Federal budget measures, especially increases in personal income and manufacturers' sales taxes, were expected to reduce consumer spending.

R. P. SETH, *Professor of Economics Mount Saint Vincent University, Halifax*

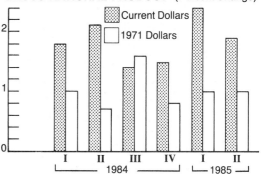

GROSS NATIONAL PRODUCT (Percent Change)

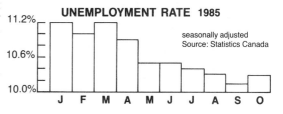

UNEMPLOYMENT RATE 1985

seasonally adjusted
Source: Statistics Canada

The Arts

Faced with cuts of more than C$100 million in federal government assistance in 1985, Canadian artists became more organized and lobbied more strongly than before. But, although they obtained some concessions, most of the cuts remained. The government, for its part, pointed out that in a weakened economy all sectors had to tighten their belts. The arts in turn emphasized that they themselves were a vital part of the economy, being the country's fourth biggest employer, with 307,000 people working in the arts.

The Canada Council, which makes grants to the arts, had to cut $3.5 million from its budget of $84 million. This prompted 500 artists to stage a protest on Parliament Hill in Ottawa. The federal Minister of Communications Marcel Masse, whose department funds the arts, started reviewing the whole arts picture, and in particular announced a review of the Canadian Broadcasting Corporation (CBC). But a sore point was that previously the Communications Department had given out funds that the recipients controlled as to how they were spent. Masse was criticized for appearing to abandon this "hands off" policy of the government. In September, Masse resigned from the cabinet because his spending in the 1984 election campaign was being investigated. After being cleared, he returned to the post late in the year.

The CBC, the biggest job market for artists, had $75 million cut from its government subsidy, resulting in more than 1,000 jobs being lost. The Friends of Public Broadcasting, a country-wide group of actors, writers, and others, campaigned against the cuts. A surprise was added when Allan Slaight, former president of Global Television, announced he wanted to buy the CBC's English-language TV network from the government. He was backed by the Committee for the Privatization of CBC Television, which claimed it could relieve the government of the $320 million a year it cost to maintain the CBC's English-language TV. The committee accused the CBC of wastefulness and of duplicating available services.

A bright spot in the arts scene was the prospect that Vancouver's 1986 world's fair, Expo 86, would provide numerous cultural events, and that its millions of visitors would boost attendance at performances elsewhere. Expo 86 will spend an estimated $35 million on entertainment, but it was not clear how much would go to Canadian groups.

Visual Arts. At the Montreal Museum of Fine Arts, the exhibition *Pablo Picasso: Meeting in Montreal* showed 81 works from the private collection of the artist's widow, Jacqueline Picasso, most of them never exhibited before. Also in Montreal, *Aurora Borealis* was the largest display of contemporary Canadian Art ever held. Toronto's Royal Ontario Museum displayed *The Precious Legacy: Judaic Treasures from the Czechoslovak State Collections*. The exhibition was a touching reminder of World War II's great tragedy, for almost all of it had been collected from Jews bound for concentration camps. The Art Gallery of Ontario mounted a big collection of works by the 19th-century artist Honoré Daumier. The same gallery's *The European Iceberg* was the largest showing of new European art ever held on the North American continent.

During its second year in new premises, the Vancouver Art Gallery featured an exhibition of paintings entitled *Christopher Pratt: a Retrospect.* For the months of Expo 86 the gallery plans four exhibitions: *Dutch Masters, Papal Splendor,* paintings by Norwegian Edvard Munch, and contemporary art from France. Egypt's Ramses II exhibit also will be shown at Expo 86, with a $5 million pavilion, designed by David Fischer, being built to house it. The Mackenzie Art Gallery at University of Regina organized *Space Invaders,* a show by Canadian, British, and American sculptors.

Performing Arts. At Stratford, Ont., the Stratford Festival's first play was *King Lear,* with Douglas Campbell as Lear. Well received, it was the last play produced by John Hirsch, who retired as the festival's artistic director after five seasons. John Neville replaced him. Other plays at Stratford included an appealing *Measure for Measure* in modern dress, directed by Michael Bogdanov. After the previous season, the festival faced a $2.8 million deficit. But under a capital renovation program the federal and provincial governments each contributed $2 million, and the festival was to raise an additional $2 million.

At Niagara-on-the-Lake, Ont., the Shaw Festival presented Noël Coward's *Cavalcade.* It was the first stage presentation of this play in more than 50 years. A huge play, which had a cast of 400 in its original production, *Cavalcade* is a panorama of three decades of British history, starting in 1898. Even much scaled down, the Shaw Festival version had a cast of 40 and was a daunting undertaking, but directors Christopher Newton and Duncan McIntosh were equal to it. Other shows in the festival's season included *One for the Pot,* a farce by Ray Cooney and Tony Holton that starred Heath Lamberts, and Shaw's *Heartbreak House,* staged by Christopher Newton.

John Gray, author of *Billy Bishop,* which was staged on Broadway, had his fifth play, *Don Messer's Jubilee,* open in Halifax. It concerns the country music show of the same title that was a popular TV show in the 1960s.

The $80 million Calgary Centre, containing the latest theatrical equipment, opened in Calgary. Among its features are the Max Bell Theatre, which is the locale of the Theatre Calgary company, and the Jack Singer Concert Hall, which seats 1,800.

Rudolph Barshai became Vancouver Symphony Orchestra's new music director and principal conductor. He was to make his debut conducting Mahler's *Symphony No. 9,* a work never before played in Vancouver. But this was not to be, for a contract dispute between the symphony society and its musicians ended with the latter being locked out, and the three Mahler performances were canceled. The lockout continued for nine days until Barshai offered to take a pay cut to help the society, which had an accumulated deficit of $1,709,284. His action influenced both sides to reach a settlement, with no pay increase for musicians. When the season finally opened, Barshai led a fine performance of Holst's *The Planets.* But the society's financial position was grave. To tide it over, the society asked for $1 million from private donors and from federal, provincial, and municipal governments. At the annual meeting a few days after the lockout, president John G. Smith resigned when candidates nominated by the musicians won five of the six vacant seats on the board, defeating all but one of the candidates he favored. However, a few days later Smith agreed to resume the presidency.

In Toronto, the National Ballet of Canada premiered *Blue Snake,* the remarkable new ballet of choreographer Robert Desrosiers. Vigorous and futuristic, it is a decided break from the traditional. Erik Bruhn, artistic director of the company, successfully revived the Danish ballet *Napoli.*

The Canadian Opera Company's *Die Meistersinger* was its biggest presentation ever, with 180 performers. The Canadian Music Council gave pianist John Kimura Parker its award as performer of the year. James McGillivray of Toronto won the gold medal at the world's leading piping contest at Inverness, Scotland. He and two other Ontario pipers to-

Peter Willi, Paris

"Woman with a Blue and Red Hat" was among the 81 Pablo Picasso's works shown at the Montreal Museum of Fine Arts in 1985. Many of the works were never exhibited before.

gether won five of the six events. Toronto's 17-day *Bach 300,* directed by Jane Forner, celebrated the 300th anniversary of Johann Sebastian Bach's birth. Edmonton's *TriBach* was the biggest musical event ever held in Western Canada, at a cost of $1.3 million. On a lesser scale, the country celebrated the birth, also in 1685, of George Frederic Handel. Angela Hewitt, 26, won the 1985 Bach Piano Competition.

See also LITERATURE—Canadian.

DAVID SAVAGE, *Simon Fraser University*

Sygma

Canada's motion picture industry produced the most expensive film in its history with "Joshua Then and Now." Adapted for the screen by novelist Mordecai Richler from his book, the film stars James Woods (center) in the title role.

The Caribbean sugar industry, an economic mainstay of the region, reached a low point in 1985 as the United States cut imports and spot prices stayed below 4 cents per pound.

Eddie Adams, Gamma-Liaison

CARIBBEAN

During much of 1985, Caribbean leaders expressed growing dissatisfaction with the economic policies of the United States toward the region.

In August the prime ministers of 11 Caribbean countries told President Reagan that their confidence in the U.S. Caribbean Basin Initiative (CBI) was being eroded by the lack of substantive economic benefits to the region. In a letter sent to the White House from the annual heads-of-government meeting of the Caribbean Economic Community (CARICOM), the 11 leaders also said they were concerned about a growing tendency toward protectionism in the U.S. Congress.

The region's economic indicators were mixed during the year. Exports to the United States fell by 18% in the first half of 1985, but tourism, mainly from the United States and Canada, rose by 6%. The Caribbean sugar industry was in a state of virtual collapse throughout the year. Economic austerity programs, imposed by governments at the behest of the International Monetary Fund (IMF), provoked rumbles of discontent in such countries as Jamaica and the Dominican Republic.

CBI. The CBI is a 12-year program under which Caribbean and Central American countries designated by Washington can ship a wide range of products duty-free to the United States. The program has been in effect since Jan. 1, 1984, but has been criticized by Caribbean beneficiary countries because several categories of products have been excluded from duty-free treatment.

"The most noted omissions from the program viewed in terms of their foreign exchange earnings and employment potential are textiles and garments, footwear and leather products," said the letter to President Ronald Reagan.

The Caribbean heads of government also protested "pending congressional actions which threaten to erode benefits already established under the CBI, and understandings reached with your administration." The leaders specifically cited a proposed duty increase on imports of ethanol (ethyl alcohol), lack of action on a plan to exempt from duty garments made in the Caribbean from U.S.-made textiles, and a proposed change in U.S. tax laws that would deprive firms operating in Puerto Rico of tax advantages. Puerto Rico suggested sharing the tax advantages with Caribbean countries under a "twin-plant" arrangement.

Trade War. CARICOM faced a serious challenge during the year as a disagreement over a common trade policy threatened to erupt into an interisland trade war. Four of the 13 members of CARICOM failed to meet an August 31 deadline for implementing measures to increase trade within the community. The measures would create a common tariff on goods from outside CARICOM and would dismantle barriers against intraregional commerce. The countries that have not implemented the pact are Trinidad and Tobago, St. Lucia, Antigua, and Belize. In addition, Trinidad and Tobago has imposed licensing requirements for imports from other Caribbean islands.

Partly because of the dispute and also because of depressed economic conditions throughout the region, intra-Caribbean trade has been declining in recent years. From an overall value of $577 million in 1981, the value of the trade fell to $432.5 million in 1984.

Sugar. The Caribbean sugar industry has been losing ground for several years, but it reached its lowest point in 1985. As worldwide demand for sugar has been declining, the United States—the prime market for Caribbean sugar—has been cutting its overall import quota to protect the domestic sugar industry. In October the U.S. Department of Agriculture lowered the 1986 sugar year quota by nearly 32%. The move reduced the Dominican Republic's share of the U.S. quota by 16%.

A study released by the Organization of American States (OAS) in April showed that the spot price of sugar had been below four cents a pound since December 1984. That level, the OAS study said, "in nominal terms is the lowest recorded in the last 14 years and in real terms, it is the lowest ever recorded." U.S. sugar imports in 1985 from the Caribbean and Latin America, the OAS said, were only slightly more than half the annual average recorded in the five years 1977 through 1981. The value of sugar imports from the Caribbean and Latin America fell from $1,347,300,000 in 1981 to $692.1 million in 1984, and the OAS estimated that the figure would decline to $460 million in 1985.

Politics. The political climate in Haiti thawed slightly in 1985. In a national referendum in July, Haitian voters approved constitutional changes that authorize the creation of political parties for the first time in the three-decade reign of the Duvalier family. Opponents of the Haitian regime said the referendum was meaningless since the voters also approved a provision for the continuation of Jean-Claude Duvalier as president for life and another giving Duvalier the right to name a successor without recourse to elections.

In Dominica the conservative Dominica Freedom Party (DFP), led by Prime Minister Eugenia Charles, retained a majority of 15 of the 21 seats in the island's legislature in an election held on July 1. Prime Minister Charles was a prominent supporter of U.S. intervention in Grenada in 1983 and campaigned this time on an anti-Communist platform which claimed that Moscow had targeted her for defeat in retaliation for her role in the Grenada invasion.

Grenada. The government of Grenada, elected in December 1984, proceeded with plans to attract foreign investment and to develop tourism and agriculture to rebuild the economy. Utilizing a $1.3 million loan from the Caribbean Development Bank, Grenada was building 40,000 sq ft (3 700 m²) of new factory space for light industry. The finishing touches were being put on a new international airport, which had been 80% complete at the time of the 1983 U.S. invasion. A master plan for tourism development seeks to expand the island's hotel capacity of 650 rooms. Tourism volume increased by 40,000 visitors in 1984, the highest gain in any one year; tourist expenditures reached $16.6 million.

Jamaica. Street riots in Kingston in January in protest of a 21% increase in gasoline prices claimed seven lives. In June there were short-lived protests by the two largest teachers' unions, the postal workers, and the police federation against austerity programs imposed under pressure from the IMF. Jamaicans also have been hard-pressed by currency devaluations, high unemployment, inflation, and declining foreign investment.

Severe cutbacks have been made in the bauxite and alumina industries, the mainstays of the island's economy. An Alcoa alumina plant closed in January but reopened in August. Aluminum Partners of Jamaica closed a plant that employed 100 workers, costing the economy an estimated $50 million a year. Business leaders have denounced the government's lack of attention to the manufacturing sector and its emphasis on agriculture as "poisoning the investment atmosphere in Jamaica."

Dominican Republic. The government of President Salvador Jorge Blanco negotiated a rescheduling of $127 million in debt over an 11-year period. The Inter-American Development Bank approved a two-year credit of $92.6 million for agricultural development. Nonetheless, the country suffered unrest because of stringent austerity programs. Wages and salaries are officially controlled, but the cost of living has tripled since 1983. Elections were scheduled for May 1986, and the government's Dominican Revolution Party seemed headed for defeat if the economic crisis were not solved.

RICHARD C. SCHROEDER
"Visión" Magazine

Henry Hillard, Gamma-Liaison

In the worst outbreak of violence since Prime Minister Edward Seaga took office in 1980, riots broke out in Kingston, Jamaica, after the government announced a sharp increase in fuel prices in mid-January.

In Nicaragua, still torn by civil war, "contra" leader Enrique Bermudez drills Sandinistas-turned-guerrillas.

CENTRAL AMERICA

Conditions in Central America changed little during 1985. War continued in El Salvador, Guatemala, and Nicaragua. Honduras was a not-too-eager host to U.S. troops as well as refugees from neighboring lands. All the republics faced critical economic problems. Under President Ronald Reagan's Caribbean Basin Initiative (CBI), Central American exports to the United States increased about 12%, but the growth was less than that experienced by the rest of Latin America and much less than the imports from the rest of the world. U.S. aid to Central America totaled more than $1 billion, about 80% of which was economic and the rest military.

Negotiations under the so-called Contadora process (named for the Panamanian island where the discussions first were held) stalled over a political asylum dispute between Costa Rica and Nicaragua. Then in November, Nicaragua declared that it would reject any Contadora proposal that did not prohibit U.S. military maneuvers in the region or prevent assistance to rebels. The four Contadora states— Colombia, Mexico, Panama, and Venezuela— had been trying for nearly three years to negotiate a peace treaty acceptable to both the United States and Nicaragua.

Washington was criticized widely, even among Americans, for refusing to accept a decision by the International Court of Justice regarding a Nicaraguan suit to halt the giving of aid to the "contras" and to collect damages for helping the rebels destroy life and property. The Reagan administration contended that the World Court had no jurisdiction in this case and later announced that it would cease to comply automatically with any Court ruling.

While the refugee problem was not confined to Central America, it certainly reached massive proportions among the nations of that region. Up to 1 million persons have left Central America for the United States in recent years. Since 1981, 45,000 or more Guatemalans have crossed the border into Mexico. An estimated one sixth of the population of El Salvador has left that country; up to 500,000 Salvadorans, generally peasants who have abandoned their land to escape the war, live in the United States. Whether they are true political refugees is often difficult to judge, and the decision can mean life or death to them. U.S. courts have been ruling on an increasing number of such cases, as well as the guilt or innocence of groups who give them sanctuary (*see* special report, page 441). Since 1980, as many as 33,000 Salvadorans have been deported from the United States. And more than 100,000 Nicaraguans and Salvadorans are illegally residing in Costa Rica, which has almost no facilities for absorbing them. The problem promises to continue long after the Central American civil wars have gone.

Belize. For the first time in more than 20 years, George Price was not the dominant figure in Belize. In December 1984 he lost his position as prime minister to Manuel Esquivel, a senator and physics teacher. Esquivel brought no sweeping changes to the Vermont-size nation in 1985, even though his United Democratic Party held a three-to-one majority in the lower house of the National Assembly. Like Price, Esquivel is a Catholic. He is Latin in ancestry, his wife is English, and they have three children. Because she teaches in Belize City, the family continues to reside there rather than in Belmopan, the new capital.

Belize celebrated its fourth year of independence on Sept. 21, 1985. Prime Minister Esquivel declared that he has no desire to be pulled into the orbit of either the United States or Cuba, but he does seek closer ties with Great Britain. Historically both Mexico and Guatemala have claimed portions of Belize, but Mexico is willing to give up its claims if Guatemala will do the same. The latter's reluctance to recognize the independence of the former British Honduras has prompted Britain to keep a number of troops there, at a cost of about $50 million a year.

Inflation was kept under control during the year, generally running less than 3%, but the austerity measures instituted by former Prime Minister Price did not succeed in reducing heavy unemployment or the substantial foreign debt. Production of fish, citrus, and garments all increased slightly in 1985, but their value was insufficient to balance the loss of revenue resulting from a sharp decline in sugar sales. Sugar, which normally accounts for more than half of export earnings, has declined in both production and price every year since 1980. Belize has been designated a partner in President Ronald Reagan's CBI, but since nearly half of its exports already go to the United States, a great increase in that market seems unlikely. Belize was to receive about $600,000 in military aid from the United States and about $10 million in economic assistance during 1985.

A more troublesome Belizean commerce is in marijuana. Belize is believed to be the fourth-largest supplier of the U.S. market, providing nearly 10% of consumption. The 500-member Belizean police force cannot contain the trade, and in 1984 it agreed to aerial spray-ing by the United States. The effort seemed successful but had to be suspended because of damage to the environment. Discussions ensued over spraying with a less dangerous chemical, but Prime Minister Esquivel planned to conduct tests first.

Civil war in other Central American states continued to press refugees on to Belize, with El Salvador and Guatemala each contributing as many as 10,000. Meanwhile, about 40,000 better trained and educated Belizeans, mostly blacks, fled to Canada or the United States in search of jobs.

Costa Rica. Faced with continuing economic stagnation, Costa Rica in 1985 began what the U.S. State Department called "Central America's most comprehensive reform program." Measures included reform of the exchange rate and the currency law. In March the World Bank and the International Monetary Fund (IMF) made adjustment loans of $80 million and $50 million, respectively, to assist these changes. With U.S. help, financing of rural road construction and farm credit programs was expanded, and the Costa Rican government sold off some of its enterprises. For fiscal 1985 the United States granted Costa Rica $201 million in economic aid.

The important banana business also underwent change. United Fruit, contending that its Pacific coast plantations were losing money because of a long strike in 1984 and also citing increased competition from Ecuador and Nicaragua, began phasing out plantations, some of which dated from 1938. Inasmuch as an estimated 50,000 Costa Ricans were dependent on banana production and the company paid $40 million annually in taxes, the government signed a deal to buy 4,200 acres (1 700 ha) of plantation land, plus 500 buildings, a rail line, and rolling stock for $1.4 million. Much of the public opposed the purchase, and the government faced problems in managing the land, but the government felt it must act to protect the nation's well-being. United was to help market the fruit and continue to operate its Caribbean farms.

Costa Rica's political parties began gearing up for the presidential election of February 1986. The National Liberation Party (PLN), the party of President Luis Alberto Monge Álvarez, was expected to campaign instead for

CENTRAL AMERICA • Information Highlights

Nation	Population (in Millions)	Area (sq mi)	Area (km²)	Capital	Head of State and Government
Belize	0.2	8,866	22 963	Belmopan	Elmira Minita Gordon, governor-general Manuel Esquivel, prime minister
Costa Rica	2.6	19,575	50 700	San José	Luis Alberto Monge, president
El Salvador	5.1	8,124	21 041	San Salvador	José Napoleón Duarte, president
Guatemala	8.0	42,000	108 780	Guatemala City	Marco Vinicio Cerezo Arévalo, president
Honduras	4.4	43,277	112 088	Tegucigalpa	José Azcona Hoyo, president
Nicaragua	3.0	50,193	130 000	Managua	José Daniel Ortega Saavedra, president
Panama	2.0	29,760	77 080	Panama City	Eric Arturo Delvalle, president

Oscar Arias. Major opposition will probably come from a coalition called the United Social Christian Party (PUSC), whose candidate is Rafael Angel Calderón Fournier, the son of a former president. Calderón is only 35 but has long service in Congress. He calls himself anti-Communist and a firm friend of the United States. In 1985, at least, the parties of the left were divided and disorganized.

Relations with Nicaragua did not improve in 1985. Large numbers of refugees continued to cross the border, and even though most of them were friendly to Costa Rica and merely fleeing the Sandinista regime, they proved burdensome to the employment and welfare situations. But some border crossings were not so friendly: in one attack by Sandinista forces, the first since 1978, two Costa Rican guardsmen were killed. The substantial Costa Rican antagonism prompted Nicaragua to recommend a demilitarized zone between the two nations. Both the Organization of American States (OAS) and the Contadora nations offered their cooperation in investigating the creation of such a zone.

In May, amid arguments over the extent of pressure from Washington, Costa Rica consented to the presence of two dozen U.S. military personnel to begin to train some 750 Costa Rican civil guards. To assist the program, Costa Rica received $9 million for rifles, antitank guns, and training costs. Costa Rica has no army, so some of its citizens complained of giving in to "the Yankee." The United States also commenced building a road in the northern jungle. Portions of the road, which will take two years to build, come within 5 mi (8 km) of the Nicaraguan border. It will have a social as well as military function.

El Salvador. Throughout 1985, President José Napoleón Duarte continued his tightrope act of governing El Salvador. He would not compromise with the powerful right wing and generally failed in peace talks with the left because it insisted on sharing power with him. Duarte did win an unexpected victory in the March 31 elections for the National Assembly, as his Christian Democratic Party wrested a majority from the conservative coalition. The right accused him of ballot stuffing and demanded recounts. Several dozen soldiers were killed protecting polling stations.

President Duarte's chief opponent, Roberto D'Aubuisson, resigned as head of the National Republican Alliance to lead a "political training" institution. In June hundreds of police and national guardsmen were required to end a four-week takeover of a number of government hospitals and clinics whose workers sought salary increases of as much as $75 per month. Other unions also asked for large benefits, and Duarte charged that the Communists in the unions were making impossible demands to aid the rebels. However, 100 or more disputes

© Davis, Gamma-Liaison

El Salvador's President Duarte is reunited with daughter Inés on October 24, six weeks after her kidnapping.

were settled peacefully, and little violence occurred on the labor front.

Other new guerrilla tactics were more destructive, for it seemed that as the rebels lost territory to the army, they became more desperate. In May they killed two newly elected mayors, kidnapped eight others, and burned the offices and records of some 30 other officials. The next month, leftist guerrillas dressed in army uniforms fired on crowds at outdoor cafés in San Salvador, killing 16 persons. The dead included four U.S. Marines and two American businessmen. The Central American Workers' Revolutionary Party claimed responsibility.

In mid-September, President Duarte's daughter, Inés Guadelupe Duarte Durán, and her secretary were kidnapped by the rebels, who also killed one of her bodyguards. The women were held for about six weeks, then released along with a large number of mayors and other officials in exchange for the freeing of 22 political prisoners and the evacuation of nearly 100 wounded rebels. For this deal the

president received much criticism from conservatives, who felt that he had yielded too much to save his own daughter.

The civil war dragged on, although the army clearly was doing a better job in pursuing the rebels. The latter, who had their worst year to date, tried such new tactics as creating administrative havoc by kidnapping scores of local officials and destroying their public records. One of the rebel commanders told reporters that, using small units, he would soon spread the war everywhere and bleed the economy to death. In October the rebels attacked a major training base at La Unión; it was the biggest assault in months, killing 40 Salvadorans.

According to the U.S. Embassy, six years of war have brought changes to the army, including less corruption and repression, and an improved human rights record. One local politician concluded that the change was mainly a consequence of American scrutiny: more than 100 U.S. congressmen visited El Salvador in two years.

Meanwhile, the government was not winning the economic war. In spite of nearly $1.5 million a day in U.S. aid, the unemployment figure hovered around 40%, the agrarian reform program made little progress, and new private investment was virtually nonexistent. For 1985, U.S. aid included $310 million in economic assistance, $128 million in military aid, and $21 million from the Inter-American Development Bank (IDB) to improve the water and sewage systems in the nation's rural communities.

Guatemala. For the past 30 years, the Guatemalan military has either held the presidency or controlled it completely. But when an election was scheduled for 1985, Chief of State Gen. Oscar Humberto Mejía Victores announced that the army would support the election process and abide by its outcome. Some officers feared that a civilian president might launch an embarrassing investigation into the "disappeared ones," but the army did remain neutral. The real test would come when the new president took office.

More than any other Central American administration, that of Gen. Mejía Victores had succeeded in quelling the activities of rebels—and without the financial assistance of the United States. (Charging excessive human rights violations, former U. S. President Jimmy Carter had suspended aid in 1979.) The army has been occasionally ruthless in its treatment of Indians, killing dissidents and burning their villages. But the army is now also setting up civic action programs to improve the situation. Able-bodied Indian males have been organized into civil defense patrols to keep the rebels away from the Indian villages, and 74 model villages have been built to house the thousands of homeless. The program is expensive, however, running into hundreds of millions of dollars, and may cost more than the country can afford.

In the November 3 election, some 70% of Guatemala's 2.7 million registered voters cast ballots for a president, vice-president, national congress, and 330 mayors. Eight presidential candidates received votes. Getting the plurality was the Christian Democrat, Marco Vinicio Cerezo Arévalo, with 39%; second was Jorge Carpio Nicolle of the National Union of the Center, with 20.3%; and third was Jorge Serrano Elías of the Democratic Party, with 13.8%.

Although the vote for Cerezo nearly doubled the total of his closest rival, Carpio, a runoff was scheduled for December 8 because he lacked an outright majority. In the campaign, Cerezo promised a "democratic" administration, more foreign investment, and an end to military repression. Carpio, a wealthy publisher, spent a great deal on advertising, brand-

Marco Vinicio Cerezo Arévalo ran a successful campaign to become Guatemala's first civilian president in 15 years.

Visiting Washington in May, then President Suazo of Honduras was assured protection against "communist aggression."

ing Cerezo a "leftist." Although Carpio probably held the support of the military, it was the liberal Cerezo, 42, who emerged as the overwhelming victor. Upon inauguration, scheduled for January 1986, he would become Guatemala's first civilian president in 15 years.

The behavior of the military would be watched closely in the months following Cerezo's election, both in Guatemala itself and in Washington. According to some estimates, the nation suffers 40% unemployment and the worst distribution of income and land in all of Latin America. The new administration clearly will need to institute reforms, but rapid or radical change would jeopardize the support of the army. This risk would be particularly great if the government were to begin an investigation of the oppression of recent years or if it fails to suppress renewed insurgency.

In February the United Nations made its fifth investigation in two years of Guatemala's human rights record and concluded again that while some violations still were occurring, "strong improvements" had taken place and no secret detention centers had been found. Some critics branded the report a lie; even Guatemala's Supreme Court declared that 120,000 children had lost one or more parents since 1981. The politically outspoken Archbishop Próspero Penados del Barrio, who has received many death threats, concluded that the UN survey was insufficiently critical. He claimed that some 60 Indians had been killed by the army in the previous seven months.

No serious inroads were made on the foreign debt of more than $2 billion. Drastic legislation to promote austerity was passed in March, then repealed a few days later in the face of numerous strikes. General Mejía also rolled back a 50% bus fare increase because of student rioting. It seemed as if the administration intended to leave the difficult economic decisions—concerning foreign debt, 60% inflation, and continued heavy unemployment—to the next government. In September a teacher strike closed almost all the nation's public schools.

Although the United States still refused military funds for Guatemala, it did grant $73 million in economic aid in 1985, and the IDB lent $64 million for road construction. The total value of the nation's exports declined 25% in 1985, partly from a drop in world coffee and cotton prices.

Honduras. In 1985, Honduras faced an unusual crisis, partly constitutional in nature. In March, Congress voted to expel five of the country's nine supreme court justices because of alleged corruption, and it replaced them with men unacceptable to President Roberto Suazo Córdoba. The president responded by ordering the arrest of the five new appointees on charges

of treason. The chief justice was jailed, but the other four went into hiding. Congress censored President Suazo, who charged that the legislators were attempting a coup. In fact, many groups felt that Suazo had his own plans for controlling elections scheduled for later in the year; labor threatened a general strike if he made such an attempt. After two months of bitter debate, President Suazo agreed to a compromise. He dropped the treason charges, and Congress rescinded its efforts to change the court's personnel. The legislators also agreed to a new election law, whereby anyone wishing to run could do so as an independent.

This new law led to a somewhat bewildering election result on November 24. According to the law, the winner would be the candidate receiving the most votes in the party that got the most votes. Since his Liberal Party's total vote exceeded that of the National Party, José Azcona Hoyo considered himself elected. But National Party candidate Rafael Leonardo Callejas drew 200,000 more votes than Azcona and called himself the victor—as he would be under the constitution. The outcome thus pointed up an apparent conflict between the new election law and the constitution. The decision was left to a national electoral tribunal, which ruled in Azcona's favor.

A discouraging report on the state of the economy came from a prestigious Honduran bank. Unemployment was estimated to be 20%, with underemployment at more than double that figure. Foreign debt had grown 600% since the 1970s, in spite of vast assistance from the United States; in 1985 the debt amounted to half the gross domestic product. And a variety of factors probably would force a reassessment of Honduras' economic strategy. The nation's major exports—coffee, silver, and bananas—have suffered losses for several successive years. World coffee prices were down. The price of silver was less than half that in 1982, and in January the nation's largest mine laid off 120 workers to avoid a shutdown. The production cost of bananas in Honduras exceeds that of other nations; the two major growers (both American) sought export-tax reductions, while reducing their landholdings and turning production over to natives in order to concentrate on marketing.

In 1985 the United States provided Honduras with $135 million in economic assistance and $62 million in military aid; the IDB granted several million for agricultural production, and the Agency for International Development (AID) awarded $5 million to begin computerizing the election machinery.

The Nicaraguan civil war continued to exacerbate relations between Honduras and the United States. In February the Honduran government declared that the Nicaraguan "contras" were no longer welcome to train or take refuge on Honduran soil. The "contras," half the number of the Honduran army, were of much concern to local security. When the Reagan administration contended that the training was essential to U.S. policy in the region, Honduras agreed that the "contras" could stay if they behaved themselves and if the United States provided them more economic aid.

Honduras has wanted to formalize its close ties with the United States, and presidents Suazo and Reagan met in Washington in May to discuss this and other matters. No treaty resulted; the U.S. position was that Honduras has sufficient protection under the 1947 Rio Treaty as well as the charter of the OAS. The two nations will share responsibility for maintenance of the 14 bases the United States has built in Honduras, but American troops off base have been placed under the jurisdiction of the local courts. Again in 1985, the two nations held joint military maneuvers. Between February 11 and May 3, 4,000 U.S. troops took part in Big Pine III, a joint exercise conducted only 3 mi (5 km) from the Nicaraguan border. Another set of maneuvers was held on the north coast during April and May for three weeks, involving 7,000 Americans, the largest operation in Honduras so far.

Late in the year, former Honduran army chief of staff Gen. José Bueso Rosa was arrested in Miami on charges relating to a 1984 plot to kill President Suazo, to be financed by the sale of drugs. Eight others had been indicted in January on similar charges.

Nicaragua. José Daniel Ortega Saavedra (*see* BIOGRAPHY), the leader of the Sandinista junta, was inaugurated president of Nicaragua on Jan. 10, 1985. He became the nation's first elected president since the revolution in 1979. Ortega won a six-year term in the elections of November 1984, taking 63% of the vote. In his inaugural address, President Ortega announced that 40% of the budget would be devoted to defense and that the civil war had so far cost 3,000 lives and $254 million in property damage. After six years of revolution, Nicaragua, unlike Cuba, remained partly a pluralistic society, still politically open. For example, about one third of the seats in the National Assembly were held by opposition parties. In August, President Ortega assumed greater authority by creating an executive committee—which he heads—to carry out decisions of the directorate.

The Sandinistas faced as much opposition in 1985 as they did the year before. At least 12,000 guerrillas bore arms against the administration. Most of these "contras" were under the umbrella of the Nicaraguan Democratic Force, which received all of the Nicaragua aid provided by the U.S. Central Intelligence Agency (CIA). The Democratic Force operated out of Honduras and was closely tied to the U.S. military. It was composed largely of peasants with some reason to dislike the Sandinis-

The Sandinista regime in Nicaragua was supplied with helicopters and other materiel from the Soviet Union.

tas, but it also included—especially among its officers—former National Guardsmen. Its supreme commander was Col. Enrique Bermúdez, former President Somoza's last military attaché to the United States. Still functioning close to the Costa Rican frontier and independent of both the Democratic Force and the United States was the Revolutionary Democratic Alliance, under the leadership of Edén Pastora.

All of the conflict, of course, continued to impede the flow of the economy. Approximately half of the means of production was in government hands, largely because of the confiscation of Somoza property. The gross national product was estimated to be about $2.4 billion per year, unemployment about 20%, inflation about 100%, imports about $800 million, and financial aid from the Soviet Union about $400 million. Much of the private investment remains in the hands of such firms as Exxon, Texaco, and General Foods. These multinationals probably plan to stay in Nicaragua in spite of shortages and restrictions, because it would be hard to leave without losing everything. But major fruit multinationals already have gone out of the production business in favor of marketing only. In February the government launched an austerity program that ended food subsidies and froze government spending. The córdoba was devalued, and prices of basic foods rose as much as 100%.

Foreign-exchange reserves disappeared, and production of coffee, sugar, and cotton was the lowest since 1979. Nevertheless, in June, more than 130 banks (more than half of which are owned by Americans) agreed to restructure the debt to give Nicaragua easier terms. A trade embargo imposed by the United States in May seemed to have little effect, as other Western nations bought the commodities formerly consumed in the United States. Not a great deal of trade had been left to embargo, anyway.

Since the original state of emergency was declared in 1982, human rights violations had gradually eased. But in October 1985 the government suddenly broadened the state of emergency for a one-year period "to fight U.S. sabotage." Freedom of expression, strikes, public assembly, and movement within the country all were restricted. Prior censorship of the press and TV were imposed. Even the independent human rights commission was told to fall in line.

Church-state relations became no smoother and remained quite complex. Archbishop Miguel Obando y Bravo, who continued to attack the human rights position of the Sandinistas, became the nation's first cardinal.

Relations with the United States remained tense. In January, U.S. delegates walked out of World Court hearings when that body ruled that it had jurisdiction over a Nicaraguan complaint that the United States was trying to over-

throw the government. In three years, the CIA spent $80 million on aid to the "contras," but congressional attitudes clearly changed. It took President Reagan more than a year to get a bill from Congress authorizing $27 million more in rebel aid, and the money was restricted to non-military use. Hondurans also pressured the United States to aid the "contras" on their soil.

Panama. Just as in 1984, Panama's president in 1985 was forced to resign in favor of the vice-president. Nicolas Ardito Barletta, who had been handpicked by the army and elected president in May 1984, took office in October of that year. He served only until September 1985, however, resigning under pressure not only from the army, but from business and organized labor as well. First Vice-President Eric Arturo Delvalle, a business executive and graduate of Louisiana State University, replaced him. Why had the first democratically elected president in 16 years lasted such a short time? No one questioned Ardito Barletta's financial acumen, but many charged him with ineptness and lack of political leadership. Most of all, he had failed to make even a dent in Panama's many economic problems.

Much of Panama's debt could be traced to policies of the late Gen. Omar Torrijos Herrera, who dominated the nation in the 1970s. Torrijos had borrowed heavily to support the

After the military ousted his predecessor, Eric Arturo Delvalle became the president of Panama on September 28.

AP/Wide World

military, keep government employment high, and buy off his opponents, a tricky operation that worked for several years. By 1985, however, Panama's foreign debt of nearly $4 billion was among the world's highest on a per-capita basis; the interest payments alone exceeded one third of the nation's export earnings, and the availability of more credit had dried up. Inflation remained severe. In response, Ardito had pushed through austerity measures that received much adverse reaction and had to be repealed almost immediately. He failed in efforts to freeze government wages and reduce trade subsidies but made enemies trying to do so. Then in July, at the request of the IMF, he took aim at the nation's 22% unemployment rate by seeking changes in the labor code. A general strike, however, forced him to back down again.

President Ardito's tribulations seemed to cost him the support of Gen. Manuel Antonio Noriega, the commander of Panama's Defense Force and latest strongman. The public would not accept the austerity dictated by international lending agencies, and the archbishop protested against corruption in the administration. In September a guerrilla leader and famed opponent of General Noriega, Hugo Spadafora, was brutally murdered. Then, apparently as a warning, the United States suddenly suspended $5 million in aid. Panamanians are not accustomed to much political violence, and the murder of Spadafora greatly shocked the public. By that time it seemed as if only the banks supported Ardito Barletta. On September 28, General Noriega forced the president to resign from office.

The fact remained, however, that political repression in Panama is minor in comparison with that in most of the region. Moreover, the government succeeded in getting its international debt extended to periods of as long as 12 years; Panama relies heavily on the operations of more than 100 foreign banks located on its soil. In addition, Panama was to receive $40 million in economic aid and $10.6 million in military aid from the United States during 1985, and the IDB promised $20 million more to improve the nation's school system.

Although terrorism has been no great problem, the United States and Panama began to work together in antiterrorist training. In some ways, the United States has greater freedom of movement on Panama's terrain than it did in 1979, right after the Canal Treaties were signed. For example, U.S. paratroopers in 1985 conducted maneuvers within Panama. Nearly 10,000 American soldiers still remain to defend the Canal until the year 2000, when Panama takes complete charge. This is the only long-term U.S. combat force stationed in Latin America.

THOMAS L. KARNES
Arizona State University

CHEMISTRY

While U.S. public attention in 1985 focused on the hazards of some chemicals, research advances continued in several areas, including asymmetric synthesis and polymer chemistry.

Chemical Hazards. After the December 1984 release of toxic gas from a Union Carbide chemical plant in Bhopal, India, public concern rose over the potential hazards posed by chemical manufacturing plants. This concern was heightened when a reactor vessel at Union Carbide's plant in Institute, WV, erupted on August 11, releasing almost two tons of chemicals, some hazardous, into the environment. No one was killed in the second incident, but 135 persons were treated in hospitals.

In June a judge found three managers of a small Illinois silver recovery firm guilty of murder in the death, by cyanide poisoning, of a worker. The managers were found to have allowed "totally unsafe" working conditions to exist, leading to the worker's death. Some lawyers regarded the case as a legal landmark because it carried a murder, rather than a manslaughter, conviction; others saw conditions at the plant as being too extreme for the ruling to have widespread implications.

Certain gases in the earth's atmosphere can trap radiation coming from the surface and may, over time, cause a warming of the planet's climate—the "greenhouse effect." Attention has long focused on the role of carbon dioxide, produced by burning fossil fuels, in this process, but in June 1985 a group of scientists warned that other gases, although present only in trace amounts, may also contribute significantly. These gases, including methane, nitrous oxide, ozone, and several chlorofluorocarbons, are much more effective at trapping infrared radiation from the earth's surface than is the more abundant carbon dioxide. Chlorofluorocarbons, in particular, are very stable and may build up atmospheric concentrations over long periods of time.

Asymmetric Synthesis. Many important chemicals, including a number of drugs, exist in two forms, essentially right-handed and left-handed versions of the same molecule. Often one form is biologically active and the other inactive, or possibly harmful. Most laboratory syntheses yield both forms in equal amounts, and chemists have long searched for ways to produce the desirable form without also producing its undesirable sibling. In 1985 synthetic chemists continued to assemble an arsenal of techniques to achieve this goal.

The previous year, researchers at Purdue University reported development of chiral (asymmetric, or "optically active") boranes for use in asymmetric synthesis. In 1985 chemists at Massachusetts Institute of Technology employed chiral boranes to produce chiral alcohols from olefins in high yields. Naturally oc-curring chiral compounds also can be used as starting materials to produce asymmetric products, and Stephen Hanessian of the University of Montreal described a computer program to design synthetic routes employing such chiral starting materials. In an alternative strategy, several groups of workers reported the use of asymmetric, metal-containing catalysts to produce chiral products. Taking advantage of the selectivity of nature's own catalysts, George Whitesides of Harvard University reported synthetic studies in which he utilized enzymes to obtain relatively high yields of optically pure products. In another approach, William Pirkle of the University of Illinois developed high-performance liquid chromatographic (HPLC) columns capable of separating chiral forms. The HPLC columns contain selected chiral compounds, so that one asymmetric form of a compound interacts more strongly with the column and thus takes longer to pass through than the other form.

Polymers. Polymers are large molecules formed by linking together smaller subunits. Modern plastics and synthetic textiles such as nylon and polyester are examples of polymers. At a New York meeting in May to honor polymer pioneer Herman Mark on his 90th birthday, polymer chemists assessed recent progress in the field. Charles Overberger of the University of Michigan described studies of polymer chains with nitrogenous bases, such as thymine and adenine, attached to them. The bases are components of the genetic material DNA. Some of the polymers display activity against viruses and others against tumors.

Other Developments. Chemists continued to search for better artificial sweeteners, sometimes in odd places. A research team from the University of Illinois, Chicago, uncovered a report written by a Spanish naturalist in the 16th century describing plants found in Aztec Mexico. Based on a description in the report, the Chicago workers were led to a specific plant from which they were able to isolate an intensely sweet substance, dubbed hernandulcin, said to be 1,000 times as sweet as sucrose. The team also synthesized the substance in the laboratory. Also, in May, a chemist at Research Triangle Institute in North Carolina reported the synthesis of an artificial sweetener similar to aspartame but having greater stability in liquids, making it more suitable for use in soft drinks.

Attempts to develop useful organic superconducting materials also continued. Scientists at Argonne National Laboratory in Illinois reported that a new organosulfur-gold-iodide compound is superconducting (permits current flow without resistance) at normal pressures at 5 degrees above absolute zero, the highest temperature thus far recorded for an organic compound to become superconducting.

PAUL G. SEYBOLD, *Wright State University*

CHESS

On Nov. 9, 1985, Gary Kasparov of the Soviet Union ended the ten-year reign of countryman Anatoly Karpov as the world champion of chess. At the Tchaikovsky Concert Hall in Moscow, Kasparov, playing black, forced Karpov to resign after 43 moves of the 24th game of their title match. Under the series format, a game victory was worth one point, and a draw would earn each player half a point. There would be a maximum of 24 games, and the first player to win six games or reach 12½ points would be the champion. Kasparov's final-game victory gave him 13 points. At age 22, the grandmaster from Azerbaijan became the youngest world chess champion in the history of the game.

The showdown had actually begun in September 1984, when the two Soviets began their first match for the championship. According to the original format, the first player to win six games would be declared the victor. By February 1985, after a staggering 48 games, neither player had won the required six. Karpov had won five and Kasparov three, with 40 draws. The International Chess Federation halted the match, saying the players were exhausted. Kasparov was incensed. Although he was trailing at the time, the young challenger had won two games in a row and felt that he had the champion on the run.

That set the stage for the rematch, which began on Sept. 2, 1985. Kasparov won Games 1, 11, 16, 19, and 24. Karpov managed victories in Games 4, 5, and 22. The rest were draws.

CHICAGO

Chicago's plans for a 1992 World's Fair died in August when political leaders could not agree on funding for the fair. Illinois House Speaker Michael Madigan said he could no longer support state funding on a fair that could lose money. Gov. James R. Thompson, a principal backer of the fair, conceded that without Madigan's support the fair was dead. The fair was to celebrate the 500th anniversary of the founding of America.

However, from the start there were disagreements over how to fund the fair, where to locate it in Chicago, and whether it would be a financial success. Losses at recent world's fairs in Knoxville, TN, and New Orleans, LA, also worked against the Chicago plan. Representative Madigan said he was convinced that such expositions have become obsolete. And Governor Thompson said it would be "foolish" to pursue the fair further.

Corruption. A 12-year prison sentence was given Judge Richard LeFevour after he was convicted of 59 counts of mail fraud, racketeering, and income-tax evasion. LeFevour, former chief judge of the Traffic Court and presiding judge of the First Municipal District, was the highest-ranking judge convicted of judicial corruption in the state's history. Two other judges have been sentenced to prison in the federal Operation Graylord investigation of corruption in the Cook County courts.

Politics. Former Mayor Jane Byrne announced that she would try for a political comeback and oppose Mayor Harold Washington in his 1987 reelection bid. Byrne said she wants to end the divisiveness in city government between the black mayor and the white majority bloc in the City Council. She also said that she would use fees from her recent public speeches and from television commercials in which she appears to support her election campaign.

Accidents. Seven young people, on their way to a Bruce Springsteen rock concert, died in August when their car was rammed by a Chicago Transit Authority bus. The bus driver, who was black, initially was charged with reckless homicide. Disagreement over who was at

In Chicago's Loop, the State of Illinois Center, a $100 million state government building and retail complex, was dedicated during the summer. The futuristic-style building, designed by Helmut Jahn, has become a mecca for Chicagoans and tourists alike.

State of Illinois Center

fault, and charges that racism was involved, forced the state's attorney, Richard M. Daley, to drop the charges against the driver.

Education. Chicago teachers were on strike for two days in September after failing to reach a contract agreement with the Chicago Board of Education. A contract was reached after Governor Thompson intervened in the negotiations. Twenty-eight thousand teachers were given a 6% raise in 1985 and were promised an additional 3% in 1986 if Thompson can get $50 million more in state aid for the school system.

ROBERT ENSTAD, *"Chicago Tribune"*

CHILDREN

The faces of missing children appeared everywhere in 1985—on milk cartons, buses, shopping bags, federal mail, and television—in a nationwide publicity campaign aimed at finding the thousands of U.S. children who vanish each year.

Various groups have estimated that from 500 to 20,000 U.S. children are abducted each year by strangers and from 25,000 to 750,000 by noncustodial parents. The 1985 publicity blitz, however, met with some success in finding these children. Some 300 companies and agencies helped distribute and display the photos, and the U.S. Congress passed a bill requiring a percentage of federal mail to carry them. Also, a toll-free number was available to call the National Center for Missing and Exploited Children, founded in 1984. In its first year of operation, the center succeeded in locating more than 1,600 children; in early 1985, as the photos became more widespread, the center reported a tripling of its success rate. Following the April television broadcast of the documentary *Missing: Have You Seen This Person?*, which included an appeal from President Reagan, the center was deluged with calls.

A second goal of the publicity campaign was to increase public awareness of the problem and to make parents more alert to danger. With similar goals, video stores in several areas of the country offered to make free tapes of children, for police use should the child be lost. And a number of video, slide, and film presentations were distributed to schools to teach children how to avoid abduction.

Children in Court. Reacting to increasing reports of child abuse, many states began to revamp laws governing such cases and to ease restrictions on child testimony. By early 1985 some 22 states had abolished the presumption that young witnesses are incompetent; 14 allowed young children to testify through videotape, thereby avoiding the stress of courtroom appearances; and 12 permitted "hearsay" testimony from adults about a child's report of abuse. While many people welcomed the changes, others contended that the new laws infringe on the right of a defendant to confront his or her accuser and make it difficult to separate spurious from fact-based charges.

Day Care. With more than half of U.S. mothers of children under six in the work force, employers have begun to help in the search for adequate day care. In 1985 some 2,000 corporations—three times the 1982 number—were providing some kind of day-care assistance. The solutions ranged from centers run by the company, with the firm and the parents sharing the cost, to cash benefits paid to workers to help defray child care costs. A few companies even offered home nursing for sick children. In some cases, local governments help pick up the tab, and three bills aimed at fostering government-business cooperation and improving the quality of day care were introduced in Congress.

Poverty. Poverty among children has continued to increase. Figures for 1983 showed that more than 22% of U.S. children were living in poor families. Among the reasons cited for the high rate were increases in the number of households headed by women and in the number of births to unmarried women.

Collecting child support payments has continued to be a problem for many of these parents. In 1985 many states passed new laws designed to comply with a federal statute adopted the year before. Under these laws, courts can take strong measures to collect back payments, including withholding pay and placing liens on property. Meanwhile, one study put the cost of raising a child from birth to age 17 at more than $230,000.

Health. A report issued by the U.S. Public Health Service showed that infant mortality rates are declining more slowly than in the past, a trend the service said is "cause for concern." Overall, the 1984 death rate for children under one year old was 10.6 per thousand live births, down from 10.9 in 1983. For infants older than four weeks, the rate actually increased slightly, from 3.6 to 3.8. Nine states—Florida, Georgia, Illinois, Kentucky, Michigan, Missouri, Ohio, South Carolina, and Wisconsin—and the District of Columbia had higher than average rates. Rates also were significantly higher for black infants.

Other studies pointed to sliding physical fitness among older children. One showed that children in grades 5 through 12 were fatter than their counterparts 20 years earlier; others found that performance on physical fitness tests had decreased over the previous decade. Surprising numbers of children showed risk factors for heart disease. Blame for the situation was assigned to several factors: school physical education programs, many of which have been cut back to fit tight budgets; the popularity of junk food; and long hours spent in front of the television set.

ELAINE PASCOE, *Free-lance Writer*

CHILE

In an effort to contain a scandal over police involvement in the killing of three prominent Communist professionals, the president, Gen. Augusto Pinochet Ugarte, suddenly replaced the head of the Carabinero police on August 2. Eleven opposition parties, previously divided on how to oust Pinochet, agreed on August 26 to a pact developed by Santiago Archbishop Juan Francisco Cardinal Fresno that called for a "Transition to Full Democracy."

Carabineros Reorganized. Gen. Rodolfo Stange Oelckers, 59, replaced Gen. César Mendoza, 66, a loyal Pinochet colleague, as head of the powerful 30,000-man force and as a member of Chile's ruling junta. Mendoza—who had repeatedly denied police involvement in the March 30 kidnapping and killing of Manuel Guerrero, José Manuel Parada, and Santiago Nattino Allende—resigned. He did so after Judge José Canovas Robles, a civilian, announced a four-month investigation that produced "clear evidence" that 14 Carabineros—including two colonels—were involved. The victims, with their throats slit, were dumped on a Santiago airport road.

August 26 Pact. Twenty-two politicians from 11 opposition parties called together by the 72-year-old archbishop agreed on direct presidential elections, an end to the state of emergency that replaced a state of siege June 17, election of a congress to reform the 1980 constitution, and guarantees for private property in a mixed economy. The declaration of principles represented the second effort by the archbishop to achieve national consensus on ending the authoritarian rule of Pinochet. Subsequently, Federico Willoughby, head of the National Action Movement (MAN) and former Pinochet press secretary; Gen. Gustavo Leigh Guzman, a former Air Force commander and junta member; and four other top-ranking retired military officers also signed the pact.

In August and September, Pinochet said he was determined to stay in power until 1989 and vetoed talks with the opposition.

CHILE • Information Highlights

Official Name: Republic of Chile.
Location: Southwestern coast of South America.
Area: 292,257 sq mi (756 945 km²).
Population (mid-1985 est.): 12,000,000.
Chief Cities (June 30, 1984): Santiago, the capital, 4,225,229 (including suburbs); Viña del Mar, 307,308.
Government: *Head of state and government,* Gen. Augusto Pinochet Ugarte, president (took power Sept. 1973). *Legislature*—Congress (dissolved Sept. 1973).
Monetary Unit: Peso (176.89 pesos equal U.S.$1, official rate Nov. 8, 1985).
Economic Index (Santiago, 1984): *Consumer Prices* (1980 = 100), all items, 200.7; food, 180.2.
Foreign Trade (1984 U.S.$): *Imports,* $3,191,000,000; *exports,* $3,657,000,000.

Economic Growth Slows. Gross domestic product (GDP) was expected to improve only 2–3% in 1985, down from the 6.3% registered in 1984. Chile was expected to end 1985 with a trade surplus of about $381 million, compared with a surplus of $356 million in December 1984 and $1 billion in December 1982. Exports were expected to rise only about 5% above 1984's $3.65 billion but were heavily dependent on copper prices, which remained stagnant. Mining Minister Samuel Lira Ovalle announced Rio Alex, a Canadian firm, would start a new Cerro Colorado project to produce 55,000–60,000 metric tons of copper annually. Total national production was expected to remain at about 1.29 million metric tons, about the same as 1983–84. A record 50 million cases of fresh fruit were exported from January through April despite severe earthquake damage to port facilities on March 3 and 25. Fish and fishmeal production grew by 12.3% in 1984 to about 4.6 million metric tons.

New Finance Minister Hernan Büchi continued a series of minidevaluations of the peso after taking office in a February cabinet reshuffle. The National Statistical Institute (INE) said in October that unemployment was 18.1% in urban areas, up from 16.9% in February. Gemines, a private firm, reported real wages fell the first half of 1985 to the lowest level in five years. Major commercial banks agreed to loan Chile $1.085 billion in late June to roll over portions of its $20 billion foreign debt as part of stretching out $6 billion in debts due between 1985 and 1987.

Foreign Policy. Assistant Secretary of State Langhorne Motley received few assurances from Pinochet about a return to democracy during a February 16 visit to Santiago. The United States abstained on proposed World Bank and Inter-American Development Bank loans to Chile in February and March as a consequence. Nevertheless, despite considerable domestic opposition, Chile agreed in July to let the United States use the Mataveri Airport on Easter Island for emergency landings of interplanetary space shuttles.

While Pinochet and Foreign Minister Jaime del Valle supported the call by Peruvian President Alan García to reduce military purchases by Andean countries, Defense Minister Admiral Patrício Carvajal acknowledged August 20 that "arms limitation agreements were not impossible" even if Chile were behind Peru from a military viewpoint. "Our main concern should be to prevent the production of nuclear weapons in Latin America."

Foreign Minister Del Valle signed a peace treaty with Argentine representatives in the Vatican on May 2, ending a bitter territorial dispute over the Beagle Channel at the tip of South America. Pinochet had signed ratification instruments on April 12.

NEALE J. PEARSON, *Texas Tech University*

© Peter Charlesworth, Gamma-Liaison

An April concert in Beijing by the British rock group Wham! gave further notice of the "opening up" of China.

CHINA, PEOPLE'S REPUBLIC OF

The year 1985 in the People's Republic of China (PRC) was marked by major personnel changes in the leading bodies of the Communist Party, aimed at ensuring an orderly succession when the current generation of leaders retires from office. The economy experienced a number of problems, many of them attributable to the implementation of the economic reforms announced in October 1984. Despite these problems, China's leaders reasserted their commitment to their "open door" policy of developing economic and cultural ties to Western countries.

Politics. Although Deng Xiaoping, 81, does not hold leadership positions in the party or government, he remained in 1985 the most important political figure in China. One of his principal goals has been to ensure the continuity of the policies he has implemented in China since he regained power in 1977. To accomplish this, he initiated a streamlining of the government in 1982 and a "consolidation" of the party in 1983. These reforms are designed to reduce the size of government and party organizations and to replace elderly and incompetent leaders with younger and better-educated individuals.

An important step in this process took place in September 1985, when the Fourth Plenum of the Twelfth Central Committee met to receive the resignations of more than 100 senior party figures. Ten members of the 24-member Politburo, 64 of the more than 340-member Central Committee, 36 of the 162 members of the Ad-

visory Commission, and 30 of the 129 members of the party's Discipline Commission all resigned. Most prominent among those submitting their resignations were Marshal Ye Jianying and Deng Yingchao, the widow of Zhou Enlai. In addition to Marshal Ye, more than two dozen military officers left leading positions in the party.

At a special party conference September 18–23, 1,000 delegates elected replacements for those who had resigned their offices. They also approved the Seventh Five-Year Plan, covering economic development during the period 1986–1990.

The Fifth Plenum of the reorganized Central Committee met September 24 and elected a Politburo and its Standing Committee. The Politburo was reduced from 24 to 20 members. Five of the members were new: Hu Qili, 56, reputed to be a potential successor to Party General Secretary Hu Yaobang; Deputy Premier Li Peng, 57, seen as the successor to Premier Zhao Ziyang; Deputy Premier Tian Jiyun, 56; Foreign Minister Wu Xueqian, 64; and Qiao Shi, 61. These appointments marked the culmination of an effort announced in late April to select a "third echelon" of young, technically capable individuals who would be groomed as successors to the "second echelon" now in power. During the course of the year, it was announced that more than 900,000 officials had resigned or retired since reform of the government and party were begun three years earlier. This figure amounts to a little less than 5% of the 22 million state and party cadres in the People's Republic.

The special party conference closed with a pair of speeches, one by Deng Xiaoping, the other by Chen Yun, a senior economist. Observers were startled by Chen's sharp criticisms of what he sees as an excessive use of monetary incentives and market forces in the current reforms.

Earlier in the year, Deng responded to criticisms like those of Chen Yun. Speaking to participants in the National Conference on Science and Technology in March, he said, "We must let our people, including our children, know that we are persisting in socialism and communism, and that all of the policies we adopt are for the development of socialism and the realization of communism. We cannot let our young people become captives of capitalist thinking. That is absolutely impermissible."

The reduction in military representation in the party's ruling circle was presaged by events earlier in the year: in April it was announced that 1 million members of the People's Liberation Army would be demobilized during 1985 and 1986—a 25% cut in troop strength. This cut would reduce the army to its size in the mid-1970s, prior to the buildup occasioned by China's deteriorating relations with Vietnam. At the same time, 47,000 officers (about 10% of the officer corps) were retired from service, and China's 11 military regions were consolidated into seven.

In January, Gen. John Vessey, then chairman of the U.S. Joint Chiefs of Staff, visited China to explore arms sales and military cooperation with Chinese military leaders. Later in the year, two arms sales contracts were signed, one for helicopters and the other for gas turbine engines for Chinese naval vessels.

Economy. The process of reform was underscored by an official report in June that the dismantling of China's 56,000 "people's communes," begun in late 1983, had been completed. But 1985 also saw the introduction of measures to control such problems as corruption and escalating wages and prices.

The first year following the inauguration of urban economic reforms on a national scale was a promising but problematic one. Industrial growth for the first half of 1985 reached 23%, far in excess of the planned 8% annual growth rate. Capital construction was up 44% during the same period, against an annual target of 1.1%. This growth far outstripped the 11% growth in energy production, exacerbating an already serious energy shortage. As output soared, quality control suffered in many instances, and enterprises found it difficult to market their products.

The planned move from a pricing system fixed by the state to one reflecting market conditions was begun in 1985. Factories felt the effect of these moves as prices of raw materials and energy were raised, while the price of finished goods remained regulated to protect urban consumers against the effects of inflation. Despite measures to increase enterprise efficiency, it was announced in June that 15% of urban enterprises were losing money. As a result, some smaller factories were forced to close down.

Meanwhile, food prices in urban markets were raised in May. To help mitigate the effect on their real income, urban residents were paid a monthly subsidy of 7.5 yuan (about $2.65). Rent increases were being put into effect to raise urban housing costs from about 4% of income to 6–10%. (Despite these increases, Chinese urban residents still enjoy very nominal rents thanks to state subsidies. The average urban family in the United States, for example, spends more than 25% of its income on housing.)

Although overall foreign trade was up during the year, exports during the first two quarters were down 2.3% from the same period in 1984, while imports were up 61%. This situation resulted in a trade deficit of some $6 billion for the first half of the year, compared with $1.2 billion for all of 1984. By midyear, foreign-exchange reserves were down from $17.3 billion in September 1984 to approximately $10 billion.

In Shenzen, a "special economic zone," work continued on a 54-story trade center, to be China's tallest building.
© Catherine Leroy, "Time"

Confronted with these disappointing figures, Chinese planners called for a slowdown in the signing of joint-venture contracts in the special economic zones and 14 coastal cities. Of the latter, only Dalian, Shanghai, Tianjin, and Guangzhou were to be permitted to develop at their earlier rate. In midsummer Deng Xiaoping spoke of Shenzhen as an experiment, the outcome of which is uncertain. His waning enthusiasm was attributed to the fact that too high a proportion of the investment in the zone has been domestic, too much of its output has been in the area of tourism and commerce, and too little development has taken place in high-tech industry.

Chinese leaders took pains to assure foreign investors that the cautious approach did not mean that the "open door" policy was being questioned. Nor were economic reforms being terminated. Indeed, plans to extend the reforms were announced in September: shares in state-owned enterprises would be sold to the workers in those enterprises. The workers would be permitted to own up to 49% of the enterprises in which they work, while the state would retain 51% ownership. Plans also were being made to permit mergers and takeovers of enterprises in the state sector.

The Seventh Five-Year Plan, announced at the Party Conference in September, places emphasis on the development of energy, transport, and telecommunications. Whereas the 1981–1985 plan targeted a 4–5% annual growth rate, the new plan for 1986–1990 calls for an overall annual rate of growth of 7–8% in agriculture and industry, and 10–12% in foreign trade. Observers predicted that China would increase its foreign borrowing from the current level of about $5 billion to a new level of $25 billion during the next five years.

Automobiles accounted for a growing share of imports. It is estimated that there are currently about three million vehicles on Chinese roads, of which 170,000 are passenger cars. Chinese automotive plants turned out 363,000 vehicles in 1985, but only about 5,000 were passenger cars. Some 100,000 vehicles were imported in 1984. That number was expected to reach 600,000 in 1985 and remain at least at that level through 1990. Prices for imported vehicles are fixed at a very high level. A Toyota Crown Super Deluxe, for example, sold in 1985 for the equivalent of $41,000.

CAAC, China's national airline, announced that it will give up national operations in mid-1987. It will retain a regulatory role in air traffic and air safety and will continue to negotiate major contracts for the purchase of aircraft. It will be replaced by one international and three regional carriers. Air China will fly international routes. The three regional companies will be China Eastern, based in Shanghai; China Southern in Guangzhou; and China Southwestern in Sichuan. It was anticipated that other regional carriers would be formed.

International Relations. The details of the constitution under which Hong Kong will be governed after 1997 are to be decided on by a 59-member drafting committee, which met for the first time in early July 1985. The committee is made up of 23 Hong Kong members and 36 members from the PRC. Critics of this process in Hong Kong argue that local residents should compose the majority of the drafting committee. The position of the government in Beijing (Peking), however, is that, since Hong Kong citizens are themselves Chinese people, there is no distinct set of interests that requires representation.

A further round of talks between China and the Soviet Union took place in April, and Deputy Premier Yao Yilin returned Soviet Vice-Premier Ivan Arkipov's December 1984 visit to China with a trip to the USSR in July. A five-year trade agreement was signed during Yao's visit, calling for an increase in two-way trade from the current level of $1.6 billion per year

Premier Zhao Ziyang's visit to Europe in June included a stop in Great Britain to promote economic cooperation.

© G. DeKeerle, Gamma-Liaison

China's economic reforms, which allow limited free enterprise, have led to impressive growth but created some new problems.

© Alon Reininger, Contact

to a new level of $6.4 billion by 1990. The Soviet Union agreed to assist China in building seven new factories and modernizing 17 others built with Soviet assistance during the 1950s. Academic and cultural exchanges will increase from 60 participants to 400.

In July, Chinese President Li Xiannian returned the 1984 visit to China by U.S. President Ronald Reagan, holding talks just after Reagan was released from the hospital following surgery. Questions concerning Chinese compliance with nuclear nonproliferation provisions were resolved in time for a nuclear agreement to be signed during Li's visit. The U.S. Congress had 90 days after the agreement was signed to register its disapproval. Some of those opposed to the agreement were favorably impressed when China announced at a September meeting of the International Atomic Energy Commission in Vienna that it would allow on-site inspection of certain nuclear facilities. Congress later approved the agreement and, following signature of the resolution by President Reagan, it went into effect in December.

President Li took the occasion of his visit to denounce U.S. congressional statements on China's birth control program. The first of these statements came in the form of a $10 million reduction in the U.S. contributions to the United Nations Fund for Population Activities. The reduction was based on the view of some in Congress that U.S. funds are being used to support forced abortion and forced sterilization in China. The second, an amendment to the foreign aid appropriations bill, denounced the Chinese for using what were seen as coercive measures to enforce its "one child per family" policy of population control. President Li said that these statements constituted an unwarranted interference in China's domestic affairs.

He dismissed them as "fabrications and distortions."

China and the United States exchanged new ambassadors in 1985: Han Xu became the new Chinese representative in Washington, and Winston Lord, the president of the Council on Foreign Relations, took up the post of U.S. ambassador in Beijing. Senate confirmation of Lord's appointment was held up for several months. Once again the issue was China's birth control program: Sen. Jesse Helms (R-NC) refused to approve the appointment until he received assurances on Lord's and the Reagan administration's positions.

Relations with South Korea were strained by an incident in March involving a Chinese torpedo boat on maneuvers in the Yellow Sea. Two of the boat's crew mutinied, and the boat drifted into South Korean waters after running out of gas. Chinese military ships pursued the vessel but were turned back by South Korean warplanes and ships. Seoul held the crew for five days to determine whether the mutineers were trying to defect to Taiwan. The boat and crew were returned to China.

Society. At a conference of the Chinese Writers' Association in January, members called for greater freedom of expression in literature. Hu Qili, considered by many to be a successor to Party General Secretary Hu Yaobang, spoke at the forum. Literary creation, he said, must be free of political constraints.

In May a 600-delegate conference was convened in Beijing to consider a party program for education reform. The most important problem addressed by the program was that of illiteracy. The 1982 census revealed that one third of the adult population of China is illiterate. In addition, primary and secondary schooling is far from universally available to Chinese

children. Finally, academic secondary school graduates are too numerous to be accommodated in universities and professional schools and are ill-trained to join the job force.

The reform program calls for the universalization of nine years of education in all but the least-developed sections of China by 1995. Citing the need for middle-level technicians in China's developing industrial sector, it seeks to achieve a ratio of one technical high school for every academic high school. The current ratio is 1:6. Finally, the program calls for greater autonomy for China's universities in finance, hiring and promoting of faculty, and recruitment and placement of students. One of the most immediate effects of the reform program was the replacement of the Ministry of Education with a new State Education Commission that includes economic planners among its membership.

Three demonstrations took place in Beijing during the year. In late April, several hundred people from Shaanxi carried out a sit-in demonstration demanding that they be permitted to resume urban residency; they had been sent to the countryside during the Cultural Revolution. Although they were persuaded to end the demonstration and return to the countryside, the government did issue a circular one week later authorizing Beijing enterprises to hire certain categories of individuals from the group represented by the protesters.

A month later a soccer match in which the Chinese team was defeated by a team from Hong Kong ended in rioting. Foreigners, particularly those who were or appeared to be Hong Kong Chinese, were the targets of the rioters. Some 5,000 young people were involved in the riots, of whom 127 were arrested. Five were convicted of hooliganism and sent to prison.

In September, about 1,000 young people marched in an anti-Japanese demonstration

---

CHINA • Information Highlights

Official Name: People's Republic of China.
Location: Central-eastern Asia.
Area: 3,706,564 sq mi (9 600 000 km²).
Population (mid-1985 est.): 1,042,000,000.
Chief Cities (1982 census): Beijing (Peking), the capital, 9,230,687; Shanghai, 11,859,748; Tianjin, 7,764,141.
Government: *Head of state,* Li Xiannian, president (took office June 1983). *Heads of government,* Zhao Ziyang, premier (took office Sept. 1980); Deng Xiaoping, chairman, Central Military Commission. *Legislature* (unicameral)—National People's Congress.
Monetary Unit: Yuan (2.921 yuan equal U.S.$1, August 1985).
Gross National Product (1984 est.): $309,000,-000,000.
Foreign Trade (1984 U.S.$): *Imports,* $25,495,-000,000; *exports,* $24,278,000,000.

---

marking the anniversary of the "Mukden Incident," which preceded Japanese occupation of southern Manchuria in 1931. Anti-Japanese sentiments were fanned by the commemoration in China and Japan of the 40th anniversary of the end of World War II.

Richard Ondrick, an American businessman, was arrested in Harbin in April. He was charged with the "unintentional crime" of setting a hotel fire that killed his partner, five North Korean scientists, and four hotel employees. The Chinese authorities accused Ondrick of falling asleep while smoking in bed. After being held in custody for four months, he was tried in August, fined, and sentenced to an 18-month prison term. While Chinese authorities attempted to make the trial a model of China's new legal system, they experienced conflicting pressures from the American and the North Korean governments. Ondrick was released November 28.

See also HONG KONG; TAIWAN.

JOHN BRYAN STARR
Yale-China Association

The big news in Beijing politics was the mass resignation of elderly party and government officials and their replacement with younger and better-educated individuals.

New York Mayor Ed Koch (left) and Los Angeles Mayor Tom Bradley—both of whom won re-election in 1985—promised to "rock the boat" against the Reagan tax proposal. The two mayors and other urban officials opposed the plan's efforts to limit the issuance of tax-exempt municipal bonds and to eliminate the deductibility of state and local taxes on federal returns.

CITIES AND URBAN AFFAIRS

The year 1985 was one of new challenges and responses as U.S. cities, suburbs, and metropolitan areas continued to adjust to President Ronald Reagan's "New Federalism" and a shifting economy, anticipated the impacts of proposed federal tax revisions in Congress, were stunned by restrictive Supreme Court decisions, and faced the challenges of a growing urban underclass.

Economic Pressure. In addition to the ongoing struggle to sustain economic viability in the face of declining federal grant programs, U.S. urban areas were faced with several new economic threats stemming from proposed tax revisions. Most notable were efforts to limit the issuance of tax-exempt bonds by municipalities, which would raise an estimated $5 billion for the debt-conscious Treasury Department, and a bitterly contested proposal to eliminate the deductibility of state and local taxes on federal returns. Local officials were fearful that the loss of deductibility would lead to an outbreak of tax revolts in local jurisdictions with high taxes. Deductibility is worth about $36 billion annually, about one fifth of all federal direct aid to cities. High-tax communities worried that businesses will flee to lower tax jurisdictions, making economic development that much more difficult.

One policy response in a growing number of communities has been to tap booming downtown commercial property development through "linkage" and "impact" fees. In such cities as San Francisco and Boston, each with strong downtown real-estate markets, fees are exacted from developers in exchange for project approval and are used to add low- and moderate-income housing, transportation, and recreation facilities. Such proposals have been rejected in New York, Seattle, and Oakland but were under active consideration in Chicago. In suburban communities, impact fees deemed appropriate for the infrastructure necessary to accommodate physical growth are being charged to developers.

Legal Pressure. In a landmark decision early in the year, *Garcia v. San Antonio Metropolitan Transit Authority,* the U.S. Supreme Court strengthened the power of the federal government to regulate state and local activities. The justices ruled that federal minimum wage and hour standards (established by the Fair Labor Standards Act) apply to the nation's 13 million state and local government employees. Whereas the usual practice had been to provide compensatory time for employees who work overtime in order to lighten the load on municipal budgets, *Garcia* requires that overtime be paid at the rate of time and one-half. It places an extremely heavy financial burden on state and local governments, which must find additional resources to pay police officers, firefighters, transit workers, and others who, of necessity, work in multiple shifts.

On a second legal front, U.S. cities large and small were being assaulted by a growing barrage of tort liability suits, which tripled in number over a five-year period. Since the 1960s, local communities have become less immune to civil litigation as the result of a series of federal and state legal decisions and statutes. Local officials are becoming more aware of the growing financial threat that civil suits pose and of the difficulty of protecting against them. Accidents linked to potholes, disease caused by city water systems, property values undermined by rezoning, damage caused by slipshod inspections, and errors in employment practices, among others, have the potential for litigation and dollar awards to plaintiffs sufficient to make even a large city uncomfortable. The bill in New York City for liability judgments quintupled in six years, and the per capita cost in a small town can exceed $500.

Social Pressure. Despite signs of economic resurgence in sections of many, if not most,

181

cities around the United States, attention was being focused increasingly on a new class of people who have taken root there. This class does not share the traditional values of work, money, education, home, and family; it is far removed from the mainstream of American life. This is not the lower class, which in one form or another has always been with us, but the *underclass,* the poorest of the poor. As many as 5 million persons populate the underclass, and the number is growing. The urban underclass appears to be permanent and self-perpetuating, with little progress between generations. It lives in a world of fear, where violence is often self-inflicted, living conditions compare unfavorably with some Third World nations, and economics is unrelated to the everyday world of commerce and industry.

One of the visible signs of the underclass is the increasing number of homeless persons. The figures vary between 300,000 to 3 million on any given night, with less than 100,000 shelter beds available. The homeless must compete for social services with battered women and runaway children, who tend to get priority. The demographics of the homeless population are changing: the new homeless are younger (average age, 34), with a greater percentage of minorities (44%), families with children (21%), and single women (13%). (*See also* SOCIAL WELFARE.)

Despite the economic opportunities and cultural diversity afforded only in cities and large urban areas, it was not altogether surprising that a 1985 Gallup Poll once again indicated that, given an option, almost half the U.S. population would live in places with less than 10,000 people, and only 7% would choose a city with more than 1 million inhabitants. Of those who prefer urban areas, two thirds would choose the suburbs over the central city.

LOUIS H. MASOTTI
Northwestern University

COINS AND COIN COLLECTING

Big news for collectors of U.S. coins in 1985 was the passage of legislation authorizing the minting and sale of commemoratives honoring the 1986 centennial of the Statue of Liberty. On July 9, 1985, President Reagan signed into law the Statue of Liberty/Ellis Island Commemorative Coin Act, allowing for production of gold five-dollar, silver one-dollar, and copper-nickel half-dollar issues. A portion of the proceeds from the sale of those commemoratives would be earmarked for restoration of the Statue of Liberty National Monument.

As stipulated by the authorizing law, the $5 coin commemorates the 100th anniversary of the Statue of Liberty; the $1 piece symbolizes the use of Ellis Island as a gateway for immigrants; and the half-dollar honors immigrants'

OBVERSE　　　　　REVERSE

Courtesy, Krause Publications, Inc.

The 1986 Statue of Liberty $5 Coin

contributions to America. First released in November 1985, the coins will be "minted to demand" through December 1986, after which they no longer will be produced. The legislation also authorized production of the United States' first silver bullion coin, the Liberty Coin, a one-ounce, .999 fine, legal-tender piece carrying a nominal face value of $1. The first of its kind ever issued in the United States, the coin is intended primarily for investment purposes. So as not to compete with the sale of Statue of Liberty commemoratives, bullion coins will not be distributed until after Sept. 1, 1986.

In other Mint activity, hopes for a return to the traditional 95% copper cent were dashed in midyear when officials estimated the coin's production costs at 97 cents per hundred. Though the cost of producing copper-plated zinc cents has risen almost 25% since 1983, they remain the more economical alternative, representing a savings of 23 cents per hundred over the traditional copper coin.

Olympic Issues. The Royal Canadian Mint officially launched its own Olympic coin program on September 16 to commemorate the 1988 Winter Games in Calgary, Alta. Marketed under the slogan "The Pursuit of Excellence," the first two of ten .925 sterling silver proof $20 pieces were released, one depicting the sport of downhill skiing and the other featuring speed skating. The remaining coins will be released two at a time at six-month intervals and will portray other Olympic sports. Revenues from the sale of the coins will help support Canada's Olympic athletes and offset the costs of Olympic construction.

Other News. Mexico announced plans to issue 21 precious-metal coins—6 in gold and 15 in silver—honoring its hosting of the 1986 World Cup soccer championship; the Falkland Islands, scene of a 1982 war between Great Britain and Argentina, issued a massive silver coin to mark the 100th anniversary of the island's self-sufficiency; and Australia introduced a new $1 coin made of aluminum bronze.

LISA A. SUNDERLIN, *The Numismatist*

COLOMBIA

The year 1985 was dominated by the end of the truce between the guerrillas and the government of President Belisario Betancur, which had been arranged the previous year, and the renewal of military encounters between the guerrillas and the Colombian army. Both Liberal and Conservative parties chose presidential candidates for the 1986 elections, as familiar faces and names dominated the political scene. The Colombian economy, under close scrutiny by international lending institutions, emerged with barely passing grades, mostly because of prospects in coal and oil development. On November 13, a volcanic eruption in the north unleashed mudslides and floods that killed more than 23,000 in the town of Armero.

Politics. The cease-fire arranged by President Betancur in 1984 between the government and all major guerrilla groups broke down in June, when the M-19 guerrillas began once again to attack army and police units. Alleging the failure of the government to live up to its side of the truce agreement, M-19 leader Alvaro Fayad stated that his organization would no longer remain in its remote Caquetá base. In June, more than 150 people were killed and 145 wounded in clashes between the guerrillas and government forces. On November 6, M-19 guerrillas seized the national courts building in Bogotá; about 100 persons (including several judges) died as government forces recaptured it. As the 1986 elections approached, elements within Betancur's Conservative party and in the military began to press for increased military action against the guerrillas.

Colombia's two old-line political parties began gearing up for the elections. Virgilio Barco, a longtime Liberal politician and former mayor of Bogotá, was chosen as that party's standard-bearer in August, while longtime Conservative leader Alvaro Gomez Hurtado became his party's candidate. Barco won nomination only after a major challenge by Luis Carlos Galan was beaten back by the party establishment. Galan, who had the backing of former President Carlos Lleras Restrepo, may run as a third candidate in the election, thus increasing Gomez Hurtado's chances by splitting the Liberal vote. Galan represents younger, more liberal elements in the party. Gomez, whose father Laureano Gomez is remembered as the principal author in the 1950s of the rural fighting known as *la violencia,* was soundly beaten in the 1974 elections by Liberal Alfonso López Michelsen.

Economy. The Colombian economy continued to perform adequately in 1985. Gross domestic product rose by slightly less than 5% during the year, and the nation's balance-of-payments deficit dropped from more than $1 billion in 1983 to only $200 million for the first six months of 1985. Earnings from coffee exports, which still account for almost half the country's foreign-exchange earnings, were up by 37% in the first six months of the year. Government estimates of inflation were at 22%, while private-sector estimates went as high as 25–30%. Unemployment was estimated at 18% at year's end. The continued development of the Cerrejon-Norte coal mine was good news for the future, as were June announcements by Texaco and Occidental Petroleum of new investments in oil exploration and production. Investment in petroleum was up 49% over 1984, to $59 million. Public investment continued at a high 9.5% of gross domestic product, with $1.8 billion in the mining sector.

Foreign Affairs. Colombia continued to play a leading role in efforts by the Contadora Group (Colombia, Venezuela, Panama, and Mexico) to achieve a peace agreement in Central America. During his visit to Washington, DC, in April, President Betancur at first appeared to approve President Reagan's plan for peace in the region. Several days later, however, the Colombian president changed his mind, stating that he had not been told that the Reagan plan called for renewed aid to the U.S.-backed Nicaraguan *contras.* Betancur stated on April 15 that this made the Reagan plan "no longer a peace proposal but preparation for war."

During a meeting of Latin American debtor nations—the Cartagena Group—at the inauguration of Peruvian President Alan García Pérez in August, President Betancur subscribed to a joint statement asking that debt payments be tied to growth in export earnings.

Colombia finally extradited four middle-level narcotics traffickers to the United States, but drug traffic continued to pose a problem in Colombian-U.S. relations. In August an Avianca 747 was seized by U.S. Customs in reprisal for what was claimed to be a pattern of the Colombian airline's planes being used to smuggle drugs into the United States.

ERNEST A. DUFF
Randolph-Macon Woman's College

COLOMBIA · Information Highlights

Official Name: Republic of Colombia.
Location: Northwest South America.
Area: 439,735 sq mi (1 138 914 km²).
Population (mid-1985 est.): 29,400,000.
Chief City (1985 est.): Bogotá, the capital, 4,584,-000.
Government: *Head of state and government,* Belisario Betancur Cuartas, president (took office Aug. 1982). *Legislature*—Congress; Senate and House of Representatives.
Monetary Unit: Peso (161.75 pesos equal U.S.$1, Oct. 21, 1985).
Gross National Product (1984 U.S.$): $48,000,-000,000.
Economic Index (Bogotá, 1984): *Consumer Prices* (1970 = 100), all items, 1,517.4; food, 1,853.1.
Foreign Trade (1983 U.S.$): *Imports,* $4,968,000,000; *exports,* $3,081,000,000.

COLORADO

Colorado, which in recent years has sought to diversify its traditional natural resources-based economy by attracting high-technology industries, found both its old and new economic pillars shaken by recession in 1985.

Economy. Energy development fueled much of the state's growth in the 1970s, but the worldwide oil glut led to numerous cutbacks in energy exploration and production in the Rocky Mountain region during 1985. Such retrenchments, combined with overbuilding, produced office vacancy rates of 30% in metropolitan Denver at midsummer. Meanwhile, the state's agricultural base dwindled in tandem with the national farm recession. The most notable victim was the 80-year-old Great Western Sugar Company, which went bankrupt in 1985 and closed the last of the 13 sugar refineries it once operated in Colorado.

Far from insulating Colorado from the woes afflicting its traditional economic base, the state's new information-related industries slumped as part of a nationwide slowdown in computer-industry growth. Boulder County was particularly hard hit; more than 5,000 workers were laid off at Storage Technology Corporation, and 1,100 were cut from the rolls at MiniScribe. Even the prestigious AT&T Information Systems announced that an unspecified number of Colorado employees would be laid off by year's end as part of a major nationwide layoff.

Economists found a common thread in the state's disparate economic problems by noting that about 24% of Colorado's manufacturing and agricultural output is aimed for export markets. The high value of the U.S. dollar in relation to foreign currencies undercut the state's ability to compete in foreign marketplaces.

Although such highly publicized problems slowed Colorado's economic growth, the state still added more than 25,000 new nonfarm jobs in the 12-month period ending July 1, 1985. That growth was less than half that of the previous 12-month period, but it signaled continuing strength in the state's service sectors, which added 10,400 jobs; in government employment, which rose by 9,500 jobs; and in retail sales, which added 6,600 new workers.

Defense-related industries also fared well, contributing $2.6 billion to the state economy. This amount almost equaled the $3 billion contributed by the traditional agricultural base.

Urban Developments. Denver Mayor Federico Peña campaigned vigorously for a new $137 million convention center, arguing that such a facility would create jobs in Denver and foster the redevelopment of the Platte Valley. Voters, however, rejected the proposal by 65% to 35%. The voter turnout of 94,430, 34% of the eligible electorate, was the highest ever recorded in a special election in the city.

Peña fared better on another favorite project, winning commitments from three major airlines—United, Continental, and Frontier—to help finance construction of a new airport. The three carriers are the largest tenants at the existing Stapleton International Airport, the nation's sixth-busiest airport, which is already operating well above its planned capacity. The only Denver-based airline in the trio, Frontier, avoided a corporate takeover attempt by Continental by merging with People Express, a low-cost carrier based in Newark, NJ. In another transportation-related development, the Regional Transportation district announced plans for a $41 million busway system to improve transportation between downtown Denver and its northern suburbs.

Peña scored a mixed success in still a third economic development effort when the Michigan-based Taubman Company announced a $300-million plan to redevelop and expand Denver's aging Cherry Creek shopping center. Peña had long sought to attract a prestigious high-fashion store to Denver to spur city retail sales. He won that objective when Saks Fifth Avenue agreed to become an anchor tenant at the remodeled Cherry Creek. The mayor would have preferred to attract such a store to the downtown Denver retail district, but he at least had the satisfaction of winning the prize for the core city over rival suburban shopping malls.

The Legislature and Politics. The state legislature approved a new 250-bed prison at Ordway and passed laws to reform higher education, clean up hazardous wastes, and begin catching up on a backlog of capital construction needs in such areas as highways, water storage, and state institutions.

Gov. Richard D. Lamm announced that he would not run for any office in 1986, ending speculation that he would seek a fourth gubernatorial term or campaign for the U.S. Senate if Gary Hart retired.

BOB EWEGEN, *"The Denver Post"*

COLORADO · Information Highlights

Area: 104,091 sq mi (269 595 km²).
Population (July 1, 1984 est.): 3,178,000.
Chief Cities (July 1, 1984 est.): Denver, the capital, 504,588; Colorado Springs, 247,739; Aurora, 194,772; Lakewood, 121,114.
Government (1985): *Chief Officers*—governor, Richard D. Lamm (D); lt. gov., Nancy Dick (D). *General Assembly*—Senate, 35 members; House of Representatives, 65 members.
State Finances (fiscal year 1984): *Revenues,* $4,878,000,000; *expenditures,* $4,560,000,000.
Personal Income (1984): $44,004,000,000; per capita, $13,847.
Labor Force (June 1985): *Civilian labor force,* 1,738,600; *unemployed,* 95,100 (5.5% of total force).
Education: *Enrollment* (fall 1983)—public elementary schools, 376,775; public secondary, 165,421; colleges and universities, 172,650. *Public school expenditures* (1982–83), $1,605,885,020 ($3,171 per pupil).

COMMUNICATION TECHNOLOGY

The year 1985 was marked by increasing emphasis on digital technology for generating, processing, transmitting, storing, and displaying information. Important advances were made in photonics (lightwaves), microelectronics, and computer software for communication systems. Progress also was made in the long-term development of ISDN (Integrated Services Digital Network), an end-to-end digital communications network which will provide simultaneous voice, picture, data, and signaling capabilities.

Transmission and Switching. Lightwave systems use lasers and light-emitting diodes (LEDs) as light sources and ultrapure glass fibers as the medium for high-speed, on-off pulses carrying information encoded in digital format. During the year, AT&T began shipment of the FT Series G, the fastest commercial lightwave system to date. It is capable of transmitting 1.7 billion bits per second (bps), enough capacity to handle 24,000 simultaneous phone calls over a single pair of glass fibers or to send 160 average-length books in one second.

At AT&T Bell Laboratories, engineers set a new distance record by transmitting 420 megabits per second over 126 mi (203 km) without amplification. In another experiment, information at a rate of 4 billion bits per second (4 gigabits) was sent 73 mi (117 km). This is equivalent to 62,500 two-way simultaneous voice channels or 44 broadcast-quality TV signals.

Plans were approved in 1985 for the construction of the first transpacific undersea lightwave cable. Designated Hawaii 4/Transpac 3, it will be a joint venture of 21 global communication companies and governments. It is designed to operate at 280 megabits per second, transmitted over two pairs of glass fibers.

Significant advances also were made in lightwave systems for business and residential use. The capacity of glass fiber SLC (subscriber line carrier) systems was increased by a factor of seven; 672 users could now be served over a single pair of fibers, providing high-volume data and voice services locally.

Electronic central office switching systems, both local and long-distance, were substantially improved during the year. The expansion of capacity and the addition of new features were accomplished mainly by new software components and by changes in the generic programs that control the switching systems.

Private Branch Exchanges (PBXs) made available during the year were designed to serve both voice and data communication needs, with the ability to handle the latter at rates of up to 64 kilobits per second. A new feature called packet switching—the interleaving of bursts of messages in digital form and their transmission during very short periods when the line is not being used for other purposes—was being integrated. The PBX is becoming a powerful data-switching device and an important element in the ISDN of the future.

Communication Services. In 1985 the number of users of cellular mobile radio telephones in the United States increased to more than 200,000, operating in more than 60 cities. About the same number were using cellular systems in foreign countries.

The year also brought increasing interaction between communication technology and business and personal computers. Financial transactions, purchasing, accessing of data bases, electronic mail, monitoring of security systems, reporting of alarms, and even automatic reading of utility meters were just some of the applications.

An improved emergency communication system (Enhanced 911) was being put into U.S. nationwide service in 1985. The new system instantaneously traces a 911 call and displays the address on a video screen—a vital improvement for many emergency situations. The integrated system uses computers and computer memory banks to store the needed data. About 100 U.S. cities would soon be equipped.

Three communication companies (AT&T, RCA, and Motorola) continued development of a new kind of secure telephone for the U.S. government. The device is expected to end international and corporate telephone eavesdropping. Each call is transmitted in a code based on random digits generated by a computer; the code is changed every time a call is made. The system operates by converting the voice signal to a digital format, rearranging the digits in random order for transmission, and then reversing the process at the receiving end—all without perceptible delay.

A fast-growing offshoot of satellite communication development has been the use of "small dish" antennas to receive television programming transmitted by satellite. Dish owners can pick up the signals of both broadcasting networks and cable companies. Thousands of these dishes, 6 or 8 ft (1.8 or 2.4 m) in diameter, are being sold each month in the United States. They are being erected in yards and on rooftops not only in rural locations remote from TV stations but increasingly in suburban areas as well. Legal questions are being raised by the cable companies, who normally charge for their programs but now see them being picked up for free. In 1985 more than 1.5 million private dishes were in use in the United States, with the number expected to grow to 5 million by 1990.

Electronic Publishing. Electronic publishing is the processing and distribution of information, usually in digital format, by electronic means. The information can come from large, computer-stored, on-line data banks with which the user can interact on a computer ter-

minal, or in physical form directly on magnetic tape cassettes, floppy magnetic disks, hard magnetic disks, or compact optical disks made by laser beam (CDs). The combination of high-speed digital transmission with its huge information-carrying capacity for words and pictures, the computer with its ability to store and quickly process vast quantities of information, and electronic printing devices like the laser printer and the laser-beam cylinder engraver have begun to transform the publishing world.

The business of providing on-line data bases and computer software already amounts to several billion dollars annually and is growing at a rate of more than 30% per year. The nature of the information and of the services provided is as diverse in subject matter as conventional publishing. News, financial information, market and weather reports, books, newspapers, magazines, catalogs, and bibliographies and references to scientific, technical, medical, and legal literature are just some of the examples.

Conventional print publishing itself is undergoing a revolution. Many newspapers and magazines have their writers filing stories on video data terminals, on which changes can be made much more quickly and easily.

In printing, the linotype machine has been replaced by computer-generated type. Now also, text and illustrations, in the form of electrical digital impulses, can be sent anywhere by lightwave fibers, satellites, or other wide-band communication facilities and printed locally cheaper and faster than by shipping printed documents. And in 1985 software became available that performs page makeup and page design using a variety of type styles and sizes and allowing for the incorporation of illustrations and other inserts in a multicolumn format.

Typifying the vast potential represented by electronic publishing, Grolier Incorporated in 1985 announced plans to market the *Academic American Encyclopedia* on a CD-ROM (compact disk, read-only memory). The 21-volume encyclopedia, totaling 9 million words, would be contained on a 4.72-inch (12-cm) disk.

Microelectronics and Microprocessors. The number of components that can be placed on a single silicon chip has been doubling at a rate of every 18 months. In 1985 a record one million components on a dime-size chip, the one megabit RAM (Random Access Memory), was put into manufacture. As a result, silicon memory for computers can become cheaper by a factor of four, machines will become smaller, and they will require less power to operate.

Also in 1985, AT&T announced the first single-chip programmable digital signal processor with 32-bit floating point arithmetic, capable of executing 8 million operations per second. Among its applications will be speech analysis and synthesis, speech recognition, and signal processing for the military.

M.D. FAGEN, *Formerly, Bell Laboratories*

COMPUTERS

Layoffs, reduced earnings, and falling stock prices masked the fact that the computer industry continued to grow in 1985, though not at the pace projected a few years earlier. As one market researcher said, "It's a slump relative to expectations, but it isn't a slump relative to every other industry that exists in the world." For instance, software sales climbed more than 35% for the first half of 1985 compared with the same period in 1984. The number of microcomputers owned by America's schools jumped 75% during the 1984–85 academic year. And the dollar value of the worldwide market for personal computers was expected to grow 23%. But competition for market share was stiff, and there were shakeouts and consolidations in all levels of the industry.

Micros and Minis. The market for computers aimed specifically at home users remained depressed. In January 1985, Coleco discontinued its Adam computer; two months later, IBM stopped production of the PCjr. Commodore and Atari, whose computers helped create the booming home market of the early 1980s, introduced sophisticated machines aimed at both home and business users, recognizing that most consumers who currently buy computers do so because they want to do work at home. Amiga, Commodore's new computer, has exceptionally fine color, sound, and animation capabilities. The basic machine comes with 256K RAM (Random Access Memory), expandable internally to 512K and externally to 8.5Mb (million bytes). Atari's new 520ST, with 512K RAM and excellent graphics and sound, features Digital Research's Graphics Environment Manager (GEM) operating system, which allows for integrated windowing and pull-down menus. Atari also unveiled a compact disk player that can be used with the 520ST. One disk can hold more than 500Mb of data.

The distinction between microcomputers and minicomputers continues to blur. In 1985, Plexus introduced P/20, a "supermicro" that can accommodate up to 16 terminals, and IBM introduced System/36, a desktop mini that can support up to three micros plus a printer. In each, the central machine can store data that can be shared by the system's users. Minicomputers also are finding increased use as links between a company's mainframe computer and its personal computers, so that employees can share files and gain access to data stored in the mainframe.

Supercomputers. By definition, supercomputers are the fastest computers in existence. By late 1985, the fastest of the fast was Cray-2, introduced by Cray Research at midyear. The machine has an internal memory capacity of 2Gb (billion bytes) and can do 1.2 billion arithmetic operations per second, making it 40,000 to 50,000 times faster than today's personal

An educational software analyst evaluates computer programs before they become part of the curriculum in New York City's public schools. The number of microcomputers owned by America's schools increased 75% during the 1984–85 academic year.

AP/Wide World

computers and almost unimaginably faster than computers of the past. Says Robert Borchers, associate director for computations at Lawrence Livermore National Laboratory, "What took a year in 1952 we can now do in a second."

In February 1985 the National Science Foundation announced that it would spend $200 million to create supercomputer centers at Cornell University, Princeton University, the University of Illinois, and the University of California at San Diego. Corporations were expected to match these moneys and underwrite joint research projects at the universities.

Peripherals. The year 1985 saw the introduction of miniaturized 10Mb hard disk drives that can be inserted into a personal computer and moderately priced modems that can communicate at 2,400 bits per second.

Several companies introduced image processors, devices that read photos, drawings, and text directly into a personal computer. There are several types of image processors, but the best-quality images are achieved by flatbed scanners, which look much like copying machines and which operate in a similar manner. When an image is placed in the machine, it is digitized and can be saved on disk. Such images can increase the usefulness of data bases in a variety of fields. For example, realtors can add photos to computerized listings of homes, financial institutions can quickly verify signatures, and security guards can check photos of people wishing entrance to restricted areas. The images also can be altered, making the processors useful to architects, engineers, and other designers.

X-10 (USA) Inc. introduced a peripheral that enables people to use their personal computers to control lights, appliances, heating and air conditioning, and other electrical devices in a home, office, or store. Up to 72 appliances can be plugged into special modules, which in turn are plugged into regular electrical outlets throughout the building. The person then programs the times and days that the devices should switch on and off. A similar system from General Electric does not require a computer but attaches directly to a television set.

Software. Word processing, data base management, spreadsheet, and telecommunication packages continued to be the most widely used types of business software, but other types of programs also became popular in 1985. Among these were desk accessory programs—electronic versions of such conventional desktop aids as calendars, calculators, clocks, note pads, and Rolodexes. Such a program remains in computer memory while the user works on another program. By pressing a few keys, the user can temporarily exit the main program, use the accessory program, and then return to where he or she left off in the main program.

New project management programs that run on micros help managers plan and keep track of the tasks, resources, time schedules, and costs of a particular project. Whether overseeing the production of a vintage wine or the construction of a skyscraper, a manager can chart time and sequence requirements of various parts of the project, generate budgets and reports, compare actual versus planned schedules, and so on.

Simulations designed to train employees in project management and other skills are becoming an important business tool, preferred by many managers to more traditional, lecture-based courses. In 1985, extremely realistic simulations, including sports games and a wilderness survival game, also were popular for the home market. Another genre that became popular was interactive fiction. Ray Bradbury's *Fahrenheit 451,* Douglas Adams' *The Hitchhiker's Guide to the Galaxy,* and other novels were adapted to games in which the characters remain the same but the plots vary depending on player's commands.

JENNY TESAR, *Free-lance Science Writer*

Computer Art and Animation

Images II+ from Computer Graphics Laboratories, Inc. is an expandable, multifunctional electronic graphics workstation. The modular hardware and software configuration can be used for creating high-resolution graphics and illustrations, scanning existing artwork and video, and even creating conventional animated effects.

The graphics design and display capabilities of the modern computer have found a myriad of applications in the worlds of industry and science. Engineers use computers to design automobiles, airplanes, and ships. With a few strokes of a computer key, architects can move a wall or beam. Doctors can recreate brain functions. Geologists can perform seismic analyses in the search for oil. Astronomers can depict planetary landscapes.

In addition to these important practical uses, computer-graphics systems are now also being used for purely aesthetic purposes. With its ability to store, access, and manipulate large numbers of picture elements, the computer has become the latest product of technology—following charred wood, brushes, chisels, paints, pastels, cameras, and other tools—to be used in the creation of visual art. The development of "dedicated" (specifically devoted) graphics chips, sophisticated software, and advanced animation systems has opened new creative opportunities for the gifted professional artist and the living-room dabbler alike.

Though still in its infancy, the field of computer art has progressed rapidly in terms of the clarity, complexity, and realism of image reproduction. Computer animation, a sequence of still pictures flashed 24 frames per second, has put some amazing video images on the movie and television screen. "Computerized paintbox" systems, consisting of an electronic tablet and a drawing "pen" linked to a computer, allow the rapid creation of color artwork, graphics, lettering, and other displays that easily can be manipulated and stored. Beginners can become instant electronic artists, and experts are afforded a unique and versatile new medium of artistic expression.

Ned Green, New York Institute of Technology

MAGI SynthaVision

Computer art—generated on a standard or custom "paint system" or by actual programming—is now being displayed in special exhibitions and contests. Ned Green's "Inside a Quark," above, was cited in "Popular Computing's" 1984 competition. One of the challenges facing computer artists is the rendering of natural textures; complex programming is brought to bear in the work of MAGI SynthaVision, left. And in computer animation, Lucasfilm's "The Adventures of André & Wally B." features full character animation, 3-D characters and background, and articulated motion blur.

Courtesy of Lucasfilm Ltd.

CONNECTICUT

Hurricane Gloria struck Connecticut on September 27 with winds up to 92 mph (148 km/h). The storm caused more than $92 million of damage and knocked out the electric power of more than half of the state's 1.3 million electricity customers. It took more than a week before power was fully restored. The hurricane took six lives in the state.

No property damage or injuries were reported when two earthquakes, rare in Connecticut, were recorded on October 19 and October 21. The second quake was said to be an aftershock of the first, which was centered in Mount Vernon, NY, not too far from the Connecticut border.

History. Connecticut as well as Hartford, the capital city, began observing their 350th anniversaries in 1985. The state's birthday will be celebrated through April 26, 1986, and Hartford's observance will extend through September 1986. Historians are uncertain whether the state and city were founded in 1635 or 1636.

Nathan Hale, the Coventry schoolmaster, hanged as a spy by the British during the Revolutionary War, was designated as the state hero by the 1985 session of the state legislature.

The USS *Nautilus,* the Navy's first nuclear submarine, arrived at its final berth in Groton on the Thames River on July 6 after being towed from Mare Island Naval Shipyard in California. The submarine had been decommissioned there on March 3, 1980. It will become the centerpiece of a submarine museum that is scheduled to open in April 1986 near Electric Boat, the shipyard where the *Nautilus* was built and christened in 1954.

Appointments. On July 17, John J. Kelly replaced Austin J. McGuigan as the state's chief attorney. McGuigan had held the job seven years, but the final seven months had been marked by feuding with the state police. Some state police officials felt that McGuigan had

AP/Wide World

Connecticut residents stood up well against Hurricane Gloria in September, but property damage was widespread.

taken over their role in the investigation of major crimes.

In October the U.S. Senate confirmed the appointment of Alan H. Nevas as a judge of the U.S. District Court of Connecticut. He had been U.S. attorney for Connecticut. One of Nevas' last jobs as U.S. attorney was to direct the arraignments of several alleged members of Los Macheteros, a Puerto Rican pro-independence group, who the FBI said were involved in some way in the 1983 robbery of $7 million from a Wells Fargo armored truck in West Hartford. Victor M. Gerena of Hartford, the principal suspect in the robbery, remained at large late in 1985.

Education. In the state's public university systems, John T. Casteen III became the 11th president of the University of Connecticut,

---

succeeding John A. DiBiaggio, and Dallas K. Beal became president of the four-campus Connecticut State University. Beal succeeded James A. Frost, who retired. DiBiaggio became president of Michigan State University in September. A. Bartlett Giamatti, who has been president of Yale University since 1978, said he would resign at the end of the 1986 school year. Benno C. Schmidt, Jr., 43, the dean of Columbia University Law School, was named as his successor.

Other. In March, Century Brass Products Inc., a major employer in Waterbury, filed for protection from creditors under Chapter 11 of the U.S. Bankruptcy Code.

The state legislature adopted a record $4.4 billion budget for fiscal year 1986 and also raised the legal drinking age from 20 to 21.

ROBERT F. MURPHY
"The Hartford Courant"

CONSUMER AFFAIRS

"The educated consumer of the last decade of this century and beyond will be one who is able to see that his or her individual action resonates within a context of shared humanity as well as shared consumption." These words of Hayden Green, a high school teacher of consumer education, may be most prophetic. American consumers are looking at their role as consumers in many different ways. The antimaterialistic attitude of many young people during the 1960s seems to be changing as one reads more and more about the "yuppies" (young, upwardly mobile professionals).

During 1985, due in considerable measure to an improvement in the U.S. economy, consumers were buying larger automobiles and more major appliances and furniture and were continuing to upgrade their purchases of clothing. The sellers of generic and off-brand products found that their markets were slipping as consumers were returning to the familiar name brands. Are these changes indicative of a contradiction of the high school teacher's belief?

Consumer Responsibility. However, some things being done by the government and by consumers themselves seem to indicate that there is an increasing sense of responsibility on the part of many consumers. The cigarette industry is disturbed by the decline in the per capita consumption of cigarettes and as smoking is being limited or prohibited in more and more public places.

Almost one third of the states have passed laws making it mandatory that seat and shoulder harnesses be used in automobiles. This resulted from a ruling by Secretary of Transportation Elizabeth Dole that passive restraint systems (airbags or harnesses attached to the driver's door that go into place automatically when the door is shut) would not be required in automobiles if states accounting for two thirds of the nation's population would pass mandatory seat-belt use laws before April 1, 1989. By Oct. 1, 1985, 14 states had passed such legislation.

Consumers are paying more attention to nutrition. The cereal industry has taken notice of this and is emphasizing cereals with fiber, low sodium, and low sugar content in its advertising.

Because of actions taken by the Reagan administration to deregulate certain industries, and, in some cases, to eliminate certain government rules and regulations, the consumer is being forced to become more responsible. As a consequence of the administration actions, a serious question arises as to what is the proper balance between government regulation and the interests of consumers. We need enough regulation to protect consumers, but not so much that the business community is shackled.

Federal Consumer Activity. The U.S. Department of Agriculture's Food Safety and Inspection Service began operating a toll-free Meat and Poultry Hotline during 1985. Consumers can call 1-800-535-4555, or in the Washington, DC, area, 447-3333, to get answers to questions about the quality, proper handling, and safety of meat and poultry.

The Consumer Product Safety Commission announced its five priority projects for fiscal year 1986: electrocution hazards, fire toxicity, gas-heating systems, portable electric heaters, and riding lawn mowers. These products have caused numerous injuries and deaths year after year.

The Civil Aeronautics Board ceased to exist as of Jan. 1, 1985, due to congressional action. Its consumer protection functions were transferred to the U.S. Department of Transportation.

The National Highway Traffic Safety Administration, which had discontinued the tread-wear grading of tires, was forced by a court ruling to resume tread-wear grading during the year.

The U.S. Office of Consumer Affairs set "Consumers Rate Quality" as the theme for 1986 National Consumers Week, which is held each year during the last full week of April.

UN Action. In 1985 the General Assembly of the United Nations adopted the *International Guidelines on Consumer Protection.* The guidelines deal with physical safety, promotion and protection of consumers' economic interests, standards for safety and quality of consumer goods and services, distribution facilities for essential consumer goods and services, measures enabling consumers to obtain redress, as well as guidelines on education and information programs. Other guidelines cover specific areas such as food, water, pharmaceuticals, pesticides, and chemicals.

STEWART M. LEE, *Geneva College*

The Singles Market

Donna Ferrato, Visions

The 20 million American singles are prime customers at the many health and fitness centers that have sprung up across the nation. At such establishments, the singles seek not only physical exercise but also camaraderie.

In 1985, some 20 million American adults were identified as one-person households. While this represented less than 8% of the U.S. population, the earning power, life-style, and upward mobility of the self-sustaining single adult became a magnet for businesses of all kinds and in many cases was the cornerstone of their marketing strategies.

The emergence of singles as a major consumer market arose from a number of social and demographic changes. The record divorce rate of the 1980s, the desire to postpone nuptials, and the yearning to live well on one's own swelled the ranks of the singles population. This rise had been fostered also by better education and its consequent increase in job and professional opportunities. In terms of pure population rise, the number of singles in 1984 (the latest year for which precise figures are available) increased to 19.89 million, 12% higher than in 1980.

Single people enjoy higher disposable income than marrieds, averaging about $30,000 annually as against about $22,000 for members of families. With fewer financial obligations and a freer life-style, the unattached consumer indulges his or her wants in a sort of conspicuous consumerism. They have spurned the conservative, patient buying habits of their parents, and "I want it now" is their shopping credo.

"Singles are pouring money into so many areas for self-enrichment and their own entertainment, millions will be made," Michael Hess, who owns a New York company marketing to singles, told *The New York Times.* "Singles live with credit more and tend to spend more on restaurant meals and entertainment," said Tom Biracree, the author of books on singles, in a *Times* interview.

Banks, credit-card companies, travel agencies, greeting-card makers, book publishers,

stockbrokers, cosmetics companies, and many stores have made concerted efforts to attract singles. Such large retailers as R. H. Macy & Company, Saks Fifth Avenue, Lord & Taylor, and Carson Pirie Scott have set up separate departments or sections to attract them. Hallmark, American Greetings, and Gibson cards also "singled" them out. Producers and sellers who have built into their offerings separate segments aimed at the singles market have been aided by the efforts of Madison Avenue ad agencies, which wisely deployed singles themselves to devise appropriate marketing and creative approaches.

Buying Trends. Singles are responsible consumers. In December 1984, 34,000 crowded into New York City's Madison Square Garden for a two-day event called "Single in New York." About 200 exhibitors took booths to greet and sell their wares to singles from their early 20s to late 50s who turned out to browse, shop, and mingle. Michael Hess, the young lawyer who dreamed up the show, scheduled similar events in three other U.S. cities late in 1985. Entrance fees alone for the New York show, at $10 a head, produced $340,000. Sunmakers Inc., a tanning parlor, sold $10,000 worth of tanning equipment, and the Cambridge Diet Plan reported that the two-day showing yielded its best-selling days of the year.

But while singles are responsive, they also can be fickle. While in the 1970s they tended to frequent nightclubs and bars, in the 1980s they have turned their attention to health and fitness centers. Racquetball, aerobics classes, Nautilus workouts, and other gym activities now absorb much of the time previously spent in singles bars.

Whether it was because singles proved to be independent shoppers or because what they preferred to buy was not much different from what other consumers wanted, some major producers decided not to develop anything special for them. At General Electric Company, for example, a marketing spokesman reported, "Our line of consumer electronics is so broad that we feel it contains anything singles would want. We are not marketing specifically to them but to the entire spectrum of American consumers."

Leslie Wexner, board chairman of The Limited Inc., the nation's fastest-growing chain of women's apparel stores, observed, "We aren't catering directly to singles but to young women in general. We don't think about our business in such segmented terms. Whether it's singles or young marrieds, we find their taste in clothing really doesn't vary much."

Demographics and the Future. Within the singles population, the 12% gain from 1980 to 1984 was more heavily weighted toward the

Carol Rosegg, Martha Swope Photography

New York's Madison Square Garden was the site of a major trade show displaying commercial goods for singles.

over-35 category than toward the under-35s. According to the Conference Board, a research group that works closely with the U.S. Bureau of Census, the over-35 segment grew 14.3%—from 12.9 million in 1980 to 14.8 million in 1984—while the under-35 singles population increased 5.6%—from 4.82 million to 5.09 million.

According to other statistics, only about one third of so-called "Baby Boomers"—those adults born after World War II—have remained single. The singles, however, constitute the most important buying segment of the U.S. population. In furniture, for example, they represent 38.5% of all furniture buyers, according to *Professional Furniture Merchant,* a trade publication. Based on a survey of 5,000 households, the publication found that although other consumer groups, particularly those over age 55, control much of the country's disposable dollars, "they are not acquiring home furnishings at the high rate the young singles and married couples are."

But does the greater increase in the over-35 singles population suggest a more conservative approach to consumer purchasing in the years ahead? Marketers are not sure. In any event, they agree that the singles market itself will unquestionably continue to grow, reaching 30 million by the early 1990s.

ISADORE BARMASH

CRIME

The U.S. crime rate dropped for the third consecutive year, according to nationwide figures tabulated by the Federal Bureau of Investigation (FBI). The bureau noted that the 1984 rate for "index crimes" was 1.9% lower than that of the previous year. "Index crimes" are murder and nonnegligent manslaughter, forcible rape, robbery, aggravated assault, burglary, larceny-theft, motor vehicle theft, and arson. The crime rate for 1984 was the lowest since 1978, although it remained 5% higher than in 1975; reports for the first half of 1985 indicated that the downward trend might be coming to an end. Moreover, there was clear evidence that a strong fear of crime was prevalent throughout the nation. (*See* feature article, page 44.)

The decrease was registered unevenly among types of crime. Property crime declined by 2.2%, but crimes of violence increased 1.2%. Rape was by far the major contributor to the escalation in violent crimes, registering a 6.7% increase. Rapes reported to the police rose 50.2% from 1975. Authorities remain uncertain whether there has been a dramatic outbreak of such offenses in the past decade or whether women have become less reluctant to report sexual assaults to law enforcement agencies.

Murder dropped 3.2% during the year; the 18,780 murders known to the police in 1984 constituted the lowest figure since 1975. This was a particularly meaningful development because murder is regarded as the offense least susceptible to reporting idiosyncracies.

Florida's Dade County, which includes Miami, was the murder capital of the United States. Its rate was three times the national figure, with 23.7 murders per 100,000 population. Nationwide, murders took place more often in December than in any other month, and 57% were committed by relatives or persons acquainted with the victim. Nine out of ten females and slightly more than eight of ten males were killed by men. A special study showed that 94% of black murder victims were slain by black offenders, while 89% of white victims were killed by whites. All told, Americans have one chance in 133 of being murdered at any time during their life (birth to age 89). In any given year, the odds of being murdered are 1 in 10,000; for violent crime in general, the lifetime risk of victimization is 1 in 31.

Interpreting the Statistics. Controversy continued regarding the veracity and meaning of the reported decline. The view that the downward spiral represents actual conditions was reinforced by the 1985 report of the National Crime Survey, based on interviews with members of 60,000 representative households. That survey showed also a slight drop in crime victimization for the third straight year, although 22.8 million American households—26% of the nation's total—had experienced a crime of violence or theft during 1984.

FBI Director William H. Webster suggested that several factors were involved in the drop in crime, including increased citizen interest in crime prevention, characterized by neighborhood watch patrols and telephone tips; improved training and management in police departments; the growth of computer operations in law enforcement; and a drop in repeat criminal offenders because of the record number of persons behind bars.

Such factors, however, were rated by experts participating in a conference on crime statistics in March at the University of California, Los Angeles, as far less important than changes in the nation's age structure. Albert J. Reiss, Jr., of Yale University noted that the country's median age rose to 31.2 years in 1984, compared with 27.9 in 1971; in 1984, 10% fewer persons were in the 14-to-25-year-old group, the age bracket with the highest crime rate. Daniel Glaser of the University of Southern California pointed out that with fewer youths and more older persons, there is apt to be more contact between youngsters and conventional adults and that this may help to reduce crime levels. Glaser observed, for instance, that more young people live at home today than have been doing so in the past decade.

Other conference participants insisted that too much is being made of the reported statistical decline. Barry Krisberg, head of the National Council on Crime and Delinquency, maintained that, despite crime figures, there is a growing mood of lawlessness in the country, marked by skyrocketing increases in "broken-window crimes," such as vandalism. John Irwin of San Francisco State University insisted that the portrait of crime would change dramatically if white-collar offenses and not just street crimes were counted (*see* special report, page 195). Other speakers noted that, despite the reported drop, the United States continues to show a much higher rate of criminal behavior than virtually all industrialized countries and that this is true despite an imprisonment rate believed to be exceeded only in South Africa and the Soviet Union.

Organized Crime. Federal authorities reported more successful prosecutions of persons in the higher echelons of organized crime in 1985 than ever before in U.S. history. The enforcement effort was aided notably by aggressive use of the RICO (Racketeer Influenced and Corrupt Organizations) law, enacted in 1970. Under the statute, the leader of any organization can be prosecuted if the group's members commit crimes that show a pattern of racketeering. Prosecutors do not have to prove that the leader personally committed the illegal acts, only that he supported them in some way.

White-Collar Crime

WHEN E.F. HUTTON TALKS....

....IT'S ON THE ADVICE OF HIS ATTORNEY

FRAUD CHARGES

A cartoonist pokes fun at E.F. Hutton and its legal problems. The brokerage firm pleaded guilty to federal charges stemming from manipulation of its checking accounts.

Reprinted by permission: Tribune Media Services

"I never dreamed it would ever come to an indictment. I thought at most there would be some kind of injunctive action, and then I thought the guilty plea would end it." This statement by Robert Fomon, president of the brokerage firm of E.F. Hutton & Company, typified the surprised reaction of businessmen, politicians, and professionals to an emerging national sense of outrage following the exposure of a series of white-collar crimes in 1985.

In the Hutton case, the company had defrauded banks by means of a check-kiting scheme that netted it millions of dollars in interest-free loans. Hutton pleaded guilty to 2,000 counts of mail and wire fraud, was fined $2.75 million, and agreed to reimburse the banks for the lost use of their money. No Hutton executive was prosecuted, however.

The public mood about white-collar crime was reflected in a midyear New York Times–CBS News poll. In response to the question "Do you think American corporate executives are honest, or not?" 55% said that they did not, 32% said that they did, and the remainder offered no opinion. Fifty-nine percent of respondents believed that white-collar crime occurs "very often," while 34% thought it was an "occasional" event, and only 3% thought "it hardly ever happens." Just 23% thought that the government was making a sufficient effort to catch white-collar criminals, while 68% disagreed. And 65% believed that the punishment of white-collar offenders is too lenient.

A variety of other white-collar scandals captured headlines during the year. In May the General Electric Company (GE) admitted that it had filed 108 false claims on an Air Force missile warhead contract. Among other things, GE had falsified employee time cards and transferred expenses from other contracts to make up for an overrun on the Air Force work. The company was fined $1.04 million and ordered to repay the overcharges. And General Dynamics Corporation, also accused of overcharging the Defense Department, had two Navy contracts canceled in May and suffered a ban on new contracts for two months. The company was accused of billing the government $18,500 for country club fees for a company executive, of billing for private use of the corporate airplane, and other improprieties. (*See also* special report, page 359.)

In the first case of its kind, three officials of a now-defunct Chicago company, Film Recovery Systems, were found guilty of murder in the death of an employee who had inhaled cyanide at work. The judge charged that the company's managers had ignored symptoms of illness in employees, had the skull-and-crossbones warning removed from containers of cyanide, and failed to keep an antidote to cyanide poisoning on the premises. The three company officials were sentenced to 25 years in prison and fined $10,000 each.

Fallout from the FBI's Operation Greylord continued in Cook County, IL, when Circuit Judge Richard F. LeFevour was convicted in July of accepting cash, cars, and copying machines for dismissing thousands of parking tickets and scores of drunken driving cases.

The undercover FBI operation had resulted in 28 indictments, including those of three lawyers, seven judges, and seven police officers.

In January, John A. Zaccaro, the husband of 1984 Democratic vice-presidential candidate Geraldine A. Ferraro, pleaded guilty in New York to charges of scheming to fraudulently obtain financing for a multimillion-dollar real estate deal. The charge was a misdemeanor and carried a fine of less than $1,000.

Other 1985 cases saw the sentencing to a 20-year prison term of Tennessee financier Jake Butcher for bank fraud, and that of a Houston broker, Fred Soudan, to 35 years for an oil swindle. Former U.S. Deputy Secretary of Defense Paul Thayer received a four-year sentence for insider trading of stocks, while R. Foster Winans, a former *Wall Street Journal* reporter, was found guilty of using advance knowledge of his paper's articles to make illicit profits in the stock market. In San Diego, J. David Dominelli drew a 20-year sentence to federal prison for an investment swindle that had cheated an estimated 1,000 investors of more than $80 million. And Roger Hedgecock, the mayor of San Diego, was convicted in October of 12 counts of perjury and one count of conspiracy in connection with the financing of his campaign.

In light of the year's barrage of white-collar crime cases, U.S. Attorney General Edwin Meese in September proposed legislation requiring tougher penalties for offenses involving computers and providing additional authority for federal agencies to cancel contracts linked to bribes or other improper payments.

GILBERT GEIS

In July 1985 the U.S. Supreme Court in *Sedima v. Imrex Company* strengthened the campaign against organized crime by upholding the use of civil RICO prosecutions. These allow litigants to gain awards against organized criminals without having to prove prior convictions. Nor do they have to meet the higher standards of the criminal process, such as proof "beyond a reasonable doubt." The civil RICO law allows treble damages for extortion, embezzlement, and other offenses.

In addition, provisions of the Comprehensive Crime Control Act, applied for the first time in 1985, aided the campaign against organized crime. Under the "relation-back" doctrine of the act, the government is permitted to confiscate all profits from organized crimes. The statute has been used to keep alleged offenders from retaining high-priced lawyers.

According to a report on money laundering by the President's Commission on Organized Crime, funds obtained from drug enterprises and illegal gambling are increasingly being cleansed through legitimate organizations. Hearings also focused on the movement into organized crime of more recent immigrants.

Burglary. "Burglary is potentially a far more serious crime than its classification as a property offense indicates," noted Steven R. Schlesinger, director of the Bureau of Justice Statistics (BJS), after a 1985 study on that crime. The study found that in 13% of household burglaries, someone is at home. In 30% of such instances, the burglary turns into a crime of violence, such as rape, robbery, or assault. In fact, the study learned, three fifths of all rapes and robberies, and about one third of all assaults, are committed by burglars. Forty-two percent of burglaries were committed by relatives, acquaintances, or someone else known to the victim. In 7% of the burglaries, the offender proved to be a spouse or former spouse of the victim.

Families with annual incomes of less than $7,500 were most often burglarized, while black households were victimized more often than those of whites. Households in single-family dwellings had lower burglary rates than those in multifamily dwellings. Rental units also were burglarized more than owner-occupied quarters. The BJS noted that burglary, as "an invasion of one's home, produces permanent emotional scars." It took hope, however, in the fact that the burglary rate has dropped in recent years, perhaps because "people are becoming more careful about locking their doors and windows."

Auto Theft. Persons who steal automobiles, the National Highway Traffic Safety Administration learned during the year, concentrate on cars that have high dollar value and great demand either as complete cars or for their parts. The Buick Riviera, a top-of-the-line specialty sedan, was the car most likely to be stolen; it had a theft rate for the year of just over 16 cars per 1,000 vehicles manufactured. At the bottom of the list of cars stolen in terms of number produced were the Renault Fuego, various Volvo models, and such General Motors midsize cars as the Pontiac Phoenix, Chevrolet Cavalier, and Oldsmobile Firenza. Following the Buick Riviera as cars most often stolen were the Toyota Celica Supra, Cadillac Eldorado, Chevrolet Corvette, and Pontiac Firebird. An exception to the rule that expensive cars are more apt to be stolen was the Rolls-Royce. There were no reports of stolen Rolls-Royces in the past two years, probably because the vehicle is readily identifiable and carefully protected.

GILBERT GEIS
University of California, Irvine

AP/Wide World

Cuba's President Fidel Castro addressed the opening of the "Latin America Debt is Unpayable" conference.

CUBA

The government of Cuba began 1985 with expectations of an improvement in relations with the United States, an issue of major importance for the island's political and economic life. The year ended with tension between Havana and Washington at its highest point in a decade and little prospects for a change.

Cuban-U.S. Relations. In December 1984, Cuba and the United States signed an agreement under which Havana was to take back 2,746 refugees, most of them with criminal records, and the United States was to accept as many as 20,000 Cubans a year. Two U.S. Congressmen—Bill Alexander (R-AK) and Jim Leach (R-IA)—spoke with Cuban President Fidel Castro in Havana in January. They found Castro willing to discuss other outstanding issues with the United States, among them the withdrawal of Cuban troops from Africa and Nicaragua and the release of political prisoners in Cuba.

Cuban-U.S. relations took a sharp turn for the worse on May 20, however, when the United States inaugurated Radio Marti, a regular broadcast beamed at Cuba that is part of the Voice of America. Castro denounced Radio Marti as a "cynical and provocative" attempt at subversion and suspended the December 1984 agreement with the United States.

In early July, President Ronald Reagan included Cuba in a list of five countries that he

---

CUBA • Information Highlights

Official Name: Republic of Cuba.
Location: Caribbean.
Area: 44,197 sq mi (114 471 km²).
Population (July 1985 est.): 10,105,000.
Chief Cities (Dec. 31, 1982 est.): Havana, the capital, 1,951,373; Santiago de Cuba, 348,912; Camagüey, 251,003; Holguín, 189,604.
Government: *Head of state and government,* Fidel Castro Ruz, president (took office under a new constitution, Dec. 1976). *Legislature* (unicameral) —National Assembly of People's Power.
Monetary Unit: Peso (0.936 peso equals U.S.$1, July 1985).
Foreign Trade (1984 U.S.$): *Imports,* $8,144,000,000; *exports,* $6,172,000,000.

---

said formed "a confederation of terrorist states" run by "the strongest collection of misfits, Looney Tunes, and squalid criminals since the advent of the Third Reich." Castro countered by calling President Reagan "a big liar" and "a madman, an imbecile, and a bum" who was "saying a bunch of stupidities and lunacies." At the same time, news reports from Havana indicated that there were no hopes for the early withdrawal of Cuba's 30,000 troops in Angola and 5,000 in Ethiopia.

In August and again in October, Havana protested what it called "acts of arrogance," two overflights of Cuban territory by a U.S. Air Force SR-71 Blackbird aircraft. Cuba claimed it was the fifth and sixth such "spy violation" of Cuban air space since 1983.

On October 8, President Reagan imposed new restrictions on the entry of Cuban officials into the United States. The action barred the entry of Cuban government and Communist Party officials unless they were coming exclusively to conduct business at the Cuban Interest Section in Washington, the Cuban Mission to the United Nations in New York, or the United Nations itself.

Cuba and Latin America. At the same time, Havana's relations with Latin America were improving, a process that started with the strong support given by Castro to Argentina during the Falkland Islands crisis three years earlier. Argentina was actively trading with Cuba under a $600 million agreement that runs through 1987. In April the right-of-center president of Ecuador, León Febres Cordero, visited Cuba. Uruguay, Peru, and Brazil moved toward reestablishing full diplomatic relations with Havana. Even without formal ties with Colombia, Castro maintained close rapport with President Belisario Betancur.

At the beginning of 1985, Castro began an intensive propaganda campaign against the International Monetary Fund and U.S. banks. Attending the inauguration of Daniel Ortega as Nicaraguan president in January, Castro announced that Cuba was canceling Nicaragua's $70 million debt. He urged the United States and other creditor nations to follow his example and forego Latin American debts totaling $360 billion. Castro charged that Latin America's $360 billion debt was tantamount to an "imperialist economic aggression." Initially, he suggested that the debt be repaid to the banks by the U.S. government, using funds from a 12% reduction of the U.S. military budget. Later, Castro began urging Latin Americans to declare the debt null and void.

In August, Cuba hosted a five-day conference whose theme was "The Latin American Debt is Unpayable." About 1,200 people, mostly Latin leftists, were flown to Havana at Cuban government expense to attend. But Castro's intransigent position on the debt issue was not supported by Western Hemisphere leaders.

In July the newly inaugurated Peruvian president, Alan García Pérez, said that Latin America's repayment of foreign debt should be limited to 10% of the area's export earnings. The García proposal, which found support even among leftist leaders, annoyed the Cuban president, beginning what looked like an ideological and personal rivalry for Western Hemisphere leadership between the two.

Ironically, shortly before the Havana conference, Cuba renegotiated its own $3.5 billion debt to Western lenders, an obligation it agreed to pay in full. Repayment of the Soviet debt, estimated at $22 billion, is due in 1986.

Domestic Affairs. One casualty of Castro's almost obsessive preoccupation with the Latin debt issue was the Third Congress of the Communist Party of Cuba, a major event at which policy is reviewed and goals are set. Scheduled for December, the Congress was postponed until February 1986.

There were no major changes on the domestic front. The economy continued to be heavily subsidized by the Soviet Union, whose economic aid was estimated at close to $5 billion annually and military subsidy at $500 million annually. Cuba's economic plight was made worse by the low world market price of sugar, its principal export. During 1985 the price fluctuated between 3 and 4 cents per pound, while Cuban production costs were about 15 cents a pound. In November, Hurricane Kate caused heavy damage to agriculture.

Havana tried to increase foreign tourism, but income from this source was negligible. Cuban trade with the West continued its decline as a result of a shortage of hard currency and goods suitable for export.

As of July 1985, Cuba began selling state-owned houses to their inhabitants, including the right to rent them, to pass them on to children, and to obtain government loans for repairs. This small movement toward a market economy did not affect the otherwise total power and authority of the Castro regime.

GEORGE VOLSKY, *University of Miami*

CYPRUS

For Cyprus, 1985 marked the eleventh year of its division. Turkey had occupied the north in 1974. There, the "Turkish Republic of Northern Cyprus," founded in 1983 (and recognized only by Turkey), functioned under its Turkish Cypriot president, Rauf Denktas. The internationally recognized government of Cyprus remained under Greek Cypriot control, with Spyros Kyprianou as president. Though the United Nations had failed through formal resolutions to persuade the Turks to withdraw their occupation troops, estimated at between 17,000 and 20,000 men, a UN peacekeeping force has been stationed on Cyprus since 1964.

AP/Wide World

UN Secretary-General Javier Perez de Cuellar (center) sponsored talks between Cyprus President Spyros Kyprianou (left) and Turkish Cypriot President Rauf Denktas.

UN Efforts. Initially, hopes ran high for a solution to the Cyprus stalemate when UN Secretary-General Javier Pérez de Cuéllar brought Kyprianou and Denktas together, for the first time in about six years, at the United Nations. But four days of negotiations ended without the Greek Cypriots and the Turkish Cypriots agreeing on a plan devised by Pérez de Cuéllar to turn Cyprus into a federal republic. Each side blamed the other for the failure.

Turkish Cypriot Zone. Shortly after the UN summit collapse, Denktas announced that general elections would be held in his jurisdiction on June 23; these were carried out on schedule. In May a draft constitution for the Turkish sector was adopted by referendum, and in early June, Denktas was reelected president.

Nonetheless, in October the 49 heads of state and government of the Commonwealth nations, meeting in Nassau, reiterated their stand that Cyprus should remain an independent state with its territory intact and that the Turkish Cypriot state should not be recognized.

Kyprianou's Difficulties. Kyprianou's failure to reach an accord at the January summit caused enormous repercussions for him and his minority Democratic Party. He was criticized severely by the two most important parties in the Cyprus House of Representatives, the Communist AKEL and the conservative Democratic Rally. Calls for his resignation were

---

CYPRUS • Information Highlights

Official Name: Republic of Cyprus.
Location: Eastern Mediterranean.
Area: 3,572 sq mi (9 251 km²).
Population (mid-1985 est.): 700,000.
Chief Cities (1982 est.): Nicosia, the capital, 149,100; Limassol, 107,200.
Government: *Head of state and government,* Spyros Kyprianou, president (took office Aug. 1977). *Legislature*—House of Representatives.
Monetary Unit: Pound (0.589 pound equals U.S.$1, Aug. 1985).
Gross Domestic Product (1983 U.S.$): $2,100,-000,000.
Economic Index (1984): *Consumer Prices* (1977 = 100), all items, 175.2; food, 176.1.
Foreign Trade (1984 U.S.$): *Imports,* $1,364,000,000; *exports,* $575,000,000.

made. So bitter became the dispute that the House of Representatives dissolved itself on November 1 and set new elections for December 8.

Official results of the election, however, showed the Communists in third place (previously they were the strongest party), with the Democratic Rally first and Kyprianou's Democratic Party second. Thus, the odd alliance of Communists and conservatives in forming a majority of the House failed in their objective of forcing the resignation of the president.

Larnaca Crisis. During a siege with Greek Cypriot forces lasting nearly ten hours, three assailants, originally described as Palestinians, killed three Israeli hostages on a yacht at Larnaca harbor on September 25—Yom Kippur, the Jewish Holy Day. Subsequently, one of the gunmen was identified as a Briton, and in December the three were sentenced to life in prison. Although the Palestine Liberation Organization (PLO) denied complicity, Israel retaliated by bombing a PLO base in Tunisia.

Spy Trial. The sensational "Cyprus Spy Trial" in London, in which British servicemen were cleared of passing secrets to Soviets on Cyprus, highlighted the importance of the Akrotiri base, which is under British sovereignty.

GEORGE J. MARCOPOULOS, *Tufts University*

CZECHOSLOVAKIA

A government report indicated that Czechoslovakia's economic performance during the first half of 1985 was uneven. In comparison with the first half of 1984, industrial production increased by 2.8%, productivity in industry by 3.5%, output of engineering goods by 5.4%, electricity by 3%, electronics by 6.8%, the chemical industry by 2.7%, investments by 4.2%, foreign trade by 2.3%, retail trade by 3.7%, food production by 0.3%, and average wages by 1.3%. On the other hand, construction fell by 0.4%, freight transportation by 5.2%, and exports to nonsocialist countries by 7.2%. Meat and poultry production also declined, and fewer apartments were completed than in the first half of 1984. The cost of production dropped only a disappointing 0.2%, and the quality of Czechoslovak products did not improve as much as anticipated. The number of enterprises failing to meet their planned targets increased.

Church-State Relations. The main religious event of 1985 was the commemoration of the 1,100th anniversary of the death of Archbishop St. Methodius, the Greek missionary who, with his brother Cyril, brought Christianity to the Slavs of central and southeastern Europe and devised the first Slavonic alphabet. While the government could not very well ignore the commemoration, it spared no effort to distort the true meaning of the Greek brothers' mission by overemphasizing its secular significance and downgrading its religious importance. Rather than extend an official invitation to Pope John Paul II, the government allowed only a Vatican delegation led by Agostino Cardinal Casaroli to attend the climactic July 7 celebration at Velehrad, where St. Methodius is believed to be buried. A number of foreign clergymen wishing to participate, including the primate of Poland and the archbishops of Paris and Vienna, were denied visas. About 150,000 Czechoslovak Catholics attended the July 7 event, reaffirming the strength of the church despite decades of government repression.

Party and Government. The National Assembly unanimously elected Gustáv Husák, secretary-general of the Czechoslovak Communist party, to a third five-year term as the country's president. Col.-Gen. Milan Václavík was appointed as the new minister of defense. The Central Committee decided to convoke the 17th party congress for March 24, 1986.

Foreign Relations. On April 26, Husák and the leaders of the other Communist-controlled countries of Eastern Europe affixed their signatures to a 20-year extension of the Warsaw Pact. In May, Husák paid an official visit to Moscow, where he signed a 15-year program of Czechoslovak-Soviet economic and scientific-technical cooperation. A similar agreement with Mongolia was signed in June.

Among the foreign dignitaries paying official visits to Prague in 1985 were the foreign ministers of Cyprus, France, and Great Britain; the prime ministers of Denmark and Finland; President Daniel Ortega of Nicaragua; and the Vatican representatives Cardinals Casaroli and Luigi Poggi.

The Czechoslovak media utilized the 40th anniversary of the ending of World War II in May to extol the role of the Soviet Union in Germany's defeat, downgrading the contributions of the Western allies.

EDWARD TABORSKY
The University of Texas at Austin

CZECHOSLOVAKIA • Information Highlights

Official Name: Czechoslovak Socialist Republic.
Location: East-central Europe.
Area: 49,370 sq mi (127 870 km²).
Population (mid-1985 est.): 15,500,000.
Chief Cities (Jan. 1, 1983 est.): Prague, the capital, 1,185,693; Bratislava, 394,644; Brno, 378,722.
Government: *Head of state*, Gustáv Husák, president (took office 1975). *Head of government*, Lubomír Štrougal, premier (took office 1970). *Communist party, secretary-general*, Gustáv Husák (took office 1969). *Legislature*—Federal Assembly.
Monetary Unit: Koruna (12.11 koruny equal U.S.$1, July 1985).
Economic Indexes (1984): *Consumer Prices* (1970 = 100), all items, 120.6; food, 117.2. *Industrial Production* (1983, 1980 = 100), 107.
Foreign Trade (1984 U.S.$): *Imports,* $17,080,-000,000; *exports*, $17,196,000,000.

DANCE

Variety was the predominant feature of dance in 1985. Highlights included a display of tango dancing from Argentina, an American "reconstruction" of a "lost" 19th-century Danish ballet, and a series of controversial dance-theater pieces from West Germany. Only a few premieres could be called distinguished, but for the first time in many years, American choreographers showed greater interest in exploring more personal forms of expression. And the experimental dance sector looked less homogeneous than before.

Modern Dance. The public proved ready to flock to a wide range of dance, worrying little about how dance should be defined. But the most coherent aesthetic direction continued to be felt in modern dance companies still headed by choreographers known for their strong artistic profile.

Martha Graham created a new work, *Song,* based on the Bible's *Song of Songs.* Selected lines from the love poems were recited on tape by the actor Jeremy Brett, as dancers portraying lovers performed to Romanian folk music on a shepherd's pipe. *Song* proved both poetic and erotic.

Merce Cunningham choreographed *Phrases* and *Native Green* for his company, which also performed his 1984 *Doubles* in New York for the first time. Less oriented toward technical display than the other pieces, *Native Green* radiated an unexpectedly sensuous mood. Cunningham created a hauntingly beautiful work for the Pennsylvania Ballet, called *Arcade.* Paul Taylor composed a major modern dance piece, *Last Look;* as his company danced among mirrored slabs designed by Alex Katz, they evoked a wasteland of alienated beings frightened at the sight of themselves. In *Roses,* set to the music of Wagner, Taylor offered a flowing meditation on love.

Alvin Ailey's *For Bird—With Love,* about the jazz musician Charlie (Bird) Parker, had its New York premiere. (The Alvin Ailey American Dance Theater had presented it the year before in Kansas City, MO.) Bill T. Jones and Arnie Zane were responsible for another new work in the Ailey troupe, *How to Walk an Elephant.*

Lar Lubovitch's *A Brahms Symphony,* an ensemble piece to the first three movements of the composer's Third Symphony, offered a sweeping, passionate visual equivalent to the music. This kind of neo-Romantic work signaled a change from the many pieces set to minimalist music choreographed by Lubovitch. A similar unpredictability was seen in premieres by Trisha Brown (*Lateral Pass*), Molissa Fenley (*Esperanto* and *Cenotaph*), and younger choreographers who began to attract critical notice, such as Mark Morris and Pooh Kaye.

Laura Dean, one of the first to dance to the minimalist music of Steve Reich, collaborated with him on a new work, *Impact.* Another premiere, *Transformer,* was set to music by Anthony Davis. Miss Dean's newest pieces, interesting in their exploration of partnering and movement, were more theatrical and less ritualistic than before.

Miss Dean appeared in the Brooklyn Academy of Music's "Next Wave Festival," which, after three years, became a fashionable and well-attended event. American choreographers presented premieres in this experimental series —Margaret Jenkins' *Inside Outside* and *Pedal Steal;* Carolyn Carlson's *Blue Lady;* Nina Wiener's *In Closed Time*—but interest centered on the return of Pina Bausch's Tanztheater Wuppertal and the debuts of other West German choreographers. Reinhild Hoffmann's *Callas,* performed by the Tanztheater Bremen, used images that alluded to Maria Callas' operatic career and the role of women and artists in society. Susanne Linke's program of solos was more successful, powerful in its Existential studies.

As in 1984, Miss Bausch's works were considered the sensations of the dance season. Again, many felt her dance-theater pieces were too violent, emphasizing brutality rather than tenderness in male-female relations. Yet her moment-by-moment catalog of social ills was often balanced by humor and striking theatrical settings. *Arien* was performed by a superbly disciplined company in ankle-deep water and featured a hippopotamus played by two men. *Kontakthof,* set in a dance hall, explored longings for affection and was one of Miss Bausch's best works. *On a Mountain a Cry Was Heard* was chilling in its theme that people can be forced to submit to one another but not to love each other. *The Seven Deadly Sins* was Miss Bausch's interpretation of the 1933 Kurt Weill–Bertolt Brecht theater piece.

The dynamism of new modern dance trends in other countries was evident in the number of U.S. debuts. The Japanese dance-theater genre known as Butoh was represented by one of its cofounders, the 79-year-old Kazuo Ohno, in *The Dead Sea* and *Admiring La Argentina;* by the young dancer Kuniko Kisanuki; and by Muteki-Sha, the company of Natsu Nakajima, whose moving childlike or grotesque images concerned wartime trauma and maturity.

Two French companies demonstrated a strong individual stamp. Jean-Claude Gallotta's Groupe Emile Dubois presented *The Survivors* and *The Adventures of Ivan Vaffan.* This New York debut delighted or puzzled viewers with its Rabelaisian irreverence. The experimental troupe at the Paris Opera—Groupe de Recherche Chorégraphique de l'Opéra de Paris —won over its audience at the American Dance Festival in Durham, NC, with the superb level of its dancers' technique and polish.

Juan Carlos Copes and María Nieves (center) and María and Carlos Rivarola salute the tango in "Tango Argentino."

Ballet. The ballet world was more concerned with romantic themes. Salt Lake City's Ballet West attracted international attention with *Abdallah,* a reconstruction of an 1855 ballet with an *Aladdin's Lamp* story. Toni Lander, the Danish-born ballerina, and Bruce Marks revived this ballet (unperformed since 1858) by the 19th-century Danish choreographer August Bournonville. Equally successful was the first American production of *La Fête Étrange,* a 1940 ballet by the late English choreographer Andrée Howard. The Louisville Ballet of Kentucky performed the haunting work with great sensitivity.

The premieres of the New York City Ballet unexpectedly favored romantic motifs. These included Peter Martins' *Poulenc Sonata, Valse Triste* to Sibelius, Jerome Robbins' *In Memory Of . . .* to Berg's *Violin Concerto,* and Jean-Pierre Bonnefoux's *Shadows,* with music by Frank Martin. Martins, who staged Bournonville's *La Sylphide* for the Pennsylvania Ballet, also created *Eight More* and *Eight Miniatures,* to Stravinsky. Robbins' *Eight Lines,* to Steve Reich's music, completed the premieres for the company, which revived George Balanchine's 1958 *Gounod Symphony* for the first time in 20 years.

The American Ballet Theatre staged Kenneth MacMillan's *Romeo and Juliet* and *Anastasia,* revived Antony Tudor's *Dim Lustre,* and presented the premieres of Fernando Bujones' *Grand Pas Romantique* and David Gordon's *Field, Chair and Mountain.* Gordon, a modern dance choreographer, created *Piano Movers* for the Dance Theater of Harlem, whose other new work was Domy Reiter-Soffer's *La Mer.*

The Joffrey Ballet gave its own popular version of *Romeo and Juliet,* by the late John Cranko. Gerald Arpino's *Jamboree,* commissioned by the city of San Antonio, and Philip Jerry's *Hexameron* were the premieres. Jiri Kylian's *Forgotten Land* received its American premiere with the company.

The Feld Ballet presented new works by Eliot Feld to Steve Reich's music: *The Grand Canon, Medium: Rare, Aurora I,* and *Aurora II.* Feld also choreographed *Against the Sky* and *Intermezzo No. 2.*

Visiting ballet companies included the Berlin Ballet with Natalia Makarova in the title role of Roland Petit's *The Blue Angel,* which was poorly received; Maurice Béjart's Ballet of the 20th Century; the Royal Ballet of Flanders with works by Valery Panov; the Basel Ballet; the Hamburg Ballet; and Aterballetto from Italy.

Other. No production from abroad became as popular as *Tango Argentino,* a display of the tango by professional ballroom dancers who were the toast of Broadway.

A new event was the Prix de Lausanne ballet competition, usually held in Switzerland, transferred for one time to the Brooklyn Academy of Music. The Samuel H. Scripps–American Dance Festival award went to Alwin Nikolais, whose *Crucible* had its premiere at the festival. Merce Cunningham was a recipient of the Kennedy Center Honors. The Capezio Award went to Doris Hering, director of the National Association of Regional Ballet.

The dance world was saddened by the deaths of Ben Sommers, founder of the Capezio Award; John Martin, the first official dance critic at *The New York Times* from 1927 to 1962; Toni Lander, who had been a Ballet Theater ballerina during her international career; and Karel Shook, codirector of the Dance Theater of Harlem.

Continuity was provided elsewhere. Helgi Tomasson retired as a principal dancer with the New York City Ballet to become director of the San Francisco Ballet. Bruce Marks became director of the Boston Ballet. John Hart, once with Britain's Royal Ballet, succeeded Marks at Ballet West in Utah.

ANNA KISSELGOFF
"The New York Times"

DELAWARE

Political transition and budget surpluses were the most significant factors characterizing Delaware's public life in 1985.

Political Change. Delaware's new governor, Michael N. Castle (R), took over the reins of state government from popular Gov. Pierre S. duPont IV (R), who had served the state for eight years. Governor Castle pledged to emphasize education reform, hazardous-waste cleanup, and improvements in the state's human services. A top priority for the new administration was to be the improvement of services to children, families, and persons suffering from mental disorders.

Delaware's most populous unit of local government received new leadership as Rita Justice took the oath of office as New Castle County executive. Her administration stressed better management of economic growth. Land development and transportation issues in the highly urbanized "corridor" that stretches through northern New Castle County absorbed much of the attention of the New Castle County administration.

Wilmington's newly elected Mayor Daniel Frawley placed the emphasis of his administration on stimulating the growth of "blue collar" employment through expansion of facilities at the Port of Wilmington, improved housing, and continued revitalization of the city's deteriorating areas.

Democratic Party domination of both houses of the legislature was replaced by Republican control in the House of Representatives. A political leadership split in the two chambers brought on a slowing in the pace of legislative activity. Deadlocks developed in the areas of budget adoption, tax reform, and pay for state employees. Political debate also centered on a surplus of current-year revenues. As the legislative session progressed, compromises were worked out as the new governor and legislative leaders became accustomed to working together.

Economy. In fiscal year 1984, state revenues continued to rise and outdistance expenditures. This pattern was maintained through the 1985 fiscal year and was expected to last through the next fiscal year. Past tax cutting, however, was expected to have an impact on revenue in fiscal 1987. Delaware lowered its top income tax bracket to 9.7% and increased the personal exemption to $800. The seasonally adjusted unemployment rate stood at 5.0% as of September 1985, well below the national average. More than 20 banks have moved into the state to take advantage of its Financial Centers Development Act, passed in 1981.

High-tech economic development became a goal advocated by many of the state's leaders. The University of Delaware joined in a partnership with corporate and governmental leaders

---

DELAWARE • Information Highlights

Area: 2,044 sq mi (5 295 km²).
Population (July 1, 1984 est.): 613,000.
Chief Cities (1980 census): Dover, the capital, 23,512; Wilmington, 70,195; Newark, 25,247; Elsmere, 6,493.
Government (1985): *Chief Officers*—governor, Michael N. Castle (R); lt. gov., S. B. Woo (D). *General Assembly*—Senate, 21 members; House of Representatives, 41 members.
State Finances (fiscal year 1984): *Revenues,* $1,494,000,000; *expenditures,* $1,211,000,000.
Personal Income (1984): $8,383,000,000; per capita, $13,685.
Labor Force (Sept. 1985): *Civilian labor force,* 313,444; *unemployed,* 15,774 (5.0% of total force).
Education: *Enrollment* (fall 1983)—public elementary schools, 61,181; public secondary, 30,225; colleges and universities, 31,945. *Public school expenditures* (1982–83), $294,222,012 ($3,456 per pupil).

---

to stimulate the growth of high-tech business. As part of this effort, the university announced plans for a new $25 million research program to establish a national research center for composite materials. The center, supported in part by a $7.5 million National Science Foundation Grant, will help make Delaware one of the leading research and development centers for lightweight products, similar in composition to plastic, with great strength.

The DuPont Company, in an effort to cut costs, provided its employees with an attractive early retirement incentive. More than 11,000 employees took advantage of this program. Of the total, 2,500 worked in Delaware.

The Environment. Water supply was a major concern in 1985 as a major drought developed over the middle Atlantic states. Delaware was not as hard hit as some of its neighboring states, but nevertheless was forced to adopt mandatory water restrictions late in the summer.

Hazardous waste continued to intensify as a major long-range concern for environmental officials and community groups. Federal and state authorities began remedial actions in some of the state's most critical areas.

JEROME R. LEWIS, *University of Delaware*

DENMARK

Parliamentary opposition to the Strategic Defense Initiative (SDI or "Star Wars"), labor unrest, and the withdrawal of Greenland from the European Community (EC) were among the year's major issues in Denmark.

Political Affairs. The Danish parliament (Folketing) in May strongly voiced its opposition to U.S. President Ronald Reagan's Star Wars concept with a vote of 64 to 0, with all four government parties abstaining. The parties voting against the SDI and Danish participation were the Social Democrats, the Radicals, the Left Socialists, and the Socialist People's

Party. Prime Minister Poul Schlüter's ruling coalition, consisting of the Conservatives, the Liberals, the Center Democrats, and members of the Christian People's Party, was thought to show a marked weakness in the area of security and disarmament.

Economic Affairs. A wage agreement between the Federation of Trade Unions and the Employers Federation, in effect for two years, was due to expire in March. Early talks ended in a deadlock, and the efforts of a mediator were also of no avail. The result was Denmark's biggest labor conflict since 1973, with strikes and lockouts affecting 300,000 private-sector workers. On March 27 the government announced the imposition of a settlement, subsequently approved by the Folketing 85 to 80. The settlement included a 2% increase the first year of the agreement and no more than 1.5% the second year, with a one-hour reduction in the work week to be introduced by March 1, 1987. The unions protested, and strikes continued for a short time; there were clashes with the police, and a 60,000-strong demonstration in front of Christiansborg castle, the home of the Folketing. The strikers, however, eventually returned to work at the call of union leaders.

The Faeroe Islands. In local elections in November 1984 the coalition cabinet in power in the Faeroe Islands was ousted, and a new cabinet took office in January. It was headed by Atli Dam, the leader of the Social Democrats, and included representatives of the Social Democrats, and the Republican, the Self-Government, and Christian People's parties. The new cabinet was approved with 17 affirmative votes in the 32-member Faeroese parliament (Lagting). The Faeroe Islands enjoy home rule within the kingdom of Denmark.

Greenland. The regional government of Greenland, on the basis of a referendum, had previously decided to leave the EC, and the step was made official in 1985. Greenland's relationship with Denmark was not altered, with

AP/Wide World

Denmark's Prime Minister Poul Schlüter visited with U.S. President Reagan in Washington in September. "Star Wars" was a central issue in U.S.-Danish relations.

Greenlandic representatives serving in the Danish parliament, and technical and financial assistance contributed by the mother country. Relations with the EC were not completely broken off, however, since fishermen from the EC countries would continue to operate in waters off Greenland, with the EC paying approximately $20 million for such access.

The year 1985 also marked the adoption of a separate flag for Greenland: red and white with a circular design in the middle.

Terrorism. Terrorist violence reached Denmark in July when a synagogue and a nursing home as well as the local office of Northwest Orient Airlines were bombed, with 27 persons injured. A telephone call from Beirut claimed that Islam Jihad, a Shiite organization, was responsible. In September a second Jewish edifice was bombed, with 12 persons wounded.

Refugees. The presence of approximately 10,000 refugees, mainly from the Middle East, gave rise to violent protests on the part of Danish youth. The young Danes voiced resentment at aid and work being given to refugees while many of them remained unemployed. In Kalundborg, 400 young men attacked a hotel housing 60 Iranian refugees, resulting in numerous injuries. Other attacks were made in Copenhagen, Aalborg, and Haderslev.

ERIK J. FRIIS
"The Scandinavian-American Bulletin"

DENMARK • Information Highlights

Official Name: Kingdom of Denmark.
Location: Northwest Europe.
Area: 16,632 sq mi (43 076 km²).
Population (mid-1985 est.): 5,100,000.
Chief Cities (Jan. 1, 1983 est.): Copenhagen, the capital, 1,372,019; Århus, 182,645; Odense, 137,606.
Government: *Head of state,* Margrethe II, queen (acceded Jan. 1972). *Head of government,* Poul Schlüter, prime minister (took office Sept. 1982). *Legislature* (unicameral)—Folketing.
Monetary Unit: Krone (9.39 kroner equal U.S. $1, Nov. 6, 1985).
Gross National Product (1983 U.S.$): $56,400,-000,000.
Economic Indexes (1984): *Consumer Prices* (1975 = 100), all items, 357.4; food, 231.5. *Industrial Production* (1975 = 100), 116.
Foreign Trade (1984 U.S.$): *Imports,* $16,975,-000,000; *exports,* $16,334,000,000.

AP/Wide World

Bolivian troops make a cocaine bust. The U.S. and some Latin governments have stepped up their antidrug offensive.

DRUGS AND ALCOHOL

The Reagan administration in 1985 followed the lead of the three previous presidencies by mounting intensive, highly publicized campaigns against drug abuse and illicit drug trafficking. Nonetheless, in September, Attorney General Edwin Meese III told a Senate Committee that he expected the use and availability of cocaine and other dangerous drugs to remain high. Meese added that he thought that marijuana and heroin use would decline slightly, although data compiled by the federal Drug Enforcement Administration (DEA) cast doubt on that assessment.

Meanwhile, the drive to fight drunken driving continued at the state and federal levels. During the year, Virginia became the 37th state to raise the legal drinking age to 21. Neighboring Maryland passed a law making it illegal to consume alcoholic beverages, including beer, while driving. Maryland raised its drinking age to 21 in 1982. But in the District of Columbia, which is surrounded by Maryland and Virginia, the legal age for beer and wine is 18 and for hard liquor 21, raising fears that teenagers from the suburbs would flock to the District to drink. Under a law passed in 1984, a portion of federal highway construction funds will be withheld from states that do not enact a minimum drinking age of 21 by 1987.

Federal Efforts. DEA officials say that southern Florida is the center of drug trafficking in the United States, although smuggling by air, sea, and land takes place in many other states as well. For example, about three quarters of the cocaine intercepted nationwide in 1984 was seized in the DEA's Florida-Caribbean district. To combat trafficking, Congress appropriated funds for a fleet of 104 high-speed boats to be stationed in southern Florida and manned by U.S. Coast Guard and Customs Service personnel.

Nonetheless, a report issued in June by the General Accounting Office said that current federal antidrug efforts "still fall far short of what is needed to substantially reduce the flow of illegal drugs into the United States." Drug seizures by the U.S. Customs Service lag far behind domestic consumption. In 1984, Customs impounded an all-time record amount of cocaine—27,525 lbs (12 485 kg), worth some $7.5 billion in street value. But the DEA estimated that cocaine consumption was 85 metric tons in 1984 and that the total would grow to 100 tons in 1985, more than double the estimated 45 tons consumed in 1981.

Data on marijuana and heroin show similar patterns. Marijuana consumption rose from an estimated 9,600–13,000 metric tons in 1981 to 13,600–14,000 tons in 1983, but Customs seizures of marijuana in 1984 totaled only 3.3 million lbs (1.5 million kg), valued at $2.5 billion. Heroin use increased from 3.89 tons in 1981 to 4.12 tons in 1983, while Customs impoundments of the drug in 1984 were limited to 684 lbs (311 kg), valued at $383 million. (While DEA and Customs figures indicate that overall marijuana use is still rising, data compiled by the National Institute on Drug Abuse suggest that per capita consumption may have leveled off or declined slightly. Drug experts agree, however, that data on substance abuse are, at best, imprecise.)

In August, Attorney General Meese flew to Arkansas to launch a nationwide campaign to eradicate domestic stands of *cannabis sativa* plants, the source of marijuana. Meese said

that during the coming year federal, state, and local officials would join forces to destroy millions of *cannabis* plants in all 50 states, many of them growing in national parks and forests and on other federally owned land.

Domestic *cannabis* accounts for only about 11% of the marijuana consumed in the United States, and marijuana itself is only one of a wide range of illicit drugs that plagues American society. Observers believe that Meese's Arkansas foray was in all likelihood an attempt to convince foreign governments that the United States is serious about dealing with its drug problems.

International. The DEA says that Latin America is the principal source of illicit drugs entering the United States. All the cocaine consumed in the United States comes from South America—three quarters of it from Colombia and another 20% from Peru and Bolivia. One third of the country's heroin is smuggled in from Mexico, while more than 80% of the marijuana originates in Colombia, Mexico, and Jamaica.

In recent years, the U.S. government has concentrated its international efforts in developing cooperative antidrug campaigns with those three countries. But drug law enforcement officials say that many other Latin American countries are also involved in the drug business. Cocaine refining, for example, takes place not only in Colombia but also in Argentina, Brazil, Bolivia, Ecuador, Mexico, Nicaragua, Peru, and Venezuela. Refueling, transshipment, and repair facilities for planes and boats used in the drug trade are known to exist in the Bahamas, Belize, Jamaica, the Dominican Republic, Haiti, Puerto Rico, the Turks and Caicos Islands, and other small cays and islets in the Caribbean.

Enlisting the cooperation of other governments is difficult, say U.S. officials, because the drug trade has become important to many national economies. Drug exports, for instance, are worth more to Colombia than its chief legal export, coffee. (An analogous situation exists in the United States, where marijuana has become the country's second leading cash crop, exceeded in value only by corn and well ahead of such staples as wheat, soybeans, or oranges.)

Nonetheless, important gains in international cooperation were made during the year. With help from the United States and Colombia, Peru began a major crackdown on cocaine processing laboratories and clandestine airports used for smuggling. In August the newly installed government of President Alan García arrested 37 police officers on drug charges.

Also in August, the United States began conversations with Mexico and Jamaica on expanding cooperative antidrug efforts. In July, 12 Jamaicans were sentenced to jail by a Jamaican court on drug charges stemming from an investigation that, for the first time, involved DEA agents working undercover in Jamaica. In August, an Air Jamaica jet plane suspected of carrying drugs was seized by the Customs Service at New York's Kennedy International Airport, and the same month, Eastern Airlines was fined $1.37 million following the discovery of nearly a ton of cocaine on two flights from Colombia.

Loophole. During the year, U.S. federal officials moved to close a loophole in drug laws that has permitted the manufacture of so-called "designer drugs," synthetic compounds closely resembling illegal narcotics and hallucinogens. The chemistry of such substances is sufficiently distinct from that of illicit drugs that they have been beyond the reach of existing criminal penalties in the Federal Controlled Substances Act, even though their effects are as strong or stronger than the drugs they resemble. In July the DEA invoked emergency powers to ban three of the substances, MPP and PEPAP, which are similar to the narcotic meperidine, and Ecstasy, a synthetic hallucinogen. At the same time, the Justice Department proposed to Congress an amendment to the Controlled Substances Act providing for a 15-year prison term and a $250,000 fine for persons convicted of producing or distributing "designer drugs."

Alcohol. In most parts of the United States, alcohol is a legal drug, but its use and abuse are among the most serious of American health problems. Heavy drinking is deeply ingrained in the country's history. (In 1830 the average American drinking man consumed about half a pint of liquor a day.) But, for the moment at least, American attitudes toward drinking seem to be changing. The current trend appears to be toward more temperate habits.

In May, *Time* magazine devoted a cover story to "America's New Drinking Habits," and concluded that, "People are drinking less, and seem to be proud of it." The new concern with physical fitness, *Time* said, has noticeably cut into sales of alcoholic beverages. The magazine reported that, while sales of bottled water soared in 1984, per capita consumption of distilled spirits fell from 2.88 gal (11.08 l) in 1974 to 2.46 gal (9.46 l) in 1984. Brewers registered their first sales slump since 1957, and sales of wine, which experienced strong growth in the 1970s, grew more slowly.

At its midyear meeting in Washington, the American Bar Association endorsed a sweeping program to combat teenage alcohol and drug abuse, including efforts to raise the drinking age to 21 in the 13 states and the District of Columbia that had not yet done so. But the ABA backed away from endorsing a tax increase on alcohol to pay for the prevention, treatment, and research programs it approved.

RICHARD C. SCHROEDER
Author, "The Politics of Drugs"

ECUADOR

The democratic regime of Ecuador remained intact during 1985, under conservative President León Febres-Cordero Ribadeneyra. Although during the first half of the year frequent clashes occurred between the president and Congress, which was controlled by the opposition, relations improved in June, when government backers achieved a majority in the legislature.

A major clash between the president and the opposition occurred in January. Febres-Cordero decreed 63–67% increases in the price of gas, 50% increases in urban transport fares, and other rises in basic commodities. The Frente Unitario de Trabajadores (FUT), the coalition of the country's three major trade union confederations, reacted by calling a general strike. Confrontations with police left 50 persons killed and 500 injured. In Quito 500 protesters were arrested.

In March a controversy developed between the president and Congress over a proposal, submitted by Febres-Cordero under an "urgency" procedure, to raise the minimum wage. When Congress did not pass any legislation, President Febres-Cordero enacted his own minimum wage law, which provoked a one-day general strike by the FUT.

The president scored a political victory in June, when two party deputies of the opposition Democratic Left declared themselves independents, joining forces with the administration bloc and giving it a majority. In August the new majority elected one of its own members to replace the former opposition leader as president of Congress.

But the economic situation remained uncertain. In April the government announced that economic pressures had forced it to raise oil production above the quota assigned by OPEC. Only later did Ecuador ask OPEC for an increase in its quota. In July the government oil company announced that new exploration efforts might double the country's reserves.

In March, Ecuador was granted a $110 million standby loan from the International Monetary Fund (IMF), but in September the IMF delayed disbursement of $21.3 million because Ecuador allegedly had not fulfilled all the conditions.

In April, agreement was reached on the refinancing of $200 million in debts scheduled to come due during the period 1984–87. Then in August an agreement was reached for a $200 million loan from the private banks.

The Febres-Cordero government gave strong emphasis to attracting foreign investment. Between August 1984 and July 1985, it was announced, $89 million in new investment had entered the country, compared with $44 million the previous year. Some $61 million of the new money was in the form of direct investments. The principal sources were the United States, West Germany, and Japan. Giving promise were three new oil exploration contracts signed in 1985.

ROBERT J. ALEXANDER, *Rutgers University*

ECUADOR • Information Highlights

Official Name: Republic of Ecuador.
Location: Northwest South America.
Area: 109,483 sq mi (283 561 km²).
Population (mid-1985 est.): 8,900,000.
Chief Cities (1982 census): Quito, the capital, 1,110,248; Guayaquil, 1,300,868; Cuenca, 272,397.
Government: *Head of state and government,* León Febres-Cordero Ribadeneyra, president (took office August 1984). *Legislature* (unicameral)—Congress.
Monetary Unit: Sucre (117 sucres equal U.S.$1, financial rate, Oct. 23, 1985).
Gross National Product (1983 U.S.$): $11,300,-000,000.
Economic Index (1984): *Consumer Prices* (1981 = 100), all items, 226.5; food, 285.5.
Foreign Trade (1984 U.S.$): *Imports,* $1,717,000,000; *exports,* $2,569,000,000.

AP/Wide World

President Léon Febres-Cordero and Mrs. Febres-Cordero welcomed Pope John Paul II to Quito on January 29. The pope spent three days in Ecuador.

In March public school teachers in Arkansas assembled at the Capitol in Little Rock to protest the state's teacher-testing law. Testing teachers for competency was a big issue across the nation in 1985.

AP/Wide World

EDUCATION

Reports critical of higher education programs, federal cuts in college student loans, and teacher education reform dominated U.S. educational news in 1985. The U.S. Supreme Court ruled against public school prayer and against use of public school funds to enrich religious school programs. There were fewer teacher strikes than in 1984, but the opening of the 1985–86 school year was marked by consternation over children with AIDS attending public schools.

Church-State Separation. On June 4, by a 6–3 vote, the U.S. Supreme Court declared unconstitutional Alabama's 1981 one-minute silent meditation school prayer law. The decision affected the legality of similar "moment of silence" laws in 25 states.

On July 1, the U.S. Supreme Court voted 5–4 against using public funds for teaching in religious schools. The ruling specifically struck down "shared time" programs in New York City and Grand Rapids, MI, in which public school teachers taught remedial and enrichment classes in religious schools. New U.S. Education Secretary William J. Bennett (*see* BIOGRAPHY) said he could not understand the court's "fastidious disdain for religion." The Reagan-appointed secretary, who succeeded T.H. Bell in February, wrote the 50 state school superintendents that, except for "shared time," federal and state school funds might legally be used to aid private and religious schools.

The U.S. Senate on September 10 voted 62–36 to table and thus kill a bill sponsored by Sen. Jesse Helms (R-NC) to prevent federal court challenges to organized public school prayer.

The three decisions were setbacks for the Reagan administration, which has favored public school prayer and government aid to private and religious schools.

AIDS. School and health officials in New York City decided to permit children with AIDS to attend public school, and objecting parents demonstrated vociferously. The 165 U.S. children under age 13 diagnosed as having AIDS (of whom 52 were still alive in mid-September) received the virus from their mothers before birth, from their mother's blood during delivery, or through later blood transfusions. The usually fatal disease aroused great fear throughout the country. According to one poll, half of all Americans believed that AIDS can be transmitted by casual contact, despite health experts' statements to the contrary. Such misinformation heightened parental concern as well as uncertainty among school officials. (*See* MEDICINE AND HEALTH.)

School Polls. In an August 21 National Education Association (NEA)/Gallup poll, 63% of respondents said that raising teachers' salaries would improve teacher quality; 52% (45% in 1983) favored more spending on education "even if it means higher taxes"; and 60% believed teacher competency tests would raise education quality.

A Phi Delta Kappa/Gallup poll on August 28 showed that 71% of parents with children in public schools gave those schools a grade of A or B. Of the total sample, 43% graded their community's public schools A or B; 27% graded the nation's public schools A or B. NEA President Mary Futrell said that parents had confidence in the schools they knew best. Of those surveyed, 49% gave local teachers an A or B grade, 75% supported sex education in public high schools, and 52% approved sex education in public elementary schools. Polls also showed less public support than in 1983 for school vouchers. Observers felt that greater public confidence in public schools is based on tougher courses, longer school days, stricter testing, and more homework.

Teacher Strikes/Raises. More than 20 teacher strikes (compared with 105 in 1984) were reported in early September, most notably in Chicago and Seattle, as well as in Michigan, Pennsylvania, Ohio, and Mississippi. The

decline in strikes was attributed to higher pay, with many teacher salaries 7–10% higher than in 1984. New Jersey's minimum starting salary for new teachers, $18,500, was the highest in the United States. Teachers' salaries averaged $23,582 in 1984–85.

High School Student Searches. On January 15 the U.S. Supreme Court ruled, 6–3, that public school officials can legally search students on "reasonable grounds" of violation of school rules. The decision upheld a Piscataway, NJ, public school search case involving drugs in a student's purse.

Federal Student Aid Cuts. The Reagan administration's 1986 budget proposed large federal cuts that limited Guaranteed Student Loans to students from families earning under $32,500 a year, Pell Grants to students from families earning less than $25,000 per year, and no more than $4,000 in federal aid per year per student. Opponents said the cuts would harm low-income and minority students, shift enrollment from private to cheaper public colleges, and make state taxpayers pay for more faculty and facilities. Congress resisted the amount of the proposed student loan cuts but expected to vote a limit on college student aid because of the huge federal deficit, rising college costs, and students' default in repaying federally guaranteed loans. College costs rose 7% in 1985, averaging $10,000 a year at private and $5,000 a year at public colleges and universities. Half of U.S. high school graduates go to college, compared with about 15% in Great Britain, West Germany, and Japan. Education Secretary Bennett said in August that the Internal Revenue Service would withhold tax refunds from a million college student loan defaulters who owe more than $4 billion in repayments.

U.S. Public and Private Schools

	1985–86	1984–85
Enrollment		
Kindergarten through Grade 8	30,940,000	30,950,000
High school	13,740,000	13,680,000
Higher education	12,200,000	12,350,000
Total	56,880,000	56,980,000
Number of Teachers		
Elementary and secondary	2,500,000	2,450,000
Higher	700,000	700,000
Total	3,200,000	3,150,000
Graduates		
Public and private high school	2,600,000	2,700,000
Bachelor's degrees	945,000	960,000
First professional degrees	74,000	74,000
Master's degrees	290,000	295,000
Doctor's degrees	33,000	33,000
Expenditures		
Public elementary-secondary school	$146,000,000,000	$136,500,000,000
Private elementary-secondary	13,300,000,000	12,400,000,000
Public higher	67,400,000,000	63,000,000,000
Private higher	34,800,000,000	32,500,000,000
Total	$261,500,000,000	$243,400,000,000

University of California President Emeritus Clark Kerr observed, "The federal era in higher education has clearly ended." New initiatives and money, he said, now will come from the states.

Teachers' National Test/Merit Pay. On January 29, American Federation of Teachers (AFT) President Albert Shanker called for a national "Board of Professional Education" to devise an entry-level test for licensing new teachers. As with lawyers' state bar examinations, the test would cover subject matter and education theory and would include one to three years of supervised internship. This combination, according to Shanker, would replace inadequate teacher tests, uneven state standards, and the tendency to lower teacher requirements during a serious shortage. The national test and internship plan would stimulate university schools of education to reform. With higher salaries and professional autonomy, the plan would attract the 150,000 able new teachers needed by 1988. Shanker said the 610,000-member AFT would deny membership to those who failed the test and urged the 1.7 million-member NEA to do the same.

On July 11, Shanker also endorsed a merit pay plan. Just as physician specialists are state-board certified, so also teachers with more training and experience could apply for higher pay to national certification boards in mathematics, science, and other fields.

In June, NEA President Futrell also endorsed a national test to certify new teachers. By her plan, states would decide themselves whether to use the test and would set their own passing score. As of late 1985, 31 states tested new teachers for certification. Arkansas went a step further in March, when it tested veteran teachers over the vehement objection of the NEA state affiliate; 10% failed the test.

Some educators fear that tests for new and veteran teachers will adversely affect minority teachers. Others see a danger in states certifying liberal arts and science graduates who lack teacher education courses. In 1985, New Jersey allowed such graduates to teach after 20 days of supervision; they would receive full certification after one year of teaching. Florida and Texas planned to follow suit, but the American Association of Colleges for Teacher Education objected to such programs. "It's enlightened self-interest," said a prominent educator about teacher unions' turnout in endorsing merit pay and tests for new and veteran teachers. NEA and AFT members, he said, along with the public, industry, and politicians, want real school reform, and that means higher teacher standards and performance.

Scholastic Aptitude Test (SAT). David Owen's 1985 book, *None of the Above: Beyond the Myth of Scholastic Aptitude,* charged that the SAT, taken by 1.5 million college-bound high

The U.S. Illiteracy Problem

Laubach Literacy Action

Adult illiteracy, a problem more common and less often recognized than either alcoholism or cocaine abuse, received considerable attention in 1985. Much of the credit belonged to author Jonathan Kozol, who highlighted the issue with his book *Illiterate America.*

It is difficult to take exact measure of the problem because of different definitions of varying degrees of illiteracy. But by all accounts the scope of the problem is enormous. According to official 1985 estimates, 27 million American adults, 1 in 5, were functionally illiterate, unable to fill out a simple job application or read a newspaper headline. And the situation was growing steadily worse, with two million more adults each year joining the ranks of the functionally illiterate. Kozol defined the epidemic in even broader terms and set the number of victims much higher. By his reckoning, fully one third of the adult American population, 60 million people, were unable to look up a telephone number, read health warnings on household-product containers, or effectively shop in a typical supermarket.

Along with other experts, Kozol noted that the curse of illiteracy is self-perpetuating. Illiterate parents cannot read to their children—the most often prescribed means of developing the ability and desire to read. Illiterate parents are also more likely to have low-paying jobs, or none at all; in general, children from poor families are less likely to receive a good education. Illiteracy, in short, may well be passed on.

Precisely because the American educational system is designed to provide basic literacy to all despite their backgrounds, the recognition of widespread illiteracy amounted to an indict-ment of the schools. The educational system's failures already had been well documented and had drawn intense concern through the early 1980s. Many of those problems had begun to be corrected, but educators remained concerned. They feared the fast-paced advance of technology would require even higher standards of literacy.

School reform, moreover, would come too late for the millions of American adults already living in illiteracy. Many of them appeared to manage well enough by relying on familiarity, memorization, and sheer bluff. Yet as the magnitude of the problem claimed the national spotlight, more and more illiterate adults seemed willing to come forward, admit their difficulty, and try to do something about it. Two major volunteer agencies were on hand to help: Laubach Literacy Action, with 50,000 volunteers in 600 local branches in 41 states; and Literacy Volunteers of America, with 200 programs in 36 states. Late in 1984 an umbrella organization, the Coalition for Literacy, mounted a major national campaign to publicize the plague of illiteracy. The federal government also was contributing $100 million through its Adult Basic Education initiative.

Author Kozol insisted that was not enough. He called for a national commitment of $10 billion a year for ten years, which he figured would reduce the adult illiterate population by half. It remained unlikely, however, that such a massive effort was forthcoming. A better bet was that increased publicity would give impetus to educational reforms that would help alleviate the situation.

DENNIS A. WILLIAMS

To show support for U.S. teachers, Secretary of Education William J. Bennett went on an eight-day teaching tour as the 1985–86 school year began. Bennett had previously taught on the university level.

AP/Wide World

school students annually, is badly conceived, badly written, easy to beat, and penalizes the poor and minorities who cannot afford SAT coaching. On July 30 the Educational Testing Service (ETS), which sponsors SAT, called Owen's arguments distortions. ETS took court action to bar two coaching firms from using copyrighted SAT questions illegally obtained. The dispute comes at a time of increased testing, with states having raised academic standards and legislatures demanding greater accountability. Yet SAT scores, after a 22-year decline, rose in 1985.

Anti-South Africa Protests. Columbia University students held protests April 4–25, demanding that the university sell its investments in firms doing business in South Africa. Similar student protests occurred at Syracuse, Rutgers, Princeton, Cornell, and the University of California campuses as well as at the South African embassy in Washington. Though much tamer than anti-Vietnam War protests in the late 1960s and early 1970s, the antiapartheid issue was embraced by students often said to be apathetic about social issues. Their protests helped induce the limited economic sanctions imposed by the Reagan administration in September. Since 1977, according to one report, 54 U.S. colleges and universities have withdrawn their South Africa–connected investments. (*See also* feature article, page 26.)

Higher Education Reports. In 1985 a report by the Association of American Colleges, *Integrity in the College Curriculum: A Report to the Academic Community,* blamed research-oriented faculty for allowing "fads and fashions" to dominate in "a marketplace philosophy." The Carnegie Foundation for the Advancement of Teaching, in *Corporate Classrooms: The Learning Business,* reported that U.S. firms (such as IBM, AT&T, Xerox, and others) spend $40 billion annually to educate nearly 8 million people in ways that "surpass many universities."

The College Board's *Equality and Excellence: The Educational Status of Black Americans* found a drop in college attendance, completion rates, and job opportunities for blacks, the result in part of federal cuts and rising requirements.

The Southern Regional Education Board, in *Access to Quality Undergraduate Education,* offered 15 steps to raise the "unacceptably low" quality of undergraduate education.

Momentum for teacher education reform came from a report by the Holmes Group of 23 public and private research university education deans, "Goals for Educating Teachers as Professionals." Also, the 14-member Task Force on Teaching as a Profession was appointed in May, backed by the Carnegie Corporation of New York, to report on ways to upgrade teacher education.

Blaming low school standards for a decline in U.S. industrial competitiveness, a report by the Committee for Economic Development, *Investing in Our Children: Business and the Public Schools,* called on high schools and colleges to work with the business community to improve the national economic well-being.

The noted education writer Fred M. Hechinger pointed to the conflicting views in the many reports critical of U.S. education since the landmark 1983 report *A Nation at Risk,* by the National Commission on Excellence in Education. The problem, Hechinger suggests, is that different authors use different yardsticks to measure the faults and successes of U.S. education. Once again the old argument over the purpose of American schooling is being raised: one camp wants tougher courses and tests to serve national economic and defense needs, even though many children will fail; others want a flexible school curriculum to serve the needs, capacities, and interests of all children.

FRANKLIN PARKER
West Virginia University

EGYPT

During 1985 the Egyptian government was tested by continued deterioration of the economy, a resurgence of internal political opposition, and challenges to its leadership in Middle Eastern affairs.

Domestic Affairs. A decline in income from three main sources of hard currency—remittances from Egyptian workers abroad, oil exports, and Suez Canal tolls—as well as increased consumption of imported food forced President Hosni Mubarak to seek a large increase in U.S. aid. During a visit to Washington in March, he requested that U.S. aid be stepped up from $2.1 billion to more than $3 billion in fiscal 1986. Washington indicated that an additional $200 million might be provided.

Minister of Economy and Trade Mustafa al-Said resigned in April amid increasing criticism of his policies and accusations of his involvement in a major financial scandal. With the economic erosion continuing, Prime Minister Kamel Hassan Ali and his cabinet resigned in September. Mubarak's naming of Ali Lufti, an economics professor and former finance minister, as the new prime minister was a sign of his new emphasis on the nation's economic problems.

In 1985, Islamic fundamentalists seemed to be back in larger numbers than at any time since the assassination of President Anwar el-Sadat in 1981. Prominent fundamentalist leader Sheikh Hafez Salama threatened in June that if the "law of God" were not enforced before the end of the Ramadan fast, he would lead the "Green Marchers" (pious Muslims) in a march to the presidential palace to demand immediate imposition of *sharia* (Koranic law). The government responded in mid-July with a massive antifundamentalist crackdown, ending a two-year tacit "truce." The operation led to scores of arrests, including that of Sheikh Salama, and the closing of his mosque in Cairo. The Ministry of Religious Affairs also took control of all private mosques.

Government cognizance of the growing fundamentalist wave was evidenced by support in parliament for stricter enforcement of Islamic codes and the arrest of 40 members of the Baha'i faith, considered heretical by strict Muslims. In May the government reached a compromise in the National Assembly by persuading those who demanded immediate introduction of *sharia* to accept instead the removal of all legal references contrary to Islamic law. The constitutional court did abrogate the "Jihan law" (named after the late President Sadat's wife) permitting a wife to divorce her husband if he marries another.

Foreign Affairs. In seeking support for his Mideast peace plans, President Mubarak visited the United States, Great Britain, France, Jordan, and Iraq during the year. In several conferences with Jordan's King Hussein, efforts were made to coordinate an Egyptian-Jordanian-PLO initiative calling for U.S. negotiations with a joint Jordanian-Palestinian delegation as preparatory to Arab-Israeli talks.

Egypt and Israel held talks in January on the issue of Taba, a tiny sliver of land adjoining Israel's port of Eilat in dispute between the two countries since the 1979 peace accords. The talks were continued in hopes of a meeting between President Mubarak and Israel's Prime Minister Shimon Peres. Mubarak had declared that he would be prepared to meet Peres after resolution of the Taba issue, complete Israeli withdrawal from Lebanon, and a first step in settlement of the Palestinian question. By year's end little progress had been made on the Taba issue, though one barrier to improved relations had been removed with the departure of most Israeli forces from Lebanon. Negotiations with Israel were jeopardized, however, by several incidents. In August an Israeli diplomat was assassinated in Cairo by a previously unknown group called "Egyptian Revolution." And in October, seven Israeli tourists in the Sinai were killed.

Peace efforts also were retarded by Israel's air attack on PLO headquarters in Tunis during September and by the seizure of an Italian tourist ship, the *Achille Lauro,* by a faction of the PLO off the Egyptian coast in October. The hijackers finally surrendered in Alexandria and were sent from the country on an Egyptian airliner. U.S. Navy fighter planes forced the airliner to land in Italy, seriously straining relations between Cairo and Washington. The incident also sparked demonstrations by Cairo students against both the U.S. and Egyptian governments. Then in late November, Egyptian military forces stormed an EgyptAir plane that had been hijacked by Palestinian terrorists en route from Athens to Cairo, then forced to land in Malta. The controversial Egyptian assault left nearly 60 persons dead.

DON PERETZ
State University of New York, Binghamton

EGYPT • Information Highlights

Official Name: Arab Republic of Egypt.
Location: Northeastern Africa.
Area: 386,660 sq mi (1 001 449 km^2).
Population (mid-1985 est.): 48,300,000.
Capital: Cairo.
Government: *Head of state,* Hosni Mubarak, president (took office Oct. 1981). *Head of government,* Ali Lufti, prime minister (took office September 1985). *Legislature* (unicameral)—People's Assembly.
Monetary Unit: Pound (1.25 pounds equal U.S.$1, Nov. 8, 1985).
Gross National Product (1983 U.S.$): $20,000,000,000.
Economic Index (1984): *Consumer Prices* (1970 = 100), all items, 421.4; food, 535.7.
Foreign Trade (1983 U.S.$): *Imports,* $10,274,000,000; *exports,* $3,215,000,000.

ENERGY

During the first five months of 1985, energy consumption in the United States was lower than for the same period in 1984. That this could occur during a period of economic growth was an indication of the energy conservation revolution that has occurred since the Arab oil embargo of 1973.

In the eight years prior to the 1973–74 oil crisis, energy consumption increased at an annual rate of 4.5%, thus doubling every 16 years. Growth in the U.S. economy followed a similar pattern, and it was widely believed that continued economic growth required continued growth in energy consumption. In the wake of the 1973 embargo, with the goal of assuring adequate supplies, a number of major studies of future energy needs were undertaken. Many of those studies took 1985 as their first major reference point. It is appropriate, therefore, to compare those mid-1970's projections with what has occurred during 1985.

Energy experts use a measure called the quad (quadrillion British thermal units or Btu's). A quad is a huge amount of energy, equivalent to 183 million barrels of oil. In 1973 the United States used roughly 74 quads of energy.

In 1974 during the crisis, a study funded by the Ford Foundation concluded that by 1985 it would be possible to have continued economic growth with consumption remaining level at 91 quads. When this 91-quad projection was made public, it was severely criticized by the vast majority of energy experts and leaders of the energy industry. These critics argued that energy and economic growth could not be uncoupled. To enjoy economic growth the critics said the nation would need between 100 and 116 quads in 1985. Many critics of the Ford Foundation study argued that its conclusions reflected the no-economic growth desires of its authors more than a realistic understanding of the relationship between economic growth and energy consumption.

Two years later, in 1976, using the largest computer model of the nation's energy system ever built, the federal government projected that U.S. energy consumption in 1985 would be 100 quads. This federal study concluded that, even if a maximum effort were made to conserve energy, the lowest possible consumption would be 93 quads.

In fact, energy consumption during 1985 was between 74 and 75 quads. Energy consumption was almost exactly equal to that of 1973, while the size of the nation's Gross National Product (GNP) had increased by roughly one third. The energy conservation performance of 1985, then, was 19% better than the most optimistic estimates of the middle 1970s and anywhere from 26 to 37% better than most experts believed possible. The nation's ability to use energy ever more efficiently has meant abundant supplies and stable prices. Oil has continued as the bellwether energy source, and during the first half of the year it was selling for roughly $1 a barrel less than in 1984. At $27 a barrel, the price was $8 lower than at its peak during 1981.

Consistent with its bellwether role, oil has led the consumption turnaround. During 1985, Americans used 1.5 million barrels a day less than in 1973 and 3 million barrels a day less than during the peak consumption year of 1979. Even in the face of a slight decrease in domestic production, imports were roughly 1.5 million barrels lower than 1973's 6 million barrels a day. When the Arab members of the Organization of Petroleum Exporting Countries (OPEC) declared the embargo, they provided 17% of U.S. oil. In 1985 that rate was 9%. Consumption of natural gas had declined to slightly more than 17.5 trillion cubic feet (496 billion m^3), 20% below the 1973 level.

With overall energy consumption at the 1973 level but with declines in oil and gas, another positive trend was evident. Oil and gas are the nation's premium fuels—ideally suited to transportation and home heating. The primary cause of the decline in oil and gas use was movement by the nation's electric utilities and industry to more abundant fuels—specifically, coal and nuclear energy. Consumption of coal, the nation's most abundant energy resource, was 30% higher in 1985 than in 1973. Similarly, consumption of electricity had increased by 25%.

No energy source had experienced quite as radical a change during the period as nuclear power. On the one hand, the contribution of nuclear energy to the nation's electricity supply had grown from 4.5% in 1973 to 14.6% in 1985. Given a 25% increase in electricity use, the growth of nuclear energy was quite striking. On the other hand, expectations with regard to the future of nuclear power have gone in just the opposite direction. In 1973 there were some 219 nuclear power plants operating or on order. By 1985 that number had declined to 132 with the prospect that some of the plants under construction might be canceled. Further, no nuclear plants have been ordered in the United States since the late 1970s.

What explains the striking changes in consumption over the last 12 years? First, while energy costs are stable and have declined from their peak in 1981, energy still represents something above 10% of all U.S. expenditures. Even when adjusted for inflation, energy cost Americans twice what it had in 1973, a real incentive for conservation. American industry has been very responsive to energy costs and has made the greatest strides in conservation. Industry used 13% less energy than it did in 1973, while economic activity grew one third in the same time frame.

Control room operators at Three Mile Island (PA) restart the Unit 1 nuclear reactor on October 3, a day after start-up had been cleared by a U.S. Supreme Court ruling. The undamaged reactor had been shut down since the 1979 accident at Three Mile Island Unit 2.

AP/Wide World

Similarly, improvement occurred in the transportation sector. Passenger car efficiency has increased from roughly 13 miles per gallon (5.5 km/1) to roughly 17 miles per gallon (7.2 km/1)—a 25% improvement. Unfortunately, at midyear it appeared 1985 might be the first year since the embargo when the efficiency of new cars did not improve. The reasons were lower gasoline prices and a renewed public desire for larger, more powerful cars.

Consistent with consumption patterns, U.S. coal production was roughly 35% larger than in 1973, natural gas production was down by 20%, and oil production was down by 3%. The nation's huge coal reserves mean that coal production is controlled by demand, a combination of domestic consumption, and exports. Natural gas production is controlled by domestic consumption. Domestic oil production occurred at peak capacity, since reduced consumption was met by reduced imports.

Although the United States has been able to maintain its oil production at roughly the 1973 level, that has occurred at the expense of declining proved reserves. Proved oil reserves during 1985 were 23% lower than in 1973. Energy experts agree that the nation's proved reserves will continue to decline and shortly production also will decline.

International Developments. The nation's major non-Communist industrialized allies have experienced much the same pattern with regard to energy consumption. During 1985, oil consumption in the rest of the non-Communist industrialized world was roughly 1.5 million barrels lower than in 1973. However, the industrial allies of the United States have not enjoyed oil price relief because on the international market oil is paid for in dollars.

For example, given the high value of the dollar vis-à-vis their currencies, during 1985 the French were paying 19% more for oil and the Italians 14% more than they had paid in 1981, the year prices peaked.

The same pattern of higher costs for oil was experienced by most of the less-developed nations. Less-developed nations, however, differed from America's industrialized allies in that their consumption of oil has grown. Available data suggest that consumption of oil in the less-developed and newly industrializing nations was 50% higher during 1985 than in 1973. Finally, unlike the United States, worldwide proved reserves of oil and gas increased significantly between 1973 and 1985. The increase was 11% for oil and 67% for gas.

With the world awash in oil, 1985 was a year full of repeated predictions that the Organization of Petroleum Exporting Countries (OPEC) would collapse. Member nations met repeatedly to establish production goals and prices and then proceeded to violate their agreements. Conflict characterized OPEC meetings, yet the organization continued to defy all predictions of collapse. OPEC remained the single largest reason for oil prices being as high as $27 to $28 per barrel.

Both the number and the effectiveness of Iraq's attacks on Iran's oil export capabilities increased. During August and September, the Iraqis launched successful attacks on Iran's major Kharg Island export facility. Independent observers suggested that Iraqi attacks had, at least temporarily, severely reduced Iran's ability to export. Oil exports appear key to the Iranians' ability to sustain the war with Iraq. Iran responded by capturing several ships in the Persian Gulf carrying supplies to Iraq. In

previous years this increased conflict would have sent shocks through the world oil market, but it had no impact during 1985 because of the world's excess production capacity.

U.S. Energy Policy. On Jan. 1, 1985, approximately half the nation's natural gas was removed from federal price controls. This reversed a situation that had been in effect since 1954. In response to the gas shortages of 1976 and 1977, the Congress had passed legislation that established a program of gradual decontrol. Opponents of this legislation had argued that with decontrol would come a rapid escalation in gas prices. In fact, January 1 turned out to be a nonevent. Gas prices remained steady and supplies abundant. Natural gas had disappeared as a major policy issue before the Congress.

During the year, support for the Synthetic Fuels Corporation continued to deteriorate. That corporation had been established in 1980 in response to the second oil shock triggered by the Iranian revolution and had been given an initial $22 billion to build a synthetic-fuels industry. The corporation was never able to implement a program capable of achieving the goals set in the legislation. During 1985 several members of the House of Representatives pushed strongly for the withdrawal of all but $500 million of the corporation's funding.

The one major synthetic-fuels plant built in the United States, the Great Plains Coal Gasification Plant, located in Beulah, ND, began full-scale operation during the year. With natural gas prices soft, however, the synthetic gas from that plant was not competitive. The companies that built the plant with a $1.5 billion federal subsidy announced that the plant would be closed unless additional subsidies were provided. The Reagan administration opposed subsidies. Opponents of the plant argued that it

is a waste of the taxpayers' money to continue subsidizing it. Supporters argued that the plant should be run until sufficient experience has been gained to ensure the nation has a capability to move rapidly to a commercial synfuels operation should that become necessary.

In combination, the energy surplus and the Reagan administration's belief that energy development is a responsibility of the private sector led to a major reduction in research and development (R&D). The Department of Energy's R&D budget has been reduced from nearly $5 billion in 1980 to less than $2 billion in 1985. Most evidence indicated that private sector R&D followed a similar pattern.

Restructuring of the Oil Industry. The most widely reported events with regard to energy were associated with the efforts by T. Boone Pickens (*see* BIOGRAPHY), an Amarillo, TX, oilman, and Carl Icahn, a New York investor, to take control of some of the nation's largest oil companies. Both Pickens and Icahn justified their efforts at takeover by arguing that the oil companies were being inefficiently managed. In no instance did Pickens or Icahn successfully carry out a takeover, but their actions did lead to a number of mergers and the financial restructuring of several companies. Some observers saw these developments as weakening the capacity of the companies to explore for and find new oil and gas resources. Other observers saw them as the necessary restructuring of an industry faced with lower-cost oil.

Surplus supplies resulting from increasingly efficient use made 1985 a year of energy complacency. Pessimists argued that energy surpluses and low prices were only a transitory condition and complacency was not justified. Optimists argued that surplus would continue through the end of the century.

DON E. KASH, *The University of Oklahoma*

Saudi Oil Minister Ahmed Zaki Yamani (right) and Mexico's Oil Minister Francisco Labastida meet reporters after a January meeting of OPEC in Geneva.

ENGINEERING, CIVIL

Transportation needs spurred the building of bridges, canals, and tunnels in 1985. Dams to control floods, maintain waterways, and supply water for power, irrigation, and human consumption also received special emphasis.

Bridges

United States. Virginia's bridge-building program included four new spans over the James River in the vicinity of Richmond to ease traffic congestion in the state capital's downtown area. Longest of the four is a 4,680-ft (1 426-m) six-lane, cable-stayed concrete bridge with a 630-ft (192-m) main span having a 145-ft (44-m) vertical clearance. The $34 million bridge will become part of Interstate 295. All four bridges are scheduled for completion by 1994.

Illinois was building a 32-ft (9.8-m) wide, two-lane structure over the Mississippi River south of Quincy to carry westbound traffic on U.S. 24 to Missouri. An existing parallel span, to be rehabilitated, will continue to carry eastbound traffic. The new $17 million, cable-stayed structure will have a 900-ft (274-m) main span and 440-ft (134-m) side spans, with steel composite decks and bowed twin concrete towers.

Denmark. Zealand, Denmark's main island, was being linked to Falster, an island to the south, by a 2.1-mi (3.4-km) two-bridge, four-lane crossing. The $120 million project crosses Faeroe Island in the Storstrom Channel. The 1-mi (1.6-km) section, north of Faeroe, is a low-level bridge with 262-ft (80-m) spans. From Faeroe south, the 1.1-mi (1.8-km) bridge consists of the same length spans except for the shipping channel portion. That is crossed by a cable-stayed segment of orthotropic steel-box girders with a main span of 951 ft (290 m) flanked by 394-ft (120-m) side spans. The deck passes through diamond-shaped concrete towers. The new structure replaces a two-lane 1937 crossing and will link Scandinavia with continental Europe by way of Route E4.

Japan. A record-span suspension bridge was shelved in Japan because of budget limitations, but the overall plan to link the country's four main islands by road and rail continued. Interest centered on connecting the main island of Honshu with Shikoku to the south. Still on the drawing board was a 5,933-ft (1 808-m) suspension span to go from Kobe, on Honshu, to Naruto, on Shikoku, crossing Awaji Island. But already well along in construction was a double-deck, four-lane bridge from Kojima, on Honshu, to Sakaide, on Shikoku. This crossing of Bisan Strait in the Inland Sea, due for completion in 1987, includes a pair of suspension bridges, built in tandem, with a length of 11,000 ft (3 353 m). They have a common anchorage

in 167 ft (51 m) of water. The longer of the two, at 5,743 ft (1 750 m), will have a main span of 3,667 ft (1 118 m) with a vertical clearance of 217 ft (66 m). Japan also was completing the 800-ft (244-m)-deep, 34-mi (55-km)-long Seikan railway tunnel under Tsugaru Strait joining Honshu with the northern island of Hokkaido.

Canals

United States. The Tennessee-Tombigbee ship canal, linking the Tennessee River with the deepwater port of Mobile on the Gulf of Mexico, opened in 1985 after 12 years of construction. Built by the U.S. Army Corps of En-

The Tennessee-Tombigbee Waterway, 12 years in the making, links the Tennessee River with the Gulf of Mexico.

U.S. Army Corps of Engineers

gineers at a cost of $2 billion, the 234-mi (377-km) Tenn-Tom Waterway shortens the Mississippi River route to the gulf by up to 875 mi (1 408 km). The slack water quality of the canal, contrasting with the powerful Mississippi currents, favors lower fuel costs for shipping. Ten locks are traversed; no fees are charged. Some 307 million yd³ (235 million m³) were excavated to provide the 9-ft (2.7-m) depth by 300-ft (91-m) width. From the Tennessee River, near the southern border of Tennessee, the waterway cuts 39 mi (63 km) through a geographic divide to a 46-mi (74-km) chain of lakes type of canal to the 149-mi (240-km) stretch of the Tombigbee.

Colombia. A new waterway, which would be an alternative to the Panama Canal, was proposed by Colombia. A deep-draft canal through the northern part of the country would connect the Caribbean Sea with the Pacific Ocean using portions of the Atrato and Truando rivers. The 115-mi (185-km) waterway could handle 285,000-ton vessels. The sea-level canal would have no locks. Japan indicated an interest in both the financing and the construction of the project.

Dams

United States. The U.S. Army Corps of Engineers was constructing an auxiliary dam east of Simmesport, LA, to support existing control structures designed to prevent the Mississippi River from changing its course to the Gulf of Mexico. The $147 million flood-control dam, scheduled for completion in 1986, will be 160 ft (49 m) high by 442 ft (135 m) long. Its concrete piers, built on piles, support six 500-ton rotating radial steel tainter gates that can be opened and closed individually to any position. The new dam will augment two existing barriers—a low-level structure and an overbank structure—that permit controlled flow from the Mississippi to Red River through an outflow channel. Further to the south, Old River provides another controlled flow from the Mississippi to meet with Red River. Both Red and Old rivers then join the Atchafalaya River, which takes the shortest route to the Gulf at Morgan City, LA—140 mi (225 km).

Japan. Work on Tamagawa Dam, Japan's second major roller-compacted concrete (RCC) gravity embankment, began in 1980 and will be completed in 1988. The multipurpose flood-control, water-supply, and electric-power project is located at the north end of Honshu Island. It will be 1,450 ft (442 m) long, 330 ft (101 m) high, and will cross the Tama River. The total 980,000 yd³ (749 264 m³) of concrete was being spread by tractor-dozers in three 10-in (25-cm) lifts. Each 30-in (76-cm) layer gets 12 passes with a 7-ton vibratory roller, and six passes with rubber-tired rollers to avoid segregation of the coarse aggregate. After a four-day wait another layer is placed. A savings of 10% in costs and one year in time was anticipated by using RCC over conventional mass concrete.

Malaysia. The $250 million Trengganu hydroelectric project will supply 400 megawatts (Mw) from the rural east, along the South China Sea, to the populous western areas of Malaysia, including Kuala Lumpur, the capital. The project includes damming Trengganu River with 508-ft (155-m)-high Kenvir rock-fill dam containing 24 million yd³ (18 million m³) of material. The river was diverted through two 2,800-ft (853-m) tunnels through the left abutment. The unlined tunnels are 49 by 39 ft (15 by 12 m). Four turbine generator sets were scheduled to go on line in late 1985.

Tunnels

United States. The N.Y. State Department of Transportation was given permission to build the 4.2-mi (6.8-km)-long Westway, Interstate 478, up the west side of Manhattan, New York City, from the Brooklyn-Battery Tunnel north to connect with the trans–Hudson River Holland and Lincoln tunnels. As 1985 wore on, however, legal and political battles continued, and the $2-billion project seemed doomed. Most of the six-lane route would have been tunneled through fill dredged from the Hudson River. Westway would have replaced the deteriorated elevated section of the West Side Highway that had been demolished.

Los Angeles was preparing to construct its first 4-mi (6.4-km) section of double-track subway in the downtown business district connecting five stations. Eventually, Metro Rail will consist of an 18.6-mi (30-km) subway running west along Wilshire Boulevard, north to Hollywood, and into the San Fernando Valley. Much of the line will be in deep rock tunnel. Cost of the entire project is estimated at $3.4 billion, with a 1990 completion date.

India. Calcutta completed the initial 2.4-mi (3.9-km) section of a projected 10-mi (16-km) double-track subway to relieve dense traffic conditions in the heavily populated city. This first portion of India's big construction project took 12 years to complete. The total line, with 17 stations, is scheduled for completion by 1990 at a cost of $1.3 billion. Technical help was provided by Hungary, Japan, and the Soviet Union. Some portions of the subway advanced by shield tunneling, but most of the work was done by cut-and-cover excavation within sheet piling. The sheeting was later replaced by slurry-wall construction. Excavation between the heavily braced slurry walls was handled almost entirely by some 3,000 men and women workers who used hoes and baskets to dig up and transport the soft clay subsoil from the deep cut in a former river bed.

WILLIAM H. QUIRK, *Construction Consultant*

On February 11, New York Gov. Mario Cuomo signed the Great Lakes Charter—an agreement by eight states and two Canadian provinces to protect the lakes from diversion.

AP/Wide World

ENVIRONMENT

Pollution from hazardous waste and industrial chemicals was in the news continually during 1985, both in the United States and at the international level. The danger posed by these contaminants not only to the environment but to human life was dramatized by the catastrophic December 1984 poison gas leak from a Union Carbide plant in Bhopal, India, which took more than 2,000 lives. In 1985, as criticism of Union Carbide over the Indian disaster mounted, the same company and chemical were in the news again as new leakage problems were discovered in the United States. Not all the environmental news was bleak, however, as strides were made in wildlife and environmental conservation and in gearing up coordinated programs for the future.

World Developments

Africa. Continued drought, desertification, and famine in Africa during the year lent credence to the position of international conservation groups that environmental protection is not just a matter of saving nature but of assuring the survival of human life. The umbrella group for global conservation, the International Union for the Conservation of Nature and Natural Resources (IUCN), coordinated several international programs aimed at helping African nations solve their pressing environmental problems.

The IUCN announced in June that it had formed a special task force to develop "an integrated action plan for the ecological rehabilitation of African countries affected by drought and desertification." Experts from around the world would seek scientific and technological solutions to the problem, according to IUCN spokesmen.

Africa, or at least the eastern portion of the continent, was the focus of another IUCN meeting, held in January. Conservation groups from several countries gathered at the Kenya National Museum in Nairobi to review existing programs and to plan future action to conserve wildlife in Kenya, Tanzania, and Uganda. Such groups as the New York Zoological Society, Frankfurt Zoological Society, and World Wildlife Fund assessed their various roles in East African conservation. The Frankfurt organization, for example, has stressed support for reserves in Tanzania, while the New York Zoological Society has focused on research and its applications in Kenya and Uganda. The IUCN declared that its own role should be to provide a regional overview and to coordinate the conservation efforts of governments and nongovernmental organizations in the region.

CITES. More than 450 delegates from 87 countries met in Buenos Aires, Argentina, during April for the biennial session of nations belonging to the Convention on International Trade in Endangered Species of Wild Fauna and Flora (CITES). The group meets every two years to review progress of the convention and to examine the status of species it covers.

A major action by the delegates to the 1985 meeting was the establishment of new international controls on the market in raw African elephant ivory. Under the plan, African nations exporting ivory must establish quotas and will have to mark and issue export licenses for all tusks involved. CITES nations that import ivory will accept tusks only from countries with elephant populations and no more than allowed under the quota system.

The disposal of toxic waste remained a prime environmental problem. Above, a volunteer fills large drums with toxic waste taken from the Niagara Falls, NY, sewer system.

Another CITES decision affected the Nile crocodile, which had been fully protected from commercial trade in hides. Malawi, backed by 25 African countries, asked that ranching of the species and limited trade in the crocodile's skins be allowed. The countries argued that crocodiles were increasing in number and threatening livestock and people and that some trade could be carried on without endangering the animal. The proposal was approved with a quota of just over 11,600 skins per year.

Greenpeace. The Greenpeace environmental organization, which has a long history of disrupting seal hunts, whaling operations, and nuclear waste dumping, literally came under attack in July for protesting French nuclear exercises in the South Pacific. Explosives planted on a Greenpeace protest ship, the *Rainbow Warrior,* exploded on July 10 and sank the vessel; one person, a photographer for the organization, was killed. The incident took place in the harbor of Auckland, New Zealand, where the *Warrior* was docked.

Two weeks later New Zealand police arrested a pair of French nationals and charged them with murder in the incident. The *Warrior*

episode caused a major scandal in France when, after initial denials by the French government, it was revealed that the ship had been sunk by a team of military advisers acting under orders from high government officials. The scandal led to the resignation of the country's defense minister and the dismissal of its secret service chief. (*See also* FRANCE.)

Acid Rain. In July, some 20 European nations and Canada, meeting in Helsinki, Finland, signed an agreement to reduce sulfur dioxide emissions, a major cause of acid rain.

Deer. The Père David's deer of China has been known to the Western world only since the 19th century. It was found by a French missionary, Père Armand David, in an imperial hunting park near Beijing (Peking). The big animal was described by the Chinese as having the antlers of a deer, the neck of a camel, the hooves of a cow, and the tail of a horse. Scientists believe that the deer in the park were the last survivors of a species that once roamed wetlands over a wide area of China.

After Père David found the deer, Western nations persuaded the Chinese government to send some of the animals to European zoos and preserves. Soon afterward, around the turn of the century, the deer still remaining in China perished during a series of natural calamities and wars. The species was kept alive by those in captivity in the West.

During March 1985, Chinese conservation authorities discussed plans to reintroduce the deer in their native country. Fencing of the preserve was near completion as the year drew to a close, and the Chinese hoped to receive animals and release them early in 1986.

Wild Horse. Hopes also were expressed during the year that another endangered Asiatic animal could be reestablished in the wild. Scientists from the Soviet Union, North America, Europe, and Mongolia met in Moscow during May to discuss reintroduction of the Przewalski's, or Mongolian, wild horse into its native habitat on the Central Asiatic steppes. The only true wild horse, this species is believed to be extinct in the wild, although there are reports of a few animals in remote areas. The horse has been successfully bred in captivity, and about 600 live in zoos and preserves.

Forestland. In 1985, designated International Year of the Forest, the UN Food and Agriculture Organization (FAO) rallied support for the protection and enhancement of the world's forestry resources and their role in rural development. Individual nations also took steps to protect forestland. In Canada, for example, where forestland is the most valuable natural resource, an economic mainstay, and the largest employer, the post of minister of state for forestry was revived by Prime Minister Brian Mulroney in 1984 to find ways to restore dwindling timberlands and a lagging forestry industry.

U.S. Developments

Chemical Leaks. The Union Carbide chemical plant in Institute, WV, was the focus of a major Environmental Protection Agency (EPA) report issued early in the year. The report described several leaks of methyl isocyanate, the same chemical accidentally released in the 1984 Bhopal tragedy. The report found that the Institute plant had leaked the chemical in gaseous form 28 times in five years, although no injuries other than minor eye and mouth irritations had resulted. The leaks, attributed to equipment failure and human errors, were small compared with the amount released in India; totals ranged from 1 to 840 lbs (.45 to 381 kg). The largest release occurred in January 1984, when a broken fuel line spewed out 14,000 lbs (6 350 kg) of liquid chemicals. The plant was closed temporarily, and the company spent more than $5 million making safety improvements, including a new emergency warning system.

In August 1985, however, another leak of hazardous chemicals sent toxic gas pouring into the air above the plant and over the surrounding community. The leak, of ingredients used in making a pesticide, resulted from three burst gaskets in a storage tank. Carbide officials did not warn local officials because the company believed that the leak had been contained within the plant. Not until the gas had spread were the authorities alerted and warning sirens sounded. More than 130 residents had to be treated for respiration problems, irritated eyes, nausea, or dizziness. After an investigation, the federal Occupational Safety and Health Administration (OSHA) cited Carbide for willful neglect of safety regulations. The company denied the charges, but OSHA proposed fining the company, and some members of Congress called for even stiffer penalties.

Toxic Discharge Compliance. Private industry obtained a measure of relief from toxic discharge standards when the U.S. Supreme Court ruled that EPA may, under some circumstances, exempt individual industrial plants from full compliance with nationwide limits on discharges. The decision overturned a 1983 ruling by a federal appeals court that prohibited EPA from granting individual exemptions from the provisions of the Clean Water Act. The appeal was made by the EPA, which argued that it needed flexibility, and by the Chemical Manufacturer's Association.

Appointments. Following the November 1984 resignation of EPA head William Ruckelshaus, Lee M. Thomas, the official in charge of the agency's toxic waste programs, was appointed to the post by President Ronald Reagan. Thomas had been recommended for the position by Ruckelshaus, who had earned generally high marks from environmental groups during his one and a half years as EPA head.

On May 1, 1985, Donald P. Hodel, who became secretary of the interior earlier in the year, announced the selection of William Penn Mott, Jr., to be director of the National Park Service. Mott had served as director of California's park service when Ronald Reagan was governor, president of the California State Park Foundation, and a trustee of the National Parks and Conservation Association.

Acid Rain. The controversy over acid rain and its effect on the environment heated up in September, when researchers from the Environmental Defense Fund claimed to have found a "linear" relationship between pollution from copper smelting plants in the Southwest and acid rain in the Rocky Mountains, 600 mi (966 km) downwind. According to the scientists, the concentration of acidic sulfates in the rain over the mountains varied directly in proportion to emissions from the smelting industry. Smelting emissions are much more variable than those of industries believed to cause acid rain in the East, which is why the scientists focused on the Southwestern copper facilities. Federal officials remained skeptical, however, saying that the results claimed by the researchers depended on statistical correlation rather than formal proof.

Lead Shot. A U.S. District Court Judge in Sacramento, CA, issued a preliminary injunction in August enjoining the U.S. Fish and Wildlife Service from allowing autumn waterfowl hunting in 22 counties of five states unless those states agree to require the use of nontoxic shot. Many scientists believe that lead shot is toxic to waterfowl in some areas and reduces populations of the birds. Moreover, bald eagles that feed on injured or dead waterfowl ingest the shot and seem in danger of lead poisoning from the projectiles. In many of these areas, states require hunters to use steel shot, which is nontoxic but more expensive than lead.

The court ruling was in response to a lawsuit filed by the National Wildlife Federation against the Fish and Wildlife Service and the Department of the Interior. The organization went to court because it believed that bald eagles in the areas involved were being imperiled by toxic shot. Under the Migratory Bird Treaty Act, all areas of the nation are closed to waterfowl hunting unless opened by Fish and Wildlife under regulations established each year. Fish and Wildlife declares some areas huntable only with nontoxic shot, but it must have state approval to do so. The five states involved in the lawsuit—California, Oregon, Illinois, Missouri, and Oklahoma—declined to give approval, and the court ruling demanded that Fish and Wildlife not open the season in the affected areas unless such approval is given.

See also ZOOS AND ZOOLOGY.

EDWARD R. RICCIUTI
Free-lance Environment and Wildlife Writer

U.S. Water Resources

For many Americans, the growing problems of the nation's water supply—both in quantity and quality—struck close to home in 1985. After a mild winter and relatively dry spring, the East and West coasts both experienced moderate to extreme drought; emergency rationing measures were implemented in some areas. Meanwhile, as Congress worked on renewing the 1972 Clean Water Act and 1974 Safe Drinking Water Act, there was a growing body of evidence on the extent of ground and surface water pollution. Said Sen. Dave Durenberger (R-MN), "Our nation is in a water crisis right now."

A new diversity of water-related problems, the increasing usage needs of the nation, a gradual decrease in federal moneys for water development, and the aging of the national infrastructure have forced a reexamination of how to manage the United States' water resources. Recent decades have presented new challenges and new responses—legal, financial, engineering, and technical—to sustaining clean and plentiful water supplies.

Quantity and Quality—Priorities. Until recently, the purpose and scope of water resource quality projects have been clear-cut. For the first 40–60 years of this century, Congress and the states enacted legislation to attain plentiful industrial, municipal, and agricultural water supply, water recreational facilities, storm and flood control protection, and the generation of cheap and bountiful hydroelectric power. Literally billions of dollars have been appropriated for the construction of massive water projects by the U.S. Army Corps of Engineers, Bureau of Reclamation, other federal agencies, and the individual states.

The drought of 1985 pointed up the need of maintaining and even upgrading the nation's water infrastructure—supply pipes, pumping facilities, sewer systems, treatment plants, and so on. The major cause of the dry spell was several months of abnormally dry conditions, with reservoirs dropping to dangerously low levels. In northern New Jersey, for example, water capacity fell to about 50% during the summer. There and elsewhere, rationing measures included a ban on watering lawns and washing cars. In some parts of the country, however, the threat of water shortage is chronic. Calls for new facilities, greater conservation, and a comprehensive national policy are being made with increasing urgency.

In addition, over the last 20 years, the U.S. Congress has made protection of health and environment a priority. In 1972 it enacted the Federal Water Pollution Control Act Amendments (Clean Water Act) to protect and clean up surface waters, eliminate the discharge of pollutants into waters, assist the states in combating pollution, and establish a goal of swimmable/fishable waters by the early 1980s. More than $30 billion has been appropriated for federal grants for the construction of municipal treatment works, and private industry has expended billions more for industrial cleanup. Congress also enacted legislation to assure the safety and cleanliness of drinking water supplies, manage the safe disposal of hazardous waste, and establish a program to clean up abandoned hazardous waste sites.

Search for Balance. In the course of these formidable achievements, however, the traditional purposes of water supply and protection programs have become increasingly intertwined and at times have been at cross-purposes. For example, the construction of a water resource project may violate clean water standards, while clean water requirements may inhibit the water supply potential of a reservoir or the safety requirements of a dam.

The conflict between water quantity and quality programs is perhaps best exemplified in court decisions that have sought to clarify the proper balance between the two. For example, in Colorado several years ago, two water districts sought a permit from the Corps of Engineers for the construction of a reservoir. The Corps, asserting that the reservoir would deplete the flow of water downstream and adversely affect an endangered habitat, denied the permit under its authority under the Clean Water Act. A federal appeals court rejected the districts' contention that the Corps' denial violated the state's right—also stipulated in the act—to allocate water within its boundaries. Thus, despite a state's right to use its water as it sees fit, water resource projects may be subject to greater considerations of health and the environment.

Another example of the growing legal conflict between water quantity and quality programs was a 1982 court ruling that a reservoir can be considered a source of pollution subject to permits under the Clean Water Act. The court determined that certain dams may cause the discharge of pollutants as defined by the Clean Water Act and are to be subject to the limitations, standards, and permits stipulated by the legislation. The decision was overruled by an appeal, however, thereby avoiding a subjugation of quantity needs to quality controls.

New Assumptions. Not only have the nature, scope, and purpose of water programs come under reassessment, but so too have the

DROUGHT SEVERITY

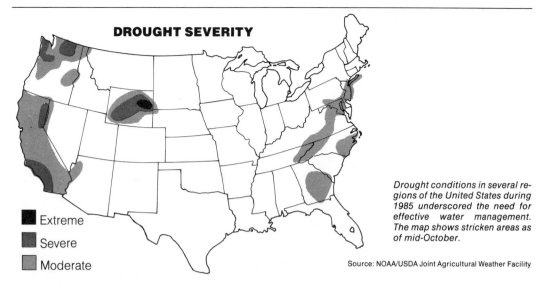

■ Extreme

■ Severe

■ Moderate

Drought conditions in several regions of the United States during 1985 underscored the need for effective water management. The map shows stricken areas as of mid-October.

Source: NOAA/USDA Joint Agricultural Weather Facility

policy and management assumptions that the experts used in the past to carry out traditional water programs. Pollution contaminants and their sources have changed in recent years and in ways that were never anticipated. The 1972 Clean Water Act established effluent limitations and treatment requirements for the most visible points of pollution—municipal sewage plants and industrial sources—and controlled the most common and obvious pollutants, such as dissolved oxygen and suspended solids. As time went on, however, it became evident that certain sources of pollution could not be traced to a particular point and that toxic substances, in addition to the so-called conventional pollutants, were also a major cause of water pollution. Untraced sources of pollution, such as urban runoff and agricultural practices, now represent the principal remaining cause of pollution in as many as six of ten Environmental Protection Regions. Thirty-nine states have reported that nonpoint source pollution is at least equal to that of point sources.

Another example of altered policy assumptions relates to groundwater supplies. When Congress passed the Clean Water Act in 1972, its ultimate objective was the protection and cleanup of surface waters. In the last few years, however, groundwater—which provides more than 96% of all fresh water in the United States —has been found to be contaminated in every state. EPA has reported that 29% of randomly selected municipal water supply systems using groundwater were found to be polluted. Numerous congressional, agency, and independent research organizations have concluded that contamination of groundwater is more severe than originally thought and that institutional, technological, and policy mechanisms must be upgraded.

Shifting Responsibilities. The conflicts between quantity and quality considerations and

the emergence of new pollution sources are compounded by a shift in the responsibility for the management of water resources. As the infrastructure "deficit" increases and as national budget constraints continue to inhibit federal expenditures, state and local governments are required to assume greater administrative control of water systems. And not only are federal environmental and water regulations geared toward greater state responsibility in the enforcement of standards, but states are also being asked to shoulder a larger burden of the costs. In debate over reauthorization of the Clean Water Act, for example, the Reagan administration called for phasing out a $2.4 billion federal grant program for construction of municipal sewage treatment plants. And for renewal of the Safe Drinking Water Act, the administration urged state responsibility for regulating drinking water and groundwater. In addition, major water resource projects bills pending in Congress would substantially increase the amount of money localities and nonfederal sponsors would pay for a dam or reservoir. As Congress adjourned in December, however, it still was deadlocked on just how the costs would be shared, and the authorizing bill was not passed.

In the last 80 years the United States has clearly shown the ability to meet the diverse challenges of managing the nation's valuable water resources. The more that is learned about water pollution and the interrelationship between water quantity and quality programs, the greater will be the capacity to formulate laws and develop programs to protect and maintain water supplies. This capacity will continue to depend on a Congress that can plan for the future, the emergence of a viable federal-state partnership, and the mobilization of the private and public sectors.

JOAN M. KOVALIC

In his new biography "Breaking with Moscow," Arkady Shevchenko, the highest-ranking Soviet official to defect to the United States, revealed that he had been a spy for the CIA during the three years prior to his 1978 defection.

ESPIONAGE

With more major espionage cases than at any time since the Cold War, 1985 might have been called the year of the spy.

The Walker Case. A major U.S. spy scandal broke in May when the wife and daughter of John Walker, a retired Navy warrant officer, reported to the Federal Bureau of Investigation (FBI) that he was passing secret documents to the Russians. Walker and his son Michael, a seaman aboard the aircraft carrier U.S.S. *Nimitz,* were arrested May 20. Also arrested were Walker's brother, Arthur, and a friend, Jerry Whitworth, both of whom were also retired from the Navy.

John Walker was charged with recruiting the others into his spy ring, which had been operating for nearly 20 years. He was said to have operated on a worldwide basis, flying to such places as Vienna and Hong Kong to meet his Soviet contacts. The motive was money.

So damaging to national security was the information that the Washington Legal Foundation called for the death penalty. Arthur Walker, the first to be convicted, was sentenced to life in prison. In October federal prosecutors accepted a plea bargain with John Walker; he would plead guilty and receive a life sentence in exchange for a reduced sentence, 25 years, for his son. Jerry Whitworth was scheduled to go on trial in January 1986.

Other U.S. Cases. In May, Thomas Patrick Cavanagh, an engineer for a U.S. defense contractor, was sentenced to life in prison for trying to sell secrets of the "Stealth" bomber to the Soviet Union. Richard Miller, a former FBI agent arrested in 1984 for conspiring to pass U.S. counterespionage secrets to the USSR, was the subject of a mistrial in October; his alleged co-conspirators, Svetlana Ogorod-

nikova and her husband, had pleaded guilty in June. In August, a former clerk for the Central Intelligence Agency (CIA) in Ghana, Sharon Scranage, pleaded guilty to identifying U.S. intelligence agents for her Ghanaian lover.

And several major cases broke late in the year. In November, Jonathan J. Pollard, a civilian employee of the Naval Investigative Service, was charged with spying for Israel; Pollard's wife also was implicated in the case. That same month, Larry Wu-Tai Chin, a retired analyst for the CIA, was accused of spying for China, and Ronald W. Pelton, a former analyst for the National Security Agency, was charged with spying for the Soviet Union. In December, Samuel Loring Morison, a former analyst for the National Intelligence Support Center, was sentenced to two years for giving classified material to the British publication *Jane's Defence Weekly*. And Randy Miles Jeffries, a messenger for a stenographic firm with ties to Capitol Hill, was arrested on charges of spying for the USSR.

Spies in Bonn. The government of West Germany was shaken in August by the defection to East Germany of Heinz Tiedge, a top official in Bonn's intelligence service. Tiedge took with him secret information on Communist spies operating in West Germany. The scandal spread as a number of secretaries in sensitive government positions either defected or were arrested before they could escape. One of the defectors was Herta-Astrid Willner, who had worked in the office of Chancellor Helmut Kohl. One of those arrested was Margarete Höke from the office of President Richard von Weizsäcker. After the initial defections, Chancellor Kohl fired Heribert Hellenbroich, his chief of intelligence.

Soviet-British Expulsions. Three Russians caused crises in Soviet and U.S. intelligence.

One, Oleg Gordievsky, had served at the Soviet embassy in Copenhagen before becoming the State Security Committee's (KGB's) top man in London. After his defection in July, it was revealed that Gordievsky had been a double agent in both Western capitals. Great Britain announced the defection in September and quickly ordered the expulsion of 25 Soviets whom Gordievsky had identified as KGB agents. Moscow retaliated by ordering 25 Britons to leave the USSR for "inadmissible activities," or spying. London expelled six more Soviets, and Moscow responded by ordering an additional six Britons out of the USSR. Because so many of its agents had been compromised by Gordievsky, the KGB reportedly was forced to undergo hasty revamping.

Defector or Double Agent? Vitaly Yurchenko of the KGB appeared to be a major catch for Western intelligence when he asked for asylum in Italy in August. He was subsequently brought to the United States, where officials said he was providing information on Soviet espionage in North America. One of the alleged spies he named was Pelton; another was Edward Howard, a former CIA agent who had been let go by the agency after failing a polygraph test for drugs. Despite FBI surveillance, Howard managed to escape from his Santa Fe, NM, home.

In November, however, it was Yurchenko who disappeared, slipping away from two CIA agents at a restaurant in Washington. Yurchenko went to the Soviet Embassy, where he declared in a news conference that he had been kidnapped by CIA agents in Rome, drugged, and transported to the United States. The U.S. State Department termed the charges "completely false." The Pelton and Howard cases seemed to prove the point, which left two other possibilities. Either Yurchenko was a genuine defector who simply changed his mind (perhaps because of an unhappy love affair), or else he was a double agent planted by the KGB and told to embarrass the United States with his fantastic story. Some members of Congress charged that, whatever the truth, the CIA had bungled the case.

Greek Drama. The third of the Russians, Sergei Bokhan, based in Athens, belonged to the Chief Intelligence Directorate of the General Staff of the Red Army (GRU). He described a Communist spy ring extending into the Greek government, the armed forces, the news media, and influential businesses. A naval officer and two businessmen were among those arrested in Athens. Sources in the United States said that Bokhan's evidence revealed how Greeks working for the GRU channeled Western technology through Greece to the USSR. Soviet agents were also said to have supported Soviet-backed terrorism while manipulating the Greek media into stressing anti-Western stories.

Greenpeace. A covert operations scandal involving France and New Zealand erupted in July when the *Rainbow Warrior,* a vessel belonging to the environmental, antinuclear group Greenpeace, was blown up in Auckland harbor. One member of the crew was killed. The trawler was due to sail for Mururoa within one week to protest a French nuclear test. An investigation by New Zealand police led to the arrest of two French intelligence agents traveling on Swiss passports. They were accused of murder and sabotage. In Paris, investigative reporters charged that a team of French military advisers had attached underwater explosives to the hull of the *Rainbow Warrior*. Ultimate responsibility was traced to high-ranking members of the French government. In September, President François Mitterrand forced the resignation of his defense minister and dismissed the head of the secret service.

Spies in the Sky. The U.S. space shuttle *Discovery* in January and *Atlantis* in October were launched on secret missions for the U.S. Defense Department. The first was believed to carry a satellite to monitor electronic signals over the Soviet Union, and the second was believed to deploy a communications satellite. The missions prompted debate over public information versus national security.

Spy Dust. On August 22 the U.S. State Department accused the KGB of monitoring the activities of Americans in Moscow by dusting doorknobs and similar objects with the chemical nitrophenylpentadienal (NPPD). Anyone touching the objects would leave traces of the "spy dust" wherever he or she went. Terming the chemical "potentially harmful," Washington demanded an end to the practice, but the Kremlin denied the whole story.

Other Cases Worldwide. Incidents of alleged spying also took place in several other countries. Taiwan arrested several of its own intelligence officials for complicity in the October 1984 murder of a dissident writer in the United States. India uncovered a spy ring, alleged to include foreign diplomats, that had penetrated high levels of government and defense. Vietnam released William Mathers, an accused American spy, after his family paid $10,000 ransom. Liberia broke diplomatic relations with Moscow, alleging spy activities by Soviet diplomats. Spain expelled three diplomats, one Russian and two Americans, on spy charges. And in Rome, the trial of Mehmet Ali Agca, the would-be assassin of the pope, continued; the big question was still if and to what extent Bulgarian intelligence was involved.

Honor. The U.S. Distinguished Service Medal was awarded posthumously to Capt. Joseph J. Rochefort for breaking Japanese naval codes in World War II, a feat that led to the decisive U.S. victory in the Battle of Midway.

VINCENT BURANELLI
Coauthor, "Spy/Counterspy"

ETHIOPIA

The extraordinary famine that continued to overwhelm Ethiopia was virtually the singular news event of the year. It overshadowed all other issues. A major airlift of Ethiopian Jews affected by the famine was initiated by Israel and the United States. At the same time Ethiopia's war against secessionist forces in the north continued.

Famine. The African famine affecting some 20 countries and about 150 million Africans ravaged Ethiopia in 1985. More than 8 million Ethiopians were classified as "at risk of starvation" by the U.S. Agency for International Development (AID). Hundreds of thousands died during the year. Food aid poured in from all over the world: The United States provided $250 million in food and development aid; more than $150 million was disbursed by Western relief agencies; India donated 100,000 metric tons of wheat, while Western Europe sent more than $100 million in government aid. In Great Britain and the United States, entertainers played a special role in raising money for Ethiopia. In fact, so much food aid was arriving in the country that the UN in June advised Western nations to pause in their shipments as a shortage of transport was causing food to rot on the docks. (*See* special report, page 90.)

To aid in the war against hunger the Ethiopian government put into place a series of edicts: fuel rationing, a 50% profit tax on the sale of businesses, limitations on housing space and building, the closing of the university during the summer so as to send students and teachers into the interior to aid famine victims, limiting to $25 the amount Ethiopians can take out of the country, and restrictions on luxury imports.

The effects of the famine also had political and social ramifications. Probably more than one million Ethiopian famine victims fled to the Sudan, Somalia, Djibouti, and Kenya, straining the economies of those countries. Early in

1985, Israel confirmed that it had airlifted 10,000 Ethiopian Jews, who had tried to flee the famine, from the Sudan to Israel; this was followed by a secret airlift by the United States of between 500 and 800 Ethiopian Jews from the Sudan to Israel. Ethiopia's demand that these "kidnapped" Ethiopians be returned by Israel fell on deaf ears. Throughout the year, Ethiopia resettled famine victims from Tigre and Eritrea, in the north, to southern regions. More than 1.5 million people were to be resettled. The secessionist liberation movements in Tigre and Eritrea and Western relief agencies condemned this activity claiming it was Ethiopia's attempt to denude the liberation movements and would cause these migrants cultural and economic distress. The Ethiopian government denied the accusations.

Toward the end of the year rain began to fall in the drought-stricken regions.

International and Domestic Affairs. Ethiopia and Sudan reestablished diplomatic relations in June, two months after a military coup took place in Sudan. The rebel wars in the north continued on an intermittent basis; in August, the strategic town of Barentu in Eritrea was recaptured by Ethiopia after having been held for two months by the rebels. The third worst train disaster in history occurred in January when about 400 people were killed as a train crossed a bridge and derailed outside the town of Awash. Paulos Tzadua, the Roman Catholic archbishop of Addis Ababa, was installed as a cardinal by Pope John Paul II in May.

PETER SCHWAB
State University of New York at Purchase

ETHNIC GROUPS

The concerns of U.S. minority groups during 1985 focused on such areas as equality in education, poverty and unemployment, business opportunity, political strategy, and land claims. Black leaders were especially concerned with U.S. policy toward the white minority government of South Africa.

Blacks. In several states there was evidence of, as well as planned remedies for, the apparent disadvantages of blacks and other ethnic groups in educational institutions. It was contended that educators with minority-group backgrounds face a particular disadvantage in hiring, competency testing, and field evaluations for merit pay increases. Arkansas Gov. William Clinton said that it is wrong to have only a small number of black teachers and administrators in a state with a large black population. In March, Arkansas became the first state to test its teachers for competency, and 905 of 28,276 teachers failed the reading, writing, and mathematics portions of the test. Governor Clinton acknowledged that there may have been some danger of racial disparity in

---

ETHIOPIA • Information Highlights

Official Name: Socialist Ethiopia.
Location: Eastern Africa.
Area: 471,776 sq mi (1 221 900 km²).
Population (mid-1985 est.): 36,000,000.
Chief Cities (July 1980): Addis Ababa, the capital, 1,277,159; Asmara, 424,532; Dire Dawa, 82,024.
Government: *Head of state and government,* Mengistu Haile-Mariam, chairman of the Provisional Military Administrative Council (took office Feb. 1977).
Monetary Unit: Birr (2.07 birr equal U.S. $1, June 1985).
Gross Domestic Product (1983–84 U.S. $): $5,000,000,000.
Economic Index (Addis Ababa, 1984): *Consumer Prices* (1970 = 100), all items, 298.7; food, 336.0.
Foreign Trade (1984 U.S. $): *Imports,* $942,000,000; *exports,* $416,000,000.

test performance, but results were not broken down by racial background. In Tennessee, Gov. Lamar Alexander revealed that 39,000 educators were to be recommended as the state's first career-ladder teachers and administrators. The president of the Tennessee Education Association, however, declared that minority educators were angry and frustrated at not being adequately informed about all aspects of the evaluation process. In Illinois, meanwhile, a program to improve the quality of undergraduate teacher education placed special emphasis on recruiting academically able minority students.

In the political arena, Tom Bradley's election to an unprecedented fourth term as mayor of Los Angeles, the reelection of mayors Coleman Young and Andrew Young in Detroit and Atlanta, respectively, and the election of L. Douglas Wilder as lieutenant governor of Virginia suggested that there was a growing coalition of voters who cast their ballots without regard to skin color.

Civil-rights groups generally welcomed the refusal of the Senate Judiciary Committee to recommend the nomination of William Bradford Reynolds for the position of associate attorney general, the number three spot in the Justice Department. Some of the committee's senators had questioned Reynolds' commitment to civil rights and the truthfulness of his remarks before the panel. Reynolds remained assistant attorney general for civil rights.

The Reagan administration, meanwhile, continued to maintain that a robust economy is much more effective than a welfare state in dealing with poverty. But U.S. Rep. Robert T. Matsui (D-CA) reported that of the 404,000 U.S. families escaping poverty, 75% were white families headed by men, while the median income for black families (some 40% of which are headed by women) did not increase significantly. The chances of a child living below the poverty line were three times greater for blacks than for whites. And the unemployment rate for black males was two to three times greater than for whites. Two out of every five black teenagers did not have a job in the summer of 1985.

In Dallas in June, the national convention of the National Association for the Advancement of Colored People (NAACP) focused on causes that must be addressed directly by the black population itself and the nation's business community. According to Fred Rasheed, the national director of the NAACP's economic development programs, "if the Reagan administration has been good for us [blacks] in any way, perhaps it's that we will have to seek the solutions to our own problems."

Native Americans. In January the National Tribal Chairmen Association voted 84–18 to reject the recommendations of the Presidential Commission on Indian Reservation Economics. The recommendations had been presented to President Reagan on Nov. 30, 1984. They included abolishing the Bureau of Indian Affairs, waiving the immunity of Indians from lawsuits on certain issues, directing Indian economic development on reservations toward private ownership and the profit motive and away from social objectives, and subordinating tribal courts to federal ones on questions involving the interpretation of law and the U.S. Constitution. The tribal chairmen issued a statement declaring that the proposals "would lead to a termination of the specific status of Indian tribes and seriously affect their sovereignty and jurisdiction over their reservation lands."

Acting as a special representative of the White House, William P. Clark failed to mediate a dispute between Navajo and Hopi Indians over reservation lands in Arizona. The former secretary of the interior tried unsuccessfully to persuade the Hopi to rent or sell to the Navajos some of the land Congress had given them in 1974, but which had been used for generations by the Navajos. Some 5,400 Navajos had moved off the disputed Hopi land but were finding it difficult to acquire new homes and adjust to new surroundings. Although Peterson Zah had been elected tribal chairman of the Navajos with a promise that he would settle the dispute, those Navajos who remained claimed that "in our tongue there is no word for relocation." Meanwhile the Hopis were divided between those "progressives" who refused to budge from the boundaries drawn by a federal court in 1979 and those who refused to evict the Navajos. By fall a settlement was still sought.

Hispanics. As in recent years, the U.S. Congress again considered new immigration legislation, an issue of prime concern to the nation's 16 million Hispanics (*see* page 440). Also in 1985, San Antonio's Mayor Henry Cisneros, the first Hispanic to be elected mayor of a large U.S. city, was reelected easily to a third term, and Xavier Suarez, a 36-year-old Harvard-educated lawyer, became the first Cuban-American to be elected mayor of Miami.

Asian Americans. Ten years after the fall of Vietnam to the Communists, the many thousands of Indochinese refugees now living in the United States continued to be assimilated into American society. Many of the Indochinese refugees were operating successful restaurants, grocery stores, computer centers, and other small businesses. In his State of the Union address, President Reagan paid special tribute to Jean Nguyen, a 1985 West Point graduate who had fled Vietnam ten years earlier. Latest government statistics showed that Indochinese refugees had earned $1.2 billion in 1982, paid taxes of nearly $115 million, and had median incomes of $9,119.

FLOYD L. BASS
The University of Connecticut

© Ronny Jaques, Photo Researchers

© Sygma

On June 12, Spain's Premier Felipe Gonzalez, above right, signed the Treaty of Accession for his country's entry into the European Community on Jan. 1, 1986. Portugal's Premier Mario Soares had signed the treaty earlier in the day. Portuguese wine, left, and other products were expected to create new competition among the EC nations.

EUROPE

For most West Europeans, 1985 was a year of moderate optimism after more than a decade of economic difficulties and psychological disillusionment. Inflation was restrained, productivity increased, and economic growth revived. After a tortuous eight-year negotiation, leaders of the European Community (EC) formally agreed to the admission of Spain and Portugal in January 1986 and began serious efforts to regain momentum toward fuller economic union. There was even a lessening of the sense of impotence in international affairs that Europeans had felt during the previous four years of heightened U.S.-Soviet tensions. The restoration of vigorous leadership in the Soviet Union under General Secretary Mikhail Gorbachev and the willingness of U.S. President Ronald Reagan to open arms negotiations with the new Moscow regime were welcomed in Europe as holding out the possibility of a new period of détente.

Reviving Economy. Just as the massive increase in the price of oil imposed in 1973 by the Organization of the Petroleum Exporting Countries (OPEC) had precipitated the long European depression, the decline in oil prices —by one third between 1981 and 1985—aided recovery. Perhaps more importantly, the increase in the value of the U.S. dollar—82% against European currencies between 1980 and 1985—enabled European exporters to undercut American producers both in the U.S. market and elsewhere. The Western European

trade surplus, which had reached $8 billion in 1984, was expected to quadruple in 1985. This export-led recovery also was helped by the long-term measures that had been undertaken in various countries during the recession years. The Socialist government of French President François Mitterrand, for example, had begun restructuring the nation's antiquated steel, shipbuilding, and mining industries despite union opposition because of the resulting unemployment; it had also helped reduce inflation and external debt by cutting government spending. Conservative Prime Minister Margaret Thatcher of Great Britain refused union demands that money-losing coal mines should be kept open despite a costly strike by miners from March 1984 to March 1985. Increasing government resistance to strike threats was beginning to persuade many union leaders to accept technological innovation as the key to improved conditions for their members. Although Western Europe lagged behind the United States and Japan in high technology, successful launches in 1984 and 1985 of the French-designed satellite-launching rocket *Ariane,* funded by the 11-member European Space Agency, dramatized Europe's ability to compete in advanced scientific fields through international collaboration.

Although Western European output was expected to increase by at least 3% in 1985, serious problems remained. Throughout Western Europe, unemployment stayed high. Even in prospering West Germany, some 9% of the work force was unemployed. In Britain the rate

reached 13%, adding fuel to the anger that erupted in riots in London in October. The economies of the Mediterranean countries were especially fragile. Italy's trade and budget deficits forced a 6% devaluation of its currency in July. Greek Prime Minister Andreas Papandreou threatened to veto the entry of Spain and Portugal into the EC unless a large modernization program was financed to enable Greece, southern France, and southern Italy to meet the increased competition within the enlarged community.

Enlarging the EC. Spain and Portugal had requested admission to the EC in 1977, after the establishment of democratic governments in both countries. The subsequent negotiations, however, were hampered by various political and economic difficulties. Many EC members wanted time to ensure that democratic government had taken firm root in both countries. Fishing interests in the EC feared competition from the Spanish fishing fleet, which outnumbered that of the rest of the Community. Producers of wine and Mediterranean fruits and vegetables feared competition from Spanish and Portuguese farmers. Industrial producers suspected that the Spanish tariff system might be used to keep out the products of northern Europe. And the actual cost of admitting the two new members also caused hesitation. Subsidies to Iberian farmers would add $1 billion to the existing $2 billion deficit in agricultural financing; aid to the Portuguese economy alone would cost $900 million. Even adding two new languages to the seven official languages of the Community would increase bureaucratic costs and slow decision-making.

Nevertheless, the prospect of expanding the EC by one third in terms of area and of increasing the internal market from 270 to 320 million people, while giving support to the new democratic regimes, ultimately proved irresistible. Meeting in Brussels in March 1985, the EC heads of government approved a ten-year program for the gradual alignment of the new members' economies with those of existing members. Within seven years, Spanish and Portuguese import duties on industrial products were to be removed, and free trade in most agricultural products was to be achieved. Spanish and Portuguese fishing fleets were to respect EC limits on their catch. The two countries would be immediately eligible for financial aid from the EC Social and Regional Funds. Spain would name two members to the European Commission and 60 members to the European Parliament, Portugal one and 25, respectively.

To assuage the opposition of Greece and France, the EC heads of government at the same time adopted "Integrated Mediterranean Programs" to provide structural improvements in the economies of Greece, southern France, and southern Italy over a seven-year period.

Renewed Plans for Unity. The imminent expansion of the EC gave further impetus to measures to turn what had been essentially a customs union into a fuller economic union. Recognizing the danger to the Community of public "Europessimism," the EC government heads, meeting in Milan in June, gave general approval to far-reaching reforms proposed by the Commission, by which the internal market would be completely integrated by 1992. The reforms included simplification and reduction of customs controls, harmonization of technical legislation, and freedom for such services as insurance or transport companies to be established in any member country. A proposal for convening a conference to amend the procedures and institutions set up in the original Treaty of Rome, which established the EC, was approved by nine members but opposed by Great Britain, Denmark, and Greece. Finally, acting on proposals by the People's Europe Committee, set up at the Fontainebleau summit of June 1984, the leaders agreed to 47 concrete steps to increase the sense of European citizenship, such as establishing a European driving license and wider educational exchanges.

Then in early December, EC leaders meeting in Luxembourg agreed on another series of measures intended to strengthen organization unity. The compromise package included steps to speed up the elimination of trade barriers, increase the authority of the European Parliament, coordinate the foreign policies of individual member nations, and commit member nations to European monetary unification.

EC members attending the May economic summit of major industrialized powers in Bonn, West Germany, however, proved unable to take a common line. France turned down a U.S. proposal supported by the other powers (Great Britain, Canada, Italy, Japan, and West Germany) for a conference on liberalization of world trade, and it received little support for a counterproposal for a monetary conference on currency fluctuations.

Pushing for Détente. Western Europeans did welcome the appointment of Mikhail Gorbachev as general secretary of the Soviet Communist Party on the death of Konstantin Chernenko in March. Gorbachev's decisive style and apparent openness to argument, which had impressed British leaders during his visit in December 1984, was equally evident during his state visit to France in October 1985. Although Britain and France both rejected Gorbachev's offer to negotiate separately on nuclear missile reductions, West European leaders were united in pressing the United States to work for meaningful détente both in arms talks that resumed in Geneva in March and in the Reagan-Gorbachev summit in November.

F. Roy Willis
University of California, Davis

The year's look of rich elegance
was exemplified by the luxurious
velvet-trimmed brocade blouson
jacket, above, worn over a wool
crepe dress, and by the floor-
length matte jersey gown, featuring cutout sleeves that seduc-
tively bared the shoulders.

Photos, Bill Blass

FASHION

A lackluster economy and complaints from manufacturers and consumers about the lack of variety of the too classic, too masculine clothes of the previous year contributed to a more imaginative and distinctive approach to fashion in 1985.

Influences. Taking their cues from television, designers mined the public's fascination with the life-styles of the rich and famous as exhibited by the wide popularity of the Carringtons of *Dynasty,* the *Dallas* set, and other fictional power families. In addition, cable's music television (MTV), with its energetic and flamboyant rock stars, inspired fashion trends, as did the exotic life of Raj India seen in *Masterpiece Theatre*'s production of *The Jewel in the Crown.*

Rich fabrics were the base for creating an elegant, moneyed look. Not only were there lush velvets, cashmeres, and plush flannels or tweeds, but ornate tapestries and brocades, often with gold or silver. Paisleys of Indian ancestry were important patterns as was chintz in florals reminiscent of English manor houses. These fancies were widely featured in all apparel categories—the tapestries and brocades in coats, vests, and jackets; the paisleys in blouses, skirts, or graceful dresses. Brocade and tapestry shoes and boots, as well as bags and belts, were major accessory looks, and leathers—tooled or embossed in paisley patterns or floral motifs—were also basic accessory materials.

The moneyed look seemed to be the catalyst for the trend to coin jewelry. Pins, necklaces, and bracelets dripped with reproductions

of ancient and current coinage. Gold chains and bangles, worn by the dozens, also were the jewelry trend seen in major designer shows.

Indian-costume influences resurrected the Nehru jacket, popular for a time in the 1960s, and introduced the dhoti, a loose wrapped pant, a novel look for both evening and casual wear. The not-for-polo jodhpur was seen in many collections but most elegantly in buttery suede by Ralph Lauren. Accessories echoed India with sari-like silk scarves, jeweled or medallion-studded belts, turbans or pillbox hats, and outrageously outsized "gems" that might have come from a Rajah's treasure house.

MTV, with its often surreal and uninhibited costuming, spawned fashion looks that ranged from copies of Prince's foppish Edwardian dress to Tina Turner's tough-strut combinations of spike heels, net tights, studded leather, and miniskirt and Cyndi Lauper's sock-hop-cum-punk style. But the pop star who inspired the most look-alikes was Madonna. Her all lace look, the corselette, bouffant skirt, headbands, mitts, and her crucifix earrings and rosary necklaces were seen often on Madonna clones.

The universal popularity of *Dynasty*'s Carrington clan precipitated a marketing dynasty. Fashion and beauty products were licensed to carry the name of the show or its characters.

There was *Forever Krystle* perfume and *Carrington* men's cologne, a line of *Dynasty* jewelry, and fashions to give every woman the opportunity to dress like her favorite character or to give her husband the successful look of the Carrington men. Joan Collins, however, with Alexis-like determination and perversity, marketed herself and competed by endorsing a hat collection, a jewelry line, and a scent called *Scoundrel*.

The fitness craze that grew from the weekly exercise class to body-building and triathlon regimens also dictated fashion changes. The woman who was spending more time and money to get a super shape wanted to show it off. To accommodate her, designers cut necklines lower, front and back. Skin was in, with bared midriffs, short skirts, and provocative cutouts. Curves returned as the waist became the focal point to be accented with darts, tucks, and wide belts. The suit lost its dress-for-success androgyny via the shaped jacket that nipped in at the waist and curved over the hip, topping a narrowed and shortened skirt.

The chemise, popular for several years, was replaced by the clinger—a dress that hugged the body from neckline to hemline and made a point of the waist with contrast cummerbunds or tucks and gathers. This figure-defining shape

Paisley prints, suggestive of the Indian influence, were important fashion news during 1985. The graceful dress, left, presented a picture of quiet elegance, while the jacket and top emphasized the richness of bold colors.

Photos, Daniel Simone, Gamma-Liaison

The rock star Madonna's unique style of dress created a fashion craze that included oversized jewelry, the bared midriff, and mitts, and was indicative of the influence of the media on fashion in 1985.

Neal Preston, Camera 5

was done to perfection by Oscar de la Renta and Yves St. Laurent. Primarily in wool or silk jersey, this silhouette was also done in such lightweight and supple fabrics as crepe, velvet, or lamé.

The well-cared-for body was also displayed in the new pants—narrow and formfitting in knits or stretch fabrics with stirrup straps to hook under the feet to maintain a long, leggy look. The tight jean was back, too, but newly done in floral printed denims or twills.

A highlight of the fall season was a new approach to the traditional turtleneck. Done in unexpected fabrics such as silk velvet and lamé or as a jersey bodysuit by Donna Karan in her first solo collection, it shed its sportswear image for new sophistication and chic.

Menswear. Menswear trends exemplified the same upscale influences as womenswear. Business wardrobes were made up of serious executive looks in gray, navy, or brown flannel of conservative cut. The occasional tweed or plaid was restrained in color and pattern while accessories tended to be traditional and limited to essentials. Even for casual wear, the jeans and running attire of former years were replaced by more "dressed up" combinations of well cut sports jackets and blazers with trousers. Here, checks and plaids were more acceptable.

The fitness trend also had an impact on menswear, particularly regarding cut. The changing male body dictated altering the form and proportions of suits, trousers, and shirts. Well-exercised males had developed wider shoulders, broader chests, more muscular legs, flatter stomachs, and trimmer waists and needed jackets and shirts that were tapered and trousers of a straighter cut. The "drop," or the difference between chest and waist measurement, went from 6 to between 8 and 10 inches (15 to 20 and 25 cm) to accommodate the fitter bodies. Three-button suits were replaced by two and even one-button models to provide the proper drape.

For the male fashion rebel, television provided a new hero—Don Johnson of *Miami Vice*. His raffish and rumpled Italian duds popularized cotton knit tank tops, silk shirts, and sweaters worn with suits in such pastels as pink and lavender. The unconstructed jackets were worn with collars up and sleeves rolled or pushed to the elbow. Pleated trousers and soft leather slip-ons completed the look.

The year 1985 had enough variety to tempt consumers of every age and life-style, but several unfashionable questions loomed before the fashion industry. Would hot trends and inventive styling be enough to win consumers back from their love affair with discount and off-price stores? Would the economy improve and trade restrictions pass Congress? The right answers perhaps would provide greater future profits.

ANN M. ELKINS
Fashion Director, "Good Housekeeping"

FINLAND

In his New Year's speech to the nation, President Mauno Koivisto reaffirmed Finland's traditional neutrality and addressed the issue of nuclear armaments. He said that the Finnish government would not accept nuclear arms on its territory, condemned the use of all types of nuclear armaments, and supported any declarations banning first use of nuclear weapons.

Foreign Affairs. The remnants of an unarmed Soviet missile that had accidentally veered off course during Soviet naval exercises and crashed into Finland's Lake Inari on Dec. 28, 1984, were returned to the USSR on February 8. There was little public comment on the incident.

Matters widely discussed by the press and the public in 1985 included the idea of creating a nuclear-free zone in Scandinavia, a reported Finnish government pledge to grant $10 million in aid to the Nicaraguan government over a three-year period, and President Ronald Reagan's Strategic Defense Initiative (SDI). U.S. officials indicated their displeasure over an April 30 speech by Prime Minister Kalevi Sorsa that sharply criticized U.S. policy in Nicaragua and the SDI.

Finland's relations with Israel were severely strained by an episode involving Finnish peacekeeping forces serving in Lebanon as part of the United Nations Interim Force in Lebanon (UNIFIL). On June 7, Finnish troops staged a mock gun battle with members of the Israeli-supported South Lebanese Army (SLA) to allow 11 SLA members to defect to Amal, the Shiite Muslim militia. In retaliation, the SLA seized 24 Finnish soldiers, holding 21 of them captive until June 15. Although President Koivisto supported his troops, there was widespread criticism of their involvement in internal Lebanese affairs and some doubt in Finland as to whether Finnish peacekeeping forces should renew their agreement to serve in the Middle East.

On July 30 the foreign ministers of 33 European nations, the United States, and Canada met in Helsinki's Finlandia Hall to mark the tenth anniversary of the signing of the Helsinki accords, which grew out of the Conference on Security and Cooperation in Europe (CSCE) held in Helsinki in 1975. Although some participants felt that the CSCE had done little to improve human rights or alleviate the tensions between East and West, Finnish Foreign Minister Paavo Väyrynen pointed to the ongoing Stockholm disarmament conference as a sign of progress.

Economy. A government report submitted to parliament on May 14 stated that tax rates would remain unchanged and recommended the continuation of the economic policies that had thus far proved effective in furthering economic development. It was expected that production would increase by 3% and inflation would be reduced by 4% over the next few years. Unemployment was expected to decline.

Cultural Affairs. On March 5 the Literary Prize of the Nordic Council was presented to young Finnish author Antti Tuuri for his recent novel *Pohjanmaa.* The annual Helsinki Festival, a celebration of Finnish and world arts, opened in August, and special events commemorating the 150th anniversary of the publication of the *Kalevala,* the Finnish national epic, were held throughout the year.

ERIK J. FRIIS
"The Scandinavian-American Bulletin"

FLORIDA

Politics attracted much attention in Florida in 1985. The legislature wrestled with vital issues such as growth management, Democrats and Republicans prepared for the 1986 elections, and Xavier Suarez became the first Cuban-American to be elected mayor of Miami in a nonpartisan November 12 runoff. The year also was marked by headline-making natural calamities.

Growth Management. Gov. Bob Graham and the legislature agreed that local planning to accommodate rapid population growth (788 persons daily in 1984) was inadequate and inconsistent. They therefore enacted a state growth plan, Growth Management Act, with which all local governments will be required to comply, to protect beaches, water supplies, and environmentally sensitive lands while providing necessary public services.

Although the cost of each new resident is estimated at $10,000, Floridians seem determined to keep taxes low. The state's $1,000-per-person expenditures for essential public services in 1983 ranked last in the nation. A special commission was appointed to study the difficult problem of financing growth and to make legislative recommendations in 1986.

FINLAND • Information Highlights

Official Name: Republic of Finland.
Location: Northern Europe.
Area: 130,160 sq mi (337 113 km²).
Population (mid-1985 est.): 4,900,000.
Chief City (Dec. 31, 1983): Helsinki, the capital, 484,480.
Government: *Head of state,* Mauno Koivisto, president (took office Jan. 27, 1982). *Head of government,* Kalevi Sorsa, prime minister (took office May 6, 1983). *Legislature* (unicameral)—Eduskunta.
Monetary Unit: Markka (5.42 markka equal U.S.$1, Dec. 2, 1985).
Gross National Product: (1983 U.S.$): $49,400,-000,000.
Economic Indexes (1984): *Consumer Prices* (1970 = 100), all items, 415.9; food, 438.0. *Industrial Production* (1980 = 100), 111.
Foreign Trade (1984 U.S.$): *Imports,* $12,443,-000,000; *exports,* $13,504,000,000.

Xavier Suarez, a 37-year-old, Cuban-born, Harvard-educated lawyer, staged a successful campaign for the mayoralty of Miami, a city with a Cuban-American population of 50%.

Office of the Mayor

Other Legislation and Politics. The legislature also tried to resolve other problems of public concern. Education was allocated 47% of the $13.9 billion 1985–86 state budget, the drinking age was raised from 19 to 21, smoking in public facilities was limited by the Clean Indoor Air Act, and new legislation required child-care workers to be fingerprinted and prohibited corporal punishment in day-care centers. A stronger law regulating the registration of farm labor contractors should give more protection to migrant workers, and growing concern about organized crime and drug smuggling convinced legislators to authorize a referendum in 1986 for the creation of a statewide prosecutor. Legislators ended the session by voting themselves a 50% salary increase and authorizing automatic future annual pay raises at the same rate given to state employees.

Historically, 75% of Florida's registered voters have been Democrats, and most regions have had no Republican candidates for local and state offices. In the wake of President Ronald Reagan's second strong victory in the state, Republicans tried to persuade voters to switch their registrations to the Republican Party. Although the expensive registration drive fell far short of its goals, the 3 to 1 advantage formerly held by Democrats is now closer to 3 to 2. The once complacent Democrats held a state convention in November that served as a workshop for candidates and provided an opportunity to focus attention on what was expected to be the key electoral battle of 1986: Democratic Gov. Bob Graham's attempt to unseat Republican U.S. Sen. Paula Hawkins.

Natural Disasters. The severe drought that hit central and south Florida in April dramatically underscored the fact that the availability of drinking water may become a limiting factor on growth. As water levels in the Florida aquifer dropped to dangerously low levels, coastal and inland counties were placed under the most extensive mandatory water restrictions ever. Dry conditions, aided by arsonists, also spawned numerous major forest fires that destroyed few homes but devastated tens of thousands of acres of forests.

Hurricane Elena brought much-needed rain over the Labor Day weekend, ending the drought. Unfortunately, Elena and the tornadoes it created battered the Gulf Coast, causing $1 billion in damages. In late October, before coastal areas could recover, Hurricane Juan caused further damage to beaches from Tampa Bay north to Pensacola. To make matters even worse, an unusually late hurricane, Kate, hit the Panhandle region in mid-November, forcing 100,000 persons to evacuate and inflicting damages in the millions.

The state's $2.5 billion-a-year citrus industry, damaged by killing frosts in four of the last five years, continued to battle the citrus canker infection that began in 1984. No nurseries were allowed to sell trees to replant freeze-damaged groves and millions of young trees were burned, with owners being partially compensated from state and federal funds.

J. LARRY DURRENCE
Florida Southern College

FLORIDA · Information Highlights

Area: 58,664 sq mi (151 939 km²).
Population (July 1, 1984 est.): 10,976,000.
Chief Cities (July 1, 1984 est.): Tallahassee, the capital, 112,258; Jacksonville, 577,971; Miami, 372,634; Tampa, 275,479; St. Petersburg, 241,294.
Government (1985): *Chief Officers*—governor, Bob Graham (D); lt. gov., Wayne Mixson (D). *Legislature*—Senate, 40 members; House of Representatives, 120 members.
State Finances (fiscal year 1984): *Revenues,* $11,896,000,000; *expenditures,* $10,320,000,000.
Personal Income (1984): $140,082,000,000; per capita, $12,763.
Labor Force (June 1984): *Civilian labor force,* 5,238,700; *unemployed,* 361,600 (6.9% of total force).
Education: *Enrollment* (fall 1983)—public elementary schools, 1,044,107; public secondary, 451,436; colleges and universities, 443,436. *Public school expenditures* (1982–83), $3,667,785,894 ($2,680 per pupil).

FOOD

Although international relief efforts had some positive effect, widespread hunger still threatened more than 30 million persons in sub-Saharan Africa during 1985. This was the only major area of the world whose food production had not increased as fast as its population growth over the previous decade. In the United States, meanwhile, a special task force reported that hunger was more widespread than at any time in the last 10–15 years. But Americans today are eating more food and taking in more calories than in the 1960s, even though per-capita consumption of animal products has declined and low-calorie foods and beverages are being consumed in record amounts. In 1985 several controversies continued over food, nutrition, and health.

Artificial Sweeteners. The American Medical Association (AMA) concluded that the artificial sweetener aspartame is safe and has no serious adverse health effects. Individuals who need to control their intake of phenylalanine, the AMA suggested, should regard aspartame as they would any other source of that acid. The Centers for Disease Control reviewed consumer complaints relating to the use of aspartame and also found no evidence of widespread, adverse health consequences. A proposal to require quantitative labeling of aspartame in soft drinks was not adopted.

The U.S. Congress voted, for the fourth time, to extend the 1977 moratorium preventing the Food and Drug Administration (FDA) from banning saccharin. The moratorium will run through May 1, 1987. The FDA reported anyway that the actual risk, if any, of saccharin to humans appears to be slight.

And finally, the National Academy of Sciences concluded that cyclamate, removed from the market in 1969, is not carcinogenic. The FDA was expected to rule on a petition for reapproval of cyclamate in 1986.

Food-Borne Illnesses. Serious outbreaks of food-related illnesses were reported in the United States during 1985. Contaminated milk from a dairy processing plant in suburban Chicago was the cause of a massive outbreak of salmonella food poisoning in several Midwestern states during late March and April. The epidemic affected some 16,000 individuals and caused several deaths.

Then in July, a total of 61 deaths and stillbirths were reported in California and six other states as a result of contaminated cheese. Authorities believed that the cheese, containing the cold-tolerant bacterium *Listeria monocytogenes,* may have been made with unpasteurized milk. Other recently recognized cold-tolerant bacteria responsible for outbreaks of illness include *camoylobacter* and *Yersinia.*

Food Irradiation. The preservation of certain foods by ionizing radiation is legal in at least 21 countries. In the United States the FDA has allowed irradiation of spices, herbs, and vegetable seasonings since mid-1983. In 1985 the FDA amended regulations to permit gamma radiation of dry enzyme preparations used as aids in the processing of food. Also approved was gamma irradiation of fresh non-heat-processed cuts of pork for control of *Trichinella spiralis,* a parasite responsible for 100–200 documented cases of trichinosis every year in the United States. The FDA also was considering a rule to allow low-dose irradiation of fruits and vegetables.

Packaging. The year saw the increased use of controlled- and modified-atmosphere food packaging. The atmosphere inside the package is controlled by the addition of an oxygen-absorbent reagent or modified by replacing some of the air with a relatively inert gas, such as nitrogen or carbon dioxide. These methods delay the growth of yeast, mold, and bacteria on foods, slow the respiration of fruits and vegetables, reduce oxidized flavors, and greatly extend shelf life.

See also feature article, The American Menu—1985 Style, page 64; AFRICA; AGRICULTURE.

KENNETH N. HALL
University of Connecticut

FRANCE

The approach of legislative elections in March 1986 provided a political backdrop for many of the events in France during 1985. The Socialist government of President François Mitterrand was criticized for the nation's weak economic performance but won wide support for its foreign policy, despite ongoing problems in New Caledonia and the *Rainbow Warrior* scandal.

Politics. On January 12 the government announced that it was sending 1,000 additional troops to the Pacific island territory of New Caledonia, where an ethnic conflict had grown increasingly violent. The move followed intensification of clashes between the island's indigenous Melanesian separatists, known as Kanaks, and French and other settlers who opposed independence from France. The issue quickly flared into a domestic political quarrel between President Mitterrand and conservative opposition leaders. Mitterrand visited New Caledonia on January 19 and met with leaders of the rival factions. The talks led to his announcement that France would hold a referendum in New Caledonia in July on the question of "independence in association with France." Opinion polls at home indicated approval for Mitterrand's handling of the issue, despite criticism from opposition leaders.

Amid continued rioting and in an effort to defuse the issue, the government on April 25

President François Mitterrand (center) visited France's troubled Pacific territory of New Caledonia in January 1985. He announced a summer referendum on "independence in association with France," but it was later postponed to 1987.

announced that it was postponing the referendum until 1987. Prime Minister Laurent Fabius disclosed a reform program under which each of four newly created regions in New Caledonia would choose its own administration in special elections. In the August balloting, French loyalists won a majority of seats in the new National Assembly, while pro-independence Melanesians won majorities in three of the four regional assemblies.

A general shift to the right among voters was confirmed by the results of runoff elections for local councils on March 17. Right-wing parties gained control of 69 of the 95 metropolitan departments, an increase of ten. Overall in the two-phase elections, the opposition obtained 54% of the vote, while the left took 46%.

On April 3 the government announced sweeping electoral changes that would substitute a system of proportional representation for the existing winner-take-all system. The proposed system would distribute seats in the National Assembly on the basis of party percentages of the total vote. If enacted, the reform would bolster the Socialists and also increase the representation of extreme left- and right-wing parties. Protesting the proposed reform, Michel Rocard resigned as minister of agriculture. Rocard was regarded as a potential rival of Mitterrand in the presidential election scheduled for 1988.

The main conservative opposition parties signed a joint declaration on April 10 stating that, if they win a majority in the parliament, they would "govern together and only to-

gether." The declaration pledged the parties to repeal the proposed electoral changes and outlined a program calling for substantial cuts in government spending, lower taxes, and deregulation of the economy, including denationalization of banks and industrial companies. Paris Mayor Jacques Chirac signed for the neo-Gaullist Rassemblement pour la République (RPR). Jean Lecanuet, a senator and a former presidential candidate, signed for the Union pour la Démocratie Française (UDF). The accord also ruled out any compromise coalition with the Socialists or with the right-wing National Front. But both Chirac and former president Giscard d'Estaing (of the UDF) said they would seek to govern with Mitterrand remaining at the Elysée Palace, an arrangement known as "cohabitation."

What became known as "the Greenpeace affair" was the stormiest and most dramatic political controversy of the year. It all started on July 10, when two explosions rocked the *Rainbow Warrior,* a protest vessel of the environmental group Greenpeace, while it was docked at Auckland, New Zealand. The boat was due to sail for Mururoa atoll within the week to protest a French nuclear test in the South Pacific. Twelve persons aboard the *Rainbow Warrior* escaped the explosions unhurt, but a Greenpeace photographer was killed. New Zealand police reported the next day that the case clearly was one of sabotage, and on July 23 they arrested a man and a woman, both carrying Swiss passports. The woman later was identified as Capt. Dominique

Prieur and the man as Maj. Alain Mafart, both members of the General Directorate of External Security, the French secret service.

On orders of the government, Bernard Tricot, a former adviser to President Charles de Gaulle, issued a 29-page report on the matter August 26. His report cleared the government and the intelligence service of involvement in the attack. Tricot did confirm that a total of six French citizens held or sought by New Zealand police were agents of the French intelligence service, but he concluded that they had been sent to New Zealand merely to gather information about Greenpeace and to infiltrate the organization. Most political observers, leaders of the opposition parties, and even some Socialists attacked the report as a whitewash. The day after it was issued, Prime Minister Fabius promised immediate action if it was proven that French citizens had committed criminal acts. Throughout September, revelations continued to appear in the French press alleging that a team of military advisers had sunk the *Rainbow Warrior* on orders of unidentified government officials.

Then on September 20, amid continuing attacks over what newspapers now were calling "the underwatergate affair," Prime Minister Fabius announced the resignation both of Defense Minister Charles Hernu and Adm. Pierre Lacoste, head of France's foreign intelligence operations. Hernu, who had repeatedly denied any prior knowledge of the bombing, declined to talk about what had actually happened. A presidential spokesman told reporters, "the affair is closed. There are no government lies." Paul Quiles became minister of defense.

As the controversy died down, France exploded a nuclear device at Mururoa on October 24. Prime Minister Fabius, who attended, reaffirmed the government's commitment to future nuclear testing. Following the explosion, Quiles and staff officers were photographed swimming in a lagoon to demonstrate the test's safety. Greenpeace members protesting the test aboard the yacht *Vega* were intercepted by French marine commandos and expelled from the area.

Economy. A paralyzing cold wave that hit Western Europe on Jan. 1, 1985, led to the deaths of nearly 40 Frenchmen described as vagrant, unemployed, or destitute. Their deaths triggered a national debate about France's "new poor." It was estimated that about 6 million of the nation's 55 million total population were living at or below the official poverty income level of about $5 a day. Growing unemployment and the virtually stagnant economy thus emerged as a key issue in the approaching legislative elections. By the end of 1985, the number of job seekers had fallen slightly to 2.3 million, or about 10% of the work force.

Overall, the French economy in 1985 was expected to post an average growth rate of about 1%, a slight drop from 1984 and one of the lowest rates among Western industrialized countries. In December the expansion rate reached 2.5%, however. Most observers felt that the government could attain its goal of 2.1% growth in 1986.

Throughout the year, conservative opposition leaders repeatedly criticized the Socialists for failing to restore significant growth to the economy. They promised that, if elected, a sweeping program of "liberalization" would be implemented to spur growth. The proposed measures included decontrolling prices, lifting exchange controls, sharply reducing government spending and taxes, and denationalizing leading banks and insurance and industrial companies.

In response to pressure from the finance ministry, which began a determined effort to stimulate investment and growth, leading banks lowered their base lending rates from 12% to 11.5% on January 9. Similar drops occurred in July and September, bringing the rate down to 9⅜%—still about 5% higher than in West Germany, France's main trading partner.

Finance Minister Pierre Bérégovoy said that he wanted lending rates, along with infla-

Amid increasing controversy over the "Rainbow Warrior" incident, Defense Minister Charles Hernu (left) resigned in September. He was replaced by Paul Quiles (right).

© Laurent Sola, Gamma-Liaison

The October visit to Paris by Mikhail Gorbachev (left) was a political high point for France's President Mitterrand (right), who was almost universally praised for his handling of the Soviet leader.

tion, to continue falling. Thanks partly to a weaker U.S. dollar, the government succeeded in reducing consumer prices. The nation began 1985 with an inflation rate of 7%, and for the first ten months of the year the rate fell to 4.5%. There were even expectations that the government could attain its goal of 3% in 1986.

President Mitterrand announced in a January 16 interview that he would support establishment of a chain of private television stations, thereby ending a state monopoly over the medium. The government on November 20 announced it was awarding the concession for a fifth channel to several French and Italian businessmen, provoking opposition from conservative leaders, publishing and film interests.

In a spectacular management shakeup, Bernard Hanon resigned as chairman of state-owned automaker Renault on January 22. The government, which ordered the ouster, immediately named as his successor Georges Besse, former head of Péchiney, the nationalized metals group. Besse had implemented a major reform plan that restored Péchiney to profitability. Besse quickly began implementing a similar plan at Renault. The automaker's losses had widened from 1.57 billion francs in 1983 to 12.5 billion francs in 1984, the most ever for a French company. Renault had slipped from its number-one position among Europe's auto producers in 1983 to sixth place in 1984. Aiming to have the company break even by 1987, Besse announced plans to lay off 21,000 workers by the end of 1986, reducing the work force in France from 98,000 to 77,000. The plan also called for cutting capacity in Western Europe from about 1.8 million cars in 1985 to 1.6 million cars by 1987. The Communist-led General Confederation of Labor (CGT) repeatedly challenged the strategy, and in late September it organized a widely publicized wildcat strike at three Renault plants. Fewer than 1,000 workers actually struck the plants, however, and most of the 16,800 employees petitioned the CGT for a return to work. By October 12 the strike was over, amid widespread recognition that the whole incident reflected a major shift in French worker attitudes toward business.

On February 27, in the first major concerted effort by Western governments to bring down the U.S. dollar, France joined the central banks of the United States, West Germany, Great Britain, Belgium, Italy, and Austria in a massive currency market intervention. In an operation estimated at between $1–$2 billion, the franc fell from 10.39 per dollar to 10.15. In a second, more sweeping action, Bérégovoy was among finance ministers and central bankers from the United States, West Germany, Japan, Great Britain, and France who on September 22 at a meeting in New York agreed to support coordinated action in world monetary markets. As the move sparked the selling of dollars, the franc on September 24 fell from 8.65 per dollar to 8.23. By the end of October, it had fallen to below 8 for the first time since 1984.

On September 18 the cabinet approved a 1986 draft budget that senior government officials and analysts said was the most rigorous in France's postwar history. Finance Minister Bérégovoy, presenting the budget to newsmen and the Socialist-dominated National Assembly (who later voted to approve the budget), said the total deficit would be kept to 3% of gross domestic product in 1986, or about 145

billion francs. Total spending was projected to rise by 3.6% from 1985, to a record 1.03 billion francs. Moderate spending increases were planned for national defense, education, and culture. To stimulate spending and investment, the government said it planned to ease some corporate taxes in 1986 and to institute an across-the-board reduction of 3% in personal income taxes. Communists and conservative opposition leaders challenged the figures and forecasts.

Foreign Affairs. In contrast to the sharp attacks on the government's failure to expand the economy, President Mitterrand was widely supported in his handling of foreign policy. On several occasions, Mitterrand challenged U.S. President Ronald Reagan and was backed at home, even by some conservatives. For example, at the Bonn economic summit of industrialized democracies May 2–4, Mitterrand refused to agree on a 1986 date for starting trade liberalization negotiations under auspices of the General Agreement on Tariffs and Trade (GATT), one of Reagan's summit goals. Mitterrand was particularly annoyed at West German Chancellor Helmut Kohl's open endorsement of the date, which came just prior to the French leader's arrival at the meeting. President Mitterrand said that he was opposed to GATT talks on agriculture, which he alleged could threaten the European Community's (EC's) common agricultural policy.

The French leader handed Reagan another setback on May 4 by publicly rejecting French participation in the administration's research program for a space-based antimissile system, known as the Strategic Defense Initiative (SDI). Other summit participants—Great Britain, West Germany, Japan, and Italy—indicated deep interest in the U.S. program, but French opposition blocked any mention of SDI in the summit's final communiqué.

A month earlier, France proposed to its West European allies another program, known as Eureka, designed to promote European cooperation in high technology. It was widely regarded as a response to SDI, but French and U.S. government officials emphasized that European companies were free to participate in both programs. Eureka was formally launched at a ministerial conference in Paris on July 17, attended by senior officials from 17 European governments and the EC Commission. Mitterrand announced that France would commit 1 billion francs to the project, but no other government followed suit. There were widespread expressions of skepticism by European business leaders and bankers whose participation was regarded as crucial. Many cited conflicts with existing EC programs. At a second ministerial meeting in Hannover, West Germany, November 5–6, however, Great Britain and Germany disclosed that they would contribute funds, though they declined to specify the

amounts. Ten Eureka projects from 14 countries were adopted at the meeting.

In a surprise move on July 24, France announced that it had suspended new investments in South Africa and recalled its ambassador to protest Pretoria's declaration of a state of emergency. French investment in South Africa amounted to about $1.6 billion, ranking behind that of Great Britain, the United States, and West Germany. South African leaders said that the French move in itself would have little impact on the economy but warned that it could encourage other Western countries to follow the example.

The October 2–5 visit to Paris by Soviet leader Mikhail Gorbachev was regarded as a significant diplomatic victory for President Mitterrand. Not even opposition leaders from the neo-Gaullist RPR could criticize his handling of the Soviet leader. Many French commentators had predicted that the Greenpeace affair would threaten Mitterrand's role as host for the visit, the first by Gorbachev to a Western capital since becoming party leader in March.

The day after his arrival in the French capital, Gorbachev proposed that the United States and the Soviet Union halve their strategic missile forces and negotiate a total ban on the development and deployment of space weapons. He also called on France and Britain to start talks with Moscow on reducing nuclear arms. The statement was widely viewed as a move to split Washington from its NATO allies. But Mitterrand said during a joint news conference with the Soviet leader that France could not agree to direct negotiations on its nuclear forces, and he urged Gorbachev to continue arms talks with the United States.

On December 4, Mitterrand met with Gen. Wojciech Jaruzelski, the Polish leader, which triggered protests from conservatives, Socialists, and labor leaders. Mitterrand did not reveal the content of their talk. Fabius reportedly offered to resign after he challenged the visit.

AXEL KRAUSE
"International Herald Tribune," Paris

FRANCE • Information Highlights

Official Name: French Republic.
Location: Western Europe.
Area: 211,207 sq mi (547 026 km²).
Population (mid-1985 est.): 55,000,000.
Chief City (1982 est.): Paris, the capital, 8,706,963.
Government: *Head of state,* François Mitterrand, president (took office May 1981). *Chief minister,* Laurent Fabius, prime minister (took office July 1984). *Legislature*—Parliament: Senate and National Assembly.
Monetary Unit: Franc (7.8080 francs equal U.S. $1, Nov. 25, 1985).
Gross Domestic Product (1983 U.S.$): $518,000,000,000.
Economic Indexes (1984): *Consumer Prices* (1970 = 100), all items, 375.2; food, 384.6. *Industrial Production* (April 1985, 1980 = 100), 104.
Foreign Trade (1984 U.S.$): *Imports,* $103,885,000,000; *exports,* $93,217,000,000.

Restrictions on water usage, caused by a severe drought in many regions of the United States, forced gardeners to resort to an old tool, the watering can.

GARDENING AND HORTICULTURE

The number one problem facing gardeners in many regions of the United States during 1985 was insufficient rainfall in water-storage areas. In such states as New York, New Jersey, Connecticut, Pennsylvania, Florida, and California, water restrictions were imposed affecting gardening practices. The most severe restrictions included absolutely no use of water for sod, flowers, and trees and shrubs, to a limit of 50 gal (189 l) of water per household per day. Automatic, overhead, and drip irrigation systems were prohibited. Watering, which was allowed for vegetable crops, had to be accomplished by hand. The old-fashioned rain barrel and watering can were reintroduced to many gardeners.

Horticulturist Honored. The American Association of Nurserymen presented the 1985 Norman Jay Colman Award to Dr. George L. Good, professor of ornamental horticulture at Cornell University. The presentation occurred in July at the 110th Annual Convention and Nursery Growers' Expo in Orlando, FL. Dr. Good received the award for outstanding achievements in horticultural research, including vital information relating to the validity of the fall planting programs being conducted throughout the United States and for the overwintering of container plants.

Award Winners. Four outstanding roses were honored by the All-America Rose Selections (AARS). "Showbiz," a brilliant scarlet floribunda, hybridized by Mathias Tantau of Ütersen, West Germany, received the only AARS award for 1985. The three AARS award winners for 1986 were "Touch of Class," "Broadway," and "Voodoo." "Touch of Class," a hybrid tea rose, produces 4.5 to 5.5 inch (11 to 14 cm) blooms of a warm pink shaded with coral and cream, hybridized by Michael Kriloff, Antibes, France. Anthony Perry of Hemet, CA, bred "Broadway," a hybrid tea rose with light reddish pink blossoms heavily suffused with yellow. "Voodoo," with 5 to 6 inch (13 to 15 cm) sweetly scented flowers, is a hybrid tea rose with a blend of yellow, peach, and orange blushing to scarlet, hybridized by Jack Christensen of Ontario, CA.

All-America Selections (AAS) 1986 winners for vegetable and flower gardens include three introductions. "Blondy" dwarf okra and "How Sweet It Is" white sweet corn are the winners in the vegetable category. "How Sweet It Is" is the first white sweet corn to receive an AAS award. The flower winner, Cosmos "Sunny Red," the first dwarf red cosmos ever, was selected for its dwarf growth habit and abundant blossoms. "Sunny Red" can tolerate heat in arid regions and is relatively immune to insect and disease problems.

Other introductions of note include Geranium "Summer Showers" F_1, the first true ivy-leaf geranium introduced from seed, and *Lisianthus* "Lion" F_1, the first double *Lisianthus* to be marketed.

Television and Computer Programs. *The Victory Garden,* a television program appearing weekly on 235 public broadcasting stations throughout the United States, developed a regional garden concept by establishing gardens and programs at Pine Mountain, GA, and Newport Beach, CA. The regional programming approach enables greater concentration on local growing conditions.

The Ortho Personalized Plant Selector, a software horticultural reference program published in 1985 by Ortho Information Services of the Chevron Chemical Co., provides a wealth of information on more than 700 different plants, from groundcovers to trees, houseplants to vines. Plant lists may be selected by botanical or common name, color, height, blooming season, or light or water requirements.

RALPH L. SNODSMITH
Ornamental Horticulturist

GENETICS

The year 1985 brought continuing advances in the field of genetics.

DNA Technology and Archaeology. The ancient Egyptians preserved a Pharaoh's body after death so that the spirit could return to it when visiting the tomb. Scientists studying these mummies have been able to establish their ages through radiocarbon dating, their skeletal diseases through X rays, and their blood types through bone samples. In the mid-1980s, Dr. Svante Pääbo, a molecular geneticist at the University of Uppsala in Sweden, was able to take some skin and underlying tissue from a 2,400-year-old mummy, extract segments of its DNA (deoxyribonucleic acid), and clone the DNA by inserting it into the plasmids of bacteria, which then proceeded to make many copies of it. Although an analysis of the DNA did not reveal anything unusual, there is the expectation that by comparing the DNA from different mummies one will be able to establish the genealogies of the various pharaonic dynasties. It is known that these families practiced incest in order to keep their heritage as pure as possible.

Gene Changes and Parasitism. The causative agent of sleeping sickness is the protozoan *Trypanosoma brucei*, which spends part of its life in tsetse flies and part of it in mammals, including human beings. When a parasite enters a mammal's blood stream, it is faced with two serious problems: the mammal's immune system and the change in host body temperature from 25°C or 77°F (insect) to 37°C or 98.6°F (mammal).

The mammalian host produces antibodies against a *glycoprotein* that is present on the parasite's surface and acts as an antigen. Dr. K.M. Esser and M.J. Schoenbechler of the Walter Reed Army Institute of Research in Washington, DC, working with mice that had been infected with trypanosomes, found that the parasites have one type of antigen when they enter the mouse's blood stream. After about four days, there is a switch to one of a number of other types of glycoproteins, thus rendering the host's antibodies harmless to the parasite. The switch occurs even if the mice are prevented experimentally from producing antibodies, indicating that the change of antigenic properties of the parasite is programmed to occur automatically.

The abrupt change in host body temperature from 25°C to 37°C brings with it a great deal of stress on the parasite's physiology and triggers changes in its development. Dr. L. H. T. Van der Ploeg and his colleagues at Columbia University found that the jump in temperature increases the activity of genes that produce proteins that aid the trypanosome in adjusting to its mammalian host. The proteins produced by this change in temperature are called heat shock proteins. They appear to be very similar to proteins produced by both *Drosophila* (a genus of two-winged flies) and yeasts when these organisms are subjected to sudden heat shock.

Genes and Development. For a long time it has been known that there are certain genes in *Drosophila,* called *homeotic genes,* that cause the development of legs where there should be antennae, or a set of wings instead of halteres. In effect these genes cause one segment to develop as if it were following the plan of another segment. Because the vertebrate skeletal, nervous, and muscle systems originate as segmented units, it is of interest to determine if homeotic genes also occur in this animal group.

Dr. Walter J. Gehring and his colleagues at the University of Basel, Switzerland, have found that at least some species of vertebrates (frogs, chickens, mice, and humans) have nucleotide sequences that closely resemble the homeotic genes of *Drosophila*. The genes in the various organisms are active during embryological development and appear to code for proteins that bind to DNA, thereby turning genes on and off. If these homeotic genes are found to be widespread among vertebrates, it would indicate a common pattern for the control of development in segmented organisms.

Microbial Insecticides. Among the many problems that confront farmers are the insects that feed on their crops. One approach to this problem has been the use of chemical insecticides that are sprayed on plants. Another method of combating insects is the use of microbial insecticides. The best-known example is the bacterium *Bacillus thuringiensis* that produces spores containing an endotoxin that, on ingestion, is released into the digestive tract of the insect and kills it. These bacteria have been sprayed on crop plants worldwide for more than 20 years and have been quite effective.

However, there are a number of insects, including black cutworm and corn earworm, whose larvae burrow in the soil and eat the roots of plants. These pests are relatively safe from sprays. In 1985, Dr. Lidia Watrud of Monsanto Company in St. Louis announced that, using recombinant DNA techniques, the endotoxin-specifying gene from *B. thuringiensis* was transferred to another bacterium *Pseudomonas fluorescens,* which lives on the surface of the roots of a number of crop plants. When root-eating insects ingest the genetically engineered *P. fluorescens,* the toxin produced by the transferred gene kills them. It is planned to add more insecticidal genes to *P. fluorescens* to increase the number of root-eating insects it could destroy. It should be possible to do the same with bacteria that normally live on other parts of crop plants, thus eventually eliminating the need for extensive spraying of insecticides.

Louis Levine, *City College of New York*

GENEVA

The announcement that President Reagan and Soviet party chairman Gorbachev would meet in Geneva in November 1985 as well as the renewal of U.S.–USSR arms talks, also in Geneva, caused international attention to focus on the French-speaking city, located in the southwestern corner of Switzerland where the Rhône River leaves Lake Geneva (Léman).

Host to two million visitors annually, yet hardly a tourist center, Geneva has emerged in recent years as the site of approximately 7,000 major and 23,000 minor conferences, both business and diplomatic, annually. Geneva also serves as headquarters for many international organizations, including the World Health Organization, the International Red Cross, the World Council of Churches, and the International Labor Organization. Designated as host city for the League of Nations, Geneva today is the official headquarters of the United Nations in Europe.

The city abounds in fine hotels and restaurants. Its atmosphere reflects the careful, considered world of the diplomat and international banker. Ranking after Zurich as a center for Swiss banking, Geneva is second in Europe only to Oslo in terms of high cost of living. Wealth abounds, but nightlife does not.

Independent, somewhat puritanical, international in outlook, and heavily business oriented, Geneva today reflects its heritage as a city that played an important role in Europe from the 16th to the 18th century. Now, as then, it goes its own way—part of, but different from, the rest of Switzerland.

PAUL C. HELMREICH, *Wheaton College, MA*

GEOLOGY

As in recent years, 1985 saw continued advance in geoscience research. Earth scientists probed the ocean floor, mapped the earth from space, monitored areas of potential volcanic and earthquake activity, and continued to ponder the causes of wholesale animal extinctions during prehistoric time.

Earthquakes. Clearly the most significant geologic event of the year was the major earthquake that devastated much of Mexico City on September 19. The quake's force—measured at 8.1 on the open-ended Richter scale—killed at least 5,600 people, injured at least 11,000 others, and left some 31,000 homeless. Although the earthquake's epicenter was located on the Pacific Coast some 50 mi (80 km) from Acapulco, Mexico City suffered far more damage because it is built on soft clay deposited in an ancient lake. The waterlogged lake sediment vibrated like a bowl of jelly as the deadly seismic waves passed through it. The capital city was jarred by a second major temblor on Fri-

day, September 20. Centered 150 mi (241 km) northwest of Acapulco and rated at 7.3 on the Richter scale, this shock collapsed dozens of previously damaged buildings and severely hampered rescue efforts.

The Mexican quakes were caused by friction between two of Earth's great crustal plates. The Cocos plate, part of the Pacific Ocean floor off Mexico, is pushing northeastward against the North American plate at the rate of about 2 to 4.5 inches (5 to 11.4 cm) per year. As the Cocos plate is thrust into the Middle Ocean Trench (a subduction zone) and dives beneath the westward-creeping North American plate, the strain involved in the relative motion of the two plates results in great stress. An earthquake occurs when the accumulated stress is released suddenly thus generating seismic (earthquake) waves.

A killer quake also struck near Santiago, Chile, on March 3. Rated at 8.0 at its epicenter near the little village of Algarrobo, the temblor caused at least 177 deaths, some 2,500 injuries, and left 150,000 homeless. Property damage was estimated to be about $2 billion. Three earthquakes hit southern Iran in February. Although they inflicted great property damage, there was minimal loss of life. Wyoming and the USSR suffered quakes in late August, and on August 23, 67 people were killed by a 7.4 magnitude shock that caused widespread damage in northwestern China. And on October 4 the strongest quake to hit Tokyo in 56 years was rated at 6.2 on the Richter scale. Fortunately there were no major injuries or damage. This is attributed to the fact that this was a deep-focus earthquake in which the seismic waves originated deep within the earth. Shallow-focus quakes (such as those in Mexico City) are more powerful. Later in October, a powerful quake measuring 6.1 struck the Soviet Central Asian republic of Tadzhikistan. It was the strongest quake to strike the USSR in nine years and caused unspecified "loss of life" as well as landslides and property damage.

Earthquake Prediction. The rash of destructive earthquakes further stimulated research in earthquake prediction. Geochemical methods were used by Japanese geologists who noted conspicuous changes in the composition of gases issuing from a fumarole (volcanic vent) near the epicenter of a 6.8 quake that shocked central Japan. It was noted that concentrations of certain chemical compounds increased sharply one week before the quake and then dropped sharply 50 days after the tremor. Similar geochemical changes may be useful in forecasting other earthquakes. California seismologists used another technique to predict that a moderate (6.0 magnitude) quake would strike the Parkfield, CA, area before 1993. Their forecast is based on the fact that a major earthquake has occurred on this part of the San Andreas Fault about every 22 years. There

have been five such quakes within the past 130 years and only the fourth was out of phase.

Volcanism. Volcanologists also are using geochemical clues in an attempt to predict hazardous volcanic eruptions. The analysis of mercury on soil particles and radon in the gases of soil at California's Long Valley Caldera has been used to distinguish current from past volcanic activity. The last known major eruption in this area occurred about 700,000 years ago. However, in 1978, unusual seismic activity, ground deformation, and uplift were observed, thus indicating that the eruption potential of the caldera is increasing.

Meanwhile, volcano-related research is yielding unexpected payoffs in providing new prospecting techniques for sources of geothermal energy. Also, laser technology used by volcanologists is now being used by gold prospectors. In addition, satellite monitoring of eruptions may soon be used to warn pilots of airborne volcanic ash that might cause crashes. Much recent volcanic research has centered around Washington's Mount St. Helens.

In Hawaii, Kilauea continued its sporadic outburst, and in Sicily, Etna spewed lava late in the year. The most damaging eruption took place in Colombia on November 13, when the reawakening volcano Nevado del Ruiz triggered avalanches of mud and water that engulfed 14 villages and towns. In one of them, Armero, more than 23,000 persons were killed.

Earth Structure. Using techniques developed for petroleum exploration, geophysicists have used seismic reflection profiling to detect the buried boundary of the North American continent and a fragment of the African continent. Now known as south Georgia and Florida, this bit of the African plate was left behind when the two continents pulled apart some 180 million years ago. Elsewhere, seismic studies have revealed the breakup of the ancient landmass of Gondwana and the drifting apart of the Antarctic and Australian continents. This evidence is preserved at the margin of east Antarctica and reveals that a submarine flood of lava poured out before seafloor spreading began.

Petroleum explorers also utilized new techniques in the search for oil and natural gas. Computer-generated structure maps are being used to locate subsurface traps for petroleum. Other computer-enhanced maps also can be used to indicate the condition and content of existing wells. And satellite imagery is revealing traces of ancient faults and plate sutures not detected by traditional techniques.

Paleontology. A number of significant fossil discoveries were reported during 1985. The well-preserved remains of a group of soft-bodied organisms were discovered near Milwaukee, WI. Estimated to be about 400 million years old, these unusual early Paleozoic fossils have provided much information about the life

AP/Wide World

A California seismologist checks the latest reading from the devastating earthquake that struck Mexico in September.

and environment of the Silurian Period. Arthropods—mostly trilobites—and worms are the predominant species. Also found was what is believed to be the first Paleozoic leech and a structure from a conodont organism.

Vertebrate fossils—especially dinosaurs—also made news. The skeleton of a 19-foot (6-m) long plateosaur, the largest reptile of Triassic time, was found in a clay pit in northern Switzerland. This was the first such discovery in that country. Meanwhile, in Petrified Forest National Park, Arizona, the bones of a plateosaurlike dinosaur were unearthed from the Chinle Formation formed some 225 million years ago. And North America's first positively identified iguanodon, a huge plant-eating reptile, was collected from Upper Jurassic rocks (135–142 million years old) near Grand Junction, CO.

Much older are probable Early Archean fossils collected in western Australia and South Africa. Found in rocks 3.5 million years old, these filamentous microfossils appear to be of definite organic origin.

Speculation continued on "mass extinctions." The effects of changing climates and so-called "nuclear winters" produced by asteroid impacts were argued by hosts of specialists. However, the asteroid impact theory of the apocalypse appears weakened by the discovery of plant-eating duck-billed dinosaurs in Alaska. Although the Alaskan climate of 65 million years ago (Cretaceous time) may have been milder, the new discovery suggests that some dinosaurs may have adapted to cooler climes.

WILLIAM H. MATTHEWS III
Lamar University

GEORGIA

The economy, business activity, and education made headlines in Georgia in 1985.

Economy. The U.S. Census Bureau announced that Georgia was the fourth-fastest-growing state, thereby documenting the tremendous economic growth that already had been noted in various other statistical indexes. Spearheading the state's growth, Atlanta was ranked the fifth-fastest-growing metropolis in the nation, the second in rate of employment growth, and the third in number of new jobs created. Georgians also organized new businesses at more than double the national rate, reflecting a high level of confidence in a strong regional economy. As a result of this surge in economic activity, personal income rose 10% making Georgia, at one point, first in national income growth.

Business. Atlanta businesses and their leaders were the focus of national attention in 1985. Led by Ted Turner, the Turner Broadcasting System (TBS) announced plans to purchase CBS Inc. When CBS presented a stock buy-back strategy, Turner failed to get an Atlanta federal judge or the Federal Communications Commission (FCC) to block it. Less than a week later Turner announced plans to acquire MGM-UA Entertainment, a company three times the size of TBS.

Nearby, another local business, Coca-Cola, was in the news. With an elaborate noonday parade in downtown Atlanta, Coca-Cola announced that it was changing the cola formula and introducing New Coke. After pressure from loyal "old coke" drinkers, the company reintroduced Classic Coke. Increased marketing expenditures generated by these products led to a slight increase only in operating income. In other news, the Coca-Cola Co. rejected a federal judge's order to reveal its legendary secret cola formulas; also, it announced plans to acquire two major television production houses. On March 7, Robert W. Woodruff, the genius behind the Coca-Cola Co. for 60 years, died at age 95.

Education. Gov. Joe Frank Harris' massive education reform package occupied the 1985 General Assembly almost exclusively. The key provisions of the Quality Basic Education Act passed by the legislature are: full-day kindergarten program; market-sensitive salaries; career ladders and stiffer standards for teachers and principals; a statewide curriculum; and a funding formula to aid poor school districts. Eventually the reform measures will cost the state more than $640 million annually. In other action, the assembly approved a $4.8 billion state budget, voted to double penalties for cocaine possession, increased workmen's compensation rates, and raised the drinking age to 20 on Sept. 30, 1985, and to 21 a year later. Rejected were bills to legalize horse racing in the state and to let voters enact laws through public initiative. The lawmakers did not act on a bill requiring silent prayer in schools.

Governor Harris remained committed to his 1982 no-tax-hike pledge made possible by economic growth that generated a record $486 million in new state revenue. Harris, however, did sign a bill allowing counties, with voters' approval, to impose a 1% local option sales tax for road construction or civic projects.

Mayoral Election. Atlanta Mayor Andrew Young won reelection by a huge margin of 80%, but only about one third of the city's registered voters went to the polls. Mayor Young said that the greatest disappointment of his past administration was the controversy surrounding the Carter presidential library and parkway.

Carter Library and Parkway. The controversy over building a road to the Carter library began in 1981 but heated up considerably in 1985. Atlanta citizens, government officials, and business leaders were embroiled in an emotional issue that pits the former president against neighborhood activists, many of whom were once among his loyal supporters. While construction began on the Carter library and the controversial presidential parkway, neighborhood residents waged a legal battle. They met with success on several fronts. A Dekalb Superior Court judge ruled that the land in question had to be used, as originally intended, for parks and not for a road. The ruling was upheld by the state Supreme Court. The eleventh U.S. Circuit Court of Appeals found that the 1984 Environmental Impact Statement on the parkway was flawed and that the Department of Transportation must research alternative routes.

Meanwhile the Carter library complex, which was about 25% complete by late 1985, was slated to open in the summer of 1986. The parkway, however, was less than 10% complete and more delays seemed inevitable.

KAY BECK, *Georgia State University*

GEORGIA • Information Highlights

Area: 58,910 sq mi (152 576 km²).

Population (July 1, 1984 est.): 5,837,000.

Chief Cities (July 1, 1984 est.): Atlanta, the capital, 426,090; Columbus, 174,824; Savannah, 145,014.

Government (1984): *Chief Officers*—governor, Joe Frank Harris (D); lt. gov., Zell Miller (D). *General Assembly*—Senate, 56 members; House of Representatives, 180 members.

State Finances (fiscal year 1984): *Revenues,* $7,458,000,000; *expenditures,* $6,699,000,000.

Personal Income (1984): $67,416,000,000; per capita, $11,551.

Labor Force (June 1985): *Civilian labor force,* 2,879,500; *unemployed,* 202,500 (7% of total force).

Education: *Enrollment* (fall 1983)—public elementary schools, 738,258; public secondary, 312,601; colleges and universities, 201,453. *Public school expenditures* (1982–83), $2,123,585,842 ($2,169 per pupil).

Chancellor Helmut Kohl addresses delegates to the economic summit of industrialized democracies in Bonn, May 4.

GERMANY

During 1985, relations between the two German states, the Federal Republic of Germany (West Germany) and the German Democratic Republic (East Germany, or DDR), continued to improve in spite of a major spy scandal. In August, West Germany's chief internal security officer defected to the DDR; that was followed a few days later by the disappearance of secretaries in the offices of the chancellor, the economics minister, and the president. (*See* ESPIONAGE.) Yet neither state allowed the security scandal to interfere with their increased economic, cultural, and political cooperation. In July, West Germany increased its limit on interest-free loans available to East Germany by about 40%. The trade volume between the two states increased by about 20% during the year. The two nations also concluded negotiations for a major cultural and educational exchange agreement, providing for visits by students, scholars, athletes, and artists. It will be the first such agreement in the history of the two German states.

Contacts between East and West Germany included a September meeting in Leipzig between East German leader Erich Honecker and Franz Josef Strauss, a key figure in West Germany's Christian Democratic Party. It was

Strauss' second trip to the DDR in three years. A few days later, the former West German chancellor and present chairman of the Social Democratic Party, Willy Brandt, also went to the DDR for talks with Honecker. It was his first trip to East Germany since he was forced to resign as chancellor in 1974 after an East German spy was discovered on his staff.

Federal Republic of Germany (West Germany)

From May 2 to 4, Bonn hosted the 11th annual economic summit conference of the seven major industrialized democracies. The meeting, however, was overshadowed by the controversy surrounding the planned May 5 visit of U.S. President Ronald Reagan to a German military cemetery in the small town of Bitburg. Reagan's visit, 40 years after the end of World War II, had been proposed by Chancellor Helmut Kohl as a symbolic gesture of German-American reconciliation. After it was discovered that the cemetery contained the remains of 49 Nazi SS troops, President Reagan came under heavy pressure from American Jewish and veterans groups, many members of Congress, and even some of his strongest supporters to cancel the visit. Reagan, however, citing his commitment to Chancellor Kohl and the strong support that this "noble gesture" had in

the Federal Republic, refused. Kohl, who was privately pressed by the White House to propose an alternative to the cemetery visit, rejected any changes in the presidential itinerary.

Bitburg provoked the sharpest sustained criticism that Kohl faced since taking office in 1982. The chancellor was charged with sloppy planning and insensitivity to the horrors of the Nazi era. But two weeks before Reagan's visit, Kohl, speaking at the site of the Bergen-Belsen concentration camp, clearly stated that "Germany bears historical responsibility for the crimes of the Nazi tyranny. This responsibility is reflected not least in never-ending shame." While the trip was popular among West Germans, it failed to help the chancellor's political fortunes. In a major state election in North Rhine–Westphalia a week after the cemetery visit, Chancellor Kohl's Christian Democratic Union lost heavily to the Social Democrats.

About three fourths of West Germany's adult population supported the Bitburg visit, with the Green as the only political party to call for its cancellation. While the Social Democrats, the major opposition party, sharply criticized the manner in which the Reagan visit was organized, they did not advocate the abandonment of the presidential gesture to Germany's war dead. Generally, Germans were surprised at the intensity of the U.S. reaction. For many Germans born since 1945, the Third Reich and World War II belong to a distant past that should no longer have any influence on West Germany's international stature and prestige. West Germany in the past 40 years, according to this view, has earned the right to be accepted as an equal within the Western community of nations.

In 1985, for the people and leadership of West Germany, the 40th anniversary of World War II's end still evoked mixed feelings. For some, May 8, 1945, was remembered as a catastrophic defeat, the collapse of long-held values of duty, patriotism, and loyalty. Surveys during 1985 found that about one fourth of the population remembered feeling this sense of defeat in 1945. The majority of the population with living memories of May 8, 1945, recalled the day as one of liberation from the Nazi regime, which had brought unprecedented death and destruction to Germany and its neighbors.

The feelings and emotions evoked by the Bitburg incident and the anniversary of the war's end also influenced a remarkable speech by Federal President Richard von Weizsäcker to the West German parliament on May 8, 1985. For the first time, a major West German political leader challenged the traditional explanation used by older, "ordinary" Germans that they "knew nothing" about the Holocaust. "Every German," Weizsäcker said, "was able to experience what his Jewish compatriots had to suffer, ranging from plain apathy and hidden intolerance to outright hatred. Who could remain unsuspecting after the burning of the synagogues, the plundering, the stigmatization with the Star of David, the deprivation of rights, the ceaseless violation of human dignity? Whoever opened his eyes and ears and sought information could not fail to notice that Jews were being deported. . . . When the unspeakable truth of the Holocaust then became known, all too many of us claimed that they had not known anything about it or even suspected anything." The address, which was widely applauded throughout Germany and Eu-

© Bob Nickelsberg, Gamma-Liaison

In São Paulo, Brazil, in late June, an international team of forensic experts confirmed that a recently exhumed skeleton was that of the notorious, long-hunted Nazi war criminal, Dr. Josef Mengele.

In a disappointing year for the Greens, the party's federal board, right, voted in January to dissolve its West Berlin provincial association. Infiltration by young neo-Nazis was cited as the reason.

AP/Wide World

rope, also made explicit mention of other groups—Communists, homosexuals, and the mentally ill—who have rarely been cited by postwar German leaders as victims of Nazism.

Politics. The year 1985 was a difficult one for the Kohl government and his Christian Democratic Party (CDU). Continued high unemployment, the spy scandal, the Bitburg incident, and new revelations of illegal fund-raising by the party took their toll, as the CDU lost two state elections and the chancellor's popularity dropped to an all-time low.

The fortunes of the opposition Social Democratic Party (SPD) dramatically improved. After suffering its worst defeat in almost 20 years at the 1983 election, the party rebounded in 1985 with decisive victories in two state elections. In March, for the first time in its history, the SPD won an absolute majority at the election in the Saar. Two months later, at the state election in North Rhine–Westphalia (by far the largest state, with almost one third of the electorate), the party again won an absolute majority of the vote. The twin victories brought two new leaders into the national political spotlight: Oskar La Fontaine from the Saar, and Johannes Rau from North Rhine–Westphalia. La Fontaine, a protégé of Willy Brandt, is a leading figure of the SPD's left wing; he favors removing West Germany from NATO's military structure. Johannes Rau is the popular minister-president (chief executive) of North Rhine–Westphalia. After the election he became the front-runner to challenge Helmut Kohl for the chancellorship in 1987. In September he formally announced his candidacy. The Social Democrats, however, had yet to present significant alternatives to the domestic and foreign policies of the Kohl government. The good showing of the party in 1985 appeared to be more the result of the mistakes of the Kohl regime than the appeal of any SPD policy proposals.

The Free Democrats (FDP), the junior partner in the Kohl government, also increased their share of the vote at the two state elections in 1985. In anticipation of the 1987 national vote, the FDP attempted to differentiate itself from the CDU through guarded criticism of, and outright opposition to, some of Kohl's policies. Foreign Minister Hans-Dietrich Genscher, for example, became identified as the major intra-governmental critic of West German participation in President Reagan's Strategic Defense Initiative, or "Star Wars," program. Genscher argued that strong West German participation in the program might have a negative impact on U.S.-Soviet arms-reduction talks in Geneva and also hinder Bonn's efforts to improve relations with Eastern Europe.

The Green party's string of electoral and political successes ended in 1985. In March the party received only 2.5% of the vote in the Saar, failing to gain representation in the state parliament; two months later, with 4.6% of the vote, the Greens were denied seats in the North Rhine–Westphalian parliament. The two defeats intensified the intraparty conflict between the fundamentalists (*Fundis*), who reject any cooperation with the established parties, and the realists (*Realos*), who are willing to form coalitions in order to achieve Green goals, if only in a piecemeal fashion. At the party's national conference in June, a compromise resolution supporting cooperation with the Social Democrats—provided that the SPD changes its policies on nuclear energy, disarmament, and environmental protection—was passed. But the resolution also condemned "power shar-

WEST GERMANY • Information Highlights

Official Name: Federal Republic of Germany.
Location: North-central Europe.
Area: 95,976 sq mi (248 577 km²).
Population (mid-1985 est.): 61,000,000.
Chief Cities (June 30, 1983): Bonn, the capital, 292,900; West Berlin, 1,860,500; Hamburg, 1,617,800; Munich, 1,284,300.
Government: *Head of state,* Richard von Weizsäcker, president (took office July 1, 1984). *Head of government,* Helmut Kohl, federal chancellor (took office Oct. 1982). *Legislature*—Parliament: Bundesrat and Bundestag.
Monetary Unit: Deutsche mark (2.6105 D. marks equal U.S.$1, Nov. 18, 1985).
Gross National Product (1983 U.S.$): $655,500,-000,000.
Economic Indexes (1984): *Consumer Prices* (1970 = 100), all items, 194.1; food, 177.6. *Industrial Production* (1980 = 100), 99.
Foreign Trade (1984 U.S.$): *Imports,* $151,246,-000,000; *exports,* $169,784,000,000.

ing" at any price, thus leaving the Greens divided on the critical question of their future relationship to the established parties. Green voters, in contrast to the party leadership, strongly support a coalition with the Social Democrats, if possible, after the 1987 national election. In October the Greens in the state of Hesse, against the opposition of the party's national leadership, finally did enter into a formal coalition with the SPD and received one ministry (environmental affairs) in the state cabinet. It marked the first time that the party assumed governmental responsibility at the state level.

Economy. With a real increase in its gross national product (GNP) of about 2.5%, West Germany in 1985 experienced its third consecutive year of modest economic growth. Inflation remained low at 2.4%, and the country's trade balance was expected to show a record surplus of almost $21 billion. But economic growth in 1985 was insufficient to produce any significant drop in unemployment, which averaged about 9% for the year. In September, Chancellor Kohl summoned top business and labor leaders to Bonn for talks on how to create more jobs. It marked the first time that major

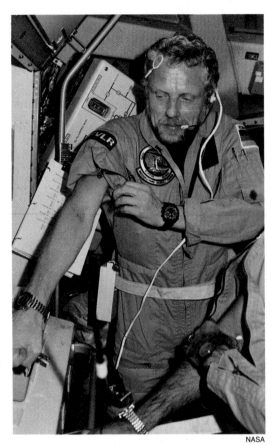

NASA

West Germany ran the early November flight of the U.S. space shuttle "Challenger." Physicist Reinhard Furrer, above, was one of two West Germans on the crew of eight.

government, business, and labor leaders met jointly to address the problem. The participants agreed on a three-pronged approach: training for unskilled workers, reducing overtime in public-sector jobs, and lengthening the unemployment insurance program for workers who have been jobless for a long period.

The government's other economic policies in 1985 continued to emphasize the improvement of supply-side conditions. The new budget limited expenditure growth to 2.4% of the previous year's outlays; the deficit of about $8.9 billion amounted to only 1.5% of the country's GNP, the lowest level since 1974. In addition, to further stimulate demand, the government passed a tax cut that would provide about $7 billion in tax relief. The cuts were to be made in two steps, in 1986 and 1988.

Environment. The Kohl government in 1985 responded to strong public concern about environmental issues with new regulations for the control of air pollution by industrial firms. The regulations, which drew the praise of many environmental groups, sharply limited industrial emissions of sulfur dioxide, nitrous oxide, lead, and cadmium. While West Germany still lags behind the United States and Japan in nuclear

Boris Becker, 17, the youngest man and first West German to win a Wimbledon tennis title, was honored in his hometown of Leimen, below, and throughout the country.

© Regis Bossu, Sygma

power plant safety measures and automobile emissions laws, its industrial air pollution measures are now the most comprehensive in the world. The Kohl government, however, was unable to secure the support of other European Community nations for its proposal to require lead-free gasoline in all automobiles produced after January 1986.

Terrorism. The year 1985 saw an increase in terrorist activities in West Germany. In February the chief executive of a major manufacturer of engines and turbines for the military was killed at his home in Munich. His company produced engines for NATO's Tornado combat plane as well as for West Germany's main battle tank, the Leopard 2. In addition, there were about 40 bombings and fires at NATO and U.S. military installations, most of which were attributed to the Red Army Faction. Government estimates placed the number of hard-core terrorists in West Germany at between 20 and 40 persons, supported by a wider circle of 100–150 sympathizers. West German terrorists appeared to act in concert with similar groups in France, Belgium, and Spain.

In September, rioting erupted in several German cities when demonstrators clashed with police and set fires at banks, police stations, and department stores. The demonstrations began in Frankfurt to protest a meeting of a minor neo-Nazi group, the National Democratic Party. But they spread, for no apparent political reason, to Berlin, Hamburg, and other major urban areas. The battles with police, which killed one person in Frankfurt, involved small urban anarchist groups that probably have some connection with the Red Army Faction.

Foreign Policy. The Federal Republic in 1985 became the leading West European supporter of President Reagan's Star Wars defense program. In spite of some opposition from Foreign Minister Genscher, the Kohl government sent a 30-member delegation to Washington in September to negotiate the details of German participation. Several German companies were expected to become major suppliers for the $26 billion program. Technology sharing, patents policy, and pricing would be determined in a formal U.S.-German agreement, expected to be concluded early in 1986.

The French plan for European technological cooperation, the "Eureka" program, also gained the support of the Federal Republic. In November, the Kohl government hosted a meeting of West European foreign and research ministers to discuss the plan, which France's President François Mitterrand envisions as a counterweight to U.S. and Japanese high-tech advances.

In the Middle East, West Germany continued its traditional policy of supporting moderate Arab states and Israel. The major issue in 1985 was military assistance to Saudi Arabia.

AP/Wide World

Chancellor Kohl (right) and Foreign Minister Genscher discuss the U.S. "Star Wars" plan during a parliamentary debate. The Kohl government gave its support to SDI.

While the Kohl government approved a major arms sale to the Saudis, it refused to include the Leopard 2 tank in the deal. The tank decision was made largely because of Israeli objections.

German Democratic Republic (East Germany)

For East Germany the 40th anniversary of the end of World War II provided yet another opportunity for the ruling Socialist Unity Party to express its loyalty and gratitude to the Soviet Union for liberating the country from the Nazis. Officially, East Germany regards the Third Reich as the inevitable result of German and international capitalism for which the DDR, as the first socialist state in German history, bears no responsibility. In spite of this official rhetoric, East Germany in 1985 continued to expand cautiously its political and economic contacts with the "capitalist West." In April, Erich Honecker became the first East German head of state ever to visit Italy, and in June, France's Prime Minister Laurent Fabius became that country's first head of government ever to make an official visit to East Berlin; other Western visitors in 1985 included the British and Italian foreign ministers. Economic and cultural agreements were concluded with all three countries. East Germany, however, continued to be a key ally of the Soviet Union, especially in the Third World states of Africa and the Middle East. The DDR had about 2,500 military advisers in 18 African and Middle Eastern countries, including almost 500 in Angola and more than 200 in Syria.

Economy. In 1985 the East German economy, considered the strongest in Eastern Europe, continued to expand. The trade balance

E. Fornacirai, Gamma-Liaison

East Germany's Erich Honecker, left, met the mayor of Rome and other officials during an April visit to Italy, the first by an East German leader to a NATO country.

showed a surplus for the third straight year, and the DDR was able to reduce its hard currency debt to less than $3 billion. While rejecting the concept of a private economic sector, East Germany has quietly introduced a variety of reforms designed to improve economic efficiency and productivity. Bureaucracy has been reduced, and factory managers have been given more independence. And a new incentive system, which rewards individual workers with premiums and salary increases rather than the work collective, has improved the quality of East German industrial products. Unlike other Eastern bloc countries, the DDR has not had difficulty securing hard currency loans. In July a consortium of 100 banks from Western Eu-

rope and Japan approved yet another $600 million credit line. Thus far, however, the strong economic performance has not brought any significant improvement in the living standard of the average East German. The drive to increase exports has in fact reduced the number of goods available for domestic consumption.

Environment. Environmental conditions in the DDR continued to worsen in 1985. A report by UNESCO, in fact, found East Germany to have the highest levels of water, air, and ground pollution of any European country. The East German leadership has put far more emphasis on increased industrial and agricultural production than on environmental protection. Chemicals such as DDT, long banned in many Western countries, are still being used in some form, and water and air pollution regulations are poorly enforced. Air pollution is particularly severe in the nation's five major urban areas: Berlin, Halle, Leipzig, Dresden, and Karl-Marx Stadt. Only about half of all cities and towns have modern sewage treatment facilities. The government-controlled press has not reported on major environmental issues. Since 1982 all environmental data have been classified secret by the government. Teachers, according to a February party directive, are forbidden to discuss the country's environmental problems in the classroom. The DDR's small environmentalist movement, which operates under the protection of the Protestant church, has had little influence. While publicly denying that there are serious environmental problems, the government in July established an "environmental inspectorate" with authority to institute unified control over all environmental questions.

West Berlin

In the divided city, 1985 was another year of political stability and steady economic improvement. Unemployment declined for the second straight year, as almost 2,000 new jobs were created largely in high-tech and industrial firms. West Berlin has been particularly successful in attracting new business through government-sponsored technology centers specializing in electronics, computer software, and environmental research.

In the March city election, the Christian Democrats retained their status as West Berlin's largest party and renewed their coalition with the Free Democrats. The Social Democrats, who dominated Berlin politics until the mid-1970s, received less than one third of the vote, their poorest performance in the postwar period. In spite of the loss of the popular and effective Richard von Weizsäcker to the federal presidency in Bonn, most Berlin voters accepted CDU claims that "Berlin was back."

DAVID P. CONRADT
University of Florida

EAST GERMANY • Information Highlights

Official Name: German Democratic Republic.
Location: North-central Europe.
Area: 41,768 sq mi (108 178 km²).
Population (mid-1985 est.): 16,700,000.
Chief Cities (June 30, 1982): East Berlin, the capital, 1,185,533; Leipzig, 558,994; Dresden, 522,532.
Government: *Head of state,* Erich Honecker, chairman of the Council of State. *Head of government,* Willi Stoph, chairman of the Council of Ministers. General secretary of the Socialist Unity (Communist) Party, Erich Honecker (took office 1971). *Legislature* (unicameral)—Volkskammer (People's Chamber).
Monetary Unit: DDR mark (3.05 DDR marks equal U.S. $1, July 1985).
Gross National Product (1983 U.S.$): $154,800,-000,000.
Economic Index (1984): *Industrial Production* (1980 = 100), 117.
Foreign Trade (1984 U.S.$): *Imports,* $22,940,-000,000; *exports,* $24,836,000,000.

The Prince and Princess of Wales were patrons of the "Treasure Houses of Britain" exhibit at the National Gallery of Art in Washington, DC. The royal couple's November visit to the U.S. capital and other cities caused a stir in social circles and in the media.

© Sygma

GREAT BRITAIN

The people of Britain may look back on 1985 and wonder whether some fundamental change came about in the character of the citizens of a country that prides itself on its tranquillity and civilized behavior. In a quiet year politically, the newspapers too often were filled with stories of British violence, of rampaging football (soccer) hooligans, of race riots that burned up inner cities, and of an unparalleled series of horrific attacks on babies and small children, all too often by their parents.

Sports Violence. British football supporters have always been notorious in Europe, and teams traveling to major European competitions always bring in their wake a group of drunken, flag-waving, obscenely shouting young fans. So it was this year, and British hometowns were terrorized as well; but the violence reached its peak with the disaster at the Heysel Stadium in Brussels, Belgium, in June, when supporters of the British champions from Liverpool attacked followers of their rivals for the European Cup, the Italian champions from Turin. A wall collapsed under the weight of a crowd running in panic from brawling fans, and 38 people were killed. The British rioters, said Prime Minister Margaret Thatcher, had brought "shame and dishonor" on British football. As a punishment, all English (as opposed to Scots, Welsh, and Northern Irish) teams were barred indefinitely from European competition. The fans were left to turn on themselves, and as late as November, for the first time in British legal history, a football fan was jailed for life for slashing open the face of a barman near the ground where his football club played.

Political Violence. The violence of a few thousand football supporters does not make a country a violent place. It was the upsurge of terror in other areas, however, that shook the country. The Irish Republican Army (IRA) kept up its campaign against British security forces in Northern Ireland and in March dealt one of its most savage blows against the Royal Ulster Constabulary when a homemade mortar exploded in a flimsy wooden police canteen in the border town of Newry, killing nine police officers. By year's end, the actual death toll in Ulster was a relatively low one, but hardly a week went by without a report of another attack on soldiers, police, or civilians.

The perpetrators of violence on both sides in Ulster argued that the bloodletting had some kind of awful logic and purpose. The IRA said that it was trying to reunite a country held apart by British force, while the British Army said that if it killed IRA men, it was protecting the majority of the community from terrorists.

Urban Riots. However, in social and political terms, the most serious violence in 1985 occurred in a series of inner city riots toward the end of the summer. The three major outbreaks of rioting were in London and the country's second-biggest city, Birmingham. All were in depressed, racially mixed areas, and all saw major confrontations between police and rioters that resulted in many injuries and vast damage to property.

Witnesses who saw the first riot, in the Handsworth area of Birmingham in September, said that they were reminded of a "blitz" air raid by German bombers in World War II. The riot was sparked by a minor incident, police trying to arrest a black youth for a motoring offense. Young blacks poured onto the streets to protest, police were called in, and petrol

bombs by the hundreds were thrown by rioters. The whole commercial center blazed, and as it did, two Asian men, trapped in their shop, were suffocated by fumes. Damage estimated at $25 million was caused as dozens of shops and houses—as well as parked cars used as street barricades—were torched.

The riots came to London in late September and early October. Both episodes, according to black leaders, were sparked by unnecessary violence used by white police toward black women. The first outbreak was caused by the shooting of an innocent black mother, who was shot and paralyzed by police who burst into her home looking for one of her sons. Once again the crowds took to the streets, burning cars and throwing Molotov cocktails. The shooting of Mrs. Cherry Groce was the second involving an innocent person within two months. It followed the shooting of a five-year-old boy in Birmingham, who was killed when a policeman's gun apparently was discharged accidentally into a bed where the boy was sleeping. The shootings drew attention to the fact that the "unarmed bobby" (policeman) is rapidly disappearing from the English scene and is being replaced by police who are increasingly both heavily armed and armored.

The third major riot, also in October, took the level of violence a notch higher. It began in a crumbling apartment block in the northern London suburb of Tottenham, after a black woman, Mrs. Cynthia Jarrett, collapsed and died after police raided her home. As crowds battled with police, rioters started to use both shotguns and at least one hand gun against police—probably the first time such a thing has occurred in a British riot. More chillingly, a police constable, Keith Blakelock, became separated from his fellow police and was beaten to death by a mob. He was the first policeman (other than in Northern Ireland) to have been killed in a riot in Britain. Police officers who saw his body afterward said they believed the rioters were trying to decapitate him.

Various theories were advanced as to why rioting had reached such levels of brutality. Opposition politicians pointed out that overall unemployment in the riot areas was especially high, at 36% in Handsworth, triple the national average, and 24% in Brixton. Unemployment among blacks was far higher than this. Labour Party politicians blamed poverty, frustration, and hopelessness for driving people to riot. They accused the government, in the words of a local Brixton area member of parliament, of "trying to police its way out of a problem." The governing Conservative Party took a much harder law-and-order line. Talking after the Handsworth riot, the newly appointed home secretary, Douglas Hurd, said sharply, "Burning and looting is crime . . . it is not social frustration."

Political Trends. This hard line may be the indication that the Conservative (Tory) Party has seen a major issue to take it through the next election—law and order. It has been a lackluster political year, in the middle of a five-year term, with the Conservative Party totally dominant in Parliament because it has a huge majority (141 seats) over all the other opposition parties combined. It is a majority that makes parliamentary debate almost meaningless. In years such as this, opposition parties usually do well in political popularity polls simply because of the electorate's boredom with its rulers. In fact, in late summer of 1985 the Tories actually trailed Labour by seven percentage points. This was a very large lead in British terms, yet by mid-November the Conservatives had regained the lead, albeit by only a couple of points. This comeback was attributed by pollsters as showing that ordinary voters are becoming increasingly disturbed by criminal and urban violence, and they see the Tories as the party most likely to take harsh measures to quell such violence.

© T. Stoddart, Gamma-Liaison

Great Britain was hit by a series of urban riots in 1985. The accidental shooting by police of a black woman in the London district of Brixton, left, precipitated a rampage by some 200 youths. At least 55 vehicles were set on fire, many stores were looted, and property was vandalized.

Certainly the Tories needed a strong issue to take the nation's mind off its major concern—unemployment. The number of unemployed remained at more than 3 million throughout the year. This figure seemed likely to remain steady at about that level, principally because of the government's steady refusal to create jobs by any sort of reflationary spending. Unemployment was the major political issue and weapon used against the government by the opposition parties. Each of the two main opposition parties—the Labour Party and the Social Democratic-Liberal Alliance—had their days in the sun in 1985.

Miners' Strike. The year began well for the Tories with the final collapse of the miner's strike in March. It had been the longest and most bitter of any major strike ever held in Britain, lasting well over a year, and hundreds of miners were arrested and equal numbers of police injured during the often savage confrontations that took place between the two sides as they met over the picket lines. The end of the strike was seen as a victory for the unyielding prime minister, Margaret Thatcher, who maintained throughout that she would never give in. Her resolute stance was finally vindicated, it seemed, because the workers went back to work with none of their objectives realized. So comprehensive was this defeat that later in the year the Nottingham miners, who had opposed the strike throughout, broke away from the National Union of Mineworkers and formed their own union. The heaviest loser of all was miners' leader Arthur Scargill, who had used the force of his rhetoric and his power as president of the union to keep his men without pay for more than a year. As it turned out, he got them nothing in return.

Scargill's humiliation was a bonus for Labour Party leader Neil Kinnock, a young (43), moderate left-winger by Labour standards, whose policies had come under heavy criticism by extreme left-wingers such as Scargill. Kinnock took something of a political gamble at his party's annual conference in October, when he launched an unexpectedly savage attack on radicals like Scargill who, he said, were not only wrecking the existing labor movement but dissuading wavering voters from joining. He lambasted various leftist factions, among them unionists and municipal leaders, and told them their antics were wrecking the party. "I'm telling you, you can't play politics with people's jobs, with their homes, and with their essential services." His bold speech silenced the left wing almost completely, and he left the conference as the labor movement's unchallenged leader. It was soon after this speech that the Labour Party leaped to its seven-point lead in the opinion polls. This was an important victory for Kinnock, who was henceforth considered to be a formidable opponent for Thatcher in a future general election—which

---

GREAT BRITAIN · Information Highlights

Official Name: United Kingdom of Great Britain and Northern Ireland.
Location: Island, western Europe.
Area: 94,200 sq mi (243 977 km²).
Population (mid-1985 est.): 56,400,000.
Chief Cities (mid-1983 est.): London, the capital, 6,754,000; Birmingham, 1,012,900; Glasgow, 751,000; Leeds, 714,000; Sheffield, 542,700.
Government: *Head of state,* Elizabeth II, queen (acceded Feb. 1952). *Head of government,* Margaret Thatcher, prime minister (took office May 1979). *Legislature*—Parliament: House of Lords and House of Commons.
Monetary Unit: Pound (0.6971 pound equals U.S.$1, Dec. 12, 1985).
Gross National Product (1983): $460,000,000,000.
Economic Indexes (1984): *Consumer Prices* (1970 = 100), all items, 481.3; food, 504.4. *Industrial Production* (1980 = 100), 103.
Foreign Trade (1984 U.S.$): *Imports,* $105,616,-000,000; *exports,* $94,538,000,000.

---

must be held no later than June 1988. Kinnock was always a compelling speaker, and he is 17 years younger than Thatcher. Until October, however, his ability and will to confront and quell his own left wing had been in question.

Social Democratic-Liberal Alliance. The Social Democratic Liberal Party alliance did not have a brilliant year. Its major success was in winning a by-election in the Welsh constituency of Brecon and Radnor, where it captured a seat that had been solidly Conservative for decades. "This confirms a major breakthrough for the alliance," said winning candidate Richard Livsey, but in fact that was the sort of rhetoric always used by the alliance in its relatively rare triumphs. The alliance's major fault was that it had great difficulty in recruiting support outside the white middle class in Britain. Although it picked up "protest" votes in by-elections from disgruntled Tories, it usually found those seats reverting back at general elections, when voters tend to vote for parties, rather than for individual candidates who get enormous television exposure when all eyes are on just one seat.

Conservative Party. The Tories, meanwhile, continued with very much the same sort of policies with which they began to govern Britain after their election victory in 1979. Thatcher has been surprisingly unadventurous in her cabinet changes over the six years of her government, preferring to change the jobs of a fixed group of cabinet ministers rather than bring in entirely new people. Thus, in her 1985 cabinet reshuffle, the most important change was to move the hesitant home secretary, Leon Brittan, to the Department of Trade and Industry, and to give his job to the cool and tough former Northern Ireland secretary, Douglas Hurd. Hurd was slated to lead the law-and-order campaign the government promised when it outlined its 1986 legislative program to Parliament in November. Prime Minister Thatcher left other major cabinet officers in

At Hillsborough Castle, County Down, Ulster, Northern Ireland, November 15, Prime Minister Margaret Thatcher of Great Britain and Prime Minister Garret FitzGerald of Ireland signed the "Anglo-Irish Agreement 1985." The accord gives Ireland a say in the administration of Northern Ireland.

© Pacemaker

place, which indicates that she approved of the financial policies of Chancellor of the Exchequer Nigel Lawson.

The Economy. Lawson has tried to adhere to a noninterventionist, strictly monetarist policy, which means no government spending to create new jobs. Carrying out this policy meant that early in the year the government did not intervene in the money markets to prop up the pound sterling, which was especially vulnerable to the soaring American dollar and to rumored weakness in the international oil market. At one point in February, the pound fell to just below $1.04 in value, and money merchants were confidently planning "parity parties" in the City of London to celebrate the day the two currencies would be equal in value. As the United States finally tried to control its own deficit and cut back on borrowing, however, the pound started a slow climb. By the end of 1985, it had risen to about $1.43.

The economy in general could hardly be said to be in good shape, especially because of the vast amounts of government money that had to be spent to pay various forms of support to Britain's 3 million unemployed. To finance its needs, the government had to use virtually all its national oil revenues to support the unemployed. A great and diminishing national asset, therefore, was doing nothing to improve the country's living standards or work prospects. The government also persisted in its policy of financing itself by selling off profitable state-run concerns such as British Airways, the national airline, and British Gas, the national gas company, just as it had already sold British Telecom, the state-owned telecommunications service. This policy disturbed many eminent Tories, none more eminent perhaps than former Prime Minister Harold MacMillan, now the Earl of Stockton, who in a speech in November compared the party's sale of assets to the action of an impoverished aristocratic family "selling off the family silver." The government's greatest economic achievement was to

get inflation down to 5.4%, but the economic cost in terms of unemployment and sale of state assets could ultimately wreck the party at a general election.

The Royal Family. The undoubted star in Britain's ruling circle was Princess Diana, whose looks, clothes, and easy manner with her future subjects have made her a media personality. As her own star has waxed, however, that of her husband, Prince Charles, the future king, has waned. More and more newspapers and magazines, both in Britain and abroad, published stories throughout the year suggesting that the couple were drifting apart. Some have claimed that she is obsessed with clothes, pop music, and her two young children, while he has withdrawn into a mystic world of herbal medicine, vegetarianism, and spiritualism. A long article featuring all these rumors in the American magazine *Vanity Fair* seemed to have goaded the royal couple into having their second-ever joint television interview in Great Britain. Their answers confirmed that she liked pop and clothes, and he was interested in unorthodox approaches to food, medicine, architecture, and sociology. But the interview also projected an image of a happy family, and shortly afterward they went on triumphant tours of Australia and the United States.

Northern Ireland. In November the British and Irish prime ministers, Margaret Thatcher and Garret FitzGerald, signed a joint agreement on Northern Ireland that could lead to the most radical changes in the administration of the troubled British province since it came into being in 1921. In an effort to combat terrorism and, more importantly, to improve civil rights for Ulster's minority Catholic population, the two leaders signed the "Anglo-Irish Agreement 1985," which in effect will give the Irish Republic a say in the way Northern Ireland will be administered.

Under the terms of the agreement, an intergovernmental conference will be established, to hold regular meetings to discuss affairs in the

north between the British government's Northern Ireland secretary, the minister now in charge of administering the province, and the Irish foreign minister. The Irish minister in this case was seen as a sort of unofficial representative of Ulster's Catholics as well as his own government. He would be able to tell his British counterpart about civil-rights abuses, miscarriages of justice, and oppressive tactics by British security forces; the most distrusted is the British army's Ulster Defence Regiment, an almost entirely Protestant force that is raised and serves only in Northern Ireland. The ministers, in turn, will be served by a permanent group of civil servants, a "secretariat," drawn from both Great Britain and Ireland. Secretariat members will have their offices in Northern Ireland, in Belfast. The agreement, although not specific, also seemed to suggest that Irish judges might serve, at least as advisers, in some Ulster trials of "terrorists."

Both sides went to great lengths to state that British sovereignty over Ulster would not be compromised in any way. Although Irish ministers could advise their British counterparts on proposed changes or reforms that they thought necessary, such changes could be made only by the British. The two leaders also said categorically that the apparent dilution of British authority was not in any way a move toward reunion of the two provinces. Such a reunion could only come about when the Protestants—who outnumber Catholics two to one, and are almost universally against reunion—voted for it.

Repeated assurances on the rights of Protestants to stay British did absolutely nothing to reassure the "Unionists" in Ulster. The agreement was greeted with almost hysterical rage by Protestants, who showed their feelings early by ringing Hillsborough Castle with demonstrators carrying signs with such slogans as "Ulster is not for sale," "No pope here," and "Ulster is British." Rev. Ian Paisley, the fiery Protestant leader, vowed that if the two governments tried to bring the Irish civil servants in the proposed secretariat to Belfast, "They will have to lower them in by helicopter." More ominously, a shadowy paramilitary group calling itself the "Ulster Freedom Fighters" issued a statement saying that it would murder any civil servants who attempted to work for the secretariat.

Despite their protests, however, the British Parliament followed their Irish counterparts by approving the agreement, in Great Britain's case by a massive vote of 473 members in favor and only 47 against. Fifteen Unionist (Protestant) members of Parliament (MPs), led by Paisley, resigned after the vote. A series of by-elections would thus have to be held in Ulster, probably in late January 1986. Unionists claimed that this vote would amount to a referendum on the agreement. Northern Ireland,

of course, would be massively against the agreement when the by-elections are held. Fortified by parliamentary approval, however, both sides seemed determined to bring fairer government to Ulster in 1986.

TONY CLIFTON
London Bureau Chief, "Newsweek"

The Arts

The public financing of Britain's arts through the national Arts Council and local government edged toward the brink of chaos during 1985. With the passage of an Act of Parliament that abolished the metropolitan councils of five major cities, including London, the £46 million (about $65 million) given by those cities to their theaters, orchestras, and museums had to be made up elsewhere. The most obvious source, the Arts Council, was expected to have to pick up the cost, and therefore asked the government for a total annual grant of £154 million (about $218 million), an increase of £49 million (about $69 million), to cover its new needs. When the respected arts minister, Lord Gowrie, suddenly resigned in September, most interpreted his departure as a signal that government support for the arts was faltering.

Theater. Amid financial altercations and the temporary closure of the Cottesloe Theatre by National Theatre director Sir Peter Hall, protesting financial strictures, a number of excellent new plays and several outstanding performances were seen during the year. Among the new plays, *Pravda,* by Howard Brenton and David Hare, scored a success at the National, with Anthony Hopkins in the leading role of a menacing newspaper tycoon. Similarly, Alan Ayckbourn delighted admirers with two new plays, *A Chorus of Disapproval* at the National and *A Woman in Mind* in Scarborough, the latter considered his blackest comedy. New plays from Michael Frayn, Peter Barnes, and Nigel Williams; a festival of Edward Bond plays at the Royal Court; and the successful transfer to the West End commercial theater of Pam Gems' *Camille* were additional evidence of the positive state of British theater.

Camille was only one of the spin-offs into commercial theater from the Royal Shakespeare Company (RSC). Also transferred to other London theaters were *Waste* and *Breaking the Silence.* At the RSC in Stratford, one of the year's highlights was Ben Kingsley in *Othello.* In its London home at the Barbican theater, the RSC drew packed houses for three top performances: Anthony Sher as *Richard III,* Roger Rees as *Hamlet,* and Kenneth Branagh as *Henry V.*

At the National Theatre, one of the year's achievements was *The Mysteries,* the cycle of

© Catherine Ashmore, Dominic Photography

A very funny production of "Orpheus in the Underworld" was a 1985 musical highlight.

medieval plays from *The Nativity* to *The Passion* to *Doomsday,* directed by Bill Bryden before a promenade audience. Sir Peter Hall directed *Martine,* with Wendy Morgan in the lead, and Philip Prowse directed an electric *Duchess of Malfi,* with Ian McKellen and Eleanor Bron. Hall also took the National's award-winning production of *Coriolanus,* with Ian McKellen, to the Athens arts festival.

Notable performances outside the main national companies included those of Diana Rigg in *Antony and Cleopatra,* Alan Bates in *Dance of Death,* Vanessa Redgrave and Jonathan Pryce in *The Seagull,* Liv Ullmann in *Old Times,* and Glenda Jackson in *Phedre.*

Music. Britain's choirs and music festivals continued to grow and in 1985 celebrated the birthdays of Bach, Handel, and Scarlatti. Near the top for quality was the Bath Festival, offering Handel's opera *Agrippina.*

In London, Stockhausen's music was much in evidence, first at a retrospective *Music and Machines* at the Barbican concert hall and later with the British premiere of *Donnerstag aus Licht,* at the Royal Opera House.

The Royal Opera House's patchy season was enlivened by the London premiere of Alexander Zemlinsky's double bill *A Florentine Tragedy* and *The Birthday of the Infanta.* Also notable was a production of *Ariadne auf Naxos,* with Jessye Norman. The English National Opera scored successes in old and new music with their production of Handel's *Xerxes* and Philip Glass's *Akhnaten,* one of the more bizarre premieres. A lively new production of Sir Michael Tippett's *Midsummer Marriage* and an uproarious *Orpheus in the Underworld* added luster to their season.

Outside London, one of the main opera events of the year was Kent Opera's *King Priam,* a Michael Tippett revival. Glyndebourne's first production of *Carmen,* directed by Peter Hall, was notable, as was Hall's version of Benjamin Britten's *Albert Herring.*

Dance. Alone among the big dance companies, the London Festival Ballet under its new director, Peter Schaufuss, pushed ahead with new dancers and prestigious guest stars, including Natalia Makarova in an outstanding *Onegin.* Schaufuss also enticed Sir Frederick Ashton into revising his *Romeo and Juliet.* Among choreographers, David Bintley's reputation continued to strengthen with his new ballet *Flowers of the Forest.*

Visual Arts. The year opened with a massive *Hommage à Chagall* exhibition at the Royal Academy of Arts and a large Renoir retrospective at the Hayward Gallery. These proved the two major draws in the first six months of the year. The Tate Gallery was dominated in the summer by a retrospective of the work of Francis Bacon. One of the liveliest events was a combined show at the Hayward of the stage designs of David Hockney and the paintings of Edward Burra. A newly refurbished Whitechapel Art Gallery, historically an outpost of modern painting in east London, reopened in September with a show of the paintings of Howard Hodgkin.

Film. During 1985, officially designated British Film Year, a campaign was started to get audiences, now at an all time low, back to the cinema. Among quality film releases were *Wetherby, Dance with a Stranger, A Passage to India,* and *Insignificance.*

MAUREEN GREEN, *Free-lance Writer, London*

GREECE

Greece during 1985 was the scene of many momentous events.

Papandreou's Policies. The year began with Prime Minister Andreas Papandreou (*see* BI-OGRAPHY) and his Panhellenic Socialist Party (PASOK) in control of Parliament as they had been since 1981. Often a strong critic of American foreign policy, Papandreou emphasized his independent ideas within NATO by a trip to the Soviet Union in February. He made the trip shortly after having stated that he would not allow American nuclear weapons to remain on Greek territory unless there was some progress in making the Balkan area nuclear-free. At the same time, Papandreou tried to point out that any quarrels with the United States were quarrels between friends. For the United States, one vexing problem was Papandreou's oft-repeated statement that he wanted eventually to close American military bases in Greece.

Resignation of Caramanlis. Papandreou stunned the Greek political world in March when he suddenly withdrew his support of the reelection of Greek President Constantine Caramanlis. Although Caramanlis had been the founder of the New Democracy Party, Papandreou's chief opposition, Papandreou had been expected to support the president for a second five-year term, in consideration of his exemplary conduct during his first five years. Caramanlis resigned the presidency on March 10. On March 29 the PASOK-dominated parliament elected by the narrowest margin a new president, Christos Sartzetakis, a supreme court judge with no real experience in political life. New Democracy's deputies refused to take part in the election and questioned the validity of the balloting.

Elections to Parliament. Elections for parliament held on June 2, 1985, resulted in PASOK winning 45.8% of the votes and 161 seats, a clear majority. New Democracy won 40.8% of the votes, giving it 125 seats. With Papandreou's victory at the polls, New Democracy gave up its challenge to the validity of Sartzetakis' election.

Impact of Economic Measures. Faced with a balance-of-payments crisis and high inflation, the Papandreou government, having had a cabinet reorganization, began on October 11 the imposition of austere economic measures and devalued the drachma by 15%. Discontent among the working classes was evident; leftist and Communist-dominated labor unions organized a series of often very disruptive strikes. That was at the time period when Papandreou was working obviously to improve relations with the United States, and left-wing elements accused him of sacrificing his socialist and independent foreign policies to court U.S. financial support. Under these circumstances

Papandreou found himself criticized not only by conservatives and middle-of-the-road politicians but also even more vehemently by leftists who previously had embraced PASOK. But he persisted, and after a late October visit to Athens by Michael Armacost, U.S. undersecretary of state for political affairs, the Greek government announced that Greece and the United States were desirous of improving relations, though Papandreou did not commit himself on the possible retention of American military bases.

November Riots. On November 17, celebrations were held commemorating a student uprising at Athens Polytechnic in 1973 against the military regime of the time. After a rally, more than 100,000 persons—echoing leftist sentiment that the dictatorship had been fostered by the United States—marched on the U.S. Embassy in Athens demanding Greek withdrawal from NATO and the removal of American military bases from Greece. Street battles broke out, and a 15-year-old youth was killed by a policeman in response to a fire-bombing incident. Severe rioting spread over the next few days from Athens to Thessaloniki, Greece's second city, as well as to the university city of Xanthi. Members of the government responsible for internal security tendered their resignations—which Papandreou refused to accept—but the country's three highest police chiefs nevertheless were suspended.

Hijackings and Violence. Athens airport in 1985 was the departure point for two separate hijacking incidents with severe international complications. The first was TWA flight 847, which was hijacked on a flight from Athens to Rome on June 14. The second, on November 23, was an EgyptAir jetliner bound from Athens to Cairo. Both involved Arab hijackers. Widespread criticism of security at Athens, including a statement from President Ronald Reagan, followed the first incident. Despite considerable changes and improvements at the airport, however, a second incident was not averted. In addition, a number of violent at-

---

GREECE • Information Highlights

Official Name: Hellenic Republic.
Location: Southwestern Europe.
Area: 50,944 sq mi (131 944 km²).
Population (mid-1985 est.): 10,100,000.
Chief Cities (1981 census): Athens, the capital, 885,136; Salonika, 402,443; Piraeus, 196,379.
Government: *Head of state,* Christos Sartzetakis, president (took office March 1985). *Head of government,* Andreas Papandreou, prime minister (took office Oct. 1981). *Legislature*—Parliament.
Monetary Unit: Drachma (150.5 drachmas equal U.S.$1, Dec. 12, 1985).
Gross National Product (1983 U.S.$): $34,900,-000,000.
Economic Indexes (1984): *Consumer Prices* (1970 = 100), all items, 813.8; food, 935.2. *Industrial Production* (1980 = 100), 97.
Foreign Trade (1984 U.S.$): *Imports*, $9,434,000,000; *exports*, $4,811,000,000.

tacks, bombings, and suspicious forest fires took place within Greece during the year.

Athens Celebrations. In 1985, Greece celebrated the 150th anniversary of Athens as the capital of modern Greece. It was during the reign of King Otho I, the first Greek king after the successful Revolution of 1821 against the Ottoman Turks, that Athens was officially designated as the capital.

GEORGE J. MARCOPOULOS, *Tufts University*

GUYANA

The unexpected death of Guyana's president, Linden Forbes Burnham, on Aug. 6, 1985, came in the midst of the most severe economic crisis the country has experienced since it became independent in 1966. Burnham, 62, had ruled Guyana for nearly 21 years. He died of a heart attack while undergoing minor throat surgery performed by two Cuban specialists. He was succeeded in the presidency by Desmond Hoyte, 56, the former vice-president, who called for December elections for president and the National Assembly. Hoyte's wide margin of victory on December 9 was denounced by opposition leaders, including Dr. Cheddi Jagan of the People's Progressive Party, who declared that the election results were rigged and invalid.

Economy. Guyana's economic problems remained formidable. The country had a foreign debt of $1.3 billion and was obliged to spend 42% of its export earnings merely to service the debt. Guyana had a foreign trade deficit estimated at $160 million in 1985 and was critically short of foreign exchange.

Guyana's credit had been suspended by virtually all international financial institutions. The government fell behind in its payments to the International Monetary Fund (IMF) and was declared ineligible for further IMF assistance. On June 16 the U.S. Agency for International Development announced a cutoff of all economic aid because of Guyana's default on principal and interest owed to U.S. creditors. The Caribbean Development Bank halted lending to Guyana because of arrears, and the World Bank did the same.

An oil credit facility extended to Guyana by Trinidad was suspended in October. The Inter-American Development Bank remained as the only major lending agency in Guyana.

During 1985, Guyana was plagued with recurring food shortages. The one bright spot in the economy was the bauxite industry, which recorded growth of 25% in 1985, on top of a 55% gain the year before. However, two other important sectors, sugar and rice, fell below government production targets.

RICHARD C. SCHROEDER, *"Visión" Magazine*

GUYANA • Information Highlights

Official Name: Cooperative Republic of Guyana.
Location: Northeast coast of South America.
Area: 83,000 sq mi (214 970 km²).
Population: 800,000.
Chief City: Georgetown, the capital.
Government: *Head of state,* Desmond Hoyte, president (took office Aug. 1985). *Legislature* (unicameral)—National Assembly.
Monetary Unit: Guyana dollar (4.3 G dollars equal U.S.$1, July 1985).

HAWAII

An airline strike, political irregularities, crime, and natural wonders highlighted 1985 in Hawaii.

Economy. Hawaii's economy received a major setback in 1985 when the Air Line Pilots' Association struck United Airlines for nearly one month, resulting in a drastic cutback in vital tourism dollars (the visitor industry is worth more than $4 billion annually to the state). United, which flies 21 round-trip flights to Hawaii daily, was forced to eliminate all but two flights a day.

The state department of economic planning and development estimated before the strike that it could result in a potential loss of $348 million in visitor expenditures. Fortunately, the loss was considerably less, although the Bank of Hawaii estimated that the strike may have cost the economy as much as $284 million. Recovery from the strike was slow, and it was uncertain whether the state achieved its goal of 5 million visitors during 1985.

Despite the strike, Hawaii's general tax revenues for the first six months of 1985 achieved their projected goal of $1.3 billion. Unemployment was nearly the same as a year earlier, with the statewide rate during August standing at 5.5%, up only 0.1% from 1984.

Politics. Although 1985 was not an election year, politics played a major role in newsmaking as the Democrats and Republicans jockeyed for power.

Charges of campaign irregularities resulted in jail sentences or severe court reprimands for several young Democrats. A key target of the prosecutors, former state Sen. Clifford Uwaine, faced possible retrial after his first trial resulted in a hung jury.

The Democrats got their chance at the Republicans when three former Democrats, veterans of the Honolulu city council, changed party affiliation and gave the GOP control of the nine-member body. Under the leadership of Patsy T. Mink, former chairman, the Democrats initiated Honolulu's first recall, resulting in the ouster of all three defectors in a special election on October 5. The defeat came despite support from President Reagan. Three Democrats won landslide victories in a special, year-end election to fill the vacancies.

HAWAII • Information Highlights

Area: 6,471 sq mi (16 759 km²).
Population (July 1, 1984 est.): 1,039,000.
Chief Cities (1980 census): Honolulu, the capital, 365,048; Pearl City, 42,575; Kailua, 35,812; Hilo, 35,269.
Government (1985): *Chief Officers*—governor, George R. Ariyoshi (D); lt. gov., John Waihee III (D). *Legislature*—Senate, 25 members; House of Representatives, 51 members.
State Finances (fiscal year 1984): *Revenues,* $2,541,000,000; *expenditures,* $2,244,000,000.
Personal Income (1984): $13,547,000,000; per capita, $13,042.
Labor Force (October 1985): *Civilian labor force,* 477,300; *unemployed,* 26,300 (5.5% of total force).
Education: *Enrollment* (fall 1983)—public elementary schools, 110,419; public secondary, 51,822; colleges and universities, 52,065. *Public school expenditures* (1982–83), $484,857,958 ($3,239 per pupil).

Hawaii Gov. George Ariyoshi (D), now serving his third and final term (he cannot run again), said he will work with the Democratic-controlled council and legislature in 1986 to push legislation important to the party.

Crime. After years of frustration, federal and state authorities finally brought suspected key members of Hawaii's underworld to trial in 1985.

The federal government was successful in its efforts to curb the activities of elements of the Japanese *Yakuza,* an underworld group that infiltrated Hawaii and attempted to share in the lucrative drug and prostitution rackets. Several suspected *Yukuza* were intercepted on arrival at Honolulu International Airport and quickly deported. Other suspected gang leaders were awaiting trial.

Natural Events. Law enforcement and political activities took a back seat briefly this year as Mother Nature flexed its muscles. Volcanic eruptions from Kilauea's flank, which have continued sporadically for several years, provided thrills for tourists and residents alike but caused no loss of property or lives. There also were two near misses from hurricanes.

CHARLES H. TURNER
Free-lance writer, Honolulu

HONG KONG

The Sino-British Joint Declaration—the agreement reached in 1984 outlining Hong Kong's future—went into effect on May 27 and was registered at the United Nations Secretariat on June 12, 1985. The Joint Liaison Group, which comprises five British and five Chinese representatives, was formed to monitor the provisions of the Declaration. The first meeting was held in July in London.

Preparation for Transfer. In 1985 the Royal Coat of Arms and the word "colony" disappeared from Hong Kong's new paper money. The government stopped recruiting Britons for the civil service as the first step in phasing out British civil servants in the territory's administration. In October the Legislative Council, Hong Kong's highest lawmaking body, included for the first time 24 elected unofficial members. The Oaths and Declarations Ordinance was amended so that Legislative Councillors have a choice of swearing allegiance to the British monarch or to the people of Hong Kong. Citizens were encouraged to participate in local politics. In September, Putonghua (Mandarin) was taught for the first time as a subject in elementary schools.

Economy. For the fourth consecutive year, the government had a budget deficit estimated at $128 million for 1985–86. As confidence in the future of Hong Kong was restored, however, the property market improved and investments began to strengthen. At the first land auction of 1985 in February, five lots of land were sold at prices 10–50% above the starting price. In the first four months of 1985, 22 foreign companies had set up factories in Hong Kong, compared with only 24 in 1984. In 1985, overseas investment amounted to about $1.5 billion—of which the United States, Japan, and the United Kingdom accounted for 54%, 21%, and 7%, respectively. Most of the foreign investments were in electronics, textiles and garments, and electrical products.

The first American-bank-affiliated financial-futures company in Hong Kong, BA Futures Inc., was set up in June 1985, in recognition of Hong Kong's importance as a financial center. In the same month, the government took over the Overseas Trust Bank and the Hong Kong Industrial and Commercial Bank to prevent their collapse. The Hong Kong Commodity Exchange is now called the Hong Kong Futures Exchange because it began in 1985 to trade in financial futures as well as commodity futures.

China has invested $4 billion in Hong Kong since 1981. About half of its 500 joint venture projects in 1984 were with Hong Kong investors. In January 1985, Hong Kong's China Light and Power Co. signed a contract with China to develop its first nuclear power plant at Daya Bay in Guangdong Province, and it was planning another joint venture hydroelectric power station in Shenzhen.

A two-lane road at Sha Tau Kok providing vehicular access to China was officially opened in February, and the Island Line of the Mass Transit Railway running along the northern shore of Hong Kong Island was opened in May.

Immigration. In the past few years, the annual average of Chinese immigrants coming to Hong Kong has numbered about 27,000. The Hong Kong government has made an agreement with China that the number of Chinese immigrants to Hong Kong be reduced from 150 persons to 75 persons per day.

DAVID CHUENYAN LAI
University of Victoria, British Columbia

Japan has introduced a new concept in modular housing. The buyer inspects models in a "housing park," makes a selection, and customizes the purchase with options, including furniture and fixtures. The building components and furniture are ordered and shipped from a factory, and assembling begins. The transaction from selection to completion takes a few months.

Massachusetts Institute of Technology Center for Real Estate Development

HOUSING

As of the mid-1980s vigorous housing production continues in the United States. Yet problems of affording housing remain, encouraging the search for less costly means of delivering shelter. This search also is seen on the international housing scene.

Production of housing in the United States often proceeds on a "boom" and "bust" cycle. In the early 1970s the number of housing starts peaked at approximately 2.3 million annually; in 1981–82 starts plummeted to 1.1 million. There was soon a dramatic turnaround; in both 1983 and 1984, declining interest rates and an improving economy stimulated housing production to 1.7 million starts. Housing starts in 1985 continued at a similar vigorous pace.

The ability to afford housing remains a problem, however. In 1970 the median monthly rent was $108; by 1984 it had tripled to $325. Over this same time period the median sales price of a new one-family home increased from $23,000 to more than $80,000. While median family income also increased dramatically during the 1970s and early 1980s, it did not match the inflation in housing costs. Many families were finding it increasingly more difficult to satisfy their shelter needs.

One response to this cost pressure has been modification of the shelter product to encompass dwellings other than a single-family detached house. In the mid-1970s, about 75% of total housing starts consisted of single-unit detached homes; as of the mid-1980s the latter share had decreased to approximately 62%. Numerous configurations of multifamily housing are becoming more commonplace and include townhouses, garden apartments, garden condominiums, and patio homes.

The growing popularity of multifamily housing is partially a result of economics—it costs less to produce an attached as opposed to a detached dwelling unit. Changing demographics are a second underlying influence. American families are having fewer children, resulting in a steady decrease in household size from 3.4 as of the 1950 census, 2.8 as of the 1980 census, and 2.7 as of 1984. This decline has diminished shelter-space needs so that the smaller detached unit is often more appropriate to today's demographics as opposed to the larger single-family home.

Public Assistance and Subsidies. The U.S. government has attempted to foster housing production and alleviate financing pressures. From the late 1960s to the early 1980s, numerous federal housing programs were available that offered low-cost mortgages, operating cost write-downs, and other assistance. There are numerous such programs today: the Community Development Block Grant (CDBG) program makes available financing for rehabilitation and other housing activities; the Housing Development Action Grant (HoDAG) subsidizes the new construction and substantial rehabilitation of rental housing; and the Rental Rehabilitation Grant provides monies for the renovation of rental properties. All of these federal programs, however, offer only a fraction of the housing subsidy available in prior decades. Moreover, in the future the current subsidies may be cut further or even eliminated.

State government has attempted to fill some of the breach. State housing and mortgage finance agencies issue tax-exempt bonds in order to make available below-market-rate financing. Some states offer other direct subsidies. New York State, for example, recently enacted an

Affordable Home Ownership Program and a Housing Trust Fund to foster the production of housing for low- and middle-income families by offering seed money grants and other assistance.

Local government also is attempting to encourage housing delivery—especially for the less advantaged. In addition to direct subsidy, some local governments have enacted inclusionary zoning ordinances. The latter mandate that a builder make available a portion of the total number of units in a development at below-market prices. This mechanism has been applied in states ranging from California to New Jersey. In a similar vein, municipalities ranging from San Francisco to Boston have required nonresidential developers to make available affordable residential dwellings.

There are further attempts to foster affordable housing production. At the federal level, the Joint Venture for Affordable Housing is searching for means to reduce housing construction costs. There are parallel efforts at the state and local government levels to revise subdivision, building code, and other regulatory standards to eliminate unnecessary building and processing costs.

Increased new housing prices and diminished public subsidy also have fostered greater investment to preserve the extant housing stock. A growing preservation ethic is highlighted by the burgeoning interest in historic preservation. As of 1955, only 20 communities in the United States had local preservation ordinances; as of the early 1980s, there were more than 1,000 such local statutes. The number of entries (individual properties and neighborhood districts) on the federal National Register of Historic Places similarly has mushroomed from 1,200 in 1968 to more than 37,000 in 1985. Rather than building anew, Americans are increasingly turning to preserving the best of the past.

International Trends. Some of the housing features prevalent in the United States are distinct from those in other countries. One striking difference is the nature of the housing stock. In the United States, it is two thirds owner-occupied, one third renter; in most other industrialized countries, this ratio is reversed. Yet, while there are other differences, many of the housing trends experienced in the United States have parallels abroad. Housing costs have been increasing. From 1970 to 1980, the cost of a new housing unit increased by approximately 10% *annually* in many industrialized countries, including Austria, Belgium, Canada, France, the Netherlands, Norway, and Sweden. Over this same period, rents have increased by roughly 5–10% annually in these same countries.

In response to rising shelter expenses, many industrialized countries have examined strategies to reduce construction costs. For ex-

ample, the Federal Republic of Germany established a Rationalization Association of the Construction Industry in order to foster building technologies and efficiency. The Dutch government has encouraged "modular coordination" as a means to encourage standardization of dimensions in the building industry.

There also has been growing interest in housing rehabilitation and historic preservation. Austria, Denmark, Finland, France, Sweden, Great Britain, and Switzerland are just some of the industrialized countries that have made grants, loans, and technical assistance available to foster the protection and upgrading of the existing stock. There also are efforts to formulate new housing subsidy mechanisms. As in the United States, available public funds for this purpose are limited—hence, the search for the most "efficient" strategy. Interestingly, both the United States and many industrialized countries—Australia, Canada, Denmark, France, the Netherlands, United Kingdom—are experimenting with housing vouchers, direct cash assistance to lower-income households to enable them to shop for and secure adequate shelter.

DAVID LISTOKIN
Rutgers University

In an attempt to sell his $143,000, three-bedroom home, an Illinoisan offers the buyer a free vacation for two.

AP/Wide World

HUNGARY

In 1985, Hungary continued to pursue its successful policy of domestic economic and political liberalization.

Political and Economic Affairs. The 13th Congress of the Hungarian Socialist Workers' (Communist) Party (HSWP) was held in Budapest, March 25–28, the first such meeting since 1980. On March 28, the 935 delegates reelected János Kádár as secretary-general (title changed from first secretary) of the central committee of the party. Károly Németh, 62, was elected to the newly created post of deputy secretary-general, raising speculations that he had been designated Kádár's heir apparent.

At the congress, discussion centered on the country's economic reform program, begun in 1968 and featuring decentralized decision making and limited free-market policies. Spokesmen emphasized that the reforms would continue. They stressed the desirability of wage differentials as work incentives, as well as the need to curb profiteering and to reorganize or close unprofitable enterprises. Grigory V. Romanov, the Soviet Union's observer at the congress, agreed with the "correctness" of Hungary's program but cautioned that socialist countries must maintain their economic independence from the West. Government newspapers called for better working conditions and higher salaries in the "state-run economic sector" to urge it to match the higher rate and quality of production in the "private sector."

In January the government adopted a policy designed to increase workers' participation in the management of their enterprises. In 25% of all companies, workers were to elect their managers directly. In another 50%, councils representing both workers and management were to select the managers and also to set wages and prices and plan investment and production strategies. The policy was to affect one third of all Hungarian enterprises during 1985 and all enterprises by the end of 1986.

Domestic economic news was mixed. In January the government warned of a 3% increase in the cost of consumer goods and services in 1985 and a rise in the consumer price index of 7%. This was attributed to the government's reduction of subsidies, in an attempt to curb domestic consumption and boost exports. Increased exports were considered vital to service the country's remaining foreign debt, estimated at $1.5–2 billion. However, Hungary's Seventh Five-Year Plan, for 1986–1990, predicted a significant rise in the country's standard of living. National income was scheduled to grow 14–17%, industrial production 13–16%, agricultural production 12–14%, and domestic consumption 13–16%. On January 10, Hungary reentered the international bond market it had abandoned in 1982, when its central bank issued a $100 million interest-bearing floating-rate note. In June the Hungarian delegation to the annual summit conference of the Council for Mutual Economic Assistance (COMECON) in Warsaw openly complained, along with Bulgarian and Romanian delegates, of the low prices received for farm products sent to the Soviet Union.

Parliamentary and municipal elections were held in June. Operating under a 1983 law mandating that at least two candidates run for every seat, 71 "independent" candidates (chosen by local selection committees but without official HSWP sponsorship) ran for and 25 won parliamentary seats. Five members of the party's central committee lost their seats, including a former premier and two other former cabinet ministers. Within the government, Col. Gen. István Olah became minister of defense; Lt. Gen. József Pacsek replaced him as chief of staff of the Hungarian People's Army; and Dr. László Medve became minister of health.

Foreign Affairs. Hungary was the site in June and July of a joint military exercise by 23,000 Soviet, Czechoslovak, and Hungarian troops of the Warsaw Pact. The Budapest Cultural Forum, an international conference held in the capital to review cultural cooperation since the Helsinki Conference on Security and Cooperation in 1975, broke up over East-West differences without agreeing on a formal statement. Heated public polemics between Hungary and Romania over the treatment of the ethnic Hungarian minority in Transylvania culminated in discussions, in Bucharest on January 21, between the foreign ministers of the two countries.

Hungarian Premier György Lázár went to Moscow in April. Nicaraguan President Daniel Ortega Saavedra visited Hungary in May, as part of a general swing through Europe to drum up support for the Sandinista regime.

JOSEPH F. ZACEK
State University of New York at Albany

HUNGARY • Information Highlights

Official Name: Hungarian People's Republic.
Location: East-central Europe.
Area: 35,900 sq mi (92 980 km²).
Population (mid-1985 est.): 10,700,000.
Chief Cities: (Jan. 1, 1984): Budapest, the capital, 2,064,374; Miskolc, 211,390; Debrecen, 206,393.
Government: *Head of state,* Pál Losonczi, chairman of the presidential council (took office April 1967). *Head of government,* György Lázár, premier (took office 1975). Secretary general of the Hungarian Socialist Workers' Party, János Kádár (took office 1956). *Legislature* (unicameral)—National assembly.
Monetary Unit: Forint (49.241 forints equal U.S.$1, Aug. 1985).
Gross National Product (1982 U.S.$): $68,800,-000,000.
Economic Indexes (1984): *Consumer Prices* (1970 = 100), all items, 201.9; food, 210.7. *Industrial Production* (1980 = 100), 109.
Foreign Trade (1984 U.S.$): *Imports,* $8,109,000,000; *exports,* $8,563,000,000.

ICELAND

In a key policy document released in late 1985, the government, a Progressive-Independence Party coalition (centrist-right) headed by Steingrímur Hermannsson, reaffirmed its commitment to roll back inflation and to curb the rise in the nation's foreign debt. The annual inflation rate at the end of 1985 was projected at some 20% with the target for the end of 1986 set at less than half that. (The figure was roughly 130% when the government took office in early 1983.) But there were signs that patience with the government's austerity program was wearing thin among the citizenry and in union ranks.

All ministries held by the Independence Party (IP), the strongest single element in Icelandic politics for many decades, changed hands in mid-October 1985—a development that gave Thorsteinn Pálsson, IP chairman since 1983, his first cabinet post (finance). Veteran IP leader Geir Hallgrímsson (foreign affairs) withdrew from the government, as of year's end, in the name of party unity.

President Vigdís Finnbogadóttir, who was reelected without contest in 1984, made official visits to Spain and the Netherlands.

Debated hotly in 1984–85 were legislative bills to repeal the state monopoly on broadcasting (passed) and a beer ban (shelved).

Fisheries. The fisheries output, the mainstay of the national economy, seemed headed for a record level in 1985, and its value was up by a notable margin at constant prices. As before, the fishing effort was subject to strict quotas; indebtedness continued to be a problem for many operators in the sector.

Economy. The terms of trade changed little from 1984. The export production headed upward, but imports more so. The foreign long-term debt rose to an estimated 53% of the gross domestic product (GDP), with payments on it put at some 21% of export revenue, down from 24% plus. Farm subsidies remained a burden, but the government sought to promote diversification in the sector, by encouraging fish- and fur-farming ventures, among other things. Unemployment was virtually nonexistent.

Energy. New electricity rates payable by a Swiss Aluminum–owned smelter were negotiated. Geothermal district heating utilities served approximately 80% of the national population.

Women's Protest. In October, thousands of women participated in a one-day strike to protest the fact that working women in Iceland earn an average of 40% less than men. President Finnbogadóttir showed her support for the cause by staying home from work.

Art Exhibits. Four exhibitions in the Reykjavík area marked the centenary of the birth of landscape painter Jóhannes S. Kjarval.

HAUKUR BÖDVARSSON
Free-lance Journalist, Reykjavík

IDAHO

State government was barely into its new fiscal year when in September Gov. John Evans ordered a 2.5% spending holdback. A slumping economy and a 1986 budget in which the legislature exceeded its own revenue projections by $2.6 million combined to necessitate the holdback. It was the fourth consecutive year in which Evans ordered a holdback.

Economy. Thirteen hundred jobs were lost when Potlatch Corporation announced closure of wood-products mills in Lewiston and Jaype. Not since the closure of the Bunker Hill mine and smelter in 1982 did a single action have such a pronounced effect on Idaho's unemployment. Champion Corporation's mill closure in Salmon (300 jobs lost) further underscored the plight of the state's timber industry.

A dry summer reduced grain harvests and produced conditions conducive to a severe infestation of grasshoppers in southern Idaho. Federal and state authorities, along with individual landowners, spent an estimated $12 million to combat the grasshoppers with pesticides. The dry conditions also made for the most costly range and forest fires since 1979. The destruction included the 30,000-acre (12 150-ha) Butte Fire, largest ever in the Salmon National Forest.

Though yields were up, the potato crop did not mark a bright spot for Idaho agriculture, as low commodity prices and high transportation costs reduced profits.

Remaining mired in its decade-long slump, the mining industry joined timber and agriculture to complete a picture of general economic stagnation. Only tourism produced increased revenues over 1984.

Legislature. The 66-day session was the shortest since a 65-day session in 1973. With both houses under firm Republican control, legislative attention focused on reducing the in-

---

ICELAND • Information Highlights

Official Name: Republic of Iceland.
Location: North Atlantic Ocean.
Area: 39,708 sq mi (102 845 km²).
Population (mid-1985 est.): 200,000.
Chief Cities (Dec. 1, 1984): Reykjavík, the capital, 88,745; Kópavogur, 14,546; Akureyri, 13,711.
Government: *Head of state,* Vigdis Finnbogadóttir, president (took office Aug. 1980). *Head of government,* Steingrímur Hermannsson, prime minister (took office May 1983). *Legislature*—Althing: Upper House and Lower House.
Monetary Unit: Krona (40.84 kronur equal U.S.$1, July 1985).
Gross National Product (1983 U.S.$): $2,100,000,000.
Foreign Trade (1984 U.S.$): *Imports,* $820,000,000; *exports,* $728,000,000.

fluence of organized labor. The "little" Davis-Bacon Act requiring federally set prevailing wages to be paid on public-works projects was repealed. A right-to-work bill, abolishing union membership as a condition of employment, was passed. It was vetoed by the governor and passed again with the two-thirds majority needed to override the veto. An emergency clause made the bill effective on passage rather than at the beginning of the new fiscal year, as is usual. The emergency clause backfired for supporters of right-to-work when the AFL-CIO challenged the provision in court and successfully delayed enforcement of the legislation pending a 1986 voter referendum.

Despite pleas from city and county officials to provide local-option taxing authority, the legislature passed no new revenue measures.

Gov. John V. Evans surveys bean fields in southern Idaho that were infested by grasshoppers during early summer.

AP/Wide World

Spending was held down by a freeze on state employee salaries.

Aryan Nations. FBI agents tracked down and arrested several members of The Order, a violent splinter group of the neo-Nazi Aryan Nations, headquartered in Hayden Lake. On April 6, David Lane was extradited from North Carolina to stand charges in Boise for alleged involvement in a $3.6 million armored truck robbery. Other members of The Order were apprehended in California, Missouri, and Washington state. The Aryan Nations were the main target of a 1984 state law prohibiting racial harassment.

M. C. HENBERG, *University of Idaho*

ILLINOIS

A convicted rapist serving his Illinois prison sentence gained international attention in 1985 when the victim of the rape recanted her story. Cathleen Crowell Webb, in going to the national media with her recantation, said she concocted her 1977 story of being raped and viciously attacked by Gary Dotson, 28, to cover up a feared pregnancy. The pregnancy never occurred. Webb said that new fundamentalist religious beliefs had caused guilt feelings over the story she said she had concocted and the unfairness to Dotson.

Others were skeptical of Webb's new story. A Circuit Court judge in Chicago refused to believe her recantation and ordered that Dotson remain in prison. Dotson, of Country Club Hills, IL, appealed to Gov. James R. Thompson for executive clemency.

Thompson, after three days of public hearings that got him national attention, denied clemency but commuted Dotson's sentence to the six years he served. "No good purpose would be served by returning Gary Dotson to prison," the governor said. Thompson said he personally believed that Webb was raped by Dotson. "Gary Dotson was proved guilty beyond a reasonable doubt," said Thompson, a former U.S. attorney for northern Illinois. "The verdict was correct."

Dotson thanked the governor for freeing him but continued his court fight to clear his name of the rape conviction. Webb and Dotson also sought movie and book rights for their separate stories.

Politics. Governor Thompson finished ten years in office in 1985 and became the longest-serving governor in Illinois history. In September he announced he would run for an unprecedented fourth term in 1986. The announcement prompted former U.S. Sen. Adlai E. Stevenson III, who narrowly lost the 1982 gubernatorial race to Thompson by 5,000 votes, to make another try for the office once held by his father. Stevenson promised a more aggressive campaign than in 1982 and said he

In Tokyo for trade talks, Gov. James R. Thompson made a pitch to Japanese businessmen for investment in Illinois.

AP/Wide World

would make a major issue of the Thompson administration's failure to stem the loss of jobs in Illinois.

Economy. Illinois politicians in both parties failed in their effort to win the new General Motors Saturn plant for the state. But they won a consolation of sorts when downstate Bloomington was selected for the $500 million auto plant to be built by Mitsubishi Motor Corp. and Chrysler Corp. The American-Japanese business venture, to be known as Diamond Star Motors Corp., will employ approximately 2,500 workers and produce 180,000 cars annually, starting in 1988.

Illinois agreed to provide $40 million to train the auto workers. Another $13 million in state and local funds was earmarked for water and sewer systems at the plant site.

Chrysler Chairman Lee Iacocca said he also expected some tax breaks for the Chrysler plant in Belvidere, IL, in return for choosing Illinois for the new plant. "If Illinois offers major incentives to win a plant half-owned by Chrysler, it must also offer incentives to a plant that is all Chrysler-owned or they will have to look the tiger in the whiskers and tell me why," said Iacocca.

Governor Thompson said the announcement should send a message to the world that Illinois has a competitive business climate. "Six years and many long, hard hours went into securing the auto plant for Illinois, and we will be reaping the benefits of it for years to come," the governor said.

Fire. A spectacular fire that leveled the Arlington Park race track in July put the future of thoroughbred horse racing in Illinois in doubt.

Track owners said they would rebuild Arlington Park, the premiere horse racing facility in the Midwest, only if they could get tax concessions from the state. In a special fall session, Illinois legislators refused to agree to the concessions.

Illinois' pari-mutuel tax is the second highest in the nation. A report prepared for the track owners said that the state's economy would lose $73.3 million annually if the track remained closed. Joseph Joyce, president of Arlington Park, called the current betting tax a significant impediment to rebuilding the facility.

See also CHICAGO.

ROBERT ENSTAD
"Chicago Tribune"

ILLINOIS • Information Highlights

Area: 56,345 sq mi (145 934 km²).
Population (July 1, 1984 est.): 11,511,000.
Chief Cities (July 1, 1984 est.): Springfield, the capital, 101,570; Chicago, 2,992,472; Rockford, 136,531.
Government (1985): *Chief Officers*—governor, James R. Thompson (R); lt. gov., George H. Ryan (R). *General Assembly*—Senate, 59 members; House of Representatives, 118 members.
State Finances (fiscal year 1984): *Revenues,* $16,470,000,000; *expenditures,* $15,050,000,000.
Personal Income (1984): $158,876,000,000; per capita, $13,802.
Labor Force (June 1985): *Civilian labor force,* 5,757,000; *unemployed,* 539,400 (9.4% of total force).
Education: *Enrollment* (fall 1983)—public elementary schools, 1,271,525; public secondary, 581,791; colleges and universities, 673,084. *Public school expenditures* (1982–83), $5,108,290,070 ($3,100 per pupil).

On July 24, India's Prime Minister Rajiv Gandhi (right) *signed an accord with moderate Sikh leader Harchand Singh Longowal (far left) to end the three-year separatist crisis in the Punjab. A month later, Longowal was assassinated by militant Sikhs.*

AP/Wide World

INDIA

The situation in India at the end of 1985 was considerably brighter than it was when the year began. Then the country, trying to recover from the most cataclysmic year since the tragedies following its independence in 1947, was faced with an uncertain future under an inexperienced leader. But Rajiv Gandhi demonstrated a capacity for vigorous and enlightened leadership. He enjoyed extraordinary personal popularity, even though his political party, the Congress (I), did not fare as well in state assembly elections in March as it did in the general elections of late December 1984. He was given a large measure of credit for the accords that were finally reached (but not fully implemented) in the three most dangerous internal crises—in the Punjab, Assam, and Gujarat. Ethnic and communal violence and tensions continued to be widespread. On the whole, the economic picture was relatively encouraging, although weak spots were noted. Foreign policy continued along well-charted lines. Gandhi made four major foreign tours and spoke out clearly on a number of international issues.

Gandhi's "Almost Bright Start." The overwhelming victory of the Congress (I) in the general elections of Dec. 24, 1984, gave Rajiv Gandhi greater political legitimacy and what he interpreted as "a mandate for change, for cleanup, for efficiency." The new look in his administration was reflected in the 39-member Council of Ministers, sworn in on the last day of 1984. He dropped several members of his interim government and brought in a number of younger, more performance-oriented persons, while retaining personal charge of nine portfolios, including external affairs, commerce, industry, science and technology, and atomic

energy. He dismissed some of his mother's personal advisers and replaced them with friends of his generation and outlook. Under his prodding, the Parliament passed a bill making political party defections more difficult.

Gandhi's reform and reorganization measures were interrupted in late January and early February by the worst spy scandal in the history of independent India. Sixteen officials, including three who held key positions in the prime minister's Secretariat, and three businessmen were arrested on charges of passing vital defense information to foreign countries. Suspicion pointed to France, the Soviet Union, East Germany, and Poland. One diplomat from each of these countries was expelled.

Gandhi's "almost bright start," to use the words of *The New York Times,* was temporarily slowed by the results of elections on March 2 and 5 for more than 2,500 seats in state assemblies in 11 of the 22 states and 1 Union Territory. The campaign, in which Gandhi participated vigorously, was marred by the worst violence in any elections to state assemblies. Although the Congress (I) retained majorities in the eight states it had previously controlled —Bihar, Gujarat, Himachal Pradesh, Madhya Pradesh, Maharashtra, Orissa, Rajasthan, and Uttar Pradesh—in almost every state its majorities were reduced. Opposition parties won majorities in Karnataka, Sikkim, and Tamil Nadu.

The Continuing Punjab Crisis. The crisis in the Punjab—whose tragic highlights in 1984 had been the storming of the Golden Temple in Amritsar by Indian Army units, with great loss of life, the assassination of Mrs. Indira Gandhi, and the bloody riots that followed—provided a severe test for Gandhi's leadership. For some weeks he vacillated on this issue, but by early March his hesitation was over. On March 8

several Sikh leaders, including Sant Harchand Singh Longowal, president of the Akali Dal, the leading Sikh party, were released from custody. They had been under detention since the Golden Temple tragedy nine months previously. Contacts were renewed between the government and Sikh leaders, and some concessions were made to Sikh demands. More radical Sikhs, however, continued to mount what the Indian home minister described as "a coordinated, well-planned operation . . . to terrorize, to create fear in the minds of citizens, and to disrupt communal peace and harmony." Sikh terrorists were alleged to be behind a series of bombings May 10–11 in New Delhi, Haryana, Rajasthan, and Uttar Pradesh that killed 79 people and injured hundreds. In such an unpropitious atmosphere negotiations between the government and the Akali Dal continued intermittently, finally leading to a historic agreement, signed in New Delhi on July 24 by Gandhi and Longowal. This agreement incorporated a number of concessions to the Sikhs, including the appointment of a commission of inquiry into the anti-Sikh riots and killings following Mrs. Gandhi's assassination, the transfer of Chandigarh to the Punjab (it had been the capital of both the Punjab and Haryana), and the restoration of normal political processes and freedoms. Several major issues in dispute were to be referred to judicial tribunals. This settlement was certainly "a tremendous achievement," as a leading Indian newspaper called it, but Gandhi was overoptimistic when he said that it "brings to an end a very critical period in the history of our country." His overoptimism was tragically demonstrated less than two months later when, on August 20—which happened to be Gandhi's 41st birthday—Longowal, who had been called a "traitor" by Sikh extremists for his "complete sellout" of the Sikhs, was assassinated.

Many of Gandhi's advisers urged him to postpone elections in the Punjab, scheduled for September 22. The prime minister insisted, however, that the elections go forward as scheduled, with a postponement of only three days. In spite of the tense atmosphere in the Punjab, the campaign was marked by relatively little violence. Ignoring the warnings of Sikh extremists to boycott the elections, more than 60% of the eligible voters went to the polls on September 25. They gave their state party, the Akali Dal, 73 seats in the state assembly, and only 32 seats to the Congress (I). The Congress (I) party, however, won almost half of the 13 seats in the Lok Sabha (the lower house of the Indian Parliament). Gandhi did not seem to be unduly disturbed by the Akali Dal victory. "We did lose the election," he commented, "but the verdict was a victory for the cause and principles of democracy and nonviolence for which we fought." On September 29, Surjit Singh Barnala, a moderate Sikh leader who had

been serving as president of the Akali Dal since Longowal's assassination, was sworn in as chief minister, at the head of an Akali Dal ministry. He pledged to "turn away from the confrontations of the past and work for solutions within the overall framework of the unity and integrity of India." The situation in the Punjab, however, remained tense.

Other Domestic Developments. In July and August, agreements were announced for resolving long-festering disputes and unrest in Assam and Gujarat. The Assam accord, between the Indian government and leaders of the long-sustained agitation in Assam, announced by Gandhi in his Independence Day speech on August 15, dealt with the foreign nationals issue. It provided that foreigners (meaning mostly Bengalis from West Bengal and Bangladesh) who arrived in Assam prior to Jan. 1, 1966, would be continued on the electoral rolls. Those who arrived from that date up to March 24, 1971, would be allowed to remain in the state but not to vote, and those who came on or after March 25, 1971, would be expelled. The Indian government agreed to assist in the economic development of Assam and to protect the cultural heritage of the Assamese people. Nevertheless, in a political setback for Prime Minister Gandhi, the Congress (I) party was defeated in Assamese state elections, held December 16.

In Gujarat, caste conflict flared up in an unprecedented level of violence and bloodshed over the issue of reservation for members of lower castes and tribes in educational institutions and the government bureaucracy. Protracted negotiations between the state government and antireservation agitation leaders led to an agreement by the latter to end the agitation. In return, the state government agreed not to implement a planned increase in reservations for "backward classes" until "a national consensus is evolved on the issue."

Human tragedies and political fallout from the toxic gas leak at the Union Carbide plant in Bhopal on Dec. 3, 1984—the worst industrial accident in history—were prominently featured in 1985. Union Carbide was faced with a spate of lawsuits. On April 8 the government of India, rejecting an offer by Union Carbide of more than $200 million as compensation for victims, filed a lawsuit against the company in a U.S. District Court in New York, claiming unspecified but substantial damages.

On September 25, Gandhi announced a major reshuffle and enlargement of the Council of Ministers, involving the reallocation of many portfolios, the dropping of several old members, and the induction of new members. Gandhi yielded the post of minister of external affairs to B. R. Bhagat, but he took direct charge of the ministries of defense, planning, science and technology, personnel and administrative reforms, and environment and forests.

The Economy. In spite of the frequently troubled political situation, the economic picture in 1985 was generally favorable. The rate of inflation, as of February 9, was 4.6%; it had been 10.8% a year previously. The overall growth rate was still too low—variously estimated between 3.5% and 5%—but there were encouraging signs that it would soon be higher. The trade deficit was still high, but it was on a downward trend. Foreign-exchange reserves increased. Food grain production reached a new high—about 150 million tons. In April the government announced a new liberalized import and export policy. Gandhi repeatedly expressed India's interest in foreign investments, especially in the area of high technology. He also voiced a determination to give ample scope to the private sector. One of his first steps was to reorganize the Planning Commission, with three new members who favored a more liberal economic policy. A report of the International Bank for Reconstruction and Development (World Bank) expressed the view that the Indian economy was moving in the right direction, but it also called attention to some "sore spots," especially in industry and exports.

The budget for fiscal year 1985–86, presented on March 16, envisaged total expenditures of Rs. 512.95 billion (about $43 billion) and receipts of Rs. 476.35 billion (about $40 billion). Aimed at "growth with stability," it included provisions for cuts in taxes for businessmen and wealthy individuals and for a reduction in government regulation of key sectors of the economy.

During the year a complete draft of the Seventh Five-Year Plan was slowly hammered out, mainly by the Planning Commission. As approved by the National Development Council in November, the plan provided for a public sector outlay of Rs. 1,800 billion (about $150 billion), an increase of about 85% over the outlay approved in the Sixth Plan, which officially ended in 1985.

In June the members of the Aid India Consortium set a target of $4.0 billion for economic assistance to India in 1985–86. It was envisaged that the World Bank and its soft-loan affiliate, the International Development Association, would make available more than half of this sum ($2.4 billion) and that the remainder would come from member countries of the consortium.

Foreign Policy. In late January, Gandhi was the host to a special summit meeting in New Delhi in which the presidents of Argentina, Mexico, and Tanzania and the prime ministers of Greece and Sweden were the other participants. At the end of their discussions they issued an appeal for "an all-embracing halt to the testing, production, and deployment of nuclear weapons and their delivery systems," with special emphasis on the need to prevent an arms race in outer space. In April, India hosted a conference in New Delhi, sponsored by the nonaligned movement (NAM), of which Gandhi was chairman, on the occupation of South-West Africa (Namibia) by South Africa, and India was represented by its minister of state for external affairs at a major NAM meeting in Angola in September.

During the year a large number of top leaders of many countries went to India on official visits. In addition to the five leaders who participated in the January meeting, these included the kings of Bhutan and Nepal; the presidents of the Maldives and Sri Lanka; the chairman of the Polish People's Republic; the prime ministers of Mauritius, New Zealand, Trinidad and Tobago, the United Kingdom, and Yugoslavia; and the vice-presidents of the United States and the Soviet Union.

Rajiv Gandhi made four major world tours during 1985. In March he led a large delegation to Moscow for the funeral of Konstantin Chernenko. This gave him an opportunity to meet with the new leader of the Soviet Union, Mikhail Gorbachev, and with a number of other world leaders. In May he returned to Moscow for an official visit and received a warm welcome. One of the fruits of the visit was an economic agreement providing for a Soviet credit of $1.2 billion and for programs of scientific and technological cooperation through the year 2000. In June an 11-day tour took him to Egypt, France, Algeria, the United States, and Switzerland. In October he went to the Bahamas for the annual Commonwealth heads of state and government conference, to the United States to join a large number of other world leaders in programs commemorating the United Nations' 40th anniversary, and to Cuba, Britain, and the Netherlands on brief official visits. During this trip he also made an unscheduled stopover in Moscow, where he conferred with Gorbachev. He made two visits to Bangladesh, one in June with President Jayewardene of Sri Lanka, the second in December to participate in the first summit meeting of the leaders of member states of the South Asian Regional Cooperation body (SARC). He also went to Bhutan in September and to Viet Nam and Japan late in the year.

India's relations with two of its South Asian neighbors, Pakistan and Sri Lanka, continued to be strained and uneasy. Meetings at various levels between representatives of India and Pakistan were held frequently throughout the year. Gandhi met with President Zia ul-Haq on six occasions—in Moscow in March; in the Bahamas, New York, and Oman in the fall; and in Dhaka and New Delhi in December. In spite of the contacts and exchanges, mutual suspicions and criticisms were more apparent than real progress in bilateral and regional cooperation. India was particularly disturbed by what it regarded as convincing evidence that Paki-

stan was moving forward in the development of a nuclear weapons capability—charges that Pakistani leaders indignantly denied—and by the substantial U.S. arms aid to Pakistan.

India's relations with Sri Lanka were particularly tense in the early months of 1985, but they improved considerably in the latter half of the year. In January a prolonged crisis was occasioned by incidents in the sea channel between the two countries. Sri Lanka continued to protest to India for the support that top Indian leaders were giving to Tamil insurgent leaders. Relations improved considerably after President Jayewardene's official visit to India in early June. His visit was followed by India's more active efforts, in which Prime Minister Gandhi took a special interest, in bringing representatives of the Tamil insurgent groups and the Sri Lankan government together. The outcome was a comprehensive proposal, embodying further concessions to the Tamils by the Sri Lankan government and the agreement of the Tamil insurgents to suspend their violent methods. In October the Indian government announced that a new cease-fire agreement had been negotiated during talks in New Delhi between the government of Sri Lanka and leaders of one major opposition Tamil group, the Eelam National Liberation Front.

The highlight of Indo-American relations in 1985 was Prime Minister Gandhi's official visit to the United States on June 11–15. The visit went very well. In his many public appearances and special meetings, including an address to a joint session of the Congress, he made a very favorable personal impression. He was frank in expressing reservations regarding or disapproval of several major U.S. policies, including the U.S. approach to the Soviet Union, the Strategic Defense Initiative, U.S. policy in Central America, and U.S. arms aid to Pakistan. In a joint statement issued at the end of his visit on June 15, he and President Ronald Reagan affirmed their desire to broaden and strengthen the ties between their two countries. Reflecting the special interest of the young Indian leader in science and technology, the statement contained an announcement that the Science and Technology Initiative, begun after Mrs. Indira Gandhi's official visit in mid-1982, would be extended for an additional three-year period.

On June 13, Gandhi officially inaugurated the Festival of India in the United States, 1985–86, an 18-month cultural extravaganza that was another result of Mrs. Gandhi's visit in 1982. The festival is an unprecedented nationwide series of programs and exhibits in some 80 cities in 33 states, designed to reveal the richness and variety of Indian culture.

Differing views on Pakistan, and to a lesser extent on Afghanistan, continued to hamper efforts to improve Indo-American relations. Indian officials were rather cool to American

AP/Wide World

The Reagans held a dinner in honor of Prime Minister Gandhi and his wife, Sonia, at the White House in June.

representatives, including Vice-President George Bush, Under Secretary of State Michael Armacost, and Donald Fortier, a member of the staff of the National Security Council, when they went to India (Bush in March, the latter two in September) to attempt to persuade the Indians that U.S. arms aid to Pakistan was not a threat to India and to suggest that India take some "regional initiatives" to avoid a nuclear arms race with Pakistan.

NORMAN D. PALMER
Professor Emeritus
University of Pennsylvania

INDIA • Information Highlights

Official Name: Republic of India.

Location: South Asia.

Area: 1,269,340 sq mi (3 287 590 km²).

Population (mid-1985 est.): 762,200,000.

Chief Cities (1981 census): New Delhi, the capital, 5,157,270; Bombay, 8,243,405; Calcutta, 3,288,148.

Government: *Head of state,* Zail Singh, president (took office July 1982). *Head of government,* Rajiv Gandhi, prime minister (took office Oct. 31, 1984). *Legislature*—Parliament: Rajya Sabha (Council of States) and Lok Sabha (House of the People).

Monetary Unit: Rupee (12.0192 rupees equal U.S. $1, Dec. 2, 1985).

Gross National Product (fiscal 1982–83 U.S. $): $150,000,000,000.

Economic Indexes (1984): *Consumer Prices* (1970 = 100), all items, 313.0; food, 302.0. *Industrial Production* (1980 = 100), 127.

Foreign Trade (1984 U.S. $): *Imports,* $13,647,-000,000; *exports,* $8,683,000,000.

On May 1, the U.S. House of Representatives voted the Democratic incumbent, Frank McCloskey, the winner of the disputed 1984 election for Indiana's 8th district.

INDIANA

Legislation enacted by the 1985 Indiana General Assembly made for one of the most historic sessions in recent decades. The longest-running contest for a U.S. congressional seat in nearly a century and a controversial decision regarding a middle school AIDS victim were also major news stories of 1985.

Legislature. In "a landmark year for environmentalists," lawmakers established a separate state environmental agency for programs formerly housed with the state board of health, raised funding for pollution control by more than $10 million, and increased taxes on hazardous-waste landfilling.

Additional historic legislation included a living-will measure allowing terminally ill patients to sign a document requesting withdrawal of life support systems and legislation creating for the first time in 50 years a new state-supported university, the University of Southern Indiana, near Evansville. A long-debated cross-county banking law permitting the formation of multibank holding companies unleashed massive changes on the Indiana banking scene.

Aimed at reducing the number of drunk drivers were two measures prohibiting establishments from lowering prices on drinks or providing two-for-one "happy hour" specials during the business day and authorizing police to make drivers involved in fatal or serious motor vehicle accidents take tests for drunkenness regardless of whether the officer has probable cause to suspect inebriation. Far more controversial was a third safety law requiring riders in the front seats of cars and buses to wear seat belts.

Defeated once again were "beer baron" measures that would have permitted exclusive sales territories for beer distributors and lethal injections as a replacement for electrocutions. Lawmakers again failed to initiate proceedings to remove a constitutional ban on state lotteries. Despite several pending federal suits attacking Indiana's party-controlled motor vehicle license branch system, the state's legislators refused to establish a schedule for reform. The General Assembly did ensure that the 1986 session would deal with the controversial issue, which lies at the heart of the parties' patronage system.

Budget. With almost unprecedented bipartisan cooperation, the legislature approved a $10 billion budget for the 1985–86 biennium. Expenditures for 1985–86 were 7.3% higher than those for 1984–85, and spending for 1986–87 was to be 6.3% more than for the first budget year. Local schools and universities claimed about 48% of the budget. Public schools were slated to receive about $2.8 billion in state funds over the next two years. Universities were to get approximately $1.3 billion, including for the first time in many years funding of universities' repair and rehabilitation projects, as well as major new buildings for each of the state's five university campuses. Mental programs and facilities received significant increases, and a designated $85.4 million honored a commitment to upgrade state employees' salaries.

INDIANA • Information Highlights

Area: 36,185 sq mi (93 720 km²).
Population (July 1, 1984 est.): 5,498,000.
Chief Cities (July 1, 1984 est.): Indianapolis, the capital, 710,280; Fort Wayne, 165,416; Gary, 143,096.
Government (1985): *Chief Officers*—governor, Robert D. Orr (R); lt. gov., John Mutz (R). *General Assembly*—Senate, 50 members; House of Representatives, 100 members.
State Finances (fiscal year 1984): *Revenues,* $7,163,000,000; *expenditures,* $6,416,000,000.
Personal Income (1984): $64,418,000,000; per capita, $11,717.
Labor Force (June 1985): *Civilian labor force,* 2,792,700; *unemployed,* 223,700 (8% of total force).
Education: *Enrollment* (fall 1983)—public elementary schools, 670,440; public secondary, 313,944; colleges and universities, 256,470. *Public school expenditures* (1982–83), $2,239,068,800 ($2,414 per pupil).

Other. From January until April citizens of Indiana's eighth congressional district were without representation in Congress because of a closely contested election between Democratic incumbent Francis X. McCloskey and Republican Richard D. McIntyre. After extensive state recounts, Republican Secretary of State Edwin J. Simcox declared McIntyre the victor, but Democrats appealed to the U.S. House of Representatives, where for the first time in 24 years a congressional task force was authorized to conduct a recount. In April the federal committee, composed of two Democrats and one Republican, recommended that McCloskey be seated, and the Democrat-controlled House concurred. The margin of victory was less than ten votes.

Local school administrators, backed by the courts, refused to allow a Kokomo seventh grader suffering from AIDS to attend the public middle school.

LORNA LUTES SYLVESTER, *Indiana University*

INDONESIA

In 1985, Indonesia experienced lower economic growth, saw the development of opposition to its government, and considered new approaches to China and Vietnam.

For the second year in a row, Indonesia experienced economic growth of slightly more than 4%, well below the average for the previous decade and a half. (*See* feature article, page 56.) Although rice production reached a record high, industry and trade—beyond the petroleum and gas sectors—failed to grow as hoped and produced neither the revenue nor the levels of employment expected. Under the 1985–86 budget, oil subsidies were cut drastically, and a number of internal taxes, including a value-added tax of 10%, were enacted or raised.

Responding in part to World Bank criticism that too many obstacles still lie in the way of export-import trade, the government announced in April a dramatic plan to restructure the existing customs system, which had long been thought a center of corruption and inefficiency. President Suharto announced 33 specific reforms, including turning over virtually all customs inspection duties to a Swiss firm noted for its honesty and careful accounting procedures. Although some criticized the reforms, others agreed with Suharto that the serious situation called for strong, pragmatic action, regardless of legal niceties.

A series of fires and riots occurred in late 1984, and there were explosions at the ancient Buddhist monument of Borobudur in January. These events made it clear that opposition to Suharto's government—whether from Muslim protesters, other civilians, or restless military figures—was capable of taking a violent turn.

INDONESIA • Information Highlights

Official Name: Republic of Indonesia.
Location: Southeast Asia.
Area: 782,659 sq mi (2 027 087 km²).
Population: (mid-1985 est.): 168,400,000.
Chief Cities (Dec. 31, 1983 est.): Jakarta, the capital, 7,636,000; Surabaya, 2,289,000; Medan, 1,966,-000; Bandung, 1,602,000.
Government: *Head of state and government,* Suharto, president (took office for fourth five-year term March 1983). *Legislature* (unicameral)—People's Consultative Assembly.
Monetary Unit: Rupiah (1,122.0 rupiahs equal U.S.$1, Nov. 12, 1985).
Gross National Product (1984 U.S.$): $90,000,-000,000.
Economic Index (1984): *Consumer Prices* (1980 = 100), all items, 151.7; food, 145.8.
Foreign Trade (1984 U.S.$): *Imports,* $13,882,-000,000; *exports,* $21,858,000,000.

It also appeared that the Indonesian public was genuinely alarmed about the prospect of an increase in such violence and was particularly shocked that the Borobudur monument should be attacked. The government prosecuted whenever it could and brought to trial a former cabinet minister, a retired general, and the former secretariat chief of the Association of Southeast Asian Nations (ASEAN). The government also continued its apparent pressuring of Islamic groups, forcing them to adhere to so-called social organization laws and accept officially the state creed of Pancasila (Five Principles) as their foundation. These and other tactics created political confusion in Muslim circles. The issue also caused comment and stirred up resentment in the military.

Foreign Affairs. The Indonesian government seemed likely to officially open direct trade relations with the People's Republic of China. Such relations would be the first since Suharto's New Order began in 1966. It was widely felt in Indonesia that China was the greatest threat to Asian peace, and for that reason it would be foolish to remain estranged from it.

Indonesia also seemed intent on improving relations with Vietnam. This policy had to be pursued very carefully by Indonesia so as not to antagonize its ASEAN neighbors—most of whom have adopted a firm stance against Vietnam as a result of that country's occupation of Cambodia.

Communications. Indonesia's vast breadth (3,200 miles, or 5 120 km), archipelagic geography, and large population (more than 168,000,000) made it one of the first nations in the nonindustrialized world to utilize space communications on a regular basis. It had its own Palapa satellite launched in 1976, and several backup satellites since then. In 1985 this system experienced its first failure, falling silent for three days and raising concerns about its dependability. However the system was working fine as the year ended.

WILLIAM H. FREDERICK, *Ohio University*

INDUSTRIAL REVIEW

Industrial production posted smaller gains in most countries in 1985 than in 1984. Aside from the mature industrialized nations, even the "tigers" of the Far East experienced considerable deceleration in their output growth.

With a wide range of U.S. manufacturing industries facing fierce competition from abroad, there was widespread concern about "deindustrialization." Pessimists pointed to problems, including the high foreign-exchange value of the dollar, faced by footwear, textile, primary metals, farm and construction machinery, automobile, semiconductor, and, yes, even photo album manufacturers and ticked off job losses in support of their argument that the United States is in danger of losing its industrial base. While conceding that the proportion of manufacturing employment as a proportion of total employment is indeed shrinking—it went from 28% in 1960 to 20% in 1985—more sanguine analysts pointed to the fairly constant share that manufacturing output has held of gross national product (GNP) over the past 25 years—24%—and the fact that manufacturing output over the long run has been rising in the United States.

U.S. Production. After rising 11.5% in 1984, preliminary data showed that U.S. industrial production increased a sluggish 2.1% in 1985, to a little over 124 (1977 = 100) on the Federal Reserve Board Index of Quantity Output.

Manufacturing posted a 2.4% gain, following a 12.4% increase in 1984. Consumer-goods output edged up 1.8%, a considerable slowdown from the 8.1% recovery in 1984. Production of business equipment, which shot up 16.9% in 1984, increased 4.7%. Defense-goods output climbed 10.3%, after posting a 13.1% gain. Production of intermediate goods slowed to a 4.2% increase, following a 12.3% growth.

Utilities output inched up by 2.3%, following a 1984 gain of 5.4%. Mining production declined 1.5%, in contrast to a 7.8% gain posted for 1984. Oil and gas extraction was especially weak in 1985, dropping nearly 2% after advancing 6.1% in the preceding year.

Production losses were widespread among manufacturing industries. Largely responsible for slower growth in 1985 were the following: farm equipment, with output plummeting over 17%, after gaining 2.8% in 1984; TV and radio production, down 14%, following an 18.3% increase; electronic components, with production down 10%, following a 29.1% hike; agricultural chemicals, which swung from a 12.1% increase to a 0.4% drop; major electrical equipment and parts, dropping nearly 9%, after a 12.5% increase; tire production declined 5%, after 11.2% growth; glass and glass products, down 0.4%, following an 8% gain; leather and leather products, down 7.5%, following a 3.8% drop; iron and steel, down 4.5%, after an 11% increase; nonferrous metals, up only 0.4%, after posting an 18.4% advance; textile mills products output lost 1% for the second year in a row; apparel output was down 1.5%, after an 8.8% gain; and tobacco products declined 2%, following a 1.8% increase; household furniture production dropped 2%, after growing 8.1%.

Star and Moderate Performers. Star performers in manufacturing were aircraft and parts, with production up about 10%, after rising 7.9% in 1984; automobile output was up 9.1%, following a 12.9% increase; railroad equipment was up nearly 9%, following an 83.2% jump in 1984; trucks, buses, and trailers showed a 7.3% gain, after 37.2% growth; mobile-home production advanced nearly 14%, after gaining 10.3%; communication equipment continued to gain, up 8.7%, building on a 16.3% increase; and fixtures and office furniture output was up 8.5%, after rolling up a 19.7% gain.

Ford minivans are produced at a St. Louis plant. All and all, it was a good year for car and truck production.

Ford Motor Company

CONSUMER PRODUCTS
The New, the Unusual, the Popular

Programmable telephones, audiobooks, and running shoes that calculate distance and calories expended are among the new products that have been influenced by recent advances in high tech. The anticipated arrival of Halley's Comet has caused a big jump in telescope sales.

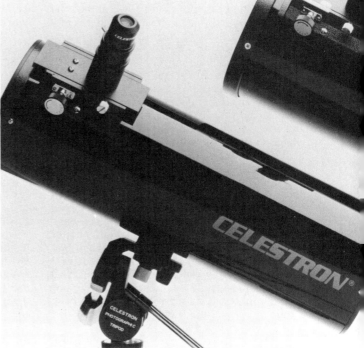

Cement and structural clay products were up 6.8%, following a 15% increase; synthetic material output rose 6.9%, after increasing 9.9%; soaps and toiletries were up 7.9%, following a 5.3% increase; hardware and plumbing supplies grew 6.5%, after gaining 15%; and construction machinery output rose 7.4%, following a brisk 28.6% gain.

More moderate production performances were by ordnance manufacturers, who recorded a 4% gain, after 8.3% growth; food products were up 3.4%, after rising 4.6%; lumber and wood products advanced 3.4%, following an 8.2% increase; paper and paper products production was unchanged, after a 7.3% growth; printing and publishing activity was up

4.4%, following a 12.7% increase; basic chemicals posted a 1.9% gain, after rising 6.1%; rubber products, excluding tires, gained only 0.6%, after increasing 13.7%; plastic products advanced 4.1%, after a 12.4% gain; metalworking-machinery producers registered a 3.5% increase, after a substantial 22.6% increase in 1984; industrial machinery was up 1.1%, following a 20.1% gain; office and service industry equipment rose 4.7%, after a 21.4% gain; ship and boat builders showed a 0.1% upward nudge, compared with a 15.4% advance; and instrument output slowed to a 2.6% gain from a 9.6% increase in 1984.

Capacity Utilization. Capacity utilization in all manufacturing was 80% in 1985, not much changed from the 80.8% of production capacity that factories used in 1984. Factory-use rate slipped from 80.4% to 79.1% for advanced processing industries. Materials producers saw their utilization rate slip from 82.4% in 1984 to 80.1% in 1985. Primary processing industries raised their rate from 81.6% to 82.1%.

Selected Industries. The automotive industry was responsible for much of the growth in manufacturing output. Production of trucks posted a 9.5% gain, making the 1985 production of 3.5 million units second best only to the record 3.7 million assemblies in 1978. But the total of both U.S. and Canadian output was 4.5 million, topping the 1978 record of 4.4 million. U.S. passenger car output rose more than 5% in 1985 to 8.2 million units. The model year of 1985 saw combined car and truck sales in the U.S. reach a record 15.6 million vehicles, including about 3.7 million imports.

U.S. aircraft producers, thanks to substantial orders from abroad, delivered 275 large airplanes in 1985 compared with 188 units in 1984.

Output of raw steel dropped about 7% in 1985 from the 92.5 million short tons produced in 1984. The industry produced at less than two thirds of capacity in 1985. Weak demand combined with an import penetration of 25% forced several of the nation's minimills out of business. In recent years minimills had fared better than large, integrated mills because of their limited product lines and production efficiencies.

Among energy producers, bituminous coal mines cut production by 3% to 865 million tons in 1985, following an increase of 15% in 1984. Crude oil output at 8.9 million barrels per day was 0.6% ahead of 1984.

The U.S. semiconductor industry was severely buffeted by competition from abroad in 1985. For instance, the Japanese grabbed about 20% of the U.S. memory chip market in 1985, and a major new product—the 256 K RAMs—is practically dominated by Japanese manufacturers. In addition, U.S. firms are rapidly helping to build up chip manufacturers in South Korea by selling or licensing technology. Already Korean firms produce microprocessors, 64K and even 256K RAMs.

Capital Outlays. American business invested $354 billion in new plant and equipment in 1984, an increase of 16.3% that followed a 1.9% drop in 1983. About 60% of the increase was accounted for by investment in passenger cars, computers, and trucks. Preliminary estimates place business investment at $384 billion for 1985, an increase of 8.3%.

Capital outlays by manufacturing rose 19.5% in 1984 and grew 10.5% in 1985 to $153 billion. Durable goods producers increased spending nearly 25% in 1984 and added 11% to their outlays in 1985 for a total of $74 billion. The motor-vehicle industry led the way with a 54% boost in 1984 and a 29% increase in 1985. Aircraft manufacturers trimmed their investment increase from 23% to just under 4% in 1985. The electrical-machinery industry held its 1985 capital outlays to a 10% growth, following a 28% expenditure increase the year before. Nonelectrical-machinery industry spending led 1984 by 4.5% compared with that year's increase of 14%. Steel-industry outlays were up 10% in 1985 compared with 9% in 1984. Nonferrous-metals producers cut capital expenditures 6% in 1985, following a 22% increase the year before. Fabricated metals pared the 1985 increase to 2.6% after a 23% boost in 1984. Stone, clay, and glass producers invested 8% more in 1985 than in 1984 when they raised capital spending by nearly 12%.

Nondurable-goods industries increased spending 15% in 1984 and 10% in 1985, to a total of $80 billion. The largest increase was by the rubber industry, up 26% in 1985 and 17% in 1984. Paper producers upped their spending by 22% in 1984 and by 13.8% in 1985. The chemical industry increased outlays by 10.8% after an 18.2% growth in 1984. Food manufacturers spent 14.6% more in 1985 than in 1984 when they added 13.3%. After a nearly 24% spending hike in 1984, the textile industry cut capital outlays by 2.6% in 1985. The petroleum industry cut its increase in half from the 10.3% growth registered for 1984.

The mining industry increased capital spending by 11% in 1984 but cut it by 4.6% in 1985 to $16 billion. Public utilities increased investment by 5.6% in 1984 and by only 1.3% in 1985 to a total of $48 billion. Electric utilities, which had shaved spending by 0.6% in 1984, reduced capital outlays by 4% in 1985. Gas utilities, in sharp contrast, raised 1985 capital expenditures by 20%, following a nearly 36% increase in 1984.

Robots and Computers. Concern with factory modernization led the Commerce Department's Census Bureau to conduct a survey of robots. It showed that in 1984, 75 companies shipped 5,535 complete robots, valued at $307 million. The automotive industry is the primary customer for industrial robots, and 27% of them were designed for welding, soldering, brazing, and cutting. Their value was $124 mil-

lion. Robots used to spray, paint, glue, and seal totaled $59 million in value. Shipments of robots used in assembly operations were valued at about $29 million.

A Census Bureau survey of computers showed that manufacturers' shipments in 1984 rose 35% to $17 billion. There were 185 companies in the business, shipping a total of 4.2 million computers. The survey provided the first breakdown of production statistics on general-purpose digital computers by suggested-retail-price categories. Nearly 88% of digital computers shipped in 1984 were priced at less than $2,500, but they accounted for only 28% of the total value of shipments. Top of the line machines—those costing $1 million or more apiece—numbered 708, valued at more than $1 billion. In addition, there were 267 companies producing peripheral equipment for computers. Their shipments increased about 13% in 1984, to $18.9 billion.

Employment. Employment in manufacturing industries was 19.5 million at year-end, about 1% lower than 12 months before. Manufacturing lost 2.3 million jobs in the recession that began in mid-1981 and has regained 1.3 million. Durable-goods industries employed 11.5 million workers at year-end 1985, 1.5% fewer than the year before. Of the 1.7 million jobs lost in the recession, they had regained 1 million as the year ended. At 7.9 million, the job count in nondurable industries was only 0.4% below the year-before level, having regained 225,000 of the 491,000 lost in the recession.

Employment in mining lagged 2.1% below the previous year-end level. At 961,000, the industry had regained 70,000 of the 145,000 jobs lost. The job count in public utilities stood at 2.2 million at year-end 1985, 0.1% above the comparable 1984 period. Still, the industry employed 46,000 fewer workers than it did before the onset of the recession.

Few manufacturing industries can boast of job counts that are above prerecession levels. Among them are lumber and wood products, now employing 712,000 compared with 678,000 in July 1981; furniture and fixtures, with a year-end 1985 job count of about 500,000 compared with 473,000; electrical and electronic equipment, with current employment at 2.2 million compared with 2.1 million; rubber and plastics, with 800,000 jobs against 750,000.

International Outlook. Among the major industrialized nations, Japan continued to set the pace in 1985. After posting an 11.1% increase in 1984, Japan's output in late 1985 was nearly 6% above the comparable 1984 period. West Germany stepped up production in 1985, with output late in the year leading the comparable 1984 period by 5%. For 1984, West Germany showed a 2.4% increase. The United Kingdom also showed signs of a production revival, with output late in 1985 about 4.5% higher than at a comparable year-before period. In 1984, the

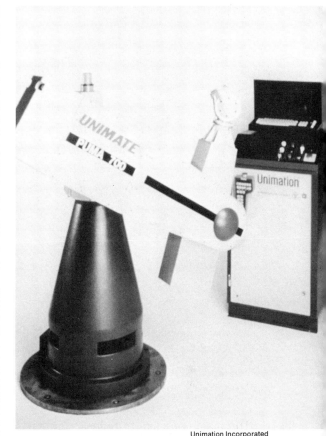

Unimation Incorporated

In planning for the future, many manufacturers are turning to the robot. Robot sales jumped 71% in 1984.

United Kingdom's industrial output rose a scant 1%. Canada posted a late 1985 gain of 2.7%, after a healthy 8.7% gain for all of 1984. Italy showed a 3.1% gain for 1984, but by late 1985 had slowed to a gain of only 0.2%. France registered a drop of 3.6% for late 1985, following a 2.6% gain in industrial production for all of 1984. The major European countries still boasted of a composite gain of 2% in late 1985 compared with a United States increase of 1.3% from late 1984.

The Soviet Union recorded a 4% gain for 1984, and it claimed a 3.7% increase for the first nine months of 1985, compared with an equivalent 1984 period. A reorientation of investment priorities may be responsible for a 4% drop in Soviet oil production in 1985, the first year since World War II to show a decline.

Some of the "tigers" of the Far East reflected the sluggish pace of industrial production in the mature industrialized countries. Thus South Korea, which had posted a 15% gain in industrial production in 1984, slowed to an increase of 4% in 1985. Singapore saw its production drop about 7% in 1985, following a 9% gain in 1984.

AGO AMBRE, *U.S. Department of Commerce*

Interior design in 1985 saw a return to formality—including colorful chintzes, area carpets, and delicate porcelains.

INTERIOR DESIGN

In what might be described as a dramatic reaction to the overwhelming popularity of the country look a few seasons back, interior design returned to formality in 1985. There now were rooms that were replete with embellished walls, colorful chintzes, intricately patterned area carpets, and delicate porcelains.

This shift to elegance, to a prettier and dressier look, in traditional decorating was matched by a new sparkle and decorative cachet in contemporary interiors as well. The totally built-in, low-key, understated, and underaccessorized approach of only a few years back has been replaced by an emphasis on greater comfort, a sense of luxury, and a more eclectic and highly individualized decor.

What interior designers were doing in 1985 was significant because even the most elaborate or expensive techniques that they might use soon would be expressed in popular design attitudes and moderately priced furnishings.

Designer showhouse rooms, which are often the barometer for the directions in which interior design is moving, are especially interesting for their architectural treatments. Molding was being applied everywhere; fireplaces were added, often as focal points, but just as often for the architectural enrichment they provide. *Faux bois* (false wood), *faux* marble, *faux* wallpaper as well as wonderful textural looks were among the fascinating things being done with mere paint to create background interest.

Elaborate window treatments also were employed to create an ornate shell for the furnishings that go within these formal interiors. Cornices, valances, swags, and every imaginable kind of trimming enhanced decorative drapery designs that were clearly evocative of an earlier and more splendid age. In addition a proliferation of gussied-up pillows and softly textured shawls combined with an exaggerated use of paintings and prints on walls, collectibles on cabinet shelves and tabletops.

The return to formality, elegance, and personalized luxe already was quite evident at the new mass-market furniture level. Many such collections were inspired by antiques found in the great houses of England and in the museum collections of the United States. A new emphasis on such 19th century design genres as Empire and Biedermeier also was noted. The Far Eastern influence was another important trend that fits in with the new emphasis on formality. Many of the latest dining room and bedroom collections expressed this theme. In contemporary furniture design, the word was lacquer. Lacquer in rich pastel colors was chosen for chair frames and sofa bases as well as for dining room and bedroom tables and cabinetry.

Fabrics also kept pace with this return to elegance, with fabulous floral chintzes embellished with ribbon motifs. Silk-look textures replaced the small scale country prints and humble homespuns that were popular a few seasons back. Softer, paler colors—going from light pastels to richer jewel tones—were favored by designers and manufacturers for fabric, carpet, and accessory collections. Lovely peach tones, pale turquoises, ivories, light buttercups, lavenders, quiet greens and blues, and a variety of subtle and warming neutrals were proliferating.

Bed linens are always expressive of new decorating trends, and prettier patterns, greater emphasis on such details as scallops and embroidery, eyelet treatment, piping, unusual shaping for pillow shams, ribbon ties, and even a softer hand for the linens themselves underscored the move toward the look and sense of luxury that was important in 1985.

GENEVIEVE FERNANDEZ
"Good Housekeeping"

INTERNATIONAL TRADE AND FINANCE

World economic recovery stretched into its third year in 1985. But it was a troubled expansion.

In the United States, growth slowed to a crawl in the first half of the year before picking up in the third and fourth quarters. The Federal Reserve System stepped on the gas, pumping out money—the fuel for the economy—at a record postwar increase of almost 12% for the year. Interest rates declined but remained high in real terms after inflation was subtracted.

In addition, the two huge American deficits were stirring up political annoyance both in the United States and abroad. The budget deficit for fiscal 1985, ending September 30, ran $202 billion. The merchandise trade deficit approached $150 billion, with the broader current account deficit—which takes into account such factors as tourism, shipping charges, services, and some capital flows—running about $125 billion.

Many economists saw the budget deficit as the root of much economic evil, soaking up such a large proportion of domestic savings that it boosted interest rates. Those high interest rates, in turn, helped attract foreign investment. The billions flowing into the United States helped finance the deficit but also raised the value of the dollar on foreign-exchange markets. That made it easier for other nations to export their goods to the United States and more difficult for Americans to export abroad.

On the positive side, this flood of imports did assist in holding down prices in the United States, with the consumer price increase staying under 4% in 1985. The imports were relatively cheap, making it difficult for American competitors to raise their prices. On the negative side, the expensive dollar swelled the trade deficit and stirred up rampant protectionism in Congress. A joint economic subcommittee was told in March by economist Roger Brinner of Data Resources Inc. that the strong dollar had cost the U.S. economy some 2 million jobs since 1980, 1.5 million of them in manufacturing. Some 300 protectionist trade bills were under congressional consideration in 1985, with measures to put a tariff surcharge on imports and to tighten quotas on textiles among the more popular. (President Ronald Reagan vetoed the latter in December.)

Alarmed by the protectionist drive in Congress, the Group of Five industrial countries—the United States, Great Britain, West Germany, France, and Japan—met in New York on September 22 to attack the problem. The dollar had already fallen some 10% from its peak in February, and the finance ministers and central bank heads agreed that "some further orderly appreciation of the main nondollar cur-

AP/Wide World

Clothing, apparel, and home furnishings sold in the United States now must include country of origin tags.

rencies against the dollar is desirable. They stand ready to cooperate more closely to encourage this when to do so would be helpful." The announcement had an immediate impact on the already nervous foreign-exchange markets. The next day the dollar plunged 5% against a trade-weighted group of currencies of the major U.S. trading partners. By selling billions of dollars on the foreign-exchange markets, the central bankers persisted in trying to keep the dollar down.

President Reagan faced not only protectionist pressure and an intractable budget deficit. He worried that major commercial banks were running a considerable risk of default on their loans to less-developed countries, on new office buildings, and on some energy loans as a result of declining oil prices. The Federal Farm Credit system's 37 principal banks were seeking a bailout on their $74 billion in farm loans, and thrifts were hoping for a similar government rescue.

Overseas, Chancellor Helmut Kohl's political prospects in West Germany suffered from high unemployment and spy revelations. The French Socialists, hurt by a weak economy and foreign policy problems, feared losing parliamentary elections in spring 1986, putting President François Mitterrand in an awkward position. The British also were getting tired of

The latest currency values are posted at a Tokyo bank. As the chart below indicates the value of the U.S. dollar was especially high early in the year and declined in the second half.

SEP. 24, 1985			
EXCHANGE QUOTATIONS			
	T.T. SELLING	T.T. BUYING	A/S BUYING
US.	229.90	227.90	227.0
STG.	330. 7	3 .	320. 3
D.M.	.84.37	82. 7	8 .
SFR	102. 3	10 .	1 .

US. CASH SELLING 231.90
BUYING 225.90

VALUE OF THE U.S. DOLLAR, 1985

	Jan. 2	March 29	June 28	Sept. 30	Dec. 30
Canada dollar	1.3220	1.3650	1.3590	1.3722	1.3972
France franc	9.7150	9.3500	9.2300	8.1805	7.5350
Great Britain pound	.8733	.8032	.7639	.7163	.6935
Italy lira	1947.00	1954.00	1928.00	1811.00	1678.00
Japan yen	251.95	250.50	248.35	216.25	200.55
West Germany mark	3.1775	3.0600	3.0355	2.6830	2.4580

high unemployment. And, faced with constant "bashing" in the West because of their large current account surpluses and highly competitive exports, the Japanese were looking for a respite. The leaders of these countries, the theory went, hoped for some relief from their troubles by speeding up their economies, even if it meant more inflation. Inflation would boost agricultural prices, putting more equity behind farm loans. Mining companies would enjoy rising metal prices. The demand for oil likely would increase, helping the Organization of the Petroleum Exporting Countries (OPEC) stabilize the price of crude. The dollar would weaken and boost commodity prices, thereby helping debtor nations service their loans. And inflation would reduce the government's flow of red ink by boosting tax revenues.

Actually, it was not so clear that the European nations would take extra measures to step up their economic pace. Largely by accident, most of Western Europe—France, Great Britain, and Italy, but not West Germany—eased monetary policy in the first half of 1985. This, economists expected, would result in a faster economic pace that, at least for a while, could trim unemployment, boost profits, and generally raise morale and the political prospects of national leaders.

In Tokyo, the ministry of finance, worried by the attacks on Japan's trade surplus, successfully attempted to boost the value of the yen by intervention on the foreign-exchange markets and by "administrative guidance." One reason for the previous weakness of the yen in relation to the dollar, despite the massive trade gap between the United States and Japan (see page 293), was the purchase of U.S. Treasury securities, corporate bonds, and other investments by Japanese pension funds and insurance companies. The money was pouring out of Japan at an annualized rate of $64.5 billion in the first seven months of 1985. On September 11, however, the ministry pointed out to these financial institutions that they were taking a "currency risk"; a stronger yen could cause them losses. Thereafter, the flow of money to the United States slowed somewhat, helping strengthen the yen.

Finance. The international capital markets continued to grow. These markets had raised an estimated $228 billion in 1984, and by the end of October 1985, total borrowing had already reached $199 billion. In addition, the capital markets were rapidly becoming more integrated and flexible. For example, the Asian Development Bank (ADB) made the first public offering of yen-dominated bonds in New York in September. The 35-billion-yen issue was equivalent to $144 million at that time. Earlier in the year, the Bank of China guaranteed more than 150 million West German marks of Eurobonds, then worth about $50 million. It was the Chinese government's first Eurobond issue.

Moreover, the capital markets were taking some loan business away from commercial

banks. Worried by the volatility of interest rates on world money markets, lenders preferred to buy securities that could be sold relatively easily. One result was that floating-rate Eurodollar bonds became more popular.

Also, underwriters developed a new borrowing technique—the Euronote issuance facility. This enables borrowers to raise effectively medium-term money (five to seven years) at the very low rates available only in the short-term money markets. The borrower issues short-term notes that are negotiable like bank certificates of deposit and can be placed with nonbank investors, such as corporate treasurers. A group of commercial banks stands ready to buy the paper at a specified price or to provide credit should the borrower be unable to find buyers for the paper when it matures. This way the borrower has the funds for the longer period. In the first eight months of 1985, $27 billion of these note issuance facilities were created, compared with $10.7 billion in the corresponding period of 1984.

Another example of capital market flexibility was seen in Philip Morris Inc.'s $5.6 billion takeover of General Foods Corporation. The deal was financed by a package involving loans from 17 domestic banks and 29 international institutions, with the foreign banks lending in dollars. Because of the massive U.S. current account deficit, foreigners were eager to find good investments for their surplus of dollars. This illustrated how corporations are increasingly shopping around the world for the cheapest or most advantageous sources of money to finance their investments or operations. Usually the most important factor is the interest rate, but there are other factors. A company might want to increase its exposure in another currency, hoping to profit from exchange-rate changes. In the Philip Morris case, the company found that foreign banks were freer to lend for a takeover than American banks were.

Trade. The volume of world trade grew by 9% in 1984, the best performance in eight years. The dollar value of trade climbed by 6%, to some $1.3 trillion. With the dollar increasing in value, trade in other currencies when measured in dollars grew more slowly. Preliminary estimates indicated that the volume of world trade in the first six months of 1985 was about 3% above that for the first half of 1984. One reason for the slower growth was the reduced economic pace in the United States and in some Asian countries. Also the volume of exports and imports by the OPEC nations fell steeply, and commodity prices weakened. An early estimate by the General Agreement on Tariffs and Trade (GATT) of the 1985 growth in world trade volume was less than 4%.

The secretariat of GATT also noted the rise of protectionist measures and other steps contravening the rules of this Geneva organization. In its annual trade report, GATT complained that market-sharing arrangements, such as those applied to Third World textile exports, Japanese automobiles, and electronics, were encumbering the international trading system.

More encouraging, after two years of haggling, the 90 member nations of GATT agreed on October 2 to open a new round of formal negotiations to liberalize world trade. Later that month a group of senior officials began examining the subjects to be negotiated. An agreement was not expected for several years. Among the more contentious issues to be resolved is the U.S. demand that the negotiations cover services, such as those provided by banks, insurance companies, consultants, engineering firms, and so on. Since tariffs are no longer such a serious barrier to trade between GATT member nations, the new round of negotiations, the eighth since World War II, will concentrate on more subtle barriers—such as subsidies, government regulations that impede imports, and informal agreements that restrict trade in sensitive areas.

At the end of September, Canada made a momentous decision to negotiate freer trade with the United States. In making the announcement, however, Prime Minister Brian Mulroney did not use the words "free trade" for political and historic reasons. Some Canadians worry about losing their national identity if ties become too close with their powerful southern neighbor; in 1911, Prime Minister Wilfrid Laurier lost an election by seeking "free trade" with the United States. Rather, Prime Minister Mulroney spoke of negotiating "the broadest possible package of mutually beneficial reductions in tariff and nontariff barriers between our two countries." Such talks could take a few years to reach a conclusion.

Commodities. Non-oil commodity prices were weak in the first half of 1985, with the International Monetary Fund (IMF) index close to its 1982 recession trough in July. Food, tropical beverages, agricultural raw materials, and metals all were weak. However, as the economic expansion ticked along in Europe and picked up in the United States during the autumn, there were signs of recovery in prices.

In the case of oil, a glut of crude weakened prices for the first nine months of 1985. This was a severe problem for OPEC, as some of its members cut their prices below the official cartel price or produced more than the cartel quotas allowed. However, just before a special meeting of OPEC ministers in Vienna in early October, Iraqi forces knocked out the oil terminal on Iran's Kharg Island. This took approximately 1 million barrels per day off the market for a time. Also, the USSR slowed its exports, and some oil companies began to rebuild inventory for the winter. As a result, crude prices strengthened substantially.

At their October meeting, the OPEC ministers had hoped to set new production quotas to

maintain prices. Saudi Arabia has long been the swing producer in OPEC, reducing output when the world market cannot absorb any more oil without the price falling. At the OPEC gathering, the desert kingdom fought to be able to pump oil at a rate closer to its OPEC quota of 4.3 million barrels per day. However, the cartel's members could reach no agreement, perhaps because the price pressure on their talks had been removed by events. Neither was there an agreement on quotas at the regular meeting in December. With the high price of oil having stimulated new production, conservation, and substitution by other energy sources, the world demand for oil remained almost constant in 1985 at about 59 million barrels per day, while non-OPEC production capacity grew. In response, at its December meeting, OPEC abandoned its pricing structure to focus on capturing a "fair" share in the world oil market.

World Debt. The major debtor nations were in the news during 1985, discussing IMF loans, rescheduling commercial debts, or complaining about austerity programs.

In late July, for example, Peru's new president, Alan García Pérez, announced that his government would limit payments on foreign debts to no more than 10% of his country's export earnings over the next 12 months while it renegotiated its $14 billion foreign debt. This prompted some concern, particularly since Cuba's Fidel Castro had invited Latin American leaders to a meeting in Havana that month to discuss the region's $350 billion in external debts. Those nations that did attend generally sent low-level officials. Latin leaders were aware that Castro was servicing his own debts while calling on them to stop servicing theirs.

The IMF in early August approved Argentina's economic austerity plan, opening the door for that country to obtain $1.4 billion in IMF funding and $4.2 billion from commercial banks. The banks later signed the deal.

In October, Brazil expressed a desire to avoid the IMF's usually strict economic austerity stipulations, wanting to assure a minimum 5% growth. With a hefty trade surplus and hard-currency reserves of about $8 billion, Brazil was in a relatively good position to bargain with the IMF.

The decline in the price of oil and a major earthquake disrupted Mexico's progress in dealing with its massive debts. Mexico figured it would need about $4 billion in fresh money in 1986 to close the gap in its international finances. This would be piled on top of the $97 billion it already owes. At the end of August, Mexico signed an agreement rescheduling $48.7 billion of that money, with payments stretched out over 14 years.

In Washington, a new U.S. Department of Treasury team led by Secretary James A. Baker determined that the debt situation was threatening political turmoil in the developing nations. And so, at the joint annual meeting of the IMF and World Bank in Seoul in early October, Secretary Baker proposed measures to step up the flow of money into the debtor nations. The trick was to devise methods of getting funds into the debtor nations without employing large amounts of U.S. government funds that would boost the budget deficit. Thus, the measures proposed by Baker were aimed at boosting loans from commercial banks and development banks (such as the World Bank) by $29 billion over the next three years. He also proposed that the IMF set aside $2.7 billion from a special fund for easy-term loans to the poorest nations, especially those in sub-Saharan Africa. The United States also indicated that it would approve a boost in the capital of the World Bank, though this would not take place until 1987. Baker also called for continued economic policy changes in debtor countries to promote long-term growth.

Economic Summit. At the 11th annual economic summit of major industrialized democracies, held in early May in Bonn, West Germany, the French delegation blocked agreement on a starting date for another round of trade negotiations. That agreement, and the start of talks, came in October. Nor did the summit participants accept a proposal by Secretary Baker for the United States to host a special international meeting on improving the world monetary system. However, the conferees did put heavy emphasis on making economic systems more adaptable and flexible. Indeed, this endorsement of the free-market, small-government philosophy of the Reagan administration by the other countries reflected a major change in attitude since President Reagan took office. "Each of our countries will exercise firm control over public spending in order to reduce budget deficits," the final communiqué said.

The Communist Nations. China moved ahead with economic reforms, extremely rapid growth, and the replacement of many aging government and party leaders with younger men and women. Meanwhile, the new leader of the Soviet Union, Mikhail Gorbachev, talked of sweeping economic reforms aimed at more efficient state control and greater emphasis on incentives to produce high-quality goods. However, there was no indication that the Soviet Union was ready to move as far as China in encouraging private initiative on farms and in factories. Indeed, if the Chinese growth rate of some 10% and the Soviet growth rate of about 3% were to extend to the year 2000, the Chinese economy would come close to matching that of the Soviet Union in size. Some observers suggested that China's progress must make the Soviets nervous.

DAVID R. FRANCIS
"The Christian Science Monitor"

IOWA

The 1985 Iowa General Assembly began the first session of the 71st Iowa Legislature in January with the Democrats in control of the Senate (29–21) and in the House (60–40). The major issue of the session was the economy. A lottery bill was enacted to increase the funds in the state treasury. Such a statute had been enacted twice in the 70th General Assembly but had been vetoed by Gov. Terry Branstad (R). However, the governor had announced before the 1985 session that he would yield to public opinion and sign a third lottery bill.

The governor's $2.2 billion budget was essentially enacted into law. In order to assure that the budget would be balanced, a number of minor taxes and fees were increased but no major tax increase was enacted. There was, however, some sentiment to again raise the sales tax one cent. The gasoline tax was increased by three cents per gallon and the 4% tax on machinery was repealed. Pay raises to state employees were limited to approximately 2% with an additional 5.5% increase assured for the 1987 fiscal year.

By October it was clear that the state's general fund was about to go into the red. Since this is prohibited by the state constitution, the governor was forced to issue an executive order that brought about an across-the-board 4% cut in all appropriations. The plans for a world trade center also were put on hold.

Agriculture. The months of April, May, June, and July were the driest in Iowa in more than 40 years. In spite of this, near-record corn and soybean crops were predicted. A harvest of 1.58 billion bushels of corn would again assure Iowa's first place in the nation in corn production. The average per acre yield was estimated at 118 bushels. The soybean crop was projected at 310 million bushels with an Iowa average of 38 bushels per acre.

The continued drop in valuation of Iowa's farmland was a major problem. In some sections of the state the value had fallen by 50% from its highest levels and in October was reported to be equal to 1970 land values. Farmers also faced problems in the fall as livestock producers were reportedly losing $100 per head on cattle. Farmers also were asserting that the price of corn and soybeans that they were receiving did not equal production costs.

On October 1, Governor Branstad issued an executive order proclaiming an economic emergency in Iowa. This brought about a one-year moratorium on all foreclosures of farmland. It was believed that this action might save as many as 10% of the 120,000 farmsteads throughout the state. (*See also* feature article, pages 36–43.)

Other. The Iowa Supreme Court handed down a $2.8 million judgment against the Iowa Department of Transportation involving a fatal

AP/Wide World

Director Ed Stanek hands out buttons promoting Iowa's new state lottery, which began operating August 22.

automobile accident. It was the largest damage award ever granted against the state.

Iowa's first pari-mutuel dog racing operation began on June 1 in Dubuque. The city-owned racing track was built with voter-approved general obligation bonds.

RUSSELL M. ROSS, *University of Iowa*

IOWA • Information Highlights

Area: 56,275 sq mi (145 753 km²).
Population (July 1, 1984 est.): 2,910,000.
Chief Cities (July 1, 1984 est.): Des Moines, the capital, 190,832; Cedar Rapids, 108,669; Davenport, 102,129; Sioux City (1980 census), 82,003.
Government (1985): *Chief Officers*—governor, Terry E. Branstad (R); lt. gov., Bob Anderson (D). *General Assembly*—Senate, 50 members; House of Representatives, 100 members.
State Finances (fiscal year 1984): *Revenues,* $4,351,000,000; *expenditures,* $4,277,000,000.
Personal Income (1984): $35,382,000,000; per capita, $12,160.
Labor Force (June 1985): *Civilian labor force,* 1,461,600; *unemployed,* 108,700 (7.4% of total force).
Education: *Enrollment* (fall 1983)—public elementary schools, 333,198; public secondary, 164,089; colleges and universities, 152,968. *Public school expenditures* (1982–83), $1,474,443,207 (3,095 per pupil).

Parliament Speaker Hashemi Rafsanjani (left) traveled to China and elsewhere to strengthen foreign relations.

IRAN

With more than five years having elapsed since the Iranian revolution, the country in 1985 seemed to have settled into the approximate stability that is the typical aftermath of revolutions. The early assumptions that the regime was inherently unstable, that it could not effectively control all of Iran's large territory, and that it would be hampered or even destroyed by internal forces of one kind or another have all proved without foundation. The threats from the *mujahedeen* on the political left and from the royalist exiles based in Paris have ceased to be credible; the *Tudeh,* the Iranian Communist party, has proved a broken reed of no particular interest even to the Soviet Union; and the threats to the territorial integrity of Iran from Kurdish or other separatist movements in the remoter provinces have alike dwindled away. The government in Tehran was in effective control of Iran, and its internal and external policies, though open to various criticisms, were far from incompetent.

If in some senses little changed in Iran in 1985, it remained true there were various hints that perhaps portended significant changes in the not-distant future. The Persian style is subtle, and it needed an attentive ear to pick up some of these signals.

Domestic Politics. The dominant figure of the dogmatic Islamic regime of Iran continued to be the Ayatollah Ruhollah Khomeini, now increasingly called by the title imam, an honorific higher than ayatollah in the Shiite Muslim hierarchy. Khomeini's exact age is unknown, but

he is in his middle eighties. However, he comes from a very long-lived family. With his previously unknown title of chief religious guide (faqih), he enjoys extraordinary authority under the new Iranian constitution, including the right to dismiss the president.

The future shape of Iranian politics became a little clearer on November 23 when it was announced that Ayatollah Hussein Ali Montazari had been formally designated as the eventual successor to Khomeini as chief religious guide. The decision was made by the 63-man Council of Experts, set up in December 1983. They were empowered to designate as successor either one man or a small panel of clergy. The succession of Montazari, 62, had long been regarded as probable. A loyal follower of Khomeini, he is thought to have shown signs of moderation in domestic matters but is an unequivocal supporter of continuing to victory the war with Iraq.

Iran's president, Mohammed Ali Khamenei, a protégé of Khomeini, was reelected on August 16 to a second four-year term. It had seemed possible he might have to face a serious challenge from Dr. Mehdi Bazargan, a secular moderate who in 1979 was the new regime's first premier. In July, however, the council of elders disqualified Bazargan on the ground that he was not a religious leader, and Khamenei was elected overwhelmingly over two opponents.

On October 28, the *Majlis* (Islamic Consultative Assembly or parliament) gave approval to premier Mir Hosein Musavi-Khamenei's new cabinet of 22 members, with some new faces but no significant changes. More surprising was the advice given by the Imam Khomeini to the new cabinet on October 31. He advised them "not to nationalize everything" and said that there was a place for committed merchants who wanted to serve the country.

One prominent and vocal opponent of excessive nationalization and something of an opponent of the premier is the speaker of the *Majlis,* the adroit and (by current Iranian standards) moderate politician Hashemi Rafsanjani. Rafsanjani's increasing importance and outspokenness—even though he has remained a close friend of Khomeini—was an interesting feature of current Iranian politics. It is evident that some degree of freedom of speech has been regained, at least by those who are within the ruling clique.

The general public, moreover, did not appear to be as totally cowed as it was in the early years of the present regime. Large demonstrations were held in April and May against the long continuance of the war with Iraq and against the clergy-dominated regime. The most extraordinary was that on May 17, when thousands of cars slowed down traffic in central Tehran. This demonstration apparently occurred in response to a radio request made

IRAN • Information Highlights

Official Name: Islamic Republic of Iran.
Location: Southwest Asia.
Area: 636,293 sq mi (1 648 000 km²).
Population (mid-1985 est.): 45,100,000.
Chief City (1982 est.): Tehran, the capital, 5,734,199.
Government: *Supreme faqih,* Ayatollah Ruhollah Khomeini. *Head of state,* Mohammad Ali Khamenei, president (took office Oct. 1981). *Head of government,* Mir Hosein Musavi-Khamenei, premier (took office Oct. 1981). *Legislature* (unicameral)—Islamic Consultative Assembly.
Monetary Unit: Rial (89.148 rials equal U.S.$1, August 1985).
Gross National Product (1984 U.S.$): $118,000,000,000.
Economic Index (1984): *Consumer Prices* (1970 = 100), all items, 658.0; food, 748.0.
Foreign Trade (1984 est. U.S.$): *Imports,* $18,500,000,000; *exports,* $15,500,000,000.

from Paris by Shahpur Bakhtiar, the Shah's last prime minister, and heard by clandestine listeners. The May 17 incident led to a few arrests, but the government made no attempt to suppress it and merely downplayed it in official comment.

Standards of Living. The demonstrators were middle class, but there was little doubt

Fresh Iranian troops assemble in Tehran before being sent to battle. The Iran-Iraq war remained stalemated.
AP/Wide World

that a mood of war-weariness was general in Iran, although the level of war casualties has been much reduced by the change to a defensive strategy in June. The middle class had much to demonstrate against. Its standard of living has been brought down sharply, and shortages of many consumer goods continued. Nor has the revolution brought much benefit to the poor. The most that can be said is that everyone has grown used to dealing with the daily difficulties, and that inflation was being kept down to about 30% per annum.

The government attempted to blame all economic difficulties on the war, but the basic problem was low productivity. However, there is no doubt Iran has foreign-exchange problems, since oil exports were running at little more than one quarter of the prewar 6 million barrels per day. In the second half of 1985 repeated bombings of Kharg Island oil terminal had threatened to reduce exports to a mere trickle. However, emergency repairs, some technical innovations, and diversion of oil to southern ports brought the figure back up to almost what it had been.

Foreign Policy. There were interesting signs that Iran was seeking to end its pariah status in world affairs. The Saudi Arabian foreign minister, at Iran's invitation, paid a landmark visit to Tehran in May. President Khamenei, moreover, has spoken of a new "open-door foreign policy." Speaker Rafsanjani traveled widely outside Iran during 1985 to create a more friendly diplomatic climate. In the most surprising development, on July 3, he called on the United States to take the initiative in restoring diplomatic relations with Iran.

ARTHUR CAMPBELL TURNER
University of California, Riverside

IRAQ

The government of Iraq remained substantially unaltered throughout 1985. The Baath (Arab Socialist Resurrection) Party has been in power in Baghdad since 1968, with Saddam Hussein Takriti as president since 1979—an impressive record of stability in a country previously plagued by insurrections and violent changes of regime. The existing National Assembly, in which the Baath Party controlled 73% of the seats, was elected on Oct. 20, 1984.

The chief element of internal division was to be found in a traditional site—in Kurdistan. There, the leader of the Kurdistan Democratic Party (KDP), Massoud Barzani, son of the great Kurdish national leader, pursued a traditional policy by forming an alliance with the government in Tehran. A series of hit-and-run raids in 1985 on police posts and other government centers in the Kurdish area proved a nuisance rather than a serious threat. The Baathist government, never gentle with rebels, con-

firmed in the fall that early in the year it had executed for treason six Kurds, ten prominent Shiites, and three Assyrian Christians.

The Economy. The Iraqi-Iranian war passed from its fifth into its sixth year in September, but the Iraqi economy seemed to be improving rather than suffering increased strain. The nadir of Iraq's economic difficulties was 1983; since then the conditions, and prospects, have grown steadily brighter. The main reasons for this were two: increased oil revenues due to increased exports and a growth in the productive capacity of heavy industry such as the production of electrical goods, fertilizers, cement, and sulfur. The government also eased the situation by extensive rescheduling of debt payments and by obliging states that want to trade with Iraq to extend credits. In addition, of course, Iraq continued to be heavily subsidized by other Arab states of the Persian Gulf sympathetic to its stand against Iranian fanaticism. It also enjoyed impartially Soviet military and economic aid and U.S. agricultural and technical assistance. U.S. aid increased in 1985, reflecting increasingly friendly relations between the two states.

The budget for 1985 passed by the National Assembly in January reflected these improvements. It envisaged an increased investment program to raise production further and increased support to keep prices of staple goods steady to ease the burdens of the poor.

Stringent new decrees were issued in February against black market activity, but this did not seem to be a major problem. Reports of observers in Baghdad indicated that the days of extreme scarcity of consumer goods seemed to be over. There were occasional spot shortages of particular items, such as eggs or imported fruits, but alternative foods were available. Even imported goods such as cigarettes, Scotch whisky, and Japanese cameras and digital watches, seldom seen in Baghdad since 1982, had reappeared in the stores by fall.

The beneficial increase in oil revenues was due primarily to the employment of a new pipeline through Turkey, which enabled Iraq in 1984 and 1985 to export some 1.5 million barrels per day—about half of the prewar flow. An additional pipeline through Turkey and one through Saudi Arabia were under construction. These were expected to enable Iraq again to approximate its prewar oil exports and to be increasingly indifferent to the fact that its Persian Gulf ports have been closed since the war began.

The resurgence of the Iraqi economy was shown not only in the growing availability of food and consumer goods, but also in the increased tempo in construction of buildings and public works, especially in Baghdad. A mood of exuberant optimism seemed to characterize the government in Baghdad, sustained by good economic news and, moreover, by the expec-

---

IRAQ · Information Highlights

Official Name: Republic of Iraq.
Location: Southwest Asia.
Area: 167,924 sq mi (434 924 km²).
Population (mid-1985 est.): 15,500,000.
Chief City (1981 est.): Baghdad, the capital, 3,400,000.
Government: *Head of state and government,* Saddam Hussein Takriti, president (took office July 1979).
Monetary Unit: Dinar (0.311 dinar equals U.S.$1, August 1985).
Gross National Product (1984 U.S.$): $27,000,-000,000.
Foreign Trade (1984 est. U.S.$): *Imports,* $13,700,-000,000; *exports,* $10,300,000,000.

---

tation that repeated attacks on Kharg Island terminal would throttle Iranian oil exports and bring Iran to the conference table. However, neither this optimism nor this expectation were entirely shared by Iraq's supporting Arab states. (*See* MIDDLE EAST.)

War casualties, of course, were a fact of Iraqi life, and public discontent from that source could certainly prove a threat to the government. Iraq, with a population only one third that of Iran, simply cannot afford to accept casualties on the same scale. But it has not had to bear them. Since 1982, Iran's strategy has been offensive, while Iraq's has been defensive. Iranian casualties, therefore, have been vastly higher. (Actual figures for either side remain unknown.) The Iranian switch to a defensive strategy in June 1985 was believed likely to result in reduced casualties for both sides.

The war occasionally has made an impact on Baghdad in the form of Iranian missile or bombing attacks. These have been sporadic and not especially destructive of life or property, though some buildings in downtown Baghdad have been damaged.

Foreign Affairs. In foreign policy, Iraq has been following an adroit and pragmatic trend that is leading to friendly cooperation with an increasing number of states. Even if the Soviet Union remains Iraq's chief arms supplier, Iraq has made a notable turn toward the West. There has been a dramatic increase in trade with Western Europe as well as with Turkey and Japan. Relations with supportive Arab states remained very good and even improved as the former Iraqi "rejectionist" stance on the questions of Israel and the Palestinians has mellowed into support of the Jordanian peace initiative. Symbolically, on March 18, when the last great Iranian mass offensive appeared to pose a serious threat, King Hussein of Jordan and President Hosni Mubarak of Egypt spontaneously flew together to Baghdad to discuss with President Saddam Hussein his military needs.

ARTHUR CAMPBELL TURNER
University of California, Riverside

IRELAND

In a courageous attempt to achieve peace, Garret FitzGerald, the Irish prime minister, flew to Hillsborough, outside Belfast, Northern Ireland, on November 15 to meet the British prime minister, Margaret Thatcher. There the two leaders signed an Anglo-Irish treaty giving the Irish Republic a formal role in consultations about the governance of Northern Ireland. Culminating months of secret talks between representatives of both governments, the treaty created the "Anglo-Irish Intergovernmental Conference," composed of cabinet ministers and other officials who would meet regularly to discuss political, legal, and security matters. The signatories also pledged to promote cooperation between the republic and the six counties of the north. In order to allay fears of a major constitutional change, the treaty reaffirmed Northern Ireland's status as an integral part of the United Kingdom until such time as a majority of those living in the north voted in favor of altering the situation. (*See also* GREAT BRITAIN.)

By agreeing to this treaty, Dr. FitzGerald risked his political future because the accord provoked Protestant militants in the north as well as the Irish Republican Army (IRA)–Sinn Fein faction to denounce what they called a "sellout." Closer to home, Charles J. Haughey, leader of the opposition Fianna Fail party, accused the prime minister of compromising the cause of Irish unity by recognizing officially the United Kingdom's legal claim to possession of the six counties. The Dail (Irish parliament) subsequently ratified the agreement by a margin of 13 votes. Prime Minister FitzGerald and his coalition government welcomed the vote.

Economy. Hoping to ease the burden of taxes on working people, Minister of Finance Alan Dukes presented a budget to the Dail on January 30 that lowered the value-added tax (VAT) on various household items. Although Dukes' plan reduced the income tax in several categories, it raised taxes on road use, gasoline, and cigarettes. The new budget also projected a decline in government borrowing from 13% of gross national product (GNP) in 1985 to 10% in 1987.

Out of the economic gloom came one piece of good news: Advanced Micro Devices, an American electronics firm, announced plans to build a new factory in Ireland costing about $175 million. When completed in 1991, this plant would employ some 1,000 workers.

The Government. In a closely fought struggle over the right of the state to legislate on questions of private morality, the government amended the Health (Family Planning) Act of 1979 so as to permit the sale of contraceptives without a prescription to anyone over the age of 18. Despite the strong opposition of the Roman Catholic Church and the Fianna Fail party to any liberalizing of the laws affecting sexual behavior, the ministry overcame several defections to win the crucial vote on February 20 by 83 to 80. Although ministers shelved plans for a national referendum on the sensitive issue of divorce, they did take steps to raise the minimum age of marriage from 14 for girls and 16 for boys to 18 for both.

The FitzGerald government scored an impressive moral as well as material victory over terrorist groups by securing the approval of both the Dail and the Senate on February 19 to an order preventing any illegal organization from using funds deposited in Irish banks. Acting on information that the Irish Republican Army (IRA) wanted to withdraw a large sum on deposit with the Bank of Ireland, the government moved swiftly to transfer control of all such accounts to the High Court. By sending to the Court almost $1,660,000 of the Provisional IRA's assets, the Bank of Ireland effectively denied these funds to the depositors. On this occasion the minister for justice described the money as derived by "extortion under threat of kidnap and murder."

Northern Ireland. Intermittent shootings and bombings in Northern Ireland during the year served as forceful reminders of the continuing conflict over the political fate of that region. Supporters of the IRA did make some substantial gains in local government elections in May, as Sinn Fein party candidates fared better than expected.

On April 30, Prime Minister FitzGerald traveled north to the city of Londonderry in the company of Foreign Secretary Peter Barry, to inaugurate a new air link with Dublin. He took advantage of this ceremony to urge voters not to support Sinn Fein candidates in the upcoming council elections. This excursion marked the first time an Irish prime minister had visited the north in 20 years.

L. PERRY CURTIS, JR., *Brown University*

IRELAND · Information Highlights

Official Name: Ireland (Eire).
Location: Island in the eastern North Atlantic Ocean.
Area: 27,136 sq mi (70 282 km²).
Population (mid-1985 est.): 3,600,000.
Chief Cities (1981 census): Dublin, the capital, 525,882; Cork, 149,792; Limerick, 75,520.
Government: *Head of state,* Patrick J. Hillery, president (took office Dec. 1976). *Head of government,* Garret FitzGerald, prime minister (took office Dec. 1982). *Legislature*—Parliament: House of Representatives (Dail Eireann) and Senate (Seanad Eireann).
Monetary Unit: Pound (0.8457 pound equals U.S. $1, Oct. 30, 1985).
Gross National Product (1983 U.S.$): $15,000,-000,000.
Economic Indexes (1984): *Consumer Prices* (1970 = 100), all items, 609.5; food, 569.6. *Industrial Production* (1975 = 100), 123.
Foreign Trade (1984 U.S.$): *Imports,* $9,663,000,000; *exports,* $9,629,000,000.

Israel's national unity government was strained but not broken in 1985. Labor's Shimon Peres (center) remained prime minister; Likud's Yitzhak Shamir (left) acted as deputy prime minister and foreign minister, and was to take over the top spot in late 1986.

AP/Wide World

ISRAEL

During 1985, disagreements over foreign policy strained the relations between the Labor and Likud members of the national unity government, although Israel's withdrawal from Lebanon removed one major bone of contention. The government managed to stabilize the economy somewhat, but it needed a substantial increase in U.S. assistance to avoid economic disaster.

Domestic Affairs. Despite Likud's threats to bring the government down because of foreign policy differences, the nine-party national unity government held throughout the year. Neither Likud nor Labor was eager for a new election; despite frequently acrimonious internal debates, compromises were found to prevent collapse of the coalition. To help alleviate tensions, an "inner cabinet" of five members each from Labor and Likud was formed in April with final say on all matters of defense, foreign affairs, and Jewish settlement in the West Bank.

Labor's position was reinforced by victory in the May elections for the 1,501 members of the Central Committee of the Histadrut labor federation. Labor won more than two thirds of the seats, an increase of 3%; Likud won less than a fifth, a loss of more than 5%. Polls conducted throughout the year confirmed Labor's lead in public opinion and wider support for its leader, Prime Minister Shimon Peres, than for Likud's Yitzhak Shamir, the foreign minister.

One issue on which there was national unity was the "ingathering" of some 10,000 Jews from Ethiopia. In January it was revealed that they had been airlifted to Israel via Sudan over several months with assistance from the United States. Once in Israel, however, they became the focus of controversy because of insistence by several orthodox rabbis that they undergo a "symbolic" ritual conversion to remove "doubts" about their Jewish origins. Many Ethiopians protested aspersions cast on their

background and staged strikes against the government and rabbinate until they were fully accepted as bona fide Jews.

Another matter that began with Likud-Labor agreement but ended in controversy was the release of 1,150 Arab prisoners in exchange for three Israeli soldiers captured in Lebanon and held by a militant Palestinian faction. Most Likud and Labor leaders agreed to the exchange, but it raised a storm in the press because of its asymmetry and because several of the released Palestinians had been convicted for murder and other terrorist acts. After the release, several Likud leaders demanded that the government balance its clemency for the Arabs with clemency for members of a Jewish terrorist ring. Some Likud leaders threatened to make the matter a test of confidence in the government, but they backed down when Peres showed determination not to connect the two issues. The Jewish terrorist trials ended in July with sentencing of 15 members of the network.

Economy. With severe austerity measures and assistance from the United States, Israel's economy seemed to stabilize by the end of 1985. In January the government, Histadrut, and manufacturers signed an eight-month wage and price agreement hailed by Peres as "almost unprecedented in a democratic society." The package called for a 7.5% decrease in worker wages within three months, required manufacturers to absorb substantial price increases, and weakened government power to make unilateral economic decisions. At the same time, subsidies on many goods and services were cut or canceled. The agreement cleared the way for unanimous cabinet approval of a $23.3 billion budget for 1985–86, a cut of nearly $2 billion from the previous year.

Because the new austerity failed to stem inflation or to end the economic crisis, the government declared an emergency in July and imposed new restrictions through emergency regulations rather than with Knesset approval. The plan included an 18.8% devaluation of the

shekel, more price increases in subsidized products, massive layoffs from public-sector institutions and companies, additional government spending cuts, and a wage and price freeze. The Histadrut strongly objected to use of emergency regulations and threatened to call a general strike. Eventually the program was approved by the Knesset, and discussions between the Histadrut and Prime Minister Peres avoided protracted labor protests.

The U.S. government praised the measures, regarding them as indications of Israel's willingness to make sacrifices in exchange for emergency assistance of $1.5 billion. Additional assistance came in a free-trade agreement, ratified in March. It was the first such agreement concluded by the United States, abolishing all protectionist measures, subsidies, and customs tariffs between the two countries over the next decade.

To help build confidence in its currency, the government issued a new shekel in September. The old shekel had fallen from 650 per dollar in January to 1,500 in July. The new shekel was worth 1,000 of the old.

By November there were signs that the government's austerity plan was beginning to work. Wages and prices were stabilized, and the value of the shekel also was holding steady. The increase in inflation slowed, exports rose, and imports declined. The uncontrolled printing of money and the policy of linking wages to the consumer price index both were halted.

Foreign Affairs. A major internal controversy was resolved by a decision early in the year to withdraw Israeli troops from Lebanon. The withdrawal took place in several stages over six months at a cost of some $60 million. Despite the withdrawal announcement, Shiite Muslim militants in southern Lebanon initiated a campaign of terror against the Israelis, resulting in ambushes of the departing troops and several assassinations. Defense Minister Yitzhak Rabin warned the Shiite guerrillas that if they persisted in their attacks he would pursue an "iron-fist" strategy. This resulted in wide searches of south Lebanese villages, a "scorched-earth" policy, and arrests and detentions of hundreds of Lebanese.

One consequence of the arrests was the hijacking of a Trans World Airlines (TWA) jetliner en route from Athens to Rome by Shiite militants on June 14. The hijackers, Shiite Muslim fundamentalists, demanded release of the prisoners held by Israel. After two weeks of negotiations, the Americans were freed, and Israel began the gradual release of its Shiite prisoners. Israel and the United States, however, denied any connection between the release of the American and Lebanese prisoners.

Although the occupation of Lebanon officially ended, several score of Israeli security advisers remained with the South Lebanese Army, a largely Maronite-officered militia that was armed, equipped, and trained by Israel to police the buffer zone in southern Lebanon.

Prime Minister Peres placed major emphasis on improving relations with Egypt, which had deteriorated into a "cold peace" since 1979. In January the two nations renewed negotiations over Taba, a disputed sliver of land adjoining the southern Israeli port of Eilat. Peres also sent Minister Without Portfolio Ezer Weizmann to Cairo on a goodwill mission in April despite Likud's opposition.

Peres won approval from Egypt and Jordan for his Mideast peace proposals. The most extensive plan was presented in his speech to the UN General Assembly in October. It called for direct negotiations with Jordan based on Security Council Resolutions 242 and 338, the formation of a Jordanian delegation to include representatives of the Palestinians, and acknowledgment of a role for the Soviet Union. The speech was considered a new departure because of the acceptance of Soviet participation in peace talks. Peres also invited Palestinian participation without directly attacking the Palestine Liberation Organization (PLO), contrary to usual Israeli policy.

But peace moves were threatened by several incidents during the year. In August an Israeli diplomat was assassinated in Cairo by a previously unknown terrorist faction; in October seven Israeli tourists were killed in Sinai by an Egyptian soldier who Cairo claimed was mentally unbalanced. In October, Israel launched an air attack on PLO headquarters in Tunis in retaliation for the murder of three Israelis in Cyprus. The raid, in which some 70 persons were killed, was condemned by Egypt and Jordan. Following an outbreak of anti-Israeli demonstrations in Cairo, President Mubarak suspended the Taba negotiations. And in late December, Jerusalem vowed revenge for Palestinian terrorist attacks against El Al travelers at Rome and Vienna airports.

DON PERETZ
State University of New York, Binghamton

ISRAEL • Information Highlights

Official Name: State of Israel.
Location: Southwest Asia.
Area: 8,000 sq mi (20 720 km²).
Population (mid-1985 est.): 4,200,000.
Chief Cities (June 4, 1983 est.): Jerusalem, the capital, 428,668 (including East Jerusalem); Tel Aviv-Jaffa, 327,625; Haifa, 235,775.
Government: *Head of state,* Chaim Herzog, president (took office May 1983). *Head of government,* Shimon Peres, premier (took office Sept. 14, 1984). *Legislature* (unicameral)—Knesset.
Monetary Unit: Shekel (1,484.00 shekels equal U.S.$1, Dec. 16, 1985).
Gross National Product (1984 U.S.$): $24,500,000,000.
Economic Indexes (1984): *Consumer Prices* (1970 = 100), all items, 179,919; food, 207,102. *Industrial Production* (1980 = 100), 116.
Foreign Trade (1983 U.S.$): *Imports,* $8,370,000,000; *exports,* $4,894,000,000.

Italy's coalition government collapsed over the ''Achille Lauro'' incident, and Prime Minister Bettino Craxi (center) tendered his resignation October 17. Weeks later, however, both Craxi and the coalition were returned to power.

AP/Wide World

ITALY

Socialist Premier Bettino Craxi (''Europe's strongman'') survived a major foreign policy crisis triggered by the Palestinian hijacking of the Italian cruise ship *Achille Lauro*. Indeed, on Nov. 15, 1985, his government set an Italian postwar record for longevity: 834 days.

Politics and Economics

Craxi versus Communists. Premier Craxi's five-party (*pentapartito*) government, composed of his own Socialists and the Christian Democrats, Social Democrats, Republicans, and Liberals, began the year by defending its anti-inflationary austerity measures. These had cut the automatic pay increases achieved by indexing of wages. The Communist Party and some of the labor unions denounced the cuts.

Regional and Local Elections. Having edged out the Christian Democrats in the June 1984 European Parliament elections, the Communists hoped to do the same in Italy's regional, provincial, and local elections in the spring of 1985. They planned then to force early parliamentary elections and demand a share in the national government. In the regional and local elections, however, held May 12–13, the Communists lost strength, trailing the Christian Democrats 30.2% to 35%. The *pentapartito* coalition got 58.1% of the vote, with Craxi's own Socialist Party accounting for 13.3%. The Republicans got 4%; the Social Democrats, 3.6%; and the Liberals, 2.2%. The neo-Fascist Italian Social Movement (MSI) polled 6.5%; the Greens (environmentalists), 2.4%; and others, 2.8%.

Several months were needed to work out the pattern of new coalition governments at the municipal and regional levels. In Rome, Christian Democrats ousted the Communists from their nine-year hold on the mayorship. Communists also lost control in Milan and Venice when their former Socialist Party allies joined the Christian Democrats. In the ''red'' region of Emilia-Romagna, Parma gained a Christian Democratic mayor, and the Communists were forced to govern alone in the cities of Bologna and Modena. In Tuscany, only Florence resisted the anti-Communist tide. With its local power base shrinking, the Communist Party appeared in danger of being deprived of influence and patronage.

Referendum on Craxi's Wage Policy. The Communists took a second drubbing June 9–10. With support from the unions, they had called a referendum in hopes of repealing the Craxi government's wage policy. But voters upheld the government's action by 54.3% to 45.7%. The anti-Communist vote was heaviest in the industrial north (59.1% to 40.9%).

Presidential Election. The seven-year term of Sandro Pertini, Italy's highly popular president, expired in midsummer. Because of his advanced age (88), the Socialist Pertini chose not to run for reelection by the Parliament. The Christian Democrats informed the Socialists that they would continue to support the Craxi government only if they could obtain the office of the presidency. Craxi agreed, and the Christian Democrats settled on Francesco Cossiga as their candidate. Only one ballot was required in the joint session of Parliament on June 24 to elect Cossiga (752 out of 977 votes).

Italy's new president (its eighth) was born in Sardinia in 1928. Trained in law, Cossiga had served twice as premier (1979–80); in 1983 he had been elected president of the Senate. Expressing the intention to be ''president of all Italians,'' Cossiga resigned his membership in the Christian Democratic Party before taking the presidential oath on July 3.

Economic Troubles. By late summer, Italy had made relative progress in coping with its economic woes. Wildcat strikes had largely ended, and inflation was down to 8%, in contrast to 10.7% in 1984. (This was still higher than Europe's average—for example, West Germany had a low 2.25%.) Italy's unemployment, on the other hand, rose from 10.4% to 12.6%, and up to 14% in the depressed south.

Italy's real GNP growth was 2.25%, down from 2.6% in 1984. The country's chief problem remained its huge public expenditures and consequent budgetary deficit—100 trillion lire, or $52 billion in 1985. This was about 16% of Italy's gross national product (GNP) (a percentage triple that of its Common Market partners). The growing trade deficit was also a serious problem.

The Craxi government was preparing to tighten its austerity program when suddenly on Friday, July 19, the lira collapsed 20% against the U.S. dollar. This fall resulted when ENI, the huge state oil company, sought to buy $125 million to repay a dollar-denominated loan.

The Common Market quickly devalued the lira by 6% and boosted by 2% the seven other currencies in the European Monetary System. The effect was to make Italian exports nearly 8% cheaper. Conversely, Italian business had to pay more for imported raw materials and technology, thus raising the specter of new inflation.

In October the Craxi government was trying to win agreement for further cuts in public spending when suddenly everything was derailed by the political fallout of the *Achille Lauro* hijacking crisis (*see* below).

Crime. The government set up special mobile police units to combat organized crime. In February a mass trial began in Naples of 639 alleged members of the Camorra organized crime group. In Milan, 72 alleged members of the Mafia were arrested on June 6. In Palermo a state of near siege occurred after the murder in August of the deputy head of the Palermo Flying Squad.

The 1981 Papal Assassination Plot. The trial of Mehmet Ali Agca and three other Turks and four Bulgarians accused of trying to assassinate Pope John Paul II in 1981 got under way in Rome in May. Agca behaved erratically and often presented confusing testimony.

Dam Collapse. On July 19 an earthen dam burst above Stava in the Dolomites. The resulting surge of water and mud buried more than 200 people and caused much property damage.

Foreign Policy

Revision of Lateran Concordat. On March 20 the Chamber of Deputies ratified a treaty revising the 1929 Lateran Concordat, which regulates church-state relations. The revision ends Roman Catholicism's status as the state religion of Italy. The vote was 350 in favor, 75 against, with 39 abstentions. The Senate had ratified the revision in August 1984.

Craxi Visit to the United States. In March, Premier Craxi made an official visit to Washington. In a speech to Congress he expressed qualified approval of the research phase of President Reagan's Strategic Defense Initiative ("Star Wars") but urged the United States to pledge that it would not violate the 1972 Anti-Ballistic Missile Treaty by deploying such a system without first negotiating with Moscow. In his talks with Reagan, Craxi warned against U.S. military intervention in Nicaragua.

Eastern Europe. In an effort to reduce tensions between East and West, Premier Craxi and Foreign Minister Giulio Andreotti mounted an Italian diplomatic foray into Eastern Europe. They visited Hungary, West Germany, Poland, and the Soviet Union. Their visit to Moscow late in May was the first by a NATO leader since Mikhail Gorbachev became the Soviet leader in March.

European Community. Foreign Minister Andreotti presided over the European Community's Council of Ministers during the first half of 1985. Italy was pleased to chair the ceremonies in Madrid on June 12 when Spain and Portugal signed a treaty of membership in the European Community, effective Jan. 1, 1986.

Somalia. In September, Craxi visited Somalia—the first Italian premier ever to visit this former Italian colony. It is the only place outside Italy where Italian is the common language.

The *Achille Lauro* Hijacking. On October 7, four Palestinian terrorists hijacked the Italian cruise ship *Achille Lauro,* with more than 400 people aboard, off the coast of Alexandria, Egypt.

Two days later, Premier Craxi announced an end to the hijacking, thanks to help from President Hosni Mubarak of Egypt and Mohammed Abbas, a Palestine Liberation Organization (PLO) diplomat. In a confused sequence of events, however, it was verified that the hijackers had murdered a 69-year-old invalid American passenger, Leon Klinghoffer, and thrown him overboard.

When President Reagan learned that Mubarak was allowing an Egyptian commercial airline to fly the four hijackers and Abbas toward PLO headquarters in Tunisia, he ordered U.S. Navy planes to intercept the aircraft. Reagan telephoned Craxi late at night on October 10, asking permission for the planes to land at the joint Italian-U.S. air base at Sigonella, Sicily. Since the planes were short of fuel, Craxi agreed. But when U.S. officials sought to fly the hijackers and Abbas to the United States, Craxi refused, insisting that Italy had jurisdiction over a crime occurring on an Italian vessel. After tense confrontation between U.S. and Italian military personnel, Reagan gave in to Craxi, who promised that the hijackers would be brought to trial.

On October 11, Italian authorities permitted the Egyptian plane with Abbas still aboard to fly on to Rome. Washington informed Rome that it had radio intercepts proving that Abbas was really the "mastermind" behind the hijacking and asked Italy to hold him for investigation and extradition. Without waiting for all

the documentation to arrive, Craxi and Foreign Minister Andreotti allowed Abbas to leave Italy for Yugoslavia. They said they had insufficient grounds to hold the PLO diplomat who was traveling on an Iraqi diplomatic passport.

Infuriated, the Reagan administration declared the Craxi government's action to be "incomprehensible." U.S.-Italian relations were strained, although in the past the Craxi government had been notably cooperative and had permitted U.S. cruise missiles to be based in Sicily. The left-wing Italian press and much of the public backed up Craxi's position.

Suddenly, however, Defense Minister Giovanni Spadolini, a former premier and the leader of the Republican Party, expressed anger that neither Craxi nor Andreotti had consulted him about the Abbas question, apparently because they felt Spadolini likely would have disapproved the decision to release Abbas. Spadolini, longtime advocate of closer ties with Israel, announced the withdrawal of his Republican Party from the government on October 16, accusing it of being soft on the PLO. It was widely known that in the late 1970s, when Andreotti was premier, a bargain had been made with PLO leader Yasir Arafat that allowed PLO personnel to pass through Italy en route to and from other countries so long as they stirred up no trouble in Italy. Craxi continued this pro-PLO tilt.

Resignation of Craxi Government. Premier Craxi went before Parliament on October 17 to set forth his version of the dispute. He announced that he was tendering the resignation of his government. President Cossiga accepted this resignation but asked Craxi to continue on as "caretaker." This was the first time in postwar Italian politics that a government had fallen over a question of foreign policy. It occurred when the 26-month-old Craxi government was only 28 days short of establishing a postwar record for longevity.

Resolution of the Crisis. As passions began to subside, President Reagan sent Deputy Secretary of State John C. Whitehead on a fence-mending mission. When Whitehead presented Craxi a conciliatory letter signed "Ron," Craxi expressed satisfaction. He announced he would be "delighted" to meet with Reagan and other leaders of the major industrialized democracies in New York, during observances of the 40th anniversary of the United Nations, the following week. There he stressed the importance of nuclear arms reductions between the superpowers.

Returning from New York, Craxi sought to persuade the same five political parties to come together again in a reinstated government. At the end of October he announced success. Spadolini, after reflection, had decided to rejoin the government on condition that Craxi sign a policy document that would call for closer consultation between the coalition parties; the doc-

---

ITALY • Information Highlights

Official Name: Italian Republic.
Location: Southern Europe.
Area: 116,302 sq mi (301 223 km²).
Population (mid-1985 est.): 57,400,000.
Chief Cities (Dec. 31, 1982): Rome, the capital, 2,834,094; Milan, 1,580,810; Naples, 1,209,086.
Government: *Head of state,* Francesco Cossiga, president (took office July 1985). *Head of government,* Bettino Craxi, prime minister (sworn in Aug. 4, 1983). *Legislature*—Parliament: Senate and Chamber of Deputies.
Monetary Unit: Lira (1,763 lire equal U.S.$1, Nov. 18, 1985).
Economic Indexes (1984): *Consumer Prices* (1970 = 100), all items, 652.6; food, 596.9. *Industrial Production* (1980 = 100), 95.
Foreign Trade (1984 U.S.$): *Imports,* $84,215,-000,000; *exports,* $73,303,000,000.

---

ument also made a small concession to the Republican Party's views on the Middle East.

By a deft constitutional procedure never before employed, President Cossiga declared that he now rescinded the resignation of the Craxi government that he had "provisionally" accepted on October 17. Speaking before the Chamber of Deputies on November 3, Craxi reaffirmed Italy's friendship with America but sharply criticized U.S. use of the NATO air base at Sigonella in the hijacking crisis. "NATO bases in Italy can be used by our allies only for specific purposes of the alliance," he declared. He also strongly defended Italy's Middle East policies. On November 6, speaking off the cuff in the Chamber, Craxi raised a new storm when he reaffirmed the "legal" right of the PLO to resort to armed struggle, even though he opposed such action. Communists and Socialists cheered him. Republicans and the extreme Right expressed disapproval.

Despite this new uproar, the Chamber gave the resurrected *pentapartito* government a 347 to 238 vote of confidence. On November 8 the Senate also voted support (180 to 102), after Craxi toned down his remarks about the "legitimacy" of Palestinian armed struggle. Thus, at last, "Europe's strongman" could turn his attention again to hammering out a 1986 budget.

Trial of the Hijackers. On November 17, after a summary trial in Genoa (which, as the *Achille Lauro*'s port, had contested jurisdiction with Siracusa, Sicily, where the hijackers landed), the four hijackers and a fifth accused confederate were convicted of gun and explosives possession and sentenced to jail terms ranging from four to nine years. They were to stand trial later for the hijacking and the murder of Klinghoffer. Two days later Italian magistrates released a list of 16 Palestinians (including those in custody) wanted for the hijacking; Mohammed Abbas headed the list.

As the year ended, terrorism struck Italy again as several travelers were attacked by gunmen at a Rome airport.

CHARLES F. DELZELL, *Vanderbilt University*

Beginning a July trip to Europe, Japan's Prime Minister Yasuhiro Nakasone (right) is welcomed in Paris by France's Premier Laurent Fabius. Later that month, Nakasone announced steps to open further Japanese markets to foreign goods. The European and U.S. reactions were cool.

JAPAN

Abroad, Japan's relations with both developed and underdeveloped nations in 1985 were dominated by the nation's record trade surplus, which in 1984 had reached a total of more than $34 billion. (See special report, page 293.) At home, Prime Minister Yasuhiro Nakasone began his second two-year term as president of the ruling Liberal-Democratic Party (LDP) with strong public support.

Nakasone originally had been boosted to power in 1983 by the support of a party faction led by former Prime Minister Kakuei Tanaka. The political scene was thrown into some confusion in February 1985 by the illness of the former prime minister. Nonetheless, in April, a Kyodo News Service survey showed that Nakasone enjoyed the highest public support (a level of 58.7%) in his 28 months in office. It seemed apparent that he would not dissolve Japan's Diet for a general election prior to expiration of his term as party president in November 1986.

Domestic Affairs

When the 102d regular session of the Diet convened in December 1984, Nakasone had sketched out a program of fiscal austerity to deal with rising public debt; administrative changes; and educational reform. Carried over from the preceding session were proposals to privatize several public industries. Among the more controversial questions of the year were defense spending and election reform.

Party Politics. After the 1983 election, the LDP had formed a government by entering a coalition with a splinter group, the New Liberal Club (NLC). In mid-1985 this coalition controlled 262 seats in the lower house of the Diet, the House of Representatives, and 139 seats in the upper House of Councillors. The chief opposition party was the Japan Socialist Party

(JSP), with 112 seats in the lower house and 42 seats in the upper house. Other parties included the Clean Government Party (Komeito), the Democratic Socialist Party (DSP), and the Japan Communist Party (JCP). Both the Komeito and the DSP continued to discuss the possibility of alliance with progressive factions of the LDP.

Within the LDP, Nakasone continued to rely on support from the powerful Tanaka faction, which embraced 123 Diet members. (In 1983, Tanaka had been found guilty of accepting bribes in the Lockheed aircraft procurement case, but he remained in the Diet and placed several members of his faction in the Nakasone cabinet. LDP Vice-President Susumu Nikaido served as acting head of the Tanaka faction.)

However, maneuvers within the LDP toward the "post-Nakasone era" already had begun in 1985, with several factions jockeying for position. Among those considered possible future leaders of the party were Foreign Minister Shintaro Abe (Fukuda faction); a former foreign minister, Kiichi Miyazawa (Suzuki faction); and Finance Minister Noboru Takeshita (Tanaka faction). On January 24 the speaker of the House of Representatives, Kenji Fukunaga, resigned. LDP Secretary-General Shin Kanemaru arranged a delicate compromise whereby Michita Sakata, who was affiliated with none of the factions, was named successor.

On February 7, Finance Minister Takeshita announced the formation of a new study group, the Soseikai, which attracted 40 members of the Tanaka faction. Takeshita's move was widely interpreted as his first step toward obtaining the prime ministership. Tanaka himself announced the move as a "defection," since it created a "faction within a faction."

Three weeks later, on February 27, Tanaka suffered a stroke. By early March his doctors had admitted that his condition was worse than had first been announced, and the former prime

minister was moved to a summer villa for rehabilitation. Nikaido, the acting faction head, appealed to LDP members to continue to seek Tanaka's political judgment. And for the moment, none of the prospective party leaders seemed prepared to make a final bid to succeed Nakasone. All were agreed, however, that Nakasone should not be permitted to amend party rules so that he could run for a third term as party president.

The Diet closed its session on June 25 without settling a controversy over public election law. On July 17 the Supreme Court ruled that the most recent election for the lower house had been unconstitutional. The court found that to win, a candidate in the most populated district had required 4.4 times as many votes as one in the least populated district. The LDP already was working on a plan, called the "6–6" plan, which would increase each of six densely populated areas by one seat and decrease each of six sparsely populated districts by one seat. On October 14 the "6–6" bill was submitted to an extraordinary session of the Diet.

Economy. The draft budget for fiscal 1985 (beginning April 1) was compiled under the strong leadership of the LDP. The party set several priorities: research on construction of new bullet-train lines, public works to increase domestic demand, and development of science and technology.

In his administrative speech to the Diet on January 25, Nakasone refused to rule out the possibility that defense spending would exceed the politically imposed ceiling of 1% of gross national product (GNP). Immediately, JSP Secretary-General Makoto Tanabe led his party in a boycott of the budget committee. In a compromise announced March 6, the LDP pledged to try to hold defense spending under the ceiling, as well as implement tax reductions for certain salaried workers, for education-related expenditures, and for the bedridden elderly.

On April 5, four days after the new fiscal year began, the Diet approved a 52.5 trillion yen (about $203 billion) budget. Partly in response to pressure from the United States, the Finance Ministry allowed defense spending to increase 5.1%, or 0.98% of estimated GNP for 1985.

For the fiscal year that ended March 31, 1985, Japan's GNP expanded 5.7%, the largest gain in 12 years. Forecasts for the fiscal year starting April 1 put the growth rate at a more moderate 4.6% (after adjustment for inflation, which in 1984 had stood at 2.2%). However, in October the government adopted measures aimed at stimulating economic growth an additional 1.27%. The measures included incentives for home construction and consumer credit and increases in public-works projects. The hope was that stimulating domestic demand would help reduce Japan's trade imbalance; but the government, faced with a long-term debt equal to 50% of GNP, stopped short of cutting taxes or increasing government spending to stimulate growth.

The government succeeded in deregulating two public corporations and drew plans for the decentralization of two others. On April 1, a private company, Japan Tobacco Incorporated, became the successor to Japan's public tobacco and salt monopoly. Lower restraints on imported cigarettes and a growing public trend to abandon smoking presented the new company with severe challenges.

Also on April 1, the old Nippon Telegraph & Telephone (NTT), a public corporation, became the new NTT Corporation (Shindenden), a joint-stock company. The government remained the sole shareholder pending release of two thirds of the stock to private investors. A planned staff reduction of one third faced stiff resistance from the 280,000 NTT union members.

The government was less successful in completing decentralization of the Japanese National Railways (JNR). In the fiscal year ending March 1984, the JNR had suffered a 1.6 trillion yen (about $6 billion) deficit and showed a cumulative debt totaling 19.9 trillion yen (about $77 billion). On July 26 a government committee recommended that the JNR be split up into 24 private companies and discontinue service on one third of its local lines. Meanwhile, on June 25, Nakasone had appointed a former vice transport minister, Takaya Sugiura, to carry out the plan for restructuring the deficit-ridden system. The government also drafted plans to privatize Japan Air Lines (JAL), a public corporation.

Social Issues. Another major issue on the Nakasone administration's agenda has been educational reform. On June 26, Michio Okamoto, chairman of the ad hoc Council on Education, presented preliminary recommendations to the prime minister. While praising the current system for its emphasis on egalitarianism, the council noted that it encouraged uniformity, placed too much emphasis on examinations, and produced students with a parochial outlook. In hearings before the council in July, Ichiro Tanaka, president of the Japan Teachers Union (Nikkyoso), attacked the proposals as designed to privatize and commercialize public education and thereby to reject the ideals of postwar educational reforms.

Equal employment rights for women were encouraged in a bill passed by the Diet in May. While the law was criticized by some groups for being "toothless," it was the first such law in Japan, which has lagged behind other industrial countries in bringing women into upper-level positions.

Japanese joined the list of victims in a rash of aircraft accidents during 1985. On June 23,

less than an hour before the loss of an Air India Boeing 747 in the Atlantic, luggage being removed from a Canadian Pacific airliner exploded at Narita International Airport in Tokyo. The blast killed two airport workers. Police surmised that the bomb was intended for transfer to an Air India flight bound for Bombay.

On August 12 a JAL Boeing 747SR, bound from Tokyo's Haneda Airport to Osaka, lost control over the sea, wandered northwest, and crashed into rugged terrain about 70 mi (110 km) from Tokyo. Only four of 524 persons aboard were rescued alive.

Although Japan's population topped the 120 million mark in March, according to the Home Ministry, the rate of growth was the lowest on record. The figure of 120,007,812 represented an increase of only 0.58% over the previous year. Of equal importance, girls born in 1984 were expected to live for 80.18 years, the first time in world records that the 80-year mark was topped in any population group. Life expectancy for Japanese males born in 1984 rose to 74.54.

On October 4, Tokyo was hit by its most severe earthquake in 62 years. The quake, which measured 6.2 on the Richter scale, shook buildings and halted trains but did little damage. Few injuries and no deaths were reported.

Expo '85. After five years of planning, the Tsukuba International Exposition (Expo '85) opened on March 17 at Tsukuba, a "science city" that already housed government research institutes. The official theme of Expo '85 was "Dwellings and Surroundings—Science and Technology for Man at Home." There were more than 100 pavilions, many sponsored by other nations and international organizations, as well as theme and history exhibits mounted by the host government. The total cost of the fair exceeded $2.5 billion. (*See also* page 79.)

Foreign Affairs

At the summit meeting of advanced industrial democracies held in Bonn, West Germany, May 2–4, Prime Minister Nakasone encountered criticism of Japan's towering trade surplus, import restrictions, and government procurement policy. While trade questions dominated U.S.-Japan relations—as they did policy toward the European Community (EC) and members of the Association of Southeast Asian Nations (ASEAN)—Japan's expanding influence as a world power was felt in other areas as well.

United States. After their election successes in 1984, Prime Minister Nakasone and President Ronald Reagan met in Los Angeles on January 2. The two leaders discussed, aside from pressing trade issues, Japan's understanding of the U.S. Strategic Defense Initiative

AP/Wide World

In the worst accident ever involving one plane, a Japan Air Lines 747 crashed outside Tokyo, killing 520 persons.

(SDI), known also in Japan as the "Star Wars" system. Back in Tokyo on January 6, Nakasone insisted that the system is defensive in character—involving conventional, not nuclear, arms—and that in cooperating, Japan must take into account its constitution, government policy, and a 1969 Diet resolution against the military use of space. On February 14 he told the Diet that Japan would follow existing agreements on Japan's transfer of high technology for military use. On May 2, in Bonn, Nakasone attached a condition for cooperation: that "Star Wars" must not alter the balance of power between the superpowers.

Meanwhile, on January 29, Vice Foreign Minister Nobuo Matsunaga was appointed ambassador to Washington. On arrival, he stated that his hardest task would be to head off protectionist moves in the U.S. Congress.

By September the United States had deployed, under the U.S.-Japan security treaty, a squadron of F-16 fighter-bombers to the American base at Misawa, Aomori prefecture. A second squadron was to arrive in 1987. Widely noted in the Japanese press, the deployment was described as a step to offset the Soviet military build-up to the north of Japan.

USSR. Although Japan normalized relations with the Soviet Union after World War II, the two powers have yet to sign a peace treaty, chiefly because of Japan's objection to continued Soviet occupation of the lower Kurile Islands. On March 4, when Nakasone was in Moscow to attend the funeral of Soviet leader Konstantin Chernenko and to meet the new leader, Mikhail Gorbachev, he again raised the question of what Tokyo calls the "northern territories" issue. Gorbachev refused to discuss the problem. However, later in the year, the

AP/Wide World

Tokyo demonstrators call for the return of the "Northern Territories," seized by the Soviet Union in 1945.

Soviets proposed talks on a peace treaty as well as on stimulating trade (which had dropped to $3.9 billion in 1984 from $5.2 billion in 1981) and on Asian security. On June 6, Japan gave the Soviets a revised draft treaty for cultural exchange. Talks on that subject had been suspended seven years earlier.

East Germany. On June 12, Foreign Minister Abe met with State Council Chairman Erich Honecker of East Germany, in Berlin. The two expressed hope for closer bilateral relations, for world peace, and for disarmament. Abe was the first Japanese cabinet minister to visit East Germany.

China, Korea, Oceania. On March 27, LDP Vice-President Nikaido left Tokyo for a week's visit to China. Thirteen years before, he had accompanied Prime Minister Tanaka on a trip to Beijing (Peking) designed to normalize relations with the People's Republic.

On July 31 in Tokyo, Foreign Minister Abe signed with his Chinese counterpart, Wu Xueqian, a nuclear-power cooperation agreement. The treaty stipulated that activities under the pact would be limited to peaceful uses of energy and that nuclear facilities would be regularly inspected by the International Atomic Energy Agency (IAEA).

Following a trip to South Korea, Chairman Yoshikatsu Takeiri of the Komeito met with Chinese senior leader Deng Xiaoping on August 1 at the resort city of Beidaihe. Takeiri delivered a message from South Korean President Chun Doo Hwan expressing hope that China would use its influence to keep peace in the Korean peninsula. (Tokyo normalized relations with Seoul in 1965 but has had only informal contacts with North Korea. China, in contrast, has had diplomatic relations with North, but not with South, Korea.)

In January, Japan lifted sanctions imposed on North Korea for the 1983 terrorist bombing of South Korean leaders in Burma. A North Korean press delegation, led by Kim Gi Nam, editor of *Rodong,* arrived in Tokyo on April 18. In talks with his host, JSP Chairman Masashi, Kim expressed hopes for improved ties between Pyongyang and Tokyo. Kim, also a member of the central committee of the Workers Party, was the highest-ranking North Korean leader to visit Tokyo since the sanctions were imposed.

Elsewhere in the Pacific region, Prime Minister Nakasone made an eight-day tour of Australia, New Zealand, Papua New Guinea, and Fiji, January 13–20. The trip was designed to promote the concept of Pacific basin cooperation. Foreign Minister Abe, at an ASEAN meeting in Kuala Lumpur in July, stated that complete withdrawal of Vietnamese troops from Cambodia would be a nonnegotiable condition of any Japanese-supported peace plan for that country.

The Middle East. Irani Foreign Minister Mojitaba Mirmehdi met with Nakasone and Abe on March 15 and 19 and asked Japan to bring about a truce in the Iran-Iraq war. Japan's subsequent appeal for a cease-fire was rejected April 1 by Iraqi Foreign Minister Tariq Aziz, who stressed that Iraq was committed to a comprehensive peace plan. Tokyo also evacuated some 250 Japanese citizens from Iran, where Japan has had extensive oil development interests.

Whaling. Japan announced on April 5 that it would withdraw its objection to the International Whaling Commission (IWC) ban on commercial whaling and would give up the activity in March 1988. The step was a response to a U.S. law that sharply reduces the quota of fish caught in American waters for any nation that does not follow the IWC ban.

See also feature article, page 56.

ARDATH W. BURKS, *Rutgers University*

JAPAN • Information Highlights

Official Name: Japan.
Location: East Asia.
Area: 143,750 sq mi (372 313 km²).
Population (March 1985): 120,007,812.
Chief Cities (Oct. 1, 1983 est.): Tokyo, the capital, 8,361,054; Yokohama, 2,893,421; Osaka, 2,624,911; Nagoya, 2,099,830.
Government: *Head of state,* Hirohito, emperor (acceded Dec. 1926). *Head of government,* Yasuhiro Nakasone, prime minister (took office Nov. 1982). *Legislature*—Diet: House of Councillors and House of Representatives.
Monetary Unit: Yen (205.1 yen equal U.S.$1, Nov. 8, 1985).
Gross National Product (1985 U.S.$): $879,000,-000,000.
Economic Indexes (1984): *Consumer Prices* (1970 = 100), all items, 265.0; food, 263.5. *Industrial Production* (1980 = 100), 117.
Foreign Trade (1984 U.S.$): *Imports,* $136,492,-000,000; *exports,* $170,132,000,000.

Japanese–U.S. Trade

"Japanese–United States ties are in a crisis situation." That's what Susumu Nikaido, vice-president of Japan's ruling Liberal Democratic Party, said in September 1985 after a meeting of senior government officials and party leaders to discuss measures for defusing an explosive trade dispute between the two nations. American officials were making similar assessments of Japanese–U.S. relations.

What troubled Washington was Japan's huge trade surplus with the United States and its view that Japan was treating imports unfairly. In 1984, Japan's excess of exports over imports amounted to nearly $34 billion. Forecasts of the surplus for 1985 ran approximately $50 billion, as the Japanese automobiles, steel, consumer and industrial electronics, and other manufactured goods pouring across the Pacific far exceeded in dollar volume the U.S. farm products, logs and lumber, computers and other high-tech goods, pharmaceuticals, aircraft, and other manufactured goods heading in the opposite direction.

The Japanese viewed their nation's surplus as the result of two factors: an overvalued U.S. dollar, making their products relatively inexpensive, and the better quality of their goods—not unfair trade practices. Nonetheless, they knew that America's trade problem could quickly become their own trade problem if it gave birth to a protectionist wave of legislation in the United States.

Japan is the largest trading partner of the United States after Canada. It is the second-largest economic power in the world after the United States. Most economists would regard a genuine trade war between the two nations as a serious threat to world prosperity. Indeed, concern in both capitals went beyond trade or economic issues to geopolitical considerations. The United States does not want to drive Japan closer to the Soviets by economic or political pressures, and Japan does not want to alienate its military protector and ally, the United States. As 1985 wore on, both President Ronald Reagan and Japanese Prime Minister Yasuhiro Nakasone came under increasing pressure to "do something" about their mutual trade problem. "Japan-bashing has become a national pastime," noted Ed Crane of the Cato Institute in Washington.

The U.S. Senate took a shot across the Japanese bow in March 1985 by approving, 92–0, a nonbinding resolution calling on the president to take steps against Japan to remedy the trade imbalance. Many legislators hold that Japan grossly restricts imports. And though experts point out that Japanese tariffs and quotas are no worse than those of most other important American trading partners, there is a more difficult question as to the significance of other restrictions on imports, termed "nontariff barriers."

At first the Reagan administration resisted the growing protectionist pressures in Congress. On March 1, for example, President Reagan announced that he would not seek an extension of the existing "voluntary" restraints on Japanese auto imports so as to spur free trade "for the benefit of the world's consumers." Though enjoying hearty sales themselves, some U.S. automakers and their employees' union, the United Auto Workers of America, wanted continued protection from the Japanese onslaught of Toyotas, Nissans, and other cars. The administration undoubtedly expected the Japanese to exercise some restraint on auto exports, and when some congressmen and industry officials raised a storm over the Reagan announcement, the Japanese government did impose its own nonnegotiated quotas. Tokyo said it would limit auto exports to the United States to 2.3 million units, an increase of about 24% from the previous level of 1.85 million.

The storm over the Japanese surplus in the United States did not die, as some in the U.S. auto industry argued that Japan's car export quotas were raised too high. But as the months rolled by, American consumers did benefit, as the president predicted, when premiums charged by some dealers on Japanese cars shrank or disappeared as shortages of the vehicles eased.

In an attempt to head off the trade storm in the United States, the Japanese on July 30 announced an "action plan" for improved foreign access to the Japanese market. Many skeptics in the United States asked if this was any different from six prior Japanese trade liberalization programs. The Japanese maintained that it was special in that it went beyond just a statement of principles and detailed specific steps that would be taken over three years. Moreover, defenders of the program noted, Prime Minister Nakasone pledged that its implementation would be overseen at the highest political levels to prevent bureaucratic foot-dragging. Nakasone even went on television to urge the Japanese people to buy more American goods.

The "action plan" included a variety of measures to overhaul Japan's restrictive standards, testing, and certification procedures, long regarded as a serious obstacle to many imports. Other sections called for the reduction or elimination of tariffs on 1,850 agricultural and

On April 9, Prime Minister Nakasone announced long-awaited measures to open up Japanese markets to more imports.

industrial products in 1986, expanded opportunities to sell to the government, and additional financial and capital market liberalization.

In Washington, the program received a cool reaction. Legislators were looking for immediate results, not pledges. Congress resumed its consideration of more than 300 bills restricting imports in some way or another. Japanese businessmen and policymakers wondered if U.S. companies would actually commit themselves to entry into the Japanese market, even if it was opened up more to imports.

In any case, by autumn Japan's politicians and businessmen felt it necessary to consider immediate measures to reduce the nation's trade surplus. These included an effort to step up domestic demand, thereby bringing in more imports; a $10 billion issue of "Nakasone bonds" in the world market, a measure intended to increase the value of the yen; an international conference to discuss stabilization of the yen-dollar relationship and other exchange rates; and an acceleration of the program to cut tariffs and simplify import procedures. In mid-October the government announced a series of incentives to stimulate the nation's economic growth rate, a move long urged by the United States as a way of curbing Japan's trade surplus. At the United Nations on October 23, Nakasone said that Japan would boost its foreign aid to a total of $40 billion from 1986 to 1992.

One reason for the continued weakness of the yen against the U.S. dollar during the spring and summer (while such other major currencies as the German mark and British pound strengthened sharply) was a flood of Japanese investments in the United States and elsewhere. Indeed, by the end of 1985, Japan was expected to become the world's largest creditor nation, with assets exceeding liabilities by perhaps $120 billion. Japanese officials were urging their nation's insurance companies and other investors to slow down their investments abroad. This had some effect.

President Reagan on September 6 attempted to calm the troubled waters by threatening to veto protectionist legislation, asking Congress to work with him to devise "a freer and fairer trading system," and launching investigations into unfair trade practices. Later that month he announced export subsidies for some goods in an effort to open foreign markets. And in talks in New York in late October, he and Prime Minister Nakasone agreed on the need to keep the yen strong.

As the year closed, Japan replaced a system of quotas on leather imports with a system of tariffs. Since the quotas were against the rules of the General Agreement on Tariffs and Trade, Japan offered the United States compensation by easing the way for imports of $236 million more in American goods. But the United States indicated that it would nonetheless impose tariffs on imported Japanese finished leather products. The incident was a sign that both the trade dispute and the trade gap between the two industrial powers would continue.

David R. Francis

JORDAN

Because of its efforts to resolve the Arab-Israeli conflict, Jordan figured prominently in the news in 1985.

Jordanian-PLO Accord. The Palestine National Council (PNC) convened its 17th congress, in Amman, in November 1984. It moved its headquarters from Damascus to Amman and elected a new PNC president and a new executive committee of the Palestine Liberation Organization (PLO), chaired by Yasir Arafat. This marked a new relationship between King Hussein of Jordan and Arafat's PLO, culminating in the accord of Feb. 11, 1985. This landmark accord included three important provisions: (1) the PLO accepted the formation of a confederation of Jordan and Palestine (East Bank and West Bank), thus dropping its former demand for an independent sovereign state; (2) the peace-negotiations team would include the PLO "within a joint Jordanian-Palestinian delegation"; and (3) the PLO accepted the basic principle of the peaceful settlement of the Arab-Israeli conflict, instead of seeking to achieve its objectives through armed struggle.

The Peace Initiative. During his visit to the United States in May, Hussein outlined his plan for four-stage Arab-Israeli talks. The first stage would involve preliminary talks between U.S. and joint Jordanian-Palestinian delegations, excluding PLO representatives; the second stage would add PLO representation to another meeting of the two sides. The third stage would be an international conference including the USSR, and the final stage would see direct Arab-Israeli negotiations.

Hussein's plan for Arab-Israeli negotiations contained elements calculated to appeal to all parties concerned in the conflict, but satisfying none completely. The first two stages of the plan are essential to obtain the support of the PLO, without which Hussein cannot proceed with his negotiations because Palestinians constitute a majority of his kingdom's population. Israeli Prime Minister Shimon Peres, however, strongly objected to those preliminary sessions between U.S. and Jordanian-Palestinian delegations, which could be construed as *de facto* U.S. recognition of the PLO. The third stage of the plan attempts to placate the Soviet Union, and especially its client-state Syria, which has been adamantly calling for an international conference. Peres has accepted a modified formula for convening an international conference linking participation of the USSR to the resumption of diplomatic relations between the latter and Israel. Finally, the fourth stage—direct negotiations between a Jordanian-Palestinian delegation and Israel—satisfies the basic demands of both Israel and the United States and harmonizes with the Camp David agreements as well as with the peace treaty between Israel and Egypt.

Two incidents occurring in October hampered the peace process. In retaliation for the slaying of three Israelis by Palestinians in Cyprus, Israel bombed the PLO headquarters in Tunisia on October 1. This act, ironically, may have increased Arafat's legitimacy; it did not undermine him. The other incident, the Palestinian hijacking of the Italian cruise ship *Achille Lauro,* did test Arafat's credibility with respect to his implicit acceptance of UN Security Council Resolutions 242 and 338 (acknowledging Israel's right to exist), which Hussein had claimed during his U.S. visit in May. Arafat tried to repair the damage in his Cairo declaration of November, which confines the PLO's operations to Israeli-occupied territories.

Jordanian-Syrian Rapprochement. As the peace process came to a standstill, Hussein tried to improve his relations with Syria. He already had prepared the ground for such an eventuality by appointing, on April 4, a new prime minister, Zaid al-Rifai, known to have good relations with Syrian President Assad. In November al-Rifai visited Damascus and met with Assad, to prepare for the visit Hussein made to Damascus on December 30. In this process of rapprochement, Hussein, in order to placate Assad, was obliged to admit that the fundamentalist Muslim Brothers had operated against Syria from Jordanian territories, without his knowledge. Concomitantly, Jordan took measures to stem the rising popularity of the Muslim fundamentalists in Jordan itself.

King Hussein had two major objectives in effecting a rapprochement between himself and President Assad. The first was to ward off the Syrian-sponsored, anti-Arafat groups who were responsible for the assassination in December 1984 in Amman of a member of the PLO executive committee as well as for numerous attacks against Jordanian diplomats abroad. The second objective is to put pressure on Arafat to be more forthcoming in his acceptance of UN Resolutions 242 and 338—and on the Palestinian representation on the joint Jordanian-Palestinian delegation.

MARIUS DEEB, *Georgetown University*

JORDAN • Information Highlights

Official Name: Hashemite Kingdom of Jordan.
Area: 37,737 sq mi (97 740 km^2), includes West Bank.
Population (mid-1985 est.): 3,600,000.
Chief Cities (Dec. 1983): Amman, the capital, 744,000; Zarqa, 255,000.
Government: *Head of state,* Hussein ibn Talal, king (acceded Aug. 1952). *Head of government,* Zaid al-Rifai, prime minister (appointed April 4, 1985). *Legislature*—Parliament: House of Representatives and Senate.
Monetary Unit: Dinar (0.36810 dinar equals U.S.$1, Dec. 30, 1985).
Economic Index (1984): *Consumer Prices* (1975 = 100), all items, 126.2; food, 118.4.
Foreign Trade (1984 U.S.$): *Imports,* $2,784,000,000; *exports,* $752,000,000.

At the winter meeting of the National Governors' Association in Washington, Gov. John Carlin of Kansas, right, chats with Senate Majority Leader Robert Dole, also of Kansas, left, and economist Alan Greenspan.

AP/Wide World

KANSAS

The Kansas economy showed the effects of the continued agricultural depression through bank failures and loan problems for individual farmers and a number of banks. (*See also* feature article, pages 36–43.) Heavy rains in central and eastern Kansas in mid-October threatened the fall harvest and caused flooding in a number of communities.

Agriculture. The 1985 wheat crop was the third largest on record and consisted of 444.6 million bushels, though the average yield per acre was 38 bushels, down 3.5 bushels from the record set in 1983. The crop was grown on 11.7 million acres (4.7 million ha) and was harvested considerably ahead of normal, due to mild temperatures and adequate rainfall. A record harvest of sorghum, corn, and soybeans was predicted, but heavy rainfall across the state in mid-October dampened prospects.

In spite of good production, prices for Kansas farm crops hit a seven-year low in September. The all-farm products index was the lowest it had been since May 1978. The price of wheat was 77 cents less and corn 78 cents less than it was in September 1984.

Bank Failures. The slumping agricultural economy contributed to the failure of 11 banks in Kansas through October 1985, and a number of others with delinquent loans were threatened. Generally the banks were located in small agricultural communities, and the failures were caused by poor agricultural loans. In most instances, individual depositors were protected by the Federal Deposit Insurance Corporation, and all but four of the 11 banks that failed in 1985 were purchased and reopened.

Legislation. The legislature dealt with a variety of issues in 1985. Gov. John Carlin signed a bill legalizing multibank holding companies in Kansas after it narrowly cleared the Kansas House. The bill set a limit of $2.8 billion on the maximum size of bank holding companies, among other restrictions. A bill prohibiting underground disposal of hazardous waste was passed, affecting all companies producing more than 55 lbs (25 kg) of waste per month. For the fourth time in six years, Governor Carlin, a Democrat, vetoed a capital punishment measure sent him by the Republican-controlled legislature. The House failed to pass a constitutional amendment allowing pari-mutuel betting, though Kansans will again vote on a constitutional amendment to allow liquor by the drink in the November 1986 general election.

KANSAS • Information Highlights

Area: 82,277 sq mi (213 098 km²).
Population (July 1, 1984 est.): 2,438,000.
Chief Cities (July 1, 1984 est.): Topeka, the capital, 118,945; Wichita, 283,496; Kansas City, 160,468.
Government (1985): *Chief Officers*—governor, John Carlin (D); lt. gov., Thomas R. Docking (D). *Legislature*—Senate, 40 members; House of Representatives, 125 members.
State Finances (fiscal year 1984): *Revenues,* $3,363,000,000; *expenditures,* $2,974,000,000.
Personal Income (1984): $32,300,000,000; per capita, $13,248.
Labor Force (June 1985): *Civilian labor force,* 1,287,700; *unemployed,* 57,200 (4.4% of total force).
Education: *Enrollment* (fall 1983)—public elementary schools, 282,389; public secondary, 122,833; colleges and universities, 141,709. *Public school expenditures* (1982–83), $1,131,758,425 ($3,058 per pupil).

Nuclear Energy. During 1985 the Kansas Corporation Commission (KCC) held rate hearings related to the $3.05 billion Wolf Creek nuclear energy plant located near Burlington, Kansas. The plant, owned by the Kansas Gas and Electric Company (KG&E) of Wichita; the Kansas City Power and Light Company (KCP&L) of Kansas City, Missouri; and the Kansas Electric Power Cooperative, Inc., of Topeka, began commercial operations in September. The three utility companies had requested a combined rate increase of $508.5 million to recover construction costs. The KCC cut their request by more than half to $212.2 million. The commission cited imprudent management leading to cost overruns and an unneeded excess generating capacity as reasons for the cut. The ruling affects an estimated 1 million consumers, primarily in the Wichita and Kansas City areas, whose utility bills are expected to increase more than 36.7% over the next three years. KG&E and KCP&L, each of which owns 47% of the plant, appealed.

PATRICIA A. MICHAELIS
Kansas State Historical Society

KENTUCKY

For the second year in a row, the major issue facing Kentucky political leaders was the effort to improve the quality of education in the state—particularly at the primary and secondary level. There was growing concern not only that Kentucky was lagging behind other states in the region, but that this lag was hurting the state's efforts to attract new business and industry.

Funding for Education. In 1984, Gov. Martha Layne Collins had failed to win legislative approval for higher taxes to improve education. In July 1985 she called a special session of the legislature and won its approval for higher funding for education and increased taxes to pay for it. The legislature overwhelmingly approved a $306 million package of improvements for education, slightly more than the governor had requested. Most of the spending would not take effect until the 1986–88 fiscal biennium.

Pay increases for teachers represented a large part of the package—annual increases of 5%, extra pay for longevity, and a small bonus for teachers with satisfactory evaluations. A proposed career ladder for teachers was set as the subject of a two-year pilot study.

Part of the educational funding was expected to come from economic growth. The rest was to come from a $215 million package of increased taxes on business, including higher corporate license fees and a repeal of anticipated investment-depreciation tax breaks. The governor failed, however, to win a five-cent-a-gallon increase in the gasoline tax to improve the state's highways.

Higher Education. While the state gave priority to primary and secondary education, leaders of higher education expressed concern that funding for the state's universities lagged behind those in other states.

The Council on Higher Education spent most of the year trying to develop a plan to streamline and rationalize the higher education system, in part by avoiding unnecessary duplication of programs. Because of the high costs of medical and professional programs, the council developed proposals for eliminating one of the state's two dental schools and one of its three law schools. By the end of the year, however, the council gave in to a variety of pressures and abandoned its plans to shut down such programs. It continued to develop plans for establishing centers of excellence, or "Commonwealth centers," in particular fields at various universities.

Politics. There were no statewide elections in Kentucky in 1985, but preparations were already under way for the 1987 governor's race, with every indication that it could be an unusually crowded one. While Lt. Gov. Steven Beshear was developing his campaign and former Gov. Julian Carroll was dropping hints about running, John Y. Brown—the most recent former governor—gained widespread attention and perhaps a position as front-runner early in the fall when he told the press that he expected to run again in 1987.

Other. In May a coal truck driver was shot and killed in an ambush in eastern Kentucky. The incident was linked to an eight-month-old strike by United Mine Workers against companies that did not endorse the union contract.

Louisville's Humana Hospital Audubon—the site of various artificial heart transplants—continued to draw national attention. The hospital's new $45 million headquarters, designed by Michael Graves, opened early in the year. (*See also* ARCHITECTURE.)

MALCOLM E. JEWELL, *University of Kentucky*

KENTUCKY • Information Highlights

Area: 40,409 sq mi (104 660 km²).
Population (July 1, 1984 est.): 3,723,000.
Chief Cities (July 1, 1984 est.): Frankfort, the capital (1980 census), 25,973; Louisville, 289,843; Lexington-Fayette, 210,150.
Government (1985): *Chief Officers*—governor, Martha Layne Collins (D); lt. gov., Steven L. Beshear (D). *General Assembly*—Senate, 38 members; House of Representatives, 100 members.
State Finances (fiscal year 1984): *Revenues,* $5,448,000,000; *expenditures,* $5,358,000,000.
Personal Income (1984): $38,347,000,000; per capita, $10,300.
Labor Force (June 1985): *Civilian labor force,* 1,714,400; *unemployed,* 141,300 (8.2% of total force).
Education: *Enrollment* (fall 1983)—public elementary schools, 454,931; public secondary, 192,483; colleges and universities, 146,503. *Public school expenditures* (1982–83), $1,233,797,475 ($2,100 per pupil).

Kenneth Matiba, Kenya's minister of culture and social services, welcomes delegates to Forum '85, a series of workshops preceding the United Nations Decade for Women Conference held in July in Nairobi.

AP/Wide World

KENYA

The consolidation of power by President Daniel arap Moi, student unrest, and a papal visit were highlights of the year in Kenya.

Presidential Power. President Moi increased his hold on power in new elections for the Kenya African National Union, KANU, the sole legal party. The June 1985 voting saw pro-Moi candidates overwhelmingly successful. The elections were accompanied by a major party recruitment drive that brought in 4 million new members. This success was tainted by massive coercion and by the requirement that all civil servants join KANU and pay the party an annual fee out of their salaries, or lose their jobs. The result was to further fasten party control on what had been East Africa's most democratic nation.

A sign of Moi's increased confidence was his granting a pardon in December 1984 for Charles Njonjo, a former cabinet minister and once Moi's chief rival. Njonjo had been broken politically by charges and trial for alleged corruption and involvement with a 1982 coup attempt. The pardon showed Moi's belief that he now had no political rivals within Kenya.

Student Unrest. The government continued its crackdown on student unrest, an aftermath of student support for the 1982 coup. In March, 14 students of the University of Nairobi were given six-month jail terms for holding illegal demonstrations, in which one student was killed by troops who broke up the protests. In April, another student was sentenced to a year in jail; three others were fined; and a fifth was acquitted. That same month, the university opened after a two-month closure. It later was divided up into separate colleges to hinder school-wide student organization and activity.

Economy. The Kenyan economy continued to stagnate in 1985, and the shilling was devalued. Crops were devastated by an infestation of army worms that destroyed more than 7,000 acres (2 835 ha). The economy also was hurt by Kenya's out-of-control birthrate, which increased population by 4.1% a year.

The new District Focus for Rural Development Program gave more decision-making power to local areas in place of central planning controls.

Visitors. As part of his African journey in August, Pope John Paul II attended the Eucharistic Congress in Nairobi, the first ever held in Africa. The pope was received warmly, though his strong opposition to birth control did not sit well with the government, which is trying to cope with the world's highest birthrate.

Kenya also was host to the United Nations Decade for Women Conference in July (*see* WOMEN).

ROBERT GARFIELD, *DePaul University*

KENYA • Information Highlights

Official Name: Republic of Kenya.
Location: East Coast of Africa.
Area: 224,960 sq mi (582 646 km²).
Population (mid-1985 est.): 20,200,000.
Chief Cities (1979 census): Nairobi, the capital, 827,775; Mombasa, 341,148.
Government: *Head of state and government,* Daniel arap Moi, president (took office Oct. 1978). *Legislature* (unicameral)—National Assembly, 170 members.
Monetary Unit: Kenya shilling (16.181 shillings equal U.S. $1, June 1985).
Gross Domestic Product (1983 U.S. $): $5,500,000,-000.
Economic Index (1983): *Consumer Prices,* (Nairobi, 1972 = 100), all items, 387.2; food, 360.6.
Foreign Trade (1983 U.S. $): *Imports,* $1,361,000,-000; *exports,* $980,000,000.

KOREA

Continuing consultations between South and North Korea highlighted the year's developments, climaxing in the first reunions of divided families in 40 years.

Republic of Korea (South Korea)

South Korea experienced its most active political year since 1960, as opposition political elements and student dissidents posed new challenges to the authoritarian government of President Chun Doo Hwan.

Politics and Government. In preparation for the February 12 parliamentary elections, the opposition succeeded in rapidly founding and consolidating the genuinely strong New Korea Democratic Party (NKDP). Many politicians—who recently had been released from political bans or who had defected from the semi-opposition parties abundantly created by the Chun government in 1980—flocked to this new political organization.

On February 8, opposition leader Kim Dae Jung returned from exile in the United States accompanied by 37 foreign sympathizers, including two American congressmen. Kim's return was given international publicity because his group was assaulted by Korean security agents. Public sympathy for Kim may have given added impetus to the opposition, which subsequently received a majority vote in the February elections. Because of divisions in the opposition, however, and a manipulative system of apportioning seats, the government party retained control. The previous main opposition Democratic Korea Party, fatally weakened by the NKDP, was then absorbed almost completely into the new party, which saw its parliamentary strength grow to 102. Although a small third party remained, a two-party system had essentially been reborn.

The start made seemed broadened by the postelection appointment of a liberal prime minister, Lho Shin-yong, by cooperation between opposition leaders, and by the release of the last chief politicians from political restraints on March 6. Kim Dae Jung's house arrest was lifted, though his suspended 1980 sentence still kept him from formal political participation. Firm government control of the Assembly, however, blunted all major opposition demands for restoration of Kim Dae Jung's civil rights, release of political prisoners, and for constitutional revisions permitting freer direct elections. The frustration of the opposition was exacerbated after October by the indictment of two opposition assemblymen for alleged participation in a student demonstration, by the failure to elect the NKDP designee as Assembly vice chairman, and by unilateral passage of the budget by the government party on December 2.

Outside the Assembly, South Korea's most widespread political problem throughout the year lay in unrelenting student violence. Student agitation was directed chiefly against the government and what dissident leaders called the "five bandit" accomplices of the government—generals, economic technocrats, business conglomerates, the controlled press, and the police. About 4,000 student rallies took place throughout the country between April and July alone. The government's December 1983 policy of keeping police off campuses, first breached in the reoccupation of Seoul National University on Nov. 15, 1984, was progressively abandoned. In early September, police were empowered to enter campuses at will to subdue demonstrations with increasingly powerful tear gas.

Pressure on the campuses also was increased by government attempts to connect student activism with Communist influence. Several smaller arrests culminated—but did not end—in the July 18 arrest of 56 "core workers of the Sammin Struggle Committee," most of whom were elected student representatives. On July 27, plans for a drastic Campus Stabilization Law were publicized. The law featured extralegal reeducation of "left-leaning" student activists in "purification camps" and the closing of universities "plagued with incessant student activism." Massive student, political, and public opposition caused the government to delay the draft law's submission to the Assembly, but its potential threat continued.

On May 27, more than 70 students occupied the Seoul United States Information Service Cultural Center for 72 hours, vainly seeking an official apology for the American role in the May 1980 Kwangju massacre. The students eventually left peacefully, but 25 of them were arrested. Twenty students were sentenced in October to 3–7 years' imprisonment after an emotional trial in which all 21 defense attorneys resigned in protest.

SOUTH KOREA • Information Highlights

Official Name: Republic of Korea.
Location: Northeastern Asia.
Area: 38,031 sq mi (98 500 km^2).
Population (mid-1985 est.): 42,700,000.
Chief City (Oct. 1984 est.): Seoul, the capital, 9,501,413.
Government: *Head of state,* Chun Doo Hwan, president (formally inaugurated March 1981). *Head of government,* Lho Shin-yong, prime minister (appointed Feb. 1985). *Legislature*—National Assembly.
Monetary Unit (886.8 won equal U.S.$1, August 1985).
Gross National Product (1983 U.S.$): $75,300,000,000.
Economic Indexes (1984): *Consumer Prices* (1975 = 100), all items, 620.2; food, 691.1. *Industrial Production* (1980 = 100), 158.
Foreign Trade (1984 U.S.$): *Imports,* $30,631,000,000; *exports,* $29,245,000,000.

The anti-American tone of this seizure reappeared in the autumn when proposed U.S. legislation restricting Korean imports caused demonstrations. On November 4, another student two-hour occupation of the Seoul American Chamber of Commerce struck a similar note. And on December 2, nine students briefly seized the U.S. Cultural Center in Kwangju.

Economic Developments. The South Korean economy caused disappointment and worry throughout the year. The gross national product (GNP) growth target of 8% was repeatedly reduced. First-half growth of 3.2% rose weakly to an indicated annual growth of 4–5%, a figure that is half that of the 1984 level. (*See also* feature article, page 56.)

Mounting world protectionism affecting nearly half of South Korea's exports, plus growing Chinese and other competition, held exports close to the 1984 level of $29.2 billion instead of a targeted 10% growth. Imports fell by 5.5%, however, reducing the current account deficit slightly. A decline in construction projects in the Middle East trimmed the number of overseas workers from 1981's 170,000 to 110,000 and reduced earnings by $540 million to $772 million. Foreign debt rose above $45.4 billion. Combined with $6 billion in overseas loans by Korean companies abroad, the total rose above $51 billion, a record indebtedness in Asia and the third highest in the world. Interest on the debt reached some $4 billion, a burden that was increasingly becoming a political issue. South Korea retained, however, a good international reputation for servicing its debt, as well as using debt constructively. The government started to open new opportunities for imports and foreign investment.

The economic disappointments of 1985 appear, however, to presage mounting difficulties with future export growth as world protectionism increases and the South Korean wage advantage decreases. Concern also began to focus on South Korea's family-controlled conglomerates, 10 of which generate more than 60% of the South Korean industrial GNP. Decreases of some 25% in profits threatened the more indebted companies. In February the Kukje Group, the sixth- largest conglomerate, collapsed under the weight of debt. Banks suffering losses from bad debts also required government support measures and pump priming.

The year 1985 also saw an undertone of labor violence against restrictions on free and representative union activity. An "illegal" strike at Daewoo Apparel was ended by force on July 11, an action that elicited sympathy strikes. A strike in Daewoo Motors, more amicably resolved, was the first to hit heavy industry. Mounting arrests and dismissals, moreover, marked the year's second half.

Despite disappointment, the year saw a great deal of progress. Trade cooperation was expanded with Pakistan, Bangladesh, the

AP/Wide World

South Korean dissident Kim Dae Jung (left) returned from exile but was barred from formal political activity.

Netherlands, Guinea Bissau, Libya, and Indonesia. Joint ventures were concluded between Samsung and Chrysler, and Daewoo and General Motors. Indirect trade with China grew toward the $1 billion level. Two thermal and one large nuclear plant were dedicated, together with roads, another Han River bridge, and a major dam in Ch'ungju. On October 18 the opening of two new subway lines essentially completed Seoul's 73-mi (116.5-km) subway network, the world's seventh longest.

Finally, with a per capita GNP of $2,010 and an $80 billion GNP, South Korea's economy now exceeds that of Denmark and approaches those of Belgium and Switzerland. Millions of South Koreans prosper.

International Relations and Security. President Chun Doo Hwan's April 25–27 visit to Washington was cordial but unproductive and was seen as disappointingly underpublicized outside South Korea. The annual joint "Team Spirit" troop exercises throughout February, March, and April successfully engaged the cooperation of 200,000 American and Korean troops but may have affected contact between the two Koreas. Periodic estimates were made that North Korean military forces were both increasing and being positioned farther forward. The sinking of a North Korean espionage ship and the smuggling from the United States and prompt deployment in North Korea of 87 Hughes helicopters helped unite the United States and South Korea. Trade frictions and, to a smaller extent, political freedom restrictions increasingly divided the two governments.

Relations with Japan were unusually cordial, marred only by a periodic reimposition of a fingerprinting requirement, which agitated

the 670,000-strong Korean population in Japan and its sympathizers in both Koreas.

Successful visits of foreign delegations to Seoul had chiefly economic results. But careful effort resulted in gradual consolidation of Seoul's position as the 1988 Olympic Games site—for socialist as well as nonsocialist nations. At the United Nations' 40th anniversary in October, Seoul again bid for admission of both Koreas over, however, Pyongyang's opposition. Seoul also raised its tally of diplomatic ties slightly, to 124.

A Chinese hydrofoil torpedo boat that inadvertently entered Korean waters on March 22 following a shooting incident among the crew was returned after a Chinese apology. The crew of a Chinese bomber that crash-landed on August 24 had to be divided, with a defecting pilot sent to Taiwan and a radioman to China. Seoul's handling of the incidents reflected its desire to increase relations with Beijing (Peking).

Unification. Relations between the two Koreas made progress in four channels: economic and trade talks; Red Cross talks; interparliamentary talks; and sports talks.

Trade discussions started most promisingly on November 15, 1984, with reinstallation of a hot line and receptiveness regarding many avenues for trade and economic cooperation, including restoration of the severed Pusan-Sinuiju railroad. Planned December talks were postponed by the unexpected November 23 defection through Panmunjom of a young Soviet trainee. Four soldiers were killed in the resulting shooting. On January 9, North Korea further delayed these and all other talks until the end of the South Korean–United States "Team Spirit" exercises. The talks resumed on May 17 at Panmunjom, but North Korea merely proposed formation of a higher-level joint economic committee of nine members headed by deputy prime ministers; specific trade issues were evaded. At a third meeting on June 20, both sides agreed in principle on a trade and economic cooperation accord. The September 18 meeting broke down over further North Korean insistence on forming six subcommittees to which trade proposals should be submitted. And a meeting on November 20 failed to produce an accord, lowering expectations.

Red Cross talks initiated November 20, 1984, on the working level suffered similar delays. The first full-dress Red Cross discussions in 12 years resumed May 28–30, however, reaching agreement in principle to exchange divided family members and art troupes. Working-level groups on July 15 and 19 reconfirmed this decision in greater detail, but the North Korean delegation limited divided families to Seoul and Pyongyang. The ninth full-dress Red Cross talks convened again August 26–29, this time in Pyongyang for the first time since 1973. Unfortunately, the negotiations broke down

when South Korean delegates walked out of militaristic exercises staged for them in Pyongyang's stadium. Nevertheless, on September 21–23, 151 South and 151 North Koreans traveled to each others' capitals. Art troupes performed in Seoul and Pyongyang, and 65 families—35 in Pyongyang and 30 in Seoul—were briefly reunited, 35 others being untraceable. A Christian service—the first since 1950—was also held in Pyongyang. Enormous emotional publicity was generated on the southern side, rather little on the northern side. Though vast differences in viewpoint were apparent, these meetings were seen as the greatest inter-Korean positive achievement since Korea's division in 1945. No further progress was made in a full Red Cross meeting in December.

In April, North Korea proposed parliamentary talks with the South's National Assembly. On July 23 and again September 25, a small working group from each Assembly met. North Korea pushed for a nonaggression pact, which Seoul's assemblymen thought the executive branch should initiate. South Korea proposed a drafting committee to start work on a new pan-Korean Constitution, a project that was not desired by the North.

An abortive inter-Korean sports meeting was also held in May and rescheduled for late in the year in Lausanne, Switzerland. Meanwhile, President Chun called in June for a joint Korean sports team for the 1988 Olympics in Seoul. In late July, however, Pyongyang called for joint hosting of the Olympics in North and South on a 50–50 basis, an idea quickly rejected by Seoul. Pyongyang continued to denounce locating the Olympic Games in Seoul. Calls by President Chun for a summit meeting with Kim Il Sung were disregarded.

Democratic People's Republic of Korea (North Korea)

Little unusual activity broke the opaque surface of North Korean development in 1985 except for progress in contacts with Seoul.

Politics and Government. The consolidation of Kim Jong Il as successor to his 73-year-old father, President Kim Il Sung, advanced steadily under a plume of rising adulation. The increasing influence of somewhat younger civilian and military leadership presumed close to the younger Kim brought him to apparent day-to-day civil and military control, although a final transition may not be completed for several years. Kim Il Sung continued in apparent health, though his domestic "on the spot" inspections seemed greatly reduced. With the death of Albania's Enver Hoxha, Kim became the senior world political leader and chief of state in the Communist world. Meanwhile, Kim Jong Il had yet to justify his incessant political mythologization with a clearly etched program and personality.

Economic Developments. On February 17 the results of the Second 7-Year Economic Plan (1978–84) were announced in customary positive tones: a 220% increase in gross industrial production (12.2% per annum) and attainment of the 10 million-ton grain production goal, achievement of which would allow a large exportable surplus. In the absence of specific statistics, however, such claims carried little conviction.

Pyongyang's 1985 budget of W27,384,000,000 (estimated at U.S.$11.5 billion), a modest 4.31% increase over 1984, may well imply economic growth of roughly similar proportions to an estimated GNP of $17.76 billion—if one accepts South Korean valuations of the North Korean won. The 14.6% of the budget officially allocated for the North's military—which Western sources place closer to 23%—explains much of the sluggishness. Despite this percentage, the South's military expenditures greatly exceed the North's.

North Korea's trade—a tiny fraction of South Korea's—continued to increase, especially with the Soviet Union, but Pyongyang still had little success in lowering or better servicing its $2–3.5 billion foreign debt. Ironically, the North's trade with China is now less than the South's. The post-Mao economic direction in China still appeared to have little influence on Pyongyang. The *People's Daily* reported, however, that North Korea's collectivized agriculture plans to allow each farmer a small plot for freely marketable produce.

Security. Kim Il Sung's trip to Moscow early in 1984 and a late November Pyongyang trip of Soviet Deputy Foreign Minister Kapitsa resulted in Soviet promises to sell to North Korea MiG-23 fighter aircraft, T-72 tanks, and a new combat helicopter. Roughly two dozen of the expected 50 MiGs reportedly arrived from May on.

Western sources gave varying estimates—from 780,000 to 880,000—of increased North Korean forces. With three times the South's tanks and assault guns, North Korea was believed to have assembled highly mobile strike forces in forward positions, with stockpiles for 60–90 days' fighting. Conditions continued relatively quiet, however, except for the capture on February 5 of two South Korean fishing boats with 21 crew members, all returned by early March, and the sinking of a North Korean spy boat near Pusan. North Korea continued to export arms to Nicaragua and the Middle East and, on July 8, was branded by President Ronald Reagan as one of five nations conspiring in a "confederation of terrorist states" that had carried out "outright acts of war against the United States." On July 29, however, Pyongyang agreed to several U.S. security details in Panmunjom. And in December, North Korea joined the 1968 nuclear nonproliferation treaty.

International Relations. Visits from and to Moscow—including Foreign Minister Kim Yong Nam's August 16–23 visit—arms transfers, and public pronouncements all indicated increased North Korean reliance on the Soviet Union. A surprise visit of Kim Il Sung to Beijing (Peking) in late November 1984 and of Chinese General Secretary Hu Yaobang to Pyongyang in early May no doubt sought to reassure China. Relations with both socialist and Third World nations remained active.

GREGORY HENDERSON, *Harvard University*

In the first civilian exchange between North and South, delegations of 151 crossed the border on September 20.

AP/Wide World

NORTH KOREA • Information Highlights

Official Name: Democratic People's Republic of Korea.
Location: Northeastern Asia.
Area: 46,768 sq mi (121 129 km²).
Population (mid-1985 est.): 20,100,000.
Chief Cities (July 1980 est.): Pyongyang, the capital, 1,445,000; Hamhung, 780,000.
Government: *Head of state,* Kim Il Sung, president (nominally since Dec. 1972; actually in power since May 1948). *Head of government.* Kang Song-san, premier (took office Jan. 24, 1984). *Legislature* (unicameral)—Supreme People's Assembly. The Korea Workers' (Communist) Party: General Secretary, Kim Il Sung.
Gross National Product (1984): $19,600,000,000.

LABOR

Persistent unemployment and its consequences continued to dominate free-world labor developments in 1985. One study by the International Labor Organization put at 1 billion the number of new jobs that would be needed by the end of the century to keep pace with burgeoning world population.

United States

Employment in the United States reached an all-time high of 109.6 million civilian workers in 1985. Another 1.6 million were serving in the armed forces. That amounts to a record 60.3% of the total population at work.

The new secretary of labor, William E. Brock III (*see* BIOGRAPHY), appointed in March, reported that the economic rebound from the bitter recession of 1982 had brought with it 10 million new jobs. Of that total, however, 8 million were in service-producing industries, and only 1.3 million were in manufacturing. All those new jobs were not enough to make serious inroads into the number of unemployed. Throughout 1985, 7% of the work force were hunting jobs every week. On average, an unemployed worker took nearly 16 weeks to find employment. Another 1.2 million workers were listed as so discouraged that they had stopped looking for jobs. Almost 5.5 million others were working at reduced incomes, unable to find full-time work.

AFL-CIO. Despite the rebounding economy, the decline in union membership preoccupied leaders of the AFL-CIO when they met in biannual convention at Anaheim, CA, in October. The meeting marked the 30th anniversary of the 1955 merger of the American Federation of Labor and the Congress of Industrial Organizations. In 1955, every third worker in the United States belonged to a trade union. In 1985, that number had dwindled to fewer than one in five (18.8%).

In convention, AFL-CIO leaders saw their movement weakened by the flight of industrial plants to warmer, nonunion climates or to foreign, low-wage countries; threatened by the influx of foreign, imported goods; and hampered, since 1981, by a hostile administration in Washington, DC. Self-examination was the theme of the 1985 convention. The executive council submitted vigorous calls for change, buttressed by the findings of two nationwide polls of union members (done by the Louis Harris and Peter Hart organizations).

The 782 delegates ratified policies and programs based on a new concept of the U.S. labor movement as it existed in 1985. Its characteristics: a majority of U.S. union members work in salaried, white-collar, and technical jobs, a minority (less than 40%) in hourly paid, blue-collar jobs; union workers are better edu-

AP/Wide World

As the AFL-CIO turned 30, President Lane Kirkland was concerned about the decline in U.S. union membership.

cated than the general population, with a higher proportion of high school and college graduates; union workers are less likely to see work as a straight economic transaction and are more likely to see it as a means of self-expression; union workers earn an average 33% more than their nonunion counterparts.

AFL-CIO President Lane Kirkland defined the union constituency as "the working middle class." Six weeks later at the University of

Largest AFL-CIO Unions
(in thousands)

1955		1985	
1. Autoworkers	1,260	State, County & Municipal Employees	997
2. Steelworkers	980	Food & Commercial Workers	989
3. Carpenters	750	Autoworkers	974
4. Machinists	627	Electrical Workers	791
5. Electrical Workers	460	Service Employees	688
6. Ladies Garment Workers	383	Carpenters	609
7. Laborers	372	Steelworkers	572
8. Hotel & Restaurant Employees	300	Communications Workers	524
9. Railway Clerks	264	Machinists	520
10. Meat Cutters	263	Teachers	470

Source: 1985 Report of the AFL-CIO Executive Council. The two largest U.S. unions, the Teamsters (1,523) and National Education Association (1,444) are unaffiliated.

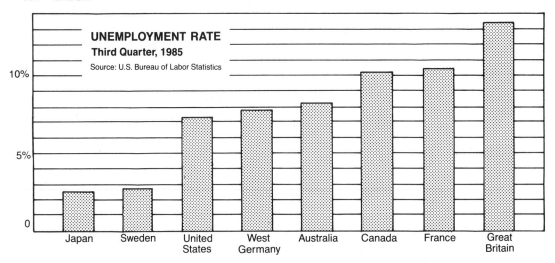

UNEMPLOYMENT RATE
Third Quarter, 1985
Source: U.S. Bureau of Labor Statistics

Japan / Sweden / United States / West Germany / Australia / Canada / France / Great Britain

Minnesota he explained: "The composition of our membership shows that we are nothing more—and nothing less—than the American middle class."

The change in the type of unions that dominate the AFL-CIO reflects changes in the U.S. work force. Whereas 30 years ago the largest unions were in manufacturing, in 1985 the biggest were organizations of public employees and employees in the service industries.

Labor-Management Relations. Evidence that a new day in labor relations was dawning for management as well as union leaders appeared in a unique, written agreement worked out by General Motors (GM) and the United Auto Workers (UAW). It will cover about 6,000 future GM employees at GM's new Saturn plant to be located at Spring Hill, TN. The plant is expected to produce 500,000 small, front-wheel drive cars using robotics and the latest computerized equipment to cut the $2,500-per-car cost advantage enjoyed by Japanese competitors.

GM and the UAW agreed to revolutionary changes in employment practices, including: elimination of the time clock, with all employees on salaries rather than hourly wages; job classifications will be cut from dozens to a single classification for all production workers, and to three to five for skilled workers; employees will work in 6- to 15-person teams, each responsible for its own maintenance, inspection, health, safety, and absenteeism; profits and productivity will be rewarded with bonuses; all employees will be treated alike regarding benefits, cafeteria, parking, entrances, and identifications; the union will have representatives on all plant committees for work unit, business unit, manufacturing complex, and corporation; and the right to strike or lock out remains, but slowdowns are banned. The agreement, approved by the UAW executive board, was branded "a sellout" by a few old followers of the late Walter Reuther.

Earnings. Most labor-management negotiations dealt with more traditional issues. Management pressure for wage cuts and other concessions continued in some industries. Annual lump sum payments replaced cost-of-living indexes in some settlements. Two-tier wage rates—with wages for new hires substantially lower than those already at work—became more common.

The Bureau of National Affairs reported a median first-year wage increase of 37 cents an hour (3.8%) in agreements negotiated through the first 46 weeks of 1985. This figure was about the same as the previous year. In construction, the median increase over the same period was 40 cents an hour (2.8%), compared with a zero median, equivalent to a wage freeze, a year earlier.

Real average weekly earnings for the entire work force actually declined by 0.2% from October 1984 to October 1985. Increases were offset by a 3.3% increase in the consumer price index. Actually, the low inflation rate for 1985 was the best since 1967.

Overtime. Congress amended the Fair Labor Standards Act (FLSA) to permit local and state governments to reach advance agreements with their employees to substitute compensatory time off for overtime pay after 40 hours a week. Compensatory time must be computed at the same time-and-one-half basis as cash payments. The issue had been in dispute since 1974, when Congress extended the FLSA to cover public employees.

Strikes. With hiring offices besieged by job applicants, strikes were few in number and quickly settled. The Bureau of Labor Statistics recorded that 50 strikes began in the first 11 months of 1985. That figure is nine fewer than in all of 1984 and an all-time record for industrial peace.

The year's most notable stoppages involved: Chrysler Corporation, National Automobile Transport Association, United Airlines,

American World Airways, Wheeling Pittsburgh Corporation, Hotel Association of New York, the Alliance of Motion Picture and Television Producers, and Yale University. First the machinists and, later in the year, the air line pilots ended their two-year strike against Continental Airlines.

Unions. The only union merger in 1985 united the 31,000-member Upholsterers with the Steelworkers, raising the latter's membership to 603,000. Five unions elected new presidents during 1985. At the Communications Workers, Morton Bahr, the union's vice-president, succeeded Glenn E. Watts who retired. Juel Drake, the secretary-treasurer of the Iron Workers, took over the organization leadership, succeeding John H. Lyons who retired. Jesse M. Calhoun retired as head of the Marine Engineers and was replaced by the vice-president, C. E. Fries. The Operating Engineers saw the retirement of J. C. Turner and the rise of Larry C. Dugan, former vice-president. John E. Lawe succeeded the late William G. Lindner as president of the Transport Workers. Late in the year, Albert Shanker announced his retirement as president of the United Federation of Teachers; he would stay on as president of the American Federation of Teachers.

International

Canada. Despite an economic upturn and a decline in immigration, 10.3% of Canada's work force was unemployed. The economy grew at a rate of 5%, the highest since 1976.

Trade union membership has been rising since 1980. In 1985 it reached 3,660,000, or 38.9% of the work force. Membership in the Canadian Labour Congress stood at 2,120,000. The rival Canadian Federation of Labour claimed 225,000.

Labor history was made in September when Canadian auto workers withdrew from the U.S.-based UAW to form UAW Canada. The separation agreement gave UAW-Canada 5% of the total assets of the UAW, $2.7 million worth of real estate, and $30 million from the UAW strike fund. Starting with 135,000 members, UAW Canada launched an aggressive organizing campaign. The 4,500-member Canadian Airline Employees Association was the first to affiliate.

Employees of Eaton's department store in Manitoba scored a first when the Manitoba Labour Board imposed on the management a "fair collective agreement" after it refused to sign an agreement with the union. Also in Manitoba, the legislature voted to require the public sector to set up a system of evaluating pay levels. The stated purpose was to determine possible discrimination against women in violation of the principles of comparable worth.

An unusual collective agreement covering 7,000 employees was reached between the Steel Workers Union and Inco Ltd., the world's largest producer of nickel. In addition to raises and employee benefits, the pact indexed wages to the world price of nickel.

Great Britain. Unemployment continued at a depression level of 13.5% of the work force. Inflation, however, moderated to an annual rate of 6%.

The year-long coal miners' strike ended in March without settlement of the main issue—the government's plan to close 20 uneconomic mines. Ten years earlier a similar strike had brought down the Conservative government of Edward Heath. The National Union of Miners (NUM) lost this time because of a world glut of energy fuels and dissension among the miners. Because of disagreements within the union membership, coal production continued in some fields. The break in miners' ranks led to secession. In October, miners in Nottinghamshire voted 17,750 to 6,972 to form a new union to challenge the NUM throughout Britain.

United Airlines' 5,000 pilots struck from May 17 to June 15 over a two-tier wage system and back-to-work issues.

AP/Wide World

NUM President Arthur Scargill, working with miners' organizations in the Soviet Union, Eastern Europe, Iran, and Syria, accepted the presidency of a newly formed International Federation of Mining and Energy Workers (IFMEW). The IFMEW intends to challenge the Miners International Federation for the allegiance of miners in the free world. Another consequence of the unsuccessful miners' strike has been fewer and shorter strikes in Great Britain. The railway union called off a strike against the London Regional Transport after one day when the majority of its 15,000 members showed up for work.

A more serious threat to the unity of British unions arose from the provisions of the 1983 Trade Union Democracy Act. That law requires a mail ballot of union members before a strike can be called and offers financing to help defray the expense. The Trade Union Congress (TUC) urged its affiliated unions to refuse such financial assistance and threatened to expel the million-member Engineers Union when it accepted such help. The powerful Electricians Union threatened to leave the TUC with the Engineers. Expulsion was postponed when the Engineers agreed to resubmit the question of financial assistance to another ballot.

The Trade Union Democracy Act required the unions to submit to mail ballot the continued use of union funds for political purposes. British trade union members voted their overwhelming approval. The main beneficiary is the Labour Party. In 1984, union contributions accounted for 80% of the party's total income.

France. The economy, having slowed down following social and economic reforms in 1981, began to pick up. Government austerity measures moderated inflation, and unemployment fell to 10% of the work force late in the year.

The French automobile industry—whether nationalized like Renault or privately owned like Peugeot—was hard hit. Both lost money during the previous three years largely because they were overstaffed. Efforts to cut back the number of workers—through attrition, early retirement, or government bonuses—failed, as did a policy of offering government bonuses to guest workers from North Africa and Portugal to induce them to return to their homelands.

Renault anticipated a loss of $1.6 billion in 1985 and was trying to reduce its staff of 98,000 by 20%. A protest strike by the Communist trade union CGT failed when police forcibly removed strikers from the LeMans plant. A one-day general strike, called by the same union on October 24, disrupted some train and port services, but most workers stayed on the job.

Federal Republic of Germany. In 1985 the reduction in working hours, fought for so bitterly a year earlier, remained an issue in collective bargaining in most industries. As a result, the regular workweek was shortened from 40 hours to 39 or 38. Some reductions to 37 hours were scheduled for 1989—in home construction, for example. Some unions—textiles, paper, oil and gas, chemical, energy, food, restaurant, and banking—opted for earlier retirement rights rather than a shorter workweek.

Legislation by the Bundestag (parliament) allowed employees to retire at age 58, on 65% of their retirement benefit, until they reach retirement age. If the retiree is replaced, the government reimburses the employer for 35% of the retirement pay. The law became effective on May 1, 1984, and will continue until 1988. In its first year, nearly 100,000 employees sought early retirement and were replaced with 80,000 new employees.

In spite of the shorter workweek and early retirement, unemployment continued high, with more than 7.9% of the work force hunting jobs. The inflation rate remained at 2.2%. Union membership stood at 7,660,000, or 42.2% of the work force.

Sweden. The worst labor conflict in five years occurred in May, when 20,000 members of the big civil service union struck for a 3.1% retroactive salary increase. The government answered by locking out 80,000 civil servants, mostly teachers. The strike paralyzed air traffic, exports, rail-freight transport, and other civil services. After 18 days the government and union agreed on a 2% salary increase, effective in December.

Unemployment moderated to 2.5%. In August, inflation was running at nearly 7%.

An agreement between the employers' federation (SAF) and the major union federation (LO, PTK) provided for more cooperation to improve productivity and profitability. In turn, employees and unions were promised more information and more participation in decision making.

Japan. Labor's annual spring offensive, known as *Shunto,* began in March with a joint-union demand for a 7% wage increase. It ended in May with an agreement for an increase of 4.97%, slightly more than in 1984. Because of increases in living costs and higher taxes, standards of living remained unchanged. Union demands for a shorter workweek met stiff management resistance and had to be dropped. Union membership amounted to only one third of the Japanese work force, but the results of *Shunto* bargaining were traditionally extended to nonunion workers.

Unions fought a government plan to partition and/or privatize the National Railway. The Labor Ministry published a white paper reporting that the number of women workers had reached 15,160,000. That is more than the number of housewives not gainfully employed outside the home.

Unemployment stood at a low of 2.5%, inflation at less than 1%.

GORDON H. COLE and JOSEPH MIRE

LAOS

An improved economy could not reverse the flow of refugees from Laos in 1985. The government improved relations with the United States but remained closely aligned with the USSR and Vietnam.

Politics. Premier Kaysone Phomvihan, 64, remained unchallenged as leader of an increasingly moderate Laotian government, but there was limited armed resistance in remote areas. In April, rebel artillery fire in the northwest downed a military helicopter and caused the death of the deputy defense minister and army chief of staff.

Refugees crossed the Mekong River into Thailand at the rate of 1,000 per month despite Thai efforts to discourage them. Most were urban middle class rather than the hill-dwelling tribesmen of earlier refugee movements.

Economy. The economy continued to improve as the country produced 1.2 million tons of rice, somewhat more than needed by the Laotian population. Coffee, maize, sugarcane, cotton, and tobacco yields also were good. Salaries for government employees in Vientiane remained low—$14 per month plus some fringes for middle-level civil servants. Small private business is allowed, and various foreign goods remain available, even if high priced and smuggled. Earnings of private merchants were three times those of government workers.

Hydroelectric power sold to Thailand was the leading export, accounting for 90% of foreign-exchange earnings.

Collectivization, which had been abandoned after its failure in the late 1970s, would not be renewed, said Deputy Premier Phoumi Vongvichit. Some 80% of agricultural output was produced on small private farms, but the government bought very little rice, allowing growers to trade the crop for consumer goods.

Foreign Relations. Relations improved markedly between the United States and Laos, the only Communist-ruled Indochinese government with which Washington had diplomatic ties ten years after the Southeast Asian war. In February, U.S. and Laotian personnel worked side by side near Pakse in southern Laos to search for the remains of 13 lost U.S. airmen from a military aircraft that crashed there 12 years earlier. In July, Washington confirmed that indeed the remains had been recovered.

LAOS • Information Highlights

Official Name: Lao People's Democratic Republic.
Location: Southeast Asia.
Area: 91,430 sq mi (236 804 km²).
Population (mid-1985 est.): 3,800,000.
Government: *Head of state,* Souphanouvong, president. *Head of government,* Kaysone Phomvihan, chairman. *Legislature* (unicameral)—National Congress of People's Representatives.
Gross National Product (1983 U.S.$): $525,000,000.

According to the Laotian vice foreign minister, the joint activity suggested "possibilities for more cooperation in the future." And there were moves in the U.S. Congress to have Laos removed from the list of countries ineligible for American aid.

Nevertheless, Laos remained closely aligned with Vietnam and the Soviet Union. Vietnamese troops in the country numbered about 40,000, along with some 3,000 Soviet advisers.

RICHARD BUTWELL
California State University, Dominguez Hills

LATIN AMERICA

After three years of virtually unrelieved gloomy news about the Latin American economies, analysts in 1985 began to find some positive developments in the hemisphere.

In the early fall, both the Inter-American Development Bank (IDB) and the World Bank issued new studies that were at least partially upbeat in their appraisals of the region. The IDB, in its annual Report on Economic and Social Progress in Latin America, found that "The favorable performance of the world economy in 1984 helped reverse the downtrend of the Latin American economy in the previous three years. The 3.1% increase in the gross domestic product (GDP) of the region, which was slightly higher than population growth, raised per capita GDP by 0.6%, after a cumulative fall of 10% in 1982–83." The IDB noted gains in agriculture and manufacturing but attributed a large part of the 1984 economic improvement to increased demand for imports in the United States and Japan, which made exports "the most dynamic component" of the region's GDP.

The World Bank, in its annual report, concurred that Latin American exports expanded substantially in 1984 and added that the increase "made possible a simultaneous increase in imports, a further strengthening of the region's trade surplus, and an accumulation of international reserves." According to the Bank, some 85% of the export increase went to the United States.

Debt. Both the IDB and World Bank warned, however, that debt service remains Latin America's principal problem. The IDB report noted that the external debt situation was somewhat relieved in 1984 by the "more flexible attitude on the part of creditor governments and financial intermediaries." Nonetheless, more capital continues to flow out of the region than enters it. The net financial outflow in 1984 amounted to $29 billion.

Throughout 1985, Latin American leaders repeatedly expressed concern about the political consequences of the rigid austerity programs they have been forced to impose in order

to honor repayment obligations. The consensus was that the harsh economic adjustment process has prevented a massive default on Latin America's $360 billion foreign debt, but that the adjustment has been made at the cost of significant damage to future growth and development prospects.

Evidence of austerity was seen throughout Latin America. Chile canceled a subway expansion project in Santiago. Mexico cut government payrolls. Venezuela raised prices and slashed imports. Peru restricted imports of products ranging from perfume to baby carriages. Argentina froze wages and prices and introduced a new currency.

The signs of unease also were widespread. In February the foreign ministers and finance ministers of the 11 most indebted Latin American countries met in the Dominican Republic and issued a call for lower interest rates and more favorable repayment terms in order to avert political and social chaos. In his inaugural address in July, Peru's new president, Alan García Pérez, said Peru would limit interest payments on its $13.7 billion debt to 10% of what it earns from exports. About the same time in Havana, Cuban President Fidel Castro held his own debt conference to urge Latin nations to declare a moratorium on repayments.

In October the Reagan administration appeared to respond to the Latin calls for a new approach to the debt problem. Speaking to the annual meetings of the World Bank and the International Monetary Fund, Treasury Secretary James Baker said that the United States was changing the emphasis of its response to the debt crisis. Henceforth, Baker said, the United States would seek ways to spur long-term Third World economic growth and to relax rigid austerity programs.

Trade. A second major concern of Latin American leaders during the year was the growth of protectionist sentiment in the United States. The huge U.S. merchandise trade deficit—projected to reach $150 billion in 1985—and a surge of low-price imports produced a spate of more than 200 trade-restricting bills in the U.S. Congress.

Latin America registered a $17.2 billion trade surplus with the United States in 1984—less than half the surplus amassed by Japan the same year—but the Latin surplus was swallowed up by debt repayments.

Health. One overlooked effect of the debt crisis has been an overall decline in Latin American health standards. Carlyle Guerra de Macedo, director of the Pan American Health Organization (PAHO), said that the state of health in Latin America and the Caribbean has "deteriorated" in recent years. Infant mortality is up in some countries, Guerra de Macedo reported, and the provision of health services has declined virtually everywhere as the hard-pressed governments of the region have had to

AP/Wide World

Argentina's President Raul Alfonsin votes in midterm elections November 3. The president's Radical Civic Union won 42% of the vote and kept its governing position.

make difficult choices in cutting public expenditures. "Social sectors are the first to be cut in times of crisis. Yet this is the time when the people need the social services the most," he said.

To Guerra de Macedo, the most serious health problem in Latin America is malnutrition. "Hunger is on the rise in the Americas, no doubt about it," he declared. "Some 130 million people in Latin America—more than one third of the population—suffer from some kind of malnutrition. Malnutrition is increasing especially among the lower income groups. The problem is not just the quality of food available to the poor, but an absolute lack of food because they cannot afford to buy it."

Politics. Democracy followed an uneven course in the hemisphere during 1985. A new civilian government was installed in Brazil on March 15, ending 21 years of military rule. President-elect Tancredo Neves was stricken with an intestinal disorder on the eve of his inauguration, and Vice-President José Sarney became acting president. Neves died on April 22, and Sarney became chief executive.

In July, Alan García was sworn in as president of Peru, succeeding Fernando Belaunde Terry in the first transition from one elected government to another since a military coup ousted Belaunde Terry in 1968. Congressional elections were held in Mexico and Bolivia in July. In both countries the balloting was peaceful but marked by charges of widespread fraud.

The Panamanian military forced President Nicolas Ardito Barletta out of office in September and installed a relatively unknown businessman, Eric Arturo Delvalle, in his place. Defense Force Chief Gen. Manuel Antonio Noriega said that the military was displeased with Ardito Barletta's handling of the country's economic crisis, but observers said Ardito Barletta was purged because he was about to approve the investigation of a murder scandal involving military intelligence agents. Chile continued to experience waves of protests against the military government of Gen. Augusto Pinochet. Opposition parties signed a pact to push for a rapid return to civilian rule.

Human Rights. Several Latin American countries condone kidnappings, torture, and murder of political opponents, according to the 1985 report of the Inter-American Commission on Human Rights. Some of the worst violations are found in Nicaragua, Cuba, El Salvador, Guatemala, Haiti, Chile, and Surinam, the commission said. Paraguay also was cited as a human rights violator, but the commission said that the situation there improved slightly from 1984.

The Inter-American Press Association contended that freedom of the press was still jeopardized in many countries of the hemisphere, citing the specific cases of Nicaragua, Haiti, Cuba, Chile, Paraguay, and Mexico.

Drugs. Latin America is the major source of illicit drugs smuggled into the United States, according to the U.S. Drug Enforcement Agency. In September the Inter-American Economic and Social Council, an arm of the Organization of American States (OAS), endorsed plans for a specialized Inter-American conference on the drug problem, to be held in 1986 or the following year. Coordinated efforts are needed to combat the drug menace, delegates to the meeting said.

Inter-American System. The Inter-American Development Bank celebrated its 25th anniversary at the annual meeting of its board of governors in Vienna, Austria, in March. It was only the second time the bank held its annual meeting outside the Western Hemisphere.

The OAS, under attack for its inaction on the Latin American debt and the strife in Central America, began debating structural reforms needed to revitalize the organization. A special OAS General Assembly on reforms to the OAS Charter was held in December in Cartagena, Colombia, but observers said any restructuring of the organization would take several years.

See also articles on individual countries; DRUGS AND ALCOHOL; THIRD WORLD.

RICHARD C. SCHROEDER, *"Visión" Magazine*

AP/Wide World

After a group of guerrillas seized the Palace of Justice in Bogotá on November 6, Colombian soldiers and police stormed the building and rescued hostages, including many judges. The confrontation resulted in an estimated 40–100 deaths.

A statue of John Marshall, chief justice of the Supreme Court from 1801 to 1835, was unveiled in Washington.

© Jose Lopez, NYT Pictures

LAW

In the United States in 1985, the dominant theme of the Supreme Court term was the relationship between government and religion, with the court reaffirming its commitment to a strict separation of church and state. There was also a strong undercurrent of concern for the health of the justices and the possibility that President Reagan would get the chance to make appointments that could reshape the court in a more conservative image. In the lower courts, there were highly publicized cases involving charges of libel (see special report, page 314), espionage charges, the indictment of a Reagan cabinet official, the trial of a sitting governor, the acquittal of Claus von Bülow, and a rape recantation. In international law, the United States announced that it was ending its policy of automatic compliance with the decisions of the World Court, though it emphasized that it was not withdrawing entirely from the Court.

United States

Supreme Court. Before its 1984–85 term, the U.S. Supreme Court seemed intent on lowering some of the traditional barriers between church and state. With the energetic support of the Reagan administration, the court, for example, had approved taxpayer sponsorship of a community Christmas Nativity display and allowed state legislatures to pay chaplains to open their sessions with daily prayer. But that trend was reversed dramatically in 1985 with a series of decisions that rebuffed the Reagan administration and heartened civil libertarians.

One of the men at the center of the controversy was Justice Lewis F. Powell, a key swing vote in the court's moderate middle. At 77, Powell was one of five members of the court older than 76. He missed nearly one third of the cases after undergoing surgery for a cancerous prostate but returned to work at the end of the term vowing to take his seat in 1985–86 if his recovery continued to be successful.

Justice Harry A. Blackmun, 76, was in the headlines when the FBI disclosed in late February that a bullet was fired through the window of his third-floor apartment in a Washington suburb. Blackmun was unharmed, and the origin of the bullet remained a mystery. The justice, author of the court's landmark 1973 ruling legalizing abortion, had received threatening letters from militant opponents of abortion.

Powell and Blackmun proved to be important justices when it came to forming a majority in controversial cases. Powell dissented from only six of the decisions in which he participated, and Blackmun cast only 12 dissenting votes.

The Supreme Court term saw four major decisions involving the volatile mix of government and religion. In June the court struck down an Alabama law that provided for daily moments of meditation or silent prayer in the state's public schools. The court said that moments of silence may be constitutional but not if state laws and school officials encourage students to use the time to pray (Wallace v. Jaffree).

Using similar reasoning, the justices overturned New York City's use of federal aid for the underprivileged to pay public school teachers to conduct classes in parochial schools (Aguilar v. Felton). In a companion case the court also barred a similar "shared time" program in Grand Rapids, MI, that used state funds to pay public school teachers to conduct classes in parochial schools (Grand Rapids School District v. Ball). Writing for the court in the New York City case, Justice William J. Brennan said, "The symbolic union of church and state . . . threatens to convey a message of state support for religion to students and to the general public."

The fourth case in which the justices reaffirmed that religion and government do not mix involved a worker who wanted to take Sundays off to observe the Sabbath. A Connecticut law asserted that an employee could not be required to work on his or her Sabbath, but the Supreme Court held that states "must take pains not to compel people to act in the name of any religion" *(Thornton v. Caldor)*.

While the religion cases attracted the greatest attention, the court also issued important rulings in criminal law. The justices departed in some cases from their general recent trend toward allowing greater leeway for police. In a ruling applauded by law enforcement officials, the court held that public school teachers and administrators do not need court warrants or the same justification that police officers need before searching students suspected of carrying drugs or weapons *(New Jersey v. T.L.O.)*. Similarly, the court ruled that a suspect's voluntary confession given after advisement of so-called Miranda rights is admissible even though an earlier confession was obtained without Miranda warnings *(Oregon v. Elstad)*.

But in two other cases, the court buttressed the rights of suspects. It said that penniless defendants whose sanity is seriously in doubt are entitled to free psychiatric help to support their insanity pleas *(Ake v. Oklahoma)*. And it ruled that police may not shoot unarmed, fleeing criminal suspects who pose no threat to the officers or the public *(Tennessee v. Garner)*.

In the area of free-speech rights and libel, the court issued four notable decisions. The justices ruled that political action committees may spend an unlimited amount of money independently to back a presidential candidate, a decision that struck down a federally imposed $1,000 maximum on such expenditures *(Federal Election Commission v. NCPAC)*. The court also ruled that lawyers may run advertisements that solicit clients for specific cases

and may use illustrations to make ads more eye-catching *(Zauderer v. Office of Disciplinary Counsel)*.

In the libel cases, the court said that free-speech protections limit the monetary damages libel defendants may be forced to pay only when the libelous statements involved a "matter of public concern" *(Dun & Bradstreet v. Greenmoss)*. It also ruled that individuals may be sued for allegedly libelous statements made in letters or in petitions to government officials *(McDonald v. Smith)*.

In a case involving the media, the court found that *The Nation* magazine violated copyright law by publishing excerpts of former President Gerald R. Ford's memoirs. The justices said use of some 300 words of verbatim quotes from the then-unpublished book was illegal even if the quotes made news *(Harper & Row v. Nation Enterprises)*.

In the area of official and governmental immunity, the justices ruled that presidential cabinet members such as former Attorney General John N. Mitchell have a limited protection against suits by citizens whose civil rights they violated. Unlike the president, cabinet officers do not enjoy absolute immunity from such suits *(Mitchell v. Forsyth)*. But the court did strengthen immunity from antitrust suits for local governments. It said that the community may not be sued for anticompetitive conduct that furthers some state policy even if the conduct in question is not ordered by the state *(Town of Hallie v. Eau Claire)*.

Local governments suffered a setback in another case in which the court gave Congress almost unlimited power to force states and communities to comply with federal law. The court allowed the federal government to order localities to pay minimum wages and overtime to employees *(Garcia v. San Antonio)*.

In the area of handicapped rights, the court ruled that the mentally retarded are not entitled

The Supreme Court ruled on one major school-prayer case in its 1984-85 term—and others appeared to be on the way.

to the same special legal protections against discrimination afforded blacks and women. But the ruling did block states and communities from basing differing treatments for the retarded on "irrational prejudice" (*Cleburne, Texas v. Cleburne Living Center*). The court also ruled that handicapped persons are not victims of illegal discrimination when cuts in Medicaid care affect them more severely than others (*Alexander v. Choate*).

In the area of labor law, the court barred unions from disciplining members who quit the union and go back to work during a strike. The justices said such retaliation violated the "voluntary unionism" required by federal law (*Pattern Makers League v. NLRB*).

And in an important business case, the court said that states have the legal authority to create regional banking systems by barring banks from outside a particular region from doing business within their borders (*Northeast Bancorp v. Board of Governors*).

The year also may have marked another important milestone for the use of the death penalty in the nation. Although there were no major Supreme Court rulings on capital punishment, the court turned aside appeals by the condemned with increasing frequency. The pace of executions increased markedly, averaging about one every two weeks.

And finally, in another case involving government powers, the court ruled that federal officials acted constitutionally in prosecuting only those young men who publicized their refusal to register for the military draft (*Wayte v. U.S.*).

Local Justice. A number of lower court cases around the United States attracted widespread attention in 1985, perhaps none more so than an alleged rape in the Chicago area going back eight years.

Cathleen Crowell Webb, who in 1977 at age 16 accused Gary Dotson of rape, filed a court affidavit recanting the charges. Webb, now married and living in New Hampshire, said she concocted the story and picked Dotson from police mug shots because she feared that she was pregnant and did not want to implicate her boyfriend. Dotson, who had served some six years of a 25-to-50-year sentence, was freed on bail after the recantation, but his troubles with the law were far from over. The judge who sentenced him originally refused to overturn the conviction, ruling that Webb's new story lacked corroboration. Finally, Illinois Gov. James R. Thompson commuted Dotson's sentence, making him a free man. But the governor did not grant a pardon to Dotson that would have cleared his record. The case stirred widespread concern among feminists, who said it would hurt the credibility of rape victims everywhere.

In Providence, RI, a jury found Danish-born socialite Claus von Bülow innocent of charges that he twice tried with insulin injections to murder his heiress wife, Martha "Sunny" von Bülow. Mr. von Bülow had been found guilty in 1982, but the conviction was overturned by the Rhode Island Supreme Court. Prosecutors said that von Bülow, 58, injected his wife with insulin and induced the comas she suffered in 1979 and 1980 at the family's Newport mansion. Mrs. von Bülow recovered from the first coma, but doctors say the second is irreversible. Von Bülow stands to inherit $14 million of his wife's $75 million utilities fortune, but the state was not allowed to introduce that fact (as it had in the first trial).

In New York City, former U.S. Labor Secretary Raymond Donovan faced trial on charges that he and nine others stole from New York City on a subway construction contract awarded prior to Donovan's appointment to the Reagan cabinet. Donovan, who resigned his federal job in March, was accused of larceny and fraud by Bronx, NY, prosecutors in connection with a project run by his construction firm in New Jersey. State prosecutors said the company overstated payments to a subcontracting company owned by a New York state senator and a reputed mobster. All the defendants denied the charges.

Spies were very much in the news in 1985, and two cases that went to trial attracted particular nationwide interest. In Los Angeles, FBI agent Richard W. Miller was accused of passing classified documents to the Soviet Union in return for a promise of $65,000 in cash and gold. Miller's Soviet lover, Svetlana Ogorodnikov, and her husband, Nikolai, pleaded guilty in the case and were serving prison sentences. In Virginia, meanwhile, the government got the so-called Walker spy case prosecution under way. The alleged mastermind of the spy ring was John A. Walker, Jr., of Norfolk, who was arrested in Maryland after federal authorities said he dropped a bag filled with classified documents beside a road. The FBI said the documents were to be picked up by a Soviet agent. Also charged in the case were Walker's older brother, his son, and a former Navy buddy. (*See* ESPIONAGE.)

Finally, in New Orleans, Louisiana Gov. Edwin Edwards went on trial on federal charges that he took part in a $10 million scheme to gain state certification for hospital corporations in which alleged co-conspirators had an interest. The government said that Edwards and his partners sought state approval for "shell corporations" that were then sold to big hospital chains. Prosecutors said Edwards put a moratorium on new hospitals and nursing homes soon after taking office and then ordered the approval of the projects in which his partners were involved. Edwards pleaded innocent. (*See* LOUISIANA.)

JIM RUBIN
The Associated Press

The International Court of Justice convened September 12 to hear oral arguments in the case brought by Nicaragua against the United States. As indicated by the empty seats (left foreground), the U.S. delegation refused to attend.

AP/Wide World

International Law

An Egyptian airliner carrying the four hijackers of an Italian cruise ship, the *Achille Lauro,* was diverted in midair by U.S. warplanes on October 10 and forced to land in Italy. It was the first such forcible U.S. response to the rising tide of international terrorism, and it raised basic questions of international law. Italy indicated that it would try the four Palestinians rather than extradite them to the United States to face charges of murdering an American passenger. Italy freed another Palestinian aboard the EgyptAir flight, Mohammed Abul Abbas, despite U.S. charges that he had planned the hijack. Later, Italian magistrates issued a warrant for Abbas' arrest, dismissing the claim that he held diplomatic immunity. The larger legal issue of the legitimacy of the U.S. diversion remained unresolved. Egypt and the Soviet Union were among the few nations that protested the U.S. action, but it won public praise in most capitals as necessary to deter potential terrorists. By comparison, when Israel kidnapped Nazi war criminal Adolf Eichmann in Argentina in 1960, the outcry had been loud and widespread. Some experts suggested that the altered response reflected an evolution of legal norms, by practice, back to the old principle of humanitarian intervention. But no consensus developed on just how far governments could go in bringing terrorists to justice.

The United States pressed in another new legal direction, under a 1984 law, by offering a $250,000 reward for the capture of three terrorists involved in the June 14 hijacking of TWA Flight 847 from Athens to Rome. The Lebanese skyjackers killed a U.S. serviceman and held 39 other Americans hostage for 16 days.

On October 7 the United States announced that it would end its 39-year acceptance of the compulsory jurisdiction of the International Court of Justice in political cases. The United States was one of only 48 nations, few of them major powers, that had agreed to be bound by World Court decisions in any case brought before the 15-judge panel at The Hague. Washing-

ton had curtailed the court's authority in 1984 by refusing to accept its jurisdiction in a suit brought by Nicaragua demanding reparations for, and an end to, U.S. support for rebel groups. The court ruled in November 1984 that it had the right to proceed, and the United States responded in January 1985 with the announcement that it would boycott the proceedings. Nicaragua presented its arguments in May and September. U.S. officials cited the Nicaragua case as the motive for the decision to end compulsory jurisdiction, saying the court was being "abused for political ends."

To show that it was not abandoning the court completely, the United States announced that it would ask a panel of World Court judges to resolve a 17-year-old commercial dispute with Italy involving the seizure of facilities owned by the Italian subsidiary of two U.S. corporations, Raytheon and Machlett Labs.

The World Court also issued a judgment on June 3 drawing a demarcation line on the continental shelf between Libya and Malta. And a five-judge panel of the court took up a frontier dispute between Mali and Burkina Faso.

The UN Commission on International Trade Law on June 21 adopted a model law on international commercial arbitration that will aid governments in standardizing their codes, thereby facilitating settlements between firms from different countries.

The UN General Assembly, in a consensus resolution on April 9, endorsed a set of global guidelines for consumer protection, providing governments with a basis for local legislation.

Canada reaffirmed on September 10 that the passages within its Arctic archipelago are "internal" waterways. It offered to accept any World Court judgment on the issue, but there was no indication that the United States, which has considered the area an international strait would mount a legal challenge.

On October 18, the 19 full members of the Antarctic Treaty agreed to restrict access to 16 areas of special scientific or environmental concern on the continent. Earlier, China and Uruguay had been granted voting status.

MICHAEL J. BERLIN, *"The Washington Post"*

Libel

Libel suits against CBS News by retired Gen. William Westmoreland, against *Time* magazine by former Israeli Defense Minister Ariel Sharon, and against other media companies by other newsworthy figures led to courtroom skirmishes that spilled over into a barrage of national newspaper headlines and nightly television coverage in late 1984 and 1985. The sensational trials highlighted the uncertainty and contradictory elements of U.S. libel law and brought calls for reform from all sides. When the smoke cleared, CBS, Westmoreland, *Time,* and Sharon each claimed victory. To understand how that can be, it is helpful to look at the historical background of contemporary U.S. libel law and at the principles as involved in each case.

Standards. In its earliest form, a libel was any writing deemed harmful to a reputation. Juries in criminal trials were told that "the greater the truth, the greater the libel." Today, nearly all libel involves civil rather than criminal law. A writer who can prove the truth of his statements, no matter how harmful to reputation they are, cannot successfully be sued for defamation. Even the author who was mistaken and cannot prove that his words were true sometimes still can win a libel suit. That is because the person who brings a libel suit against a newspaper, book publisher, television network, or any other of the mass media must prove four things: that the offending words were actually published or broadcast; that those words referred specifically to the person suing; that the words were untrue and likely to damage the plaintiff's reputation; and that the media defendant is guilty under a legal doctrine called "fault."

Within the context of the civil-rights movement of the 1960s, a case called *New York Times v. Sullivan* reached the U.S. Supreme Court. The high court's 1964 ruling in that case radically changed the rules of U.S. libel law. L.B. Sullivan, the police commissioner of Montgomery, AL, sued the *Times* for running an ad that criticized the way his police department had treated Martin Luther King, Jr., and other civil-rights workers. The Alabama courts awarded Sullivan $500,000, but the U.S. Supreme Court overturned that decision. Justice William Brennan said the 1st Amendment required "a federal rule that prohibits a public official from recovering damages for a defamatory falsehood relating to his official conduct unless he proves that the statement was made with 'actual malice'—that is, with knowledge that it was false or with reckless disregard of whether it was false or not."

The *Sullivan* ruling was based on the idea that citizens in a democratic system must be exposed to the open discussion of current events in order to carry out responsibly the duties of self-governance, such as voting. Truth can sort itself out in the marketplace of ideas only if all ideas have the chance to be heard. To uphold the constitutionally mandated freedoms of speech and press, the court reasoned, the risk of honest mistakes would have to be tolerated.

By 1966 the federal "actual malice" test had been applied to cases involving public "figures" as well as public officials. A public official is a person elected or appointed to a government office; a public figure is a person outside the government who voluntarily enters the public limelight in one way or another to influence public opinion. Public figures have included citizens who spoke out on environmental and consumer issues as well as athletes and movie stars. In 1974 the Supreme Court ruled that the 1st Amendment also requires "private persons" suing the media for libel to prove at least a minimum level of fault called "simple negligence." Simple negligence is usually defined as a lack of reasonable care.

The lines between public officials, public figures, and private persons can be difficult for juries to distinguish. Even more difficult can be the application of the legal definitions of actual malice and simple negligence. Some critics say this part of libel law is so ill defined and so complex that juries are unable to make correct decisions. They point to the fact that nearly two thirds of libel suits decided by juries are decided against the media, but that two thirds of those decisions are then overturned by judges when media defendants appeal.

Sharon v. Time. Recognizing the complexity inherent in a libel suit filed by a foreign official against a U.S. magazine, the judge in the Sharon case took a novel tack. Sharon sued *Time* for $50 million over an article about the September 1982 massacres at two Palestinian refugee camps in West Beirut, Lebanon. The magazine reported that, after the assassination of Prime Minister Bashir Gemayel two days before, Sharon had discussed the need for revenge with Gemayel's family.

Sharon clearly was a public figure, and Judge Abraham Sofaer instructed the jury to decide the case in three stages. Following his instructions, the jury first decided that *Time* indeed had defamed Sharon. Then it decided that the defamation was not true. But finally, the jury concluded that *Time*'s level of fault did

not reach actual malice; it did say that *Time* had acted "negligently and carelessly." From a purely legal standpoint, *Time* won the libel suit because Sharon could not prove actual malice. At the same time, the jury in effect cleared Sharon's name and cast a shadow on *Time*'s reporting.

The *Sharon* case underscored one of the loudest criticisms of U.S. libel law: a public figure, even if he can prove he was libeled, can still lose his suit because of the fault requirement. Scholars argue that Judge Sofaer's innovative three-verdict approach should be adopted as a matter of course in future libel cases. That way the courts might help a person clear his reputation without unduly challenging the freedom of the press. Others say the *Sharon* case points up the need for new kinds of libel laws. They say that a person should be able to sue without having to prove actual malice or even simple negligence if the suit is brought simply to clear a reputation and not to collect monetary damages. In such an action, the only issue would be the truth or falsity of an injurious article, without regard to whether the defendant was negligent.

Westmoreland v. CBS News. As if to underscore the problems of libel law, the $120 million libel suit against CBS by General Westmoreland ended close on the heels of the *Sharon* case—and this time without a verdict for either side. After four months in court, the general withdrew his claim in mid-February 1985. The case had begun with a CBS-TV documentary, "The Uncounted Enemy: A Vietnam Deception." The show suggested that as commanding general in Vietnam, Westmoreland condoned reports that underrepresented the military strength of the North Vietnamese and Viet Cong. The case ended with a joint press conference at which the general said he respected the rights of journalists to "examine the complex issues of Vietnam." CBS, while adhering to the position that its documentary was accurate, said that it respected the general's service and did not believe that he "was unpatriotic or disloyal in performing his duties as he saw them."

Some libel experts say the Westmoreland case demonstrates the inadequacy of the courts as an arena for arguing public policy. They point out that libel suits can cost hundreds of thousands of dollars in legal fees and that, in cases like Westmoreland's, it is impossible to prove the truth one way or the other. As trial judge Pierre Leval told the jury when he dismissed them, "It may be for the best that the verdict is left to history." Finally, some fear that forcing journalists to bear the cost of long trials may discourage publishers and broadcasters from tackling controversial issues in the first place.

Other Cases. While the Sharon and Westmoreland cases ended without clear-cut victors, a third sensational libel case continued to crawl through the judicial process. It began in 1980, when William Tavoulareas, the president of Mobil Oil Co., filed a $2.05 million suit against *The Washington Post* over an article that said he had "set up his son in the petroleum business." Tavoulareas won the suit the first time it went to trial, but in May 1984 the decision was overruled on grounds that "actual malice" had not been proved. Then in April 1985, a three-judge panel of the U.S. Court of Appeals for the District of Columbia reinstated the initial jury award, ruling that indeed there had been "actual malice." In June the court announced that the case would be reconsidered again.

Yet another notable libel case involved businessman and former Massachusetts gubernatorial candidate John R. Lakian, who sued *The Boston Globe* for an article about his business practices and personal background. Lakian sought $50 million in damages from the newspaper and the reporter who wrote the article. In an unusual verdict, the jury in August 1985 decided that Lakian had been libeled by five paragraphs in the article but that the article as a whole was not libelous; it therefore awarded no damages. Subsequently the judge in the case dismissed all charges against the paper and the reporter.

Issues. Few would disagree that a libel suit is an expensive, time-consuming, and often unsatisfying way to settle questions of damaged reputation. Researchers at the University of Iowa, in fact, reported in 1985 that most libel trials concentrate very little on truth, falsity, or harm to reputation. Instead attention is concentrated on fault. Concurrently, communication researchers at Stanford University began to raise questions about how much plaintiffs actually are damaged by articles considered libelous. One school of thought holds that damages for libel should be awarded only after specific proof of harm. On the other side, however, are those who argue that "actual malice" rules make it too hard for those damaged by the media to fight back.

While there is little to indicate that the 1st Amendment "actual malice" rule will be substantially modified any time soon, it seems likely that some modification of U.S. libel law will remain on the agenda for the nation's attorneys, judges, journalists, and media law researchers. In August 1985, Congress took steps to ensure further discussion of the issues, as the House Civil and Constitutional Rights Subcommittee announced plans to hold future hearings on "current libel law and alternatives to it."

JEREMY COHEN

Although the last of Israel's combat units were withdrawn from Lebanon in June, some patrols and observers stayed.

LEBANON

The year 1985 in Lebanon began with Israel announcing a plan to remove its forces and ended with an agreement among rival militias to end ten years of civil war. Nevertheless, it was another difficult and convulsive year, with bitter rivalries and complex issues still unresolved. Syria expanded and fortified its control; international terrorist attacks were carried out by Lebanon-based groups; and the nation's economy suffered the consequences of political turmoil.

Israeli Withdrawal. The failure of talks between Lebanon and Israel on security arrangements for the withdrawal of Israeli forces from Lebanese territory, held at the border town of Naqura from November 1984 to January 1985, did not bode well for Lebanon. Israel did decide on a plan for withdrawal (except from a southern buffer zone, to be controlled by the Israeli-backed South Lebanon Army) but without any coordination with Lebanese authorities.

The first phase of the Israeli withdrawal, from the port city of Sidon and adjacent regions, began January 20 and was completed February 16. The immediate deployment there of the Lebanese army was welcomed by Sidon residents, as was a February 17 visit by President Amin Gemayel and Prime Minister Rashid Karami. It seemed clear that legitimate government authority was still preferred to foreign occupation or the rule of local militias. The next day, however, partisans of the Party of God (*Hizballah*) were sent to Sidon on a rampage to undermine the new peace.

Hopes for implementing a security plan in which the Lebanese army would be deployed from the Awali River in southern Lebanon to the Batrun region in northern Lebanon were soon dissipated when fighting broke out between the Christian Lebanese forces and the Muslim militias of Sidon. And when the Lebanese forces were pulled out from the Kharrub and Zahrani regions near Sidon in April, tens of thousands of Christians either fled or were evicted from their homes.

The second and third phases of the Israeli withdrawal, conducted from April through June, were accompanied by attacks against the evacuating forces and were followed by intensified conflicts among the Lebanese factions. Despite public statements by Syria in support of the deployment of the Lebanese army on the heels of the withdrawing Israeli troops, every effort was made by pro-Syrian militias to prevent such a deployment.

Syrian Control. The failure of the Lebanese army to take a central role prepared the ground for an expanded Syrian presence. Over several months, in East Beirut, West Beirut, Tripoli, and Zahle, Syrian troops were deployed after car bombing incidents. The residents of Zahle actually invited the Syrian army to return in September, five years after it had been forced to evacuate. In Tripoli, on the other hand, the leader of the Islamic Unification Movement, Sheikh Saeed Shaaban, refused to accept the return of the Syrian army. Consequently, Syria's President Hafez al-Assad unleashed the militias of the Lebanese Communist Party, the Syrian Social Nationalist Party, the pro-Syrian Baath Party, and the Alawi Arab Democratic

Party against Shaaban. Important parts of Tripoli were destroyed, and the Syrian army, after an absence of more than three years, reentered the city in October. In short, the Syrian regime in 1985 launched a gradual and protracted offensive aimed at reoccupation of Lebanon or a return to the *status quo ante* of December 1976–February 1978. This time, however, the domination of Lebanon was expected to be more complete because previous countervailing powers are no longer there. These included Yasir Arafat's Palestine Liberation Organization (PLO), forced out in 1983; Israel, which withdrew to the southern security zone in 1985; and the United States, France, and Saudi Arabia, forced out in 1984.

Tripartite Agreement. After three months of negotiations under the sponsorship of Syria, leaders of Lebanon's major rival militia forces signed an agreement December 28 designed to end ten years of fighting. The agreement was signed in Damascus by Nabih Berri, leader of the Shiite Muslim movement called Amal; Walid Jumblat, head of the Druze Progressive Socialist Party; and Elie Hobeika, commander of the Christian militia called the Lebanese Forces. The reforms called for in the agreement were essentially those stipulated in the Constitutional Document of February 1976. The seats in Lebanon's legislature, the National Assembly, would be divided equally between Christians and Muslims. The prime minister would be selected by the National Assembly rather than by the president, whose power would be curbed. The number of seats in the legislature would be doubled to 198, with new and vacant seats filled by nomination or election.

The power-sharing arrangements between Muslims and Christians represented only one section of the agreement. The other provided mechanisms for ending the civil war. By the accord, all militias would be disarmed and disbanded, to be replaced by the Lebanese Internal Security Forces. The central government would regain control of the country for a period of 12 months, though the Lebanese army would be sent back to the barracks for retraining by the Syrian army. Until the Lebanese army could be restructured, Syria would provide military assistance in maintaining law and order in the regions previously controlled by the three factions.

It is perhaps important to note that the December accord was signed only by militia leaders whose mainstays of power were in regions of Lebanon not controlled by Syria. Forces based in the Syrian-controlled areas, such as the *Hizballah,* the Syrian Social Nationalist Party, and the militia of former President Suleiman Franjieh, were not party to the accord. Thus, it appeared that the agreement was designed primarily to legitimize the protracted reoccupation of Lebanon by Syria rather than

to settle disputes or divide power among the various factions in Lebanon.

Terrorism. As Syria became the dominant power in Lebanon and as Iran's influence also increased during the year, terrorism loomed large in Lebanese affairs. Both of those countries were accused of sponsoring terrorism in the Middle East. Islamic Jihad, which is believed to be the operational arm of the *Hizballah* and operates primarily from Lebanon, has very strong links with Iran. The mainstay of its political and military power is in the Syrian-controlled Baalbak area of the Bekaa Valley. Although the *Hizballah* has given the impression of pursuing its own ends, it has worked within parameters set by Syria and Iran. Attacks by the Islamic Jihad on U.S. and French military and diplomatic installations from 1982 to 1984 all served Syrian and Iranian interests in Lebanon and the Middle East as a whole. The United States and France had been the two major powers calling for the withdrawal of non-Lebanese forces from Lebanon, namely the PLO, the Israeli army, and the Syrian army. To Iran, the United States represents the great Satan, while France has been the greatest source of arms to Iraq from the West, as well as a haven for prominent anti-Khomeini Iranians. Thus, with Syria and Iran having common interests against U.S. and French policies in the Middle East, it is not surprising that the Islamic Jihad has singled out those two countries for terrorist attacks and kidnappings.

All the hostages being held in Lebanon by the Islamic Jihad in 1985 were either U.S. or French citizens. The release of two American hostages, journalist Jeremy Levin in February and the Rev. Benjamin Weir in September, took place directly or indirectly through the good offices of Syrian authorities. However, while Levin and Weir were set free during the

With Syria's presence in Lebanon increasing, President Gemayel (left) met often with Syria's President Assad.

In November and December, Terry Waite, a special envoy of the archbishop of Canterbury, traveled to Beirut in a humanitarian attempt to gain the release of Americans held hostage in Lebanon.

AP/Wide World

year, two other Americans were kidnapped: David Jacobsen, the head of the American University of Beirut Hospital, in May; and Thomas Sutherland, a dean at the American University of Beirut, in June.

The hijacking of a TWA jetliner from Athens to Beirut in June by partisans of the *Hizballah* was another hostage incident played out in Lebanon. President Assad of Syria was able to gain the release of the final 39 hostages after two weeks, showing that Syria could prevail over the *Hizballah* to serve its own interests.

A French parliamentary delegation that visited Iran in December was told that the release of French hostages in Lebanon and any improvement in French-Iranian relations required a change in French policy, especially regarding military and financial support for Iraq. In short, the taking of hostages is intended to force a change in the policies of the United States and France in the entire region.

Economy. The year 1985 was a disastrous one for the Lebanese economy. This was reflected in the exchange rate of the Lebanese pound, which fell from 8.86 per U.S. dollar in December 1984 to 18.4 in December 1985. (In December 1982 it had been 3.88.) The reasons for the economic problems are not difficult to discern. Because of the ongoing conflict, there has been a major flight of capital, foreign investment has been discouraged, and remittances from Lebanese working abroad, especially in the oil-rich countries of the Middle East, have been invested elsewhere. One of the major consequences of Syria's protracted offensive has been the undermining of Leba-

non's central government and its institutions. That, along with the growing supremacy of militias in various regions of the country, has reduced the treasury's revenues from taxes, customs, and such public utilities as electricity and telephone. Moreover, until the curtailment of gasoline subsidies in December, the Lebanese treasury was incurring losses of some 10 billion pounds annually.

Another consequence of Lebanon's turmoil with long-term economic consequences has been a "brain drain" among professionals in all religious sects. Physicians at the American University of Beirut Hospital, for example, have been driven away by the continuing conflict in Beirut and even harassed by unruly militias.

See also MIDDLE EAST; SYRIA; TERRORISM.

MARIUS DEEB
Georgetown University

LEBANON • Information Highlights

Official Name: Republic of Lebanon.
Location: Southwest Asia.
Area: 4,000 sq mi (10 360 km^2).
Population (mid-1985 est.): 2,600,000.
Chief Cities (1980 est.): Beirut, the capital, 702,000; Tripoli, 175,000.
Government: *Head of state,* Amin Gemayel, president (took office Sept. 1982). *Head of government,* Rashid Karami, prime minister (took office May 1984). *Legislature* (unicameral)—National Assembly.
Monetary Unit: Lebanese pound (18.400 pounds equal U.S.$1, Dec. 27, 1985).
Foreign Trade (1983 U.S.$): *Imports,* $3,300,000,000; *exports,* $690,000,000.

LIBRARIES

Libraries in 1985 found themselves more than ever at odds with the Reagan administration, which tried again to scuttle federal aid to libraries, put restrictions on the flow of information, cut back on government publications, took the U.S. out of UNESCO, pushed for tax changes that could hurt libraries, and temporized on South Africa while libraries and library associations were divesting themselves of U.S. firms doing business there.

On the other hand, some libraries tried to adapt by playing up their services to the private sector, engaging in friendly projects with the Communist Chinese, and making unfriendly statements about the Communist Russians. At the August meeting in Chicago of the International Federation of Library Associations and Institutions, Librarian of Congress Daniel Boorstin welcomed Russian librarians with anti-Soviet remarks.

Literacy. The library attack on illiteracy gained greater funding at several levels of government in 1985, notable examples being the governments of the states of Illinois and Texas and the city of New York. Great efforts and expenditures continue to be made, especially in the recruitment and training of volunteer tutors, but to date, no quantitative evaluation of the results achieved by library programs has been reported. (*See also* page 209.)

Automation, Networking, and Video. Libraries of all types continue to commit large sums to automation, moving now from the automation of library housekeeping tasks to the automated manipulation of information, most of which is held in remote databanks and tapped by telecommunications. Libraries, however, are starting to access information held locally on discs, a development encouraged by rising telecommunications costs. Automation, besides saving money by reducing library staffs, is changing the makeup of library staffs. Low-level clerical workers as well as skilled catalogers are being replaced with middle- to upper-level clerical workers.

School libraries are now joining networks, both of other school libraries and of public and academic libraries. New York State is a leader in funding this area. The Online Computer Library Center (OCLC), the engine that powers most networking in the United States, is moving still further from its beginnings as a vendor of catalog information to become an independent entrepreneur in the information marketplace. Utilities like OCLC, however, now are threatened by optical disc technology, which could reduce their core income from the sale of cataloging information.

Videotapes first appeared on public library shelves in the early 1980s, but their circulation has become a major activity, even rivaling book lending in some cases. The annual circulation of one New York library (300,000) includes 176,000 loans of videotapes.

Conservation, Staffs, and Public Libraries. The struggle against book decay intensified in 1985. Work started on a deacidification facility for the Library of Congress. Ohio was exploring construction of one for all of the state's libraries. Other libraries, especially research libraries, are operating small deacidification plants. The year also saw publication of a permanent paper standard.

Staff development is a major concern of academic libraries, especially in the areas of user education and access to computerized information. Medical research libraries are leading the way here, with efforts to move the librarian higher on the ladder of medical information handling.

New emphasis is being placed on service to the aged and rural people. Funding uncertainties continue to spur exploration of alternative sources of income. In some communities, however, support for libraries is being won again by vigorous librarians and boards, and new building projects are proliferating.

Associations. At the 104th annual conference of the American Library Association (ALA) in Chicago in July, incoming president Beverly Lynch urged a more rigorous inquiry into the principles that govern librarianship and its role. Also at the meeting, the Commission on Freedom and Equality of Access to Information gave its draft report, and Thomas J. Galvin, dean of the School of Library and Information Science at the University of Pittsburgh, served as executive director designate.

President Judith McAnanama chose "Information is Power: Yesterday's Prophecy, Today's Reality, Tomorrow's Economy" as her theme at the 40th annual conference of the Canadian Library Association (CLA). The meeting was held in Calgary, Alta., June 13–18.

KARL NYREN, *"Library Journal"*

LIBRARY AWARDS OF 1985

Beta Phi Mu Award for distinguished service to education for librarianship: Robert M. Hayes, Graduate School of Library and Information Science, University of California–Los Angeles

Randolph J. Caldecott Medal for the most distinguished picture book for children: Trina Schart Hyman, *Saint George and the Dragon*

Melvil Dewey Award for recent creative professional achievement of a high order: Joseph H. Howard, National Agricultural Library

Grolier Foundation Award for unusual contribution to the stimulation and guidance of reading by children and young people: Mary K. Chelton, coeditor of Voice of Youth Advocates and director of programming and community relations, Virginia Beach, VA

Joseph W. Lippincott Award for distinguished service to the profession of librarianship: Robert G. Vosper, university librarian and professor emeritus, University of California–Los Angeles

John Newbery Medal for the most distinguished contribution to literature for children: Robin McKinley, *The Hero and the Crown*

AP/Wide World

Libyan athletes display photo of Mr. Qaddafi, their longtime national leader, at the University Games in Japan.

LIBYA

The continuing decline in world oil prices in 1985 had severe adverse consequences for Libya. The troubled state of the economy fueled political discontent, which was reflected in the activities of opponents of the regime both at home and abroad. President Muammar el-Qaddafi's support for revolutionary movements throughout the world brought criticisms and attempted reprisals from the United States. While remaining on poor terms with many African and Arab states, Libya successfully mended fences with Sudan, with which it had been carrying on a bitter propaganda battle.

Economic Stress. The Organization of the Petroleum Exporting Countries (OPEC) sought to halt the drop in crude oil prices occasioned by producer competition and consumer conservation by implementing a new pricing structure in 1985. Libya was one of only three OPEC members to oppose these efforts, adamantly objecting to plans to lower the ceiling price of high quality crude oil, the primary product of its fields. Libyan oil revenues, which had risen to $20 billion at the start of the decade, were projected to reach only about $8 billion in 1985. Libya's consistent stand against the OPEC arrangement was designed to prevent oil income from dipping any lower.

Workers' Expulsion. In the fall, Libya deported many foreign workers, including more than a quarter of the 100,000 Tunisians employed in the country. President Qaddafi characterized the expulsions as part of a policy to encourage Libyan self-reliance, but, in reality, the weakened economy could no longer absorb so many imported laborers. The Tunisian government interpreted Libya's action as a deliberate attempt to destabilize and embarrass it by compounding its political and economic problems. It had been the underdevelopment of southern Tunisia that had compelled so many workers to seek jobs abroad to begin with, and no new opportunities existed there for the persons forced to leave Libya. Tunisia retaliated by expelling several hundred Libyans accused of espionage and plotting acts of sabotage. Late in September, the two countries broke diplomatic relations. Amid this furor, rumors persisted that units of the Libyan army had mutinied rather than obey orders to invade Tunisia.

Coup Attempts. Earlier in the year, military officers had mounted at least two assassination attempts against Qaddafi. As many as 75 soldiers died in these abortive coups or were executed in their aftermath. Discontent within the military stemmed from rivalries between the traditional officer corps and members of revo-

lutionary committees charged by the president with overseeing the army after a foiled coup in 1984. Outside Libya, opposition groups claimed credit for the murders of representatives of the government, while anti-Qaddafi exiles were themselves the targets of gunmen in several European cities.

Foreign Relations. In Middle Eastern affairs, Libya did not deviate from the hard line normally characterizing its policy. It boycotted an emergency meeting of the Arab League during the summer to avoid participating in a discussion. of moderate approaches to Middle Eastern problems. Qaddafi attacked Palestine Liberation Organization leader Yasir Arafat's apparent willingness to seek a negotiated settlement of the differences between Israel and the Arabs. He harshly criticized the attack by Shiite and Druze militias on Palestinian refugee camps in Beirut in June, accusing Syria of failing to protect the Palestinian civilians in the camps adequately. In general, however, Syria and Libya pursued many of the same objectives, as reflected in their support for Iran in its war with Iraq. This Libyan policy drew fire from many Arab states.

Elsewhere in the Arab world, Libya enhanced its relations with several former enemies. In the furtherance of its unity agreement with Morocco, initiated in 1984, Libya granted more than $100 million in development loans. In view of Libya's own economic troubles, this represented a substantial commitment to the concept of the union, as did the continuing absence of Libyan support for Polisario guerrillas in their fight with the Moroccan army in the Western Sahara. Morocco and Libya also set up a joint legislative body to explore and implement additional aspects of unity.

Shortly after a military coup ousted Jaafar al-Nemery from the Sudanese presidency in April, Libya and Sudan resumed diplomatic ties after a four-year hiatus. During that time, Libya had provided arms and money to rebels in the southern Sudan, while the Khartoum government had permitted anti-Qaddafi groups to operate freely in Sudan, often providing them with access to the state radio to beam propaganda broadcasts into Libya. The new Sudanese military rulers hoped that improved relations with Libya would cut the rebels off from a critical external source of supply, fatally damaging the movement. Qaddafi, on the other hand, viewed a thaw in relations with Sudan as useful not only in terms of closing down a sanctuary for his critics, but also as a means of lessening Egyptian and American influence in the country. The Libyan leader visited Sudan in the spring, and in July the two nations signed a military agreement suggesting the emergence of still closer ties. By the terms of the pact, Libya was to provide training and logistical support for the Sudanese military. An even more important aspect of the agreement, however, was a Libyan promise to supply badly needed oil and foodstuffs, particularly crucial items in the famine-stricken Sudan, to its new ally.

In February, Libya released four Britons imprisoned in 1984 in retaliation for the expulsion of Libyan diplomats from the United Kingdom. Although this paved the way for some improvement in relations, guilty verdicts rendered in the cases of Libyan students on trial for committing acts of terrorism in Britain kept contacts between the two states cool.

The United States attacked Libya for its promotion of revolutionary movements directed against pro-Western governments. Libyan aid to the Sandinista regime in Nicaragua was singled out for particularly vehement criticism by President Reagan. But Qaddafi also was accused of supporting opposition forces in the Caribbean, particularly on the island of Dominica, and in Africa, where his criticism of Zaire's President Mobutu Sese Seko had been especially bitter. In July, President Reagan included Libya on a list of "terrorist states" that were said to be organizing acts of violence against American citizens and installations overseas.

The alleged involvement of Libyan-backed Palestinians in major terrorist incidents late in the year heightened tensions with both Egypt and the United States, as well as much of the Western world. Egyptian officials blamed Qaddafi for backing the November 23 hijacking of an Egyptair flight from Athens to Cairo, which was forced to land in Malta. In the aftermath, Egypt reinforced and mobilized its forces along the border with Libya. Then, as the year came to a close, Washington accused Qaddafi of supporting the December 27 Palestinian attacks at the Rome and Vienna airports, which left 16 persons dead. Calling Qaddafi a "pariah" for his "longstanding involvement in terrorism," President Reagan on Jan. 7, 1986, announced plans to break all U.S. economic ties with Libya and ordered all remaining Americans in Libya to leave by February 1.

KENNETH J. PERKINS
University of South Carolina

LIBYA · Information Highlights

Official Name: Socialist People's Libyan Arab Jamahiriya ("state of the masses").
Location: North Africa.
Area: 679,359 sq mi (1 759 540 km²).
Population (mid-1985 est.): 4,000,000.
Chief Cities (1980 est.): Tripoli, the capital, 1,223,000; Benghazi, 530,000.
Government: *Head of state*, Muammar el-Qaddafi (took office 1969). *Legislature*—General People's Congress (met initially Nov. 1976).
Monetary Unit: Dinar (0.296 dinar equals U.S. $1, Aug. 1985).
Gross Domestic Product (1984 est. U.S.$): $26,900,000,000.
Foreign Trade (1984 U.S.$): *Imports*, $8,000,000,000; *exports*, $10,000,000,000.

University of California Press

Huck Finn turned 100, its author 150.

LITERATURE

Mark Twain was irked by the observance of anniversaries, but in 1985 he was celebrated for three of them. Sinclair Lewis, who in the American classic *Main Street* satirized life in his Midwestern hometown, was thrown a parade there on the occasion of his 100th birthday. New works by Hemingway, a resurgence of some popular old genres, and the awarding of the Nobel Prize to a longtime practitioner of the French *nouveau roman* provided further links between the old and the new in the world of letters.

Anniversaries. "What ought to be done to the man who invented the celebrating of anniversaries?" Twain once wrote. "Mere killing would be too light." Whether he would have liked it or not, the great American author and humorist was honored on the 150th anniversary of his birth, the 75th anniversary of his death, and the 100th anniversary of the publication of *The Adventures of Huckleberry Finn.* But in addition to all the special events in his honor—

exhibits, marathon readings, stage productions, and so on—there was also heated debate over his masterpiece, *Huck Finn.* The ever-controversial book was denounced by many as openly racist and removed from the shelves of some schools and public libraries. Defenders of the book insisted it was an *attack* against racism and slavery.

In Sauk Centre, MN, the prototype for Lewis' narrow-minded, self-satisfied fictional town of Gopher Prairie, local folk nonetheless turned out with pride and affection to remember a native son who became America's first Nobelist in literature (1930). A parade down the main street, an official birthday dinner, and other hoopla marked the occasion.

Familiar Themes. A new book by Ernest Hemingway, called *The Dangerous Summer,* is the edited version of an unwieldy epilogue he wrote for his treatise on bullfighting *Death in the Afternoon.* And five previously unpublished short stories by a youthful Hem touched on similarly familiar themes—idealism, courage, adversity, and personal codes.

A previously unknown poem by Shakespeare was discovered at Oxford University in England. It is a nine-stanza love lyric probably written between 1593 and 1595.

In a more contemporary vein, two standard genres in popular American fiction were booming again. Crime and detective novels (*see* special report, page 433) were selling well, and the western novel also was riding high.

Nobelist. The Nobel Prize for Literature once again was awarded to a relative unknown, the 72-year-old French novelist Claude Simon. The author of 15 novels—including *Le tricheur* (1945), *Le vent* (1957), *L'herbe* (1958), *La route des Flandres* (1960), *Le palace* (1962), *Histoire* (1967), *Tryptyque* (1973), and *Les Géorgiques* (1981)—Simon is considered a key figure in the school of the abstract "new novel."

French novelist Claude Simon won the Nobel Prize.
AP/Wide World

American Literature

Contemporary American literature was severely criticized in two new books, Charles Newman's *The Post-Modern Era* and Joseph Epstein's *Plausible Prejudices*. Both decried the influence of the marketplace and lamented various concerns of the modern novel—politics, sex, popular media, the nature of art, and the elusiveness of reality.

In fact 1985 seemed like a lively year. Established writers produced interesting work, new writers emerged, the short story revival continued, and there were some signs of a resurgence of interest in poetry.

Novels. Mary Gordon's *Men and Angels,* a powerful and·beautifully observed story, tells of an educated young woman who, while doing research on a woman painter of a previous generation, finds out a great deal about herself. Anne Tyler's *The Accidental Tourist* demonstrates her continued growth as a novelist. The hero is a wonderfully sad, comic character, a man who has tried to insulate himself from the surprises of life: he makes a living by writing travel books for businessmen who want only the familiar and predictable no matter where in the world they might be.

The odd dislocations of modern life attracted a number of writers. Frederick Barthelme's *Tracer* catches a spirit of aimlessness and lack of purpose. Ann Beattie's *Love Always* renders close attention to surfaces. Bobbie Ann Mason's *In Country,* about the legacy of the Vietnam War, depicts the loss of tradition in modern America. Elizabeth Tallent's *Museum Pieces* deals with the effects of the breakdown of relationships. And in Janet Burroway's *Opening Nights,* art seems more real than life. These authors seem less interested in capturing the psychology of individuals than the rhythms of the culture itself.

Another way of accomplishing that is to take up a position in the future and look back at the present. Tim O'Brien's *The Nuclear Age* begins in 1995 in order to comment on the preceding decades. Denis Johnson's *Fiskadoro* starts some 80 years in the future, after World War III, but its subject is our contemporary spiritual condition. Kurt Vonnegut's *Galápagos* also is post-apocalyptic; here an isolated group of survivors suggests what man is likely to become.

Questions having to do with the nature of the novel are often asked by deliberately avantgarde writers, as in, for example, Gilbert Sorrentino's *Odd Number.* But Garrison Keillor's beguiling *Lake Wobegon Days* unself-consciously raises similar issues through his invention of a Minnesota community with a topography, a population, and a history that creates an indisputable but rather unclassifiable work of art. A more complex and ambitious work in the same vein, Hugh Nissenson's *The*

© Jim Brandenburg
Radio storyteller Garrison Keillor came out with "Lake Wobegon Days," about his fictional Midwestern town.

Tree of Life, purports to be a diary of a New Englander in an 1811 Ohio community. E. L. Doctorow's *World's Fair* amalgamates autobiography and fantasy in what he provocatively called "a story about memory." William Gaddis' brilliant *Carpenter's Gothic* tests the possibility of a successful novel existing almost entirely as dialogue.

The traditional novel has by no means been forgotten. John Hersey's *The Call* movingly tells the life story of a missionary in China. William Wharton's *Pride* keeps deliberately to a simple style in his tale of family life. Larry McMurtry's epic *Lonesome Dove* follows a cattle drive. Herman Wouk's *Inside, Outside* is about the protagonist's attempt to balance his personal faith with his outside, workaday life. And James Michener's *Texas* is another massive social history in the style he has made famous.

A number of new novels deal successfully with political and social concerns. Philip Roth's *Zuckerman Bound* adds to the trilogy about the troubled writer with a novella, *The Prague Orgy,* which has Zuckerman recognize that under a dictatorship art often has dire consequences. Russell Banks' sensitive *Continental Drift* grew out of his reading about Haitian refugees. Louis Auchincloss' *Honorable Men* dramatizes the effects of the Vietnam War on "establishment" life. Don DeLillo's *White Noise* is about an industrial accident in a small Midwestern town. And John Irving's *The Cider House Rules* deals with some of the complex problems raised by abortion.

Short Stories. The South continues to be one of the most fruitful sources of important short fiction. More than 30 years of the haunting, poetic stories by the highly admired but relatively unknown Texas writer William Goyen are collected in *Had I a Hundred Mouths.* Though *The Collected Stories of William Humphrey* are set mostly in Texas, they are more concerned with the inevitable sadness

© Mary Ellen Mark

© John Kings

JOHN
IRVING

CIDER
HOUSE
RULES

Morrow & Co.

John Irving, above left, published his sixth novel, "Cider House Rules," an exploration of the passions and principles involved in the abortion issue. James Michener, above right, produced another fictionalized history on a grand scale, the 1,100-page "Texas." Both titles hit the top of the hardcover bestsellers list.

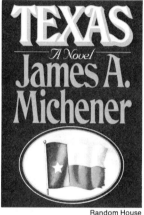
Random House

in human relationships than with locale. Peter Taylor elegantly continues to explore Virginia gentility in *The Old Forest*. The late Tennessee Williams' *Collected Stories* sensitively captures crucial moments in the lives of the outcasts of society. And Barry Hannah's *Captain Maximus* captures the underside of Southern character.

On the other hand, Grace Paley's *Later the Same Day* brilliantly captures the rhythms and speech of urban Northerners. Alice Adams' *Return Trips* tends to deal with the memories and feelings of educated, mature women. Mary Morris' *The Bus of Dreams* ranges over North and South America. R. M. Berry's *Plane Geometry and Other Affairs of the Heart* seems to take place entirely inside his characters' minds.

And short fiction continued to attract writers known for their work in other forms. The poet Mark Strand collected his idiosyncratic stories in *Mr. & Mrs. Baby*. Frank Conroy, the author of *Stop-Time* (1967), a beautifully rendered autobiographical memoir, brought together eight deeply observed stories in *Midair*.

Poetry. The richness and continuity in American poetry is often underestimated. Despite their relatively small audience, poets tend to remain devoted to their art throughout their lives. Robert Penn Warren's *New and Selected Poems 1923–1985* attests to the grace of a poet who has enriched our sense of mystery for more than 60 years. Kenneth Koch's *Selected Poems 1950–1982* establishes the achievement of one of the liveliest voices in American poetry. *The Collected Poems of Wendell Berry 1957–1982* balances his irritation at human stupidity with a love of the land that is an abiding source of strength. And Charles Simic's *Selected Poems 1963–1983* focuses attention on an inventive poet who has not been recognized to the extent that he deserves.

American poetry continues to be marked by the use of a highly personal, often overtly autobiographical mode that nonetheless addresses the universal problems of life and death. Galway Kinnell's *The Past*, Maxine Kumin's *The Long Approach*, and Philip Levine's *Sweet Will* all exemplify this voice while speaking in their own distinct styles.

But other approaches also flourish. Robert Bly's *Loving a Woman in Two Worlds* sees universals in the forms of nature. John Updike's *Facing Nature* derives its energy from the poet's sense of the immanence of art and language in all perceptions. Michael S. Harper's

Healing Song for the Inner Ear uses music, especially jazz. Hayden Carruth's *Asphalt Georgics* reinterprets classical forms. Gjertrud Schnackenberg's *The Lamplit Answer* makes use of history and myth. James Merrill's *Late Settings* tends toward the mystical. Laura Jensen's *Shelter* owes much to magic. And X. J. Kennedy's *Cross Ties* reverts to the style of 18th-century satire in his witty dissections of contemporary mores.

Several younger poets produced volumes that balance audacity and subtle craftsmanship. Amy Clampitt's *What the Light Was Like,* Louise Gluck's *The Triumph of Achilles,* and Robert Peterson's *The Only Piano Player in La Paz* are all fresh and distinctive.

But perhaps the most important event for the new generation was *The Morrow Anthology of Younger American Poets,* a diverse collection of 104 poets born after 1940 who have published at least one book.

Criticism. Significant texts and letters became available in 1985. Ernest Hemingway's *The Dangerous Summer* was to be the epilogue to a new edition of Hemingway's classic on bull fighting, *Death in the Afternoon* (1932). Starting in 1959, he became engrossed in the project and produced an unpublishable manuscript almost 700 pages long. A new edition, edited by Michael Pietsch and introduced by James Michener, judiciously reduces the text to half its original length.

William Carlos Williams' *Something to Say,* a compilation by James E. B. Breslin of reviews and commentaries on other poets, makes clear Williams' commitment to the use of the American idiom as an artistic medium and his generosity in encouraging young writers.

Houston A. Baker, Jr.'s *Blues, Ideology, and Afro-American Literature* argues persuasively that American literature has neglected to acknowledge its debt to black language and culture.

Louis Rubin's *The History of Southern Literature,* a collection of essays by numerous scholars, is a major attempt to describe and define the past, present, and future of the literature of the American South.

Sandra M. Gilbert and Susan Gubar's *The Norton Anthology of Literature by Women* provides an important record of the feminist literary tradition.

History and Biography. The interest in Ernest Hemingway continued to be strong in 1985. Jeffrey Meyers' biography *Hemingway* discloses many of the novelist's personal inadequacies and problems. Peter Griffin's account of Hemingway's early years, *Along With Youth,* presents a more attractive figure vigorously devoting himself to his art.

Peter Manso's *Mailer: His Life and Times* is not so much a biography as an oral history told by people who know him. Elizabeth Frank's *Louise Bogan* is a fine biography of an important American poet. Tennessee Williams was the subject of Dotson Rader's touching memoir *Tennessee: Cry of the Heart* and of David Spoto's sympathetic biography *The Kindness of Strangers.* David Stuart's *Ogden Nash* tries to get under the surface of the man whose ingenious rhymes made him one of America's funniest and most memorable poets.

John Hope Franklin's *George Washington Williams* details the life of the fascinating black abolitionist who fought in the Civil War, lectured eloquently, corresponded with Longfellow, and exposed the inhuman treatment of the natives in the Belgian Congo.

Barbara M. Solomon's excellent *In The Company of Educated Women* traces the achievements and ironies of women's higher education in America. Richard Slotkin's *The Fatal Environment* is a penetrating critique of the effects of the myth of the frontier on American development. And in *The Lively Audience,* Russell Lynes, best known for his analysis of highbrow, middlebrow, and low-

On the strength of only two collections since 1959, Grace Paley had been regarded as one of America's most skillful short story writers. A new volume in 1985, "Later the Same Day," added to that reputation.

© Dorothy Marder

LATER THE SAME DAY

GRACE PALEY

Farrar, Straus and Giroux

brow tastes, wittily examines America's performing and visual arts in the 20th century.

One of the most acclaimed new books of the year was J. Anthony Lukas' *Common Ground: A Turbulent Decade in the Lives of Three American Families*. The study deals in particular with Boston from 1968 to 1978, focusing on the city's racial problems and school crisis as they affected three real families. The issues and attitudes, however, are societal in scope, and Lukas' account provides an insightful view of racial conflict in America.

JEROME STERN
Florida State University

AMERICAN LITERATURE: MAJOR WORKS | 1985

NOVELS

Auchincloss, Louis, *Honorable Men*
Banks, Russell, *Continental Drift*
Barthelme, Frederick, *Tracer*
Beattie, Ann, *Love Always*
Berger, Thomas, *Nowhere*
Burroughs, William S., *Queer*
Burroway, Janet, *Opening Nights*
Charyn, Jerome, *War Cries Over Avenue C*
DeLillo, Don, *White Noise*
DeVries, Peter, *The Prick of Noon*
Doctorow, E. L., *World's Fair*
Elkin, Stanley, *The Magic Kingdom*
Friedman, Bruce Jay, *Tokyo Woes*
Gaddis, William, *Carpenter's Gothic*
Gordon, Mary, *Men and Angels*
Hawkes, John, *Adventures in the Alaskan Skin Trade*
Hersey, John, *The Call*
Irving, John, *The Cider House Rules*
Johnson, Denis, *Fiskadoro*
Keillor, Garrison, *Lake Wobegon Days*
Le Guin, Ursula, *Always Coming Home*
Lelchuk, Alan, *Miriam in Her Forties*
Mason, Bobbie Ann, *In Country*
McInerney, Jay, *Ransom*
McMurtry, Larry, *Lonesome Dove*
Michener, James, *Texas*
Nissenson, Hugh, *The Tree of Life*
O'Brien, Tim, *The Nuclear Age*
Roth, Philip, *Zuckerman Bound*
Sarton, May, *The Magnificent Spinster*
Smith, Lee, *Family Linen*
Sorrentino, Gilbert, *Odd Number*
Tallent, Elizabeth, *Museum Pieces*
Tyler, Anne, *The Accidental Tourist*
Vonnegut, Kurt, *Galápagos*
Wambaugh, Joseph, *The Secrets of Harry Bright*
Wharton, William, *Pride*

SHORT STORIES

Adams, Alice, *Return Trips*
Baxter, Charles, *Through the Safety Net*
Berry, R. M., *Plane Geometry and Other Affairs of the Heart*
Boyle, T. Coraghessan, *Greasy Lake*
Calisher, Hortense, *Saratoga, Hot*
Conroy, Frank, *Midair*
Garrett, George, *An Evening Performance*
Giles, Molly, *Rough Translations*
Goyen, William, *Had I a Hundred Mouths*
Hannah, Barry, *Captain Maximus*
Hempel, Amy, *Reasons to Live*
Humphrey, William, *The Collected Stories of William Humphrey*
Matthews, Jack, *Crazy Women*
Moore, Lorrie, *Self-Help*
Morris, Mary, *The Bus of Dreams*
Norris, Helen, *The Christmas Wife*
Painter, Pamela, *Getting to Know the Weather*
Paley, Grace, *Later the Same Day*
Robison, James, *Rumor*
Strand, Mark, *Mr. & Mrs. Baby*
Taylor, Peter, *The Old Forest*
Williams, Tennessee, *Collected Stories*
Wolff, Tobias, *Back in the World*

POETRY

Bartlett, Amy, *Afterwards*
Berry, Wendell, *The Collected Poems of Wendell Berry 1957–1982*
Bly, Robert, *Loving a Woman in Two Worlds*
Carruth, Hayden, *Asphalt Georgics*
Carver, Raymond, *Where Water Comes Together With Other Water*
Clampitt, Amy, *What the Light Was Like*
Ginsberg, Allen, *Collected Poems 1947–1980*
Glück, Louise, *The Triumph of Achilles*
Graham, Matthew, *New World Architecture*
Hacker, Marilyn, *Assumptions*
Harper, Michael S., *Healing Song for the Inner Ear*
Hayden, Robert, *Collected Poems*
Jarolim, Edith, ed., *The Collected Poems of Paul Blackburn*
Jensen, Laura, *Shelter*
Jones, Robert L., *Wild Onions*
Kennedy, X. J., *Cross Ties*
Kinnell, Galway, *The Past*
Koch, Kenneth, *Selected Poems 1950–1982*
Kumin, Maxine, *The Long Approach*
Levine, Philip, *Sweet Will*
Lieberman, Laurence, *The Mural of Wakeful Sleep*
Merrill, James, *Late Settings*
Moss, Howard, *New Selected Poems*
Pastan, Linda, *A Fraction of Darkness*
Peterson, Robert, *The Only Piano Player in La Paz*
Piercy, Marge, *My Mother's Body*
Schnackenberg, Gjertrud, *The Lamplit Answer*
Simic, Charles, *Selected Poems 1963–1983*
Smith, Dave, *The Roundhouse Voices*
Smith, Dave, and Bottoms, David, eds., *The Morrow Anthology of American Younger Poets*
Updike, John, *Facing Nature*
Warren, Robert Penn, *New and Selected Poems 1923–1985*
Williams, Norman, *The Unlovely Child*

CRITICISM AND CULTURE

Aaron, Daniel, ed., *The Inman Diary*
Baker, Houston, *Blues, Ideology, and Afro-American Literature*
Baldwin, James, *The Evidence of Things Not Seen*
Baldwin, James, *The Price of the Ticket: Collected Nonfiction, 1948–1985*
Breslin, James E. B., ed., *Something to Say: William Carlos Williams on Younger Poets*
Epstein, Joseph, *Plausible Prejudices*
Gallup, Donald, ed., *The Journals of Thornton Wilder, 1939–1961*
Gilbert, Sandra M., and Gubar, Susan, *The Norton Anthology of Literature by Women*
Hemingway, Ernest, *The Dangerous Summer*
Kidder, Tracy, *House*
Lukas, J. Anthony, *Common Ground: A Turbulent Decade in the Lives of Three American Families*
McCarthy, Mary, *Occasional Prose*
Newman, Charles, *The Post-Modern Era*
Peck, Abe, *Uncovering the Sixties: The Life and Times of the Underground Press*
Rubin, Louis, ed., *The History of Southern Literature*
West, James L. W., ed., *Conversations with William Styron*
Young, Thomas Daniel, and Core, George, eds., *Selected Letters of John Crowe Ransom*

HISTORY AND BIOGRAPHY

Ferraro, Geraldine, *Ferraro: My Story*
Frank, Elizabeth, *Louise Bogan*
Franklin, John Hope, *George Washington Williams*
Griffin, Peter, *Along with Youth: Hemingway, the Early Years*
Higham, Charles, *Orson Welles: The Rise and Fall of an American Genius*
Levy, David, *Herbert Croly of The New Republic*
Lynes, Russell, *The Lively Audience: A Social History of the Visual and Performing Arts in America 1890–1950*
MacShane, Frank, *Into Eternity: the Life of James Jones, Writer*
Manso, Peter, *Mailer: His Life and Times*
Meyers, Jeffrey, *Hemingway*
Philip, Cynthia Owen, *Robert Fulton: A Biography*
Rader, Dotson, *Tennessee: Cry of the Heart*
Sheed, Wilfrid, *Frank and Maisie: A Memoir with Parents*
Slotkin, Richard, *The Fatal Environment: The Myth of the Frontier in the Age of Industrialization*
Solomon, Barbara M., *In the Company of Educated Women: A History of Women and Higher Education in America*
Spoto, Donald, *The Kindness of Strangers: The Life of Tennessee Williams*
Stuart, David, *Ogden Nash: A Biography*

Children's Literature

Important shifts in the marketplace continued to affect the children's books area of publishing. School and public libraries once accounted for 90% of trade-book sales, but the bookstore (nonlibrary) market share has grown significantly, and publishing trends reflected that fact. There was an upsurge in toy and board books for babies, toddlers, and older preschoolers as parents exposed their children to books at an earlier age. New editions of old classics was another area where numbers were growing, and paperback series, whether they were mystery, romance, or adventure, abounded.

Awards. In 1985 the American Library Association's John Newbery Medal was awarded to Robin McKinley for her high fantasy, *The Hero and the Crown*. The novel is a sequel to *The Blue Sword* and presents a strong heroine in Princess Aerin. The ALA's Randolph Caldecott Medal went to Trina Schart Hyman for her elegant illustrations in *Saint George and the Dragon*, a legend retold by Margaret Hodges.

Recommended Books. Picturebooks in 1985 offered a rich lode of pleasurable reading for young children. Among the best are Eric Carle's *The Very Busy Spider*, notable both for its appealing story of a spider spinning her web and its bright illustrations that employ a raised line for the spider's web so that blind children may also experience the fun. Tomie dePaola's *Mother Goose* is an exceptionally handsome edition of this childhood classic, and Steven Kellogg offers a particularly funny revisionist version of the familiar Henny Penny story in his *Chicken Little*, which has the fox getting his just deserts.

Excellent nonfiction was also available for this young age group. Colleen Stanley Bare's *Guinea Pigs Don't Read Books* is a cleverly informative and imaginative introduction of these animals to very young children. Linda Walvoord Girard's *Who Is a Stranger and What Should I Do?* is an especially good treatment of the subject of strangers for very young children and is one of a growing number of books aimed at arming children against kidnapping and sexual abuse.

Outstanding titles for middle-grade readers (ages 8 to 12) spanned a satisfying range of genres. Roald Dahl's *Boy* is a funny and sometimes macabre memoir of this famous writer's boyhood and his attendance at strict British boarding schools. Solid contemporary drama is found in Janet Taylor Lisle's *Sirens and Spies*, a compelling story of a girl who discovers a disturbing secret in her violin teacher's unhappy past, and Newbery-Award-winning author Virginia Hamilton offers a series of black folktales in *The People Could Fly*. Fans of fantasy delighted in Mary Stolz' *Quentin Corn*,

about a pig who masquerades as a man, and in Dick King-Smith's nimble, entertaining *Babe: the Gallant Pig*.

Of interest in nonfiction was Russell Freedman's *Cowboys of the Wild West* and James Lincoln Collier's memorable biography *Louis Armstrong*.

Junior high and high school readers will find a witty, sobering story of teenage suicide in Richard Peck's *Remembering the Good Times*, and Robert Cormier presented a sequel to his classic *The Chocolate War* in *Beyond the Chocolate War*. A young woman struggles to forgive the mother who abandoned her as a baby in Colby Rodowsky's *Julie's Daughter*. Bruce Brooks' stylistically innovative *The Moves Make the Man* was a Newbery honor book.

DENISE M. WILMS
Assistant Editor, "Booklist"

SELECTED BOOKS FOR CHILDREN*

Preschool–Age 6
Brown, Marc, *Hand Rhymes*
Gibbons, Gail, *The Milk Makers*
Hoban, Tana, *A Children's Zoo*
Hoban, Tana, *1, 2, 3*
        What Is It? (companion books)
Isadora, Rachel, *I Hear*
    I See
    I Touch (companion books)
Johnston, Tony, *The Quilt Story*
Jonas, Ann, *The Trek*
Levinson, Riki, *Watch the Stars Come Out*
Rockwell, Anne, *First Comes Spring*
Rylant, Cynthia, *The Relatives Came*
Van Allsburg, Chris, *The Polar Express*

Ages 7–10
Carrick, Carol, *Stay Away from Simon*
Feldman, Alan, *Lucy Mastermind*
Herman, Charlotte, *Millie Cooper, 3B*
Herzig, Alison Cragin and Mali, Jane Lawrence, *Thaddeus*
MacLachlan, Patricia, *Sarah, Plain and Tall*
Simon, Seymour, *Jupiter*
    Saturn (companion books)
Wolf, Bernard, *Cowboy*

Ages 9–12
Byars, Betsy, *Cracker Jackson*
Callen, Larry, *Who Kidnapped the Sheriff?*
Fritz, Jean, *China Homecoming*
Fleischman, Paul, *Coming-and-Going Men*
Krementz, Jill, *How It Feels When Parents Divorce*
Lasky, Kathryn, *Puppeteer*
Lauber, Patricia, *Tales Mummies Tell*
Meltzer, Milton, *Dorothea Lange*
Naylor, Phyllis Reynolds, *The Agony of Alice*
Paterson, Katherine, *Come Sing, Jimmy Jo*
Paton Walsh, Jill, *Gaffer Samson's Luck*
Rylant, Cynthia, *A Blue-Eyed Daisy*
St. George, Judith, *The Mount Rushmore Story*

Young Teens
Bernbaum, Israel, *My Brother's Keeper*
Cross, Gillian, *On the Edge*
Edmonds, Walter D., *The South African Quirt*
Highwater, Jamake, *Ceremony of Innocence*
Howker, Janni, *Badger on the Barge*
Kincaid, Jamaica, *Annie John*
Matsubara, Hisako, *Cranes at Dusk*
Meltzer, Milton, *Ain't Gonna Study War No More*
Parnall, Peter, *The Daywatchers*
Stone, Bruce, *Half Nelson, Full Nelson*
    *Works not cited in article.

Canapress Photo Service

Pierre Berton and wife Janet launch "The Berton Family Cookbook." He also issued a novel, under a pseudonym.

Canadian Literature: English

Canadian readers encountered a number of new books in 1985 that either recalled their past or told them how to improve their present.

Nonfiction. In the first category are histories, a biography, and memoirs. Books honoring the 75th anniversary of the birth of the Royal Canadian Navy include Hal Lawrence's *Tales of the North Atlantic*, Graeme Arbuckle's well-illustrated *Customs and Traditions of the Canadian Navy*, Marc Milner's *North Atlantic Run: The Royal Canadian Navy and the Battle for the Convoys*, and Michael L. Hadley's *U-Boats Against Canada*.

Desmond Morton's *A Military History of Canada* details Canada's wars from earliest colonial days. William Arthur Bishop's *Courage of the Early Morning* is the biography of his father Billy Bishop, a top World War I Allied fighter pilot who shot down 72 enemy planes. Memoirs include those of diplomat George Ignatieff, *The Makings of a Peacemonger*, and *Jack of All Trades: Memoirs of J.V. Clyne* that tells of the author's life from cowboy and sailor to a British Columbia Supreme Court judge and lumber executive. *Mr. Speaker—The Man in the Middle*, by James Jerome, speaker of the House of Commons (1974–79), gives an interesting view of Pierre Elliott Trudeau and other political leaders. *So Very Near* is the reminiscences of former federal Conservative cabinet minister Donald L. Fleming. Poet Irving Layton's first of two volumes of memoirs is entitled *Waiting for the Messiah*.

In the category of self-improvement are Janis Ford's *Get to Work*, which tells how to get either a first or a better job; Dr. John Wright's *Survival Strategies for Couples;* and Judylaine Fine's *Your Guide to Coping with Back Pain*. Best-selling author Pierre Berton joined with his wife in producing *The Berton Family Cookbook*, about how family members can cooperate in preparing meals. Dr. Peter C. Hanson's *The Joy of Stress* is subtitled *How to Live Well Past 100*. Brenda Rabkin's *Loving and Leaving: Why Women Are Walking Out on Marriage* suggests that marriage should be more a partnership of equals.

Columnist Richard Gwyn's fourth book, *Nationalism Is Not Enough*, claims that Canada's economy is falling seriously behind that of the United States and that Canada must find a new means of dealing with the problem in order to halt further economic and political assimilation. *New York Times* correspondent Andrew Malcolm's thoroughly researched *The Canadians* was a well-received survey of Canada and its people. Also well received and a brisk seller was the three-volume *Canadian Encyclopedia*, with 8,000 articles.

Poetry. Joe Rosenblatt shows his range in *Poetry Hotel: Selected Poems 1963–1983*. Lorna Crozier's *The Garden Going on Without Us*, has most of the poems set in the Prairies, her home. *An Exchange of Gifts*, edited by Robert Gibbs, presents 200 of the late Alden Nowlan's poems. Other volumes are two by Richard Outram, *Selected Poems 1960–1980* and *Exile;* Susan Musgrave's *Cocktails at the Mausoleum;* J. R. MacSween's *Called from Darkness;* and George Whipple's *Life Cycle*. *The New Canadian Poets: 1970–1985*, edited by Dennis Lee, presents works by 45 writers.

In *Advice to My Friends*, Robert Kroetsch's poems give advice to various other poets who are his friends. Fred Candelaria contributes *Poems New and Selected*, and Tom Wayman's latest work is *The Face of Jack Munro*. *Essential Words*, edited by Seymour Mayne, collects poems by Canadian Jews. Two other collections are Volume II of *The Atlantic Anthology*, edited by Fred Cogswell, and *The Contemporary Canadian Poem Anthology*, edited by George Bowering. Richard Lemm's second volume is *A Difficult Faith*, and J. Michael Yates offers *The Completely Collapsible Portable Man*.

Fiction. Morley Callaghan's *Our Lady of the Snows* has a prostitute for its main character. Brian Moore's fifteenth novel, *Black Robe*, concerns Jesuit missionaries in New France in the 1630s. Pierre Berton was revealed as the author of *Masquerade*, which had been published some weeks earlier under the pseudonym Lisa Kroniuk. Berton's first novel, it is subtitled *15 Variations on a Theme of Sexual*

Fantasy. Ted Wood's third novel, *Live Bait,* is about a policeman's action-packed adventures. Anna Porter's *Hidden Agenda* is about the murder of a publisher. Margaret Atwood's latest novel, *The Handmaid's Tale,* takes place in the near future, when the United States has become a theocracy called the Republic of Gilead. Robert Harlow's *Making Arrangements* is set in the world of the racetrack. Ann Ireland's *A Certain Mr. Takahashi* tells how a Japanese influences the lives of two sisters. *Helmet of Flesh,* by Scott Symonds, concerns a prominent Canadian whose life is changed radically by a trip to Morocco. In her third novel, *Borderline,* Janet Turner tells of two strangers who meet at a border crossing into Canada and become involved with a South American refugee trying to get across the border.

Among short story collections are *Fatal Recurrences,* edited by Hugh Hood and Peter O'Brien, an anthology of stories by Montreal writers; *Glass Canyons,* edited by Ian Adam, collecting short stories and poetry from 30 Calgary writers; Ray Guy's Newfoundland stories, *This Dear and Fine Country;* and *Double Bond,* edited by Carol Heath, comprising stories by Prairie women.

DAVID SAVAGE, *Simon Fraser University*

Canadian Literature: French

In 1985, novels and essays dominated the literary scene. Jacques Godbout received the Quebec government's Prix David, while Governor-General's Awards went to Nicole Brossard for her poetry volume *Double Impression* and to the poet Jacques Brault for his first novel *Agonies.*

Nonfiction. The centennial of Louis Riel's hanging (November 1885) aroused wide public interest. Bernard Saint-Aubin's biography *Louis Riel, un destin tragique* and Gilles Martel's *Le Gibet de Regina* offer general information. Martel's major essay, *Le Messianisme de Louis Riel,* provides new insights based on the insurgent's diaries. A three-volume series, *L'Identité usurpée,* by Jean Morisset, uses Riel as a focal point to discuss the federal government's treatment of native peoples.

Three titles described francophone minorities living outside Quebec province. Jean-Bernard Robichaud discusses Acadians' intentions to preserve their language in *Objectif 2000.* Francophones of Western Canada are the subject of Grant MacEwan's bilingual volume, *French in the West/Les Franco-Canadiens dans l'Ouest.* A series of essays comments on their culture in *La langue, la culture et la société des francophones de l'Ouest.* Novels of a French immigrant to Canada's West provide the basis of Jean Papen's study, *Georges Bugnet, homme de lettres canadien.*

Political essays continued to interest Québécois readers. Jean Chrétien, a former Cabinet minister, published his memoirs of the Trudeau years in *Dans la fosse des lions.* A most colorful volume is *Les Coqs du village,* in which Jean-Louis Gagnon, a former journalist, recreates Quebec politics of the 1920s.

Books about writers or their works were numerous and varied in 1985. In *Yves Thériault se raconte,* André Carpentier provides unpublished interviews with this recently deceased novelist. M. G. Hesse offers the author's choice of her own writings in *Gabrielle Roy par elle-même.* The prolific Madeleine Ouellette-Michalska reminisces about tours of Canada and the United States in *La Tentation de dire.*

Two journals deserved special comment. Jean Pettigrew launched the first volume of *L'Année de la science-fiction et du fantastique québécois.* René Dionne marked the tenth anniversary of the death of a major poet in *Alain Grandbois* (volume 8 of *Histoire littéraire du Québec et du Canada français*).

Variety and scholarship characterized a number of excellent literary studies. Laurent Mailhot and Benoît Melançon provide a rich anthology, *Essais québécois, 1837–1983,* while Richard Giguére explores the poetry of English and French Canada (1925–1955) in *Exil, révolte et dissidence.* Semiotic interpretations of Quebec literature are found in Louis Françoeur's *Les signes s'envolent,* and Pierre Lavoie's study of theatrical sources provides pertinent materials in *Pour suivre le théâtre au Québec.* André Brochu's essay *L'Evasion tragique* analyzes Andre Langevin's novels. In *Le Jour,* Victor Teboul studies Jean-Charles Harvey's newspaper.

Fiction. *Les Corridors,* by the editor Gilbert Larocque, appeared prior to his untimely death. Gerard Bessette's *Les Dires d'Omer Marin* and Denis Bombardier's *Une Enfance à l'eau bénite* are autobiographical accounts. V. L. Beaulieu's *Stéven le herault,* Claude Jasmin's *Une Duchesse à Ogunquit* and *C'est pour quand le paradis* by Claude Le Bouthillier vied for attention with Suzanne Paradis' *Un aigle dans la basse-cour,* Yolande Villemaire's *La Constellation du cygne,* and Alice Parizeau's *Ils se sont connus à Lwow.*

Poetry. Among significant new works of poetry are Cécile Cloutier's *L'Echangeur,* Jacques Godbout's *Souvenir Shop,* Louky Bersianik's *Axes et eau,* Gilles Vigneault's *Assonances,* and Denis Vanier's *Cette langue dont nul ne parle.* Editions des Forges produced a deluxe edition of *Ode du Saint-Laurent.*

Theater. Successful plays included Maryse Pelletier's *Duo pour voix obstinées,* Marie Laberge's *Deux tangos pour toute une vie,* Elizabeth Bourget's *En Ville,* and Jean-Raymond Marcoux's *Bienvenue aux dames, Ladies welcome.*

RAMON HATHORN, *University of Guelph*

English Literature

The art of fiction was thriving in Britain during 1985. Anthony Burgess produced *The Kingdom of the Wicked*, set in the years of early Christianity in Rome. The book was variously received by critics, some of whom were dismayed by the author's admission that he had researched the tale while putting together a television series. A. S. Byatt published her sequel to *The Virgin in the Garden* under the title *Still Life*. It was welcomed as an excellent work, perhaps even superior to the first book, continuing a portrait of British cultural circles in the 1950s.

Many reviewers found John Fowles' new work, *A Maggot*, set among dissenters in 18th-century England, to be his most imaginative since *The French Lieutenant's Woman*, although some thought it showed this author's difficulties in providing a conclusion as brilliant as his beginnings. A "lost" Graham Greene, *The Tenth Man*, surfaced from the archives of the film studio MGM, where it had lain collecting dust for 40 years. Lawrence Durrell, at age 73, completed *Quinx*, the fifth novel of his *Avignon Quintet*, which he declared to be his farewell to the novel form. Doris Lessing returned from her interlude of science-fiction novels with *The Good Terrorist*, set in London and polemical in character. In a new novel *The Good Apprentice*, Iris Murdoch continued to examine the complexities of good and evil at work in today's world. *Unexplained Laughter*, a mocking new work by Alice Thomas Ellis, and *Hawksmoor*, by Peter Ackroyd, were among other notable works.

When the short list of novels being considered for the Booker McConnell prize for fiction, Britain's most prestigious annual literary prize, was published, many were disappointed to see that only two of the above-mentioned works were included, the novels of Doris Lessing and Iris Murdoch. John Fowles had requested not to be listed, but the omission of some other names was hard to justify. Nonetheless, the Booker prize was awarded to Keri Hulme for her novel *The Bone People*.

Nonfiction. The year also was rich in biographies. Michael Scammell's *Solzhenitsyn*, a vast work, was hailed as one of the outstanding works of the decade. The book not only pieces together in its 1,000 pages the tumultuous life story of one of the most extraordinary of modern writers, but asks what Scammell calls "the question of the age"—whether Communist Russia is a temporary aberration of European culture, like Nazism, or the start of the general collapse of its civilization. One of the few studies that did not pale beside this large work was Tim Hilton's first part of his biography of John Ruskin, *John Ruskin: The Early Years*. The result of 20 years of scholarship, it was praised for maintaining the flavor of Ruskin's passion and extravagance. More straightforward was *Mountbatten*, the official life of Earl Mountbatten of Burma by Philip Ziegler, with its revelations of the marriage of the Mountbattens and his charmed life at the center of British politics. A new Bloomsbury biography was published, this time the life of *Brett: From Bloomsbury to New Mexico*, written by Sean Hignett. The work provided a new light on the Bloomsbury circle from the point of view of Dorothy Brett who ended her days with D.H. Lawrence.

Another literary oddity was investigated in *With Friends Possessed: A Life of Edward FitzGerald*, by Robert Bernard Martin, the life of a complex, rich drifter who attained fame by his translations of the *Rubaiyat of Omar Khayyam*. *The Selected Letters of E.M. Forster*, edited by Mary Lago and P.N. Furbank, also threw light on the private life of the writer and his novel *A Passage to India*. In a letter to William Plomer in 1934 he wrote, "I tried to show that India is an unexplainable muddle by introducing an unexplained muddle, Miss Quested's experience in the cave." Most moving was *Dylan Thomas: The Collected Letters*, edited by Paul Ferris, witness of the poet's hardships and joys.

Among works of reference, the new edition of *The Oxford Companion to English Literature*, edited by Margaret Drabble, was warmly welcomed.

Poetry. Britain experienced a considerable poetry revival during the year, with increased membership of The Poetry Society and other organizations and a new interest in poetry competitions and readings. The Arvon international poetry prize was won by a young Englishman, Oliver Reynolds, with *Rorschach Writing*, a poem written after working as a porter in a mental hospital. Oliver Reynolds' first book of poetry, *Skevington's Daughter*, sold out within a few months and signaled the arrival of a new voice in English poetry.

Also in 1985, the doyen of English poetry writers, Geoffrey Hill, published his *Collected Poems*, an event that established his position as one of the premier poets in the English language. Douglas Dunn's *Elegies*, a series of poems written after the death of his wife, was also highly praised. Roy Fuller's *New and Collected Poems* and R.S. Thomas' *Ingrowing Thoughts* established two elder statesmen, English and Welsh. Fierce in its concentration on mankind's atrocities was Peter Reading's *Ukelele Music*. Other titles well received were Irish poet Michael Langley's *Poems 1966–1983*, Anne Stevenson's *The Fiction Makers*, and Hugo Williams' *Writing Home*. Two important anthologies made an impact—the controversial *Making for the Open*, a book of postfeminist poetry edited by Carol Rumens, and *The Bloodaxe Book of Contemporary Women Poets*, edited by Jenny Couzyn.

MAUREEN GREEN, *Free-lance Writer, London*

Joyce Ravid

R.K. Narayan, India's most notable fiction writer, produced "Under the Banyan Tree and Other Stories."

World Literature*

The year 1985 was a strong one for literature in virtually all the principal regions and languages of the world, notably in French, Spanish, German, the Slavic tongues, and several areas of the so-called Third World.

Near Eastern. From the Near East, for example, came excellent translations of the two finest practicing Egyptian authors, Yusuf Idris and Tawfiq al-Hakim, and of Turkey's perennial Nobel candidate Yashar Kemal. *Rings of Burnished Brass* offers a well-chosen selection of Idris' stories and novellas from all periods of his 30-year career, and al-Hakim's *Theater of Society* gathers several Shaw-like dramas of ideas by the Arab world's greatest dramatist. *The Sea-Crossed Fisherman* shows Kemal at his most exotic and exuberantly colorful best in a near-mythic novel of Istanbul's lower depths during the prolonged civil unrest of the 1970s. Hanan el-Sheikh's novel *Zahra* (the name means "flower" in Arabic) presents an intimate, realistic portrait of a young Shiite girl's maturation amid the recent Lebanese civil war, the blooming of a "flower" within a world become a desert. Three Israeli novels, two by Amos Oz (*A Perfect Peace, Elsewhere Perhaps*) and one by David Shahar (*Nin-Gal*), center on the isolation and confinement of the kibbutz as metaphor for an Israel beset by continual threats to its existence.

*Titles translated

Oriental. The Orient also was well represented with new works and new translations. Linda Ty-Casper, firmly established as a novelist and short-story writer in the Philippines, had to publish her sixth novel in the United States for political reasons. *Awaiting Trespass* revolves around a wake for the aged playboy Don Severino Gil and the rampant speculation among the guests as to why his coffin must remain sealed. The appearance of *The Fall of the House of Nire* in translation completed for Western readers Morio Kita's darkly comic saga spanning three generations of the ordinary, middle-class Nire family of Japan and their representative fortunes through the end of World War II. *A Tired Horse Trots On* by prizewinning Vietnamese refugee writer Nguyen Mong Giac contains 13 stories written during confinement in an Indonesian relocation camp and examining mainly the effect of defeat and loss on the author's perceptive but modest fellow Central Vietnamese. The youngest generation of Chinese writers (from Taiwan, Hong Kong, and abroad as well as from the People's Republic) is introduced to the West in the English-language anthology *Trees on the Mountain*, which offers poetry, drama, and criticism, in addition to an extensive selection of short fiction.

Eastern and Central European. From the Soviet Union and the Russian diaspora came several important new works and translations by established figures and newcomers alike. Popular songwriter-singer and poet Bulat Okudzhava's novel *Poor Avrosimov* details the investigation and execution of one of the leaders of the 1825 Decembrist uprising, with many implicit parallels to contemporary Soviet circumstances. Poet Yevgeny Yevtushenko's novel *Ardabiola* presents a lively account of a creative, optimistic scientist who develops a miraculous curative plant that succeeds mainly in bringing a series of disasters upon him from all directions, particularly from the oppressive bureaucracy he encounters in pursuing his ambitious plans for the little creation. Émigré novelist Vassily Aksyonov brought out both a collection of his recent stories in English translation (*Surplussed Barrelware*) and a new novel in Russian, *Say Cheese!*, a fictionalized account of the developments culminating in the 1980 publication of the "unofficial anthology" *Metropole*, which ultimately led to his expulsion from the USSR. Selections of previously untranslated stories by Yuri Nagibin and the late regionalist writer Vassily Shukshin appeared in English during 1985, and the most recent stories and essays by Siberian native Valentin Rasputin were gathered in *Live and Love Forever*. The most surprising hit, however, was *Metro* by émigré first novelist Alexander Koletski, a "colorful, fast-paced ride through the world of secret dissident meetings, black-market transactions, and subversive art-

Peru's Mario Vargas Llosa won the Ritz Paris Hemingway Award for his novel "The War of the End of the World."

ist circles for a rare look at how the upper class lives in a 'classless' society."

The rest of Eastern and Central Europe was well represented in quality if not quantity in 1985. The Czech expatriate writer Milan Kundera's novel *The Unbearable Lightness of Being,* a huge success in English and French a year earlier, finally appeared in the Czech original, as did the latest story collection by his countryman Ivan Klíma, *My First Loves.* Another collection by Klíma, *My Merry Mornings,* was issued in translation, thus exposing to Western readers the author's deft ironic touch and bemused observations on a world that is often harsh and absurd. *Report from the Besieged City* became the fourth major collection by Polish poet Zbigniew Herbert to appear in the West, taking as its theme the categorical imperative of bearing faithful witness to the truth of events and experience. *Hourglass,* by the Yugoslav novelist Danilo Kiš, gradually reveals itself as a horrifying account of the last months and weeks in the life of a Hungarian Jew before his deportation to a death camp. And in the story collections *Invitation to an Official Concert* and *In the Shadow of a Fleur-de-Lys* the French continued to spread the colorful, kaleidoscopic work of, respectively, Albanian author Ismail Kadare and the fantastic tales of Romanian-born theologian and fiction writer Mircea Eliade.

Spanish. Quality also characterized the Spanish-speaking world's principal publications during the year. The most important event from a historical perspective was the release of *War in Spain,* the long-lost and only

recently rediscovered Goyaesque reports and intellectual meditations on the years 1936–53 by Spain's 1956 Nobel laureate, the late Juan Ramón Jiménez. A starkly different view of the early Franco decades is provided by the celebrated but renegade novelist Juan Goytisolo in *Game Preserve,* the revealing account of his own difficult childhood and adolescence during the 1940s and 1950s: alienation from pro-fascist parents, radicalization by university schooling, and victimization by the prejudices of the neo-Catholic social system that arose under Franco. From Spanish America came two new works by leading fiction writers: *The Old Gringo* by Mexico's Carlos Fuentes recreates the final days in the life of American author Ambrose Bierce during the Mexican revolution of 1910; and *The Real Life of Alejandro Mayta* by Mario Vargas Llosa deals with a revolutionary figure from the history of the writer's native Peru. Two posthumous dramatic sketches by the late Argentine fabulist Julio Cortázar were published jointly as *Nothing to Pehuajó and Adios to Robinson,* the latter recounting a disillusioning return by Robinson Crusoe to the now-civilized island where he once was stranded.

French. The French literary scene was practically awash in important new books during 1985, not the least of which were two volumes of previously unreleased correspondence by the earlier masters Marcel Proust and Stéphane Mallarmé; the Proust volume proved particularly revelatory, covering the surprisingly difficult trials and tribulations involved in the publication of *Remembrance of Times Past.* A miscellany of hitherto unpublished verse and prose by the late Henri Michaux appeared under the title *Displacements, Disengagements.* One of the more surprising developments was the release of a new book by Alain Robbe-Grillet after a lengthy absence from nonfilm writing; *The Mirror That Reflects* is as much autobiography as it is fiction in its oblique remembrance of early childhood, the author's "first approximation at his literary autobiography," written "to destroy, by describing them with precision, the nocturnal monsters which threaten to invade my waking life"—namely, the life-draining, vampirish presences of such literary greats as Flaubert, Proust, Sartre, and Breton, under whose shadows he writes. Philippe Sollers followed up his 1984 success, *Women,* with *Portrait of a Player,* which tantalizingly interweaves several themes: the eye-opening return home of a former provincial, the cruelly comic confrontation of pre-1968 and post-1968 generations in Paris, and oblique verbal eroticism à la 18th-century French literature. The young Patrick Modiano's latest novel, *Lost District,* follows a successful writer's inadvertent investigation into a dispiriting chain of events of 20 years before among the idle rich of Paris who gave him his

start. Modiano's contemporary, J.M.G. Le Clézio, indulged in an almost anachronistic neoromanticism with *The Treasure Hunter,* in which a young adventurer's quest for pirate gold in the primeval wilds of Mauritius is derailed by the horrors of World War I. Popular successes were scored by the late Simone Signoret with *Good-bye Volodia,* a sprawling novel about two families of East European Jews during the interwar years, and by Françoise Sagan, whose novel *The Program* tracks the loves and adventures of a young Egyptian girl in Paris.

German. All four of the German-speaking nations produced noteworthy works in 1985, though the proportions were far from balanced. From Switzerland came the excellent but slight novella *Indian Summer* by Urs Widmer, a tale of five artists and one writer unable to confront the chaos of the modern metropolis and who seek, via separate paths, the solace of a spiritual "Indian summer" in the "happy hunting grounds" of remote, primitive reservations. The clown prince of Austrian literature, poet H.C. Artmann, produced his own unique creation story in *The Sun Was a Green Egg,* containing "tales which recapture much that Moses and Darwin hid from us: Yea, so might it have come to pass as the world began, and so might it have been told in wigwams and igloos." In a more serious vein, Thomas Bernhard's dark comedy *Old Masters* features an 82-year-old protagonist, Reger, whom the young narrator recognizes as a true intellectual genius and therefore without fame in Austria: "Genius and Austria cannot stand each other." Through years of study, the arts critic and philosopher Reger has always found, to his despair, some imperfection in every artwork, every performance, even every social and political activity; with the death of his dear wife, however, his whole mental construct collapses, for "all art is nothing in comparison to a single beloved person. . . . The Old Masters cannot replace a human being."

Émigrés produced the year's most interesting works by writers of East German origin. The late Uwe Johnson, whose four-volume magnum opus *Anniversaries* was completed only a year earlier, was paid posthumous tribute via publication of his first novel, *Ingrid Babendererde: Final Exam 1953,* written in the mid-1950s but never before published; its detailed yet disheartening account of the political ruination and virtual expatriation of two aspiring high school seniors presents a stark picture of the 1950s' cultural struggles in the East and the mixed feelings of many who, like the author, left their homeland only reluctantly for a system and a country they did not consider superior. Stefan Heym's novel *Schwarzenberg* portrays the same 1950s' struggle for East Germany's soul and future direction on a larger scale, using less individualized, more archetypal characters who are actually in positions to set or at least affect society's course in the unsettled postwar years; in one critic's words, Heym's *Schwarzenberg* is "a game with invented figures in a very real setting; it has the magic of something dreamed that would almost become reality."

It was from West Germany, however, that the largest number of first-rate new books emerged, including novels by Peter Härtling (*Felix Guttmann*) and Martin Walser (*Surf* and *Messmer's Thoughts*), a highly idiosyncratic novella by writer-filmmaker Herbert Achternbusch (*Way*), and short-story collections by Gert Hofmann (*The Blind Man's Fall*), Hubert Fichte (*The Departure for Turku*), and the inimitable Gabriele Wohmann (*The Mad Guest*). Topping the list, though, was the final completed work by 1972 Nobel laureate Heinrich Böll, who died in July. *Women Before a River Landscape* takes present-day Bonn as its setting and the network of human and political ties that bind the city's inhabitants as its theme. Particular focus is placed on the wives of the capital's politicians, women whose relative freedom of movement serves as a kind of corrective to much of the ingrained scheming, deception, and outright corruption that characterize the world of their husbands. The unspoken aspects of West German politics thus are fictionally placed in public view by a writer who has often been referred to as the Federal Republic's postwar conscience. The novel will stand as a fitting capstone to Böll's long and distinguished career.

WILLIAM RIGGAN
"World Literature Today"

The last work of West German novelist Heinrich Böll, who died in July, was "Women Before a River Landscape."

Alain Mingam, Gamma-Liaison

LONDON

The year 1985 was a historic one for the city of London, as the Conservative national government of Prime Minister Margaret Thatcher won passage of the Local Government Act in both houses of Parliament. The law called for the abolition of Britain's main metropolitan councils, including the Greater London Council (GLC), the city's governing body. Though the Conservatives' built-in majority secured an easy passage in the House of Commons, every clause was bitterly contested in the House of Lords. On four major points—the future of the Inner London Education Authority (ILEA); the Green Belt policy, which prohibits building on a ring of country land around the capital; waste disposal; and highway planning—the government was forced to reformulate its program. On two of those issues, the future of ILEA and the future of the Green Belt, Parliament insisted that no change be made without referring the issue back for further debate.

The GLC will be disbanded on March 31, 1986. Of its 42 present functions, 32 will go to joint boards and "quangos" (quasi-autonomous nongovernmental organizations, appointed by the central government), and ten will devolve to the borough council level. Of the GLC's overall budget, only 17% will be directed to borough councils, suggesting that the running of the city will be done largely by central appointees rather than by local councillors.

Confusion over the new arrangement is widespread, and Londoners are uncertain how they will fare as the only capital city in the Western world without its own elected government. Artistic, charitable, and other types of organizations await their future with anxiety. The confusion is not lessened by a promise from the Labour Party that, if returned to power at the next general election, it will reconstitute the GLC, albeit in a new form.

The one figure to achieve national recognition from the long battle against GLC's demise was its left-wing leader, Ken Livingstone. He secured his adoption as Labour candidate in the next general election for the north London parliamentary constituency of Brent East.

MAUREEN GREEN, *Free-lance Writer, London*

LOS ANGELES

The city of Los Angeles in 1985 reelected a mayor, argued over the value and safety of a subway, and closed down its ballet.

Politics. On April 9, Mayor Tom Bradley received more than 67% of the vote in winning election to an unprecedented fourth term. In a light voter turnout (30%), Bradley defeated City Councilman John Ferraro and seven other candidates. Bradley, a liberal Democrat, was expected to try again for the governorship against the Republican incumbent George Deukmejian in 1986. City voters also approved several ballot measures, including an amendment limiting campaign contributions in municipal elections to $1,000.

Safety and the Subway. In March a methane gas explosion and fire injured 21 persons in a Fairfax district shopping center. The gas, believed to be from an abandoned oil field, threatened further delay of the city's beleaguered subway project. But after a compromise providing for additional safety precautions and the avoidance of tunneling in the dangerous area, the U.S. House of Representatives passed its first appropriation for the system—$429 million of a projected cost of at least $3.3 billion. Opponents of the subway think it will be ineffective and possibly unsafe.

Education. With the teacher surplus of only a few years earlier having turned into a severe shortage, the school district drew criticism for hiring nearly half of its new teachers from among applicants who had not yet completed work on their credentials. Critics said the practice threatened teacher standards; defenders said on-the-job training would be effective. Also, with the end of the economic recession and the imposition of a state-required fee, there was a decline in community college enrollments—13% lower than in fall 1984—thus complicating the financing of the system.

Crime. Another so-called serial killer, suspected by the police of 16 murders and many other major crimes, haunted the area for seven months. Journalists dubbed him the "Night Stalker." Finally on August 31, Richard Ramirez, 25, was arrested and charged with several of the crimes.

Religion. The Most Rev. Roger M. Mahony was installed in September as head of the Roman Catholic archdiocese of Los Angeles. At age 49 he became the youngest Roman Catholic archbishop in the United States. He succeeded Timothy Cardinal Manning, 76, who retired. With more than 2.6 million parishioners in Los Angeles, Santa Barbara, and Ventura counties, the archdiocese is the largest in the country.

Fine Arts. The year 1985 marked a beginning and an end in the city's fine arts. The Los Angeles Philharmonic welcomed Andre Previn as its new music director. But after ten years of financial and other troubles, the Los Angeles Ballet company was dissolved.

Sports. LA sports fans had much to cheer about. The Lakers won the National Basketball Association championship by defeating the rival Boston Celtics, four games to two, in the play-off finals. The University of Southern California defeated Ohio State, 20–17, in the 1985 Rose Bowl. And in baseball, the Dodgers won the Western Division of the National League.

CHARLES R. ADRIAN
University of California, Riverside

LOUISIANA

The governor on trial, economic difficulties, and three hurricanes were the focuses of attention in Louisiana during 1985.

Politics. In his third term, Democratic Gov. Edwin Edwards was indicted by a federal grand jury in February on charges of conspiracy and wire and mail fraud. (Edwards had served two terms beginning in 1972 but was prevented by the state constitution from succeeding himself for a third consecutive term in 1980. He was returned to office with a landslide victory in 1983.) The charges against Edwards —along with his brother Marion, his nephew, and five others—pertained to a hospital development scheme in which he allegedly received $2 million. He was accused of helping to form a business enterprise but hiding his role, so as to profit from state approval of hospitals. As governor, prosecutors said, he imposed a moratorium on approval of new hospitals but allowed and fostered the approval of health care projects proposed by his partners. He was accused of making the money through his share of ownership in the projects. Governor Edwards called the accusations against him a political "vendetta."

The trial began on September 17 and dragged on throughout the fall, capturing state and national attention. Among the more interesting allegations were prosecution contentions that Edwards needed the money to pay off huge gambling debts he had accumulated in Las Vegas.

Finally on December 18, after six days of jury deliberations, the federal court judge declared a mistrial. The jurors were unable to reach a unanimous verdict, although they had voted 11–1 and 10–2 to acquit Edwards on the various charges. The jury was unable to reach a complete verdict on four other defendants, including the governor's brother (who was found not guilty on many, but not all, counts). The judge had ordered the acquittal of the three other defendants prior to the start of jury deliberations.

Jurors said after the trial that the defendants were merely businessmen trying to make money. Some pointed to the fact that Edwards became involved with the firms while still a private citizen, making his role that of a businessman rather than a government official. Because the hung jury leaned so heavily in favor of acquittal, Edwards claimed the outcome as an affirmation of his innocence. Federal prosecutors, however, said they may bring the governor to trial again. Edwards vowed to seek another term in 1987, but opinions differed on how the trial will affect the future of the once immensely popular governor.

Edwards was not the only state official in legal trouble during 1985. Education Superintendent Thomas Clausen was indicted for malfeasance and payroll fraud. His deputy and three others also faced charges in the alleged scheme.

New Orleans Mayor Ernest "Dutch" Morial was dealt a political defeat late in the year when voters overwhelmingly turned down a city charter amendment that would have allowed him to seek a third consecutive term. Morial said he would run for a city council seat instead, but his forced departure from the mayor's race left that contest wide open.

Economy. Political and legal problems notwithstanding, Edwards' biggest challenge was dealing with the state's economic difficulties. The slowdown in the oil industry has severely damaged the economy in the southern part of Louisiana, and the state's unemployment rate hovered around 11% through the year. One state official estimated that Louisiana's oil industry lost 117,000 jobs since 1982. For the year ending June 30, 1986, Louisiana faces a deficit of $100 million, with an anticipated shortfall of $200 million for the 1986–87 fiscal year.

The state's economic outlook received a further blow in late 1985, when the U.S. Congress refused to turn over up to $800 million in federal money as part of a settlement over offshore mineral revenues. At year's end, Governor Edwards promised to call a special legislative session for early 1986 and present a bold plan for economic recovery.

Hurricanes. Louisiana was struck by three hurricanes in 1985, believed to be the most ever to hit the state in one year. The first two, Danny in August and Elena in September, caused relatively little damage. Hurricane Juan in late October, however, caused hundreds of millions of dollars in property and crop damage. Juan also killed 14 persons in the state's nearby Gulf waters.

JOSEPH W. DARBY III
"The Times-Picayune/States-Item"

LOUISIANA • Information Highlights

Area: 47,752 sq mi (123 677 km^2).
Population (July 1, 1984 est.): 4,462,000.
Chief Cities (July 1, 1984 est.): Baton Rouge, the capital, 368,571; New Orleans, 559,101; Shreveport, 219,996; Houma, 101,998.
Government (1985): *Chief Officers*—governor, Edwin W. Edwards (D); lt. gov., Robert L. Freeman (D). *Legislature*—Senate, 39 members; House of Representatives, 105 members.
State Finances (fiscal year 1984): *Revenues,* $7,201,000,000; *expenditures,* $7,664,000,000.
Personal Income (1984): $48,233,000,000; per capita, $10,808.
Labor Force (June 1985): *Civilian labor force,* 1,981,400; *unemployed,* 226,900 (11.5% of total force).
Education: *Enrollment* (fall 1983)—public elementary schools, 561,181; public secondary, 221,253; colleges and universities, 179,647. *Public school expenditures* (1982–83), $1,954,086,520 ($2,739 per pupil).

MAINE

As workers struck the state's largest industrial employer, environmentalists clashed with the pulp and paper industry, and no less than 15 candidates said they intended to run for governor, Maine moved steadily through 1985, continuing the pattern of quiet growth maintained since the start of the decade.

Economy. The net gain in Maine's population for the year was 7,500, a figure that continues the annual growth rate at about one percentage point. The slow but steady increase has allowed the state's economy an equally stable transition from a dependence on the pulp and paper industry to a more diverse mix that has seen the number of in-state high-tech jobs double during the decade, according to the Maine Labor Department. In response to this more balanced, stable situation, the state's unemployment was lower in 1985 than it had been in more than 20 years. In southern Maine, the jobless rate was under 4%, while the state average was less than 5%.

In the face of this stability, the 14-week strike at the Bath Iron Works seemed to run against the economic grain. Yet when they walked out in June, the 4,500 members of the shipbuilders union felt they should resist management's request for a wage freeze that it claimed would ensure competitive bidding for U.S. Navy contracts. When the same shipbuilders voted on October 8 to return to work, they approved a two-year contract that included the original wage-freeze proposal.

Despite one of the driest, sunniest summers in more than 80 years, the annual tourist takeover of Maine's coastal resorts was not quite so vigorous as it had been in other, recent years. While more than 3 million visitors arrived, the gain over 1984 was not quite in keeping with projections. The lag was attributed to the strong U.S. dollar versus a more volatile Canadian currency. This imbalance in the exchange rate may have discouraged visits by Canadians, many of whom traditionally vacation in Maine.

Environment. Along the southern Maine oceanfront, unusual visitors made headlines during July and August: schools of menhaden clogged rivers and harbors from Kittery to Christmas Cove. So numerous were the multitudes of silver fish, and so savage the hordes of bluefish that pursued them, that vast fish kills were reported as the menhaden depleted oxygen in rivers already undernourished by drought. Cooler weather and autumnal rains provided a natural solution to the glut.

The state's Land Use Regulatory Commission made a decision certain to extend the life of a debate that has continued for years. By voting to grant the Great Northern Paper Company the right to dam the West Branch of the Penobscot River, the commission ensured the

continuation of efforts by environmental groups to preserve the wild, white water at Ripogenus Gorge and Big Ambejacknockamus ("Big A") Falls, some of the wildest rapids left in the northeast, according to its defenders. The battle then moved to the courts.

Politics. Meanwhile, the number of possible contestants in the 1986 elections grew larger. With Democratic Gov. Joseph E. Brennan's constitutionally limited two terms coming to an end, 15 candidates expressed interest in his job. First District GOP Congressman John R. McKernan was the favorite in a field that included two Independents, two more Republicans, and ten Democrats.

JOHN N. COLE, *Portland Press Herald*

MALAYSIA

An election upset and schisms within the main Chinese party in the ruling National Front delayed plans for national elections.

Politics. In Sabah, independent Kadazan leader Joseph Pairin Kitingan's by-election victory in December 1984 prompted the ruling Berjaya party to call state elections in April 1985. In March, Kitingan registered a new opposition party, Parti Bersatu Sabah (PBS), and it won 25 of 48 seats to topple the Berjaya party, which had been in power for nine years.

The PBS's narrow victory was immediately challenged by defeated chief minister Harris Salleh and his former bitter enemy Tun Mustapha Harun, leader of the United Sabah National Organization (USNO). The two schemed to have the state governor swear in Mustapha as the new chief minister. Within hours, the governor renounced his action, claiming to have been coerced, and administered a new oath to Kitingan as chief minister. Court challenges by Berjaya and USNO were pending late in the year. The PBS petitioned for admission to the National Front, but its dependence on Catholic, Kadazan, and Chinese votes

As of mid-1985, no one had been executed under Malaysia's mandatory death penalty for possession of heroin or morphine, instituted in 1983. In recent years, however, 31 have been executed under noncompulsory legislation, and 50 others have had commutations of death sentences.

AP/Wide World

raised questions about its multiethnic commitment and the question was tabled.

In neighboring Sarawak, the governor and former state leader, Rahman Yakub, relinquished the titular governorship to challenge the chief minister and National Front leader in the state, his nephew Taib Mahmud, for the leadership of the Partai Pesaka Bumiputra Bersatu.

The largest Chinese party in Peninsular Malaysia, the Malaysian Chinese Association (MCA), continued in turmoil as factions led by party president Neo Yee Pan and former vice-president Tan Koon Swan struggled for control of the party. A third faction emerged when Neo's choice for vice-president, Mak Hon Kam, held a meeting in which Neo was replaced as president by Mak. Neo responded that the meeting was not legal and dismissed Mak and party secretary general Tan Tiong Hong from their positions. As an alternative to expelling the party from the National Front, Prime Minister Mahathir bin Mohamad fired Neo as cabinet minister and engineered an agreement for party elections late in the year.

The National Front's concern is that the disarray in the largest Chinese party will lead to massive disaffection among Chinese voters in national elections, which it is planning for early 1986. During 1985 the opposition Parti Islam, primary challenger for Malay votes to the United Malays National Organization (UMNO), which dominates the National Front, sought to moderate its extremist image among non-Malay voters who hold the key swing votes in many election contests between the two parties.

Economy. Banking remained a political as well as an economic issue. The scandal lingered over loans in Hong Kong by the government-backed Bank Bumiputra's Bumiputra Malaysian Finance as former directors were sued to repay some of the defaulted loans. Finance Minister Daim Zainnuddin solidified his control of the financial sector when he picked the chairman of Malayan Banking, Jaffar Hussein, as the governor of the national bank.

In September, Malaysia's national automobile, the Proton Saga, officially rolled off the assembly line and put in a prominent appearance at the dedication of a bridge to provide a road link between the island of Pinang and the mainland. The new car, a joint venture between Mitsubishi and a government-backed company, had a backlog of domestic orders but eventually would be available for export.

K. MULLINER, *Ohio University*

MALAYSIA • Information Highlights

Official Name: Malaysia.
Location: Southeast Asia.
Area: 128,597 sq mi (333 065 km²).
Population (mid-1985 est.): 15,700,000.
Chief City (1980 census): Kuala Lumpur, the capital, 937,875.
Government: *Head of state,* Sultan Mahmood Iskandar (elected Feb. 9, 1984). *Head of government,* Mahathir bin Mohamad, prime minister (took office July 1981). *Legislature*—Parliament: Dewan Negara (Senate) and Dewan Ra'ayat (House of Representatives).
Monetary Unit: Ringgit (Malaysian dollar) (2.46 ringgits equal U.S.$1, July 1985).
Economic Indexes (July 1984): *Consumer Prices* (1980 = 100), all items, 125.4; food, 126.0. *Industrial Production* (1984, 1980 = 100), 142.

MANITOBA

The year in Manitoba was marked by three major events. These were the decision by Canada's Supreme Court to invalidate all Manitoba legislation passed since 1890; the decision by the provincial government to proceed with a major power-generating project in Manitoba's north; and the apparent recovery of the provincial government from a long series of political setbacks.

Legislation Invalidated. When Manitoba was formed in 1870, the population was about half French- and half English-speaking. The Manitoba Act, or provincial constitution, stated that either English or French could be used in legislative or judicial proceedings. But by 1890, less than 10% of the population spoke French, and in that year the Manitoba legislature decreed that thenceforth all legislation would be in English only.

In the 1970s the Franco-Manitoban Society (SFM), backed by the Canadian federal government, tested the validity of Manitoba's unilingual legislation. In 1979 the Canadian Supreme Court ruled in favor of the SFM on the test cases. In an expansion of its 1979 judgment, the Supreme Court ruled in June 1985 that all unilingually enacted acts of the legislature of Manitoba—virtually all of the province's 4,500 laws—were invalid.

To prevent legal chaos, the Supreme Court gave the province a period of grace for translation. The Manitoba government argued that it would take years of effort and millions of dollars to translate the laws.

This controversy cost the New Democratic Government (NDP) much support among its non-French-speaking electors, who felt that the NDP had given too many concessions to the French-speaking minority. The Progressive Conservative opposition (PCs) failed to gain from the NDP, however, since their national leader, Brian Mulroney, endorsed the Manitoba government's stand. The provincial PCs opposed both Mulroney and the NDP on the issue.

Power Project. A second notable event of 1985 in Manitoba was the sale of hydroelectric power to the North States Power (NSP) company of Minneapolis. The price to the NSP was to be 89% of NSP's cost of generating power by the use of coal. In order to generate the hydro power, the Manitoba government committed itself to building a dam at Limestone, in northern Manitoba, at a cost of C$2.1 billion.

Expert opinion was divided about the timing of this agreement, since it appeared that Manitoba could be charged $200 million a year in interest payments for several years before any power sales took place. However, the provincial treasurer arranged partial financing at just over 7%, from Japanese investors.

Provincial Government. A surprising development of 1984–85 was the resurgence of the NDP government. A year earlier, it had seemed to be on the verge of defeat, since it was more than 30% behind the PCs in opinion polls, and an NDP candidate had come in a poor third in a by-election.

However, during 1984–85, the government adopted a very cautious policy in relations with the public, and deemphasized its role in the French-language question. By October 1985, it was leading the PCs in opinion polls, won a provincial by-election, and appeared to be heading for victory in the expected provincial general election.

MICHAEL KINNEAR
The University of Manitoba

MARYLAND

A major upheaval in the state's savings and loan (S&L) industry dominated the year in Maryland.

Savings and Loan Troubles. The problems began in May when the Maryland Savings-Share Insurance Corp. (MSSIC), private insurer of 102 state-chartered S&Ls with $6.7 billion in deposits, ordered changes in the management of a large thrift, Old Court Savings and Loan Association. Within days there was a run on deposits at Old Court, and it quickly spread to several other S&Ls.

A judge placed Old Court into the hands of a conservator. Another S&L, Merritt Commercial, asked to be placed under conservatorship. MSSIC, set up by the state after the collapse of several S&Ls in the 1960s, did not have the funds to cover the losses at Old Court and Merritt.

Gov. Harry Hughes placed a limit of $1,000 a month per account on withdrawals from all state-chartered S&Ls insured by MSSIC. All accounts at Old Court and Merritt were frozen, and the panic subsided.

MANITOBA • Information Highlights

Area: 251,000 sq mi (650 090 km²).
Population (April 1985 est.): 1,067,900.
Chief Cities (1981 census): Winnipeg, the capital, 564,473; Brandon, 36,242; Thompson, 14,288.
Government (1985): *Chief Officers*—lt. gov., Pearl McGonigal; premier, Howard Pawley (New Democratic Party). *Legislature*—Legislative Assembly, 57 members.
Provincial Finances (1985–86 fiscal year budget): *Revenues,* $3,122,000,000; *expenditures,* $3,618,-000,000.
Personal Income (average weekly earnings, June 1985): $388.38.
Labor Force (August 1985, seasonally adjusted): *Employed workers,* 15 years of age and over, 478,000; *Unemployed,* 45,000 (8.6%).
Education (1985–86): *Enrollment*—elementary and secondary schools, 218,850 pupils; postsecondary (full-time, 1985–86)—universities, 21,000; community colleges, 3,810.
(All monetary figures are in Canadian dollars.)

MARYLAND · Information Highlights

Area: 10,460 sq mi (27 092 km²).
Population (July 1, 1984 est.): 4,349,000.
Chief Cities (1980 census): Annapolis, the capital, 31,740; Baltimore (July 1, 1984 est.), 763,570; Rockville, 43,811.
Government (1985): *Chief Officers*—governor, Harry R. Hughes (D); lt. gov., J. Joseph Curran, Jr. (D). *General Assembly*—Senate, 47 members; House of Delegates, 141 members.
State Finances (fiscal year 1984): *Revenues,* $7,296,000,000; *expenditures,* $6,880,000,000.
Personal Income (1984): $62,906,000,000; per capita, $14,464.
Labor Force (June 1985): *Civilian labor force,* 2,289,800; *unemployed,* 102,100 (4.5% of total force).
Education: *Enrollment* (fall 1983)—public elementary schools, 451,716; public secondary, 231,775; colleges and universities, 239,232. *Public school expenditures* (1982–83), $2,118,972,417 ($3,445 per pupil).

The General Assembly met in special session May 17 and established the Maryland Deposit Insurance Fund to replace the defunct MSSIC. Laws were drawn up to provide limited, temporary state help for larger S&Ls to qualify for the Federal Savings and Loan Insurance Corp. (FSLIC) and to encourage mergers or sales of small thrifts that could not hope to qualify for FSLIC.

In August, accounts were frozen at Community and First Maryland savings and loans.

Conservators and officials of Chevy Chase Savings and Loan, working together to manage Old Court, estimated the thrift might be $175 million in the red. Old Court was placed in receivership November 8. Officials of Old Court were under investigation by state and federal authorities because of allegations they profited personally from mismanagement.

On October 17 the General Assembly met again in special session. It wrangled five days before barely passing a bill to authorize Chase Manhattan Bank to take over Merritt, estimated to be $65 million in the red, and two healthier S&Ls to turn them into commercial banks. The state agreed to provide about $25 million toward Merritt's debts.

Politics. Two key political announcements in Congress set off a domino effect toward the fall 1986 election. Sen. Charles McC. Mathias, a moderate Republican, and Rep. Parren J. Mitchell, a Democrat representing the Baltimore area and a former chairman of the Congressional Black Caucus, announced that they would not run for new terms.

Mathias' seat attracted the interest of Rep. Michael Barnes (a Democrat representing the Washington suburbs), Rep. Barbara Mikulski (a Democrat from Baltimore), and Governor Hughes, who by law cannot seek another term in the statehouse. Candidates lined up for the House seats Barnes and Mikulski would vacate and for Baltimore City Hall, as Mayor William Donald Schaefer prepared to run for governor.

Other. After several years of poor investment return and high payouts for damage settlements, the troubles of the insurance industry spilled over onto such diverse groups as obstetricians and nurse-midwives, small towns, and companies that remove asbestos from buildings. The groups complained they were unable to get coverage or faced premiums as much as ten times higher than those of previous years.

PEGGY CUNNINGHAM
"Baltimore News American"

MASSACHUSETTS

Economic developments, state and municipal politics, and education tended to dominate the headlines in Massachusetts in 1985.

Economy. Business in the Bay State continued to grow rapidly. In September, unemployment was only 3.4%—one of the lowest jobless rates in the nation. In certain areas, such as office work, employment shortages developed and employers had to pay premium wages and other incentives to fill jobs.

The strong economy did not, however, extend to some of the state's largest high-technology firms—which have for many years led economic growth. Many Massachusetts computer companies, particularly those specializing in personal microcomputers and software, were hit by a national decline in the industry. Major high-tech employers, such as Wang, Computer-vision, Data General, Teradyne, and LTX, laid off substantial numbers of workers. A recovery for the industry, forecast for midyear, failed to emerge at year's end.

The economic growth also swelled the state treasury, creating an unprecedented surplus and prompting a debate on how to spend the money. A strong movement began to repeal the 7.5% surtax on incomes—a measure passed in 1975 to deal with a large deficit. The issue was a difficult one for Democratic Gov. Michael S. Dukakis, who had pushed for enactment of the surtax in his first term (1975–79). Now in his second term (since January 1985), Dukakis initially opposed the surtax repeal but by autumn gave way to mounting pressure.

The economic boom was not without its problems. One effect of rapid growth was a surge in real-estate prices. Housing prices in the Boston Metropolitan area grew faster than anywhere else in the country. By June, the median resale price of homes was $131,000, the third highest in the nation. High housing prices created serious problems for first-time home buyers and also threatened the supply of moderate-priced houses and rental units.

In another area, a state report cited the growth of childhood poverty in recent years. The number of Massachusetts children below the poverty line had grown by more than 17% since 1970.

MASSACHUSETTS · Information Highlights

Area: 8,284 sq mi (21 456 km²).
Population (July 1, 1984 est.): 5,798,000.
Chief Cities (July 1, 1984 est.): Boston, the capital, 570,719; Worcester, 159,843; Springfield, 150,454.
Government (1985): *Chief Officer*—governor, Michael S. Dukakis (D). *General Court*—Senate, 40 members; House of Representatives, 160 members.
State Finances (fiscal year 1984): *Revenues,* $10,253,000,000; *expenditures,* $9,736,000,000.
Personal Income (1984): $85,709,000,000; per capita, $14,784.
Labor Force (June 1985): *Civilian labor force,* 3,139,100; *unemployed,* 123,400 (3.9% of total force).
Education: *Enrollment* (fall 1983)—public elementary schools, 578,306; public secondary, 300,538; colleges and universities, 423,348. *Public school expenditures* (1982–83), $2,792,652,742 ($3,378 per pupil).

Politics. After a tense showdown, George Keverian of Everett was elected speaker of the Massachusetts House of Representatives in January, defeating Thomas McGee of Lynn, who had held the key post for a decade. In March, former representative and majority whip Vincent Piro was acquitted of extortion charges at the end of a second trial. A scramble among a dozen politicians for the nomination to fill the U.S. House of Representatives seat being vacated in 1986 by Speaker Thomas P. O'Neill sparked considerable interest.

Boston. Schools in the state's capital and largest city had been under the direct control of the federal courts for 11 years. In September, federal judge W. Arthur Garrity, Jr., formally withdrew from the stormy desegregation case, returning full authority to the school committee. The troubled school system also received a new superintendent, Laval S. Wilson, formerly head of schools in Rochester, NY. Wilson became the first black to head the Boston schools.

In city government, several persons in the buildings department were indicted on corruption charges in August. The indictments were the first brought against officials of the two-year-old administration of Mayor Raymond L. Flynn. The 1984 population estimates of the U.S. Census Bureau showed that the city of Boston increased in size for the first time in decades. At the same time, many suburban communities in the Boston area experienced declines or sharply curtailed growth.

Other Events. The state's financial community was startled when the Bank of Boston, the largest in New England, pleaded guilty to violations of federal currency regulations because it failed to report large cash transactions. The incident prompted investigation of several other banks that might have assisted in "money laundering" for illegal activities.

In an unusual lawsuit, businessman and former Republican gubernatorial candidate John Lakian sued *The Boston Globe* for libel in connection with stories questioning Lakian's statements about his qualifications. After a lengthy trial, no libel was found in the case, which was seen as a test of "freedom of the press."

HARVEY BOULAY, *Rogerson House*

The new Basketball Hall of Fame, a museum of "The American Game," opened in Springfield, MA, on June 30.
Basketball Hall of Fame

MEDICINE AND HEALTH

AIDS, a disease discovered only four years earlier, continued to dominate medical headlines through 1985. As researchers tried to learn more about the disease—its cause, prevention, and treatment—they also had to deal with public anxiety over the disease. Other medical problems growing at alarming rates also made headlines, as experts stressed the need to prevent such diverse illnesses as skin cancer and obesity. Meanwhile, experimental procedures, from artificial hearts to robot-assisted surgery, offered hope to patients whose illnesses had been untreatable.

AIDS. By late 1985 the number of known victims of Acquired Immune Deficiency Syndrome (AIDS) was doubling every nine months. More than 14,000 cases had been reported in the United States, and smaller numbers of cases had been reported in at least 70 other nations. AIDS suppresses the body's immune system and in an estimated 30% of patients damages the brain or spinal cord, resulting in dementia and other mental illnesses. There is no known cure for the disease, which is believed to be always fatal. To date, evidence indicates that AIDS can be transmitted only via blood and semen, even though some AIDS viruses have been found in victims' saliva and tears. In the United States and other Western nations, the disease affects primarily male homosexuals and intravenous drug users. But in central Africa, where almost as many women as men have been struck by the disease, it appears that the virus is spread by conventional heterosexual intercourse.

Though much is still unknown about AIDS and how it may be transmitted, some of the public's fears appeared to be unjustified. Evidence indicates that the disease only spreads through intimate sexual contact and transfers of blood. For instance, there have not been any documented cases of infection among family members of AIDS victims or among doctors and nurses who have treated AIDS patients. Nonetheless, some undertakers refused to embalm the remains of AIDS victims. There were school boycotts by parents protesting attendance of children with AIDS and, in one case, attendance of a healthy boy whose adopted sister had an AIDS-related disorder. Lawmakers proposed laws that, among other things, would quarantine AIDS victims, require food handlers to be tested for the AIDS virus, and make it a felony for any person in a high-risk group to donate blood.

In March the U.S. government approved two screening tests for blood contaminated by AIDS viruses. In July the Food and Drug Administration (FDA) reported that the tests were 99.8% accurate. In October the U.S. Defense Department announced that it would use the

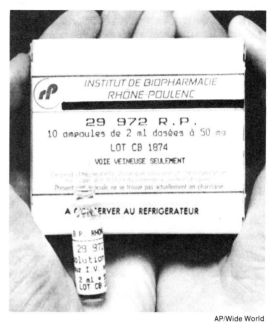

AP/Wide World

French researchers introduced a new drug, HPA-23, that appears to inhibit reproduction of the AIDS virus.

tests to screen all military personnel for AIDS infections; individuals found to have the disease would be given treatment and honorable discharges.

"Neither a vaccine nor an effective treatment is on the immediate horizon," reported James O. Mason, the U.S. acting assistant secretary of health. Although some drugs showed promise in at least temporarily controlling the AIDS virus, serious side effects often developed. Late in 1985, physicians at the Laennec Hospital in Paris reported that Cyclosporine-A, a drug ordinarily used to prevent the body's rejection of transplanted organs, appeared to halt the progression of the disease by paralyzing cells infected with the AIDS virus, thereby giving the body an opportunity to rebuild its immune system.

Other STDs. AIDS is not the only sexually transmitted disease (STD) that poses a serious health threat. According to Dr. Ward Cates, director of the STD Division of the Centers for Disease Control in Atlanta, an estimated 25–40 million Americans have genital warts (human papilloma virus), 5–20 million are infected with genital herpes, and 3–4 million are thought to have chlamydia. The prevalence of gonorrhea and syphilis has declined in developed nations, largely because of improved surveillance campaigns, but is widespread in other countries. All these diseases have enormous economic repercussions and can lead to serious complications, particularly in babies born to infected women.

Early in 1985 the FDA approved the first capsule for the treatment of genital herpes. The

drug, acyclovir, relieves symptoms associated with recurrent outbreaks of the disease and reduces the period during which the afflicted person is contagious.

Heart Disease. Following the review of seven large-scale studies, the FDA endorsed the prescription of aspirin for patients who have had previous heart attacks and for people suffering from unstable angina. Six of the studies, involving more than 11,000 heart attack victims, indicated that an aspirin a day reduced the chance of a subsequent heart attack by about 20%. The remaining study, of 1,266 men suffering from unstable angina, found that aspirin cut the risk of having a heart attack in half, from 12% to 6%. (Aspirin is believed to inhibit cells that play a role in the formation of blood clots, which can block the flow of blood to the heart and thus cause a heart attack.)

The FDA also approved the use of a device that can be surgically implanted in patients suffering from abnormally rapid or irregular heartbeat, problems that pose the risk of cardiac arrest. When arrest occurs, the device, called a defibrillator, generates an electrical pulse that shocks the heart back to normal.

A long-term study conducted by scientists at Johns Hopkins University School of Medicine indicates that people who drink five or more cups of coffee a day are 2.8 times more likely to develop heart problems than people who do not drink coffee. The findings contradict most previous studies, which found no link between coffee consumption and heart disease.

Artificial Hearts. Eight men and one woman, the first ever, received artificial hearts during 1985. In three cases, the hearts were implanted as permanent devices; in the other six cases, the implantations were performed as stopgap measures to keep the patients alive until suitable human donor hearts became available. Four of the patients died. Others suffered severe strokes, as did William Schroeder, who received a permanent artificial heart in November 1984. Other complications of the operation have included blood clots, internal bleeding, kidney and respiratory problems, recurrent infections, and suppression of the immune system. Designers of the artificial hearts were modifying their devices in efforts to reduce the risk of such problems.

Cancer. President Ronald Reagan's operation in July for the removal of a colon polyp focused attention on colorectal cancer, the second-largest cancer killer in the United States, taking some 60,000 lives annually. The American Cancer Society estimated that 75% of these lives could be saved through early detection and prompt treatment of the disease. Also receiving increased attention was skin cancer, in part because of a new American Cancer Society educational campaign—with the slogan "Fry now, pay later"—that stressed the link between suntanning and skin cancer.

Late in the year, the National Cancer Institute (NCI) in Bethesda, MD, reported promising results from a study of a new treatment technique for cancer. Called immunotherapy, it is a complex technique designed to rally the body's own immunological forces to destroy malignant cells. Dr. Steven Rosenberg, who headed the NCI team, emphasized that the results were only preliminary and that immunotherapy "is certainly not a cancer cure in 1985."

And in its own battle against cancer, the American Medical Association (AMA) in December called for a complete ban on the advertising of tobacco products, as well as laws banning vending machine sales of cigarettes and setting a minimum legal age of 21 for buying tobacco products.

Medical Technology. A new era in medical history began in March when the first operation using a robot was performed at Long Beach (CA) Memorial Medical Center. Doctors used a computerized robotic arm to assist in brain surgery. The procedure was faster, more accurate, and less invasive than traditional surgical methods. After the surgeons located a suspected tumor deep inside a patient's brain and determined the safest path to it, the robotic arm directed a surgical drill that bored a tiny hole through the skull. The arm then inserted a biopsy needle which removed a tissue sample from the suspected tumor.

Blue Cross and Blue Shield of Maryland announced the development of a card that can carry a person's medical history. Similar in size to a credit card, LifeCard can hold the equivalent of 800 pages of printed information, including a digitized photograph of the person, copies of electrocardiograms and X rays, drug allergies, and information on previous medical care. Computers and laser optics technology are used to encode and read the information on LifeCard. A complex series of codes protects confidentiality by preventing unauthorized access to the data.

Drug Shortages. In addition to the serious legal and economic issues raised by the burgeoning number of medical malpractice cases (*see* special report, page 345), product liability suits against pharmaceutical companies have led to shortages of vaccines and other critical drugs. In early 1985 a shortage of whooping cough vaccine developed after two of the three U.S. manufacturers halted production. The vaccine, which is given to nearly every infant, causes severe brain damage in 3.2 children out of every million inoculated. Multimillion-dollar court judgments against the manufacturers made production of the vaccine unprofitable for the pharmaceutical companies.

Similarly, only one company now produces polio vaccine, which previously had been made by three, and only one company produces measles vaccine, which previously had been made by six. In July a committee appointed by the

© Gary L. Kieffer, "U.S. News & World Report"

Walk-In Medical Clinics

In recent years, some 3,000 walk-in medical centers have opened in the United States, inducing both applause and criticism. Though controversial, the centers already have had a significant impact on traditional health-care providers.

Walk-in clinics, which usually are located in shopping centers or on busy highways, offer an alternative to doctors' offices and hospital emergency rooms. Staffed by physicians, nurses, and other licensed health personnel, they advertise quick, immediate care at reasonable cost. Most are open 12–18 hours a day, seven days a week; some stay open for treatment around the clock. No appointment is necessary.

Although most of the clinics are equipped to treat heart attacks and other emergencies, the emphasis has been on treating minor illnesses and injuries, such as fevers, sore throats, poison ivy, and twisted ankles. Some clinics, however, are increasing their range of services in an effort to establish ongoing doctor-patient relationships.

Supporters like the convenience and cost-effectiveness of the centers. Some critics say the trend will result in medical care of poorer quality, though health officials have found no evidence that this has occurred. Another concern is that the centers, which usually require immediate payment for their services, cater only to the well-to-do and middle class, leaving nonprofit community hospitals to treat the poor.

Among those who support the centers are insurance carriers. "We view the availability of competing settings for health care as a favorable development," says Gerry Schade of Aetna Life & Casualty Company. Indeed, in response to the competition from walk-in centers, some hospitals have reduced rates and formed walk-in clinics of their own; and some private physicians have expanded their hours and services.

JENNY TESAR

Institute of Medicine, a branch of the National Academy of Sciences, warned that "precarious" vaccine supplies posed a "threat to the public's health."

Stroke. The third leading cause of death in the United States after heart attacks and cancer, stroke afflicts some 400,000 Americans each year and kills approximately 160,000 of them. Cerebral bypass surgery, performed about 3,000 times a year, has been used since the mid-1960s to circumvent a common cause of strokes—a blockage in an artery carrying blood to the brain. In 1985, however, after an eight-year study by the National Institute of Neurological and Communicative Disorders and Stroke (NINCDS), it was reported that the cerebral bypass procedure does not reduce the incidence of stroke. In some patients, in fact, it may actually increase the risk. The study involved 1,377 patients who had experienced a minor stroke or clear warning signal. All of them received medical treatment, with about

half assigned to undergo bypass surgery. The surgical group experienced 14% more strokes than the nonsurgical group. Although doctors seemed to agree that some patients may need the operation, the study gave strong reason for caution.

Contraception. A new contraceptive for women developed by scientists at the Population Council "provides an effective and reversible long-term method of fertility regulation," according to a report from the World Health Organization. Called Norplant, the device consists of six silicone capsules that are implanted under the skin, usually on the inside of a woman's upper arm. Small quantities of a contraceptive hormone are gradually released into the bloodstream, inhibiting ovulation and blocking the passage of sperm into the uterus. The Norplant implant is effective for at least five years, though it can be removed whenever a return to fertility is desired. It is believed to be safer than the pill and less likely to fail than any other form of birth control except sterilization.

Two studies published in April found that the use of an intrauterine device (IUD) seems to double a woman's risk of infertility. The risk is greater among users of plastic IUDs than among women who use copper-covered devices.

Weight and Obesity. A panel convened by the National Institutes of Health concluded that obesity is a health-threatening condition that significantly increases the risks of diabetes, cardiovascular disease, certain cancers, gall bladder disease, arthritis, respiratory problems, and premature death. The panel noted that any excess weight—even 5–10 lbs (2.3–4.5 kg)—may impair health, but that people who weigh 20% or more above the desirable weight for their height are particularly at risk. For instance, such individuals are three times more likely than normal-weight people to have high blood pressure or diabetes.

According to the panel, approximately 34 million Americans are 20% or more overweight. Particularly alarming, they said, is the increasing number of obese children. Some researchers have found that more than one fifth of American teenagers are at least 20% overweight.

To determine one's desirable weight, the panel suggested using the 1983 Metropolitan Life Insurance Company tables of height and weight standards. But these tables have been challenged by Dr. Reubin Andres, clinical director of the Gerontology Research Center of the National Institute on Aging. He contended that "the age of the individual makes a very large difference in the estimate of what the best weight should be." Andres, who analyzed the same statistics used by Metropolitan Life, says the lowest death rates are found among individuals who were lean in their 20s, then experienced moderate weight gains into middle age.

In a study of cancer incidence among 8,006 Hawaiian-Japanese men, researchers found that those men who gained weight after age 25 had a significantly greater risk of colon cancer at age 55 and older. Population studies cited by the researchers found that Japanese men living in Hawaii are some 18 lbs (8.2 kg) heavier and have more than three times greater risk of colon cancer than Japanese men in Japan.

Animal studies by David Kritchevsky of the Wistar Institute in Philadelphia have demonstrated a relationship between obesity and certain types of cancer. In one experiment, 24 female rats were allowed to eat as much as they wanted; another 24 were on diets with 40% fewer calories. After all the rats were given a carcinogenic chemical, 14 of the first group developed breast cancer but none of those on the restricted diet got the disease. In a colon cancer experiment, Kritchevsky studied two groups of 19 male rats. All 19 that ate as much as they wanted got cancer, while only 10 of the 19 receiving 40% fewer calories got cancer.

Epidemiological studies in Sweden showed that people with pot bellies have a greater risk of developing diabetes and cardiovascular disease than people whose excess weight is elsewhere in the body. For instance, said Dr. Ulf Smith, chairman of medicine at the University of Göteburg, "the 20% of women with the highest waist-to-hip ratios had eight times the stroke risk of the 20% with the lowest ratios." The studies indicated that a man's disease risk increases if his waist is as big, or bigger than, his hips; a woman's increases if her waist measurement is 80% or more than that of her hips.

See also article on back pain, page 51.

JENNY TESAR, *Medicine and Science Writer*

Patti Frustaci became the first American to bear septuplets. But only three of the babies survived, and barely.

AP/Wide World

Malpractice

In March 1985, a doctor in Albany, NY, used the wrong drug when giving a spinal injection to a pregnant cancer patient; weeks later the young woman and her baby died. Earlier that month, a retired newspaper photographer lay brain-dead in Miami after doctors accidentally injected a toxic chemical during surgery. And in another 1985 incident, an improperly administered anesthetic in an Illinois hair-transplant clinic left the patient brain-damaged and paralyzed.

Tragic accidents like these continue to occur with alarming frequency, despite a lot of talk about better medical risk management. The results are: more medical malpractice suits, higher awards when these cases get to court, huge increases in malpractice insurance premiums, and, inevitably, a higher medical care tab for consumers and their employers.

Million-dollar awards, unheard of prior to the early 1960s, now are commonplace. Jury Verdict Research, Inc. (JVR), a collector of such data, found that 70 of the 253 plaintiff verdicts in medical malpractice cases during 1983 were for more than $1 million. Indeed the average value of a malpractice verdict soared from $166,165 in 1974 to nearly $1 million in 1984; and that does not include the many pre-trial out-of-court settlements that near or exceed $1 million. The reasons for these higher awards, says JVR, include "the escalating cost of medical care, the increased ability of trial lawyers, and the passion or prejudice of the jurors."

The publicity about such large rewards in turn contributes to the rise in the number of malpractice suits. A 1984 study by the American Medical Association found that 16 of every 100 U.S. doctors were sued in 1983, up from 3% in 1978. In New York, more than 50% of obstetrics-gynecology specialists have been sued three or more times.

A 1983 study by the Institute for Civil Justice at the Rand Corporation found that some pro-patient changes in the 1960s contributed to the crisis. These included abolition of the "locality rule," which judged a doctor's competence by local standards, and the adoption of informed-consent standards, which require that a patient be informed beforehand of the risks in a medical procedure. States that adopted such changes by 1970 had claim costs in 1976 more than twice as high as states that did not.

Some state reforms, however, actually helped. Key provisions of a package enacted in California a decade ago were upheld by that state's Supreme Court in 1985. The provisions included a cap on attorney's fees, ranging downward from 40% of the first $50,000 in awards to 10% of anything over $200,000; penalties for frivolous suits; and a $250,000 limit on pain and suffering awards. Another reform, installment payment of awards greater than $150,000, is something many insurers would like to see spread to other states, along with termination of payment after the patient recovers or dies.

The insurance availability crisis of the mid-1970s spawned a host of reforms, some of which—such as caps on rewards and mandatory arbitration panels—have been struck down by state courts. Others, such as doctor- or hospital-owned malpractice mutuals, have proven largely inadequate. Many such units are running up huge underwriting deficits and have imposed premium increases as large as 100% in the case of hospitals. Nevertheless, these mutuals now provide some 60% of all U.S. medical malpractice coverage.

Several states have mandated programs that pick up all malpractice awards above a certain amount, usually at least $100,000, for participating physicians. But now these, too, are in trouble. The Patients' Compensation Fund in Wisconsin projected a 1985 deficit of $48 million. In 1985, some 88 Florida hospitals had to kick in $44 million to pay malpractice claims owed by the now-defunct Florida Patients' Compensation Fund.

The swelling tide of litigation and underwriting losses is driving some of the biggest players out of the malpractice insurance market. Aetna Life & Casualty Co., for example, which insured 14,000 doctors and 300 hospitals in 1978, covered only 2,500 doctors and 65 hospitals in 1984.

Some high-risk specialties—such as obstetrics, anesthesiology, and neurology—are becoming particularly difficult to insure. In 1985, CIGNA Corp. informed the American College of Obstetrics and Gynecology that it would not renew coverage for 750 of its 15,000 members. Because of this problem, about 10% of the nation's obstetricians have withdrawn from practice, and more are cutting back.

A big part of America's health tab today, anywhere from $15 billion to $40 billion, goes to "defensive medicine," the host of tests that doctors order to protect themselves. And now doctors have a new defense—the computer. Those who subscribe to the services of the Docket Search Network in Chicago can learn whether a new patient has a history of medical malpractice litigation.

RESA W. KING

Dentistry

Because of rapid advances in preventing tooth decay and improved equipment and materials that reduce treatment time, the average private practicing dentist in the United States in 1985 was less busy than at any time during the previous five years. The incidence of tooth decay has declined an estimated 50% in two decades, and a 1985 study by the National Institute of Dental Research (NIDR) showed that nearly 40% of children aged 5–17 have no cavities. In reaction, general dental practitioners have turned increasingly to services once referred to specialists, such as oral surgery, root-canal work, and cosmetic dentistry. Meanwhile enrollments in U.S. dental schools are declining rapidly—down 20% from 1978 to 1985. The American Dental Association (ADA) did note, however, that enrollments by women and minorities have risen sharply.

Anti-Cavity Vaccine. Development of an anti-cavity vaccine, which has been going on since the early 1960s, focuses on a bacterial strain called *streptococcus mutans,* considered to be the main cause of dental caries (cavities). Scientists at NIDR have already been able to protect rats, hamsters, and monkeys from caries. Other vaccine research is being conducted at the Forsyth Dental Center in Boston, where scientists are working on a formula for a bacterial enzyme called glucosyl transferase, believed to be a deterrent in the decay-producing process. And British researchers are experimenting with a vaccine that would not only fully mobilize decay-fighting antibodies in human saliva but also prime the body's immune system to produce the antibodies more quickly.

Other. New technologies also are aiding dental treatment in many ways. For patients suffering the various bite-related jaw pains known collectively as TMJ (temporomandibular joint syndrome), computerized tomography scans—or CT—have helped dentists pinpoint the source of the problem and provide more effective treatment. And at Northwestern University, dental researchers are using lasers to vaporize severe gum overgrowth, a side-effect of commonly prescribed epilepsy medicine.

LOU JOSEPH
Hill and Knowlton

Mental Health

The National Institute of Mental Health (NIMH) has funded 14 projects, totaling close to $2 million, for research on the psychiatric, behavioral, psychological, and social aspects of Acquired Immune Deficiency Syndrome (AIDS). NIMH has expanded its research efforts into the psychological reactions of persons who receive positive results from blood tests for antibodies to the HTLV-III virus, the probable cause of AIDS.

Through publications and press releases, the NIMH tried to educate the public regarding the psychological aspects of the disease. New directions in prevention programs were being sought. Studies on changing patterns of intimacy and behavior among members of the high-risk group as well as relationships between immune function and mental status were underway.

Teenage Suicide. Suicide ranks as the third leading cause of death among U.S. teenagers, and it is on the increase. Many theories as to the basic causes of adolescent suicide have been formulated. They are complex and often interrelated. They include the stresses of adolescence, the association of mental disorders, the presence of a family history of suicide or a psychiatric disorder, and the meaning of death for adolescents (that death is reversible).

Behavior changes, life changes, loss, and precipitating events lead to self-destructive behavior in young people. Some of the behavioral clues to suicidal behavior are: a drastic change in personal appearance, inability to concentrate, feelings of worthlessness, weight change, sleep disturbance, excessive and inappropriate guilt, emotional outbursts, preoccupation with death, hopelessness, giving away prized possessions, loss of interest in usual activities, and suicidal talk and ideas.

Electroconvulsive Therapy. Electroconvulsive Therapy (ECT) is a treatment for severe mental illness in which electricity applied to the scalp passes through the brain, producing a generalized convulsion. Although the procedure has been in use for more than 45 years, it remains controversial. In June 1985 a consensus development conference was held to better understand the treatment. A panel of psychiatrists, psychologists, neurologists, epidemiologists, as well as a lawyer and a consumer heard presentations by experts as well as testimonials by former patients.

The panel found that ECT is demonstrably effective for a narrow range of severe psychiatric disorders, especially acute major depression, acute mania, and certain schizophrenic syndromes. However, there may be significant side effects, notably acute transient confusional states and memory dysfunction as well as persistent memory deficits for events during the months surrounding the treatment. The panel agreed, however, that proper administration of the procedure can reduce potential side effects. Panel members also agreed that the physician's decision to offer ECT to a patient, and the patient's decision to accept it, should be based on a complex consideration of advantages and disadvantages of ECT compared with alternative treatments.

SHERVERT H. FRAZIER, M.D., *Director*
National Institute of Mental Health

METEOROLOGY

Meteorologists in 1985 made advances in understanding nuclear winter, acid rain, wind shear, cloud seeding, and global climate changes. The year also marked the 25th anniversary of weather satellites.

Nuclear Winter. Computer models of the climate conducted at Los Alamos National Laboratory and the National Center for Atmospheric Research (NCAR) have strengthened and clarified the conclusions reached previously about the climatic effects of large-scale nuclear war. For the first time, calculations have included the effects of solar heating of soot particles, the transport of smoke by the wind, and the removal of smoke and soot by rainfall. The results show that for a war conducted during the summer, a third of the smoke that would result from burning cities would remain in the upper atmosphere for much longer than previously believed. The resulting cold and dark at the earth's surface—"nuclear winter"—would cause such a disruption to agriculture that conditions would resemble the present-day famine in Ethiopia and the Sudan.

Acid Rain. With increasing evidence of damage to forests, lakes, and buildings, both Canada and the state of New York took the unprecedented step of enacting legislation to reduce emissions that might contribute to acid rain. Because of new understandings regarding the distance of environmental impact and frustrated by the efforts of the Reagan administration, seven Northeastern states sued the U.S. Environmental Protection Agency (EPA) demanding that it restrict emissions from states in the Ohio Valley. In a study conducted by the National Oceanic and Atmospheric Administration (NOAA), natural sources in the Gulf of Mexico were shown to be an insignificant source of air pollution compared with even one coal-fired power plant burning low-sulfur coal.

Wind Shear. The August crash of a Delta Airlines jet in Dallas, believed to be caused by a microburst (a highly localized wind shift), focused attention on the inadequacy of the wind-shear detection system currently installed in many U.S. airports. The common Low Level Wind Shear Alert System has anemometers so widely spaced that many microbursts go undetected. Furthermore, the current system produces so many false alarms that it is being ignored by air traffic controllers and pilots. A joint research program of NCAR and the Federal Aviation Administration (FAA) at the Denver airport has demonstrated the usefulness of a sophisticated Doppler radar system that can detect wind shear more reliably.

Satellites. As NOAA celebrated the 25th anniversary of the weather satellite, only one U.S. geostationary satellite remained operational, reducing the ability of the National Weather Service (NWS) to monitor storms. A new satellite was planned for launch in early 1986. NOAA-8, one of the polar orbiting satellites, also experienced problems during the year, reducing the ability of NOAA to monitor the global atmosphere.

Forecasting. Studies have shown that the accuracy of NOAA temperature, wind, and precipitation forecasts has continued to rise since computers were first used decades ago. A new Nested Grid forecast model, running on the new CYBER 205 supercomputer, has begun to contribute even further to weather forecasting skills. The best weather forecasts come from the European Centre for Medium Range Weather Forecasting in Reading, England, which will soon install a Cray XMP-48 supercomputer, the world's fastest.

In an unprecedented ruling, a U.S. federal judge ruled in 1985 that the NWS was responsible for the deaths of three fishermen near Boston who relied on a forecast that turned out to be wrong. The ruling, based on evidence of an improperly maintained buoy, set a precedent that may require all forecasts to contain a warning that they are based on imperfect data. NWS appealed the case.

Two new large-scale observational projects were being planned to help in the understanding and forecasting of storms. One, called GALE (Genesis of Atlantic Lows Experiment), will use a research ship, eight airplanes, sounding balloons, buoys, and radars to study winter storms that batter the East Coast. The other, called STORM (Stormscale Operational and Research Meteorology), will use 80 automatic weather stations, 10 radars, and 20 balloon launching sites to study severe thunderstorm complexes and lightning.

Cloud Seeding. A review by NOAA scientists of Project Stormfury, an unsuccessful 20-year attempt to modify hurricanes by seeding the eye wall (where the winds are strongest), indicated the reasons for the project's failure. Hurricanes, they found, have too little supercooled water and too much natural ice for the seeding particles to induce any further production of ice. Also, hurricanes have proven to be so variable that any changes observed after seeding cannot be distinguished from what might have occurred anyway.

Climate Variations. The El Niño ocean and weather phenomenon of 1982–83 has prompted a ten-year international research program called Tropical Ocean Global Atmosphere, involving drifting buoys, sophisticated satellite data, and complex computer models of the ocean and atmosphere.

An NCAR study has shown that trace gases —including Freon, ozone, methane, and nitrous oxide—emitted by industry and other human activities are as important as carbon dioxide in their potential for producing a warmer global climate in the near future.

ALAN ROBOCK, *University of Maryland*

The Weather Year

The 1985 weather year in the United States was characterized by a record cold winter in the Plains and an extraordinary number of tropical storms during the hurricane season.

December 1984–February 1985. Winter season temperatures were lower than average in the western half of the United States and near normal in the East. Precipitation was heavy in the Mississippi Valley and upper Great Lakes.

In December 1984 sharply contrasting patterns were observed across the country. More than twice the average precipitation blanketed a large area from the Southwest to the southern Plains into the Great Lakes region, while the Northwest and Southeast were unseasonably dry. Monthly temperatures were unusually high in the East and relatively low in the West.

January was cold and dry over most of the country, with a number of cities hitting record-low temperatures. At mid-month, the worst storm in a century in central Texas dumped 10–13 inches (25–33 cm) of snow on San Antonio. Much of Florida's citrus and vegetable crops were damaged by a freeze.

Winter's fury continued during the first half of February. Freezing temperatures reached into the Gulf of Mexico, southern California, and Arizona. Snow and freezing rain plagued the area from Arkansas and Missouri northward to the Great Lakes. On February 1 the temperature at Peter Sink, UT, plunged to −69.9°F (−56.6°C), a record low for the contiguous 48 states. Rapid warming and heavy rain in the latter half of the month caused flooding in the Mississippi Valley.

March–May. Dry weather prevailed on both coasts during the spring, and seasonal temperatures were generally above average. In March, nearly twice the normal rainfall was recorded from south central Texas through Oklahoma, southeastern Texas, and southern Mississippi. Record warmth blanketed the East Coast early in the month, while an intense storm dumped heavy snow on the northern Plains. In late March a powerful Pacific storm battered the West Coast, eventually producing heavy snow in the Rockies.

April was extremely dry over much of the country, and monthly temperatures were 6–8°F (3–4°C) higher than average in many areas. Much-needed rain fell on the Northeast in May, but reservoir levels remained below normal. Dry weather persisted in the Southeast. At mid-month, violent thunderstorms hit the Midwest, while record high temperatures exacerbated dry conditions in Florida. Late in the month, moderate showers eased the dryness in the northern Plains. Tornadoes caused extensive damage and several deaths in western Pennsylvania, New York, and Ontario.

June–August. Summer was warm and dry across the Intermountain region but cooler than normal in most other areas. Thunderstorms rumbled through the Plains and Southeast almost daily during June. Early in the month, warm air in the Southeast pushed temperatures to more than 100°F (38°C), establishing many new all-time highs.

July rainfall was above normal in much of the nation. Average temperatures were normal or slightly below everywhere except the Pacific Northwest. Late in the month, Tropical Storm Bob moved across southern Florida and northward to the South Carolina coast.

August was cold and wet over most of the country. Hurricane Danny brought torrential rains and flooding to Louisiana, Mississippi, and Alabama. As the month ended, Hurricane Elena buffeted the Florida panhandle.

September–November. Autumn precipitation was above average in most of the United States. Temperatures were below average early in the season, while the latter part was marked by record cold in the West and record warmth in the East.

September was a busy month for tropical storms. Hurricane Elena weakened to tropical storm strength by the time it hit land near Biloxi, MS, but it spread heavy showers from the Mississippi Delta to southern Illinois. Late in the month, Tropical Storm Henri and Hurricane Gloria belted the East Coast. Gloria was one of the most intense Atlantic hurricanes on record.

In mid-October, the remnants of Hurricane Waldo spread Pacific moisture into the Plains. Torrential rains caused flooding from Texas to Missouri. High winds and heavy rain buffeted the Northwest later in the month. And as the storm moved inland, it brought heavy snow to the Cascades, Sierras, and northern Rockies. At month's end, Hurricane Juan caused severe flooding in Louisiana.

November temperatures were 4–8°F (2–4°C) above average in the eastern half of the country and 4–16°F (2–8°C) colder in the western half. Precipitation was generally above average. Early in the month, heavy rain produced serious flooding in North Carolina, Virginia, and West Virginia. A series of winter storms spread heavy snow across the Northwest and Upper Plains at mid-month. And Hurricane Kate, an unusual late-season storm, hit the Florida panhandle the following week.

See also ACCIDENTS AND DISASTERS.

IDA HAKKARINEN

MEXICO

Devastating earthquakes, continuance of severe economic problems, and political controversies marred the year for Mexico. The nation remained politically stable, however, and President Miguel de la Madrid received a warm reception during his European diplomatic tour.

Earthquakes. The most serious earthquake of the 20th century, measuring 8.1 on the Richter scale, shook the nation on the morning of September 19, killing thousands and destroying billions of dollars worth of property. Worst hit was the central part of Mexico City, where hotels, hospitals, and apartment buildings collapsed, trapping an unknown number in the rubble. The tragedy worsened on Friday night when a second quake, an aftershock of the first, struck Mexico City with a force of 7.3 on the Richter scale. Published estimates counted 4,600 dead, but the number may have been higher in the densely packed city. At least 3,000 buildings collapsed or were so severely damaged that they had to be demolished. Destroyed were seven 13-story apartment buildings, two of the city's largest hospitals, more than 200 schools, nine hotels, and numerous government and private office buildings. Long-distance telephone communications were disrupted for weeks when transmitter towers collapsed. More than 50,000 people had to live in temporary shelters or improvised camps on public land.

The rescue effort was slow, laborious, and controversial. City residents immediately began rescue efforts voluntarily and saved many lives. The government mobilized police forces and the military. The instability of many buildings and the lack of sufficiently trained personnel and heavy equipment prolonged rescue efforts even after the government swung into action. The Mexican government initially rejected all but trivial aid from other countries, asserting, in a burst of nationalism, that the nation was capable of dealing with the disaster by itself. Relatives of those missing or known to be trapped grumbled that the government's false pride was risking lives. When the grumbling turned to loud cries of protest after the second quake struck, the government began accepting much larger quantities of financial and material aid from numerous countries. Many lives were saved during the first week after the quakes, as the international news media focused attention on dramatic rescue efforts. Such attention created problems for the government when it had to decide to cease rescue efforts and begin clearing sites to prevent the spread of disease. Many Mexicans argued that the government had badly mishandled the disaster by not accepting massive foreign assistance sooner and not coordinating rescue efforts better.

Protest marches against governmental inefficiency in handling the disaster continued into November. The slowness of the government to

A Mexico City resident anxiously reads the latest news regarding the tragic earthquakes that struck Mexico in September.

AP/Wide World

find housing for the very visible thousands of homeless was a constant source of criticism. In late October the government responded by expropriating private property in the city with the promise to distribute it to the homeless. This act, however, frightened all private-property owners and brought criticism from the political center and right. Many critics demanded that the Mexico City government be democratized, noting that the average citizen had responded to the crisis more quickly and effectively than had the government.

The long-term political implications of the disaster were not immediately clear. On the one hand, it diverted attention from the severe national economic crisis and electoral controversies. On the other hand, it revealed that the government, in spite of its highly centralized control, was incapable of acting decisively in the face of a major national disaster in the seat of its own power. It was unlikely that the government would make more than cosmetic changes in the political system, however. At best, Mexico City residents might be given a slightly greater voice in municipal affairs.

Economy. Economic policy sought to meet the austerity requirements of the International Monetary Fund (IMF) while also meeting domestic political needs. Goals included reduction of deficit spending, slowing the growth rate of the foreign public debt, lowering the inflation rate, promotion of exports and limitation of imports, stimulation of industrial production, and maintenance of a realistic exchange rate for the peso. Protection of industry was reduced, while importation of items necessary for industrial production was eased. Further, President Miguel de la Madrid sought increased governmental efficiency by beginning the sale, transfer, or liquidation of 236 of the 900 government-owned corporations, many of which operated at a loss. The state-owned banking system continued divesting itself of the nonbanking companies it acquired in the 1982 bank nationalization. Government agencies also were consolidated.

As part of the austerity plan, the national budget was projected at 18.4 trillion pesos (about $37 billion), a figure the government claimed was only 38% higher than estimated 1984 expenditures and considerably less than the 59% inflation rate for that year. Other economists, however, noted that the government had significantly increased expenditures at the end of 1984 for political reasons and that the new budget was actually close to the anticipated 58% inflation rate for 1985. Education, regional development, health, and social security received budgetary increases as the government sought to mitigate some of the effects of a falling standard of living for the average person. More than one third of the budget was destined for debt service, severely limiting the government's options.

The economy continued in crisis, producing such revenue shortfalls that the government took further austerity measures during the year. During the first quarter of the year, bank deposits and financing fell, nonpetroleum exports decreased 11.1%, petroleum exports were 18% less than they were for the same period the previous year, and the trade surplus was only $2.4 billion compared with $4 billion for the first quarter of the previous year. Mexico was forced to lower its petroleum prices in February and July to remain competitive in world markets, moves that cost the nation $350 million in earnings. Growth in the tourism industry, the second-largest source of foreign exchange, lagged behind expectations, and net earnings were reduced by a 30% increase in the number of Mexicans traveling abroad. The government increased the rate of the daily peso devaluation in March and then, in July, devalued it 20%. Public expenditures were cut in February, March, and May by freezing job vacancies and postponing major public works programs.

In early October, Mexico deferred its scheduled $950 million payment in its foreign debt and announced that new rates and terms would be fixed within six months. This decision, made in consultation with the World Bank and the United States, freed money for earthquake relief. Mexico, successful during the year in renegotiating its almost $100 billion foreign debt, reiterated its promise to meet its debt obligations.

Politics. The government and its Institutional Revolutionary Party (PRI) showed concern over the growing strength of the National Action Party (PAN) in northern border states. In Chihuahua and Coahuila municipal elections in December 1984, the government annulled elections rather than recognize PAN victories. PAN members protested, sometimes violently, but to little avail. That PRI agreed to govern Monclova, Coahuila, jointly with PAN was tacit admission that PAN had won the annulled elections in that city. Many domestic and foreign observers expected PAN to win the gubernatorial elections in Sonora and possibly Nuevo León, but the PRI claimed substantial majorities in the July elections while PAN cried fraud. In Chihuahua, the all-PRI state electoral commission annulled the election of PAN's Juan Saldana Rodríguez to the state legislature to keep PAN victories to five and prevent loss of two-thirds control of a state legislature. The 1983 election of Saldana Rodríguez also had been annulled.

The seriousness of PAN's challenge to PRI dominance of the northern border area brought concerted efforts to reduce PAN's support. The leftist Mexican United Socialist, Peoples' Socialist, and Mexican Workers parties accused PAN of conspiring with John Gavin, the U.S. ambassador, and demanded his expul-

AP/Wide World

President Miguel de la Madrid casts his vote in July elections, which were called fraudulent by the opposition.

sion. Government periodicals printed articles asserting that PAN had close ties with the Republican Party in the United States and that PAN victories would result in the "Texicanization" of the northern border. Shortly before the elections, President de la Madrid announced a 153-billion-peso (about $300 million) Northern Border Development Program and the creation of free trade zones in Baja California and parts of Sonora.

In the July elections the government and PRI made it clear they were still in control even if fraud had to be used in some cases. In spite of de la Madrid's promises of moral renovation and honest elections, it appeared that the government, afraid to show weakness during the economic crisis, manipulated results in some races. PRI candidates were declared victorious in all seven gubernatorial races, but PAN charged fraud in Sonora and Nuevo León. For the regular 300 congressional seats, the PRI took 290, PAN eight, and the Authentic Mexican Revolutionary Party two. In the parallel election for the 100 seats in the five regional congressional districts, eight opposition parties received seats, five of which are guaranteed to any party receiving at least 1.5% of the total vote and less than 50 regular seats. Through this election, PAN received another 32 seats; the Mexican United Socialist, the Socialist Workers, and the Mexican Democratic parties 12 each; the Peoples' Socialist Party 11; the Authentic Mexican Revolutionary and the Workers parties 6 each. Government encouragement of new leftist parties, which received seats, reduced PAN's congressional representation while pacifying leftist critics.

Although PRI could claim 65% of the votes cast, the almost 50% abstention rate indicated dissatisfaction with the government.

Opposition to PRI rule in Chihuahua forced the resignation of the governor and the state university rector in September. Students seized Chihuahua city buses and barricaded streets to force the resignation of the university rector, who, openly backed by PRI, had sought reelection. The student upheaval, PAN strength, and opposition from Fidel Velasquez, national head of the Mexican Workers Federation, forced the resignation of the governor and the eventual appointment of the state treasurer in his place.

Foreign Policy. Mexican foreign policy followed its traditional lines but was limited in its effectiveness by domestic problems. The nation supported a nuclear freeze, lower interest rates for debtor nations (of which it is a major one), and the efforts of the Contadora Group seeking a negotiated peace in Central America. Although Mexico is a member of the Contadora Group and has sold oil at discount prices to its Central American neighbors, it suspended sales to Costa Rica and Nicaragua in March because they were behind on their payments. Relations between Mexico and Guatemala remained strained because thousands of Guatemalans have fled to safety in Mexico to escape repression at home. Illegal aliens, principally from Central America, now number 1 million in southern Mexico, putting a severe strain on the economy. President de la Madrid sought European support for the Contadora process when he made state visits to major European nations but concentrated his efforts on obtaining European trade and investments to help the Mexican economy.

Relations with the United States remained good in spite of Mexican opposition to the militarization of space and complaints about sensationalist publicity concerning drug murders of several U.S. citizens.

DONALD J. MABRY
Mississippi State University

MEXICO • Information Highlights

Official Name: United Mexican States.
Location: Southern North America.
Area: 761,601 sq mi (1 972 547 km²).
Population (mid-1985 est.): 79,700,000.
Chief Cities (1979 est.): Mexico City, the capital (1980 census), 9,377,300; Guadalajara, 1,906,145; Monterrey, 1,090,009.
Government: *Head of state and government,* Miguel de la Madrid Hurtado, president (took office Dec. 1982). *Legislature*—Congress: Senate and Federal Chamber of Deputies.
Monetary Unit: Peso (505 pesos equal U.S.$1, floating rate, Nov. 18, 1985).
Gross Domestic Product (1983 U.S.$): $121,200,-000,000.
Economic Indexes (1984): *Consumer Prices* (1972 = 100), all items, 2,841; food, 2,738. *Industrial Production* (1980 = 100), 102.
Foreign Trade (1984 U.S.$): *Imports,* $11,207,-000,000; *exports,* $23,462,000,000.

MICHIGAN

Detroit's economy continued to improve under the impetus of a continuingly profitable auto industry. Several major building projects were started or completed in Detroit. Detroit Mayor Coleman A. Young was elected easily to a fourth four-year term.

Economy. The major auto firms continued to report impressive—if reduced from 1984—profits. General Motors reported profits of $2.7 billion for the first nine months of 1985, off 24% from $3.6 billion in the same period of 1984. Ford Motor Co. reported profits of $1.8 billion for the first nine months, down from 1984's $2.19 billion. Chrysler Corp. had nine-month earnings of $1.4 billion, down from $1.5 billion in the 1984 period.

Chrysler Corp. and the United Auto Workers (UAW) reached a three-year agreement that gave 70,000 Chrysler workers parity with Ford Motor and General Motors. Ratification of the contract on October 27 ended a strike that began October 16.

The Millender Center opened in downtown Detroit and was hailed as another sign of Detroit's "renaissance." The $73.5 million complex, across the street from the riverfront Renaissance Center, comprised the 20-floor, 258-room Omni Hotel, a 38-story residential tower, offices, and a parking garage.

Ground was broken October 29 on a $200 million expansion of Cobo Hall, the city's convention center. The larger facility was to offer 750,000 sq ft (67 500 m²) in five exhibit halls and 100 meeting rooms, including 650,000 sq ft (58 500 m²) on one level. The expansion was to be partly financed by an increase in taxes on hotel rooms and state whiskey taxes. Mayor Young predicted the larger structure would spark construction of 3,000 new hotel rooms and provide jobs for 20,000 people.

Gannett Co. Inc., the nation's largest newspaper chain, agreed to buy the Evening News Association (ENA), publisher of *The Detroit News,* for $717 million, ending 112 years of family ownership of the ENA. The merger, announced on August 30, culminated the ENA's five-week effort to find a friendly buyer to stave off a hostile takeover by television producer Norman Lear and associates.

Legislation. Soaring medical malpractice insurance premiums prompted legislative efforts to make insurance cheaper and more readily available to doctors. On October 23, more than 10,000 doctors and other health-care professionals demonstrated in front of the capitol in Lansing, the largest demonstration since May 14, 1970, when Michigan State University students protested the Vietnam War.

The legislature also passed a bill requiring seat belts to be worn by car drivers and front-seat passengers. A fine of $10 was imposed, to be increased to $25 on Jan. 1, 1986.

MICHIGAN · Information Highlights

Area: 58,527 sq mi (151 586 km²).

Population (July 1, 1984 est.): 9,075,000.

Chief Cities (July 1, 1984 est.): Lansing, the capital, 127,972; Detroit, 1,088,973; Grand Rapids, 183,000; Warren, 152,035; Flint, 149,007; Sterling Heights, 109,440.

Government (1985): *Chief Officers*—governor, James J. Blanchard (D); lt. gov., Martha W. Griffiths (D). *Legislature*—Senate, 38 members; House of Representatives, 110 members.

State Finances (fiscal year 1984): *Revenues,* $17,071,000,000; *expenditures,* $15,368,000,000.

Personal Income (1984): $114,408,000,000; per capita, $12,607.

Labor Force (June 1985): *Civilian labor force,* 4,399,400; *unemployed,* 449,800 (10.2% of total force).

Education: *Enrollment* (fall 1983)—public elementary schools, 1,132,701; public secondary, 603,180; colleges and universities, 515,760. *Public school expenditures* (1982–83), $5,351,619,530 ($3,307 per pupil).

Detroit. In the mayoral election, incumbent Coleman A. Young won easily over Thomas Barrow, an accountant and cousin of former heavyweight boxing champion Joe Louis.

Mayor Young attracted criticism from some local leaders for rebuilding downtown Detroit at the expense of the neighborhoods suffering most from a lack of police protection. The mayor recommended a 1985–86 budget that would allow the hiring of 720 police officers. However, crime remained a recurrent issue, heating up just before the city's November election with a series of shootings near city schools in which several students were shot, including six wounded at a high school football game. Because of continuing violence in public schools, Detroit instituted unannounced electronic searches at high schools. Forty-seven students were arrested and nearly 75 weapons were confiscated before the American Civil Liberties Union, challenging the constitutionality of mass searches, filed suit to halt them.

People Mover. Problems continued to threaten construction of the People Mover, a 2.9-mi (5-km) railway designed to link major elements of downtown Detroit. Federal officials threatened to cut off funding unless the city and state acted to halt cost overruns, which totaled $73 million with stations still to be built and rail cars still to be purchased. The project, originally under the direction of the Southeast Michigan Transportation Authority, was turned over to a new quasi-public corporation, Detroit Transportation Corp., with the city and state pledging to assume liability for further cost overruns.

Silverdome. On March 4 the 10-acre (4-ha) roof of the Pontiac Silverdome, home of the Detroit Lions, collapsed under the weight of tons of snow, ice, and water during a snow and sleet storm that also closed 135 state school districts. The roof was replaced by fall.

CHARLES THEISEN, *"The Detroit News"*

MICROBIOLOGY

The year 1985 saw a number of exciting discoveries in the field of microbiology.

Cancer Vaccines. A completely successful vaccine for a virus-induced cancer must provide both for resistance to the invading organism, *prevention,* and for destruction of any already formed cancer cells, *therapy.* In order to do this the vaccine must have two different antigenic properties. One antigen must be virus-specific and reflect the proteins that form the coat of the virus, while the other must be tumor-specific and reflect one or more characteristics of the surface of already transformed cells.

Dr. Richard Olsen of Ohio State University in Columbus developed a vaccine against a form of leukemia that affects cats. This is the first vaccine developed against any cancer in mammals. The virus involved is called *feline leukemia virus* (FLV), and it annually kills about 1 million of the 50 million pet cats in the United States. Infected cats spread the virus to other cats through saliva by grooming each other or by sharing food dishes. The vaccine contains two components, one that stimulates an immune reaction against FLV itself and another that destroys any cancerous tissue present if the cat already has been infected.

Prospecting for Ores. Microorganisms have been used for a long time as indicator species in exploring for oil. In the mid-1980s, however, one species of bacteria has been found to be extremely abundant near ore deposits. Dr. John Watterson of the U.S. Geological Survey (USGS) in Denver, CO, has discovered that the bacterium *Bacillus cereus* is 100,000 times more prevalent in the earth above a big copper deposit in Montana than in the surrounding topsoils. Dr. Nancy Parduhn, also of the USGS, found a similar situation in a soil survey near gold deposits in California.

Whether *B. cereus* uses the same physiological mechanism to avoid being killed by heavy concentrations of the different metals remains to be discovered. Further, whether one can use the presence of the bacterium to identify ore-rich deposits deep in the earth would require investigations of untested areas.

Toxic Chemicals. Virtually every technological advance has produced waste products that require disposal. Unfortunately, many of these chemicals are poisonous to organisms, including humans, and persist in the environment for long periods of time. PCBs (polychlorinated biphenyls), a group of compounds that are used as coolants in electrical transformers, have been found to damage the reproductive systems of laboratory animals and are suspected of causing birth defects in human beings.

Dr. William A. Chantry of the University of Wisconsin in Madison has selectively cultured bacteria, including species of *Pseudomonas* and *Nocardia,* that can break down these environmental pollutants. Interestingly, another group of scientists, led by Dr. Steven D. Aust at Michigan State University in East Lansing, found that the fungus *Phanerochaete chrysosporium* can do the same. It remains to be seen which organism proves to be the most practical to use in waste-disposal systems, and whether genetic engineering can improve the efficiency of the organism.

Antibiotics in Animal Feed. In order to increase beef production, small amounts of antibiotics usually are mixed with animal feed. Although the levels of antibiotics are considered subtherapeutic when compared to doses used to combat human diseases, the effect of the antibiotics in animal feed has been to kill off drug-sensitive microbes in the intestinal tracts of cattle and to promote the growth of drug-resistant strains. In the subsequent slaughtering of the animals, these microbes are released and are able to infect the beef that later is sold to humans.

A study by Dr. Scott A. Holmberg and his colleagues of the Centers for Disease Control in Atlanta, GA, found that an outbreak of food poisoning caused by the bacterium *Salmonella newport* could be attributed to eating meat that originated at a farm that routinely added an antibiotic to the animals' feed.

Other studies involving the bacterium *Campylobacter jejeuni* and the use of antibiotics in the feed of chickens revealed a similar situation in causing diarrheic illness. The findings give support to those who want passage of federal legislation banning the use of antibiotics in animal feed.

Algae Below Sea Level. The amount of light that penetrates the ocean decreases dramatically with increasing depth. This severely limits the ability of photosynthetic plants to live very far below the surface of the water. Prior to 1985, it generally was believed that photosynthesis could not take place at depths where the amount of light was less than 1% of that at the surface. Because of this limitation, 180 m (590 ft) was considered the deepest point in the ocean at which photosynthetic plants could live.

Dr. Mark M. Littler of the Smithsonian Institution in Washington, DC, led a group of scientists in a study of a gradually sloping underwater land area off San Salvador Island in the Bahamas. They discovered a new species of algae living at 268 m (879 ft) below the surface. At this depth the light intensity is 0.0005% of its value at the ocean surface. Subsequent laboratory studies showed that these plants, under artificial laboratory conditions, are 100 times more efficient in carrying on photosynthesis than their shallow-water counterparts.

LOUIS LEVINE
City College of New York

© Zohrab, Sygma

In a year of intense diplomatic activity, Jordan's King Hussein (left) *and Egypt's President Hosni Mubarak* (right) *flew to Baghdad in March for a briefing from Iraq's President Saddam Hussein* (center) *on the Iran- Iraq war.*

MIDDLE EAST

Turmoil, tension, and terrorism characterized the Middle East in 1985, and there was little if any perceptible movement toward a resolution of the many conflicts that plague the region. There was plenty of diplomatic activity and a considerable number of international visits by heads of state and government, but the net effect of all this did not suffice to change the situation substantially. Internally, no changes occurred in the political structure and alignment of states, with the exception of the Sudan, where a major change took place.

The Palestinians: Peace Moves? The key performers in the diplomatic process were King Hussein of Jordan and the leader of the Palestine Liberation Organization (PLO), Yasir Arafat. They have been engaged in delicate, curious, inconclusive off-and-on negotiations since 1953. However little they may resemble each other in most respects, these two individuals have at least some attributes in common. They have both demonstrated extraordinary ability as survivors, and both are masters of ambiguity in their actions and public statements.

It is difficult to conceive of any resolution of the Palestinian problem that does not involve Hussein and Arafat. On the other hand, it is equally difficult to imagine any possible resolution that would be satisfactory, or even acceptable, to both. It is still more difficult to imagine any outcome satisfactory to both Hussein and Arafat that also would be acceptable to an Israeli government, whether led by the Likud or Labor parties. Yet all three political

elements are essential parts of any hypothetical solution.

These basic obstacles emerged clearly in the year's negotiations. Any sincere negotiations have as a major condition an unequivocal acceptance by the PLO of Israel's existence, yet this acceptance has never yet been forthcoming. A genuinely independent Palestinian state, moreover, would have little appeal to King Hussein. The only solution acceptable to the Israelis—a West Bank Palestinian entity under some kind of joint Israeli-Jordanian supervision and control—would be anathema to Arafat. Finally, a solution of the Palestinian problem would rob Arafat of his long-running political role as spokesman for a grievance. On the Israeli side, there is very little reason to believe that Israel will ever be ready to trade territory for peace—as it did in giving the Sinai back to Egypt—by surrendering the other territories acquired in the 1967 war. The loss of the Sinai did not make Israel vulnerable as the loss of the West Bank would.

The Hussein-Arafat Initiative. The year began with talks in early January between Arafat on one side and King Hussein and Crown Prince Hassan on the other. It was announced on February 11 that agreement on a peace initiative had been reached between Arafat and King Hussein at talks in Amman, the Jordanian capital. This was to be based on the idea of trading territory for peace, and on the establishment of a confederated relationship between an autonomous Palestinian entity and Jordan. In response Shimon Peres, the Israeli prime minister, confirmed his willingness to have talks with Jordan without preconditions,

but he reiterated that there was no possibility of entering into talks with the PLO.

The full text of the accord was released on February 23. But this did not clear up all ambiguities. The text called for "the achievement of a just and peaceful settlement of the Middle East crisis" based on "total Israeli withdrawal from the territories occupied in 1967" in terms of "United Nations and Security Council resolutions." A Jordanian spokesman explained this as meaning the PLO accepted UN Resolution 242—which implies Israel's right to exist. The PLO's executive committee, however, had explicitly rejected Resolution 242 at its meeting on February 20.

The agreement envisaged that the Palestinian "right of self-determination" would be achieved "within the context of the formation of the proposed confederated Arab states of Jordan and Palestine" (an ambiguous phraseology). Syria immediately denounced the agreement as an attempt to liquidate the Palestinian cause. Egyptian President Hosni Mubarak welcomed the proposal, and Prime Minister Peres of Israel stated his readiness to hold talks with a Jordanian-Palestinian team, provided the latter contained no PLO representatives.

Thus was launched the much-publicized "peace process," which involved much diplomatic coming and going for the rest of the year, without specific results. King Fahd of Saudi Arabia was in Washington, DC, on February 11–12, concurrently with the Amman meetings. President Mubarak also visited Washington a few weeks later. King Hussein visited Washington, May 29–31, had talks with President Ronald Reagan and Secretary of State George Shultz, and said that Jordan and the PLO were in agreement on holding talks with Israel under the "umbrella" of an international conference. King Hussein said that the PLO had agreed, on the basis of UN Resolutions 242 and 338, to acknowledge Israel's right to exist. (This hearsay version of PLO policy, however, hardly had the force or validity of a statement.)

The international conference "umbrella" concept was one of those involved in the diplomatic maneuvering of the remainder of the year. The United States and Israel, though wary of a procedure that would necessarily bring in the Soviet Union, were both inclined to cautious acceptance. Peres, risking the wrath of hard-liners in the Likud party, indicated this in his September speech at the United Nations. But he also showed his strong long-term preference for direct negotiations with Jordan.

Arafat's prestige declined later in the year because of his assumed involvement in the piracy on the Italian cruise ship *Achille Lauro*. All this, strangely, did not inhibit a warm reunion between Arafat and Hussein in Jordan at the beginning of November. In a speech on that occasion Arafat refused to renounce violence and equally refused to recognize UN Resolution 242 or Israel's right to exist.

On these matters the year ended inconclusively. On December 18 an unnamed U.S. State Department spokesman acknowledged that American efforts to bring about peace talks between Israel and Jordan in 1985 had failed. The spokesman claimed, however, that considerable progress had been made. He argued that the positions of the parties had converged on a number of points, particularly on the idea of an international conference, though its precise form remained undecided.

Aborted Arms Sales. There can be little doubt that the influence wielded in the Middle East by the United States was diminished during the year by failure to implement the proposed sale of arms to Saudi Arabia and Jordan. The transaction, contemplated by the U.S. administration at the beginning of the year, concerned $2 billion worth of F-15 aircraft for Saudi Arabia and $1.5 billion in assorted arms for Jordan. Congress made its opposition clear early on, so the administration never ventured to push the issue hard.

Jordan and Syria. A curious feature of Jordanian diplomacy was the strong tendency, shown in the second half of the year, to draw toward Syria. That nation's hard-line anti-Israeli policy and support of Iran in the war with Iraq have little in common with Jordan's aims. Ministerial meetings in Saudi Arabia in the summer led to a December visit to Jordan by the Syrian premier, Abdel Raouf al-Kassem. King Hussein, moreover, visited Syria at the end of December and conferred at length with President Hafez al-Assad. Among the advantages to Syria of a rapprochement would be, presumably, involvement by Syria and also its patron, the Soviet Union, in any international conference on the Arab-Israeli issue. The benefits for Jordan are less clear, though they might include less Syrian support for subversion inside Jordan.

Terrorist Spectaculars. Much of the world's attention during the year was focused not on actions of Middle East states, but on terrorist phenomena. The first major incident, the hijacking of TWA Flight 847, occurred on June 14 and lasted until the surviving 39 hostages were freed on June 30. One of the most publicized of several incidents in which Israelis were murder victims occurred in Cyprus. On September 25, three pro-Palestinian gunmen (one of whom was British) stormed aboard a yacht in the port of Larnaca and shot to death three Israelis. Cyprus refused Israel's request to extradite the accused. By December, however, the three had been tried, found guilty, and sentenced to life imprisonment. In retaliation for the Cyprus murders, Israel—which blamed the murders on the PLO—mounted an air raid on October 1 on PLO headquarters in far-off Tunisia. Buildings were destroyed and

Yasir Arafat (second from right), chairman of the Palestine Liberation Organization (PLO), joined Mohammad Abul Abbas (third from right), leader of the pro-Arafat faction of the Palestine Liberation Front (PLF), at a PLF congress in September. Although Arafat's role in the hijacking of the cruise ship "Achille Lauro" was debated, Abbas was accused of masterminding the terrorist attack.

at least 36 people were killed. The action was intended to show that distance did not confer immunity from Israeli retaliation. In the cycle of reprisals that followed, Palestinian gunmen seized and held captive for 51 hours an Italian cruise ship, the *Achille Lauro,* murdering an elderly American who was among the passengers. This time events took a new and better turn. The plane on which the ship hijackers were making their escape from Egypt was intercepted and forced down in Malta by U.S. jets in a flawless operation. President Mubarak, much criticized in the West for his timid role in the *Achille Lauro* affair, tried to make up for it on November 24 by ordering decisive action when an Egyptian plane was ambushed to Malta. The rescue attempt by Egyptian troops resulted in the deaths of 60 out of 98 persons aboard.

Lebanon. Lebanon at year's end saw some hope for the restoration of normal order and civil government. Under the supervision of Syrian Vice-President Abdel Halim Khaddam, the leaders of Lebanon's three contending military groups signed an agreement in Damascus on December 28 to end the ten-year civil war. Syria, which has become the major external power in Lebanon, viewed the agreement optimistically, but many Lebanese were skeptical, having seen earlier peace accords collapse.

Iraqi-Iranian War. The five-year-old war between Iraq and Iran continued to drag on. Casualties were much lower than they were in the first two or three years, and observers concluded that both sides lacked the military means—or will—to achieve their goals. There was only one major offensive, that mounted on March 12 by Iran in the marshy country north of Basra. It followed the usual pattern of heavy Iranian casualties for minimal gains and had petered out by mid-March. Sporadic bombing

of cities and of shipping by both sides continued. The 50 or more Iraqi attacks on Iran's Kharg Island terminal temporarily disrupted Iran's oil exports and led to long-term plans to build pipelines to export points farther south on the Persian Gulf.

Diplomatic Changes. Diplomatic links in the region underwent some significant changes. On September 27, Tunisia broke diplomatic links with Libya, accusing Libyan dictator Muammar el-Qaddafi of chronic aggression. Israeli links with other powers were, or are about to be, considerably strengthened. Spain announced in September its intention to exchange embassies with Israel. Hungary and Poland are about to establish "interests sections" in Israel, and there were persistent rumors that the USSR might restore normal links with Israel, which were broken in 1967. The restoration of Israeli links with African states took a long step forward when on December 18 Prime Minister Peres and President Félix Houphouët-Boigny of the Ivory Coast held a surprising meeting in Geneva and announced their intention to restore diplomatic links.

Sudan. After 16 years of rule, President Jaafar al-Nemery was ousted from office. Nemery had been pro-Western and pro-Egyptian but had recently alienated the non-Islamic south of the Sudan by changing the Sudan's legal system to conform to Islamic principles.

Missiles. In the last weeks of the year, two developments concerning missiles created tension. One was the emplacement by Libya of Soviet-made missiles on its eastern border. The other was the installation of anti-aircraft missiles by Syria on or beyond its border with Lebanon. Israel called the missile action provocative and dangerous to the peace.

ARTHUR CAMPBELL TURNER
University of California, Riverside

MILITARY AFFAIRS

The Strategic Defense Initiative (SDI), or "Star Wars," a plan proposed by U.S. President Ronald Reagan in spring 1983 to develop a space-based defense system against ballistic missile attack, grew in 1985 to dominate the debate on military affairs in the United States and to become the principal military dispute between Washington and Moscow. The heart of the SDI debate in domestic circles was whether it would be technologically possible and politically desirable to augment, and perhaps later replace, the current nuclear retaliation doctrine with strategic defensive capabilities. The purposes and effects of such a system were a major bone of contention at the U.S.-Soviet arms control talks in Geneva and in the verbal exchanges between the White House and the Kremlin (*see* ARMS CONTROL).

Other issues and developments in U.S. military affairs during 1985 included debate over defense spending, MX missile funding, the introduction of new weapons, outlays for military pensions, and the appointment of a new chairman of the Joint Chiefs of Staff.

SDI—Rationale and Research. As President Reagan explained it, a successful Strategic Defense Initiative would mean that in the event of nuclear war, missiles—not people—would be killed. Being able to prevent nuclear attack would render nuclear weapons "impotent and obsolete." Such a system, he maintained, would provide an alternative to the dangerous doctrine of Mutual Assured Destruction (MAD), the strategy of deterring nuclear attack by promising unacceptable retaliation.

As presently envisioned, SDI would provide a multilayered defense against incoming nuclear warheads launched by intercontinental ballistic missiles (ICBMs) and submarine-launched ballistic missiles (SLBMs). Such a defense would consist of satellites placed in geosynchronous orbit above the Soviet Union to provide early warning of a missile attack and to monitor and manage the evolving battle matrix. Other satellites in lower orbits would be used to fire lasers and particle beams at the Soviet vehicles during the boost phase, post-boost phase, and midcourse phase of their flight path. These would be augmented by ground-based stations that would fire lasers and kinetic "kill" vehicles at the warheads when they are in the terminal phase of their flight.

In 1985 the U.S. Department of Defense supported research to explore the effectiveness of a number of "kill" mechanisms that would become part of this layered defense against ballistic missiles. The laser—a device that produces a coherent beam of radiation in the infrared, visible, ultraviolet, and X-ray regions of the electromagnetic spectrum—is one such mechanism. In order to be destructive, a laser

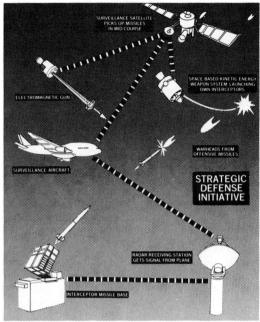

AP/Wide World

The Strategic Defense Initiative would provide a multi-layered shield against nuclear ballistic missile attack.

beam must be focused on a target sufficiently long to deposit a lethal amount of energy. Types of lasers currently under investigation include chemical, excimer, free-electron, and X-ray. A variant of the latter is one of the most exotic kill mechanisms now under study. A nuclear-pumped X-ray laser weapon would receive its energy from a small nuclear explosion. The energy thus generated would be used to send multiple X-ray laser beams toward enemy missiles high above the earth's atmosphere. A disadvantage of this system is that the laser unit is destroyed in the process of detonation of the nuclear explosion and thus can be used only once. Another disadvantage is that some laser beams are less effective in the atmosphere and tend to spread over long distances.

Another family of kill mechanisms is particle beams. Differing from laser beams, which are pure energy, particle beams consist of very small pieces of matter, such as protons, electrons, neutral atoms, and heavy ions. These can be propelled by particle accelerators at nearly the speed of light in the form of a beam. Various kinds of particle beams could penetrate a missile or warhead and render its electronic brain inoperative, thus preventing the enemy vehicle from functioning as programmed. Disadvantages of particle beam weapons are that they do not work well in the atmosphere and that the beams tend to be bent by the earth's magnetic field.

A third type of kill mechanism is kinetic energy weapons. These are the best understood

and closest to being deployed of the SDI possibilities to date. The effectiveness of such weapons is based on the fact that a high-velocity target, such as an approaching missile warhead, will disintegrate if it collides with another object traveling at a different speed. Current kinetic kill systems consist of high-acceleration rockets fired from the ground or from satellites. A successful test of the former was conducted by the U.S. Army in June 1984. Research is being conducted on an alternative technology that would launch kinetic kill interceptors at much higher velocities than now possible. This device is called an electromagnetic railgun. Using intense magnetic fields, a railgun hurls projectiles at speeds estimated in excess of 20 km (12 mi) per second.

A major component of the SDI system would be the one that electronically senses an attack, tracks the Soviet missiles, guides the U.S. defense effort, and assesses the damage. Such capabilities would involve the rapid processing of enormous amounts of data within the 30 minutes that it would take a Soviet missile to reach targets in the United States. Currently, neither the computer hardware nor software exists to perform the integrated functions required for successful missile defense. With regard to software, a government team studying the battle management, communications, and data processing facets of SDI wrote in 1984 that "specifying, generating, testing, and maintaining the software for a battle management system will be a task that far exceeds in complexity and difficulty any that has yet been accomplished in the production of civil or military software systems."

SDI—Opposition. In 1985, as members of the Reagan defense team lobbied Congress and the public in support of SDI, others worked to defeat what they derisively called "Star Wars." Chief among the opponents were the Union of Concerned Scientists and the Federation of American Scientists, both of which include scientists who had worked on the U.S. atomic bomb effort during World War II but who now oppose Star Wars on technical and political grounds.

The opposition groups set forth five arguments for their position. First, an American SDI would be too easily negated by Soviet countermeasures, which also would tend to be less expensive. Second, the development and deployment of an SDI would provoke the Soviets into joining and exacerbating the arms competition in space, resulting in much higher defense costs but no great increase in the security of either superpower. Third, although the cost of technologies still under research cannot be estimated, the final bill for an SDI likely would be economically ruinous. Fourth, the presence of a unilaterally built SDI would be dangerous because the Soviets might view it as the prelude to an American first-strike de-

signed to reduce Soviet retaliatory capability; opponents point out that even if both nations had an SDI, the situation would be unstable because of the temptation for one nation to strike first and rely on its SDI to negate the opponent's response. Finally, SDI opponents argue that the system would violate one of the major treaties between the United States and Soviet Union, the Anti-Ballistic Missile Treaty.

SDI—Soviet View. Late in the year, the Soviets admitted that they were already engaged in SDI-type research, as Washington had charged. Moscow also stated that if the United States began development of an SDI, the Soviet Union would follow with its own system, even if it meant significant economic belt-tightening. In the fall, Soviet leader Mikhail Gorbachev traveled to France prior to his November meeting with President Reagan, lobbying against SDI and predicting dire consequences should there be an SDI race between the two superpowers.

ASAT Debate. Related to the SDI research, but much further developed technically, is the U.S. antisatellite (ASAT) system. This weapon consists of a modified F-15 jet fighter that carries a two-stage rocket to approximately 60,000 ft (18 300 m). There the rocket is fired toward an enemy satellite, which is destroyed when struck by the second stage of the rocket. In September 1985, using an old scientific satellite as a target, the United States successfully tested such a system. The Reagan administration justified ASAT development and testing, criticized by arms controllers, on the grounds that the Soviet Union already possesses such a weapon, albeit a relatively crude one.

MX Funding. Also pressed by the Reagan administration was continued congressional support for the MX (Missile Experimental) program. The White House contended that the intercontinental MX was essential as bargaining leverage in the U.S.-Soviet talks at Geneva. Many members of Congress, however, particularly House Democrats, rejected President Reagan's logic. Instead they argued that building the MX would be destabilizing for two reasons. One was that placing the missiles in fixed silos, which currently hold Minuteman ICBMs, would leave the MX vulnerable to a Soviet first strike. The second argument was that the ten-warhead MX, which is claimed to be accurate to within 300 ft (90 m), would appear to the Soviets to be a first-strike weapon that could threaten their ICBMs. Thus it was contended that MX development would create a situation in which the Soviets would be tempted to fire their ICBMs first or risk losing them to a U.S. first strike. Late in the year, a compromise was struck between the White House and Congress. It gave the president less than he wanted, but it was considerably more favorable to him than

Defense Contracting—Waste and Abuse

The most quoted portion of President Dwight D. Eisenhower's farewell address to the American people, delivered as the former five-star general left office in 1961, was a warning about the problems inherent in maintaining the huge "military-industrial complex" that was required by the presence of the Soviet military capability. The president said: "This conjunction of an immense military establishment and a large arms industry is new in the American experience. The total influence—economic, political, even spiritual—is felt in every city, every state house, every office of the federal government. We recognize the imperative need for this development. Yet we must not fail to comprehend its grave implications. . . . In the councils of government, we must guard against the acquisition of unwarranted influence, whether sought or unsought, by the military-industrial complex. The potential for the disastrous rise of misplaced power exists and will persist."

In 1985, Eisenhower's warning was highlighted by congressional investigations of wrongdoing by several of the nation's largest defense contractors. In the spring the House of Representatives' Energy and Commerce Subcommittee on Oversight and Investigations, chaired by Congressman John Dingell (D-MI), accused the General Dynamics Corporation of improperly charging the government for entertainment expenses, including country club fees, and lobbying expenses. The corporation was even accused of putting the cost for keeping an executive's dog in a kennel on the government's bill. The disclosure prompted Secretary of Defense Caspar Weinberger to order the suspension of overhead payments to General Dynamics for nearly five months, and to push harder on his campaign to improve management efficiency in the Pentagon.

Stung by reports of various defense contractors charging $7,600 for coffee brewers and $659 for ashtrays, Secretary Weinberger sought to reassure the taxpayers by delivering a hard-hitting speech before the American Legion. Weinberger stated that all contractors would be required to certify under penalty of perjury that their claims are properly allocable to the government and do not include any political or entertainment expenses.

Secretary of the Navy John Lehman fined General Dynamics for providing thousands of dollars in gratuities to ADM. Hyman Rickover, retired head of the Navy's nuclear submarine building program. Lehman also sent a letter of censure to Rickover. In response to the condemnation, Rickover issued a statement that read, "My conscience is clear. . . . No gratuity or favor ever affected any decision I made."

In another case the General Electric Company pleaded guilty to defrauding the government in regard to the Minuteman ICBM program. General Electric was fined $1.04 million and was required to repay $800,000 in overcharges that it had billed the Pentagon. Dingell questioned whether, "a $1 million fine means much to a company such as GE which did 4,000 times that amount of business with the federal government in just one year." Others on Capitol Hill also were critical of what was perceived as overly light treatment of the large defense contractor. On the other hand, Pentagon officials pointed out that the government is so dependent on major defense production firms, such as GE and General Dynamics, that it would be impractical to completely suspend business with them.

Late in the summer Secretary Weinberger startled many in the Army, but pleased critics of excessive defense spending, when he announced that he was canceling further production of a new air defense gun on which $1.8 billion had already been spent. Weinberger stated that the weapon's performance was "not worth the additional cost." Weinberger's action saved approximately $3 billion that had been appropriated but not spent for the twin cannon gun unit mounted on a tank chassis. The weapon, officially known as the DIVAD (Division Air Defense System), also was called the Sergeant York.

In the fall the subcommittee that had made the original accusations opened new and extensive hearings on waste, fraud, and abuse in Department of Defense purchasing procedures, and on the business practices of defense contractors. The hearings began with an examination of how General Dynamics tried to bill the government $9,609 for a small wrench used to repair F-16 fighter plane radars. The subcommittee also was scheduled to examine the possible use of foreign consultants to sell American military equipment overseas, and the possibility of bribery and other inducements being used to reward foreign governments for purchasing U.S.-made military products.

And in December, General Dynamics again came under fire. James M. Beggs, a former officer and now the administrator of NASA, and three company executives were charged with conspiring to commit fraud by improperly billing the government under the DIVAD contract. General Dynamics was temporarily suspended from obtaining new defense contracts.

ROBERT M. LAWRENCE

Adm. William J. Crowe, Jr. (second from right) was sworn in October 1 as chairman of the Joint Chiefs of Staff, replacing Gen. John W. Vessey, Jr. Also present at the White House ceremony were Crowe's wife Shirley, Secretary of Defense Caspar Weinberger (extreme right), and President Reagan. Crowe urged cooperation among the service branches.

the "zero-MX" favored by some Congressmen: Congress decided to fund 50 MXs for initial deployment in 1986.

Other Weapons and Systems. Although overshadowed by the SDI controversy and debates over ASAT and the MX, other military events in 1985 were worth noting. These included the launching by the United States of its eighth Trident submarine, a new class of vessel that carries 24 SLBMs; and the delivery to the Air Force of the first B-1B strategic jet bomber, designed to replace the aging fleet of B-52s currently in service.

The Soviets, meanwhile, deployed a new mobile ICBM, the SS-25. U.S. Defense Secretary Caspar Weinberger alleged that the new missile violated a SALT agreement limiting the Soviets to only one new ICBM, which had already been deployed. The Soviets responded that the SS-25 is merely an updated version of the old SS-13. In addition, they were expected soon to deploy a new multiwarhead ICBM, the SS-24, which would be somewhat comparable to the U.S. MX.

Pensions and the Budget. In the ongoing effort by Congress and the White House to cut the federal budget, one area that came under close scrutiny in 1985 was the military retirement system. Attention was focused early in the year when then Budget Director David Stockman told the Senate Budget Committee that the current program is a "scandal" and an "outrage." Stockman charged that "Institutional forces in the military are more concerned about protecting their retirement benefits than

they are about protecting the security of the American people." Secretary of Defense Caspar Weinberger and various veterans groups were quick to respond. Weinberger accused Stockman of defaming "men and women in uniform who endure great personal hardships and make many sacrifices for the security of the United States." Stockman later resigned as budget director, leaving the effort to reform military pensions in the hands of the new chairman of the House Armed Services Committee, Congressman Les Aspin (D-WI).

One of the most controversial aspects of the military retirement system is the provision allowing for retirement at half pay after only 20 years of service.

Late in December, President Reagan signed a defense authorization bill for $281.6 billion. The administration originally had requested $322 billion.

New Head of Joint Chiefs. On October 1, Gen. John W. Vessey, Jr., retired as chairman of the Joint Chiefs of Staff eight months short of completing his second two-year term. He was succeeded by Adm. William J. Crowe, Jr., a 43-year Navy veteran. The 60-year-old former submarine commander called on the Army, Navy, Air Force, and Marines to put aside rivalries and cooperate more closely. He said that "the need for joint operations, joint thinking, and joint leadership has never been greater" as the military faces the end of vast budgetary expansion.

ROBERT M. LAWRENCE
Colorado State University

Canterbury Downs

Canterbury Downs, a new horse racing track in suburban Shakopee, had a successful first season. Some one million enthusiasts wagered a total of $84 million.

MINNESOTA

Distress on the farms and the Iron Range, an $800 million tax cut, and a protracted fight over locating a state-supported convention center dominated events in Minnesota.

Economy. With farm income at its lowest level since 1970—falling $10–$15 billion below 1984's $34.6 billion—distress in rural Minnesota was escalating. High costs and steep declines in farm prices forced widespread foreclosures. Anticipation of good crops forced further market drops. Meanwhile, unemployment on the Iron Range continued to be severe, with iron ore plants running at greatly reduced capacity.

In contrast to rural Minnesota, the Twin Cities metropolitan area experienced relatively low unemployment. Some firms, most notably Control Data, reported sharp drops in earnings, but generally economic conditions appeared stable. Concern was expressed that Minnesota was heading for a dual economy, prosperous in the larger cities, poor in the rest of the state.

Tax Cut. Under pressure from business to counter the state's high-tax image, the legislature in May voted an $800 million slash in personal income taxes and provided a $450 million "rainy day" fund. By late fall, revenues were down, and the contingency fund was eroding. If a deficit materialized, the state faced the prospect of an automatic increase in income taxes with suspension of indexing.

Convention Center. After the legislature refused to provide a state subsidy to help Minneapolis build a $135 million convention center, suburban Bloomington announced plans to build a $1.2 billion mega-mall designed to rival Disneyland as a national attraction. The city sought substantial development aid, in the form of tax forgiveness, for a convention cen-

ter as part of the mall, claiming the project would generate 40,000 new jobs. This set the stage for a protracted round of claims and counterclaims involving the governor, legislative leaders, city officials, and the developers.

Ouster Attempt. Kathleen Morris, Scott County attorney, was a center of attention throughout the year. A commission appointed by Gov. Rudy Perpich held hearings on an ouster petition after Morris dismissed charges against 30 families she had accused of child abuse. Accepting the commission's recommendation, the governor decided against the ouster.

New Race Track. Thoroughbred horse racing enjoyed a successful opening season at Canterbury Downs, in suburban Shakopee, the state's first race track. In its 83-day season it drew one million customers. The track was authorized following adoption of a constitutional amendment legalizing pari-mutuel betting.

MINNESOTA • Information Highlights

Area: 84,402 sq mi (218 601 km²).
Population (July 1, 1984 est.): 4,162,000.
Chief Cities (July 1, 1984 est.): St. Paul, the capital, 265,903; Minneapolis, 358,335; Duluth (1980 census), 92,811.
Government (1985): *Chief Officers*—governor, Rudy Perpich (DFL); lt. gov., Marlene Johnson (DFL). *Legislature*—Senate, 67 members; House of Representatives, 134 members.
State Finances (fiscal year 1984): *Revenues,* $8,826,000,000; *expenditures,* $7,536,000,000.
Personal Income (1984): $55,129,000,000; per capita, $13,247.
Labor Force (June 1985): *Civilian labor force,* 2,267,100; *unemployed,* 112,600 (5% of total force).
Education: *Enrollment* (fall 1983)—public elementary schools, 466,579; public secondary, 238,663; colleges and universities, 214,219. *Public school expenditures* (1982–83), $2,075,572,146 ($3,085 per pupil).

Open Enrollment. The 1985 legislative session gave high school juniors and seniors the opportunity to take college courses for high school credit, with school districts paying the college tuition. During the fall term 1,000 students took advantage of the program, which was heading for review in the 1986 session.

Meatpacking Strike. In November a strike of 1,500 workers at the Geo. A. Hormel & Co. meatpacking plant in Austin was entering its 12th week with no sign of settlement. The striking United Food and Commercial Workers union attempted to broaden the dispute by picketing seven other Hormel plants not being struck.

Mayors Reelected. Minneapolis Mayor Don Fraser and St. Paul Mayor George Latimer, both Democrats, were reelected. Fraser won a third term in office, Latimer an unprecedented sixth.

ARTHUR NAFTALIN, *University of Minnesota*

MISSISSIPPI

An unprecedented teacher strike, a disappointing legislative session, and quadrennial municipal elections were events of particular interest to Mississippians in 1985. An economy that generated less-than-hoped-for tax revenues and a costly Labor Day hurricane were other items of major interest and concern.

Teacher Strike. When the legislature convened in January, there seemed to be general agreement that teachers deserved a substantial pay raise and that state House and Senate leaders could reach an early compromise on the amount. An agreement was not forthcoming, however, provoking the Mississippi Association of Educators to call for a statewide strike protesting the nation's lowest pay scale for teachers. Over a two-week period beginning February 25, some 10,000 teachers in 57 of 154 school districts left their classrooms. The issue was resolved in mid-March when legislators overrode Gov. Bill Allain's veto of a $4,400 increase financed by a "grab bag" tax package that relied heavily on alcohol and tobacco taxes.

Legislative Session. In addition to voting a teacher pay raise, lawmakers granted home rule to municipal governments, reluctantly raised the minimum drinking age for beer and light wine from 18 to 21, and repealed the provision of the 1982 Education Reform Act that required the Educational Finance Commission to prepare a school consolidation plan. Measures to restructure or eliminate existing blue laws were defeated, as were attempts to find a solution to the continuing problem of prison overcrowding. A bill that could have led to pari-mutuel betting in two counties was killed when the president pro tempore of the Senate was arrested by federal officers on February 28 and charged with extorting money from the Mississippi Horse Racing Association. He did not resign his post until his conviction in June.

Municipal Elections. In June elections, held in nearly all 292 municipalities, ward voting replaced at-large balloting for aldermen/councilmen/commissioners in a number of jurisdictions. The switch to wards was the result of lawsuits or threatened lawsuits and, as in the case of Jackson, sometimes reflected a change in the form of government. Democrats continued to dominate municipal offices, but Republicans increased their numbers by about 30%. The number of black officeholders increased, and blacks were elected to governing boards in some cities for the first time in the 20th century.

Economic Conditions. Mississippi's economy continued to show weakness, as reflected by unemployment levels and tax collections. In early November the Fiscal Management Board ordered major budget cuts for state agencies. This marked the fourth time in five years that cuts, freezes, and other budget adjustments were necessary.

Storm Damage. After threatening areas from Louisiana to Florida, Hurricane Elena hit the Mississippi gulf coast on September 2 with winds in excess of 100 mph (161 km/h). No lives were lost, but the storm and the tornadoes it spawned caused property damage in the hundreds of millions of dollars. Pascagoula and Moss Point were especially hard hit. Two months later, Hurricane Juan brushed the Mississippi coast, producing serious flooding.

Other Happenings. The $2 billion Tennessee-Tombigbee Waterway was officially dedicated in June 1 ceremonies in Columbus; the first unit of the Grand Gulf Nuclear Station began its commercial start-up on July 1; and on July 2 the Navy announced plans to base four of its warships at Pascagoula.

DANA B. BRAMMER
The University of Mississippi

MISSISSIPPI • Information Highlights

Area: 47,689 sq mi (123 515 km²).
Population (July 1, 1984 est.): 2,598,000.
Chief Cities (1980 census): Jackson, the capital (July 1, 1984 est.), 208,810; Biloxi, 49,311; Meridian, 46,577.
Government (1985): *Chief Officers*—governor, William A. Allain (D); lt. gov., Brad Dye (D). *Legislature*—Senate, 52 members; House of Representatives, 122 members.
State Finances (fiscal year 1984): *Revenues,* $3,641,000,000; *expenditures,* $3,351,000,000.
Personal Income (1984): $22,802,000,000; per capita, $8,777.
Labor Force (June 1985): *Civilian labor force,* 1,114,500; *unemployed,* 113,900 (10.2% of total force).
Education: *Enrollment* (fall 1983)—public elementary schools, 327,509; public secondary, 140,235; colleges and universities, 109,728. *Public school expenditures* (1982–83), $812,671,198 ($1,849 per pupil).

In the fall of 1985, Missourians were deeply divided: the state's two baseball clubs were fighting for the World Series crown. In a classic comeback, the Royals defeated the St. Louis Cardinals, bringing joy to Kansas City.

AP/Wide World

MISSOURI

Despite the fact that 1985 was not an election year, Missouri politicians campaigned actively. The major office at stake in 1986 would be the U.S. Senate seat now held by Thomas F. Eagleton (D), who has announced his retirement at the end of his third term. Lt. Gov. Harriet Woods appeared to be the front-runner for the Democratic nomination, and it seemed likely that former Gov. Christopher S. Bond would be unopposed in the Republican primary.

The state court system, educational innovations, and an all-Missouri baseball World Series were other headline items.

The Court System. The state's nonpartisan judicial selection process, known as the Missouri plan, may have succumbed to creeping partisanship. For 45 years the Missouri plan has been regarded as a model for the nation in respect to the choice on a merit basis of judges for the higher courts of a state.

Rumblings of dissatisfaction surfaced in June when Gov. John D. Ashcroft (R) picked his 33-year-old chief of staff, Edward D. Robertson, who lacked judicial experience, as a judge of the state Supreme Court. The action followed months of bickering among the judges of the court.

The Missouri Bar and the state Senate each appointed special committees to review the operation of the nonpartisan plan. In testimony

before the Senate committee, former Republican State Committee chairman John Powell alleged that he and Supreme Court Judge Albert L. Rendlen (R) attempted in 1982 to arrange the appointment of three high court judges, two of whom were actually named by then-Governor Bond, but that Rendlen "double-crossed" Powell by failing to support the third person included in the package deal.

In other testimony Judge Robert T. Donnelly (D) of the high court admitted that in 1982 he discussed with Bond "a dozen potential

---

MISSOURI • Information Highlights

Area: 69,697 sq mi (180 516 km²).
Population (July 1, 1984 est.): 5,008,000.
Chief Cities (July 1, 1984 est.): Jefferson City, the capital (1980 census), 33,619; Kansas City, 443,075; St. Louis, 429,296; Springfield, 136,939; Independence, 112,121.
Government (1985): *Chief Officers*—governor, John Ashcroft (R); lt. gov., Harriett Woods (D). *General Assembly*—Senate, 34 members; House of Representatives, 163 members.
State Finances (fiscal year 1984): *Revenues,* $5,964,000,000; *expenditures,* $5,263,000,000.
Personal Income (1984): $60,847,000,000; per capita, $12,151.
Labor Force (June 1985): *Civilian labor force,* 2,497,500; *unemployed,* 165,400 (6.6% of total force).
Education: *Enrollment* (fall 1983)—public elementary schools, 546,155; public secondary, 249,298; colleges and universities, 248,329. *Public school expenditures* (1982–83), $1,772,111,337 ($2,468 per pupil).

nominees to the court.'' Donnelly subsequently resigned as chairman of the Appellate Judicial Commission, charging that both Rendlen and another judge, Warren D. Welliver (D), were lobbying on behalf of candidates for the court.

The Legislature. Despite the fact that the 83d General Assembly had a solid Democratic majority, it and the Republican governor maintained a considerable degree of harmony. A high priority was an "excellence in education" act that provided among other things for entry-level testing and exit monitoring for students in teacher education. Implementation of programs for professional development of teachers and evaluation of administrators outlined in the legislation was left to the Department of Elementary and Secondary Education; however, funding for these innovations awaited later appropriations.

In 1984 the Coordinating Board for Higher Education had made numerous recommendations for reorganization of the state's universities and four-year colleges in an effort to end duplication in programs and to upgrade academic standards. An item on the list, designating Northeast Missouri State University as a statewide liberal arts university, was enacted by the 83d General Assembly. Most of the other proposals aroused a storm of protest, and the legislature backed away from them.

In the closing hours of the session, a bill making a number of minor changes in criminal statutes went to the governor with a clerical error that could have been construed as repealing the law against rape. To rectify the error, the state Supreme Court quickly ruled the measure void. Consequently, provisions establishing penalties for failure to return library books or for snatching cable television programs out of the sky failed to become law, but rape remained a crime in Missouri.

RUTH W. TOWNE
Northeast Missouri State University

MONTANA

Before 1985 was a week old, the stage had been set for what was to become one of the worst years on record for agriculture in eastern Montana. However, the year was profitable for utilities and encouraging for the sagging mining industry.

Farming. Three branches of the Production Credit Association, one of the state's major farm lenders, folded during the first week of the year, prompting proposals to merge all federal farm-lending agencies in the Northwest into one association. The proposal eventually died because members of one Idaho lender voted it down.

While farmers worried about their finances, the weather turned cold and dry, killing winter wheat that was planted the autumn before.

MONTANA · Information Highlights

Area: 147,046 sq mi (380 848 km²).
Population (July 1, 1984 est.): 824,000.
Chief Cities (1980 census): Helena, the capital, 23,938; Billings, 66,798; Great Falls, 56,725.
Government (1985): *Chief Officers*—governor, Ted Schwinden (D); lt. gov., George Turman (D). *Legislature*—Senate, 50 members; House of Representatives, 100 members.
State Finances (fiscal year 1984): *Revenues,* $1,538,000,000; *expenditures,* $1,385,000,000.
Personal Income (1984): $8,690,000,000; per capita, $10,546.
Labor Force (June 1985): *Civilian labor force,* 426,600; *unemployed,* 29,000 (6.8% of total force).
Education: *Enrollment* (fall 1983)—public elementary schools, 108,268; public secondary, 45,378; colleges and universities, 37,877. *Public school expenditures* (1982–83), $456,518,613 ($3,289 per pupil).

Those who reseeded found little moisture in the soil to germinate their new crops.

Spring runoff peaked a month earlier than normal in eastern Montana, thanks to a light winter snowpack in the mountains. That was the harbinger of the fourth consecutive drought year. By the middle of July, many rivers were too low to provide farmers with irrigation water. The Missouri River ran at its lowest level in 40 years.

Grasshoppers spread through the region starting in May and were blamed for leveling the forage on pastures and cropland throughout the state. The federal government declared all but one of Montana's 56 counties disaster areas because of the drought and grasshopper onslaught. The winter-wheat harvest in July was 44% of normal.

Utilities and Mining. Montana Power Company, which earlier was denied a $96.4 million electrical rate increase to pay for its Colstrip 3 coal-fired power plant, took its case to the Montana Supreme Court and won. The court ruled that the state Public Service Commission failed to consider the future need for power when it decided that the power plant was an unnecessary burden on ratepayers. The commission later allowed the entire increase.

Montana's economically depressed mining region had reason for optimism late in 1985. Dennis Washington, president of a Missoula heavy-construction conglomerate, bought the closed Anaconda Company open-pit copper mine at Butte and promised to open it—four years after it closed—sometime in 1986. Montana Power Company scrambled to reduce some industrial power rates to encourage Washington to open the mine and smelter.

Legislation. The Montana legislature, trying to reduce its biennial budget, cut all able-bodied persons younger than 35 from the state welfare roles and limited the amount of time that older Montanans could collect welfare. The law was temporarily overturned by a state-court injunction the day it took effect, how-

ever. The issue remained unsettled late in the year.

The legislature also approved a buffalo hunting season, which the state had not had for several decades. The decision was prompted by herds of the animals leaving Yellowstone National Park during the winter and spreading diseases to cattle. State game wardens killed nearly 50 buffalo on private land north of the park in January. Brucellosis was found in several of the dead animals.

ROBERT C. GIBSON
Regional Editor, "The Billings Gazette"

MOROCCO

King Hassan II suffered a series of diplomatic setbacks in 1985 in his struggle with the Polisario Front for control of the Western Sahara. The completion of the final segment of Morocco's 1,550-mile (2 400-km) wall through the territory was considered a strategic success, however.

Foreign Affairs. Morocco ended its ninth year of war against the Polisario Front and its guerrilla forces by claiming military dominance over nearly two thirds of the Western Sahara, the area enclosed by the wall. An estimated 80,000 Moroccan troops are stationed along the massive sand and stone barrier. In March the king said that Morocco could sustain the war with $1 billion in modern weapons to be purchased over the next five years.

Morocco was less successful in building diplomatic support for its claim to the Western Sahara. The foreign ministers of the nonaligned nations, meeting in Angola in September, approved a resolution containing Polisario's basic premises and rejected Morocco's efforts to amend it. There was little interest in Morocco's proposal for a unilateral cease-fire and a referendum on self-determination in the Western Sahara, presented to the UN in October.

Morocco's relations with the United States were strained early in the year when Algerian President Chadli Benjedid, who supports Polisario, received a warm reception in Washington. In July, however, Morocco and the United States signed a trade treaty that gives American investors the same legal rights as their Moroccan counterparts and ensures compensation for expropriation as well as free transfer of capital and profits. Morocco was attempting to develop new trade links, anticipating the loss of markets when Spain and Portugal join the European Community (EC) in January 1986.

Relations between Morocco and Spain deteriorated after the Spanish foreign minister stated that Spain broadly supports Algeria's policy in the Western Sahara. A long-standing dispute between the two nations was rekindled when Hassan compared Spain's efforts to recover Gibraltar from Britain to Morocco's claim to Ceuta and Melilla, two Spanish ports on the north coast of Morocco. Spain rejected Morocco's claim, stressing that the two enclaves have never been part of the modern state of Morocco and that their populations are primarily Spanish.

Politics and the Economy. The four center-right parties that have a majority in Parliament gained greater representation in the cabinet after a reshuffle in April. Two parties that had grown increasingly critical of the government —the nationalist Istiqlal and the Socialist Union of Popular Forces—were excluded from the new coalition.

Mohamed Karim Lamrani, reconfirmed as prime minister, announced his intention to push the economic reform program supported by the International Monetary Fund (IMF). Measures include increasing the efficiency of Morocco's public enterprises, transferring some of them to the private sector, and liberalizing foreign exchange. The prices of basic foods and minimum wages were increased in early September. These efforts were expected to improve the position of the *dirham,* Morocco's currency, which fell sharply in value during the year.

The massive $13 billion national debt and the heavy cost of the war continued to seriously strain the economy. After the IMF granted $315 million in special drawing rights to the Moroccan government in September, the Paris Club agreed to favorable conditions for a rescheduling of 90% of approximately $1 billion of Morocco's debt to Western governments. Good harvests and an increase in tourism in 1985 helped ease the debt burden.

Fourteen Moroccans were sentenced to death in September after being convicted of a plot to overthrow the monarchy and establish an Islamic regime. Nine of them were tried in absentia. An additional 12 received sentences ranging from five years to life imprisonment. They were accused of receiving arms and money from the Algerian military.

PAULA M. HIRSCHOFF, *"Africa Report"*

MOROCCO • Information Highlights

Official Name: Kingdom of Morocco.
Location: Northwest Africa.
Area: 172,413 sq mi (446 550 km²).
Population (mid-1985 est.): 24,300,000.
Capital: Rabat.
Government: *Head of state,* Hassan II, king (acceded 1961). *Head of government,* Mohamed Karim Lamrani, prime minister (took office Nov. 1983). *Legislature* (unicameral)—National Assembly.
Monetary Unit: Dirham (10.212 dirhams equal U.S.$1, July 1985).
Gross Domestic Product (1984 U.S.$): $11,900,-000,000.
Economic Indexes (1984): *Consumer Prices* (1974 = 100), all items, 254.5; food, 258.4. *Industrial Production* (1983, 1980 = 100), 105.
Foreign Trade (1984 U.S.$): *Imports,* $3,861,000,000; *exports,* $2,095,000,000.

MOTION PICTURES

Actresses frequently complain about the lack of worthy roles for women, but 1985 brought some of cinema's foremost actresses, and numerous newcomers, colorful roles in major films. Meryl Streep again showed her skills, this time both in Fred Schepisi's adaptation of David Hare's play *Plenty* and in Sydney Pollack's *Out of Africa,* about the Danish writer Isak Dinesen. Jessica Lange gave an extraordinary performance as the late country singer Patsy Cline in Karel Reisz's *Sweet Dreams.* Kate Nelligan became a Greek peasant in the title role of *Eleni,* directed by Peter Yates and based on journalist Nicholas Gage's personal story of how he tracked down the truth about his mother's execution during the Greek Civil War.

Kathleen Turner further enhanced her growing reputation with her role as a Mafia hit woman (opposite Jack Nicholson as another mob executioner) in John Huston's *Prizzi's Honor,* a film in which Anjelica Huston also gave a memorable performance as a Mafia boss' daughter. Turner saw double duty, returning in *The Jewel of the Nile,* Michael Douglas' sequel to *Romancing the Stone.* Another actress seen in two films was Glenn Close. She played a lawyer in Richard Marquand's thriller *Jagged Edge* and both a secretary to a San Francisco bishop and the spirit of a silent-film flapper in *Maxie.*

Agnes of God, directed by Norman Jewison from John Pielmeier's play pitting faith against reason, featured three star performances. Meg Tilly was luminous as the young nun, Anne Bancroft captured the fervor of the mother superior, and Jane Fonda was outstanding as the persevering court psychiatrist. Ellen Burstyn stood out as the abandoned wife in Bud Yorkin's *Twice in a Lifetime,* and in the same film, Ann-Margret was exceptional as the other woman.

Sissy Spacek gallantly battled corruption in Roger Donaldson's *Marie,* the true story of a woman who exposed the selling of pardons and paroles in Tennessee. Sally Field (*Places in the Heart*) again was cast as a struggling woman in Martin Ritt's *Murphy's Romance.* Mia Farrow was funny, romantic, and generally delightful as the obsessed movie fan in Woody Allen's imaginative *The Purple Rose of Cairo.*

A powerful film debut was made by British actress Miranda Richardson in Mike Newell's *Dance with a Stranger,* about the last woman to be hanged in England. Another outstanding newcomer, Argentine actress Norma Aleandro, triumphed as a woman coming to terms with past political persecutions in Argentina in Luis Puenzo's *The Official Story.* Madonna displayed comedic acting ability as the costar with Rosanna Arquette in Susan Seidelman's

Tri-Star Pictures

In "Sweet Dreams," Jessica Lange gives one of the year's best performances as the late singer Patsy Cline.

exuberant *Desperately Seeking Susan.* Whoopi Goldberg also received her first movie break as the star of Steven Spielberg's *The Color Purple,* adapted from Alice Walker's novel.

The Men. Actors were not short of their own opportunities. Veteran Gene Hackman gave one of his finest performances as the 50-year-old steelworker who exits from his marriage of 30 years in *Twice in a Lifetime.* He also was good in the less demanding role of a former CIA agent in Arthur Penn's suspense movie *Target.* Jack Nicholson's performance in *Prizzi's Honor* ranked as one of his best, and William Hickey brought originality to the part of the elderly Mafia don in the same film. William Hurt and Raul Julia were especially effective as the persecuted cell mates in Brazilian director Hector Babenco's *Kiss of the Spider Woman.*

Harrison Ford, mainly thought of as the action movie hero of *Star Wars* and *Raiders of the Lost Ark,* impressively widened his scope as the detective in Peter Weir's *Witness.* There was also a new perspective on Don Johnson, enormously popular as the costar of television's *Miami Vice* series. He demonstrated that he could handle demanding dramatic roles as the troubled war veteran in the impassioned film *Cease Fire.*

One of the year's most remarkable performances was that of Klaus Maria Brandauer in Istvan Szabo's *Colonel Redl,* a fictional treatment of the mystery surrounding the suicide of a military officer accused of espionage in the Austro-Hungarian empire. In a lighter vein, Alan Arkin was both hilarious and touching as the brash former convict in Ted Kotcheff's *Joshua Then and Now,* based on Mordecai Richler's novel. Don Ameche and Hume Cronyn were picture stealers as the rejuvenated codgers in Ron Howard's *Cocoon.*

Sylvester Stallone, in addition to surfacing again as his standby hero in *Rocky IV,* became a new money-making force in *Rambo: First Blood Part II.* The action film, exploiting lingering resentments over defeat in Vietnam, grossed more than $150 million at the box office. Chuck Norris continued his climb as an action hero in *Code of Silence* and *Invasion USA,* and Clint Eastwood upheld his tough-guy image with the Western *Pale Rider.*

Old Masters. There is always something exciting about a great director proving himself anew. Veteran Japanese director Akira Kurosawa, age 75, who had struggled for ten years to finance and film his epic *Ran,* finally presented what turned out to be a masterwork. Set in 16th-century Japan, it borrowed plot aspects from Shakespeare's *King Lear* and honed them into a spectacular and enthralling drama about a warlord and his feuding heirs.

Like Kurosawa, John Huston has had more than one man's share of successes. At the age of 78, he returned with his witty, gallows-humor treatment of the Mafia in *Prizzi's Honor.* Critics predicted that it would rank along with his classics—*The Maltese Falcon, The Treasure of the Sierra Madre,* and *African Queen.*

Although Kurosawa and Huston are in special categories, other important directors also left their imprint. Martin Scorsese's *After Hours* was a Kafka-esque descent into New York at night. Paul Schrader examined the bizarre life and death of fanatical Japanese author Yukio Mishima in the film *Mishima: A Life in Four Chapters.* Richard Attenborough (*Gandhi*) accepted the challenge of adapting the Broadway musical *A Chorus Line.* Robert Altman made a movie from Sam Shepard's play *Fool for Love.* Louis Malle made the first-rate but underappreciated *Alamo Bay,* about tension between Vietnamese immigrants and Texas fishermen.

Eyes were particularly on Michael Cimino in the aftermath of his *Heaven's Gate* (1981) debacle. His movie *Year of the Dragon* was a dud, but it was completed on schedule and within budget, enabling Cimino to demonstrate that he could be counted on for a professional job.

Controversy. Director Jean-Luc Godard, a leader of the French "New Wave" 25 years ago, made waves of controversy with *Hail Mary,* to which many Catholics objected. Pope John Paul II deplored the movie. John Cardinal O'Connor attacked it from his pulpit in New York, and pickets protested its showing at the New York Film Festival and elsewhere. Godard's work was a modern parallel of the Immaculate Conception and birth of Jesus Christ. His Mary was a young woman who worked as a gas station attendant; his Joseph was a taxi driver. Many did not find the film at all anti-Catholic. There were even those who saw reverence in Godard's outlook, but nude shots of Mary and the everyday treatment of the church's virgin mother were in themselves offensive to many.

Teenage Films. Executives and viewers alike found their patience tried by the glut of teen-oriented films released during the summer vacation months. Robert Zemeckis's *Back to*

"Prizzi's Honor," a wickedly funny film about the Mafia, has excellent performances from Jack Nicholson and Kathleen Turner, who portray a husband and wife who happened to be "hit men."

In "Kiss of the Spider Woman," Raul Julia (left), as a heterosexual revolutionary, and William Hurt, a homosexual window dresser, must share a South American prison cell where they move from an alienation of one another to understanding. For his performance, William Hurt won the Cannes Film Festival best actor award.

Island Alive

the Future, starring Michael J. Fox in a delightful story about a teenager who travels back in time and alters the lives of his parents-to-be, met with general approval. *Goonies,* directed by Richard Donner, also had wide appeal. But little value could be found in such similar-sounding movies as *Weird Science, My Science Project,* and *Explorers.* Their failure at the box office sent a strong message to Hollywood executives.

In the realm of family movies, *The Journey of Natty Gann,* released by the Disney studio and directed by Jeremy Kagan, was a surprise. Most family films are set in bland surroundings or some exotic place. This one, about a teenage girl who sets out to find her father, takes place in the 1930s depression and offers a bleak portrait of an America in which the unemployed were hungry, evictions were commonplace, the homeless rode the rails, and shantytowns were destroyed by goons. The film did resort to standard Disney emotional ploys, and Natty, the heroine, acquired a pet wolf. But the Disney release showed that an appealing family movie could deal with weighty reality.

Documentaries. A monumental film by Frenchman Claude Lanzmann outshone all other documentaries. Working ten years on his project and filming 350 hours of interviews in 14 countries, Lanzmann created *Shoah,* an in-depth, revealing study of Hitler's extermination program that claimed the lives of 6 million Jews. The film was nine and one-half hours long and was shown in two parts. Never before had the Holocaust been explored with such detail that revealed the intricacies of the death camps and their assembly-line manufacture of death.

Cassette Revolution. A dramatic statistic made the movie industry take notice of chang-

ing times. Income from videocassettes now reached grosses almost equal to that for movies shown in theaters. The estimated total for 1985 was $3.3 billion from cassettes and $3.7 billion at theaters. Another revelation was found in the marketplace. Certain films that had failed in theaters were becoming cassette hits. Among the examples were *Cotton Club, Dune, Red Dawn,* and *The Pope of Greenwich Village.* Reasons for the contradiction could be found in impulse rentals based on counter displays and posters, the relatively small investment needed to satisfy curiosity, and the diminished expectations of casually watching a film in one's living room.

Business. Hollywood and the broadcasting industry were paying close attention to a possible new trend. Tycoon Rupert Murdoch's 20th Century–Fox purchase and Ted Turner's buy into MGM/UA pointed to an interesting situation. Major movie companies controlled by those who also owned television stations could be in the advantageous position of having their own products given preferential television treatment. Could this be a situation comparable to that of studios owning their own theaters, a condition that was abolished by a 1948 antitrust ruling of the Supreme Court?

Awards. One film stood out as the major Oscar winner of the 1984 crop. It was *Amadeus,* adapted from Peter Shaffer's play and directed by Milos Forman. It won for best picture, director, screenplay, and actor. (*See also* PRIZES AND AWARDS.)

At the Cannes Film Festival, still the leader among the world's film gatherings, there was a surprise winner. A little-publicized film from Yugoslavia, *When Father Was Away on Business,* walked off with the top honor.

WILLIAM WOLF, *Gannett News Service*

"Rambo," the summer box-office hit, starred Sylvester Stallone (left) as a Vietnam veteran on a POW search mission.

MOTION PICTURES | 1985

AFTER HOURS. Director, Martin Scorsese; screenplay by Joseph Minion. With Griffin Dunne, Rosanna Arquette, Teri Garr, John Heard.

AGNES OF GOD. Director, Norman Jewison; screenplay by John Pielmeier. With Jane Fonda, Anne Bancroft, Meg Tilly.

ALAMO BAY. Director, Louis Malle; screenplay by Alice Arlen. With Amy Madigan, Ed Harris, Ho Nguyen, Donald Moffat.

BACK TO THE FUTURE. Director, Robert Zemeckis; screenplay by Mr. Zemeckis and Bob Gale. With Michael J. Fox.

BRAZIL. Director, Terry Gilliam; screenplay by Mr. Gilliam, Tom Stoppard, Charles McKeown. With Jonathan Pryce, Kim Griest, Michael Palin, Robert De Niro.

THE BREAKFAST CLUB. Written and directed by John Hughes. With Molly Ringwald, Anthony Michael Hall.

CEASE FIRE. Director, David Nutter; screenplay by George Fernandez. With Don Johnson, Lisa Blount.

A CHORUS LINE. Director, Richard Attenborough; screenplay by Arnold Schulman, based on the stage play by James Kirkwood and Nicholas Dante. With Michael Douglas, Alyson Reed.

CLUE. Director, Jonathan Lynn; screenplay by Mr. Lynn. With Eileen Brennan, Tim Curry, Madeline Kahn.

COCOON. Director, Ron Howard; screenplay by Tom Benedek, story by David Saperstein. With Don Ameche, Hume Cronyn, Maureen Stapleton, Jessica Tandy, Gwen Verdon.

COLONEL REDL. Director, Isván Szabó; screenplay by Mr. Szabó and Péter Dobai. With Klaus Maria Brandauer.

THE COLOR PURPLE. Director, Steven Spielberg; screenplay by Menno Meyjes, based on the novel by Alice Walker. With Whoopi Goldberg, Danny Glover, Adolph Caesar, Margaret Avery, Rae Dawn Chong.

COMMANDO. Director, Mark L. Lester; screenplay by Steven E. deSouza. With Arnold Schwarzenegger.

COMPROMISING POSITIONS. Director, Frank Perry; screenplay by Susan Isaacs. With Susan Sarandon, Raul Julia, Judith Ivey, Edward Herrmann, Mary Beth Hurt.

DANCE WITH A STRANGER. Director, Mike Newell; screenplay by Shelagh Delaney. With Miranda Richardson, Ian Holm, Rupert Everett.

DANGEROUS MOVES. Director, Richard Dembo; screenplay by Mr. Dembo. With Michel Piccoli, Leslie Caron, Alexander Arbatt, Liv Ullmann.

DESPERATELY SEEKING SUSAN. Director, Susan Seidelman; screenplay by Leora Barish. With Rosanna Arquette, Madonna.

THE DOCTOR AND THE DEVILS. Director, Freddie Francis; screenplay by Ronald Harwood. With Timothy Dalton, Jonathan Pryce, Twiggy, Stephen Rea.

ELENI. Director, Peter Yates; screenplay by Steve Tesich. With Kate Nelligan, John Malkovich.

ENEMY MINE. Director, Wolfgang Petersen; screenplay by Edward Khmara. With Dennis Quaid, Louis Gossett, Jr.

THE FALCON AND THE SNOWMAN. Director, John Schlesinger; screenplay by Steven Zaillian, based on the book by Robert Lindsey. With Timothy Hutton, Sean Penn.

A FLASH OF GREEN. Director, Victor Nuñez; screenplay by Mr. Nuñez, based on John D. MacDonald. With Ed Harris, Blair Brown, Richard Jordan.

FLETCH. Director, Michael Ritchie; screenplay by Andrew Bergman, based on the novel by Gregory McDonald. With Chevy Chase, Jo Don Baker.

FOOL FOR LOVE. Director, Robert Altman; screenplay by Sam Shepard, based on his play. With Mr. Shepard, Kim Basinger.

THE GIG. Written and directed by Frank D. Gilroy. With Wayne Rogers, Cleavon Little.

THE GOONIES. Director, Richard Donner; screenplay by Chris Columbus, story by Steven Spielberg.

GRACE QUIGLEY. Director, Anthony Harvey; screenplay by A. Martin Zweiback. With Katharine Hepburn.

HAIL MARY. Part 1: *The Book of Mary*—director, Anne-Marie Miéville, with Rebecca Hampton; Part 2: *Hail Mary*—director, Jean-Luc Godard, screenplay by Mr. Godard, with Myriem Roussel, Thierry Rode.

THE HOME AND THE WORLD. Director, Satyajit Ray; screenplay by Mr. Ray, based on the novel by Rabindranath Tagore. With Soumitra Chatterjee, Victor Banerjee, Swatilekha Chatterjee.

INSIGNIFICANCE. Director, Nicholas Roeg; screenplay by Terry Johnson. With Michael Emil, Theresa Russell, Tony Curtis, Gary Busey, Will Sampson.

INTO THE NIGHT. Director, John Landis; screenplay by Ron Koslow. With Jeff Goldblum, Michelle Pfeiffer.

JAGGED EDGE. Director, Richard Marquand; screenplay by Joe Eszterhas. With Glenn Close, Jeff Bridges.

THE JEWEL OF THE NILE. Director, Lewis Teague; screenplay by Mark Rosenthal and Lawrence Konner. With Michael Douglas, Kathleen Turner.

JOSHUA THEN AND NOW. Director, Ted Kotcheff; screenplay by Mordecai Richler, based on his novel. With James Woods, Alan Arkin, Michael Sarrazin.

KEY EXCHANGE. Director, Barnett Kellman; screenplay by Kevin Scott and Paul Kurta, based on the Kevin Wade play. With Brooke Adams, Ben Masters, Daniel Stern.

KING DAVID. Director, Bruce Beresford; screenplay by Andrew Birkin and James Costigan. With Richard Gere.

KISS OF THE SPIDER WOMAN. Director, Hector Babenco; screenplay by Leonard Schrader, based on a novel by Manuel Puig. With William Hurt, Raul Julia.

LA CHÈVRE. Written and directed by Francis Veber. With Pierre Richard, Gérard Depardieu.

LOST IN AMERICA. Director, Albert Brooks; screenplay by Mr. Brooks and Minica Johnson. With Albert Brooks, Julie Hagerty, Garry K. Marshall.

MACARONI. Director, Ettore Scola; screenplay by Ruggero Maccari, Furio Scarpelli, and Mr. Scola. With Marcello Mastroianni, Jack Lemmon.

MAD MAX BEYOND THUNDERDOME. Directors, George Miller and George Ogilvie; screenplay by Terry Hayes and Mr. Miller. With Mel Gibson, Tina Turner.

MARIA'S LOVERS. Director, Andrei Konchalovsky; screenplay by Mr. Konchalovsky, Gerard Brach, Paul Zindel, Marjorie David. With Nastassja Kinski, John Savage, Robert Mitchum, Keith Carradine.

MARIE. Director, Roger Donaldson; screenplay by John Briley, based on the book *Marie: A True Story*, by Peter Maas. With Sissy Spacek, Jeff Daniels.

MASK. Director, Peter Bogdanovich; screenplay by Anna Hamilton Phelan, based on the true story of Rocky Dennis. With Cher, Sam Elliott, Eric Stoltz.

MAXIE. Director, Paul Aaron; screenplay by Patricia Resnick, based on *Marion's Wall* by Jack Finney. With Glenn Close, Mandy Patinkin, Ruth Gordon.

MIXED BLOOD. Written and directed by Paul Morrissey. With Marilia Pera, Richard Ulacia.

MURPHY'S ROMANCE. Director, Martin Ritt; screenplay by Irving Ravetch and Harriet Frank, Jr. With Sally Field, James Garner.

1918. Director, Ken Harrison; screenplay by Horton Foote. With Hallie Foote, Matthew Broderick.

NINETEEN EIGHTY-FOUR. Written and directed by Michael Radford, based on the novel by George Orwell. With John Hurt, Richard Burton, Suzanna Hamilton.

THE OFFICIAL STORY. Director, Luis Puenzo; screenplay by Mr. Puenzo and Aïda Bortnick. With Hector Alterio, Norma Aleandro.

OUT OF AFRICA. Director, Sydney Pollack; screenplay by Kurt Luedtke, based on the writings of Isak Dinesen; With Robert Redford, Meryl Streep.

PALE RIDER. Director, Clint Eastwood; screenplay by Michael Butler and Dennis Shryack. With Clint Eastwood, Michael Moriarty, Carrie Snodgress.

PERFECT. Director, James Bridges; screenplay by Aaron Latham and Mr. Bridges. With John Travolta, Jamie Lee Curtis, Laraine Newman.

PLENTY. Director, Fred Schepisi; screenplay by David Hare. With Meryl Streep, Tracey Ullman, John Gielgud, Charles Dance.

PRIVATE FUNCTION. Director, Malcolm Mowbray; screenplay by Alan Bennett. With Michael Palin, Maggie Smith.

PRIZZI'S HONOR. Director, John Huston; screenplay by Richard Condon, Janet Roach. With Jack Nicholson, Kathleen Turner, William Hickey, Anjelica Huston.

THE PURPLE ROSE OF CAIRO. Written and directed by Woody Allen. With Mia Farrow, Jeff Daniels, Danny Aiello, Ed Herrmann, Van Johnson, Zoe Caldwell.

RAMBO: FIRST BLOOD PART II. Director, George P. Cosmatos; screenplay by Sylvester Stallone, James Cameron, story by Kevin Jarre, based on characters created by David Morrell. With Sylvester Stallone.

RAN. Director, Akira Kurosawa; screenplay by Mr. Kurosawa, Hideo Oguni, Masato Ide. With Tatsuya Nakadai.

THE RETURN OF THE SOLDIER. Director, Alan Bridges; screenplay by Hugh Whitemore, based on a novel by Rebecca West. With Glenda Jackson, Julie Christie, Ann Margret, Alan Bates.

REVOLUTION. Director, Hugh Hudson; screenplay by Robert Dillon. With Al Pacino, Donald Sutherland, Nastassja Kinski.

ROCKY IV. Written and directed by Sylvester Stallone. With Mr. Stallone, Dolph Lundgren, Talia Shire, Burt Young.

RUNAWAY TRAIN. Director, Andrei Konchalovsky; screenplay by Djordje Milicevic, Paul Zindel, Edward Bunker, based on the script by Akira Kurosawa. With Jon Voight, Eric Roberts, Rebecca DeMornay.

SANTA CLAUS: THE MOVIE. Director, Jeannot Szwarc, screenplay by David Newman. With Dudley Moore.

SHOAH. Director, Claude Lanzmann. (Documentary on the Holocaust of World War II).

THE SHOOTING PARTY. Director, Alan Bridges; screenplay by Julian Bond, based on the novel by Isabel Colegate. With James Mason, John Gielgud, Edward Fox.

SILVERADO. Director, Lawrence Kasdan; screenplay by Lawrence and Mark Kasdan. With Kevin Kline, Scott Glenn, Rosanna Arquette, Jeff Goldblum, Linda Hunt.

SPIES LIKE US. Director, John Landis; screenplay by Dan Aykroyd, Lowell Ganz, Babaloo Mandel. With Chevy Chase, Mr. Aykroyd.

SUBWAY. Director, Luc Besson; screenplay by Mr. Besson, Pierre Jolivet, Alain Le Henry, Sophie Schmit. With Christopher Lambert, Isabelle Adjani.

THE SURE THING. Director, Rob Reiner; screenplay by Steven L. Bloom and Jonathan Roberts. With John Cusack, Daphne Zuniga.

SWEET DREAMS. Director, Karel Reisz; screenplay by Robert Getchell. With Jessica Lange, Ed Harris.

TARGET. Director, Arthur Penn; screenplay by Howard Berk and Don Petersen. With Gene Hackman, Matt Dillon.

TO LIVE AND DIE IN L.A. Director, William Friedkin; screenplay by Mr. Friedkin and Gerald Petievich. With William L. Petersen, Willem Dafoe.

THE TRIP TO BOUNTIFUL. Director, Peter Masterson; screenplay by Horton Foote, adapted from his play. With Geraldine Page, John Herald, Carlin Glynn.

TWICE IN A LIFETIME. Director, Bud Yorkin; screenplay by Colin Welland. With Gene Hackman, Ann Margret, Ellen Burstyn, Amy Madigan.

WETHERBY. Written and directed by David Hare. With Vanessa Redgrave, Ian Holm, Judi Dench.

WHEN FATHER WAS AWAY ON BUSINESS. Director, Emir Kusturica; screenplay by Abdulah Sidran. With Moreno d'e Bartolli, Miki Manojlović, Mirjana Karanović.

WHITE NIGHTS. Director, Taylor Hackford; screenplay by James Goldman, Eric Hughes. With Mikhail Baryshnikov, Gregory Hines, Isabella Rossellini.

WITNESS. Director, Peter Weir; screenplay by Earl W. Wallace and William Kelley. With Harrison Ford.

YEAR OF THE DRAGON. Director, Michael Cimino; screenplay by Oliver Stone and Mr. Cimino, based on a novel by Robert Daley. With Mickey Rourke.

YOUNG SHERLOCK HOLMES. Director, Barry Levinson; screenplay by Chris Columbus. With Nicholas Rowe.

© Doc, Gamma-Liaison

The rock star Madonna (left) and Rosanna Arquette are the stars of the off-beat "Desperately Seeking Susan." The film, which marked Madonna's debut in motion pictures, is the work of Susan Seidelman, a young director of promise, and involves two women, from Greenwich Village and New Jersey, and their escapades in and around New York.

On a 15-city summer tour marking its 100th anniversary, the Boston Pops played outdoors in the nation's capital.

MUSIC

Baroque, Broadway, and the Boston Pops had much to celebrate in 1985. Baroque pieces were heard everywhere, as orchestras all over the world commemorated the 300th birthdays of three period masters—the German-born composer Johann Sebastian Bach (*see* special report, page 375), the German-English composer George Frideric Handel, and the Italian composer Domenico Scarlatti. For Broadway musical buffs, 1985 saw a spate of special tributes and retrospectives marking the 100th birthday of the American composer Jerome Kern. And though nobody wore black ties, there was a special festive flair at Symphony Hall in Boston for a gala centennial concert by another musical bastion—the Boston Pops.

Though their own anniversaries were somewhat overshadowed by that of Bach, Handel (1685–1759) and Scarlatti (1685–1757) nevertheless were recognized as giants of the late Baroque whose works have endured, resoundingly, for three centuries. Indeed, while Bach remained an obscure provincial composer until after his death, Handel became a wealthy international celebrity. In 1985, Handel's works were no less eminent, as crowds gathered in concert halls, churches, and opera houses to hear *Messiah, Water Music,* and scores of other choral and instrumental compositions. Scarlatti also was renowned during his own lifetime, both as a harpsichordist and as a composer. His modern reputation rests on his more than 600 sonatas and other keyboard pieces.

New York–born Jerome Kern (1885–1945) was remembered as the musical creator of melodic, buoyant musical stage shows, including *Oh, Boy!* (1917), *Leave it to Jane* (1917), *Oh, Lady! Lady!* (1918), *Sally* (1920), *Sunny* (1925), *Showboat* (1927), and numerous others. Among Kern's songs that have become classics are "Ol' Man River," "Can't Help Lovin' Dat Man," "The Song Is You," and "Smoke Gets in Your Eyes." His 100th birthday was commemorated with a new U.S. 22¢ stamp and a series of concert, radio, and TV tributes. An off-Broadway revue about his life, *Ladies and Gentlemen . . . Jerome Kern,* debuted in June.

The Boston Pops, one of the most famous orchestras in the world, kicked off its new century of "a lighter kind of music" with a 15-city transcontinental tour. For the gala opening, Boston's Symphony Hall was hung with mirrors, baubles, and balloons in the cabaret style. The program, conducted by John Williams, included a Berlioz overture, a musical tribute to Judy Garland, and the premier of a "newly discovered" spoof by P.D.Q. Bach (Peter Schickele) called *The 1712 Overture.* And following a special White House performance in July, first lady Nancy Reagan expressed the sentiments of many: "to one of America's oldest and most enjoyable cultural institutions—thank you, again, and a very happy birthday."

The Ordway Music Theatre

In St. Paul, MN, the Ordway Music Theatre, the new home of the St. Paul Chamber Orchestra, the Minnesota Opera, and the Shubert Club, opened in January. It includes the 1,800-seat Main Hall (above) and a 315-seat studio theater.

Classical

The stylistic current in new concert music flowed consistently toward greater listener accessibility. Even among composers noted for the complexity of their music, many seemed to be easing off. A comparable accommodation to the realities of the concert hall could be observed among experimental composers and in the "new music festivals" at the opposite end of the spectrum.

In consequence, new works—both in premieres and, significantly, repeat performances—appeared on subscription series with increasing regularity and as a matter of normal course. There was a more natural balance in the concert scene, and major modern works from earlier in the century took a firmer place in the working repertory as recognized classics.

Symbolic of this development, Aaron Copland was honored in his 85th year in concerts and nationally televised programs. On Copland's birthday, November 14, tribute was paid him with an all-Copland concert by the New York Philharmonic. Three days later he was honored in a concert that also honored William Schuman's 75th and David Diamond's 70th birthday, by the American Composers Orchestra. Schuman's distinguished contribution was recognized in performances by more than 100 organizations, and with a Special Citation from the Pulitzer Prize Committee.

New Music. The favorable climate did not necessarily bring out distinguished and highly original works as much as it welcomed compositions created with a certain fluency in a broad and easy mix of styles. Ellen Taaffe Zwilich followed up on her 1983 Pulitzer Prize–winning first symphony with a Symphony No. 2, *Cello Symphony*, that was conservatively fashioned, light in texture and substance. It received its premiere on November 13 by the San Francisco Symphony, which had commissioned it, with Edo de Waart conducting.

The influence of jazz in music of those composers with the popular idiom in their backgrounds ranged widely. With Donald Erb the presence is subtle, as in his *Contrabassoon Concerto,* premiered on March 15, by the Houston Symphony, Greg Henegar soloist, Sergiu Commissiona conducting. Jazz is more evident in the free and improvisatory idiom of the younger composer William Thomas McKinley whose *Clarinet Concerto* was introduced by Richard Stoltzman and the American Composers Orchestra in Alice Tully Hall, New York City, on February 21.

Other distinctive premieres included: Toru Takemitsu's *Piano Concerto* by the Los Angeles Philharmonic, Peter Serkin soloist, Simon Rattle conducting, on January 10; Bernard Rands' *Ceremonial* by the San Diego Symphony, David Atherton conducting, on November 7 at the opening of its new Symphony Hall,

converted from a 1929 movie palace; Aulis Sallinen's Symphony No. 5, *Washington Mosaics,* by the National Symphony, Mstislav Rostropovich conducting, on October 10; Gunther Schuller's *Viola Concerto,* by the New Orleans Symphony, Thomas Riebl soloist, the composer conducting, on December 17.

Charles Wuorinen, long noted for his intense, richly textured counterpoint, and in the forefront of American composition, was widely performed. His *Concertino* for 14 winds, introduced by the Winds of Parnassus in New York City's Alice Tully Hall on February 5, was described as highly volatile and energetic. *Rhapsody* for violin, given its premiere on January 15 by the San Francisco Symphony, Daniel Kobialka soloist, was a work in free fantasy; and his *Crossfire* by the Baltimore Symphony, David Zinman conducting, on May 9, was outgoing in nature.

Opera. The American operatic scene continued to be conservative even with respect to new works. A single exception was John Eaton's *The Tempest,* to a libretto on Shakespeare's play by Andrew Porter, given its premiere by the Santa Fe Opera on July 27. The opera was fanciful and highly original, its music a fusion of various styles intensified by microtonal treatment and sophisticated electronics.

Thea Musgrave's *Harriet, The Woman Called Moses,* an opera about Harriet Tubman, the black slave who became an abolitionist leader and organizer of the Underground Railway, was given its premiere by the Virginia Opera Company in Norfolk, VA, on March 1. The opera was Musgrave's sixth and was criticized for its undistinguished music and conventional operatic treatment. In the first of two opera collaborations between the Minnesota Opera and the St. Paul Chamber Orchestra, Dominick Argento's critically praised *Casanova's Homecoming* was given its premiere on April 12. On November 12 it was produced by the New York City Opera. Argento's 13th

opera deals with the return of the old Casanova to Venice after a long exile.

On September 27 the Minnesota Opera and St. Paul Chamber Orchestra, with Pinchas Zukerman conducting, produced the American stage premiere of a novelty work—the British composer Oliver Knussen's 45-minute fantasy opera based on writer Maurice Sendak's *Where the Wild Things Are.* Sendak created the set and costumes.

Wagner's *Der Ring des Nibelungen* was presented three times by the San Francisco Opera in June. The "Götterdämmerung" was the final addition to the newest *Ring,* a $5.4 million venture begun with "Das Rheingold" in 1983. John Conklin's sets returned to the romantic design tradition, drawing on 19th-century paintings by Caspar David Friedrich and set designs by Karl Schinkel, but within this frame, Niklaus Lehnhoff's production concepts were original. The outstanding singers were James Morris as Wotan in the first two operas, Thomas Stewart as Wotan in "Siegfried" and Eva Marton as Bruennhilde in "Götterdämmerung."

Two other American *Ring* cycles, both modern production conceptions, were initiated with a strange "Die Walküre" at the Seattle Opera in July, and a successful "Das Rheingold," using sets borrowed from the Dallas Opera, at Artpark, Lewiston, NY, June 27, with Christopher Keene conducting.

Los Angeles Music Center Opera Association, headed by Peter Hemmings with Placido Domingo as adviser, announced it would produce operas with international casts beginning in 1986 with five productions. Heretofore, the association had been a sponsor of visiting companies, the last of which was the Deutsche Oper Berlin in September. Two months later, the Los Angeles Opera Theater, which had been presenting American casts for five years, closed because of a lack of funds.

Dresden's famous Semper Opera House, completely rebuilt in its original highly decora-

The line was long as New York's Symphony Space offered an eight-hour free concert to mark the 300th birthday of Domenico Scarlatti. A premiere performance of one of Scarlatti's unpublished solo contatas was a highlight.

© James Heffernan

The opening of the Metropolitan Opera's 1985–86 season featured "Tosca" with Luciano Pavarotti as Cavaradossi and Montserrat Cabelle as Tosca.

tive splendor, was reopened 40 years after its destruction by Allied bombers. The opening opera was Carl Maria von Weber's *Der Freischuetz,* the last work performed there before the house was closed by the Nazis in 1944.

Leontyne Price, 57, concluded her illustrious 29-year career on the opera stage on January 3, with a farewell performance of Verdi's *Aïda,* nationally televised, at New York's Metropolitan Opera.

Festivals and Special Observances. There was an unprecedented celebration of Handel's long-neglected operatic glory. The rediscovery in the production of so many of his 40 operas was the major achievement of the Handel Tercentenary year. In New York City's Carnegie Hall alone, there were performances of *Orlando, Ariodante, Semele, Alessandro* (the U.S. premiere occurred earlier at the John F. Kennedy Center, Washington, DC, with Stephen Simon conducting the Handel Festival Orchestra), and in concert, *Deidama* and *Agrippina,* besides the oratorios *Theodora, Belshazzar,* and *Israel in Egypt.*

Handel operas in other cities included a lively and witty staging of *Agrippina* in Fort Worth, TX, *Rodelinda, Tamerlano,* and a much edited and primarily decorative *Ariodante* at the Spoleto Festival, Charleston, SC, produced by the Concert Royal and the New York Baroque Dance Company. In early June, the Boston Early Music Festival's production of *Teseo,* conducted by Nicholas McGegan, was highly praised as a historical reconstruction of exceptional integrity. The complete *Giulio Cesare* in a strikingly original production by Peter Sellars was given eight performances at the PepsiCo Summerfare Festival in Purchase, NY. The San Francisco Opera produced *Orlando,* with Marilyn Horne in the title role, Charles Mackerras conducting, on September 14.

The Tercentenary of Domenico Scarlatti also was observed widely, mainly in recitals featuring his harpsichord sonatas of which

there are more than 550. On his birthday, October 26, 100 of them were played in an eight-hour free concert broadcast nationally from New York City's Symphony Space.

American Music Week (November 4–10) was celebrated in more than 40 states by 200 organizations. The major observance of the centennial of Alban Berg's birth on Feb. 9, 1885, was held at Oberlin (OH) College.

Two major contemporary festivals were held in Los Angeles. The California Institute of the Arts, Valencia, produced as the main offering five concerts between March 7 and 11, each one dedicated to a single composer, including the Californians Mel Powell, Robert Erickson, and Paul Dresher; Toru Takemitsu of Japan; and Louis Andriessen of Holland. The more extensive seventh annual New Music America Festival involved 12 arts organizations including the Los Angeles Philharmonic.

Appointments and Other News. Herbert Blomstedt began his tenure as the San Francisco Symphony's music director conducting his first concert in that capacity on October 2. His predecessor, Edo de Waart, was meanwhile appointed the new music director of the Minnesota Orchestra, as of 1986. Andre Previn, whose appointment as the Los Angeles Philharmonic music director officially would start January 1986, conducted the season's opener on October 10. Semyon Bychkov was appointed music director of the Buffalo Philharmonic beginning with its 50th anniversary season, 1985–1986.

Henry Fogel was appointed executive director of the Chicago Symphony; Stephen Klein succeeded Fogel in the top position at the National Symphony.

The Ordway Music Theatre, a $45 million facility with a main theater seating 1,800 persons and a studio theater seating 315 in St. Paul, MN, was inaugurated with a festival series of concerts January 8–12.

Awards. Pianist Marc-Andre Hamelin, 24, of Montreal, Canada, took the first prize in the Carnegie Hall International American Music Competition. The Bach International Piano Competition in Toronto on May 11 was won by Angela Hewitt, 26. Hugh Wolff, newly appointed music director of the New Jersey Symphony, and Kent Nagano, music director of the Berkeley (CA) Symphony, were cowinners of the Affiliate Artists' first Seaver Conducting Award. Margaret Wray and Robynne Redmon, mezzo sopranos, won the G. B. Dealey Awards in Dallas, TX, competition, in June. Violinist Nai-Yuan Hu took the first prize in the Queen Elisabeth of Belgium International Music Competition in July.

See also BIOGRAPHY—Bumbry, Grace; OBITUARIES—Ormandy, Eugene; PRIZES AND AWARDS.

ROBERT COMMANDAY
Music Critic, "San Francisco Chronicle"

Johann Sebastian Bach (1685–1985)

© David Relas, Courtesy of the New York Philharmonic

The New York Philharmonic and Westminster Choir marked Bach's 300th birthday with eight special performances.

The tercentenary of the birth of Johann Sebastian Bach was the dominant feature of the musical year. Musical organizations and institutions worldwide celebrated Bach on their regular programs and with special or festival observances. The universal tributes acknowledged that Bach represents the trunk of the tree from which music has since grown and is the one musician upon whom subsequent musicians depend.

A new understanding of many aspects of Bach emerged. The bulk of his church music now seems to have been composed before 1730, not as previously believed, between 1723–1744. Bach's exploratory impulse later in life and the continuity of his stylistic development were revealed by such studies as those that found both conservative and modernist, and operatic inclinations in the later contatas. One quality examined and valued was Bach's urge to be comprehensive, represented in his *Art of Fugue, Well-Tempered Clavier,* and his other famous sensational or "collection" works. Another quality was his compulsion to learn and incorporate music and periods that established the compositional tradition of valuing and drawing on the musical past.

The parent Bach festival occurred, logically, in Leipzig, East Germany, Bach's home and musical empire for the last 27 years of his life. From March 19 to March 27 several thousand performers, scholars, and musical pilgrims from 18 countries participated in 55 concerts and conferences of the combined Fifth International Bach Festival and 60th Bachfest of the new Bach Society.

The first major event was an inspiring performance in Bach's own principal church, St. Thomas, of *B-minor Mass* with the current cantor, Hans-Joachim Rotszch, conducting the St. Thomas Choir Boys and the Leipzig Gewandhaus Orchestra. Bach's 300th birthday, March 21, was celebrated by a performance of the *St. Matthew Passion* in the new Gewandhaus with Kurt Masur conducting the Gewandhaus orchestra's distinguished soloists and a splendidly trained East German youth choir of 150.

In America the festivals included an International Symposium at Hofstra University (NY), October 24–26; the Minnesota Bach Society—coordinated performances in the Minneapolis-St. Paul area of more than 150 Bach choral works during the year; 200 Bach concerts held in Birmingham, AL; and a festival entitled "TriBach" in Edmonton, Alberta, March 21–April 6.

A tercentennial monument was the revelation performance and publication of 33 previously unknown chorale preludes by Bach, subsequently dubbed the Arnstadt Chorale Preludes. Christoph Wolff, eminent Bach expert and chairman of the Harvard University Music Department who discovered them in a collection at the Yale University Library, believes Bach composed them in the first decade of the 18th century just before his *Little Organ Book.*

ROBERT COMMANDAY

Benny Goodman made a surprise appearance at the 1985 Kool Jazz Festival to honor the music of John Hammond.

Jazz

In 1985 the most prevalent and successful formulas utilized in jazz music were eclectic musical collaboration and the blending of musicians and styles. For his *Dream of the Blue Turtles* album, the pop star Sting used jazz saxophonist Branford Marsalis and pianist Kenneth Kirkland, both of the Wynton Marsalis group; Omar Hakim of Weather Report; and the Miles Davis bass player Darryl Jones. Such pop-jazz collaborations, as well as the multidirectional, musical-spectrum big bands of Laurence "Butch" Morris, David Murray, and Lester Bowie, provided a contemporary setting for traditional, gospel, Latin, rhythm and blues, and bebop jazz.

Jazzman Miles Davis helped to define the direction of contemporary jazz music as well with his album *You're under Arrest*. Considered to be his first pop album, *You're under Arrest* blended Davis' past musical statements with current pop, punk, and funk dance music.

The eclectic approach also was apparent in the programs of the 1985 jazz festivals, particularly those of the Kool Festival in New York and the Festival International de Jazz de Montreal. To broaden the scope of the Kool festival, Spanish, Brazilian, and African artists were featured. The Montreal festival offered something for everyone with $2 million worth of entertainment, ranging in musical style from Wynton Marsalis, to Tony Bennett, to Art Blakey, to Dr. John. This sort of balanced programming gave the majority of the 1985 jazz festivals commercial feasibility.

In 1985 the big-band renaissance was evident in the current jazz movement and featured innovative as well as traditional musicians. Also making an important comeback was the modern jazz quartet. A jazz messenger alumni group toured during the year, giving credence to a movement back to the basic and versatile standard bebop quintet and sextet format. The best of these groups was the Phil Woods Quintet, featuring trumpeter Tom Harrell.

Within the jazz community there was a continued resolve to build stronger support systems for jazz through organizing and coordinating activities and information. The 1985 jazztimes convention in New York presented a varied program of lectures, concerts, and panel discussions. The panel discussions focused on coordination of jazz organizations, the jazz video market, and the publishing of a jazz repertoire. The newly formed National Jazz Service Organization, with David Baker as its president, proposed a national center for jazz to provide a permanent center for jazz archives and activities. As part of the Congressional Black Caucus Foundation's 15th annual legislative weekend, Michigan Congressman John Conyers, Jr., lobbied to have jazz officially recognized as America's music.

Awards. The winners in *Down Beat* magazine's 33d Annual International Critics Poll included: Zoot Sims—Hall of Fame; *That's the Way I Feel Now*—record of the year; Sun Ra —big band; Art Ensemble of Chicago—acoustic group; Miles Davis —electric group; Carla Bley—composer; Gil Evans—arranger; Wynton Marsalis—trumpet; Jimmy Knepper—trombone; Steve Lacy—soprano sax; Phil Woods—alto sax; Sonny Rollins—tenor sax; Pepper Adams—baritone sax; Stephane Grappelli—violin; Cecil Taylor—acoustic piano; Jim Hall—guitar; Charlie Haden—acoustic bass; Max Roach—drums; Joe Williams—male singer; Sarah Vaughan—female singer; Manhattan Transfer—vocal group.

DOMINIC SPERA, *Indiana University*

Photos by © Neal Preston, Camera 5

Madonna (left) and Prince captured the imaginations of rock fans with their highly individualistic approaches to music. Madonna won new success in the film "Desperately Seeking Susan," and Prince worked on new film and video projects.

Popular

A return to social and political consciousness reminiscent of popular music in the 1960s distinguished pop music in 1985.

Do They Know It's Christmas?, recorded in 1984 by a group of 40 British superstars collectively known as Band Aid to raise funds for the starving in Africa, spawned numerous similar charitable recordings and performances in 1985. The most significant of these was the *We Are the World* recording and video, which brought together 45 of the world's best-known artists. Dubbed "USA for Africa," the group included Bruce Springsteen, Michael Jackson, Bob Dylan, Tina Turner, Willie Nelson, Lionel Richie, Cyndi Lauper, and Harry Belafonte and generated millions of dollars for African relief. The song dominated the airwaves, and on Good Friday it was broadcast simultaneously by 8,000 radio stations throughout the world. It also gave birth to Live Aid, a benefit rock concert broadcast from JFK Stadium in Philadelphia and Wembley Stadium in London on July 13. Live Aid reached 1.6 billion people worldwide, earned more than $70 million, and featured more than 60 artists in exciting combinations. Duets by Mick Jagger and Tina Turner, Sting and Phil Collins, Bob Dylan with members of the Rolling Stones, and the reunions of Led Zeppelin and the Who were highlights. Rocker Bob Geldof, originator of these events, became the first entertainer ever nominated for the Nobel Peace Prize.

Live Aid was followed by an avalanche of charitable concerts and recordings. In September, Willie Nelson, John Cougar Mellencamp, and Neil Young organized the Farm Aid concert to benefit American farmers. Latin artists headed by Julio Iglesias united to record *Cantaré Cantaras* and to stage a telethon to aid Mexican earthquake victims. Political causes inspired musical events as well. Chief among these was the antiapartheid *Sun City,* recorded by 30 artists led by Steve Van Zandt.

Bruce Springsteen ended his 15-month-long global "Born in the U.S.A." tour. (*See also* BIOGRAPHY.) His enthusiastic reception and massive record sales elevated him to the status of the original king of rock, Elvis Presley, whose 50th birthday was celebrated posthumously in January.

The influence of women in pop music became even stronger in 1985. Madonna captured a vast audience with her erotic rock performances. Her first major concert tour swept the United States, and she proved a charismatic actress in the popular movie *Desperately Seeking Susan.* Rock doyenne Tina Turner echoed these achievements in music and film with her "Private Dancer" tour and her film performance in *Mad Max Beyond Thunderdome.* Cyndi Lauper, Pat Benatar, Sheena Easton, the Pointer Sisters, Laura Branigan, Chaka

Khan, Annie Lennox of Eurythmics, and Sade peppered the chart with hits.

The British invasion continued, spearheaded by the internationally recognized artists Wham!, Phil Collins, Tears for Fears, Dire Straits, and Paul Young. Wham! became the first major Western pop group to perform in China.

After two years of total domination of popular music, Michael Jackson faded from public view. Prince, who picked up Jackson's mantle in 1984, completed his spectacular "Purple Rain" tour, released a successful follow-up album, *Around the World in a Day,* and continued to work on film and video projects.

A minor soul revival occurred, accompanied by reissues of early recordings by vocal greats Sam Cooke and Jackie Wilson. Soul queen Aretha Franklin retook her throne with her chart-topping album *Who's Zoomin' Who.* New York's legendary Apollo Theatre celebrated its 50th anniversary with a concert featuring nearly every soul star of the decade. A concert by Hall and Oates with former Temptations Eddie Kendricks and David Ruffin in June marked the reopening of the famed Harlem landmark.

Hand in hand with the soul revival came a new ascendency of the human voice in pop music. The vocal prowess of newcomers Sade, Whitney Houston, and Freddie Jackson gained them instant popularity.

New artists with widely divergent pop styles took a bigger-than-ever chunk of the charts and concert audiences, as evidenced by the success of neophytes Julian Lennon (son of Beatle John), 'Til Tuesday, Simple Minds, Hooters, Katrina and the Waves, Hüsker Dü, the Mary Jane Girls, Full Force, and Lisa Lisa and Cult Jam. Go-go music, a variation on funk, spiraled out from Washington, DC. Run-D.M.C., the Fat Boys, Whodini, and Kurtis Blow filled the airwaves with the street sounds of rapping and beat music and produced a controversial movie, *Krush Groove.* Heavy metal still drew huge teen audiences.

Country music as defined by the slick Nashville Sound declined in popularity, although American legends of the stature of Willie Nelson and Dolly Parton endured. The greatest successes were achieved by rock-tinged country acts like Alabama, by new wavers Jason and the Scorchers and Lone Justice, and by new traditionalists Ricky Skaggs, George Strait, and the Judds.

Video remained an essential tool in a popular musician's career and became a powerful disseminator of regional music to a broader audience.

The Broadway musical season was dismal. *Big River* swept the Tony Awards.

See also PRIZES AND AWARDS; RECORDINGS.

PAULETTE WEISS, *Free-lance Journalist*

Live Aid, the largest live-television event ever, raised money for the famine victims in Africa.

© Neil Leifer, Camera 5

Music Videos

Music videos, the union of rock music and mesmerizing images, came into their own as an entertainment medium with the birth of the cable channel MTV (music television) in 1981. By 1985 music videos were being sold directly to consumers like records, but the number fell below the predictions of optimistic recording-industry pundits. In the booming home-video market, movies garnered 74% of home-video-cassette sales; special-interest programming, including exercise tapes and other how-to items, accounted for 15%; while music videos captured 11%. The music-video percentage was well below the 25% share predicted for 1986.

Nevertheless the trade magazine *Billboard* noted the growing market strength of music videos in August 1985 when for the first time in the history of its Top 40 videocassette sales chart, four of the Top 10 were music videos. These were: *Prince and the Revolution Live, We Are the World—the Video Event,* Tina Turner's *Private Dancer,* and *Wham! The Video.*

Vestron's *Making Michael Jackson's Thriller* remained the biggest-selling music videocassette to date, while RCA/Columbia's *We Are the World* exploded into second place with a number one debut on *Billboard*'s charts. Holding third and fourth places were the Rolling Stones' *Video Rewind* and *The Compleat Beatles.*

These mixed sales reports hardly reflected the powerful influence music videos had on pop culture in the early 1980s. Videos set the style for film, advertising, television programming, and fashion. Their influence was international, disseminated by broadcast and cable television, in clubs and movie theaters. The revolutionary television series *Miami Vice* took its character from music videos; teenage girls worldwide dressed like flamboyant video rock songstress Madonna; and USA for Africa's video *We Are the World* helped unite the globe in a charitable cause.

Film and video intermingled, epitomized by rocker Prince's hugely popular 1984 movie *Purple Rain,* essentially a series of videos tied together by a thin plot. Other fledgling rock artists with a flair for the theatrical rocketed to stardom driven by video power, among them Duran Duran, Madonna, Cyndi Lauper, and Huey Lewis and the News. As video-oriented music artists reaped the benefits of the phenomenon, directors, producers, cinematographers, and performing artists of many kinds expanded into the infant medium. Music videos left their mark on technology as well, through their experiments with animation,

MTV Networks Inc.

Annie Lennox and Dave Stewart of the Eurythmics perform at the Second Annual MTV Music Video Awards.

computer graphics, lighting, robotics, and lasers. At the same time, however, music videos were being criticized by some as too violent and sexually explicit.

As the influence of music videos grew, so did the number of programs devoted to them on broadcast and cable TV. Although MTV, now under new ownership, was reaching 24 million American homes, by 1985 two dozen music video shows, including *Friday Night Videos, Radio 1990,* and *Night Flight,* were broadcast nationally and hundreds of shows sprang up locally.

Almost as impactful as radio in selling records, these largely rock-oriented programs were soon joined by country, rhythm and blues, and "adult contemporary" video-music shows. The Nashville Network carried *Video Country* and *Country Clips,* the Black Entertainment Network had *Video Soul,* and in January 1985, MTV gave birth to VH-1, a sister video channel with the smoother sounds of such artists as John Denver, Linda Ronstadt, and Kenny Rogers.

PAULETTE WEISS

As March ended, the city of Omaha was hit by 7½ in (19 cm) of snow—the area's heaviest spring snowfall in 40 years.

AP/Wide World

NEBRASKA

Agricultural hardship, economic problems, and school district consolidation dominated state news in 1985.

Agriculture and the Economy. Reversing a weather pattern of preceding years, growing conditions were excellent, and record crop yields seemed certain. But prices for farm products, already low, were down from 1984, and farm land values for the year ending April 1 declined by 28%.

The ripples from agricultural depression were felt throughout the state. Meatpacking plants and farm support businesses closed or suffered losses, the housing market in much of the state was depressed, unemployment increased, rural school enrollments declined, and property tax delinquency was up.

Another effect of the troubled farm economy was closing of banks because of defaulted farm loans. By mid-September nine banks had failed in Nebraska, the largest number since the Great Depression and more than 10% of the year's bank failures in the entire nation.

The 1983 closing of Nebraska's largest industrial loan and investment firm, Commonwealth Savings Company of Lincoln, continued to have repercussions in 1985. The last court cases ended with the conviction of the fourth member of the family charged with practices that led to the Commonwealth collapse, and Nebraska Attorney General Paul Douglas, convicted of felony perjury in the Commonwealth investigation, resigned his office effective Jan. 1, 1985. A special session of the state legislature met in September to finalize an appropriation of $8.5 million for partial reimbursement of Commonwealth losses.

The Legislature and State Government. Given the depressed state of the economy, Gov. Robert Kerrey began seeking ways to cut his proposed budget even before it was formally presented to the legislature. When tax revenues fell sharply below projections in April, both governor and legislature sought extensive budget cuts in order to avoid a tax increase. State aid to local government was reduced, and in the autumn Kerrey asked local governments to cut expenses and return some funds to the state.

During its regular session, the legislature passed a highly controversial school consolidation measure requiring school districts having only kindergarten through eighth grade classes to merge with districts that have high schools. The bill included a provision to reduce property-tax support of public schools to 45% of the total, with a 1% increase in the state sales tax to make up the difference. The measure was challenged by a petition drive to put the bill before the voters in 1986.

The legislature also passed a mandatory seat belt law. Although traffic deaths in August fell to their lowest level since 1948 (even before the bill went into effect), another petition drive put repeal of the seat belt law on the 1986 ballot.

NEBRASKA • Information Highlights

Area: 77,355 sq mi (200 350 km²).
Population (July 1, 1984 est.): 1,606,000.
Chief Cities (July 1, 1984 est.): Lincoln, the capital, 180,378; Omaha, 332,237; Grand Island (1980 census), 33,180.
Government (1985): *Chief Officers*—governor, J. Robert Kerrey (D); lt. gov., Donald McGinley (D). *Legislature* (unicameral)—49 members (nonpartisan).
State Finances (fiscal year 1984): *Revenues,* $2,047,-000,000; *expenditures,* $1,884,000,000.
Personal Income (1984): $19,962,000,000; per capita, $12,430.
Labor Force (June 1985): *Civilian labor force,* 830,400; *unemployed,* 42,400 (5.1% of total force).
Education: *Enrollment* (fall 1983)—public elementary schools, 185,941; public secondary, 81,057; colleges and universities, 95,162. *Public school expenditures* (1982–83), $759,197,398 ($2,984 per pupil).

Governor Kerrey. Nebraskans enjoyed speculating about the much-publicized romance of Governor Kerrey and actress Debra Winger. In October the popular governor announced that he would not seek reelection to a second term, prompting speculation about his future plans. His current term would end in January 1987.

WILLIAM E. CHRISTENSEN
Midland Lutheran College

NETHERLANDS

Despite a slow but significant improvement of economic conditions, the Netherlands faced in 1985 a political conflict of an intensity unmatched since the end of World War II.

Political Unrest. The chief issue involved was the decision of the government of Prime Minister Rudolf (Ruud) F. M. Lubbers on November 1 to go ahead with the installation of 48 cruise missiles carrying nuclear warheads as part of the strategic plans of the North Atlantic Treaty Organization (NATO). The decision of the cabinet—which the parliament (States General) confirmed on December 1—was taken upon the expiration of a period of a year and a half during which a final determination was delayed. The delay was intended to give the Soviet Union an opportunity to hold the number of its SS-20 missiles at or below 378, the number at the time of the original decision, and to allow time for the Soviet Union to reach an arms-limitation agreement with the United States. The failure of the USSR to meet these conditions clearly and unequivocally, although it prompted the decision of the Dutch government, did not diminish a wide movement of protest.

In this movement the left political parties, most importantly the Labor party, were joined by a vigorous peace movement of church peace activists. A petition protesting the pending cruise missile decision was signed by a very large segment of the population. Protesters argued that the cabinet and parliament violated the constitution by going ahead in the face of such widespread opposition, and claimed that the decision, as equivalent to a treaty, required a two-thirds vote in parliament. The protests arose not from support of the USSR, which was rare, but from general antipathy to nuclear power, even for peaceful uses. The protest also tended to reflect a feeling of frustration and exasperation that the Netherlands, a small country, seemed to be unable to determine its own fate. There was talk of civil disobedience and a continuation of disruptive demonstrations at Woensdrecht, the airbase where the missiles would be installed, and elsewhere.

Politically more important was the prospect, indicated by public opinion polls, that the Liberal (conservative) party, one of the two partners in the coalition government, would suffer a major loss of seats in the parliamentary elections to be held in the spring of 1986, while the Labor party would gain strongly. The Christian Democrat Party of Prime Minister Lubbers was divided on the issue of installing cruise missiles, although the large majority of its deputies supported the government.

Economy and Domestic Affairs. Measures taken by the government to cut back expenditures and to reduce the national budget deficit began to show some success in reviving economic activity. The number of unemployed dropped from more than 800,000 to under 750,000 during 1985. The extensive welfare program of the Dutch state, although remaining intact, was made less generous in its provisions. The major change in principal was the uncoupling of welfare payments from the minimum wage structure as set by law.

Although Dutch contributions to international programs for assistance to less-developed countries remained high, the government tightened requirements for entry of refugees, notably Tamils from Sri Lanka.

The tensions within the Roman Catholic Church in the Netherlands between liberals and the conservative forces backed by the Vatican were displayed before the world when Pope John Paul II visited the country in May. Hostile public demonstrations by antireligious fringe groups occurred, and meetings between the pontiff and some members of his own church were marked by often passionate appeals to the pope to change his conservative course in matters such as abortion and marriage of priests.

The Netherlands government continued to be bedeviled by a number of scandals, including the failure of the minister of economic affairs to inform the parliament fully and candidly of his role in subsidizing the huge Rijn-Schelde-Verolme shipbuilding and machine concern, which subsequently went bankrupt.

HERBERT H. ROWEN, *Rutgers University*

NETHERLANDS • Information Highlights

Official Name: Kingdom of the Netherlands.
Location: Northwestern Europe.
Area: 15,770 sq mi (40 844 km^2).
Population (mid-1985 est.): 14,500,000.
Chief Cities (Jan. 1984 est.): Amsterdam, the capital, 676,439; Rotterdam, 555,349; The Hague, the seat of government, 445,213.
Government: *Head of state,* Beatrix, queen (acceded April 30, 1980). *Head of government,* Ruud Lubbers, prime minister (took office Nov. 1982). *Legislature*—States General: First Chamber and Second Chamber.
Monetary Unit: Guilder (2.8125 guilders equal U.S.-$1, Dec. 2, 1985).
Economic Index (1984): *Consumer Prices* (1980 = 100) all items, 243.7; food, 116.9.
Foreign Trade (1984 U.S.$): *Imports,* $62,136,-000,000; *exports,* $65,881,000,000.

NEVADA

Increased state support for education, a thriving economy, and Sen. Paul Laxalt's decision not to run for reelection in 1986 were the news highlights in Nevada in 1985.

Education. Democratic Gov. Richard Bryan stole a march on the Republicans in November 1984 by calling for no general tax increase; however, a healthy surplus in the state general fund allowed him to recommend a 20% increase in state funding for the public schools and a 27% increase for the University of Nevada system. The 1985 Nevada legislature cut the public schools slightly but increased the university budget over the governor's proposal. University faculty and state employees received an 11% salary increase, after receiving only a token increase during the 1983–85 biennium.

Other Legislative Actions. The legislature enacted an omnibus child-protection law that permits the use in court of videotaped depositions by sexual abuse victims and child witnesses. The legislators opted for a study of rising hospital costs rather than enact the governor's cost-containment proposal. The tax increases that were enacted with a "sunset" provision to meet the financial crisis were continued, with the exception of the controversial tax on soft drinks. Small increases in the property tax to help pay for rising costs for indigent medical care and in the motor vehicle fuel tax to support road repair were also approved by the legislature. On the whole, Governor Bryan's legislative program fared well, and he was not displeased that the legislators increased his budget proposals for welfare (ADC) and prisons. The attempt of the Republican Assembly to scuttle the governor's plan to pay a bonus to teachers and state employees from the state surplus boomeranged after a large number of schoolteachers descended on the legislative chambers; the Republicans quickly rescinded their opposition but may have alienated many teachers by their previous action.

Economy. Nevada's economy continued on the upswing during 1985. Gambling-tax and sales-tax revenues were up 8 and 10%, respectively, over the 1983–84 fiscal year. The economic diversification campaign led by Governor Bryan met with considerable success, as many new non-gaming businesses were attracted to the state. Unemployment fluctuated between a low of 7.4% in February to a high of 8.5% in July.

The mining industry continued to boom in Nevada in 1985. Nevada again was the leading gold-producing state, as 58% of the nation's gold was mined in the 400-plus mining operations in the state. Nevada's mines also produced 100% of the magnesium ore in the nation, 99% of the mercury, and 83% of the barite.

Laxalt's Announcement. U.S. Sen. Paul Laxalt, President Ronald Reagan's "first friend," announced on August 19 that he would not run for a third term. Several possible candidates showed initial interest in the seat; by fall the Democratic leadership had united behind Congressman Harry Reid, while the Republicans were split among three possible candidates, including former four-term Democratic Congressman James Santini, who switched parties in late August.

DON W. DRIGGS
University of Nevada, Reno

NEW BRUNSWICK

New Brunswick was in the national limelight in 1985 as seldom before—and not in especially flattering ways. Politics, real and threatened police strikes, and a fish scandal all figured prominently in the news.

Political. For better or worse, it was the year of Premier Richard Hatfield—long a source of fascination and even titillation for

Canapress Photo Service

Richard Hatfield, New Brunswick's 54-year-old premier, was one of Canada's major newsmakers throughout 1985.

New Brunswickers and Canadians. Canada's longest-serving premier was acquitted January 29 in Fredericton of possessing marijuana. Police had discovered 35 grams of the drug in his suitcase just before a Fredericton-Moncton flight Hatfield made with Queen Elizabeth on Sept. 25, 1984, during the royal tour. The judge ruled that the prosecution had not proved its case beyond a reasonable doubt.

Hatfield hardly had time to breathe easier when, in early February, various newspapers carried stories alleging that he had smoked marijuana with three teenagers at his Fredericton home in 1981. Hatfield denied the allegations, and no charges were made.

As the year wore on, it seemed to become more and more apparent that Hatfield was living, politically speaking, on borrowed time. On April 29 the Liberal Party candidate, Hubert Seamens, defeated the candidate of Hatfield's ruling Conservative Party, Scott MacGregor, by a better than two-to-one margin in a by-election in Riverview constituency. It was the first time in 33 years that the Liberals had won Riverview. The victory provided an advance spirit lifter for the new Liberal leader, Frank McKenna, who was elected at a convention in Moncton five days later.

In October, Hatfield tried to revive his sagging fortunes by shuffling his cabinet and streamlining the government. But the moves failed to appease his critics, including a rebel group of Conservative backbenchers, who, however, failed in their first major attempt—November 9—to bring about a leadership review.

Police Strife. The police forces of New Brunswick's two largest cities, Saint John and Moncton, were poised to go on strike in early May, but the provincial cabinet passed last-minute decrees ordering them to stay on the job. At about the same time, a police walkout in Chatham ran its course for two weeks—spawning a number of violent incidents in the streets—before the government stepped in with a back-to-work order. In each case, provision was made for binding arbitration of the policemen's pay demands.

Aroma of Scandal. A canning plant in St. Andrews gained notoriety in September when it was revealed that the federal fisheries minister, John Fraser, had ordered a million tins of its tuna released for public sale—even though his own departmental inspectors had found it decomposing and unfit for human consumption. The resulting furor in the Canadian Parliament forced Fraser to order the suspect tuna removed from store shelves. Shortly after that, Fraser resigned.

Nuclear Power. Plans for a second nuclear power plant at Point Lepreau were suspended in February. Maritime Nuclear, a federal-provincial corporation, said that markets for the output of the proposed C$1.4 billion plant would take longer to develop than thought.

JOHN BEST, *"Canada World News"*

NEWFOUNDLAND

High unemployment, public salary freezes, and little money for new programs were sufficient to overcome the good news in Newfoundland in 1985. The good news was the settlement, after many years, of the dispute between Canada and Newfoundland as to the ownership and management of offshore oil and gas resources. In February, Prime Minister Brian Mulroney and provincial Premier Brian Peckford signed the "Atlantic Accord." The province was to have final say on the mode of development for its offshore resources.

Politics and Government. On the strength of this agreement, Peckford called a provincial election for April, just three years after the last

---

NEWFOUNDLAND • Information Highlights

Area: 156,185 sq mi (404 519 km²).
Population (April 1985 est.): 579,700.
Chief Cities (1981 census): St. John's, the capital, 83,770; Corner Brook, 24,339.
Government (1985): *Chief Officers*—lt. gov., W. Anthony Paddon; premier, A. Brian Peckford (Progressive Conservative). *Legislature*—Legislative Assembly, 52 members.
Provincial Finances (1985–86 fiscal year budget): *Revenues,* $2,377,000,000; *expenditures,* $2,450,000,000.
Personal Income (average weekly earnings, June 1985): $390.82.
Labor Force (August 1985, seasonally adjusted): *Employed workers,* 15 years of age and over, 178,000; *Unemployed,* 46,000 (20.5%).
Education (1985–86): *Enrollment*—elementary and secondary schools, 143,080 pupils; postsecondary (full-time, 1985–86)—universities, 9,450; community colleges, 3,050.
(All monetary figures are in Canadian dollars.)

election. The results were disappointing for him. The premier's Progressive Conservatives (PCs) won 36 seats and 48.6% of the popular vote, eight seats fewer than before. The Liberals won 15 seats with 36.8% of the vote, and the New Democratic Party (NDP) captured its first seat in the provincial legislature with a 14.4% share of the vote. The shift in voting was generally attributed to labor strikes and teacher dissatisfaction with a two-year wage freeze. In Labrador, where the NDP won, voters reacted to a reduction in the Iron Ore of Canada's operations.

The budget, brought down in May, projected expenditures of C$2.45 billion and a deficit of $73.0 million. Although it included no new taxes, it nevertheless managed to paint a grim future in the short run.

Royal Commissions. Two Royal Commissions made the news. The joint federal-provincial commission established in 1982 to investigate the "Ocean Ranger" oil rig accident off the Grand Banks ruled that design and human factors accounted for the more than 80 deaths and called for a safe evacuation system for offshore rigs. In January a provincial Royal Commission on Employment and Unemployment was established.

Hibernia. The Hibernia oil field continued to gain attention. In July, Mobil Oil decided to use fixed concrete platforms at Hibernia rather than floating ones. The choice was seen as a victory for the provincial government.

SUSAN MCCORQUODALE
Memorial University

NEW HAMPSHIRE

The year in New Hampshire proved to be one of continuity and important transition.

Economy. While much of the nation experienced economic problems or only moderate growth, New Hampshire had another exceptionally fine year. The state's economy continued to expand, while the state budget showed a surplus. Employment gains remained at near-record levels, while unemployment was well below the regional and national average. The unemployment rate stood at 4.4% in June and 5.1% in July. The positive employment picture stemmed from the role of defense-related industries and the fact that older industries such as shoe manufacture were a much smaller percentage of total labor force. In addition, high-tech jobs did not decline here as much as nationally.

Environment. Growth, however, does not come without some despoilment. The Environmental Protection Agency (EPA) warned the state that air quality in the Nashua area was below acceptable limits. Most agreed that this condition was caused by traffic congestion and the rapid population increase in the metropolitan area. Both threatened the life-style that many came to the state to enjoy. The problems of the Nashua region were symptomatic of the urgent need for the development of plans addressing the inadequacies of the road system in congested parts of the state.

Seabrook. Another recurring problem during 1985 centered on the Seabrook nuclear power plant. In 1984 many were predicting that Public Service Co. would go bankrupt because of huge cost overruns. But 1985 witnessed a turnaround for the troubled project. Under the direction of William Derrickson, construction costs were brought under control. Other contributing circumstances were the successful sale of securities and the approval by New Hampshire Public Service Commission to increase weekly construction spending from $5 million to $8 million. After January, work on Unit I progressed smoothly with completion set for October 1986. But the plant's possible impact on electric rates caused growing concern. Some predicted it would be generating the most costly electric power in New England.

Population Growth. Perhaps nothing demonstrated major transition more dramatically than the announcement at midyear that the estimated population of the state exceeded 1 million. Throughout the 1980s, New Hampshire has been the third-fastest-growing state east of the Mississippi, with a growth rate of 6.1%.

State Government. The state government entered some unchartered areas in 1985. For the first time since 1877 the legislature began to hold annual sessions after approval of a constitutional amendment in 1984. In September, Maine, New Hampshire, and Vermont inaugurated the Tri-State Megabucks lottery, first in the nation. Its purpose was to offer larger prizes than any of the states could do alone so as to compete with the huge prizes offered in Massachusetts. The drinking age went back to 21, reverting to the level it had been before the changes arising from the activism of the 1960s.

WILLIAM L. TAYLOR
Plymouth State College

NEW HAMPSHIRE • Information Highlights

Area: 9,279 sq mi (24 032 km²).
Population (July 1, 1984 est.): 977,000.
Chief Cities (1980 census): Concord, the capital, 30,400; Manchester, 90,936; Nashua, 67,865.
Government (1985): *Chief Officer*—governor, John H. Sununu (R). *General Court*—Senate, 24 members; House of Representatives, 400 members.
State Finances (fiscal year 1984): *Revenues,* $1,276,000,000; *expenditures,* $1,128,000,000.
Personal Income (1984): $12,885,000,000; per capita, $13,192.
Labor Force (June 1985): *Civilian labor force,* 543,200; *unemployed,* 24,100 (4.4% of total force).
Education: *Enrollment* (fall 1983)—public elementary schools, 106,303; public secondary, 52,727; colleges and universities, 53,143. *Public school expenditures* (1982–83), $402,306,643 ($2,750 per pupil).

NEW JERSEY

Gubernatorial politics dominated events in New Jersey in 1985.

Elections. During his first term, Gov. Thomas Kean gained enormous popularity by presenting an image of a moderate Republican opposed to the Reagan administration's cuts in spending for social programs. Further enhancing Kean's reputation was the improved economic climate of the state, measured by a low unemployment rate compared with the national average; the growth of a high-tech corridor centered between Princeton and New Brunswick; the revitalization of the Hudson River waterfront; and the plans for commercial real-estate development in such older cities as Newark and Jersey City. Early in the year, Kean announced that he would seek reelection, and no other Republicans opposed him.

Five Democratic aspirants threw their hats in the ring: Essex County Executive Peter Shapiro, Newark Mayor Kenneth Gibson, former state Sen. Stephen B. Wiley, former federal prosecutor Robert J. Del Tufo, and state Senate Majority Leader John F. Russo. In the June 4 primary, Shapiro was the winner with 31% of the vote, compared with 27% for Russo and 26% for Gibson. Overall, only about 4% of eligible voters participated.

Kean's strategy in the election campaign was to run on his record as much as possible. On a number of issues he took positions and called for programs that were similar to those previously endorsed by the Democratic-controlled legislature. This was especially true with environmental protection: in his State of the State message in January, Governor Kean proposed a $450 million environmental trust fund, to be used for cleaning toxic-waste dumps and establishing more efficient means for solid-waste disposal. Another prominent issue stressed by Kean was educational re-

AP/Wide World

Gov. Thomas Kean, who easily won a second term in November, publicizes New Jersey's mandatory seat-belt law.

form, including the state's $18,500 minimum salary for teachers (highest in the nation) and an alternative teacher certification program that would allow qualified people to work in the classroom without having completed the standard college-level education. For his part, Shapiro criticized Kean for overstating his successes in toxic-waste cleanup, making that the major issue in the campaign.

Expectations of a Republican sweep were realized in the results of the November 5 election. With about 60% of the eligible voters going to the polls, Kean received 70% of the vote, the largest margin ever recorded in a New Jersey gubernatorial contest. Results of the elections for the 80-member House of Assembly demonstrated the length of Kean's coattails, as Republicans gained control for the first time since 1971. Taken all together, the election outcomes made Kean a potential power in national Republican politics.

Various public questions also were on the November 5 ballot. The one that received the most publicity involved simulcasting horse

---

NEW JERSEY • Information Highlights

Area: 7,787 sq mi (20 169 km²).

Population (July 1, 1984 est.): 7,515,000.

Chief Cities (July 1, 1984 est.): Trenton, the capital (1980 census), 92,124; Newark, 314,387; Jersey City, 223,004; Paterson, 138,818; Elizabeth, 107,455.

Government (1985): *Chief Officer*—governor, Thomas H. Kean (R). *Legislature*—Senate, 40 members; General Assembly, 80 members.

State Finances (fiscal year 1984): *Revenues,* $14,677,000,000; *expenditures,* $12,635,000,000.

Personal Income (1984): $116,029,000,000; per capita, $15,440.

Labor Force (June 1985): *Civilian labor force,* 3,900,900; *unemployed,* 214,300 (5.5% of total force).

Education: *Enrollment* (fall 1983)—public elementary schools, 761,194; public secondary, 386,377; colleges and universities, 314,468. *Public school expenditures* (1982–83), $4,340,959,702 ($4,007 per pupil).

races; it was approved by a wide margin. A constitutional amendment allowing for legislative veto of certain executive actions was voted down.

Accidents. A major fire in Passaic and a plane collision near the Hudson River also made headlines during the year. On September 2, fire broke out at a chemical plant in downtown Passaic, engulfed a four-block industrial complex, and then spread to homes and apartment buildings. There were no serious injuries, but the neighborhood had to be evacuated, and several factories, homes, and other buildings were destroyed. Arson was suspected.

On November 10, two small planes collided and fell in flames over the towns of Fairview and Cliffside Park in northeastern New Jersey. Burning wreckage set off fires in several residential and commercial buildings. Two persons in one plane, three persons in the other, and a sixth on the ground were killed.

Miscellaneous. A poll conducted by the Eagleton Institute at Rutgers University during the summer showed that New Jersey residents had a more positive image of their state than in recent years. The New Jersey Sports and Exposition Authority was empowered to locate an appropriate site for a major league baseball stadium.

HERMANN K. PLATT, *St. Peter's College*

NEW MEXICO

In 1985, New Mexicans mourned the death of one of their state's best-known citizens, Albuquerque businessman and balloonist Ben Abruzzo. He was killed in February in the crash of a private plane. Abruzzo, with Maxie Anderson and Larry Newman, gained worldwide attention in 1978 when they became the first men to complete a transatlantic balloon flight. Anderson died in a ballooning accident in West Germany during the summer of 1983.

Politics. The 1985 legislative session was virtually paralyzed by partisan politics. Two special sessions called by Gov. Toney Anaya (D) in an effort to enact pending legislation met with only marginal success. A conservative coalition of Democrats and Republicans that ruled the state Senate was in constant conflict with the liberal policies of the Anaya administration. The 42-member Senate initially was evenly divided between the two parties, but Democrat Les Houston of Albuquerque formed a coalition with the Republicans to defeat the governor's bills. In August, Houston announced that he was switching his membership to the Republican Party, giving it clear control of the Senate in the next session.

Meanwhile, Governor Anaya faced problems in other areas. His special-projects director was indicted in a bribery and fraud scheme involving disaster relief contracts. Two of his

---

NEW MEXICO • Information Highlights

Area: 121,593 sq mi (314 925 km²).
Population (July 1, 1984 est.): 1,424,000.
Chief Cities (1980 census): Santa Fe, the capital, 48,953; Albuquerque (July 1, 1984 est.): 350,575; Las Cruces, 45,086.
Government (1985): *Chief Officers*—governor, Toney Anaya (D); lt. gov., Mike Runnels (D). *Legislature*—Senate, 42 members; House of Representatives, 70 members.
State Finances (fiscal year 1984): *Revenues,* $3,338,000,000; *expenditures,* $2,833,000,000.
Personal Income (1984): $14,610,000,000; per capita, $10,262.
Labor Force (June 1985): *Civilian labor force,* 647,300; *unemployed,* 59,300 (9.2% of total force).
Education: *Enrollment* (fall 1983)—public elementary schools, 191,824; public secondary, 77,887; colleges and universities, 66,094. *Public school expenditures* (1982–83), $713,500,218 ($2,901 per pupil).

---

top financial officials were convicted of extortion and conspiracy. And an investigation was launched into the granting of a permit to a hospital corporation that contributed to Anaya's campaign.

Health. In late summer Dr. Thomas Tomasi, director of the University of New Mexico Cancer Center, announced "a development that could be very significant in the field of cancer diagnosis and treatment." He and his colleague, Dr. William Anderson, after three years of research discovered a way to shield laboratory-produced antibodies allowing them to ward off the natural hazards of the human body and go directly to the killing of cancer cells. The Cancer Center research has advanced from testing the modified antibodies in test tubes to trials in mice.

Economy. New Mexico's farming, ranching, and mining sectors continued to show signs of slowing down. Brian McDonald, director of the Bureau of Business and Economic Research, declared, "The state, with little manufacturing, is underdeveloped." Thousands of miners have lost jobs since the collapse of the uranium industry in the early 1980s and a recent decrease in coal mining. Criticism mounted that state government has produced no plan for economic development.

In another area, the U.S. Soil Conservation Service in Albuquerque released a report showing that wind erosion—causing damage to homes, landscaping, machinery, and recreational facilities—costs the state an estimated $514 million a year. Moreover, the rate of soil erosion is increasing sharply. In a one-year period, 857,000 acres (347 000 ha) in New Mexico suffered serious wind damage.

Moncor, Inc., headquartered in Hobbs and the state's fourth-largest banking institution, filed for bankruptcy. It was the first failure of a major bank in New Mexico since the Great Depression.

MARC SIMMONS
Author, "New Mexico, A History"

NEW YORK

For New York State, 1985 was a year when a $39 billion state budget included something for almost everyone, and there was money left over to cut taxes as well. But despite a continued healthy economy, politicians spoke of the growing gap between the rich and the poor.

For the first time in a decade, the governor and the legislature were able to pass a budget without the constraints that had overshadowed spending plans since the New York City fiscal crisis of 1975. The state spent more money than ever before on education and aid to local governments, began a $50 million housing program, continued efforts to protect the environment and house the homeless, and increased the size of the basic welfare grant. At the same time, it enacted a three-year plan to cut personal income taxes by more than $1 billion to reduce New York's double-digit tax rates and improve the business climate in the state.

Gov. Mario Cuomo led the fight to retain federal deductions for state and local taxes. His national reputation continued to grow, and he began a series of 90-second national radio commentaries, alternating every weekday with former Sen. Howard Baker, a Tennessee Republican. Although Cuomo continued to express interest only in seeking reelection in 1986, rumors of his possible presidential candidacy in 1988 spread as polls showed his popularity increasing, with favorable ratings as high as 75% in New York State. Although the Republicans had fielded no gubernatorial candidate, Cuomo had raised more than $9 million by the end of 1985 in preparation for his reelection campaign.

In another political development of major interest, Geraldine Ferraro, the 1984 Democratic vice-presidential candidate, announced that she would not run against Sen. Alfonse D'Amato in 1986. The incumbent Republican was expected to seek a second term.

Legislation. The threat of a cutoff of federal highway funds prompted the state legislature to raise the legal drinking age from 19 to 21. A mandatory seat-belt law also became effective in 1985. An amnesty program allowing individuals and small businesses to pay back taxes without penalty was coupled with much more stringent penalties for future tax evaders.

Legislators continued to struggle with problems caused by rising insurance rates, particularly for doctors. A new law aimed at curbing medical malpractice premiums set limits on attorney fees and allowed insurance companies to pay out some verdicts over a longer period of time. Other insurance problems loomed as 1986 approached, with everyone from municipal and school officials to day-care-center owners and architects saying that skyrocketing insurance rates might force them to drop coverage. The insurance crisis was one of the key factors prompting Governor Cuomo to call a largely unproductive special session of the legislature in December.

A number of measures to help businesses in the state were adopted, including a reduction in the bank tax rate and a sweeping law aimed at making hostile corporate takeovers more difficult. Voters approved a doubling, from $300 million to $600 million, in the bonding capacity of the state Job Development Authority, which lends money to businesses that promise to keep or create new jobs.

Energy. Energy issues, including the fate of the Long Island Lighting Company's Shoreham nuclear plant, remained unresolved. The Lilco plant received a license to begin low-power testing despite the opposition of the county legislature and the governor and the refusal of the local government to participate in an evacuation drill. Anger over rising rates and the amount of time it took to restore power in the wake of September's Hurricane Gloria gave rise to a growing movement for a public takeover of the utility. State legislators supported the move, and Cuomo said his staff was exploring the feasibility of some sort of state takeover.

Other Matters. The number of homeless people in the streets, particularly families with children, increased greatly. Advocates for the homeless criticized local and state officials for failing to provide adequate housing.

The deadly disease AIDS became increasingly controversial as the number of reported cases rose, prompting Governor Cuomo to institute public health regulations allowing local officials to shut down establishments, like homosexual bath houses, where the disease might be spread. Gay rights groups took the government to court in an effort to overturn the new rules.

MIRIAM PAWEL
Albany Bureau Chief, "Newsday"

NEW YORK • Information Highlights

Area: 49,108 sq mi (127 189 km²).
Population (July 1, 1984 est.): 17,735,000.
Chief Cities (July 1, 1984 est.): Albany, the capital, 100,048; New York, 7,164,742; Buffalo, 338,982; Rochester, 242,562; Yonkers, 191,234; Syracuse, 164,219.
Government (1985): *Chief Officers*—governor, Mario M. Cuomo (D); lt. gov., vacant. *Legislature*—Senate, 61 members; Assembly, 150 members.
State Finances (fiscal year 1984): *Revenues,* $42,412,000,000; *expenditures,* $35,917,000,000.
Personal Income (1984): $253,934,000,000; per capita, $14,318.
Labor Force (June 1985): *Civilian labor force,* 8,289,200; *unemployed,* 548,900 (6.6% of total force).
Education: *Enrollment* (fall 1983)—public elementary schools, 1,735,517; public secondary, 939,301; colleges and universities, 1,022,521. *Public school expenditures* (1982–83), $10,985,-513,938 ($4,686 per pupil).

Up for reelection in 1985, New York City's Mayor Edward Koch (center) greets his opponents in the Democratic primary, City Council President Carol Bellamy and Assemblyman Herman Farrell. After winning his party's nod, Mayor Koch had little difficulty winning a third term in the general election in November.

AP/Wide World

NEW YORK CITY

A hurricane, a drought, an earthquake, and stormy battles over Acquired Immune Deficiency Syndrome (AIDS) and the Westway project made headlines in New York City in 1985. Mayor Edward I. Koch won a third term by a landslide. Two libel trials, a hotel strike, and crimes and scandals were also in the news.

Hurricane Gloria roared across the metropolitan region on September 27, driving people from coastal areas and knocking out power to more than one million homes. The city escaped catastrophe, but Long Island bore the brunt of $285 million in losses. The storm added little water to the city's upstate reservoirs, and a drought that afflicted New York City all summer and fall—prompting many water-use restrictions—was expected to continue in 1986. On October 19 a predawn earthquake, the largest to hit the metropolitan area in years, shook homes and roused thousands from sleep but caused no injuries or major damage.

Anxiety over AIDS touched schools, hospitals, and other institutions where carriers of the disease were admitted. The city had a third of the nation's cases of AIDS, which was still largely confined to homosexuals and intravenous drug users. Another controversy, a ten-year fight over Westway, ended in defeat for the $4.2 billion Manhattan highway project. Stymied by lawsuits and other obstacles, Mayor Koch, Gov. Mario M. Cuomo, and other advocates agreed not to build Westway and opted for a trade-in to get $1.7 billion in federal funds for mass transit and a more modest West Side roadway.

In municipal elections, Koch became the fifth mayor in the city's history to win a third term, easily defeating rivals in the heavily Democratic city. Manhattan Borough President Andrew J. Stein won the number two post of city council president and Harrison J. Goldin was reelected city comptroller.

In federal courts, Ariel Sharon, Israel's former defense minister, lost a libel suit against *Time* magazine, and William C. Westmoreland, who had commanded American forces in Vietnam, dropped a libel suit against the Columbia Broadcasting System (CBS) without a verdict, damages, or a retraction. (*See* LAW—Libel.)

A 27-day strike by 16,000 workers against 53 Manhattan hotels in June inconvenienced visitors and cost the hotels $16.2 million and the city economy even more. Broadway theaters had their worst season in a decade. But the city enjoyed its healthiest economy in years. One poll found New Yorkers more satisfied with city life; another said crime was their chief worry. The most prominent crime case was that of Bernhard Goetz, who in late 1984 shot four youths on a subway train after they asked him for five dollars. (*See* feature article, page 44.) Allegations that a prisoner had been tortured at a police station in Queens led to a shakeup of the police department.

One of the nation's best-known churchmen, Dr. Norman Vincent Peale, resigned as rector of Marble Collegiate Church, ending a 52-year career of religious leadership. In appointments and resignations, City Budget Director Alair A. Townsend was named deputy mayor, replacing Kenneth Lipper, who ran unsuccessfully for city council president. The city's Chief Medical examiner, Dr. Elliot M. Gross, took a leave to defend himself against state charges of incompetence and negligence.

In sports, the Mets and the Yankees lost close pennant races. Tom Seaver, a longtime Met pitching star, won his 300th major league game on the mound for the Chicago White Sox, a 4–1 victory over the Yankees. The Knicks, after years of lackluster basketball, signed the nation's top rookie, Georgetown's 7-foot (2.1-m) center, Patrick Ewing, to a six-year, $17-million contract.

ROBERT D. MCFADDEN
"The New York Times"

NEW ZEALAND

Throughout the year revolutionary changes pending in the tax system, the rift with the United States over visits by nuclear warships, and the sinking of a Greenpeace protest vessel by French secret service agents competed for attention in New Zealand.

The Economy. Economic indicators gave a confused picture of the nation's condition. By October prime lending rates had climbed to 25%, and inflation had stubbornly settled at about 16%. However, after the New Zealand dollar was floated in March, it appreciated remarkably, by October standing at U.S.$0.60 as against an original U.S.$0.44. This allowed an unprecedented two 10% decreases in the price of gasoline in two months. Unemployment, running at 8% of the work force in February, had dropped to 6% by August. Although the economy and unemployment continued to head polls on matters of national concern (29% and 16% in midyear), joint reports by the Organization for Economic Cooperation and Development (OECD) and the International Monetary Fund (IMF) warmly welcomed the firm monetary policy of Roger Douglas, the minister of finance, and his commitment to deregulation of the economy and reduction of the internal deficit.

The budget was presented in two stages. The first announced sizable leaps in defense, health, and education spending, but was primarily a holding operation. The second unveiled the introduction of a 10% goods and services tax from Oct. 1, 1986. To compensate, substantial cuts in income tax—25% at the average wage rate—and in wholesale taxes were promised.

NEW ZEALAND • Information Highlights

Official Name: New Zealand.
Location: Southwest Pacific Ocean.
Area: 103,736 sq mi (268 676 km²).
Population (mid-1985 est.): 3,300,000.
Chief Cities (March 31, 1983 est.): Wellington, the capital, 342,500; Auckland, 882,000; Christchurch, 322,700; Hamilton, 167,700.
Government: *Head of state,* Elizabeth II, queen, represented by Archbishop Sir Paul Reeves, governor-general (took office Nov. 1985). *Head of government,* David Lange, prime minister (took office July 26, 1984). *Legislature* (unicameral)—House of Representatives.
Monetary Unit: New Zealand dollar (1.7452 N.Z. dollars equal U.S.$1, Nov. 8, 1985).
Gross National Product (year ending March 1984): $16,200,000,000.
Economic Index (1984): *Consumer Prices* (1970 = 100), all items, 496.0; food, 492.0.
Foreign Trade (1984 U.S.$): *Imports,* $6,010,000,000; *exports,* $5,358,000,000.

External Issues. After permission was refused for the U.S.S. *Buchanan* to visit in February, efforts were made to resolve the nuclear warships ban. However, the United States called off reciprocal visits and joint defense exercises and stopped providing certain military intelligence; in March the ANZUS (Australia, New Zealand, United States Defense Treaty) alliance summit was canceled. Later, a draft no-nuclear bill was prepared, and there were even hints that the government might contemplate scrapping the ANZUS treaty itself.

By the time Prime Minister David Lange departed for the Commonwealth Heads of Government meeting in the Bahamas and a visit to the United States in October, the deadlock was unbroken. An opinion poll in September revealed that while 59% of the populace

The Greenpeace protest vessel "Rainbow Warrior," sunk by French agents in Auckland harbor July 10, was salvaged.

© Gil Hanly, Sygma

opposed port visits by nuclear armed ships, an overwhelming majority—71% to 14%—wished New Zealand to stay a partner in ANZUS.

On July 10 the *Rainbow Warrior,* flagship of the Greenpeace protest flotilla preparing to sail for the French nuclear tests site in the Mururoa Atoll, was sunk at its berth in Waitemata Harbour, Auckland, by limpet mines. French involvement was quickly suspected, and a touring couple, later identified as officers in the French secret service, were arrested and charged with sabotage and murder. After initially denying being implicated, the French government finally admitted that its agents were responsible. In November the two agents were allowed to plead guilty to lesser charges of manslaughter, thus eliminating the need for a trial.

Domestic Affairs. The governing Labour Party and its chief opposition, the National Party, seesawed in popularity. However, in a June by-election brought about by the death of Sir Basil Arthur, the speaker of parliament, National won with an 11% swing. Opinion polls showed an astounding degree of support for Sir Robert Muldoon, deposed National Party leader.

GRAHAM BUSH, *University of Auckland*

NIGERIA

The economic and political controls implemented by Gen. Mohammad Buhari's military government failed to solve the country's massive economic problems and were primarily responsible for the overthrow of his 20-month-old regime by Gen. Ibrahim Babangida, one of his associates in the 1983 coup.

Economic Developments. Faced with a critical reduction in demand for petroleum, which provides 97% of Nigeria's foreign exchange; mounting external debts estimated at $25 billion; and an inflation rate of more than 50%, the Buhari government imposed stringent controls on the economy. Imports were cut by 28%, money and credit controls established, public spending slashed, and the naira devalued. Despite protests by the Organization of the Petroleum Exporting Countries (OPEC), petroleum prices were lowered. Buhari closed Nigeria's borders and declared war on smuggling. Many public servants suspected of corruption were arrested, tried, and sentenced. Buhari's economic program was partially successful: the inflation rate was cut by 25%, external reserves improved, foreign borrowing was curbed, and his reallocation of resources pointed toward a more realistic use of funds. But there was a price to pay for Buhari's "war against indiscipline." An estimated 150,000 jobs were wiped out, adding to the already high unemployment rate; many thousands more were forced to take pay cuts; and higher taxes

bankrupted many businessmen and small traders. In combination with the political decrees and social unrest, Buhari's stringencies by mid-1985 had made his government extremely unpopular. His refusal to accept the recommendations of the International Monetary Fund (IMF), particularly its suggestion to devalue the naira by 50%, meant postponement of $2.5 billion in credits.

Internal Affairs. Two decrees issued in early 1985 alienated large segments of the population. One made criticism of any public officials a criminal offense; the other allowed the imprisonment without trial of anyone deemed by the government to be subversive. In July the regime banned all debate on the political future of Nigeria. Imprisonment of journalists was only one unpopular action. In March a three-week strike by doctors resulted in the outlawing of their organizations. The military also clashed with students in various states. Buhari ordered the immediate expulsion of illegal aliens in May. Unplanned, the forced exodus of more than 750,000 caused great hardship and embittered Nigeria's relations with its neighbors.

Disagreement developed in the Supreme Military Council with Buhari's harsh, ineffectual policies. General Babangida, chief of staff of the Army, was one spokesman for moderation. On August 27, while both Buhari and his second in command, Gen. Tunde Idiagbon, were away from Lagos, Babangida and his associates overthrew the unpopular regime. Their bloodless coup immediately led to the release of political prisoners, abrogation of the two most unpopular decrees, a promise by Babangida of moderation in attacking the nation's problems, and a decision to cooperate with the IMF.

Foreign Policy. Nigeria maintained its support for the antiapartheid movement in South Africa and for the liberation of Namibia. The government's relations with the United States and the European Community (EC), while friendly, were colored by its financial problems and the huge debt owed the West.

HARRY A. GAILEY, *San Jose State University*

NIGERIA • Information Highlights

Official Name: Federal Republic of Nigeria.
Location: West Africa.
Area: 356,667 sq mi (923 768 km²).
Population (mid-1985 est.): 91,200,000.
Chief City: Lagos, the capital.
Government: *Head of state and government,* Maj. Gen. Ibrahim Babangida, leader, federal military government (took office Aug. 27, 1985). *Legislature*—Senate and House of Representatives.
Monetary Unit: Naira (0.895 naira equals U.S.$1, July 1985).
Economic Index (June 1984): *Consumer Prices* (1975 = 100), all items, 465.9; food, 486.6.
Foreign Trade (1983 U.S.$): *Imports,* $13,440,-000,000; *exports,* $11,317,000,000.

NORTH CAROLINA

Even in a nonelection year, politics provided the main topic of discussion in North Carolina in 1985.

Politics. James G. Martin, the second Republican elected governor in the 20th century, received mixed reviews. He cheered state employees by significantly reducing the number of posts open to the spoils system, and he drew heavily on staffers who had served under Jim Holshouser, the moderate Republican governor in the 1970s. However, he failed to build the bipartisan administration that many of his Democratic supporters had expected, and he fared only tolerably well with his legislative program. The Democratic-controlled General Assembly refused to propose a constitutional amendment to allow the gubernatorial veto. However, it exempted Martin from the provisions of another amendment that, if approved by plebiscite, would bar future governors from two successive elected terms. The Democrats also rewrote Martin's ambitious tax proposals, thus sharing credit for reductions. A "comparable worth" study was canceled, a seat belt law was enacted, the legal drinking age was changed to 19, and a strict antipornography law sent video, film, and magazine dealers scurrying to clear their shelves of X-rated materials before the October 1 enforcement date.

Shock waves ran through both parties when U.S. Sen. John East (R) announced that he would retire due to ill health and former governor Jim Hunt (D) revealed that he would not seek the office. With the blessing of the conservative Congressional Club, David B. Funderburk, former ambassador to Romania, threw his hat into the ring; the Republican moderates persuaded Congressman James Broyhill to challenge him.

Economy. In the fiscal year ending in June, general-fund revenues totaled $4.33 billion, up nearly 14%, but the highway fund suffered a 1% drop, and there was talk of increasing the gasoline tax in 1986. Antismoking campaigns and problems with the federal tobacco program resulted in virtual panic among agricultural and political leaders, none of whom appeared willing to face the prospect of the eventual demise of tobacco as the state's major crop. Meanwhile, both textile manufacturers and their workers clamored for trade barriers to limit the importation of competing products. Employees of Cannon Mills decisively rejected representation by the Amalgamated Clothing and Textile Workers Union.

Crime. Murders in Kentucky and North Carolina were solved following a bizarre incident in which the bodies of Frederick Klenner, his cousin and girlfriend Susie Newsom Lynch, and her two sons were found in an exploded van near Winston-Salem. Investigation revealed that the children had been poisoned and shot prior to the explosion. Officers traced to Klenner and Lynch a conspiracy that killed her parents, grandmother, and estranged husband's mother and sister.

History. The commemoration of the Roanoke colonies of 1585–87 continued with major exhibits in the North Carolina Museum of History and the New York Public Library; the 50th anniversary of the Blue Ridge Parkway was observed; and the first state marker to a Confederate regiment—the 26th North Carolina—in 80 years was dedicated at Gettysburg. Historian William S. Powell was recipient of the North Caroliniana Society Award, and the University of North Carolina dedicated its $22 million central library.

H. G. JONES
University of North Carolina at Chapel Hill

NORTH DAKOTA

North Dakotans witnessed a court battle over control of the governor's office in 1985. The future grew clouded for a major water project and a pioneering energy plant, and lawmakers met in a biennial session marked by fiscal austerity.

Politics. George Sinner won the governorship in the 1984 elections, but he ran into trouble when trying to assume his new duties. Sinner said he had constitutional authority to take office on January 1, but former Gov. Allen Olson argued that the office was his until the first Monday of the month—January 7. The state Supreme Court ruled against Olson, allowing Sinner to take office on January 4.

Legislature. State lawmakers met and hammered out a $2.47 billion budget for 1985–87, up approximately 15% from the previous budget. Spending for primary and secondary education increased just 4.8% for the period.

Lawmakers also approved a "Family Farm Survival Act," allocating up to $100 million from the state-owned Bank of North Dakota

---

NORTH CAROLINA • Information Highlights

Area: 52,669 sq mi (136 413 km²).
Population (July 1, 1984 est.): 6,165,000.
Chief Cities (July 1, 1984 est.): Raleigh, the capital, 169,331; Charlotte, 330,838; Greensboro, 159,-314; Winston-Salem, 143,366; Durham, 101,997.
Government (1985): *Chief Officers*—governor, James G. Martin (R); lt. gov., Robert B. Jordon III (D). *General Assembly*—Senate, 50 members; House of Representatives, 120 members.
State Finances (fiscal year 1984): *Revenues,* $8,735,000,000; *expenditures,* $7,588,000,000.
Personal Income (1984): $66,891,000,000; per capita, $10,850.
Labor Force (June 1985): *Civilian labor force,* 3,115,000; *unemployed,* 170,200 (5.5% of total force).
Education: *Enrollment* (fall 1983)—public elementary schools, 761,053; public secondary, 328,553; colleges and universities, 301,675. *Public school expenditures* (1982–83), $2,231,620,811 ($2,162 per pupil).

for low-interest farm loans. A separate bill appropriated $2 million to help farmers faced with foreclosure save their farmsteads.

Garrison. U.S. Interior Secretary William Clark in early January endorsed a federal study commission's recommendations for sweeping changes in the Garrison Diversion project. The commission, formed by Congress to iron out disputes over the massive Missouri River water project, had recommended a major cutback in project irrigation of farmland and a new emphasis on the delivery of water to cities and rural water systems. But the project became mired in controversy again as project supporters and opponents in Washington argued over language to write the commission recommendations into law. Congress approved a $41.3 million appropriation for fiscal 1986 but stipulated that the money would be taken back if a bill authorizing the commission recommendations were not approved by March 30, 1986. Sinner entered into protracted negotiations with the National Audubon Society, the leading opponent of the Garrison project.

Great Plains. The $2.1 billion Great Plains coal gasification plant, the nation's first commercial-size synthetic fuels plant, fell into the hands of the U.S. Department of Energy when a consortium of private developers defaulted on $1.5 billion in government-guaranteed construction loans. A Government Accounting Office report estimated that a shutdown of the plant could cost state, federal, and local governments nearly $255 million in increased costs and lost revenue over a seven-year period. U.S. Energy Secretary John S. Herrington promised to operate the plant at least until the spring of 1986 while the department studies its options.

Agriculture. Continuing low prices dimmed what would have been a bright year for farmers. Wheat production was expected to total 304.4 million bushels, the third-largest harvest on record.

JIM NEUMANN, *"The Forum," Fargo*

NORTHWEST TERRITORIES

The selection of Nick Sibbeston as the new government leader was the major political development in the Northwest Territories.

Politics. Sibbeston, a Metis lawyer born in the small Mackenzie Valley community of Fort Simpson, has served in the Legislative Assembly of the Northwest Territories for ten years. He was chosen by a caucus vote of all members of the assembly to replace Richard Nerysoo. The planned review of all cabinet members took place in October 1985, after completion of the first two years of the assembly's term.

Shortly after Sibbeston's appointment, it was announced that the elected government leader would take on increased responsibility, mainly the chairing of the executive council (cabinet) and authority for the department of personnel. Both functions have been handled by the federally appointed commissioner. These steps were seen as further evolution toward fully responsible government. There was less progress on division of the Northwest Territories into two jurisdictions.

Economy. A highlight on the economic front was the completion and official opening of Esso Resource's Norman Wells oil field expansion and pipeline project in May. The C$1 billion project provided about 4,200 short-term jobs. Once full production is reached, Norman Wells will be the third-largest producing oil field in Western Canada. Severe negative economic effects of the European seal skin boycott continued to be experienced in the Arctic regions.

Culture. A task force was established to protect and ensure increased usage of aboriginal languages. The government amalgamated all culturally related programs into one department, and an advisory council was established to recommend policy and evaluate grants for the visual and performing arts.

Youth. Youth Forum, held in association with the United Nations' International Youth Year, brought delegates together from across the Northwest Territories to discuss their aspirations and recommend a plan of action to improve the role of youth in the territories.

ROSS M. HARVEY
Government of the Northwest Territories

NORWAY

The three-party, Conservative-led coalition headed by Prime Minister Kåre Willoch barely escaped defeat in the September 9 parliamentary elections. Having commanded a majority in the old, 155-seat Storting (parliament), it was returned for a new four-year period as a minority government.

Elections. In a close finish, the Conservative/Christian Democrat/Center Party alliance secured a total of 78 seats, only one seat more than the Socialist opposition: Labor, with 71 seats, plus the Socialist Left Party, with 6. This left the far-right Progress Party holding the balance of power, with two seats (the new Storting, after some revision of constituency boundaries, had 157 representatives).

The voters' verdict came as a shock to the dominant Conservative Party. With the economy enjoying a boom, inflation slowing, and unemployment falling, party leaders had initially expected a triumph at the polls. Instead, the coalition's share of the popular vote fell to 45.3%, from 47.8% in the previous (1981) general election, while Labor and its allies (the Socialist Left and Liberal parties) boosted their share to 49.3%, from 46%. The workings of the electoral system deprived the small Liberal Party of its two seats in the Storting, despite the fact that it polled 3.1% of the vote.

The coalition's near defeat was due to widespread dissatisfaction with the state of Norway's health and social services. Labor and its allies made this a major campaign issue, arguing that the Norwegian welfare state was under threat.

Budget. The budget for 1986 tabled by the minority coalition on October 14 showed it had heeded the voters' message. It provided for a 12.6% boost in expenditure to 222.3 billion Norwegian kroner (Nkr), or about $28 billion. This left a deficit before loan transactions of Nkr 948 million (about $118 million), compared with a forecast surplus of almost Nkr 19.3 billion (about $2.4 billion) in 1985. Over one third of total spending was earmarked for the Social Affairs ministry, which allocates funds for health, as well as social services.

The opposition claimed, however, that the proposed increases were inadequate. They also maintained that the government was deliberately underestimating 1986 revenues from the country's offshore oil and gas, in order to make the budget appear more expansionist than it was. Norwegian petroleum output in 1986 was expected to be about the same as in 1985—just over 63 million tons of oil equivalent—but the finance ministry forecast a sharp fall in tax take from the offshore sector, because of weaker oil prices and the falling value of the U.S. dollar, the currency in which petroleum is traded.

Oil and Gas Exploitation. Plans to exploit Norway's extensive offshore gas resources suf-

---

NORWAY · Information Highlights

Official Name: Kingdom of Norway.
Location: Northern Europe.
Area: 125,181 sq mi (324 219 km²).
Population (mid-1985 est.): 4,160,000.
Chief Cities (Jan. 1, 1984): Oslo, the capital, 447,257; Bergen, 207,332; Trondheim, 134,143.
Government: Head of state, Olav V, king (acceded Sept. 1957). Head of government, Kåre Willoch, prime minister (took office October 1981). Legislature—Storting: Lagting and Odelsting.
Monetary Unit: Krone (7.9 kroner equal U.S. $1, Oct. 23, 1985).
Gross National Product (1983 U.S.$): $55,100,-000,000.
Economic Indexes (1984): Consumer Prices (1970 = 100), all items, 325.8; food, 332.7. Industrial Production (1980 = 100), 113.
Foreign Trade (1984 U.S.$): Imports, $13,890,-000,000; exports, $18,911,000,000.

---

fered a setback in February, when the British government vetoed the purchase by the British Gas Corporation of gas from the Norwegian Sleipner field. To fill the investment gap created by the loss of Sleipner and prevent a sharp decline in petroleum output and earnings in the 1990s, Norway's oil ministry ordered Statoil, the state oil company, to speed development of Gullfaks phase 2, a major oilfield project.

Meanwhile, talks were in progress with potential customers in Continental Europe for gas from an even larger Norwegian field, Troll. However, because of technical problems—deep water and difficult seabed conditions—Troll gas would be expensive to produce. It was far from certain that the European gas companies would be prepared to pay the high price needed to justify the field's development.

On the country's oldest oil and gas field, Ekofisk, a new problem emerged. The seabed was found to be sinking at the rate of about 20 inches (50 cm) per year, threatening the safety of field installations. The subsidence, which by mid-1985 had reached an estimated 8 ft (2.5 m), was caused by compaction of the main Ekofisk reservoir, some 10,000 ft (3 000 m) beneath the seabed. To counter it, gas exports had to be cut by a quarter and much of the gas produced reinjected, to maintain reservoir pressure.

Spy Trial. The trial on spying charges of former Norwegian diplomat and politician Arne Treholt attracted wide international media coverage. In June a tribunal sentenced him to 20 years in prison for espionage on behalf of the USSR and Iraq.

THOR GJESTER, Editor, "Økonomisk Revy"

NOVA SCOTIA

The year 1985 brought Nova Scotians news about a major setback on the oil and gas exploration front, a high unemployment rate, increased sales and tobacco taxes, and the first-time enforcement of seat belt laws.

World Trade and Convention Centre

The new World Trade and Convention Centre in downtown Halifax offers 104,000 sq ft (9 662 m²) of exhibit space.

Economy. Despite high unemployment and collapse in offshore gas exploration, the Nova Scotian economy showed signs of strong growth. Capital spending in the province was expected to increase by 13.8%, well above the national average of 9.4%. Brisk construction activity was accompanied by a dramatic upturn in real estate sales. The Halifax-Dartmouth area alone recorded gross sales of $235 million from September 1984 to September 1985. Higher consumer spending; a rise in farm cash receipts, fish landings, and pulpwood production; coupled with a boisterous export sector gave additional impetus to economic recovery.

Government and Legislation. With 55,000 unemployed, the government of Premier John Buchanan concentrated on strengthening resource industries and encouraging industry efforts that promote job creation in the province. The Nova Scotian Training and Education Program has offered wage subsidies to small companies if they provide training programs for their employees. However, the closure of two heavy water plants in Glace Bay and Port Hawkesbury during the summer months left 700 people unemployed, and developments such as these dampened somewhat the impact of the job creation policy. On the other hand, other events provided examples of confidence in Nova Scotia's potential for providing additional jobs during the coming years. An additional $500 million of construction activity in the Halifax-Dartmouth area was envisaged, and Pratt and Whitney decided to locate a $50 million plant in the province to manufacture aircraft components. The government also hoped to foster creation of 4,000 new jobs during the next five years as yearly exports were expected to double to more than $2 billion. To symbolize this export potential the government opened a new $24 million Trade and Convention Centre—an attractive addition to the Halifax skyline.

In 1985 the government introduced 101 bills in the Legislative Assembly, of which 79 became law. These statutes covered a wide variety of subjects, including trade unions, municipal financing, residential tenancies, human rights, foreign trade, and agriculture.

Energy. On the energy front, most Nova Scotians were keeping their fingers crossed, hoping that all obstacles in the way of developing the Venture Gas Project would be overcome. In the meantime, however, the federal government's decision to withdraw the Petroleum Incentive Program reduced the number of drilling rigs operating in the waters of the Scotian Shelf from nine to three. The provincial government, however, remained optimistic about the commercial viability of existing as well as potential gas reserves. The successful exploitation of these reserves, government spokesmen believed, could move Nova Scotia into the ranks of Canada's "have" provinces.

R. P. SETH
Mount Saint Vincent University, Halifax

NOVA SCOTIA • Information Highlights

Area: 21,425 sq mi (55 491 km²).
Population (April 1985 est.): 879,600.
Chief Cities (1981 census): Halifax, the capital, 114,594; Dartmouth, 62,277; Sydney, 29,444.
Government (1985): *Chief Officers*—lt. gov., Alan R. Abraham; premier, John Buchanan (Progressive Conservative). *Legislature*—Legislative Assembly, 52 members.
Provincial Finances (1986 fiscal year budget): *Revenues,* $2,518,000,000; *expenditures,* $3,124,-000,000.
Personal Income (average weekly earnings, May 1985): $373.89.
Labor Force (July 1985, seasonally adjusted): *Employed workers,* 15 years of age and over, 335,000; *Unemployed,* 56,000 (14.3%).
Education (1985–86): *Enrollment*—elementary and secondary schools, 177,380 pupils; postsecondary (full-time, 1985–86)—universities, 23,070; community colleges, 2,880.
(All monetary figures are in Canadian dollars.)

OBITUARIES[1]

LODGE, Henry Cabot

U.S. politician: b. Nahant, MA, July 5, 1902; d. Beverly, MA, Feb. 27, 1985.

Henry Cabot Lodge was a Republican senator from Massachusetts when he helped persuade Dwight D. Eisenhower to seek the presidency. So involved did Lodge become in the 1952 Eisenhower campaign that he neglected his own reelection race. As a result he narrowly lost his Senate seat to John F. Kennedy. For the next eight years, Lodge represented the United States at the United Nations. Then in 1960 he was chosen to be Richard M. Nixon's running mate on the Republican ticket. The Nixon-Lodge opponents were John Kennedy and Lyndon B. Johnson. Once again the race was extremely tight, with the Democrats winning a squeaker.

In June 1963 in a "deft political move," President Kennedy named his former political opponent U.S. ambassador to South Vietnam. Lodge arrived in Saigon just a few months prior to the overthrow of President Ngo Dinh Diem.

After winning the 1964 New Hampshire primary as a write-in candidate, the moderate Republican supported William Scranton in his unsuccessful attempt to stop Sen. Barry M. Goldwater from winning the GOP nomination. At the request of President Johnson, Lodge returned to Saigon in 1965 and remained as ambassador until 1967. During that time, U.S. troop strength in Vietnam grew and the war escalated. After serving as an ambassador at large (1967–68) and ambassador to West Germany (1968–69), he led the U.S. delegation at the Paris peace talks on Vietnam for ten months. From 1970 until 1977, he was a special presidential envoy to the Vatican.

Background. The son of George Cabot Lodge, a poet, and Mathilda Elizabeth Frelinghuysen, and the grandson of Sen. Henry Cabot Lodge, the future politician and diplomat was graduated *cum laude* from Harvard University in 1924. After eight years as a reporter for the New York *Herald Tribune,* Lodge served in the Massachusetts General Court (1933–36) and was elected to the U.S. Senate in 1936. After winning reelection in 1942, he resigned his seat to serve in the U.S. Army during World War II. Lodge's military service earned him several decorations, and he later rose to the rank of major general in the Army Reserve. He was returned to the Senate in 1946.

Lodge married Emily Sears, the daughter of a Boston physician, on July 1, 1926. They had two sons. He was the author of *The Storm Has Many Eyes* (1973) and *As It Was* (1976).

JAMES E. CHURCHILL, JR.

CHERNENKO, Konstantin Ustinovich

Soviet leader: b. Bolshaya Tes, Krasnoyarsk region, Siberia, Sept. 24, 1911; d. Moscow, March 10, 1985.

Konstantin U. Chernenko's 13 months as general secretary of the Soviet Communist Party and 11 months as the USSR's president were considered a period of transition between the stagnant stability of the Leonid Brezhnev years and the changes to come with a new generation of younger leaders. It is believed that Chernenko did not govern the Soviet Union but simply went along with the decisions of the ruling, collective leadership.

Although illness frequently kept Chairman Chernenko away from the public scene, the campaign against corruption, inefficiency, and bureaucratic inertia begun by his predecessor, Yuri Andropov, continued. Relations between the Soviet Union and its two principal adversaries, the United States and China, remained extremely cool. However, in December 1984 the USSR and China signed a series of commercial, scientific, and technological agreements, and in January 1985 the USSR and the United States agreed to resume arms talks.

Background. Konstantin Ustinovich Chernenko left school at the age of 12 to work as a farmer. He joined Komsomol, the young Communist League, in 1926 and the Communist Party five years later. He held several party positions in Krasnoyarsk, becoming regional secretary in 1941. Chernenko was transferred in 1948 to the new Moldavian Republic, where two years later his future mentor, Leonid Brezhnev, became party leader.

In 1956, Chernenko followed Brezhnev to Moscow and was named propaganda chief of the Central Committee apparatus. When Brezhnev became chairman of the presidium (president) in 1960, Chernenko became a member of that body. In 1964, Brezhnev succeeded Khrushchev as party secretary, and Chernenko was made head of the important General Department of the Central Committee. In 1971, Chernenko became an actual member of the Central Committee. In 1976 he joined the party Secretariat, and in 1978 he was made a full member of the Politburo.

Brezhnev was thought to favor Chernenko as his successor, but when he died in November 1982, the Politburo majority chose Chernenko's rival, Andropov. Observers believed that Chernenko's career had ended, and his 1984 rise to power came as a surprise.

Chernenko was survived by his wife, Anna Dmitriyevna, and their daughter, Yelena Konstantinovna.

RONALD GRIGOR SUNY

[1] Arranged chronologically by death date

CBS

ORMANDY, Eugene

Hungarian-born American music director: b. Budapest, Nov. 18, 1899; d. Philadelphia, March 12, 1985.

Eugene Ormandy, whose 44 years at the helm of the Philadelphia Orchestra constituted the longest music directorship in the history of American symphonies, died on March 12 in his home in Philadelphia at the age of 85, of pneumonia.

After becoming the Philadelphia's codirector (with Leopold Stokowski) in 1936 and sole director two years later, Ormandy immediately made the orchestra his own and made it still greater. Ormandy's orchestra became a smooth virtuoso instrument renowned for the "Philadelphia sound." He himself regarded this

UPI/Bettmann News Photos

Jim Kalett

ERVIN, Samuel James, Jr.

U.S. senator: b. Morganton, NC, Sept. 27, 1896; d. Winston-Salem, NC, April 23, 1985.

When Sam J. Ervin, Jr., was appointed to the U.S. Senate in 1954, a local newspaper advised, "Let's not label Judge Ervin—yet." When he retired from the Senate 20 years later, he was still without a consensus label, for his adherence to the Constitution—interpreted literally—resulted in a consistency that to a changing society often appeared to be a continuum of contradictions. For example, Ervin opposed passage of many civil-rights bills, yet he was acclaimed as a civil libertarian. He was a traditionalist, wedded to the prerogatives of senators, but as a freshman he was influential in the censure of a colleague, Joseph R. McCarthy. A conservative Democrat, he often

WHITE, E(lwyn) B(rooks)

American writer and stylist: b. Mount Vernon, NY, July 11, 1899; d. North Brooklin, ME, Oct. 1, 1985.

One of the leading essayists and literary stylists of his time, E.B. White edified and entertained readers for 60 years with his wry, uncluttered, often irreverent commentaries on the vagaries of modern American life. His sketches, poems, and editorial essays for *The New Yorker* magazine (including the "Notes and Comments" column for 12 years) helped set the tone and reputation of that publication from its founding in 1925. His three classic books for children—*Stuart Little* (1945), *Charlotte's Web* (1952), and *The Trumpet of the Swan* (1970)—still sell tens of thousands of copies every year. And his revised, expanded

blended tone of rich strings and full, singing winds as the Ormandy sound.

A diminutive but commanding man, he was anything but flamboyant. His technique was conservative, straightforward, and clear. His interpretations were models of integrity and lucidity. Mr. Ormandy learned his scores quickly and typically conducted them from memory.

Although he conducted 20th century music liberally, he was most impressive in music of Romantic composers with performances noted for big gestures and glowing warmth. Ormandy's skills as an accompanist were legendary. Leading artists insisted on recording with him.

Background. Eugene Ormandy was born Jenö Blau in Budapest on Nov. 18, 1899, and at age 3 started studying the violin. At 5, he entered the Royal Academy of Budapest; at 9, he became a pupil of the great Jenö Hubay after whom he had been named; and at 14, he received his diploma. He traveled to the United States at 21 and began work in the pit of the Capitol Theater in New York City. In two years, he was the conductor there and quickly became a U.S. citizen. He conducted the New York Philharmonic and Philadelphia Orchestra in summer concerts and was music director of the Minneapolis Symphony (1931–36).

By the time poor health compelled him to retire in 1980, more people had heard his Philadelphia orchestra than any other, thanks to its extensive touring and more than 400 long-playing records. Even after retiring, he continued to appear as a guest conductor worldwide. His final concert was at New York's Carnegie Hall in January 1984.

Ormandy was survived by his second wife, Margaret Frances Hitsch, whom he had married in 1950, and two brothers.

ROBERT COMMANDAY

voted for Republican-sponsored legislation but never for a Republican candidate. By nature the self-ascribed "country lawyer" was a gentle mountaineer, exuding Southern graces and biblical quotations, but when provoked by defiant witnesses and mounting evidence of criminal misconduct in the Watergate affair, he helped bring down no less a figure than the president of the United States, Richard Nixon.

Background. The son of an attorney, Samuel James Ervin, Jr., grew up in Morganton, NC. He attended the state university at Chapel Hill, was twice wounded and four times decorated for valor in World War I, and earned a law degree from Harvard in 1922. As a state legislator, he helped defeat a bill that would have outlawed the teaching of evolution "as a fact" in the schools. He also was a county judge, U.S. representative, and state supreme court justice before joining the Senate.

Ervin soon acquired a reputation as the Senate's authority on the Constitution despite his frequent minority stands on civil-rights bills, which, he argued, subordinated individual liberties to the demands of special groups. On the other hand, he opposed governmental surveillance over private habits of citizens, denial of bail or legal counsel to indigent criminal suspects, and admission of evidence obtained by illegal searches.

Millions watched on television during the Watergate hearings as the senator, his jowls quivering and his eyebrows bobbing, relentlessly unraveled the story of political espionage and obstruction of justice. To many Americans, Sam Ervin became the personification of "Uncle Sam." His story is told in his books, including *The Whole Truth: The Watergate Conspiracy* and *Preserving the Constitution*.

H. G. JONES

edition of Prof. William Strunk, Jr.'s *The Elements of Style* (1959) has become a standard manual for writing in the English language.

Background. The son of a piano manufacturer and his wife, E.B. White attended public schools in Mount Vernon, NY. He enrolled at Cornell University in 1917 but left a year later to serve in the Army. Returning to Cornell, he served as editor in chief of *The Daily Sun* and received a B.A. in English in 1921. After one year as a reporter for the *Seattle Times* and a stint as a ship's messboy, White wound up back in New York, where he took a job as a production assistant and copywriter in an advertising agency. He felt "ill at ease."

When *The New Yorker* was founded, White began contributing stories, articles, and other pieces, which earned him an invitation to join the staff in 1926. Working with James Thurber and other notables at the magazine's Manhattan offices, White attracted admirers for his sophisticated, cleanly styled verse and prose.

In 1937, White moved with his wife—*The New Yorker* editor Katharine Sergeant Angell —to an old farmhouse in North Brooklin, ME. He continued writing for *The New Yorker* on a free-lance basis and sent in a monthly column to *Harper's Magazine* called "One Man's Meat." His first book was a volume of poems titled *The Lady is Cold* (1929), followed by satirical essays with Thurber called *Is Sex Necessary?* (1929). Other books include *Every Day Is Saturday* (1934); *Here is New York* (1949); *The Second Tree from the Corner* (1953); and *The Points of My Compass* (1962).

White's many honors include a Presidential Medal of Freedom in 1963, a National Medal for Literature in 1971, and, in 1978, a special Pulitzer Prize for the body of his work.

JEFFREY H. HACKER

Photo Trends

WELLES, Orson

American director and actor: b. Kenosha, WI, May 6, 1915; d. Los Angeles, CA, Oct. 10, 1985.

Orson Welles was never able to equal the achievement of his seminal movie *Citizen Kane,* released in 1941 just before his 26th birthday. But it was enough to guarantee him a lasting place in the history of cinema.

The film was both his triumph and his albatross. Everything he did thereafter in his life would be measured against *Kane,* which he produced, directed, and cowrote, and in which he played the title role. Directors and students the world over still study the film for its technical virtuosity. Welles built upon the visual foundations of the silent era and explored the new opportunities of the sound age, taking both to an exciting, challenging level.

Citizen Kane has been praised lavishly for its ingenious camera angles; dazzling use of composition and sets; fluidity and economy of editing; depth-of-field photography, enabling the viewer to simultaneously observe sharply focused action in the foreground and background; realistic sound effects; and other achievements. But *Kane* was not merely a technical showcase. It was born of the fervor of the 1930s Depression. Its content, fictional but obviously inspired by the life of controversial newspaper tycoon William Randolph Hearst, dealt with power, politics, the Ameri-

can dream, and the betrayal of that dream, and it had a candor unusual for movies of the time.

Background. George Orson Welles, born to the former Beatrice Ives and Richard Head Welles, was observed to be a child prodigy by the family doctor, who encouraged his interest in music, acting, painting, and learning magic tricks. The boy's parents were divorced, and his mother died when he was nine. His father, a manufacturer and inventor, took him abroad on frequent trips. As a schoolboy Welles began to develop his acting talent, and at the age of 16 he managed to get roles in the Gate Theater of Dublin, Ireland. By 19 he was playing Tybalt on Broadway in Katharine Cornell's *Romeo and Juliet.* He also began acting in radio and became the voice of *The Shadow* in the series.

Greater opportunities grew out of the Federal Theater, established under the Works Progress Administration to help alleviate unemployment during the 1930s Depression. Welles had brashness and vision to go with his versatility. His productions of *Macbeth,* with a black cast, and a modern-dress *Julius Caesar,* set in a fascist state, triumphed. He cofounded the Mercury Theater with John Houseman, and its production of Marc Blitzstein's pro-labor *The Cradle Will Rock* became a cause célèbre after attempts were made to suppress it.

It was the Mercury Theater of the Air, however, that made Welles internationally famous. On Oct. 30, 1938, his radio enactment of H. G. Wells' *War of the Worlds* was so realistic that thousands of listeners fled their homes because they believed Martians had indeed landed.

Armed with his "boy wonder" reputation, Welles took his Mercury troupe to Hollywood to film *Citizen Kane.* He was given a level of artistic freedom (though short-lived) rare for Hollywood. He disowned his second film, *The Magnificent Ambersons,* after it was reedited. He was dogged throughout his career by accusations that he was extravagant and unreliable. His defenders called him a victim of a system that has no tolerance for genius. He acted prolifically in the films of others, and in recent years he did wine commercials on television. Despite his difficulties, Welles directed an impressive array of films that include *Touch of Evil, Lady From Shanghai, The Trial, Macbeth, Chimes at Midnight* (also *Falstaff*), and the unfinished *The Other Side of the Wind.* In 1975 he was honored with the Lifetime Achievement Award of the American Film Institute, and in 1984 he received The Directors Guild of America's D. W. Griffith Award.

Welles had three marriages, first to Virginia Nicholson, then to Rita Hayworth, and next to Paola Mori. He had three children, one from each marriage. In his later years Welles grew increasingly obese, and his size further added to the legend of a great director and cinema genius who was larger than life.

WILLIAM WOLF

The following is a selected list of prominent persons who died during 1985.
Articles on major figures appear in the preceding pages.

Photo Trends   AP/Wide World   AP/Wide World   AP/Wide World

Laura Ashley   Anne Baxter   James Beard   Yul Brynner

Abruzzo, Ben (54), balloonist; in 1978 was one of three men who first crossed the Atlantic in a balloon. In 1981 he was one of four balloonists who first crossed the Pacific: d. Albuquerque, NM, Feb. 11.

Adams, Tom (born John Michael Geoffrey Manningham) (53), prime minister of Barbados (1976–85): d. Bridgetown, Barbados, March 11.

Arends, Leslie (89), U.S. representative (R-IL, 1935–75); served as the Republican House whip from 1943 until retirement: d. Naples, FL, July 16.

Ashley, Laura (60), British designer; built an international fabric and clothing empire with her English country designs. Her first retail store opened in London in 1969: d. Coventry, England, Sept. 17.

Austin, J. Paul (70), chairman of the Coca-Cola Company (1970–81); he had become president of the company in 1962 and chief executive officer in 1966. During his tenure Coke was introduced to mainland China (1978). Then he introduced Fanta Orange into the USSS, ending Pepsi-Cola's monopoly of American soft drink sales there: d. Atlanta, GA, Dec. 26.

Bacchelli, Riccardo (94), Italian writer; best known for the three-volume novel *The Mill on the Po*: d. Monza, Italy, Oct. 8.

Balogh, Thomas (Lord Balogh) (79), British economist: d. London, Jan. 20.

Baxter, Anne (62), actress; won an Academy Award as best supporting actress in the film *The Razor's Edge*. She recently appeared on the television series *Hotel*: d. New York City, Dec. 12.

Bayer, Herbert (85), Austrian-born painter, architect, and graphic and industrial designer; one of the "masters" of the Bauhaus, the design school founded by Walter Gropius in Weimar, Germany. Bayer came to the United States in 1938. He was a design consultant, helping to develop the town of Aspen, CO, and later worked as art and design consultant for Atlantic Richfield Company: d. Montecito, CA, Sept. 30.

Beard, James (81), cooking authority and writer; was a foremost champion of American cooking. He wrote or cowrote 24 books and hundreds of articles, as well as a syndicated column, on gastronomic subjects and also was a consultant to several restaurant chains and food and wine suppliers: d. New York City, Jan. 23.

Beck, Julian (60), actor, painter, and writer; along with his wife he founded the Living Theater in 1947: d. New York City, Sept. 14.

Beckerman, Bernard (64), professor of dramatic literature at Columbia University; he was a noted Shakespeare scholar: d. Manhasset, NY, Oct. 7.

Blackwell, Betsy Talbot (79), editor of *Mademoiselle* magazine, was a fashion editor in 1935 when the magazine was founded. Two years later she became editor in chief, a position she held until 1971: d. Norwalk, CT, Feb. 4.

Blake, Eugene Carson (78), Protestant leader; he was stated clerk (executive director) of the Presbyterian Church in the U.S.A. and its successor group, the United Presbyterian Church, U.S.A. (1951–66). He served as president (1954–57) and general secretary (1966–72) of the World Council of Churches: d. Stamford, CT, July 31.

Blanding, Sarah Gibson (86), president of Vassar College (1946–64); she was the first woman president of the college: d. Newtown, PA, March 3.

Blood, Johnny (born John Victor McNally) (82), National Football League football player. He led the Green Bay Packers to four league championships and was inducted into the Hall of Fame in 1963: d. Palm Springs, CA, Nov. 28.

Blough, Roger M. (81), chairman and chief executive of U.S. Steel (1955–69). As head of U.S. Steel he was involved in 1962 in a dispute over steel prices with President John Kennedy: d. Hawley, PA, Oct. 8.

Böll, Heinrich (67), West German novelist; wrote of Germany in World War II and of postwar West Germany. He was awarded the 1972 Nobel Prize for literature. He was a corporal in the German infantry during World War II. His first novel, *The Train Was on Time*, came out in 1949. His other books include *Traveler, If You Come to Spa* (1950), a short-story collection; and the novels *Adam, Where Art Thou* (1951), *Billiards at Half-Past Nine* (1959), *The Clown* (1963), and *Group Portrait With Lady* (1971): d. near Bonn, West Germany, July 16.

Boulting, John (71), British filmmaker; worked as director, writer, and producer in films. Along with his twin brother Roy, he formed an independent film company in 1937. His films include *Fame Is the Spur, The Guinea Pig, Private's Progress, Brother's in Law, I'm All Right Jack, Heavens Above!, The Family Way,* and *There's a Girl in My Soup*: d. Sunningdale, Berkshire, England, June 17.

Boyle, William Anthony (Tony) (83), United Mine Workers president (1963–72). In 1969 he was challenged in the union election for president by Joseph A. Yablonski. Mr. Boyle emerged the winner, but soon thereafter Yablonski, his wife, and daughter were murdered, and eventually Boyle was connected with the murders. He was convicted and began serving three life sentences in 1978: d. Wilkes-Barre, PA, May 31.

Brady, Scott (born Jerry Tierney) (60), Broadway, motion picture, and television actor; he was seen most recently in the films *China Syndrome* and *Gremlins*: d. Woodland Hills, CA, April 17.

Braudel, Fernand (83), French historian and author; wrote *The Mediterranean and the Mediterranean World in the Age of Philip II* (1949) and *Civilization and Capitalism, 15th–18th Century* (1979): d. Paris. Nov. 28.

Brooks, Louise (78), silent-movie actress; she made the short bobbed hair, popular in the 1920s, her signature. Her films include *American Venus* (1926) and *Pandora's Box* (1929). Her memoir *Lulu in Hollywood* was published in 1982: d. Rochester, NY, Aug. 8.

Bryant, Sir Arthur (85), British pilot and historian; was a member of the Royal Flying Corps fighters over France during World War I. Later he wrote popular history books. He also was a biographer and wrote on Charles II and Samuel Pepys: d. Salisbury, England, Jan. 22.

Brynner, Yul (65), actor; became strongly identified with the role of the King of Siam in the Rodgers and Hammerstein musical *The King and I*. He gave 4,625 performances in the role over a 30-year period and last appeared in the role on Broadway during 1985. He won an Academy Award in the 1956 film version of the musical. He made a number of other films, including *The Ten Commandments, Anastasia, The Brothers Karamazov, The Sound and the Fury,* and *The Magnificent Seven*: d. New York City, Oct. 10.

Burnet, Sir (Frank) MacFarlane (85), Australian microbiologist and virologist; was renowned for his work on the nature of viruses and the body's immune system. He was awarded the Nobel Prize in 1960. Knighted in 1951, he retired from Melbourne University in 1965 and subsequently wrote 16 books on science and medicine: d. Melbourne, Australia, Aug. 31.

Burnham, Linden Forbes Sampson (62), leader of Guyana (1964–85): d. Georgetown, Guyana, Aug. 6.

Burrows, Abe (74), librettist, director, author, and comic; best known for writing the book for the Broadway show *Guys and*

Dolls (1950) and for writing and directing *How to Succeed in Business Without Really Trying* (1961): d. New York City, May 17.

Byrnes, John W. (71), U.S. representative (R-WI, 1945–73): d. Marshfield, WI, Jan. 8.

Caldwell, (Janet Miriam) Taylor (84), author; one of the world's best-selling authors. Her works include *Dynasty of Death* (1938), about a family of munitions makers over a 60-year period; *Dear and Glorious Physician* (1959), based on the life of St. Luke; *Captains and Kings* (1972); and *Answer Like a Man* (1981): d. Greenwich, CT, Aug. 30.

Calvino, Italo (61), Italian novelist of international standing; considered a master of the allegorical fantasy. Most of his work was translated into English. His books include *The Path to the Nest of Spiders, The Baron in the Trees, The Non-Existent Knight, Italian Folk Tales, Marcovaldo, Cosmicomics, If On a Winter's Night a Traveler,* and *Mr. Palomar:* d. Siena, Italy, Sept. 19.

Canaday, John (78), art critic; worked for *The New York Times* for 17 years from 1959 to 1977. He served in the Pacific during World War II and began writing mysteries during that time under the name of Matthew Head. Between 1953 and 1959 he was education director of the Philadelphia Museum. His books on art include *Metropolitan Seminars on Art, Lives of the Painters,* and *Mainstreams of Modern Art:* d. New York City, July 19.

Chagall, Marc (97), Russian-born French painter—*see* ART, page 116: d. St. Paul de Vence, France, March 28.

Charlotte of Luxembourg (89), Grand Duchess of Luxembourg; acceded to the throne in 1919 and served until 1964, when she resigned in favor of her son: d. Fischbach Castle, Luxembourg, July 9.

Chase, James Hadley (born Rene Raymond) (79), British-born mystery writer: d. Corseaux, Switzerland, Feb. 6.

Chase, Stuart (97), economist and member of Franklin D. Roosevelt's "brain trust," was responsible for coining the phrase "New Deal": d. Redding, CT, Nov. 16.

Claire, Ina (92), stage and film actress; renowned for her comedic talents: d. San Francisco, Feb. 21.

Clarke, Kenny (Klook) (71), jazz drummer; in the 1940s he made a major contribution to the development of the rhythms that became be-bop: d. near Paris, France, Jan. 25.

Clements, Earle C. (88), governor of Kentucky (1947–50) and U.S. senator (1951–57). A Democrat, Clements also was a member of the U.S. House of Representatives (1945–47): d. Morganfield, KY, March 12.

Clinton, Larry (75), orchestra leader, composer, and arranger of the big-band era. His tune *The Dipsy Doodle* was a top hit of the late 1930s. Later in his life he became a music publisher: d. Tucson, AZ, May 2.

Colasanto, Nicholas (61), stage, film, and television actor; well known as the "Coach" on the popular television series *Cheers:* d. Los Angeles, Feb. 12.

Cole, Lester (81), screenwriter; was one of the ten Hollywood figures jailed for contempt of Congress and blacklisted for refusing to testify before a House committee investigating Communist influence. His screenplays include *Objective Burma, High Wall,* and *The House of Seven Gables:* d. San Francisco, Aug. 15.

Colin, Paul (92), French posterist; in his career he designed more than 1,200 posters and about 700 stage and film sets: d. Nogent-sur-Marne, France, June 18.

Collingwood, Charles (68), news correspondent; was with CBS News in various capacities from 1941 until his retirement in 1982; thereafter, he was a special CBS correspondent. He began his career as a reporter for the United Press in London in 1939. He joined Edward R. Murrow's staff in London in 1941 and in 1959 succeeded Murrow as the host of television's *Person to Person* series: d. New York City, Oct. 3.

Cooper, Irving S. (63), neurosurgeon who developed successful surgical techniques for treating Parkinson's disease and other crippling neurological disorders: d. Naples, FL, Oct. 30.

Coots, John Frederick (J. Fred) (87), composer; wrote the music for many songs, including *Santa Claus Is Coming to Town:* d. New York City, April 8.

Cowles, Gardner, Jr. (82), publisher; the cofounder and publisher of *Look* magazine (1937–71). He was head of a family communications empire that included newspapers, notably *The Des Moines Register and Tribune;* magazines; book publishing; and television stations: d. Southampton, NY, July 8.

Crespi, Count Rodolfo (61), international fashion magazine executive; was international director of Vogue Brasil and editorial director of Vogue Mexico: d. New York City, Sept. 6.

Creston, Paul (born Giuseppe Guttoveggio) (78), composer; his first published work was *Five Dances for Piano* (Op. 1) (1932). His Symphony No. 1 won the New York Music Critic's Circle Award in 1943. His last major work was Symphony No. 6. Creston was an organist in New York City from 1934 to 1967: d. San Diego, Aug. 24.

Cushman, Robert E. (70), former commandant of the Marine Corps and deputy director of the Central Intelligence Agency. He was drawn into the Watergate scandal of the 1970s because he initially had approved CIA assistance in the burglary of Daniel Ellsberg's psychiatrist's office: d. Fort Washington, MD, Jan. 2.

Davidson, David (77), novelist and author; wrote about 100 teleplays during the early and mid-1950s. His novels include *The Steeper Cliff* (1947), *The Hour of Truth* (1949), *In Another Country* (1950), and *The Quest of Juror 19* (1971): d. New York City, Nov. 1.

Day, Robert (84), cartoonist and illustrator. His work appeared mainly in the *New Yorker* magazine between 1931 and 1976: d. St. Louis, MO, Feb. 7.

Deckers, Jeanine (52), Belgian Roman Catholic nun; was known as the "Singing Nun," she became famous in 1963 for her song *Dominique.* She left the Dominican order during 1966: d. Wavres, Belgium, April 1 (found dead, an apparent suicide).

Delacour, Jean (95), French ornithologist and aviculturist; he owned the world's largest private zoo and aviary on his estates in Normandy. He was director of the Los Angeles County Museum (1952–60): d. Los Angeles, CA, Nov. 5.

de Quay, Jan E. (83), prime minister of the Netherlands (1959–63): d. Beers, Holland, July 4.

Desmond, Johnny (born Giovanni de Simone) (65), singer and actor; was a vocalist with Glenn Miller's swing band. He had begun his career with Bob Crosby's band, then was with Gene Krupa's orchestra. He appeared on Broadway in *Say, Darling* and *Funny Girl* and in 1958 on the television series *Your Hit Parade:* d. Los Angeles, CA, Sept. 6.

Diamond, Selma (64), comedy writer and actress. She wrote for both radio and television, working for Groucho Marx, Milton Berle, Garry Moore, Tallulah Bankhead on *The Big Show,* and Sid Caesar. As an actress she was seen most recently in the television series *Night Court:* d. Los Angeles, CA, May 13.

Donghia, Angelo (50), interior designer; created a contemporary look through the use of gray flannel-covered, oversized furniture, lacquered walls, and bleached floors: d. New York City, April 10.

Douglas-Home, Charles (48), British journalist; editor of *The Times of London* (1982–85): d. London, Oct. 29.

Downey, Morton (83), Irish tenor and composer; was popular on the radio and in nightclubs in the 1930s and 1940s: d. Palm Beach, FL, Oct. 25.

Dubuffet, Jean (83), French painter and sculptor; was an advocate of L'art brut. Among his outstanding works are the *Métro* series (1944), the *Corps du Dame* series (1950), and the *Hourloupe* series (1962–66): d. Paris, May 12.

Forbes Burnham   *Taylor Caldwell*   *Italo Calvino*   *Nicholas Colasanto*

Photos, AP/Wide World

Charles Collingwood

Gardner Cowles, Jr.

Jeanine Deckers
"The Singing Nun"

Jean Dubuffet

Photos, AP/Wide World

Duvivier, George (64), musician; a string bassist, he played with the bands of Jimmie Lunceford, Coleman Hawkins, and Benny Goodman: d. New York City, July 11.

Eisenhower, Milton (85), diplomat and educator; brother of President Dwight Eisenhower. An adviser to six presidents, he helped President Harry Truman reorganize the Agriculture Department, negotiated with Fidel Castro for President Kennedy, and headed commissions and study groups for Presidents Johnson and Nixon. He began government service in 1926, serving with the Department of Agriculture for 16 years. In 1942 he became director of the War Relocation Authority, involved in resettling residents of Japanese descent. In 1943 he became president of Kansas State College, his alma mater. On a part-time basis he served with UNESCO. He also served as president of Pennsylvania State University and twice at Johns Hopkins University: d. Baltimore, May 2.

Enders, John F. (88), Nobel Prize–winning virologist and former professor at Harvard University. His discoveries led to vaccines against polio, measles, German measles, and mumps and contributed to the fight against cancer and genetic advances. He received the Nobel Prize in medicine in 1954: d. Waterford, CT, Sept. 8.

Erlander, Tage F. (84), prime minister of Sweden (1946–69): d. Huddinge, Sweden, June 21.

Fetchit, Stepin (born Lincoln Theodore Perry) (83), black entertainer; was the first widely known black actor in films: d. Los Angeles, CA, Nov. 19.

Flory, Paul J. (75), Nobel laureate in chemistry; was a pioneer in polymer chemistry and professor at Stanford University. He won the Nobel Prize in 1974 and used his prize money in behalf of human rights: d. Big Sur, CA, Sept. 9.

Foster, Phil (72), stand-up comedian; later became an actor on stage and in television. Perhaps he was best known as the father of Laverne DeFazio in the series Laverne and Shirley (1976–83): d. Rancho Mirage, CA, July 8.

Garbuzov, Vasily (74), Soviet finance minister (1960–85): d. Moscow, Nov. 12.

George-Brown, Lord (born George Alfred Brown) (70), British politician. As foreign secretary under Prime Minister Harold Wilson (1966–68), he was the author of the UN Security Council Resolution 242, adopted in 1967, implying Israel's right to exist. After losing his seat in Parliament in 1970, he was made a life peer. He resigned from the Labour Party, of which he had been deputy leader, in 1976 and joined the newly formed Social Democratic Party in 1981: d. Cornwall, England, June 2.

Gerasimov, Sergei (79), Soviet film director: d. Nov. 28.

Gernreich, Rudi (Rudolph) (62), fashion designer; famous for the topless swimsuit of the 1960s: d. Los Angeles, CA, April 21.

Giacometti, Diego (82), Swiss-born craftsman and furniture designer. The high point of his career came when he was commissioned to do the tables, chairs, and chandeliers for the new Picasso Museum in Paris. He and his brother Alberto, the famed sculptor and painter, were inseparable for 40 years, and Diego modeled constantly for his brother until Alberto's death in 1966: d. Paris, July 15.

Gilels, Emil (68), Soviet pianist: d. Moscow, Oct. 14.

Gomberg, Harold (68), principal oboist of the New York Philharmonic (1943–77): d. Capri, Sept. 7.

Gordon, Ruth (born Ruth Gordon Jones) (88), actress and writer, she debuted on the Broadway stage in 1915. In her first starring role in Seventeen, she was panned by the critics for her performance, but in 1925 the turning point in her stage career came with Holding Helen. She turned to films in 1940 with Abe Lincoln in Illinois, but from 1943 until 1966 she did not act in films. She and her husband, Garson Kanin, wrote successful screenplays, including A Double Life, and the Hepburn-Tracy classics Adam's Rib and Pat and Mike. With Rosemary's Baby (1968), for which she won an Academy Award, Miss Gordon was introduced to a new generation of filmgoers. She wrote the books Myself Among Others and My Side and three plays, including The Actress: d. Edgartown, MA, Aug. 28.

Gould, Chester (84), cartoonist; creator of detective strip Dick Tracy: d. Woodstock, IL, May 11.

Graves, Robert (90), British poet and classical scholar. His poetry was considered traditional in form, and he felt that the function of poetry was foremost to convey meaning. His major writings include the autobiography Goodbye to All That (1929), I, Claudius (1934), and The White Goddess (1947). He also was a professor of poetry at Oxford (1961–66): d. Deyá, Majorca, Dec. 7.

Gromov, Mikhail (85), Soviet air pioneer. In 1937, along with a copilot and navigator, he flew nonstop across the North Pole to an emergency landing in California. He established many long-distance flying records during the 1930s: d. Moscow, Jan. 22.

Groppi, James E. (54), former Roman Catholic priest who led more than 200 marches for open housing in Milwaukee during the 1960s. He formally broke with the Roman Catholic Church in April 1976: d. Milwaukee, WI, Nov. 4.

Gurney, John Chandler (Chan) (88), U.S. senator (R-SD, 1939–51): d. Yankton, SD, March 9.

Hamilton, Margaret (82), actress; best known as the Wicked Witch of the West in The Wizard of Oz. She played character roles in more than 70 films: d. Salisbury, CT, May 16.

Hanley, James (84), British writer of novels, short stories, and plays. His works include Drift, Boy, Against the Stream, and the plays Say Nothing and The Inner Journey: d. London, Nov. 11.

Hannaford, Mark W. (60), U.S. representative (D-CA, 1975–79): d. Lakewood, CA, June 2.

Hardy, Sir Alister (89), British marine biologist; winner of the 1985 Templeton Prize for Progress in Religion: d. Oxford, England, May 23.

Harlech, Lord (Sir William David Ormsby Gore) (66), British ambassador to the United States during the Kennedy and Johnson administrations; he was a close friend of the Kennedy family. He entered Parliament in 1950 and held several foreign office posts prior to going to Washington: d. Shrewsbury, England, Jan. 26.

Harper, John D. (75), aluminum manufacturing company executive; president (1963–75), chief executive officer (1965–75),

Milton Eisenhower

UPI/Bettmann Newsphotos

Ruth Gordon

© Derek, Photo Trends

AP/Wide World

Robert Graves

AP/Wide World

Margaret Hamilton

© S. Norris, Photo Trends

Lord Harlech

UPI/Bettmann Newsphotos

Patricia Harris

and chairman of the board (1970–75) of the Aluminum Company of America. From 1979 until 1983 he was chairman of the Communications Satellite Corporation: d. Pittsburgh, PA, July 26.

Harris, Patricia Roberts (60), lawyer, educator, civil-rights activist; she was the first black woman to serve as a U.S. ambassador (to Luxembourg, 1965–67) and to be a member of a president's cabinet—secretary of housing and urban development (1977–79) and of health, education and welfare/health and human services (1979–81). She was also a professor of law and dean at Howard University Law School: d Washington, DC, March 23.

Harteck, Paul (82), chemist; codiscoverer of tritium (the heaviest form of hydrogen) in 1934 and co-designer of the world's largest atmospheric simulation chamber. Dr. Harteck was professor of physical chemistry at Rensselaer Polytechnic Institute (1953–82): d. Santa Barbara, CA, Jan. 21.

Hathaway, Henry (86), motion picture director; his films include *The Real Glory, The Lives of a Bengal Lancer, The Desert Fox, Nevada Smith,* and *True Grit:* d. Los Angeles, CA, Feb. 11.

Hayes, Alfred (74), poet, novelist, and screenwriter; his best-known novel was *The Girl on the Via Flaminia* (1949). He worked on the screenplays of several classic Italian films, including *Paisan* and *Bicycle Thief.* He wrote the poem *Joe Hill,* which became well known when it was later set to music: d. Sherman Oaks, CA, Aug. 14.

Hayward, Louis (75), South African–born motion picture actor; was best known for his roles in such films as *Man in the Iron Mask* and *Son of Monte Cristo:* d. Palm Springs, CA, Feb. 22.

Hecht, Harold (77), film producer; along with actor Burt Lancaster formed one of the first independent film producing companies in Hollywood. The company's productions included the Academy Award–winning *Marty* (1955): d. Beverly Hills, CA, May 25.

Hewitt, Foster William (83), Canadian sports announcer; was a radio and television broadcaster for the Toronto Maple Leafs. He began broadcasting hockey games in the mid-1920s: d. Toronto, April 21.

Holland, Jerome H. (69), black educator and civil-rights advocate; was president of two predominantly black colleges—Hampton Institute and Delaware State College. He served as U.S. ambassador to Sweden (1970–1972). Later he became the first black member of the New York Stock Exchange. In May 1985 he was awarded posthumously the U.S. Presidential Medal of Freedom: d. New York City, Jan. 13.

Enver Hoxha

Rock Hudson

© Haley, Sipa Special Features

Photo Trends

Holt, John (62), teacher; wrote the books *How Children Fail* (1964) and *How Children Learn* (1967) as well as several others. His first book sparked a national debate in the 1960s in U.S. schools: d. Boston, MA, Sept. 14.

Horrocks, Sir Brian (89), British World War II general; helped take North Africa from the Germans at the battle of El Alamein in 1942. He later was knighted and became a member of the House of Lords. He also was a historian and a British television personality: d. Fishbourne, England, Jan. 6.

Hough, Henry Beetle (88), longtime owner and editor of *The Vineyard Gazette* of Edgartown, MA, one of America's best-known weeklies. He also wrote some 20 books and was a staunch environmentalist: d. Edgartown, MA, June 6.

Hoxha, Enver (76), first secretary of the Albanian Workers' (Communist) Party (1944–85)—*see* ALBANIA: d. Tiranë, Albania, April 11.

Hudson, Rock (born Roy Scherer, Jr.) (59), actor; particularly well known for his role in *Giant* (1956), for which he received an Academy Award nomination, and for a series of comedies with actress Doris Day, including *Pillow Talk* (1959), *Lover Come Back* (1962), and *Send Me No Flowers* (1964). He also appeared in two television series—*McMillan and Wife* (1971–76) and *The Devlin Connection* (1982). Hudson, who was the first major public figure to acknowledge that he was suffering from AIDS, was instrumental in focusing public attention and concern on the disease: d. Los Angeles, Oct. 2.

Hutchinson, Edward (70), U.S. representative (R-MI, 1963–77): d. Naples, FL, July 22.

Ingersoll, Ralph (84), journalist, author, and publisher; he founded the newspaper *PM* in 1940 and worked on *The New Yorker, Fortune,* and *Life* magazines. He also wrote several books: d. Miami Beach, FL, March 8.

Jenkins, Walter W. (67), aide to Lyndon Johnson from 1939 until 1964 when he resigned following arrest on a morals charge relating to homosexual behavior: d. Austin, TX, Nov. 23.

Jenner, William E. (76), U.S. senator (R-IN, 1944–45; 1947–59); an archconservative, he accused both Harry Truman and George Marshall of aiding Communists. He was elected to fill out the remaining few weeks of the term of Sen. Frederick Van Nuys, who had died, before being elected to his first full term in office: d. Bedford, IN, March 9.

Johnson, Paul B., Jr. (69), governor of Mississippi (1964–68); a Democrat, he campaigned as a segregationist, but in office was a moderate who guided his state toward desegregation: d. Hattiesburg, MS, Oct. 14.

Johnston, S. Paul (86), director of the National Air and Space Museum of the Smithsonian Institution (1964–69). He was an editor for *Aviation* magazine and wrote books on aviation history: d. Easton, MD, Aug. 9.

Jones, Jo (73), jazz drummer; worked with Count Basie's band from 1935 to 1948, and thereafter performed with numerous jazz groups: d. New York City, Sept. 3.

Jones, Philly Joe (born Joseph Rudolph) (62), jazz drummer; was a member of Miles Davis' quintet between 1952 and 1958; thereafter, he played with John Coltrane, Johnny Griffin, Art Pepper, Jackie McLean, and others. He lived and taught drums in Europe from 1967 until 1972. In the 1980s he was leader of a repertory group called Dameronia: d. Philadelphia, PA, Aug. 30.

Kaussen, Guenther (57), West German real estate tycoon; thought to have been West Germany's biggest landlord. He also owned apartments in San Francisco and Atlanta: d. Cologne, April 15.

Kelly, Charles E. (64), U.S. Army sergeant and World War II hero known as Commando; was the first enlisted man to receive the Medal of Honor in the war: d. Pittsburgh, PA, Jan. 11.

Kelly, John B., Jr. (57), recently elected president of the U.S. Olympic Committee; he was a leading advocate of amateur

sports. His sister was the late Princess Grace of Monaco: d. Philadelphia, PA, March 2.

Kertész, André (91), Hungarian-born photographer; one of the acknowledged innovators of 20th-century photography. Among his important pictures are "Satiric Dancer" and a Cubist-inspired view of Mondrian's studio, as well as "Reading" and "Wandering Violinist." During the 1920s, Kertész lived in Paris and did some magazine photography. In 1929, museums began to buy his work. He came to the United States in 1936 with the intention of returning to Europe, but World War II intervened, and he did not return. He became a U.S. citizen in 1944: d. New York City, Sept. 27.

Kimball, Spencer (90), president and foremost leader of the Mormon Church. He was selected as the 12th president of the church by the church's Council of Twelve Apostles on Dec. 30, 1973. Under his leadership black men were allowed in the Morman priesthood: d. Salt Lake City, Nov. 5.

King, Wayne (84), saxophonist and bandleader; became known as the "Waltz King." He played the Aragon Ballroom in Chicago from 1927–35. His band was featured on radio in *The Lady Esther Serenade* (1931–38), and in the late 1940s and early 1950s he performed on television: d. Paradise Valley, AZ, July 16.

Koo, V. K. Wellington (97), Chinese diplomat who was chairman of China's delegation to the 1919 Paris Peace Conference. He was prime minister and foreign minister of China (1926–27) and ambassador from China to France (1936–41) and to Great Britain (1941–46) and from Nationalist China to the United States (1946–56). He was a judge and vice-president of the International Court of Justice at The Hague (1957–67): d. New York City, Nov. 14.

Koopmans, Tjalling (74), Dutch-born economist; was the cowinner of the 1975 Nobel Prize for economics for his theories on the optimal allocation of resources: d. New Haven, CT, Feb. 26.

Kuznets, Simon (84), economist; won the Nobel Prize for economics in 1971 for pioneering the measurement of national income and economic growth. He taught at the University of Pennsylvania (1930–54), with service during World War II as director of the War Production Board's Bureau of Planning and Statistics; Johns Hopkins University (1954–60); and Harvard (1960–71): d. Cambridge, MA, July 8.

Kyser, Kay (James King Kern) (79), band leader during the "swing-era." His band, which performed on the radio, was known as the Kollege of Musical Knowledge: d. Chapel Hill, NC, July 23.

Lander, Toni (born Toni Pihl Petersen) (53), Danish ballerina with the Royal Danish Ballet, the London Festival Ballet, and New York's American Ballet Theatre: d. Salt Lake City, May 19.

Lang, Harold (64), ballet dancer, became a musical comedy star; was with the Ballet Russe de Monte Carlo (1941–43) and the American Ballet Theatre (1943–45). His Broadway shows included *Pal Joey*, in which he played the title role in a 1952 revival: d. Chico, CA, July 26.

Langer, Susanne K. (89), philosopher; her work in aesthetics affected 20th-century thought in psychology and the social sciences. She believed that the artist does not seek to arouse or convey feeling but to show the nature of feeling. Her books include *The Practice of Philosophy* (1930), *Philosophy in a New Key: A Study in the Symbolism of Reason, Rite, and Art* (1942), and *Mind: An Essay on Human Feeling*, 3 volumes (1967–82): d. Old Lyme, CT, July 17.

Larkin, Philip (63), British poet; his works include *The Less Deceived* (1955), *The Whitsun Weddings* (1964), and *High Windows* (1974): d. Hull, England, Dec. 2.

Lindbergh, Pelle (26), Swedish hockey player; was with the National Hockey League's Philadelphia Flyers and was the top goaltender in 1984: d. Stratford, NJ, Nov. 12.

List, Eugene (66), American pianist; made his New York debut in 1935. In 1945, as a performer at the Potsdam conference, he played for the World War II Allied leaders Truman, Churchill, and Stalin, winning international fame: d. New York City, March 1.

Lodge, John Davis (82), Republican governor of Connecticut (1951–55); also had served as a member of the U.S. House of Representatives from Connecticut (1947–51) and as ambassador to Spain (1955–61), Argentina (1969–74), and Switzerland (1983–85). A lawyer by profession, he had also been an actor for a time in the 1930s. He was the younger brother of Henry Cabot Lodge, Jr.: d. New York City, Oct. 29.

London, George (born George Burstein) (64), operatic bass-baritone singer; began his international career in 1949 in Vienna. He made his debut at New York's Metropolitan Opera in 1951: d. Washington, DC, March 24.

Long, Gillis (61), U.S. representative (D-LA, 1963–65; 1973–85): d. Washington, DC, Jan. 20.

Lon Nol (72), Cambodian general; assisted in the overthrow of Prince Sihanouk in 1970 and headed a pro-American military government for five years until it was overpowered by Khmer Rouge forces: d. Fullerton, CA, Nov. 17.

MacInnes, Helen (77), Scottish-born novelist; wrote international espionage fiction. Among her 21 novels are *Above Suspicion, Assignment in Brittany, The Venetian Affair, The Salzburg Connection,* and *Ride a Pale Horse:* d. New York City, Sept. 30.

Mahon, George H. (85), U.S. representative (D-TX, 1935–79): d. San Angelo, TX, Nov. 19.

Maldonado Gonzalez, Jose (85), president (1970–77) of Spain's Republican government in exile, based in Mexico. He dissolved the government when Spain returned to democratic government: d. Oviedo, Spain, Feb. 11.

Maris, Roger (51), baseball player; as a New York Yankee he set the major league record for the most home runs (61) in a single season (1961), which overturned Babe Ruth's record, although Maris played eight more games than did Ruth. During his 12-year career with the Cleveland Indians, Kansas City Athletics, the Yankees, and the St. Louis Cardinals, he batted .260 and hit 275 home runs. While with the Yankees, he was named the American League's most valuable player in 1960 and 1961: d. Houston, TX, Dec. 14.

Marks, Johnny (75), composer; wrote the well-known Christmas song *Rudolph the Red-Nosed Reindeer,* which was first recorded by Gene Autry in 1949. Worldwide, the song sold 150 million records and more than 8 million sheet-music copies: d. New York City, Sept. 3.

Marriott, J. Willard (84), founder of the Marriott Corporation, a diversified business that includes hotels, restaurants, and airline catering services. Marriott started with a root beer stand and from there built a business empire: d. Wolfeboro, NH, Aug. 13.

Marshall, Fred (79), U.S. representative (D-MN, 1949–63): d. Litchfield, MN, June 5.

Mathews, Mitford (94), linguist and lexicographer; was editor of *A Dictionary of Americanisms on Historical Principles,* the first dictionary composed entirely of American contributions to the English language: d. Chicago, IL, Feb. 14.

Mayer, Sir Robert (105), German-born British financier, philanthropist, and patron of Britain's youth concerts, which carry his name: d. London, Jan. 9.

McKell, Sir William (93), Australian politician; served as governor-general (1947–53). He also had been premier of New South Wales for six years: d. Jan. 11.

Médici, Emilio Garrastazú (79), president of Brazil (1969–74): d. Rio de Janeiro, Brazil, Oct. 9.

Miller, Arnold R. (62), president of the United Mine Workers of America (1972–79): d. Charleston, WV, July 12.

André Kertész

Pelle Lindbergh

Lon Nol

Roger Maris

Photos, AP/Wide World

Montagu, Ewen (84), writer; during World War II he led a counter-espionage unit that was responsible for a hoax to deceive the Nazis regarding landings in the Mediterranean. He wrote of the hoax in the best-selling *The Man Who Never Was:* d. London, July 19.

Montet, Numa François (93), U.S. representative from Louisiana (1929–37): d. Thibodaux, LA, Oct. 12.

Mooney, Michael (55), author and editor; wrote *The Hindenberg* (1972): d. Washington, DC, Nov. 18.

Morante, Elsa (67), Italian writer. Among his books are *History: A Novel, House of Liars, Arturo's Island,* and *Aracoeli:* d. Rome, Nov. 25.

Morse, Philip McCord (82), physicist and educator; was founding director of Brookhaven National Laboratory: d. Concord, MA, Sept. 5.

Moskalenko, Kirill (83), Soviet army marshal, helped develop the Soviet strategic missile forces. He was deputy defense minister from the early 1960s until he retired in 1983: d. USSR, June 17.

Mungo, Van Lingle (73), baseball pitcher, was in the major leagues for 14 seasons, 11 with the Brooklyn Dodgers and three with the New York Giants. A man with a combative personality, he was thought to have paid more fines than any other player of his era: d. Pageland, SC, Feb. 12.

Murray, Pauli (74), priest, lawyer, writer, and civil-rights activist; the first black woman ordained to the Episcopal priesthood (1977). She studied law at the University of California at Berkeley, and in 1946 became a deputy attorney general of California. In 1948 she was admitted to the New York bar. She taught at various universities, including Brandeis, Yale, and Ghana University in Accra. Her books include *State Laws on Race and Color* (1951), *Proud Shoes* (1956), and *The Constitution and Government of Ghana* (1961), the last cowritten with Leslie Rubin. She also wrote poetry: d. Pittsburgh, July 1.

Nagel, Ernest (83), philosopher and professor at Columbia University from 1930 until 1973 except for a year in the 1960s when he taught at Rockefeller University. His best-known work is probably *The Structure of Science:* d. New York City, Sept. 20.

Naipaul, Shiva (40), Trinidad-born novelist and journalist; brother of the novelist V. S. Naipaul. His books include *Fireflies* (1971), *The Chip-chip Gatherers* (1973), *North of South* (1979), *Love and Death in a Hot Country* (1984), and *Beyond the Dragon's Mouth* (1985): d. London, Aug. 13.

Nathan, Robert (91), novelist; his career spanned more than 70 years. During much of his career he wrote one or two books per year. His novels include *Portrait of Jennie* (1940): d. Los Angeles, May 25.

Nelson, Ricky (45), singer and television performer on *The Adventures of Ozzie and Harriet* (1952–66). His popular songs include *Mary Lou, Travelin' Man,* and *Garden Party:* d. near De Kalb, TX, Dec. 31.

Nemon, Oscar (79), British sculptor; well known for his likenesses of Winston Churchill: d. Oxford, England, April 14.

Neves, Tancredo (75), Brazilian president-elect—*see* BRAZIL: d. São Paulo, April 21.

Nolan, Lloyd (83), actor in films, theater, and on television; his career spanned more than 50 years and included numerous performances in grade B movies prior to his receiving critical acclaim in *The Caine Mutiny Court Martial.* His films include *Bataan* (1943), *A Tree Grows in Brooklyn* (1944), and *The House on 92d Street* (1945). He also appeared on television in the series *Julia:* d. Los Angeles, Sept. 27.

North, John Ringling (81), head of the Ringling Brothers and Barnum & Bailey Circus for some 26 years: d. Brussels, Belgium, June 4.

O'Brien, Edmund (69), actor; his first recognition came from a role in the 1949 film *White Heat.* In 1955 he won the Academy Award for best supporting actor in *The Barefoot Contessa:* d. Inglewood, CA, May 9.

O'Brien, George (85), film actor; appeared in 75 films including the silent *Sunrise* and the Westerns *Fort Apache* and *Iron Horse:* d. Broken Arrow, OK, Sept. 4.

Olson, Johnny (75), television announcer on such programs as *The Price Is Right, What's My Line,* and *To Tell the Truth:* d. Santa Monica, CA, Oct. 12.

O'Malley, J. Pat (80), Irish-born character actor; best known for his work in television in such series as *My Three Sons, The Twilight Zone, My Favorite Martian,* and *Gunsmoke:* d. San Juan Capistrano, CA, Feb. 27.

O'Malley, Jerome F. (53), commander of the U.S. Air Force Tactical Air Command. He had served in Vietnam and had flown in 116 combat missions: d. Scranton, PA, April 20.

Oppenheimer, Frank (72), nuclear physicist; brother of J. Robert. In 1949 he testified before the House Un-American Activities Committee to having been a member of the American Communist Party before World War II. He thus aided in ending his brother's government career: d. Sausalito, CA, Feb. 3.

Orkin, Ruth (63), photojournalist and filmmaker; her black-and-white photos of celebrities and street life were regularly in *Life, Look, Ladies' Home Journal* and other publications between the 1940s and the 1960s. Between 1952 and 1955 she codirected two films, including *The Little Fugitive:* d. New York City, Jan. 16.

Payson, Charles (86), financier, sportsman, and philanthropist. A native of Portland, ME, he contributed millions of dollars to the Portland Museum of Art: d. Lexington, KY, May 6.

Pereira, William L. (76), architect and urban planner; designed the Transamerica building in San Francisco and master-planned the community of Irvine, CA: d. Los Angeles, CA, Nov. 13.

Philaret, Metropolitan (born George Nikolaevich Voznesensky) (82), Russian-born archbishop of New York and Eastern America and Primate of the Russian Orthodox Church Outside Russia (1964–85): d. New York City, Nov. 21.

Podoloff, Maurice (95), first president of the National Basketball Association; headed the league from 1946 until 1963: d. New Haven, CT, Nov. 24.

Pritikin, Nathan (69), nutritionist and writer; he advocated exercise and a salt-free, low-cholesterol diet and became internationally known for his program. His most widely known book is *The Pritikin Program for Diet and Exercise:* d. Albany, NY, Feb. 21.

Quinlan, Karen Ann (31), comatose patient who was the focus of a 1976 right-to-die law case when her parents successfully petitioned the court to disconnect a life-sustaining respirator. Miss Quinlan lived for ten years after the respirator had been disconnected: d. Morris Plains, NJ, June 11.

Ramgoolam, Sir Seewoosagur (85), prime minister of Mauritius; he led his nation to independence from the British in 1968 and remained prime minister until 1982 when he was defeated by a left-wing alliance in a general election. He became governor-general in 1983: d. Port Louis, Mauritius, Dec. 15.

Redgrave, Sir Michael (77), British stage and film actor. In 1936 he joined the Old Vic Company and made his debut in *Love's Labour's Lost.* He continued to perform Shakespearean roles in the 1950s and 1960s. He also won high praise for his work in *Uncle Vanya* and *The Master Builder.* Sir Michael's films include *The Lady Vanishes, A Stolen Life, Dead of Night, The Browning Version,* and *The Loneliness of the Long Distance Runner:* d. Denham, England, March 21.

Riboud, Jean (65), French chairman of Schlumberger Ltd. (1965–85). Under his leadership the oilfield services corporation was often called one of the world's best: d. Paris, Oct. 20.

Richter, Charles (85), pioneer in seismology; in 1935 he helped create, along with Beno Gutenberg, a scale, which now bears

Arnold Miller

Ricky Nelson

Lloyd Nolan

Edmund O'Brien

Photos, AP/Wide World

Camera Press/Photo Trends

Sir Michael Redgrave

UPI/Bettmann Newsphotos

Charles Richter

UPI/Bettmann Newsphotos

Carlos Romulo

AP/Wide World

Simone Signoret

his name, to gauge the magnitude of earthquakes: d. Pasadena, CA, Sept. 30.

Rico, Donato (Don) (72), cartoon artist; wrote and illustrated such comic books as *The Claw, Captain America, Captain Marvel,* and *Daredevil:* d. Los Angeles, CA, March 27.

Riddle, Nelson (64), composer and arranger; best known for his song orchestrations for Frank Sinatra. His 1983 album *What's New* with Linda Ronstadt sold more than 3.5 million copies: d. Los Angeles, CA, Oct. 6.

Rifai, Abdel Monem (68), prime minister of Jordan in 1969 and again in 1970. In 1973 and 1974 he served as a special adviser on international affairs to King Hussein: d. Amman, Jordan, Oct. 17.

Robinson, Julia Bowman (65), mathematician at the University of California (Berkeley). In 1976 she became the first woman mathematician elected to the National Academy of Science: d. Oakland, CA, July 30.

Romulo, Carlos (86), Filipino diplomat; a cofounder of the United Nations in 1945, he saw to it that its charter explicitly endorsed the independence of colonies. In World War II he was chosen to accompany the U.S. invasion of the Philippines in 1944. He rose to the rank of brigadier general in the U.S. Army. He was the first Asian president of the UN General Assembly (1949, 1950) and was the Philippine chief delegate (1945–54). Other posts that he held included ambassador to the United States (1952–53; 1955–62), foreign minister (1950–52; 1968–84), director of the education ministry (1966–68), and president of the University of the Philippines (Manila) (1962–68): d. Manila, Philippines, Dec. 15.

Rosenstock, Joseph (90), conductor and general manager of the New York City Opera (1952–55). He conducted at the Metropolitan Opera House and for orchestras in Germany and Japan: d. New York City, Oct. 17.

Rothstein, Arthur (70), photojournalist and editor; well known for his pictures of the Dust Bowl during the Great Depression of the 1930s. He was director of *Look* magazine for 25 years: d. New Rochelle, NY, Nov. 11.

Roy, Maurice Cardinal (80), Roman Catholic primate of Canada (1956–81) and a former archbishop of Quebec: d. Montreal, Canada, Oct. 24.

Ryskind, Morrie (89), writer of plays and screenplays of the 1920s, 1930s, and 1940s. His screenplays included *My Man Godfrey, Room Service,* and *Penny Serenade* and such collaborations with George S. Kaufman as the Marx Bros. films *A Night at the Opera, Coconuts,* and *Animal Crackers.* For the stage he collaborated with Kaufman and George and Ira Gershwin to produce *Strike Up the Band, Let 'em Eat Cake,* and *Of Thee I Sing,* for which he shared a Pulitzer Prize: d. Washington, DC, Aug. 24.

Sandman, Charles (63), U.S. representative (R-NJ, 1967–75): d. Cape May Court House, NJ, Aug. 26.

Sarkis, Elias (60), president of Lebanon (1976–82): d. Paris, June 27.

Sattar, Abdus (79), Bangladesh president (1981–82); was the only elected civilian president in Bangladesh's 13-year history; was elected in November 1981 and deposed five months later: d. Dhaka, Bangladesh, Oct. 5.

Schneider, Mischa (81), cellist with the Budapest String Quartet for 38 years: d. Buffalo, NY, Oct. 3.

Scoville, Herbert, Jr. (70), nuclear arms expert; helped develop nuclear weapons with the U.S. Defense Department's Armed Forces Special Weapons Project (1948–55). He was with the Central Intelligence Agency (1955–63) and then in the Arms Control and Disarmament Agency until 1969. After leaving government service he became an advocate of arms control: d. Washington, DC, July 30.

Selden, Armistead, Jr. (64), U.S. representative (D-AL, 1953–69): d. Birmingham, AL, Nov. 14.

Sessions, Roger (88), music composer and professor; was a composer of symphonies, opera, and chamber music. Mr. Sessions, known for the difficulty of his music, was on the faculty of several colleges and universities, including Princeton and The Juilliard School. Among his major musical pieces is the opera *Montezuma:* d. Princeton, NJ, March 16.

Shaughnessy, Mickey (born Joseph C.) (64), comedian and actor; appeared in 41 movies, including *The Marrying Kind* (1952) and *From Here to Eternity* (1953). He performed his nightclub act until near the end of his life: d. Cape May Court House, NJ, July 23.

Shivers, Allan (77), governor of Texas (1949–57); was a Democrat who gained national attention when he supported Republican Dwight Eisenhower for president: d. Austin, TX, Jan. 14.

Shklovsky, Iosif S. (68), Soviet astrophysicist; well known in the United States for his speculations about extraterrestrial life. *Intelligent Life in the Universe,* an English-language version of his 1962 book on the subject, was published in 1966: d. Moscow, March 3.

Shook, Karel (64), dancer and ballet master; cofounder of the Dance Theater of Harlem. Originally a dancer, he began to teach ballet in 1952. His book *Elements of Classical Ballet* was published in 1977: d. Englewood, NJ, July 25.

Signoret, Simone (born Simone Kaminker) (64), French film actress; won an Academy Award for her performance in *Room at the Top* (1958). Among her other films are *Diabolique* (1955), *Ship of Fools* (1965), and *Madame Rosa* (1978). She wrote a volume of memoirs, *Nostalgia Isn't What It Used to Be,* and the best-selling novel *Adieu, Volodia:* d. Eure, France, Sept. 30.

Silvers, Phil (born Philip Silversmith) (73), comedian; best known as Sgt. Ernie Bilko from the television series *The Phil Silvers Show* (also known for a time as *You'll Never Get Rich*) that ran 1955–59. He was awarded a Tony award for his performance in the 1972 revival of *A Funny Thing Happened on the Way to the Forum:* d. Los Angeles, CA, Nov. 1.

Sims, Zoot (John Haley) (59), jazz swing saxophonist: d. New York City, March 23.

Sloane, Eric (Everard Jean Hinrichs) (80), painter and author; wrote and illustrated many books including *I Remember America* (1971). He designed the Hall of Atmosphere in the American Museum of Natural History and painted a six-story-high mural of a skyscape for the Smithsonian Institution: d. New York City, March 6.

Smith, Samantha (13), Maine schoolgirl who wrote a letter to the Soviet leader Yuri Andropov about peace and subsequently was invited to the USSR for a visit. She recently became a television actress and was filming the series *Lime Street:* d. near Auburn, ME, Aug. 25.

Sondergaard, Gale (86), actress; appeared in numerous movies of the 1930s and 1940s, often playing a villain. She made her film debut in 1936 in *Anthony Adverse.* She later was black-listed: d. Woodland Hills, CA, Aug. 14.

Sparkman, John (85), U.S. senator (D-AL, 1946–79); he also had served as a U.S. representative (1937–46) and was the Democratic vice-presidential nominee in 1952: d. Huntsville, AL, Nov. 16.

Spender, Sir Percy Claude (87), Australian political figure; held a number of government posts, including minister of external affairs and territories, and was his nation's ambassador to the United States between 1951–58. From 1958 until 1967 he was on the bench of the International Court of Justice: d. May 3.

Spiegel, Sam (84), producer of such films as *The African Queen, On the Waterfront, The Bridge on the River Kwai,* and *Lawrence of Arabia;* for the latter three he won an Academy Award as best picture of the year. Other important films that he produced were *The Stranger* (1946), *Suddenly, Last Sum-*

AP/Wide World

Phil Silvers

AP/Wide World

Samantha Smith

AP/Wide World

John Sparkman

UPI/Bettmann Newsphotos

Potter Stewart

mer (1959), *Nicholas and Alexandra* (1971), *The Last Tycoon* (1976), and *Betrayal* (1983): d. St. Martin, Caribbean, Dec. 31.

Spota, Luis (60), Mexican author, journalist, and television news commentator; published more than 30 novels. Many were translated into other languages: d. Mexico City, Jan. 20.

Springer, Axel (73), West German publisher; headed the Axel Springer Publishing Group, one of Europe's biggest publishing concerns: d. West Berlin, Sept. 22.

Stenberg, Leif (53), Swedish artificial heart recipient. He lived 229 days with the artificial heart: d. Stockholm, Nov. 21.

Sterling, J. E. Wallace (78), president of Stanford University (1949–68): d. Woodside, CA, July 1.

Stewart, Potter (70), U.S. Supreme Court justice; served for 23 years on the court before his retirement in June 1981. For half of his tenure he was a conservative and a frequent dissenting member of the court of Earl Warren. After Warren Burger became chief justice, Stewart moved more to the center in his judicial opinions. A graduate of the Yale Law School, he briefly practiced law in New York and then joined a leading Cincinnati law firm. He held political posts in that city before being appointed to the U.S. Court of Appeals for the Sixth District in 1954. He was appointed to the Supreme Court in 1958: d. Hanover, NH, Dec. 7.

Stringfellow, William (56), lawyer, author, and Episcopalian lay theologian; active in radical politics in the 1960s. His books include *My People Is the Enemy* (1964) and *Dissenter in a Great Society* (1966): d. Providence, RI, March 2.

Sturgeon, Theodore (born Edward Hamilton Waldo) (67), American science-fiction writer; his works include the short-story anthology *Without Sorcery* (1948), the collections *E Pluribus Unicorn* (1953) and *The Worlds of Theodore Sturgeon* (1972), and the novels *The Dreaming Jewels* (1950) (later renamed *The Synthetic Man;* 1961), *More Than Human* (1953), *Venus Plus X* (1960), and *Some of Your Blood* (1961). He wrote short stories under his own name and under the pseudonyms E. Hunter Waldo and Fredrick R. Ewing. He also wrote plays and teleplays for *Star Trek, The Invaders,* and *Wild, Wild West:* d. Eugene, OR, May 8.

Terry, Luther L. (73), surgeon general of the United States (1961–65); was instrumental in preparing a 1964 report indicating that cigarette smoking was linked to lung cancer and certain respiratory ailments: d. Philadelphia, PA, March 29.

Thuy, Xuan (73), vice chairman of Vietnam's National Assembly and North Vietnam's chief diplomat at the Paris peace talks that led to the withdrawal of American forces from Vietnam: d. Hanoi, June 18.

Tillstrom, Burr (68), creator and puppeteer of the popular television show *Kukla, Fran & Ollie* (1947–57): Palm Springs, CA, Dec. 6.

Trevelyan, Humphrey (Lord Trevelyan) (49), British diplomat who served as ambassador to Moscow from 1962 to 1965: d. Feb. 8.

Turner, Joseph Vernon (Big Joe) (74), blues singer; he first became popular in the 1930s. His famous jump-blues songs include *Shake, Rattle, and Roll* and *Corrina, Corrina:* d. Englewood, CA, Nov. 24.

Van Niel, Cornelis Bernardus (87), Dutch-born microbiologist; in the 1930s he was the first scientist to explain the chemical basis for photosynthesis: d. Carmel, CA, March 10.

Vassalo e Silva, Manuel António (86), colonial governor of Portuguese India who surrendered the territory to India in 1961 despite the orders to the contrary of the dictator Antonio de Oliveira Salazar: d. Lisbon, Aug. 11.

Vinci, Piero (73), Italian diplomat, served as Italy's representative to the United Nations in the 1960s and 1970s. He was instrumental in admitting mainland China to the United Nations: d. Ischia, Italy, July 17.

Visser 't Hooft, Willem Adolf (84), secretary-general of the World Council of Churches (1948–66): d. Geneva, Switzerland, July 4.

Wambsganss, Bill (91), baseball player; played on the 1920 world champion Cleveland Indians team. He is the only man in baseball who made an unassisted triple play in a World Series: d. Lakewood, OH, Dec. 8.

Waterhouse, Sir Ellis (80), author and historian of British art: d. Oxford, England, Sept. 7.

Welch, Robert H. W., Jr. (84), a founder (1958) of the right-wing John Birch Society. He retired as the group's president in 1983. He also was involved in candy manufacturing (1922–56) and was president of Robert Welch, Inc., publishers since 1956: d. Winchester, MA, Jan. 6.

Willcox, William (77), historian and editor of the papers of Benjamin Franklin at Yale University. In 1965 he was a recipient of a Bancroft Prize in American history for his book *Portrait of a General: Sir Henry Clinton in the War of Independence:* d: North Haven, CT, Sept. 15.

Williams, Cootie (Charles) (77), trumpet player; was a member of Duke Ellington's Orchestra from 1928 to 1940, when he joined Benny Goodman's orchestra. A year later he formed a group of his own: d. New York City, Sept. 15.

Williams, Lynn A. (76), Chicago lawyer and industrialist; was a founder of the Great Books Foundation: d. Evanston, IL, April 21.

Wirkkala, Tapio (69), Finnish sculptor and designer; he first won international acclaim for Chantarelle, a group of glass vases produced by Iittala Glassworks: d. Espoo, Finland, May 19.

Wolfenden, Lord (John Frederick) (78), educator and British social reformer, was chairman of a government committee from 1954 to 1957 that investigated male homosexuality and female prostitution. The Wolfenden Report recommended that private homosexual acts between consenting male adults be decriminalized and that female prostitution remain legal if not involving street solicitation. The recommendations were adopted in 1967. He also was chairman of the University Grants Committee (1963–68) and director of the British Museum (1969–73): d. London, Jan. 18.

Wood, Joseph (Smoky Joe) (95), baseball pitcher; in 1912 compiled a 34–5 won-lost record for the Boston Red Sox, including 16 straight victories for an American League record: d. West Haven, CT, July 27.

Woodruff, Robert (95), former head of the Coca-Cola Company. He became president of Coca-Cola in 1923, retiring from the company in 1955, but he remained as a director and chairman of the finance committee of the board of directors until 1981 when he became chairman emeritus: d. Atlanta, GA, March 7.

Wright, Olgivanna Lloyd (85), wife of architect Frank Lloyd Wright; she was a keeper of his legacy in the years after his death in 1959: d. Scottsdale, AZ, March 1.

Xu Shiyou (80), Chinese military leader: d. Nanjing, Oct. 22.

Yepishev, Aleksei (77), chief political commissar of the Soviet armed forces from 1962 until his retirement in 1984: d. Sept. 15.

Yutkevich, Sergei (80), Soviet filmmaker; known in the USSR for his series of films about Lenin: d. Moscow, April 23.

Zaslofsky, Max (59), basketball player, considered one of the best two-handed shooters of all time: d. New Hyde Park, NY, Oct. 15.

Zimbalist, Efrem, Sr. (94), Russian-born violinist; was an alumnus of Leopold Auer's famed violin classes in Czarist St. Petersburg. He made his first American appearance in 1911 with the Boston Symphony Orchestra. In 1928 he joined the faculty at the Curtis Institute in Philadelphia and was its director from 1941 until 1968. He was also a composer: d. Reno, NV, Feb. 22.

OCEANOGRAPHY

Worldwide climate and weather are closely tied to the oceanic system. The ongoing World Climate Research Program (WCRP) includes the ten-year Tropical Ocean and Global Atmosphere (TOGA) study, which involves an attempt to understand the atmosphere's southern oscillation, the *El Niño* phenomenon in the Pacific Ocean, and their joint effect on climate at midlatitudes. The second major WCRP project is the World Ocean Circulation Experiment (WOCE), designed to determine the general circulation of the ocean in three dimensions. And still another program, the Marginal Ice Zone Experiment (MIZEX), focuses on the extent, characteristics, and variability of sea ice and of water locked in glaciers and ice shelves. Employing seven ships and eight aircraft, MIZEX was conducted in the northern Greenland Sea in summer 1984 at the period of greatest ice retreat. Scientists from Canada, Denmark, West Germany, Finland, France, Ireland, Norway, Sweden, the United Kingdom, and the United States obtained data to define features of the Atlantic currents under ice in the Fram Strait. Among those features were mesoscale eddies, measuring 16–31 mi (25–50 km) in diameter, which were followed along the ice edge by aircraft and by satellite remote sensing. Turbulence experiments measured fluctuating currents, temperature, and salinity at several levels beneath the ice.

To improve the understanding of winter storm patterns, a program called the Genesis of Atlantic Lows Experiment (GALE) was to undertake intensive field work along the Carolina coast in winter 1986. GALE would seek to develop and test improved predictive models for such storms, employing a network of surface and airborne instruments as well as satellite observations. The response of the ocean to actions in the atmosphere will be surveyed, and several coastal marine sites have been instrumented to relay weather conditions to land via satellite. As the storms move northeast away from the GALE area and drift toward the coast of Nova Scotia, they will be monitored by the Canadian Atlantic Storm Project (CASP).

In 1985 the Ocean Drilling Program (ODP) began operating a new drilling vessel, the *Joides Resolution*. This 470-ft (143-m) drill ship has a 200-ft (61-m) derrick and a 7-story laboratory complex for the study of cores, including their chemical, gas, and physical properties and their paleontological, petrological, paleomagnetic, and sedimentological aspects. Marine geophysical research is conducted while the ship is under way, between drill stations. The ship's drilling system can handle 30,000 ft (9 144 m) of drill pipe and can drill in water depths of up to 27,000 ft (8 230 m). The first cruises included drilling off the coast of Spain, in the Norwegian Sea, and at high latitudes in the North Atlantic that could not be studied previously because of the ice conditions. In the area of Baffin Bay, drilling was planned in a dead rift, a site at which the North Atlantic originally began to open before the present rift on the other side of Greenland developed. ODP is an international cooperative effort by Canada, France, West Germany, Japan, and the United States. The United Kingdom and a research consortium of European countries were expected to join the effort.

New seabed communities of animals associated with hydrothermal vents—unique large clams, mussels, and worms—continue to be found. The latest additions include one on a Pacific Ocean sea mount at a depth of 5,150 ft (1 570 m) on Juan de Fuca ridge and two in the Gulf of Mexico, at a depth of 10,715 ft (3 266 m) near Florida and at a depth of some 2,300 ft (700 m) at a petroleum seep in the central Gulf. The latter communities are associated with cold sulfide seeps; the other vent populations are at much higher temperatures. Additional undersea vents associated with the mid-Atlantic rift system have been located, and at least one of these sites appears to harbor a characteristic vent community.

The organisms in deep seabed communities exist by bacterial synthesis of energy from the sulfides and other minerals of the vent or seep. The general pattern that is emerging is of a fauna with many similarities from place to place. The occurrence of this fauna over such wide distances raises many questions. The forms apparently survive by rapid growth and by widespread dispersal of larvae to colonize new vents as they occur. There is fossil evidence of vent communities in the Paleozoic and Mesozoic eras, and some barnacles thought to be extinct since the Mesozoic era have been recognized.

A recent survey near San Salvador Island in the Bahamas with a manned submersible produced surprising evidence of vigorous algal growth at depths of up to 879 ft (268 m). Previously, a depth of 656 ft (200 m) was thought to represent the point at which solar energy becomes so attenuated that it can no longer stimulate photosynthesis. A new species of purple crustose alga was found to need much less than the 1% of surface sunlight previously thought to be required for growth. The new form, which belongs to the group of Red Algae, is the only known macrophyte (plant visible to the unaided eye) that can grow at this depth.

By means of a tethered, unmanned, camera-equipped, submersible craft, U.S. and French scientists succeeded in locating the sunken ocean liner *Titanic* (*see* special report, page 408). The underwater vessel, called *Argo*, is said to be the most advanced unmanned system ever developed for exploring the ocean.

DAVID A. McGILL
U.S. Coast Guard Academy

"Titanic" Found

AP/Wide World

Dr. Robert Ballard, leader of the expedition that located the sunken ocean liner "Titanic," believes that massive loss of life might have been averted if a nearby ship, the "Californian," had moved to rescue stranded passengers.

The sinking of the S.S. *Titanic,* the most technologically advanced oceangoing vessel of its day, was perhaps the most unexpected and most mythologized tragedy of the 20th century. Because of its state-of-the-art double hull and 16 watertight compartments, the 900-ft (274-m) luxury liner had been proudly declared "unsinkable." But on the night of April 14, 1912, on its maiden voyage from Southampton, England, to New York City, the fabled steamship struck an iceberg some 370 mi (595 km) off the coast of Newfoundland and sank 2½ hours later. Of the 2,200 passengers on board, more than 1,500 lost their lives; among them were some of the wealthiest personages of the era, including the financier John Jacob Astor and the industrialist Benjamin Guggenheim. The exact location of the sinking was never determined, and for 73 years the *Titanic* lived only in books, movies, songs, and the collective memory.

The discovery of the sunken vessel on Sept. 1, 1985, also employed some of the most advanced ocean technology of its day and also came as something of a surprise. The find was made by scientists testing a state-of-the-art deep-sea research craft and only incidentally interested in the *Titanic* wreck. A team of 13 investigators from the Woods Hole (MA) Oceanographic Institution sailed on the U.S. Navy vessel *Knorr* and joined forces with a group of French scientists on board the *Suroit,* operated by the Research Institute for Exploitation of the Sea (IFREMER) in Paris. Both ships carried sophisticated equipment for tracing and exploring the ocean floor. The *Knorr* carried a submersible, unmanned photographic "sled" called the *Argo,* which could descend to depths of 20,000 ft (6 096 m) and remain underwater indefinitely. The search for the *Titanic* was, first and foremost, a scientific sea trial of the *Argo.*

The first evidence of "something down there" was an echo recorded by a high-resolution sonar device aboard the *Suroit.* The *Argo* was then deployed, and within one week it was sending up images of the *Titanic.* The ship was resting upright on the ocean floor at a depth of more than 13,000 ft (3 962 m). Two of its four smokestacks were missing and there was serious damage at the stern, but some 75% of the famed ocean queen remained intact. And at that depth, many of the ship's relics—unopened bottles of wine, luggage, china plates, and other items—had been preserved by the absence of sunlight, heat, and parasitic life. Said Robert Ballard, the expedition leader from Woods Hole, "It is a museum piece."

The excitement of the scientists quickly gave way to solemnity, however, as they recalled the more than 1,500 victims. No human remains were located among the *Titanic*'s debris, and the researchers felt that the entire vessel should be left undisturbed. Nevertheless, tangled legal questions were raised over who owns the ship and any valuable items that might be retrieved from it. Several salvage operations already were being planned.

OHIO

The chill of a March 4 default by ESM Government Securities, a Florida financial firm, shivered Ohio citizens for weeks, particularly depositors of Home State Savings Bank of Cincinnati. The scandal also provided anxious months for the Ohio legislature and Gov. Richard F. Celeste, who froze Home State operations after customers withdrew some $90 million. Home State had invested millions in ESM, and its loss was estimated at between $90 million and $140 million. The losses threatened to deplete Ohio's $136 million private-insurance pool for nonfederally insured savings and loans banks. When thrift customers statewide began lining up to make withdrawals, Governor Celeste closed down 70 such institutions for ten days to halt the run. (*See also* BANKING.)

Home State was owned by Marvin L. Davis, an associate of ESM officials and a major fund raiser for Celeste's 1982 election campaign. In late May, Home State was taken over by American Financial Corporation. The purchase was facilitated by a subsidy from the State of Ohio of up to $43 million.

Tax Breaks. Finances of a different sort figured in an important action by the Ohio legislature. A compromise general fund budget for 1986–87 of nearly $20 billion authorized cuts in the state's income tax of 5% on 1985 income and 10% on 1986 income. The succeeding biennium would see more reductions if employment conditions warrant.

Deaths. Frederick D. Holliday, 58, who had been appointed Cleveland's public school superintendent 27 months earlier, shocked the community by fatally shooting himself on Jan. 26, 1985. In a typewritten note he charged that "petty politics" within the elected school board and elsewhere were blocking plans for further improvement of the schools and that this had "sickened" him. Holliday was the city's first black school superintendent; the second is his successor, Ronald A. Boyd, 44, who assumed office September 23.

On July 30, Lt. Gov. Myrl H. Shoemaker died of cancer. The position will not be filled until January 1987.

Politics. Cleveland's Mayor George V. Voinovich, a Republican, took 63.6% of a nonpartisan primary vote on October 1, then faced a runoff on November 5 against Democrat Gary Kucinich, who finished second in the primary voting with 25.5%. Voinovich was the easy winner on Election Day, taking 72% of the vote. Statewide, voters approved a constitutional amendment allowing issuance of up to $100 million of general obligation bonds for research on coal desulfurization. An efficient method would mean many new jobs.

Water. On February 5 the chief executives of Ohio, seven other states, and the Canadian provinces of Ontario and Quebec signed the Great Lakes Charter. The pact obligated them to gather data on lake water use and to work together to tighten controls. It also warned Western states against lobbying for pipelines or for federal approval to siphon off Great Lakes water. Meanwhile, the reappearance of fish in many Ohio River tributaries was evidence of the success of antipollution efforts by the Ohio Valley Water Sanitation Commission.

Energy. Cleveland Electric Illuminating and Toledo Edison asked shareholders late in 1985

Gov. Celeste signs a bill March 20 allowing Ohio S&Ls to reopen. Fears of a run had forced a closedown.

AP/Wide World

OHIO • Information Highlights

Area: 41,330 sq mi (107 044 km²).

Population (July 1, 1984 est.): 10,752,000.

Chief Cities (July 1, 1984 est.): Columbus, the capital, 566,114; Cleveland, 546,543; Cincinnati, 370,481; Toledo, 343,939; Akron, 226,877; Dayton, 181,159.

Government (1985): *Chief Officers*—governor, Richard F. Celeste (D); lt. gov., vacant. *General Assembly*—Senate, 33 members; House of Representatives, 99 members.

State Finances (fiscal year 1984): *Revenues,* $18,682,000,000; *expenditures,* $16,348,000,000.

Personal Income (1984): $132,842,000,000; per capita, $12,355.

Labor Force (June 1985): *Civilian labor force,* 5,156,600; *unemployed,* 440,200 (8.5% of total force).

Education: *Enrollment* (fall 1983)—public elementary schools, 1,240,344; public secondary, 586,956; colleges and universities, 535,592. *Public school expenditures* (1982–83), $4,600,474,824 ($2,676 per pupil).

to approve affiliation in Centerior Energy Corporation, to be headquartered in Cleveland. The David-Besse nuclear plant near Port Clinton, jointly owned by Cleveland Electric and Toledo Edison, was shut down by the U.S. Nuclear Regulatory Commission on June 9 because of an operating malfunction.

Retardation Probe. Mistreatment of mental patients under state care in Cincinnati, Cleveland, and Columbus led to the resignation of the director of the state mental health department. The Cleveland *Plain Dealer* cited unreported deaths, rapes, and beatings at various institutions. Reports of especially bad conditions in northeastern Ohio resulted in the resignation of the regional superintendent.

Tornadoes. A late afternoon storm on May 31 spawned numerous tornadoes that killed at least 85 persons and injured hundreds in the Niles-Newton Falls area of Ohio, Pennsylvania, and New York. In four Ohio counties, damage to property was estimated at $34 million.

JOHN F. HUTH, JR., *Former Reporter*
"The Plain Dealer," Cleveland

OKLAHOMA

The Oklahoma legislature adjourned on July 20, 1985, on its 90th legislative day ending with a 21-hour marathon budget session. The issues of reform and economic development dominated the early days of the session. Passage of the largest tax package in state history and appropriations decisions came late.

Major reforms resulted from submission of constitutional amendments to the voters in April. Approved were changes in the budget balancing amendment, to free $121 million in funds, and a five-year *ad valorem* tax exemption for new or expanding industries. Also passed were a new financial disclosure law for legislators, a change in the Prevailing Wage Act, a four-year driver's license law, and a new state "immunity" law.

Oklahoma gained the distinction of authorizing the largest percentage tax increase of any state in 1985. Following three years of steady decline in state revenues, the legislature, led by House Speaker James Barker, Muskogee Democrat, passed a $415 million tax increase package. The sales tax was increased to 3.25%; corporate income tax went to 5%; and excise taxes were raised on autos, airplanes, and boats. The gasoline tax was raised to 10¢ per gallon; smokeless tobacco was taxed; license fees increased for nonfarm trucks; and domestic insurance company premiums were taxed.

The budget was funded at $2.55 billion; $1.368 billion going to operations and capital outlays for educational institutions. Seventy-one percent of new revenues went to education. Teachers were granted a raise in base sal-

aries to $15,600, and an average $2,000 increase. State employees received 6–8% increases, and college and university faculty received averages of 8–10%. State correctional facilities received increased funds.

Other legislation included a "living will" or natural death statute, a fair housing law barring discrimination, stricter guidelines on the "home arrest" program, a mandatory seat belt law, tightened state tax collection, and a state holiday to honor Martin Luther King, Jr.

Education. A Higher Education Task Force, which would include the governor, legislators, and lay members, was mandated. The task force was to focus on the link of higher education to economic development. Such issues as having too many institutions, duplication of programs, and missions were to be investigated.

Frank E. Horton, chancellor of the University of Wisconsin-Milwaukee, became the 11th president of the University of Oklahoma.

The Economy. Oklahoma still was suffering from recession in the oil industry and depressed farm prices. Bankruptcies, especially on farms, were up. Housing sales were off. Surveys found a slight decrease in population. Banks continued to fail. An International Development Office was established in Japan. Gov. George Nigh and industrial leaders visited the Orient to attract trade partners.

Other. More than one third of 77 counties legalized liquor-by-the-drink sales following passage in 1984 of a local option constitutional amendment. Complex new laws regulated sales. Governor Nigh signed an executive order authorizing early release for 1,856 nonviolent offenders to reduce prison overcrowding.

The Oklahoma Horse Racing Commission voted to limit horse racing to one major track. Earlier the legislature increased the share of the take for racetrack owners, reducing the state share.

JOHN W. WOOD, *University of Oklahoma*

OKLAHOMA • Information Highlights

Area: 69,956 sq mi (181 186 km²).
Population (July 1, 1984 est.): 3,298,000.
Chief Cities (July 1, 1984 est.): Oklahoma City, the capital, 443,172; Tulsa, 374,535; Lawton (1980 census), 80,054.
Government (1985): *Chief Officers—*governor, George Nigh (D); lt. gov., Spencer Bernard (D). *Legislature—*Senate, 48 members; House of Representatives, 101 members.
State Finances (fiscal year 1984): *Revenues,* $5,064,000,000; *expenditures,* $4,708,000,000.
Personal Income (1984): $38,438,000,000; per capita, $11,655.
Labor Force (June 1985): *Civilian labor force,* 1,582,400; *unemployed,* 112,900 (7.1% of total force).
Education: *Enrollment* (fall 1983)—public elementary schools, 420,913; public secondary, 170,476; colleges and universities, 174,171. *Public school expenditures* (1982–83), $1,560,103,477 ($2,805 per pupil).

David Peterson, a 41-year-old Liberal from London, Ontario, became the province's first non-Conservative premier in 42 years. The former businessman pledged to promote job creation, equality for women, pollution control, and educational reform.

Canapress

ONTARIO

The year 1985 was a memorable one in Ontario politics. The Progressive Conservative Party (PC) was finally ousted after more than 40 years in power.

Political Developments. Former Treasurer Frank Miller succeeded William Davis as premier late in January after winning the leadership of the Progressive Conservative Party, a win widely interpreted as a victory for the right wing. With public opinion polls showing a conservative lead, Miller sought a mandate by calling an election in May. A lackluster campaign, right wing in tone, saw the PC representation in the Legislative Assembly reduced to 52 seats. Liberal Party candidates—who campaigned on funding to Roman Catholic high schools, the extension of rent control, an end to extra billing by doctors in medicare, and equal pay for work of equal value—took 48 seats in the legislature. The New Democratic Party (NDP) won 25 seats. But Miller's government was defeated on the Speech from the Throne, which is a statement of policy by the party in power. The NDP meanwhile had signed a controversial agreement to support a Liberal administration on condition that it immediately proceed on its promises on rent control, extra billing, and Catholic school funding. The Liberal government headed by David Peterson took office on June 26.

Issues. Unquestionably, the subject of extending full funding to Catholic schools is a major issue in Ontario. The election call aborted a debate on Conservative funding proposals in the legislature. Since all three parties supported it in principle, it was not aired publicly during the election campaign. The proposal is opposed by public school teachers, school trustees, and many religious groups. There is doubt about its constitutionality and fear that it could lead to a total fragmentation of the public school system, since other religious groups could demand funding for their own schools. Apparently the question was a major factor in the Conservatives' election defeat, since PC voters opposed to the proposi-

tion failed to vote. Premier Peterson is going forward but has referred the constitutional issue to the Ontario Court of Appeal for a ruling. In the meantime, he has delayed the introduction of legislation, relying on executive action as a stopgap measure.

With his party badly divided and falling in popularity, Opposition Leader Frank Miller resigned in September. He was succeeded by former Treasurer Larry Grossman.

The new government faced the problem of carrying out its promises to increase spending on education, health services, and job creation—while maintaining Ontario's triple-A bond rating. Tax hikes seem inevitable in the first Liberal budget. While proceeding with schemes for equal pay for work of equal value in the public sector, loud outcries from business have made the government delay a similar move in the private sector. The new government also has seemed to hesitate on its promised ban on extra billing by physicians, instead challenging pharmacists over high drug costs. These moves may, however, jeopardize the alliance with the NDP.

Other Events. A PCB spill near Kenora contaminated more than 160 mi (250 km) of the

---

ONTARIO • Information Highlights

Area: 412,582 sq mi (1 068 587 km²).
Population (April 1985 est.): 9,047,900.
Chief Cities (1981 census): Toronto, the provincial capital, 599,217; Ottawa, the federal capital, 295,163; North York, 559,521; Mississauga, 315,056; Hamilton, 306,434; London, 254,280.
Government (1985): *Chief Officers*—lt. gov., Lincoln Alexander; premier, David Peterson (Liberal). *Legislature*—Legislative Assembly, 125 members.
Provincial Finances (1985–86 fiscal year budget): *Revenues,* $30,483,000,000; *expenditures,* $32,-696,000,000.
Personal Income (average weekly earnings, June 1985): $423.28.
Labor Force (August 1985, seasonally adjusted): *Employed workers,* 15 years of age and over, 4,400,000; *Unemployed,* 384,000 (8.0%).
Education (1985–86): *Enrollment*—elementary and secondary schools, 1,850,660 pupils; postsecondary (full-time, 1985–86)—universities, 185,900; community colleges, 96,200.
(All monetary figures are in Canadian dollars.)

TransCanada highway, closing it for four days, raising questions about the transportation of hazardous substances, and leading to issuance of new regulations.

A strike by brewery workers in March deprived the province of beer for three weeks. The Liberals made the sale of beer and wine in corner grocery stores a campaign issue. In April, Hyundai of South Korea announced that it would build an automobile parts plant north of Toronto costing C$25 million.

Looking beyond its borders, Ontario banned further purchases by provincial liquor stores of wines and spirits from South Africa. Premier Peterson took a strong line at the Premiers' Conference. He disagreed with most of the other provincial premiers and opposed schemes for greater free trade with the United States, expressing concern that such a policy would harm Ontario as Canada's preeminent manufacturing region.

PETER J. KING, *Carleton University*

OREGON

Oregon's economy, heavily resource-based, continued to wallow in recession. Though unemployment showed some improvement, wood-products mill closures continued.

Economy. In January, Champion International Corporation announced the closure of most of its wood-products operations in the Pacific Northwest. Included were five plants in Oregon, representing 1,288 jobs with a combined annual payroll of $27.1 million. The company blamed the shutdowns on high labor, timber, and tax costs in the region. At the same time, Weyerhaeuser Company announced the closing of its plywood mill in Springfield, idling another 164 workers.

The annual Alexander Grant "manufacturing climate" survey rated Oregon 44th among the 50 states, a slight improvement over 1984. The Naisbitt Group, however, stated that while Oregon's timber industry continues to suffer, new electronics firms are keeping Oregon's economy moving. The U.S. Navy announced it had chosen Portland as a home port for four of its vessels, and the Port of Astoria was picked for the berthing of four small minesweepers. Lease and payroll monies for the Portland port will amount to an estimated $450,000. In addition, ship repair contracts amounting to $42.5 million were awarded to Portland firms by the U.S. Navy.

Declining interest rates, a third-quarter increase in building starts, and the prospect of increasing protectionist sentiment in the U.S. Congress have prompted some guarded optimism among Oregon timber interests.

Education. After several years of declining enrollments, colleges and universities reported modest increases in September. Western Oregon State College in Monmouth led state institutions, with a gain of almost 18% over the previous year. For the first time since 1981, the Oregon legislature appropriated funds for faculty salary increases—amounting to 5%—for Oregon's eight institutions of higher learning.

Fifty-three school districts, representing 31% of the state's precollege enrollment, had been unable to pass operating levies when schools opened in September. The number of Oregon school districts in difficult financial straits was greater in September 1985 than ever before. While inadequate tax bases and increasing property taxes were ordinarily cited as causes for levy defeats, the 1985 ballot included a sales-tax initiative, which was beaten back by a better than four-to-one margin. Many commentators blamed the large number of levy defeats on an unusually high negative voter turnout prompted by the sales tax initiative. By mid-October, several districts were still without operating budgets, and the threat remained of a shutdown of some schools before year's end. Impending teacher strikes in several other districts jeopardized future school sessions.

Other. In Antelope, OR, the state's largest commune, led by the Baghwan Shree Rajneesh, a guru from India, was rocked by controversy. The Baghwan accused his former secretary and several other members of absconding with several million dollars of the commune's assets. Other alleged crimes involved with the commune included arson and attempted murder. Rajneesh, an alien, under investigation by the state and several federal agencies, was arrested as a fugitive in North Carolina in October. Under a plea bargain arrangement with federal authorities, Rajneesh pleaded guilty in November to two counts of violating U.S. immigration law. He was fined $400,000, received a suspended sentence, and left the United States.

L. CARL AND JoAnn BRANDHORST
Western Oregon State College

OREGON • Information Highlights

Area: 97,073 sq mi (251 419 km²).
Population (July 1, 1984 est.): 2,674,000.
Chief Cities (July 1, 1984 est.): Salem, the capital (1980 census), 89,233; Portland, 365,861; Eugene, 101,602.
Government (1985): *Chief Officers*—governor, Victor Atiyeh (R); secretary of state, Barbara Roberts (D); *Legislative Assembly*—Senate, 30 members; House of Representatives, 60 members.
State Finances (fiscal year 1984): *Revenues,* $4,981,000,000; *expenditures,* $4,443,000,000.
Personal Income (1984): $31,052,000,000; per capita, $11,611.
Labor Force (June 1985): *Civilian labor force,* 1,335,600; *unemployed,* 125,200 (9.4% of total force).
Education: *Enrollment* (fall 1983)—public elementary schools, 307,121; public secondary, 139,988; colleges and universities, 141,172. *Public school expenditures* (1982–83), $1,417,392,505 ($3,504 per pupil).

OTTAWA

Despite a slump in the high-technology industry and a restraint on civil-service growth imposed by the new Conservative government, Ottawa enjoyed a relatively prosperous year in 1985.

With declining enrollment, several city high schools were to be closed. Under intense local pressure, the trustees were unable to agree on which schools to choose. The problem was compounded by uncertainties created by full funding for Roman Catholic high schools, which may attract students from the reduced public system. Proposals to amalgamate the city and county public schools boards were revived again.

A severe shortage of rental accommodation, with consequent high rents, has hit lower income groups very hard. How best to face the problem has been a major concern of the city council. Attempts have been made to restrict the conversion of rental units into condominiums, and an official report in September suggested that the city itself purchase apartment buildings for rental.

Mayor Marion Dewar decided not to run for reelection. After a hard-fought election contest between two aldermen—Marlene Catterall, representing the "progressive" wing, and Jim Durrell—Durrell was the winner and new mayor following the November election.

A building boom transforming the downtown area did not slacken in 1985. Many new buildings were finished, and others were under construction. The city government announced that a new city hall would be built and the regional government would build a new headquarters. The new National Gallery and the new Museum of Man under construction by the federal government were facing huge cost overruns.

Transportation, a contentious issue in the past, was less so in 1985. Although costs on the Transitway soared from C$60 million to over $300 million, the Regional Council's refusal to permit an audit has upset many.

The regional city of Kanata, center of the high-tech industries, found itself embarrassed financially when the Continental Bank, which held many of its funds, failed in September.

PETER J. KING, *Carleton University*

PAKISTAN

In accordance with President Mohammad Zia ul-Haq's civilianization program, parliamentary and provincial elections were held in February 1985, for the first time since the declaration of martial law in 1977. Although the elections were held on a nonparty basis and opposition leaders were prohibited from publicizing their call for a boycott, turnout was relatively strong, and the elections were generally regarded as fair, unlike the nationwide referendum held two months earlier. Although voters generally ignored the boycott call of the 11-party opposition Movement for the Restoration of Democracy (MRD), they also registered their displeasure with the military regime by defeating seven of General Zia's ministers.

General Zia named veteran Sindhi politician Mohammad Khan Junejo prime minister, but his choice for assembly speaker, Khwaja Muhammad Safdar, was defeated by former cabinet member Fakhr Imam. Imam's wife, Abida Hussein, was the only woman elected to the National Assembly from a nonreserved constituency.

Civilianization. Throughout the remainder of the year several steps were taken to devolve power and responsibility gradually on the civilian government and elected representatives. In March a constitutional order was issued by President Zia, which restored much of the 1973 constitution, though in amended form. Despite Zia's earlier ideological opposition to political parties, the members of the assembly debated the reestablishment of legal parties. In October they passed amendments to the constitution preparatory to the promised lifting of martial law by the end of 1985. Some of these changes gave legal protection to Zia and the military for actions taken during the martial law period, but another abolished the provision for a military council, which Zia had earlier introduced.

These developments served, at least in the short run, to isolate the MRD leaders who had sat out the elections in expectation of a successful boycott. The opposition politicians continued to portray the activities of the elected representatives as a shadow play and to predict that the civilianization process would be derailed just as elections had been in 1977 and 1979. Both Zia and the elected officials readily admitted that steady progress toward the lifting of martial law and the restoration of a fully civilian order would be needed in order to maintain the credibility of the process.

PAKISTAN · Information Highlights

Official Name: Islamic Republic of Pakistan.
Location: South Asia.
Area: 310,403 sq mi (803 943 km²).
Population (mid-1985 est.): 99,200,000.
Capital (1981 census): Islamabad, 201,000.
Government: *Head of state,* Mohammad Zia ul-Haq, president (took power July 5, 1977). *Head of government,* Mohammad Khan Junego, prime minister (installed April 10, 1985). *Legislature*— Parliament: Senate and National Assembly.
Monetary Unit: Rupee (15.98 rupees equal U.S.$1, Nov. 4, 1985).
Gross National Product (1984 U.S.$): $31,000,-000,000.
Economic Index (1984): *Consumer Prices* (1977 = 100), all items, 175.4; food, 173.1.
Foreign Trade (1984 U.S.$): *Imports,* $5,884,000,000; *exports,* $3,219,000,000.

President Mohammad Zia ul-Haq deposits his ballot in February parliamentary and provincial elections—Pakistan's first since the declaration of martial law in 1977.

AP/Wide World

Pakistan People's Party leader Benazir Bhutto returned to Pakistan to handle the funeral ceremonies for her brother Shahnawaz, who died under mysterious circumstances in France in August. Although General Zia had previously given assurances that she would be safe, she was placed under house arrest shortly after the funeral, held for two months, and expelled from the country.

At year-end, Zia declared an end to martial law and urged his critics to give the new government a chance.

Ethnic Issues. Sporadic ethnic violence erupted in Karachi between two immigrant groups, Urdu-speaking Biharis and Muhajirs and Pushtu-speaking Pathans, when, in mid-April, a bus, carelessly driven by a Pathan, killed two female students and injured several others. It took days for police to restore order, and violence erupted again between the same groups a month later. Sunni-Shia clashes in Quetta in early July resulted in more than 20 deaths and 600 arrests and led to a curfew and the closing of educational institutions. Regional tensions were manifested in a water dispute between Punjab and Sind, which interrupted agricultural production, and in a set of demands by opposition leaders, both in Pakistan and in exile, for the replacement of present constitutional arrangements with a confederal system that would allocate most governmental functions to the four Pakistani provinces.

Economy. Pakistan's economy grew by about 8.5% in 1984–85, less than the predicted 10% but considerably better than the 3.5% the year before. Pakistan's real growth of more than 6% annually during the 1980s has brought the country to the threshold of middle-income status. Although inflation was held to about 7.5%, Pakistan suffered increased budgetary deficits, further depreciation of the rupee against the U.S. dollar, and deterioration in the balance of payments.

Bad weather led to a decline in wheat production and the first wheat imports in four years. Imports, estimated at about 1 million tons in 1984–1985, were expected to increase.

Foreign Relations. Pakistan endured pressures on both its Afghan and Indian borders. Continued incursions of Afghan and Soviet aircraft led Pakistan to acquire hand-held Stinger anti-aircraft missiles from the United States. The Soviet Union maintained diplomatic pressure on Pakistan, especially during Zia's visit to Moscow in the spring. The Geneva talks on Afghanistan proceeded without tangible progress.

Dialogue with India over normalization of relations was interrupted several times by India's accusations and alarms concerning Pakistani support to dissident Sikhs in Punjab and Pakistan's alleged nuclear weapons program. Potentially more serious were continued skirmishes among Pakistani and Indian troops in Kashmir, particularly over control of the undemarcated Siachin Glacier.

WILLIAM L. RICHTER
Kansas State University

PARAGUAY

Municipal elections, speculation on the political succession, economic problems, and a postponed diplomatic trip were the principal news topics in Paraguay in 1985.

Politics and Government. Municipal elections were held throughout Paraguay on October 20. The official Colorado Party claimed a landslide victory, with its candidates winning some 700,000 votes. Loyal opposition parties received fewer than 90,000 of the ballots tallied, and election critics alleged that widespread electoral fraud had occurred.

Party activity was dominated by a deepening split among the ruling Colorados. Opposing factions within the party—denominated "traditionalists" and "militants"—aspired to name the party's standard-bearer once that role is relinquished by Gen. Alfredo Stroessner, 73,

PARAGUAY · Information Highlights

Official Name: Republic of Paraguay.
Location: Central South America.
Area: 157,046 sq mi (406 750 km²).
Population (mid-1985 est.): 3,600,000.
Chief City (1982 census): Asunción, the capital, 455,517.
Government: *Head of state and government,* Gen. Alfredo Stroessner, president (took office 1954). *Legislature*—Congress: Senate and Chamber of Deputies.
Gross Domestic Product (1984 U.S.$): $2,500,-000,000.
Foreign Trade (1983 U.S.$): *Imports,* $506,000,000; *exports,* $284,000,000.

who has exercised executive power since 1954. Traditionalists maintained that Stroessner should retire at the end of his current term, which ends in 1988; they unofficially favored a civilian, Luis Argaña, president of the supreme court, as Stroessner's successor. Meanwhile, the "militants" favored yet another presidential term for Stroessner and announced in August their preference for Gustavo Stroessner, an air force lieutenant colonel, to succeed his father.

Economy. An adamant government refused to devalue the guaraní. Upper echelons of the central bank were replaced in September after requesting a devaluation. It had been suggested to the government that the 1986 budget be prepared using a devalued exchange rate of 240 guaranís to the dollar for payments on the external debt and 320 guaranís to the dollar for governmental imports. Because of uncertainty over the value of the guaraní, there were runs on commercial banks, and the central bank was losing $50 million of its reserves each month. The free market rate for available dollars had topped 1,000 guaranís by September.

With construction completed on the giant Itaipú hydroelectric facility, economically depressed Paraguay urged a start-up on the construction phase of Yacyretá, another long-delayed hydroelectric project on the Paraná River, to be built jointly with Argentina. The U.S. Export-Import bank signed a $400 million agreement with both Paraguay and Argentina in March to help finance purchases of American-built power plant turbines. Argentina's economy minister, however, was opposed to Yacyretá. The Argentine head of the binational project claimed in June that the only way to save Yacyretá was to reduce its cost. Such action would require a renegotiation of the 1974 construction agreement and an accord on a more realistic exchange rate for the guaraní.

While investments severely declined because of a deteriorating economic climate, the government expressed optimism over oil exploration. Two U.S. corporations, Anschutz and Chesapeake International, were awarded exploratory contracts for areas near the Bolivian and Argentine borders. Aimed at covering the domestic demand for wheat, a 1985 national program called for placing 370,500 acres (150-000 ha) under cultivation.

Foreign Relations. President Stroessner's long-planned state visit to West Germany, homeland of his father, was postponed until sometime in 1986. The invitation to the Paraguayan leader had come through the intercession of Franz Josef Strauss, head of the Bavarian state government. Some officials of West German Chancellor Helmut Kohl's government did not want the visit to take place, charging that Stroessner was internationally scorned because of his record on human rights and friendship with Nazi fugitives and drug smugglers.

LARRY L. PIPPIN, *University of the Pacific*

PENNSYLVANIA

The economy was the dominant public concern in Pennsylvania in 1985. With no major elections (except in Pittsburgh, where Mayor Richard Caliguiri easily won reelection), public attention focused on money and jobs.

Economy. No single picture of the state's economy emerged in 1985. Some areas, primarily eastern counties associated with service industries, recovered strongly from the recession of the early 1980s. Other areas, mostly rural counties and western counties associated with Pennsylvania's traditional smokestacks and steel mills, continued to suffer.

Agriculture is the state's largest single industry, but low prices for farm products and heavy debt burdens threatened many Pennsylvania farmers with bankruptcy. The manufacturing sector, especially durable goods, also did poorly in 1985. Manufacturing employment declined 2.6% and steel production dropped below one million tons per month. Pennsylvania's share of America's steel production fell

PENNSYLVANIA · Information Highlights

Area: 45,308 sq mi (117 348 km²).
Population (July 1, 1984 est.): 11,901,000.
Chief Cities (July 1, 1984 est.): Harrisburg, the capital (1980 census), 53,264; Philadelphia, 1,646,713; Pittsburgh, 402,583; Erie, 117,461; Allentown, 103,899.
Government (1985): *Chief Officers*—governor, Richard L. Thornburgh (R); lt. gov., William W. Scranton III. *Legislature*—Senate, 50 members; House of Representatives, 203 members.
State Finances (fiscal year 1984): *Revenues,* $18,985,000,000; *expenditures,* $16,601,000,000.
Personal Income (1984): $146,545,000,000; *per capita,* $12,314.
Labor Force (June 1985): *Civilian labor force,* 5,685,000; *unemployed,* 517,300 (9.1% of total force).
Education: *Enrollment* (fall 1983)—public elementary schools, 1,130,767; public secondary, 607,185; colleges and universities, 545,112. *Public school expenditures* (1982–83), $5,465,364,449 ($3,329 per pupil).

from 15.7% in mid-1984 to 12.9% in mid-1985. The Pittsburgh-based Wheeling-Pittsburgh Steel Corporation filed for bankruptcy on April 16.

Although employment overall rose 3.3% in the year and unemployment was down to 7.5% by August, these figures reflected a shift in jobs from the relatively high-paying manufacturing sector to the generally lower-paying service sector.

Budget and Taxes. During the recession of the early 1980s, Republican Gov. Richard L. Thornburgh had raised taxes and cut state support for many programs. By 1985, however, the state had a projected budget surplus of $200 million. Thornburgh and the divided legislature (a Democratic House and a Republican Senate) thus debated program enhancements and tax cuts rather than which programs should be slashed and whose taxes should be raised.

The $9.3 billion budget approved at the July 1 start of the fiscal year cut personal income taxes from 2.35% to 2.2% as of Jan. 1, 1986, gave businesses certain tax benefits, and slightly increased the budgets of most programs and departments. A new "rainy day" fund to offset the need for tax increases during hard times was allocated $25 million, and another $25 million was allocated to a "sunny day" fund to pay for new efforts to attract industries to the state. The state's emergency food aid program was increased to $9 million after the Democrats defeated Thornburgh's recommendation to eliminate the program.

Regional Cooperation. In 1985, Pennsylvania signed the Great Lakes Charter, in which the eight Great Lakes states, Ontario, and Quebec agreed to consult one another on proposed major projects involving diversion or consumption of lake water, and joined Maryland and Virginia as a member of the Chesapeake Bay Commission, which recommends measures to manage the bay.

Nuclear Power. Over the objections of antinuclear groups and the state government, the Nuclear Regulatory Commission approved the restart of the undamaged reactor at Three Mile Island; it produced electricity for the first time since the 1979 accident on October 3.

Other Events. On March 14, the worst system of tornadoes to hit the United States since 1974 struck hardest in northwestern Pennsylvania, where 64 people died and 12 counties were declared eligible for federal disaster aid.

John J. Torquato, Jr., the founder of Computer Technology Associates, was among those convicted of bribing public officials to gain contracts. Although testimony at the trial implicated Republican State Treasurer R. Budd Dwyer, only lower-level officials were convicted.

A May 13 police assault on a Philadelphia house containing members of the radical MOVE group caused a fire that left 11 MOVE members dead and destroyed 61 houses. (*See also* PHILADELPHIA.) In Pittsburgh, a downtown subway officially opened on July 3.

ROBERT E. O'CONNOR
The Pennsylvania State University

PERU

On July 28, 36-year-old Alan García Pérez was sworn in as president of Peru, succeeding 72-year-old Fernando Belaúnde Terry. In his inaugural address, García said Peru would limit payments on its $13.6 billion foreign debt to 10% of the nation's export earnings, seek an end to the five-year war with Sendero Luminoso (Shining Path) guerrillas, and combat the illegal cocaine industry.

Election Returns. García, leader of the center-left American Popular Revolutionary Alliance (APRA), won 3,457,030 votes, or 47.7% of an estimated 7,200,000 votes. This was more than twice the total for the candidate of the United Left coalition (IU), Alfonso Barrantes Lingán, mayor of Lima. Javier Alva Orlandini, candidate of Belaúnde's Popular Action Party (AP), won only 6.3%, an indicator of widespread dissatisfaction with the government whose election in 1980 ended 12 years of military rule.

The APRA also won 32 seats in the 60-member Senate to 16 for the IU coalition and 107 seats in the 180-member Chamber of Deputies to 48 for IU, 18 for the Popular Christian Party, and 7 for AP.

Optimism and Reformist Zeal. Exuding self-confidence, García frequently appeared on a balcony of the presidential palace to engage in lively exchanges with passing crowds. In one appearance in August he announced an $800 ceiling on monthly salaries of government employees. He also informed the enthusiastic crowd that gathered that he had ordered a reduction in personnel assigned to embassies abroad and was selling expensive diplomatic residences in Washington, DC, and New York.

In an effort to clean out police corruption, 21 of 43 generals in the Civil Guard and 16 of 53 generals in the Peruvian Investigative Police (PIP) were retired.

Human Rights Concern. In a decision without precedent, García removed Gen. César Enrico Praeli, chief of the Armed Forces Joint Command, September 26 as part of a change in strategy to combat the Sendero Luminoso and the Tupac Amaru Revolutionary Movement, an urban guerrilla group that surfaced in 1984. Army generals Sinesio Jarama and Wilfredo Mori, commanders in the Central Andes Second Military Region and Ayacucho, respectively, were relieved of their commands after a military investigation found an army patrol guilty of the August 19 massacre of 40 peasants in Purayacu, north of Ayacucho. It was the first

time that a civilian government or its military admitted that soldiers had killed civilians not directly linked to the Sendero Luminoso.

Drugs Combated. Deputy Interior Minister Augustín Mantilla announced in August that Colombia and the United States had cooperated in dismantling three cocaine laboratories and airstrips in the Amazon region. Police also arrested two Peruvians boarding a Venezuelan airliner bound for Italy with a cargo of pure cocaine worth an estimated $130 million. In March, 59 persons were arrested in Peru, Southern California, and Miami, FL.

Papal Visit. At the Ayacucho Airport on February 3, Pope John Paul II urged rebels to lay down their arms and "seek the roads of dialogue and not . . . violence." He exhorted Peruvian officials to correct social injustices.

Economic Measures. García said Peru would repay its foreign debt but pointed out that export earnings, estimated at $3.1 billion in 1985, were not enough to cover interest and principal of $3.7 billion due in 1985. Foreign banks rolled over $1.85 billion in interest, which fell due May 13 after Peru made token payments in January, March, and May to avoid a "value-impaired status." Negotiations began September 13 to roll over other debts due.

Oil exploration contracts with Occidental Petroleum and Belco Petroleum were canceled August 29 on the grounds that the companies had failed to use 1980 tax reductions to boost exploration. Production was estimated at 185,000 barrels per day (bpd), but domestic consumption increased to 120,000 bpd.

On August 1 the government increased the minimum wage to about $38 a month from just over $26, increased the prices of many basic foodstuffs to stimulate agricultural productivity, and then froze wages and prices. Interest rates were lowered from 260% to 110% and the sol was devalued. Later, García announced Peru was reducing to 13 the 26 Mirage-2000 fighters ordered in 1982 from France.

NEALE J. PEARSON, *Texas Tech University*

PHILADELPHIA

The building boom in downtown Philadelphia continued in 1985, when ground was broken for a controversial 60-story office complex —the first downtown structure that will rise higher than City Hall. Despite a strike against the city's two major newspapers that hurt local businesses, the unemployment rate continued to decline, although nearly two thirds of the metropolitan area work force now is employed in the suburbs rather than in the city proper. Racial tensions flared in the predominantly white Elmwood neighborhood, where a state of emergency was imposed on November 22.

The most widely discussed event of the year, however, was the May 13 police assault on a house occupied by members of a radical group known as MOVE. The incident attracted national attention and reduced public confidence in the administration of Mayor W. Wilson Goode, previously considered one of the nation's most promising black politicians.

The small antiestablishment, antitechnology MOVE group had long posed problems for city officials; a similar confrontation in 1978 led to the death of a police officer and murder convictions for nine MOVE members. Some members of the group later moved into a middle-class neighborhood in West Philadelphia, where they broadcast threats and obscenities over loudspeakers, fortified their house, and violated numerous health and building codes. Residents urged city authorities to act.

Early on the morning of May 13, after unsuccessful negotiations, police evacuated the neighborhood and issued an eviction notice. Attempts to dislodge the armed MOVE members with water cannon, gunfire, and tear gas failed. At 5:27 P.M., a police helicopter dropped a bomb onto the building's rooftop bunker. By the time the ensuing fire was declared under control, a two-block area lay in ruins and 11 persons in the MOVE house, including at least four children, were dead.

It remained unclear why the bomb was dropped in a city neighborhood, why firefighters waited so long to begin to battle the blaze, and why more efforts were not made to encourage the MOVE adults to permit the children to leave the building. City Managing Director Leo A. Brooks and Police Commissioner Gregore J. Sambor subsequently resigned, and the officials involved made contradictory statements during a televised inquiry by a commission appointed by Mayor Goode. The commission's report was due early in 1986. Kevin M. Tucker, a native of Brooklyn, NY, was named police commissioner, effective Jan. 1, 1986.

Meanwhile, the city is rebuilding the 61 row houses destroyed by the fire and repairing 82 other homes in the neighborhood, at an estimated total cost of $10 million.

ROBERT E. O'CONNOR

PHILIPPINES

The 20-year rule of Philippine President Ferdinand E. Marcos, 68, was challenged on two fronts in 1985: a rapidly escalating Communist insurgency and an increasingly active political opposition. And the 1983 murder of Marcos' chief rival, Benigno Aquino, Jr., continued to have reverberations.

Aquino Trial. The trial of Gen. Fabian Ver, on leave as armed forces chief, and 25 military codefendants for Aquino's murder began in February and lasted seven months. The Supreme Court, meanwhile, had thrown out much of the evidence against Ver, a close Marcos confidant. When the verdict finally was handed down in December, there was little surprise. General Ver and the other defendants were found not guilty. As early as February, President Marcos had stated that the general would automatically be reinstated as chief of staff if acquitted.

Insurgency. The rebel New People's Army grew by an estimated 20% during the year, reaching some 16,500 combatants. Through October, according to the military, 4,500 persons died as a result of the rebellion—2,100 Communists, 1,200 government soldiers, and 1,200 civilians. For the first time, the insurgents engaged the 200,000-strong Philippine armed forces in company- and battalion-size operations. At least 20% of Philippine villages were believed to be in the hands of the insurgents, who had a military presence in 62 of 73 provinces. The rebels' political arm, the National Democratic Front, had some 1 million members. U.S. officials foresaw a "strategic stalemate" in three to five years, but President Marcos predicted victory within the year if additional aid were forthcoming from the United States.

Politics. The non-Communist opposition also continued to resist Marcos' continuance in power. A move in the legislature to have him impeached was blocked in August, but demonstrations continued throughout the year. August 21, the anniversary of Aquino's murder, saw especially large rallies. September 19–21, the 13th anniversary of the declaration of martial law, saw the year's most violent incidents. In Negros province, police fired into a crowd of 15,000 anti-Marcos demonstrators, killing 20.

In early November, before the situation worsened further, President Marcos asked for a presidential election in January 1986. An election was not constitutionally scheduled until 1987, but Marcos said he was anxious to demonstrate his popular support. The legality of moving up the vote was questioned, but a date of February 7 was set. In December, after extended talks, two leading opposition figures announced that they would join forces on a single ticket. Corazon Aquino, the widow of the Laban party's Benigno Aquino, would run as president; Salvador (Doy) Laurel of the Unido party would run as vice-president.

Economy. The Philippine economy continued to falter. The gross national product, which fell by 5.5% in 1984, was expected to decline another 3.5% for 1985. One positive aspect of the retrogression, however, was a reduction in the country's previously spiraling inflation. The impact of the failing economy was felt most dramatically by the already poor, especially in rural areas. Unemployment rose as high as 30%. Negros province was especially hard hit by a decline in sugar exports. The government contended that the economic problems were caused in part by conditions attached to a December 1984 loan by the International Monetary Fund (IMF). U.S. involvement in the Philippine economy remained substantial, as the total American private investment reached some $2 billion, or about half the foreign investment in the Philippines. Most of the nation's $26 billion debt was owed to U.S. or U.S.-financed institutions.

Foreign Relations. With the two largest U.S. overseas military bases—Clark Air Force Base and Subic Bay Naval Base—located in the Philippines, Washington expressed growing concern over the expanding insurgency. Further U.S. concern resulted from a Soviet naval and air buildup at Cam Ranh Bay across the South China Sea in Vietnam.

The United States remained obligated to provide the Philippines with $180 million annually as part of the pact (which expires in 1991) for use of the Clark and Subic Bay bases. In November the U.S. Senate approved a military construction bill providing $104 million for improvements at the bases.

Washington also was concerned with the welfare of U.S. nationals in the Philippines; 15 Americans had been killed in two years of insurgency, two by government forces.

RICHARD BUTWELL
California State University, Dominguez Hills

PHILIPPINES · Information Highlights

Official Name: Republic of the Philippines.
Location: Southeast Asia.
Area: 116,000 sq mi (300 440 km²).
Population (mid-1985 est.): 56,800,000.
Chief Cities (1980 census): Manila, the capital, 1,630,485; Quezon City, 1,165,865; Davao, 610,375; Cebu, 490,281.
Government: *Head of state,* Ferdinand E. Marcos, president (took office Dec. 30, 1965). *Head of government,* César Virata, premier (appointed April 8, 1981). *Legislature* (unicameral)—National Assembly.
Monetary Unit: Peso (19.1 pesos equal U.S.$1, Dec. 31, 1985).
Gross National Product (1984 U.S.$): $32,093,-000,000.
Economic Index (1984): *Consumer Prices,* (1972 = 100), all items, 286.4; food, 271.4.
Foreign Trade (1984 prelim. U.S.$): *Imports,* $5,928,000,000; *exports,* $5,348,000,000.

PHOTOGRAPHY

The year 1985 saw the long-awaited introduction of the world's first production-line auto-focusing single-lens reflex (SLR) camera, the Minolta Maxxum 7000, which features the most complete automation of any camera ever. And the burgeoning of electronic photography —evident in both video products and still-camera exploration, as well as silver-image hybrid devices—continued relentlessly.

In the fine-art sphere, museum-quality photography spread out from New York, as evidenced by impressive collections in institutions throughout the country. Photographic art using computer technology, though still evident in New York showplaces, took a backseat to photojournalism, which made a comeback not in magazines but in galleries and art museums.

Equipment. Not since the introduction of the Canon AE-1 in 1976, which ushered in the automatic-exposure age, has any camera generated as much interest as Minolta's 35mm Maxxum. This fastest auto-focusing marvel has multimode, multiprogrammed operation, with automatic film loading, motorized film transport and rewinding, and DX film cartridge reading for the film speed. Its greatest claim to fame is that it has an AF motor built into the camera body rather than individual lenses, the 12 "dedicated" (specifically devoted) optics embracing focal lengths from 24mm to 300mm, including five macro zooms. The Program Flash 2800 AF and 4000 AF were also new in 1985. And in the 35mm rangefinder arena, the classic camera appears in the latest stage of its legendary evolution, the Leica M6.

In the meantime, at the annual Photographic Manufacturers Association (PMA) show, independent lens makers brought out longer, lighter, more compact zooms than ever before: Soligor introduced a 35–200mm f/3.5–4.8 one-touch zoom that is 124mm long and weighs 23 oz (.65 kg). Of particular interest on the PMA trade-show floor were hundreds of telescopes offered for the astro-photographic event of a lifetime, the coming of Halley's Comet.

In the video sphere, compactness was also the virtue of Sony's tiny new Video 8 system, the smallest video yet. At 2.2 lbs (1 kg) and measuring 2.2 x 4.3 x 8.5 inches (5.6 x 10.9 x 21.6 cm), it is not much longer than the videotape itself and can fit into a purse or small camera case. The Mini-8 camera and Mini-8 portable player together cost $1,800. And from Fuji and Konica came prototype electronic still cameras with plenty of video accessories.

Last but not least in the hardware arena was a new state-of-the-art enlarger head for 4x5 enlargers. The Beseler/Minolta 45A Enlarger Light Source combines in a single unit the functions of a color head, color analyzer, and voltage stabilizer. Also for the darkroom, but in the software sphere, no less than seven new color-printing papers were shown by four manufacturers, including Agfacolor Type 8 Paper, Agfa-Gevaert's newest entry in the color-print-from-a-color-negative race, and its Agfachrome Color Reversal Paper, for making prints from slides. And in black-and-white, a new but old-fashioned contact paper came from Pal of California and Frankfurt am Main, West Germany—a silver chloride paper said to be slightly faster and far more inexpensive than Kodak's classic Azo.

Exhibitions and Books. At the Museum of Modern Art (MoMA) in New York, to complete the four-part exhibition series of the work of the 19th-century photographer Eugène Atget (started in 1981 and supported by Springs Industries) parts III and IV were on view simultaneously: "The Work of Atget—The Ancien Régime" (1901–27), lyrical views of the châteaus and gardens owned by French aristocracy; and "Modern Times" (1898–1927) with straightforward depictions of ordinary commerce and everyday amusements in Parisian

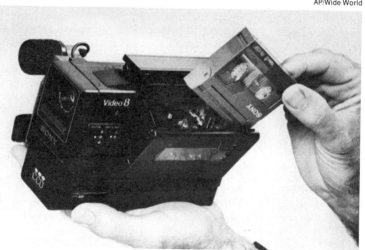

Sony introduced the Video 8 system, an 8mm portable video camera recorder.

AP/Wide World

"Meudon, 1923" was a highlight of an André Kertész retrospective in Chicago and later in New York City.

society as it moved into the 20th century. Also available were two companion books, with the same names as the exhibitions, coauthored by John Szarkowski and Maria Morris Hambourg. (In 1985, Hambourg became the Metropolitan Museum's new curator of photography, replacing Weston Naef, who moved to the J.P. Getty Museum in Malibu, CA.)

The active West Coast photography scene was highlighted by the Getty Museum, which in one sensational purchase of four leading photography collections ensured that Los Angeles would become an important international center of photographic studies. Meanwhile, at the San Francisco Museum of Art, three exhibitions from its 20th-century collection demonstrated that it, too, is a photographic institution of international scope and standing.

Back in New York, master photographers received kudos. "Aaron Siskind: 50 Years," a stunning retrospective, was held at the International Center of Photography (ICP). That 11-year-old museum, the first in the United States to be devoted exclusively to photography, also held its first annual Awards Dinner on April 23. The 91-year-old Hungarian-born André Kertész was the recipient of its first Master of Photography award. A retrospective of his ephemeral images, called "André Kertész of Paris and New York," was on view at the Art Institute of Chicago during the summer and later moved to the Metropolitan Museum in New York. The celebrated photographer died in New York City on September 27. Meanwhile, Abbeville Press published his autobiography.

The photography world also mourned the death in late 1984 of Lee Witkin, who created the first successful wholly photographic gallery in recent times, the Witkin Gallery in New York. The work of Robert Frank, however, another man who triggered a photographic revolution, once again graced gallery walls. In the mid-1950s, the Swiss-born émigré, armed with a Leica and Guggenheim grant, set out on a photographic odyssey that resulted in a book called *The Americans,* which did as much to change the face of photography as any single collection of pictures before or since. In 1985 one New York gallery showed his vintage prints from the 1940s and 1950s; another gallery, in a show called "Home Improvements," exhibited some of his more recent 20 x 24–inch (51 x 61–cm) Polaroids, which reflected a more spontaneous and improvisational approach.

Images using computer-based technology—teleprinters, X rays, high voltage dischargers, and photocopy machines—also made their appearance in New York. Seventeen "artists using advanced technology" were shown at the Fashion Institute of Technology, while "Simulacra: Forms without Substance," computer-generated portraits by Nancy Burson at ICP, was the first in a series there called "New Directions." Many of these photographic images, which bear absolutely no connection to any external reality, were regarded by critics as elementary in impact despite their technical sophistication.

The contrasting trend, and one that possibly reflects a renewal of social consciousness, was the incorporation in the fine art field of photojournalism—images made primarily for the sake of reportage, not personal expression. Major retrospectives were held for the legendary Robert Capa at ICP and for W. Eugene Smith at the Philadelphia Museum of Art. The primary interest in such exhibitions was historical, with attention focused on work from the 1930s to the 1950s.

Of particular interest were Richard Avedon's "In the American West," sponsored by the Amon Carter Museum in Fort Worth, TX, consisting of life-size and larger portraits of miners, drifters, and drinkers; "The Indelible Image: Photographs of War, 1846 to the Present" at New York University; "A Summer's Day," colorful sweet-sad images by Joel Meyerowitz at the Brooklyn Museum; and, at the Corcoran in Washington, DC, the final installment of a three-part series on photojournalism called "The New York School," with work by Diane Arbus and Bruce Davidson.

Also in Washington, at the National Gallery of Art, a 75-print "museum set" of what the late photographer considered his greatest work appeared in a show called "Ansel Adams: Classic Images."

BARBARA L. LOBRON
Free-lance Writer, Editor, and Photographer

PHYSICS

In 1985 a huge new accelerator was proposed, new neutron scattering facilities were near completion, and neutral atoms were trapped.

Elementary Particle Physics. With the discoveries of the W and Z particles at the European Center for Nuclear Research (CERN) in Geneva, Switzerland, in 1983 and the top quark in 1984, the electroweak theory seemed confirmed. Quarks are considered the basic components of matter, with such exotic properties as fractional electric charge. There are now six quarks—up and down, strange and charm, bottom and top. In the electroweak theory the intermediate vector bosons (W^+, W^-, and Z^0) transfer the force for the weak interactions, just as the photon does for the electromagnetic interaction. Emphasis now has turned to detailed studies of the W and Z particles. At CERN a new large electron-positron ring with a 16.7-mi (27-km) circumference was under construction in 1985, while at Stanford, CA, a 2-mi (3.2-km) linear accelerator was being modified to function as a colliding beam machine. Both projects are designed to produce large numbers of Z^0 particles.

Superconducting Super Collider. Many theorists believe that new advances in particle physics will require significantly higher energies. The proposed Superconducting Super Collider (SSC) would be the biggest and most expensive accelerator ever built. The American design calls for two colliding beams of protons of 20 TeV each (1 TeV = 10^{12}eV). The circumference of the beam's orbit would be at least 62 mi (100 km). The cost has been estimated at more than $5 billion. According to President Reagan's science adviser, G. A. Keyworth II, the SSC would "stimulate interest in science and excellence far across society." Many U.S. scientists fear, however, that for the SSC to be built, compensating cutbacks in other research areas would be required.

Such an accelerator would require international cooperation. CERN physicists proposed an accelerator that would be similar to the SSC but would use higher-powered superconducting magnets in the tunnel being built for the electron-positron collider. By using existing facilities, CERN physicists claim that their accelerator could perform the same experiments as the SSC but for less than $1 billion.

Neutron Scattering and Condensed Matter. Neutron scattering provides information that complements that obtained by charged particles and photons. Thermal neutrons have been used for a generation in structural investigations of materials. Thermal neutrons have wavelengths of an angstrom (10^{-8}cm) and energies about 1/40 eV. Such wavelength and energy are ideally suited for the study of many features of solids. Early work emphasized the use of reactors, and high flux reactors continue to be important for condensed matter studies.

Another approach to the production of neutrons is spallation, the production of neutrons by a high energy beam of charged particles striking a target. A spallation source produces a much larger component of high energy neutrons than does a reactor. A major spallation source at the Rutherford Laboratory in Oxford, England, produced its first neutron irradiation in 1985. When fully operational, the Rutherford facility would be the world's leading source of pulsed neutrons. Shortly after the English success, researchers at Los Alamos National Laboratory stored a beam in the Proton Storage Ring (PSR). The Los Alamos Meson Physics Facility (LAMPF) is an 800 MeV proton linear accelerator nearly 0.6 mi (1 km) long. A neutron research laboratory (WNR) was added to LAMPF to produce neutrons for defense and materials research. This laboratory is being upgraded. PSR will take 1 of every 10 LAMPF pulses and produce short pulses of high maximum intensity. The combination—linear accelerator plus storage ring—will produce almost as intense a beam as the one from Rutherford Laboratory source.

Trapped Ions and Atoms. The trapping of ions and elementary particles has reached a new level, with a single electron confined for nearly a year in a combined electric and magnetic field. Now neutral atoms have been stopped and trapped by the two groups of National Bureau of Standards (NBS) scientists.

For ions, the emphasis has been on the trapping of single particles in small orbits in a combined electric and magnetic field. With single particles in a small volume, new levels of precision are possible. Protons, electrons, and positrons already have been trapped. There is now a proposal to trap an antiproton and measure its parameters as precisely as those for protons.

For spectroscopic studies the ideal would be a group of atoms or molecules at rest. Since the trapping methods work only for very low velocities, the crucial step is to slow the atoms. The required velocities correspond to a temperature of about 1°K, while normal room temperature is about 300°K. Atomic beams have been slowed by laser radiation pressure. The atom absorbs thousands of laser photons before reaching the required velocity of 33 ft (10 m) per second. As the atoms slow, the frequency for resonance photon absorption changes. One has to change the laser frequency to compensate for the decreasing velocity or change the magnetic field in which the atom is decelerating. Both methods now have been applied successfully by NBS scientists. Ultimately such trapped atoms can be used to make much better atomic clocks.

GARY MITCHELL
North Carolina State University

The trial of the accused murderers of Jerzy Popieluszko, a Roman Catholic priest and Solidarity supporter, dominated news in Poland early in 1985. For their roles in the crime, Capt. Grzegorz Piotrowski (left) and police lieutenant Leszek Pekala (center) were sentenced to 25 and 15 years in prison, respectively.

POLAND

Political conflict, government repression, and economic hardships characterized life in Poland during 1985.

The Popieluszko Trial. News in Poland during the early part of the year was dominated by the trial of the accused murderers of the Roman Catholic priest and Solidarity supporter Jerzy Popieluszko. Among those sentenced in February were Security Forces' Capt. Grzegorz Piotrowski and Col. Adam Pietruszka, each of whom received 25 years in prison; and two police lieutenants, Leszek Pekala and Waldemar Chmielewski, who received 15 and 14 years' imprisonment, respectively. The media coverage of the trial of the four secret police officials was without precedent in Poland or any Communist state. Nevertheless, the trial failed to establish, or expose, the involvement of any security personnel beyond Colonel Pietruszka, although the testimony of some of the defendants implied such knowledge and involvement.

Church-State Relations. The murder of Father Popieluszko and the trial of his accused killers fueled church-state conflict to a degree rare even in Communist Poland. In February, Josef Cardinal Glemp charged that government and Communist party authorities were waging a malicious campaign against the church, and he denied the claims of the regime that many priests engaged in subversive activities. Glemp defended the late Father Popieluszko against charges that he had acted illegally, and he pledged to defend the right of clergymen to speak out on religious and moral issues. Meantime, a barrage of charges and threats against the Roman Catholic Church was leveled by various government figures. In mid-February a government spokesman, Jerzy Urban, accused the church of "viciously attacking Poland's socialist system," and of stirring up "hatred." In April, proposals to seize church buildings that were being used for antiregime sermons by priests surfaced in certain party-controlled newspapers. According to one suggestion, the

Gdansk church attended by Lech Walesa (St. Brigida's) and its pro-Solidarity pastor, Henryk Jankowski, were appropriate targets of government shutdowns. In May the minister for religious affairs, Adam Lopatka, declared publicly that there was a "worsening anti-socialist mood" among the nation's priests since the murder of Popieluszko.

There were some signs of an attempt by both church and state in the second half of the year to improve relations, but these did not appear to be very successful. Foreign Minister Stefan Olszowski traveled to the Vatican in June in an attempt to establish full diplomatic relations between Poland and the Holy See. Pope John Paul II declined Poland's offer and reproached its regime for human rights violations.

Economy. Most of the economic news during the year was adverse. Poland's difficulties were compounded by a very harsh winter, which, according to official data released in March, seriously hurt industrial production largely because of energy and raw material shortages.

The government backed away from some harsh price increases on food, fuel, and other basic items that had been discussed in February. The decision to delay or lessen price increases seemed linked to widespread popular unrest and Solidarity plans to protest price hikes with strike actions.

Nevertheless, the government imposed a series of price increases in March, with ten basic food items—including bread, milk, tea, and sugar—rising in price anywhere from 11–75%. The increases averaged 35% of the February price level of those commodities. Shortages of goods in government-run stores led to a great upsurge in black market activity throughout the country and also to increased importance of smuggling of foreign goods from abroad. According to an official report published in December, Poland was experiencing the most acute environmental crisis in Europe, with more than 90% of its rivers too polluted for safe human consumption.

The Solidarity Opposition. Although still outlawed, the Solidarity movement continued as a formidable antagonist to Poland's Communist regime. The year began with most Solidarity activists, led by Lech Walesa himself, rejecting a government amnesty that would require them to give up oppositional activity. In early February, Walesa and other leaders called for a 15-minute symbolic strike to take place on February 28 as a protest against threatened price increases. The government responded by arresting three Solidarity leaders, Wladyslaw Frasyniuk, Adam Michnik, and Bogdan Lis. Walesa was threatened with prosecution and interrogated for alleged incitement to the illegal strike, but he was never prosecuted. (Early in June the three arrested leaders received jail terms ranging from 2½ to 3½ years.) In early May, Solidarity demonstrations, which generally met with violent government response, occurred in several locations in Poland, most notably at the birthplace of Solidarity in Gdansk.

It was officially reported that Miroslaw Milewski, the Politburo member charged with security matters (and apparently involved in the Popieluszko murder), was dismissed from that body and placed under house arrest. On the other hand, the government announced in June new and harsher policies of censorship and curbs on freedom of expression in the universities.

Probably the largest Solidarity demonstration of the year occurred at Czestochowa in mid-September, where some 50,000 Poles joined Lech Walesa in an outdoor rally at the Jasna Gora monastery. The regime's response was a series of arrests among Solidarity leaders and activists. In September, police used clubs and tear gas to disperse Warsaw crowds commemorating the murder of Jerzy Popieluszko. In November the government brought forward new charges of slander against Lech Walesa for allegedly accusing Polish election officials of issuing fraudulent voting reports. Again, Walesa escaped trial and continued in his special, anomalous role—a defiant leader of an illegal movement who was himself at liberty. The government promised to release most of the arrested Solidarity activists after the October parliamentary elections, but the new amnesty appeared to exclude Michnik, Frasyniuk, and Lis, among others. As for Walesa, the regime seemed to be fearful of the consequences of jailing him. In late November the regime fired more than 30 top academicians, apparently as punishment for their political views.

Parliamentary Elections. On October 13, Poland held its first parliamentary elections since 1980, with the opposition Solidarity movement calling for a boycott by the country's 26 million eligible voters. General Jaruzelski, on the other hand, promised an amnesty for 280 (acknowledged) political prisoners if the turnout in the election exceeded 75%. Jaruzelski appealed to the people to "boycott the boycott." The actual result of the voting for Poland's unicameral 460-member parliament (Sejm) was never in doubt. The Communist party controlled the nomination of all the candidates on the ballot and directly assigned itself and its two adjunct parties (Peasant and Democratic) 85% of the seats. In most districts, voters were given a choice between two candidates, but in such cases they were always of the same party or pro-regime orientation.

In the aftermath of the election, the government claimed a turnout of about 78%, which was the lowest official figure since the first parliamentary election under the Communist system in 1947. Solidarity sources claimed the actual turnout was closer to 65%. Elections were marred by Solidarity protests and demonstrations in various locations throughout Poland. The regime interpreted the results as an indication of success for its "social stabilization" policies, and it called on the Western powers to restore normal economic and political relations with Poland.

Party and Government Changes. The most visible change in the Polish regime occurred in November, when Gen. Wojciech Jaruzelski gave up his post of premier, a position then assumed by 56-year-old Deputy Premier Zbigniew Messner. The latter, an economist, was politically identified as a loyal follower of the general. Jaruzelski retained his most critical position, that of first secretary of the Polish United Workers' (Communist) Party and was believed to be devoting more time to the task of revitalizing the organization and rank and file of the party. The party lost about one third of its membership (nearly one million) since the imposition of martial law in 1981. While relinquishing the premiership, Jaruzelski assumed the largely titular office of president of the council of state from Henryk Jablonski. Within

---

POLAND · Information Highlights

Official Name: Polish People's Republic.
Location: Eastern Europe.
Area: 120,700 sq mi (312 612 km²).
Population (mid-1985 est.): 37,300,000.
Chief Cities (Dec. 1983): Warsaw, the capital, 1,641,300; Lodz, 848,500; Cracow, 735,100.
Government: *Head of state,* Gen. Wojciech Jaruzelski, chairman of the Council of State (took office Nov. 6, 1985) and first secretary of the Polish United Workers' Party (took office Oct. 1981). *Head of Government,* Zbigniew Messner, chairman of the Council of Ministers (took office Nov. 6, 1985). *Legislature* (unicameral)—Sejm.
Monetary Unit: Zloty (156.000 zlotys equal U.S.$1, July 1985).
Gross National Product (1983 U.S.$): $203,700,-000,000.
Economic Indexes (1984): *Consumer Prices* (1980 = 100), all items, 341.8; food, 401.9. *Industrial Production* (1980 = 100), 95.
Foreign Trade (1984 U.S.$): *Imports,* $10,585,-000,000; *exports,* $11,697,000,000.

a week of the change at the top, five vice premiers and 13 of the 30 cabinet ministers were fired from their posts. Among those fired was Foreign Minister Stefan Olszowski, who also lost his position in the party's Politburo. Olszowski was replaced by Marian Orzechowski at the foreign ministry. The changes were generally interpreted in Poland as strengthening Jaruzelski's leadership within the party and the government and also as reflective of the regime's reluctance toward any sweeping liberalization policies.

Foreign Relations. In an April meeting held in Warsaw, Poland participated with the Soviet Union and other signatories in a 20-year renewal of the Warsaw Pact, a defense agreement originally concluded in 1955. Soviet leader Mikhail Gorbachev made his first visit to Poland for this meeting. In late April, Poland and the United States agreed to resume regular commercial flights between the two countries suspended since the imposition of martial law in Poland in 1981. Other U.S. sanctions, including a freeze on new credits and denial of most-favored-nation trading status, continued in effect. In February, U.S.-Polish relations were severely strained when Polish authorities detained and then expelled as spies the U.S. military attaché in Warsaw and his wife. A series of reciprocal diplomatic expulsions followed, and Poland suspended air courier service to the American Embassy in Warsaw in May.

In May, Nicaraguan President Daniel Ortega visited Poland as an honored guest. In September, however, there were reports of Polish arms sales to U.S.-backed "contras" in Nicaragua, a transaction apparently prompted by Poland's acute dollar shortage.

Polish representatives attended the Warsaw Pact conference in Prague in November, where Soviet leader Gorbachev reported on the U.S.-Soviet summit. Early in December, President Jaruzelski visited France for talks with President François Mitterrand. It was the first such high-level contact with a Western country since Solidarity was outlawed in 1981.

ALEXANDER J. GROTH
University of California, Davis

POLAR RESEARCH

Antarctic. More than 300 U.S. scientists conducted 99 projects in Antarctica during the 1984–85 austral summer. They worked at three U.S. stations, at remote camps, aboard two U.S. Coast Guard icebreakers, and aboard the research ship *Polar Duke* and the British ship *John Biscoe.*

In January 1985, U.S. Navy pilots, part of the U.S. Antarctic program, flew French glaciologists to the Soviet station Vostok, near the south geomagnetic pole. Part of an international program participated in by the United States, France, and the Soviet Union, the flight enabled French scientists to retrieve an ice core drilled by Soviet scientists from east Antarctic ice near Vostok. Initial testing by French and Soviet scientists indicated that the ice core included a climate record for more than 150,000 years. This record covered a complete cycle, including the last major glacier age and interglacial age, and was expected to help scientists learn more about why glacial ages begin and end.

Between November 1984 and January 1985, two groups of solar astronomers studied the sun to learn about its dynamics and structure from telescopes at the South Pole. In January 1985 the National Academy of Sciences sponsored an international workshop on Antarctica and the Antarctic Treaty. The conference took place at a camp near the Beardmore Glacier in the Transantarctic Mountains.

On Nov. 8, 1984, U.S. President Ronald Reagan signed into law an act that implemented for the United States the Antarctic Treaty Convention on the Conservation of Antarctic Marine Living Resources. This convention, signed by 15 nations in 1980, establishes a conservation standard to ensure the continued health of Antarctic marine organisms.

Arctic. In February 1985, scientists from the National Oceanic and Atmospheric Administration (NOAA) Pacific Marine Environmental Laboratory began studying a polynya (open water in the park ice) near St. Lawrence Island in the Bering Sea. The 2,000-sq mi (5 200-km^2) polynya is a source of heat in an extremely cold area. Coupled with heat transferred between the ocean and the air, the persistence of a polynya strongly affects regional weather and possibly weather in a much larger area. The scientists used instruments placed on the ice and ocean bottom, a research ship, and NOAA weather satellites. They hoped to learn more about weather patterns, wind behavior in the Northern Hemisphere, and ocean currents.

In June 1985, scientists began searching for a drilling site on the Greenland ice sheet. This project, a cooperative effort by U.S., Swiss, and Danish scientists, followed up the three-year project completed in 1981 during which an ice core was drilled through the ice sheet to bedrock. Drilling was scheduled to begin in 1986.

As a result of the Arctic Research and Policy Act of 1984, President Reagan appointed a commission to develop and recommend an integrated Arctic research policy. This group was to work with the Interagency Arctic Research Policy Committee to prepare a comprehensive five-year research plan. The commission held its first meetings in Barrow, Fairbanks, and Anchorage, Alaska, in late June 1985.

WINIFRED REUNING
National Science Foundation

PORTUGAL

The victory of the Social Democratic party (PSD) in fall parliamentary elections brought centrists to power just as the economy, purged of its worst external problems, seemed poised on the brink of recovery.

Politics and Government. The June 13 resignation of 19 PSD ministers and secretaries of state brought down a coalition headed by the Socialist Prime Minister Mário Soares, precipitating the October 6 contests. The middle-of-the-road PSD, successful in downplaying its participation in previous governments, emerged from the balloting with 30% of the vote and 88 of the parliament's 250 seats.

Even though the Social Democrats fell far short of a majority, Gen. Antonio Ramalho Eanes, the hugely popular chief executive, asked PSD leader Anibal Cavaco Silva to form a new government, the country's 16th in 11 years. The aloof, 46-year-old former finance minister, who took over his party at its congress in May, enjoys a reputation for his strong will, self-confidence, and competitiveness. He is a professor of economics at the Catholic University in Lisbon and the author of four books on economic affairs.

Even as the PSD expanded by 3% its share of the vote over the 1983 election, the traditional parties of the left and the right lost ground. The Socialists, the largest party since the establishment of democracy in 1974, lost nearly 1 million votes as they gained the support of only 21% of the electorate compared with 36% two years before. Economic orthodoxy and 30 months of belt-tightening austerity supervised by the International Monetary Fund drove a wedge between the Socialists and their working-class constituents. This factor would weigh on Soares' chances to capture the presidency in elections that were scheduled for January 1986.

The Moscow-oriented Communists suffered a 3% decline to 15.5% of the votes. Similarly, the right-center Christian Democrats, eclipsed by the PSD, experienced a 3% drop in support to less than 10% of the electorate. This setback precipitated a quest for a new leader to replace Francisco Lucas Pires.

The Democratic Renewal Party (PRD) provided the greatest surprise in the "new faces" election. This party, emphasizing both its newness and links to President Eanes, came from nowhere to finish third, obtaining 18% of the vote and 45 seats. Trading on widespread disillusionment with traditional politicians, it could grow even more in 1986 if Eanes, after completing his term, grasps the PRD's reins. This ideologically eclectic party's position on cooperating with Cavaco Silva will determine the fate of his legislative program.

Economy. An admirer of West German–style Social Democracy, the new prime minister has urged the return of much of state industry to private hands, while calling for higher pensions and other social benefits. Thanks to a Soares-directed stabilization scheme, the real purchasing power of workers remained stable in 1985, after a 10% drop the year before. Cavaco Silva's ability to excite confidence for his economic plan should determine whether investment and growth take place. He must reform intricate laws that militate against reform: Only with great difficulty can employers either dismiss workers or declare bankruptcy; and tens of thousands of employees have gone without wages for months because their employers lacked funds to meet payrolls.

A 1.5% growth in exports proved a bright spot in an otherwise gloomy economic picture as the trade deficit—$520 million in 1984—narrowed to $200 million.

European Community. Following eight years of negotiations, Portugal entered the ten-member European Community (EC) on Jan. 1, 1986, pursuant to a pact signed seven months before. Soares said of the event: "Now that the imperial era has closed, we shall symbolically make a new departure, with Portugal returning to the European fold and playing its rightful part in Europe's dynamism and progress."

The Treaty of Accession provided for a ten-year transition period after which Portugal (along with Spain) would be fully integrated into the EC. The country will receive a net transfer of resources from Brussels; however, as the Greek government learned, Community membership is no panacea for a struggling economy. Indeed, favorable admission terms aside, some economists fear that joining the European Community will rekindle price increases in an economy where the inflation rate dropped from 21.5% in December 1984 to 17% one year later.

See also EUROPE.

GEORGE W. GRAYSON
College of William & Mary

PORTUGAL • Information Highlights

Official Name: Portuguese Republic.
Location: Southwestern Europe.
Area: 35,553 sq mi (92 082 km²).
Population (mid-1985 est.): 10,300,000.
Chief Cities (1981 census): Lisbon, the capital, 812,400; Oporto, 327,368; Amadora, 95,518.
Government: *Head of state,* Antonio Ramalho Eanes, president (took office July 1976). *Head of government,* Anibal Cavaco Silva, prime minister (took office November 1985). *Legislature* (unicameral) —Assembly of the Republic.
Monetary Unit: Escudo (162.5 escudos equal U.S. $1, Oct. 21, 1985).
Gross National Product (1983 U.S.$): $20,700,000,000.
Economic Indexes (1984): *Consumer Prices* (1976 = 100), all items, 534.2; food, 564.2. *Industrial Production* (1980 = 100), 106.
Foreign Trade (1984 U.S.$): *Imports,* $7,797,000,000; *exports,* $5,184,000,000.

POSTAL SERVICE

The fiscal strategy of the United States Postal Service (USPS) in recent years has been to gain surpluses during the first year or two of a typical three-year rate cycle and balance these against a loss the third year. With a surplus figure of $143 million for fiscal year (FY) 1984, ending September 30—setting a modern record of three surpluses in a row—the service's finances appeared secure. However, the USPS in fact ran a deficit of more than $400 million in the last half of FY 1985, during which it was also in marathon bargaining sessions with its labor unions.

Problems. An enormous volume increase of 12 billion pieces during FY 1984 caused service difficulties in major cities. This prompted the use of more overtime than usual and the employment of several thousand added personnel. Inflation and built-in wage increases from prior wage contracts were adding to costs.

In 1985 the difficulties mounted. Deregulation of the airlines industry continued to cause massive transport dislocations for the mail. President Ronald Reagan recommended ending by late 1985 the usual revenue subsidy of some $900 million, which compensated for the below-cost rates for nonprofit organizations. The U.S. Office of Management and Budget then pushed for an added 2% contribution of several hundred million dollars to the federal retirement system on behalf of postal workers. Volume increased another 7.5 billion pieces during FY 1985, totaling a record 139 billion.

Meanwhile, the lengthy bargaining over wages during 1984 went to arbitration in the winter of 1984–85. Final awards raised wages 2.7% annually and renewed prior cost-of-living bonuses, producing a total average annual increase of 5% during the three-year contract. However, the USPS received approval of a partial two-tier pay system, reducing pay rates for new employees some 20%, with no catch-up to previous scales for six years.

Rates. The USPS had taken out some fiscal insurance by requesting a general rate increase of 15% in late 1983. The Postal Rate Commission approved an average rise of about 9% for all classes of mail. The USPS accepted this revision, and the new rates (including 22 cents for a first-class letter) took effect Feb. 17, 1985. The added revenue helped, but cumulative and prospective problems caused the new postmaster general (PMG), Paul Carlin (took office Jan. 1, 1985), to predict in May a $500 million deficit for FY 1985. At the same time, he and his new deputy PMG, Jackie A. Strange, the first woman to hold a top post in the USPS, announced a broad plan to hold down costs.

Economy Measures. Carlin and 33 other top postal managers took pay cuts of 3.5%. Planned pay raises of 3.3% for 714 other senior managers were deferred. New hires at management levels were suspended. All managers were ordered to reduce costs, especially of expensive overtime. Several thousand more new employees were hired at the new reduced pay rates to help with distribution problems. New air freight contracts were negotiated. Plans were made for a possible 41% rise in nonprofit mail rates in late 1985, and the Postal Board of Governors approved the borrowing of $1 billion for capital investment during 1986, the first such action in nine years.

In October 1985, PMG Carlin announced considerable cost-cutting success, reinstated full pay for managers, and predicted an FY 1985 deficit reduction to less than $300 million. Carlin said that the economy efforts would continue and that he hoped they might permit FY 1986 finances to approach a break-even point.

Other Developments. Productivity continued to rise. Obtaining no acceptable offer for its first domestic electronic mail effort, begun in 1982, the USPS terminated E-COM on Sept. 3, 1985. By the end of FY 1985, only the Belgian first-class rate was lower than that of the United States.

Canada. The New Canada Post Corporation continued to stress economy, closing its FY 1985 (ending March 31) with a deficit of $357 million. Collective bargaining during the spring ended in pay raises averaging 3% for some 50,000 of its 63,000 employees. Rate increases, including a first-class rise from 32 to 34 cents (Canadian), came in the summer of 1985, with no further increases expected for two years. Unlike the United States, Canada has encouraged its postal system to enter and compete in the electronic communications field.

Paul P. Van Riper, *Texas A&M University*

PRINCE EDWARD ISLAND

Residents of Prince Edward Island (P.E.I.) got some relief in 1985 from the highest electricity rates in Canada. The provincial government was involved in a controversial real-estate transaction. Premier James Lee shuffled his cabinet, possibly in preparation for an early election.

Power Comes Down. Island electricity consumers will pay up to 25% less for their power as a result of a federal-provincial agreement signed September 13, and an earlier ruling by the National Energy Board. All residential and nonresidential customers received a 17% reduction under the agreement, which incorporated a range of federal and provincial initiatives valued at more than C$50 million. One key element was a federal undertaking to provide up to $20 million to pay off P.E.I.'s outstanding debt on the underwater electrical cable that carries power from New Brunswick.

Only a month earlier, a federal ruling denied the right of New Brunswick to continue selling

PRINCE EDWARD
ISLAND · Information Highlights

Area: 2,184 sq mi (5 657 km²).
Population (April 1985 est.): 127,000.
Chief Cities (1981 census): Charlottetown, the capital, 15,282; Summerside, 7,828.
Government (1985): *Chief Officers*—lt. gov., Robert Lloyd MacPhail; premier, James Lee (Progressive Conservative). *Legislature*—Legislative Assembly, 32 members.
Provincial Finances (1985–86 fiscal year budget): *Revenues,* $476,500,000; *expenditures,* $481,000,000.
Personal Income (average weekly earnings, June 1985): $338.29.
Labor Force (July 1985, seasonally adjusted): *Employed workers,* 15 years of age and over, 52,000; *Unemployed,* 7,000 (12.2%).
Education (1985–86): *Enrollment*—elementary and secondary schools, 25,070 pupils; postsecondary (full-time, 1985–86)—universities, 1,740; community colleges, 900.

(All monetary figures given in Canadian dollars.)

electricity to power-short P.E.I. at rates higher than those New Brunswick charges the New England states. The ruling saves P.E.I. about $4 million a year.

Takeover. One of the most controversial buildings ever erected in P.E.I.—the Prince Edward Island Hotel and Convention Centre in Charlottetown—was taken over by the provincial government in late August for $5.1 million. The 200-room complex, which cost $30 million to build, had been in financial difficulty from the moment it opened in February 1984. The $5.1 million paid for the complex was in addition to nearly $5 million the government already had spent as a result of loan guarantees to Dale Corp., the builder. The federal government was an even bigger loser, paying out an estimated $17 million in guarantees. Liberal party critics predicted that the subject would become a major issue in the pending provincial election.

Job Switch. Robert Lloyd MacPhail, former longtime Conservative member of the legislature and former finance minister, was sworn in July 30 as P.E.I.'s 23d lieutenant governor. He succeeded Joseph Doiron, who had served in the post since 1980.

Cabinet Touch-Up. Premier Lee carried out a minor cabinet shuffle on August 13, naming Gordon Lank to succeed MacPhail as finance minister and minister of tourism. To succeed Lank as minister of transportation and public works, Lee named Peter Pope, the rebel backbencher who sat as an independent member from February until May. Pope had frequently charged that the government neglected his district in Prince county.

Promotion in Ottawa. The island's representative in the federal cabinet, Tom McMillan, got a promotion in August when Prime Minister Brian Mulroney moved him from a junior minister's post (tourism) to the job of environment minister. McMillan replaced Mrs. Suzanne

Blais-Grenier, who had become estranged from the environmental community for—it was alleged—paying insufficient attention to ecological concerns.

JOHN BEST, *"Canada World News"*

PRISONS

The situation in U.S. prisons, overcrowded and often violent, remained grim. Public sentiment for harsher sentences appeared to remain high, while voter support for the construction of new prisons remained low. Private corporations cautiously moved into the construction and management of prisons. For the 12th year in a row, the prison population reached another record high, and executions continued at the rate of several a month.

Overcrowding. Longer sentences and an increasing rate of imprisonment pushed the nation's jails and prisons to beyond 120% of capacity. The federal and state prison population on any given day in 1985 approached 475,000, with an additional 200,000 behind bars in local jails. Conditions in many institutions were described as "a slow-motion riot." In California's Folsom Prison, designed for 1,782 prisoners but holding more than 3,000, inmate stabbings averaged 19 a month, double the number of the previous year. Overall, homosexual rape was described as commonplace, and racial conflict was widespread.

In June, more than 65 prisoners in the Los Angeles County prison rioted for hours. Three officers and more than 50 inmates were injured in the battle, which broke out as guards tried to remove a half-dressed inmate from the lunch line. In July a ruling in Tennessee that prisoners would be required to wear striped uniforms led to uprisings that spread to four prisons in the state. Hostages were taken, and one inmate was killed and five others injured. The looting and burning of buildings resulted in an estimated $11 million in damages.

The Texas prison system, the second largest in the country following California, continued in a state of unrest. In June, Raymond K. Procunier, brought in a year earlier to reorganize the state's troubled, 37,000-inmate system, resigned. Before leaving he achieved settlement of a legal suit brought by inmates charging brutality and excessive overcrowding, won substantial budget increases from the legislature, and replaced half the wardens. The Texas prison population continued to grow by 240 inmates each month, but the violence—more than 500 stabbings, 38 fatal, in 1984—appeared to be diminishing. Prisons in almost 40 states and more than 150 counties were operating under federal court orders that declared them in violation of the prisoners' constitutional rights due to deteriorating and overcrowded conditions.

Complaining of overcrowding, bad food, and the issuing of striped uniforms, inmates at four Tennessee prisons rioted July 1-2. At the state facility in Nashville, left, several guards were taken hostage.

AP/Wide World

Economics. Governments at the federal, state, and local levels spend more than $10 billion a year on jails and prisons. In several states the cost of confining a prisoner exceeded $20,000 a year. As voters defeated prison construction bond referendums, officials looked for new ways to provide facilities for those sentenced by law to prison.

"Privatization," the construction and management of prisons by private corporations under contract to government agencies, made some gains, although questions about prisons for profit continued to be raised.

By 1985, more than 20 major prisons were being operated by private groups. In February, U.S. Sen. Alfonse M. D'Amato (R-NY) introduced legislation to increase tax benefits for private investors in prison construction. In March the National Governors Association passed a resolution, with reservations, that endorsed the private operation of public prisons. In Jefferson County, Colorado, where voters twice rejected prison bond referendums and officials were faced with a federal court order to construct a new jail to ease overcrowding, private funds were raised to construct a $30.2 million county jail and sheriff's facility. In several states, bondlike notes were sold to the public through private brokerage houses and gave investors the advantages of real-estate tax shelters and tax-free interest earnings for a secure investment. The Correction Corporation of America, based in Nashville, TN, expanded into several states, including Texas, and offered privately built and operated detention facilities, charging governments a per diem rate for each inmate. Although highly regulated, private corporations are able to operate with substantial savings, in part because they can avoid civil-service benefits and pension plans for personnel. All indications are that privatization will increase in the future, but questions such as liability in the case of riots or escapes remain to be determined. In Hamilton County, TN, officials were required by contract to pay $200,000 more than anticipated when the prison population increased beyond expectations.

Technology, developed and supervised by private companies, gave some promises of substituting electronic supervision for jail time. A transmitter strapped to the leg allows constant supervision through a black box that monitors the movements of a person convicted of a serious traffic violation or other misdemeanor, thereby freeing jail space for more dangerous offenders. Electronically monitored in-house supervision is now being used on more than 10,000 persons in Florida, and supporters claim that it can save taxpayers significant sums of money by freeing up much-needed cell space. But this technology also raises questions of the extent of supervision that a government should enforce.

Capital Punishment. As of Oct. 1, 1985, 1,590 men and women were on death rows in 37 states. The largest numbers were in Southern states, including 221 in Florida and 211 in Texas. The rate of executions again accelerated from 21 in 1984 to almost 50 in 1985, but by becoming almost routine, the executions drew little public attention.

In October, William Vandiver was executed after having instructed his lawyers to cease any appeals on his behalf. Attorneys for death row defendants increasingly reported that more of their clients were asking them to stop legal proceedings. On September 11, Charles Rumbaugh, 27, was executed in Texas for a murder he committed at 17 years of age while legally a juvenile. Thirty-two others on death row had been sentenced for crimes committed before they were 18.

DONALD GOODMAN
John Jay College of Criminal Justice

PRIZES AND AWARDS

NOBEL PRIZES[1]

Chemistry: Herbert A. Hauptman, Medical Foundation of Buffalo (NY), and Jerome Karle, Naval Research Laboratory, Washington, DC, cited "for their outstanding achievements in the development of direct methods for the determination of crystal structures."

Economics: Franco Modigliani, Massachusetts Institute of Technology, for his "pioneering work in analyzing the behavior of household savers and the functioning of financial markets," deemed by the committee to be "extremely important." (*See* page 137.)

Literature: Claude Simon, French novelist. (*See* page 322.)

Peace Prize: International Physicians for the Prevention of Nuclear War, cited because the organization had "performed a considerable service to mankind by spreading authoritative information and by creating an awareness of the catastrophic consequences of atomic warfare." (Award given to the two cofounders, Dr. Yevgeny I. Chazov of the USSR and Dr. Bernard Lown of the United States.)

Physics: Klaus von Klitzing, Max Planck Institute for Solid State Research, Stuttgart, West Germany, cited because he has "opened up a new research field of great importance and relevance" through his 1980 discovery that electrical resistance takes place in extremely precise units.

Physiology or Medicine: Michael S. Brown and Joseph L. Goldstein, University of Texas, cited for "a milestone in cholesterol research" that has "drastically widened our understanding of the cholesterol metabolism and increased our possibilities to prevent and treat atherosclerosis, or hardening of the arteries, and heart attacks."

[1] about $225,000 in each category

ART

American Academy and Institute of Arts and Letters Awards

Academy-Institute Awards ($5,000 ea.): art—James Bohary, Kim Jones, Scott Pfaffman, George Sugarman, Esteban Vicente; music—Gheorghe Costinescu, Donald J. Erb, John Stewart McLennan, Ezra Sims

Nathan and Lillian Berliawsky Award ($5,000): The Group for Contemporary Music

Arnold W. Brunner Memorial Prize in Architecture ($1,000): William Pedersen and Arthur May

Distinguished Service to the Arts: Sen. Claiborne Pell

Gold Medal for Distinguished Achievement in Music: Leonard Bernstein

Walter Hinrichsen Award: Louis S. Karchin

Charles Ives Fellowship ($10,000): Thomas Oboe Lee

Charles Ives Scholarships ($5,000 ea.): William E. Coble, Glen Cortese, Paul D. Kozel, James Primosch, Robert Steven Rouse, Michael Torke

Goddard Lieberson Fellowships ($10,000 ea.): Todd Brief and Sheree Clement

Richard and Hinda Rosenthal Foundation Award for Painting ($5,000): David Kapp

Special Citation for Service to the Arts: William Shawn, *The New Yorker*

American Institute of Architects Honor Awards: (*See* ARCHITECTURE.)

Capezio Dance Award: Doris Hering

Dance Magazine Awards: Charles (Honi) Coles, Richard Cragun, Frederick Franklin, Heather Watts, Walter Sorell

George Eastman Prize: Claude Baker, *Homages and Fantasies* (musical composition)

Grawemeyer Award ($150,000): Witold Lutoslawski for Symphony No. 3 (musical composition)

John F. Kennedy Center Honors for career achievement in the performing arts: Merce Cunningham, Irene Dunne, Bob Hope, Alan Jay Lerner, Frederick Loewe, Beverly Sills

MacDowell Colony Medal: Robert Motherwell

National Academy of Recording Arts and Sciences Grammy Awards for excellence in phonograph records

Album of the year: *Can't Slow Down*, Lionel Richie (singer and producer), James Anthony Carmichael (producer)

Classical album: *Amadeus*, Neville Mariner (conductor), Academy of St. Martin in the Fields, John Strauss (producer)

Country music song: *City of New Orleans*, Steve Goodman

Jazz vocal performance: *Nothin But the Blues*, Joe Williams

New artist: Cyndi Lauper

Record of the year: *What's Love Got to Do with It*, Tina Turner, Terry Britten (producer)

Song of the year: *What's Love Got to Do with It*, Graham Lyle, Terry Britten (songwriters)

National Medal of Arts: Elliott Carter, Ralph Ellison, Jose Ferrer, Martha Graham, Louise Nevelson, Leontyne Price, Georgia O'Keeffe, Dorothy Buffum Chandler, Lincoln Kerstein, Paul Mellon, Alice Tully, Hallmark Cards, Inc.

Naumburg Chamber Music Awards: Meloira Quartet (based at the Eastman School of Music)

Pritzker Architecture Prize ($100,000): Hans Hollein

Pulitzer Prize for Music: Stephen Albert, *Symphony, River Run*

(special citation)—William H. Schuman

Samuel H. Scripps-American Dance Festival Award ($25000): Alwin Nikolais

Leopold Stokowski Conducting Award ($5,000): Jo Ann Falletta

Van Cliburn International Piano Competition ($12,000): José Feghali

JOURNALISM

George Polk Memorial Awards

Environmental reporting: Tom Harris, Jim Morris, *The Sacramento Bee*

Foreign reporting: Mark Fineman, *The Philadelphia Inquirer*

Local reporting: Ellen Whitford, *The Norfolk Virginian-Pilot*

Magazine reporting: John Vinocur, *The New York Times Magazine*

Medical reporting: William R. Ritz, John Aloysius Farrell, *The Denver Post*

National reporting: Robert Parry, The Associated Press

News photography: Ozier Muhammad, *Newsday*

Special interest reporting: Lois R. Ember, *Chemical & Engineering News*

Special award: "Amnesty International Report," Amnesty International

Foreign television reporting: Michael Buerk, Mohammed Amin, BBC and VisNews, Televised by NBC News

Local television reporting: Rick Nelson, Joe Collum, KPRC TV, Houston

National television reporting: Alex Kotlowitz, Kwame Holman, Susan Ades, *MacNeil/Lehrer NewsHour*, WNET, New York, and WETA, Washington, DC

Maria Moors Cabot Prizes ($1,000 ea.): Shirley Christian, *The New York Times;* William H. Heath, Associated Press, Buenos Aires; Rafael Herrera, editor of *Listin Diario* of Santo Domingo, Dominican Republic; Aldo Zuccolillo, founder of ABC Color, Asunción, Paraguay. Special citations to: Richard and Dery Dyer, *Tico Times*, San José, Costa Rica; Rev. Andrew Morrison, *The Catholic Standard*, Georgetown, Guyana

National Magazine Awards

Design: *Forbes*

Essays and criticism: *Boston Magazine*, for Howard Carr and his "incisive and elegant re-creation of the character and spirit of Boston's changing political scene."

Fiction: *Playboy*, for stories by Andre Dubus 3d, Gabriel Garcia Marquez, and the late John Gardner

General excellence awards: *Time, American Health, American Heritage, Manhattan, inc.*

Photography: *Life*

Overseas Press Club Awards

Book on foreign affairs: Kevin Close, W. W. Norton, *Russia and the Russians*

Business news reporting from abroad: (magazines and books)—Peter Koenig, *Institutional Investor*, for "Anatomy of a Eurobond Scandal"; (newspapers and wire services)—no award given

Cartoon on foreign affairs: Don Wright, *The Miami News*

Daily newspaper or wire service interpretation of foreign affairs: Drew Middleton, *The New York Times*, for "Return to Normandy"

Daily newspaper or wire service reporting from abroad: Jeff Sommer, *Newsday*, for "India Coverage"

Economic reporting from abroad: (magazines and books)—John Pearson, Carla Anne Robbins, Sarah Bartlett and Team, *Business Week*, "Will Mexico Make It?"; (newspapers and wire services)—William Montalbano,

Juan DeOnis, Juan Vasquez, *Los Angeles Times,* for "Mexican Economy"
Magazine story on foreign affairs: V. S. Naipaul, *Harper's Magazine,* for "Grenada: An Island Betrayed"
Magazine reporting from abroad: Scott Sullivan, *Newsweek,* for "The Decline of Europe"
Photographic reporting from abroad: (magazines and books)—David Burnett, Contact Press Images for *Time;* (newspapers and wire services)—Larry Price, *Philadelphia Inquirer*
Radio interpretation of foreign affairs: Alan Berlow, National Public Radio, for "Hotel Intrigue"
Radio spot news from abroad: Cameron Swayze, Philip Till, NBC Radio News, for "Beirut Coverage"
Television interpretation or documentary on foreign affairs: Garrick Utley, Bryant Gumbel, NBC-TV, for "The New Cold War"
Television spot news reporting from abroad: Mohamed Amin, Visnews, for "Ethiopian Famine"
Robert Capa Gold Medal: James Nachtwey, Black Star for *Time* magazine, for "Photos of El Salvador"
Madeline Dane Ross Award: Stan Grossfeld, photographer, and Colin Nickerson, correspondent, *The Boston Globe,* for "Ethiopia: Famine and Flight"
Pulitzer Prizes
Commentary: Murray Kempton, *Newsday*
Criticism: Howard Rosenberg, *The Los Angeles Times*
Editorial cartooning: Jeff MacNelly, *The Chicago Tribune*
Editorial writing: Richard Aregood, *The Philadelphia Daily News*
Explanatory journalism: Jon Franklin, *The Baltimore Evening Sun*
Feature photography: Stan Grossfeld, *The Boston Globe*
Feature writing: Alice Steinbach, *The Baltimore Sun*
General news reporting: Thomas Turcol, *The Virginian-Pilot, The Ledger-Star,* Norfolk, VA
International reporting: Josh Friedman, Dennis Bell, Ozier Muhammad, *Newsday*
Investigative reporting: William K. Marimow, *The Philadelphia Inquirer;* Lucy Morgan, Jack Reed, *The St. Petersburg Times*
National reporting: Thomas J. Knudson, *The Des Moines Register*
Public service: *The Fort Worth Star-Telegram*
Specialized reporting: Randall Savage, Jackie Crosby, Macon (GA) *Telegraph and News*
Spot news photography: *The Register,* Santa Ana, CA

LITERATURE

American Academy and Institute of Arts and Letters Awards
Academy-Institute Awards ($5,000 ea.): Alan Dugan, Maria Irene Fornés, George Garrett, Carolyn Kizer, Gilbert Sorrentino, Paul West, John Williams, Paul Zimmer
The American Academy in Rome Fellowship in Literature: Oscar Hijuelos
Award of Merit for the Novel ($5,000): Richard Stern
Witter Bynner Prize for Poetry ($1,500): J. D. McClatchy
Gold Medal for Distinguished Achievement in Poetry: Robert Penn Warren
Sue Kaufman Prize for First Fiction ($2,500): Louise Erdrich
Richard and Hinda Rosenthal Foundation Award for Fiction ($5,000): Janet Kauffman
Jean Stein Award ($5,000): George W. S. Trow, Jr.
Harold D. Vursell Memorial Award ($5,000): Harriet Doerr
Morton Dauwen Zabel Award ($2,500): Stanley Cavell
American Book Awards ($10,000 ea.)
Fiction: Don DeLillo, *White Noise*
First fiction: Bob Shacochis, *Easy in the Islands*
Nonfiction: J. Anthony Lukas, *Common Ground: A Turbulent Decade in the Lives of Three American Families*
Bancroft Prizes ($4,000 ea.): Suzanne Lebsock, *The Free Women of Petersburg: Status and Culture in a Southern Town, 1784–1860;* Kenneth Silverman, *The Life and Times of Cotton Mather*
Bollingen Prize in Poetry ($2,500 ea.): John Ashbery, Fred Chappell
Canada's Governor-General Literary Awards
English-language awards:
Drama—Judith Thompson, *White Biting Dog*
Fiction—Josef Skvorecky, *Engineer of Human Souls*

Nonfiction—Sandra Gwyn, *The Private Capital: Ambition and Love in the Age of MacDonald and Laurier*
Poetry—Paulette Jiles, *Celestial Navigation*
French-language awards:
Drama—Rene-Daniel Dubois, *Ne Blamez jamais les Bédouins*
Fiction—Jacques Brault, *Agonies*
Nonfiction—Jean Hamelin, Nicole Gagnon, *Le XXᵉ Siècle histoire du catholicisme québécois*
Poetry—Nicole Brossard, *Double Impression*
Miguel de Cervantes Prize ($50,000): Ernesto Sabato
Alfred Harcourt Award ($10,000): Ernst Pawel, *The Nightmare of Reason: A Life of Franz Kafka*
Jerusalem Prize for Literature on the Freedom of Man in Society: Milan Kundera
Robert F. Kennedy Memorial Books Awards ($2,500):
Raymond Bonner, *Weakness and Deceit: U.S. Policy and El Salvador*
Honorable mention: David Haward Bain, *Sitting in Darkness: Americans in the Philippines;* Joel Williamson, *The Crucible of Race*
National Book Critics Circle
Fiction: Louise Erdrich, *Love Machine*
Nonfiction: Freeman Dyson, *Weapons and Hope*
Poetry: Sharon Olds, *The Dead and the Living*
Biography: Joseph Frank, *Dostoevsky: The Years of Ordeal 1850–1859*
Criticism: Robert Hass, *Twentieth Century Pleasures: Prose on Poetry*
P.E.N./Faulkner Prize ($5,000): Tobias Wolff, *Barracks Thief*
Pulitzer Prizes
Biography: Kenneth Silverman, *The Life and Times of Cotton Mather*
Fiction: Alison Lurie, *Foreign Affairs*
General nonfiction: Studs Terkel, *The Good War: An Oral History of World War II*
History: Thomas K. McCraw, *The Prophets of Regulation*
Poetry: Carolyn Kizer, *Yin*
Ritz Paris Hemingway Award ($50,000): Mario Vargas Llosa, *The War of the End of the World*
(See also Libraries.)

MOTION PICTURES

Academy of Motion Picture Arts and Sciences ("Oscar") Awards
Actor—leading: F. Murray Abraham, *Amadeus*
Actor—supporting: Dr. Haing S. Ngor, *The Killing Fields*
Actress—leading: Sally Field, *Places in the Heart*
Actress—supporting: Dame Peggy Ashcroft, *A Passage to India*
Cinematography: Chris Menges, *The Killing Fields*
Costume design: Theodore Pistek, *Amadeus*
Director: Milos Forman, *Amadeus*
Film: *Amadeus*
Foreign-language film: *Dangerous Moves* (Switzerland)
Music—original score: Maurice Jarre, *A Passage to India*
Music—original song score or adaptation: Prince, *Purple Rain*
Music—song: Stevie Wonder, *I Just Called to Say I Love You*
Screenplay—original: Robert Benton, *Places in the Heart*
Screenplay—adaptation: Peter Shaffer, *Amadeus*
Gordon E. Sawyer Technical Award: Linwood G. Dunn, special effects cameraman
Jean Hersholt Humanitarian award: David Wolper, producer
Honorary awards: James Stewart, National Endowment for the Arts
Special Achievement, Sound Effects Editing: Kay Rose, *The River*
American Film Institute's Life Achievement Award: Gene Kelly
Cannes Film Festival Awards
Golden Palm award (best film): Emir Kusturica, *Otac Na Sluz benom Putu* (Papa Is on a Business Trip) (Yugoslavia)
Special jury grand prize: Alan Parker, *Birdy*
Special jury awards: John Bailey, Eiko Ishioka, Philip Glass, *Mishima;* Istvan Szabo, *Colonel Redl*
Best actor: William Hurt, *Kiss of the Spider Woman*
Best actress: (shared) Cher, *Mask;* Norma Aleandro, *La Historia Oficial*

Best director: André Techine, *Rendez-vous*
Best short film: *Jenitba*

PUBLIC SERVICE

American Institute for Public Service Jefferson Awards:
Greatest public service by an elected or appointed official: James A. Baker III
Greatest public service by a private citizen: Lee Iacocca
Greatest public service benefiting the disadvantaged: Betty Ford
Greatest public service by an individual 35 or under: Trevor Ferrell
Public Service benefiting local communities: Linda Barker, Frank McGlone, Arturo Montoya, Jean Kennedy Smith, Mary Beth Tober
Winston Churchill Award: H. Ross Perot
Companion of the Order of Canada for "outstanding achievement and service to Canada": Anne Murray, Oscar Peterson, Floyd Chambers, Alex Baumann
Congressional Gold Medal (presented by President Ronald Reagan, March 26, 1985): Harry Truman (posthumously)
Jabotinsky Prize-Defender of Jerusalem Award ($100,000): Jeane J. Kirkpatrick and Operation Moses
Roosevelt Freedom Medals: Claude Pepper, Kenneth B. Clark, John Kenneth Galbraith, Elie Wiesel, Isidor I. Rabi
Templeton Prize for Progress in Religion ($185,300): Sir Alistair Hardy
Harry S. Truman Public Service Award: Sen. Thomas Eagleton
U.S. Presidential Medal of Freedom (awarded by President Ronald Reagan on May 23): Jacques-Yves Cousteau, Sidney Hook, Jeane J. Kirkpatrick, S. Dillon Ripley, Mother Teresa, Frank Sinatra, James Stewart, Gen. Albert Coady Wedemeyer, Charles E. Yeager; (posthumously) Count Basie, Jerome Holland, George M. Low, Frank Reynolds (posthumously).
World Methodist Peace Award: President Jimmy Carter

SCIENCE

Bristol-Myers Award for distinguished achievement in cancer research ($50,000): William S. Hayward, Philip Leder (shared)
General Motors Cancer Research Foundation Awards ($130,000 ea.): Paul C. Lauterbur, John Christopher Wagner, Robert T. Schimke
Louisa Gross Horwitz Prize for research in biology or biochemistry ($22,000 shared): Mark Ptashne, Harvard University, Boston, MA; Donald D. Brown, Carnegie Institution of Washington, Baltimore, MD
Albert Lasker Awards ($15,000 ea.)
Basic research: Michael S. Brown, Joseph L. Goldstein, University of Texas Health Science Center
Clinical research: Bernard Fisher, University of Pittsburgh
Public service: Lane Adams, American Cancer Society; Eppie Lederer (Ann Landers), syndicated columnist

TELEVISION AND RADIO

Academy of Television Arts and Sciences ("Emmy") Awards
Actor—comedy series: Robert Guillaume, *Benson* (ABC)
Actor—drama series: William Daniels, *St. Elsewhere* (NBC)
Actor—limited series or a special: Richard Crenna, *The Rape of Richard Beck* (ABC)
Actress—comedy series: Jane Curtin, *Kate & Allie* (CBS)
Actress—drama series: Tyne Daly, *Cagney & Lacey* (CBS)
Actress—limited series or a special: Joanne Woodward, *Do You Remember Love* (CBS)
Children's program: *Displaced Person (American Playhouse)* (PBS)
Classical program in the performing arts: *Tosca (Live from the Met)* (PBS)
Comedy series: *The Cosby Show* (NBC)
Drama series: *Cagney & Lacey* (CBS)
Informational series: *The Living Planet: A Portrait of the Earth* (PBS)
Informational special: *Cousteau: Mississippi* (Syndicated)
Limited series: *The Jewel in the Crown (Masterpiece Theatre)* (PBS)
Special drama: *Do You Remember Love* (CBS)
Supporting actor—comedy series: John Larroquette, *Night Court* (NBC)
Supporting actor—drama series: Edward James Olmos, *Miami Vice* (NBC)
Supporting actor—limited series or a special: Karl Malden, *Fatal Vision* (NBC)
Supporting actress—comedy series: Rhea Perlman, *Cheers* (NBC)
Supporting actress—drama series: Betty Thomas, *Hill Street Blues* (NBC)
Supporting actress—limited series or a special: Kim Stanley, *Cat on a Hot Tin Roof* (PBS)
Variety, music, or comedy program: *Motown Returns to the Apollo* (NBC)
George Foster Peabody Awards
Radio: Brigham Young University, Provo, UT, *Bradbury 13;* Protestant Radio and Television Center, *The Protestant Hour;* KFGO, Fargo, ND, for coverage of a blizzard; KNX Newsradio, Los Angeles, CA, *The Immigration Problem;* WAFX Radio, Ft. Wayne, IN, *D-Day: 40 Years Later;* WFMT, Chicago, and Ray Nordstrand; WNYC AM/83, New York, NY, *Small Things Considered*
Television: ABC News Closeup, *To Save Our Schools, To Save Our Children;* ABC Theater, *Heartsounds;* Roone Arledge, ABC, NY, for significant contributions to television news and sports programming; Central Independent Television of England, *Seeds of Despair;* CBS Entertainment and The David Gerber Company, *George Washington;* The Corporation for Entertainment and Learning, Inc./Bill Moyers, *A Walk Through the 20th Century with Bill Moyers;* Frontline, Boston, MA, for overall excellence; Granada Television of England, *The Jewel in the Crown;* Ted Koppel/*Nightline,* NY; KDFW-TV, Dallas, TX, for investigative reports on the Dallas Fire Department; KGW-TV, Portland, OR, *Rajneesh Update;* NBC and MTM Enterprises, *St. Elsewhere;* "Roger Rosenblatt Essays," from the *MacNeil/Lehrer NewsHour;* Showtime, *Faerie Tale Theatre;* Turner Broadcasting System, Atlanta, GA, *Costeau/Amazon;* WCAX-TV, Burlington, VT, *Patterns of Practice;* WCCO Television, Minneapolis, MN, *The Hollow Victory: Vietnam Under Communism;* WCVB, Boston, MA, *Somerville High;* WDVM-TV, Washington, DC, *Eyewitness News;* WMAQ-TV, Chicago, IL, *Political Parasites;* WNET/Thirteen, NY, *The Brain;* WNET/Thirteen, NY, *Heritage: Civilization and the Jews*
Humanitas Prizes
Long-form category ($25,000): Hume Cronyn, Susan Cooper, *The Dollmaker*
One-hour category ($15,000): John Masius, Tom Fontana, episode of *St. Elsewhere*
One-half-hour category ($10,000): John Markus, episode of *The Cosby Show*

THEATER

Susan Smith Blackburn Prize ($3,000): Shirley Gee, *Never in My Lifetime*
New York Drama Critics Circle Awards
Best new play: *Ma Rainey's Black Bottom*
Foreign play: No award
Musical: No award
Antoinette Perry ("Tony") Awards
Actor—drama: Derek Jacobi, *Much Ado About Nothing*
Actor—musical: no award
Actress—drama: Stockard Channing, *A Day in the Death of Joe Egg*
Actress—musical: no award
Director—drama: Gene Saks, *Biloxi Blues*
Director—musical: Des McAnuff, *Big River*
Featured actor—drama: Barry Miller, *Biloxi Blues*
Featured actor—musical: Ron Richardson, *Big River*
Featured actress—drama: Judith Ivey, *Hurlyburly*
Featured actress—musical: Leilani Jones, *Grind*
Musical: *Big River*
Musical—book: William Hauptman, *Big River*
Musical—score: Roger Miller, *Big River*
Play: *Biloxi Blues*
Reproduction of a play or musical: *A Day in the Death of Joe Egg*
Special awards: Steppenwolf Theater of Chicago, New York State Council on the Arts, Yul Brynner, Edwin Lester
Pulitzer Prize for Drama: Stephen Sondheim, James Lapine, *Sunday in the Park with George*

PUBLISHING

All segments of the U.S. publishing industry posted gains in revenues, sales, and profits in 1985. Major trends for book publishing, magazines, and newspapers included growing industry concentration and a variety of new applications for computer technology.

Books. Book sales in 1985 were expected to top the $9.4 billion recorded in 1984 by about 4.5%. Disposable personal income continued to grow, as did funding for schools and libraries. The best performers in 1984 were trade paperbounds, juvenile books, and school textbooks. Mass-market paperbacks, which posted a small increase in 1984, declined sharply in the first quarter of 1985. New authors had a more difficult time getting published; not a single new fiction author sold 100,000 copies of a book in 1984.

Total book title output in 1984 was 51,000, about 2,000 below the 1983 figure and 4.5% below the record 1953 total. Mass-market paperback output was 1% below the 1983 total, but trade, or quality, paperbacks increased more than 8%. In best-sellers, the fiction list was dominated by veteran authors. Business, how-to, and cookbooks led the nonfiction best-sellers, with biography, history, and inspirational books also strong. Paperback best-sellers included business, romance, and humor books. A total of 107 mass-market best-sellers passed one million copies by the end of 1984. Away from the best-seller lists, average print runs per title were down (from 7,000–9,000 in recent years to the 2,000–5,000 range), and mass-market publishers offered lower prices for paperbound rights. The trend toward paperbound books continued. In 1984 about 25% of sales came from paperbounds, compared with 21% in 1977. Textbooks continued to sell strongly, constituting about 31% of total shipments in 1984. There was more price discounting for books. Nearly 25% of paperbacks were bought at a discount in 1984.

A Gallup survey of book buyers in 1984 reported that about 6 of every 10 adults bought one book or more during any three-month period. One in four adults reported buying five or more books in a three-month period. Among fiction books, heavy purchasers were most likely to buy mysteries and romances, while in the nonfiction category they preferred history books, reference works, and biographies.

Exports of U.S. books increased by about 10% in 1984, with sales of technical books up by about 30%.

In the development of technology applications, more computer software became available in 1985 to meet the special needs of a relatively small and diverse industry with many different discount, royalty, and returns policies. After a late start relative to other U.S. industries, most publishing houses by 1985 had automated their operations for order processing and fulfillment.

More than a dozen computer systems were available to publishers, with other services and software designed for booksellers, especially for inventory control. By 1985 many publishers had developed links with their warehousing and distribution centers, as well as with their contract printers, wholesalers, and major bookstore accounts.

For writers, the computer continued to open a new market known as interactive fiction or the electronic novel. Companies began to follow pioneer Infocom's lead ("Zork") with releases of games, adventure stories, and mysteries, many with graphics and music.

In another merging of electronic and printed information and entertainment, some publishers became involved in the sale and production of videocassettes. Companies such as Western (publisher of children's Golden Books), Random House, Crown Publishers, Simon and Schuster, and others looked at videocassette sales as a lucrative market with original material, as well as tapes based on previously published books.

Some publishers who had tried to reach out to the book-buying public with development of software groups pulled out of the production and marketing of computer software; these companies included John Wiley, Harper & Row, and Reader's Digest.

Other industry trends included an increase in merger and acquisition activity during 1984–85. Gulf & Western, already the owner of Simon & Schuster, bought Prentice-Hall for more than $700 million. Gulf also bought Esquire, Inc., an educational publisher. And Macmillan paid about $15 million in stock for Scribner Book Companies. Macmillan also bought the Four Winds children's line from Scholastic, acquired Harper & Row's school division, and increased its holdings in Addison-Wesley. As a result of these consolidations, the largest U.S. book publisher became the Simon & Schuster and Prentice-Hall combination. After a long contest to dominate the U.S. market with romance books, Pocket Books' Silhouette line was acquired by Canadian-based Harlequin Books. Other acquisitions included Times Books by Random House, and the SFN Companies by a group of investors. At the bookseller end of the industry, Waldenbooks, the largest U.S. bookstore chain (900 outlets), was bought by the K-mart chain of general discount stores for $295 million.

Despite these major consolidations, new industry statistics suggested that the number of individual book publishers continued to grow. Nearly 17,000 individual book publishers had works in print in 1984, with about 200 new publishers added each month.

Magazines. U.S. magazines continued to be a growth industry in 1985, and further expan-

Mysteries and Crime Thrillers

"The nephew did it."

Eric Burgin, Rothco

One need not be Sherlock Holmes, Nero Wolfe, or Miss Jane Marple to detect the phenomenon. A glance at the best-seller lists, a stop at the supermarket book rack, and maybe a quick survey around the pool or ski lodge make the deduction elementary. Crime fiction —from the whodunit murder mystery to the gritty police thriller—is booming.

Invented in 1841 by Edgar Allan Poe with "The Murders in the Rue Morgue," the detective story has enjoyed increasing popularity over the decades. Works by Sir Arthur Conan Doyle, Dorothy Sayers, Dashiell Hammett, Raymond Chandler, Rex Stout, and others helped bring literary respectability to the genre. And in recent years, mysteries and crime thrillers have enjoyed unprecedented commercial success. Surveys show that more than half of America's college graduates are frequent readers of mysteries; many other people find them an occasional escape from the pressures of daily life. Consequently, specialty bookstores with names like Murder Ink and Sherlock's Home are doing a lively business. New authors, new detectives, and new formulas are finding their way into print by the hundreds.

Leading the way in 1985 were works by such popular and prolific mystery/crime writers as Elmore Leonard (*Glitz*), John D. MacDonald (*The Lonely Silver Rain*), Dick Francis (*Proof*), and Ed McBain (*Eight Black Horses*). The works of George Higgins, Donald E. Westlake, William Diehl, P. D. James, and, of course, Agatha Christie were as popular as ever. Even Norman Mailer got into the act, as his 1984 Cape Cod murder mystery, *Tough Guys Don't Dance*, was a paperback best-seller.

One interesting aspect of the new wave in detective fiction has been the emergence of ethnically and culturally diverse sleuth heroes. The hard-boiled private eyes of the Philip Marlowe and Sam Spade generation have given way to hip professors, gays, a Navajo Indian, rabbis and priests, yuppies, and professionals of almost every variety. An especially notable trend has been the new breed of woman detective, brought to life by such authors as Sara Paretsky, Martha G. Webb, Marcia Muller, Sue Grofton, Mickey Friedman, and Marcia Biederman.

Indeed the conventional whodunit has taken on new commerical twists, as well. Several publishers have had success with open-ended murder mysteries and the offering of a $10,000– $15,000 prize for the first or best solution. Then there are the electronic media spin-offs. A New York company called IntraVision introduced a $500,000 contest called *Treasure,* in which clues are made available in a paperback book, videocassettes, and videodiscs. Infocom's "Deadline" is an interactive computer software package in which players have 12 hours to solve a homicide. If the amateur sleuth is looking for still other cases to crack, there are "mystery weekends," in which guests pay $300 or more to witness a mock murder, track down clues, and name the culprit. There also is television. Among the 1985 selections were CBS-TV's *Murder, She Wrote,* starring Angela Lansbury as a mystery writer and happenstance crime solver, and PBS' *Mystery,* a seven-part series of Sherlock Holmes stories— with a paperback tie-in. And as the year drew to a close, mystery aficionados were awaiting eagerly the screen appearance of Colonel Mustard, Miss Scarlett, and their cohorts from the longtime popular board game "Clue."

JEFFREY H. HACKER

sion was predicted for 1986. Records were set in 1985 for the number of magazines published, the number of copies sold, and the total amount of revenue generated by advertising income. The big growth area of the industry came from specialized magazines in such areas as computers, health, food, sports, and hobbies.

A record 11,090 periodicals were published in 1985, compared with 9,657 ten years earlier. More than 313 million magazines were sold in 1984, about eight million more than in 1983. Total circulation in 1984 was up by 33 million compared with 1980.

Subscription sales accounted for the growth, with single-copy sales continuing to decline. Industry leaders believed the slump in single-copy sales was caused by the decline of mass-appeal magazines (which rely heavily on single-copy sales), the fact that there were fewer newsstands and supermarkets serving as distribution outlets, and promotion of subscription sales by publishers.

The large-circulation magazines continued to account for a major part of total circulation, with 15% of the titles producing 70% of total circulation. The eleven largest circulation magazines (five million and above) accounted for one third (or almost 105 million) of all magazine circulation in the second half of 1984.

The top-circulating magazines were: *Reader's Digest, TV Guide, Modern Maturity, NRTA/AARP News Bulletin, National Geographic, Better Homes & Gardens, Family Circle, Woman's Day, McCall's, Good Housekeeping,* and *Ladies Home Journal.* However, six of these top magazines lost circulation in the second half of 1984, and the only large gains were made by *Modern Maturity* and the *NRTA/AARP News Bulletin.*

Meanwhile, the largest individual percentage gains were made by more specialized magazines, including *Sylvia Porter's Personal Finance Magazine, Compute!'s Gazette, Sun, Family Computing, Inside Sports, Denver Magazine, Circus, Pro Bass, Video Review,* and *Fins and Feathers.* The business press, which distributed about 72 million copies of magazines in 1984 and was a large part of the total magazine market, posted significant gains.

In 1984, for the second year in a row, magazines increased their share of the advertising market as compared with broadcasting. Total advertising revenue for magazines hit $4.7 billion in 1984, up by 18.5% from the previous year. In 1985 the number of advertising pages was estimated to rise by 6% and advertising dollars by 10%.

In the first half of 1985, advertising revenues climbed again, by 8.2% to $2.4 billion. General-interest magazines went up by 10% and women's magazines by 9.8%. The top five revenue leaders in the first half of 1985 were *Time, TV Guide, Newsweek, People Weekly,* and *Sports Illustrated.* The number of advertis-

ing pages also increased, as did the advertising cost per page per thousand.

The cost of magazines to the reader increased by about 4% in 1984. The ratio of advertising to editorial linage was 53–47 in 1984, about the same ratio as in the previous five years.

The merger trend continued, with multimedia corporations leading the way. The largest merger in 1985 to affect the magazine industry was the $3.5 billion acquisition of the American Broadcasting Companies (ABC) by Capital Cities Communications, creating a media empire worth close to $1 billion. ABC Publishing included business magazines, farm publications, the city magazine *Los Angeles,* and consumer magazine divisions, including ABC Leisure Magazines and the COMPUTE! group. The magazine interests of Capital Cities included the Fairchild group, the monthly *Institutional Investor,* as well as newspapers and electronic publishing businesses.

A large media merger in late 1984, the CBS purchase of Ziff-Davis properties, involved 12 magazines for the price of $362.5 million, believed to be a record for a magazine group. Ziff-Davis also sold eight magazines to Rupert Murdoch.

A number of magazines were born in 1985, and a number failed or were merged. The area of computer technology continued to provide opportunities for many publishers (although the failure rate was high) as did the health and fitness field. Periodicals about business, such as *New York City Business, California Business,* and the *Kansas City Business Journal,* continued to grow.

Electronic publishing was seen by many industry leaders as a natural outgrowth of magazine publishing. Most saw the electronic future as a development of such supplementary services as the supply of data bases and interactive forms of communication. Pioneer experiments continued with the translation of magazine material to cable television, such as the *Good Housekeeping* experiment. (*See also* COMMUNICATION TECHNOLOGY.)

New computer technology was applied to magazine distribution, incorporating distributors and wholesalers into an information-exchange network. This industry-wide project was expected to result in faster and more detailed information on sales from products advertised in magazines.

Newspapers. U.S. newspaper credibility came under serious scrutiny by industry associations in 1985, while revenues and profits reached new highs.

Advertising volume in 1984 increased by more than 15% for the second year in a row. Employment rose to a new high of 443,000, an increase of 15,000 within one year. Circulation rose slightly, although the number of daily newspapers decreased by 13.

In a year highlighted by media company mergers and acquisitions, editorial staff of the "Des Moines Register" await a board decision on offers from several top newspaper groups. The "Register" ended up going to the Gannett Company.

Studies of credibility were commissioned by two major groups, the American Society of Newspaper Editors (ASNE) and the Associated Press Managing Editors (APME). The ASNE study showed that three fourths of all adults have some doubts about media credibility. Critics of daily newspapers were also critical of television news. One fifth of all adults surveyed had even stronger feelings about the media and were reported to "deeply distrust their news media." On the other hand, approximately half of the people in the survey said that daily newspapers were accurate, while 15% said that they were inaccurate. About seven in 10 believed that "the news media usually try to correct their mistakes."

The follow-up study by APME, expected to be released late in 1985, was designed to determine attitudes of working journalists toward credibility issues. One leading publisher noted that editors and publishers were responsible for restoring public confidence and that "credibility is directly related to our future," in terms of readership.

Other editorial concerns of newspapers in 1985 included the large number of libel suits (*see* special report, page 314) and a growing concern about the employment of minorities in the newsroom. Fewer than 6% of editorial jobs were held by minorities in 1984.

Industry profit margins increased in 1984 despite greater competition for advertising by the broadcast media. The daily newspaper share of advertising revenue was down slightly, to 27%, as compared with 29.2% for television and radio. Local advertising revenues showed strong gains, but national advertising weakened. Competition with direct-mail advertisers was keen. Evening newspapers continued to show declines in circulation. Morning circulation rose by 1.8 million. Total daily circulation posted a 700,000 gain to 63.3 million but did not keep pace with household formation. Weekly newspapers showed a healthy gain of 5.9 million in circulation, up 14% to 49 million. The largest circulation gains were recorded by Sunday newspapers.

Newsprint prices rose by 7%, and the prices of some newspapers also increased. Newsprint consumption in 1984 was at a record high, up 8% from the previous year. This trend continued into 1985, with consumption for the first half of the year rising another 2%.

Mergers and acquisitions in 1985 underlined the long-term trend toward greater concentration in the industry, especially by the multimedia corporations. At the end of 1984, 543 independent daily newspapers were left in the United States, 13 fewer than in 1983. Group publishers accounted for about 78% of total circulation. Major acquisitions in 1985 by the Gannett Company included the *Des Moines Register,* the Evening News Association, and *Family Weekly.* And Rupert Murdoch's media interests were enlarged and broadened when he bought Metromedia television stations and a half interest in 20th Century-Fox Film Corporation.

Antitakeover measures were adopted by many media companies, including Dow Jones & Company, the Tribune Company of Chicago, A.H. Belo Corporation of Dallas, Gannett, and the Knight-Ridder newspapers of Miami, as well as smaller, family-owned groups.

For the rest of the 1980s, media analysts predicted that advertising rates would continue to rise somewhat faster than the rate of inflation. They expected circulation to grow by about 1% a year, slower than the growth in households, making an increase in readership the major challenge for the remainder of the decade. Futurists continued to predict that newspapers would be published on a computer-readable medium within a decade and that many other providers of information by electronic means would emerge.

Elizabeth S. Yamashita
University of Oklahoma

PUERTO RICO

Puerto Rico mourned the death of some 180 people in devastating floods that swept the island early in October. Hardest hit was the poor squatter community of Barrio Mameyes near the southern coast city of Ponce. An estimated 127 people were buried under tons of debris there after a massive mudslide sent flimsy wooden houses hurtling down a large hill. The mudslide stirred new awareness of the plight of the island's many ill-housed poor. Officials estimated that up to 200,000 may be living in shantytown conditions, and the administration of Gov. Rafael Hernández Colón vowed to place a higher priority on their needs.

Tax Issue. Gov. Hernández Colón, who took office for a second term (after an eight-year hiatus) on Jan. 1, 1985, spent much of the year trying to avert a disaster on the economic front. Commonwealth officials warned that the island's economy would be "devastated" if the U.S. Congress approved a provision in the Reagan administration's proposed tax reform that would phase out tax benefits for U.S. corporations operating on the island. The governor traveled back and forth to Washington trying to persuade congressmen that ending Section 936 of the Internal Revenue Code would wreak havoc on the island's already fragile economy.

Section 936 offers U.S. firms setting up factories in Puerto Rico close to a 100% tax exemption and the right to take home profits tax-free after investing them for a time in the local economy. It has been the principal incentive for attracting industry and badly needed jobs to the island, where the unemployment rate in 1985 exceeded 20%. The U.S. Treasury Department, however, sees 936 as a widening loophole that costs some $1.7 billion per year. The Reagan tax plan, to replace 936 in five years with a wage-credit plan, appeared headed for defeat as the House Ways and Means Committee in November approved a compromise calling for only slight reductions in tax benefits.

Hernández Colón proposed that 936 funds held in Puerto Rico's Government Development Bank be tied into the Reagan administration's Caribbean Basin Initiative (CBI) through investment in "twin-plant" projects, where manufactured goods would be started at newly established factories in a CBI country and finished in Puerto Rico.

Criminal Cases. The notorious Cerro Maravilla case entered its final stages with the conviction in March of ten policemen on charges of perjury and conspiracy to obstruct justice. The policemen were sentenced to up to 35 years for their roles in the cover-up of the slayings of two young supporters of Puerto Rican independence on the Cerro Maravilla mountaintop in July 1978. The ten also faced murder charges in a local court, and in October seven other policemen also were charged with mur-

---

PUERTO RICO • Information Highlights

Area: 3,421 sq mi (8 860 km²).
Population (mid-1985 est.): 3,300,000.
Chief Cities (1980 census): San Juan, the capital, 434,849; Bayamon, 196,206; Ponce, 189,046.
Government (1985): *Chief Officer*—governor, Rafael Hernández Colón (Popular Democratic Party). *Legislature*—Senate, 27 members; House of Representatives, 51 members.

---

der. The two *independentistas*, supposedly on a mission to sabotage communications towers, were led into a police trap and allegedly shot to death after having surrendered.

In another case with political overtones, the FBI on August 30 arrested 11 suspected members of the Macheteros, a pro-independence Puerto Rican terrorist organization, in connection with the $7 million robbery of a Wells Fargo depot in West Hartford, CT, in 1983. The suspects were arrested in Puerto Rico and extradited to stand trial in Connecticut.

ROBERT FRIEDMAN, *"The San Juan Star"*

QUEBEC

The cause of Quebec independence flickered and died in 1985. The predominantly French-speaking province of 6.5 million commenced the process of rejoining the mainstream of Canadian political life. The transition was dramatized, but by no means instigated, by the return of a Liberal government after nine years of Parti Québécois (PQ) rule.

Sovereignty Renounced. On a cold, overcast Saturday in midwinter—January 19—delegates to a special PQ convention in Montreal resoundingly approved the proposal of their leader, Premier René Lévesque, to drop the goal of sovereignty from the party's electoral platform.

The 921–495 vote sparked a massive walkout from the convention hall by party hard-liners. In the following weeks a number of PQ supporters—cabinet ministers, backbenchers, and constituency organizers—resigned in protest. This left the government in an increasingly precarious position in the National Assembly, or provincial legislature.

The situation deteriorated further on June 3, when the opposition Liberals defeated the PQ in four by-elections, bringing to 26 straight the number of by-elections lost by the PQ since it first took office in 1976. (The PQ also lost the 1980 independence referendum, but it was nevertheless reelected in 1981.)

Lévesque's Resignation. A weary and embattled Premier Lévesque announced on June 20 his intention to resign, paving the way for a leadership contest that was eventually won by Pierre Marc Johnson. Johnson, minister of jus-

In a year of political transition for Quebec, Robert Bourassa and the Liberal party were returned to power in December provincial elections. Bourassa, 52, had served as premier from 1970 to 1976.

Canapress Photo Service

tice in the Lévesque cabinet, defeated five other candidates on the first ballot September 29. He was a logical choice to take the helm as PQ leader and premier, since it was he who had prevailed on Lévesque to drop the sovereignty option many months earlier.

Nonetheless, Johnson was not in an enviable position. He inherited a party still deeply divided over the independence battle, a party whose once-comfortable majority had diminished as a result of defections and by-election defeats. He had to decide fast whether to call a quick election or wait until the PQ's mandate ran out in April 1986—and thereby risk defeat meanwhile in the legislature.

To nobody's surprise, on October 23—three weeks after taking office—Johnson called an election for December 2. The result was a Liberal landslide: 99 Assembly seats to the PQ's 23. Johnson did have the satisfaction of gaining personal reelection in Montreal Anjou, while Liberal leader Robert Bourassa suffered a humiliating defeat in the Montreal-area constituency of Bertrand.

Premier-elect Bourassa thus had to form a government while hoping that one of the winning Liberal candidates would give up his seat to allow Bourassa to run for it.

A Province Transformed. Lévesque's victory over the PQ hard-liners in Montreal, his subsequent resignation, Johnson's accession, and finally the Liberal return to power—all were part of an evolutionary and creative process in Quebec politics and society. No longer is Quebec the defensive, excessively inward-looking province that welcomed the separatist-minded PQ in 1976. It is more mature economically and driven increasingly by an assertive class of business leaders rather than by politicians in liaison with the Catholic Church, as was once the case. Part of the reason for the Liberal victory in December was that the electorate regarded that party as more surefooted than the PQ in the areas of economics and sound administration.

The new Quebec is also more at home with the rest of Canada and less obsessed about pre-serving its distinctive cultural identity, which, in fact, looks more robust than ever.

Constitutional Issues. Premier Lévesque, in a broadcast May 17 on the provincial TV network, outlined sweeping demands for the revision of Canada's federal constitution. The effect would be to exempt Quebec from most provisions of the Canadian Charter of Rights and Freedoms if and when the province accepts the 1981 constitution, of which the charter forms part. The premier also asked that Quebec be given exclusive jurisdiction over language, as well as control over economic development and a voice in international relations.

Lévesque called the list a "starting position." These demands will likely be on the table in future federal-provincial constitutional negotiations. It is likely that the staunchly pro-federalist Liberals will be as aggressive as the PQ in standing up for provincial rights.

Power Exports. Hydro-Quebec will sell 70 billion kilowatt-hours of electrical power to New England under a ten-year agreement signed on October 14 in Montreal. The accord is expected to earn the provincially owned utility $3 billion (U.S.).

JOHN BEST, *"Canada World News"*

QUEBEC • Information Highlights

Area: 594,860 sq mi (1 540 687 km²).
Population (April 1985 est.): 6,572,300.
Chief Cities (1981 census): Quebec, the capital, 166,474; Montreal, 980,354; Laval, 245,856; Longueuil, 124,320.
Government (1985): *Chief Officers*—lt. gov. Gilles Lamontagne; premier, Robert Bourassa (Liberal). *Legislature*—National Assembly, 122 members.
Provincial Finances (1985–86 fiscal year budget): *Revenues,* $24,155,000,000; *expenditures,* $27,250,000,000.
Personal Income (average weekly earnings, July 1985): $410.53.
Labor Force (September 1985, seasonally adjusted): *Employed workers,* 15 years of age and over, 2,814,000; *Unemployed,* 368,000 (11.6%).
Education (1985–86): *Enrollment*—elementary and secondary schools, 1,164,740 pupils; post-secondary (full-time, 1985–86)—universities, 111,700; community colleges, 156,800. (All monetary figures are in Canadian dollars.)

RECORDINGS

The runaway popularity of the compact disc (CD), a ratings system for pop music, and the international gathering of superstars to record for charity were the major developments in the recording industry in 1985.

Classical. The 300th anniversaries of the births of Johann Sebastian Bach, George Frideric Handel, and Domenico Scarlatti made 1985 a big Baroque-music year for classical record companies. There were major releases of Bach, but Handel and Scarlatti releases were fewer. Deutsche Grammophon issued a 130-disc Bach Edition. Delos imported the Capriccio label's multi-disc Leipzig Bach Edition from East Germany.

Classical record collectors bought compact discs with so much enthusiasm that by the end of the year there was a shortage. Denon, a Japanese company, emerged as an important supplier in the United States. Delos, a small American digital pioneer, abandoned the vinyl LP and released only compact discs.

Many companies released CDs that were earlier LP releases, particularly recordings by such famous conductors as Ernest Ansermet (London), Otto Klemperer (Angel), and Fritz Reiner (RCA). Angel released on CD its famous 1950s' *Tosca* with Maria Callas. Complete 1960s' recordings of Wagner's *The Ring of the Nibelung* were issued on CD by London, Philips, and Deutsche Grammophon.

Popular. Although the compact disc had greatest visibility in the classical sector, it was a significant force in pop recording as well. Here too, production fell short of demand. A major factor stimulating pop CD sales was the effort of labels to release simultaneously all formats—LP, CD, cassette, and video—of a new album. Besides enhancing the sales of major labels, CDs became the lifeblood of small labels. Compleat Records became the first label to produce rock recording only on CD. The GRP label's jazz sales were rejuvenated by the compact disc.

Recordings in all formats sold well in 1985, as evidenced by the Recording Industry Association of America's (RIAA) creation of a new certification for multimillion unit sales. This certification attested to the renewed vigor of the industry after its disastrous 1979–1982 slump.

Censorship of pop recordings became a heated issue as the Parents' Music Resource Center pressed for a ratings system for records and videos. The group, which includes the wives of some major politicians, cited lyrics of a sexually explicit or violent nature in the works of Mötley Crüe, Prince, Sheena Easton, and Madonna. The RIAA offered to apply warning stickers to "offensive" discs.

Based on the success of Bob Geldof's 1984 Band Aid project, musicians gathered to record for charitable causes. The *We Are the World* recording was the first and largest such effort in 1985. A group of 45 pop superstars, dubbed USA for Africa, recorded this song, which earned millions for African relief and topped all charts. Political causes benefited from the new social consciousness as well. Steve Van Zandt organized artists to record the antiapartheid *Sun City*. The sixth New Music seminar, the industry's largest event, featured apartheid and record ratings as its focal topics.

The industry saw old high-water marks topped in 1985. Bruce Springsteen's *Born in the USA* became Columbia's biggest-selling album of all time. Madonna's seven Top-10 singles made her the fifth female in 30 years with such a string of hits. Stevie Wonder achieved his 26th Top-10 single. Only the Beatles and Elvis Presley had more. Tina Turner swept the 1985 Grammy Awards. Her *Private Dancer* album won in best female rock performer, record of the year, and song of the year categories. British recordings appeared on American charts in increasing numbers. New artists shared the charts with superstars. Julian Lennon (son of the late John Lennon), Sade, Tears for Fears, Wham!, 'Til Tuesday, Katrina and the Waves, the Hooters, and many others had enormous success with their debuts as well. Superstar solo debuts by The Rolling Stones' Mick Jagger, the Police's Sting, and Van Halen's David Lee Roth were hits as well. Members of Duran Duran regrouped to record as Power Station and Arcadia.

To celebrate what would have been the King's 50th birthday, RCA released several Elvis Presley titles in LP and CD formats. Popular vocal recordings by Whitney Houston, Freddie Jackson, and Aretha Franklin inspired many classic soul releases, among them RCA's *Sam Cooke Live at the Harlem Square Club* and Epic's *The Jackie Wilson Story, Vol. 2.* In jazz, Capitol Records revived Blue Note, perhaps the most important jazz label in history.

Dropping from a 20% to a 10% share of all money spent on recordings in the United States in 1984, country sales plummeted even lower in 1985. The audience for the Nashville Sound averaged over 50 years of age. Most records were purchased in 1985 by consumers in their teens through the early 30s in age, a group whose tastes were decidedly pop and rock oriented.

Although video recordings proved disappointing as a consumer item, the promotional clips shown on Music Television (MTV) and other music video channels had enormous impact on record sales. In fact, MTV, by putting a premium on the performer's visual as well as musical talents, has designated some for stardom who perhaps would not otherwise have made it.

PAULETTE WEISS
Free-lance Journalist

CLASSICAL

BACH/HANDEL: *Bach/Handel 300*, Graziano Mandozzi, synthesizer (Deutsche Grammophon).
BEETHOVEN: Piano Sonatas 1–32, Daniel Barenboim, piano (Deutsche Grammophon).
BRUCKNER: Symphony No. 3, Bavarian Radio Symphony Orchestra, Rafael Kubelik, conductor (London).
IVAN DAVIS: Piano Music of Grieg, Czerny, and Liszt (Audiofon).
DVOŘÁK: Symphony No. 9 (*From the New World*), Berlin Philharmonic Orchestra, Klaus Tennstedt, conductor (Angel).
HANDEL: *Messiah*, soloists, Amsterdam Baroque Orchestra, Ton Koopman, conductor (Erato).
LISZT: Sonata in B Minor and other works, John Browning, piano (Delos).
MOZART: Divertimento in E-flat (K.563), Gidon Kremer (violin), Kim Kashkashian (viola), Yo-Yo Ma (cello) (CBS).
MOZART: Piano Sonatas in C Major and F Major, Rondo in A Minor, Mitsuko Uchida, piano (Philips).
PUCCINI: *Manon Lescaut*, Mirella Freni, Placido Domingo, other soloists, Philharmonia Orchestra, Giuseppe Sinopoli, conductor (Deutsche Grammophon).
ROSSINI: *Maometto Secondo*, Samuel Ramey, June Anderson, other soloists, Philharmonia Orchestra, Claudio Scimone, conductor (Philips).
SCARLATTI: Twelve Sonatas, Narciso Yepes, guitar (Deutsche Grammophon).
VIVALDI: *The Four Seasons*, John Holloway (violin), Taverner Players, Andrew Parrott, conductor (Denon).

JAZZ

LESTER BOWIE'S BRASS FANTASY: *I Only Have Eyes for You* (ECM).
CHICK COREA: *Septet* (ECM).
RICKY FORD: *Shorter Ideas* (Muse).
MICHAEL FRANKS: *Skin Dive* (Warner Bros.).
STEPHANE GRAPPELLI/STUFF SMITH: *Violins No End* (Pablo).
HERBIE HANCOCK & FODAY MUSA SUSO: *Village Life* (Columbia).
EARL HINES/JAKI BYARD: *Duet* (Verve/MPS).
AL JARREAU: *In London* (Warner Bros.).
JEAN LUC-PONTY: *Fables* (Atlantic).
MANHATTAN TRANSFER: *Vocalese* (Atlantic).
WYNTON MARSALIS: *Black Codes* (From the Underground) (Columbia).
MARK MURPHY: *Sings the Nat King Cole Songbook*, Vol. 1 (Muse).
NEWPORT JAZZ FESTIVAL ALL-STARS: (Concord Jazz).
DIANE SCHUUR: *Schuur Thing* (GRP).
ARCHIE SHEPP: *Down Home in New York* (Soul Note).
WAYNE SHORTER: *Atlantis* (Columbia).
L. SUBRAMANIAN/STEPHANE GRAPPELLI: *Conversations* (Milestone).
SARAH VAUGHAN: *Lover Man* Vol. 3 (Musicraft).
MAL WALDRON/DAVID FRIESEN: *Encounters* (Muse).

MOVIES, BROADWAY

BACK TO THE FUTURE: soundtrack (MCA).
BEVERLY HILLS COP: soundtrack (MCA).
BIG RIVER: original cast (MCA).
THE BREAKFAST CLUB: soundtrack (A&M).
FOLLIES: original cast (RCA).
WHOOPI GOLDBERG: original cast (Geffen).
KRUSH GROOVE: soundtrack (Warner Bros.).
MIAMI VICE: soundtrack (MCA).
MISHIMA: film soundtrack (Nonesuch).
ST. ELMO'S FIRE: soundtrack (Atlantic).
VISION QUEST: soundtrack (Geffen).

POPULAR

A-HA: *Hunting High and Low* (Warner Bros.).
ALABAMA: *40 Hour Week* (RCA).
PHILIP BAILEY: *Chinese Wall* (Columbia).
GEORGE BENSON: *20/20* (Warner Bros.).
LAURA BRANIGAN: *Branigan 2* (Atlantic).

BRONSKI BEAT: *The Age of Consent* (MCA).
KATE BUSH: *Hounds of Love* (EMI-America).
ERIC CLAPTON: *Behind the Sun* (Warner Bros.).
PHIL COLLINS: *No Jacket Required* (Atlantic).
THE COMMODORES: *Nightshift* (Motown).
SAM COOKE: *Feel It! Live at the Harlem Square Club* (RCA).
DEBARGE: *Rhythm of the Night* (Gordy).
DEPECHE MODE: *Some Great Reward* (Sire).
DIRE STRAITS: *Brothers in Arms* (Warner Bros.).
BOB DYLAN: *Biograph* (Columbia).
SHEENA EASTON: *A Private Heaven* (EMI-America).
EURYTHMICS: *Be Yourself Tonight* (RCA).
THE FIRM: *The Firm* (Atlantic).
JOHN FOGERTY: *Centerfield* (Warner Bros.).
FOREIGNER: *Agent Provocateur* (Atlantic).
ARETHA FRANKLIN: *Who's Zoomin' Who?* (Arista).
AMY GRANT: *Unguarded* (A&M).
MERLE HAGGARD: *Kern River* (Epic).
DARYL HALL & JOHN OATES: *Live at the Apollo with David Ruffin & Eddie Kendrick* (RCA).
COREY HART: *Boy in the Box* (EMI-America).
HEART, *Heart* (Capitol)
DON HENLEY: *Building the Perfect Beast* (Geffen).
HOOTERS: *Nervous Night* (Columbia).
WHITNEY HOUSTON: *Whitney Houston* (Arista).
JULIO IGLESIAS: *Libra* (Columbia).
FREDDIE JACKSON: *Rock Me Tonight* (Capitol).
MICK JAGGER: *She's the Boss* (Columbia).
JESSE JOHNSON'S REVUE: *Jesse Johnson's Revue* (A&M).
HOWARD JONES: *Dream into Action* (Elektra).
STANLEY JORDAN: *Magic Touch* (Blue Note).
KATRINA & THE WAVES: *Katrina & the Waves* (Capitol).
KOOL & THE GANG: *Emergency* (De-Lite/PolyGram).
HUEY LEWIS & THE NEWS: *Picture This* (Chrysalis).
LISA LISA/CULT JAM WITH FULL FORCE: (Columbia).
LOS LOBOS: *How Will the Wolf Survive?* (Slash/Warner Bros.).
MARY JANE GIRLS: *Only Four You* (Motown).
MAZE: *Can't Stop the Love* (Capitol).
JOHN COUGAR MELLENCAMP: *Scarecrow* (Riva/PolyGram).
MÖTLEY CRÜE: *Theatre of Pain* (Elektra).
WILLIE NELSON: *Half Nelson* (Columbia).
OLIVIA NEWTON-JOHN: *Soul Kiss* (MCA).
TOM PETTY & THE HEARTBREAKERS: *Southern Accents* (MCA).
ROBERT PLANT: *Shaken 'n' Stirred* (Es Paranza/Atlantic).
POINTER SISTERS: *Contact* (RCA).
THE POWER STATION: *The Power Station* (Capitol).
PRINCE & THE REVOLUTION: *Around the World in a Day* (Paisley Park/Warner Bros.).
RATT: *Invasion of Your Privacy* (Atlantic).
R.E.M.: *Fables of the Reconstruction* (I.R.S.).
REO SPEEDWAGON: *Wheels Are Turnin'* (Epic).
LIONEL RICHIE: *Can't Slow Down* (Motown).
DIANA ROSS: *Eaten Alive* (RCA).
DAVID LEE ROTH: *Crazy from the Heat* (Warner Bros.).
RUN:DMC: *King of Rock* (Profile).
SADE: *Diamond Life* (Portrait/Epic).
STARSHIP: *Knee Deep in the Hoopla* (Grant/RCA).
STING: *The Dream of the Blue Turtles* (A&M).
GEORGE STRAIT: *Something Special* (MCA).
BARBRA STREISAND: *The Broadway Album* (Columbia).
TALKING HEADS: *Little Creatures* (Sire/Warner Bros.).
TEARS FOR FEARS: *Songs from the Big Chair* (Mercury/PolyGram).
TEENA MARIE: *Starchild* (Epic).
THE THOMPSON TWINS: *Here's to Future Days* (Arista).
'TIL TUESDAY: *Voices Carry* (Epic).
UB40: *Little Baggariddim* (Virgin/A&M).
USA FOR AFRICA: *We Are the World* (Columbia).
U2: *Wide Awake in America* (Island).
LUTHER VANDROSS: *The Night I Fell in Love* (Epic).
HANK WILLIAMS, JR: *Five-O* (Warner Bros.).
GEORGE WINSTON: *Autumn* (Windham Hill/A&M).
STEVIE WONDER: *In Square Circle* (Tamla/Motown).
PAUL YOUNG: *The Secret of Association* (Columbia).
ZZ TOP: *After Burner* (Warner Bros.).

REFUGEES AND IMMIGRATION

The world's refugee population, estimated at 11 million in 1984, swelled significantly in 1985 as natural disasters and civil strife forced hundreds of thousands of new victims from their homes across national borders.

Africa. The worst refugee problem was in Africa, where the devastating drought of 1984 and early 1985 brought famine to several countries. The United Nations Food and Agriculture Organization (FAO) said early in 1985 that 18 African countries would need major food assistance from the Western world if their people were to avert starvation.

Ethiopia was perhaps the most severely affected. In that country alone, more than 8 million suffered the effects of drought. Thousands of Ethiopians fled to neighboring Sudan and Somalia in search of food and water. At midyear, an estimated 150,000 Ethiopians were in refugee camps in Somalia. The situation was exacerbated by the Ethiopian government, which closed a major famine relief center, forcibly expelling as many as 100,000 refugees.

Other African countries also experienced massive refugee flows, but in many cases the cause was politics rather than natural disasters. In April, Nigeria ordered 700,000 illegal aliens —nearly half of them from Ghana—to leave the country by May 10. By that deadline 50,000 Ghanaians had left, but thousands were stranded when Nigeria closed its borders. Thousands more were rounded up in detention camps, where rioting broke out because of lack of food.

In August and September, Libya evicted more than 30,000 Tunisian nationals because of rising tension between the two countries. And in Uganda, hundreds of foreign citizens fled growing violence in that country after the overthrow of President Milton Obote in July.

Bloodshed. Violence against refugees was not confined to Africa. In Lebanon, Shiite Muslims laid siege to three Palestine refugee camps housing 25,000 persons. Hundreds were killed and thousands wounded in fighting between Palestinians and Shiites during May and June.

In Central America, Honduran troops raided a refugee camp near the border of El Salvador in search of suspected guerrillas in September. International relief workers charged that at least two people were killed, 13 wounded, and 25 beaten with rifle butts. The Honduran army acknowledged one death and ten arrests but maintained that the raid had been merely an "inspection."

Elsewhere in Central America, guerrilla warfare continues to displace thousands. By one estimate, 90,000 Guatemalans are now in refugee camps in southern Mexico. In 1984 the Mexican government began to resettle the refugees in the sparsely populated states of Campeche and Quintana Roo in the Yucatan peninsula. The United Nations said that of the 42,000 refugees it aids in Mexico, 18,000 had been resettled and that the 99 camps in the state of Chiapas had been reduced to 75.

Asia also continued to suffer from enormous refugee problems. The ongoing war between Afghan guerrillas and occupying Soviet troops kept an estimated 4 million Afghans in refugee camps outside the country, mainly in Pakistan. Thailand harbored more than 250,000 Cambodians pushed out of their country by Vietnamese forces. Under a program begun in 1982, 2,927 Amerasian children fathered by Americans stationed in Vietnam during the Indochinese War had been brought to the United States by late 1985.

Immigration Bill. In the United States the Congress struggled, as it had for several years, with proposed legislation to reform the country's immigration laws. In September the Senate approved, 69–30, a bill introduced by Sen. Alan K. Simpson (R-WY) that would impose fines of $100 to $2,000 on employers for each illegal alien they hire; the fines would rise to $3,000 to $10,000 for repeat offenders. The bill would grant permanent resident status to illegal aliens who entered the United States before Jan. 1, 1980. In a highly controversial section, the Simpson bill would permit 350,000 alien workers to enter the country temporarily to harvest perishable crops. The aliens would be allowed to stay in the United States for up to nine months a year and move from farm to farm within a defined area. The "guest worker" provision would remain in effect for three years.

Immigration legislation also was introduced in the House of Representatives by Rep. Peter W. Rodino, Jr. (D-NJ). The Rodino bill would grant resident status to aliens entering the country before Jan. 1, 1982, and would provide both civil and criminal penalties for employers who hire illegal aliens. The House version contained no guest-worker provision, and observers foresaw difficulty in reconciling the two bills.

The scope of U.S. immigration problems was highlighted in a report released by the Immigration and Naturalization Service (INS) on its fiscal year 1985 operations. In the year ending Sept. 30, 1985, the INS Border Patrol apprehended a record 1,265,054 illegal aliens, more than 95% of whom were Mexicans. Of the remainder, more than three fourths were from Central America. The INS predicted that total apprehensions, including seizures in the interior of the country, would reach 1.32 million by year's end, compared with 1.24 million in 1984.

In May, Cuban President Fidel Castro canceled a major immigration exchange agreement with the United States to protest the start-up of Radio Martí, a new U.S. broadcast service aimed at Cuba.

RICHARD C. SCHROEDER, *"Visión" Magazine*

The Sanctuary Movement

The Casa Oscar Romero in San Benito, TX, shelters some 200 Central American refugees.

AP/Wide World

Since mid-1982, more than 200 churches across the United States have joined together in a loose coalition known as the sanctuary movement. The aim of the movement is to provide help and shelter for illegal immigrants, principally Salvadorans, in defiance of U.S. immigration law. In addition to the churches, several cities—Berkeley, CA; Cambridge, MA; and Chicago, IL, and New York, NY—have declared themselves sanctuaries for illegal immigrants from Central America.

During the same period, the U.S. Immigration and Naturalization Service (INS) has mounted a campaign to thwart the movement. INS efforts were capped in 1985 by the indictments and convictions of a number of sanctuary workers on charges of transporting or sheltering illegal Salvadoran aliens.

Those participating in the sanctuary movement see the immigrants they assist as political refugees who would face persecution and even death if they were returned to their homelands. The INS insists that the illegals are economic refugees in search of jobs and better living conditions and are not entitled to asylum. U.S. immigration laws stipulate that asylum may be granted only to persons who flee outright persecution or have a "well-founded fear of persecution."

Moreover, says INS Commissioner Alan C. Nelson, there has been "absolutely no evidence" of harm to any of the illegal aliens who have been deported or who have returned voluntarily to their countries. The sanctuary movement is essentially an exercise in "civil disobedience" aimed at changing U.S. policy in Central America, the INS says.

Adherents of the movement justify their activities by pointing out how infrequently asylum is granted to immigrants who ask for it. The INS gave political asylum to 503 Salvadoran immigrants in 1984 but denied more than 13,000 applications.

The INS, on the other hand, says that appeals of the denials can delay actual deportations for years, during which time most applicants are given permission to work. INS data show that apprehensions of illegal Salvadoran aliens are on the increase, rising from 14,000 in 1982 to nearly 19,000 in 1984, while actual deportations have declined from 5,500 in 1982 to 3,900 in 1984. The INS estimates that there are between 300,000 and 500,000 illegal Salvadorans in the United States and says that 71% of the illegals who have been apprehended are still in the country.

The sanctuary movement has ancient roots, dating from Egyptian, Greek, Roman, and biblical times. Christian churches were recognized as sanctuaries from the early 4th century through the end of the Middle Ages. Criminals who reached a place of worship before being detained could not be apprehended by civil authorities lest they commit a sacrilege. The concept of church sanctuary fell into disuse with the rise of the nation-state and the supremacy of secular authorities over criminal matters, but it lived on in international law and diplomacy. The modern sanctuary movement in the United States began in May 1982, when several churches established themselves as havens for illegal aliens from Central America.

The most celebrated sanctuary prosecution was the 1985 trial of a dozen persons in Arizona, including a nun, two priests, and two Protestant ministers, on charges of transporting illegal aliens and hiding them in a church. A federal judge in the case ruled that the defendants could not use religious arguments to justify their illegal acts. At year's end the highly publicized trial was still going on.

RICHARD C. SCHROEDER

As in any year, various administrative changes occurred in the world religions in 1985. In the Roman Catholic archdiocese of Los Angeles, Archbishop Roger Mahony (right) *succeeded Timothy Cardinal Manning.*

RELIGION

In 1985 the National Council of Churches reported an increase of nearly 1% in mainline church membership in 1983 and revealed that women constituted more than 25% of the seminarians in the United States and Canada in the fall of 1984. According to a new report on "Religion in America" by George Gallup, Jr., "9 in 10 [Americans surveyed] state a religious preference, 7 in 10 are church members, and 6 in 10 attend religious services in a given month." A majority told the Gallup organization that "they are more interested in religious and spiritual matters today than they were five years ago." On the other hand, Gallup noted that "widespread cheating is found on all levels of society, and two thirds of Americans hold the view that the level of ethics in the United States has declined during the past decade."

Far Eastern

There has been controversy among scholars concerning the nature of Confucianism. Some have said it is not a religion, but an ethic or a humanistic philosophy. Confucius was critical of certain religious practices that were to him too absorbed in the supernatural, or not valuable to social well-being. Yet he was supportive of religious belief and practice, setting an example that became, until China's Cultural Revolution of the 1960s, the Chinese ideal. Recently there have been attempts to rehabilitate the significance of Confucianism to the Chinese way of life.

Although the spiritual leader of Tibetan Buddhism, the Dalai Lama, canceled plans to visit his homeland in 1985, there were stirrings of reconciliation between the Chinese government and the Tibetans. Two hundred tons of Buddhist relics seized during the Cultural Revolution were returned to monasteries for restoration, and a three-member delegation representing the Dalai Lama had visited Peking in the fall of 1984. The Chinese also agreed to repair Buddhist temples atop Mt. Wutai.

India. The struggle between Sikh minorities and the Hindu majority continued in India. The April 19 shooting of Raghunandan Lal Bhatia, general secretary of the ruling Congress (I) party, caused government security forces to raid residences near the Sikh Golden Temple at Amritsar, site of the June 1984 carnage. This time forces did not enter the shrine but made arrests and seized weapons. The only Sikh member of the national cabinet, Agricultural Minister Buta Singh, was excommunicated by Sikh high priests for his support of government policy in the restoration of the Golden Temple. Later in the summer, Harchand Singh Longowal, the leader of the predominantly Sikh Akali Dal party, was assassinated. Sikhs seek autonomy for the Punjab, where most of them live, and have demanded greater freedom for the militant All-India Sikh Students Federation and an end to popular Hindu hostility.

Also in India, the lingering effects of the ancient Hindu caste system continued to produce conflict. The state had decided to increase the quotas of lower caste Hindus in government jobs and in public institutions such as universities. Rival higher castes have agitated for similar preferential considerations. The resultant conflict led to riots and loss of lives in the western state of Gujarat.

Sri Lanka. In June, Tamil separatist guerrillas and the Sri Lankan government agreed to a "cessation of hostile incidents." Violence between the separatists and government troops had escalated in mid-May. On May 23 nearly 500 Buddhist monks demonstrated in protest of the massacre of about 150 civilians in Anuradhapura, indicating a more active political role on the part of the Buddhist establishment. Tamils are predominantly Hindu and, along with Muslims, are minorities in the Singhalese state, where Buddhists are in the majority.

RICHARD E. WENTZ
Arizona State University

Islam

During 1985 many of the world's Muslims expressed a desire to establish fully Islamic frameworks for their lives. Because Muslims view Islam as a total system regulating all aspects of their lives, not simply their religious obligations, they do not make the distinction between matters of "church" and "state" normally drawn in Western societies. Consequently, several Muslim countries adjusted their legal systems to bring them into conformity with Islamic law (*sharia*). In a few countries with sizable Islamic minorities, the assertiveness of some Muslims brought them into conflict with their fellow citizens of other faiths.

In an attempt to adhere to the admonition in the Koran (Quran), Islam's sacred scripture, against usury, Pakistani authorities enacted legislation forbidding banks, including those owned by non-Muslims, to charge or pay interest. Instead, borrowers were to pay service charges, while depositors were to share in the bank's profits or losses.

In Sudan, where punishments specifically prescribed in the Koran had been in force for over a year, President Jaafar al-Nemery ordered the execution, in January, of the leader of the Republican Brothers, a religious organization opposed to applying the Koranic penalties. In April, however, Nemery was deposed in a military coup. Sudan's new rulers refrained from enforcing the Koranic prescriptions, accusing the previous regime of having used them as a political weapon against its opponents.

A major controversy over the *sharia* arose in Egypt in 1985. For some time, conservative Muslims had urged the state to bring its laws immediately into complete conformity with the Koran. In May the parliament voted to review the legal system gradually and to consider revisions of those sections not in agreement with the Koran. Fundamentalists demonstrated their displeasure in a series of protests that led to the jailing of many Muslim militants.

Also in the spring, Egypt's Constitutional Court struck down a women's rights law popularly known as the Jihan Law, after Anwar el-Sadat's widow, who had been a prime mover in its passage in the late 1970s. The law had lessened the traditionally great control husbands exercised over their wives. In July, however, parliament passed new legislation that, while permitting polygyny, restored to women some rights guaranteed in the recently abrogated bill.

In Indonesia, tensions between the Muslim majority and Buddhist minority resulted in several violent incidents. Despite the fact that Indonesia is the world's largest Muslim country, President Suharto moved quickly to curb the rise of extremism. He imposed a ban on public expressions of any ideology other than the sectarian principles, known as *Pancasila,* of the ruling political party. Competition between the Muslim and non-Muslim communities (largely composed of Indonesians on the one hand and ethnic Chinese on the other) for opportunities in the troubled economy, however, allowed for only an uneasy peace between religious groups.

In the United States the American Muslim Mission, founded in the 1930s as the Nation of Islam, formally disbanded in 1985, encouraging its members to move into the mainstream of the Islamic faith. The decision represented a final break with the movement's political activities begun by its founder, Elijah Muhammad. His son, Warith Deen Muhammad, has emphasized the need for American Muslims to use religion, education, and economic advancement as means of improving their lives.

KENNETH J. PERKINS
University of South Carolina

Judaism

For world Jewry, 1985 was a year of dramatic developments.

Ethiopian Jews. First came an announcement in January that the government of Israel had airlifted thousands of Ethiopian Jews from that famine-stricken country and relocated them to Israel. It was a historic event seen by them as divine fulfillment of centuries-old prayers and by others as the return of an ancient Hebrew tribe to its ancestral homeland. Calling themselves "Beta Israel" (House of Israel), the Ethiopian Jews are a remnant of an independent kingdom that thrived for a thousand years in a mountain fastness bordered by the Takkaze River in northern Ethiopia. Defeated by neighboring Christian tribes, the group had been a persecuted minority in Ethiopia for centuries. In Israel the arrival of tens of thousands of these malnourished immigrants, many with unfamiliar diseases and without modern skills, came as a shock to the country's unstable economy. Contributions of money, clothing, and other supplies from Jews throughout the world helped ease the initial hardships. In September several hundred of the Ethiopian Jews staged a three-week sit-down demonstration opposite Jerusalem's great synagogue to protest the Chief Rabbinate's insistence that young Ethiopians wishing to marry must undergo ritual immersion as a reaffirmation of their Jewishness.

Anti-Soviet Protest. In an unprecedented coordinated action dubbed "Operation Redemption," Christian clergy joined hundreds of rabbis and Jewish students in a series of protest demonstrations at Soviet diplomatic facilities in New York, San Francisco, and Washington, DC, against "the new spiritual genocide" of Jews in the Soviet Union. Some protesters wrapped themselves in prayer shawls, carried

Torah scrolls, recited psalms, and blew rams' horns to dramatize the religious nature of Soviet oppression. Meanwhile, imprisonment in the Soviet Union of Hebrew teachers and others observing Jewish religious ritual rose to a rate of one per week, and Jewish emigration from the USSR dropped to an all-time low. The 14th annual May solidarity march for Soviet Jewry in New York drew 240,000 people.

Holocaust Reminders. The solidarity march coincided with President Ronald Reagan's May 5 visit to a West German military cemetery at Bitburg where, among regular German army soldiers, 49 of the Third Reich's notorious Waffen-SS lie buried. Hundreds of protesters from the United States and Europe lined the road to Bitburg cemetery; others assembled at other sites in Germany and the United States to voice their bitterness over the president's choice of this gesture to mark the 40th anniversary of the end of World War II and of U.S.–German reconciliation. The same day, President Reagan visited the Bergen-Belsen Nazi concentration camp to honor victims of the Holocaust. (*See also* BIOGRAPHY—Wiesel, Elie.)

Another agonizing reminder of World War II was the intensified search for Josef Mengele, the fugitive Auschwitz death camp doctor. The quest culminated in June with the discovery of Mengele's bones in a grave in Brazil and confirmation by an international team of forensic experts that they were indeed his remains.

Anti-Semitism. A worldwide increase in anti-Semitic incidents was attributed in large part to anti-Israeli agitation by the Soviet Union and the Arab bloc. Jewish leaders in Great Britain were especially alarmed by a drastic rise in anti-Semitic rhetoric in various forms of literature. They believed that the Lebanon war of 1982 had opened a floodgate of anti-Israeli hostility, resulting in publications that blurred the long-maintained distinction between anti-Zionism and anti-Semitism.

Jewish representatives at the UN Decade for Women Conference in Nairobi, Kenya, in July experienced a similar extension of anti-Israeli sentiment to include all Jews. Jewish women from the United States, Canada, Europe, and Israel were equally exposed to harassment, isolation, and abuse.

Cries of protest arose from many Jewish circles in May, when Israel released 1,150 mostly Palestinian prisoners, including 167 convicted terrorists, in exchange for three Israeli soldiers held in Syrian jail. In the months that followed, Arab terrorism escalated to unprecedented heights. Bombings and kidnappings; bus, plane, and even ship hijackings; the killing of hostages; and random murder became almost daily occurrences in Israel and elsewhere. Although Jews and Jewish institutions were the most frequent targets, the epidemic of violence claimed many other victims throughout the Middle East and Europe.

AP/Wide World

Amy Eilberg was ordained May 12 as the first woman rabbi in the century-long history of the Conservative movement.

Other. After years of debate, the worldwide governing body of Conservative Judaism, the Rabbinical Assembly, announced its decision in February 1985 to admit women as rabbis. The first candidate, Amy Eilberg, 30, of New York City, was ordained in May.

In September the Vatican issued its third "Guidelines" concerning Jews and Judaism. Many Jewish leaders were disappointed with its contents, feeling that the 1985 document, unlike its 1965 and 1975 predecessors, strengthened theological differences between the two religions. They objected primarily to the Vatican's mere passing reference to the Holocaust and its direction to Catholics to view modern Israel in a political rather than a religious perspective. In November, Catholic and Jewish leaders announced agreement on a program "to overcome the residues of indifference, resistance, and suspicion."

And 1985 was designated by UNESCO as the Year of Maimonides, the great medieval Jewish philosopher. The series of events marking the 850th anniversary of Maimonides' birth opened in Paris in March and continued in Jerusalem in July. In September an international congress marked the event in Cordova, Spain, Maimonides' birthplace, followed by scholarly sessions in Fez, Morocco, where he completed a major portion of his scholarly work.

LIVIA E. BITTON-JACKSON
Herbert H. Lehman College, CUNY

Orthodox Eastern

Ignatius IV, Orthodox Patriarch of Antioch and All the East, made his first visit to North America in 1985. The spiritual leader of millions of Arab Orthodox Christians began his Western journey in Latin America. He was welcomed to the United States and Canada in May by Metropolitan Philip Saliba, head of the 350,000-member Antiochian Orthodox Christian Archdiocese, who accompanied the patriarch in his meetings designed "to communicate with the people about the life of the church." While in America, the 65-year-old prelate, who is involved in Christian-Muslim dialogue, also was received by Archbishop Iakovos of the Greek Orthodox Archdiocese and by Metropolitan Theodosius of the Orthodox Church in America.

Appointments and Meetings. Nicholas Smisko, titular bishop of Amisus in the Ecumenical Patriarch of Constantinople, was elected primate of the Carpatho-Russian Orthodox diocese with its headquarters in Johnstown, PA. Nathanael Popp was elected bishop of Detroit within the Orthodox Church in America (OCA) with episcopal leadership over the Romanian Orthodox Episcopate in the United States and Canada.

The Synod of Bishops of the Greek Orthodox Archdiocese in America voted to limit programs at its Hellenic College in Brookline, MA, to Greek and pretheological studies. The synod also reaffirmed the need for Greek language study and worship at its Holy Cross School of Theology, also in Brookline. The Holy Cross School hosted an international conference of Eastern and Oriental Orthodox Churches in June concerning the "reception process" of the WCC Faith and Order Statement on *Baptism, Eucharist and Ministry*. The representatives of the churches greeted the statement with cautious enthusiasm. The international Lutheran-Orthodox Consultation met in May in Allentown, PA, with its participants joining in the 80th anniversary celebration of St. Tikhon's Monastery in South Canaan, PA.

In addition to bilateral discussions with Catholics and Protestants, Orthodox participated in the first meeting of the newly appointed Faith and Order Commission of the World Council of Churches in Stavanger, Norway, in August. For the first time an American woman theologian, Dr. Kyriake FitzGerald of Cambridge, MA, was among the Orthodox commissioners.

The USSR. The Eastern Orthodox Church in the USSR continued preparations for the celebration of the 1,000th anniversary of Christianity in its land in 1988. The Monastery of St. Daniel in Moscow is being restored to house the offices of the Moscow patriarchate.

While the new Gorbachev regime appeared to support the Orthodox Church whose state-confirmed leaders back the government's foreign policy programs and its efforts toward internal reform, certain influential church leaders, including Archbishop Kyril of Vyborg, the rector of the Leningrad Theological Academy, and Bishop Chrysostom of Kursk, were moved to less powerful positions.

Anniversary. The 1,100th anniversary of the death of St. Methodius, the missionary who with his brother Cyril brought Christianity to the Slavs, was celebrated in ceremonies in Thessalonica, Greece, their native city, as well as in Sophia, Bulgaria, and Prague, Czechoslovakia.

Obituary. Metropolitan Philaret, archbishop of New York and Eastern America and primate of the Russian Orthodox Church Outside of Russia, died in late November.

THOMAS HOPKO, *St. Vladimir's Seminary*

Protestantism

Church-led activism to exert pressure for change in South Africa's racial-separatist policies was the most significant story of 1985 in U.S. Protestantism. Protests of church leaders at South African diplomatic offices, decisions to disinvest holdings in companies doing business in South Africa, and campaigns to halt U.S. sales of the gold coin called the Krugerrand were among the actions taken.

Three South African clerics—Desmond Tutu, installed in February as the first black Anglican bishop of Johannesburg; mixed-race Reformed leader Allan Boesak; and white Reformed activist and top South African Council of Churches executive C.F. Beyers Naude—were outspoken in their opposition to apartheid. (*See* feature article, pages 26–35.)

Other activist themes in the year's news included attention to the nuclear arms race and the struggle between church and state over the movement to give sanctuary to illegal aliens from Central America. (*See* special report, page 441.)

Problems in Central America and the Middle East also caused concern. Protestants clashed over U.S. policy in Nicaragua, with the neoconservative Washington-based Institute on Religion and Democracy issuing strong condemnations of liberal Protestant groups that favored the Sandinista government. The continuing conflict in Lebanon particularly involved Protestant groups with historic missionary ties in the Middle East. In September, Presbyterian missionary Benjamin Weir was released by a group of Muslim extremists who had kidnapped him in May 1984 in Beirut.

Religion and U.S. Politics. Conservative Protestants were critical of a Supreme Court action striking down an Alabama law mandating a moment of silent prayer in public schools. A yet-to-be-decided case would determine

Hawaii's Episcopal Bishop Edmond Lee Browning addresses the Episcopal Church's governing convention September 11 in Anaheim, CA, after being elected presiding bishop. By coincidence, the day also marked his 32nd wedding anniversary with wife Patricia (left).

whether a student religious club at a Pennsylvania public high school was unconstitutionally discriminated against when school officials refused it permission to meet during school hours at a time designated for meetings of other extracurricular groups.

Evangelical television host M.G. "Pat" Robertson was considering a race for the Republican U.S. presidential nomination on the basis of statistics showing rising numbers of "born-again" voters.

Denominational News. The country's largest Protestant denomination, the 14-million-member Southern Baptist Convention (SBC), continued its six-year struggle between so-called "moderate" and "ultra-conservative" factions. Atlanta pastor Charles Stanley, a leader of the fundamentalist or "biblical inerrancy" group, was reelected SBC president. A 22-member "peace committee" was named to find solutions to the continuing conflict. Meanwhile, moderates predicted that college and seminary professors and agency staffers would be fired if continued victories by the fundamentalists shifted the balance of power on trustee boards.

Three Lutheran bodies planning to unite in 1988—the Lutheran Church in America, the American Lutheran Church, and the Association of Evangelical Lutheran Churches—tentatively picked Chicago as their headquarters city.

Two Protestant denominations—the United Church of Christ and the Disciples of Christ—decided not to commit themselves to a proposed church union. Instead they established an "ecumenical partnership" to encourage shared worship and joint mission efforts.

Leaders. The Episcopal Church elected a 56-year-old liberal with overseas missionary experience—Bishop Edmond Browning of Hawaii—to a 12-year term as its new presiding bishop.

The National Council of Churches installed a new leader, 49-year-old Reformed clergyman Arie Brouwer, and began an ambitious process of restructuring itself and revamping its financial operations to quiet criticisms that the 31-denomination council had been unresponsive to church opinion at the grass-roots level.

An activist Clairton, PA, pastor, D. Douglas Roth, was deposed from the ministry of the Lutheran Church in America. His case, and the cases of two other pastors, pitted the church and major corporate interests against a small group of clergy and labor union members who used confrontational, often highly offensive, tactics to dramatize the plight of unemployed workers in a depressed steel-producing region.

Other News. Anglicans in both England and Australia squabbled over the question of ordaining women to the priesthood, but support of the idea appeared to be gaining ground in both countries.

The National Council of Churches, traditionally a foe of movie censorship, issued a report from its study of sex and sexual violence in the media, warning that television (both commercial and cable), film, and home-video industries could avoid the threat of censorship only if they policed themselves to eliminate pornographic content. The report called for measures to protect children from exposure to such programming and supported a renewal of a regulatory role for the Federal Communications Commission.

Lovers of church music had three birthdays to celebrate with festive services and concerts—the 300th birthdays of J.S. Bach and George F. Handel and the 400th birthday of Heinrich Schütz. By far the most enthusiastic attention was given to the music of Bach, the German organist-choirmaster, who composed his greatest works for Lutheran congregations.

JEAN CAFFEY LYLES
Associate Editor, Religious News Service

Archbishop Jan Schotte of Belgium (right) served as general secretary of the world Synod of Bishops, called by Pope John Paul II to review the Second Vatican Council. The synod met Nov. 25–Dec. 8, 1985.

Roman Catholicism

The extraordinary world Synod of Bishops, called by Pope John Paul II near the end of 1985 to evaluate the Second Vatican Council, dominated the year's Catholic events.

The Synod. Despite the synod's advisory status, the deliberations and statements, widely covered in the world media, received significant attention, particularly with respect to questions of church authority, shared responsibility, and a reaffirmation of Vatican II teachings. The unprecedented two-week meeting in Rome involved delegates from every bishops' conference worldwide. Among its expected results were: new efforts toward fuller implementation of Vatican II; the development of a compendium or catechism based on council teachings; and a new thrust toward Christian unity and evangelization.

The Pope and the Vatican. The year also witnessed trips by the pope to Latin America, the Benelux countries, Africa, and the tiny state of Liechtenstein. In almost all settings, the pope took a dual approach, speaking out on the need for deeper unity and spirituality among Catholics and on behalf of human rights, especially freedom of religion.

Among the controversies affecting the worldwide church were the publication of a so-called "Pope's column" by an international syndicate, which was repudiated by the Vatican; Vatican intervention in a dispute over clergy and religious signing an ad in *The New York Times* that claimed valid alternatives to church teaching regarding abortion; a Vatican-inspired probe of complaints about church life in the Seattle archdiocese; and statements by Joseph Cardinal Ratzinger, head of the Vatican doctrinal congregation, suggesting Vatican II has been a failure thus far.

Church and State. In Poland, homeland of the pope, the conviction of the killers of a popular Polish priest did little to alleviate tensions and fears engendered by the country's state of martial law. Twenty of Poland's leading university educators later were fired by the government in what some observers called a political purge. The action was denounced by Pope John Paul.

The kidnapping of an American Servite priest, Lawrence Martin Jenco, by Muslim extremists in Beirut, Lebanon, and his continuing detention was a developing story throughout 1985, as various efforts were mounted to free him and other U.S. hostages taken in Lebanon.

In Nicaragua, relations between the Marxist Sandinista regime and the Catholic bishops deteriorated. But the U.S. bishops continued to call for peace talks and urged the U.S. government to halt aid to rebel "contra" forces.

The 1983 shooting of Filipino leader Benigno Aquino and the subsequent exoneration of his alleged killers caused a widening split between church leaders and the regime of President Ferdinand Marcos. During 1985, several priests were killed, and bishops increasingly spoke out against the government.

In South Africa, Catholic leaders joined other Christian churchmen in denouncing the country's apartheid (racial segregation) policies and called for economic boycotts of South Africa by foreign nations.

The sanctuary movement in the United States, which involved Catholic clergy and religious in providing refuge for illegal aliens from Central America, caused strains between some church elements and the government.

Jews and Catholics. Celebrations and discussions were held in the United States, Rome, and elsewhere to mark the 20th anniversary of the Vatican II statement on the Jews, *Nostra Aetate*. Meeting under the auspices of the Vatican and in conjunction with the anniversary, Jewish and Catholic leaders agreed to a joint program "to overcome the residues of indifference, resistance, and suspicion."

Administration. Archbishop John O'Connor of New York and Archbishop Bernard Law of Boston were among 28 new cardinals named by the pope. And the U.S. bishops approved the second draft of their controversial pastoral on the economy. Bishop Roger M. Mahony was named to head the Los Angeles archdiocese.

ROBERT L. JOHNSTON, Editor
"The Chicago Catholic"

RETAILING

American retailing in 1985 had an exciting but agonizing time. Merchants found themselves buffeted by an erratic sales trend; sharp price cutting to stimulate business, which severely cut profit margins; new forms of competition; and constant battling with protectionists seeking to limit imports. They often wondered what had happened to the economic recovery that Washington predicted.

The disappointing 1984 Christmas season spilled over into 1985, both in terms of sluggish business and heavy price-cutting. Mixed financial results were reported by most big chains during the year, and hopes for a sound second half began fading. But in late summer the sales tempo quickened, and retailers found reason to expect a better final quarter.

The pressures led to many corporate developments. The biggest was the decision by Montgomery Ward, a division of Mobil Corporation, to close its century-old, losing catalog business, thereby giving up 25% of sales. Earlier, Mobil said that the barely profitable Ward's would be pruned and its stores remodeled to increase profits. Mobil also said it planned to eventually spin off Ward, presumably to Mobil shareholders, as a separate company.

Another major event was the purchase by The Limited Inc. of Lerner Stores, the second-largest chain of shops selling popularly priced apparel, from McCrory Corporation, owned by Rapid-American Corporation. McCrory itself appeared headed in a new direction when its parent named Stephen L. Pistner, Montgomery Ward's chief executive, as McCrory chairman.

The new Limited-Lerner combination promptly made a dramatic move. It abruptly canceled all outstanding orders to the apparel trade in an effort, as Leslie H. Wexner, Limited's chairman, put it, to "consolidate Lerner's paperwork and inventories." But the stoppage produced widespread resentment among suppliers and led to a number of court suits.

F. W. Woolworth took two major actions. It closed 17 stores or half of its J. Brannam off-price apparel chain amid strong hints that it would close that unprofitable subsidiary. The company also set up 11 test projects in the specialty-store field—including footwear, stationery, and drug discounting—hoping they would be major profit contributors.

Mergers and Acquisitions. Ames Department Stores bought the G. C. Murphy Company, a chain of variety and discount stores. Zayre Corporation, a discount and off-price operator, purchased Gaylords National Corporation, a discounter. Associated Dry Goods Corporation sold its Powers Dry Goods division to Allied Stores Corporation. And Hutzler Brothers, a ten-store department-store company in Baltimore, bought the retail business of B. Altman & Company, New York.

But the most significant factor for retailers remained the on-again, off-again mood of American consumers. The pervasive price-cutting plagued retailers who wanted to curtail it but were afraid they might lose market share. Upgrading merchandise, better service, more store labels did not seem to help much. The debt-laden consumer was sending a clear signal: "I'll buy when I'm ready."

ISADORE BARMASH
"The New York Times"

Montgomery Ward

Montgomery Ward announced that it would phase out its 113-year-old catalog business by the end of 1986. Instead, the company hopes to become more profitable by increased sales at its remodeled stores.

RETAILING / SPECIAL REPORT

The Flood of Coupons

Jane DiMenna

In July 1985, Coupons a la Carte, an in-store vending machine operator, found itself compelled to file for protection from its creditors under the Chapter XI provisions of the U.S. bankruptcy act because it could not raise the funds to make its northern New Jersey debut.

The reason behind the insolvency was the queasiness of venture capitalists and other investors to stake the new company. It was a major disappointment for the two sponsors, Electronic Advertising Network, Dallas, and New York Subways Advertising Company, New York. They already had obtained contracts from retailers for placement of free-coupons machines and from product makers for purchase of space on the system. The problems of this latest wrinkle in the rapidly flourishing practice of offering discount coupons may have been symptomatic of that binge itself.

With an estimated 155 billion of cents-off coupons distributed in 1985, it was obvious that consumers loved them. But a variety of problems had dampened industry's ardor. Retailers were resisting the coupons' eight-cents handling fee from producers because it did not offset the cost. Handling itself, with consumers hoarding the coupons until they had a stack, created an uneven flow. Misredemption, fraud, and even counterfeiting also tended to dismay producers who liked coupons to test new products or jog sales of old ones.

Yet, with all those headaches, the flood of coupons in 1985 appeared endless. Consumers, both young and old, clipped them from newspapers, four-color inserts, and package mail to their homes. They even swapped them with one another. With many, clipping coupons became as much a hobby as saving recipes. Discounting of all sorts was in during 1985, and coupons met the national mood.

The coupon craze began about 1898 with the C. W. Post Company distributing penny-off coupons to spur the sale of cereals. It remained a small but enduring part of the American shopping process for decades. But it has been only in the last decade that coupons have boomed as newspapers and women's magazines have sought to increase their circulation and attract more advertising by expanding reader services. This has meant a corresponding demand by producers of all types of goods to increase the tonnage of their merchandise via the coupon method.

Coupons offer consumers a discount at the cash register that can range from a few cents to as much as 20% off the standard price. In most cases, the product involved is a branded one. Inevitably, as the food stores compete, they frequently double or triple the face value of the coupon discount to spur traffic. It has been said that 9 of every 10 American families redeem at least one coupon weekly. But American customers, an informal survey showed, either love the coupons or completely spurn them.

Some harried merchants have suggested that producers simply lower their prices so that coupons would not be needed. But producers have countered that coupons represent only a temporary cut and serve to induce immediate business.

ISADORE BARMASH

RHODE ISLAND

The year 1985 was one of contrasts in Rhode Island, but they were hardly tranquil. January 1 saw the inauguration of the first Republican governor in 16 years, of the nation's first woman attorney general, and the start of the General Assembly session. Predictions that the new governor, Edward DiPrete, would move with vigor but meet stiff resistance in the heavily Democratic legislature were only partially correct. The surprise was the general aura of cooperation between the two branches.

The governor's promised retroactive tax cut was passed quickly; his budget with its hefty package of agency and program reorganizations was compromised amicably; and the long-controversial law allowing strikers to collect unemployment benefits was repealed in the name of improving the business climate, with a surprising amount of Democratic support.

Further tax cuts were enacted for the new fiscal year, and increased aid to cities and towns for local education was provided. Adjournment did not come until late June, five or six weeks later than usual, but the session was applauded as a great success on all sides.

The Economy. Tax cuts were made possible by the impressive performance of the state's economy. The unemployment rate started out at 4.8%, rose slightly to 5.2% by midyear, but dropped to 4.1% by autumn, the lowest level in 16 years and substantially below the national average. New business incorporations had increased at a record rate in 1984, it was announced in July 1985, and the number of business failures was down. In October the governor revealed that tax revenue had exceeded projections by $17 million.

Trials and Investigations. The year brought the reenactment of the celebrated trial of Claus von Bülow. He had won a new trial from the State Supreme Court on his conviction of attempting to murder his wife by insulin injection. This time he was acquitted.

Publication of allegations late in 1984 that Chief Justice Joseph A. Bevilacqua had maintained friendships with underworld figures while on the bench escalated into a major controversy early in 1985. Following an investigation by the Commission on Judicial Tenure and Discipline, Bevilacqua was censured and agreed to a four-month suspension without pay. As the time for his return to the bench on November 1 approached, there were calls for his resignation from the governor and assembly leaders of both parties. Refusal seemed certain to trigger legislative procedures for his impeachment.

The state was also agitated by revelations of wrongdoing at the Rhode Island Housing and Mortgage Finance Corporation. The executive director was under indictment, and a bank vice president and others were charged with receiving or improperly providing mortgages to political friends. A wide-ranging investigation went on all year.

Constitutional Convention. Delegates to a convention approved by the voters in November 1984 were selected at a nonpartisan election on November 5. The convention was scheduled to meet in January 1986. Several proposals for constitutional change have been suggested, including four-year terms for state officials, strengthening the powers of the governor, and generally updating the present constitution, which dates from 1843.

Hurricane. The first major hurricane in 30 years struck the state in late September. Hurricane Gloria did less damage than anticipated and caused only two deaths but left nearly all of the state without electric power for periods up to a week in some cases. The aftermath brought severe criticism of the power companies for delays in restoring power, and an estimated total of $20 million in damage.

ELMER E. CORNWELL, JR.
Brown University

ROMANIA

In 1985, Romanians continued to endure severe economic hardship, while their government suffered harsh condemnation from abroad for its political repression.

Domestic Affairs. At its congress in November 1984, the Romanian Communist Party (RCP) unanimously reelected Nicolae Ceauşescu, 67, its secretary-general. On March 29, 1985, the Grand National Assembly also unanimously reelected Ceauşescu to a new five-year term as president of the republic. Twenty years after he came to power, Ceauşescu, his personality cult, and his Stalinist regime seemed totally secure. In the general elections of March 17, only 2.27% of the nation's 16 million voters opposed the single list of officially sponsored candidates.

Romania's Nicolae Ceaușescu (far right) *joined other leaders of the Warsaw Pact nations for a summit in Sofia, Bulgaria, in October. Ceaușescu in 1985 marked his 20th year in power.*

The country remained in the grip of a severe economic crisis, with serious shortages of foodstuffs and energy and a large foreign debt. Food rationing and a 50% cut in the use of electricity, initiated in 1984, continued, although private cars were permitted back on the roads in April. In February all electric power stations were placed under military command, and the deputy premier in charge of the energy sector and several associated ministers were dismissed. Ceaușescu defended his harsh austerity measures and restrictions on imports as necessary to fuel the country's ambitious industrialization program and retire its foreign debt, estimated at $8 billion. For 1985, exports were mandated to increase by 85%, imports to decline by 18%, as compared with 1984. In September, the RCP decreed that when an enterprise failed to meet its export or raw-material-extraction quota, all of its personnel as well as the responsible minister and deputy premier and their staffs would suffer salary cuts of up to 50%. However, the new Eighth Five-Year Plan, for 1986–1990, promised Romanians a 44-hour workweek, an 8% annual rise in national income, and liquidation of the foreign debt.

A massive demolition program began in October in the center of Bucharest, destroying many important structures to make space for a grandiose new party and government center.

Foreign Relations. In the international arena, Romania came under sharp attack for its domestic human-rights violations, especially those of religious and intellectual dissidents and of the almost 2 million ethnic Hungarians in Transylvania. Heated polemics over the latter issue in the Hungarian and Romanian press resulted in a meeting of the foreign ministers of the two countries in Bucharest on January 21. Romania's civil-rights policies were criticized on January 15 by the Helsinki Watch and Americas Watch groups and the Lawyers Committee for International Human Rights. In May, David B. Funderburk resigned as U.S. ambassador to Romania, accusing the U.S. administration of exaggerating Romania's independence from the Soviet Union and ignoring its repressive domestic policies. A resolution calling for self-determination for Transylvania was introduced in the U.S. Congress, and the U.S. delegation to a 35-nation conference on human rights in Ottawa denounced Romania.

During a brief visit to Canada in April, Ceaușescu discussed arms control and the sale of Canadian nuclear-reactor technology.

Foreign visitors to Bucharest in 1985 included British Foreign Secretary Sir Geoffrey Howe, Israeli Premier Shimon Peres, Nicaraguan President Daniel Ortega Saavedra, and U.S. Secretary of State George Shultz.

JOSEPH F. ZACEK
State University of New York at Albany

ROMANIA • Information Highlights

Official Name: Socialist Republic of Romania.
Location: Southeastern Europe.
Area: 91,700 sq mi (237 499 km²).
Population (mid-1985 est.): 22,800,000.
Chief Cities (1983 est.): Bucharest, the capital, 1,834,377; Brașov, 290,722; Cluj-Napoca, 270,820.
Government: *Head of state,* Nicolae Ceaușescu, president (took office 1967) and secretary-general of the Communist Party (1965). *Head of government,* Constantin Dascalescu, premier (took office May 1982). *Legislature* (unicameral)— Grand National Assembly.
Monetary Unit: Leu (16.490 lei equal U.S.$1, Aug. 1985).
Gross National Product (1983 U.S.$): $109,700,-000,000.
Foreign Trade (1983 U.S.$): *Imports,* $9,959,000,000; *exports,* $13,241,000,000.

SASKATCHEWAN

Although the year 1985 was the 80th anniversary of Saskatchewan's founding and the centenary of the North West Rebellion (an uprising of Indians and *métis*, persons of mixed French-Canadian and Indian blood), Premier Grant Devine and his Progressive Conservative (PC) administration had little time for musing on the past.

Politics and Government. The Pioneer Trust Company of Regina collapsed February 7, following the withdrawal by the province of a C$35 million preferred share issue guarantee. Minister of Finance Bob Andrew refused the Opposition's demand for a judicial inquiry into alleged conflicts of interest and mismanagement. The province's response was the passage in May of a depositors' assistance act that covered uninsured depositors and complemented the more financially significant federal safeguards.

A severe prairie drought continued from 1984, leading to a crisis atmosphere in the agricultural sector. The premier defused some of the worry in July by announcing changes in the federal-provincial crop insurance program and a cash-advance program for cattle, and by pressuring the federal Farm Credit Corporation to depreciate certain loans. Later, in August, at the annual Premiers' Conference, Devine committed Saskatchewan to preparation of a "national agricultural policy" for November, to be based on interest-group and interprovincial consultation.

Some surprises as to indications of party support surfaced. A poll by the University of Manitoba's Institute for Social and Economic Research conducted in March showed Conservative support at 50.4% of decided voters, the New Democratic Party (NDP) at 40.5%, and the Liberals at about 9%. A September poll by the institute, however, showed NDP growth at 46.3% of decided voters, a PC retreat to 43.8%,

and Liberal stability at 9.3%. In the March by-election in the Thunder Creek constituency, won by the Conservatives, Liberal support had climbed from 3.1% to 27.1%, largely at the cost of the Conservative vote. After the PC candidate was defeated in a November by-election, Devine revised his cabinet. The number of ministers was reduced from 23 to 19. Rumors of a provincial election abounded.

Fiscal and Economic Issues. Andrew continued and elaborated on his social-consensus approach to budget making. The 1985–86 budget included a five-year plan to pump $1.5 billion in developmental funds into agriculture, education, employment development, and health care. The budget also called for a 1% flat tax, a 5% sales tax on used vehicles, and the elimination of various property tax rebate programs. The C$3.46 billion budget included the forecast of a $291 million deficit (this government's fourth such deficit), which would push the accumulated deficit to $1.245 billion.

Resources. In June, Devine announced yet another extension of the controversial oil-royalty holiday program until the end of 1986. The program, first introduced in 1982, exempts new primary wells from royalties in the first year of production. The picture for other resources was mixed. China and the Soviet Union were expected to import less grain, driving down wheat prices. Saskatchewan potash held its European and non-Communist market share against international competitors but faced a puzzling slump in demand from a major customer, China. Uranium prices were low, but the government predicted they had bottomed out.

CHRISTOPHER DUNN
University of Saskatchewan

SASKATCHEWAN • Information Highlights

Area: 251,700 sq mi (651 903 km²).
Population (April 1985 est.): 1,018,200.
Chief Cities (1981 census): Regina, the capital, 162,613; Saskatoon, 154,210; Moose Jaw, 33,941.
Government (1985): *Chief Officers*—lt. gov., F. W. Johnson; premier, Grant Devine (Progressive Conservative). *Legislature*—Legislative Assembly, 64 members.
Provincial Finances (1985–86 fiscal year budget): *Revenues,* $3,175,400,000; *expenditures,* $3,446,-700,000.
Personal Income (average weekly earnings, June 1985): $394.91.
Labor Force (August 1985, seasonally adjusted): Employed workers, 15 years of age and over, 450,000; Unemployed, 40,000 (8.2%).
Education (1985–86): *Enrollment*—elementary and secondary schools, 215,240 pupils; postsecondary (full-time, 1985–86)—universities, 19,600; community colleges, 3,380.
(All monetary figures are in Canadian dollars.)

SAUDI ARABIA

Saudi oil production fell and government revenues from oil decreased as the Saudi economy faced a substantial decline in 1985.

Oil and Finance. Saudi oil production has declined for four years in a row, as world demand for oil held steady and other countries entered into production. In December 1984 the Organization of the Petroleum Exporting Countries (OPEC) named Saudi Arabia its watchdog to monitor adherence to OPEC production quotas. Saudi production fell from 4.1 million barrels per day in October 1984, to 2.5 million the following June, and to a 20-year low of 2.2 million in August.

Prices for Saudi oil on the "spot" market, where there are no long-term contracts, gradually eased downward in 1985. The Saudis, who reportedly were tired of bearing the burden of falling prices and production for the benefit of other OPEC countries, secured a reduction from $29.00 to $28.00 per barrel in Saudi light

King Fahd of Saudi Arabia welcomes Britain's Prime Minister Margaret Thatcher to Riyadh, April 14. The two leaders discussed economic relations and a variety of world issues.

AP/Wide World

crude oil at an OPEC meeting in January. In July and October, however, Saudi threats to double production of oil unless OPEC agreed to cut quotas were ignored by the other member states. Oil Minister Ahmed Zaki Yamani increased Saudi production to 3 million barrels per day in September and sold U.S. oil companies 800,000 barrels per day at below the official prices.

Saudi oil revenue in 1984 was only $43 billion, about 40% of what it had been in 1981. As a result, government payments to foreign contractors were often delayed, subsidies to Saudis for crops such as wheat were cut, and overtime pay for government workers was limited. Imports decreased and new construction fell, as attention was transferred to maintenance and full use of existing facilities. Private-sector companies saw that the great boom was over.

The fiscal 1984–85 budget had a $13 billion deficit. For 1985–86, a budget balanced at $55 billion was predicted. The Saudi government, moreover, pledged not to draw on its substantial foreign reserves that amounted to more than $100 billion. The new Five Year Plan emphasized spending on the military, education, and industrial plants for the desalinization of water. The plan also envisaged an increase in nonpetroleum-related revenues.

Foreign Affairs and the Military. As the nearby war between Iran and Iraq entered its sixth year, Saudi Arabia was intent on staying out of the fighting while continuing to send Iraq financial aid. On Nov. 29, 1984, Saudi Arabia and its five smaller partners in the Gulf Cooperation Council (Bahrain, Kuwait, Oman, Qatar, and the United Arab Emirates) agreed to set up a temporary rapid deployment force for mutual defense.

Arms purchases from abroad were crucial to ensure continued Saudi noninvolvement in the wars plaguing much of the Middle East. King Fahd visited Washington, DC, in Febru-

ary to arrange arms purchases and to present Saudi views on Arab-Israeli peace proposals. In 1984 the United States sold Saudi Arabia about $3 billion worth of weapons—an amount second only to U.S. arms sales to Turkey. On February 25 the Boeing Corporation announced a $1.2 billion contract to supply the Saudis with a ground network for aircraft warning and control systems (AWACS), which would become part of the Saudi "Peace Shield" defensive system. In March the U.S. Senate and House of Representatives foreign affairs committees placed limits on the delivery of AWACS airplanes that had been ordered by Saudi Arabia in 1981. New U.S. sales to Saudi Arabia were further hampered by the August foreign aid authorization bill that allowed Congress to hold up arms transfers unless Saudi Arabia openly supported American pro-Israeli peace initiatives.

To avoid these restrictions on its freedom to conduct foreign policy and to bypass another bruising battle with the U.S. Congress, Saudi Arabia turned to Great Britain for military supplies. In April, British Prime Minister Margaret Thatcher visited Riyadh, and in August she and Saudi Minister of Defense Prince Sultan secretly met in Austria to discuss arms sales.

SAUDI ARABIA • Information Highlights

Official Name: Kingdom of Saudi Arabia.
Location: Arabian peninsula in southwest Asia.
Area: 829,996 sq mi (2 149 690 km²).
Population (mid-1985 est.): 11,200,000.
Capital: Riyadh.
Government: *Head of state and government,* Fahd bin 'Abd al-'Aziz al Sa'ud, king and prime minister (acceded June 1982).
Monetary Unit: Riyal (3.6495 riyals equal U.S.$1, Oct. 24, 1985).
Gross Domestic Product (fiscal year 1984 U.S.$): $108,000,000,000.
Economic Index (first quarter 1984): *Consumer Prices* (1970 = 100), all items, 370.6; food, 288.6.
Foreign Trade (1983 U.S.$): *Imports,* $39,206,000,000; *exports,* $46,941,000,000.

With the tacit approval of President Ronald Reagan, the largest sale of British weapons ever was announced on September 26. The Saudis were to purchase 72 Tornado combat jets as well as 60 trainer fighters at a cost of about $4.5 billion. Delivery was to be made by 1989. The British government did not restrict the basing of the aircraft, as had the United States for earlier sales, and Great Britain accepted part of the payment in the form of oil.

Government. Although King Fahd stated in December 1984 that a consultative assembly would be established soon, no progress on this question was made, and few basic changes took place in Saudi politics. Two bomb blasts in Riyadh in May were isolated incidents with no repercussions. The most notable event affecting the prestige of the royal family was the flight of Prince Sultan bin Salman, a nephew of the king, on the U.S. space shuttle *Discovery* in June. Prince Sultan, the first Arab and the first Muslim in space, returned to earth as a national hero.

WILLIAM OCHSENWALD
Virginia Polytechnic Institute

SINGAPORE

In late 1984 the ruling People's Action Party (PAP) again easily won the national elections, but growing opposition to some policies and a sagging economy marked a change from past years.

Politics. Despite the continued PAP dominance, opposition parties won two seats, the first victories in national elections since independence, capturing 36% of the popular vote. Victorious were J. B. Jeyaretnam, leader of the Workers' Party, who retained the seat he won in a 1981 by-election, and Chiam See Tong, leader of the Singapore Democratic Party.

Accelerating the transition to a new generation of leaders, Goh Chok Tong was named first deputy prime minister, replacing Goh Keng Swee who, like many in the party's old guard, stepped down before the election. Goh Chok Tong was considered the clear front-runner to succeed Prime Minister Lee Kuan Yew, who has talked of retiring when he reaches 65 in 1988. Lee's son, Lee Hsien Loong, who resigned a senior military post to enter politics, won a seat and was named to a minor cabinet post. Naming Goh Chok Tong as the heir apparent quieted but did not eliminate speculation about a Lee family dynasty.

In March, President C. V. Devan Nair was forced to resign when the prime minister revealed in parliament that Nair was a chronic alcoholic. Shortly after, Nair left for treatment in the United States. In August, Wee Kim Wee, a former journalist and the head of state broadcasting, was named to the presidency, a largely ceremonial position.

Reinforcing statements that Lee was serious about retiring as prime minister, the government indicated that the duties of the president would be enlarged. These duties would include veto power over legislation that would reduce the substantial financial reserves accumulated under Lee and former economic czar Goh Keng Swee. Should Lee retire, it was believed that he would be named president, permitting him to oversee the next regime.

Economy. After a decade of having one of the fastest growing economies in the world, the economy in 1985 stumbled into negative growth. High wage costs, resulting from an intentional policy to discourage labor-intensive industries, led some international corporations to make products at home or to concentrate on other countries with cheap labor. The decline affected nearly every part of Singapore's economy, since exports had become less competitive and construction had stalled after years of overbuilding. Shipbuilding and petroleum refining industries were particularly hit.

Singapore, as a city-state dependent on trade, remained vulnerable to international economic developments. The stalled recovery of the U.S. economy and the failure of other Western economies to take up the slack led to layoffs and cutbacks. This was the case even in the touted high-tech industries as world computer markets failed to boom as expected. Regionally, other member nations of the Association of Southeast Asian Nations (ASEAN) imposed surtaxes and special charges on their citizenry for the short vacations or shopping trips to Singapore, sharply cutting into one of the mainstays of retailers.

Singapore's currency—which had maintained its strength against the U.S. dollar through the recent international recession—came under attack from speculators in September. Government intervention was required to stabilize it. The government also sought to regain competitiveness by winning from unions an agreement to forego the annual midyear wage increases.

K. MULLINER, *Ohio University*

SINGAPORE • Information Highlights

Official Name: Republic of Singapore.
Location: Southeast Asia.
Area: 239 sq mi (618 km²).
Population (mid-1985 est.): 2,600,000.
Capital: Singapore City.
Government: *Head of state,* Wee Kim Wee, president (took office August 1985). *Head of government,* Lee Kuan Yew, prime minister (took office 1959). *Legislature* (unicameral)—Parliament.
Monetary Unit: Singapore dollar (2.135 S. dollars equal U.S.$1, Oct. 23, 1985).
Gross Domestic Product (1983 U.S.$): $16,000,-000,000.
Economic Index (1984): *Consumer Prices* (1970 = 100), all items, 218.7; food, 240.3.
Foreign Trade (1984 U.S.$): *Imports,* $28,712,-000,000; *exports,* $24,108,000,000.

SOCIAL WELFARE

Sluggish economic growth continued to affect much of mankind during 1985. In most industrial nations, unemployment either rose or stayed at the high level of 1984. In Western Europe, which had enjoyed lower jobless rates than the United States in the 1960s and 1970s, unemployment ranged still higher, from 8% for West Germany to more than 16% for Turkey and 20% for Spain. Only Scandinavia and Austria had rates lower than the U.S. rate of 7% (which by European counting methods would have been about 9%). The costs of holding down the rates in Sweden raised social tensions. Strikes and lockouts there involved civil-servant unions protesting lower real wages, while critics demanded more reductions in welfare spending.

In Britain, like Sweden a founder of the modern welfare state, the government retreated further from welfarism in proposing "reforms" that would cut several across-the-board benefits and target them for the needy only, while also slashing housing benefits for more than 3 million people. A bitter coal strike, a jobless rate of more than 13%, and a series of racial incidents added rancor to the ongoing policy debate. A consensus arose on raising penalties against the narcotics traffic, which was rapidly becoming a major problem in Britain, with reported addicts more than double those reported in 1980. Even in West Germany's "wonder" economy, the jobless held mass demonstrations against both layoffs and cuts in welfare programs.

Third World. In the Third World the major welfare problem was continued famine in Africa. Rains broke the worst of the drought in the Sahel, and international relief efforts for starving Ethiopians and Sudanese became both fashionable and more effective. But the devastating effects of widespread hunger were still nightmarishly evident, and persistent shortages still threatened more than 30 million persons in Africa south of the Sahara, the only large area of the globe that had not increased its food production over the last decade at rates faster than population growth.

In China, India, parts of Latin America, and the Pacific Rim, the so-called Green Revolution had prevented the worldwide shortages predicted at the 1974 UN-sponsored World Food Conference in Rome. In much of Latin America and a few Asian nations, however, pressure to meet payments on massive government debts to private banks were forcing the imposition of greater economic burdens and lower living standards on the citizens of these countries. In Brazil a new government sought to allay some of the pain by passing a law to distribute more than 100 million acres (40.5 million ha) of land to poor families over the next four years. In October the annual meeting of the World Bank and the International Monetary Fund (IMF) in Seoul, South Korea, heard U.S. delegates propose a special fund from which those nations restoring sound financial policies could draw to refinance their loans. If successful, the fund would help prevent further cuts in real income for those nation's citizens. On the other hand, the sharpest decline in living levels outside Africa probably took place in the Philippines, where rising opposition to the regime of President Ferdinand Marcos seemed linked to disastrous economic failure.

United States. In the United States, both the jobless rate and many emergency welfare costs were still high. In terms of aid to the homeless and health care, state and local governments began taking up the slack from further cuts in federal programs. Texas increased its benefits

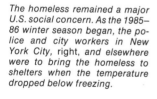

The homeless remained a major U.S. social concern. As the 1985–86 winter season began, the police and city workers in New York City, right, and elsewhere were to bring the homeless to shelters when the temperature dropped below freezing.

scale, extended unemployment coverage to farm workers, and authorized $18.5 million to feed the poor, in addition to special funds for health care in counties without public hospitals. Pennsylvania took similar steps to plug gaps in the "safety net."

The median family income in the United States rose a bit during the year, yet the share of the poor in the population also grew. A vigorous debate, carried over from 1984, spread among social critics, economists, and administrators of programs over the extent and reasons for poverty. Charles Murray's closely reasoned book, *Losing Ground*, recommended scrapping much of the federal-welfare and income-support structure for working-age persons, including Aid to Families with Dependent Children (AFDC), Medicaid, food stamps, disability insurance, and subsidized housing. The book became one of the most discussed tracts on the subject in years. It gave new life to the numbers in a series of Census Bureau studies issued during the summer, indicating an increase in the proportion of the population below the federally defined poverty line, from slightly more than 10% in 1970 to a bit more than 15% in 1983. The rates were higher in the Eastern and Midwestern cities—24% in New York, 25% in Philadelphia, 27% in Chicago, and 38% in Detroit. Poverty also was unevenly distributed among different population groups: it was concentrated among blacks and Hispanics and was worse among women and children. The so-called feminization of poverty derived in part from the rise in female-headed single-parent families, with young unwed mothers (often unable to care for their children) contributing an ever larger share to that category. The worst off were children, whose numbers among the poor rose by 3 million between 1968 and 1983, even as their share of the national population shrank by 6 million. More than 70% of the children of unwed mothers lived in poverty, the largest factor in making 22% of those under 18 fall below the poverty line. By contrast, Social Security and private savings were reducing the share of poor among the elderly, defined as those over 65, to only 14%, while among those Americans between 18 and 65 only 12% were poor.

The continued high levels of divorce since the 1970s also meant that the number of single-parent families in white households—a large share from middle-class backgrounds—almost doubled over the previous decade and currently accounted for 17% of the nation's families. One improvement for some of them was the passage of the Retirement Equity Act late in 1984, which in 1985 began opening the way for judges to award a share of the husband's pension to the wife in a divorce.

A more serious problem for pension holders was the tendency by large corporations to restructure their pension plans and drain off many of the assets tied up in those plans for their own refinancing solutions. The Pension Benefit Guaranty Corporation, the federal agency created in 1974, had the abandoned plans of more than 1,000 companies on their hands; with the dumping of the Wheeling-Pittsburgh Steel Company pension obligations on the agency in November, the agency's deficit more than doubled, amid cries that it was helping that corporation avoid the bite of competition.

For most Americans, the Social Security Act was still the basic foundation of their pension claims. As the nation observed the 50th anniversary of the act, many of the recent fears about its viability had subsided. There were many assurances that the old-age pension funds were not only sacrosanct, but sound enough in fiscal terms to last at least another half century without major adjustments. The consensus in support of the system, which held firm during the year's worst wrangling over the budget and federal deficit, could not shield certain features of Social Security from modifications by the administration that went further than charging recipients for a larger share of their costs under Medicare. Efforts persisted to reduce disability payments and scrutinize recipients more strictly for eligibility and led judges in one state after another to issue orders for reinstatement. In one instance, a federal judge fined Social Security officials for failure to comply with such an order. Congressional critics also protested plans to close as many as 700 field offices across the nation, and to lay off up to 17,000 workers in them, although the key House Committee admitted the closings met the criteria they had themselves defined. At year-end, concern remained that these and other steps might end with drawing the system and its "entitlements" into future budget battles; therefore, the Senate by a 4–1 vote ordered the drafting of a bill that would isolate Social Security funds from the rest of the federal budget, as was the case during much of its earlier history.

An even more divisive welfare issue that surfaced during the year at every level of politics was family planning and abortion. In several states, efforts to control abortions by restrictions on doctors ran afoul of federal appeals court judges, who used the 1973 landmark Supreme Court decision *Roe v. Wade* as grounds for striking out many provisions of such laws. In July the Reagan administration urged the Supreme Court to review those decisions, and its own position, by accepting the cases. The court agreed and was expected to hand down a ruling during 1986. Meanwhile, the question of making antiabortion laws legal was placed on the ballots in two New England municipal elections, and vigorous campaigns by "pro-life" groups were launched on their behalf, but they were narrowly defeated at the polls in November. At the congressional level,

several of the major groups—among them the Moral Majority, the American Life Lobby, and the National Right to Life Committee—mounted a drive for passage of the Kemp-Hatch bill, which would prohibit federal funding for any agency providing information on abortions and related services. Pro-choice advocates saw this as an effort to kill the effectiveness of federally funded planning agencies but were also relieved that violent assaults on planned parenthood clinics had dropped off with the indictment and conviction of several "pro-life" bombers responsible for the previous outrages.

The plight of the hungry and homeless in America continued to worsen and to attract the attention of the public. In February the Physician Task Force on Hunger in America reported on its two-year nationwide study, concluding that hunger was more widespread (affecting about 20 million) and serious than at any time in the last 10 or 15 years, largely because of "governmental failure." The House of Representatives formed a Select Committee to investigate the problem; by October, testimony at hearings was verifying the findings. By then, a disparate group of entertainers, sports figures, and other celebrities, moving beyond the model of popular music concerts to raise relief funds, scheduled a Hands Across America program for Memorial Day weekend in 1986, in which at least 6 million people would literally link hands across a 4,000-mi (6 440-km) route in a human chain designed to raise funds and attention to the plight of the poor. Church-affiliated groups such as the Bread for the World Educational Fund joined in publicizing the problem.

One of the consequences of hunger was its impact on health. The poor, and the minority groups that account for a disproportionate share of them, were increasingly vulnerable to illness at a time when cuts in Medicaid and Medicare funds, and pressures to keep costs of hospital care under control, made such care less accessible. In fact, health insurance costs for workers and retirees had continued to rise so steeply that they drove more and more businesses, including some of the nation's largest, to adopt self-insurance plans. The best-known example of such recasting of this critical fringe benefit was at Chrysler Corporation, where former Health and Human Services (HHS) Secretary Joseph Califano headed the firm's health insurance system while contributing eloquently to a national discourse on the subject.

In November, Robert M. Hayes, the former Wall Street lawyer heading the National Coalition for the Homeless, reported that a new wave of destitute people were using the modest facilities his group and others provided. A large share of these clients were children and infants. Along with other child welfare organizations and the Legal Aid Society, he had brought suit against New York City twice during the year, to force the provision of counseling and other preventive steps for the parents of such children so they would not be placed routinely in foster homes. He won his first suit, which also required the authorities to provide supervision for youngsters between 18 and 21 in an effort to keep a second generation from falling into the cycle of poverty and homelessness that had often been their fate as children. Hayes estimated that of the 60,000 homeless in New York City alone, 12,000 were children, a ratio common across the country. According to him, the average age of the homeless had dropped to the early 30s from about 55 a decade before, and only 10 or 20% of them were mentally ill. This profile was quite different from the stereotypical images of the shopping bag lady or the Skid Row derelict. New York City also responded by turning over selected city-owned vacant buildings to 24 nonprofit groups for rehabilitation with city grants or low-cost loans for conversion to housing for their clients. In Washington the charismatic Mitch Snyder continued to battle for more aid for the homeless, and one of his refuges was reportedly being fortified to resist eviction at year's end by federal agencies. The standoff gave way in the headlines for a time, while HHS Secretary Margaret Heckler, who reportedly was either too poor an administrator or too sympathetic to poor citizens, was replaced amid considerable fanfare by Dr. Otis R. Bowen, a former governor of Indiana. By year's end the spokespersons for HHS were challenging once more the estimates on the number of homeless that went as high as 3 million nationally, claiming instead it did not exceed 350,000.

The numbers of homeless, from whatever source, did not include the roughly 1 million children, with a median age of 15, who ran away from their mostly middle-class homes each of the past three years. At least one third of them, according to the director of the National Network of Runaway and Youth Services, were victims of incest or other physical abuse. The National Center for Child Abuse and Neglect claimed that by the most conservative estimates at least 1 million children were victims of adults annually.

At the other end of the spectrum, the House Subcommittee on Health and Long Term Care estimated that 1.1 million people over the age of 65—nearly 4% of all elderly Americans—were abused, neglected, or exploited each year. On the more positive side, at least 5 million Americans were caring for a more-or-less helpless parent, and the nation as a whole was doing better than ever for an older population that was living much longer and requiring more attention both in and out of nursing homes than ever before.

MORTON ROTHSTEIN
University of California, Davis

SOUTH AFRICA

Even as domestic violence and foreign sanctions in opposition to South Africa's apartheid policy had the nation reeling (*see* feature article, page 26), the Pretoria government and its military forces were embroiled in another often violent conflict—the dispute over Namibia (South-West Africa). In mid-April, President Pieter W. Botha announced that South Africa would unilaterally establish an interim government in Namibia. At the same time it was announced that the last South African troops had been withdrawn from Angola, where they had been conducting operations for nearly a decade against SWAPO (South-West Africa People's Organization) and ANC (African National Congress) guerrillas fighting for Namibian independence with Angolan assistance. In May, however, Pretoria admitted that it had launched a secret foray into Angola's northern Cabinda province; Angola reported that several South African commandos had been killed or captured trying to sabotage a major oil installation there. Then in late June and again in mid-September, South African forces crossed into Angola in pursuit of SWAPO guerrillas. On the entire matter, Pretoria stood virtually alone in the world community. The Soviet Union stepped up arms supplies to Angola. The United States condemned the raids. And the Nonaligned Movement called for economic sanctions.

One positive development was heavy February rain in previously parched regions. The downpours, however, caused serious flooding.

SOUTH CAROLINA

Newsworthy events in the state during 1985 included the first execution in more than 20 years, the repeal of Sunday blue laws, and a near-encounter with two hurricanes.

Government. During a long session, the General Assembly enacted laws raising the drinking age to 21, increasing significantly state and local funds for medical care for the indigent, authorizing the federal form for state income taxes, and permitting the allocation of water during droughts. The legislature also stiffened sentences for burglary and other crimes, opened the way for adopted children to identify their birth parents, created a bill of rights for nursing home patients, and established the Heritage Land Trust Fund. After compromises, Sunday blue laws were repealed. All businesses are now allowed to open after 1:30 P.M., and alcoholic beverages may be sold if approved by local referendums. Constitutional amendments limiting the growth of state spending and numbers of employees were affected. Actions were taken to restrict the dumping of nuclear wastes.

Education. The objectives of the 1984 Public Educational Improvement Act were met on schedule. Overall, students improved scores on state-developed basic skill tests, the Scholastic Aptitude Tests (SATs), and others. Average daily attendance increased and the teacher absentee rate declined. Programs for talented and gifted students, teacher evaluation, certification of principals, identification of outstanding school districts, and reduction of paperwork for teachers were stressed. State staff worked directly with local school districts that were classed as educationally impaired. Tuition loans were provided for future math and science teachers. The educational television network continued to make exceptional achievements in its public and school programming. Vocational education in high schools and technical colleges was evaluated by a special committee. Teacher pay was expected to reach the southeastern U.S. average in 1986.

Industry and Agriculture. Despite the continued closing of textile and apparel plants, unemployment (6.1%) remained below the

national average, although it was alarmingly high in several counties. In comparison with recent years new industry lagged, both in levels of investment and number of jobs. Three of the largest banking institutions merged with other southeastern banks. The Springs and Lowenstein textile chains merged. Extension of Interstate Highway 20 from Florence to Myrtle Beach was approved, and development began on rustic Daufuskie Island near Hilton Head.

Late freezes and drought reduced yields in some crops, and South Carolina shared in the national decline in agricultural prices. Although tobacco and soybean acreages decreased, yields nevertheless increased. Partly as a reflection of the near-extinction of the boll weevil, cotton acreage increased. "Pick your own" vegetable and fruit farms multiplied.

General. A 50th-year anniversary celebration of the opera *Porgy and Bess* was performed in Charleston. Construction of the long-awaited downtown complex in historic Charleston began. The University of South Carolina broke ground for a $15 million performing arts center. With special ceremonies and performances, the state honored Dizzy Gillespie and Brooks Benton, both native sons.

ROBERT H. STOUDEMIRE
University of South Carolina

SOUTH DAKOTA

A package of education reforms passed by the state legislature and the continuing problems of farmers dominated news in South Dakota.

Legislation. The quality of education was a prime concern of legislators. At the added cost of $3.25 million in the 1986 fiscal year, their bill limited the absence of teachers from class and lengthened the school term by five days. It lowered the compulsory school age from 7 to 6 years and offered parents the option of sending children from low enrollment districts into better systems nearby without the payment of tuition. It tightened regulation on advancement and tenure of teachers to improve their performance and provided for multiple-district cooperation for offerings in special and vocational education.

The legislators enlarged the allocations of state funds less than 7% over the previous year and gave most of the increase to education (nearly 15%), while freezing or lowering nearly all other categories of expense.

Economy. For many years, South Dakotans have ranked in the lower 20% among state groups on national scales of per capita income. Through the early 1980s, they have suffered increasing depression in their agricultural sector.

Agriculture retained its place as mainstay in the state's economy, although it continued to diminish in importance. By 1985 it had slipped

as employer of 30% of the work force in 1960 to half that percentage. Officials believed that as many as 20% more would leave the land in the next year.

Farm Rally. On February 12, some 6,000 farmers and ranchers assembled in Pierre during the legislative session to complain of economic hardships. They spoke in a single voice about their distress, but opinions diverged over proper remedies. Officers in the liberal Farmers Union, National Farmers Organization, and American Agriculture Movement voiced preference for larger price supports, while spokesmen for the conservative Farm Bureau and South Dakota Stock Growers Association preached a free enterprise credo.

Later in February state legislators traveled en masse to Washington, DC, to lobby for increases in farm aid. (*See* page 36.)

Native Americans. The 10% of the population that is of Indian extraction formed an element of society under even greater stress. Tribal elections changed leadership abruptly, betraying frustration over the nearly 90% unemployment on some reservations. Withdrawals of federal funds to sustain housing developments and tribal industries have removed alternatives. Reductions in social services by governmental agencies at all levels have driven some families into gradual starvation.

Higher Education. While legislators dwelled on the improvement of education for grades K through 12, public agencies struggled for betterment in higher education. The Board of Regents awarded faculty members the 4% increase given to all state employees plus increments for merit, and increases to bring them closer to averages paid by other institutions in the region. The Regents required exit examinations of graduating seniors to measure quality by national standards, and they increased contact hours per semester.

HERBERT T. HOOVER
The University of South Dakota

SOUTH DAKOTA · Information Highlights

Area: 77,116 sq mi (199 730 km²).

Population (July 1, 1984 est.): 706,000.

Chief Cities (1980 census): Pierre, the capital, 11,973; Sioux Falls, 81,343; Rapid City, 46,492.

Government (1985): *Chief Officers*—governor, William J. Janklow (R); lt. gov., Lowell C. Hansen II (R). *Legislature*—Senate, 35 members; House of Representatives, 70 members.

State Finances (fiscal year 1984): *Revenues,* $999,000,000; *expenditures,* $953,000,000.

Personal Income (1984): $7,813,000,000; per capita, $11,069.

Labor Force (June 1985): *Civilian labor force,* 364,900; *unemployed,* 19,300 (5.3% of total force).

Education: *Enrollment* (fall 1983)—public elementary schools, 86,324; public secondary, 36,736; colleges and universities, 34,879. Public school expenditures (1982–83), $292,102,189 ($2,486 per pupil).

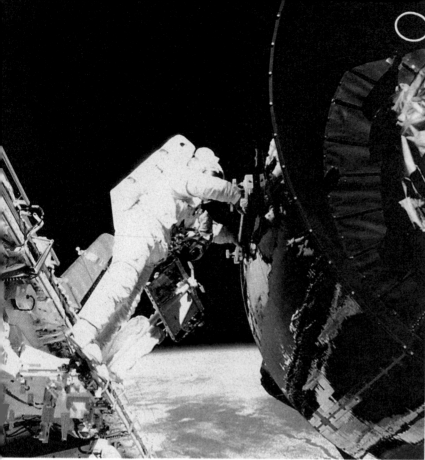

During the eight-day mission of *Discovery* in late August and early September, astronauts William F. Fisher, left, and James D. van Hoften exited the shuttle to retrieve the Leasat-3 satellite.

NASA

SPACE EXPLORATION

In 1985 the first direct exploration of a comet was carried out by the International Cometary Explorer (ICE), which flew through the tail of Comet Giacobini-Zinner and provided a detailed characterization of the dynamics and constituents within the plasma tail. Three space probes—the European Space Agency's (ESA's) Giotto and Japan's Suisei and Sakigake spacecraft—were launched to join the Soviet Union's Vega 1 and Vega 2 toward an encounter with Halley's Comet in 1986. In manned space exploration, *Atlantis* joined *Columbia, Challenger,* and *Discovery* as part of the U.S. space shuttle fleet, and a total of nine shuttle missions were flown. The Soviet Salyut 7 space station was reoccupied in June, and the station was continuously manned for 168 days until a cosmonaut's illness forced a return to Earth.

Manned Space Flight. Nine U.S. space shuttle missions were conducted in 1985, as *Atlantis,* the last of four planned operational orbiters, joined *Columbia, Challenger,* and *Discovery* as part of the fleet. Two of these missions, STS-15 (Space Transportation System Mission 15) and STS-21, carried classified Department of Defense payloads that were lofted into geosynchronous orbit by booster rockets. The STS-15 mission of *Discovery,*

launched on January 24 from Kennedy Space Center (KSC) at Cape Canaveral, FL, was commanded by Thomas K. Mattingly, assisted by Loren J. Shriver, Ellison S. Onizuka, James F. Buchli, and Gary E. Payton. STS-21, the first flight of *Atlantis,* was launched from KSC on October 3 and landed at Edwards Air Force Base (EAFB), CA, on October 7; the mission was commanded by Karol J. Bobko, supported by Ronald J. Grabe, Robert C. Stewart, David C. Hilmers, and William A. Pailes.

STS-16, *Discovery*'s fourth flight, was launched on April 12 with a crew of seven, including Sen. Jake Garn (R-UT), the first public official to fly aboard the shuttle. The other crew members were mission commander Karol J. Bobko, Donald E. Williams, M. Rhea Seddon, Jeffrey A. Hoffman, S. David Griggs, and Charles D. Walker. The mission was marked by the successful deployment of Canada's Anik C-1 and the Hughes Aircraft Company's Leasat-3 (Syncom IV-3) satellites from *Discovery*'s payload bay. However, the free-flying Leasat-3 spacecraft failed to activate, and Griggs and Hoffman performed an unscheduled space walk to attach a snaring device to *Discovery*'s manipulator arm to be used to trip an electrical activation lever on the Leasat-3. The snaring device contacted the lever on the spinning satellite, but the satellite still failed to activate. STS-16 ended April 19.

Discovery was launched again on August 27 on an eight-day mission (STS-20) to perform an on-orbit repair on the inactive Leasat-3 spacecraft. Following rendezvous with Leasat-3, James D. van Hoften and William F. Fisher exited the orbiter and attached a grappling fixture to the satellite, which allowed it to be retrieved by *Discovery*'s manipulator arm. Over the next two days, Fisher and van Hoften installed a new electrical activation circuit on Leasat-3, then redeployed the activated satellite. Leasat-3 was subsequently boosted to geosynchronous orbit by an on-board propulsion system. Three communication satellites were also deployed on the STS-20 mission and lofted to geosynchronous orbit by booster rockets— ASC-1 for American Satellite Company, Aussat-1 for Australia, and Leasat-4 for Hughes Aircraft Company. Other crewmen on the mission were Joe H. Engle, Richard O. Covey, and John M. Lounge.

Three missions were flown by *Challenger* in 1985, all carrying the Spacelab mission equipment developed by the European Space Agency. The seven-day STS-17/Spacelab-3 mission, launched April 29, utilized the high-quality microgravity environment in the manned Spacelab module for scientific investigations in crystal growth, materials and fluid processing, and life sciences studies. The crew consisted of mission commander Robert F. Overmyer, Frederick D. Gregory, Donald L. Lind, Norman Thagard, William A. Thornton, Taylor Wang, and Lodewijk van den Berg.

The STS-19/Spacelab 2 mission, launched July 29 and ending with a landing at EAFB on August 6, carried a seven-man crew composed of mission commander C. Gordon Fullerton and pilot Roy D. Bridges, Jr., supported by Anthony W. England, Karl G. Henize, F. Story Musgrave, Loren W. Acton, and John-David F. Bartoe. The mission utilized the Spacelab's experiment mounting structure to carry several large telescopes for scientific investigations in solar physics, infrared astronomy, and high-energy astrophysics.

The seven-day STS-22/Spacelab D-1 mission, launched October 30, was totally paid for and dedicated to a payload provided by West Germany. A crew of eight was carried, the largest ever flown in space: mission commander Henry W. Hartsfield; pilot Steven R. Nagel; mission specialists James F. Buchli, Guion S. Bluford, and Bonnie J. Dunbar; and payload specialists Reinhard Furrer and Ernst Messerschmid of West Germany and Wubbo Ockels of the Netherlands. The scientific portion of the mission, focusing on microgravity research in materials science, life sciences and technology, and communications and navigation, was controlled from the German Space Operations Center at Oberpfaffenhofen, West Germany.

STS-18, *Discovery*'s fifth flight, was launched June 17 with a crew of seven: Daniel C. Brandenstein, John O. Creighton, Steven R. Nagel, John M. Fabian, Shannon W. Lucid, Patrick Baudry of France, and Sultan Salman al-Saud, the first Saudi Arabian astronaut. Three communication satellites were deployed: Morelos-A for Mexico, Arabsat-A for the Arab Satellite Communications Organization, and Telstar 3-D for the American Telephone & Telegraph Company (AT&T). The highlight of the mission was the deployment of the Spartan payload carrier for studies of galactic X-ray emissions and the subsequent retrieval of the carrier and its return to Earth on board the shuttle on June 24.

The techniques necessary for the construction of large structures in space were tested by astronauts Jerry L. Ross and Sherwood C. Spring on *Atlantis*' second flight, STS-23, launched November 26. Three communications satellites also were deployed and boosted to geosynchronous orbit by payload assist modules—Morelos B for Mexico, Aussat-2 for Australia, and Satcom K-2 for the Radio Corporation of America (RCA)—and materials-processing experiments were conducted using

Sen. Jake Garn (R-UT), a "congressional observer" aboard Discovery *in April, was monitored for motion sickness.*

NASA

Tass from Sovfoto

Cosmonauts Grechko, Volkov, and Vasyutin (l-r) *were launched to the Salyut 7 space station in September.*

the low-gravity environment. Other crew members on the mission were mission commander Brewster H. Shaw, Jr., Bryan D. O'Connor, Mary L. Cleave, Charles D. Walker, and Mexico's first astronaut, Rudolfo Neri. The mission, the last of 1985, was successfully completed with a landing at KSC on December 3.

Soviet development of a reusable spaceplane continued with the fourth flight test of an unmanned subscale model on the Cosmos 1614 mission. The spaceplane performed a wingborne reentry and landed in the Black Sea, as in the third flight test in 1983. Meanwhile, the technical definition and architectural planning phase for a permanently manned U.S. space station continued; Japan, Canada, and the ESA continued to assess participation in the development and operation of the station.

The Soviet Union's Salyut 7 space station, which had been unoccupied since October 1984, was reactivated and reoccupied by mission commander Vladimir Dzhanibekov and Viktor Savinykh on June 8, following the launch of their Soyuz T-13 spacecraft the previous day. Over the next ten days, the two cosmonauts repaired and restored the station to full operational capability. Using equipment supplied by an unmanned Progress 24 transport launched on June 21, Dzhanibekov and Savinykh performed a five-hour space walk on August 2 to install additional solar panels on the station for added electrical power. An instrument provided by France also was mounted to the exterior of the station to collect dust particles from Comet Giacobini-Zinner when the Earth passed through the comet's orbit in October.

A new three-man cosmonaut crew—mission commander Vladimir Vasyutin, Georgi Grechko, and Alexander Volkov—was launched to the station on board Soyuz T-14 on September 17 for a partial crew exchange. On September 26, Grechko and Dzhanibekov returned to Earth aboard the Soyuz T-13 spacecraft, leaving Vasyutin, Volkov, and Savinykh on board the station. A new unmanned module was docked to the station on September 27, nearly doubling the station's size to a length of 115 ft (35 m) with a mass of 103,000 lbs (46 800 kg). On November 21 mission commander Vasyutin became ill, and the three cosmonauts returned to Earth in the Soyuz T-14 spacecraft. After landing in the Republic of Kazakhstan, USSR, Vasyutin was hospitalized for treatment.

Scientific Satellites. The first direct exploration of a comet occurred on September 11, when the International Cometary Explorer intercepted the Comet Giacobini-Zinner and penetrated the tail 4,880 mi (7 850 km) downstream from the nucleus. Data on the comet's interaction with the solar wind and the dynamics and constituents within the tail were acquired. Following the encounter, the spacecraft was retargeted to pass 18.6 million mi (30 million km) upstream of Comet Halley in 1986.

In 1985 three space probes were launched to join the Soviet Union's Vega 1 and Vega 2 missions, launched in 1984, toward an encoun-

ter with Comet Halley when it reappears in 1986 after an absence of 76 years. The European Space Agency's Giotto mission was launched July 2 on a French Ariane 1 booster; two Japanese spacecraft, Sakigake and Suisei, were launched on MU-3S2 boosters on January 8 and August 19, respectively. All the encounters were scheduled to occur in March 1986.

On June 11 and June 15, respectively, as the Vega 1 and Vega 2 spacecraft swung by Venus on their way to Comet Halley, each deployed a descent module containing a balloon probe and a lander into the Venusian atmosphere. The balloons remained aloft for two days and acquired data on the atmospheric circulation; the landers obtained information on the atmospheric properties during descent and, after landing, on the surface composition.

In November, Voyager 2 entered the observatory phase of data acquisition as it neared Uranus, with the spacecraft targeted to pass within 62,000 mi (100 000 km) of the planet in January 1986.

The Soviet Union launched two scientific satellites into Earth orbit in 1985. On April 26, a Prognoz 10 Intercosmos spacecraft was launched with a joint Soviet-Czechoslovakian payload to study the interaction of the solar wind with the Earth's magnetosphere. The Cosmos 1667 Biosatellite was launched on July 10 carrying two rhesus monkeys, one of which was instrumented with sensors provided by the United States. The spacecraft returned to Earth on July 17, and flight data were provided to U.S. investigators for analysis.

Application Satellites. The Landsat-5 remote sensing satellite continued to provide data for a variety of Earth resources applications in agriculture, forestry, urban studies, and geological mapping. In 1985, ownership and operation of the U.S. land remote sensing system was transferred from the government to a commercial organization, the Earth Observation Satellite Company.

Two Soviet electronic-imaging natural-resources spacecraft continued operations in 1985. In addition, six Earth-resources film-return satellites were launched to acquire data during the agricultural season.

In the area of meteorological satellites, only one spacecraft was launched in 1985, a Soviet Meteor 2 on February 7 to join the Soviet constellation of low, near-polar orbiting meteorological spacecraft.

Communication Satellites. In addition to the 10 geosynchronous communication satellites launched by the space shuttle, 12 civil communication satellites were placed in geosynchronous orbit by expendable launch vehicles in 1985. Of these 12, three were launched by the United States, four by France, and five by the USSR. Atlas-Centaur vehicles were used by the United States to launch three Intelsat V's for Intelsat: on March 22, June 29, and September 28. French Ariane 3 growth vehicles were used to launch dual communication satellite payloads: Arabsat-1 and Brasilsat S-1 on February 8 and a GTE-Spacenet G-Star 1 and a French Telecom 1-B on May 7. In addition, two communication satellites were lost on September 12—a GTE-Spacenet F3 and a European Space Agency/Eutelsat ECS-3—when the Ariane 3 launch vehicle malfunctioned.

The five domestic communication satellites placed in geosynchronous orbit in 1985 by the USSR include two Radugas, two Gorizont, and one Ekran television relay spacecraft.

WILLIAM L. PIOTROWSKI

AP/Wide World

As shown in an artist's conception, right, the Voyager 2 space probe began its approach to the planet Uranus late in the year.

SPAIN

Napoleon's assertion that Africa begins at the Pyrenees was refuted in 1985 as Spain prepared to join the European Community (EC) on Jan. 1, 1986. Otherwise, it was a year of political ferment and economic austerity that left in doubt whether the Socialist Party of Prime Minister Felipe González could retain its governing majority after upcoming elections.

Politics and Government. After 31 months in office with the same ministerial team, González reshuffled his cabinet in midyear. Three horrible air disasters in four months sparked removal of the transport minister; a penchant for leaking government decisions to the press sealed the fate of the public-works minister; and ineffectiveness proved the undoing of the minister for local government, who—in an astute move—was replaced by a politician of mixed Basque and Catalan parentage.

Also ousted was Foreign Minister Fernando Morán, who had distinguished himself in Spain's protracted negotiations over EC affiliation, in paving the way for a French-Spanish declaration of cooperation and friendship, and in striking a deal with Great Britain over reopening the border with Gibraltar. Still, González, who has reversed field to become a champion of his nation's continued membership in the North Atlantic Treaty Organization (NATO), worried about Morán's halfhearted support for this position. The issue loomed especially large in view of a referendum on Spain's relationship to the Western alliance promised for 1986.

González chose as Morán's successor Francisco Fernández Ordóñez, a pro-NATO Social Democrat, who—as a member of the center-right government of former Prime Minister Adolfo Suárez—had ingratiated himself with the left by sponsoring bills to reform the fiscal system and legalize divorce. It would fall to Fernández Ordóñez to persuade Spaniards both to remain in NATO and keep a strong U.S. military presence in the country. Success in these tasks may be achieved by scheduling the referendum to coincide with general elections, which must be held by October 1986. Public opinion polls taken in 1985 showed a large majority favoring withdrawal from the American-led collective security pact.

The most surprising cabinet change was the resignation of Miguel Boyer as minister of economy, finance, and commerce. Anxious to nudge the Socialist government even nearer the center, Boyer used the forced departure of his colleagues to seek the additional title of deputy prime minister, thereby placing him on an equal footing with his rival Alfonso Guerra, a González confidant. At Guerra's urging, the prime minister spurned the request, and Boyer resigned—to be replaced by Carlos Solchaga, the moderate minister for industry and energy.

This shake-up deflected attention from a bitter dispute over strategy within the Communist Party that triggered the April 19 expulsion of its former leader, Santiago Carrillo, from its central and executive committees. This action exacerbated a profound breach in a party eager to expand its slice of the electorate, only 4% in the 1982 parliamentary contests.

Economy. Trade-union leaders applauded the departure of Boyer, whose high-handed implementation of an austerity program had seen the unemployment rate climb from 17% in 1982 to 22% in 1985. Critics ridiculed his failure to create 800,000 new jobs, once pledged by González. Meanwhile, the gross national product (GNP) grew only 2% in 1985, down from 3% the year before. Labor resentment, sharpened by a government plan to trim pension benefits, spurred Communist-headed unions to call a June 20 work stoppage, the first effective general strike in half a century.

In restructuring the steel and shipbuilding industries, Economy Minister Solchaga eliminated 60,000 jobs. Yet, with elections on the horizon, he would have to extend the olive branch to organized labor, particularly the Socialist-dominated General Union of Workers (UGT), whose leaders have excoriated the harshness of the prime minister's belt-tightening measures.

Foreign Affairs. Pursuant to a bilateral agreement, the border between Spain and the British crown colony of Gibraltar was reopened on Feburary 5. (*See* accompanying special report.)

Although promising to abide by the Gibraltans' wishes, London has indicated a willingness to discuss the question of its continued sovereignty over the citadel. Such possible negotiations are complicated by the insistence of Morocco's King Hassan II that his country obtain Ceuta and Melilla, Spanish enclaves in North Africa, once the Rock is returned to Spain.

Gibraltar

© Thierry Campion, Gamma-Liaison

On Feb. 5, 1985, Spain fully reopened its border with the British crown colony of Gibraltar, closed on June 8, 1969, by Generalissimo Francisco Franco, who hoped to starve the British off what is known as "the Rock."

The closure failed to ingratiate Spain with the residents of the 2.5-sq-mi (5-km²) peninsula that towers over the eastern entrance to the narrow Strait of Gibraltar, which links the Mediterranean with the Atlantic and separates Europe from Africa. London supplied the 25,000 Gibraltans by sea and air, and they exhibited a strong preference for retaining their ties to Great Britain—which first occupied the citadel in 1704 during the War of Spanish Succession—rather than become part of Spain. Little had changed since 1967 when residents—by a vote of 12,138 to 44—endorsed the existing relationship with Britain.

Spanish sensitivity to Gibraltar surfaced when King Juan Carlos declined an invitation to attend the wedding of Prince Charles to Lady Diana Spencer because the newlyweds planned to begin their honeymoon by flying to a yacht anchored there.

Merchants in the nearby Spanish town of Ceuta rejoiced over the frontier opening. Strained Anglo-Spanish relations had worked an acute economic hardship on the town's population, which increasingly suffered massive unemployment and the rise—along with neighboring La Línea—of drug smuggling.

The opening will facilitate cooperation between Britain and Spain over the latter's entry into the European Community on Jan. 1, 1986. Especially important to Prime Minister Felipe González is British support on agricultural questions at a time when the Italian and French governments wish to protect their farmers from competition from Iberian producers.

Gibraltar once symbolized the British empire and its renowned fleet. Yet, the advent of modern security systems and weapons has diminished the importance of the missile-infested Rock, under which a British submarine base is tunneled.

Claims to Spanish holdings in North Africa complicate the possibility of Britain's returning Gibraltar to Spain, now both a Common Market and NATO ally. Morocco's King Hassan has said that if Spain recovered Gibraltar, his country expected to recover Ceuta, a Spanish enclave opposite Gibraltar, as well as Melilla, 150 mi (241 km) down the Mediterranean coast. The presence of 13,000 Spanish troops at Ceuta affirms Madrid's determination to protect its possessions.

GEORGE W. GRAYSON

Doubtless, Hassan can count on the support of Libya and other Arab states for his position should Spain establish diplomatic ties with Israel—an action that Foreign Minister Fernández Ordóñez insisted would occur before the 1986 elections. Exchanging ambassadors with Israel would shatter a deal dating from the Franco era whereby Arab leaders backed both Spain's admission to the United Nations and its claims to Gibraltar in return for Madrid's advocacy of Arab causes, including nonrecognition of Israel. Falling oil prices have contributed to a new Spanish Middle East policy.

GEORGE W. GRAYSON
College of William & Mary

Sept. 11, 1985: Pete Rose singles to left for the 4,192nd hit of his career, breaking Ty Cobb's all-time record.

An Overview

Rose and Gooden, Gretzky, Spinks, Becker and Mandlikova, Montana, Cram and Slaney, Abdul-Jabbar and the Villanova Wildcats. An all-Missouri World Series, a new heavyweight champ, sweet revenge for the Lakers, Stanley Cup II for "The Great One," world records in the mile, a whiz kid at Wimbledon, and an edge-of-your-seat college roundball final.

The heroes and headlines of 1985 would have been enough to fill the sports pages with all the color and drama that any fan could hope for. But as the *business* of sport had an ever-growing effect, directly or indirectly, even the most enthusiastic rooter could hardly ignore the sometimes discouraging developments off the courts and outside the stadiums. "Scandal" and "strike," "cleanup" and "reform" also made sports headlines.

Cheering for the national pastime was interrupted twice during the 1985 season. On August 6, major league baseball players went on strike over terms of a new five-year contract, but an agreement was reached the following day, and play resumed on August 8. Then in September, a former caterer for the Pittsburgh Pirates, Curtis Strong, went on trial in federal district court on charges of selling cocaine to players from 1980 to 1983. Seven former and current major leaguers testified that they had bought from the defendant. Strong was convicted. In the aftermath of the trial, Baseball Commissioner Peter Ueberroth asked all major league players to undergo voluntary drug tests beginning in 1986.

Scandal struck college basketball on April 4, when eight people, including three members of the Tulane University team, were indicted for alleged point shaving during the 1984–85 season. The school ended up scrapping its entire basketball program. At a convention in New Orleans of the 80-year-old National Collegiate Athletic Association (NCAA), delegates talked about an "integrity crisis" in collegiate sports. The 797-member body overwhelmingly approved the strongest sanctions ever against colleges and coaches who violate rules concerning recruiting, academic standards, and amateurism. Also announced at the June convention was the creation of the 12-member National Consortium of Colleges and Universities, with the aim of promoting academic excellence among athletes.

Promoting academic excellence was also the purpose of a new rule in the state of Texas that barred from athletic competition any high school student who receives a failing grade in any subject.

In another area of progress, doors were *opened* for women at almost every level of competition. A judge in New Jersey ruled that 15-year-old Elizabeth Balsley could not be barred from playing on her high school football team. At the college level, in the 13th year since Title IX of congressional civil rights legislation, the number of women participating in athletics reached more than 150,000 (compared with 16,000 in 1972), and the number of scholarships available to women athletes rose to more than 10,000. And finally, the Harlem Globetrotters, the "clown princes" of basketball, welcomed a princess. Lynette Woodard, the 5'11" (1.80 m) captain of the 1984 U.S. Olympic squad, was selected as the first woman member of the Trotters.

The obituary list for 1985 was headed by the North American Soccer League, which finally met its demise after 17 down-up-and-down years. If anyone needed a good laugh, they could always turn to professional wrestling, which—of all things—was booming. (*See* special report, page 490.)

JEFFREY H. HACKER

Focus on Sports

Nancy Lopez won the LPGA Championship en route to record earnings. Boris Becker, age 17, triumphed at Wimbledon.

Steve Powell, All-Sport

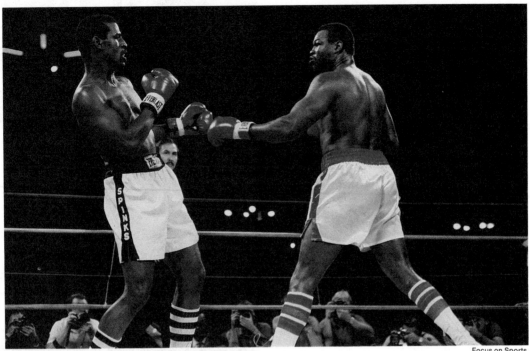

Focus on Sports

Steve Powell, All-Sport

Overview, cont. *Michael Spinks* (above left) *became the first light heavyweight champion also to take the heavyweight crown, as he outpointed previously undefeated Larry Holmes. Britain's middle-distance runner Steve Cram set three world records—in the mile; the 1,500 m, below left, and the 2,000 m; his mark in the 1,500, however, was eclipsed by Morocco's Said Aouita. And Wayne Gretzky found new ways to dazzle hockey fans in leading the Edmonton Oilers to their second straight Stanley Cup.*

Richard Pilling

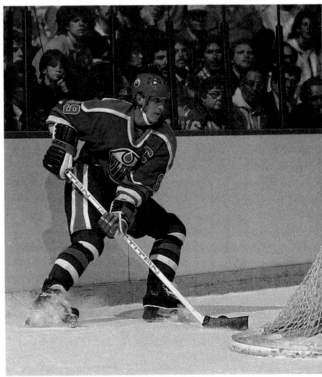

Auto Racing

Alain Prost of France, who had finished second in the overall standings two years in a row and who had won a record-tying seven Formula One Grand Prix races in 1984, finally won the World Driving championship in 1985. Taking the checkered flag in five 1985 Grand Prix races, the Team McLaren driver became the first Frenchman ever to capture the world title.

Defending champion Mario Andretti won three of the first four events in the CART-PPG Indy Car series but then faded in the stretch. Danny Sullivan won the 69th Indy 500 despite a 360-degree spin on the 120th lap. But it was steady Al Unser of the Penske team who won the CART-PPG championship, for the third time. At age 46 he became the oldest driver ever to earn the crown. Big Al took the title by only one point (151–150) over his son, Al Unser, Jr. Little Al, 23, who had won two CART-PPG events during the season, was attempting to become the youngest driver ever to capture the championship.

Bill Elliott won an impressive 11 races on the 28-event NASCAR Grand National Stock Car racing schedule, including the Daytona 500. That victory, along with first-place finishes in the Southern 500 and Winston 500, earned Elliott a $1 million bonus from the R. J. Reynolds Tobacco Company. The prize had been promised to any racer who won three of the four Big Four events. Nevertheless, the 1985 NASCAR champion was Darrell Waltrip, who consistently finished near the top. It was Waltrip's third NASCAR title.

DUSTY BRANDEL, *American Auto Racing Writers and Broadcasters Association*

AUTO RACING
Major Race Winners

Indianapolis 500: Danny Sullivan
Michigan 500: Emerson Fittipaldi
Pocono 500: Rick Mears
Daytona 500: Bill Elliott

1985 Champions

World Championship: Alain Prost (France)
CART: Al Unser (Sr.)
NASCAR: Darrell Waltrip

**Grand Prix for
Formula One Cars, 1985**

Australia: Keke Rosberg (Finland)
Austria: Alain Prost
Belgium: Ayrton Senna (Brazil)
Brazil: Alain Prost
Canada: Michele Alboreto (Italy)
Detroit: Keke Rosberg
Europe: Nigel Mansell (Great Britain)
France: Nelson Piquet (Brazil)
Germany: Michele Alboreto
Great Britain: Alain Prost
Italy: Alain Prost
Monaco: Alain Prost
Netherlands: Niki Lauda (Austria)
Portugal: Ayrton Senna
San Marino: Elio De Angelis (Italy)
South Africa: Nigel Mansell

Baseball

For Pete Rose, Rod Carew, Tom Seaver, and Phil Niekro, 1985 was the year of the milestone. For the Kansas City Royals, it was the year of the comeback. For baseball fans, it was a year of cocaine scandal, labor unrest, and an expanded seven-game league championship series.

Play-offs and World Series. Though they finished next-to-last in the American League (AL) in batting, runs scored, and on-base percentage, the Kansas City Royals relied on a young pitching staff and the timely hitting of George Brett to finish first in the AL West for the second consecutive season. As late as October 2, Kansas City trailed the California Angels, who led the division for most of the summer. But the Royals came from behind to defeat the Oakland Athletics, 5–4, on October 5, clinching the title and making them the first repeat divisional winner since the 1980–81 New York Yankees.

The Yankees, like the Royals, finished strong in 1985, but they just missed catching the Toronto Blue Jays, who led the East for most of the season. Toronto went into its first post-season competition as a heavy favorite and took a three-games-to-one lead in the American League Championship Series (ALCS). But Kansas City came back to win three straight games—the last two in Toronto —to win a berth against the St. Louis Cardinals in the first all-Missouri World Series since 1944.

Surviving a last-week scare from the second-place New York Mets, the speedy Cards finished the season with 101 victories, the most in baseball. The Cardinals had relied on their running game for the entire season, but they won the National League Championship Series (NLCS) with an unexpected display of power. After leading the majors with 314 stolen bases, St. Louis used ninth-inning home runs by light-hitting Ozzie Smith in Game 5 and by Jack Clark in Game 6 to defeat the Los Angeles Dodgers, winners of the Western Division title, four games to two.

Unfortunately for the Cardinals, the catalyst of their running game, NL Rookie of the Year Vince Coleman, suffered an injured knee when he was accidentally pinned by an automatic tarpaulin at Busch Stadium prior to the fourth play-off game. Without Coleman, who had stolen a rookie-record 110 bases to lead the majors, the St. Louis offense became anemic. Cardinal hitters managed only a .185 batting average, the lowest ever in the World Series. That allowed Kansas City again to overcome a 3–1 deficit, even with the final two games in St. Louis.

The pitching aces of both teams, John Tudor of St. Louis and Bret Saberhagen of Kansas City, each won two games in the Oc-

tober Classic, but the 21-year-old Royal right-hander defeated the veteran Card lefty in Game 7, 11–0. Saberhagen, a second-year player, was named Most Valuable Player (MVP) of the World Series.

The Cards, behind Tudor, had taken the Series opener, 3–1, in Kansas City, and then won Game 2 there, 4–2, scoring all their runs in the ninth inning. The Royals rebounded for a 6–1 triumph in Game 3 at St. Louis, but Tudor tossed a 3–0 shutout for the Cards in Game 4. The Royals stayed alive with a 6–1 triumph in Game 5 and then, back in Kansas City, evened the Series with a dramatic 2–1 victory in Game 6. The winning hit was a one-out, bases-loaded single by pinch-hitter Dane Iorg in the bottom of the ninth. The finale was decided when Tudor, who led both leagues with ten shutouts, suffered a third-inning knockout, his earliest in 41 pitching appearances. Two innings later Cardinal right-hander Joaquin Andujar was ejected from the game after charging and bumping home plate umpire Don Denkinger during a heated argument over ball-and-strike calls. As a result, Andujar was suspended for the first ten games of 1986 by Commissioner Peter V. Ueberroth.

In his first full season on the job, Ueberroth also appointed former President Richard M. Nixon as arbitrator of a dispute by umpires seeking increased compensation because of the expanded play-off format. Nixon awarded the umpires a 40% pay hike.

Regular Season. Personal mediation by Ueberroth helped curtail a potentially devastating player strike that began on August 6. After two days of games were lost, Ueberroth announced a settlement that included an increased contribution by owners to the players' pension plan, an increase in the minimum player salary to $60,000, an end to the free-agent reentry draft and professional compensation for lost players, withdrawal by owners of demands for a salary cap, and an increase in player eligibility for salary arbitration from two to three years of service.

Following the September 20 conviction of Philadelphia caterer Curtis Strong on 11 counts of selling cocaine to athletes, the commissioner also asked the players to submit to voluntary drug testing. Granted immunity from prosecution, players who admitted past use of cocaine included Keith Hernandez and Dave Parker.

On the field, two pitchers—Tom Seaver of the Chicago White Sox and Phil Niekro of the New York Yankees—won their 300th games, the former at New York on August 4 and the latter at Toronto on October 6. Two hitters also made history: Pete Rose, player-manager of the Cincinnati Reds, passed Ty Cobb as the career hit leader with No. 4,192—a first-inning single against the San Diego Padres on September 11; and Rod Carew of the California Angels notched his 3,000th hit on August 4.

Season-long highlights included the pitching of Dwight Gooden of the Mets and the hitting

Kansas City pitcher Bret Saberhagen (left) won two games in the World Series and the AL Cy Young Award; teammate George Brett batted .335. Fireballing Dwight Gooden of the Mets posted a 1.53 ERA and took NL Cy Young honors.
Photos © Richard Pilling, Inc.

of Wade Boggs of the Boston Red Sox. At age 21, Gooden earned the NL Cy Young Award by winning a rare Triple Crown of pitching: major league leadership in wins, strikeouts, and earned run average (ERA). Gooden was 24–4 with 268 strikeouts and a 1.53 ERA, the latter being best in the majors since Bob Gibson's record 1.12 in 1968. Tudor, Andujar, and Cincinnati rookie Tom Browning also were 20-game winners in the NL.

Ron Guidry of the Yankees led AL pitchers with 22 wins, while Toronto's Dave Stieb posted a league-best 2.48 ERA. But AL Cy Young honors went to Saberhagen, who went 20–6 and 2.87. Bert Blyleven of the Minnesota Twins led the majors with 24 complete games and the AL with 206 strikeouts and five shutouts. Leaders in saves were Dan Quisenberry of the Royals with 37 and the Montreal Expos' Jeff Reardon with 41.

No pitcher seemed too tough for Boggs, whose 28-game hitting streak, 240 hits, .368 batting average, and .450 on-base percentage led the majors. George Brett was second in the AL batting race at .335 and led both leagues with a .585 slugging percentage. But that was not enough to keep Don Mattingly of the Yankees from winning league MVP honors. Mattingly led the majors with 145 runs batted in (RBIs), finished second in the league in hits and slugging, third in batting, and fourth in home runs. He was helped enormously by new teammate Rickey Henderson, who led the AL with 80 stolen bases and 146 runs scored and became the first American Leaguer to steal at least 50 bases and hit at least 20 homers in the same season.

The AL home-run king was a surprise: 38-year-old Darrell Evans of the Detroit Tigers. He not only led the majors with 40 home runs but became the oldest American Leaguer to hit that many and the first man to reach that level in both leagues. Dale Murphy of the Atlanta Braves led the NL with 37 homers and 118 runs scored and was second in RBIs to Cincinnati's Dave Parker, who knocked in 125. Pedro Guerrero of the Dodgers tied a record by hitting 15 home runs in June, then went on to lead the league with a .577 slugging percentage and a .422 on-base average. Guerrero was second in batting and third in homers but close to batting champion Willie McGee of St. Louis in the MVP voting. McGee's .353, the highest average ever posted by a National League switch-hitter, was accomplished with 216 hits, including 18 triples, both NL highs. He also stole 56 bases, won a Gold Glove for fielding excellence, and knocked in two runs to help the NL win the July 16 All-Star Game, 6–1.

Two former Cardinals, Lou Brock and Enos Slaughter, were among four players enshrined in the Baseball Hall of Fame; Hoyt Wilhelm and the late Arky Vaughan also were inducted.

There was one ownership change during the year: the financially troubled Pittsburgh Pirates were sold by the Galbreath family to a group of local investors.

DAN SCHLOSSBERG, *Baseball Writer*

BASEBALL

Professional—Major Leagues
Final Standings, 1985

AMERICAN LEAGUE

Eastern Division	W	L	Pct.	Western Division	W	L	Pct.
Toronto	99	62	.615	Kansas City	91	71	.562
New York	97	64	.602	California	90	72	.556
Detroit	84	77	.522	Chicago	85	77	.525
Baltimore	83	78	.516	Minnesota	77	85	.475
Boston	81	81	.500	Oakland	77	85	.475
Milwaukee	71	90	.441	Seattle	74	88	.457
Cleveland	60	102	.370	Texas	62	99	.385

NATIONAL LEAGUE

Eastern Division	W	L	Pct.	Western Division	W	L	Pct.
St. Louis	101	61	.623	Los Angeles	95	67	.586
New York	98	64	.605	Cincinnati	89	72	.553
Montreal	84	77	.522	Houston	83	79	.512
Chicago	77	84	.478	San Diego	83	79	.512
Philadelphia	75	87	.463	Atlanta	66	96	.407
Pittsburgh	57	104	.354	San Francisco	62	100	.383

Play-Offs—American League: Kansas City defeated Toronto, 4 games to 3; National League: St. Louis defeated Los Angeles, 4 games to 2.

World Series—Kansas City defeated St. Louis, 4 games to 3. First Game (Royals Stadium, Kansas City, Oct. 19, attendance 41,650): St. Louis 3, Kansas City 1; Second Game (Royals Stadium, Oct. 20, attendance 41,656): St. Louis 4, Kansas City 2; Third Game (Busch Memorial Stadium, St. Louis, Oct. 22, attendance 53,634): Kansas City 6, St. Louis 1; Fourth Game (Busch Memorial Stadium, Oct. 23, attendance 53,634): St. Louis 3, Kansas City 0; Fifth Game (Busch Memorial Stadium, Oct. 24, attendance 53,634): Kansas City 6, St. Louis 1; Sixth Game (Royals Stadium, Oct. 26, attendance 41,628): Kansas City 2, St. Louis 1; Seventh Game (Royals Stadium, Oct. 27, attendance 41,658): Kansas City 11, St. Louis 0.

All-Star Game (Metrodome, Minneapolis, July 16, attendance 54,960): National League 6, American League 1.

Most Valuable Players—American League: Don Mattingly, New York; National League: Willie McGee, St. Louis.

Cy Young Memorial Awards (outstanding pitchers)—American League: Bret Saberhagen, Kansas City; National League: Dwight Gooden, New York.

Managers of the Year—American League: Bobby Cox, Toronto; National League: Whitey Herzog, St. Louis.

Rookies of the Year—American League: Ozzie Guillen, Chicago; National League: Vince Coleman, St. Louis.

Leading Hitters—(Percentage) American League: Wade Boggs, Boston, .368; National League: Willie McGee, St. Louis, .353. (Runs Batted In) American League: Don Mattingly, New York, 145; National League: Dave Parker, Cincinnati, 125. (Home Runs) American League: Darrell Evans, Detroit, 40; National League: Dale Murphy, Atlanta, 37. (Hits) American League: Boggs, 240; National League: McGee, 216. (Runs) American League: Rickey Henderson, New York, 146; National League: Murphy, 118.

Leading Pitchers—(Earned Run Average) American League: Dave Stieb, Toronto, 2.48; National League: Dwight Gooden, New York, 1.53. (Victories) American League: Ron Guidry, New York, 22; National League: Gooden, 24. (Strikeouts) American League: Bert Blyleven, Minnesota, 206; National League: Gooden, 268. (Shutouts) American League: Blyleven, 5; National League: John Tudor, St. Louis, 10. (Saves) American League: Dan Quisenberry, Kansas City, 37; National League: Jeff Reardon, Montreal, 41.

Stolen Bases—American League: Rickey Henderson, New York, 80; National League: Vince Coleman, St. Louis, 110.

Professional—Minor Leagues, Class AAA

American Association: Louisville
International League: Tidewater
Pacific Coast League: Vancouver

Amateur

NCAA: Miami
Little League World Series: Seoul, South Korea

Veteran center Kareem Abdul-Jabbar led the Lakers to an NBA championship with his patented —and virtually unstoppable— ''sky hook.'' He also became the all-time leading scorer in playoff competition.

Noren Trotman

BASKETBALL

The Los Angeles Lakers, who had failed to beat the Boston Celtics in eight previous championship-round attempts, emerged as professional basketball's best team in 1984–85 by defeating the Celtics in the National Basketball Association's (NBA's) final play-off series, four games to two. It was the Lakers' third NBA title in six years.

In one of the most stunning upsets in the history of college basketball, the Villanova Wildcats defeated the heavily favored Georgetown University Hoyas, 66–64, in the 47th National Collegiate Athletic Association (NCAA) championship. UCLA won the National Invitation Tournament (NIT), and Old Dominion won the women's NCAA title.

The Professional Season

The NBA, which had been plagued by falling attendance, out-of-control salaries, and poor television ratings, had a rebirth in 1984–85. Ratings and attendance both increased mark-

edly, with interest peaking for the championship-round series between longtime rivals Boston and Los Angeles. In addition, two other pro leagues were attracting fans: the Continental Basketball League, which served as a developing ground for the NBA, and the fledgling United States Basketball League, which played its games in the spring and summer.

Boston and Los Angeles of the NBA had been closely matched all season. Boston finished with the best regular-season record (63–19), and Los Angeles was close behind (62–20). The Lakers were the top team in the Western Conference, finishing ten games ahead of Denver, which took the Midwest Division title. The Houston Rockets, with 7'0" rookie center Akeem Olajuwon joining 7'4" second-year pro Ralph Sampson, won 48 games, 19 more than it managed in 1983–84. Sampson and Olajuwon became the first teammates to average 20 points and 10 rebounds in the same season since Elgin Baylor and Wilt Chamberlain of the Lakers did it in 1969.

In the Eastern Conference, the Celtics and Philadelphia '76ers staged another of their

PROFESSIONAL BASKETBALL

National Basketball Association
(Final Standings, 1984–85)

Eastern Conference

Atlantic Division	W	L	Pct.
*Boston	63	19	.768
*Philadelphia	58	24	.707
*New Jersey	42	40	.512
*Washington	40	42	.488
New York	24	58	.293
Central Division			
*Milwaukee	59	23	.720
*Detroit	46	36	.561
*Chicago	38	44	.463
*Cleveland	36	46	.439
Atlanta	34	48	.415
Indiana	22	60	.268

Western Conference

Midwest Division	W	L	Pct.
*Denver	52	30	.634
*Houston	48	34	.585
*Dallas	44	38	.537
*San Antonio	41	41	.500
*Utah	41	41	.500
Kansas City	31	51	.378
Pacific Division			
*L.A. Lakers	62	20	.756
*Portland	42	40	.512
*Phoenix	36	46	.439
L.A. Clippers	31	51	.378
Seattle	31	51	.378
Golden State	22	60	.268

*Made play-offs

Play-Offs
Eastern Conference

First Round	Boston	3 games	Cleveland	1
	Detroit	3 games	New Jersey	0
	Milwaukee	3 games	Chicago	1
	Philadelphia	3 games	Washington	1
Semifinals	Boston	4 games	Detroit	2
	Philadelphia	4 games	Milwaukee	0
Finals	Boston	4 games	Philadelphia	1

Western Conference

First Round	Denver	3 games	San Antonio	2
	Los Angeles	3 games	Phoenix	0
	Portland	3 games	Dallas	1
	Utah	3 games	Houston	2
Semifinals	Denver	4 games	Utah	1
	Los Angeles	4 games	Portland	1
Finals	Los Angeles	4 games	Denver	1
Championship	Los Angeles	4 games	Boston	2
All-Star Game	West 140, East 129			

Individual Honors

Most Valuable Player: Larry Bird, Boston
Most Valuable Player (play-offs): Kareem Abdul-Jabbar, Los Angeles
Most Valuable Player (all-star game): Ralph Sampson, Houston
Rookie of the Year: Michael Jordan, Chicago
Coach of the Year: Donald Nelson, Milwaukee
Leading Scorer: Bernard King, New York, 32.9
Leader in Assists: Isiah Thomas, Detroit, 13.9 per game
Leading Rebounder: Moses Malone, 13.1 per game
Leader in Field Goal Percentage: James Donaldson, L.A. Clippers, .637

close races for the Atlantic Division title, which Boston finally won by five games after the '76ers suffered a series of second-half injuries. The surprise team of the season was the Milwaukee Bucks, who had been picked as an also-ran after the retirement of center Bob Lanier but instead ran away with the Central Division championship. The Cleveland Cavaliers also performed better than expected, making the play-offs despite being picked for last place.

The Clippers spent their first season in Los Angeles after moving from San Diego, and in another franchise change the Kansas City Kings played their final season in that city before moving to Sacramento, CA, for the 1985–86 schedule.

Boston's Larry Bird was named the league's most valuable player after a brilliant season in which he averaged 28.7 points and 10.5 rebounds per game and made 52% of his field goal attempts. But Bird was not the only player who stood out. Rookie Michael Jordan of the Chicago Bulls became an instant star, dazzling fans and players alike with his leaping ability and daring drives to the basket; so spectacular was Jordan's play that his team recorded an 87% increase in attendance. The league's top guards, Detroit's Isiah Thomas and the Lakers' Magic Johnson, finished one-two in assists (13.9 to 12.6 per game), with Thomas setting a new NBA season record of 1,123. New York's Bernard King led in scoring (32.9) despite suffering a late-season knee injury, and Philadelphia's Moses Malone again was the leading rebounder (13.1).

The play-offs had few surprises, with both Boston and Los Angeles breezing to the final round. This was the matchup basketball fans had been anticipating since the previous season, when the Lakers lost control of the championship series and fell in seven games. This time Los Angeles proved more durable. After a 148–114 trouncing in the opening game on Memorial Day, the Lakers bounced back behind the leadership of Kareem Abdul-Jabbar, the 38-year-old veteran center. Playing like a man ten years younger, Abdul-Jabbar averaged 25.5 points and nine rebounds and earned Most Valuable Player honors for the series.

The Lakers rebounded from that opening game loss by winning Game 2, 109–102, also at Boston Garden; Abdul-Jabbar scored 30 points and grabbed 17 rebounds. It was Boston's first home play-off defeat in 1985 and gave the Lakers a decided advantage as the series moved to Los Angeles for the next three games.

With forward James Worthy scoring 29 points and Abdul-Jabbar getting 26, the Lakers coasted to a 136–111 win in the third game. Abdul-Jabbar, who already held the NBA regular-season career scoring record, also became the all-time career play-off scoring leader during the game, breaking the record held by Jerry West, now the Lakers' general manager. Boston evened the series at two games apiece by beating the Lakers, 107–105, in Game 4, as guard Dennis Johnson made an 18-foot jump shot at the buzzer. Bird, who had been bothered by a sore right elbow during the entire series, scored 26 points and had 11 rebounds. But the Lakers came back from that heartbreaking defeat as well, running past Boston in Game 5, 120–111. Abdul-Jabbar played splendidly once more, scoring 36 points.

The Villanova Wildcats squeezed past heavily favored Georgetown, 66-64, in an exciting NCAA final. Center Ed Pinckney (shooting) was named MVP of the tournament. Georgetown center Patrick Ewing (falling) was regarded as the nation's top collegiate player.

AP/Wide World

The sixth game of the series was played at Boston Garden. The Celtics made a very poor 38% of their field-goal attempts and were outplayed by the quicker, deeper Lakers, 111–100. The loss prevented Boston from becoming the first NBA team to win back-to-back championships since 1969.

The College Season

Georgetown University, led by towering center Patrick Ewing, and St. John's University, featuring star guard-forward Chris Mullin, were the two dominant teams during the 1984–85 college basketball season. But it was another Big East Conference squad, Villanova University, that became the collegiate champion at the end of the annual NCAA tournament.

Georgetown was the preseason favorite, and, except for a brief time after losing to St. John's in a January matchup, the Hoyas were ranked No. 1 in the country during the regular season. The competitiveness of the Big East, which had such other powerful teams as Syracuse and Boston College, helped fuel the continuing growth in popularity of college basketball. The Atlantic Coast Conference—with Duke, North Carolina, and Georgia Tech—and the Big 10—with Michigan, Illinois, and Iowa—also were very strong. Other standout teams included Louisiana Tech, Oklahoma, Memphis State,

Nevada-Las Vegas, and Virginia Commonwealth.

Wichita State's Xavier McDaniel made history by leading the nation in both scoring (27.2 points per game) and rebounding (14.8) during the regular season. But Ewing and Mullin, both stars of the 1984 U.S. Olympic basketball team, were acknowledged as the top players in the nation. Ewing was a dominating shot blocker and rebounder who also became a more dangerous scorer in his senior season. Mullin was an accurate shooter and uncanny passer who ranked among the country's top scorers. Other All-Americas included Wayman Tisdale of Oklahoma, Keith Lee of Memphis State, Mark Price of Georgia Tech, Ed Pinckney of Villanova, Johnny Dawkins of Duke, Benoit Benjamin of Creighton, David Robinson of Navy, Kenny Walker of Kentucky, Joe Kleine of Arkansas, Brad Daughtery of North Carolina, and Jon Koncak of Southern Methodist.

Amid all the excitement and accomplishments, however, came news of a point-shaving scandal allegedly involving players at Tulane University. It eventually resulted in the resignation of the head basketball coach, Ned Fowler, and grand jury indictments against a number of Tulane players and students. Among those arrested was John (Hot Rod) Williams, Tulane's leading scorer, rebounder, and shot blocker as well as the Metro Conference player

COLLEGE BASKETBALL

Conference Champions*

Atlantic Coast: Georgia Tech
Atlantic-10: Temple
Big East: Georgetown
Big Eight: Oklahoma
Big Sky: Nevada-Reno
Big Ten: Michigan
East Coast: Leigh
ECAC Metro: Fairleigh Dickinson
ECAC North: Northeastern
ECAC South: Navy
Ivy League: Pennsylvania
Metro: Memphis State
Metro Atlantic Athletic: Iona
Mid-American: Ohio University
Mid-Continent: E. Illinois
Mid-Eastern Athletic: North Carolina AT&T
Midwestern City: Loyola, IL
Missouri Valley: Wichita State
Ohio Valley: Middle Tennessee
Pacific Coast Athletic: Nevada-Las Vegas
Pacific-10: Washington and USC (tie)
Southeastern: Auburn
Southern: Marshall
Southland: Louisiana Tech
Southwest: Texas Tech
Southwestern Athletic: Southern
Sun Belt: Virginia Commonwealth
Trans America Athletic: Mercer
West Coast Athletic: Pepperdine
Western Athletic: San Diego State
   * Based on postseason conference
    tournaments, where applicable

Tournaments

NCAA: Villanova
NIT: UCLA
NCAA Div. II: Jacksonville State
NCAA Div. III: North Park
NAIA: Fort Hays State
NCAA (women's): Old Dominion

of the year in 1983–84. It was the first such scandal in college basketball since one involving Boston College in 1981.

Georgetown was seeded No. 1 in the expanded 64-team NCAA tournament. The Hoyas, who had won the NCAA title in 1983–84, had little trouble advancing to the tournament's Final Four round. But Michigan, the No. 2 seed, was not quite so fortunate. The Wolverines were upset by Villanova, 59–55, in the Southeast Regional. Villanova then advanced to the Final Four by downing North Carolina State, 56–44. St. John's, the best team in the West Regional, made it to the Final Four by defeating North Carolina State, 69–60. The other team in the Final Four was Memphis State, which had squeezed out a victory over Oklahoma, 63–61.

In the Final Four at Lexington, KY, Georgetown and St. John's, playing for the fourth time since the beginning of the season, met in one of the semifinal games. The Hoyas, playing brilliantly, ran away with an easy 77–59 victory and became heavy favorites to capture the championship—especially after Villanova upset favored Memphis State in the other semifinal. Georgetown was especially effective on defense, holding Mullin to just eight points. Villanova, which was unranked after the regular season and had a 23–10 record entering the tournament, had lost twice previously to Georgetown and was much smaller than Mem-

phis State. But the Wildcats neutralized the Memphis State height advantage with outstanding defenses and smart court play. Memphis State also was hurt when its star player, Lee, fouled out with ten minutes left in the game.

Georgetown, meanwhile, was widely regarded as one of the best teams ever in college basketball. The Hoyas were a bigger, deeper team than Villanova, and Ewing had become one of the most heralded players ever to play the game. Entering the final, Georgetown had recorded 17 straight victories. But the Wildcats overcame those deficits and defeated Georgetown, 66–64, for the NCAA title. It was a finely played game, one of the most exciting and memorable in NCAA tournament history. Georgetown played well enough to win most games, shooting 54% from the floor and forcing 17 turnovers. But Villanova was even better. The Wildcats made a magnificent 78.6% of their field goal attempts, an NCAA record, to offset 14 points by Ewing and 16 by forward David Wingate. Every time Georgetown would try to catch up in the second half, Villanova would make the pressure basket to stay ahead. Pinckney, the Villanova center, had 16 points and was named most valuable player of the tournament; forward Dwayne McClain had a game-high 17 points; and guard Howard Jensen, a substitute, had 14 points, including the basket that put his team ahead for good. Villanova coach Rollie Massimino, who said the championship was "the greatest thing that ever happened to me," later considered signing a contract with the New Jersey Nets of the NBA but changed his mind and stayed at Villanova.

After the season, Ewing became the first player selected in the NBA college draft, chosen by the New York Knicks. Tisdale, who decided to skip his senior year at Oklahoma, was chosen by the Indiana Pacers. Benjamin passed up his senior year at Creighton and was drafted by the Clippers.

UCLA, which once dominated the NCAA tournament, won the New York City–based NIT by defeating Indiana, 65–62, at Madison Square Garden. UCLA, which had a poor 3–6 record earlier in the regular season, was led by forward Reggie Miller, who scored the winning basket. His sister, Cheryl, was named the player of the year in women's college basketball. A standout on the U.S. women's Olympic basketball team in 1984, Cheryl played her collegiate ball at the University of Southern California. The top women's team in the country, however, was Old Dominion, which defeated Georgia, 70–65, in the finals of the women's NCAA tournament. Forward Tracy Claxton of Old Dominion was selected as the tournament's most valuable player after scoring 17 points in the final.

PAUL ATTNER
"The Sporting News"

Boxing

The watchful eyes of boxing fans in 1985 were on Larry Holmes, the International Boxing Federation (IBF) heavyweight champion who was pursuing the late Rocky Marciano's career record of 49 victories without a defeat. Holmes, who won the World Boxing Council (WBC) heavyweight title from Ken Norton on June 9, 1978, and defended it 17 times, relinquished it on Dec. 11, 1983, and then was recognized as champion by the IBF.

Holmes started the year with a tenth-round knockout of David Bey on March 15 in Las Vegas, raising his record to 47–0. Then on May 20, he was extended to 15 rounds by Carl (The Truth) Williams but won a unanimous decision to keep the crown. Williams was surprisingly effective against the 35-year-old champion, whose lackluster victory seemed to signal that age was beginning to catch up with him.

On September 21 at Las Vegas, Holmes' quest to equal Marciano's record came to an abrupt end when he lost a unanimous 15-round decision to Michael Spinks. It was the 28th victory for the unbeaten Spinks, who became the first light heavyweight champ to win the heavyweight title. Eight other light heavyweights in a total of 13 bouts had fought for the heavyweight crown. After the bout with Spinks, Holmes announced his retirement; his record stood at 48–1, with 34 knockouts.

Spinks gave up his undisputed light heavyweight crown in November to fight exclusively as IBF heavyweight champion; that division, he felt, would offer more challengers and larger purses. As the light heavyweight champ, the 28-year-old Spinks had defended his title ten times, twice in 1985—against David Sears in February and Diamond Jim MacDonald in June. As a heavyweight, however, Spinks had his work cut out for him, since two other men also claimed a share of the title. On April 29 in Buffalo, NY, Tony Tubbs of Cincinnati used superior hand speed to dethrone Greg Page as World Boxing Association (WBA) heavyweight champ with a unanimous 15-round decision. The other champion was Pinklon Thomas, also unbeaten, who retained his WBC title on June 15 in Las Vegas with an eighth-round knockout of Mike Weaver.

A much-anticipated fight, matching perhaps the two best fighters in the world, took place in Las Vegas on April 15, when Marvelous Marvin Hagler, the undisputed middleweight champion, risked his title against Thomas (Hitman) Hearns, the WBC junior middleweight champ. Despite the interest in the heavyweight division, the Hagler-Hearns matchup was widely considered the fight of the year. Hagler (60–2–2) had not lost a fight in nine years and was unbeaten in his last 35. Hearns (40–1) had lost previously only to Sugar Ray Leonard in the 14th round of a 1981 welterweight title fight. In a furious battle, regarded as one of the most exciting ever, Hagler, who had been cut above and below his right eye in the first round, knocked out Hearns at 1 minute and 49 seconds of the third round with a right to the chin. It was Hagler's 11th defense since winning the title in 1980. He was to fight again in November against John Mugabi, but he suffered a broken nose in training and the bout was postponed until 1986.

Livingstone Bramble, the WBA lightweight champion who stopped Ray (Boom Boom) Mancini to win the title in 1984, proved that the triumph was no fluke by taking a 15-round decision in a brutal rematch on February 16. Mancini announced his retirement in August.

Nationalistic fervor accompanied the arrival on the world featherweight scene of Barry McGuigan of Northern Ireland, who dethroned Eusebio Pedroza of Panama for the WBA title June 8 in London. Pedroza had reigned for seven years and had defended his title 19 times before the loss. The popular 24-year-old McGuigan was born in the Irish Republic but now lives in Northern Ireland and fights as a British citizen. He made his first defense in Belfast in September, defeating Bernard Taylor in the eighth round.

Donald Curry, the WBA and IBF welterweight titleholder, became the undisputed champion when he knocked out Milton McCrory, the WBC champ, in the second round of a unification bout in Las Vegas on December 6. GEORGE DE GREGORIO, *"The New York Times"*

World Boxing Champions*

Junior Flyweight—Yoo Myong Woo, South Korea (1985), World Boxing Association (WBA); Chang Chong Koo, South Korea (1983), World Boxing Council (WBC); Dodie Penalosa, Philippines (1984), International Boxing Federation (IBF).

Flyweight—Santos Laciar, Argentina (1982), WBA; Sot Chitalada, Thailand (1984), WBC; Soon Chung Kwon, South Korea (1984), IBF.

Junior Bantamweight—Khaosai Galaxy, Thailand (1984), WBA; Jiro Watanabe, Japan (1984), WBC; Elly Pical, Indonesia (1985), IBF.

Bantamweight—Richard Sandoval, United States (1984), WBA; Miguel Lora, Colombia (1985), WBC; Jeff Fenech, Australia (1985), IBF.

Junior Featherweight—Victor Callejas, Puerto Rico (1984), WBA; Lupe Pintor, Mexico (1985), WBC; Loris Stecca, Italy (1985), IBF.

Featherweight—Barry McGuigan, Northern Ireland (1985), WBA; Azumah Nelson, Ghana (1984), WBC; Min Keun Oh, South Korea (1984), IBF.

Junior Lightweight—Wilfredo Gomez, Puerto Rico (1985), WBA; Julio Cesar Chavez, Mexico (1984), WBC; Barry Michaels, Australia (1985), IBF.

Lightweight—Livingstone Bramble, United States (1984), WBA; Hector Camacho, Puerto Rico (1985), WBC; Jimmy Paul, United States (1985), IBF.

Junior Welterweight—Ubaldo Sacco, Argentina (1985), WBA; Lonnie Smith, United States (1985), WBC; Aaron Pryor, United States (1984), IBF.

Welterweight—Donald Curry, United States (1983), WBA, WBC, IBF.

Junior Middleweight—Mike McCallum, Jamaica (1984), WBA; vacant, WBC; Carlos Santos, Puerto Rico (1984), IBF.

Middleweight—Marvin Hagler, United States (1980), WBA, WBC, IBF.

Light Heavyweight—vacant, WBA; J.B. Williamson, United States (1985), WBC; Slobodan Kacar, Yugoslavia (1985), IBF.

Cruiserweight—Dwight Muhammad Qawi, United States (1985), WBA; Bernard Benton, United States (1985), WBC; Lee Roy Murphy, United States (1984), IBF.

Heavyweight—Tony Tubbs, United States (1985), WBA; Pinklon Thomas, United States (1984), WBC; Michael Spinks, United States (1984), IBF.

* As of Dec. 10, 1985; year of achieving title in parentheses.

Football

In the National Football League (NFL), 1985–86 was the Year of the Bear. Led by the league's top defense, Chicago's "Monsters of the Midway" compiled a 15–1 record, tying San Francisco's 1984–85 mark for the most regular-season wins in NFL history. Then, to the delight of championship-starved Chicago fans, the Bears rolled to their first Super Bowl appearance and completely overwhelmed the year's "Cinderella" team, the New England Patriots, 46–10. With an awesome defense that limited the Patriots to minus-19 yards in the first half, the Bears established Super Bowl records for points scored and margin of victory. Chicago's defensive end Richard Dent was named the game's most valuable player. A crowd of 73,818 persons witnessed Super Bowl XX in the Superdome in New Orleans.

In the United States Football League (USFL), Baltimore's Stars, who had moved from Philadelphia before the season, won their second consecutive league championship. In the title game, played on July 14, the Stars downed the Oakland Invaders, 28–24, behind the running of Kelvin Bryant. His three-touchdown, 103-yard performance earned Bryant the game's MVP award. The USFL was playing its final spring-summer schedule, planning to compete head-to-head against the NFL beginning in the fall of 1986.

The British Columbia Lions won the Grey Cup, symbolic of the championship of the Canadian Football League (CFL), with a 37–24 victory in the November 24 title game against the Hamilton Tiger-Cats.

And on the college level, the Oklahoma Sooners emerged as national champions after handing Penn State its first loss of the season, 25–10, in the Orange Bowl. Auburn's stellar running back Bo Jackson narrowly outpointed Iowa quarterback Chuck Long in the closest-ever balloting for the Heisman Trophy.

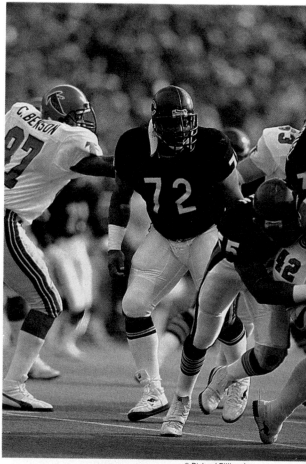

© Richard Pilling, Inc.

Chicago's William "the Refrigerator" Perry (72), a 308-lb rookie, became a celebrity on and off the field.

National Football League

Having last won an NFL championship in 1963 and having come within one victory of a Super Bowl appearance in 1984–85, the Bears were a hungry team as the new season began. In the fighting spirit of Coach Mike Ditka, himself a star tight-end in the 1960s, the Chicagoans powered their way to 12 straight wins before succumbing to the Miami Dolphins, 38–24, in Week 13 at Miami. Then, having already clinched the National Football Conference (NFC) Central Division title, the Bears tuned up for the play-offs with three more victories.

Spearheading the Chicago attack, running back Walter Payton, the NFL's all-time leading rusher, set a league record by gaining 100 or more yards in nine straight games; he ended the regular season with a total of 1,551 yards, sec-ond in the NFC to Gerald Riggs' 1,719 for Atlanta. Complementing the Payton ground attack was the passing and ball-handling of Jim McMahon, the Bears' tough, agile, and free-spirited quarterback. On defense, Chicago was led by such standouts as linebacker Mike Singletary, right end Richard Dent (who led the entire league in quarterback sacks with 17), and pro football's celebrity of the year, William "the Refrigerator" Perry. A 6'2", 308-lb rookie defensive tackle, Perry caught the imagination of fans everywhere with his *scoring* exploits. With Coach Ditka using him in the offensive backfield in several goal-line situations, the Refrigerator lumbered for two touchdowns and caught a pass for a third.

The other play-off teams in the NFC were the Western Division champion Los Angeles Rams (11–5); the defending Super Bowl champion San Francisco 49ers (10–6), who featured the first player, Roger Craig, ever to gain 1,000 yards rushing and 1,000 yards receiving in a single season; the Eastern Division champion Dallas Cowboys (10–6); and the New York Giants (10–6). The two "wild card" teams,

New York and San Francisco, matched up in the first play-off contest, with the Giants forging a 17–3 victory. The following week, however, the Giants met their match at windy Soldier Field in Chicago, where the Bears blew to an impressive 21–0 triumph. The same weekend, Los Angeles recorded an equally impressive win over Dallas, 20–0, with Ram running back Eric Dickerson rushing for a play-off record 248 yards.

The result was a Bears-Rams showdown for the NFC championship—which proved to be just another day at the office for the hard-driving Chicagoans. Their 24–0 trouncing of L.A. marked the first time that an NFL team had recorded back-to-back shutouts in play-off competition. Jim McMahon ran for one touchdown and passed for another, while the defense held the Rams to only 130 yards in total offense and took in a fumble for the Bears' final score. Fittingly, the new George S. Halas Trophy was awarded to the team after the game as symbolic of the National Conference title. Halas, who died in 1983 at age 88, had been a pioneering figure in pro football as the longtime owner and coach of the Bears. Coach Ditka's squad had dedicated their 1985–86 season to his memory.

In the American Conference (AFC), three of the five play-off teams hailed from the hotly contested Eastern Division: the perennial champions, the Miami Dolphins (12–4), highlighting the passing of Dan Marino; the New York Jets (11–5), led by the league's top-rated quarterback, Ken O'Brien; and the New England Patriots (11–5), featuring a strong defense. Also claiming post-season berths were the Central Division champion Cleveland Browns (8–8), who boasted two 1,000-yard rushers, rookie Kevin Mack (1,104) and Earnest Byner (1,002); and the always-tough Los Angeles Raiders (12–4), who relied heavily on Marcus Allen—he had led the NFL in rushing with 1,759 yards and matched Payton's feat by slashing for 100 or more yards in nine straight games.

The Patriots began their unlikely drive to the Super Bowl with a 26–14 victory over the favored Jets in the AFC "wild card" game. An upset of a larger magnitude was in store the following week, as New England took advantage of six turnovers by the Raiders and came from behind to win, 27–20. Also coming from behind that weekend were the Dolphins, who eked out a 24–21 victory over Cleveland with three touchdowns in the second half.

The AFC championship game thus pitted Miami against New England, with the Patriots again the underdog. The game was played at Miami's Orange Bowl, where the Pats had lost 18 straight games beginning in 1966. But the Dolphins proved uncharacteristically generous, turning the ball over six times, and New England rolled to a 31–14 triumph. Quarterback Tony Eason tossed three touchdown passes, and halfback Mosi Tatupu sealed the victory by scoring the Patriots' final touchdown on a one-yard run. New England had well earned its first AFC title and a trip to Super Bowl XX.

The two weakest teams in the league during the regular season were the Buffalo Bills and Tampa Bay Buccaneers, each finishing with a 2–14 record. Buffalo got a new coach at mid-season, as Hugh Bulough replaced Kay Stephenson. At New Orleans (5–11), Bum Phillips stepped down and his son, Wade, took over. Other coaches who were out by the end of the regular season were Hugh Campbell of Houston (5–11), Marion Campbell of Philadelphia (7–9), and Jim Hanifan of St. Louis (5–11).

While the NFL record book did not quite undergo the assault that it had the previous year (when Dan Marino, Eric Dickerson, Walter Payton, and others established major new single-season and career standards), the 1985–86 campaign did see its share of stellar individual performances. San Diego's Lionel "Little Train" James accounted for an NFL-record 2,535 all-purpose yards (rushing, receiving, and punt and kick returning), eclipsing the 1975 mark of 2,462 by St. Louis' Terry Metcalf. James also set a record for most receiving yards by a running back in one season, with 1,027. The Raiders' Marcus Allen accounted for a total of 2,314 combined yards from scrimmage (rushing and receiving), breaking Dick-

Quarterback Tony Eason signals touchdown as his Patriots defeat the Miami Dolphins for the AFC crown.

AP/Wide World

PROFESSIONAL FOOTBALL

United States Football League

Final Standings

Eastern Conference

	W	L	T	Pct.	Points For	Against
Birmingham	13	5	0	.722	436	299
New Jersey	11	7	0	.611	418	377
Memphis	11	7	0	.611	428	337
Baltimore	10	7	1	.583	368	260
Tampa Bay	10	8	0	.556	405	422
Jacksonville	9	9	0	.500	407	402
Orlando	5	13	0	.278	308	481

Western Conference

	W	L	T	Pct.	Points For	Against
Oakland	13	4	1	.750	473	359
Denver	11	7	0	.611	433	389
Houston	10	8	0	.556	544	388
Arizona	8	10	0	.444	276	405
Portland	6	12	0	.333	275	422
San Antonio	5	13	0	.278	296	436
Los Angeles	3	15	0	.167	266	456

PLAY-OFFS

Baltimore 20, New Jersey 17
Birmingham 22, Houston 20
Memphis 48, Denver 7
Oakland 30, Tampa Bay 27
Baltimore 28, Birmingham 14
Oakland 28, Memphis 19

CHAMPIONSHIP GAME: Baltimore 28, Oakland 24

National Football League

Final Standings

NATIONAL CONFERENCE

Eastern Division

	W	L	T	Pct.	Points For	Against
Dallas	10	6	0	.625	357	333
N.Y. Giants	10	6	0	.625	399	283
Washington	10	6	0	.625	297	312
Philadelphia	7	9	0	.438	286	310
St. Louis	5	11	0	.313	278	414

Central Division

	W	L	T	Pct.	Points For	Against
Chicago	15	1	0	.938	456	198
Green Bay	8	8	0	.500	337	355
Minnesota	7	9	0	.438	346	359
Detroit	7	9	0	.438	307	366
Tampa Bay	2	14	0	.125	294	448

Western Division

	W	L	T	Pct.	Points For	Against
L.A. Rams	11	5	0	.688	340	277
San Francisco	10	6	0	.625	411	263
New Orleans	5	11	0	.313	294	401
Atlanta	4	12	0	.250	282	452

PLAY-OFFS

N.Y. Giants 17, San Francisco 3
Chicago 21, N.Y. Giants 0
L.A. Rams 20, Dallas 0
Chicago 24, L.A. Rams 0

AMERICAN CONFERENCE

Eastern Division

	W	L	T	Pct.	Points For	Against
Miami	12	4	0	.750	428	320
N.Y. Jets	11	5	0	.688	393	264
New England	11	5	0	.688	362	290
Indianapolis	5	11	0	.313	320	386
Buffalo	2	14	0	.125	200	381

Central Division

	W	L	T	Pct.	Points For	Against
Cleveland	8	8	0	.500	287	294
Cincinnati	7	9	0	.438	441	437
Pittsburgh	7	9	0	.438	379	355
Houston	5	11	0	.313	284	412

Western Division

	W	L	T	Pct.	Points For	Against
L.A. Raiders	12	4	0	.750	354	308
Denver	11	5	0	.688	380	329
Seattle	8	8	0	.500	349	303
San Diego	8	8	0	.500	467	435
Kansas City	6	10	0	.375	317	360

PLAY-OFFS

New England 26, N.Y. Jets 14
New England 27, L.A. Raiders 20
Miami 24, Cleveland 21
New England 31, Miami 14

SUPER BOWL XX: Chicago 46, New England 10

erson's record of 2,244 the year before. In the last game of the regular season, wide receiver Stephone Paige of the Kansas City Chiefs caught eight passes against San Diego for a record 309 yards, breaking the previous best of 303 by Jim Benton of Cleveland in 1945. With nine pass interceptions, Dallas' Everson Walls topped the league for a record third time. Henry Ellard of the Rams set a new NFL record for punt return average in a single season with 13.5, while the Raiders' Fulton Walker established a new standard for total punt return yardage in a season with 692.

Among the season's other statistical leaders and outstanding performers were Giants running back Joe Morris, who scored 21 touchdowns (and rushed for a team record 1,336 yards); 49ers quarterback Joe Montana (*see* BIOGRAPHY), who was the NFC's top-rated passer; Colts punter Rohn Stark, who averaged 45.9 yards per kick; Bears kicker Kevin Butler, who led the league with 144 points; New England linebacker Andre Tippett, who topped the AFC with 16.5 sacks; and Cincinnati quarterback Boomer Esiason, everybody's choice for rookie of the year.

All in all, it was a successful, high-visibility year for the NFL, with television ratings back on the rise and the "Refrigerator phenomenon" expanding fan appeal. Appropriately enough, the Pro Football Hall of Fame in Canton, OH, on August 3 inducted its most glamorous class. The newest members were quarterbacks Joe Namath and Roger Staubach, running back O.J. Simpson, NFL Commissioner Pete Rozelle, and center Frank Gatski, who was named by a special committee considering old-time players.

The College Season

In another topsy-turvy race for the unofficial national championship of college football, it took until the major bowl games on New Year's Day (1986) for the matter to be settled. The Oklahoma Sooners (11–1), who had been the preseason choice in both wire-service polls as the best team in the country, took back the top ranking from Penn State with a 25–10 victory in the Orange Bowl. Coach Barry Switzer's Sooners, the champions of the Big Eight and boasting the nation's stingiest defense (190.6 yards per game), completely shut down the Nittany Lions in the second half. The Sooners scored their 25 points on a 71-yard touchdown pass from Jamelle Holieway to

Keith Jackson, a 61-yard touchdown run by Lydell Carr, and four field goals—an Orange Bowl record—by Tim Lashar.

Oklahoma's only loss had come at the hands of Miami (10–2) in the fourth game of the season, 27–14. Iowa (10–2), the Big Ten champion, stayed at the top of the polls for several weeks, until a 22–13 loss to Ohio State (9–3). Joe Paterno's Penn State team, meanwhile, was maintaining a perfect record, even if five of its victories had been by a margin of four points or less. By beating Penn State in the Orange Bowl, Oklahoma was the consensus choice as national champion. Its two main rivals to that claim, Miami and Iowa, both were upset on New Year's Day. The Hurricanes were whipped 35–7 by Tennessee (9–1–2) in the 52d Sugar Bowl, and the Hawkeyes were outscored, 45–28, by Pac Ten champion UCLA (9–2–1) in the 72d Rose Bowl. In the other major New Year's Day games, Texas A&M (10–2) defeated Auburn (8–4), 36–16, in the 50th Cotton Bowl, and Michigan (10–1–1) beat Nebraska (9–3) in the Fiesta Bowl, 27–23.

The bowl game results fixed identical top-four rankings in the final polls of both the AP and UPI: Oklahoma, Michigan, Penn State, and Tennessee. Other final top-ten teams included Florida, Texas A&M, UCLA, Air Force, Miami, Iowa, and Nebraska.

Perhaps the strongest conference in the nation was the Big Ten, with six of its teams earning bowl invitations. The conference ended up with a 3–3 record in postseason play: in addition to Iowa's loss in the Rose Bowl (the 11th defeat in 12 years for the Big Ten representative) and Michigan's victory in the Fiesta Bowl, Ohio State (9–3) beat defending national champion Brigham Young (11–3) in the Florida Citrus Bowl, 10–7; Minnesota (7–5) defeated Clemson (6–6) in the Independence Bowl, 20–13; Michigan State (7–5) lost to Georgia Tech (9–2–1) in the All-American Bowl, 17–14; and Illinois (6–5–1) was defeated by Army (9–3) in the Peach Bowl, 31–29.

The U.S. service academies had one of their best seasons ever. Employing a wishbone offense, the Air Force Falcons tied Brigham Young for the Western Athletic Conference championship and wrapped up a 12–1 season with a 24–16 victory over Texas in the Bluebonnet Bowl and a top-ten national ranking. Army's victory in the Peach Bowl gave it one of the best records among the major independent schools. And though Navy finished with a disappointing 3–8 mark, the Midshipmen scored an upset by defeating the Cadets, 17–7.

It was another frustrating year at Notre Dame (5–6), whose beleaguered coach, Gerry Faust, announced his resignation prior to the team's last game. Faust and the Irish suffered a final humiliation in that contest, falling to the unrelenting Miami Hurricanes, 58–7. Minnesota's Lou Holtz was named to replace Faust.

One of the year's biggest stories in college football had to do with another, more successful head coach. On October 5, Grambling's Eddie Robinson earned the 324th victory of his

Oklahoma's tight end Keith Jackson takes a 71-yard pass in for a score as the Sooners defeat Penn State in the 1986 Orange Bowl and take top ranking in both the AP and UPI polls.

Although a shoulder separation cut down his playing time, Auburn's running back Bo Jackson was named winner of the 51st Heisman Trophy in a close vote.

© Dan Helms, Duomo

career with a 27–7 win over Prairie View A&M. At age 66, Robinson became the winningest coach in college football history, surpassing the late Paul (Bear) Bryant.

The balloting was never closer in the 51-year history of the Heisman Trophy, as Auburn's Bo Jackson outpolled Iowa's Chuck Long by 45 votes. During the regular season, Jackson rushed 278 times for 1,786 yards and 17 touchdowns; he capped his collegiate career with a 133-yard effort in the Tigers' Cotton Bowl loss. Long, in addition to having the best name ever for a quarterback, completed 66% of his passes for 2,978 yards and 26 touchdowns. The Outland Trophy and Lombardi Award for the nation's top lineman went to Boston College nose guard Mike Ruth and Oklahoma nose guard Tony Casillas, respectively.

There were a host of other outstanding performers: Brigham Young quarterback Robbie Bosco passed for 4,273 yards and 30 touchdowns. Michigan State's Lorenzo White led the country in rushing with 1,908 yards (173.5 per game). Navy's Napoleon McCallum topped the list in all-purpose yardage with 2,330, including 219 yards rushing against Army. UCLA's John Lee, the most accurate field-goal kicker in National Collegiate Athletic Association (NCAA) history, nailed 23 straight in an 11-game stretch. And running back Joe Dudek of tiny Plymouth (NH) State ended his four-year career with an all-time collegiate record of 79 touchdowns (shattering Walter Payton's mark of 66 for Jackson State) and a Division III record of 5,570 yards.

Scandals surfaced during the year at two Southwest Conference schools, Southern Methodist University (SMU) and Texas Christian University (TCU). SMU was placed on probation by the NCAA for illegal recruiting practices. And at TCU, Coach Jim Wacker suspended six players, including a star running back, when he learned that they had accepted cash payments from school boosters. Early in the year, the University of Georgia was placed on one-year probation because of recruiting violations.

Jeffrey H. Hacker

COLLEGE FOOTBALL

Conference Champions	Atlantic Coast—Maryland Big Eight—Oklahoma Big Ten—Iowa Pacific Coast—Fresno State Pacific Ten—UCLA Southeastern—Tennessee Southwest—Texas A&M Western Athletic—Brigham Young, Air Force (tie)
NCAA Champions	Division I-AA—Georgia Southern Division II—North Dakota State Division III—Augustana
NAIA Champions	Division I—Wisconsin-Lacrosse Division II—Central State (AR), Hillsdale (MI) (tie)
Individual Honors	Heisman Trophy—Bo Jackson, Auburn Lombardi Award—Tony Casillas, Oklahoma Outland Trophy—Mike Ruth, Boston College

Major Bowl Games

All-American Bowl (Birmingham, AL, Dec. 31)—Georgia Tech 17, Michigan State 14
Aloha Bowl (Honolulu, Dec. 28)—Alabama 24, USC 3
Bluebonnet Bowl (Houston, TX, Dec. 31)—Air Force 24, Texas 16
California Bowl (Fresno, CA, Dec. 14)—Fresno State 51, Bowling Green 7
Cherry Bowl (Pontiac, MI, Dec. 21)—Maryland 35, Syracuse 18
Cotton Bowl (Dallas, TX, Jan. 1)—Texas A&M 36, Auburn 16
Fiesta Bowl (Tempe, AZ, Jan. 1)—Michigan 27, Nebraska 23
Florida Citrus Bowl (Orlando, FL, Dec. 28)—Ohio State 10, Brigham Young 7
Freedom Bowl (Anaheim, CA, Dec. 30)—Washington 20, Colorado 17
Gator Bowl (Jacksonville, FL, Dec. 30)—Florida State 34, Oklahoma State 23
Holiday Bowl (San Diego, Dec. 22)—Arkansas 18, Arizona State 17
Independence Bowl (Shreveport, LA, Dec. 21)—Minnesota 20, Clemson 13
Liberty Bowl (Memphis, TN, Dec. 27)—Baylor 21, Louisiana State 7
Orange Bowl (Miami, Jan. 1)—Oklahoma 25, Penn State 10
Peach Bowl (Atlanta, Dec. 31)—Army 31, Illinois 29
Rose Bowl (Pasadena, CA, Jan. 1)—UCLA 45, Iowa 28
Sugar Bowl (New Orleans, Jan. 1)—Tennessee 35, Miami 7
Sun Bowl (El Paso, TX, Dec. 28)—Georgia 13, Arizona 13

Golf

Success on the men's Professional Golfers' Association (PGA) Tour was fragmented in 1985, with Lanny Wadkins winning Player of the Year honors, Curtis Strange winning the money title, and four others winning the major championships. So the biggest news in U.S. golf during 1985 was created by women's star Nancy Lopez and senior Peter Thomson.

Returning to full-time play on the Ladies Professional Golf Association (LPGA) Tour three years after giving birth to a daughter, Lopez won five tournaments, including her second LPGA championship. She finished in the top ten a remarkable 21 times in 25 events entered. She earned a record $416,473, collected the Vare Trophy with a record-low scoring average of 70.73, won the Rolex Player of the Year award (for the third time), and took the Mazda-LPGA Series trophy.

Thomson, the Australian veteran who has won five British Open championships but had never made a mark in the United States, corrected that during 1985 with an astounding nine victories on the PGA Senior Tour, earning a record $386,724 in official money plus $125,000 from the Senior Tour's Mazda Bonus Pool.

Pat Bradley won three events and finished second on the LPGA money list with $387,378. Alice Miller, who dominated the women's tour with four victories in the first part of the year, finished third with $334,526. Amy Alcott also won three tournaments. Penny Hammel, who won the Jamie Farr Toledo Classic and $71,192, was named the LPGA's Rookie of the Year. Kathy Baker survived a duel with Judy Clark over Baltusrol's Upper Course to win the U.S. Women's Open.

Back on the men's side, Wadkins got off to a fast start with two early victories and closed with a late triumph to win $446,893 and the PGA's Player of the Year award. But Strange, whose three victories included a $171,000 payday in the Panasonic Las Vegas Invitational, accumulated a record $542,321 in earnings. Strange, who also won the Canadian Open, nearly won the Masters but slipped on the final holes to let West Germany's Bernhard Langer claim the championship in a dramatic finish. Andy North came back from several injury-ridden seasons to win his second U.S. Open Championship at Oakland Hills in Detroit. Scotland's Sandy Lyle overcame challenges by Tom Kite, David Graham, and Langer at Royal St. George's to win the British Open. And former U.S. Open winner Hubert Green completed his comeback with a triumph in the PGA Championship at Cherry Hills in Denver. One of the highlights of the PGA Tour was the victory by amateur Scott Verplank in the Western Open. Verplank became the first amateur in 29 years to win a Tour event.

LARRY DENNIS, *"The Golf Club"*

GOLF

PGA 1985 Tournament Winners

Bob Hope Classic: Lanny Wadkins (333)
Phoenix Open: Calvin Peete (270)
Los Angeles Open: Lanny Wadkins (264)
Bing Crosby National Pro-Am: Mark O'Meara (283)
Hawaiian Open: Mark O'Meara (267)
Isuzu-Andy Williams San Diego Open: Woody Blackburn (269)
Doral-Eastern Open: Mark McCumber (284)
Honda Classic: Curtis Strange (275)
Hertz Bay Hill Classic: Fuzzy Zoeller (275)
USF&G Classic: Severiano Ballesteros (205)
Panasonic Las Vegas Invitational: Curtis Strange (338)
Tournament Players Championship: Calvin Peete (274)
Greater Greensboro Open: Joey Sindelar (285)
Masters: Bernhard Langer (282)
Sea Pines Heritage Classic: Bernhard Langer (273)
Houston Open: Ray Floyd (277)
MONY Tournament of Champions: Tom Kite (275)
Byron Nelson Golf Classic: Bob Eastwood (272)
Colonial National Invitation: Corey Pavin (266)
Memorial Tournament: Hale Irwin (281)
Kemper Open: Bill Glasson (278)
Manufacturers Hanover Westchester Classic: Roger Maltbie (275)
U.S. Open: Andy North (279)
Georgia-Pacific Atlanta Golf Classic: Wayne Levi (273)
St. Jude Memphis Classic: Hal Sutton (279)
Canadian Open: Curtis Strange (279)
Anheuser-Busch Golf Classic: Mark Wiebe (273)
Miller High Life Quad Cities Open: Dan Forsman (267)
Sammy Davis, Jr.–Greater Hartford Open: Phil Blackmar (271)
Western Open: Scott Verplank (279)
PGA Championship: Hubert Green (278)
Buick Open: Ken Green (268)
World Series of Golf: Roger Maltbie (268)
B.C. Open: Joey Sindelar (274)
Bank of Boston Classic: George Burns (267)
Greater Milwaukee Open: Jim Thorpe (274)
LaJet Classic: Hal Sutton (273)
Texas Open: John Mahaffey (268)
Southern Open: Tim Simpson (264)
Walt Disney World Golf Classic: Lanny Wadkins (267)
Pensacola Open: Danny Edwards (269)
Seiko-Tucson Match Play: Jim Thorpe

LPGA 1985 Tournament Winners

Mazda Classic: Hollis Stacy (280)
Elizabeth Arden Classic: JoAnne Carner (280)
Sarasota Classic: Patty Sheehan (278)
Circle K Tucson Open: Amy Alcott (279)
Samaritan Turquoise Classic: Betsy King (280)
Uniden LPGA Invitational: Bonnie Lauer (277)
Women's Kemper Open: Jane Blalock (287)
GNA Classic: Jan Stephenson (290)
Nabisco Dinah Shore: Alice Miller (275)
Kyocera Inamori Classic: Beth Daniel (286)
J&B Scotch Pro-Am: Patty Sheehan (275)
S&H Golf Classic: Alice Miller (272)
Moss Creek Women's Invitational: Amy Alcott (284)
United Virginia Bank Golf Classic: Kathy Whitworth (207)
Chrysler-Plymouth Classic: Nancy Lopez (210)
LPGA Corning Classic: Patti Rizzo (272)
LPGA Championship: Nancy Lopez (273)
McDonald's Championship: Alice Miller (272)
Rochester International: Pat Bradley (280)
Mayflower Classic: Alice Miller (280)
Lady Keystone Open: Juli Inkster (209)
Mazda Hall of Fame Championship: Nancy Lopez (281)
U.S. Women's Open: Kathy Baker (280)
Boston Five Classic: Judy Clark (280)
du Maurier Classic: Pat Bradley (278)
Jamie Farr Toledo Classic: Penny Hammel (278)
Henredon Classic: Nancy Lopez (268)
Nestlé World Championship of Women's Golf: Amy Alcott (274)
MasterCard International Pro-Am: Muffin Spencer-Devlin (209)
LPGA National Pro-Am: Pat Bradley (284)
Rail Charity Classic: Betsy King (205)
Portland Ping Championship: Nancy Lopez (215)
Safeco Classic: JoAnne Carner (279)
Konica San Jose Classic: Val Skinner (209)
Mazda Japan Classic: Jane Blalock (206)

Other Tournaments

British Open: Sandy Lyle (282)
U.S. Men's Amateur: Sam Randolph
U.S. Women's Amateur: Michiko Hattori
U.S. Men's Public Links: James Sorenson
U.S. Women's Public Links: Danielle Ammaccapane
U.S. Senior Men's Open: Miller Barber (285)
Mid-Amateur: Jay Sigel
U.S. Senior Men's Amateur: Lew Oehmig
U.S. Senior Women's Amateur: Marlene Streit
U.S. Junior Boys: Charles Rymer
U.S. Junior Girls: Dana Lofland
World Match Play: Severiano Ballesteros
NCAA Men: Houston
NCAA Women: Florida
Walker Cup: United States 13, Great Britain/Ireland 11
Ryder Cup: Great Britain-Europe 16½, United States 11½

A son of Nijinsky II and half-brother of 1977 Triple Crown winner Seattle Slew fetched a record bid of $13.1 million at the Keeneland July Selected Yearling Sale.

AP/Wide World

Horse Racing

D. Wayne Lukas, training a powerful stable led by such standouts as Lady's Secret, Tank's Prospect, Twilight Ridge, and Life's Magic, enjoyed a banner year in 1985. He won the Eclipse Award as the top U.S. trainer. His horses set a record for earnings in one season ($11.1 million). And he won two of the seven races on the Breeders' Cup $10 million card: Twilight Ridge won the Breeders' Cup Juvenile Fillies, and Life's Magic took the Breeders' Cup Distaff.

Spend a Buck, trained by Cam Gambolati, scored a 5¼-length victory in the Kentucky Derby, running the mile and a quarter in 2:00 ⅕, the third-fastest winning time in the race's 111-year history. Spend a Buck bypassed the other two legs of the Triple Crown, the Preakness and Belmont, and instead ran in the $1 million Jersey Derby. His victory in that race earned an additional $2 million bonus, offered to a horse that won the Cherry Hill Mile, Garden State Stakes, Kentucky Derby, and Jersey Derby. Spend a Buck was the year's leading money winner ($3,552,704).

Tank's Prospect rallied under Pat Day's handling to win the Preakness in track-record time of 1:53 ⅖ for the mile and three sixteenths. Creme Fraiche provided trainer Woody Stephens with an unprecedented fourth straight victory in the Belmont Stakes. Chief's Crown, the beaten favorite in all three Triple Crown races, nonetheless had an outstanding season, with six victories in 12 starts.

Other outstanding horses of 1985 were: Proud Truth, who won the $3 million Breeders' Cup Classic and a total of seven races in 11 starts; Vanlandingham, who won the Suburban Handicap, Jockey Club Gold Cup, and Washington DC Handicap; Mom's Command, who won New York's Triple Crown for fillies (Acorn, Mother Goose, and Coaching Club American Oaks); Lady's Secret, who triumphed in 10 of 17 starts, including eight in a row; and Precisionist, who won the Strub Series (Malibu Stakes, San Fernando Stakes, and Charles H. Strub Stakes) as well as the Breeders' Cup Sprint.

Harness Racing. Nihilator set records for earnings in a single season ($1,864,286) and career ($3,225,653) by a standardbred. The son of Niatross paced the fastest race-mile of all time (1:49 ⅗) and won 23 of 25 starts in 1985.

JIM BOLUS, *"The Louisville Times"*

HORSE RACING

Major U.S. Thoroughbred Races

Belmont Stakes: Creme Fraiche, $512,900 (value of race)
Breeders' Cup Classic: Proud Truth, $3,000,000
Breeders' Cup Distaff: Life's Magic, $1,000,000
Breeders' Cup Juvenile: Tasso, $1,000,000
Breeders' Cup Juvenile Fillies: Twilight Ridge, $1,000,000
Breeders' Cup Mile: Cozzene, $1,000,000
Breeders' Cup Sprint: Precisionist, $1,000,000
Breeders' Cup Turf: Pebbles, $1,926,000
Budweiser-Arlington Million: Teleprompter, $1,000,000
Californian: Greinton, $307,100
Charles H. Strub Stakes: Precisionist, $324,300
Coaching Club American Oaks: Mom's Command, $251,000
Flamingo: Chief's Crown, $265,000
Florida Derby: Proud Truth, $300,000
Hollywood Futurity: Snow Chief, $1,172,000
Hollywood Gold Cup Handicap: Greinton, $500,000
Hollywood Turf Cup: Zoffany, $500,000
Jersey Derby: Spend a Buck, $1,000,000
Jockey Club Gold Cup: Vanlandingham, $861,000
Kentucky Derby: Spend a Buck, $581,800
Man o' War: Win, $324,000
Marlboro Cup Invitational: Chief's Crown, $500,000
Mother Goose: Mom's Command, $198,000
Preakness: Tank's Prospect, $545,700
Santa Anita Derby: Skywalker, $354,500
Travers: Chief's Crown, $333,500
Turf Classic: Noble Fighter, $718,500
Washington D.C. International: Vanlandingham, $400,000
Woodward: Track Barron, $334,000
Yellow Ribbon: Estrapade, $400,000

Major U.S. Harness Races

Cane Pace: Chairman of the board, $600,000
Governor's Cup: Barberry Spur, $1,357,500
Hambletonian: Prakas, $1,272,000
Kentucky Futurity: Flak Bait, $185,000
Little Brown Jug: Nihilator, $350,730
Meadowlands Pace: Nihilator, $1,018,000
Messenger: Pershing Square, $483,560
Peter Haughton Memorial Trot: Express Ride, $1,000,000
Roosevelt International: Lutin D'Isigny, $250,000
Sweetheart Pace: Follow My Star, $1,000,000
Woodrow Wilson Pace: Grade One, $1,344,000
World Trotting Derby: Prakas, $553,750
Yonkers Trot: Master Willie, $440,840

Ice Hockey

The 1984–85 National Hockey League (NHL) season was the longest in history, winding up May 30, 1985. After winning just 3 of their final 12 regular-season games, the Edmonton Oilers turned it on in the play-offs, losing just 3 times in 18 games for their second consecutive Stanley Cup title. They won the title with a 4-games-to-1 victory over the league's youngest team, the Philadelphia Flyers—the club that had the most points (113) in regular-season play.

Regular Season. Oiler center Wayne Gretzky won the scoring crown for the fifth straight time with 208 points. It was the third time in his six-year NHL career that he had scaled the 200-point plateau. En route to his smashing seasonal total, Gretzky became the youngest player to reach 1,000 career points. He accomplished the feat in just 424 games. Linemate Jari Kurri was runner-up for the Art Ross (scoring) Trophy with 135 points. The Finnish winger had 71 goals, 2 less than Gretzky, but nevertheless became the first European to score more than 60 goals in a single season. He also was only the third player to score 70 goals in one campaign. (Gretzky and retired Boston center Phil Esposito were the other two.) Defenseman Paul Coffey was fifth in league scoring with 121 points, as the Oilers took 3 of the first 5 scoring places.

In all, there were 16 players with 100 points or more, including Pittsburgh's Mario Lemieux (100), the most highly touted youngster since Gretzky. Nine players had 50 goals or more. One of those was Washington's Bobby Carpenter (53), who became the highest-scoring American-born player in history. New York Islander winger Mike Bossy had 58 goals, a record eighth straight time that he had scored more than 50. In the voting for the Hart Trophy as the league's most valuable player (MVP), Gretzky won for the sixth consecutive time. Winnipeg captain Dale Hawerchuk was a distant second.

In a surprising move, the Patrick Division Flyers finished first overall, four points ahead of the Smythe Division Oilers (109). Montreal and St. Louis won the Adams and Norris divisions, respectively.

Play-offs. Gretzky also won the Conn Smythe Trophy as MVP of the play-offs, during which he had a staggering 47 points. He tied an NHL play-off record with 7 points (4 goals and 3 assists) in the Smythe Division series clincher over the Winnipeg Jets. Coffey set a record for defensemen with 12 goals and 37 points. Oiler goalie Grant Fuhr tied Islander goalie Billy Smith's record with 15 play-off wins.

The Oilers started their march to a second league title by sweeping their Smythe Division opponents. They beat Los Angeles in three

ICE HOCKEY

National Hockey League
(Final Standings, 1984–85)

Wales Conference

Patrick Division	W	L	T	Pts.	Goals For	Goals Against
*Philadelphia	53	20	7	113	348	240
*Washington	46	25	9	101	322	240
*N.Y. Islanders	40	34	6	86	345	312
*N.Y. Rangers	26	44	10	62	295	345
New Jersey	22	48	10	54	263	346
Pittsburgh	24	51	5	53	276	385
Adams Division						
*Montreal	41	27	12	94	309	262
*Quebec	41	30	9	91	323	275
*Buffalo	38	28	14	90	290	237
*Boston	36	34	10	82	303	287
Hartford	30	41	9	69	268	318

Campbell Conference

Norris Division	W	L	T	Pts.	Goals For	Goals Against
*St. Louis	37	31	12	86	299	288
*Chicago	38	35	7	83	309	299
*Detroit	27	41	12	66	313	357
*Minnesota	25	43	12	62	268	321
Toronto	20	52	8	48	253	358
Smythe Division						
*Edmonton	49	20	11	109	401	298
*Winnipeg	43	27	10	96	358	332
*Calgary	41	27	12	94	363	302
*Los Angeles	34	32	14	82	339	326
Vancouver	25	46	9	59	284	401

*Made play-offs

Stanley Cup Play-Offs
Wales Conference

First Round	Montreal	3 games	Boston	2
	N.Y. Islanders	3 games	Washington	2
	Philadelphia	3 games	N.Y. Rangers	0
	Quebec	3 games	Buffalo	2
Semifinals	Philadelphia	4 games	N.Y. Islanders	1
	Quebec	4 games	Montreal	3
Finals	Philadelphia	4 games	Quebec	2

Campbell Conference

First Round	Chicago	3 games	Detroit	0
	Edmonton	3 games	Los Angeles	0
	Minnesota	3 games	St. Louis	0
	Winnipeg	3 games	Calgary	1
Semifinals	Chicago	4 games	Minnesota	2
	Edmonton	4 games	Winnipeg	0
Finals	Edmonton	4 games	Chicago	2

Championship

Edmonton	4 games	Philadelphia	1

Individual Honors

Hart Trophy (most valuable player): Wayne Gretzky, Edmonton
Ross Trophy (leading scorer): Wayne Gretzky
Vezina Trophy (top goaltender): Pelle Lindbergh, Philadelphia
Norris Trophy (best defenseman): Paul Coffey, Edmonton
Selke Award (best defense forward): Craig Ramsay, Buffalo
Calder Trophy (rookie of the year): Mario Lemieux, Pittsburgh
Lady Byng Trophy (sportsmanship): Jari Kurri, Edmonton
Conn Smythe Trophy (most valuable in play-offs): Wayne Gretzky
Adam Trophy (coach of the year): Mike Keenan, Philadelphia

All-Star Game

Wales Conference 6, Campbell Conference 4

NCAA: RPI

games, winning two in overtime, and defeated Winnipeg in four games. The Flyers, who had not won a play-off game since 1982, took the Patrick Division with relative ease. They got past the New York Rangers in three games and ended the proud Islander dream in five games. The Adams playdowns produced an early loss for the highly rated Buffalo Sabres; they fell to

the Quebec Nordiques in five games. Montreal got past Boston in the same number, setting up another "battle of Quebec." In 1984 the Canadiens shocked the Nordiques, but Quebec gained a measure of revenge this time with a seven-game victory to reach the Wales Conference finals.

In the NHL's worst division, the Norris, the St. Louis Blues bowed to Minnesota in three straight. Chicago, dogged by injuries in 1984, blasted Detroit in similar fashion. In a high-scoring series, Chicago outlasted Minnesota in six games as Hawks captain Darryl Sutter scored two overtime winners along the way.

In the Wales Conference final, the Flyers got superb goaltending from Swedish netminder Pelle Lindbergh and got past Quebec in six games. The Oilers ripped Chicago with an NHL record 11 goals in the fourth game of the Campbell Conference final but needed six games to reach the championship for the third consecutive time. (They had lost to the Islanders in 1983.)

The Cup final was a match of contrasting styles—the offensive might of the Oilers against the stingy defense of the Flyers. In the opener, the Flyers stifled the Oilers, 4–1, limiting them to just 26 shots. Gretzky was held without a point or a shot by Flyers' center Ron Sutter, who scored a game-winner on a breakaway on Fuhr in the third period. The Oilers beat the Flyers at their own defensive game with a 3–1 victory in game two in Philadelphia.

The Flyers never saw their home fans again, as the Oilers swept the next three games in Edmonton. The Oilers led all the way to take game three, 4–3, as the Flyers scored two third-period goals to make it interesting. Game four belonged to Fuhr. He stopped a penalty shot by Sutter in the first period, deflating the Flyers who led 3–2 after one period. Gretzky had the game-winner and insurance maker as the Oilers rallied against Lindbergh, in what turned out to be his last game. He had been playing with a partially torn tendon in his knee since the Wales final, and it finally gave out on him. In the final game, the Oilers clobbered the Flyers, 8–3, as Jari Kurri tied the NHL record of 19 play-off goals, set by Philadelphia's Reggie Leach in 1976. Gretzky had four points and Coffey got two goals as the Oilers recorded the most goals in a Stanley Cup final.

Other. The Soviet Union's seven-year domination of the World Ice Hockey Championship ended as Czechoslovakia defeated Canada, 5–3, to take the crown. The Soviets, however, captured the bronze medal with a 10–3 victory over the United States.

Rensselaer Polytechnic Institute (RPI) defeated Providence College by a score of 2–1 to capture the NCAA's hockey crown in Detroit. Providence's goalie Chris Terreri was the game's MVP.

JIM MATHESON, *"Edmonton Journal"*

Skiing

European skiers again dominated the World Cup competition in 1985.

Marc Girardelli, a native of Austria who competes for Luxembourg, swept the slalom (125 points) and giant slalom (120) competitions en route to the men's overall championship (262 points). He capped his season at Heavenly Valley, CA, late in March with a victory in the slalom. It was his seventh triumph of the season in that event, tying the record set in 1977 by Sweden's Ingemar Stenmark. The 21-year-old Girardelli also won four giant slalom events on the 1984–85 World Cup circuit. He clinched the overall crown in mid-March, as Pirmin Zurbriggen, the defending champion, faltered in several races and fell far behind in points. Helmut Hoeflehner of Austria took the men's downhill title with 110 points. Americans failed to place among the top ten in any category.

Among the women, Michela Figini, 18, a gold medalist at the 1984 Olympics, led a Swiss parade of stars as she won the downhill and overall World Cup championships. She also tied with Maria Kiehl of West Germany in the giant slalom standings (118 points), but Kiehl won the title under a tie-breaking formula. Another Swiss, Erica Hess, the 1984 overall champion, took the slalom crown, beating out Tamara McKinney of Lexington, KY. American women were strongest in the giant slalom, with 17-year-old Diann Roffe of Williamson, NY, the youngest skier on the circuit, finishing ninth; Eva Twardokens of Squaw Valley, CA, finishing 10th; and McKinney taking 11th place. In the overall standings, the Swiss finished first, second, and third: Brigette Oertli was second (219 points) to Figini (259), with Maria Walliser third (197). McKinney, the 1983 overall champion, finished eighth overall.

In the World Alpine Championships at Bormio, Italy, in February, young Roffe scored one of the major upsets of the season by winning the gold medal in the giant slalom. A member of the U.S. "B" team, Roffe had won her first World Cup giant slalom race at Lake Placid, NY, only a week before. Figini captured the downhill title at Bormio, Perrine Pelen of France was first in the slalom, and Hess earned the overall crown. In men's competition, Markus Wasmaier of West Germany won the giant slalom, with Zurbriggen taking the downhill and combined titles. Jonas Nilsson of Sweden gained the slalom crown.

In the U.S. Alpine Championships, held at Copper Mountain, CO, Felix McGrath of Norwich, VT, and Ann Melander of the University of Wyoming won the slalom events; Tiger Shaw of Stowe, VT, and Twardokens were the giant slalom champions; and Brian Stemmle of Canada and Holly Beth Flanders of Arlington, MA, finished first in the downhill.

GEORGE DE GREGORIO

At Heysel Stadium in Brussels just prior to the European Cup final, rioting broke out between overzealous fans of Liverpool and Turin. Dozens were killed and hundreds injured.

Syndication International/Photo Trends

Soccer

It was a year of tragedy and disappointment for the sport of soccer.

The tragedy occurred in two separate international incidents, one of which will leave its mark on the game for years to come. On May 29 in Brussels, Belgium, prior to the European Cup final between Liverpool of England and Juventus of Turin, Italy, some 40 persons were killed and 260 injured in stadium rioting among supporters of the two teams. As a result of the incident, British soccer teams were temporarily banned from participating in world competition outside of England. Countries around the world began to focus on the problem of fan violence.

The other incident did not involve fan violence but had similar tragic overtones. A total of 54 persons were killed and more than 200 injured as fire swept through the wooden grandstands at Bradford, England, during a Third Division match on May 11. A cigarette was blamed for igniting the fire, which burned down the grandstands in four minutes.

The two incidents detracted from a World Cup qualifying year in which the 24 countries for the 1986 World Cup tournament in Mexico were determined. The United States will not be among the 24, having been eliminated in second-round qualifying at the CONCACAF (Confederation of North Central American and Caribbean Federations) regional level. The United States was ousted in a three-team round robin with Trinidad and Tobago and Costa Rica, losing 1–0 to Costa Rica at Torrance, CA, in the final game of the competition on May 31. The United States has not qualified for the World Cup since qualifying procedures were instituted in 1954. After the defeat, the United States Soccer Federation failed to renew the contracts of National Coach Alkis Panagoulias and Director of Coaching Karl-Heinz Heddergott.

Elsewhere in USSF-sponsored activities, the United States finished seventh in a 12-team field at the World University Games in Kobe, Japan, in September. The U.S. Women's National Team, playing abroad for the first time, came in last in a four-team tournament in Italy.

In the collegiate ranks, UCLA defeated American University, 1–0, in an eight-overtime game to win the NCAA championship.

On the professional scene, the North American Soccer League (NASL) suspended operations for 1985 after seeing its once 24-team league (1978–80) dwindle to two clubs. That left the United Soccer League as the only outdoor league in the United States, but it, too, folded prior to the opening of its regular season in May. By year's end, the only professional league still in existence was the Major Indoor Soccer League (MISL), which began its 1985–86 season with 12 teams and a new commissioner—newspaper publisher Francis Dale.

In the 1984–85 MISL season, the San Diego Sockers won their fourth straight indoor championship (two in the MISL and two in the NASL) by defeating the Baltimore Blast, four games to one, in the championship round. Forward Steve Zungul of the Sockers won the league scoring title with 136 points (68 goals, 68 assists) and was also named the league's most valuable player. San Diego's Kevin Crow was named defender of the year and the L.A. Lazers' Peter Wall was coach of the year.

As 1986 began, it appeared as though professional outdoor soccer was dead in the United States, at least for the time being. Still, there was increased popularity for the sport at the youth and senior amateur levels. An estimated 9 million Americans were actively involved in soccer.

JIM HENDERSON, *Soccer Writer*

Swimming

Matt Biondi, a 6'6" (1.98 m), 19-year-old freestyle sprinter from Moraga, CA, emerged as a prominent figure in swimming during 1985, setting (or helping set) world records four times during the year. A sophomore/junior at the University of California, Biondi also has been a member of the school's championship water polo team for two years.

On August 6, at the U.S. Long Course Championships in Mission Viejo, CA, Biondi twice lowered the world standard for the 100-m freestyle. His time of 49.24 seconds in the preliminaries trimmed .12 off the previous mark set by Rowdy Gaines in 1981. That night in the final, Biondi broke the 49-second barrier with a clocking of 48.95. The following day, he established a new U.S. record in the 200-m with a time of 1 minute, 47.89 seconds.

Biondi had first won notice in the 1984 Olympics as the fourth member of the U.S. 400-m freestyle relay team, which set a world record (3:19.03). A year later, on Aug. 17, 1985, at the Pan Pacific championships in Tokyo, Biondi was the anchorman in a new world record performance—3:17.08—with Scott McCadam, Mike Heath, and Paul Wallace. And the following day, in the same meet, Biondi anchored the U.S. 400-m medley relay team to a world record of 3:38.28, again eclipsing the mark established by the 1984 U.S. Olympic team. Biondi's teammates were Rick Carey, John Moffet, and Pablo Morales.

At the World University Games in Kobe, Japan, during the summer, Biondi and butterfly specialist Mary T. Meagher won four gold medals each, as U.S. swimmers took 15 of 30 events.

Michael Gross, the 6'7½" (2.02 m) Olympic champion from West Germany, also set several world records during an outstanding season. In late June at the West German National Swimming Championships in Remscheid, Gross swam the 400-m freestyle in 3:47.80, bettering by .52 seconds the 1983 mark of Vladimir Sal-

nikov of the USSR. In the same meet, Gross swam the 200-m butterfly in 1:57.01, erasing the previous standard of 1:57.04 established by Australia's Jon Sieben at the 1984 Olympics. And then in mid-August at the European Championships in Sofia, Bulgaria, he lowered the record still further, to 1:56.65. In addition, Gross still held the world records in the 200-m freestyle (47.44) and the 100-m butterfly (53.08), both set in the 1984 Olympics.

Another world record that did fall was in the 200-m backstroke. In a Soviet–East German meet in early March at Erfurt, East Germany, Igor Polyansky of the Soviet Union established a new mark of 1:58.14.

Among the women, only one world standard was toppled during the year. In the East German championships June 5 in Leipzig, Silke Hoerner clocked 2:28.33 in the 200-m breaststroke to break the six-year-old record of the USSR's Lina Kachushite.

GEORGE DE GREGORIO

TENNIS

Boris Becker, a callow and combative West German, was the year's stunner, not only the first of his country to capture Wimbledon but, at 17, the youngest male ever to rule that oldest and most prestigious of tennis tournaments. Until Becker beat Kevin Curren in the final— 6–3, 6–7, 7–6, 6–4—no unseeded player had ever won at Wimbledon. It was all an astounding jumbling of form, since the South African-born Curren had been the first player to conquer three-time champion John McEnroe (in the quarterfinals) and two-time champion Jimmy Connors (in the semifinals) in a major event.

Nearly as surprising was the inability of the Number One players of 1984—McEnroe and Martina Navratilova—to continue as dominant forces. For the first time since 1968, the dawn of the open-tennis era, six different players won the year's six most important singles ti-

American freestyle sprinter Matt Biondi twice set world records in the 100 m and set a U.S. standard in the 200 m. He also helped establish new world marks in the 400-m relay and the 400-m medley relay.

tles: Becker and Navratilova, Wimbledon; Ivan Lendl (*see* BIOGRAPHY) and Hana Mandlikova, U.S. Open; and Mats Wilander and Chris Evert Lloyd, French Open.

In scoring the first European double in the U.S. Open, the Czechoslovaks Lendl and Mandlikova both dethroned the reigning champions. Lendl unseated McEnroe—7–6, 6–3, 6–4—after Mandlikova ousted Navratilova—7–6, 1–6, 7–6. The latter match's five-point margin made it the closest major final in history. Moreover, in taking their first U.S. Open titles, Hana and Ivan brought about only the second double dethroning in 79 years (the first in 23 years). The gifted yet so frequently erratic Mandlikova at last put together her attacking game for six sets in back-to-back wins over Evert Lloyd and Navratilova, who had met in both the French and Wimbledon finals. Although Becker fell in the fourth round at Flushing Meadow, another German juvenile popped up impressively, 16-year-old Steffi Graf, the youngest foreign semifinalist in women's annals.

Despite falling short in London and New York, 30-year-old Evert Lloyd was still the epitome of high-quality durability, maintaining her remarkable record of winning at least one Grand Slam championship for a 12th consecutive year. It happened in Paris where Chris topped the incumbent, Navratilova—6–3, 6–7, 7–5—to register a record sixth French Open title. It was also Evert Lloyd's 137th career title, an all-time record that she stretched to 142 by season's end. Paris also witnessed the rise of that tourney's youngest semifinalist

TENNIS

Davis Cup: Sweden
Federation Cup: Czechoslovakia
Wightman Cup: United States

Major Tournaments

U.S. Open—men's singles: Ivan Lendl (Czechoslovakia); men's doubles: Ken Flach and Robert Seguso; women's singles: Hana Mandlikova (Czechoslovakia); women's doubles: Claudia Kohde-Kilsch (West Germany) and Helena Sukova (Czechoslovakia); mixed doubles: Heinz Gunthardt (Switzerland) and Martina Navratilova; men's 35 singles: Bob Lutz; women's 35 singles: not held; junior boys: Tim Trigueiro; junior girls: Laura Garrone (Italy).
U.S. Clay Courts—men's singles: Ivan Lendl; men's doubles: Ken Flach and Robert Seguso; women's singles: Andrea Temesvari; women's doubles: Manuela Maleeva (Bulgaria) and Katerina Maleeva (Bulgaria).
U.S. National Indoor—men's singles: Stefan Edberg (Sweden).
Grand Prix Masters—men's singles: John McEnroe; men's doubles: McEnroe and Peter Fleming.
Virginia Slims (New York)—women's singles: Martina Navratilova; women's doubles: Navratilova and Pam Shriver.
World Championship Tennis (Dallas)—Ivan Lendl.
Wimbledon—men's singles: Boris Becker (West Germany); men's doubles: Heinz Gunthardt (Switzerland) and Balazs Taroczy (Hungary); women's singles: Martina Navratilova; women's doubles: Kathy Jordan and Liz Sayers Smylie (Australia); mixed doubles: Martina Navratilova and Paul McNamee (Australia).
French Open—men's singles: Mats Wilander (Sweden); women's singles: Chris Evert Lloyd; men's doubles: Mark Edmondson (Australia) and Kim Warwick (Australia); women's doubles: Martina Navratilova and Pam Shriver; mixed doubles: Navratilova and Heinz Gunthardt (Switzerland).
Italian Open—men's singles: Yannick Noah (France); men's doubles: Mats Wilander (Sweden) and Anders Jarryd (Sweden).
Canadian Open—men's singles: John McEnroe; men's doubles: Ken Flach and Robert Seguso; women's singles: Chris Evert Lloyd; women's doubles: Martina Navratilova and Gigi Fernandez.
Australian Open—men's singles: Stefan Edberg; men's doubles: Paul Annacone and Christo Van Rensburg (South Africa); women's singles: Martina Navratilova; women's doubles: Navratilova and Pam Shriver.

N.B. All players are from the United States, unless otherwise noted.

Hana Mandlikova of Czechoslovakia beat Chris Evert Lloyd and Martina Navratilova en route to a U.S. Open title.

AP/Wide World

ever, a 15-year-old Argentine, Gabriela Sabatini.

A month later, however, Martina resumed a slight edge in her rivalry with Evert Lloyd (34–32 since 1973) by defeating Chris—4–6, 6–3, 6–2—for a sixth Wimbledon crown. Not since the Frenchwoman Suzanne Lenglen from 1919 to 1925 had anyone won so many Wimbledon titles without dropping a final.

If the tall, redheaded Becker was green at Wimbledon, the bearish Swede Mats Wilander wasn't much older in winning his second French championship—3–6, 6–4, 6–2, 6–2—over the defender, Lendl. His Parisian feats coupled with Australian titles in 1983 and 1984 sent Wilander one title ahead of the precocious pace of countryman Björn Borg: four Grand Slam titles at age 20.

Becker and Wilander led their countries to the Davis Cup final in Munich, where the Swedes, blessed by superior depth, retained the 85-year-old trophy despite the efforts of flaming Boris, a month past his 18th birthday.

The female counterpart, the 22-year-old Federation Cup, went to Czechoslovakia for a third consecutive year. At Nagoya, Japan, Mandlikova completed her country's 15th straight match win in a 2–1 final-round defeat of the United States.

The most majestic of all tennis winning streaks, 109 matches in a row (through 23 tournament victories), ended on Wimbledon's Centre Court when the doubles team of Navratilova and Pam Shriver fell in the final to the U.S.-Australian coalition of Kathy Jordan and Liz Sayers Smylie, 5–7, 6–3, 6–4.

Singular as a triple threat, Navratilova remained the game's biggest winner. She won 12 singles titles in 1985 for a career total of 111; she also added the French doubles (with Shriver) and the U.S. and French mixed (with Heinz Gunthardt), for a grand total of 37 Grand Slam titles—tied for third on the all-time list.

Failing to win a tourney for the first time since his rookie year of 1972, Connors sat on his men's career record of 105, while McEnroe—winning eight to reach 66—and Lendl—with ten raising him to 61—took aim.

BUD COLLINS, *"The Boston Globe"*

Track and Field

Steve Cram of Great Britain and Mary Decker Slaney of the United States broke world records in the mile, track and field's glamor event, as some 20 new world standards were entered in the record book during 1985.

Cram had an exceptional summer, breaking three world marks in 19 days. On July 27 at the Bislett Games in Oslo, Norway, the 24-year-old from Jarrow, England, shattered the four-year-old record for the mile with a time of 3:46.31; that was 1.02 seconds faster than the previous mark set by countryman Sebastian Coe. Billed as the "Dream Mile" because of the strong field, the Oslo race featured three other runners who finished under 3:50: José-Luis Gonzalez of Spain (3:47.79); Coe (3:49.22); and Steve Scott of the United States (3:49.93).

Cram had begun his assault on the record book 11 days earlier at Nice, France, where he registered a 3:29.67 world mark for the 1,500 m. That record lasted only a little more than a month, however, as Said Aouita of Morocco surpassed it with 3:29.45 in West Berlin on August 23.

Cram's third big effort came on August 4 in the 2,000 m at Budapest, Hungary, where he turned in a blistering 4:51.39 to better the nine-year-old mark of John Walker by .01.

Aouita, who also enjoyed a banner season, lowered the world mark in the 5,000 m on the same day that Cram set the mile record. Aouita's time of 13:00.40 broke Dave Moorcroft's three-year-old standard by .01.

Mary Decker Slaney (*see* BIOGRAPHY) became the record holder in the women's mile with a posting of 4:16.71 in Zurich, Switzerland, on August 21. That toppled the mark of 4:17.44 set by Romania's Maricica Puica in 1982.

Earlier, in July, Slaney defeated Zola Budd of Great Britain in the 3,000 m at the Crystal Palace in London; it was their first confrontation since the two runners collided in the 1984 Olympics. But Budd did go on to set a new world record in the 5,000 m on August 26 in London, with a time of 14:48.07.

At the World Cup meet in Canberra, Australia, on October 6, East Germany's Marita Koch broke the world mark in the 400 m; her time of 47.60 seconds snapped the record of 47.99 set by Jarmila Kratochvilova of Czechoslovakia in 1983. In the final outdoor appearance of her career, Kratochvilova finished fifth in Canberra. The World Cup also saw a new record in the women's 400-m relay, 41.37, set by East Germany. In the team competition, the United States beat the Soviet Union, 123–115, for the men's title, and East Germany ran away with the women's title.

On June 16, Willie Banks became the first American since Dan Ahearne in 1911 to set a world record in the triple jump, when he leaped 58'11½" (17.97 m) at the U.S. outdoor championships in Indianapolis. The high jump record was broken twice during a three-week period: Rudolf Povarnitsyn of the Soviet Union jumped 7'10½" (2.40 m) on August 11, but on September 5 countryman Igor Paklin did 7'10¾" (2.41 m) at the World University Games in Kobe, Japan. And in the pole vault, Sergei Bubka of the Soviet Union, who had set the world record several times in 1984, raised the standard to 19'8¼" (6.00 m) on July 13 in Paris.

Three other world records were broken by East German athletes at a meet in East Berlin on September 22: Ulf Timmerman tossed the shot put 74'1¾" (22.60 m); Sabine Busch recorded a time of 53.56 seconds in the women's 400-m hurdles; and Heike Drechsler set a new mark in the women's long jump with a leap of 24'5" (7.44 m). And one other women's event in which a record was set was the javelin, as East Germany's Petra Falka registered a throw of 247'4" (75.40 m) on June 4.

Although no official world records are kept for the marathon, best-ever times were recorded for both men and women in April. Carlos Lopes of Portugal, the 1984 men's Olympic champion, recorded a time of 2 hours, 7 minutes, 11 seconds in Rotterdam, the Netherlands, on April 20. The following day in London, Ingrid Kristiansen of Norway posted a time of 2:21.06. The 1985 Boston Marathon was won by Geoff Smith of Great Britain and Lisa Larsen Weidenbach of the United States. Ahmed Saleh of Djibouti and Katrin Dorre of East Germany won the World Cup event at Hiroshima. Steve Jones of Wales and Joan Benoit Samuelson won in Chicago. And Orlando Pizzolato of Italy and Grete Waitz of Norway triumphed again in New York, he for the second time and she for the seventh time.

GEORGE DE GREGORIO

Pro Wrestling's New Hold

Boxing's Muhammad Ali (left) and pianist Liberace join Hulk Hogan, the champ of pro wrestling, in preparing for Wrestle-Mania. The pro wrestling extravaganza attracted a full house at New York's Madison Square Garden March 31.

AP/Wide World

On March 31, 1985, the World Wrestling Federation (W.W.F.) sponsored WrestleMania, an exhibition wrestling card at New York City's Madison Square Garden. Featuring such wrestling luminaries as champions Hulk Hogan and Wendi Richter, the lineup also included celebrities from television, motion pictures, music, and legitimate sports. Television's Mr. T appeared as Hogan's partner against Rowdy Roddy Piper and Paul (Mr. Wonderful) Orndorff; rock star Cyndi Lauper served as Richter's ringside manager; pianist Liberace was an official timer; boxing's Muhammad Ali lent his fame as a referee; and Billy Martin, the in and out manager of the New York Yankees, was a ring announcer. This carnival-like fusion of acrobatics and theater was seen by a live audience of some 18,000 persons, who paid up to $100 for ringside seats, and was televised across the country and to 26 other nations on closed circuit and cable.

Indeed the exhibition represented the high point in the development of pro wrestling. In fact, professional wrestling had become so popular by 1985 that some 10 million persons were attending W.W.F. matches annually. In addition, the weekly television audience for such displays was estimated at 25 million, and four of cable television's ten most popular programs were wrestling shows. Unlike previous years when the wrestling audience was for the most part an unsophisticated one, today's wrestling promotions are aimed at more cultivated spectators. It also is interesting that 40% of 1985's wrestling fans were women.

A cross between sport and entertainment, with almost all results predetermined, today's pro wrestling is related only very distantly to the freestyle and Greco-Roman wrestling of the Olympic Games. It does, however, dramatize the conflict between good and evil. The heroes and villains are stereotypical. The heroes manifest the virtue of endurance. The villains are drawn from the newspapers and American folklore. They can be evil foreigners (for example, the Iron Sheik or Nikolai Volkoff) or black-hat–wearing hired guns from Western sagas. The villains win most matches until their heroic opponents triumph in one with some finalizing stipulation. Lavish robes, overdressed managers, championship belts, treacherous attacks, and heroic rescues add to the drama.

Today three major promotions, including the W.W.F., compete for talent. Each group proclaims its own champion. Wrestlers work on short-term contracts in various regions to help maintain fan interest. Today's top wrestlers earn yearly salaries as high as $500,000.

The W.W.F.'s Vince McMahon has played a major role in wrestling's media renaissance. Working out of Greenwich, CT, McMahon has attracted major stars as well as a national audience for his farce-oriented exhibition. McMahon now has a stable of some 200 men and women wrestlers. According to the 39-year-old third-generation promoter, he is simply "filling a marketing niche for a wholesome show at a reasonable cost."

GERALD W. MORTON

SPORTS SUMMARIES[1]

ARCHERY—U.S. Champions: men: Richard McKinney, Glendale, AZ; women: Terri Pesho, Tempe, AZ.

BADMINTON—U.S. Champions: men's singles: Chris Jogis, Tempe, AZ; men's doubles: John Britton and Gary Higgins, Manhattan Beach, CA; women's singles: Judianne Kelly, Garden Grove, CA; women's doubles: Pam Brady, Grand Blanc, MI, and J. Kelly.

BIATHLON—U.S. Champions: men: Lyle Nelson, San Francisco; women: Julie Newman, Mercer Island, WA.

BILLIARDS—World Champions: men: Mike Sigel, Towson, MD; women: Belinda Bearden, Austin, TX; three-cushion: Raymond Ceulemans, Belgium.

BOBSLEDDING—U.S. Champions: 2-man: Brent Rushlaw, Saranac Lake, NY, and Ed Card, Claverack, NY; 4-man: Matt Roy, Saranac Lake, NY, Avni Tuemer, Walnut City, CA, Tom Hatton, Shaker Heights, OH, Dan Rock, Morrisonville, NY.

BOWLING—Professional Bowlers Association: national champion: Mike Aulby, Indianapolis; Tournament of Champions: Marshall Williams, Beaumont, TX; men's world cup: Alfonso Rodriguez, Mexico; women's world cup: Marjorie McEntree, Ireland. **American Bowling Congress:** singles: Glenn Harbison, Pittsburgh; doubles: Howard Higby and Clyde Gibson, Lake Jackson, TX; all-events: Barry Asher, Anaheim, CA; masters: Steve Wunderlich, St. Louis; team: Terry's Pro Shop, Solon, OH. **Women's International Bowling Congress:** singles: Polly Schwarzel, Cheswick, PA; doubles: Linda Graham, Des Moines, and Melody Philippson, Coalfax, IA; all-events: Aleta Sill, Cocoa, FL.

CANOEING—U.S. Champions (flatwater): kayak: men's 500 m, 1,000 m, 10,000 m: Greg Barton, Homer, MI; women's 500 m: Leslie Klein, Lexington, KY. Canoe: men's 500 m, 1,000 m: Bruce Merritt, Ridge, MD.

CRICKET—World Series: Pakistan.

CROSS COUNTRY—World Champions: men: Carlos Lopes, Portugal; women's: Zola Budd, Great Britain. **U.S. Athletics Congress:** men: Pat Porter, Alamosa, CO; women: Lynn Jennings, Durham, NH.

CURLING—World Champions: men: Al Hacker, Canada; women: Linda Moore, Canada.

CYCLING—Tour de France: Bernard Hinault, France. **World Professional:** road: Joop Zoetemelk, The Netherlands. **World Amateur:** road: Lech Piasecki, Poland; sprint: Lutz Hessich, East Germany.

DIVING—U.S. Indoor: men's 1m, 3m, 10m: Greg Louganis, Malibu, CA; women's 1m, 10m: Michelle Mitchell, Phoenix; 3m: Kelly McCormick, Columbus, OH. **U.S. Outdoor:** men's 1m, 3m, 10m: G. Louganis; women's 1m: Wendy Lucero, Orlando, FL; 3m: K. McCormick; 10m: M. Mitchell.

DOG SHOWS—Westminster: best-in-show: Ch. Braeburn's Close Encounter, Scottish Terrier owned by Sonnie Novick, Plantation Acres, FL.

FENCING—U.S. Fencing Association: men's foil: Michael Marx, Portland, OR; épée: Robert Marx, Portland, OR; saber: Peter Westbrook, New York; women's foil: Molly Sullivan, North Andover, MA; épée: Cathy McClellan, Marblehead, MA.

FIELD HOCKEY—NCAA (Division 1): University of Connecticut.

FIGURE SKATING—World Champions: men: Alexandr Fadeev, USSR; women: Katarina Witt, East Germany; pairs: Elena Valova and Oleg Vasiliev, USSR; dance: Natalia Bestemia and Andrei Bukin, USSR. **U.S. Champions:** men: Brian Boitano, Sunnyvale, CA; women: Tiffany Chin, Toluca Lake, CA; pairs: Jill Watson, Bloomington, IN, and Peter Oppegard, Hacienda Heights, CA; dance: Judy Blumberg, Tarvana, CA, and Michael Seibert, Washington, PA.

GYMNASTICS—NCAA (Division 1): men: Ohio State; women: Utah.

HANDBALL—U.S. Handball Association: men's one-wall: Ed Golden, New York; four-wall: Naty Alvarado, Hesperia, CA; women's one-wall: Anna Calderone, New York; four-wall: Glorian Motal, Martinez, CA.

HORSE SHOWS—U.S. Equestrian Team: dressage: Hilda Gurnry, Moorpark, CA, riding Keen; three-day event: Derik di-Grazia, Pebble Beach, CA, riding Sasquatch (spring); Karen Lende, Uppervile, VA, riding Castlewellan (fall); show jumping: Leslie Burr Lenehan, Westport, CT, riding McLain. **World Cup:** Conrad Homfeld, Southampton, NY, riding Abdullah.

JUDO—U.S. Champions, Senior Nationals: men's 132-lbs: Edward Liddie, Colorado Springs; 143: Douglas Tono, Chicago; 156: Nick Yonezuka, Cranford, NJ; 172: Brett Barron, San Bruno, CA; 189: Tommy Martin, Stockton, CA; under 209: Lee White, U.S. Army; over 209: Steve Cohen, Chicago; open: James Brewster, Thompson, CA; women's 106-lbs: Jo Quiring, Colorado Springs: 114: Janet Trussel, Colorado Springs; 123: Eve Aranoff, New York; 134: Lynn Roethke, New York; 145: Grace Jividen, Dayton, OH; 158: Diana Bridges, Colorado Springs; over 158, open: Margaret Castro, New York.

LACROSSE—NCAA (Division 1): men: Johns Hopkins; women: New Hampshire.

LUGE—U.S. Champions: men: Miroslav Zajonc, Annapolis, MD; women: Cammy Myler, Willsboro, NY.

MODERN PENTATHLON—World Champions: men: Attila Mizser, Hungary; women: Barbara Kotowska, Poland. **U.S. Champions:** men: Mike Burley, Berea, OH; women: Kim Dunlop, Tallahassee, FL.

PADDLEBALL—U.S. Champions—men's four-wall open: Steve Wilson, Flint, MI; women's four-wall open: Carla Teare, Clarkston. MI.

POLO—International Gold Cup: Fountains Boca Raton. **World Cup:** White Birch, CT.

RACQUETBALL—U.S. Champions: men's open: Ed Andrews, Huntington Beach, CA; women's open: Cindy Baxter, Lewiston, PA.

ROWING—World Open Champions: men's single sculls: Finland; double sculls: East Germany; quadruple sculls: Canada; women's single sculls: East Germany; doubles: East Germany; quadruple sculls: East Germany.

RUGBY—National Club: Milwaukee. **National Collegiate:** University of California, Berkeley.

SHOOTING—Olympic Style Champions: men's air rifle: Matts Suggs, Eugene, Or; small-bore rifle, three-positions: Lones Wigger, Ft. Benning, GA; skeet, trap: Dan Carlisle, Conroe, TX; free pistol: Don Hamilton, Kingston, MA; sport rifle: Ruby Fox, Parker, AZ; women's air rifle: Pat Spurgin, Billings, MT; small-bore rifle, three positions: Deena Wigger, Ft. Benning, GA; skeet: Ellen Dryke, Sequim, WA; trap: Frances Strodtman, Jackson, MT.

SOFTBALL—U.S. Champions: men's major fast pitch: Pay 'n Pack, Bellevue, WA; major slow pitch: Blantons, Fayetteville, NC; women's major fast pitch: Hi-Ho Brakettes, Stratford, CT; major slow pitch: Key Food Lady Mustangs, Pensacola, FL.

SPEED SKATING—U.S. Champions: men's outdoor: Andy Gabel, Northbrook, IL; women's outdoor: Betsy Davis, Lavallette, NJ.

SQUASH RACQUETS—World Pro: men: Janhangir Khan, Pakistan; women: Susan Devoy, New Zealand.

VOLLEYBALL—World Cup: United States; **NCAA (Division 1)** men: Pepperdine; women: Pacific University.

WEIGHT LIFTING—U.S. Weightlifting Federation: men's 52 kg: Stephen Bartlett, Albany, GA; 56: Brad Wickersham, Louisville, OH; 60: Brian Miyamoto, Honolulu; 67.5: Mike Jacques, Warner Robbins, GA; 75: John Orlando, San Francisco; 82.5: Arn Kritsky, Vienna, VA; 90: Curt White, Charleston, IL; 100: Ken Clark, Pacifica, CA; 110: Jeff Michels, Chicago; plus 110: Mario Martinez, San Franciso; women's 44 kg: DeAnna Hammock, Cumming, GA; 48: Rachel Silverman, San Francisco; 52: Michele Evris, Garfield, OH; 56: Colleene Colley, Tucker, GA; 60: Giselle Shepatin, San Francisco; 67.5: Glenda Ford, Livermore, CA; 75: Ann McKinnon, Knoxville, TN; 82.5: Carol Cady, Stanford, CA; plus 82.5: Karyn Tarter, Pelham, NY.

WRESTLING—NCAA (Division 1): team: Iowa.

YACHTING—U.S. Yacht Racing Union: championship of champions: Steve Rosenberg, Long Beach, CA; Mallory Cup: Scott Young, Austin, TX, YC; Adams Trophy: Cory Fischer, Severn Sailing Association, Annapolis.

[1] Sports not covered separately in pages, 466–90.

SRI LANKA

Trends of recent years that have transformed Sri Lanka from one of the most tranquil to one of the most troubled developing countries continued throughout 1985, with an unprecedented level of violence in the first half of the year. Prolonged talks between representatives of the Sinhalese-dominated government and major Tamil insurgent groups followed limited cease-fire agreements in June and in October. The deepening ethnic crisis undermined support for the government headed by President Junius R. Jayewardene. The turmoil hampered economic development, created new strains in relations with India, and raised doubts about the possibility of a solution within the framework of a united Sri Lanka.

Ethnic Violence. During the five months following the collapse of talks between representatives of the government and Tamil insurgent groups in December 1984, more than 700 people were killed, either by the Sri Lankan army or by Tamil guerrillas. Nearly one half of the army was stationed in Tamil-majority areas in the north and east. Moderate Tamils were overshadowed and terrorized by more militant Tamil groups, some of which demanded a separate Tamil nation (*Tamil Eelam*). The worst violence occurred in May, when Tamil guerrillas disguised as soldiers staged a violent assault in Anuradhapura, the first major attack in a Sinhalese-majority area, killing about 150 people. In retaliation, Tamils were killed in various parts of the country.

In the following month the situation seemed to improve. In mid-June the government announced an agreement with major Tamil guerrilla groups for a cease-fire for three months. This was followed by two prolonged rounds of talks, in July and August, between representatives of the government, led by Hector Jayewardene, brother of Sri Lanka's president, and four major Tamil insurgent groups, in Thimpu,

capital of Bhutan. After the talks were adjourned without agreement in August, Hector Jayewardene and other Sri Lankan official representatives spent ten days in New Delhi in conferences with Indian leaders. These talks led to a comprehensive proposal, based on further government concessions to Tamil demands and agreement by Tamil groups to end the violence and drop their most extreme demands. In mid-October a group representing four Tamil resistance factions asked for a new cease-fire as a first step toward their goal of more self-rule in Tamil-majority areas.

The Economy. The adverse effects of ethnic violence were reflected in the virtual suspension of the development program in Tamil-majority areas, a decline in the production of tea, a substantial increase in defense spending, and a sharp decline in the tourist industry. But in some respects the economic picture was quite favorable. Economic development programs continued outside of the troubled Tamil-majority areas. The Mahaveli River Valley Development Project, Sri Lanka's largest, neared completion. The rate of inflation, moreover, went down to zero (it had been as high as 35% in 1980), and the country maintained a surplus in balance of payments and a satisfactory position in its foreign-exchange reserves.

Foreign Policy. Cooperation and tensions with India dominated Sri Lanka's foreign relations. The tensions were caused mainly by long-standing Sri Lankan suspicions of India's policies and intentions, aggravated by alleged Indian sympathies with and support of Tamil insurgency movements in Sri Lanka. President Jayewardene and other government spokesmen publicly stated that without Indian assistance the Tamil insurgency would not have reached the dimensions of a threat to the stability and unity of the country.

Indian–Sri Lankan cooperation was manifested through continuing contacts and exchanges, and especially through joint efforts to prevent the ethnic tension in Sri Lanka from developing into a major threat to regional as well as internal stability and peace. President Jayewardene's official visit to New Delhi in early June led to a noticeable improvement in relations. On June 2, he and India's Prime Minister Rajiv Gandhi traveled to Bangladesh to demonstrate their sympathy with the government and people of that country for the human and physical devastation caused by a major cyclone-flood disaster. Lengthy talks between the two leaders led to a more active mediatory role for India in negotiations between the Sri Lankan government and Tamil insurgents. Other highlights in foreign policy were President Jayewardene's official visit to Pakistan (March–April), and the visit of British Prime Minister Margaret Thatcher to Sri Lanka in April.

NORMAN O. PALMER
University of Pennsylvania

SRI LANKA · Information Highlights

Official Name: Democratic Socialist Republic of Sri Lanka.

Location: South Asia.

Area: 25,332 sq mi (65 610 km²).

Population (mid-1985 est.): 16,400,000.

Chief Cities (1982 est.): Colombo, the capital, 602,000; Dehiwala–Mount Lavinia, 177,000; Jaffna, 121,000; Kandy, 107,000.

Government: *Head of state,* Junius R. Jayewardene, president (took office Feb. 1978). *Head of government,* Ranasinghe Premadasa, prime minister (took office Feb. 1978). *Legislature* (unicameral) —Parliament.

Monetary Unit: Rupee (27.250 rupees equal U.S.$1, July 1985).

Gross Domestic Product (1983 U.S.$): $4,900,-000,000.

Economic Index (Colombo, 1984): *Consumer Prices* (1970 = 100), all items, 400.2; food, 438.0.

Foreign Trade (1984 U.S.$): *Imports,* $1,846,000,000; *exports,* $1,449,000,000.

F. A. Bartholdi, Statue of Liberty Sculptor

The new F.A. Bartholdi commemorative incorporated computer techniques in stamp designing for the first time.

STAMPS AND STAMP COLLECTING

Shortly after it was authorized to hike domestic first-class postage rates to 22 cents, the U.S. Postal Service began issuing stamps bearing the letter "D" until denominated ones could be produced. The various other rate hikes gave Washington problems because of the numerous regular stamps that had to be made in addition to previously authorized special and commemorative issues. So many new regulars were needed that several planned stamps had to be postponed or scrapped. To buy just a single example of all 1985 issues, collectors had to spend $27.61.

The stamp world was shocked by the year's many criminal activities. In addition to an increasing number of burglaries, there were several crimes of a more serious nature. Early in the year, The Philatelic Foundation discovered that a computer clerk had altered about 250 certificates for stamps that the Foundation's Expert Committee found to be either counterfeited or faked. It alerted the Federal Bureau of Investigation and U.S. Attorney's Office, which found that the clerk had been bribed by a wealthy California dealer who had doctored inexpensive stamps to make them look like rarities worth at least $5,000 each. Further investigation revealed that several members of the American Stamp Dealers Association, including its president, had taken part in the fraud; they were arrested and brought before a grand jury.

In another case, U.S. Postal Inspectors arrested several persons who had removed the postmarks from some half a million used stamps and sold the stamps at a discount to buyers who put them on mail a second time.

In late 1985 the U.S. Customs Service settled an $850,000 case against a midwestern merchandising firm for avoiding import duties seven years earlier. At the time the firm imported a huge stock of stickers produced on thin gold foil for a privately owned island off the coast of Scotland. The customs declaration described the stickers as postage stamps, on which no duty is charged. In offering them to the gullible public, however, the firm called them "gold stamps," a description the government noticed. Checking the port of entry records, Customs officers spotted the deception and initiated the suit. The firm agreed to pay $45,150 immediately and an additional $120,000 via a note payable over three years.

On the international scene, classic rarities were bought by collectors for record prices, but the rest of the market remained generally soft. The gaudy Third World pictorials of the last few decades were especially weak sellers.

Major international competitions were held in Argentina, Israel, Italy, and Switzerland.

ERNEST A. KEHR
Stamp News Bureau

Selected U.S. Commemorative Stamps, 1985

Subject	Denomination	Date
Jerome Kern	22¢	Jan. 23
Abraham Baldwin	7¢	Jan. 25
Alden Partridge	11¢	Feb. 12
L. & E. Sperry	39¢	Feb. 13
Alfred Verville	33¢	Feb. 13
Pacific Airmail	44¢	Feb. 15
China Clipper	33¢	Feb. 15
ADM. Nimitz	50¢	Feb. 22
Mary Bethune	22¢	March 5
Grenville Clark	39¢	March 20
Sinclair Lewis	14¢	March 21
Duck Decoys	4x22¢ block	March 22
Special Olympics	22¢	March 25
Stanley Steamer	12¢	April 2
Seashells	5x22¢	April 4
Love	22¢	April 17
J. J. Audubon	22¢	April 23
Express Mail	$10.75	April 29
Rural Electrification	22¢	May 11
AMERIPEX 86	22¢	May 25
Abigail Adams	22¢	June 14
F. A. Bartholdi	22¢	July 18
Korean Veterans	22¢	July 26
Social Security	22¢	Aug. 14
Junipero Serra	44¢	Aug. 22
WWI Veterans	22¢	Aug. 26
End Hunger	22¢	Sept. 7
Horses	4x22¢	Sept. 25
Public Education	22¢	Oct. 1
Youth Year	4x22¢	Oct. 7
Christmas contemp.	22¢	Oct. 30
Madonna & Child	22¢	Oct. 30
Mark Twain	36¢	Nov. 30

STOCKS AND BONDS

The U.S. stock market climbed to record highs in 1985, extending a bull market unlike anything seen on Wall Street since the soaring 1960s. For the first time, the Dow Jones average of 30 industrials surpassed 1,300, 1,400, and 1,500 during the year. In fact the index reached an all-time high of 1,553.1 on December 16. By the close on December 31, it stood at 1,546.67, up 335.1 points, or 27.66%, from year-end 1984. Other, broader indicators, such as the New York Stock Exchange (NYSE) composite index and Standard & Poor's 500-stock index, also established new highs. (*See* page 546.)

As the rise in stock prices progressed, annual trading volume records were set both at the NYSE and in the National Association of Securities Dealers' automated over-the-counter market. Volume on the Big Board amounted to 27.51 billion shares, topping the previous high of 23.07 billion recorded in 1984.

The impressive showing on Wall Street came against a surprisingly subdued background in the U.S. economy. Growth in business activity and corporate profits proved to be disappointing. Government officials and legislators struggled to resolve the problem of the federal budget deficit. Proposals to overhaul the tax system moved in Congress.

But the stock market got a great deal of support from inflation, which set an annual pace of less than 5%, and interest rates, which fell substantially. Lower rates go hand-in-hand with a strong bond market. In November, the yield on long-term Treasury bonds dropped below 10% for the first time in five years. As recently as 1983, it had been above 13%.

Many Wall Streeters gave a large measure of credit for reduced inflation and declining interest rates to the Federal Reserve and its chairman, Paul Volcker, who opted to pursue a relatively expansive credit policy despite a spell of rapid growth in the nation's basic money supply. Lower interest rates gave Wall Streeters hope for a stronger economy in 1986.

Mutual Funds. The drop in interest rates also contributed to the biggest year ever for the mutual fund industry, which serves as a means of investing in diversified securities portfolios for millions of individuals and institutions. Through the first nine months of 1985, according to the Investment Company Institute, sales of mutual fund shares (excluding short-term funds) reached $77 billion. The previous high for a full year was $45.9 billion in 1984.

Savers who had grown accustomed to two-digit yields in bank money-market deposit accounts, Treasury bills, or money market funds watched returns on those vehicles slip to 9%, 8%, and then 7%. In their search for higher yields, many turned to mutual funds, investing in longer-term securities such as Treasury bonds, mortgage-backed securities, and even so-called "junk" bonds with comparatively speculative credit ratings.

Mutual fund managers, at the same time, were busy innovating. They offered more and more new choices—international funds, specialized bond funds, and "sector" funds—concentrating on stocks of a single industry or category of companies. All this provoked some controversy; many observers questioned whether buyers of the new funds were getting a clear and full understanding of the risks they might be taking. There was no disputing, however, that mutual funds as a group were enjoying an unprecedented popularity.

New Investment Strategies. For sophisticated investors, the year was marked by the expanding use of complex strategies involving stocks and options or futures contracts based on stock-market indexes. In these maneuvers, a trader might simultaneously sell a futures contract and buy a basket of stocks closely matching the makeup of the index represented by the futures contract. The intent was to profit from temporary disparities in the price of the futures contract and the present level of the market index itself. A problem with this arbitrage strategy arose, critics said, when options or futures contracts approached their expiration dates, and it was time for traders to "unwind" their positions. The resultant rush of trading, it was said, often caused volatile swings in stock prices—as on March 15, when the Dow Jones industrials fell 12.70 points, or on June 21, when the average jumped 24.75.

There was much debate, as well, about the continued torrid pace of corporate takeovers and buyouts. (*See* page 151.) Beyond the merger, it was a big year for deals known as leveraged buyouts (LBOs). In this type of transaction, the acquiring party gains control of its target with a small cash outlay and a large amount of borrowed money, typically obtained by pledging assets of the acquired company as collateral. LBOs were conducted or proposed for such prominent companies as Beatrice, R. H. Macy, and Storer Communications.

Many analysts voiced concern that LBOs and junk-bond financing were adding to an already worrisome mountain of debt. There was much talk about what future strains this debt might exert on the banking and financial system, especially if a recession were to develop.

International. Enthusiasm for international investing was heightened by strong markets in just about all major financial capitals. Stock indexes for eight countries showed all posting gains for the year through late November. The leader was West Germany, up 62.9%; followed by Hong Kong, up 45.9%; Switzerland, up 44.9%; Australia, up 38.1%; France, up 26.1%; Britain, up 19.9%; Canada, up 16.3%; and Japan, up 7.5%.

CHET CURRIER, *The Associated Press*

In Cairo, Egypt, expatriate Sudanese rallied in support of the regime that overthrew Jaafar al-Nemery, the president of Sudan for more than 15 years.

SUDAN

After more than 15 years of increasingly erratic and repressive rule, President Jaafar al-Nemery was ousted in a bloodless coup. The armed forces seized power on April 6, after anti-Nemery demonstrations broke out among students, workers, and professionals. Maj. Gen. Abdel Rahman Suwar el Dahab, minister of defense under Nemery, took over as head of state. The new regime's top priorities included reviving the economy, alleviating the famine, and ending warfare between the predominantly Christian south and Arab-Muslim north.

Politics. The ruling Transitional Military Council promised to promote political pluralism and to transfer power to civilians in April 1986. A temporary constitution was approved in October, providing for political parties and the election of a parliament that will develop a permanent constitution. A decision on whether to retain Islamic law had yet to be made.

Power struggles and policy disputes in the military council and the civilian cabinet and confusion as to the division of power between them immobilized the new government. Within months, the joy that had seized the country at Nemery's overthrow turned to frustration at the lack of progress toward easing Sudan's complex and deep-rooted problems.

John Garang, leader of the Sudanese People's Liberation Army (SPLA), the major guerrilla group, repeatedly rejected Suwar el Dahab's peace overtures. Demanding an immediate transfer of power to civilians, he stepped up guerrilla activity soon after the coup. His well-trained forces defeated a government offensive in July.

Lacking the resources for a heavier military commitment, the new government turned to the SPLA's main rival, Anya Nya II, named after a force that fought in the civil war before Nemery negotiated peace in 1972. The military council began supplying Anya Nya II, which in turn agreed to stop attacking government outposts.

In late September a small number of government troops mutinied in Khartoum, apparently in response to government plans to send them into the war zone. The government arrested 160 persons, many of them low-ranking soldiers from the west and south.

Foreign Relations. The military regime reestablished relations with Libya after an 11-year hiatus and received promises of aid as well as a Libyan commitment to stop assisting the SPLA. In addition, Sudanese workers were spared when Libya expelled thousands of North African guest laborers. The U.S. government received assurances of Sudan's continuing friendship, in spite of the restoration of links with Libya. In November, however, the United States warned Americans not to travel to Khartoum, charging that Libyan and other terrorists had established bases there. Ethiopia continued to be the SPLA's chief source of support, despite Suwar el Dahab's efforts to negotiate with Ethiopian leader Lt. Col. Mengistu Haile Mariam.

Relations between Sudan and Egypt were strained after the coup, particularly when Egypt refused to yield to demands for Nemery's extradition. Under Egyptian law and tradition, political fugitives are protected. The Sudanese government tried the former leader

---

SUDAN • Information Highlights

Official Name: Democratic Republic of the Sudan.
Location: Northeast Africa.
Area: 967,495 sq mi (2 505 813 km²).
Population (mid-1985 est.): 21,800,000.
Chief Cities (1983 census): Khartoum, the capital, 476,218; Omdurman, 526,287; Khartoum North 341,146.
Government: *Head of state,* Abdel Rahman Suwar el Dahab, chairman, Transitional Military Council (took over April 6, 1985). *Head of government,* El Gizouli Datalla, prime minister (sworn in April 25, 1985). *Legislature* (unicameral)—National People's Assembly.
Monetary Unit: Pound (2.5 pounds equal U.S.$1, Aug. 1985).
Foreign Trade (fiscal year 1984 U.S.$): *Imports,* $1,800,000,000; *exports,* $790,000,000.

in absentia. Tensions eased, however, when Dahab met President Mubarak in October.

The Economy. Sudan was verging on economic collapse when Suwar el Dahab took over, but little progress was made toward recovery in 1985. Interest due on the $10 billion external debt to Arab and Western creditors exceeded the country's annual export earnings, and payments were not being made.

Chevron's oil explorations and pipeline construction in the south, interrupted with the resurgence of civil war in 1983, did not resume, nor did work on the Jonglei Canal, a major joint irrigation project with Egypt.

The war exacerbated the drought-caused famine in the south, displacing entire communities and preventing the cultivation of crops in some areas. Hundreds of thousands of famine victims crowded into towns and relief camps. Countless numbers died as relief supplies backed up in Port Sudan.

In July and August, rainfall was heavier than it had been in several years, ensuring that the harvest of sorghum, the staple food, would be adequate in regions where people were able to plant. The rains, however, also washed out roads, bridges, and railroad tracks vital to the transport of supplies to remote areas. An estimated 1 million refugee immigrants fleeing famine and warfare in Chad, Ethiopia, Uganda, and Zaire further strained Sudan's resources.

PAULA M. HIRSCHOFF, *"Africa Report"*

SWEDEN

The Swedish Parliament celebrated its 550th anniversary on May 24, 1985, in the city of Arboga. King Carl XVI Gustaf and Queen Silvia, together with members of the government and the Riksdag (parliament), attended the commemoration. It was in Arboga that the early forerunner of the Riksdag met in 1435.

Elections. Swedish voters went to the polls on September 15 to select 349 members of the one-chamber Riksdag for a three-year term.

SWEDEN • Information Highlights

Official Name: Kingdom of Sweden.
Location: Northern Europe.
Area: 173,731 sq mi (449 964 km²).
Population (mid-1985 est.): 8,300,000.
Chief Cities (Dec. 31, 1983): Stockholm, the capital, 650,952; Göteborg, 424,186; Malmö, 229,380; Uppsala, 150,579.
Government: *Head of state,* Carl XVI Gustaf, king (acceded Sept. 1973). *Head of government,* Olof Palme, prime minister (took office Oct. 7, 1982). *Legislature* (unicameral)—Riksdag.
Monetary Unit: Krona (7.87 Kronor equal U.S.$1, Nov. 8, 1985).
Economic Indexes (1984): *Consumer Prices* (1970 = 100), all items, 345.8; food, 400.7. *Industrial Production* (1980 = 100), 110.
Foreign Trade (1984 U.S.$): *Imports,* $26,401,-000,000; *exports,* $29,382,000,000.

The election resulted in a seven-seat loss for the ruling Social Democrats as well as losses for the Conservatives, the Center Party, and the Communists. The Liberals were the big winners with an additional 30 seats in Parliament, rising from 21 to 51. The Social Democrats, with 159 seats, lost their majority but remained in power with the support of minor parties. Olof Palme remained prime minister.

Economic Affairs. February 8 marked the conclusion of the first major agreement in 1985 between industry and labor. Covering 600,000 blue-collar workers in private industry, the agreement recommended that wage increases be restricted to 5%.

On March 18 a wage agreement for 200,000 workers in the metal and engineering industries specified no pay increases except for adjustments, retroactive to February 1, calling for a five-cent increase per hour subject to local negotiations.

A strike of 20,000 white-collar government workers erupted on May 2, affecting major sectors of the country's economic life. Involved were civil air-traffic controllers, customs clearance staff, postal supervisors, and meat inspectors. The National Collective Bargaining Office, supervising the wage negotiations, retaliated with a lockout of 80,000 additional government employees, mainly teachers, beginning on May 11. A final settlement was reached on May 20, preceded by secret talks between Prime Minister Palme and union leaders. A small retroactive adjustment in wages was part of the settlement.

International Affairs. The fifth session of the Conference on Confidence- and Security-Building Measures and Disarmament in Europe took place in Stockholm January 29–March 23. The 35 participating nations included all the European states (except Albania), the United States, and Canada. Three additional sessions were held during the year, the results indicating that further ground had to be broken.

Neutral and nonaligned states were represented at a meeting in Stockholm, April 29–30, at the invitation of Foreign Minister Lennart Bodström. The ministers discussed the work of the Stockholm Conference and matters connected with the Conference on Security and Cooperation in Europe. The European nonaligned states comprise Sweden, Cyprus, Finland, Yugoslavia, Liechtenstein, Malta, San Marino, Switzerland, and Austria.

Since 1960, Sweden has given more than 100 billion kronor in aid to developing countries, reaching the target of 1% of gross national product (GNP). Eight billion kronor (about $1 billion) was allocated for 1985–86. Begun during the year was a process of extensive restructuring of Sweden's development assistance.

ERIK J. FRIIS
"The Scandinavian-American Bulletin"

SWITZERLAND

Antipollution measures and a major step forward in the civil emancipation of women highlighted developments in Switzerland during 1985.

Environmental Controls. On Jan. 1, 1985, a new federal law established mandatory national principles for environmental control. Initially, regulations were imposed only on heating system emissions, but on September 16 the government announced that beginning in 1987, new cars registered in Switzerland would have to meet emission control standards similar to those in effect in the United States since 1983. Reflecting deep concern about the effect of air pollution on Switzerland's forests, Swiss standards will be far more severe than those anywhere else in Europe.

Women's Rights. On September 22, 54.7% of approximately 1 million voters approved a referendum proposal abolishing laws that had assured male supremacy within the institution of marriage. Struck down were regulations that allowed a husband to keep his wife from holding a job and gave him exclusive right to determine the couple's place of residence and to manage her inheritance and personal savings.

The new law mandates shared information within the marriage on income, property, and debts. It outlaws all references to a "head of household," or a single decision maker. However, the depth of opposition was readily apparent, for the measure was rejected in 12 of Switzerland's 36 cantons. Even in Bern, the capital, it passed by only 97 votes out of more than 250,000 cast.

Economic Developments. On January 1 the Swiss imposed a tax on all vehicles using Swiss highways, this despite strenuous opposition and protest from Swiss truck drivers who were fearful that other nations would impose similar taxes on them as a retaliatory gesture. These concerns proved to be well founded, for within two months France, Hungary, and West Germany had established tariffs on Swiss trucks traveling within their borders.

AP/Wide World

Some 2,000 soldiers and 1,300 police provided security during the Reagan-Gorbachev summit in Geneva, November 19–21. The city spent more than $1 million on the event.

On September 9 the Union Bank of Switzerland revealed that it would continue to grant credits to South Africa. In a related matter, it was announced on September 26 that Fritz Leutwiler, former chairman of the Swiss Central Bank and the Bank for International Settlements, had agreed to serve as an "honest broker" in renegotiating a major part of South Africa's $24 billion foreign debt obligations. This became necessary because many non-Swiss banks were reluctant to negotiate directly with the Pretoria government because of growing antiapartheid sentiment in their countries.

In comparison with 1984, exports for the first half of 1985 declined 7.1% to $12,386,000,000; however, imports were reduced 8.6% to $14,109,000,000.

PAUL C. HELMREICH, *Wheaton College, MA*

SWITZERLAND • Information Highlights

Official Name: Swiss Confederation.
Location: Central Europe.
Area: 15,918 sq mi (41 228 km²).
Population (mid-1985 est.): 6,500,000.
Chief Cities (Jan. 1983 est.): Bern, the capital, 143,847; Zurich, 363,648; Basel, 179,684.
Government: *Head of state,* Kurt Furgler, president, (took office Jan. 1985). *Legislature*—Council of States and National Council.
Monetary Unit: Franc (2.1215 francs equal U.S.$1, Nov. 25, 1985).
Gross National Product (1983 U.S.$): $100,200,000,000.
Economic Indexes (1984): *Consumer Prices* (1970 = 100), all items, 193.7; food, 203.6. *Industrial Production* (1980 = 100), 97.
Foreign Trade (1984 U.S.$): *Imports,* $29,474,000,000; *exports,* $25,864,000,000.

SYRIA

In his 15th year in power, Syria's President Hafez al-Assad in 1985 emerged in a stronger position than at any time in the 1980s.

Domestic Affairs. The problem of succession, which had come up during Assad's illness in late 1983 and early 1984, was shelved, as the

497

president regained his health. The heir apparent, his brother Rifaat al-Assad, was reprimanded for the forceful manner in which he pursued his own ambitions. Although Rifaat was deprived of his "defense companies," he was nevertheless appointed vice-president for security affairs. Perhaps the clearest indication of President Assad's recovery and his complete control of the country was his reelection, with 99.9% of the votes, in a February plebiscite. On March 13 he was sworn in for a third seven-year term.

After a lapse of five years, the ruling Baath Party held a congress, its eighth, in Damascus in January. The 800 delegates to the congress elected a new 90-member central committee, which in turn elected a 20-member regional command. The congress devoted half its sessions to discussion of economic matters, reflecting ongoing problems. Especially troublesome were the inefficiency of the public sector and rampant corruption.

On April 8, President Assad accepted the resignation of the government of Prime Minister Abdel Raouf al-Kassem and announced the formation of a new one. Kassem remained prime minister, but several other ministries changed hands.

Foreign Affairs. Syria capitalized on the Israeli withdrawal from Lebanon during the first half of the year, launching a major "offensive" to recover territory it had lost from 1978 to 1982. This offensive was a gradual and protracted one, involving both military means (conventional and terrorist) as well as political means. The Syrian objective was twofold: to expand military presence on Lebanese territory, and to render the local and national leaders of Lebanon's major religious sects dependent on the Assad regime, so as to better control the country internally.

In September, for instance, when the Sunni militants of Tripoli refused to accept the deployment of Syrian troops in their city, President Assad unleashed the militias of the Lebanese Communist Party, the Syrian Social Nationalist Party, and the Alawi Arab Democratic Party. After a considerable part of Tripoli was destroyed, the Sunni militants handed over their arms to the Syrian army, which reentered the city in October. Similarly, in the wake of a car bomb incident in Zahle, Syrian troops were invited to redeploy in that city in September.

The Sunni leaders of West Beirut and Sidon, who had links to the Palestine Liberation Organization (PLO) or wanted to remain independent, also were forced to toe the line behind Syria. In West Beirut, the Shiite Amal and Druze militias undermined the Sunni's power and crushed their militias, leaving them with no other option than to seek Assad's help. And in Sidon, a car bomb incident in January that almost killed the local Sunni leader forced the Sunnis to support the Syrian "option" in Lebanon.

Even the Christian Lebanese Forces, whose uprising in March had been defiantly anti-Syrian, drastically changed its course. In May it elected Elie Hobeika, who fully backed the Syrian role in Lebanon, as its leader.

All in all, Syria in 1985 continued to loom large in regional politics, playing an indispensable role as mediator in incidents involving the superpowers. President Assad often demonstrated his ability to manipulate conflicts and use them in his favor. For example, by virtue of its alliance with Iran, the Assad regime convinced the Iranian government to put an end to the hijacking of a Kuwaiti airliner to Tehran in December 1984; Syria's mediation was praised by King Fahd of Saudi Arabia and other leaders. Syria also assisted in arranging a visit to Iran by the Saudi foreign minister in May, which was followed by the release of the Saudi consul in Beirut, who had been held by pro-Iranian Shiite militants for more than a year.

And Assad timed his actions to suit his own purposes. In February, Syria turned over the U.S. journalist Jeremy Levin, who had "escaped" from Lebanon after a year of captivity, to the American ambassador in Damascus. That move coincided with Saudi King Fahd's visit to Washington and the first phase of the Israeli withdrawal from Lebanon. And perhaps Assad's greatest coup was arranging the release of the TWA hostages in June 1985, taking credit for it (bypassing the Lebanese authorities), and extracting from the U.S. State Department a statement expressing favor for Syria's domination of Lebanon.

Assad's struggle against Yasir Arafat's PLO continued unabated. In Damascus in March, six Palestinian groups opposed to Arafat formed the Palestinian National Salvation Front. Assad's opposition to the PLO-Jordanian accord of February did not change despite rapprochement with Jordan.

MARIUS DEEB, *Georgetown University*

SYRIA • Information Highlights

Official Name: Syrian Arab Republic.
Location: Southwest Asia.
Area: 71,498 sq mi (185 180 km²).
Population (mid-1985 est.): 10,600,000.
Chief Cities (Dec. 1982 est.): Damascus, the capital, 1,036,920; Aleppo, 905,944; Homs, 414,401.
Government: *Head of state,* Lt. Gen. Hafez al-Assad, president (took office officially March 1971). *Head of government,* Abdel Raouf al-Kassem, prime minister (took office Jan. 1980). *Legislature* (unicameral)—People's Council.
Monetary Unit: Pound (3.925 pounds equal U.S.$1, August 1985).
Gross Domestic Product (1983 U.S.$): $19,700,-000,000.
Economic Index (1984): *Consumer Prices* (1970 = 100), all items, 448.0; food, 471.0.
Foreign Trade: (1984 U.S.$): *Imports,* $4,116,-000,000; *exports,* $1,853,000,000.

In April a Taipei district court judge sentenced Chen Chi-li and his aide Wu Tun to life imprisonment for their roles in the October 1984 murder of Chinese-American author Henry Liu.

AP/Wide World

TAIWAN (Republic of China)

It was a troublesome year for the government of Taiwan. A series of embarrassing episodes eroded confidence in the government at home and abroad, and economic performance did not match the encouraging levels of 1984.

Politics. Taiwan's reaction to the signing of the agreement between Great Britain and the People's Republic of China (PRC) on the future status of Hong Kong in December 1984 was strongly negative. The government-controlled press denounced Great Britain for having negotiated the agreement with an illegitimate Chinese government and for having "betrayed the 5.5 million Hong Kong people." The government announced that it "will do everything it can" to help Hong Kong residents resettle in Taiwan and that it will sever all ties between Taiwan and Hong Kong in 1997, when Great Britain will relinquish Hong Kong.

In late February a financial scandal erupted that undermined confidence in the government and resulted in changes in the composition of the cabinet under Premier Yu Kuo-hwa. Tsai Chen-chou and five other officers of the Tenth Credit Corporation were arrested, charged with fraud, forgery, and the writing of bad checks. Tsai was one of the so-called "golden oxes"—wealthy and influential Kuomintang (ruling Nationalist Party) members serving in the Legislative Yuan. The ensuing investigation revealed that Tenth Credit had written illegal loans to individual employees of the Tsai family's Cathay business group, Taiwan's second-largest corporation with holdings of $2.5 billion in more than 100 subsidiary firms. State-controlled banks were directed to assume responsibility for the outstanding obligations of Tenth Credit Corporation.

The investigation also revealed that government officials had known of the illicit practices at Tenth Credit for as long as two years. As a result, just prior to the arrests, Tsiang Yen-shih, secretary-general of the Kuomintang, resigned and was replaced by Ma Soo-lay, 76, Taiwan's informal "ambassador" to Japan.

Prior to his resignation, Tsiang had been regarded as a possible successor to President Chiang Ching-kuo, who is 75 and in poor health. Shortly thereafter, Economics Minister Hsu Li-teh resigned and was replaced by Lee Ta-hai, chairman of the Chinese Petroleum Corporation. Finally, in August, Robert Chien replaced Loh Jen-kong as finance minister.

In April a second trial began that embarrassed the government and adversely affected its relations with the United States. Chen Chi-li, a leader in the criminal organization known as the Bamboo Union, stood trial together with Wu Tun and Tung Kuei-sen. The three were accused of the October 1984 murder of Henry Liu, the Chinese-American author of an unflattering biography of President Chiang Ching-kuo, outside his home in Daly City, CA. Although the U.S. government had requested the extradition of Chen and Wu (Tung was still at large), the government of Taiwan refused.

At the trial, Chen testified that he had been ordered to kill Liu by Vice Adm. Wong Hsi-ling, head of the Ministry of National Defense Intelligence Bureau. Chen and Wu were sentenced to life imprisonment. Wong, meanwhile, was dismissed and put on trial before a military tribunal. Wong admitted having told

---

TAIWAN (Republic of China) · Information Highlights

Official Name: Republic of China.
Location: Island off the southeastern coast of mainland China.
Area: 12,456 sq mi (32 260 km²).
Population (mid-1985 est.): 19,358,000.
Chief Cities (Dec. 31, 1983): Taipei, the capital, 2,388,374; Kaohsiung, 1,261,743; Taichung, 636,-406; Tainan, 622,073.
Government: *Head of state,* Chiang Ching-kuo, president (installed May 1978). *Head of government,* Yu Kuo-hwa, premier (took office, June 1984). *Legislature* (unicameral)—Legislative Yuan.
Monetary Unit: New Taiwan dollar (39.46 NT dollars equal U.S. $1, Dec. 31, 1984).
Gross National Product (1984 est. U.S. $): $56,600,-000,000.
Foreign Trade (1984 est. U.S.$): *Imports,* $21,600,-000,000; *exports,* $30,400,000,000.

Chen that Liu needed "teaching a lesson" but denied having ordered Liu killed. Nonetheless Wong was sentenced to life imprisonment.

Finally, an arrest in September caused some to question Taiwan's commitment to procedural justice. Lee Ya-ping, a permanent resident of the United States and editor of a Chinese-language newspaper in Los Angeles, was arrested by the Garrison Command while visiting Taiwan and accused of following a seditious editorial policy in her newspaper. The U.S. State Department formally protested Lee's arrest, referring to the illegitimate "intimidation and harassment" of U.S. residents by the Taiwan government.

In local and provincial elections on November 16, the Kuomintang retained its dominance, winning 146 of the 191 contested seats. But all 11 opposition candidates won in Taipei, suggesting that the scandals cost the government support in the capital.

Economy. Whereas the overall growth rate for 1984 reached 11%—the best performance since 1978—predictions for 1985 were adjusted downward midyear from 8.5% to 6.3%, and many observers felt that the growth rate would not reach even 5%. Figures for the first eight months of 1985 showed foreign trade down by 1.3% over the comparable period in 1984.

Despite the overall downturn, direct and indirect trade with the mainland increased substantially in 1985. Indirect trade through Hong Kong and Singapore, together with the illegal direct trade carried out by smugglers, was projected to exceed $1 billion for the year. Taiwan firms also made investments in mainland enterprises through Hong Kong third parties, including two factories in Fujian Province.

See also CHINA, PEOPLE'S REPUBLIC OF.
JOHN BRYAN STARR, *Yale—China Association*

TANZANIA

The retirement of President Julius K. Nyerere and continued economic problems were the main developments in Tanzania in 1985.

Nyerere Retires. President Nyerere, who had led Tanganyika from 1961 to 1964 and Tanzania (the union of Tanganyika and Zanzibar) since 1964, retired on Nov. 5, 1985. He remained chairman of the Chama Cha Mapinduzi, Tanzania's sole political party, which chose Vice-President Ali Hassan Mwinyi as his successor in August. Mwinyi received 92% of the vote in October 27 elections. Reviewing his years in power, Nyerere called the survival of Tanzania as a nation, its program of African socialism, and its 85% literacy rate his greatest achievements.

Reform in Zanzibar. Mwinyi's victory was due in large part to his activities as president of Zanzibar, a post he had held since January 1984. He reduced secessionist demands there by restoring civil liberties, returning parts of the economy to private ownership, and attempting to diversify the clove-based economy. A $43 million grant was obtained to rebuild Zanzibar's historic Old Town. It was hoped that the restoration, coupled with a luxury hotel being constructed by a French company, would attract badly needed tourist dollars.

Economy. The low Tanzanian standard of living continued to decline in 1985. The fact that 85% of the population lives in relatively self-sufficient communal *ujamaa* villages has helped the economic situation somewhat, but agriculture was adversely affected by a prolonged drought. When the rains returned in mid-1985, farmers lacked adequate storage and transportation facilities and found few goods to buy with their earnings. Oil alone made up 60% of imports, and a severe shortage of foreign exchange kept Tanzania from importing medicines, spare parts, and other needed goods. In desperation, the country resorted to barter arrangements in its foreign trade.

Although Nyerere sharply criticized the drastic economic changes demanded by the International Monetary Fund in return for credits to help Tanzania pay its large foreign debts, the economic crisis has led to quiet modifications in Tanzania's socialist policies. Restrictions on small private enterprises have eased, and some money-losing quasi-governmental corporations have been allowed to collapse or have merged with more successful operations.

Foreign Affairs. Nyerere, long one of Africa's most respected leaders, was chairman of the Organization of African Unity for 1984–85. Tanzania joined other frontline states in calling for the imposition of economic sanctions against South Africa, and efforts to restore economic ties to Kenya and Uganda continued. In July, Tanzania and Uganda agreed to construct a power line from Owen Falls Dam in Uganda to Tanzania and to reopen rail lines and resume ferry service across Lake Victoria.

ROBERT GARFIELD, *DePaul University*

TANZANIA · Information Highlights

Official Name: United Republic of Tanzania.
Location: East coast of Africa.
Area: 363,947 sq mi (942 623 km²).
Population (mid-1985 est.): 21,700,000.
Chief City (1980 est.): Dar es Salaam, the capital, 900,000.
Government: *Head of state,* Ali Hassan Mwinyi, president (took office Nov. 1985); *Head of government,* Joseph Warioba, prime minister (took office Nov. 1985). *Legislature* (unicameral)—National Assembly, 239 members.
Monetary Unit: Tanzanian shilling (17.097 shillings equal U.S.$1, Aug. 1985).
Gross Domestic Product (1984 U.S. $): $4,200,-000,000.
Economic Index (1984): *Consumer Prices* (1970 = 100), all items, 1,035.3; food, 1,222.2.
Foreign Trade (1984 U.S.$): *Imports,* $831,000,000; *exports,* $396,000,000.

TAXATION

The potentially adverse effects of high tax rates and inequitable tax systems on individuals, businesses, and the economy at large received growing recognition. Accordingly, several major industrialized nations began moves toward significant revisions in tax policies.

The United States

Congressional Action. On May 30, President Ronald Reagan presented to Congress a sweeping set of proposals to redesign the federal income tax system, with the announced goals of achieving fairness, growth, and simplicity. Congressional consideration of the proposals began in late May. In December the House of Representatives approved a bill modifying the president's proposals but retaining many of the basic principles. The Senate was expected to consider the legislation in 1986.

The president's plan would reduce sharply the rates of individual and corporate income taxes in exchange for curtailing or eliminating more than 65 categories of deductions and credits. Designed to be "revenue neutral" overall, the plan would cut individual taxes by an estimated 5% and raise corporate taxes by 23% over five years.

For individuals, the plan would eliminate the present system of 14 income brackets with rates ranging from 11% to 50%. In its place would be a three-bracket system with tax rates of 15%, 25%, and 35%. The personal exemption for taxpayers and dependents would rise from $1,080 (in 1986) to $2,000, and standard deductions would be increased. Also liberalized would be the earned income tax credit for the working poor and deductions for Individual Retirement Accounts (IRAs) by spouses who do not work outside the home.

For individuals, the most costly of the tax allowances that the plan would repeal is the deduction for state and local taxes, which now saves taxpayers more than $30 billion a year. The proposal would also eliminate special deductions for a married couple when both work, abolish income averaging, limit deductions for entertainment and business meal expenses, repeal the partial exclusion for unemployment compensation benefits, repeal the political contributions credit, replace the child and dependent care credit with a deduction, and terminate the charitable deduction allowance for those who do not itemize. Further, the plan would restrict deductions for interest payments on home mortgages other than the taxpayer's principal residence, impose tax on a portion of employer-paid health benefits, repeal the $100 dividend exclusion ($200 for joint returns), and curtail deductions for employee business expenses.

For corporations, the administration's proposal would cut the top income tax rate from 46% to 33%, while maintaining lower graduated rates for small corporations. It would mitigate the double taxation of corporate income by instituting a corporate-level deduction for 10% of the previously taxed corporate earnings paid out as dividends.

Sizable increases in corporate taxes would result from other provisions. The investment tax credit, which now saves corporations $26 billion a year in taxes, would be repealed. The present accelerated cost recovery system, enacted in 1981, would be replaced by a far less generous system of write-offs for new plant and equipment investment. The plan also includes a recapture provision that would prevent owners of old assets, which still would be depreciated under present accelerated rates, from receiving a windfall as a result of the lower rates.

Proposed revisions in the rules for taxing foreign source income would raise U.S. taxes of multinational corporations, mainly by placing a tighter limit on the amount of taxes paid in foreign countries that a business can use to reduce its U.S. tax bill.

Many specific industries also would be subjected to curtailment or repeal of tax incentives allowed under present law, including the oil and gas industry, banking and insurance companies, the timber industry, the commercial real estate business, and the homebuilding industry.

Other provisions in the plan would restrict tax benefits for retirement savings, repeal the tax exemption of private-purpose bonds issued by state and local governments, revise the taxation of capital gains, and impose stiffer minimum taxes on both individuals and corporations who sharply reduce their taxable income by using certain tax rules.

Supreme Court. The major tax cases decided by the court dealt with the powers of the Internal Revenue Service (IRS) to enforce federal tax laws and with the validity of state laws under the Equal Protection Clause of the 14th Amendment to the U.S. Constitution.

In *U.S. v. Boyle,* the court sided with the IRS in holding that failure to file a tax return on time is not excused by the taxpayer's reliance on a lawyer. Boyle, executor of his mother's will, retained an attorney to handle the estate and provided all relevant information for filing a federal estate tax return. Apparently because of a clerical oversight in the attorney's office, the return was filed three months late. Returns filed late are subject to a penalty unless the late filing is due to "reasonable cause and not due to willful neglect." In this case, the only issue was whether the late filing was due to reasonable cause. When the IRS assessed the penalty, the respondent paid it and filed suit for a refund, contending that his failure to file on time

Rep. Dan Rostenkowski (left), chairman of the House Ways and Means Committee, Treasury Secretary James Baker (right), and Rep. Fortney Stark enjoy a laugh before hearings on tax reform. Rostenkowski, an ally of the administration on the subject, had asked Americans to "write Rosty" urging tax legislation.

AP/Wide World

was due to reasonable cause, that is, to reliance on his attorney. Two lower courts had absolved Boyle from the filing penalty. The Supreme Court, however, said that Congress had placed the burden of prompt filing on the taxpayer and that an executor's duty to meet the filing deadline cannot be delegated.

In *Tiffany Fine Arts, Inc. v. U.S.,* the court's decision strengthened the hand of the IRS in its pursuit of allegedly abusive tax shelters. The question in the case involved the type of procedure required by the IRS in serving a summons affecting unnamed persons. Tiffany Fine Arts is a holding company for subsidiaries that promote tax shelters. During an audit of the company, an IRS agent issued summonses requesting the names and other information about persons who had acquired licenses from the firm to distribute a certain medical device. Tiffany refused to comply, holding that since the other taxpayers (licensees) were unknown, the law requires the IRS to apply to a district court for approval of a John Doe summons. The Supreme Court, however, upheld the IRS claim that its summons procedure was valid. The IRS need not comply with the John Doe summons procedures, the court said, when it seeks the records of a tax shelter promoter as a known taxpayer and at the same time also seeks the names of unknown clients who are potential targets of tax investigations.

In *U.S. v. National Bank of Commerce,* the court also sided with the IRS in its effort to collect unpaid taxes without recourse to the courts. Federal law allows the IRS to collect unpaid taxes either by a lien-foreclosure suit in a federal court or by administrative levy, which typically does not require a lawsuit. The case

against the bank grew out of a tax assessment of Roy J. Reeves of Pine Bluff, AR, and an IRS levy on joint accounts held in the National Bank of Commerce by Reeves, his wife, and his mother. Contending that it did not know how much of the joint account belonged to the taxpayer, the bank refused to comply with the levy. The IRS accordingly brought suit against the bank for the amount of the delinquent taxes ($856.61). Lower courts upheld the bank's refusal, ruling that the IRS could not levy on the joint accounts without first quantifying the rights of the co-depositors in a court proceeding, joining all co-depositors as defendants. The Supreme Court held that the bank had no basis for refusing to honor the levy. In its ruling, the court made it clear that the IRS's administrative levy was only a provisional remedy, and that co-depositors of the account still have the right to bring a civil action against the IRS or employ other means to have their property returned.

The court invalidated three state statutes—in Alabama, New Mexico, and Vermont—as unconstitutional. All three of the laws distributed benefits unequally on the basis of residence. The court found that the distinction among beneficiaries did not "rationally further a legitimate state purpose" and the laws were therefore in violation of the Equal Protection Clause of the 14th Amendment.

Metropolitan Life Insurance Co. v. Ward involved an Alabama insurance law that imposes a substantially lower gross premiums tax rate on domestic insurance companies than on out-of-state (foreign) firms. Foreign firms are permitted to reduce but not eliminate the differential by investing in Alabama assets. The state

asserted that the purposes of the discriminatory rates were the promotion of local business and the encouragement of investment in Alabama. Ruling that these purposes were not legitimate, the court said that a state may not constitutionally favor its own residents by taxing foreign corporations at a higher rate solely because of their residence.

Hooper v. Bernalillo County Assessor involved a New Mexico law that granted a tax exemption to certain Vietnam veterans. The statute exempts from the state's property tax $2,000 of the taxable value of property of honorably discharged veterans who served on active duty during the Vietnam War for at least 90 continuous days and who were residents of New Mexico before May 8, 1976. Alvin D. Hooper, who with his wife established residence in the state in 1981, met all requirements for the exemption except the residency rule. The Hoopers applied for the tax exemption for the 1983 tax year, but their claim was denied. The Supreme Court upheld the taxpayer's claim, reasoning that the residence test of the law bears no rational relationship to the state's asserted objectives, which were to encourage veterans to settle in the state and to serve as an expression of the state's appreciation to its own citizens for honorable service. "Neither the Equal Protection Clause, nor the court's precedents, permit the state to prefer established resident veterans over newcomers in the retroactive apportionment of economic benefits," the court said.

On similar grounds, the court invalidated Vermont's motor vehicle use tax law (*Williams v. Vermont*). Two taxpayers bought their cars outside of Vermont before becoming Vermont residents. In registering their vehicles in Vermont after moving to the state, they were required to pay Vermont's 4% use tax, even though they had already paid sales taxes where the cars were purchased. Since Vermont residents are allowed a credit for payment of an out-of-state sales tax, the taxpayers contended that the state's failure to grant a similar credit to nonresidents was discriminatory. The Supreme Court agreed, stating that no legitimate purpose is served by the discriminatory provisions of the tax and that the residence distinction bears no relation to the statutory purpose of raising revenues for the maintenance and improvement of Vermont roads.

State and Local Taxes. State and local governments collected $339,480,000,000 in taxes during the 12 months ending March 31, 1985, an increase of $29,433,000,000 or 9.5% over the previous year.

State legislatures in 1985 reduced state taxes by about $1.3 billion annually, on a net basis. While 21 states raised taxes by $1.0 billion, the increases were more than offset by reductions totaling $2.3 billion in 16 other states. Almost 90% of the reductions were accounted for by personal income tax cuts in 14 states.

International

Canada. In May, Minister of Finance Michael H. Wilson presented a budget that included temporary tax increases to reduce the projected deficit, along with tax reductions to spur investment. Tax increases include surcharges on taxes paid by higher-income individuals and corporations. For 1986, individuals will pay a surcharge of 5% on federal income taxes between C$6,000 and $15,000 and 10% on higher amounts. For corporations, the surtax is 5%. There were also increases in the federal sales tax and in gasoline and cigarette levies. Reductions include a personal tax exemption for capital gains up to a lifetime limit of $500,000, a phaseout of the petroleum and gas tax, and a variety of tax incentives to finance research and development by small businesses. The net effect of the budget proposals, as subsequently amended, would be to raise taxes by about $2.5 billion in calendar year 1986.

Europe. Great Britain's budget for 1986, announced by Chancellor of the Exchequer Nigel Lawson in March, includes a modest easing of taxes through a 10% increase in tax-free allowances, extension of the 15% value-added tax to newspaper advertising, and major changes in the rates and structure of national insurance contributions. The budget introduced a graduated scale of insurance contributions, cutting the costs of employing lower-paid workers, while boosting sharply employer contributions for higher-income employees.

The West German Bundestag (parliament) approved a two-stage tax relief totaling 20.2 billion Deutsche marks (about $7.75 billion) for the years 1986 through 1988. Effective in 1986, personal income taxes will be lowered by raising tax-free allowances and child deductions. Beginning in 1988, income tax rates will be cut, with relatively greater reductions for lower income classes and taxpayers with children.

The French government submitted its 1986 budget to the parliament in September. The major changes include personal income tax cuts of 3%, in addition to inflation adjustments; a slight reduction in the net wealth tax; and a lowering of the corporate income tax rate on retained earnings from 50% to 45%.

The Italian government will consider reducing personal income taxes by raising the tax brackets and personal allowances, in an effort to counteract fiscal drag.

Japan. Tax measures adopted by the Japanese cabinet include increases in tax rates on nonprofit corporations, discontinuing the exemption of mass media industries from the enterprise tax, and granting investment credits for many high-tech industries.

ELSIE M. WATTERS, *Tax Foundation, Inc.*

TELEVISION AND RADIO

"Television '85 could be Television '55," noted one critic at the opening of the 1985 fall season.

At first glance, that statement might have appeared sarcastic. After all, the increasingly steamy subject matter of the nighttime soap operas—such as *Dallas, Dynasty,* and *Falcon Crest*—would have caused an uproar during the Eisenhower administration. And some of the more graphic police/action series would have been unthinkable 30 years earlier. The National Coalition on Television Violence issued a report stating that 61% of all viewing hours had violent themes. *Lady Blue, Our Family Honor,* and *The Equalizer* were cited as chief offenders among new series.

But the controversies about sex and violence were carryovers from previous seasons; what was new in 1985, as the critic noted, was a return to family settings and traditional values. Observers noted that *The Cosby Show,* which had sparked a general resurgence of the National Broadcasting Company (NBC) the previous season, received the sincerest form of flattery from the new fall shows that directly or indirectly imitated it. Examples were: the Columbia Broadcasting Company (CBS) comedy *Charlie & Company,* starring Flip Wilson and Gladys Knight as unstereotyped black parents dealing with sensitive family matters; NBC's *Hell Town,* starring Robert Blake as a priest aiding his inner-city parishioners; and the American Broadcasting Companies (ABC) comedy *Growing Pains,* starring Alan Thicke as a psychiatrist who keeps his practice in the family home. Even the private eye of ABC's *Spenser for Hire,* played by Robert Urich, declined the offer of a tryst in one episode by making a brief speech against "instant gratifications."

TV also returned to the '50s in its new 1985 suspense programs. New editions of the classic anthologies *Twilight Zone* on CBS and *Alfred Hitchcock Presents* on NBC were introduced. With a flashy new Steven Spielberg production, *Amazing Stories,* also joining NBC, *Variety* magazine dubbed 1985–86 the "Year of the Anthology."

At the same time, however, many critics were troubled by what they saw as a corresponding conservative swing in TV news and documentaries, noting that recent challenges to the power and accuracy of TV news had "chilled" aggressive journalism.

Network Ratings and Programming. CBS finished first in the A. C. Neilsen ratings for the sixth consecutive year in the 1984–85 season (ending April 1985). NBC, after years in the cellar, made a comeback to topple ABC for second place in 1984–85 and won the ratings war in five of the first eight weeks of the 1985–86 season.

CBS had more than a resurgent NBC to worry about. The short-lived assignment of Phyllis George as a *CBS Morning News* anchor was a major embarrassment to Van Gordon Sauter's presidency of the news division. And though the plan by cable TV impresario Ted Turner and conservative action groups to purchase a controlling interest in CBS was never considered feasible by financial analysts, CBS still bought enough of its own stock, as a defensive measure, to cause the elimination of 125 new jobs. Concerned over the new emphasis of style over journalistic substance, anchorman Dan Rather and a group of news executives proposed buying the news division and setting it up as a private, independent operation.

NBC continued to be regarded by critics as the innovator in quality programming. *Golden Girls,* an NBC comedy, was named by *The New York Times* as the "lone exception" in an otherwise formulaic crop of new 1985 shows, an opinion echoed by the National Council of Working Women. *Girls* joined such critically acclaimed NBC shows as *Cheers, Hill Street Blues,* and *St. Elsewhere.*

Bea Arthur, Rue McClanahan, Betty White, and Estelle Getty (clockwise from left) are NBC's "Golden Girls."

AP/Wide World

Cable Television. *Variety* reported the results of a study that predicted cable TV would increase its reach from 34 million American households in 1984 to nearly 48 million households by 1990, and that the industry's after-tax profits would triple to $1.7 billion by that year. *The New York Times* reported that programming produced exclusively for cable was the major factor in the three networks' slippage in total audience share to 70% in 1985.

Still, critics were disappointed at cable's general failure to originate the enlightened programming that had been so enthusiastically predicted up to the early 1980s. Ironically, it was the lightest entertainment that appeared the most influential. The success of Music Television (MTV) spawned imitator programs that were syndicated to over-the-air stations, and critics noted that MTV was changing the complexion of the pop-music industry. Cable was given credit for its ability to resuscitate intelligent programs killed by the rating wars on commercial TV; Showtime brought back *The Paper Chase,* and USA Network created a new weekly talk show for ABC/PBS veteran Dick Cavett.

Cable executives were not so happy about another *Variety* projection that four million home satellite dishes would be in operation by 1990, allowing "free riders" to pick up programs without paying subscriptions. Home Box Office (HBO) and Cable News Network (CNN) were among major cable services studying techniques to "scramble" their signals to prevent such video piracy.

Public Television. In what some critics saw as an unfortunate step toward commercialism, the Corporation for Public Broadcasting loosened guidelines for identifying corporate sponsors, allowing brief "enhanced underwriting messages" on public TV and radio that stopped just short of being conventional advertisements. *Variety* noted that a few major corporations had in effect rescued the Public Broadcasting Service (PBS) from its financial crisis of the early 1980s and "have assumed the role of programmers and dictate what types of broadcasts they will underwrite and support."

But while critics mourned PBS' increased political cautiousness, they still applauded its excellent cultural programming that was absent from commercial TV. *The New York Times* called *The Nadine Gordimer Stories: Scenes from South Africa* a "memorable achievement," and Athol Fugard's powerful drama of apartheid, *Master Harold . . . and the boys* with Matthew Broderick, was acclaimed as a superb adaptation of the Broadway production.

"Magazine" Programming. *The New York Times* said Paramount Television's syndicated magazine of news and gossip *Entertainment Tonight* had "irrevocably changed television and added a new word—*infotainment*—to the vocabulary of the medium." Capitalizing on the show's success, Paramount entered a more ambitious magazine, *America,* into syndication in September, with sex therapist Ruth Westheimer joining the anchor team of McLean Stevenson, Sarah Purcell, and Stuart Damon.

Many TV observers saw the issue of gossip versus journalism crystallized in the controversy surrounding the shelving of ABC's *20/20* segment about a possible relationship between Robert F. Kennedy and Marilyn Monroe in the days leading up to her apparent suicide. Co-anchors Hugh Downs and Barbara Walters publicly criticized ABC News President Roone Arledge for the decision to cancel, and Geraldo Rivera, an original *20/20* correspondent with 15 years on the network, resigned two weeks after the showdown. The CBS magazine *West 57th,* a new fall entry featuring four stylish reporters in their thirties, was widely criticized as "yuppie" entertainment masquerading as news.

TV and Public Issues. In an unprecedented move, PBS allowed Accuracy in Media, the conservative media watchdog, to use two hours of broadcast time on June 26 to air its own report, *Inside Story: Vietnam Op-Ed,* a rebuttal of PBS' acclaimed 1983 series *Vietnam: A Television History.* Critics saw it as part of a recent pattern of public resistance to the power of the news media, though *The Wall Street Journal* noted that both reports sidestepped "the real problem, which is that the making of documentary films seems to require taking liberties with the historical materials. . . ."

And there was more fallout from TV's Vietnam retrospectives. In the wake of Gen. William Westmoreland's libel suit against CBS for its report *Vietnam: The Uncounted Enemy* (*see* special report, page 314), it became more difficult and expensive for documentary producers to obtain insurance against lawsuits. *Variety* observed that the trend "could have a far-ranging and damaging effect on the future of investigative journalism."

NBC's *An Early Frost,* about a victim of Acquired Immune Deficiency Syndrome (AIDS), was praised as one of the increasingly rare TV dramas addressing a public issue with candor and sensitivity.

People. Dustin Hoffman's performance in the CBS adaptation of the Broadway revival of *Death of a Salesman* was critically hailed as a television milestone. Lucille Ball was praised for the integrity of her portrayal of a "bag lady" in the CBS movie *Stone Pillow.* And Kirk Douglas tackled the gutsy, unglamorous lead in *Amos,* an NBC movie about neglect of the elderly. On less weighty subjects: Don Johnson of NBC's *Miami Vice* supplanted Tom Selleck of CBS's *Magnum, P.I.* as TV's favorite "beefcake." Charlton Heston became a regular on *The Colbys,* joining the ranks of mature stars reviving their careers on evening serials. Mary Tyler Moore had an emotional homecoming at CBS in the new comedy *Mary.* And

George C. Scott shaved his head for the title role in the NBC movie *Mussolini: The Untold Story*. Hoping to reverse its ratings slide by adding Joe Namath to the anchor team of Frank Gifford and O. J. Simpson, ABC's *Monday Night Football* suffered an extra bruise when former anchor Howard Cosell lashed out at Gifford and his other former colleagues in his book *I Never Played the Game*. Cybill Shepherd made a comeback in the new ABC series *Moonlighting*, and the starlet also won acclaim for her role in the NBC movie *The Long Hot Summer*.

Radio. The debate over violent and sexually explicit rock-music lyrics became a subject for congressional hearings in 1985, and naturally the debate affected American radio. The Associated Press (AP) reported that when a major Los Angeles station, KKHR, bowed to public pressure and pulled Prince's *Erotic City* off the air, it was the first such backlash since the Federal Communications Commission (FCC) had

The Broadway revival of "Death of a Salesman" came to television, with Dustin Hoffman starring as Willy Loman.

Photo Trends

AP/Wide World

Lucille Ball won plaudits for her portrayal of a New York "bag lady" in the made-for-TV movie "Stone Pillow."

fined two stations in the early 1970s for playing what the FCC called "titillating" songs. AP quoted an FCC spokeswoman as saying federal statutes against such songs were rarely invoked. *Erotic City* prompted the Cleveland City Council to pass a resolution urging stations not to play explicit songs. The National Council of Churches blamed the FCC and radio networks for "moral pollution of the airwaves." Sheena Easton's *Sugar Walls* and Animotion's *Obsession* were also frequently cited as offensive by parents and community leaders.

The conservativism of broadcast rulings under the Reagan administration continued with a U.S. Court of Appeals reversal of a 1978 FCC resolution granting women an advantage over men in competing for FM radio licenses.

Variety noted a general decline in the number of minutes that affiliate stations carried national news broadcasts by the ABC, CBS, NBC, and RKO radio networks, opting instead for local news or more music.

DAN HULBERT
"The Dallas Times Herald"

TELEVISION | 1985
Some Sample Programs

Aaron Copeland's 85th Birthday with the New York Philharmonic—A tribute to the composer. With Zubin Mehta conducting a program of the composer's work. PBS, Nov. 14.

A.D.—Five-part miniseries dramatizing the rise of Christianity in the Roman world following the death and resurrection of Christ. With James Mason, Ava Gardner, Colleen Dewhurst, Anthony Andrews, Richard Kiley. NBC, March 31.

Aïda—Live from New York's Metropolitan Opera, the Verdi opera marks the operatic farewell appearance of Leontyne Price. PBS, Jan. 3.

American Caesar—Five-hour documentary about Gen. Douglas MacArthur, based on William Manchester's biography. Independent, March 3.

Amos—A 1985 TV-movie about a disabled athlete confined to a nursing home. With Kirk Douglas, Elizabeth Montgomery. CBS, Sept. 29.

Anna Bolena—A *Live from Lincoln Center* three-hour concert version of Donizetti's opera. With Joan Sutherland. PBS, Nov. 25.

Arch of Triumph—A 1985 TV-movie adaptation of the Erich Maria Remarque novel. With Anthony Hopkins, Lesley-Anne Down, Donald Pleasence. CBS, May 29.

Arthur the King—A TV dramatization of the legend of King Arthur. With Malcolm McDowell, Candice Bergen, Dyan Cannon. CBS, April 26.

The Atlanta Child Murders—Two-part miniseries drawn from the real-life murders of mostly black children that occurred in Atlanta between 1979 and 1981. With James Earl Jones, Martin Sheen, Percy Rodrigues, Calvin Levels, Jason Robards, Ruby Dee. CBS, Feb. 10.

Christopher Columbus—A two-part 1985 TV-movie on the life of the explorer Christopher Columbus. With Gabriel Byrne, Oliver Reed, Faye Dunaway, Eli Wallach, and Nicol Williamson. CBS, May 19.

Cousteau: The First 75 Years—Documentary on Jacques-Yves Cousteau and his achievements on the occasion of his 75th birthday. Independent, June 24.

Crisis in Central America—A four-part *Frontline* series documentary on Central America; segments include *The Yankee Years*, *Castro's Challenge*, *Revolution in Nicaragua*, and *Battle for El Salvador*. PBS, April 9.

A Death in California—A 1985 TV-movie broadcast in two parts and based on an actual murder case in California. With Cheryl Ladd. ABC, May 12.

Death of a Salesman—Television adaptation of the Arthur Miller play. With Dustin Hoffman, John Malkovich, Stephen Lang, Kate Reid, Charles Durning. CBS, Sept. 15.

Do You Remember Love?—A 1985 TV-movie about a college professor who contracts Alzheimer's disease. With Joanne Woodward, Richard Kiley. CBS, May 21.

Evergreen—Three-part miniseries about a Jewish immigrant who arrives in America in 1909. With Leslie Ann Warren, Armand Assante, Ian McShane. NBC, Feb. 24.

Florence Nightingale—A TV-movie biography of the English woman who revolutionized nursing. With Jaclyn Smith, Claire Bloom, Jeremy Brett. NBC, April 7.

The Gordimer Stories—Seven-part series based on the short stories of Nadine Gordimer, including *Six Feet of the Country*, *A Chip of Ruby Glass*, *City Lovers*, *Praise*, *Good Climate, Friendly Inhabitants*, *Oral History*, and *Country Lovers*. PBS, July 1.

Go Tell It on the Mountain—A television adaptation of James Baldwin's first novel. With Paul Winfield, Olivia Cole, Ruby Dee. PBS, Jan. 14.

The Heart of the Dragon—Twelve-part series examining the history of the People's Republic of China. PBS, May 6.

Hiroshima Plus 40 Years . . . and Still Counting—A *CBS Reports* telecast on the dropping of the atomic bombs on Hiroshima and Nagasaki. CBS, July 31.

Honor, Duty, and a War Called Vietnam—Documentary on the American involvement in Vietnam, commemorating the 10th anniversary of the fall of Saigon. With Walter Cronkite. CBS, April 25.

The Importance of Being Ernest—An adaptation of the Oscar Wilde play. With Wendy Hiller. PBS, Dec. 6.

Intercom: Cuba—25 Years of Revolution—Two-part documentary on Cuba. PBS, July 25.

Jamaica Inn—Two-part dramatization of the Daphne Du Maurier novel set in 19th-century England. With Jane Seymour, Billie Whitelaw. Independent, June 3.

John and Yoko: A Love Story—A dramatization of the relationship between singer John Lennon and artist Yoko Ono. With Kim Miyori, Mark McGann. NBC, Dec. 2.

Kane and Abel—A three-part dramatization of the Jeffrey Archer novel about rivalry between two Boston business tycoons. With Peter Strauss, Sam Neill, Ron Silver, David Dukes. CBS, Nov. 17.

The Key to Rebecca—Two-part dramatization of the Ken Follett novel, set in World War II Cairo. With Cliff Robertson, David Soul, Season Hubley, Robert Culp, David Hemmings. Independent, April 29.

La Rondine—A *Live from Lincoln Center* telecast of the Puccini work. With the New York City Opera Company; Alessandro Siciliani conducting. PBS, Oct. 30.

Live Aid: Concert to End World Hunger—Eleven-hour benefit performance featuring more than 50 of the top rock recording artists. Independent and ABC, July 13.

The Long Hot Summer—A two-part adaptation of William Faulkner's *Hamlet* and the 1958 film. With Don Johnson, Jason Robards, Cybill Shepherd, Judith Ivey, Ava Gardner. NBC, Oct. 6.

Love's Labour's Lost—Shakespeare's comedy, the final play offered in the seven-year series of Shakespeare's plays. With Jonathan Kent, Maureen Lipmen. PBS, May 31.

Master Harold . . . and the boys—A television adaptation of the Athol Fugard play. With Matthew Broderick. PBS, Nov. 15.

Murder: By Reason of Insanity—A 1985 TV-movie about a woman afraid that her husband will kill her. With Candice Bergen, Hector Elizondo. CBS, Oct. 1.

Murder with Mirrors—This 1985 TV-movie is an Agatha Christie whodunit. With Helen Hayes, Bette Davis, John Mills. CBS, Feb. 20.

Mussolini: The Untold Story—Three-part television drama on the life of the Italian Fascist leader. With George C. Scott. NBC, Nov. 24.

North and South—A six-part miniseries dramatizing the novels of John Jakes about a Northern and Southern family and their lives in the decades leading up to the American Civil War. With Patrick Swayze, David Carradine, Parker Stevenson, Lesley-Anne Down. ABC, Nov. 3.

Promises to Keep—A drama about a man who returns to his home and family after having deserted them 30 years before. With Robert Mitchum. CBS, Oct. 15.

The Rape of Richard Beck—A drama about a tough cop who gets sexually assaulted and the ensuing trauma. With Richard Crenna, Meredith Baxter Birney. ABC, May 27.

Rigoletto—A 1983 Jean-Pierre Ponnelle film adaptation of Verdi's opera. With Luciano Pavarotti. PBS, March 15.

Simon Boccanegra—A *Live from the Met* presentation of the Verdi opera; James Levine conducts. PBS, April 17.

Snowstorm in the Jungle—Jacques Cousteau explores South America's Amazon region and the cocaine culture found there. TBS, Jan. 16.

Soundstage: Tina Turner—Concert. PBS, July 16.

Space—A five-part miniseries, adapted from the James Michener novel, about the American space program. With James Garner, Beau Bridges, Bruce Dern. CBS, April 14.

Stone Pillow—A drama about the relationship that develops between a "bag lady" and a young social worker. With Lucille Ball. CBS, Nov. 5.

Strangers and Brothers—*Masterpiece Theatre*'s seven-part dramatization of the C. P. Snow novel. PBS, May 5.

Terrorism: War in the Shadows—A documentary examining what the American response to terrorism ought to be. With Walter Cronkite. CBS, June 19.

13 at Dinner—A television adaptation of the Agatha Christie novel. With Peter Ustinov, Faye Dunaway, Lee Horsley. CBS, Oct. 19.

Three Sovereigns for Sarah—A three-part docudrama, based on the Salem (MA) witch trials of 1692. With Vanessa Redgrave. PBS, May 27.

Titus Andronicus—From the series of Shakespeare Plays. With Trevor Peacock, Anna Calder-Marshall, Eileen Atkins. PBS, April 19.

The Woman in White—A five-part dramatization on the *Mystery* series of the early British detective novel by Wilkie Collins. With Diana Quick, Ian Richardson. PBS, May 2.

TENNESSEE

Industrial development was big news in Tennessee when in late July General Motors announced plans to locate a $3.5 billion Saturn plant at a site 30 mi (48 km) south of Nashville. It was to be the biggest single industrial development in the state's history. Six thousand workers would be employed initially, with another 10,000 jobs generated from support facilities. Not long after this announcement, Nissan told of plans for a new $5 million supply plant in Winchester, and Toyota talked seriously of a $500 million plant for the state.

Legislation. On Capitol Hill, legislators developed a $5.6 billion budget to provide for a continuation of state functions and small salary increases for teachers and government workers. After year-long hearings on tax reform held by a special legislative committee, legislators surprised no one by leaving taxes pretty much as they were. The sales tax continued to be one of the nation's highest. In addition, a two-cent increase on gasoline sales, expected to generate $645 million, was earmarked for road improvement and maintenance. Other new legislation opened Tennessee's banking business to 13 other states (which will provide reciprocal arrangements), permitted parents to teach their children at "home schools," and expanded benefits to children of poor families.

Prison Problems. Summer riots in four prisons caused more than $11 million in damages and served to focus attention on the state's prison needs. At midyear, newly appointed Corrections Commissioner Steve Norris unfolded plans for a sweeping overhaul of the state's correctional system.

Crops and Weather. Seasonal rains in most of the state and a warm summer sun brought an above-average harvest. An increase in tobacco acreage, particularly in the north-central and eastern counties, caused that crop to exceed soybean production for the first time in more than a decade. Farmers harvested the smallest wheat crop since 1979, as planters turned to the production of grain sorghum instead. Fruit growers suffered considerably, as hundreds of acres of peach and other fruit trees failed to survive the severe winter.

Government and Politics. Finance Commissioner Hubert McCullough, the chief cabinet official, resigned to reenter private business and was replaced by Donald Jackson. Kathryn Celauro was named revenue commissioner, bringing the number of women in Gov. Lamar Alexander's cabinet to four—the most in the state's history. Nashville businessman Joe Rodgers became ambassador to France.

Crime. Two-time gubernatorial candidate and wealthy Knoxville businessman Jake Butcher, responsible in 1983 for the nation's third-largest commercial bank failure since the 1930s, was imprisoned after he admitted to guilt involving bank fraud and failure to report more than $38 million in income taxes. A plea bargain arrangement provided that his several sentences will run concurrently and cannot exceed 20 years. A close associate, Jesse Barr, was sentenced to 18 years.

ROBERT E. CORLEW
Middle Tennessee State University

TERRORISM

From skyjackings to seajackings, from kidnappings of Americans and Soviets to the abduction of the daughter of a Central American president, 1985 was indeed a dramatic year in international terrorism. While terrorists made their presence felt in virtually all corners of the globe, governments intensified their efforts to combat this growing threat. The midair interception of a plane carrying suspected terrorists, retaliatory raids against terrorist headquarters, and explicit warnings to states that sponsor terrorist activities were among the counterterrorist measures adopted during the year.

Middle East. Three major hijackings in the Middle East resulted in the murder of three Americans. On June 14, Lebanese Shiite terrorists hijacked a Trans World Airlines (TWA) jetliner out of Athens and held 39 Americans captive in Beirut for more than two weeks. Their major demand was the release of 766 Lebanese prisoners, mostly Shiites, being held in Israel. The hostages finally were freed on June 30 after Syria helped mediate a solution. One U.S. Navy diver had been murdered during the early stages of the hijacking.

The second major hostage episode that resulted in the murder of an American was the seizure on October 7 of the Italian cruise liner *Achille Lauro* off the coast of Egypt. Palestinian terrorists hijacked the vessel and shot an

American tourist, throwing his body overboard. Although their demand for the release of Palestinian prisoners in Israel was not met, they surrendered to Palestinian and Egyptian officials in Egypt. What followed was indicative of the complexities involved in trying to resolve a terrorist incident. A group of U.S. F-14 jet fighters intercepted the plane carrying the suspected terrorists out of Egypt and diverted it to Italy, touching off a diplomatic furor between Washington and Cairo. U.S.-Italian relations also suffered a setback when Italy allowed the alleged mastermind of the hijacking, Palestinian guerrilla leader Mohammed Abbas, to leave the country.

The third hostage incident was the bloodiest. On November 23, Palestinian terrorists hijacked an Egyptian airliner en route from Athens to Cairo. The plane, the same one that had been intercepted by U.S. fighters in the aftermath of the *Achille Lauro* incident, was forced to land in Malta. There the terrorists began shooting the passengers one by one until Egyptian commandos stormed the plane. The hijackers detonated three grenades during the counterterrorist assault, and when the smoke cleared 59 people were dead, including an American woman who had been executed earlier by the terrorists. Egypt accused Libya of sponsoring the hijacking.

Other terrorist incidents in the Middle East included the kidnapping of Americans and other foreigners in Lebanon by Islamic Jihad. The main demand of that organization was the release by Kuwait of a number of Shiite terrorists being held for the 1983 bombing of the U.S. and French embassies there. Kuwait refused to accede to the demands. Meanwhile, in a clear indication that terrorists find their victims among all nationalities, four Soviet officials were abducted in Beirut, with one of them eventually being murdered. Islamic Jihad took credit for the kidnapping, demanding that Moscow put pressure on Syria to end its support for pro-Syrian militias fighting fundamentalist Muslims in Tripoli. Soon after the kidnapping, Syrian troops entered Tripoli and enforced a cease-fire between the warring factions. The remaining three Soviet hostages were subsequently released. Two Americans, a journalist and a clergyman, both of whom had been held hostage in Lebanon for several months, were released in 1985, but another U.S. official was believed to have been executed.

Europe. The year's most serious terrorist incidents in Europe occurred on December 27, when Palestinian gunmen simultaneously attacked the check-in counters of El Al Israeli Airlines at airports in Rome and Vienna. A total of 16 persons were killed.

Otherwise, terrorism in Europe during the year centered on East-West relations rather than on issues of religious fundamentalism and the Arab-Israeli conflict. A wave of anti-U.S. and anti-NATO bombings that had begun in late 1984 continued into the new year with NATO oil pipelines, ships, headquarter buildings, and bases falling victim to terrorist attack in several countries. Among the more active terrorist groups were the Communist Combatant Cells in Belgium, the Red Army Faction (RAF) and Revolutionary Cells in West Germany, and the Direct Action in France. Direct Action and the RAF issued a joint communiqué in January announcing the coordination of future activities. Shortly thereafter, the head of France's arms export program was killed in Paris, while a West German industrialist involved in the manufacture of NATO tank and aircraft engines was assassinated in Munich.

U.S. servicemen in Europe also were singled out for attack. A club catering to Americans from Hellenikon Air Base in Athens was bombed in February, and a café frequented by U.S. servicemen from Torrejon Air Base near

AP/Wide World

In October, Palestinian guerrillas held more than 400 persons, including six British dancers (right), *hostage for two days aboard the Italian cruise ship "Achille Lauro."*

Madrid was bombed during April. Scores of Americans were injured in both attacks, with 18 being killed in the Madrid incident. U.S. service personnel also were killed during the summer, when a car bomb went off at Rhein-Main Air Base near Frankfurt; the RAF took credit for that attack. Especially noteworthy about this incident was the claim by the RAF that it had murdered a U.S. serviceman in Weisbaden in order to use his identity papers to gain access to the base. This represented a new departure in terrorist tactics.

Several European countries experienced terrorism associated with separatist movements. In Spain, ETA guerrillas fighting for Basque independence were active in a number of major attacks during the year, including the assassination in July of the director of policy for the defense ministry. In Northern Ireland, the Irish Republican Army launched a mortar attack early in the year against a police station in Newry, killing nine officers. A September mortar attack west of Belfast injured 30 people.

Asia. The year 1985 was an unusually violent one in Asia, as Sikhs in India, Tamil separatists in Sri Lanka, the New People's Army (NPA) in the Philippines, and Kanak separatists in New Caledonia utilized a variety of terrorist tactics to achieve their objectives. Sikh extremists in the Punjab waged a violent campaign of bombings and assassinations in support of their demand for independence of the region. Sikh extremists also were suspected of placing a bomb aboard an Air India jet out of Canada, which exploded over the Atlantic on June 23, killing all 329 persons aboard. And a plot by Sikhs to assassinate Prime Minister Rajiv Gandhi on a visit to the United States in June was uncovered. In Sri Lanka, Tamil separatists engaged in a terrorist war against the Sinhalese majority throughout the year, with train bombings and police station raids as some of their tactics.

Most attention in Asia during 1985, however, focused on the Philippines, where President Ferdinand Marcos faced mounting opposition. Like many other insurgent groups in recent years, the Communist NPA mixed terrorist tactics with guerrilla warfare in its struggle to topple the Marcos regime. Among the terrorist incidents attributed either to the NPA or other anti-Marcos groups were the assassinations of several mayors throughout the country, the throwing of grenades into a crowded movie house on the island of Mindanao, and the setting of fires at hotels in Manila.

Latin America. One of the most audacious kidnappings of the year occurred in El Salvador, where rebels abducted the daughter of President José Napoleon Duarte on September 10. She was released one month later after the government agreed to free several political prisoners and provide safe passage to more than 90 guerrillas wounded during the war. As part of the agreement, the rebels also released a number of small-town mayors whom they had abducted during the year. In a separate incident, leftist rebels opened fire on a café in San Salvador in June, killing four U.S. Marines, two U.S. businessmen, and other civilians.

Meanwhile, other left-wing and right-wing terrorism rocked the region, with Peru, Chile, Colombia, Argentina, and Guatemala experiencing the brunt of the attacks. Of particular note were the activities of the Maoist Sendero Luminoso guerrillas in Peru, who attacked both urban and rural targets, often blacking out the capital. A bombing campaign in the spring was aimed at disrupting the national election, while the inauguration of President Alan García Pérez in July was marked by a series of car bombings in Lima. In Chile, bombings occurred throughout the year, including one that blacked out much of the country in September on the 12th anniversary of the military coup that brought President Augusto Pinochet to power. Right-wing violence in Argentina included a bombing campaign to coincide with the trial of former military leaders for alleged crimes during the rule of the junta, while in Guatemala a number of terrorist incidents were reported as the country prepared for fall presidential elections.

A major incident in Ecuador involved the kidnapping during the summer of the country's leading banker. An attempt by police and government troops to free him failed, as both the banker and those who abducted him, which included members of the Alfaro Vive organization and Colombia's M-19 guerrillas, were killed in the raid. Meanwhile, in Colombia, M-19 guerrillas seized the Palace of Justice in Bogotá during November, taking several judges and civilians hostage.

The growing link between terrorism and drug trafficking also was evident during 1985, as traffickers abducted and killed a U.S. Drug Enforcement Agent in Mexico, and a $350,000 bounty was reported to be offered by drug traffickers in Colombia for the kidnapping of the head of the U.S. Drug Enforcement Agency. Mexico was the scene of a shoot-out between police and drug traffickers during the fall, with more than 20 policemen killed.

North America and Africa. Terrorism remained at a rather low level in North America and Africa, although there were a number of incidents in the latter region associated with the political violence in South Africa, the ongoing insurgencies in Angola, Uganda, Mozambique, Ethiopia, and Sudan, and the guerrilla war in Namibia (South-West Africa).

In the United States, the major incidents involved attacks on abortion clinics, right-wing terrorism associated with the neo-Nazi movement, and a bombing that killed the regional director of the Arab-American Anti-Discrimination Committee in the wake of the hijacking

of the *Achille Lauro*. In Canada, the major terrorist incident was the March 12 seizure of the Turkish Embassy in Ottawa by the Armenian Revolutionary Army (ARA), whose main target had been the Turkish ambassador. The ambassador escaped during the assault, and all the hostages were released when the ARA members surrendered.

JEFFREY D. SIMON
The Rand Corporation

TEXAS

In a year not dominated by state or national elections, the economy remained the principal matter of concern in Texas. Great numbers of illegal immigrants entering Texas from Mexico contributed to the high level of unemployment, while judicially mandated bilingual education in the public schools also sparked controversy. Unfortunately, the devastating earthquake in Mexico City seemed likely to increase the number of immigrants seeking refuge in Texas. Texans, nevertheless, responded with their usual generosity in sending aid and supplies to the beleaguered city.

Economy. The downward spiral in world oil prices severely affected the Texas economy. A decline in exploration and thus greater unemployment among oil-field workers was the result. A greater number of rigs than ever before stood idle while more oil-field equipment companies were forced into bankruptcy. Houston, the state's leading petrochemical center, was particularly hard hit. Rising unemployment, depressed real-estate values, and empty office space throughout Houston were all testimonials to the flagging Texas economy. The picture in Dallas and San Antonio was less gloomy. Austin continued to experience steady growth. As the leading high-tech center and sustained by the presence of the state government and principal state university, its future seemed assured. Along with most of the rest of the nation, Texas farmers suffered from a combination of declining prices and continued adverse weather conditions.

Politics. With no major statewide races scheduled in 1985, Texans began to gear up for the 1986 gubernatorial contest. Gov. Mark White, a conservative Democrat, will very likely seek vindication of his record in office. Texas Republicans will probably choose between former Congressman Kent Hance and former Gov. William Clements. Both have already attacked White for his failure to grant state employees a promised pay raise and for lack of imagination in combating the state's economic malaise. Clements, in particular, stressed the possibility that Texas will be facing huge annual deficits within ten years. To offset this, liberal Democrats have called for the enactment of a state income tax or increased taxes on corporations. However, these alternatives are unlikely since among all the "Sunbelt" states, Texas has traditionally granted the most concessions to new businesses.

Houston Mayor Kathy Whitmire (D) was elected to a third two-year term.

Education. Reflecting statewide economic conditions, the 1984–85 session of the state legislature slashed funding for higher education. In addition to a substantial tuition increase for residents and nonresidents alike, appropriations for individual state universities also were cut. Support for pure research was reduced greatly, thereby jeopardizing ambitions in the field of high-tech development. With long-range planning in mind, the legislature mandated the establishment of a "blue ribbon" Committee on Higher Education to consider such matters as the merger of existing institutions where possible, faculty tenure policies, and expansion of the junior and community college system.

On a public school level, a uniform "exit" test as a condition for graduation from high school was administered for the first time. While admittedly not very difficult, the results were gratifying to school authorities. Some public school districts continued to experience teacher shortages, particularly in the area of bilingual education, but throughout Texas there were no teacher strikes.

And in 1985 the state instituted a "no pass, no play" rule regarding high school extracurricular activities. If a student fails only one course, he or she is barred from participating in sports, band, debate, drama, and the like for six weeks. While bitterly opposed by some football coaches and parents, the ruling was upheld by the Texas Supreme Court. The "no pass, no play" rule was expected to be an issue in the next gubernatorial campaign.

STANLEY E. SIEGEL, *University of Houston*

TEXAS • Information Highlights

Area: 266,807 sq mi (691 030 km²).
Population (July 1, 1984 est.): 15,989,000.
Chief Cities (July 1, 1984 est.): Austin, the capital, 397,001; Houston, 1,705,697; Dallas, 974,234; San Antonio, 842,779; El Paso, 463,809; Fort Worth, 414,562; Corpus Christi, 258,067.
Government (1985): *Chief Officers*—governor, Mark White (D); lt. gov., William P. Hobby (D). *Legislature*—Senate, 31 members; House of Representatives, 150 members.
State Finances (fiscal year 1984): *Revenues,* $18,912,000,000; *expenditures,* $16,880,000,000.
Personal Income (1984): $201,013,000,000; per capita, $12,572.
Labor Force (June 1985): *Civilian labor force,* 8,055,000; *unemployed,* 624,000 (7.7% of total force).
Education: *Enrollment* (fall 1983)—public elementary schools, 2,155,012; public secondary, 834,784; colleges and universities, 795,741. *Public school expenditures* (1982–83), $7,442,158,754 ($2,731 per pupil).

THAILAND

During 1985 a financial scandal and a failed military coup underscored three important points about Thai politics. First, the five-year-old government of Prime Minister Prem Tinsulanonda is strong because it has strengthened Thailand's democratic institutions. Second, by opening up the economy to free market forces and reducing the deficit, the government has achieved high economic growth—although not all Thai people have benefited equally. Third, although the military has allowed its political and economic role to be sharply curtailed in recent years, it is still a potent political force.

Domestic Affairs. The major financial scandal of the year concerned a revolving fund—somewhat like a chain letter—that was operated by a former government clerk named Chamoy Thipyaso. Over a ten-year period, she persuaded thousands of people—mostly Thai military officers—to invest their savings in her fund. The government became concerned that this and other unregulated funds were controlling a large share of the country's wealth. In March 1985, after King Bhumibol Adulyadej had issued a royal decree banning revolving funds, Chamoy disappeared from her home and stopped making interest payments to her customers.

Three months later, she reappeared at a Royal Thai Air Force facility and announced that she could only repay depositors a fraction of what she owed them. It was widely believed that she had already repaid her most influential military protectors. Chamoy was jailed by the police, and many air force officers complained that they had been cheated—not by her but by the government.

Meanwhile, the government was busy fending off a vote of no confidence in parliament. The opposition tried to oust four economic ministers from the cabinet because of economic policies that included austerity measures aimed at trimming the deficit. The long-term effect of these policies was to strengthen the economy, but the short-term effect was to cut the spending power of urban workers. Nevertheless, the government emerged from the battle victorious. Prime Minister Prem even felt strong enough to amend the constitution to reduce the role of active-duty military officers in the parliament and government.

In August the annual promotion list of senior military officers rewarded Gen. Chaovalit Yongchaiyut and others who had supported government policies. Gen. Pichit Kullavanich, the main rival of Chaovalit, was not promoted. This led to a hasty effort to form an antigovernment alliance including senior officers who had not been promoted, those who had lost out because of the government's austerity measures, and those who blamed the government for the collapse of Chamoy's revolving fund.

On September 9 the test of strength came. Col. Manoon Roopkachorn, who had been cashiered from the army for leading an unsuccessful coup in 1981, tried once again to overthrow the government with a force of only 500 supporters and 22 tanks. Although he held the Supreme Command headquarters in Bangkok for ten hours and killed a number of civilians, no military units, workers, or students rallied to his side. After firing a last few rounds of artillery into the city, Manoon surrendered in return for safe conduct from the country.

A few retired generals—including one former prime minister—who supported the coup claimed to have been coerced. The government, nevertheless, charged them with sedition. If convicted, they could be punished by life imprisonment or death. This was a departure from the past practice of forgiving those who launched unsuccessful coups. But Manoon's action was also a departure from the Thai tradition of "bloodless" coups. It was seen to have harmed not only the reputation of the military but that of the entire nation as well. Some observers feared that the government might face more challenges unless it found a way to provide more jobs for a growing number of unemployed workers and college students.

International Events. In foreign affairs, the government was criticized by members of the coup group for its tough policy of resisting Vietnamese control of Cambodia and Laos. Thai leaders met with leaders of the Lao and Vietnamese governments, but the Thai authorities also defended their border vigorously and continued to call for the removal of all Vietnamese troops from Cambodia. In November, Thailand and the other members of the Association of Southeast Asian Nations (ASEAN) again persuaded most of the members of the United Nations to vote for the withdrawal of "foreign" (meaning Vietnamese) forces from Cambodia.

PETER A. POOLE
Author, "The Vietnamese in Thailand"

THAILAND • Information Highlights

Official Name: Kingdom of Thailand (conventional); Prathet Thai (Thai).
Location: Southeast Asia.
Area: 198,772 sq mi (514 820 km²).
Population (mid-1985 est.): 52,700,000.
Chief City (Dec. 1984 est.): Bangkok, the capital, 5,018,327.
Government: *Head of state,* Bhumibol Adulyadej, king (acceded June 1946). *Head of government,* Gen. Prem Tinsulanonda, prime minister (took office March 1980).
Monetary Unit: Baht (26.85 baht equal U.S.$1, Aug. 1985).
Gross National Product (1983 U.S.$): $40,300,-000,000.
Economic Index (Bangkok, 1984): *Consumer Prices* (1970 = 100), all items, 309.7; food, 322.5.
Foreign Trade (1983 U.S.$): *Imports,* $10,235,000,000; *exports,* $7,414,000,000.

THEATER

Each new season looks like Broadway's last, and 1985 did little to relieve its baleful prospects. Higher costs continued to discourage innovativeness, revivals provided many of the season's pleasures, and new material seldom challenged the technical expertise of those presenting and performing it.

Musicals. This outlook was particularly true for the musical season, which contained a few more entries than in 1984 but none so distinguished as 1984's best, *Sunday in the Park with George,* by Stephen Sondheim. *Big River,* a musical adaptation of Mark Twain's *Huckleberry Finn,* won most of the musical Tony Awards but, in the view of many observers, by default rather than the compelling or commanding nature of its music and lyrics (by Roger Williams) or book (by William Hauptman). *Big River,* in fact, represents something of a throwback to the days before *Oklahoma!,* which taught us to expect the songs to be integrated into the story and accompanied by lively dancing. Williams' country and western songs often are pretty—*River in the Rain* and *Muddy Water* are the best—but they are free-floating; they seem like hit singles that could have been dropped into, or taken from, the Billboard charts.

The Mystery of Edwin Drood, based on Charles Dickens' unfinished mystery, moved to Broadway from Central Park, where Joseph Papp's New York Shakespeare Festival unveiled it during the summer. Rupert Holmes' score is another one that does not abound in musical riches, but the boisterous, outgoing nature of the show conceals its slender means better than the often plaintive *Big River* can manage. What puts *Edwin Drood* across is Wilford Leach's idea to stage it as a Victorian music-hall entertainment. Such sure-handed veterans as George Rose and Cleo Laine are given the chance to charm the audience with their plummy embrace of both the period and the material before coming to an ending in which the audience chooses the guilty party.

Andrew Lloyd Webber, the British composer who gave Broadway such hits as *Evita* and the still-running *Cats,* returned with a reworked version of his less-successful London outing of a few years earlier, *Tell Me on a Sunday.* Reshaped by Richard Maltby, Jr., and given a new second act, it was rechristened *Song & Dance.* The story deals with the travails of an English girl in New York (Bernadette Peters) and the American boy who deserts her (Christopher d'Amboise). The show's two halves are uneasily joined; it is Peters' sparrowlike pluck that puts the songs across, most notably *Tell Me on a Sunday.*

The season's big surprise was not the usual sort of musical at all, but a cabaret-style dance concert, *Tango Argentino.* The show presented

© Martha Swope

Broadway's big hit was "Big River," with Daniel Jenkins (center) as Huck Finn and Ron Richardson (rear) as Jim.

sexy, razor-sharp dancing from virtuosic couples whose very looks left no doubt about the tango's origins as a working-class diversion.

Several personalities had their musical innings, too. Yul Brynner added to his record-breaking total of appearances in the starring role of a musical, another revival of Rodgers and Hammerstein's *The King and I,* and was universally mourned when he died in October. New York's ubiquitous Mayor Edward I. Koch was celebrated in song and dance, too, as Charles Strouse set Koch's autobiographical memoir, *Mayor,* to music at the Latin Quarter. Ellie Greenwich, the girl from Levittown, NY, who wrote all those doo-wop songs for female groups of the 1960s, came to Broadway in *Leader of the Pack,* but no effective way was found to integrate her songs with her life story, and the show flopped. So did *Grind,* a Harold Prince outing with music by Larry Grossman and lyrics by Ellen Fitzhugh, about a 1930s burlesque house in Chicago and starring Ben Vereen. Paul Schierhorn's *The News,* a rock 'n' roll look at a tabloid very much like *The New York Post,* also vanished quickly. *Singin' in the Rain,* a sodden stage version of the beloved 1952 M-G-M movie musical, proved more remarkable for its perseverance than for its entertainment value. Refusing to be doomed by mostly negative reviews, it hung on and still was running at year's end.

Plays. Broadway maintained its franchise as a dispenser of drama, but the season's two most distinguished plays were staged off-Broadway: Sam Shepard's *A Lie of the Mind*

The latest from Neil Simon was the autobiographical "Biloxi Blues." Considered by some critics to be his best work, "Biloxi Blues" won the Tony Award for best play.

and David Hare's *A Map of the World.* The former is too diffuse to be ranked with Shepard's best plays, but its story of two families linked by a terrible marriage is filled with wonders—lines that burrow deep into the American psyche and striking visual metaphors, such as Harvey Keitel looking for his father's love in a box containing the latter's ashes. At four hours, it lacks the sustained depth and bite of such other of Shepard's works as *Buried Child* or *The Curse of the Starving Class* (revived off-Broadway in 1985). But it does carry forward Shepard's preoccupation with the American West as a place of spiritual exhaustion (the play unfolds in California and Montana) and his drive to believe that family wounds can be healed. For its performers—especially Geraldine Page, Amanda Plummer, Ann Wedgeworth, and Will Patton, in addition to Keitel—it is a feast.

Hare's *A Map of the World,* imported by the New York Shakespeare Festival from England's National Theatre, focuses on the family as the arena for conflict. *A Map of the World* is the kind of play Shaw might have written if he were alive today, and angry enough. It unfolds in India during a world conference on hunger, and it boils down to a debate between the Left and the Right, as the Third World hovers, aggrieved, in the distance. Hare had the dramatic shrewdness to make the right-winger, Roshan Seth, the charmer and give him most of the good lines. The play is long but intellectually and verbally scintillating.

The theater's most intense tackling of issues focused on Acquired Immune Deficiency Syndrome (AIDS). William Hoffman's *As Is* opened off-Broadway and soon moved to Broadway, and Larry Kramer's *The Normal Heart* ensconced itself off-Broadway at the New York Shakespeare Festival's Public Theatre. *As Is* examines the AIDS phenomenon from a domestic perspective, showing a dying man comforted by a former lover when the latter hears the news. *The Normal Heart* is less interested in tender compassion than in abrasive polemics, excoriating the government for not financing more AIDS research.

The best of the new Broadway plays was Neil Simon's *Biloxi Blues,* continuing the autobiography he began with *Brighton Beach Memoirs.* Matthew Broderick again plays a stand-in for the young Simon, this time thrown together with a barracks full of ill-matched buddies in 1943. The play has the nostalgic compassion of Eugene O'Neill's *Ah, Wilderness!,* and it won Simon his third Tony (*see* BIOGRAPHY).

The year's most brilliant new nonmusical material on Broadway was performed by Lily Tomlin in the one-woman *The Search for Signs of Intelligent Life in the Universe,* by Jane Wagner. Tomlin's character observation is deeper than ever and informed by touchingly rueful compassion, whether embodying a Manhattan bag lady or, in the evening's most extended sketch, a California woman whose life is emblematic of the 1960s and 70s. From England came Hugh Whitemore's *Pack of Lies,* about a woman's conflict between friendship and patriotic duty when she learns that the couple next door is suspected of being spies. David Wiltse's *Doubles,* about the ups and downs of four guys whose routine at a Connecticut health club remains the only consistent aspect of life, proved a solid commercial comedy.

BROADWAY OPENINGS | 1985

MUSICALS

Big River, music and lyrics by Roger Miller, book by William Hauptman; directed by Des McAnuff; with Daniel H. Jenkins, Ron Richardson, Rene Auberjonois, Bob Gunton; April 25–.

Grind, music by Larry Grossman, lyrics by Ellen Fitzhugh, book by Fay Kanin; directed by Harold Prince; with Ben Vereen, Stubby Kaye, Timothy Nolen, Leilani Jones; April 16–June 22.

Harrigan 'n Hart, music by Max Showalter, lyrics by Peter Walker, book by Michael Stewart; directed by Joe Layton; with Harry Groener, Mark Hamill; Jan. 31–Feb. 3.

Jerry's Girls, music from various Jerry Herman musicals; directed by Larry Alford; with Dorothy Loudon, Chita Rivera, Leslie Uggams; Dec. 18–.

The King and I, music by Richard Rodgers, book and lyrics by Oscar Hammerstein II, based on the Margaret Landon novel *Anna and the King of Siam;* directed by Mitch Leigh; with Yul Brynner, Mary Beth Peil; Jan. 7–June 30.

Leader of the Pack, music and lyrics by Ellie Greenwich and friends; liner notes by Anne Beatts, additional material by Jack Heifner, original concept by Melanie Mintz; directed and choreographed by Michael Peters; with Dinah Manoff, Patrick Cassidy, Darlene Love; April 8–July 21.

The Mystery of Edwin Drood, by Rupert Holmes, suggested by the novel by Charles Dickens; directed by Wilford Leach; with George Rose, Betty Buckley; Dec. 2–.

The News, music and lyrics by Paul Schierhorn; story by Mr. Schierhorn, David Rotenberg, and R. Vincent Park; directed by Mr. Rotenberg; with Frank Baier, Jeff Conaway; Nov. 7–9.

Singin' in the Rain, based on the M-G-M film, screenplay and adaptation, Betty Comden, Adolph Green; directed by Twyla Tharp; songs by Nacio Herb Brown, Arthur Freed; with Don Correia, Mary D'Arcy, Peter Slutsker; July 2–.

Song and Dance, music by Andrew Lloyd Webber; lyrics by Don Black; with Bernadette Peters, Christopher d'Amboise; Sept. 18–.

Take Me Along, music and lyrics by Bob Merrill; book by Joseph Stein and Robert Russell, based on the play *Ah, Wilderness!* by Eugene O'Neill; directed by Thomas Gruenewald; with Robert Nichols, Kurt Knudson, Beth Fowler; April 14.

Wind in the Willows, music by William Perry, lyrics by Mr. Perry and Roger McGough, book by Jane Iredale; directed by Edward Berkeley; with Vicki Lewis, David Carroll, Nathan Lane; Dec. 19–22.

PLAYS

Aren't We All?, by Frederick Lonsdale; directed by Clifford Williams; with Claudette Colbert, Rex Harrison, Lynn Redgrave, Jeremy Brett; April 29–July 21.

Arms and the Man, by George Bernard Shaw; directed by John Malkovich; with Kevin Kline, Glenne Headly; May 30–Sept. 1.

As Is, by William M. Hoffman; directed by Marshall W. Mason; with Jonathan Hogan, Jonathan Hadary; May 1–.

Benefactors, by Michael Frayn; directed by Michael Blakemore; with Sam Waterston, Glenn Close, Mary Beth Hurt, Simon Jones; Dec. 22–.

Biloxi Blues, by Neil Simon; directed by Gene Saks; with Brian Tarantina, Matthew Broderick, Barry Miller, Alan Ruck, Matt Mulhern, Bill Sadler, Geoffrey Sharp, Randall Edwards, Penelope Ann Miller; March 28–.

Blood Knot, written and directed by Athol Fugard; with Mr. Fugard, Zakes Mokae; Dec. 10–.

The Boys of Winter, by John Pielmeier; directed by Michael Lindsay-Hogg; with D. W. Moffett, Matt Dillon, Wesley Snipes, Tony Plana, Andrew McCarthy, Thomas Ikeda; Dec. 1–8.

Dancing in the End Zone, by Bill C. Davis; directed by Melvin Bernhardt; with Matt Salinger, Pat Carroll, Laurence Luckinbill, Dorothy Lyman; Jan. 3–26.

Doubles, by David Wiltse; directed by Morton Da Costa; with John Cullum, Ron Leibman, Austin Pendleton, Tony Roberts; May 8–.

Hay Fever, by Noël Coward; directed by Brian Murray; with Rosemary Harris, Roy Dotrice, Mia Dillon, Robert Joy; Dec. 12–.

Home Front, by James Duff; directed by Michael Attenborough; with Carroll O'Connor, Frances Sternhagen, Christopher Fields; Jan. 2–12.

The Iceman Cometh, by Eugene O'Neill; directed by José Quintero; with Barnard Hughes, Jason Robards, Donald Moffat; Sept. 29–Dec. 1.

I'm Not Rappaport, by Herb Gardner; directed by Dan Sullivan; with Judd Hirsch, Cleavon Little; Nov. 19–.

Joe Egg, by Peter Nichols; directed by Arvin Brown; with Jim Dale, Stockard Channing, Tenney Walsh, Joanna Gleason, John Tillinger, Margaret Holton; March 27–June 23.

The Loves of Anatol, adapted by Ellis Rabb and Nicholas Martin from the work by Arthur Schnitzler; directed by Mr. Rabb; with Philip Bosco, Stephen Collins, MaryJoan Negro; March 6–April 14.

The Marriage of Figaro, by Pierre Augustin Caron de Beaumarchais; directed by Andrei Serban; with Anthony Heald, Mary Elizabeth Mastrantonio, Dana Ivey, Christopher Reeve; Oct. 10–Dec. 15.

The Octette Bridge Club, by P. J. Barry; directed by Tom Moore; with Nancy Marchand, Elizabeth Franz, Peggy Cass, Gisela Caldwell, Elizabeth Huddle, Anne Pitoniak, Bette Henritze, Lois de Banzie, Nicholas Kaledin; March 5–23.

The Odd Couple, by Neil Simon; directed by Gene Saks; with Rita Moreno, Sally Struthers; June 11–.

Pack of Lies, by Hugh Whitemore; directed by Clifford Williams; with Patrick McGoohan, Rosemary Harris, George N. Martin; Feb. 11–May 25.

Requiem for a Heavyweight, by Rod Serling; directed by Arvin Brown; with John Lithgow, George Segal; March 7–9.

Strange Interlude, by Eugene O'Neill; directed by Keith Hack; with Glenda Jackson, Edward Petherbridge, Tim Aldredge, Brian Cox, James Hazeldine; Feb. 21–May 5.

Other Entertainment

The Search for Signs of Intelligent Life in the Universe, by Jane Wagner; production supervised by Charles Bowden; with Lily Tomlin; Sept. 26–.

Tango Argentino, conceived and directed by Claudio Segovia and Hector Orezzoli; Oct. 9–.

Herb Gardner's *I'm Not Rappaport* threw together in funny and sentimentally feisty fashion two old timers who regularly inhabit the same Central Park bench—Judd Hirsch as an old Jew whose social conscience will not retire, and Cleavon Little as a wary old black survivor.

Several of the Broadway failures were deserved. John Pielmeier's *The Boys of Winter* was filled with Vietnam and battlefield platitudes that a cast including teenage heartthrobs Matt Dillon and Andrew McCarthy could do nothing to salvage. James Duff's *Home Front* cast Carroll O'Connor as a Texan Archie Bunker whose resentment of his Vietnamveteran son's self-righteousness was not altogether unfounded. Similarly, the self-righteousness of the collegiate protagonist in Bill C. Davis' *Dancing in the End Zone,* who discovers moral impurity in athletics and quits his team on the eve of the big game, nullified that play's appeal.

But some of the failures deserved better. P. J. Barry's *The Octette Bridge Club,* which

originated at the Actors Theatre in Louisville, was only mildly eventful, dealing with the lives of eight grown Catholic sisters who meet monthly to play bridge in their Rhode Island town; but it was an enjoyable vehicle for such veterans as Nancy Marchand, Peggy Cass, Bette Henritze, and Anne Pitoniak. And Rod Serling's *Requiem for a Heavyweight,* made famous as a 1962 film starring Anthony Quinn, was all anyone could ask, carried by John Lithgow's admirable pug and George Segal's venal manager.

Perhaps *Requiem for a Heavyweight* would have fared better if it had been advertised as a revival and aroused different expectations. Certainly Broadway's growing role as a dramatic museum was inescapable in 1985. Eugene O'Neill, America's play-writing giant, in fact had two revivals during the year: *Strange Interlude* and *The Iceman Cometh.* The first was an English import starring Glenda Jackson as the bitch-goddess Nina Leeds, who leads the others in speaking their thoughts not from behind masks, as O'Neill prescribed, but as asides. This minimized the rough edges and dated aspects of the dialogue and turned O'Neill's unwieldy yet deeply felt experiment into something of a drawing-room comedy, with agony replaced by irony. *The Iceman Cometh,* with Jason Robards in the lead role of Hickey, the character bent on stripping the illusions of a stage full of barflies, was quite simply the dramatic peak of the Broadway year. Jose Quintero's staging—his patient building of atmosphere and refusal ever to patronize O'Neill's sometimes clumsy, slang-ridden lingo —paid off magnificently. The play came from the new American National Theatre at Wash-

The American Repertory Theatre in Cambridge, MA, staged Pirandello's "Six Characters in Search of an Author."

© Richard Feldman

ington's Kennedy Center, but its commercial failure cast a dark shadow over the possibility of further distinguished revivals appearing on Broadway.

From Yale University came another season high, a revival of Athol Fugard's *The Blood Knot,* with the playwright and Zakes Moake as two brothers—one white, the other black— whose impossible predicament remains an aching metaphor for South Africa. The saucy candor behind Noel Coward's wit found triumphant expression in a revival of *Hay Fever,* starring Rosemary Harris as the grande dame of a family whose stagy egocentricity drives weekend guests mad. Frederick Lonsdale's *Aren't We All?,* an even older country-weekend comedy, proved an agreeably light-handed returnee, too, with a cast headed by Rex Harrison and Claudette Colbert. Neil Simon's *The Odd Couple* came back in a gender-switch revival headed by Rita Moreno and Sally Struthers. Peter Nichols' *Joe Egg,* about a couple pretending that their handicapped child is not ripping their marriage apart, was affectingly reprised by Stockard Channing and Jim Dale.

And then there were the annual revivals at the Circle in the Square. Anatol Schnitzler's *The Loves of Anatol* was lumpish, and Beaumarchais' *Marriage of Figaro* seemed gimmicky. Shaw's *Arms and the Man,* with Raul Julia and Kevin Kline, was the Circle's most accomplished offering, making the comedy work simply by presenting it straightforwardly.

The latter production was directed by John Malkovich, whose presence reflected Chicago's growing influence on the New York theater scene. Malkovich and Gary Sinise brought the Steppenwolf Theater production of Sam Shepard's *True West* to New York, and the Steppenwolf presented another new play off-Broadway, Lyle Kessler's *Orphans,* a powerful Pinter-like exercise about three criminals locked in a house in Philadelphia. The Steppenwolf's visceral style won it a special Tony.

The year also saw increased recognition for the American Repertory Theatre (ART) of Cambridge, MA. *Big River* originated at the ART, which regularly stages premieres by such avant-garde mainstays as Robert Wilson and Philip Glass. ART artistic director Robert Brustein's staging of Pirandello's *Six Characters in Search of an Author* was a 1985 dramatic high. On balance, however, it was Chicago's year. The season closed with the news that another Chicago director, Gregory Mosher of the Goodman Theater, would try to rejuvenate Lincoln Center's troubled Vivian Beaumont Theatre. As the year ended, Mosher was preparing to open two new plays by David Mamet, whose Pulitzer Prize–winning *Glengarry Glen Ross* he brought to New York in 1984.

JAY CARR
Critic-at-Large, "The Boston Globe"

Various Third World leaders—including Argentina's President Raúl Alfonsín (second from left), Tanzania's President Julius Nyerere (second from right), and India's Prime Minister Rajiv Gandhi (right)—met in Delhi, India, in January. The leaders called for a halt to the testing of nuclear weapons and a ban on the development of space weapons.

AP/Wide World

THIRD WORLD

Amid mounting protectionism in industrialized nations, the United States took the lead in devising means to spur economic advancement in less-developed countries (LDCs) beset by huge foreign debts.

International Debt. Leaders of the world's developing nations, which by the end of 1985 collectively owed international banks and lending agencies nearly $1 trillion, listened attentively to proposals to lighten their burdens. Brazil's former Finance Minister Celso Furtado championed joint action through a "debtors' cartel"; Peruvian President Alan García Pérez advocated limiting debt repayment to 10% of a country's export earnings; and Cuban President Fidel Castro urged repudiation of "illegitimate" external obligations. Complementing these ideas was stinging criticism of the belt-tightening plans required before the International Monetary Fund (IMF) dispenses short- and medium-term credits.

Recognizing that default by a major debtor would jolt, if not topple, the world's financial system, U.S. Treasury Secretary James A. Baker III backed a shift from quick fixes to long-range development of Third World economies. Announced at the annual IMF–World Bank meeting in Seoul, South Korea, in October, the U.S. initiative called for a three-year infusion of $29 billion in new loans, of which $9 billion would come from the World Bank and $20 billion from commercial banks.

The Multilateral Investment Guarantee Agency (MIGA), set up by the World Bank in September, was intended to help overcome the private bankers' reluctance to extend fresh credit. The MIGA would protect investments against contingencies beyond ordinary business failure: government expropriation, inconvertibility of funds into hard currencies for repatriation, breach of contract without effective recourse, and civil unrest or war.

As evidenced by an August general strike in Argentina to protest austerity measures, continued insistence on IMF-style stabilization schemes poses a threat to fragile democracies. An emphasis on increased monies for long-term growth was the hoped-for approach of the next World Bank president, to succeed A.W. Clausen. In October 1985, Clausen announced that he would step down at the end of his term the following July.

Oil Prices and Protectionism. Sagging oil prices throughout the year cheered heavy energy importers—such as Argentina, Brazil, India, and Pakistan—which form a vast majority of LDCs. But the decline imperiled the economic recuperation of such key petroleum-exporting states as Algeria, Indonesia, Iran, Nigeria, Venezuela, and Mexico. In particular, diminished oil earnings complicate efforts to rebuild the portions of Mexico City devastated by two September earthquakes.

Uniformly upsetting to the Third World was the escalating mood of protectionism in the United States, especially regarding the textile industry. U.S. imports of fabrics and clothes, largely from LDCs, doubled between 1976 and 1984. A protectionist textile bill passed the House of Representatives (262 to 159) in October, and some 200 parallel measures had been proposed.

Women's Conference. Representatives of 159 nations traveled to Nairobi, Kenya, in July to attend the UN Decade for Women Conference. Many of the 350 proposals approved at the meeting focused on the developing world. Among these were demands for equal employment, sharing of household work and child care, expanded participation by women in local and national government, and relieving the burden on women of the task of fetching water.

See also articles on individual countries; INTERNATIONAL TRADE AND FINANCE.

GEORGE W. GRAYSON
College of William & Mary

TRANSPORTATION

A relatively robust national economy was no assurance of palmy days for the U.S. transportation industries in 1985. The one bright spot for all transportation companies was the continuing decline in oil prices, which translated into lower costs for both aviation fuel and the diesel fuel used by trucks and railroads. The continuation of the structural shift toward a service-based economy gave a boost to transport sectors, particularly passenger airlines, susceptible to the same cycles as other industries dependent on personal consumption. With intercity bus lines continuing to lose traffic to cut-rate airlines, Greyhound decided it would rather switch than fight and began hauling passengers to airports to catch cheap flights.

Intense price competition in the recently deregulated transportation industries helped depress profits and added further pressure to reduce costs. Cost cutters' prime target was, once again, the industries' big bill for wages and benefits. The efforts met with mixed success, at least partially because industrial workers have been resisting concessions more strongly since the end of the recession.

Tiger International, representing the first ambitious effort at creating a one-stop transportation supermarket—with disastrous results—continued shedding trucking and railcar acquisitions. By year's end it was once again fully dependent on its original air cargo business. There its mainstay Pacific traffic was under attack from newcomer Nippon Cargo Airlines, whose 19 owners controlled the bulk of Japanese air cargo shipments.

Tiger's experience notwithstanding, the year saw an acceleration in the growth of multimodal transportation companies. The U.S. Interstate Commerce Commission (ICC) approved the acquisition of North American Van Lines from PepsiCo by Norfolk-Southern Corporation, which already owned 17.6% of Piedmont Aviation. The holding company for the Burlington Northern railroad bought a clutch of smaller truckers. United Airlines bought rental car giant Hertz Corporation from RCA, and both United and Northwest Airlines got into the tour business.

Consolidation within modes of transport continued as well. Citing competitive problems, the ICC gave the nod to a $570 million offer from the Soo Line to acquire the 3,100 mi (5 000 km) core of the bankrupt Milwaukee Road over a $787 million bid from Chicago & Northwestern Transportation Company. The ICC also concluded hearings on the merger of the Santa Fe and Southern Pacific railroads; it was expected to approve the combination early in 1986, with some restrictions. Justice Department objections notwithstanding, United Airlines struck a deal to buy Pan American World Airways' Pacific division for $900 million, but

Texas Air Corporation's bid to become the nation's third-largest airline company by adding Trans World Airlines (TWA) to its Continental Airlines and New York Air units was defeated. TWA was acquired instead by corporate raider Carl C. Icahn.

Airlines. The airline industry in 1985 will be remembered for a string of disastrous accidents, accelerating consolidation of airline companies, new deep discounts that sent traffic soaring, and labor unrest.

The year began inauspiciously with the crash of an Eastern Airlines jetliner in Peru just three hours into the new year. The hijacking of a TWA plane from Athens; terrorist attacks against airline offices in Madrid, Frankfurt, and elsewhere; the mysterious explosion of an Air India Boeing 747 jumbo jet over the Atlantic Ocean south of Ireland; the fire in a Pratt & Whitney engine that consumed a British tour operator's Boeing 737 in Manchester, England; the crash of a Japan Air Lines Boeing 747 in Japan; several commuter airline accidents; and other incidents made 1985 the worst year ever for airline safety. The U.S. Federal Aviation Administration (FAA) came under scathing attack for its record of monitoring airline safety practices. Its levying of a $1.5 million fine against American Airlines in September for poor maintenance practices associated with the big carrier's rapid expansion did little to mollify the agency's critics. Legislators, airlines, and others also assailed the FAA's inadequate management of the nation's air traffic control system. Late in the year, U.S. carriers proposed a federal corporation to take over from the FAA the running and financing of air traffic control.

Takeover fever hit the airline industry after the United Airlines–Pan Am deal in April. Next up for a change in ownership was TWA. Investor Carl C. Icahn opened the bidding in May and was soon joined by Texas Air and casino-operator Resorts International. It looked like Texas Air would win the battle until TWA's unions promised big wage concessions to Icahn in return for his reentering the fray to save them from Texas Air President Frank Lorenzo, an arch foe of airline labor. Fast-growing Southwest Airlines Company bought Muse Air Corporation. Piedmont struck a deal to buy Empire Airlines, a small jet operator in upstate New York, and People Express agreed to purchase Denver-based Frontier Airlines. Late in the year Ozark Airlines was known to be on the block. Consolidation among smaller carriers accelerated as more commuter airlines allied themselves with large operators and in some cases—including USAir's purchase of Pennsylvania Airlines and Republic Airlines' acquisition of a piece of Simmons Airlines—sold out to them.

American Airlines dreamed up the "ultimate supersaver" fare—a deep discount with

stringent advance-purchase restrictions and cancellation penalties—to grab back leisure traffic from discount airlines. Quickly adapted by other carriers, the "ultimate supersaver" expanded the travel market and helped push traffic up more than 12% through August. With effective cost controls, most carriers posted record profits through midyear, but expansion, fare slashing, and softening traffic in the fall made it doubtful that they would be able to say the same at year's end. And although it was another banner year for travel to Europe, poor management and inability to control discounts at Pan Am and TWA, the two biggest U.S. carriers across the Atlantic, left them in red ink.

Airline labor rates in 1984 were lower than the previous year for the first time ever. But employee distrust of management's profit projections, among other factors, led to month-long strikes in the first half of 1985 by the Transport Workers Union at Pan Am, the International Association of Machinists at Alaska Airlines, and the Air Line Pilots Association at United Airlines.

Trucking. It was no banner year for U.S. trucking. Inventory adjustments, particularly inventory liquidation among retailers, coupled with very small gains in industrial production kept tonnage from rising much more than 2%. Increases in less-than-truckload shipments were offset by continuing weakness in truckload freight, a segment of the industry under attack from nonunion operators.

With not much optimism about tonnage growth, rates and costs held an even bigger key to future profitability. Weak traffic made it unlikely that a 3% across-the-board rate increase on July 1 would stick. But a new national contract with the International Brotherhood of Teamsters, allowing lower rates for new employees and making it tougher for unionized lines to form new nonunion subsidiaries—a practice known as "double breasting"—should help truckers' profits. Truck lines held wage-and-benefit hikes in the new three-year contract to about 9%, a rate of increase that should slow the loss of business to nonunion haulers. With nearly one third of its 300,000 truckdriver members out of work, the Teamsters gave work-rule concessions that should offset much of the increase. Similar changes have cut payroll costs an average 1% annually at companies that got concessions in side deals with the Teamsters since 1982.

Skyrocketing insurance rates are a growing worry for truck lines. Larger carriers saw rates rise 30%–40% in 1985 and expected the same in 1986. Smaller lines, which are not self-insured, could be squeezed out of business altogether by rate hikes of 200% and more.

The Reagan administration in 1985 submitted legislation to complete trucking deregulation by removing all controls on rates and entry, but Congress did not take up the issue.

Some $7 billion for the Highway Trust Fund, authorized in 1984, was finally freed for spending. Squabbles over the pet projects of certain congressmen had held up its disbursement. More than 40 states had used money from general funds to finance road construction before they were able to pressure Congress into disbursing the Highway Trust money.

Railroads. The stories of the year for U.S. railroads were the Reagan administration's effort to eliminate subsidies for Amtrak (*see* special report, page 520) and the government's failure to sell its 85% stake in Conrail. In the dealings over Conrail (a freight carrier), the Transportation Department endorsed a $1.2 billion offer from Norfolk Southern. But that deal was stymied by a proposal from investment banker Morgan Stanley & Company, which put together a syndicate to buy Washington's share and resell it to the public. In September, Norfolk Southern loosened its restrictions on granting trackage rights to competitors after a merger, a move seen as increasing its chances of winning Conrail.

Legislation to increase the ICC's role in railroad rate making, introduced in the spring, was expected to be acted on in 1986. Shippers who lost the ability to bring antitrust actions against railroads over ICC-approved rates in the 1920s thus made progress in winning back that right. They argued that they effectively have had no antitrust protection because the ICC has been all but out of the rate-making business.

Slim to no increases in industrial production hurt railroad profits in 1985. Despite extensive cost-control programs, rail company earnings were down 24.5% in the first half. With oil, wheat, copper, and other basic commodities in excess supply, railroad carloadings were off 6% through mid-September. The biggest drop —20.8%—was in grain loadings. The only bright spot was shipments of motor vehicles and related equipment, up 6.6%.

The United Transportation Union rejected a new contract in August, largely over the old issue of abolition of the fireman's job—even though the last coal-fired locomotive was retired decades ago. A later compromise allowed for elimination of the job by attrition.

Shipping. In another poor year for the U.S. maritime industry, excess capacity and slow tonnage growth led to massive rate cutting, even in the long-profitable Pacific trade. And with new liners scheduled to add to capacity through 1986, the outlook was for the situation to get worse. The Shipping Act of 1984, intended to revitalize the U.S. Merchant Marine by granting some freedom in rate setting and routes served, instead aggravated the plight of shipping lines by giving customers more leverage in winning low rates during hard times.

REGGI ANN DUBIN
Transportation Consultant

The U.S. Passenger Railroad

Jose R. Lopez, NYT Pictures

The 20,000 intercity passenger trains that thundered over the railroads of the United States scarcely half a century ago now have dwindled to about 250. These doughty survivors of a bygone era wear the red, white, and blue livery of the National Railroad Passenger Corporation, better known as Amtrak. While they are only distant relations of such glamorous all-Pullman trains of the past as the New York–Chicago "Twentieth Century Limited" and the Los Angeles–Chicago "Super Chief," they nonetheless provide efficient, all-weather service to 510 towns and cities. Some of Amtrak's trains—for example, the premium-fare 120-mph (193-km/h) "Metroliner" between Washington and New York and the double-deck "Empire Builder" that links Chicago and Seattle—stand proud among the world's premier passenger trains.

But Amtrak's trains operate with a heavy federal subsidy, which has been as high as $900 million a year. They carry only about 20 million passengers a year, about half of the number carried by United Airlines, the nation's largest air carrier, or by the Greyhound Corp., the busiest bus line.

When David Stockman, then director of the Office of Management and Budget (OMB), was searching for ways to reduce the federal budget late in 1984, Amtrak must have looked like an easy target—a costly anachronism preserved for a handful of die-hard train buffs. President Reagan enthusiastically accepted Stockman's recommendation that the new federal budget eliminate Amtrak's subsidy, which was $684 million for fiscal year 1985. Less enthusiastic about zero-budgeting Amtrak was Secretary of Transportation Elizabeth Hanford Dole, who in closed-door White House councils pleaded for a reprieve. She was unsuccessful, and it fell to her lot to announce, early in 1985: "At a time when deficit reduction is our highest national priority, we can no longer afford to provide railroad subsidies that primarily benefit passengers in the middle- and upper-income brackets." She also dutifully reported Stockman's finding that every time a passenger boarded an Amtrak train, it cost U.S. taxpayers $35.

As it turned out, OMB Director Stockman and President Reagan were dead wrong in assessing the mood of the country with respect to passenger trains, and Mrs. Dole was right. On Oct. 1, 1985, the first day of the new fiscal year—a day when Amtrak President W. Graham Claytor, Jr., had warned that he might have to close down the railroad—all of Amtrak's trains were still running.

The successful battle that Amtrak partisans waged in the intervening months illuminated the role that passenger trains still perform in space-age America; if anything, it strengthened the affectionate ties that Americans maintain with trains, even those Americans who seldom, if ever, ride those trains. The Amtrak "lobby," which quickly spread from the

grass roots to the halls of Congress, immediately attacked the two linchpin arguments of the anti-Amtrak faction. Without disputing the $35-a-head subsidy that Stockman said Amtrak required, they were able to establish, to the satisfaction of most members of Congress, that airline passengers were enjoying nearly the same amount of federal largess in the form of hidden subsidies.

The Passenger. As for Amtrak passengers representing a relatively affluent slice of society, studies were trotted out suggesting that the reverse was the case. In a comparison of railroad, airline, and private-automobile travelers, Amtrak riders came out at the bottom of the income heap: 14% had total family incomes of less than $10,000 a year; 26% were in the $10,000–$20,000 range; 22%, $20,000–$30,000; and 38%, more than $30,000.

Why do people ride trains? Amtrak's own study showed that 37.1% were visiting family or friends, 24.1% were on vacation, 14.8% were on business trips, 13.7% were commuting to or from work, 7.6% were on personal business, and 2.7% were traveling to or from school.

Amtrak also found out that more than one third of its long-haul riders were 55 or older and more than one fifth were at least 65.

While conceding that it carried only a fraction of all U.S. intercity travelers, Amtrak scored a telling point by informing Congress that in the congested Washington–New York portion of the Northeast Corridor, whose skies have hardly room for one more airplane, Amtrak has been carrying 46% more people than all of the airlines combined.

Subsidy. Amtrak President Claytor, who is widely respected as the former head of the Southern Railway, one of the world's most profitable freight railroads, and as a former secretary of the Navy, had other arguments that helped carry the day in Congress. He pointed out that Amtrak in 1985 was covering 58% of its costs out of revenues, against 56% in 1984

and 54% in 1983. As a result, he said, Amtrak's federal subsidy in constant dollars had dropped by nearly $400 million from its peak. In 1986, Amtrak expects revenues to meet 60% of its costs.

With a loss of its federal subsidy, Claytor argued, Amtrak would not only have to halt 250 daily trains serving communities in 44 states, including some communities not served by any other passenger common carrier; it also would have to scrap $3 billion worth of passenger equipment, facilities, and tracks for about ten cents on the dollar; it would have to deprive 25,000 people of jobs; and the federal government would become liable for the payment of $2.1 billion in labor protection payments.

Claytor emphasized that the proposed elimination of the Amtrak subsidy differed from other deficit-reducing proposals in one important aspect: "Most of the other cuts simply suspend programs, or hold the line until, perhaps at some future time, they can be restored or expanded. But with Amtrak the whole investment and the entire operation is eliminated once and for all. This is an irreversible decision. We would never be able to bring passenger service back again."

Congress did not make that irreversible decision, and Amtrak emerged from the budget battle of 1985 a little leaner but with its train operations intact. While the new budget of about $616 million would require deferral of certain capital improvements, a reduction in nonsafety-related maintenance, and reduced service on some major routes, the basic Amtrak system was unchanged. That system includes trains that operate over about 24,000 route miles (38 600 km) of track. (The only track owned outright by Amtrak is that in the Northeast Corridor; elsewhere, its trains run over the lines of freight railroads.) Amtrak's operating fleet as fiscal 1985 began was 284 locomotives and 1,741 railcars.

LUTHER S. MILLER

TRAVEL

The great American exodus continued in 1985 as U.S. travelers once again headed for foreign destinations in record numbers. It seemed there was just no keeping Americans at home, for they were rediscovering their own country along with overseas ports. What kept the mood from being totally optimistic was the intrusion of a new travel reality: travelers are easy targets for political terrorists worldwide. Security became *the* top issue within the travel industry.

All the same, Americans did not hesitate to take advantage of a strong U.S. dollar by traveling abroad. The final tally was expected to

show that nearly 13 million Americans had gone overseas by year's end, a jump of 10% over the previous year. Close to 5 million people applied for U.S. passports during the government's fiscal year ending September 30, an increase of 9% over 1984 and another record.

Europe was again the destination of choice, attracting an estimated 6.6 million U.S. travelers—15% more than the year before. Low-priced travel packages and attractive exchange rates kept America's love affair with Europe going strong, and even the first signs of an anticipated drop in the value of the dollar did not seem to be a deterrent. Furthermore, what was once a strongly seasonal destination was becoming a year-round one, as roughly 40% of

Europe's American visitors chose the "off-season" months of October to March for their trips.

In addition, some 12 million Americans visited Canada during the year, an increase of 3%. But Mexico, with an expected final count of under 4 million American visitors, registered a 4% decrease. Mexico's devastating September earthquakes discouraged some travelers, though an immediate 30% drop in tourists to Mexico was soon reversed.

Concerns about personal safety made Americans think twice about some destinations. Dramatic terrorist hijackings in the eastern Mediterranean of both a TWA jetliner and an Italian cruise ship carrying many American passengers cast a cloud over the region—and perhaps changed the complexion of leisure travel forever. Airlines and cruise lines alike were faced with the necessity of developing new approaches of security, and the idea of travel as a carefree escape may never be quite the same again.

For the airline industry, 1985 proved to be a year of economic stability despite a series of air disasters worldwide that made flight safety another prominent topic of concern for travelers. U.S. air carriers toted up healthy passenger loads for the year, and travelers continued to benefit from competitive fares.

U.S. Travel. After concentrating on previously postponed purchases like automobiles for a couple of years, Americans now seemed to feel economically secure enough to spend money on travel. In 1985 they were going farther and staying longer as they traveled around their own country.

Amtrak reported a record year in revenue and its second-best ridership figures ever, topped only by the gasoline-problem year of 1980. Final figures were expected to show some 20.9 million Amtrak passengers for the fiscal year ending in October, and the usual dropoff in riders after Labor Day just did not materialize. Similarly, the American Automobile Association received 8% more requests for trip routings and other services.

Foreign tourism to the United States regained ground lost in 1984, with 21.7 million arrivals representing a 4% increase from the previous year and a return to 1983 levels. Half of the total foreign visitors came from Canada. One of the strongest areas of growth was Asia, which sent nearly 2.5 million visitors to the United States, a 9% increase. Some 1.5 million of those came from Japan (6% more than in 1984), and their choice of Hawaii as a favorite destination was a significant factor in helping the islands show an overall increase in tourists for the year despite a July strike by United Airlines pilots that put a big dent in airline capacity from the mainland. Amtrak also reported substantial growth in rail passengers from Asian countries besides Japan.

Cruising. More Americans than ever before set sail on cruise ships, continuing a pattern that has resulted in 300% growth in the cruise industry in North America since 1970. It was estimated that 1.8 million North Americans would be counted as cruise passengers by year's end, a 12.5% increase over the previous year. Californians accounted for nearly 20% of these sailors.

With a number of new ships intensifying the competition for passengers, travelers found themselves lured seaward in new ways. Expanding on the popular "theme cruise" idea of the past several years, cruise lines brought top name personalities on board to serve as lecturers on all sorts of topics from wine to history. Passengers could come face to face with household names in broadcasting, politics, and entertainment, all serving as shipboard experts. Well-known astronomers were lined up to star aboard Halley's Comet cruises starting late in the year and continuing in 1986, positioning passengers for good views of the celestial performance.

This was all part of a movement toward enhancing the cruise product itself rather than cutting prices to win passengers. Instead of dollar discounts, extras ranging from mink coats to free shore excursions might be had on various cruises. Nonetheless, free airfare had become almost standard for cruises departing domestic ports, and many overseas programs also included it. And promotional fares could still be found in the highly competitive cruising arena of the Caribbean.

Several new cruise ships made their maiden voyages during 1985, among them Carnival Cruise Lines' 1,450-passenger *Holiday,* Costa Cruises' 1,100-passenger *CostaRiviera,* Regency Cruises' 708-passenger *Regency,* Sea Goddess Cruises' 120-passenger *Sea Goddess II,* and Sundance Cruises' 990-passenger *Stardancer.* U.S.-registered American Hawaii Cruises expanded beyond what its name would indicate with the December introduction of French Polynesia cruises aboard the 715-passenger *Liberté.*

Trends. The computer, now firmly established as a necessary component of the travel industry for transportation services and travel agencies, moved increasingly into use by individual travelers. Personal computers were used by more and more people in their own homes to obtain travel information and to use data base resource services to benefit from other travelers' experiences.

In contrast, and perhaps as a reaction to the increasing technological orientation of modern life, adventure travel continued to grow in popularity. Adventure touring specialists took Americans on touch-the-earth journeys that ran the gamut from rugged mountaineering experiences to easy floats on lazy rivers.

PHYLLIS ELVING, *Free-lance Travel Writer*

TUNISIA

The year 1985 was fraught with tension for the government of President Habib Bourguiba. Relations with the powerful General Union of Tunisian Workers (UGTT) deteriorated after the midyear collapse of wage negotiations. Conflict with Libya intensified in August as Col. Muammar el-Qaddafi expelled 30,000 Tunisian migrant workers. A few weeks later, an Israeli raid on Palestine Liberation Organization (PLO) headquarters in Tunis seriously strained the traditionally close relations between Tunisia and the United States.

Foreign Relations. Libya's expulsion of Tunisian workers began early in the year, reaching a peak in late August. Approximately one third of the more than 90,000 Tunisians working in Libya were ordered to leave the country. The returning migrants reported that their bank accounts had been frozen and their property confiscated in Libya. Many said they had been detained, denied food, or tortured after rejecting Libyan offers of Arab citizenship.

When Libyan fighter planes flew into southern Tunisia, Bourguiba ordered a military alert and eventually deported more than 280 Libans, including four diplomats accused of mailing letter bombs to local journalists. In late September, Bourguiba severed diplomatic ties with Libya. In response to the crisis, Algeria expressed solidarity with Tunisia. The United States reiterated a pledge, made during Bourguiba's June visit to Washington, DC, to defend Tunisia's security and territorial integrity.

Only days later, Tunisians were questioning the U.S. commitment to the pledge in light of a White House statement condoning the Israeli bombing of PLO headquarters. The raid provoked anti-American and anti-Israel reactions in Tunis. In an effort to mend the rift, the Reagan administration toned down the official statement and praised Tunisia for encouraging peace in the Middle East.

Labor Relations and Politics. A series of labor strikes early in the year culminated in a

---

TUNISIA • Information Highlights

Official Name: Republic of Tunisia.
Location: North Africa.
Area: 63,170 sq mi (163 610 km²).
Population (mid-1985 est.): 7,200,000.
Chief City (1984 census): Tunis, the capital, 596,654.
Government: *Head of state,* Habib Bourguiba, president for life (took office 1957). *Chief minister,* Mohamed Mzali, prime minister (took office April 1980). *Legislature* (unicameral)—National Assembly.
Monetary Unit: Dinar (.824 dinar equals U.S.$1, July 1985).
Gross National Product (1984 U.S.$): $8,300,-000,000.
Economic Indexes (1984): *Consumer Prices* (1977 = 100), all items, 182.6; food, 191.3. *Industrial Production* (1983, 1980 = 100), 112.
Foreign Trade (1984 U.S.$): *Imports,* $3,171,000,000; *exports,* $1,793,000,000.

UGTT boycott in May of municipal elections. Opposition parties also refused to participate, citing a lack of guarantees that the elections would be fair. Salary negotiations reached an impasse in June. The government held that wage rises should be linked to increased productivity, while the UGTT insisted that they should be indexed to the cost of living. Prime Minister Mohamed Mzali accused UGTT Secretary-General Habib Achour of collusion with Libya after a UGTT strike coincided with the start of the expulsions from Libya. A few weeks later, the government closed down the union's headquarters and took over its regional offices, arousing fears for the UGTT's autonomy. The crisis peaked in November, when the government placed Achour under house arrest, accusing him of seeking violent confrontations to deflect attention from mismanagement in the union.

The aging Bourguiba reconfirmed before the ruling Destour Socialist Party in March that Prime Minister Mohamed Mzali was his designated successor. Strong criticism of the administration's policies, especially its pro-U.S. stance, weakened Mzali's standing, however, and he began meeting with opposition leaders.

The Economy. A good rainfall produced record crops, and growth was recorded in tourism, light manufacturing, and construction, but inflation and unemployment remained high. Heavy debt service payments and the rising trade deficit forced Mzali to order that budget expenditures be frozen in 1986. Parliament continued efforts to privatize public enterprises, which suffer from management problems and chronic deficits.

PAULA M. HIRSCHOFF, *"Africa Report"*

TURKEY

The year 1985 was generally quiet politically in Turkey. The government of Prime Minister Turgut Ozal, elected in 1983, continued with only minor cabinet changes. In August a pending merger was announced between the Populist Party, which holds 113 Assembly seats, and the Social Democrat Party, which had not run in the parliamentary election of 1983 but had done well in the 1984 local elections. The proposed political merger was regarded as a move to prepare for the next national election, constitutionally scheduled for no later than 1988.

With regard to internal security, trials of accused separatists and terrorists continued. More than 100 Kurds were convicted in January, and the government acknowledged that some 7,000 to 8,000 persons were still in prison on political charges stemming from the crises that led to the military intervention of 1980–83. The security situation was deemed good enough, however, to lift martial law in March

---

TURKEY · Information Highlights

Official Name: Republic of Turkey.
Location: Southeastern Europe and southwestern Asia.
Area: 301,381 sq mi (780 576 km²).
Population (mid-1985 est.): 52,100,000.
Chief Cities (1980 census): Ankara, the capital, 1,877,755; Istanbul, 2,772,708; Izmir, 757,854.
Government: *Head of state*, Gen. Kenan Evren, president (took office Nov. 10, 1982). *Head of government*, Turgut Ozal, prime minister (took office Dec. 13, 1983). *Legislature*—Grand National Assembly.
Monetary Unit: Lira (547.9 liras equal U.S. $1, Oct. 23, 1985).
Gross National Product (1983 U.S.$): $51,000,-000,000.
Economic Index (1984): *Consumer Prices* (1982 = 100), all items, 195.0; food, 246.2.
Foreign Trade (Ankara, 1984 U.S.$): *Imports,* $10,822,000,000; *exports,* $7,086,000,000.

---

in an additional 11 provinces. Martial law was removed in six more provinces in July—including Ankara and Izmir—leaving only 17 of the nation's 63 provinces under military jurisdiction.

Economic Affairs. The economy continued to be a subject of major attention. At midyear, inflation had been brought down to 40%, and exports in 1984 rose significantly over the 1983 level. Of the total exports, 52% were to countries in the Organization for Economic Cooperation and Development (OECD), 41% to Islamic nations, and 4.6% to the Eastern bloc. The good progress toward economic recovery again brought Turkey several large World Bank credits and a declaration by OECD officials that Turkey "no longer needs first aid."

Several steps were taken toward continued liberalization of the economy. Measures were announced to ease restrictions on foreign investment and to abolish some state monopolies. Legislation was also enacted to create several free-trade zones. In the area of large-scale development, public sale of shares for an additional large Keban dam was begun, and the foundation for a second bridge across the Bosphorus (to be named the Fatih Sultan Mehmed Bridge) was laid. Ground was broken for an airplane engine factory near Eskisehir and for three new hydroelectric dams in Erzurum, Agri, and Samsun. Canadian and Turkish government representatives signed a preliminary agreement to build a nuclear power plant near Mersin. Costs of the plant were estimated at $1.3 billion, and it was planned for completion in 1991. The government announced that 41 new oil exploration licenses had been issued in the first half of 1985, compared with 25 licenses in all of 1984.

During 1985 the Turkish government signed trade and cooperation protocols with Japan, China, India, Saudi Arabia, Morocco, Romania, Czechoslovakia, West Germany, Austria, the United States, and others.

Foreign Affairs. During 1985, Prime Minister Ozal paid a state visit to the United States, where new agreements for military and economic aid were negotiated and the U.S.-Turkish bases agreement was renewed. The prime minister also visited China, where agreements were signed for large trade increases and cultural exchange. As a result of the visit, the first Chinese consulate in Istanbul was opened. Official visits also were made by Ozal to Japan, West Germany, and Saudi Arabia, and President Kenan Evren visited Romania. Foreign officials who made state visits to Turkey included Egyptian President Hosni Mubarak, German Chancellor Helmut Kohl, and Indonesian President Suharto. A Turkish parliamentary delegation traveled to the USSR.

There was little change in the stalemated Cyprus situation, despite some attempts by United Nations officials to ease tensions on that divided island. One result of the lack of progress was that the Turkish Republic of Northern Cyprus—which had declared its independence in 1983—moved to consolidate its position by promulgating a new constitution. Little progress was noted in easing tensions with Greece over problems in the Aegean.

Turkish diplomatic establishments abroad continued to be targets of terrorist groups. In March a group of Armenians took several hostages at the Turkish Embassy in Ottawa, Canada. Before the attackers were finally subdued by Canadian police, a Canadian security guard was killed.

A major dispute flared with Bulgaria over its insistence that the estimated 900,000 ethnic Turks living in Bulgaria take Slavic family names. Violent resistance reportedly occurred, and throughout 1985, Turkey attempted to bring the situation to the attention of world public opinion and to pressure Bulgaria to reverse its policy. Toward the end of 1985, however, there were no signs that Bulgaria's policy had altered, and tensions remained high.

Other Matters. An unusually large number of archaeological sites were active in Turkey in 1985. Restoration work on rock mural paintings in Goreme (Cappadocia) was begun in cooperation with UNESCO. A commemoration was held in conjunction with the 70th anniversary of the Allied landings in Gallipoli during World War I. Deaths in 1985 included Afet Inan, the adopted daughter of Ataturk.

WALTER F. WEIKER
Rutgers—The State University of New Jersey

UGANDA

A sudden military coup d'état and continued civil violence during 1985 highlighted the year in Uganda.

Military Takeover. After years of mounting violence and civil disorder, the Uganda army

Lt. Gen. Tito Okello (center) was named chairman of the military council that took the reins of power in Uganda after the July 27 overthrow of President Milton Obote and his civilian government. The coup was commanded by Brig. Basilio Olara Okello (right), no relation.

AP/Wide World

staged a coup d'état on July 27, overthrowing the regime of President Milton Obote. The immediate cause of the revolt was the rivalry within the army of the Lango and Acholi tribes. President Obote, a Lango, had been promoting his kinsmen to high office in the armed forces and the Acholi officers resented this. Deeper causes of the revolt included the allegedly fraudulent 1980 election that brought Obote to power, his often-brutal crackdown on opposition, and the continued violence that has seen 300,000 Ugandans killed since 1980.

After the coup, Obote and his family fled to Kenya. Massive looting immediately broke out in Kampala, with soldiers as well as civilians and common criminals all taking part. Obote's hometown of Lira was virtually destroyed by gangs of pro- and anti-coup soldiers and civilians. The town's 20,000 inhabitants fled into the bush.

New Government. The leader of the coup was Brig. Basilio Okello, an Acholi and commander of the army's northern brigade. The rebels formed a Military Council, which named 71-year-old Lt. Gen. Tito Okello (no relation) as head of state. Obote's vice-president, Paulo Muwanga, was initially named prime minister but was dismissed in late August. Muwanga was replaced by Abraham Waligo, the former finance minister. The leader of the opposition Democratic Party, Paul Ssemogerere, was named interior affairs minister. Ssemogerere is a member of the large and powerful Ganda tribe that had been severely persecuted by Obote. His appointment was taken as a gesture of reconciliation by the new government. The Military Council announced plans for an election and a return to civilian rule in July 1986.

Opposition to the Coup. The main military opponent of Obote, Yoweri Museveni's National Resistance Army (NRA), welcomed the coup but continued its guerrilla war in the countryside. The NRA demanded admission to the new government as an equal partner with the military. Toward the end of 1985 the 8,000 troops of the NRA had taken control of most of western Uganda. The survival of the new government in Kampala was therefore by no means assured.

Continued Violence. Both before and after the coup, constant violence afflicted Uganda. Bandits, ill-disciplined soldiers, rebels, and urban gangs all stole, robbed, beat, and killed at will. By late 1985, nearly half a million Ugandans had fled the country and another 800,000 were internal refugees.

The new government released more than 1,400 political prisoners and promised to end the violence. Much of the killing had been done by Obote's security police forces, which were disbanded. More than 1,000 police were put under arrest.

Economy. The Ugandan economy had been slowly recovering from the Idi Amin years when the coup occurred. After the initial chaos had subsided, merchants were able to bring food and fuel into Kampala and other cities, indicating that the modest economic recovery might survive the coup and its aftermath.

ROBERT GARFIELD, *DePaul University*

UGANDA • Information Highlights

Official Name: Republic of Uganda.
Location: Interior of East Africa.
Area: 91,075 sq mi (235 885 km²).
Population (mid-1985 est.): 14,700,000.
Chief Cities (1980 census): Kampala, the capital, 458,423; Jinja, 45,060.
Government: *Head of state,* Lt. Gen. Tito Okello, president (named July 29, 1985). *Head of government,* Abraham Waligo, prime minister (appointed Aug. 25, 1985). *Legislature* (unicameral) —National Assembly.
Monetary Unit: Uganda shilling (600.0 shillings equal U.S. $1, June 1985).
Foreign Trade (1983–84 U.S.$): *Imports,* $509,-000,000; *exports,* $380,000,000.

General Secretary Mikhail Gorbachev (right) realigned the Moscow leadership after taking power in March. Nikolai Ryzhkov (left) was made prime minister, and Andrei Gromyko (center) was elevated to the position of president.

USSR

Domestically the most important development in the USSR in 1985 was the emergence of a new and vigorous leadership team headed by 54-year-old Mikhail Sergeyevich Gorbachev (*see* BIOGRAPHY). His major effort was to invigorate the faltering economy by emphasizing increased labor productivity and modernization of industry. In foreign policy the principal concern was to improve relations with the United States, something made more imperative because of President Ronald Reagan's Strategic Defense Initiative (SDI), his plans for a defensive nuclear umbrella, known popularly as "Star Wars." After initial meetings in January between Soviet Foreign Minister Andrei Gromyko and U.S. Secretary of State George Shultz, talks between the superpowers on arms control were reinstituted in Geneva. In November, Gorbachev and Reagan met at the first summit conference since the Brezhnev-Carter meeting in Vienna in 1979. The year ended with optimism about future relations.

Domestic Affairs

Leadership. Just as 1983 had been the year of Yuri Andropov and 1984 the year of Konstantin Chernenko, so 1985 came to be regarded as the year of Mikhail Gorbachev. Indeed 1985 appeared to mark the beginning of a new generation of leadership and perhaps an era of reform. After the death of General Secretary Chernenko (*see* OBITUARIES) on March 10, it took the Politburo only 24 hours to recommend Gorbachev to the Central Committee as his replacement. Gorbachev had been the major spokesman for Soviet policy and the apparent heir to power since the deterioration of Chernenko's health in late 1984. He was formally nominated as party chief by the dean of the older generation, then-Foreign Minister Andrei Gromyko, and power at long last began to pass to men of a different life experience. The new generation, led by Gorbachev, had been too young to fight in World War II and rose through the party ranks during the erratic reforms of Nikita Khrushchev and the conservative retrenchment of Leonid Brezhnev.

During 1985, Gorbachev appeared to be a moderate reformer in the mold of Yuri Andropov. In agriculture he pushed for reorganization of the work force. Labor brigades were permitted to work out contracts with farm management for tools and seeds. Productivity was to be rewarded by higher income. The new party leader spoke out against "dogmatic ideas" and called for greater rationality and practicality in economic decision making. "Inertia and conservative thinking" ought to be replaced, he argued, by "new methods" of working. But after several months of Gorbachev's administration, the new ways of working were not very clear. Obviously the energetic young politician, willing to innovate, was faced by more conservative and entrenched forces within the ruling bureaucracy that made the pace of reform painfully slow.

In the months following his election, the new general secretary took steps to enhance his power. Nearly a dozen government ministers and two dozen regional party secretaries lost their jobs. In April he promoted three men to full membership in the Politburo—Yegor Ligachev, Nikolai Ryzhkov, and Viktor Chebrikov, the head of the state police, the KGB. Later in the year, Nikolai Talyzin, the new head of Gosplan, the highest planning agency in the USSR, was raised to candidate membership in the Politburo. And on July 1, Gorbachev's major rival, Grigory Romanov, formerly the party chief in Leningrad, was removed

from the Politburo and replaced by the head of the Georgian Communist Party, Eduard Shevardnadze. The next day Shevardnadze was named foreign minister, replacing Gromyko, who had held the post since 1957. Gromyko, in turn, was elevated to the presidency of the Soviet Union. In addition, three new national secretaries were appointed to head the party bureaucracy—Viktor Nikonov; Lev Zaikov, Romanov's successor in Leningrad; and Boris Yeltsin, a protégé of Ryzhkov. Then, on September 27, the aging and ill Nikolai Tikhonov retired as prime minister and was succeeded by Ryzhkov, the youngest member of the Politburo after Gorbachev. Finally, in December, Viktor Grishin, 71, was removed as the party chief of Moscow, likely to be followed by his retirement from the Politburo.

Thus, within a year of coming to power, Gorbachev had installed a new team of key players. His Politburo was weighed in favor of a new generation of party leaders—Gorbachev (54), Ryzhkov (56), Shevardnadze (57), Vitaly Vorotnikov (59), Heidar Aliev (61), Chebrikov (62), and Ligachev (65). Left among the older generation were Vladimir Shcherbitsky (67), Mikhail Solomentsev (72), Dinmukhamed Kunaev (73), Gromyko (76), and Tikhonov (80). Gorbachev was already in a position to reshape the top levels of the Soviet bureaucracy as the older officials retire or die.

Particularly impressive to Western observers was Gorbachev's toughness combined with charm and graciousness. A new style of leadership—more open and practical, less rhetorical and confrontational—characterized Gorbachev. For the first time in years, the Soviet Union had a vigorous, physically fit, and energetic leader, one who was confident enough to give press conferences and interviews to Western journalists and who lightened his more somber words with flashes of humor. His fashionable wife, Raisa, proved to be an asset in his diplomatic forays abroad, and much debate in the American press centered on the question of which side was winning the "media" war.

Economy. The success or failure of the Gorbachev regime will depend on its ability to improve the rate of economic growth. The economy grew during 1985, but slowly. Industry as a whole increased by 3.9%. The Soviet Union continued to be the largest producer in the world of both oil and steel, but output of both lagged behind the previous year's levels. Agriculture also was mixed. Fruit and vegetable production fell 5% because of poor weather, but meat production rose. Labor productivity in industry rose about 3% in the first half of the year, and national income grew by 3.8% in 1985.

In various speeches during the year, Gorbachev revealed some of his ideas about revitalizing the economy. Instead of proposing deep structural changes or replacing central planning with greater reliance on markets, he emphasized increased labor productivity, more effective investment, improvements in quality of products, and modernization of plants. He criticized those ministers who spent vast sums of money for new construction without considering new technologies. Not every sector, he told the June plenum of the Central Committee, but only the most productive would receive capital investments. Allocation of capital, he said, would not be like giving "earrings to each sister." Automation, increased use of computer technology, and better mechanical engineering were the ways to boost output and efficiency.

At the plenary meeting of the Party Central Committee in October, Gorbachev introduced the draft for the next five-year plan (1986–90). The growth in national income, he said, would come entirely from improvement in worker output. Labor productivity was projected to increase by 130–150%. National income would almost double in the next 15 years,

The Kremlin launched a major campaign to combat the Soviet Union's most serious social problem—alcoholism.

Reuters/Bettmann Newsphotos

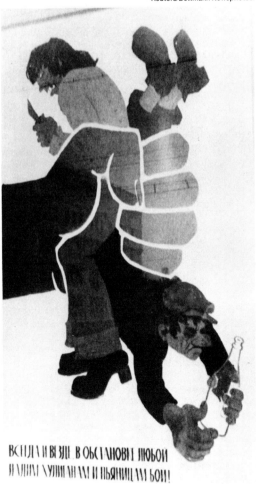

ВСЦ ЈI \ I БІ ЗЈІ В ОбС I \ЛЮВІ I ЈIЮЬОІІ
ЈI \ЈІЈI \ \ЈIІ \ЛІ \І I ІІ ІІЬЯІІІІІ I \І ЬОІІ!

AP/Wide World

The SS-21, a tactical short-range nuclear missile, is shown publicly for the first time at a Moscow parade marking the 40th anniversary of the end of World War II. The arms buildup continued to dominate relations with the West.

he promised, requiring an average annual growth rate of 4.7%. And, as Gorbachev's close associate Ligachev announced, this growth was to occur "without any shift toward the market economy or private enterprise." The reforms taking place in Hungary or China would not be imitated in the USSR.

Gorbachev placed much emphasis on stimulating workers to a higher level of productivity. The 50th anniversary of the Stakhanovite movement—a campaign during the Stalin period to praise and promote workers who set new production records—was formally recognized in 1985. Like Andropov, Gorbachev emphasized greater discipline among workers, punishment for absenteeism, and a campaign against alcoholism. In August, prices for vodka, hard liquor, and beer were raised, a move that was met with much grumbling by the Soviet citizenry. Gorbachev promoted the 1983 Law on Work Collectives, which was intended to increase the role of workers in the management of industrial enterprises. Yet at the same time he admitted that managers were reluctant to bring issues before the labor collectives and that workers themselves did not exercise their new rights with great vigor. Gorbachev repeatedly spoke of deepening and extending socialist democracy in the Soviet Union, and this apparently meant expanding the role of workers in enterprises.

Relying more on rational economic decisions than on appeals to ideological principle, the Gorbachev program adopted reforms based on experiments in reorganization that had been carried out in Georgia and other regions. The number of separate agencies dealing with agri-culture had been reduced in these localities, and the entire system of agricultural production, from sowing through food processing, had been integrated under a single authority. In November it was announced that five all-union ministries and one state committee dealing with agriculture had been merged into a single State Committee for the Agro-Industrial Complex. A protégé of Gorbachev from Stavropol, Vsevolod Muralkhovsky, was appointed to head this superagency. The bureaucracy in agriculture, it was estimated, would be reduced by 3,000 persons, and the lines of command would be made clearer.

Foreign Affairs

The year 1985 saw a significant improvement in East-West relations, despite the depth of the differences between the Reagan White House and the Gorbachev Kremlin. The tone was set in the January discussions between Foreign Minister Gromyko and Secretary of State Shultz in Geneva, which revived the arms-control talks broken off by the Soviets in November 1983. The major issue dividing the two sides was the question of Star Wars, the U.S. proposal to create a defensive shield to protect itself from Soviet nuclear missile attack. The Soviets wished to continue to rely on deterrence, the threat of mutual assured destruction (MAD), to keep both sides from launching a first strike. They considered the introduction of nuclear weapons into space to be a serious escalation of the arms race. Moreover, they claimed that the deployment of missiles to protect U.S. long-range missiles would

violate the 1972 Anti-Ballistic Missile (ABM) Treaty. The Reagan administration interpreted the treaty as permitting development of SDI. These issues, plus the continuing matters of long-range strategic and short-range tactical weapons, were discussed through the year by the new delegations sent to Geneva, but no agreement emerged from the talks.

The USSR was at a considerable disadvantage vis-à-vis the United States in 1985. American economic and technological superiority forced the USSR to spend much more of its resources just to keep up with the current arms race, not to mention the new race in space. A U.S. effort to develop Star Wars would require a huge investment by the Soviets to expand research and development of a new generation of weapons and would preclude certain expenditures for domestic economic development. Secondly, the United States had already deployed Cruise and Pershing II missiles in Western Europe and thereby had shortened the flying time of sophisticated nuclear weapons to the Soviet Union. But Soviet buildup of its counterforce antagonized and frightened the Western Europeans. In 1985 the Soviets began to scale down their missile fleet in the European sector in a futile attempt to lure the Europeans away from the Americans.

In an April interview with *Pravda,* Secretary Gorbachev mentioned a Soviet proposal for a moratorium on the development of strike space weapons and a freeze on strategic offensive arms while the negotiations in Geneva proceeded. The USSR halted deployment of intermediate-range missiles in the European theater in an effort to win over West European public opinion. In July the general secretary announced a moratorium on all nuclear testing by the USSR for the remainder of the year—and longer if the United States also refrained from testing. But the United States considered the Soviet proposals to be propaganda ploys and rejected them. The Soviet arms-control campaign was made against the background of a year-long observance of the 40th anniversary of the end of World War II. The celebrations marking "Victory Day" in May emphasized the Soviet Union's commitments both to peace and to military strength.

The summer saw some improvement in Soviet relations with the West. On July 2 it was announced that Reagan and Gorbachev would meet in a summit at Geneva. Later that month, newly appointed Foreign Minister Eduard Shevardnadze made his first major address at the Helsinki Conference marking the tenth anniversary of the signing of the Helsinki Accords. Shevardnadze, a Georgian and a local party boss rather than a product of the central bureaucracy, was still an unknown factor in international affairs, but he quickly impressed Western diplomats with his open manner. He met with Shultz in Helsinki and then at the United Nations in late September, after which he traveled to Washington to meet with President Reagan. Shevardnadze met again with Shultz several times before the Reagan-Gorbachev summit.

In early October, Gorbachev made his own first visit to the West since becoming general secretary, meeting with French President François Mitterrand in Paris. The nuclear arms race and France's role in it was a primary topic of discussion. Pleased by Mitterrand's opposition to participation in Star Wars, Gorbachev announced that Soviet SS-20 missiles aimed at Europe had been reduced to 243, the same number as in June 1984. He urged both France and Great Britain to hold arms-control talks separate from those of the United States, but Paris and London both rejected the invitation.

Though arms control and Star Wars remained at the center of Soviet concern in 1985, the thorny problem of dissent within the USSR became a factor in foreign policy. In answer to questions from French television journalists about Jewish persecutions in the Soviet Union, Gorbachev said sharply, "If there is a country where political and other rights have been gained by Jews more than in ours, I would be very happy to hear about it." But both in France and later in Geneva, the Soviet leader was confronted with protests against human rights violations. Questions about imprisoned dissidents, such as Anatoly Shcharansky, and the exiled Nobel prize winner Andrei Sakharov

Yelena Bonner, the wife of dissident Andrei Sakharov, was allowed to travel to the West for medical treatment.

AP/Wide World

plagued Soviet officials. In December, Yelena Bonner, Sakharov's wife, was permitted to travel to the West for medical treatment, but revelations about Sakharov's poor treatment by the Soviet authorities only reinforced the Western impression that the Soviet record on human rights was dismal. As the time approached for the summit meeting, however, the top officials in the U.S. government decided not to attack the USSR publicly on this vulnerable point.

The Summit. From November 19 to 21, President Reagan and General Secretary Gorbachev held a series of face-to-face discussions in Geneva on subjects ranging from arms control and Star Wars to Afghanistan, Africa, and Central America. The talks, held in private with no releases to the press until they had concluded, were intense, often heated, but friendly. The disagreements remained, and no accord was reached beyond a number of minor cultural exchange agreements. Neither side moved from its position on space weapons. And on the matter of regional conflicts, Reagan told Gorbachev: "You have no right to be in Afghanistan, Ethiopia, Angola. No right! This is Soviet aggression. It is destabilizing." Gorbachev replied: "There is no basis for this! None at all! These are people struggling for national liberation."

Difficulties arose in preparation of the final communiqué. The United States proposed 50% cuts in comparable weapons systems but wished to exclude all but land-based missiles. This meant that bombers, which the Americans had in greater numbers than the Soviets, and European submarines would not be included. The Soviets wanted to include a statement against the expansion of the arms race into space, but the Americans refused. A compromise finally was reached, one that each side was able to interpret in its own way. Much more important than the vaguely written communiqué, however, was an agreement to hold a series of follow-up meetings, the first in 1986 in the United States, the next in 1987 in the USSR. At the end of the conference, Reagan said that he thought Gorbachev sincerely wanted peace, and Gorbachev characterized the talks as "very frank," "very, very likely indeed," and "to a certain extent productive."

Third World. As a global power, the Soviet Union maintained its clients in various parts of the world and continued its support of "national liberation movements." In Asia its most trusted ally was Vietnam, a country alienated from its powerful neighbor China and isolated from other nations because of its occupation of Cambodia. Soviet troops continued to fight in Afghanistan but seemed no closer to crushing the Islamic rebellion. The war in Afghanistan, in its sixth year, had now ground on longer than the Soviet struggle against Nazi Germany in World War II.

In Africa the Soviets supplied material to Angola, which continued its fight against internal guerrillas backed by South Africa and the United States; Cuban and Soviet troops were active in the campaign against the rebel forces. The Soviet Union sent food and military aid to the government of Ethiopia, which was faced with a devastating famine. Relations were improved with the government of Zimbabwe, whose Marxist leader, Robert Mugabe, visited the USSR.

In the Middle East the Soviet Union attempted to remain neutral in the war between Iraq and Iran, but the Iranian revolutionary regime continued to persecute the left and was vigorously criticized in the Soviet press. Israel's raid against PLO headquarters in Tunisia on October 1 was condemned by the Soviets, and Syria remained Moscow's closest ally in the region.

Tensions over the revolutions and counterrevolutions in Central America divided the Soviet Union and United States almost as much as the arms-control issue. The USSR increased its arms supplies to the Sandinista government of Nicaragua, to the annoyance of the United States; Nicaragua's President Daniel Ortega visited the Soviet Union in April. The Soviet government also endorsed Fidel Castro's call for repudiation of debts owed by poorer Third World countries to the principal lending nations.

In Eastern Europe the Soviets were faced with ongoing public discontent with the military government in Poland. Gorbachev celebrated the 30th anniversary of the formation of the Warsaw Pact, the Soviet bloc's answer to NATO, with a visit to the Polish capital in March. Leaders of the Warsaw Pact nations approved a 20-year extension.

RONALD GRIGOR SUNY
University of Michigan

USSR • Information Highlights

Official Name: Union of Soviet Socialist Republics.
Location: Eastern Europe and northern Asia.
Area: 8,649,498 sq mi (22 402 200 km²).
Population (mid-1985 est.): 278,000,000.
Chief Cities (Jan. 1, 1984 est.): Moscow, the capital, 8,546,000; Leningrad, 4,832,000; Kiev, 2,411,000.
Government: *Head of state,* Andrei A. Gromyko, chairman of the Presidium of the Supreme Soviet, president (elected July 2, 1985). *Head of government,* Nikolai I. Ryzhkov, premier (took office Sept. 1985). General secretary of the Communist Party, Mikhail S. Gorbachev (elected March 11, 1985). *Legislature*—Supreme Soviet: Soviet of the Union Soviet of Nationalities.
Monetary Unit: Ruble (0.809 ruble equals U.S.$1, September 1985—noncommercial rate).
Gross National Product (1983 U.S.$): $1,843,-000,000.
Economic Indexes (1983): *Consumer Prices* (1970 = 100), all items, 108.2; food, 109.9. *Industrial Production* (1984, 1980 = 100), 115.
Foreign Trade (1984 U.S.$): *Imports,* $80,624,-000,000; *exports,* $91,649,000,000.

Life Today

AP/Wide World

Within hours of the death of Konstantin Chernenko on March 10, 1985, the Soviet Politburo announced that it had turned for leadership to its youngest member, 54-year-old Mikhail S. Gorbachev. Intelligent, energetic, and personally engaging, Gorbachev represented the first of a new generation of Soviet leaders—men in their 50s and 60s who had been too young to fight in World War II and had climbed the party ladder under Nikita Khrushchev and Leonid Brezhnev. Though sweeping changes in Soviet society were unlikely, a mood of optimism seemed to follow Gorbachev's election. In one Moscow office, a woman beamed at the news. "At last we have a young leader," she said.

Whatever the hopes of the Soviet people, however, Gorbachev will need more than youthful vigor and style to cope with the challenges he inherits. The Communist Party points with great pride to the strides the country has made since the Bolsheviks seized power in 1917, and indeed these are impressive. The Soviet Union has the world's second largest economy and a huge and potent military machine. It provides cradle-to-grave security, including guaranteed employment, free health care and education, and cheap housing and transportation. But as Gorbachev acknowledged in his first speeches after taking power, serious problems continue to hamper the quality of life. Economic growth has slowed markedly in recent years. Many of the goods produced by Soviet factories are so shoddy that no one will buy them. Production is stymied by waste, inefficiency, and poor work habits. There is a chronic shortage of housing. Many basic commodities are in short supply. And drunkenness is a pervasive social problem. The average life expectancy for Soviet men has declined from 66 to 62 in less than two decades. All in all, the material quality of life in the Soviet Union lags far behind that in Western Europe or the United States.

Housing. The first problem facing the average Soviet citizen is finding a place to live. By law, rent cannot exceed 3% of a person's income. With the average salary at about 200 rubles ($250) per month, the rent of six rubles per month in state flats is thus eminently affordable. The problem is getting a flat. Despite ambitious construction projects over many years, some 20% of the urban population still lives in communal apartments, in which several families share a bathroom and kitchen. In cities like Moscow, the lucky family of four with a sepa-

Editor's Note: In spring 1985, Robert B. Cullen, the author of this report, completed a 2½-year assignment as Moscow bureau chief for *Newsweek*.

rate apartment usually makes do with two rooms and a kitchen in one of the huge housing projects that ring the older sections of the city. The parents sleep on a daybed in the living room, and the children share the bedroom. In the countryside, a farm worker may have a detached house, but typically it has no running water. Winter entails many cold walks to the well and the outhouse.

The shortage of housing has inspired a variety of ploys which the Soviets describe as *na levo*—literally translated as "on the left," roughly translated as "under the table." Some people inherit control of a deceased relative's apartment and rent it out for as much as 150 rubles per month. Others trade to get bigger flats. An alley in Moscow called Bathhouse Lane features a long brick wall lined with tattered ads for apartment exchanges. On summer evenings one can see men and women pacing up and down the alley, calling out softly, "I have an apartment, a lovely apartment. Isn't anyone interested in a trade?"

Still other people resort to fraudulent marriages to get better housing. Students from the hinterlands who study at Moscow institutes and universities are often reluctant to return to the provinces. But it is very difficult to obtain a permit to live in Moscow, and without one it is illegal to move there. Unless graduates can come up with a valid reason for staying in the capital, the government will assign them to jobs in rural areas. Thus, these students are willing to pay thousands of rubles to native Muscovites, who are entitled to stay in the city; the purported spouse also is allowed to claim

residence there. And just as there are paper marriages, so there are paper divorces. A young, single Moscow woman named Lena told this correspondent that her parents had recently gotten a sham divorce to enable her to get a small apartment of her own. Once the divorce went through, the woman's father used his seniority at a factory to claim a one-room apartment for himself. Instead, he continued to live with Lena's mother, while Lena moved into the new apartment.

Food and Clothing. Next on the list of daily necessities that require ingenuity and patience to obtain are food and clothing. The Soviet Union is far from being a Third World country, and it would be a mistake to imagine people there going hungry or shivering for lack of a warm coat. The problem is to eat and dress well. Clothes produced by the Soviet textile industry always seem dowdy and a few years behind the times compared with Western apparel. Women's winter boots, for example, are easy to distinguish from Western imports: they all have zippers up the inside of the calf because Soviet leather is not supple enough for boots that slip over the foot. Consequently, boots without zippers, brought into the country by people with connections abroad, are hot items on Moscow's *na levo* clothing market. So are genuine blue jeans, which command anywhere from 80 to 150 rubles on the black market. (The state is the only legal importing agent. Because of restrictions on foreign travel and laws that prohibit spending rubles overseas, Soviets cannot legally buy what they want from abroad.) The Soviet press in 1984

Despite major new construction, housing remains modest and in short supply in Murmansk, below, and other cities.

© Dilip Mehta, Contact

At an outdoor market in Moscow, shoppers are quick to snap up the best available produce and other foods.

told of the triumphs of customs inspectors at the railroad yard in Brest, where trains from the West cross the border. The inspectors regularly impounded cargoes, ranging from blue denim to brass rivets, destined for *na levo* jeans makers.

Fresh bread, sometimes even hot, is always available, and it is very cheap. The government makes sure of that, even if it has to import 35 million tons of grain to do it. Beyond that, however, filling the larder is a matter of chance. In the state-operated stores, sometimes there is sausage, sometimes there is chicken, and sometimes there are nice cuts of beef. Occasionally, vendors on Moscow's winter streets have oranges from Egypt or Morocco. But just as often they do not. It varies from day to day. In many parts of the country, the government issues ration cards so that when meat or butter is available shoppers cannot snatch it all up. As with housing and clothes, scarcity gives rise to a black market. Store workers set aside choice items for friends who remember them with periodic gifts or favors. Sometimes the gifts are very lucrative. In 1984 the former director of a large grocery store on Moscow's Gorky Street was executed for bribery. His well-connected customers had descended into his basement offices, where the right "fee" brought them steak, caviar, and champagne. The customers above stood on line and grumbled about the shortages.

Partly because the government-operated system cannot always put vegetables on the table, the state tolerates a limited form of free enterprise in food production. Peasants are permitted to grow vegetables on small private plots, generally one acre or less. Whatever they do not eat they can take to city markets and sell for whatever price the market will bear. Even in winter, therefore, it is possible to buy tomatoes in Moscow. Peasants from southern regions like Georgia and Tadjikistan bring suitcases and crates packed with tomatoes to sell in the big city. The only problem is price. For a kilogram (2.2 pounds) of tomatoes in January, Muscovites will pay about 15 rubles—more than $8 per pound.

Work. If nothing else, men and women in the Soviet Union enjoy virtually guaranteed employment. Because of a long-standing labor shortage, even the few workers who get fired from their jobs usually find another one in a short time. For those who work hard there are rewards, such as inexpensive holidays at public resorts or even supervised trips abroad. Men can retire at age 60 and women at 55, with pensions of 60% to 70% of their peak salaries.

But the average Soviet worker hardly can be described as content and productive. It is virtually impossible to change careers, and there is no profit incentive to work hard. Even the official Soviet press has characterized the average worker as sloppy, wasteful, and unpro-

The latest reforms in the Soviet educational system place greater emphasis on vocational and computer training.

ductive. Considerable time is spent away from the workplace, selling goods on the black market or tracking down food, clothing, and other consumer items. It has been estimated that the Soviet work force is only about 55% as productive as those in the West.

Health, Education, and Religion. Health care is theoretically not a problem for the Soviets, as a national network of neighborhood polyclinics provides free treatment. Over the past year, however, articles in the Soviet press have documented problems in health care delivery. Doctors are careless, facilities lack proper equipment, and prescription medicines are impossible to find in some cities. The press has also revealed an interesting side effect of the problems in health care delivery: in some cities faith healers are back in vogue, treating hundreds of sick people who have despaired of getting help from the official system.

Education also is free, up through the university level. But here again the problem is getting access. Entrance to institutes and universities is highly competitive; the state's educational plan calls for about 20% of the young people to get higher educations and the rest to take job-oriented courses to prepare them for the labor market. In 1984 the party launched a major educational reform aimed at making vocational education more attractive. And in 1985 it decreed that computer education will be offered to ninth and tenth graders.

The problem is that there are not enough computers to go around, so that the vast majority of pupils will be learning about computers without ever touching one.

Although the state endorses and promotes atheism, a peculiarly Soviet kind of religious life still flourishes. In the immediate postrevolutionary period, churches were destroyed and clerics were persecuted. Such practices have stopped, but believers say that in certain ideologically oriented occupations, such as teaching, church members are handicapped. Churches and mosques continue to operate in most Soviet cities today, but to do so they must accept certain written and unwritten state requirements. Congregations must register with the state, they cannot proselytize, and any printed material has to be formally approved. Beyond that, the churches—particularly the Russian Orthodox Church—often urge their congregations to be good patriots and to support the government's frequent "peace initiatives."

Entertainment. To divert themselves from their problems, the Soviets have only a limited array of entertainment. State-operated television has three channels, which present a somewhat stodgy mix of entertainment and public affairs programming, all tailored to the state's interest. TV movies stress patriotic themes like World War II heroism. Variety shows are heavy on Ukrainian folk dancers and

hefty sopranos, while rock ensembles are rarely seen. At 9 P.M. each evening, all three channels broadcast *Vremya* (Time), the centrally produced national news program. The larger cities have professional theaters and dance troupes, but getting into their performances is a problem. Tickets are cheap but hard to come by for a popular play or a ballet performance at the Bolshoi Theater. Outside the theater, even on freezing winter nights, crowds gather to beseech the lucky ones entering the theater with the words *"Lishniye bileti?"* ("Extra tickets?").

The Problem of Alcoholism. Both in the workplace and throughout Soviet society, one of the top concerns of the new Kremlin leadership is alcohol abuse. There are no official statistics on the total number of alcoholics, presumably because they would embarrass the government; published figures only hint at the extent of alcohol abuse. The depth of the problem, however, is evidenced in many areas of ordinary life. In the European parts of the USSR, for example, the divorce rate approaches 50% of all marriages. According to published research, about half of the divorced women cite drunkenness on the part of their former husbands as a cause of the divorce. (The rate of divorce is itself a government concern. Many divorced women have only one or no children, contributing to an extremely low birth rate and the chronic labor shortage.)

In a survey conducted in a timber-cutting region of Siberia, one third of the population acknowledged getting drunk at least several times a week. An American expert on the subject calculated that the legal alcohol consumption in the USSR had doubled during the 1970s. Alcoholism is the third most prevalent health problem in the nation, after heart disease and cancer. It accounts for an estimated 50,000 deaths per year.

Only two months after coming to power, in May 1985, the Gorbachev regime announced a series of measures to combat the alcohol problem. The legal drinking age would be raised from 18 to 21. Liquor stores would not open until 2 P.M., near the end of the first work shift. Prices would be raised, and the production of vodka and other liquors would be gradually cut. Penalties for public drunkenness would be increased, and vodka would no longer be served at official functions.

Policies and Politics. As ever, it remains difficult to determine how average Soviet citizens evaluate their new leader and his efforts to improve the quality of life. There is no Soviet equivalent of the Gallup poll for gauging a leader's popularity. Elections are sterile affairs in which voters choose simply to endorse or not endorse single party candidates to the local and national soviets (councils). No candidate ever loses these elections, and the only suspense is whether the party will turn out a favorable vote by an even more overwhelming percentage than in the previous election—usually more than 99% of the vote. In any case, the soviets themselves make no policy decisions. These are left to the Communist Party, whose officials are appointed.

Visitors to the Soviet Union nevertheless come away with the feeling that most citizens basically support the system. The thinking seems to be that a strong, tough leadership is necessary to create a better standard of living without exposing the society to the vagaries of Western-style freedom, such as crime and unemployment. A young female barber in Moscow named Tanya is perhaps typical. "People want to feel confidence in the strength of the leader," she said. And as for the details of politics, she went on, "I don't need to know. Normal people don't. We have a saying: 'The less you know, the better you sleep.' "

AP/Wide World

Fashionable clothes and accessories are at a premium in the USSR. Quality leather goods, from supple boots to soft handbags are hard to come by—and afford—for the average citizen.

UNITED NATIONS

The United Nations celebrated its 40th anniversary on October 24, the date in 1945 that the UN Charter went into effect. The ceremonies began on October 10 and attracted 84 kings, presidents, and prime ministers to New York City in the largest such gathering ever. During the ten-day celebration, at least, the organization was the center of global attention, a status envisioned for it by its founders.

Much of the year was spent in soul-searching by UN officials and government leaders over the crisis of confidence in the institution and how to make it better able to fulfill its primary purpose—in the words of the UN Charter, "to save succeeding generations from the scourge of war." Secretary-General Javier Pérez de Cuéllar summed up the event by saying: "We have heard beautiful speeches. But what we need now is action."

The UN's frustrations were symbolized by the failure of delegates to agree on a declaration of UN accomplishments and goals, a document that was to have been the candle in the birthday cake. The sticking point was an Arab demand, rejected by the United States, that the text include a call for Palestinian rights.

Many world leaders used the UN anniversary as a stage to demonstrate their will for peace. In a speech to the General Assembly on October 24, U.S. President Ronald Reagan proposed enlarging the agenda of his upcoming summit meeting with Soviet leader Mikhail Gorbachev to include regional issues. Soviet Foreign Minister Eduard Shevardnadze criticized Reagan's so-called "Star Wars" defense initiative.

Prime Minister Shimon Peres moderated Israel's policy by offering a role for an international conference under UN auspices as part of the Middle East peace process. King Hassan II of Morocco offered a cease-fire and a referendum to rebels in the territory of Western Sahara. In one of many bilateral meetings that the UN event made possible, the leaders of India and Pakistan held talks to ease their historic differences.

The anniversary overshadowed other UN achievements, such as its coordinating role in easing the famine in Africa, and post-summit cooperation between the United States and the Soviet Union that resulted in the adoption of landmark condemnations of terrorism by the General Assembly and Security Council.

The year also was marked by continuing American success in UN forums. "There were a number of positive achievements," said U.S. Ambassador Vernon Walters, who replaced Jeane Kirkpatrick as chief U.S. delegate in May (*see* BIOGRAPHY). "The voting pattern and the tone of debate were more balanced and less confrontational, a return to the older and better traditions of the UN."

Yet Washington continued to show its irritation with the UN. The Reagan administration withdrew from compulsory jurisdiction of the World Court on political disputes and cut back voluntary funding for UN population programs. The U.S. Congress mandated restrictions on the movement of UN staffers from the Soviet Union and other nations, and it set funding cuts starting in 1986 on its contributions to the regular UN budget (20%) and the UN peace force in Lebanon (50%).

General Assembly. The 39th General Assembly session, which had begun in 1984, reconvened in April and adopted by consensus a set of guidelines for consumer protection. The 40th Assembly opened on September 17 and elected Jaime de Piniés, the ambassador from Spain, as its president.

The anniversary fete was briefly threatened by a motion inviting Palestine Liberation Organization (PLO) chief Yasir Arafat to participate. It was withdrawn only after President Reagan threatened to boycott.

Amid the formal speeches, Nancy Reagan and 30 other first ladies held an informal meeting on drug abuse. Two months later, the Assembly unanimously called for a larger UN role in stemming the international drug traffic and set a world conference on the issue for 1987.

Turning to its first substantive business early in November, the Assembly adopted by the largest margins ever resolutions calling for the withdrawal of Vietnamese troops from Cambodia (114 to 21, with 16 abstentions) and Soviet troops from Afghanistan (122 to 19, with 12 abstentions). Later, the Assembly acted for the first time to express concern over massive violations of human rights in Afghanistan. It

Secretary-General Pérez de Cuéllar addresses diplomats in San Francisco celebrating the UN's 40th anniversary.

AP/Wide World

Entertainer Stevie Wonder was awarded a citation by the UN General Assembly's Special Committee Against Apartheid. At the ceremony May 13, he performed a song, "The Bell for Freedom," which he wrote especially for the occasion.

AP/Wide World

also criticized rights violations by South Africa, Israel, Iran, Chile, El Salvador, and Guatemala.

The United States was isolated on a resolution calling for it to end the trade embargo it imposed on Nicaragua on May 1. The United States criticized eight major allies for backing the proposal, which was adopted by a vote of 91–6, with 49 abstentions.

Washington and Moscow worked together on a number of issues. They joined a December 9 consensus on a resolution condemning terrorist acts as criminal, "wherever and by whomever committed." They and 30 other parties to the Antarctic Treaty refused to participate in voting on resolutions calling for equal sharing by all nations in the profits from the continent's resources and for the exclusion of South Africa from the treaty.

The United States and Soviet Union also acted jointly on a number of resolutions seeking to limit UN costs and to reform budget procedures. Both were among those voting against the UN budget for 1986 and 1987, which was adopted on the Assembly's last day, 127 to 10, with 11 abstentions. It appropriated $1,663,-341,600 for those two years. Virtually the entire 13% ($190 million) increase over the 1984–85 budget derived from inflation and currency shifts.

Another major issue in 1985 was the status of South Africa. Several resolutions urged sanctions on the white minority government there because of its domestic policies and its refusal to grant independence to Namibia (South-west Africa). The Assembly scheduled international conferences on Namibia and on the sanctions issue for 1986. The United States was successful in deleting seven critical references to it and to Israel from the resolutions on Namibia.

More than a score of resolutions were adopted on the Arab-Israeli dispute, but little new ground was broken. Once again the Assembly voted to shelve a resolution that would have ousted the Israeli delegation (80 to 41, with 20 abstentions). Resolutions also were passed on disarmament, the Falklands, Western Sahara, and the Law of the Sea.

The 40th session was suspended on December 18, having adopted 259 resolutions overall. Ten of the 148 agenda items—including Central America, Cyprus, the Iran-Iraq war, and talks on economic issues between rich and poor nations—were held over until 1986.

Security Council. The UN Security Council continued in 1985 to experience frustration in its attempts to keep or restore peace between nations. On most issues it was deadlocked by differences among the major powers, and it either made no attempt to take action or had resolutions blocked by American vetoes. Those resolutions that were adopted had little practical impact on the disputes involved. This weakness was the focus of a special Council meeting attended by 13 foreign ministers on September 26. Each of the Council members offered suggestions on how to improve the body's performance.

The Security Council's most important actions of 1985 were theoretical rather than practical. On October 9, after the hijacking of the Italian cruise ship *Achille Lauro*, the Council issued a unanimous statement condemning all acts of terrorism, including hostage-taking. Two months later, a unanimous resolution drafted jointly by the Soviets and Americans detailed the condemnation of hostage-taking and demanded the immediate release of all kidnap victims.

Earlier, the United States vetoed two resolutions critical of actions by Israeli occupation

ORGANIZATION OF THE UNITED NATIONS

THE SECRETARIAT

Secretary-General: Javier Pérez de Cuéllar (until Dec. 31, 1986)

THE GENERAL ASSEMBLY (1985)

President: Jaime de Piniés, Spain
The 159 member nations were as follows:

Afghanistan	Cape Verde	German Demo-	Laos	Papua New	Surinam
Albania	Central African	cratic Republic	Lebanon	Guinea	Swaziland
Algeria	Republic	Germany, Federal	Lesotho	Paraguay	Sweden
Angola	Chad	Republic of	Liberia	Peru	Syria
Antigua and	Chile	Ghana	Libya	Philippines	Tanzania
Barbuda	China, People's	Greece	Luxembourg	Poland	Thailand
Argentina	Republic of	Grenada	Madagascar	Portugal	Togo
Australia	Colombia	Guatemala	Malawi	Qatar	Trinidad and Tobago
Austria	Comoros	Guinea	Malaysia	Romania	Tunisia
Bahamas	Congo	Guinea-Bissau	Maldives	Rwanda	Turkey
Bahrain	Costa Rica	Guyana	Mali	Saint Christopher	Uganda
Bangladesh	Cuba	Haiti	Malta	and Nevis	Ukrainian SSR
Barbados	Cyprus	Honduras	Mauritania	Saint Lucia	USSR
Belgium	Czechoslovakia	Hungary	Mauritius	Saint Vincent and	United Arab Emirates
Belize	Denmark	Iceland	Mexico	The Grenadines	United Kingdom
Belorussian SSR	Djibouti	India	Mongolia	São Tomé and	United States
Benin	Dominica	Indonesia	Morocco	Principe	Uruguay
Bhutan	Dominican	Iran	Mozambique	Saudi Arabia	Vanuatu
Bolivia	Republic	Iraq	Nepal	Senegal	Venezuela
Botswana	Ecuador	Ireland	Netherlands	Seychelles	Vietnam
Brazil	Egypt	Israel	New Zealand	Sierra Leone	Western Samoa
Brunei Darussalam	El Salvador	Italy	Nicaragua	Singapore	Yemen
Bulgaria	Equatorial Guinea	Ivory Coast	Niger	Solomon Islands	Yemen, Democratic
Burkina Faso	Ethiopia	Jamaica	Nigeria	Somalia	Yugoslavia
Burma	Fiji	Japan	Norway	South Africa	Zaire
Burundi	Finland	Jordan	Oman	Spain	Zambia
Cambodia	France	Kenya	Pakistan	Sri Lanka	Zimbabwe
Cameroon	Gabon	Kuwait	Panama	Sudan	
Canada	Gambia				

COMMITTEES

General. Composed of 29 members as follows: The General Assembly president; the 21 General Assembly vice presidents (heads of delegations or their deputies of the Bahamas, Barbados, Burkina Faso, China, Costa Rica, Cyprus, France, Gabon, Kenya, Lesotho, Malta, Pakistan, Philippines, Qatar, Romania, Senegal, Tunisia, USSR, United Kingdom, United States, Yemen, Democratic); and the chairmen of the following main committees, which are composed of all 159 member countries.

First (Political and Security): Ali Alatas (Indonesia)
Special Political: Keijo Korhonen (Finland)
Second (Economic and Financial): Omer Y. Birido (Sudan)
Third (Social, Humanitarian and Cultural): Endre Zador (Hungary)
Fourth (Decolonization): Javier Chamorro Mora (Nicaragua)
Fifth (Administrative and Budgetary): Tommo Monthe (Cameroon)
Sixth (Legal): Riyadh Al-Qaysi (Iraq)

THE TRUSTEESHIP COUNCIL

President: Peter Maxey (United Kingdom)

China[2] France[2] USSR[2] United Kingdom[2] United States[1]

[1] Administers Trust Territory. [2] Permanent member of Security Council not administering Trust Territory.

THE SECURITY COUNCIL

Membership ends on December 31 of the year noted; asterisks indicate permanent membership.

Australia (1986)	Ghana (1986)	United Arab Emirates
Bulgaria (1987)	Madagascar (1986)	(1987)
China*	Thailand (1986)	United Kingdom*
Congo (1987)	Trinidad and	United States*
Denmark (1986)	Tobago(1986)	Venezuela (1987)
France*	USSR*	

THE INTERNATIONAL COURT OF JUSTICE

Membership ends on February 5 of the year noted

President: Nagendra Singh (India, 1991)
Vice-President: Guy Ladreit De Lacharrière (France, 1991)

Roberto Ago (Italy, 1988)	Kéba Mbaye (Senegal, 1991)
Mohammed Bedjaoui (Algeria, 1988)	Ni Zhengyu (China, 1994)
Taslim O. Elias (Nigeria, 1994)	Shigeru Oda (Japan, 1994)
Jens Evensen (Norway, 1994)	José María Ruda (Argentina, 1991)
Robert Y. Jennings (United Kingdom, 1991)	Stephen Schwebel (United States, 1988)
Manfred Lachs (Poland, 1994)	José Sette Camara (Brazil, 1988)
	Nikolai Konstantinovich Tarasou (USSR, 1988)

THE ECONOMIC AND SOCIAL COUNCIL

President: T. Kobayashi (Japan)
Membership ends on December 31 of the year noted.

Argentina (1986)	Guinea (1987)	Rwanda (1986)
Australia (1988)	Haiti (1987)	Senegal (1987)
Bangladesh (1987)	Iceland (1987)	Sierra Leone (1988)
Belgium (1988)	India (1987)	Somalia (1986)
Brazil (1987)	Indonesia (1986)	Spain (1987)
Byelorussian Soviet	Iraq (1988)	Sri Lanka (1986)
Socialist Republic	Italy (1988)	Sweden (1986)
(1988)	Jamaica (1988)	Syrian Arab Republic
Canada (1986)	Japan (1987)	(1988)
China (1986)	Morocco (1987)	Turkey (1987)
Colombia (1987)	Mozambique (1988)	Uganda (1986)
Djibouti (1988)	Nigeria (1987)	USSR (1986)
Egypt (1988)	Pakistan (1988)	United Kingdom
Finland (1986)	Panama (1988)	(1986)
France (1987)	Papua New Guinea	United States
Gabon (1988)	(1986)	(1988)
German Democratic	Peru (1988)	Venezuela (1987)
Republic (1988)	Philippines (1988)	Yugoslavia (1986)
Germany, Federal	Poland (1986)	Zaire (1986)
Republic of (1987)	Romania (1987)	Zimbabwe (1987)

INTERGOVERNMENTAL AGENCIES

Food and Agricultural Organization (FAO); General Agreement on Tariffs and Trade (GATT); International Atomic Energy Agency (IAEA); International Bank for Reconstruction and Development (World Bank); International Civil Aviation Organization (ICAO); International Fund for Agricultural Development (IFAD); International Labor Organization (ILO); International Maritime Organization (IMO); International Monetary Fund (IMF); International Telecommunication Union (ITU); United Nations Educational, Scientific and Cultural Organization (UNESCO); United Nations Industrial Development Organization (UNIDO); Universal Postal Union (UPU); World Health Organization (WHO); World Intellectual Property Organization (WIPO); World Meteorological Organization (WMO).

forces in Lebanon and the West Bank. On October 4 the United States abstained as the Council "vigorously condemned" a raid by Israeli jets against PLO headquarters in Tunisia three days earlier. The Israelis acted after a PLO terrorist squad killed three Israelis vacationing on Cyprus.

During the year there were 13 separate debates on issues involving South Africa. Nine resolutions were adopted, condemning the Pretoria government for raids on Angola and Botswana, for refusing to free the territory of Namibia, and for imposing a state of emergency and taking other actions against its own citizens. Great Britain and the United States, however, cast their vetoes to block a November 15 resolution that would have imposed mandatory sanctions.

The Security Council members also extended into 1986 the mandates for peacekeeping forces in Cyprus, Lebanon, and the Golan Heights, the Syrian territory occupied by Israel in 1967. Debates also were held on Chad and Nicaragua, and two statements were issued on the Iran-Iraq war.

Secretariat. The use of the secretary-general's office to mediate international disputes was an innovation not envisaged in the UN Charter. But Secretary-General Pérez de Cuéllar has taken this function a step further, contending in a 1985 speech that under international "common law" his office is the appropriate channel to deal with all disputes that have stymied the Security Council. During 1985, Pérez de Cuéllar offered to act as a catalyst in disputes over the Falklands, Cambodia, Cyprus, Namibia, Central America, Afghanistan, the Persian Gulf, and Israel.

He came frustratingly close to success at a January summit meeting between Greek Cypriot President Spyros Kyprianou and Turkish Cypriot leader Rauf Denktas. In the end Denktas accepted the secretary-general's proposals, but Kyprianou demanded changes, and the opportunity was lost. Pérez de Cuéllar produced two more compromise drafts without success but vowed to renew his efforts in 1986.

During a trip to Indochina in late January, the secretary-general concluded that the positions of the disputants in Cambodia were still "too far apart" to warrant active mediation, but he was able to ease relations between Vietnam and the United States.

After a visit to Tehran and Baghdad in April, the secretary-general reported that Iraq had refused to continue imposing "humanitarian" limits on the use of chemical weapons and artillery attacks on civilian population centers unless the negotiating agenda also included an end to the fighting. Iran, however, rejected any discussion of a cease-fire. Pérez de Cuéllar urged the Security Council to invite both nations to a debate on the Persian Gulf war, but the Council failed to act.

Talks on Afghanistan in June, August, and December produced tentative agreements on side issues but deadlocked at year's end on the key issue of Soviet troop withdrawal and reciprocal guarantees that aid to rebel fighters would stop. A new round was set for Geneva in February 1986.

Alec Collett, a British journalist working for the UN in Beirut, was kidnapped on March 25 and remained in custody through the end of the year. In June, 21 Finnish soldiers in the UN peace force in southern Lebanon were kidnapped by militiamen allied with Israel after they had helped 11 members of the militia to desert; the 21 were freed after one week.

The year's most effective UN staff action was coordinating the global response to the African famine by determining what was needed, where it could be found, and how it might be shipped. The UN team reported that 5.5 million tons of food was sent to the 20 countries involved, at a cost of $3 billion, and that some 35 million lives had been saved. It said another $1 billion in aid would be needed in 1986.

Bradford Morse, an American who headed the Africa team and ran the UN Development Program, and Brian Urquhart, a Briton who had worked for the UN for 40 years and ran its peacekeeping operations, both announced their retirements.

Specialized Agencies. Great Britain and Singapore quit the UN Educational, Scientific and Cultural Organization (UNESCO) at the end of 1985, following the example of the United States in 1984. Their action worsened UNESCO's political and financial crisis, and it was forced to trim its budget by 25%.

The UN Children's Fund (UNICEF) announced in December that a joint campaign with the World Health Organization (WHO) had saved the lives of more than 1 million Third World children in 1985 through inoculations and oral rehydration therapy to relieve diarrhea. The UNICEF-WHO objective was to make the techniques universal by 1990 and thereby save the lives of half the 15 million children who die each year in developing countries.

After a hotly contested lobbying campaign, Jean-Pierre Hocke of Switzerland, a man with a reputation for efficiency as chief of the International Committee of the Red Cross, was named on December 10 to succeed Poul Hartling as UN High Commissioner of Refugees.

An 11-member panel set up by the UN Center on Transnational Corporations held hearings on the corporate role in South Africa. The group, headed by former Australian Prime Minister Malcolm Fraser, recommended in October that governments should enforce divestment if South Africa's apartheid system is not dismantled by the end of 1986.

MICHAEL J. BERLIN
"The Washington Post"

With the Republicans in control of the Senate and the Democrats having the upper hand in the House, the first session of the 99th Congress did not adjourn until well into the Christmas season. Highlights of the session included new farm legislation and a budget deficit reduction act.

UNITED STATES

Domestic Affairs

In a nationally televised State of the Union Address on Feb. 6, 1985, two weeks after being sworn in for a second presidential term, Ronald Reagan outlined plans for what he called "a Second American Revolution of hope and opportunity," with a sweeping proposal for reform of the federal income tax code as its centerpiece. But events of the year belied President Reagan's early optimism. Though the economy continued to perform reasonably well, it failed to grow fast enough to overcome the huge federal deficit, and the changes the president had contemplated in his blueprint for a Second American Revolution were overshadowed by a drastic change in government machinery intended to stem the tide of red ink.

The Deficit. Concern over the deficit was heightened right after the New Year when the administration disclosed that the deficit, originally estimated at well below $200 billion, would more likely reach $218 billion in fiscal 1985 and keep climbing to $235 billion in 1988.

On January 3, Robert Dole, the new Republican leader in the Senate, introduced a bill aiming at a $100 billion deficit by 1988, the same goal previously set by the White House. But Dole warned that achieving this objective would be difficult unless the president agreed to scale down his plans for increases in Pentagon spending.

But the president's budget proposal submitted to Congress on February 4 called for a $31.2 billion increase in military spending over 1985 levels, part of a $973.7 billion spending package with a projected 1986 deficit of $180 billion. The president called for spending cuts that would trim the deficit by $51 billion in 1986, a figure similar to the goal of Senate Republicans. But the estimated deficit for 1988 was far higher than the $100 billion objective announced by the Senate Republicans.

On April 4, Senate Republicans appeared to have reached agreement with the White House on a plan that would trim defense spending increases, restrict cost-of-living adjustments (COLAS) in Social Security benefits, and make deep cuts in domestic spending with the result of cutting the expected 1986 deficit to $175.3 billion and trimming the 1988 deficit below $100 billion. A legislative package embodying most

of these points passed the Senate by a 50 to 49 vote on May 10.

Meanwhile the House, controlled by Democrats, approved its own approach to deficit reduction that differed from the Senate most notably by freezing military spending in 1986 while allowing for Social Security COLAS to rise. After House-Senate negotiations on their different budget plans collapsed, the president, in an effort to break the deadlock, announced that he would accept a "framework for agreement" on the budget that included the House's rejection of a freeze on Social Security COLAS. Ultimately the president's decision paved the way for House and Senate approval on August 1 of a joint budget resolution that purportedly would cut the deficit by $55.5 billion in 1986. The package allowed military spending authority in 1986 to increase, but only at the rate of inflation and granted Social Security beneficiaries their customary cost-of-living increases. But passage left many Senate Republicans unhappy because they felt the president had backed away from an understanding with them to support a freeze on Social Security COLAS, after they had taken the politically dangerous step of supporting such a freeze. GOP senators, and some Democratic lawmakers too, also contended that the budget resolution would fall short of achieving the savings it promised.

Seeking a longer-term solution, Senate Republicans, with some Democratic support, turned to an ambitious legislative scheme that promised to reduce the deficit to zero by fiscal 1991 through a series of mandated annual reductions. Proposed in late September by Republican senators Phil Gramm of Texas and Warren B. Rudman of New Hampshire, along with Democratic Sen. Ernest Hollings of South Carolina, the plan passed the Senate on October 9, while the Democratic-controlled House adopted its own version of the scheme. A compromise version passed both chambers on December 11 and was signed by President Reagan. The new law gives Congress and the White House time each year to reach agreement on a deficit reduction package. But if the legislators and the executive fail to meet the preordained deficit reduction goals set by the law, automatic spending cuts would be imposed. The mandatory cuts would come from defense spending and domestic programs on a 50–50 basis. But the law specifically exempts from the automatic cuts Social Security and a group of programs for the poor, including Medicaid, Aid to Families with Dependent Children, and food stamps.

The constitutionality of the law was challenged immediately in the federal courts on grounds that it amounted to an abdication of congressional responsibility. Critics also argued that the spending cuts decreed by the new law would endanger national defense and crip-

ple many domestic programs. Many of its supporters acknowledged the law's potential dangers but contended that the deficit crisis left them little choice.

Meanwhile, though, the lawmakers continued to demonstrate how hard it was for them to actually cut the deficit when they adjourned for the year on December 20 after failing to reach agreement on a three-year $74 billion deficit reduction package. This measure had been designed to achieve a substantial portion of the deficit reduction contemplated by the budget resolution Congress had passed earlier in the year.

Congress. Apart from the deficit, the most consequential issue faced by the 99th Congress in its first session was tax reform, proposed by President Reagan in fulfillment of the promise he made to voters in his 1984 reelection campaign. In announcing the details of his plan in a televised address on May 28, Reagan promised that it would make the tax system fairer and simpler, thus encouraging economic growth. Among the significant changes were: reducing the number of tax brackets from 14 to 3 and cutting the maximum tax rate from 50% to 35%; increasing the personal exemption from $1,080 to $2,000 for all taxpayers; disallowing deductions for state and local taxes; eliminating the investment tax credit for business; and reducing the benefits for depreciation of new equipment.

Republicans complained that reducing tax advantages for business would slow economic growth. Democrats, led by New York Gov. Mario Cuomo, charged that disallowing deductions for state and local taxes would make it difficult for big states to meet their responsibilities to their citizens, all the more so since the federal government was cutting back on many of its programs. And some in both parties complained because the plan was ostensibly revenue neutral and thus would not produce any additional funds to meet what many considered the nation's most urgent problem, the budget deficit.

But for all the controversy it caused, some Republican strategists saw the idea as a weapon to help their party achieve majority

---

UNITED STATES • Information Highlights

Official Name: United States of America.
Location: Central North America.
Area: 3,618,770 sq mi (9 372 614 km^2).
Population (mid-1985 est.): 238,900,000.
Chief Cities (July 1, 1984 est.): Washington, DC, the capital, 622,873; New York, 7,164,742; Los Angeles, 3,096,721; Chicago, 2,992,472; Houston, 1,705,697; Philadelphia, 1,646,713; Detroit, 1,088,973.
Government: *Head of state and government,* Ronald Reagan, president (took office for second term, Jan. 20, 1985). *Legislature*—Congress: Senate and House of Representatives.
Monetary Unit: Dollar.

status, and Democrats were reluctant to allow the GOP to claim credit for what they contended was originally a Democratic idea. It was a Democrat, Illinois Rep. Daniel J. Rostenkowski, chairman of the House Ways and Means Committee, who proved to be Reagan's most potent ally in the battle for tax overhaul. "Rosty," as he urged citizens to call him, presided over prolonged committee hearings and then intensive bargaining sessions as the Democratic-dominated panel rewrote Reagan's initial proposal and submitted its own version of tax overhaul to the full House.

Like the original Reagan plan, the committee bill shifted some of the tax burden to business from individual taxpayers. But the committee gave larger benefits to low- and middle-income taxpayers and smaller ones to the more affluent than the president's proposal. Other differences were that the committee retained the deduction for state and local taxes; established four brackets instead of three, with the highest rate at 38%, instead of 35%; and gave taxpayers who itemize deductions—usually the wealthier taxpayers—only a $1,500 personal exemption instead of the $2,000 granted non-itemizers.

Though unhappy with some of these changes, the president called on Republicans in the Democratic-controlled House to support the bill, contending that it could be improved on by the Republican-controlled Senate. Angered by what some regarded as the president's cavalier treatment of them, House Republicans at first rejected this advice and helped to defeat a procedural motion needed to bring the bill to the House floor for a vote. But after the president made an unusual personal visit to the Hill, urging Republicans to back the measure and promising ultimately to veto any tax revision proposal that did not lower the top rate to 35% and did not grant the $2,000 exemption to all taxpayers, House Republicans gave their support to the bill. It passed the House on December 17, by a voice vote. However, its prospects for enactment in 1986 were uncertain because it was unclear whether Senate Republicans would make the changes the president wanted, and it seemed unlikely that House Democrats would accept the bill if the president did get his way.

In dealing with another major problem, the economic crisis confronting American farmers, Congress adopted two measures whose combined impact represented a sweeping change in federal farm policy. One bill lowered income and price supports to farmers, the first such reduction since that program was established in 1933. The other measure reorganized and strengthened the Farm Credit System, the nation's largest agricultural lender. The new laws were expected to spur the prevailing trend toward reducing the number of farmers, and some growers were expected to suffer hard-

ships as a result of the policy changes. Nevertheless, supporters of the legislation claimed that in the long run, driving down price support floors for domestic crops would make them more competitive overseas and help restore the health of the agricultural economy.

Concern about the trade deficit, which totaled $30.5 billion in the third quarter of 1985, also prompted Congress to pass legislation that would sharply restrict imports of shoes, textiles, and copper. But the president, who in response to the outcry in Congress about the trade deficit earlier had launched his own program to help U.S. trade, vetoed the import restriction bill on grounds that it would provoke foreign retaliation. Congressional leaders chose not even to attempt to override the veto.

The Presidency. The most dramatic event affecting Ronald Reagan's presidency in 1985 had nothing to do with the normal course of politics and government, though it did underline some of the qualities that have made Reagan such a potent political figure. This was the abdominal surgery for removal of a cancerous growth that the president underwent on July 13. The malignancy had been discovered on July 12 during what had been thought to be a routine operation for removal of a benign polyp from the president's lower intestine at the Bethesda, MD, Navy Medical Center just outside Washington. Because of the operation the president temporarily transferred the powers of his office to Vice-President George Bush. The transfer was in effect for only eight hours, while the president was undergoing the 2-hour and 53-minute operation and immediately afterward. Though the White House said the president had not formally invoked the 25th amendment to the constitution, the procedures followed conformed to those established by the amendment that covers presidential disability and succession.

With the eyes of the nation riveted on him, Reagan displayed grit, determination to get back on the job, and humor in the face of grim adversity. He quipped that he had told one of his doctors "that if Congress can't make the spending cuts we need, I'm going to send him up to Capitol Hill to do some cutting." The president left the hospital on July 20, only a week after his surgery, and on July 25 he signaled his readiness to return to his normal duties by convening a cabinet meeting. His approval rating climbed in opinion polls, much as it had after the assassination attempt he survived in the first weeks of his presidency.

Despite his continued high popularity, Reagan could not entirely avoid the problems of being a lame duck, particularly the attrition rate among his cabinet secretaries and other key aides, some of whom seemed eager for change after four years on the job. Early in the year it was announced that two key figures in the administration, White House Chief of Staff

Changes in the Reagan team (l-r): Edwin Meese III became attorney general after lengthy confirmation hearings; Donald Regan took over as White House Chief of Staff, and Otis Bowen was named secretary of health and human services.

James A. Baker III and Treasury Secretary Donald T. Regan, would exchange jobs. Baker's talent and experience were put to good use at the Treasury where he assumed much of the responsibility for promoting tax reform on Capitol Hill. But at times his shrewd political instincts were missed at the White House where critics complained that Regan's abrasive style caused unnecessary irritation. (*See* BIOGRAPHY.)

In other changes, William P. Clark, another Reagan confidant, resigned as Interior Secretary, to be replaced by Energy Secretary Donald P. Hodel, who was in turn replaced by John S. Herrington, White House personnel director. William J. Bennett, chairman of the National Endowment for the Humanities, succeeded Terrel H. Bell, who had announced his resignation as education secretary late in 1984.

One of the most prominent women in the administration, Jeane J. Kirkpatrick, resigned as United Nations ambassador to return to private life and was replaced by Lt. Gen. Vernon A. Walters (*see* BIOGRAPHY), who had served as deputy director of the Central Intelligence Agency in the Nixon and Ford administrations. Edwin Meese III, whose 1984 nomination to be attorney general, replacing William French Smith, touched off prolonged controversy over his handling of his personal finances, was finally confirmed by the Senate. But a new cabinet opening was created when Labor Secretary Raymond T. Donovan, who in 1984 had become the first cabinet officer to be indicted while holding office, resigned after a New York State judge denied a motion to dismiss the charges against him. Donovan was replaced by William E. Brock III (*see* BIOGRAPHY), who had been Reagan's U.S. trade representative.

Next to leave was David A. Stockman, director of the Office of Management and Budget, who joined a New York investment

banking firm. He was replaced by James C. Miller III, chairman of the Federal Trade Commission. Also leaving the cabinet was Health and Human Services Secretary Margaret Heckler, whose departure was preceded by frequent reports that she was out of favor with White House Chief of Staff Regan. Heckler, who became ambassador to Ireland, was succeeded by former Indiana Gov. Otis R. Bowen, a physician as well as a politician. And late in the year, Robert C. McFarlane gave up his post as national security adviser. His deputy, Vice Adm. John M. Poindexter, took over the post.

One unanticipated problem for the Reagan administration was posed by the unprecedented disclosures of widespread spying against the United States. In a series of investigations the Federal Bureau of Investigation arrested 11 persons on espionage charges during the year. Perhaps the most damaging of the spying activities uncovered was a Navy family spy ring, involving former Navy Chief Warrant Officer John Anthony Walker, Jr., and his son Navy Seaman Michael Lance Walker, both of whom pleaded guilty to espionage, along with John Walker's brother, Arthur James Walker, a retired Navy lieutenant commander who was convicted of espionage. Also allegedly involved in the ring was a retired Navy Chief Petty Officer and friend of John Walker, Jerry A. Whitworth. Though the members of the Walker spy ring and most of the other espionage suspects apprehended were accused of passing classified documents to the United States' chief adversary, the Soviet Union, one person arrested, Jonathan Jay Pollard, a civilian analyst for the Navy, was charged with selling classified documents to one of the United States' closest allies, Israel. (*See also* ESPIONAGE.)

As part of an effort to combat espionage, the president ordered a far-reaching program

In July, Nancy Reagan toured the aircraft carrier "USS America" and learned about the Navy's anti-drug and alcohol campaign. Such programs remained a principal interest of the first lady.

AP/Wide World

of polygraph, or lie detector, tests, for government personnel and employees of civilian contractors handling sensitive information. However, when Secretary of State George P. Shultz publicly threatened to resign if he were forced to take such a test, the administration decided to limit the lie detector program and to use it in conjunction with other security measures.

Politics. With the political scene in ferment following President Reagan's landslide reelection in 1984, both parties faced significant challenges in 1985. For the Democrats the imperative was to develop a new alliance to replace the old New Deal coalition after its apparent demise in the 1984 elections. To help lead them the Democrats chose as their national chairman Paul G. Kirk, Jr., a Washington lawyer and former aide to Massachusetts Sen. Edward M. Kennedy. Though Kirk had been opposed by some Democrats from the South and West on the grounds that he was too

Vice-President George Bush is sworn in for a second term. There was talk that he would run for the top spot in '88.

AP/Wide World

liberal, the new chairman quickly set about to reassure them. He took steps to restrict the influence of the interest group caucuses in the national committee, which many complained had tarnished the party's image. He also publicly urged the AFL-CIO leadership to refrain from endorsing a contender for the party's presidential nomination, in order to avoid the divisiveness that the labor federation's endorsement had caused in 1984.

As for the Republicans, they had the task of taking advantage of the opportunity created by Reagan's popularity and the Democratic weakness to make themselves into a new majority party. They did succeed in persuading a number of local Democratic leaders to convert to the GOP ranks. But overall, Republicans were hindered by general voter apathy toward either political party, a trend that some analysts said suggested political de-alignment rather than realignment.

Republicans were disappointed at their inability to capture an open congressional seat in a conservative House district in east Texas, which had been traditionally Democratic. In the August 3 vote Democratic candidate Jim Chapman narrowly defeated Republican Edd Hargett, though Hargett outspent him by more than $1 million and had Vice-President Bush campaign for him.

The two statewide elections in November were equally inconclusive about the balance of political party power. In New Jersey popular Republican incumbent Thomas H. Kean won a landslide victory over little-known Democratic challenger, Peter Shapiro, and helped his party take control of the lower house of the state legislature. On the other hand, in Virginia, a Democratic ticket headed by state Attorney General Gerald L. Baliles and including a woman and a black swept the three top state offices. The Democratic candidate for lieutenant governor, State Sen. L. Douglas Wilder, became the first black elected to an executive post statewide in the South since reconstruction. The two elec-

Big election news in Virginia: L. Douglas Wilder (center)), a black state senator from Richmond, and Mary Sue Taylor (left), a lawyer-legislator from Patrick County, were chosen lieutenant governor and state attorney general, respectively. Gerald L. Baliles (right), a former state attorney general, headed the winning Democratic ticket.

Richmond Newspapers

tions left the Democrats in control of 34 governors to 16 for Republicans.

In mayoral elections, incumbents Edward I. Koch in New York and Coleman Young in Detroit, both Democrats, and George Voinovich in Cleveland, a Republican, easily won reelection. In Houston another incumbent, Democrat Kathy Whitmire, was also reelected in a campaign marked by an attempt by her challenger, former Mayor Louie Welch, to exploit public concern about Acquired Immune Deficiency Syndrome (AIDS) against Whitmire, who had the support of Houston's gay community. In Miami, six-term Mayor Maurice Ferre was unseated by a Harvard-trained lawyer, Xavier Suarez, who became the city's first Cuban American mayor. Earlier in the year Los Angeles Mayor Tom Bradley captured an unprecedented fourth term without difficulty.

In referenda of note, Oak Park, IL, citizens voted to keep a ban on handguns; voters in Boulder, CO, and Oberlin, OH, approved propositions designating their communities as "nuclear-free zones"; and voters in three New England communities—Bristol, CT; Dover, NH; and Derry, NH—endorsed the Supreme Court decision Roe v. Wade, giving a woman the right to an abortion.

Although the 1986 midterm elections were still a year away, early maneuvering was already underway for the 1988 presidential election. On the Republican side, opinion polls indicated that Vice-President George Bush was the front-runner, with New York Congressman Jack Kemp and Republican Senate leader Bob Dole of Kansas among his rivals. On the Democratic side, Senator Kennedy, who had been considered a strong contender for the presidential nomination he sought in 1980, surprised many political observers by announcing in December that he would not seek the White House in 1988. With Kennedy out of the picture, Colorado Sen. Gary Hart appeared to be

the Democratic front-runner, on the basis of his strong race against Walter F. Mondale in 1984.

Allegations of illegal and improper behavior by public officials cast a shadow over the political scene. Former New York Congresswoman Geraldine Ferraro, the 1984 Democratic vice-presidential candidate, announced that she would not seek her party's Senate nomination in New York to challenge Republican incumbent Alfonse D'Amato, because of uncertainty about the outcome of a Justice Department investigation into her financial background. In New Orleans the fraud and racketeering trial of Louisiana Democratic Gov. Edwin W. Edwards ended in a hung jury after a week of deliberations.

ROBERT SHOGAN
Washington Bureau, "Los Angeles Times"

Campaigning for tax reform, President Reagan receives the endorsement of North Carolina State University's mascot.

AP/Wide World

The Economy

To the surprise of many economists and the great satisfaction of almost everyone, the U.S. economy found a reserve of strength early in the year that enabled it to skirt the edge of recession and remain moderately strong as the year wore on. It was a remarkable performance, considering the pitfalls that pocked the road ahead, and as the year ended economists were as busy analyzing the past as they were with forecasting the future. By their reasoning, the economic times were not supposed to have been so good, and they wanted to know the reason why.

Confidence. Moreover, in spite of the old obstacles, such as a $200 billion-plus budget deficit once again, the good times were expected to continue. Statements from the White House repeatedly were upbeat, and they were matched by comments in millions of homes. Business looked for rising profits, and consumer surveys showed great confidence among buyers. The stock market confirmed the feeling, with all stock indexes rising to record highs.

"The picture that emerges is of an economy in little danger of faltering in 1986," said Morgan Guaranty Trust. "An improving economy and a promising outlook for next year offer several reasons for rejoicing this Christmas season," said CIGNA, a big insurer. Merrill Lynch, the brokerage house, said that it expected the gross national product (GNP) to grow more in 1986 than it did in 1985. To many people, it was the good old days, and some compared the feeling to that of the soaring 1960s.

"Over the past five years," said Richard Curtin of the University of Michigan's Survey Research Center, "the confidence index has not only posted a larger net increase than following any of the recessions of the 1970s, but it has remained near peak levels for an unusually extended time." The center's midyear survey showed that the highest proportion of American families in more than 30 years held favorable attitudes toward buying conditions for large household durables, such as furniture. More than 60% of families thought it was a good time to buy cars, and 53% thought it was a favorable time to buy houses, which equaled the survey's peak figure, recorded two years earlier. Late in the year the Census Bureau announced that 26.4 million of the 83.9 million U.S. households were sufficiently affluent to live comfortably and have money remaining—$10,525 on average—to save or spend on luxuries. It was a gain of one million since 1981.

Data Resources, Inc., an economic numbers factory used by many of the nation's top institutions, documented some of the reasons for the confidence. On the expansion's third anniversary in December, it reminded clients that "inflation has been brought under control, nominal interest rates are less than half what they were just four years ago, and over 8 million people are back at work since unemployment peaked at 10.6% in 1982." The number employed rose 2.2 million to 107.2 million in 1985, and most of them were women. The civilian jobless rate fell to 7.2% from 7.5% a year earlier.

The mood was a distinct contrast to the nervousness with which the year began. In January, after two years of growth from perhaps the deepest recession since the Great Depression of the 1930s, most Americans were expecting a pronounced downturn. The slowdown did seem to come; in the first three months of the year, according to the Commerce Department, the GNP—based on constant or 1972 dollars to reduce the distortions of inflation—grew at only 0.3%, compared with 10.1% in the same quarter a year earlier. Economists said the tiny expansion documented what they termed a "growth recession," or growth insufficient to reduce jobless rates and raise personal income.

Indexes. Even the stock market got caught in the mood, and the Dow Jones industrial average recorded its lowest reading of the year, 1,184.96 points, on January 4. Then, reaffirming the maxim that investor actions foretell the weakness or strength of the economy, it began rising. After breaking one record high after another, it reached a pinnacle of 1,553.1 points on December 16, and remained above 1,500 points as the year ended. Helping to put it there was a spree of mergers, acquisitions, and takeovers, based in part on the desire of corporate management to restructure itself for more competitive international markets. (*See* page 151.)

The rise in GNP, or total production of goods and services, seemed to quicken to an annual rate of 1.9% in the second quarter and then, according to early figures, leaped to a 4.3% pace in the third quarter. Revisions made just before the year ended, however, pushed

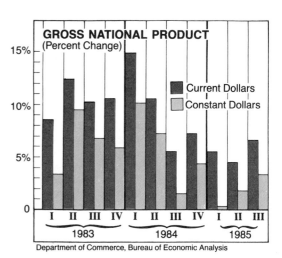

GROSS NATIONAL PRODUCT
(Percent Change)

Current Dollars
Constant Dollars

I II III IV   I II III IV   I II III
1983   1984   1985

Department of Commerce, Bureau of Economic Analysis

DOW JONES INDUSTRIAL (30 stocks) AVERAGE 1985 (Friday closing figures)

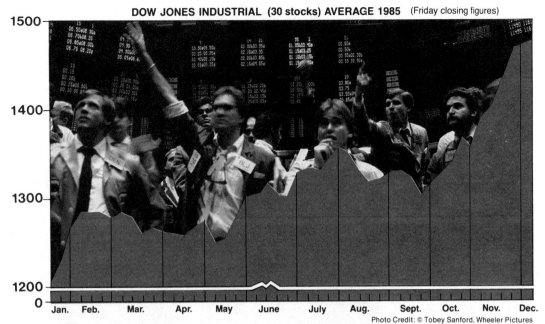

The Dow Jones industrial average set new marks—1,300 on May 20, 1,400 on November 6, and 1,500 on December 11.

Photo Credit: © Tobey Sanford, Wheeler Pictures

the first-quarter rate up to 3.7% and brought the third quarter down to 3%. Almost simultaneously, a Commerce Department "flash estimate" indicated the final quarter of the year was moving ahead at a 3.2% rate, higher than most analysts had anticipated. For the year, the GNP rose to nearly $1,680 billion, 2.4% or $40 billion more than a year earlier, based on constant (1972) dollars. Prices rose only 3.5% for the year, a slight improvement over 1984. It was the third straight year of relative stability.

It was the same with interest rates: good news. A slow decline throughout the year, and the expectation of a continuation, helped almost all areas of investing, but none more than housing. The lessening of inflation, a mortgage rate decline to between 10% and 12% (the lower figure being for variable as opposed to fixed rate loans), and a 2.2% rise in disposable personal income made it possible. The number of existing home sales approached 3 million by year's end, while new-housing starts rose to about 1.75 million units, slightly higher than in 1984.

Cars did even better, helped in part by offers from the Big Three—General Motors, Ford, and Chrysler—of below-market financing. In some instances the interest rate was only 7.9%, while credit-card users continued to pay rates at least double that. In all, 11.1 million cars were sold in 1985, with 8.3 million of them domestic makes.

Credit. Many economists were disturbed by the amount of credit used. E. Gerald Corrigan, president of the Federal Reserve Bank of New York, said "the pervasiveness of credit might mean it is symptomatic of a cultural revolution about debt." People who had spent a lifetime

accumulating equity now were accumulating debt. "Credit use has virtually exploded," said Morgan Guaranty Trust. "Credit growth no longer is moving in close step with economic growth, as it did for decades."

Morgan statisticians estimated that the credit demand from the federal government rose 14.8%, from municipalities floating tax-exempt issues by 20.2%, and from consumers by 20.8%. Business borrowing rose 10.6%, and the amount needed to finance mortgages rose 9.1%. The total new demand for credit came to $1.87 trillion, up 12.8% in one year.

In spite of such spending, corporate profits after taxes fell about 3% to just over $140 billion from nearly $146 billion a year earlier. But Merrill Lynch forecast a sharp rise in 1986.

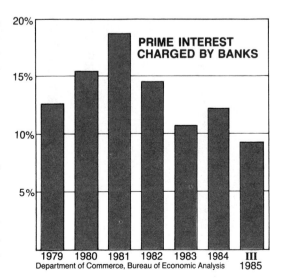

PRIME INTEREST CHARGED BY BANKS

Department of Commerce, Bureau of Economic Analysis

1979 1980 1981 1982 1983 1984 III 1985

Senators Phil Gramm (R-TX), left, and Warren Rudman (R-NH) successfully sponsored a bill which calls for the elimination of the budget deficit by fiscal 1991. The constitutionality of the new legislation was to be tested in the federal courts in 1986.

AP/Wide World

Disappointments and Outlook. There were big disappointments. Farmers continued to lose their lands because of low prices and heavy mortgages. (*See* page 36.) The growing wealth seemed unevenly distributed; the number of people considered to be living in poverty hardly shrank at all and even grew by some estimates. While Congress managed to pass the Gramm-Rudman balanced budget bill, it failed to agree on tax legislation. And, while the trading value of the dollar was finally falling, as had been hoped for many months, it had yet to make an impact on the U.S. balance-of-payments deficit.

These were serious problems, and persistent ones, and they were bound to undo the economic expansion if not attended to. But as the year ended, the optimists seemed to be in control. Had not the economy escaped the consequences in 1985? The mood seemed to be: it can be done again.

JOHN CUNNIFF, *The Associated Press*

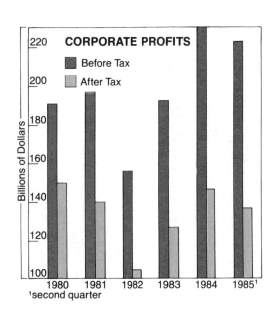

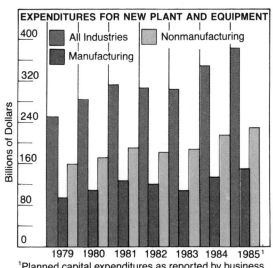

¹Planned capital expenditures as reported by business
Department of Commerce, Bureau of Economic Analysis

REPORT

State Lotteries

...ited States
...ornia opened
...ober 3, and New
...jackpot in August.
...ted lotteries in 1985,
...st Virginia readied for
...e five new lotteries were
...s in 1984, with Iowa's com-
...85 legislature. With the new
...ates and the District of Colum-
...al lotteries. Montana is scheduled
...a lottery in November 1986, and Ne-
...also is considering one. In Florida a
...ide petition drive to vote on a lottery in
...ember 1986 is under way.

Lotteries in the United States date from the Revolutionary War period. Scandals resulted in bans, however, which lasted until 1964, when New Hampshire started a state-run sweepstakes. As other states recognized lotteries as an alternative to increased taxes, the number of games and tickets sold grew steadily. From July 1, 1984, to June 30, 1985, total state lottery sales reached an estimated $9 billion and represented the fastest-growing segment of the U.S. gaming industry, with a market share of 22%. Illinois, New York, and Pennsylvania each have lottery sales in excess of $1 billion annually.

The trend in lotteries is toward lotto games, in which players typically pick six out of 40 or so numbers with a drawing determining the winner. New lotteries typically start with rub-off instant game tickets and later add lotto and other numbers games. Many states have computerized on-line games for lotto, and Illinois is testing video lottery games.

California authorized 20,000 retail outlets to sell the 400 million tickets printed for its first instant game. With expected sales of $1.4 billion, the lottery could bring in $475 million for education during its first year of operation. Iowa sold $11.5 million in instant tickets during the month following its start on August 22, with annual revenues expected to reach $100 million. Oregon opened on April 25 and predicted its sales to be $110 million annually.

From state to state, lottery revenues range from less than 1% of general fund revenues to more than 6% (in Maryland). Lottery revenues go to general funds in ten states and to education in five. In the other states, revenues are dedicated to purposes ranging from transportation to parks. Among the new entrants, California will be devoting its lottery revenues to education, while Oregon and Iowa will use the money for economic development; Iowa also will designate a portion of the revenues to a

AP/Wide World

Joseph Moore of Brooklyn won a one-third share of the record $41 million jackpot in New York's Lotto 48 game in August. A total of 36,112,626 tickets were sold for the drawing. The winning combination? 14-17-22-23-30-47.

gamblers assistance fund. And in Missouri and West Virginia, profits will go to the general fund.

Oregon planned to start a lotto game early in 1986 using on-line computer retail terminals in order to compete with Washington, the first Western state to offer on-line lotto games. California also planned to offer on-line games in 1986.

In the East, Maine, New Hampshire, and Vermont opened the first regional lottery on September 3 in a move to build bigger jackpots to compete with New York. The New York lottery's record $41 million jackpot in August was split among three tickets, including one held jointly by 21 factory workers. According to a survey of 1,000 lottery winners by H. Roy Kaplan, a sociology professor at the Florida Institute of Technology, most retain a strong "work ethic" after winning the big prize. He found that only 40% of $1 million winners subsequently quit working or retired.

ELAINE S. KNAPP

In Geneva, November 21, President Reagan and Soviet Chairman Gorbachev (second row, left) *watched intently as their foreign ministers, George Shultz and Eduard A. Shevardnadze* (left) *signed documents ending the summit conference.*

Foreign Affairs

In 1985, U.S. foreign policy confronted the same issues that had concerned the nation during the previous few years. Relations with the Soviet Union—bad since 1979—improved as the two sides held a series of talks culminating in a summit meeting between President Ronald Reagan and Soviet Chairman Mikhail Gorbachev in November. Central America continued to provoke anxiety in Washington and the country at large. Progress toward peace in the Middle East was interrupted by hostage crises in June and October. In the spring the president suffered an embarrassment when he commemorated the 40th anniversary of the end of World War II. Congress and an aroused public tried to force stronger U.S. action against South Africa's apartheid system.

Organization of Personnel. The principal figures in charge of American foreign policy remained for the most part the same for much of the year. George Shultz and Caspar Weinberger continued as secretaries of state and defense, respectively, and Robert McFarlane remained assistant to the president for national security affairs until December. Then on December 4 the White House announced that McFarlane was giving up the post "to move on to new personal and professional challenges." He was succeeded by Vice Adm. John M. Poindexter, 49, who had been serving as McFarlane's deputy. Early in the year, Jeane Kirkpatrick resigned as ambassador to the United Nations and left the administration. She was replaced by Gen. Vernon Walters (*see* BIOGRAPHY).

On the Senate side, Richard Lugar (R-IN) became head of the Foreign Relations Committee and Barry Goldwater (R-AZ) took over the leadership of Armed Services. Sen. David Durenberger (R-MN) replaced Goldwater as head of the Intelligence Committee. In the House of Representatives, Rep. David Obey (D-WI) chaired the important Foreign Operations Subcommittee of the Appropriations Committee, and Dante B. Fascell (D-FL) remained chairman of the Foreign Affairs committee. Perhaps the most significant change in House personnel took place in January when the Democratic caucus voted to strip Rep. Melvin Price (D-IL) of the chairmanship of the Armed Services Committee. His replacement, Rep. Les Aspin (D-WI), 46, represented a new breed of younger Democratic representatives.

Soviet Relations. The United States and the Soviet Union held a series of talks during 1985 aimed at improving relations between the two countries and capping the arms race. By the conclusion of the November summit, it was not clear if the negotiations had borne fruit.

Secretary of State George Shultz and Soviet Foreign Minister Andrei Gromyko met in Geneva January 7–8 and agreed to open talks on the arms race and space weapons. By the end of that month the two governments had agreed to send delegates to three related sets of talks to be held in Geneva commencing in March. President Reagan named Max M. Kampelman (*see* BIOGRAPHY) to be the overall director of the American delegation. The president selected Maynard W. Glitman as the chief American delegate to the intermediate-range ballistic missile talks, and retired Sen. John B. Tower

(R-TX) became the official American delegate to the Strategic Arms Reduction Talks.

Before the negotiators assembled in Geneva in March, another change took place at the top of the leadership of the Soviet Union. Party leader Konstantin U. Chernenko died on March 10. He was replaced almost immediately by Mikhail Gorbachev. After several months of negotiations, the United States and the Soviet Union agreed to a summit meeting on neutral ground in Geneva in the middle of November. Before the meeting took place, Andrei Gromyko was succeeded as foreign minister by Eduard Shevardnadze.

At the Geneva arms-control negotiations, the Soviets insisted that the United States stop work on its Strategic Defense Initiative (SDI). For its part the United States was just as adamant in insisting that it could not link work on SDI with other arms-control issues. Instead, the American negotiators called on the Soviets to reduce their missile force in Eastern Europe and make a good faith effort at capping the number of heavy ballistic missile launchers.

President Reagan and General Secretary Gorbachev held their summit conference November 19–21. They met privately with only interpreters present for more than six hours and spent an additional five hours in plenary sessions in the presence of senior advisers. At the end of their conversations they signed agreements on cultural exchanges, consulates, and air safety in the North Pacific. Most significantly, they agreed to regular meetings, with Gorbachev coming to Washington in 1986 and Reagan traveling to Moscow in 1987. The two leaders restated their opposition to the spread of nuclear weapons and their hopes for a ban on chemical weapons. They pledged international cooperation on research in fusion energy, and they promised to study the creation of a joint crisis center to reduce the risks of nuclear war. They made less obvious progress on the divisive issues of arms control, human rights, and regional conflicts. They pledged continued efforts at an arms-control agreement, did not comment on the extension of the 1979 Strategic Arms Limitation Treaty (SALT II), and made no joint statements on human rights.

Central America. In Central America, Nicaragua and El Salvador presented difficulties. The United States continued to support the counterrevolutionary armies fighting to overthrow the Sandinista government in Nicaragua. In El Salvador, however, the United States maintained its support of the Christian Democratic government of José Napoleón Duarte against a revolution led by the Democratic Revolutionary Front (FDR).

In the case of Nicaragua, the administration found its position assailed abroad and in trouble at home. On January 18 the State Department announced that it would not participate in the World Court case brought by Nicaragua against the United States.

Congress attempted to block funding for the counterrevolutionaries. In April the Senate voted to continue to provide some $14 million in so-called humanitarian aid for the counterrevolutionaries. In the Democratic-controlled House, however, the administration had more trouble receiving support. After President Reagan warned of "a new danger" in Central America from support of Nicaragua by Iran, Libya, and the Palestine Liberation Organization (PLO), Democratic representatives worried that war might be imminent. The House voted by a narrow margin on April 24 to stop all support for the counterrevolutionaries.

Immediately after this rebuff of the president, Nicaragua's President Daniel Ortega visited Moscow. Some Democrats in the House of Representatives reacted with alarm to Ortega's presence in the Soviet capital. Accordingly, in June the House reversed itself and voted $27 million in nonmilitary aid over the next nine months.

The Allies. The 11th annual economic summit conference of the seven major industrial nations of the non-Communist world (Canada, France, West Germany, Great Britain, Italy, Japan, and the United States) was held in the West German capital of Bonn at the beginning of May. Instead of a triumphal tour of Western European capitals to mark the 40th anniversary of the end of World War II, the president became embroiled in a nasty altercation over Germany's responsibility for its Nazi past.

Earlier the president had agreed to a request from Chancellor Helmut Kohl to visit a cemetery containing the graves of Germany's war dead. Unfortunately, no American war dead lay in rest at the Bitburg cemetery the president intended to visit. Even worse, among the 2,000 German soldiers were 49 members of the elite Waffen SS troops. In the face of opposition from American Jewish and Veterans' groups, the president went forward with his scheduled visit on May 5. He spent only ten minutes at the cemetery and did not speak there. Instead, the highlight of the day was a moving ceremony at the German concentration camp of Bergen-Belsen. The remainder of the president's European tour—including stops in Spain and Portugal and an address before the European Parliament—was overshadowed by the controversy over the visit to Bitburg.

Nor did the economic summit prove to be a success for the American objective—a definite date for a new round of trade talks. President Reagan's counterparts complained that the high price of the U.S. dollar, which had risen to its highest levels in five years in March, had made it difficult for them to purchase U.S. goods. The overvalued dollar and the huge U.S. federal budget deficit were seen as the principal causes of the U.S. trade deficit.

The Middle East. The United States resumed its efforts to broker an agreement between Israel and its neighbors. Much activity took place, but little progress was evident.

Prospects seemed promising at the beginning of the year, when the new coalition government in Israel signaled its willingness to improve relations with Egypt and reach an agreement with Jordan and, possibly, Syria. Prime Minister Shimon Peres wanted to remove Israel's troops from their three-year occupation of southern Lebanon. To achieve these ends, Peres received Assistant Secretary of State Richard Murphy who toured the Middle East in April. Peres did not rule out Israel's participation in a peace conference, but he did want to make certain that the joint Palestinian-Jordanian delegation did not contain any avowed members of the PLO. Israel's army also departed from Lebanon by early June.

Progress stopped abruptly, however, on June 14 when several Shiite Muslim gunmen commandeered TWA's Flight 847 out of Athens. The hijackers murdered an American seaman, Robert Stethem. Once the plane finally stopped in Beirut, the gunmen kept the remaining 39 American men as hostages. The Shiites demanded that the United States force Israel to release 766 prisoners it had captured during its occupation of Lebanon and taken back with them to Israel proper.

Throughout the hostage crisis, echoes reverberated of the earlier Iranian captivity of 1979–81. President Reagan observed, "I have to wait it out," when asked if he would use armed force. The United States used Syria's President Hafiz al-Assad and Lebanon's Justice Minister and Shiite leader Nabih Berri as intermediaries. After days of frantic conversations, a deal was struck. On June 30 the hostages were released to the custody of Syria. The United States made no public claim on Israel to release its prisoners, but Israel did let all of them go over the next three months.

President Reagan consolidated his public popularity by his handling of another Mideast hijacking in October. On October 7, four Palestinian gunmen commandeered an Italian cruise ship, the *Achille Lauro,* off the Egyptian coast. They murdered a 69-year-old disabled American, Leon Klinghoffer, before surrendering to Egyptian authorities. Cairo promised the hijackers safe passage out of Egypt, but U.S. navy jets intercepted their airliner and forced it to land in Sicily. There, Italian police arrested the terrorists. Unfortunately, relations between the United States and Italy and Egypt became badly strained in the aftermath. (*See also* TERRORISM.)

Turmoil in South Africa. The U.S. administration was caught by surprise by fast-moving events in South Africa. By the end of the summer, public outrage in the United States over the racist policy of apartheid had forced the

AP/Wide World

President Reagan announced in December that John M. Poindexter (right) *would succeed Robert McFarlane* (left) *as presidential assistant for national security affairs.*

State Department and the president to substantially alter their policy of "constructive engagement" with the Pretoria government. The public and Congress took the lead in forcing changes. At Thanksgiving-time 1984, opponents of apartheid threw up a picket line around the South African embassy in Washington. These demonstrations soon spread.

During the summer, riots erupted in South Africa itself as blacks in the shantytowns surrounding the white cities took to the streets. In late July the South African government responded by imposing a state of emergency, banning demonstrations of all kinds, but unrest continued. Congress considered the imposition final proof that constructive engagement had failed. Both houses considered legislation imposing sanctions against South Africa. The House passed a sanctions bill before adjourning for its August recess. The Senate seemed ready to pass similar legislation.

Alarmed at the prospect of losing control of foreign relations, the Reagan administration looked for other ways to force changes in South Africa. In August, National Security Adviser McFarlane met with South African officials in Vienna who promised him that President P. W. Botha would soon announce significant reforms. When Botha spoke to a gathering of his Nationalist Party, however, he deflated these hopes.

An angry Sen. Robert Dole promised swift action on the sanctions bill. Left with little choice, the president issued an executive order imposing some sanctions. (*See also* feature article, page 26.)

ROBERT D. SCHULZINGER
University of Colorado, Boulder

U.S.-Soviet Summitry

The post World War II history of U.S.-Soviet summitry has been one of both substantive accomplishment and political posturing, hostility and détente. When U.S. President Ronald Reagan and Soviet Communist Party General Secretary Mikhail Gorbachev met in Geneva on Nov. 19–21, 1985, it marked the tenth summit conference between leaders of the two superpowers since the mid-1950s. Their talks did not result in any agreements on the central issues of arms control, but they did produce some tangible results, including an agreement to exchange visits over the next two years. In short, the 1985 summit was neither so chilly as the Vienna meeting between John F. Kennedy and Nikita Khrushchev in 1961, nor so concretely successful as the three conferences between Richard M. Nixon and Leonid Brezhnev.

The 1950s and 1960s. After World War II, in the early days of the Cold War, no summits were held while the Soviet dictator Joseph Stalin was still alive. After his death in 1953, Great Britain's Prime Minister Winston Churchill encouraged the new U.S. president, Dwight D. Eisenhower, to open a dialogue with Stalin's successors, and a meeting was arranged for Geneva in the summer of 1955. Eisenhower electrified the gathering with a call for "open skies" to monitor each side's atomic tests. That plan came to naught, but the optimistic "spirit of Geneva" seemed to portend a lessening of tensions. In September 1959, Eisenhower met again with Nikita Khrushchev, and the two men promised to continue their conversations. Nine months later, however, Khrushchev abruptly canceled a meeting in Paris after the Soviets shot down an American U-2 spy plane over their territory.

President Kennedy's only Soviet summit was held in Vienna in June 1961. Khrushchev confronted him over the Berlin issue and insisted that the two sides sign a treaty with East Germany. Shortly after the summit, Kennedy called for a large buildup of U.S. forces and Khrushchev presided over construction of the Berlin Wall.

President Lyndon B. Johnson met with Premier Aleksei Kosygin at Glassboro, NJ, in June 1967, immediately following the Six-Day Arab-Israeli war. They could not resolve differences, including Vietnam, but they did set in motion lower-level talks on arms control.

The 1970s. President Nixon's three summits with Leonid Brezhnev marked the high point of concrete accomplishments in the era of détente. At the first one, in Moscow in May 1972, a logjam was broken over strategic weapons, and the two leaders thereupon signed the Anti-Ballistic Missile (ABM) treaty and the Interim Agreement on Strategic Arms Limitations (SALT I). At their next meeting, in Washington in June 1973, Nixon and Brezhnev agreed to reach a new arms treaty by 1974. When Nixon went to Moscow in late June of that year, he brought back the Treaty on Limitation of Underground Nuclear Weapon Tests and a ten-year economic pact. President Gerald Ford had one summit with Brezhnev, in November 1974. He was unable to nail down a SALT II treaty, but a tentative arrangement was reached on missiles and bombers.

President Jimmy Carter abandoned the arms-limitations positions of the Ford administration, and the Soviets reacted coolly to the U.S. reversal. It therefore took more than two years of hard bargaining before a SALT II treaty was ready. This document became the centerpiece of the Vienna summit between Carter and Brezhnev in June 1979. But conservative opposition at home and the Soviet invasion of Afghanistan forced Carter to remove the agreement from consideration by the Senate.

The 1980s. Ronald Reagan campaigned for the U.S. presidency in 1980 opposing détente, SALT II, and the practice of regular summit meetings. For most of his first term, he resisted calls to meet with Soviet leaders, denouncing the USSR as "the focus of evil in the modern world." But as the election of 1984 approached, Reagan became more conciliatory, agreeing to meet with Soviet Foreign Minister Andrei Gromyko in September 1984. He dispatched Secretary of State George Shultz to Geneva in January 1985 to resume arms-control negotiations that had broken off 13 months earlier. And when Soviet party leader Konstantin Chernenko died in March 1985, U.S. Vice-President George Bush attended the funeral. He carried an invitation to the new Soviet leader, Mikhail Gorbachev, to meet President Reagan in the United States.

Gorbachev demurred at traveling to Washington, but by July he agreed to a meeting in Geneva in November. For the rest of the summer and fall, each side tried to shape public expectations for the upcoming talks. The Soviets tried to make arms control and the Strategic Defense Initiative the centerpiece, while the Americans tried to reduce public optimism. Where once Reagan had derided any "get acquainted" meeting, now his advisers stated that U.S.-Soviet relations would improve merely if the two men met, sized each other up, and agreed to continue their dialogue. The Geneva summit fulfilled these lowered hopes.

ROBERT D. SCHULZINGER

URUGUAY

Restoration of an elected constitutional civilian government, after a dozen years of military dictatorship, was the most important event in Uruguay during 1985.

Political Affairs. On February 15 the parliament, which had been elected on Nov. 25, 1984, was sworn in. On March 2, President Julio Maria Sanguinetti took office. Some 500 foreign representatives from 73 countries attended his inauguration.

The new democratic regime saw the re-emergence of the major political forces that had predominated before the installation of the military regime in 1973. President Sanguinetti had been elected by the traditional Colorado Party, and his first cabinet was made up principally of members of that party, although there were minority representatives of the pro-Catholic Civic Union Party. In parliament the Colorados had the largest representation, but the major opposition Blanco Party also had substantial membership, as did the Wide Front coalition of Socialists, Communists, Christian Democrats, and dissident Colorados.

The Sanguinetti government moved quickly to dismantle the apparatus of the military dictatorship. The first cabinet meeting ended the legal ban on the Communist Party and restored legal status to the Convencion Nacional de Trabajadores (CNT) labor confederation and the Students Federation.

The new regime also sponsored in Congress a political amnesty. Just before Sanguinetti took office, a court had freed 111 political prisoners, 99 of whom had been charged with subversion. Subsequently, an amnesty law exonerated all those convicted of political offenses since 1962. The former terrorists of the Tupamaro group responded positively to their amnesty and release. They pledged that they would continue their revolutionary struggle by peaceful means, not terrorism.

The relationship of the new regime with the still-powerful military establishment remained touchy. Although there had been a tacit agreement by many of the civilian politicians not to try to bring the military to account for their behavior during the dictatorship, it was not entirely clear that such would be the case. In July, denunciations in Congress, particularly by members of the Wide Front, of tortures and murders by military and police members during the dictatorship brought "concern" from the armed forces.

Economy. The economic situation remained precarious. By March 31 the country had a foreign debt of $4.6 billion. An interim agreement had been reached with foreign banks in December 1984, providing for a six-month rollover of $120 million due in the first half of 1985. In June and July, the Minister of Economy and head of the Central Bank undertook negotiations with the International Monetary Fund and foreign banks for more long-term arrangements.

However, the country's international position was made more difficult by the fact that its foreign trade surplus dropped 70% during the first five months of the year. But the situation was helped in September, when Uruguay received a $45 million loan from the World Bank to finance energy projects.

Finance Minister Ricardo Zerbino presented an overall government economic plan calling for growth in the gross domestic product (GDP) of 2–4% annually, a "realistic" exchange rate, and a cut in inflation to 60% a year. He also called for a reduction in the government's fiscal deficit, an expansion of exports, and an increase in investments of 6% by the public sector.

The government's economic program aroused some negative reaction from the CNT labor confederation. Early in June, it announced a state of mobilization in the form of strikes and marches because of "inadequate" wage increases decreed by the government.

Foreign Policy. The Sanguinetti government conducted an aggressive foreign policy. In August, when Gen. Hugo Banzer threatened an insurrection to thwart election of Victor Paz Estenssoro as president of Bolivia, Sanguinetti joined Argentine President Alfonsín and Colombian President Betancur in going to La Paz to dissuade the general. In that month, Uruguay also joined the Contadora Support Group to seek a peaceful solution to Central American problems.

ROBERT J. ALEXANDER
Rutgers University

URUGUAY • Information Highlights

Official Name: Oriental Republic of Uruguay.
Location: Southeastern coast of South America.
Area: 68,037 sq mi (176 215 km²).
Population (mid-1985 est.): 3,000,000.
Capital: Montevideo
Government: *Head of state,* Julio Maria Sanguinetti, president (took office March 2, 1985). *Legislature*—National Congress: Senate and House of Deputies.
Monetary Unit: Peso (117.2 pesos equal U.S.$1, Oct. 30, 1985).
Gross Domestic Product (1983 U.S.$): $5,400,000,000.
Economic Index (Montevideo, 1984): *Consumer Prices* (1970 = 100), all items, 48,073.9; food, 49,728.9.
Foreign Trade (1983 U.S.$): *Imports,* $788,000,000; *exports,* $1,045,000,000.

UTAH

Bizarre criminal acts, a ski resort explosion, and a political surprise were among the unusual events that occurred in Utah in 1985.

Crime. Bombing attacks that killed two people and critically injured a prime suspect in the

Spencer W. Kimball (left), president of the Church of Jesus Christ of Latter-day Saints, and Ezra Taft Benson, president of the Church's Quorum of the Twelve Apostles, confer at an April meeting. Mr. Kimball died at the age of 90 on November 5 and was succeeded as Mormon leader by Mr. Benson, the 86-year-old former secretary of agriculture in the Eisenhower administration.

AP/Wide World

case shocked the citizens of the state. On Oct. 15, 1985, sophisticated bombs designed to detonate at the slightest touch separately killed a Salt Lake City businessman, Steven F. Christensen, and Kathleen W. Sheets, the wife of a former business associate of Christensen. Police at first suspected that the bombings were the result of a failed business venture and were performed by a "hired assassin." However, on Oct. 16, 1985, a third person, Mark Hoffman, was critically injured in a car explosion in downtown Salt Lake City. After obtaining the appropriate warrants, police found in the wreckage of Hoffman's car and in his home items similar to those used in the previous bombings. Also found were documents related to activities of the Church of Jesus Christ of Latter-day Saints (LDS), and indications of questionable business dealings related to those documents involving Christensen and the husband of Mrs. Sheets. (It was speculated that the bomb that killed Mrs. Sheets was intended for her husband; the package, in fact, was addressed to him.) In addition to the documents, almost $250,000 in money orders and checks payable to Hoffman was recovered. The money apparently was connected with the purchase of rare historical documents pertaining to the LDS Church. Hoffman, a dealer in historical documents, had recently been involved in the sale of controversial discoveries concerning the founder of the LDS Church, Joseph Smith. Hoffman had been in contact with various church officials, especially concerning the sale of certain letters sold to Christensen.

Fatal Blast. On March 16, 1985, a blast killed two persons and injured six others at Alta, one of Utah's famed ski resorts. One victim, a 12-year-old girl from Wisconsin, was saved after eight hours of effort by emergency crews. The accident was caused by a propane gas tank explosion that collapsed the floors of the four-story structure.

Politics. After ten years as mayor of Salt Lake City, Ted L. Wilson resigned his position to assume the directorship of the Hinckley Institute of Politics at the University of Utah. Mayor Wilson wished to return to teaching and working closely with young people who plan to seek political careers or service in government. The city's public works director, Palmer DePaulis, was named interim mayor and was elected to a two-year term in November.

Sports. The University of Utah's women's gymnasts won their fifth straight NCAA championship. Brigham Young's football team, undefeated and rated number one after the 1984 season, ended 1985 by going to the Florida Citrus Bowl.

LORENZO K. KIMBALL, *University of Utah*

UTAH • Information Highlights

Area: 84,899 sq mi (219 889 km²).
Population (July 1, 1984 est.): 1,652,000.
Chief Cities (1980 census): Salt Lake City, the capital (July 1, 1984 est.), 164,844; Provo, 74,108; Ogden, 64,407.
Government (1985): *Chief Officers*—governor, Norman Bangerter (R); lt. gov., W. Val Oveson (R). *Legislature*—Senate, 29 members; House of Representatives, 75 members.
State Finances (fiscal year 1984): *Revenues,* $2,877,000,000; *expenditures,* $2,446,000,000.
Personal Income (1984): $16,074,000,000; per capita, $9,733.
Labor Force (June 1985): *Civilian labor force,* 743,400; *unemployed,* 44,400 (6% of total force).
Education: *Enrollment* (fall 1983)—public elementary schools, 281,649; public secondary, 97,416; colleges and universities, 103,324. *Public school expenditures* (1982–83), $702,033,143 ($2,013 per pupil).

VENEZUELA

Unlike many other developing nations, Venezuela was able to cope with its debt crisis in 1985 without having to suffer high inflation, a severe drop in the standard of living, or burdens imposed by the International Monetary Fund. Lower oil prices were offset by increased agricultural production and severe import restrictions.

Economy Rebounds. Finance Minister Manuel Azpurus Arreaza finished renegotiating the $21.1 billion public debt in May—the first such agreement by a Latin American nation. Petroleum export sales were expected to drop to $12 billion in 1985, compared with $15.3 billion in 1984 and $19 billion in 1981, as a result of reduced exports and lower prices. Crude prices for heavy and high-sulfur oil dropped to between $23–$24 a barrel in the last half of 1985, compared with $24.65–$25.75 in January to June 1985 and $26.71–$27.55 in mid-1984. Venezuela's decision in August to lower prices an average $1.78 per barrel was strongly influenced by Mexico's June decision to sell heavy Maya crude to the United States for $23.50 a barrel, or $2.00 a barrel less than Venezuelan crude.

Imports were reduced from $12 billion in 1983 to $7.39 billion in 1984, while nontraditional exports increased 21%. This enabled the country to go from a $4.2 billion current account deficit in 1982 to a surplus of $4.2 billion in 1984, with international reserves at a comfortable $13 billion. These developments allowed Venezuela to participate in a 12-nation $483 million bridging loan to Argentina to pay overdue interest on its foreign debt.

Self-sufficiency was reached in corn and cotton production as the result of a combination of institutional changes in policy-making, credit, lower fertilizer prices, and bans on the importation of processed foods, poultry, and pork. *Gabinetes agricolas* (agricultural cabinets)—made up of farmers, cattlemen, and peasants in cooperatives and industrialists—tackled price and production problems in each state. Interest rates were reduced from 14% to 8%, and loan-processing time was reduced

from seven months to two, allowing many farmers to buy new machinery in time for the 1985 harvest.

After the collapse of the Venezuelan Bank of Commerce in June, the Ministry of Finance prohibited the creation of new banks, credit institutions, and insurance firms. The government intervened in the Banco Hipotecario Centro-Occidental in September when its debts grew to 28 times the amount of its assets. It was the ninth intervention in four years.

Minimum Wages Increased. Campaign pledges in 1983 were fulfilled in March with an increase in the minimum wage for agricultural workers from 750 bolívars ($57.25 per month at the free market rate) to 1,200 bolívars ($91.60). The salaries of urban workers were raised from 900 bolívars ($68.70) to 1,500 bolívars ($114.50).

Papal Visit. Pope John Paul II opened a 12-day South American tour in Caracas on January 26 quoting Christopher Columbus and hoping to encourage social justice in the region. At an outdoor Mass in Caracas attended by 1 million persons January 27, he strongly condemned contraception, sterilization, abortion, and divorce. He was critical of liberation theology in homilies in Caracas and at an outdoor Mass in Merida in the Andes.

Foreign Policy. Normalization of diplomatic relations with Cuba was more likely after the visit by Cuban Foreign Minister Isidoro Malmiera to a United Nations Symposium on Education for Peace in Caracas June 5–6.

Rear Admiral Wolfgang Larrazabal, provisional president in 1958, was one of a few former Latin American presidents attending a meeting in Havana July 30–August 3 to discuss the Latin American debt crisis. President Lusinchi rejected Fidel Castro's proposal that Latin America not pay its foreign debt.

Venezuela tried to avoid taking sides or becoming militarily involved in Central America while also defending pluralism where it tenuously existed. In May, President Lusinchi criticized Nicaraguan President Daniel Ortega's trip to Moscow and the Reagan administration's embargo on trade with Nicaragua.

Venezuela increased its pressure on Guyana by announcing it would issue identity cards to residents in the disputed Essequibo border region starting in July.

NEALE J. PEARSON, *Texas Tech University*

VENEZUELA · Information Highlights

Official Name: Republic of Venezuela.
Location: Northern coast of South America.
Area: 352,143 sq mi (912 050 km²).
Population (mid-1985 est.): 17,300,000.
Government: *Head of state and government,* Jaime Lusinchi, president (took office Feb. 2, 1984). *Legislature*—Congress: Senate and Chamber of Deputies.
Monetary Unit: Bolívar (14.5 bolívars equal U.S.$1, Oct. 30, 1985).
Gross Domestic Product (1983 U.S.$): $66,400,000,000.
Economic Index (Caracas, 1984): *Consumer Prices* (1970 = 100), all items, 339.8; food, 514.6.

VERMONT

Rock-ribbed Vermont has always been as much an image as a place. By the mid-1980s the image was changing from museum piece to Yuppie chic: the recreational and gourmet capital of the Northeast, writers' hangout, and the first state in the nation to elect a foreign-born woman governor, Democrat Madeleine M.

AP/Wide World

Burlington's Bernie Sanders, the only Socialist mayor in the United States, was elected to a third term in March. He also expressed interest in seeking higher state office.

Kunin. To emphasize this transition, the Vermont House, despite a narrow Republican majority, elected a Democratic speaker, and the Senate, with its first Democratic majority ever, elected its first Democratic president pro tem.

The Legislature. The 1985 legislative session was burdened by a commitment to pay off the unprecedented $44 million deficit inherited from the previous administration. Nevertheless, the legislature expanded the state's property tax rebate program, increased state aid to education by $7.8 million, and mandated kindergartens in all towns. Revenue measures included extension of the sales tax to cigarettes and participation in a tri-state lottery with Maine and New Hampshire. Refusal to raise the state's legal drinking age from 18 to 21, however, jeopardized future receipts of federal highway funds.

Vermont's traditional concern with the environment was highlighted in 1985 with legislative acts to protect groundwater quality, clean up hazardous waste dumps, and notify localities of hazardous waste shipments. The Kunin administration and Vermont's congressional delegation led the call for national action to deal with acid rain.

Politics. As anticipated, a number of women were among Governor Kunin's cabinet-level appointments. Republicans charged her with creating an antibusiness climate, citing the assessment for $17 million in taxes sent to People Express airlines in an effort to impose the state's sales tax on commercial airlines. Governor Kunin revoked the assessment and dismissed her secretary of administration who had approved the tax commissioner's plan without informing her.

In the March local elections, Socialist Bernard Sanders easily bested half a dozen rivals to win a third term as mayor of Burlington. Acknowledging interest in higher state office while continuing in his condemnation of U.S. foreign policy, Sanders was the only elected U.S. official to attend Nicaragua's independence day celebration in July.

Local News. Burlington and other communities rejected school tax increases. In Bennington, alleged fraud and budget irregularities led to criminal charges against the ousted superintendent of schools and the resignation of the town manager. Hinesburg, near Burlington, experienced the most prolonged school strike in the state's history. Striking teachers were replaced by the local school board, but the state Labor Relations Board ruled in August that the school board must allow the striking teachers to reclaim their jobs even if replacements had to be fired.

South Africa. A stock divestiture movement to protest apartheid in South Africa, urged by students and professors at the University of Vermont, came to a head in September in a dramatic tie vote among the university trustees, broken by the chairman's vote against divestiture. President Lattie F. Coor incurred criticism for abstaining in the vote.

ROBERT V. DANIELS AND SAMUEL B. HAND
University of Vermont

VERMONT • Information Highlights

Area: 9,614 sq mi (24 900 km²).
Population (July 1, 1984 est.): 530,000.
Chief Cities (1980 census): Montpelier, the capital, 8,241; Burlington, 37,712; Rutland, 18,436.
Government (1985): *Chief Officers*—governor, Madeleine M. Kunin (D); lt. gov., Peter Smith (R). *General Assembly*—Senate, 30 members; House of Representatives, 150 members.
State Finances (fiscal year 1984): *Revenues,* $992,000,000; *expenditures,* $941,000,000.
Personal Income (1984): $5,723,000,000; per capita, $10,802.
Labor Force (June 1985): *Civilian labor force,* 272,200; *unemployed,* 13,300 (4.9% of total force).
Education: *Enrollment* (fall 1983)—public elementary schools, 63,452; public secondary, 26,964; colleges and universities, 31,306. Public school expenditures (1982–83), $266,700,052 ($3,051 per pupil).

In Ho Chi Minh City (once Saigon), April 30, 1985, Politiburo members and foreign dignitaries watch a colorful parade marking the tenth anniversary of the victory of the Communists in the Vietnam war.

Matsumoto, Sygma

VIETNAM

In April 1985, Vietnam marked the tenth anniversary of North Vietnam's conquest of the southern half of the country. It was a celebration that Vietnamese officials hoped would end the country's political isolation and get the sluggish economy moving again.

Hundreds of visiting Western journalists found only a few reminders of the war and not much hostility toward Americans by ordinary people or Communist officials. Most of the bombed buildings have been repaired, and bomb craters in the countryside are overgrown with dense vegetation. Rusty artillery pieces and parts of airplanes serve as war memorials in many towns. And thousands of unexploded bombs and shells are embedded in the fields.

But there still is a striking contrast between the northern and southern halves of Vietnam. The north is much poorer in part because it is much more crowded than the south. The economy of the north has been under state control for 30 years, and it has hardly grown at all in that period. However, farmers and fishermen now are allowed to sell surplus food for profit. As a result a farmer may earn up to five times as much as an office worker in Hanoi. And with some help from the occupied neighboring countries of Laos and Cambodia, Vietnam is producing enough food to feed itself.

In Ho Chi Minh City (formerly Saigon), the shops are full of consumer goods. Some are manufactured locally or imported legally, but many items are smuggled in from abroad with the aid of corrupt officials. Even senior bureaucrats in Ho Chi Minh City "moonlight" at private trades in order to give their families a more comfortable life. While there is no organized political dissidence in the south, 500,000 people have applied officially to leave under the United Nations "orderly departure" program, and about 300 leave each week.

Foreign Affairs. The year saw a series of diplomatic gestures by Vietnam and its opponents in the seven-year war for control of Cambodia. Relations improved between China and the Soviet Union—Vietnam's main ally. This made it easier for Vietnam and China to discuss their differences. Vietnam also announced it would withdraw its troops from Cambodia by 1990. There were meetings between diplomats from Vietnam and the Association of Southeast Asian Nations. But by late 1985 they had not been able to find an acceptable compromise.

Meanwhile, in August, a group of American officials flew to Hanoi to seek an accounting for U.S. servicemen who were missing or killed in action. The Vietnamese side reportedly showed greater interest than in the past in establishing diplomatic and economic relations with the United States.

PETER A. POOLE
Author, "Eight Presidents and Indochina"

VIETNAM • Information Highlights

Official Name: Socialist Republic of Vietnam.
Location: Southeast Asia.
Area: 127,300 sq mi (329 707 km^2).
Population (mid-1985 est.): 60,500,000.
Chief Cities (1985 est.): Hanoi, the capital, 2,000,000; Ho Chi Minh City, 3,500,000.
Government (1985): Communist Party secretary, Le Duan; State Council chairman, Truong Chinh; Council of Ministers, chairman, Pham Van Dong.
Monetary Unit: Dong (10.7 dongs equal U.S.$1, November 1984).
Gross National Product (1983 U.S.$): $14,800,000,-000.
Foreign Trade (1983 U.S.$): *Imports,* $1,550,000,000; *exports,* $652,000,000.

The Ten Years Since Saigon's Fall

When the North Vietnamese army occupied Saigon in 1975, they felt they were entering the capital of an enemy country. They expected resistance from the South Vietnamese army and people, who had stubbornly resisted a Communist takeover for 13 years. It had been one of the longest and bloodiest wars of the 20th century, claiming the lives of 57,718 Americans and more than 1 million Vietnamese, Lao, and Cambodians.

But in April 1975 the war was finally over. Most of the South Vietnamese people seemed to accept the Communist victory with resignation though not with enthusiasm. Only a few South Vietnamese soldiers held out against the new regime. Most of the military and civilian officials surrendered to the Communist victors, and they were sent to reeducation camps, some for periods of only a few weeks but others for many years.

When the North Vietnamese found that resistance in the south was slight, they decided to speed up the timetable for unifying Vietnam and turning it into a single Communist state. They gradually replaced the military occupation in the south with a civilian administration —composed almost entirely of North Vietnamese officials. They held elections throughout the country for a National Assembly in 1976, and they began cautiously to reorganize the south's free market economy into a centralized, state-controlled economy. Yet the task of rebuilding the country proved to be even greater than people in Hanoi imagined.

Food Shortage. The most immediate problem was a desperate shortage of food. During the war, many southern peasants left their farms and fled to the comparative safety of the cities. This meant that much less food was grown than the country needed. The deficit had to be made up by emergency shipments from abroad. Moreover, the entire economy was in a state of collapse. The Chinese merchants who traditionally managed the food distribution system in the south were now the object of deep suspicion by North Vietnamese officials. Not only were they capitalists but they were also suspected of being sympathetic to China, Vietnam's new enemy.

Vietnam had no money with which to import food and few friends it could turn to for aid. The United States and other Western governments provided relief through the United Nations. China continued to provide the same amount of aid it had provided during the war. Eventually, the Soviet Union and other Eastern bloc states increased their aid to an estimated $1 million a day. This helped pay for food and other vital imports and made it possible for Hanoi to invade Cambodia, beginning in 1977, and maintain a large occupation force in that country.

Unemployment. With food still scarce and millions of urban dwellers unemployed, Hanoi took steps to open up new lands on the plateaus that rise behind the densely settled coastal areas. In the first year after the war, Hanoi sent 500,000 people from South Vietnamese cities to live and work in what were called "new economic zones."

Many of the people who were sent were considered socially undesirable by the new regime. Some were common criminals, others were simply unemployed, and many were members of the Chinese minority. All of them found conditions in the new economic zones extremely harsh. They had to build their own housing and clear the land of dense tropical vegetation. They had little in the way of medical care or other amenities. Some contracted malaria and died as a result of the ordeal. Others returned illegally to the cities, where they were not allowed jobs or ration cards.

Although food production gradually increased after the regime began to allow some market incentives, unemployment in the cities has remained a serious problem. The closing of war industries, the lack of foreign investment, and the inefficiency of the Vietnamese bureaucracy all contributed to this problem. A further cause has been the partial breakup of those sectors of the southern economy that were traditionally dominated by the ethnic Chinese, known as Hoa.

Plight of the Hoa. Until 1975, Chinese businessmen dominated the rice trade in South Vietnam and played a prominent role in banking, foreign trade, and many kinds of manufacturing. The Hoa community in the south numbered about 1 million and was concentrated in the city of Cholon, a suburb of Saigon. After their victory in 1975, the Vietnamese Communists tried to keep most of the Chinese businessmen and technicians in their jobs in order to maintain production. However, as the traditional hostility between China and Vietnam reemerged, Hanoi began to rethink this policy.

In 1978, as Hanoi was forging an alliance with Moscow (China's enemy at the time), new steps were taken by Hanoi to break the Chinese hold on South Vietnam's economy. Hoa businesses were seized, and many Hoa residents were strongly "encouraged" to leave the country. Those who left North Vietnam fled to China. Many Hoa in the south left on small, overcrowded boats and tried to sail to neigh-

G. Spengler, Sygma

Billy Ford, Photoreporters

In Vietnam today, the north, top, remains a predominantly agricultural society, while black market shops continue to sell highly sought consumer goods in Ho Chi Minh City, right. Although the nation now produces enough food to feed itself, food production has consistently fallen below government goals. Meanwhile the Vietnam children, above, of American soldiers who fought in the war are treated as second-class citizens.

Sygma

boring countries. Thousands died in shipwrecks or at the hands of pirates. Vietnamese Communist officials often collected large sums of money to allow these departures, but Hanoi claimed it made no profit on the "boat people" and that it was more humane to let them leave than to force them to stay. By 1985, only about 500,000 Hoa remained in Vietnam.

War in Cambodia. Meanwhile, Vietnamese forces invaded Cambodia in December 1978 and quickly occupied the towns and main highways. Thousands of Cambodian refugees streamed across the border into Thailand, adding to the tensions between Vietnam and its neighbors. China invaded Vietnam in early 1979 to "teach Hanoi a lesson." Vietnam claimed that the trouble was started by China, which had supported the previous Cambodian regime in raids against Vietnam.

Most members of the United Nations sided against Vietnam on these issues. The UN response was led by China and the Association of Southeast Asian Nations (ASEAN)—Thailand, Malaysia, Singapore, Indonesia, the Phil-

ippines, and, since 1984, Brunei. In the fall of 1979 and each year thereafter, the ASEAN states mustered lopsided majorities for resolutions condemning Vietnam's occupation of Cambodia. Most UN members also voted to seat a Cambodian government in exile composed of rebel forces opposing the Vietnamese occupation of their country.

Foreign Relations. Like all states, Vietnam feels the need for friendly neighbors and secure borders. Like many other countries, Vietnam also needs foreign capital to develop its economy. The problem is how to achieve these goals without sacrificing Vietnam's independence or its Communist revolution. The alliance with Moscow has brought added military strength but questionable security. The alliance also has brought Hanoi enough aid to survive though not enough to expand economically.

The United States has voted with the ASEAN states and China on the Cambodian issue at the United Nations. The United States also has provided some humanitarian aid to the Cambodians who seek to oust the Vietnamese from Cambodia. However, the United States does not want to see a major war break out between the Soviet Union and China, because this could easily become another world war. Thus, Washington officials tended to be relieved when Sino-Soviet and Sino-Vietnamese tensions eased in 1984 and 1985.

The Vietnam War and the United States. The Vietnam War produced the greatest divisions in American society since the U.S. Civil War. It undermined respect for all the great institutions of American life—and for a while people wondered if the pendulum would ever swing back again. By 1985, it was possible to say that much of the respect for American institutions that was lost during the war had been regained. And although the war itself was more unpopular than ever, Americans now have added a new folk hero to their culture. The Vietnam veteran is being celebrated in books, songs, movies, and television series. He is usually shown as a sturdy, somewhat cynical loner who perseveres and does his duty even when he is not certain he has support from his superiors.

Most Americans now view their country's involvement in the Vietnam War as a tragic mistake. According to a 1985 *New York Times* poll, 73% of adult Americans held this view while 19% opposed. Yet the same poll shows that about half of all American adults believe their government will tend to make the right decisions all or most of the time. Interestingly, the age group that expressed the greatest confidence in its government was the 18- to 22-year-olds. Fifty-nine percent expressed confidence, compared with only 47% of American adults as a whole.

The positive feelings of the American people toward their Vietnam veterans were symbolized by the building of Vietnam memorials in Washington and New York and by special tenth anniversary parades honoring these men and women. Americans have also generally given a cordial welcome to the Indochina refugees who have arrived since 1975. Beyond that, however, the lessons learned from the war tend to vary with the individual. Some would say the war taught us that the military should be free of all political restraints. Others would say that a democratically elected government should not try to send soldiers into battle without first explaining where and why they are going and securing the consent of Congress and the support of the general populace.

PETER A. POOLE

Jodi Buren, Sygma

In New York City, May 7, some 25,000 Vietnam veterans were honored with a ticker-tape parade. In the ten years since the war's end, the Vietnam vet has become an American folk hero.

VIRGINIA

The 1985 elections made stunning history in Virginia, as voters in the Old Dominion selected the first black and the first woman ever to hold elected statewide office.

Elections. In choosing L. Douglas Wilder, a lawyer and state senator from Richmond, as its lieutenant governor, Virginia became the first Southern state since Reconstruction to elect a black to a top state job. And lawyer-legislator Mary Sue Terry of Patrick County, who won a landslide victory, became only the second elected female attorney general in the United States.

The two Democrats were elected on a ticket headed by Gerald L. Baliles who easily beat his Republican opponent, Wyatt B. Durrette, by a 55–45% margin. The Democratic sweep in a state that voted overwhelmingly for President Ronald Reagan in 1984 attested to the popularity of incumbent Gov. Charles S. Robb, who could not run for another term.

The election also was historic in that it appeared to end the dominance of Virginia politics by heirs of the segregationist "machine" of the late Sen. Harry E. Byrd. The campaigning on behalf of the Republicans by former Gov. Mills E. Godwin (R), godchild of the organization and the most powerful figure in the state during the 1970s, was perceived widely as a negative influence.

Floods. The drama of election week was heightened because torrential rains in the western part of Virginia resulted in the state's worst flooding in more than a decade. The Roanoke, Shenandoah, and James rivers all crested their banks; the death toll hit close to 20, and damage estimates ranged beyond $700 million.

The Legislature. Education was a prime concern of the state's legislators in 1985. The lawmakers increased educational appropriations for fiscal 1986 by an average of $296 per pupil. Funds were allocated to institute programs to improve the quality of teacher education, to prevent school dropouts, and to assist communities in evaluating prospective school principals. The legislature also approved plans to improve correctional officer job classification and training requirements and mental-health care for prison inmates.

Espionage. In May, Virginians, together with Americans from the rest of the country, were shocked by the arrest of John A. Walker, Jr., of Norfolk and his brother and son on charges Walker had operated the most damaging espionage ring in recent history.

John Walker had been stationed with the Navy in Norfolk and ran a detective agency there. His brother, Arthur, a former Navy lieutenant commander, worked for a defense contractor in Chesapeake and lived in Virginia Beach. John Walker's son, Seaman Michael Walker, was arrested aboard the U.S.S. *Nimitz,* a carrier stationed at the Norfolk Naval Base.

Arthur Walker was convicted in August and sentenced to life in prison. In October, John Walker entered into a plea bargain with the government. Under the arrangement, he would receive a life sentence—but could be eligible for parole in ten years—and in return his son would receive a reduced sentence, 25 years. Pentagon officials said they agreed to the plea bargain in order to ensure John Walker would tell the government all he knew about the spy ring and his Soviet contacts. He also would be the key witness in any trial of the fourth man, Jerry Whitworth of California, arrested in the case.

Other Headline Items. Virginians had cause to train their eyes toward the Middle East and the Atlantic Ocean during 1985. Some of the 39 civilians and servicemen on the TWA flight hijacked to Lebanon in June were from or had families or friends in the Norfolk area, and the hostages were welcomed back enthusiastically to the United States after 17 days as hostages.

The welcoming for the reproduction ship *Godspeed* at Jamestown was more subdued than originally planned. The tiny wooden vessel had set sail from England on April 30 in an attempt to recreate the 1607 voyage that brought the first permanent settlers to the New World. But problems with weather and disagreements among the amateur crew caused the voyage to be aborted in the Virgin Islands. The boat was finally towed into the Jamestown docks on October 23.

The well-known Richmond drug company A. H. Robins Co., beset by mammoth payouts and pending lawsuits against its defective Dalkon Shield intrauterine device, filed for protection and reorganization under federal bankruptcy law.

ED NEWLAND
"The Richmond Times-Dispatch"

VIRGINIA • Information Highlights

Area: 40,767 sq mi (105 586 km²).

Population (July 1, 1984 est.): 5,636,000.

Chief Cities (July 1, 1984 est.): Richmond, the capital, 219,056; Virginia Beach, 308,664; Norfolk, 279,683; Newport News, 154,560; Chesapeake, 126,031.

Government (1985): *Chief Officers*—governor, Charles S. Robb (D); lt. gov., Richard J. Davis (D). *General Assembly*—Senate, 40 members; House of Delegates, 100 members.

State Finances (fiscal year 1984): *Revenues,* $8,171,000,000; *expenditures,* $7,096,000,000.

Personal Income (1984): $74,694,000,000; per capita, $13,254.

Labor Force (June 1985): *Civilian labor force,* 2,929,100; *unemployed,* 156,800 (5.4% of total force).

Education: *Enrollment* (fall 1983)—public elementary schools, 674,016; public secondary, 292,094; colleges and universities, 288,588. *Public school expenditures* (1982–83), $2,381,954,532 ($2,620 per pupil).

WASHINGTON

Booth Gardner became Washington's 19th governor on Jan. 16, 1985. He immediately launched an economic development campaign, the Washington Plan, designed to foster cooperation between the public and private sectors in a drive for balanced economic expansion in the state.

Economy. Although the state's unemployment rate dropped from 1984, it still remained higher than the national rate and was ranked tenth in the country. Also ominous was the decline of personal income to a level below the national average. Only during the Depression and the Boeing bust of 1970 did the state's personal income dip below the national figure.

Sluggish or stagnant growth had a strong impact on public-sector finances. Although the state's tax base was climbing, the rate of climb was much less than expected. The state budget had very little reserve monies set aside for emergencies in 1986. Increasing demands were heard during the year for overhaul of the state's tax system. Proponents of a state personal income tax emerged, as did business people calling for a restructuring of the sales tax and of the business and occupation tax, which is a tax on revenues rather than profits.

Legislature. In June, after a regular and a special session, the legislature adjourned. Among its actions it guaranteed a tax break for new corporations and approved a $286 million package of bond-financed construction projects.

WPPSS. In August the Bonneville Power Administration and four Washington private utilities finally reached an agreement on a new power-swap plan to settle a $2 billion lawsuit over the mothballing of Washington Public Power Supply System (WPPSS) nuclear plant 3. Construction was halted on the plant in 1983 due to WPPSS financial problems.

WASHINGTON • Information Highlights

Area: 68,139 sq mi (176 479 km²).
Population (July 1, 1984 est.): 4,349,000.
Chief Cities (July 1, 1984 est.): Olympia, the capital (1980 census), 27,447; Seattle, 488, 474; Spokane, 173,349; Tacoma, 159,433.
Government (1985): *Chief Officers*—governor, Booth Gardner (D); lt. gov., John A. Cherberg (D). *Legislature*—Senate, 49 members; House of Representatives, 98 members.
State Finances (fiscal year 1984): *Revenues,* $8,833,000,000; *expenditures,* $8,139,000,000.
Personal Income (1984): $55,633,000,000; per capita, $12,792.
Labor Force (June 1985): *Civilian labor force,* 2,142,600; *unemployed,* 173,800 (8.1% of total force).
Education: *Enrollment* (fall 1983)—public elementary schools, 503,551; public secondary, 232,688; colleges and universities, 229,639. *Public school expenditures* (1982–83), $2,206,230,814 ($3,211 per pupil).

Closures and Openings. The changes in the state's economy were evidenced by a number of closures and openings. Champion International closed two wood-products mills, and Weyerhaeuser closed three. Aluminum and shipbuilding industries were struggling during the year, burdened by the effects of higher energy costs, high interest rates, and new sources of competition. A bright note was RCA-Sharpe's decision to locate a $200 million semiconductor plant in Clark County that would employ more than 600 people. Also noteworthy was the Navy's decision to make Everett home port to a 15-ship battle group led by aircraft carrier U.S.S. *Nimitz*.

Comparable Worth. Advocates of comparable worth were dealt a blow when a federal court overturned a lower court ruling that Washington state had discriminated against women employees because their wages were generally lower than that of men's in comparable jobs. The court found that prevailing labor market rates existed and that a case of deliberate sex discrimination did not exist. In a similar case, a federal court dismissed a suit of University of Washington nursing faculty.

Crime. The Federal Bureau of Investigation entered the investigation of the Green River, King County, murders, which remained unsolved in 1985. In Seattle the racketeering trial of several neo-Nazi members of the Order of Silent Brotherhood began.

JEREMIAH J. SULLIVAN
Pacific Northwest Executive

WASHINGTON, DC

A record cold wave, with below-zero temperatures, disrupted the quadrennial presidential inauguration ceremony and festivities in the U.S. capital in January. The arctic air forced President Ronald Reagan to move his second oath of office and inaugural address indoors to the Capitol rotunda. Fears of health risks to participants and spectators caused cancellation of the inaugural parade for the first time in history.

Amendment and Statehood. The DC Voting Rights Amendment, which would permit DC residents to elect full voting representation in Congress, officially expired on August 22. Only 16 of the necessary 38 states had approved the proposed U.S. constitutional amendment within the seven-year time frame set by Congress.

Bills on statehood for the district were reintroduced into the new Congress. A subcommittee of the House DC Committee held hearings in May.

New Legislation. Banks in the district were permitted to purchase or merge with those in 11 southeastern states having reciprocal agreements.

Drivers and passengers in the front seat of a motor vehicle were required to wear seat belts or face possible $15 fines.

Health-care professionals, police officers, social workers, and others were required to report cases of abuse, neglect, or exploitation of the elderly.

Rent control was extended another six years. The new act exempted single-family homes owned by individuals, buildings that are at least 80% vacant, and dilapidated properties. Tenant associations, however, petitioned the rent-control exemption provisions to a referendum election, the first held in the city. The referendum was successful.

Shelter for the Homeless and Employment. The 1984 initiative guaranteeing overnight shelter for homeless people was struck down by a DC Superior Court judge, who ruled that the measure was improperly allowed on the ballot because it required the city to spend money. The judge argued that the electorate did not have the power to appropriate public funds, an action reserved for the City Council.

The city ranked second highest in a national census of the number of public employees per residents (39,000 full-time workers, or about 1 for every 16 of its 622,823 residents), and paid its employees the second-highest salaries in the country (an average of $21,442 annually).

Royal Visit. A social highlight of the Washington year was the three-day visit in November of the Prince and Princess of Wales. The royal couple came to the United States to promote British products and preside at the opening of the "Treasure House of Britain" exhibition at Washington's National Gallery of Art. The exhibit showed treasures, ranging from paintings to furniture, from the stately country homes of Britain.

Other. Four new stations and 7 mi (11 km) of track were added to the Metrorail network to complete one end of the Red Line from the district into suburban Maryland.

Alvaro Corrada del Rio was installed as the first bishop of Hispanic origin in the Roman Catholic archdiocese of Washington.

MORRIS J. LEVITT, *Howard University*

WEST VIRGINIA

Republican Gov. Arch Moore faced a 103–31 Democratic majority in the state legislature, but his political experience carried virtually all of his "must" legislation through to approval in 1985. As the year ended, the public's decision on the effectiveness of the program designed by Moore to "get our fellow West Virginians back to work" was still uncertain.

Legislation. Key legislation included the creation of an energy department, combining the departments of mines and natural resources in an attempt to put decisions up to political

---

WEST VIRGINIA · Information Highlights

Area: 24,231 sq mi (62 759 km²).
Population (July 1, 1984 est.): 1,952,000.
Chief Cities (1980 census): Charleston, the capital, 63,968; Huntington, 63,684; Wheeling, 43,070.
Government (1985): *Chief Officers*—governor, Arch A. Moore, Jr. (R); secy. of state, Ken Hechler (D). *Legislature*—Senate, 34 members; House of Delegates, 100 members.
State Finances (fiscal year 1984): *Revenues,* $3,547,000,000; *expenditures,* $3,136,000,000.
Personal Income (1984): $18,991,000,000; per capita, $9,728.
Labor Force (June 1985): *Civilian labor force,* 758,300; *unemployed,* 90,600 (12% of total force).
Education: *Enrollment* (fall 1983)—public elementary schools, 263,254; public secondary, 107,997; colleges and universities, 83,202. *Public school expenditures* (1982–83), $957,532,433 ($2,764 per pupil).

---

appointees rather than to normally less pliable civil-service personnel. The program admittedly was designed to make the agency more sympathetic to coal interests. However, public outcry greeted the appointment of key mining-related individuals, who were later forced to divest themselves of their holdings after permits were issued to companies with which they were or had been connected.

One of the more controversial measures tion (B&O) tax with a combination of new levies, to go into effect in 1987. Coal, oil, and gas industries, along with marginal small businesses, would be the main beneficiaries of the change. Most of the opposition was against any change in view of the B&O tax's role as one of the principal generators of income.

The commerce department was reestablished as the state's principal economic development agency, with several new types of tax credits approved to support its work. The inheritance tax was repealed; a hotel-motel occupancy tax of 3% was adopted, half to go to local governments and half to the promotion of tourism; and teachers received about a 5% raise—all measures designed to stimulate economic recovery and to increase cash flow.

The legislature also approved a school construction amendment of $200 million to go on a 1986 ballot. Another bill moved the primary from June back to May beginning in that year.

Much public debate was reserved for the delayed start-up on a state lottery, approved by the electorate in 1984 and set for November 1985 by the legislature. But one snarl after another threatened to delay the actual issuance of tickets, climaxed by a closed-door meeting of the commission at which an operating contract was awarded to other than the low bidder. A court-ordered open session confirmed the original decision, but by late October the date had been moved back to January 1986, despite the fact that the 1985–86 budget included a substantial anticipated piece of income from the lottery.

Economy. But it was fear of toxic leaks in the Kanawha (Chemical) Valley and the continuing economic slump that captured most of the headlines. West Virginia continued to have the highest unemployment rate in the nation. A 90-day strike against the Wheeling-Pittsburgh Steel Co. ended in October with more than 20% concessions by thousands of northern panhandle workers. A persistent deadlock between the United Mine Workers and the Massey Coal Co. crippled the already depressed bituminous industry in the south.

And in early November, what officials termed the worst flood in the state's history devastated 29 of the state's 55 counties, leaving as many as 48 dead and damage estimated as high as $250 million. Several towns were simply swept away.

DONOVAN H. BOND
West Virginia University

WISCONSIN

Politics, economic development, and sometimes even sports combined in different ways in Wisconsin in 1985.

State Government. Amid continued complaints from business about the state's tax climate, and with a reelection campaign only a year away, Gov. Anthony Earl called a special session of the legislature to deal with economic development. Even Republicans rallied to the Democratic governor's call, and all 17 of his bills were passed with only minor adjustments. The most significant was a measure to allow utilities to create new parent holding companies as subsidiaries. The utilities will be able to plow stockholder profits into new ventures, creating new jobs, and making even more money. The utilities were ready to invest about $500 million in the newly-instituted diversification program.

WISCONSIN • Information Highlights

Area: 56,153 sq mi (145 436 km²).
Population (July 1, 1984 est.): 4,766,000.
Chief Cities (July 1, 1984 est.): Madison, the capital, 170,745; Milwaukee, 620,811; Green Bay (1980 census), 87,899.
Government (1985): *Chief Officers*—governor, Anthony S. Earl (D); lt. gov., James T. Flynn (D). *Legislature*—Senate, 33 members; Assembly, 99 members.
State Finances (fiscal year 1984): *Revenues,* $9,572,000,000; *expenditures,* $7,530,000,000.
Personal Income (1984): $59,453,000,000; per capita, $12,474.
Labor Force (June 1985): *Civilian labor force,* 2,407,100; *unemployed,* 157,200 (6.5% of total force).
Education: *Enrollment* (fall 1983)—public elementary schools, 500,778; public secondary, 273,868; colleges and universities, 277,751. *Public school expenditures* (1982–83), $2,308,552,461 ($3,237 per pupil).

Other bills passed in the special session included one to support technology development, another to set up a regulatory mechanism for monitoring and regulating diversion of fresh water, and a third to encourage in-state investment of public pension funds.

Legislature. In approving a $18.7 billion 1985–87 budget bill, the legislature adopted an innovative tax idea. Starting with tax returns for 1986 income, the state will convert its income-tax system from one of mainly deductions to one of mainly credits. The switch to credits was part of a trade-off that also restored some politically popular tax deductions that were to be curtailed.

After weeks of wrangling, the legislature reached a compromise on a bill designed to reduce unwanted teenage pregnancies. The bill includes a pregnancy and sex counseling grant program, a more restrictive standard for allowing abortions, and an adoption hotline. It also makes parents financially liable for support costs for babies born to their teenagers until the teenage parent reaches age 18.

Milwaukee Arena Dispute. In a mix of sports and politics, Milwaukee spent much of the year debating where a new sports arena would be built. The issue rose early in the year when the Milwaukee Bucks of the National Basketball Association (NBA), after a threat to leave the city, were sold to Milwaukee developer Herbert Kohl. Having almost lost the team, Milwaukeeans sought to build a new arena for the team, which had been playing in the smallest house in the NBA. Within days, in a totally unexpected and dramatic gesture, Jane Pettit, the daughter of a Milwaukee industrialist, and her husband said they would donate a multimillion-dollar sports and entertainment center to the city.

Then more infighting began. The Pettits wanted to build the center near the Milwaukee County Stadium, where the Brewers baseball team plays. Mayor Henry Maier wanted to have it downtown, where the Bucks have played and which is in the midst of renewal. The mayor's forces lost against the argument that the gift could not be jeopardized. Meanwhile the Brewers were in court fighting a state proposal to build a new prison on another nearby site.

Economy. Economic growth was strong in the first half of 1985, though it tapered off to modest rates in the second half. Current employment at the end of the year was higher than the previous peak in the last quarter of 1979, and total employment growth for 1985 was estimated at 2.6%. Agricultural cash receipts were up slightly, but net farm income declined. Throughout 1985, prices received by farmers continued to be generally lower than a year earlier.

PAUL SALSINI, *"The Milwaukee Journal"*

Some 2,200 delegates from 159 nations assembled in Nairobi, Kenya, in July for the United Nations Decade for Women Conference. The meeting unanimously passed a nonbinding report, "Forward-Looking Strategies."

AP/Wide World

WOMEN

The year 1985 marked the end of the United Nations Decade for Women, proclaimed in 1975 to focus attention on women's problems. At a closing convention held in Nairobi, Kenya, in July, delegates drew up strategies for future progress. In the United States, new leadership of the National Organization for Women (NOW) promised to take stronger stands in fighting for equal rights.

The Nairobi Conference. The UN Decade for Women Conference was attended by more than 2,200 delegates from 159 countries, while some 10,000 other women converged on Nairobi for unofficial meetings and workshops. The various meetings were highly charged politically, with discussions spilling over to include such international issues as apartheid, space weapons, and the Palestinian question. The U.S. delegation, headed by Maureen Reagan (daughter of President Reagan), lost an early bid to force the conference to pass any resolution unanimously, but it did prevail in its desire for a consensus on the meeting's final document.

The conference and its final document dealt mainly with the problems faced by women around the world. At the root of these problems, according to a UN report, was the fact that a woman's role as wife and mother "is underpaid and undervalued." In Africa, women do 75% of the agricultural work in addition to domestic chores, but they rarely own land. In developed countries, women spend an average of 56 hours per week on unpaid domestic work. The report also found women to be vastly underrepresented in government and managerial positions.

The UN did report some progress during the decade: increases in the number of government bodies dedicated to the advancement of women, in the number of countries with legal equality for women, and in the number of countries with equal-pay laws.

The conference's final document outlined wide-ranging goals for women through the year 2000. These included setting an economic value on domestic work; better child care and flexible working hours for parents; equal pay for work of equal worth; government funding for women's organizations; and improved minimum wage standards and insurance benefits for women. Other sections called for an end to laws that discriminate against women in such areas as inheritance, property ownership, and child custody.

U.S. Issues. Women in the United States were able to report some progress. For example, women made up 14.7% of state legislators in 1985, compared with 8% in 1975. Nevertheless, problems remained. Poverty among families headed by women showed a slight decline —from 36.1% in 1983 to 34.5% in 1984—but was still substantial. Affirmative action programs were attacked, and the concept of "comparable worth" met with resistance. Women were divided over other issues. Some women campaigned for laws that would make pornography a violation of women's civil rights, while others said such laws would restrict free speech. And the debate on abortion continued, with the Reagan administration asking the Supreme Court to overturn its 1973 decision establishing a constitutional right to abortion.

Divisions aside, many women felt that gains made early in the decade were being eroded by pressure from conservative political groups. The election of Eleanor Smeal as president of NOW may have reflected that concern. Taking an activist approach, Smeal had headed the group from 1977 to 1982, when she turned over the presidency to the more moderate Judy Goldsmith. In the early 1980s, however, NOW began to lose members and money. Smeal won back the office in the July 1985 election with promises of active campaigns for an equal rights amendment, abortion rights, and equality in pay, insurance rates, and other areas.

ELAINE PASCOE, *Free-lance Writer*

Comparable Worth

Comparable worth is a policy that seeks to narrow the earnings gap between women and men workers. The U.S. General Accounting Office has defined comparable worth as "the general formulation that employees in jobs held predominantly by females should be paid the same as jobs of comparable worth to the employer held predominantly by males."

In 1985 in the United States, the average full-time female worker's earnings were about 65% that of her male counterpart. Most often cited as sources of this wage gap are differences between women's and men's education and work experience and the fact that women are concentrated in a relatively small number of low-paying sex-segregated or female-dominated jobs such as secretary, nurse, teacher, and sales clerk. Another possible reason for the gap is systematic sex discrimination. While not necessarily intentional, discrimination reflects employers' adherence to long-established practices that regard women's work as being of secondary importance compared with that performed by men. Comparable worth proponents argue that sole reliance on market forces and prevailing wages to set pay results in the perpetuation of both discrimination and the male-female earnings gap.

As a remedy, they propose more widespread use of job evaluation to set pay, specifically the point-factor method. With this method, jobs are rated and ranked according to a number of factors—skills, effort, responsibilities, and working conditions—as the basis for making comparisons between disparate jobs, such as librarian and maintenance worker. Once jobs have been rated on all factors, the relative importance of each factor with regard to the job's pay is determined by application of a complex statistical approach. Wage data are taken from the employer or prevailing wage standards in the relevant labor market. The resulting pay-setting model can then be used to gauge the pay of jobs.

The application of job evaluation methods has revealed a pattern whereby the jobs in which women are concentrated have smaller salaries relative to comparably evaluated male-dominated jobs. This has led unions and other groups to endorse comparable worth.

Developments. Forty-five states have taken steps to address pay equity. Minnesota has been phasing in pay adjustments worth $39 million over a four-year period since 1983. Numerous municipalities have also implemented comparable worth.

Considerable comparable worth activity occurred in 1985. In April the U.S. Civil Rights Commission rejected the idea of comparable worth and of using job evaluation to set pay. In May the City of Los Angeles became the first major municipality to implement comparable worth voluntarily. In June the Equal Employment Opportunity Commission, responsible for enforcing equal employment laws, issued a decision that failure to pay the same wage for comparably evaluated male and female jobs did *not* constitute a violation of Title VII, the major equal employment statute. In September the U.S. Court of Appeals overturned a landmark comparable worth victory against the State of Washington that had found the state guilty of sex discrimination and ordered millions in back pay. In sum, despite major setbacks, 1985 was a year of continued progress at the state and local levels.

The Debate. Critics of comparable worth argue that it would disrupt the free market system of wage determination based on supply and demand. They question the existence of market-based sex discrimination and point to existing laws as sufficient to address any problem. They further contend that the policy would be expensive and inflationary, resulting in higher wages without a corresponding increase in productivity. It would lead, they say, to higher unemployment among women, since employers would be forced to dismiss women workers if their wages were raised. Job evaluation, central to implementation of the policy, is criticized as being inherently subjective and unreliable.

Comparable worth advocates, on the other hand, cite the importance of the policy at a time when poverty among women, especially heads of households, is increasing. They claim that raising the pay of undervalued women's jobs will benefit employers by increasing their ability to attract and retain the best work force. They further argue that comparable worth can decrease sex segregation by making female jobs more attractive to men. Advocates challenge the idea of a free market, contending that the policy would be no more disruptive than other interventions—for example, existing legislation to prohibit employment discrimination, minimum wage laws, and so on. They defend the validity of job evaluation based on its widespread use in government and industry.

Comparable worth—called the issue of the 1980s—is highly charged politically. Regardless of the intrinsic merits of the arguments on either side, its future progress will undoubtedly be decided primarily in the political arena.

PAMELA STONE CAIN

WYOMING

In Wyoming during 1985 the economy remained distressingly flat, and flash floods ripped through Cheyenne on August 1.

Legislation. To cover state expenses through July 1986, the Republican-controlled legislature approved a budgetary supplement of $60 million, half of which was drawn from the state's budgetary reserve. Laws granted future tax breaks to oil recovery and oil mining projects to stimulate oil production, but a bill granting similar breaks to "wild cat" oil wells was vetoed by Gov. Ed Herschler on the grounds that it would immediately erode the state's tax base. Although legislation to permit the sale of water rights to maintain minimum water levels in rivers and streams that sustain fish again failed to pass, the in-stream flow initiative qualified for the November 1986 ballot. It was supported by environmentalists and opposed by agricultural and industrial interests. A bill to place carbon dioxide in the state's severance tax structure failed to pass. Some state officials believe the gas, which would soon be produced in enormous quantities at a new Exxon plant in western Wyoming, is taxable under present law. Exxon disagrees, and the question seems headed for the courts. Other new laws allow cities to negotiate with suppliers for cheaper natural gas, permit school districts the option of a four-day school week, and designate the American bison (buffalo) the state mammal.

Property Tax Reform. Historically, the state has assessed different types of property at different tax rates. The complex resulting "tiered" system is open to legal challenge because the constitution mandates equal and uniform taxation. After rejecting a bill that would legitimize the existing pattern, the legislature considered a constitutional amendment to do the same thing. In addition, a joint legislative committee explored modifications to the present system that would meet both revenue and legal objectives, and a state-wide property census and evaluation was completed in 1985.

The Economy. Unit prices for most of Wyoming's minerals remained well below the levels reached in the early 1980s. As current prices tend to dictate how much oil, coal, natural gas, trona, and bentonite will be produced in the state, none of these commodities showed a strong upward trend in production. The agricultural sector remained depressed, with severe drought in the northern half of the state during 1985 adding to the problem. Despite a 2% decline in the labor force, state-wide unemployment stood at 6% in August, one point higher than a year earlier.

Other Developments. On August 1, a summer storm dumped more than 6 in (15 cm) of rain and hail on the capital city in less than four hours. Flood waters rose to 6 ft (2 m) in some areas. The record storm left 12 persons dead and caused property damage estimated in the millions.

Construction on MX installations near Cheyenne continued on schedule, with the first ten missiles scheduled for deployment late in 1986. After lenders foreclosed on a huge ranch Gov. Ed Herschler had purchased with three partners in 1977, the chief executive became the first governor in Wyoming's history to file for bankruptcy.

H. R. Dieterich, *University of Wyoming*

YUGOSLAVIA

In 1985, Yugoslavia continued to be plagued with serious domestic problems, economic and political.

Economy. In May, Prime Minister Milka Planinc (president of the Federal Council) publicly detailed the country's economic woes—stagnant production, frightening rates of unemployment and inflation, a falling standard of living, a mediocre export performance, and a heavy foreign debt. In 1985, Yugoslavia had Europe's highest rate of unemployment (15%) and a rate of inflation of more than 75%. Its foreign indebtedness was estimated at $19 billion. In November, the country's nine-member collective presidency formally warned Planinc that a major economic crisis seemed imminent.

The government sought, by various means, to head off such a disaster, though without conspicuous success. On January 16, talks in London between Yugoslavia and its leading bank creditors over the rescheduling of Yugoslavia's $3.5 billion commercial debt were broken off. On April 29 the International Monetary Fund (IMF) did approve a $300 million loan to Yugoslavia. In return, the latter was required to abolish almost all price controls and subsidies, which led to a sharp rise in the rate of inflation. In late May, Planinc traveled to the United States, where she met with President Ronald Reagan, Secretary of State George Shultz, Commerce Secretary Malcolm Baldrige, and

---

WYOMING • Information Highlights

Area: 97,809 sq mi (253 326 km²).
Population (July 1, 1985 est.): 511,000.
Chief Cities (1980 census): Cheyenne, the capital, 47,283; Casper, 51,016; Laramie, 24,410.
Government (1985): *Chief Officers*—governor, Ed Herschler (D); secretary of state, Thyra Thomson (R). *Legislature*—Senate, 30 members; House of Representatives, 64 members.
State Finances (fiscal year 1984): *Revenues,* $1,802,000,000; *expenditures,* $1,415,000,000.
Personal Income (1984): $6,252,000,000; per capita, $12,224.
Labor Force (June 1985): *Civilian labor force,* 268,700; *unemployed,* 16,400 (6.1% of total force).
Education: *Enrollment* (fall 1983)—public elementary schools, 73,861; public secondary, 27,104; colleges and universities, 23,844. *Public school expenditures* (1982–83), $382,181,627 ($4,045 per pupil).

YUGOSLAVIA · Information Highlights

Official Name: Socialist Federal Republic of Yugoslavia.

Location: Southeastern Europe.

Area: 98,766 sq mi (255 804 km²).

Population (mid-1985): 23,100,000.

Chief Cities (1981 census): Belgrade, the capital, 1,470,073; Osijek, 867,646; Zagreb, 768,700.

Government: *Head of state,* collective state presidency, Radovan Vlajković, president (took office May 1985). *Head of government,* Milka Planinc, prime minister (took office May 1982). *Legislature* —Federal Assembly: Federal Chamber and Chamber of Republics and Provinces.

Monetary Unit: New Dinar (286.412 dinars equal U.S.$1, August 1985).

Gross National Product (1983 U.S.$): $122,300,000,000.

Economic Indexes (1984): *Consumer Prices* (1970 = 100), all items, 2,272.7; food, 2,494.9. *Industrial Production* (1980 = 100), 111.

Foreign Trade (1984 U.S.$): *Imports,* $11,996,000,000; *exports,* $10,255,000,000.

Paul Volcker, chairman of the Federal Reserve Board, as well as officials of the IMF and the World Bank. She received assurances of continued U.S. support for Yugoslavia's economic stabilization program, adopted in 1983.

Dissent and Ethnic Relations. Yugoslav domestic life was strained by persistent challenges from political dissenters and disgruntled ethnic minorities. In April 1984, six Serbian intellectuals were arrested for attending a sociology seminar in Belgrade at which Milovan Djilas, the noted author and dissident, had lectured. They were put on trial for "counter-revolutionary conspiracy" in November 1984. In January 1985 the charges were dropped against one of the accused, and on February 4 three others received relatively mild sentences of one-to-two years' imprisonment for "disseminating hostile propaganda." In November, all three convicted defendants appealed their sentences. One was acquitted, and the sentences of the other two reduced to eight-to-18 months' imprisonment. On February 5, in another case, a professor of philosophy in Belgrade was sentenced to 18 months' imprisonment for "antistate activities."

The repeated reductions of charges and sentences suggested that the leadership of the Yugoslav Communist party (League of Communists of Yugoslavia—LCY) was badly divided over how to deal with intellectual dissidents. It was asserted that the trials had been engineered by neo-Stalinist Croatian Communists in an effort to embarrass their more liberal Serbian counterparts. Negative international publicity included a charge by Amnesty International on May 28 that Yugoslavia was convicting more than 500 persons a year for "political offenses."

On May 15, Radovan Vlajković, a Serb from Vojvodina province, became the titular head of state, a post rotating annually among the collective state presidency. Sinan Hasani, an ethnic Albanian from Kosovo province, became the new vice-president and president-elect for 1986. But ethnic relations were not as smooth at other levels as they appeared to be within the collective leadership. Stirring ethnic Albanian nationalism in Kosovo, supported by charges from Albania that Yugoslavia was trying to "liquidate" its kinsmen, spurred the LCY to adopt a tough stand against such nationalistic expressions, coupled with recommendations for more generous government spending in Kosovo and the granting of full republic status to the autonomous region.

In March-April, the Yugoslav and Bulgarian media exchanged polemics over the status of the Socialist Republic of Macedonia within Yugoslavia and its relationship to Bulgaria. During the year, dogmatic ideologists in Croatia and Bosnia-Hercegovina launched a campaign against Serbian party liberals, charging that they were distorting and destroying the heritage of the deceased national leader, Tito.

JOSEPH F. ZACEK
State University of New York at Albany

AP/Wide World

During a three-day visit to Yugoslavia, Nicaragua's President Daniel Ortega (left) was received by the then president, Veselin Djuranović. The two nations signed a cultural, scientific-technical, and educational pact.

YUKON

In 1985 the Yukon Territory elected a new leader. The economy continued to lag, although there were some signs of improvement.

Government. A territorial election held on May 13, 1985, resulted in the formation of a minority New Democratic Party (NDP) government under the leadership of Tony Penikett. In the popular vote, the Conservatives received 47%, the NDP 41%, and the Liberals 8%. The NDP was still the winner, however, capturing 8 of 16 legislative seats. The Progressive Conservatives took six seats and the Liberals won two seats. The Conservatives lost one seat in September when Whitehorse Conservative legislative member Andy Philipsen died in a highway accident.

Economy. The Yukon economy remained in a recession, and unemployment was high, but there were signs of improvement. With tourists spending an estimated C $82 million in 1984, and with 1985 promising to be an even better year, tourism provided some help. Mining industry figures for 1984 indicated that the Yukon produced $60 million in minerals, $40 million in placer gold, and $15 million in silver.

Cyprus Anvil Mine, the large lead and zinc producer near Faro, may resume production during the winter. Curragh Resources Corporation Ltd. signed a conditional agreement to buy the idle mine from Dome Petroleum. The purchase hinges on a number of conditions such as cheaper transportation and power rates. Cyprus Anvil ceased production in 1982 and was on the verge of closing permanently late in the year.

Indian Land Claims. The Yukon Indian Land Claims negotiations have been undergoing a one-and-a-half-year hiatus with no movement being made toward a final land claims agreement. The federal government requested that a memorandum of understanding be drawn up to embody the principles necessary for negotiations to resume. The federal and territorial governments and the Council for Yukon Indians have been studying the elements of the agreement.

DON SAWATSKY, *Whitehorse*

ZAIRE

Economic factors continued to dominate the affairs of Zaire.

Economic Developments. Pressured by the International Monetary Fund (IMF), President Mobutu Sese Seko's government attempted to rectify the most obvious deficiencies. Among the accomplishments were dismantling *Sozacom,* the inefficient government company that marketed all minerals; devaluation of the currency; establishment of a floating exchange rate; spending cutbacks; and reorganizing the government. These actions did not satisfy the IMF; however, creditors did reschedule payments on $3.2 billion of Zaire's $4 billion external debt, servicing of which costs $900 million per year. Inflation, although lower than the 100% level of 1984, remained double-digit, and wages failed to keep pace. Acute shortages of staples remained in all cities, and black markets thrived.

Domestic Affairs. President Mobutu, after beginning his third seven-year term in December 1984, retained his prime minister, Kengo Wa Dondo, while reorganizing the central and territorial administrations. He also reduced the size of the Central Committee of the ruling *Mouvement populaire de la révolution* (MPR) and banned those members from belonging to the cabinet. Mobutu reorganized his government twice more, attempting to meet the demands of the IMF; forced the resignation of 20 senior military officers; and created a new Inspector General's Office. The government crushed an armed uprising in Shaba Province in June, and Mobutu closed Kisangani University because of student protests.

Foreign Affairs. Relations with Zambia continued strained because of expulsion of aliens in 1984. Angolan relations improved after the visit of President dos Santos in February, and a state visit by Mobutu to Gabon in August produced a pronouncement of continued friendship. Zaire's recognition of Israel in 1982 paid dividends with the announcement of a future $400 million investment. In August, Pope John Paul II visited Kinshasa.

HARRY A. GAILEY
San José State University

YUKON · Information Highlights

Area: 207,037 sq mi (536 223 km²).
Population (June 1985): 24,734.
Chief City (1985 est.): Whitehorse, the capital, 17,265.
Government (1985): *Chief Officers*—commissioner, Douglas Bell; government leader, Tony Penikett. *Legislature*—16-member Legislative Assembly.
Public Finance (1984–85 fiscal year budget est.): *Revenues,* C$152,320,000; *expenditures,* C$148,-214,000.
Personal Income (average weekly earnings, May 1985): $491.61.
Education (1985–86): *Enrollment*—elementary and secondary schools, 4,790 pupils.

ZAIRE · Information Highlights

Official Name: Republic of Zaire.
Location: Central equatorial Africa.
Area: 905,563 sq mi (2 345 409 km²).
Population (mid-1985 est.): 33,100,000.
Chief City (1980 est.): Kinshasa, the capital, 3,000,000.
Government: *Head of state,* Mobutu Sese Seko, president (took office 1965). *Legislature* (unicameral)—National Legislative Council.
Monetary Unit: Zaire (50.65 Zaires equal U.S.$1, June 1985).
Foreign Trade (1983 U.S.$): *Imports,* $498,000,000; *exports,* $1,134,000,000.

ZIMBABWE

The elections held in June and July marked the end of the first five years of Zimbabwe's independence. Much was accomplished during that period: public education and health care were both expanded, and the guerrilla armies, as well as blacks in the Rhodesian military, were integrated into one Zimbabwean army. Despite a devastating drought, Zimbabwe had good harvests in 1985. However, the country continued to have ethnic, race, clan, and ideological divisions, and these remained a threat to its long-term stability.

On June 27, Ian Smith's Conservative Alliance of Zimbabwe (CAZ) won a decisive victory of 15 out of 20 seats in the separate election for Zimbabwe's 35,000 registered white voters. Twenty seats in the House of Assembly were reserved for whites under the Zimbabwe Constitution adopted in 1979, which brought independence and black rule after a protracted guerrilla war. The extent of the June victory entitled the Smith group to appoint ten whites to the 40-member Senate. The Zimbabwe Independence Group, a loose organization of former CAZ members, won four seats. One seat was won by Chris Anderson, who referred to himself as "an independent Independent." The CAZ won 55% of the votes cast and the Zimbabwe Independence Group 44%. Many of the seats won by the CAZ were by extremely small margins.

Prime Minister Mugabe's immediate response was that whites, by continuing to support Smith, had rejected his policy of reconciliation. There was speculation that he would immediately seek to punish whites by abolishing their seats in Parliament, even though under the Constitution this would not be possible.

In July the 2.9 million registered African voters (out of a potential African electorate of 3.2 million) voted for 79 of the 80 seats in the House of Assembly. Only 79 seats were contested at the election due to a by-election made necessary because of the death of a candidate, Robson Manyika, a deputy minister. In the previous Parliament the ruling Zimbabwe African National Union–Patriotic Front (ZANU-PF) held 57 seats, Joshua Nkomo's opposition Zimbabwe African People's Union (ZAPU) 20 seats, and Bishop Abel Muzorewa's United African National Council 3. In the campaign before the election it was clear that Prime Minister Mugabe particularly hoped to reduce or eliminate Nkomo's 20 seats in Parliament. Earlier in the year Nkomo's supporters in Matabeleland had been subjected to intimidation and even abduction, but in the months before the elections much of the violence stopped, and the elections took place in a free environment.

The final results of the election were that ZANU-PF won 64 seats, 6 more than in the 1980 election but short of the 70 seats needed to bring about one-party rule by 1987 when, under the constitution, major changes would be possible if approved by 70% of those in Parliament. Until then changes could only be made with 100% agreement. ZAPU won all 15 seats in Matabeleland, a clear indication that the ruling ZANU-PF had no support in Nkomo's Ndebele stronghold.

Bishop Abel Muzorewa's United African National Council lost all three of the seats it held in the previous Parliament, but the Zimbabwe African National Union (not to be confused with the ruling ZANU-PF), led by the exiled Rev. Ndabaningi Sithole, won one seat.

After the heat of the election was over, it was clear that Mugabe's primary concern was to neutralize Nkomo and ZAPU. As far as the white seats were concerned, the Mugabe approach seemed to be that they "would be dealt with when the time came."

The one surprising change in the cabinet reshuffle following the election was Mugabe's dismissal of the former agriculture minister, Denis Norman, who was highly respected and a nonpolitical appointment. Enos Nkala was appointed to the important Ministry of Home Affairs, which is in charge of the police. The only white remaining in the Cabinet was Chris Anderson, who retained his post as minister of public service.

The white population of Zimbabwe was estimated at 100,000, less than half of what it was at independence in 1980 and less than 2% of the total population of the country. White emigration continued, and it was estimated that the white population would ultimately stabilize at approximately 70,000. Despite the vote for CAZ, Mugabe's attempts at reconciliation had been successful. White political power had been neutralized, although whites still dominated commerce and industry. Mugabe's major political trouble continued to be the opposition of ZAPU and Joshua Nkomo.

PATRICK O'MEARA, *Indiana University*

ZIMBABWE • Information Highlights

Official Name: Republic of Zimbabwe.
Location: Southern Africa.
Area: 151,000 sq mi (391 090 km²).
Population (mid-1985 est): 8,600,000.
Chief Cities (provisional census, Aug. 1982): Harare (formerly Salisbury), the capital, 656,000; Bulawayo, 413,800; Chitungwiza, 172,600.
Government: *Head of state,* Canaan Banana, president (took office April 1980). *Head of government,* Robert Mugabe, prime minister (took office March 1980). *Legislature*—Parliament: Senate and House of Assembly.
Monetary Unit: Zimbabwe dollar (1.548 Z dollars equal U.S.$1, July 1985).
Economic Indexes (Oct. 1984): *Consumer Prices* (1970 = 100), all items, 192.1; food, 207.3. *Industrial Production* (May 1984, 1980 = 100), 95.
Foreign Trade (1984 U.S.$): *Imports,* $959,000,000; *exports,* $1,088,000,000.

ZOOS AND ZOOLOGY

Major exhibits started and opened by zoos and aquariums in the United States during 1985 demonstrated that these institutions are increasingly evolving from menageries featuring as many different species as possible to environmental education centers that use live animal displays to dramatize ecological concepts to the public. Zoos and aquariums also made continued progress in their efforts to propagate rare species, in many cases destined for eventual reintroduction into the wild.

Exhibits. A new building at Birmingham (AL) Zoo exemplifies the trend toward specialized exhibits. Opened in March, the facility is devoted entirely to predator species; it is the first to cover predators on virtually all rungs of the taxonomic ladder. The Predators, as the building is called, displays not only predatory birds and mammals but also insects, fish, amphibians, and reptiles. Walking along a corridor that winds through the building, visitors see lions, tiger beetles, coral shrimp, bald eagles, Arctic foxes, and other predators in their natural settings. Design of the building, by Jerry M. Johnson, Inc. of Boston, was especially difficult because of the vastly differing needs of the various animals. Designers also were challenged by the problems of weaving a wide spectrum of animal life into the building's central theme—the importance of predators in the

A growing number of American ranchers are providing havens for rare animals. The Fossil Rim Ranch, above, is one of more than 600 sanctuaries in Texas alone. Meanwhile, 12 Golden Lion Tamarin monkeys were returned to the Brazilian rain forest from the Washington National Zoo.

overall scheme of nature and the need for their conservation.

While the Birmingham building focuses on a specific group of animals, a facility that opened in June at the Bronx (NY) Zoo concentrates on a specific ecological area, the jungles of Asia. JungleWorld is the largest and most detailed of the Bronx Zoo's major exhibit buildings. Covering 17,000 sq ft (1 580 m²), it simulates portions of tropical jungle ecosystems such as a mangrove swamp in Borneo, a rain forest in southeast Asia, and a volcanic scrub forest in Indonesia. Among the animals in the exhibit, the final element in the zoo's Wild Asia complex, are proboscis monkeys, white-handed gibbons, monitor lizards, and great hornbills. These and many other animals live in a mix of natural and artificial surroundings that blend into dioramas difficult to tell from the real wild. Living trees, flowers, and vines are interspersed with those made of artificial materials. The building has waterfalls, cliffs, riverbeds, and many other natural features of the Asian jungle.

One of the most ambitious projects underway during the year was the construction of a new zoo in Indianapolis. Scheduled to open in 1988, the new zoo will be three times the size of the existing facility. Among the exhibits to be featured is a water complex, to include aquatic animals from both Indiana and around the world.

Breeding. Most of the publicity given to the breeding of rare species focuses on creatures that are relatively well known, such as Siberian tigers and gorillas. However, many breeding programs also stress lesser-known creatures that are no less important to the balance of nature. For example, ten zoos worldwide are striving to breed the rare Puerto Rican crested toad, an imperiled amphibian found only in a few areas of Puerto Rico. The U.S. zoos involved are Brookfield (Chicago), Buffalo, Cincinnati, Columbus, Fort Worth, Indianapolis, Toledo, and Mayaguez (Puerto Rico). Toads also are at the Metro Toronto Zoo in Canada and the Frankfurt Zoo in Germany. In September, the American Association of Zoological Parks and Aquariums reported that the Toronto Zoo had recorded the first natural breeding of the crested toad outside of its Puerto Rican range.

Among the other notable breeding successes during 1985 were of a rare giant Galápagos tortoise at the Gladys Porter Zoo in Brownsville, TX, an endangered black rhinoceros at Brookfield, and lowland gorillas at Oklahoma City and Columbus.

The Sea World aquarium in San Diego made headlines with the birth of a male Commerson's dolphin in February. Officials at the aquarium said that the birth probably was the first ever in captivity. Isolated populations of these rare sea mammals are found off the

Jane DiMenna

JungleWorld, a major new exhibit at the Bronx Zoo in New York, features a series of simulated tropical environments and a variety of animals from the jungles of Asia.

southern tip of South America and the Falkland Islands, as well as around the Kerguelen Islands in the Indian Ocean.

Research. Sea mammals also figured in the plans of the Mystic (CT) Marinelife Aquarium during the year. The aquarium began a campaign to build a major facility for research into whales and dolphins. The $4.3 million Whale Study Center will be designed to provide students from southern New England with a chance for classroom and field experience with marine mammals and to serve as a base for laboratory and field studies.

A New York Zoological Society study of Magellanic penguins in southern Argentina has provided some disheartening news for conservationists. Ecologist Dee Boersma, who returned to the United States from Argentina in March, reported one of the worst mass fatalities ever observed in a penguin colony. Almost half a million young penguins perished because of unusual cold and storms during the Southern Hemisphere summer, when the chicks normally hatch. The freak weather prevented the normal upwelling of nutrient-rich bottom waters off the coast, which in turn diminished the amount of fish and squid eaten by the adult penguins. Consequently, the adults had to roam far at sea for food, leaving their young exposed to the difficult weather.

EDWARD R. RICCIUTI
Free-lance Environment and Wildlife Writer

Statistical and Tabular Data

NATIONS OF THE WORLD

A Profile and Synopsis of Major 1985 Developments

Nation, Region	Population in millions	Capital	Area Sq mi (km²)	Head of State/Government
Angola, S.W. Africa	7.9	Luanda	481,351 (1 246 700)	José Eduardo dos Santos, president

Fighting continued between Angolan government forces, aided by Cuban troops, and guerrillas of the National Union for the Total Independence of Angola (UNITA). In April, following an agreement signed in 1984, South Africa withdrew the last of the troops it had sent into Angola to support UNITA and to pursue guerrillas of the South West African People's Organization (SWAPO), who had staged raids on Namibia (South West Africa) from bases in Angola. It was hoped that the move would foster dialogue between Angola and South Africa; however, relations soured when South African troops again crossed the border in May and repeatedly through 1985. In September, Angola was reported to be turning the tide against UNITA with the help of increased Soviet aid. In August, President Reagan signed a foreign-aid bill, lifting the ban against U.S. assistance to anticommunist insurgents in Angola. In response, the Angolan government broke off diplomatic contacts with the United States. On February 9, Angola and Zaire signed a security and defense agreement. President José Eduardo dos Santos was reelected to a second five-year term, and Afonso Van Dunem Mbinda was appointed foreign minister. In April, Angola signed the Lomé Convention, gaining preferred trade status with the European Community. Foreign Trade (1984): Imports, $636 million; exports, $2.03 billion.

Nation, Region	Population in millions	Capital	Area Sq mi (km²)	Head of State/Government
Antigua and Barbuda, Caribbean	0.1	St. John's	171 (443.6)	Sir Wilfred E. Jacobs, governor-general Vere C. Bird, prime minister

Noting that interregional trade had fallen off in recent years, Antigua and Barbuda joined other members of the Caribbean Community and Common Market (CARICOM) at a July 1–4 meeting in pledging to stimulate trade and establish a common tariff. Gross Domestic Product, GDP (1982): $129.5 million. Foreign Trade: Imports (1982), $138.1 million; exports (1985), $34.5 million.

Nation, Region	Population in millions	Capital	Area Sq mi (km²)	Head of State/Government
Bahamas, Caribbean	0.2	Nassau	5,380 (13 934)	Sir Gerald C. Cash, governor-general Lynden O. Pindling, prime minister

The Bahamas joined with other members of the Nonaligned Movement in urging economic sanctions against South Africa as a means of ending that country's policy of apartheid. Gross National Product, GNP (1982): $1.4 billion. Foreign Trade (1984): Imports, $3.03 billion; exports, $2.38 billion.

Nation, Region	Population in millions	Capital	Area Sq mi (km²)	Head of State/Government
Bahrain, W. Asia	0.4	Manama	261 (676)	Isa bin Sulman Al Khalifa, emir Khalifa bin Salman Al Khalifa, prime minister

Representatives of Bahrain gathered with delegates from 15 other Arab League nations in an "emergency" summit in Casablanca, Morocco, in August. The emir discussed the Iran-Iraq war and other issues with Great Britain's Prime Minister Margaret Thatcher in London in April. In June, British police arrested eight Arabs for allegedly plotting to overthrow Bahrain's government. Declining oil revenues adversely affected the national economy. A causeway, linking Bahrain and Saudi Arabia, was due to be completed in December. GDP (1982 est.): $4 billion. Foreign Trade (1984): Imports, $3.53 billion; exports, $3.14 billion.

Nation, Region	Population in millions	Capital	Area Sq mi (km²)	Head of State/Government
Barbados, Caribbean	0.3	Bridgetown	166 (430)	Sir Hugh Springer, governor-general Bernard St. John, prime minister

Prime Minister John M. G. Adams died suddenly of a heart attack March 11; Bernard St. John, former leader of the Labour Party, was sworn in to replace him. Elections were expected within 15 months. On July 1–4, Barbados hosted a CARICOM summit meeting, at which St. John warned of the dangers protectionism held for the Caribbean region. GDP (1982): $997.5 million. Foreign Trade (1984): Imports, $659 million; exports, $391 million.

Nation, Region	Population in millions	Capital	Area Sq mi (km²)	Head of State/Government
Benin, W. Africa	4.0	Porto Novo	43,483 (112 622)	Mathieu Kérékou, president

Thousands of Ghanian and Togolese workers expelled from Nigeria were stranded in transit camps along the Benin-Nigeria border in April and May, after the Benin government initially refused to let them cross its territory. Most of the workers had returned to their home countries by the end of May. GNP (1982): $1.1 billion. Foreign Trade (1982): Imports, $590.3 million; exports, $304.3 million.

Nation, Region	Population in millions	Capital	Area Sq mi (km²)	Head of State/Government
Bhutan, S. Asia	1.4	Thimphu	18,000 (46 620)	Jigme Singye Wangchuck, king

GDP (fiscal year 1982–83): $150 million. Foreign Trade (fiscal year 1982–83): Imports, $58.5 million; exports, $16.7 million.

Nation, Region	Population in millions	Capital	Area Sq mi (km²)	Head of State/Government
Botswana, S. Africa	1.1	Gaborone	231,804 (600 372)	Quett Masire, president

South Africa accused Botswana of aiding African National Congress (ANC) guerrillas and on June 14 raided Gaborone, attacking what it called the "nerve center" of the ANC. At least 16 people were killed. Botswana protested the strike, and the United Nations Security Council condemned it on June 21. Throughout the year, Botswana continued to suffer from a three-year drought. GDP (1982): $722 million. Foreign Trade (1983): Imports, $740 million; exports, $640 million.

Nation, Region	Population in millions	Capital	Area Sq mi (km²)	Head of State/Government
Brunei	0.2	Bandar Seri Begawan	2,226 (5 765)	Sir Hassanal Bolkiah, sultan and prime minister

British Prime Minister Margaret Thatcher visited Brunei on April 9, just over a year after the sultanate assumed full sovereignty from Great Britain. GDP (1981): $4.3 billion. Foreign Trade (1983): Imports, $728 million; exports, $3.39 billion.

Nation, Region	Population in millions	Capital	Area Sq mi (km²)	Head of State/Government
Burkina Faso, W. Africa	6.9	Ouagadougou	92,741 (240 200)	Thomas Sankara, head of state

Burkina Faso, formerly Upper Volta, was among the African countries most heavily afflicted by drought and famine in 1985. Burkina Faso was engaged in a year-end border war with Mali. GDP (1984): $66 million. Foreign Trade (1983): Imports, $288 million; exports, $57 million.

Nation, Region	Population in millions	Capital	Area Sq mi (km²)	Head of State/Government
Burundi, E. Africa	4.6	Bujumbura	10,747 (27 834)	Jean-Baptiste Bagaza, president

In a symptom of worsening church-state relations, ten Roman Catholic missionaries were expelled from Burundi in March, after the government claimed that clerics were encouraging opposition to its policies. President Bagaza denied on July 21 charges that his government was aiding rebels in neighboring Zaire. GDP (1983): $1.12 billion. Foreign Trade (1984): Imports, $186 million; exports, $99 million.

Nation, Region	Population in millions	Capital	Area Sq mi (km²)	Head of State/Government
Cameroon, Cen. Africa	9.7	Yaounde	183,567 (475 439)	Paul Biya, president

Thousands of Cameroon workers were among 700,000 illegal aliens expelled from Nigeria in April and May. On August 11, Pope John Paul II visited Cameroon, urging a dialogue with Islam and opposition to apartheid. GDP (1983): $6.7 billion. Foreign Trade (1984): Imports, $1.11 billion; exports, $883 million.

Cape Verde, W. Africa	0.3	Praia	1,560 (4 040)	Aristides Pereira, president Pedro Pires, prime minister

In March, President Pereira dismissed the ministers for foreign affairs and planning, assuming those duties himself. GNP (1982): $106 million. Foreign Trade (1983): Imports, $68 million; exports, $1.6 million.

Central African Republic,
Cen. Africa	2.7	Bangui	240,534 (622 984)	André-Dieudonne Kolingba, president of the Military Committee for National Recovery

The Central African Republic's elephant population was reported severely reduced by poachers, including Sudanese rebel groups who were financing their operations through ivory sales. GDP (1983): $616 million. Foreign Trade (1982): Imports, $127 million; exports, $109 million.

Chad, N.- Cen. Africa	5.2	Ndjamena	495,753 (1 284 000)	Hissèin Habré, president

Chad remained partitioned, with sections of the country under the control of Libyan-backed forces loyal to former president Goukouni Oueddi. Drought was a problem throughout the year. GDP (1980): $500 million. Foreign Trade (1982): Imports, $109 million; exports, $58 million.

Comoros, E. Africa	0.5	Moroni	838 (2 171)	Ahmed Abdallah Abderemane, president

In January, Mozambique charged Comoros with aiding rebels of the Mozambique National Resistance (MNR). GNP (1982): $107 million. Foreign Trade (1982): Imports, $19 million; exports, $18 million.

Congo, Cen. Africa	1.7	Brazzaville	132,046 (342 000)	Denis Sassou-Nguesso, president Ange Edouard Poungui, prime minister

Congo was among members of the Nonaligned Movement urging economic sanctions against South Africa. GDP (1984 est.): $1.8 billion. Foreign Trade (1983): Imports, $806 million; exports, $1.07 billion.

Djibouti, E. Africa	0.3	Djibouti	8,494 (22 000)	Hassan Gouled Aptidon, president Barkat Gourad Hamadou, premier

GDP (1983): $369 million. Foreign Trade (1983): Imports, $179 million; exports, $108 million.

Dominica, Caribbean	0.1	Roseau	291 (752.7)	Clarence A. Seignoret, president Mary Eugenia Charles, prime minister

In elections on July 1, Prime Minister Charles won a second five-year term as her Dominica Freedom Party secured 15 of the legislature's 21 seats. Former Prime Minister Patrick R. John, awaiting trial on charges of attempting to overthrow the government, was also among those who won a seat. GNP (1983): $56.4 million. Foreign Trade (1982): Imports, $48.5 million; exports, $24.7 million.

Dominican Republic,
Caribbean	6.2	Santo Domingo	18,816 (48 734)	Salvador Jorge Blanco, president

Gasoline and food price hikes announced on January 25 sparked riots and a general strike on February 11; two people were killed and several leftist leaders arrested. The government rolled back increases on some items February 12. Riots broke out again in June after wage increases for public workers were vetoed, and the government again backed down. The austerity measures were accompanied by currency devaluation in an attempt to win International Monetary Fund (IMF) approval for a $67 million loan. The Dominican Republic succeeded in rescheduling its foreign debt, estimated at $2 to $3 billion, in July. In a primary held November 24 by the ruling Revolutionary Party to choose a candidate for the 1986 presidential election, two men—Senate President Jacobo Majluta and Mayor José Francisco Pena Gomez of Santo Domingo—claimed victory. Vote counting was halted after violence broke out between their supporters. GNP (1982): $7.6 billion. Foreign Trade (1984): Imports, $1.26 billion; exports, $876 million.

Equatorial Guinea
Cen. Africa	0.3	Malabo	10,830 (28 051)	Teodoro Obiang Nguema Mbasogo, president Christino Seriche Bioko, premier

GNP (1983): $75 million. Foreign Trade (1982): Imports, $41.5 million; exports, $16.9 million.

Fiji, Oceania	0.7	Suva	7,095 (18 376)	Sir Penaia Ganilau, governor-general Sir Kamisese Mara, premier

Fiji was one of eight members of the 13-country South Pacific forum that formally declared their region a nuclear-free zone in August. The signers of the treaty agreed to ban the manufacture, testing, and basing of nuclear arms and the dumping of nuclear waste. Japanese Prime Minister Nakasone visited Fiji in January and offered assurances that his country would delay plans to dump atomic waste in the Pacific. Fiji also was visited by Chinese Communist Party Secretary Hu Yaobang (in April) and by U.S. Secretary of State George Shultz (in July). GDP (1982): $1.85 billion. Foreign Trade (1984): Imports, $450 million; exports, $256 million.

Gabon, Cen. Africa	1.0	Libreville	103,346 (267 667)	El Hadj Omar Bongo, president Léon Mébiame, premier

GDP (1983): $3.4 billion. Foreign Trade (1983): Imports, $853 million; exports, $1.98 billion.

Gambia, W. Africa	0.8	Banjul	4,361 (11 295)	Sir Dawda Kairaba Jawara, president

In January, Louise Njie became minister of education, youth, sports, and culture, the first woman to hold a cabinet post in Gambia. A law adopted in February required all Gambians over the age of 18 to carry identity cards. GDP (1984): $138 million. Foreign Trade (1984): Imports, $98 million; exports, $47 million.

Ghana, W. Africa	14.3	Accra	92,100 (238 538)	Jerry Rawlings, chairman, Provisional National Defense Council

On May 17, Ghana lodged official protests over the use of force by Nigeria in expelling Ghanian workers as illegal aliens; however, the workers, many of whom had previously been expelled from Nigeria but returned to that country nonetheless, got a cool welcome from their government. In other developments, a Ghanian national, Michael Agbouti Soussoudis, was arrested in the United States on espionage charges; and in November, Ghana sentenced two of its citizens to prison terms for spying for the U.S. Central Intelligence Agency. Ghana became a nonpermanent member of the United Nations Security Council in October. GNP (1982): $10.5 billion. Foreign Trade (1983): Imports, $2.53 billion; exports, $2.03 billion.

Nation, Region	Population in millions	Capital	Area Sq mi (km²)	Head of State/Government
Grenada, Caribbean	0.1	St. George's	133 (344)	Sir Paul Scoon, governor-general Herbert A. Blaize, prime minister

The United States announced on February 7 that all foreign troops would leave Grenada by September. (Some 250 U.S. troops and 450 members of a Caribbean peacekeeping force had remained on the island after a U.S.-led invasion in 1983 drove out Marxists who deposed and killed Prime Minister Maurice Bishop.) A visit by Great Britain's Queen Elizabeth II in October marked the mending of relations between Grenada and Britain. GDP (1983): $119 million. Foreign Trade (1983): Imports, $56.2 million; exports, $19.1 million.

Guinea, W. Africa	6.1	Conakry	94,964 (245 957)	Lansana Conté, president

President Conté foiled a coup attempt July 4–5 by former Prime Minister Diarra Traoré, who had been demoted in December 1984. The rebels seized the radio station but failed to take the capital. Eighteen people were killed and 18 arrested. Traoré was thought to have been executed. GDP (1983): $1.51 billion. Foreign Trade (1984 est.): Imports, $403 million; exports, $537 million.

Guinea-Bissau, W. Africa	0.9	Bissau	14,000 (36 260)	João Bernardo Vieira, president

President Vieira dismissed Attorney General M. Nicandro Barreto, accusing him of supporting an antigovernment plot. On February 23, Guinea-Bissau and Gabon signed a "treaty of cooperation and friendship." GDP (fiscal year 1983): $154 million. Foreign Trade (1982): Imports, $50 million; exports, $12 million.

Haiti, Caribbean	5.8	Port-au-Prince	10,714 (27 749)	Jean-Claude Duvalier, president

Charges of human-rights abuse continued to be leveled at the Duvalier regime. In May, 36 political prisoners were released, and the government was said to be holding none for the first time in memory. However, on July 20, two days before a referendum that granted Duvalier the title president-for-life, six journalists were arrested; other Duvalier opponents were arrested later in July. Interior Minister Roger Lafontant, who had been charged with torturing prisoners, was dismissed September 10 in response to U.S. criticism. Nevertheless a wave of anti-Duvalier protests—which at times led to harsh government action—was sweeping Haiti late in the year. GNP (1982): $1.5 billion. Foreign Trade (1983): Imports, $314 million; exports, $187 million.

Ivory Coast, W. Africa	10.1	Yamoussoukro	124,503 (322 463)	Félix Houphouët- Boigny, president

On October 10 the legislature abolished the post of vice-president, ending, for the moment, speculation over who might succeed 80-year-old President Houphouët-Boigny. Houphouët-Boigny, who had led the country since its independence from France in 1960, was the sole candidate in an October 27 presidential election and won 99% of the vote. Following a mid-December meeting in Geneva, President Houphouët-Boigny and Israel's Prime Minister Shimon Peres announced that the two nations would restore diplomatic relations. GDP (1982): $7.6 billion. Foreign Trade (1983): Imports, $1.81 billion; exports, $2.07 billion.

Jamaica, Caribbean	2.3	Kingston	4,244 (10 991)	Florizel Glasspole, governor-general Edward Seaga, prime minister

Riots broke out January 15–16 after the government announced fuel price hikes; eight were killed in the worst violence during Seaga's four years in power. A general strike called June 24 to protest job layoffs and a high cost of living ended July 1 pending talks with the government. Seaga said the austerity measures that sparked the unrest were necessary to aid the country's troubled economy, which had been dealt a further blow in February when Alcoa announced it would close its Jamaican bauxite refinery. (Bauxite makes up two thirds of Jamaica's exports.) The government struck a deal with the company to take over the plant, which employs 800. GNP (1982): $3 billion. Foreign Trade (1984): Imports, $1.18 billion; exports, $777 million.

Kiribati, Oceania	0.06	Tarawa	ca. 266 (690)	Reginald Wallace, governor-general Ieremia Tabai, president

Kiribati agreed to grant the Soviet Union fishing rights in its territorial waters in exchange for annual payments of $1 million, a move that left some Western nations concerned that Kiribati would become subject to Soviet pressure. In other developments, Kiribati was one of eight Pacific Forum nations who declared a nuclear-free zone in August. (See also Fiji.) GDP (1983): $20.4 million.

Kuwait, W. Asia	1.9	Kuwait	6,880 (17 818)	Jabir al-Ahmad Al Sabah, emir Saad al-Abdallah Al Sabah, prime minister

The emir narrowly escaped death May 25, when a suicide bomber drove a car filled with explosives into his motorcade. The Shiite group Islamic Holy War claimed responsibility, demanding the release of 17 prisoners being held for a series of 1983 bombings. However, Iran, Iraq, and the U.S. Central Intelligence Agency also were blamed by various sources. On November 24, a Kuwaiti cargo ship was seized by Iranian gunboats in the Gulf of Oman. GDP (1983): $26.7 billion. Foreign Trade (1983): Imports, $7.2 billion; exports, $11.2 billion.

Lesotho, S. Africa	1.5	Maseru	11,761 (30 460)	Moshoeshoe II, king Leabua Jonathan, prime minister

Friction between the government and members of the Pan African Congress (PAC), an underground group opposing white rule in South Africa, increased in March, after Lesotho security guards killed six PAC members near its border. The government threatened PAC members with expulsion for aligning themselves with Lesotho opposition parties. In October, King Moshoeshoe II, addressing the United Nations, called for an end to white South African rule but warned that his country must be protected from the effects of any economic sanctions imposed on South Africa. GNP (1982): $640 million. Foreign Trade (1983): Imports, $450 million; exports, $124 million, including $94 million in remittances of Basotho workers in South Africa.

Liberia, W. Africa	2.2	Monrovia	43,000 (111 370)	Samuel K. Doe, president

Samuel K. Doe, who came to power in a 1980 coup, was elected president October 2 in Liberia's first multiparty election. However, charges of widespread intimidation and election fraud placed continued U.S. aid to Liberia's tottering economy in jeopardy. On November 12, Doe foiled a coup attempt led by former military commander Thomas Qwiwonkpa; Doe had escaped an April 1 assassination attempt by the chief of his personal guard. With President Doe charging that participants in the attempted coup had trained in neighboring Sierra Leone, Liberia closed its border and recalled its ambassador to Sierra Leone. A few days later, Doe introduced severe austerity measures. On July 18, Liberia severed relations with the Soviet Union, charging the Soviet embassy in Monrovia with espionage; in October, Eastern European and Muslim nations blocked Liberia's election as a nonpermanent member of the United Nations Security Council. GDP (1982): $1.06 billion. Foreign Trade (1983): Imports, $415 million; exports, $429 million.

Liechtenstein, Cen. Europe	0.03	Vaduz	62 (160)	Franz Josef II, prince Hans Brunhart, prime minister

Luxembourg, W. Europe	0.4	Luxembourg	998 (2 586)	Jean, grand duke Jaques Santer, prime minister

Luxembourg took over the presidency of the European Communities Council from Italy in July and was also a participating member of Eureka, the European research agency launched July 18 by 17 European countries to enhance their part in the U.S. Strategic Defense Initiative (Star Wars plan). The country's former constitutional ruler, Grand Duchess Charlotte, died July 9 at age 89; she had ruled from 1919 to 1964, when she abdicated in favor of her eldest son, Jean. GNP (1983): $4.7 billion.

Nation, Region	Population in millions	Capital	Area Sq mi (km²)	Head of State/Government
Madagascar, E. Africa	10.0	Antananarivo	228,919 (592 900)	Didier Ratsiraka, head of government Desire Rakotoarijaona, premier

Government troops July 31–August 1 attacked the Antananarivo headquarters of an underground kung fu organization, killing the leader and 19 followers and arresting 208 others. The government said the group was behind urban crimes and terrorism. In October, Admiral Ratsiraka addressed the United Nations and called for a debt strike by Third World nations. GDP (1984): $2.5 billion. Foreign Trade (1984): Imports, $356 million; exports, $328 million.

Malawi, E. Africa	7.1	Lilongwe	45,747 (118 484)	Hastings Kamuzu Banda, president

Heavy rains fell in January and February, bringing relief to drought-stricken areas for the first time in three years. GDP (1982): $1.34 billion. Foreign Trade (1984): Imports, $279 million; exports, $292 million.

Maldives, S. Asia	0.2	Malé	115 (298)	Maumoon Abdul Gayoom, president

The Maldives became a member of the Commonwealth in June. GDP (1982): $74 million. Foreign Trade (1982): Imports, $46 million; exports, $17.3 million.

Mali, W. Africa	7.7	Bamako	478,764 (1 240 000)	Moussa Traoré, president

Mali was among the African nations seriously affected by drought in 1985 and was the recipient of international aid. U.S. Vice-President George Bush, on a visit March 9–10, announced that Mali would be the first to receive funds in an experimental program designed to encourage free-market agricultural policies. In other news, an Air Mali passenger jet crashed February 22 in Timbuktu, killing 50 people including former Finance Minister Attaher Maiga. Mali charged Burkina Faso with torturing villagers during a year-end border war. GDP (1982): $1 billion. Foreign Trade (1983): Imports, $344 million; exports, $167 million.

Malta, S. Europe	0.4	Valletta	121 (313)	Agatha Barbara, president Karmenu Mifsud Bonnici, prime minister

An Egypt Air passenger jet en route to Cairo from Athens was hijacked November 23 and forced to land in Malta. The hijackers, believed to be radical Palestinians, shot several American and Israeli passengers, killing two. On November 24, Egyptian commandos stormed the plane; the hijackers retaliated by throwing hand grenades at the remaining passengers. About 60 persons were killed in the incident. GDP (1982): $1.12 billion. Foreign Trade (1984): Imports, $717 million; exports, $394 million.

Mauritania, W. Africa	1.9	Nouakchott	397,954 (1 030 700)	Maaouiya Ould Sidi Ahmed Taya, president and prime minister

In April, Mauritania and Algeria agreed on a common border, ending three years of negotiations. The country also reestablished diplomatic relations with Morocco (broken in 1981) and with Libya (broken in 1984). President Taya, who had taken power in a coup in December 1984, reshuffled his cabinet three times in his first six months in office. GNP (1982): $730 million. Foreign Trade (1984): Imports, $194 million; exports, $294 million.

Mauritius, E. Africa	1.0	Port Louis	720 (1 865)	Sir Seewoosagur Ramgoolam, governor-general Aneerood Jugnauth, prime minister

Laws adopted in March would fine or imprison any person who publishes or speaks false information or information, true or false, judged prejudicial to government. GDP (1983–84 est.): $1.1 billion. Foreign Trade (1984): Imports, $472 million; exports, $373 million.

Monaco, S. Europe	0.03	Monaco-Ville	0.7 (1.9)	Ranier III, prince Jean Herly, minister of state
Mongolia, E. Asia	1.9	Ulan Bator	604,100 (1 564 619)	Jambyn Batmonh, chairman of the Presidium Dumaagiyn Sodnom, chairman, Council of Ministers

Mongolia was represented at a COMECON summit in Warsaw on June 25–27.

Mozambique, E. Africa	13.9	Maputo	302,328 (783 030)	Samora Moises Machel, president

Many areas of Mozambique suffered famine; rains broke a long drought in February but brought flooding. The U.S. Congress granted economic aid to Mozambique's private sector but barred other help, including a proposal for $1 million in military aid. Economic reforms introduced in June seemed to indicate that President Machel was backing off the socialist course he had followed since taking office in 1975. Meanwhile, the government continued to battle guerrillas of the Mozambique National Resistance (MNR); South Africa, failing to abide by a March 1984 nonaggression pact with Mozambique, was said to be helping the rebels. GNP (1983 est.): $2 billion. Foreign Trade (1982): Imports, $836 million; exports, $229 million.

Nauru, Oceania	0.008	Nauru	8 (20.7)	Hammer DeRoburt, president

President DeRoburt lost a seven-year-long libel suit brought in U.S. courts against the Pacific Daily News, a Guam newspaper, over two articles that linked him to a controversial loan to Marshall Islands separatists in 1978. The jury, sitting in Honolulu, found that DeRoburt had been defamed but that the paper had not acted out of malice.

Nepal, S. Asia	17.0	Katmandu	54,359 (140 791)	Birendra Bir Bikram, king Lokendra B. Chand, prime minister

Opposition groups pressed for the lifting of a ban on political parties that had been instituted in 1960. Several hundred members of banned parties were arrested in protests in late May and early June, and two newspapers were closed. Soon after, on June 20, five bombs exploded at the king's palace, the National Assembly, and other sites in Katmandu, killing seven people. Some 1,400 people were said to have been arrested after the incident. GDP (fiscal year 1983–84): $2.4 billion. Foreign Trade (1982–83): Imports, $431.8 million; exports, $79.2 million.

Niger, W. Africa	6.5	Niamey	489,189 (1 267 000)	Seyni Kountché, president Hamid Algabid, prime minister

As one of the nations most heavily hurt by famine in 1985, Niger received emergency international aid. Adding to the country's problems, some 100,000 Niger workers returned home after being expelled as illegal aliens by Nigeria in April and May. GDP (1982): $2 billion. Foreign Trade (1982): Imports, $442 million; exports, $333 million.

Oman, W. Asia	1.2	Muscat	ca. 82,000 (212 380)	Qaboos bin Said, sultan and prime minister

Construction neared completion on four military bases at the entrance to the Persian Gulf, funded at a cost of $255 million by the United States. The bases were to remain under Omani control, with an agreement allowing the United States to use them in the event of a military emergency. Long one of the staunchest U.S. allies in the Persian Gulf region, Oman announced in September that it and the Soviet Union would reestablish diplomatic relations broken 15 years earlier. The country also marked the 15th year of the current sultan's rule with nationwide celebrations. GNP (1982): $6.8 billion. Foreign Trade (1983): Imports, $2.5 billion; exports, $4.25 billion.

Nation, Region	Population in millions	Capital	Area Sq mi (km²)	Head of State/Government
Papua New Guinea, Oceania	3.3	Port Moresby	178,259 (461 691)	Sir Kingsford Dibela, governor-general Paias Wingti, acting prime minister

In November, Michael Somare was ousted as prime minister in a no-confidence motion over his economic policies. Paias Wingti was named head of a caretaker government until elections are held in 1987. A clash between rebels in Papua New Guinea's remote Western Province and an Indonesian border survey team was reported in November. Among foreign dignitaries visiting Papua New Guinea in 1985 were Japanese Prime Minister Yasuhiro Nakasone in January, Chinese Communist Party General Secretary Hu Yaobang in April, and Australia's Foreign Minister Bill Hayden in November. GNP (1982): $2 billion. Foreign Trade (1983): Imports, $974 million; exports, $813 million.

Nation, Region	Population in millions	Capital	Area Sq mi (km²)	Head of State/Government
Qatar, W. Asia	0.3	Doha	4,247 (11 000)	Khalifa bin Hamad Al Thani, emir and prime minister

As two years of disagreement on oil prices continued, Qatar delegates walked out of the semiannual meeting of the Organization of the Petroleum Exporting Countries (OPEC) on July 6 in Vienna, when it was clear that members would not reach an agreement on cutting prices. A second meeting, held two weeks later in Geneva, produced a price-cutting agreement that Qatar approved; however, OPEC's October 4 meeting in Geneva again broke up without reaching agreements on output or pricing. GNP (1983): $7.6 billion. Foreign Trade (1983): Imports, $1.5 billion; exports, $3.3 billion.

Nation, Region	Population in millions	Capital	Area Sq mi (km²)	Head of State/Government
Rwanda, E. Africa	6.3	Kigali	10,169 (26 338)	Juvénal Habyarimana, president

Libyan leader Muammar el-Qaddafi, visiting Rwanda on May 16–18, called for a "holy war" to end the Mobutu regime in neighboring Zaire. Rwanda later disavowed Qaddafi's remarks and denied that it was aiding rebels in Zaire. GDP (1983): $1.5 billion. Foreign Trade (1984): Imports, $290 million; exports, $83 million.

Nation, Region	Population in millions	Capital	Area Sq mi (km²)	Head of State/Government
Saint Christopher and Nevis, Caribbean	0.04	Basseterre	101 (261)	Clement A. Arrindell, governor-general Kennedy A. Simmonds, prime minister

Saint Christopher and Nevis joined with other members of the Caribbean Community and Common Market (CARICOM) in urging freer trade among countries of the Caribbean. (See also ANTIGUA AND BARBUDA; BARBADOS.) GNP (1982): $41.6 million. Foreign Trade (1983): Imports, $47.3 million; exports, $30.6 million.

Nation, Region	Population in millions	Capital	Area Sq mi (km²)	Head of State/Government
Saint Lucia, Caribbean	0.1	Castries	239 (619)	Sir Allen Lewis, governor-general John Compton, prime minister

Saint Lucia joined with other CARICOM members in urging freer trade among Caribbean countries. GDP (1983): $141.4 million. Foreign Trade (1982): Imports, $119 million; exports, $42 million.

Nation, Region	Population in millions	Capital	Area Sq mi (km²)	Head of State/Government
Saint Vincent and the Grenadines, Caribbean	0.1	Kingstown	150 (389)	Joseph Lambert Eustace, governor-general James F. Mitchell, prime minister

Saint Vincent and the Grenadines also joined with other CARICOM members in urging freer trade among Caribbean countries. The island nation became a full member of the Commonwealth in June. GNP (1981): $69.6 million. Foreign Trade (1982): Imports, $61.6 million; exports, $32.7 million.

Nation, Region	Population in millions	Capital	Area Sq mi (km²)	Head of State/Government
San Marino, S. Europe	0.022	San Marino	24 (62)	Co-regents appointed semiannually

Nation, Region	Population in millions	Capital	Area Sq mi (km²)	Head of State/Government
São Tomé and Principe, W. Africa	0.1	São Tomé	372 (963)	Manuel Pinto da Costa, president

São Tomé and Principe celebrated its tenth year of independence from Portugal on July 12. In February, President da Costa dismissed the ministers of foreign affairs and planning and assumed their duties.

Nation, Region	Population in millions	Capital	Area Sq mi (km²)	Head of State/Government
Senegal, W. Africa	6.7	Dakar	75,750 (196 192)	Abdou Diouf, president

Addressing the United Nations in October, President Diouf called for international economic sanctions to end apartheid in South Africa. Opposition leader M. Abdoulaye Wade was arrested in August and accused of "unauthorized demonstration in a public place." The nation was hit by another cholera epidemic early in the year. GDP (1983 est.): $2.5 billion. Foreign Trade (1983): Imports, $1.04 billion; exports, $543 million.

Nation, Region	Population in millions	Capital	Area Sq mi (km²)	Head of State/Government
Seychelles, E. Africa	0.1	Victoria	108 (280)	France Albert René, president

Former president Gérard Hoareau, who had left the Seychelles in 1977 when Albert René took power in a coup, was shot and killed in London on November 29. His supporters blamed the Seychelles government, which denied the charge. GDP (1983): $150 million. Foreign Trade: Imports (1983), $80.9 million; exports (1982), $2.8 million.

Nation, Region	Population in millions	Capital	Area Sq mi (km²)	Head of State/Government
Sierra Leone, W. Africa	3.6	Freetown	27,699 (71 740)	Joseph Momoh, president

On November 28, Siaka Stevens, who had led the country since 1961, turned over the presidency to Joseph Momoh, thus becoming only the fourth African leader in 25 years to voluntarily resign. Momoh, the armed-forces commander and Stevens' hand-picked successor, had won 99% of the vote in a one-candidate election in October. GDP (1983–84 est.): $1 billion. Foreign Trade (1984): Imports, $166 million; exports, $148 million.

Nation, Region	Population in millions	Capital	Area Sq mi (km²)	Head of State/Government
Solomon Islands, Oceania	0.3	Honiara	11,500 (29 785)	Sir Baddeley Devesi, governor-general Sir Peter Kenilorea, prime minister

The Solomon Islands rejected a Soviet offer, similar to that accepted by Kiribati, to allow Soviet ships to fish its waters in exchange for payment. A U.S. ban on imported Solomon fish, stemming from a 1984 incident in which an American boat was impounded after being caught fishing in Solomon waters, was lifted. GNP (1980): $110 million. Foreign Trade (1983): Imports, $61 million; exports, $61 million.

Nation, Region	Population in millions	Capital	Area Sq mi (km²)	Head of State/Government
Somalia, E. Africa	6.5	Mogadishu	246,200 (637 657)	Mohamed Siad Barre, president

Somalia's ability to increase farm yields in recent years, despite drought that caused famine in some areas, was cited by U.S. Vice-President George Bush on a March visit as a product of the country's free-market agricultural policies. Ties to the United States were evidenced by the completion of a military base, built with U.S. funds, which the United States will have access to for emergency use. Relations with neighboring Ethiopia remained tense; in October, Somalia said it had repulsed two attacks by Ethiopian troops. GDP (1982): $1.9 billion. Foreign Trade (1983): Imports, $407 million; exports, $101 million.

Nation, Region	Population in millions	Capital	Area Sq mi (km²)	Head of State/Government
Surinam, S. America	0.4	Paramaribo	63,037 (163 265)	Desire Bouterse, head of National Military Council Willem Udenhout, prime minister

A 31-member National Assembly was appointed on January 1 and charged with drafting a new constitution. Surinam received $100 million in aid from Libya, following a visit to that North African nation by Lt. Col. Desire Bouterse and Prime Minister Willem Udenhout. GDP (1983): $1.3 billion. Foreign Trade (1983): Imports, $446 million; exports, $345 million.

Nation, Region	Population in millions	Capital	Area Sq mi (km²)	Head of State/Government
Swaziland, S. Africa	0.6	Mbabane	6,704 (17 363)	Ntombi Thwala, queen regent Prince Bhekimpi Dlamini, prime minister

Skirmishes between Swazi forces and guerrillas opposed to white rule in South Africa continued to increase following the 1984 announcement of a secret 1982 nonaggression pact between Swaziland and South Africa. Late in 1984 and early in 1985, African National Congress (ANC) guerrillas staged a series of raids on Swazi police stations. Swaziland benefited from rains that broke a three-year-drought in February. GDP (1983): $580 million. Foreign Trade (1983): Imports, $464 million; exports, $330 million.

Togo, W. Africa	3.0	Lomé	22,000 (56 980)	Gnassingbé Eyadéma, president

Pope John Paul II, on a tour of African nations, visited Togo on August 8–9 and urged religious tolerance. GNP (1982 est.): $950 million. Foreign Trade (1983): Imports, $284 million; exports, $162 million.

Tonga, Oceania	0.1	Nuku'alofa	385 (997)	Taufa'ahau Tupou IV, king Prince Fatafehi Tu'ipelehake, premier

GNP (1980): $50 million. Foreign Trade (1983): Imports, $38 million; exports, $6 million.

Trinidad and Tobago, Caribbean	1.2	Port-of-Spain	1,980 (5 128)	Ellis Clark, president George Chambers, prime minister

Trinidad and Tobago's heavy duties and restrictions on imports, aimed at protecting its dwindling hard currency reserves, came under fire from other CARICOM members at the organization's July 1–4 summit in Barbados. In April it was reported that Texaco had sold its Trinidad and Tobago petroleum refinery to the government in a deal valued at $182.2 million. Prime Minister George Chambers reshuffled his cabinet on February 28. Pope John Paul II visited the island early that same month. GNP (1982): $7.3 billion. Foreign Trade (1984): Imports, $2.1 billion; exports, $2.2 billion.

Tuvalu, Oceania	0.008	Funafuti	10 (26)	Sir Fiatau Penitala Teo, governor-general Tomasi Puapua, prime minister

Tuvalu was among eight South Pacific Forum members who declared their region a nuclear-free zone in August. The country also declined a Soviet offer to allow Soviet ships to fish its waters in exchange for payment.

United Arab Emirates, W. Asia	1.3	Abu Dhabi	32,278 (83 600)	Zayid bin Sultan Al Nuhayyan, president Rashid bin Said Al Maktum, prime minister

The United Arab Emirates opened diplomatic relations with the Soviet Union on November 14, becoming the third of the small Persian Gulf states (after Kuwait and Oman) to do so in recent years. Delegates from the United Arab Emirates, urging cuts in petroleum prices, quit OPEC's semiannual meeting in Vienna on July 6. (See also QATAR.) GDP (1983): $27.5 billion. Foreign Trade (1983): Imports, $8.3 billion; exports, $15.3 billion.

Upper Volta (*See* BURKINA FASO.)

Vanuatu, Oceania	0.1	Port-Vila	5,700 (14 763)	George Ati Sokomanu, president Walter Lini, prime minister

Foreign Trade (1984): Imports, $67 million; exports, $44 million.

Vatican City, S. Europe	0.001	Vatican City	0.17 (0.438)	John Paul II, pope

Italy and the Vatican officially exchanged documents ratifying the 1984 Concordat regulating their relations. São Tome and Principe and the Vatican established diplomatic relations.

Western Samoa, Oceania	0.2	Apia	1,133 (2 934)	Malietoa Tanumafili II, head of state

Western Samoa was among the eight South Pacific Forum members who declared their region a nuclear-free zone in August. Following a general election on February 22, Tofilau Eti was unopposed for the premiership. However, a year-end budget dispute led to his resignation. Opposition leader Vaai Kolone was to take office early in 1986. Foreign Trade (1984): Imports, $50 million; exports, $20 million.

Yemen, North, S. Asia	6.1	San'a	75,000 (194 250)	Ali Abdallah Salih, president Abdel Aziz Abd al-Ghani, prime minister

The Arab Monetary Fund agreed to lend North Yemen $11.5 million. North Yemen boycotted the Arab League summit on Middle East issues August 7–9. GNP Per Capita (1982): $500. Foreign Trade (1982): Imports, $1.5 billion; exports, $39 million.

Yemen, South, S. Asia	2.1	Aden	124,698 (322 968)	Ali Nasir Muhammad al-Hasani, chairman, Supreme People's Council Presidium Haydar Abu Bakr al-Attas, chairman, Council of Ministers

After Ali Nasir Muhammad al-Hasani resigned as chairman of the Council of Ministers in February, a new cabinet, headed by Haydar Abu Bakr al-Attas, took office. Muhammad remained head of state and secretary general of the ruling Yemen Socialist Party. President Muhammad visited Syria, Algeria, and Libya, February 27–March 7. A delegation from South Yemen attended the Arab League summit in August. GNP Per Capita (1982): $470. Foreign Trade (1980): Imports, $670 million; exports, $38 million.

Zambia, E. Africa	6.8	Lusaka	290,585 (752 614)	Kenneth David Kaunda, president Kebby Musokotwane, prime minister

The African National Congress (ANC), exiled from South Africa for its opposition to apartheid, held a "council of war" June 16–23 in Kabwe, Zambia, at which it vowed to step up its attacks on South Africa's government. Among those visiting Zambia to talk with both ANC and Zambian leaders were U.S. Sen. Edward Kennedy (D-MA) and delegations of white South African businessmen and opposition legislators. Zambia, which had suffered a three-year drought, benefited when heavy rains fell in mid-February. Minister of General Education and Culture Kebby Musokotwane formed a new cabinet in May. President Kaunda visited Cairo in February, and a joint Egypt-Zambia cooperation committee was formed. GDP (1981): $2.9 billion. Foreign Trade (1984): Imports, $566 million; exports, $648 million.

Compiled by ELAINE PASCOE

WORLD MINERAL AND METAL PRODUCTION

	1983	1984
ALUMINUM, primary smelter		
(thousand metric tons)		
United States	3,353	4,099
USSR[e]	2,000	2,100
Canada	1,091	1,222
West Germany	743	777
Norway	715	761
Australia	478	758
Brazil	401	412
Venezuela	332	386
Spain	358	381
China[e]	380	380
France	361	342
Yugoslavia	284	302
United Kingdom	252	288
Japan	256	287
Other countries[a]	2,941	3,153
Total	13,945	15,648
ANTIMONY, mine[b] (metric tons)		
China[e]	15,000	15,000
USSR[e]	9,200	9,300
Bolivia	9,951	9,281
South Africa	6,302	7,660
Mexico	2,519	3,064
Thailand	1,193	1,275[e]
Yugoslavia	950	945
Turkey	840	850[e]
Peru	713	700[e]
Austria	659	565
Other countries[a]	3,209	4,330
Total	50,536	52,970
ASBESTOS[c] (thousand metric tons)		
USSR[e]	2,250	2,300
Canada	858	922
South Africa	221	170[e]
Zimbabwe	153	165[e]
China[e]	160	160
Brazil	159	160[e]
Italy	139	140[e]
Other countries[a]	267	246
Total	4,207	4,263
BARITE[c] (thousand metric tons)		
China[e]	1,000	1,000
United States	684	703
USSR[e]	520	540
India	323	415[e]
Mexico	357	365[e]
Morocco	282	300[e]
Ireland	200	200[e]
Other countries[a]	2,064	2,204
Total	5,430	5,727
BAUXITE[d] (thousand metric tons)		
Australia	24,540	29,300[e]
Guinea	12,421	13,160
Jamaica	7,683	8,734
USSR[e]	6,185	6,185
Brazil	7,199	5,239[e]
Surinam	2,886	3,454
Yugoslavia	3,500	3,347
Hungary	2,917	2,994
Greece	2,455	2,800[e]
India	1,923	1,994
China[e]	1,600	1,600
Guyana	1,791	1,556
France	1,716	1,528
Other countries[a]	3,630	4,359
Total	80,446	86,250
CEMENT[c] (thousand metric tons)		
USSR	128,156	130,000[e]
China	108,250	121,080
Japan	80,891	78,851
United States	64,725	71,395
Italy	39,217	40,000[e]
West Germany	30,466	31,500
Spain	30,638	30,000[e]
India	25,356	29,030
Brazil	20,870	25,000[e]
France	24,352	24,000[e]
South Korea	21,282	20,413
Mexico	17,068	18,000[e]
Poland	16,200	16,700
Other countries[a]	307,351	324,487
Total	914,822	960,456
CHROMITE[c] (thousand metric tons)		
South Africa	2,232	3,006
USSR[e]	2,940	3,000
Albania[e]	900	870
Turkey	512	608
Zimbabwe	432	450[e]
India	422	440[e]
Brazil	276	280[e]
Philippines	267	270[e]
Finland	246	254
Other countries[a]	289	322
Total	8,516	9,500

	1983	1984
COAL, anthracite and		
bituminous[c] (million metric tons)		
United States	665	750
China	688	736
USSR	554	551
Poland	191	192
South Africa	146	150[e]
India	135	142[e]
Australia	120	125
West Germany	90	84
United Kingdom	119	51
Canada	37	48
North Korea[e]	36	36
Other countries[a]	165	168
Total	2,946	3,033
COAL, lignite[cf]		
(million metric tons)		
East Germany	278	296
USSR	162	160
West Germany	124	127
Czechoslovakia	102	105
Yugoslavia	58	65
United States	52	57
Poland	43	50
Australia	34	35
Other countries[a]	193	203
Total	1,046	1,098
COPPER, mine[b] (thousand metric tons)		
Chile	1,257	1,290
United States	1,038	1,091
Canada	718	784
USSR[e]	570	590
Zambia	574	541
Zaire	535	540[e]
Peru	322	364
Poland	349	360
Australia	262	236
Philippines	273	226
South Africa	205	198
Mexico	196	180[e]
China[e]	175	180
Papua New Guinea	202	164
Other countries[a]	1,257	1,165
Total	7,933	7,909
COPPER, refined, primary and		
secondary (thousand metric tons)		
United States	1,584	1,509
USSR[e]	915	939
Japan	1,092	935
Chile	833	879
Zambia	575	522
Canada	497	504
Belgium	405	397
West Germany	420	379
Poland	360	372
China[e]	310	310
Zaire	227	224
Peru	191	219
Australia	193	197
Spain	159	156
South Africa	139	156
Other countries[a]	1,217	1,374
Total	9,117	9,072
DIAMOND, natural (thousand carats)		
Zaire	11,982	18,459
Botswana	10,731	12,914
USSR[e]	10,700	10,700
South Africa	10,311	10,143
Australia	6,155	5,690
Angola	1,034	1,000[e]
China[e]	1,000	1,000
Namibia	963	930
Other countries[a]	2,943	2,994
Total	55,819	63,830
FLUORSPAR[g] (thousand metric tons)		
Mongolia[e]	700	700
Mexico	605	699
China	550	650
USSR[e]	540	550
South Africa	274	321
Spain	232	240[e]
Thailand	207	220[e]
France	196	195[e]
United Kingdom	131	160[e]
Other countries[a]	851	870
Total	4,286	4,605
GAS, natural[h] (billion cubic feet)		
USSR	18,929	20,799
United States	16,657	17,935
Netherlands	2,703	2,800[e]
Canada	2,465	2,506
Algeria	1,581	1,700[e]
Indonesia	1,032	1,367
United Kingdom	1,296	1,340
Mexico	1,274	1,194
Romania[e]	1,100	1,120
Other countries[a]	8,531	9,206
Total	55,568	59,967

	1983	1984
GOLD, mine[b] (thousand troy ounces)		
South Africa	21,847	21,905
USSR[e]	8,600	8,650
Canada	2,363	2,614
United States	1,956	2,059
China	1,850	1,900
Brazil	1,750	1,750[e]
Australia	984	1,200
Papua New Guinea	582	835
Philippines	812	773
Other countries[a]	4,138	4,349
Total	44,882	46,035
GYPSUM[c] (thousand metric tons)		
United States	11,688	12,282
Canada	7,507	8,709
Japan	5,845	6,080[e]
Spain	5,098	5,600[e]
France	5,544	5,440
Iran	5,400	5,000
USSR[e]	4,900	4,900
China[e]	4,265	4,810
United Kingdom	2,967	3,000[e]
Mexico	2,958	2,995[e]
West Germany	2,485	2,177
Australia	1,800	1,995
Romania[e]	1,630	1,800
Italy	1,388	1,270[e]
Other countries[a]	14,882	15,155
Total	78,357	81,213
IRON ORE[c] (thousand metric tons)		
USSR	245,000	247,000
Brazil	89,200	90,000[e]
Australia	71,625	90,000[e]
China[e]	71,000	75,000
United States	38,165	50,459
India	38,800	41,026
Canada	30,326	37,785
South Africa	16,605	24,496
Sweden	13,212	17,556
Liberia	14,937	15,100[e]
France	15,966	15,030
Venezuela	9,715	12,723
Other countries[a]	80,807	83,492
Total	735,358	799,667
IRON, steel ingots (thousand		
metric tons)		
USSR	152,514	154,000
Japan	97,179	105,586
United States	76,762	83,940
China	39,950	43,370
West Germany	35,729	39,389
Italy	21,674	24,026
France	17,623	18,996
Brazil	14,659	18,385
Poland	16,236	16,500[e]
United Kingdom	14,986	15,121
Czechoslovakia	15,024	14,831
Canada	12,828	14,715
Spain	12,731	13,484
South Korea	11,915	13,033
Romania	12,593	13,000[e]
Belgium	10,157	11,292
India	10,305	10,084
South Africa	7,004	7,827
Mexico	6,978	7,543
East Germany	7,219	7,500[e]
Other countries[a]	68,521	73,730
Total	662,587	706,352
LEAD, mine[b] (thousand metric tons)		
Australia	481	446
USSR[e]	435	440
United States	466	333
Canada	252	259
Peru	205	196
Mexico	184	195
China[e]	160	160
Morocco	98	101
Yugoslavia	114	100
Other countries[a]	971	960
Total	3,366	3,190
LEAD, refined, primary and secondary[i]		
(thousand metric tons)		
United States	1,018	979
USSR[e]	745	755
Japan	322	366
West Germany	348	357
United Kingdom	322	331
Canada	242	254
Australia	223	218
France	214	207
China[e]	195	195
Mexico	194	195
Spain	145	148
Italy	126	128
Other countries[a]	1,160	1,157
Total	5,254	5,290

MAGNESIUM, primary (thousand metric tons)

	1983	1984
United States	105	144
USSR[e]	83	85
Norway	30	50[e]
France	12	11
Canada	6	8
Italy	8	7
Japan	6	7
Other countries[a]	10	12
Total	260	324

MANGANESE ore[c] (thousand metric tons)

	1983	1984
USSR	9,876	10,100
South Africa	2,886	3,049
Brazil	2,092	2,200
Gabon	1,867	2,119
Australia	1,353	1,700
China[e]	1,600	1,600
India	1,320	1,300[e]
Other countries[a]	863	955
Total	21,857	23,023

MERCURY (76-pound flasks)

	1983	1984
USSR[e]	64,000	64,000
Spain[e]	41,075	40,000[e]
China[e]	20,000	20,000
United States	25,070	19,048
Algeria[e]	10,000	10,000
Other countries[a]	20,679	21,440
Total	180,824	174,488

MOLYBDENUM, mine[b] (metric tons)

	1983	1984
United States	15,400	47,021
Chile	15,264	16,861
USSR[e]	11,000	11,200
Canada	10,194	10,965
Peru	2,628	3,100
China[e]	2,000	2,000
Other countries[a]	7,294	3,520
Total	63,780	94,667

NATURAL GAS LIQUIDS (million barrels)

	1983	1984
United States	571	615[e]
Algeria	180	192
USSR[e]	145	160
Canada	114	139
Saudi Arabia	125	120[e]
Mexico	95	100[e]
Other countries[a]	239	255
Total	1,469	1,581

NICKEL, mine[b] (thousand metric tons)

	1983	1984
USSR[e]	170	175
Canada	122	174
Australia	77	75
Indonesia	49	62
New Caledonia	40	41
Cuba[e]	38	32
South Africa[e]	20	25
Dominican Republic	21	24
Other countries[a]	120	137
Total	657	745

NITROGEN, content of ammonia (thousand metric tons)

	1983	1984
USSR	14,500	15,000[e]
China	13,800	13,970
United States	10,248	12,074
India	3,525	3,715
Canada	2,374	2,872
Romania	2,600	2,650
France	1,900	2,350
Netherlands	1,747	2,318
West Germany	1,703	1,964
United Kingdom	1,720	1,836
Other countries[a]	23,267	25,526
Total	77,384	84,275

PETROLEUM, crude (million barrels)

	1983	1984
USSR	4,528	4,486
United States	3,159	3,193
Saudi Arabia	1,834	1,714
Mexico	973	983
United Kingdom	817	893
China	774	836
Iran	892	791
Venezuela	657	658
Canada	495	560
Indonesia	490	517

PETROLEUM, crude (cont'd)

	1983	1984
Nigeria	452	502
United Arab Emirates	409	424
Iraq	400	410
Libya	402	391
Other countries[a]	3,130	3,145
Total	19,412	19,503

PHOSPHATE ROCK[c] (thousand metric tons)

	1983	1984
United States	42,573	49,197
USSR[e]	31,600	31,900
Morocco	20,106	21,245
China[e]	12,500	11,800
Jordan	4,749	6,263
Tunisia	5,924	5,346
Brazil	3,208	3,855
Israel	2,969	3,312
Togo	2,081	2,696
South Africa	2,742	2,585
Other countries	10,813	12,372
Total	139,265	150,571

POTASH, K$_2$O equivalent basis (thousand metric tons)

	1983	1984
USSR	9,294	9,500[e]
Canada	6,938	7,685
East Germany	3,431	3,450
West Germany	2,419	2,280
United States	1,429	1,564
France	1,536	1,500
Other countries[a]	2,379	2,659
Total	27,426	28,638

SALT[c] (thousand metric tons)

	1983	1984
United States	31,393	34,803
USSR[e]	16,200	16,500
China[e]	16,100	16,000
West Germany	10,402	11,200[e]
Canada	8,602	10,294
India	7,013	7,500[e]
France	6,951	7,130
United Kingdom	6,311	6,500[e]
Mexico	5,703	6,000[e]
Australia[e]	5,000	5,000
Romania	4,596	4,500[e]
Italy	4,554	4,255
Brazil	4,187	4,250
Netherlands	3,124	3,650
Other countries[a]	29,132	29,559
Total	159,268	167,141

SILVER, mine[b] (thousand troy ounces)

	1983	1984
Mexico	63,607	67,800
Peru	55,878	56,534
USSR[e]	47,200	47,400
United States	43,415	44,440
Canada	35,559	37,568
Australia	33,849	32,000[e]
Poland	21,798	22,000[e]
Chile	15,055	15,000[e]
Japan	9,877	10,403
South Africa	5,559	6,997
Sweden	5,491	5,500[e]
Bolivia	6,025	4,920
Other countries[a]	48,955	47,992
Total	392,268	398,554

SULFUR, all forms[j] (thousand metric tons)

	1983	1984
United States	9,290	10,652
USSR[e]	9,390	9,340
Canada	6,573	6,609
Poland	5,349	5,350[e]
China	2,850	2,650
Japan	2,613	2,572
Mexico	1,702	1,925
France	1,931	1,900[e]
West Germany	1,322	1,490
Spain	1,204	1,230
Other countries[a]	8,091	8,166
Total	50,315	51,884

TIN, mine[b] (thousand metric tons)

	1983	1984
Malaysia	41,367	41,307
USSR[e]	35,000	36,000
Thailand	19,943	21,920
Indonesia	26,553	21,530
Bolivia	25,278	19,911
Brazil	13,418	16,021

TIN, mine[b] (cont'd)

	1983	1984
China[e]	15,000	15,000
Other countries[a]	34,094	34,964
Total	210,653	206,653

TITANIUM MINERALS[c] [k] (thousand metric tons)

ILMENITE

	1983	1984
Australia	909	1,119
Norway	544	550
USSR[e]	435	440
Finland	164	165
India	150	150[e]
China[e]	145	145
Other countries[a]	353	325
Total	2,700	2,894

RUTILE

	1983	1984
Australia	158	175
Sierra Leone	72	91
South Africa	50	49
Other countries[a]	27	26
Total	307	341

TITANIFEROUS SLAG

	1983	1984
Canada	612	625
South Africa	400	390
Total	1,012	1,015

TUNGSTEN, mine[b] (metric tons)

	1983	1984
China[e]	12,500	12,500
USSR[e]	9,100	9,100
South Korea	2,480	2,500[e]
Bolivia	2,449	2,100[e]
Australia	2,015	1,843
Austria	1,405	1,500[e]
Portugal	1,185	1,200[e]
Burma	930	1,096
Brazil	1,000	1,000[e]
United States	980	1,000[e]
France	832	850
Other countries[a]	4,490	4,880
Total	39,366	39,569

URANIUM OXIDE (U$_3$O$_8$)[l] (metric tons)

	1983	1984
Canada	8,423	12,700[e]
United States	9,344	6,800
South Africa	6,840	6,760
Namibia	4,379	4,350
Australia	4,354	4,350[e]
Niger	4,010	4,000[e]
France	3,857	3,800[e]
Other countries[a]	2,195	2,204
Total	43,402	44,964

ZINC, mine[b] (thousand metric tons)

	1983	1984
Canada	988	1,207
USSR[e]	805	810
Australia	703	667
Peru	576	568
Mexico	266	289
United States	297	278
Japan	256	253
Spain	168	228
Sweden	203	207
Ireland	186	206
Poland	149	191
China[e]	160	160
Other countries[a]	1,403	1,433
Total	6,160	6,497

ZINC, smelter, primary and secondary (thousand metric tons)

	1983	1984
USSR[e]	930	945
Japan	701	754
Canada	617	685
West Germany	356	356
United States	305	331
Australia	303	307
Belgium	263	271
France	250	259
Spain	190	205
Netherlands	188	185
Mexico	175	185
China[e]	175	185
Poland	170	176
Finland	155	159
Other countries[a]	1,423	1,445
Total	6,201	6,448

[a] Estimated in part. [b] Content of concentrates. [c] Gross weight. [d] Includes calculated bauxite equivalent of estimated output of aluminum ores other than bauxite (nepheline concentrate and alunite ore). [e] Estimate. [f] Includes coal classified in some countries as brown coal. [g] Gross weight of marketable product. [h] Marketed production (includes gas sold or used by producers; excludes gas reinjected to reservoirs for pressure maintenance and that flared or vented to the atmosphere which is not used as fuel or industrial raw material, and which thus has no economic value). [i] Excludes bullion produced for refining elsewhere. [j] Includes (1) Frasch process sulfur, (2) elemental sulfur mined by conventional means, (3) by-product recovered elemental sulfur, and (4) elemental sulfur equivalent obtained from pyrite and other materials. [k] Excludes output in the United States, which cannot be disclosed because it is company proprietary information. [l] Excludes output (if any) by Albania, Bulgaria, China, Czechoslovakia, East Germany, Hungary, North Korea, Mongolia, Poland, Romania, and Vietnam.

Compiled by Charles L. Kimbell primarily from data collected by the U.S. Bureau of Mines, but with some modifications from other sources.

EDUCATION AND HEALTH: SELECTED COUNTRIES (1981)

	Primary		Secondary		Higher		Hospitals	Physicians
	Teachers	Students	Teachers	Students	Teachers	Students		
Afghanistan	37,537	1,198,286	7,532[1]	136,898[1]	1,448[3]	22,974[3]	64	1,215
Algeria	94,216	3,178,192	47,771	1,154,709	8,962[1]	79,351[1]	367[3]	6,881[3]
Argentina	206,535[2]	4,197,372[2]		1,366,444	47,637	527,596		
Australia	91,280[1]	1,688,121[1]	85,340[1]	1,095,610[1]	20,687	334,030	2,369[5]	26,140[1]
Austria	27,561	384,986	65,747	713,106	——	140,720	——	17,028
Bahamas	——	32,854[1]	1,018[1]		——		6[1]	197[1]
Bahrain	2,577[1]	48,451[1]	1,184[1]	26,528[1]	159[1]	1,908[1]	12[1]	363[1]
Bangladesh	188,234	8,236,526	111,927[1]	2,407,888	12,329[3]	232,780[3]	504	10,065
Barbados	1,473*	30,728	1,231	27,787	317[1]	4,033[1]	10[1]	201[3]
Belgium	45,130	821,059	——	835,177		196,153[1]	521	25,629
Benin	10,381	404,297	——	87,648[1]		3,003[3]	131[1]	204[1]
Brunei	1,800	31,677	1,538	17,869	51[3]	436[3]	5	97
Bulgaria	57,682	1,029,747	25,684	306,240	13,910	98,915	——	22,088
Canada		2,296,996	——	2,340,255	44,466	924,445	1,226[4]	43,192[3]
Central African Rep.	4,130[1]	246,174[1]	——	45,824[1]	303	2,450		99[1]
Chile	——	2,139,319	——	554,749	——	145,497[1]	300[1]	5,671[3]
China	5,580,000	143,328,000	3,008,800	50,145,900	249,876	1,295,047	65,911	518,089[1]
Colombia	137,721	4,217,800	88,103	1,891,530	34,844	318,293	849[1]	12,720[5]
Costa Rica	10,556	348,616	6,955	133,909	——	60,990[1]	39[1]	1,506[3]
Cuba	83,113	1,409,765	86,578	1,056,763	10,680[1]	151,733[1]	305[3]	13,531[3]
Czechoslovakia	90,282	1,930,634	33,364	393,343	21,842	198,784	580	43,246
Djibouti	382	18,896	——	3,123[4]			24	56
Egypt	167,821[1]	4,662,816[1]	121,999[1]	2,929,168[1]			1,521	53,342
Ethiopia	37,844	2,374,362	——		1,137	14,985	86[1]	428[1]
Finland	26,664	365,418	34,248	441,232	——	123,165[1]	——	9,538
France		4,506,604	256,369[1]	5,050,028	——	1,076,717[1]	3,548[5]	91,442[5]
Germany, Dem. Rep.	170,115	2,106,463	——	506,412[1]	40,835	404,618	——	33,894[1]
Germany, Fed. Rep.	273,556[1]	4,776,000*	298,277[1]	4,300,740[1]	171,708[1]	1,223,221[1]	3,234[1]	139,431[1]
Grenada	587[3]	18,076[1]	——		77[3]	614[3]	6[1]	25[4]
Guinea-Bissau	3,256	83,155	462[1]	11,341				108
Haiti	14,927	658,102	4,392[1]	101,519			52[1]	600[3]
Honduras	16,385[1]	601,337[1]	4,489[1]	127,293[1]	1,653[1]	25,825[1]	35[1]	1,141[3]
Hungary	78,053	1,213,465	——	218,188	13,843	102,564	——	27,431
Iceland	——	24,809	——	26,769	——	4,383	46[1]	488[1]
India	1,345,376[1]	72,687,840[1]	——		231,233[4]	4,456,198[4]	8,626	268,712
Iran	192,719	5,283,377	——		15,453[5]	155,811[5]	585	15,182
Iraq	98,422	2,637,023	35,825	1,110,655	6,515[1]	102,430[1]	205	7,634
Ireland	14,636[1]	419,998[1]	20,965[1]	300,601[1]	——	54,746[1]	209[1]	4,443
Israel	42,068	641,668	——	210,047	——	88,786[3]	80[1]	9,800[1]
Italy	——	4,335,911	——	5,299,462	——	1,117,742[1]	1,832[3]	164,555[†1,3]
Japan	477,101	11,924,653	553,684	10,011,340	213,537[1]	2,412,117[1]	9,224	154,578
Jordan	14,891	467,696	13,539	281,192	——	36,549[1]	35	1,966
Kenya	102,489*[1]	3,930,991*[1]	17,081[1]	431,327[1]	——	12,797[1]	——	1,466[4]
Kiribati	450[2]	13,836[2]	•108[2]	1,774[2]	——	741[4]	——	16
Korea, Rep. of	122,727	5,586,494	113,185	4,396,984	24,357	786,354	——	26,875
Kuwait	8,385	154,772	15,342[1]	181,882[1]	1,110	15,725	——	2,133
Libya	36,591[1]	662,843[1]	24,323[1]	20,327[1]	——	15,267[3]	74	4,690
Luxembourg	1,765[1]	24,628[1]	1,927[1]	24,171[1]	250[1]	748[1]	25	495
Malaysia	65,227[2]	1,701,944[2]	42,512	977,613[2]	4,644	67,368	163	3,514[1]
Mauritius	6,447	130,145	——		192	901	29[1]	503[1]
Mexico	400,417	14,981,028	301,939	5,332,131	82,967	966,228		
Morocco	63,675	2,309,696	43,455	895,743	——		143	1,153
Mozambique	18,751	1,376,865	3,388	107,849	347[1]	1,852	321[1]	309[1]
Nepal	27,805[1]	1,067,912[1]	16,376[1]	512,434[1]	2,918[1]	38,450[1]	68[1]	487[1]
Netherlands	51,399	1,269,868	——	1,412,714	——	371,515	788[1]	25,947[3]
Norway	46,604[3]	390,186[1]	——	370,597[1]	7,624[3]	79,211[1]	928	8,311
Oman	4,399*[2]	116,591*[2]	1,957*[2]	27,180*[2]	——		35	605
Pakistan	148,000*[1]	7,039,000*[1]	117,885*[3]	2,652,429[3]	6,239[4]	153,536[4]	——	26,668
Papua New Guinea	10,236[2]	326,021[2]	2,289	49,334	638[1]	5,039*[1]	390[1]	192[1]
Philippines	264,241[1]	8,033,642[1]	85,779[1]	2,928,525[1]	43,770[1]	1,276,016[1]	——	7,378
Poland	233,004	4,255,678	138,888	1,608,017	——	544,895	1,086[3]	61,460[3]
Qatar	2,303	32,618	1,755	17,158	198	2,981	4	186
Romania	157,709	3,285,073	49,394	1,168,829	14,354	190,903	——	34,440
Rwanda	13,043	743,067	984	12,505	229[1]	1,243[1]	232	1,182
Saudi Arabia	55,836	994,901	30,604*	385,583	7,448[1]	62,074[1]	95	3,576
Singapore	9,505	285,179	9,162	190,239	2,270[1]	23,256[1]	25	2,219
Solomon Islands	1,148[1]	28,870[1]	257[1]	4,030[1]	——		130	32[5]
Spain	——	3,633,713	——	4,039,580	42,831[1]	681,022[1]	1,135[3]	96,569
Sri Lanka	131,656	2,132,596	——		4,818[1]	42,694[1]	488	1,964
Sudan	46,437	1,524,381	18,689	426,932	——	33,309	160	2,169
Surinam	3,068[4]	85,060[4]	.1,867[4]	34,372[4]	118[5]	900[5]	17[1]	214[4]
Sweden	——	662,581	——	606,152	——	205,431	711[1]	18,300[1]
Syria	59,110	1,642,888	34,533	635,355	——	135,077[1]	151	4,165
Thailand	304,400[1]	7,370,846[1]	——	1,912,621[1]	35,731	911,166	714[1]	6,867[1]
Tunisia	28,764	1,088,822	15,937	331,487	4,031[1]	32,832	98[1]	1,800[1]
Turkey	212,795	5,859,711	117,644	2,310,113	22,223	240,719	831	28,411
Uganda	38,422[1]	1,407,158	——	94,614	——	6,192[3]	485	611
USSR	2,810,100	26,648,000	——	19,899,900	363,300[1]	5,284,500	23,100[1]	995,600[†1]
United Arab Emirates	4,838	103,937	——	39,868	208[1]	2,519[1]	22	1,491
United Kingdom	260,283[1]	4,910,724[1]	——	5,341,849[1]	——	832,106[1]	3,438[1]	90,628*[1]
United States	1,351,000[1]	27,448,000[1]	1,100,000*[1]	14,556,000*[1]	395,992[1]	12,371,672	7,051[1]	414,916[1]
Vanuatu	1,076	24,061	188*	2,480	——		21[1]	22
Venezuela	97,045	2,591,051	——	884,233	28,052[1]	307,133[1]	444[4]	14,771[4]
Vietnam	204,104[1]	7,887,439[1]	——		17,242[1]	114,701[1]	11,550	13,517
Yemen, North	10,576[1]	460,630[1]	——		157[1]	4,519[1]	28	896
Yemen, South	10,832	270,167	2,016	31,705	386[1]	3,469[1]	48[1]	258[1]
Yugoslavia	60,264	1,446,228	134,360	2,412,814	24,449[1]	411,995[1]	——[1]	33,444
Zambia	21,455[1]	1,041,086[1]	4,431[3]	94,782[4]	717[3]	7,340[3]	636	821
Zimbabwe	49,588[2]	1,907,225[2]	6,148	149,018	——		——	1,148[1]

Source: *UN Statistical Yearbook* 1982 (latest available edition).
Note: * estimate.   † including dentists.   [1] 1980.   [2] 1982.   [3] 1979.   [4] 1978.   [5] 1977.

THE UNITED STATES GOVERNMENT

(selected listing, as of Dec. 31, 1985)

President: Ronald Reagan   **Vice-President:** George Bush

Executive Office of the President
The White House

Chief of Staff and Assistant to the President: Donald T. Regan

Assistant to the President and Press Secretary: James S. Brady

Assistant to the President and Director of Communications: Patrick J. Buchanan

Counsel to the President: Fred R. Fielding

Assistant to the President for National Security Affairs: John M. Poindexter

Assistant to the President for Legislative Affairs: M. B. Oglesby

Assistant to the President and Principal Deputy Press Secretary: Larry Speakes

Assistant to the President for Policy Development: John Svahn

Assistant to the President and Director, Office of Intergovernmental Affairs: Mitchell E. Daniels, Jr.

Deputy Counsellor to the President: Richard H. Hauser

Office of Management and Budget, Director: James C. Miller III

Council of Economic Advisers, Chairman: Beryl W. Sprinkel

Office of United States Trade Representative, U.S. Trade Representative: Clayton Yeutter

Council of Environmental Quality, Chairman: A. Alan Hill

Office of Science and Technology Policy, Director: (vacant)

Office of Administration, Director: Christopher Hicks

The Cabinet

Secretary of Agriculture: John R. Block[1]

Secretary of Commerce: Malcolm Baldrige

Secretary of Defense: Caspar W. Weinberger
Joint Chiefs of Staff, Chairman: Adm. William J. Crowe, Jr.
Secretary of the Air Force: Russell A. Rourke
Secretary of the Army: John O. Marsh, Jr.
Secretary of the Navy: John Lehman

Secretary of Education: William J. Bennett

Secretary of Energy: John S. Herrington

Secretary of Health and Human Services: Otis R. Bowen
National Institutes of Health, Director: James B. Wyngaarden
Surgeon General: C. Everett Koop
Commissioner of Food and Drugs: Frank E. Young

Social Security Administration, Acting Commissioner: Martha McSteen

Secretary of Housing and Urban Development: Samuel R. Pierce, Jr.

Secretary of the Interior: Donald Paul Hodel

Department of Justice, Attorney General: Edwin Meese III
Federal Bureau of Investigation, Director: William H. Webster

Secretary of Labor: William E. Brock III
Women's Bureau, Director: Lenora Cole-Alexander
Commissioner of Labor Statistics: Janet L. Norwood

Secretary of State: George P. Shultz

Secretary of Transportation: Elizabeth H. Dole

Secretary of the Treasury: James A. Baker III
Internal Revenue Service, Commissioner: Roscoe L. Egger, Jr.

Independent Agencies

ACTION, Director: Donna M. Alvarado

Central Intelligence Agency, Director: William J. Casey

Commission on Civil Rights, Chairman: Clarence M. Pendleton, Jr.

Commission of Fine Arts, Chairman: J. Carter Brown

Consumer Product Safety Commission, Chairman: Terrence M. Scanlon

Environmental Protection Agency, Administrator: Lee M. Thomas

Equal Employment Opportunity Commission, Chairman: Clarence Thomas

Export-Import Bank, President and Chairman: William H. Draper III

Farm Credit Administration, Chairman: William D. Wampler

Federal Communications Commission, Chairman: Mark S. Fowler

Federal Deposit Insurance Corporation, Chairman: William Seidman

Federal Election Commission, Chairman: John Warren McGarry

Federal Emergency Management Agency, Director: (vacant)

Federal Home Loan Bank Board, Chairman: Edwin J. Gray

Federal Labor Relations Authority, Acting Chairman: Henry B. Frazier III

Federal Maritime Commission, Chairman: Edward V. Hickey, Jr.

Federal Reserve System, Chairman: Paul A. Volcker

Federal Trade Commission, Chairman: Terry Calvani

General Services Administrator: Terence C. Golden

Interstate Commerce Commission, Chairman: Reese H. Taylor, Jr.

National Aeronautics and Space Administration, Administrator: James M. Beggs (on leave)

National Foundation on the Arts and Humanities
National Endowment for the Arts, Chairman: Francis S. M. Hodsoll; National Endowment for the Humanities, Chairman: (vacant)

National Labor Relations Board, Chairman: Donald L. Dotson

National Science Foundation, Chairman: Roland W. Schmitt

National Transportation Safety Board, Chairman: James E. Burnett

Nuclear Regulatory Commission, Chairman: Nunzio J. Palladino

Peace Corps, Director: Loret M. Ruppe

Postal Rate Commission, Chairman: Janet D. Steiger

Securities and Exchange Commission, Chairman: John S. R. Shad

Selective Service System, Director: Thomas K. Turnage

Small Business Administrator: James C. Sanders

Tennessee Valley Authority, Chairman: Charles H. Dean, Jr.

U.S. Arms Control and Disarmament Agency, Director: Kenneth L. Adelman

U.S. Information Agency, Director: Charles Z. Wick

U.S. International Trade Commission, Chairman: Paula Stern

U.S. Postmaster General: Paul N. Carlin[1]

Veterans Administrator: Harry N. Walters

The Supreme Court
Chief Justice, Warren E. Burger

William J. Brennan, Jr.	Byron R. White	Thurgood Marshall	Harry A. Blackmun
Lewis F. Powell, Jr.	William H. Rehnquist	John Paul Stevens	Sandra Day O'Connor

[1] Resigned in early January 1986.

UNITED STATES: 99th CONGRESS
Second Session

SENATE MEMBERSHIP

(As of January 1986: 53 Republicans, 47 Democrats) Letters after senators' names refer to party affiliation—D for Democrat, R for Republican. Single asterisk (*) denotes term expiring in January 1987; double asterisk (**), term expiring in January 1989; triple asterisk (***), term expiring in January 1991.

Alabama
*** H. Heflin, D
* J. Denton, Jr., R

Alaska
*** T. Stevens, R
* F. H. Murkowski, R

Arizona
* B. Goldwater, R
** D. DeConcini, D

Arkansas
* D. Bumpers, D
*** D. Pryor, D

California
* A. Cranston, D
** P. Wilson, R

Colorado
* G. Hart, D
*** W. Armstrong, R

Connecticut
** L. P. Weicker, Jr., R
* C. J. Dodd, D

Delaware
** W. V. Roth, Jr., R
*** J. R. Biden, Jr., D

Florida
** L. Chiles, Jr., D
* P. Hawkins, R

Georgia
*** S. Nunn, D
* M. Mattingly, R

Hawaii
* D. K. Inouye, D
** S. M. Matsunaga, D

Idaho
*** J. A. McClure, R
* S. Symms, R

Illinois
* A. J. Dixon, D
*** P. Simon, D

Indiana
** R. G. Lugar, R
* D. Quayle, R

Iowa
* C. E. Grassley, R
*** T. Harkin, D

Kansas
* R. J. Dole, R
*** N. Kassebaum, R

Kentucky
* W. H. Ford, D
*** M. McConnell, R

Louisiana
* R. B. Long, D
*** J. B. Johnston, D

Maine
*** W. Cohen, R
** G. Mitchell, D

Maryland
* C. M. Mathias, Jr., R
** P. S. Sarbanes, D

Massachusetts
** E. M. Kennedy, D
*** J. F. Kerry, D

Michigan
** D. W. Riegle, Jr., D
* C. Levin, D

Minnesota
** D. Durenberger, R
*** R. Boschwitz, R

Mississippi
* J. C. Stennis, D
*** T. Cochran, R

Missouri
* T. F. Eagleton, D
** J. C. Danforth, R

Montana
** J. Melcher, D
*** M. Baucus, D

Nebraska
** E. Zorinsky, D
*** J. J. Exon, Jr., D

Nevada
* P. Laxalt, R
** C. Hecht, R

New Hampshire
*** G. Humphrey, R
* W. Rudman, R

New Jersey
*** B. Bradley, D
** F. R. Lautenberg, D

New Mexico
*** P. V. Domenici, R
** J. Bingaman, D

New York
** D. P. Moynihan, D
* A. D'Amato, R

North Carolina
*** J. Helms, R
* J. P. East, R

North Dakota
** Q. N. Burdick, D
* M. Andrews, R

Ohio
* J. H. Glenn, Jr., D
** H. M. Metzenbaum, D

Oklahoma
*** D. Boren, D
* D. Nickles, R

Oregon
*** M. O. Hatfield, R
* B. Packwood, R

Pennsylvania
** J. Heinz, R
* A. Specter, R

Rhode Island
*** C. Pell, D
** J. H. Chafee, R

South Carolina
*** S. Thurmond, R
* E. F. Hollings, D

South Dakota
*** L. Pressler, R
* J. Abdnor, R

Tennessee
* J. Sasser, D
*** A. Gore, Jr., D

Texas
** L. M. Bentsen, D
*** P. Gramm, R

Utah
* E. J. Garn, R
** O. Hatch, R

Vermont
** R. T. Stafford, R
* P. J. Leahy, D

Virginia
*** J. Warner, R
** P. S. Trible, Jr., R

Washington
* S. Gorton, R
** D. J. Evans, R

West Virginia
** R. C. Byrd, D
*** J. D. Rockefeller IV, D

Wisconsin
** W. Proxmire, D
* R. W. Kasten, Jr., R

Wyoming
** M. Wallop, R
*** A. Simpson, R

HOUSE MEMBERSHIP

(As of January 1986, 253 Democrats, 182 Republicans) "At-L," in place of Congressional district number means "representative at large." * Elected in special 1985 election.

Alabama
1. H. L. Callahan, R
2. W. L. Dickinson, R
3. W. Nichols, D
4. T. Bevill, D
5. R. Flippo, D
6. B. Erdreich, D
7. R. Shelby, D

Alaska
At-L. D. Young, R

Arizona
1. J. McCain, III, R
2. M. K. Udall, D
3. B. Stump, R
4. E. Rudd, R
5. J. Kolbe, R

Arkansas
1. W. V. Alexander, Jr., D
2. T. Robinson, D
3. J. P. Hammerschmidt, R
4. B. Anthony, Jr., D

California
1. D. H. Bosco, D
2. E. A. Chappie, R
3. R. Matsui, D
4. V. Fazio, D
5. S. Burton, D
6. B. Boxer, D
7. G. Miller, D
8. R. V. Dellums, D
9. F. H. Stark, Jr., D
10. D. Edwards, D
11. T. Lantos, D
12. E. Zschau, R
13. N. Y. Mineta, D
14. N. Shumway, R
15. T. Coelho, D
16. L. E. Panetta, D
17. C. Pashayan, Jr., R
18. R. Lehman, D
19. R. J. Lagomarsino, R
20. W. M. Thomas, R
21. B. Fiedler, R
22. C. J. Moorhead, R
23. A. C. Beilenson, D
24. H. A. Waxman, D
25. E. R. Roybal, D
26. H. L. Berman, D
27. M. Levine, D
28. J. Dixon, D
29. A. F. Hawkins, D
30. M. G. Martinez, Jr., D
31. M. Dymally, D
32. G. M. Anderson, D
33. D. Dreier, R
34. E. Torres, D
35. J. Lewis, R
36. G. E. Brown, Jr., D
37. A. McCandless, R
38. R. K. Dornan, R
39. W. Dannemeyer, R
40. R. E. Badham, R
41. W. D. Lowery, R
42. D. Lungren, R
43. R. Packard, R
44. J. Bates, D
45. D. L. Hunter, R

Colorado
1. P. Schroeder, D
2. T. E. Wirth, D
3. M. L. Strang, R
4. H. Brown, R
5. K. Kramer, R
6. D. Schaefer, R

Connecticut
1. B. Kennelly, D
2. S. Gejdenson, D
3. B. Morrison, D
4. S. B. McKinney, R
5. J. G. Rowland, R
6. N. L. Johnson, R

Delaware
At-L. T. R. Carper, D

Florida
1. E. Hutto, D
2. D. Fuqua, D
3. C. E. Bennett, D
4. W. V. Chappell, Jr., D
5. B. McCollum, R
6. K. H. MacKay, D
7. S. M. Gibbons, D
8. C. W. Young, R
9. M. Bilirakis, R
10. A. Ireland, R
11. B. Nelson, D
12. T. Lewis, R
13. C. Mack, 3d, R
14. D. A. Mica, D
15. E. C. Shaw, Jr., R
16. L. Smith, D
17. W. Lehman, D
18. C. Pepper, D
19. D. B. Fascell, D

Georgia
1. R. L. Thomas, D
2. C. Hatcher, D
3. R. Ray, D
4. P. L. Swindall, R
5. W. Fowler, Jr., D
6. N. Gingrich, R
7. G. Darden, D
8. J. R. Rowland, Jr., D
9. E. L. Jenkins, D
10. D. Barnard, Jr., D

Hawaii
1. C. Heftel, D
2. D. K. Akaka, D

Idaho
1. L. Craig, R
2. R. Stallings, D

Illinois
1. C. A. Hayes, D
2. G. Savage, D
3. M. Russo, D
4. G. M. O'Brien, R
5. W. O. Lipinski, D
6. H. J. Hyde, R
7. C. Collins, D
8. D. Rostenkowski, D
9. S. R. Yates, D
10. J. Porter, R
11. F. Annunzio, D
12. P. M. Crane, R
13. H. W. Fawell, R
14. J. E. Grotberg, R
15. E. R. Madigan, R
16. L. Martin, R
17. L. Evans, D

18. R. H. Michel, R
19. T. L. Bruce, D
20. R. Durbin, D
21. C. M. Price, D
22. K. J. Gray, D

Indiana
1. P. J. Visclosky, D
2. P. R. Sharp, D
3. J. Hiler, R
4. D. Coats, R
5. E. H. Hillis, R
6. D. Burton, R
7. J. T. Myers, R
8. F. McCloskey, D
9. L. H. Hamilton, D
10. A. Jacobs, Jr., D

Iowa
1. J. Leach, R
2. T. Tauke, R
3. C. Evans, R
4. N. Smith, D
5. J. R. Lightfoot, R
6. B. W. Bedell, D

Kansas
1. C. P. Roberts, R
2. J. Slattery, D
3. J. Meyers, R
4. D. Glickman, D
5. B. Whittaker, R

Kentucky
1. C. Hubbard, Jr., D
2. W. H. Natcher, D
3. R. L. Mazzoli, D
4. G. Snyder, R
5. H. Rogers, R
6. L. Hopkins, R
7. C. C. Perkins, D

Louisiana
1. R. L. Livingston, Jr., R
2. C. C. Boggs, D
3. W. J. Tauzin, D
4. C. E. Roemer III, D
5. T. J. Huckaby, D
6. W. H. Moore, R
7. J. B. Breaux, D
8. *C. Long, D

Maine
1. J. R. McKernan, Jr., R
2. O. Snowe, R

Maryland
1. R. Dyson, D
2. H. D. Bentley, R
3. B. A. Mikulski, D
4. M. S. Holt, R
5. S. Hoyer, D
6. B. Byron, D
7. P. J. Mitchell, D
8. M. Barnes, D

Massachusetts
1. S. O. Conte, R
2. E. P. Boland, D
3. J. D. Early, D
4. B. Frank, D
5. C. G. Atkins, D
6. N. Mavroules, D
7. E. J. Markey, D
8. T. P. O'Neill, Jr., D
9. J. J. Moakley, D
10. G. E. Studds, D
11. B. Donnelly, D

Michigan
1. J. Conyers, Jr., D
2. C. D. Pursell, R
3. H. Wolpe, D
4. M. Siljander, R
5. P. B. Henry, R
6. B. Carr, D
7. D. E. Kildee, D
8. B. Traxler, D
9. G. Vander Jagt, R
10. B. Schuette, R
11. R. Davis, R
12. D. E. Bonior, D
13. G. Crockett, Jr., D
14. D. Hertel, D
15. W. D. Ford, D
16. J. D. Dingell, D
17. S. Levin, D
18. W. S. Broomfield, R

Minnesota
1. T. J. Penny, D
2. V. Weber, R
3. B. Frenzel, R

4. B. F. Vento, D
5. M. Sabo, D
6. G. Sikorski, D
7. A. Stangeland, R
8. J. L. Oberstar, D

Mississippi
1. J. L. Whitten, D
2. W. Franklin, R
3. G. V. Montgomery, D
4. W. Dowdy, D
5. T. Lott, R

Missouri
1. W. L. Clay, D
2. R. A. Young, D
3. R. A. Gephardt, D
4. I. Skelton, D
5. A. Wheat, D
6. E. T. Coleman, R
7. G. Taylor, R
8. W. Emerson, R
9. H. L. Volkmer, D

Montana
1. P. Williams, D
2. R. Marlenee, R

Nebraska
1. D. Bereuter, R
2. H. Daub, R
3. V. Smith, R

Nevada
1. H. Reid, D
2. B. Vucanovich, R

New Hampshire
1. R. C. Smith, R
2. J. Gregg, R

New Jersey
1. J. J. Florio, D
2. W. J. Hughes, D
3. J. J. Howard, D
4. C. Smith, R
5. M. Roukema, R
6. B. J. Dwyer, D
7. M. J. Rinaldo, R
8. R. A. Roe, D
9. R. G. Torricelli, D
10. P. W. Rodino, Jr., D
11. D. A. Gallo, R
12. J. Courter, R
13. H. J. Saxton, R
14. F. Guarini, D

New Mexico
1. M. Lujan, Jr., R
2. J. Skeen, R
3. W. B. Richardson, D

New York
1. W. Carney, R
2. T. J. Downey, D
3. R. J. Mrazek, D
4. N. F. Lent, R
5. R. McGrath, R
6. J. P. Addabbo, D
7. G. L. Ackerman, D
8. J. H. Scheuer, D
9. T. J. Manton, D
10. C. E. Schumer, D
11. E. Towns, D
12. M. R. Owens, D
13. S. J. Solarz, D
14. G. V. Molinari, R
15. B. Green, R
16. C. B. Rangel, D
17. T. Weiss, D
18. R. Garcia, D
19. M. Biaggi, D
20. J. J. DioGuardi, R
21. H. Fish, Jr., R
22. B. A. Gilman, R
23. S. S. Stratton, D
24. G. B. H. Solomon, R
25. S. L. Boehlert, R
26. D. Martin, R
27. G. C. Wortley, R
28. M. F. McHugh, D
29. F. Horton, R
30. F. J. Eckert, R
31. J. Kemp, R
32. J. J. LaFalce, D
33. H. J. Nowak, D
34. S. N. Lundine, D

North Carolina
1. W. B. Jones, D
2. T. Valentine, D

3. C. O. Whitley, D
4. W. W. Cobey, Jr., R
5. S. L. Neal, D
6. H. Coble, R
7. C. Rose, D
8. W. G. Hefner, D
9. J. A. McMillan III, R
10. J. T. Broyhill, R
11. B. Hendon, R

North Dakota
At-L. B. Dorgan, D

Ohio
1. T. A. Luken, D
2. W. D. Gradison, Jr., R
3. T. Hall, D
4. M. Oxley, R
5. D. L. Latta, R
6. B. McEwen, R
7. M. DeWine, R
8. T. N. Kindness, R
9. M. Kaptur, D
10. C. E. Miller, R
11. D. E. Eckart, D
12. J. R. Kasich, R
13. D. J. Pease, D
14. J. F. Seiberling, D
15. C. P. Wylie, R
16. R. Regula, R
17. J. A. Traficant, Jr., D
18. D. Applegate, D
19. E. F. Feighan, D
20. M. R. Oakar, D
21. L. Stokes, D

Oklahoma
1. J. R. Jones, D
2. M. Synar, D
3. W. W. Watkins, D
4. D. McCurdy, D
5. M. Edwards, R
6. G. English, D

Oregon
1. L. AuCoin, D
2. R. F. Smith, R
3. R. Wyden, D
4. J. Weaver, D
5. D. Smith, R

Pennsylvania
1. T. Foglietta, D
2. W. Gray, III, D
3. R. A. Borski, Jr., D
4. J. P. Kolter, D
5. R. T. Schulze, R
6. G. Yatron, D
7. B. Edgar, D
8. P. H. Kostmayer, D
9. B. Shuster, R
10. J. M. McDade, R
11. P. E. Kanjorski, D
12. J. P. Murtha, D
13. L. Coughlin, R
14. W. Coyne, D
15. D. Ritter, R
16. R. S. Walker, R
17. G. W. Gekas, R
18. D. Walgren, D
19. W. F. Goodling, R
20. J. M. Gaydos, D
21. T. J. Ridge, R
22. A. J. Murphy, D
23. W. Clinger, Jr., R

Rhode Island
1. F. J. St Germain, D
2. C. Schneider, R

South Carolina
1. T. Hartnett, R
2. F. D. Spence, R
3. B. C. Derrick, Jr., D
4. C. Campbell, Jr., R
5. J. Spratt, Jr., D
6. R. M. Tallon, Jr., D

South Dakota
At-L. T. Daschle, D

Tennessee
1. J. H. Quillen, R
2. J. J. Duncan, R
3. M. Lloyd, D
4. J. Cooper, D
5. W. H. Boner, D
6. B. Gordon, D
7. D. Sundquist, R
8. E. Jones, D
9. H. E. Ford, D

Texas
1. *J. Chapman, D
2. C. Wilson, D
3. S. Bartlett, R
4. R. Hall, D
5. J. Bryant, D
6. J. Barton, R
7. B. Archer, R
8. J. Fields, R
9. J. Brooks, D
10. J. J. Pickle, D
11. J. M. Leath, D
12. J. C. Wright, Jr., D
13. E. B. Boulter, R
14. D. M. Sweeney, R
15. E. de la Garza, D
16. R. Coleman, D
17. C. Stenholm, D
18. M. Leland, D
19. L. Combest, R
20. H. B. Gonzalez, D
21. T. Loeffler, R
22. T. DeLay, R
23. A. G. Bustamante, D
24. M. Frost, D
25. M. Andrews, D
26. R. Armey, R
27. S. P. Ortiz, D

Utah
1. J. Hansen, R
2. D. S. Monson, R
3. H. C. Nielson, R

Vermont
At-L. J. M. Jeffords, R

Virginia
1. H. H. Bateman, R
2. G. W. Whitehurst, R
3. T. Bliley, Jr., R
4. N. Sisisky, D
5. D. Daniel, D
6. J. R. Olin, D
7. D. F. Slaughter, Jr., R
8. S. Parris, R
9. F. C. Boucher, D
10. F. Wolf, R

Washington
1. J. Miller, R
2. A. Swift, D
3. D. L. Bonker, D
4. S. Morrison, R
5. T. S. Foley, D
6. N. D. Dicks, D
7. M. Lowry, D
8. R. Chandler, R

West Virginia
1. A. B. Mollohan, D
2. H. O. Staggers, Jr., D
3. R. E. Wise, Jr., D
4. N. J. Rahall, II, D

Wisconsin
1. L. Aspin, D
2. R. W. Kastenmeier, D
3. S. Gunderson, R
4. G. D. Kleczka, D
5. J. Moody, D
6. T. E. Petri, R
7. D. R. Obey, D
8. T. Roth, R
9. F. J. Sensenbrenner, Jr., R

Wyoming
At-L. R. Cheney, R

AMERICAN SAMOA
Delegate, Fofó Sunia, D

DISTRICT OF COLUMBIA
Delegate, W. E. Fauntroy, D

GUAM
Delegate, Ben Garrido Blaz, R

PUERTO RICO
Resident Commissioner
J. B. Fuster, D

VIRGIN ISLANDS
Delegate, Ron de Lugo, D

585

AMBASSADORS AND ENVOYS [1]

From U.S.	Countries	To U.S.	From U.S.	Countries	To U.S.
(vacant)	AFGHANISTAN	M. Haider Req [2]	Reginald Bartholomew	LEBANON	Abdallah Bouhabib
L. Craig Johnstone	ALGERIA	Mohamed Sahnoun	S. L. Abbott	LESOTHO	L. A. Thoahlan
Thomas H. Anderson, Jr.	ANTIGUA AND BARBUDA	Edmund Hawkins Lake	Edward J. Perkins	LIBERIA	G. Toe Washington
			Jean B. S. Gerard	LUXEMBOURG	Paul Peters
Frank V. Ortiz, Jr.	ARGENTINA	Lucio Garcia Del Solar	Robert B. Keating	MADAGASCAR	Leon M. Rajaobelina
L. W. Lane, Jr.	AUSTRALIA	F. Rawdon Dalrymple	Weston Adams	MALAWI	T. S. Mangwazu
Helene A. von Damm	AUSTRIA	Thomas Klestil	Thomas P. Shoesmith	MALAYSIA	Dato' Lew Sip Hon
Lev E. Dobriansky	BAHAMAS	Reginald L. Wood	James W. Spain	MALDIVE IS.	(vacant)
Donald Charles Leidel	BAHRAIN	G. M. Algosaibi	Robert J. Ryan, Jr.	MALI	Lassana Keita
H. B. Schaffer	BANGLADESH	A.Z.M. Obaidullah Khan	Gary L. Matthews	MALTA	Lawrence Farrugia [2]
T. H. Anderson, Jr.	BARBADOS	Peter D. Laurie	Robert L. Pugh	MAURITANIA	Abdellah Ould Daddah
Geoffrey Swaebe	BELGIUM	J. Raoul Schoumaker	George R. Andrews	MAURITIUS	C. Jesseramsing
James L. Malone [3]	BELIZE	Edward A. Liang	John A. Gavin	MEXICO	Jorge Espinosa de los Reyes
George E. Moose	BENIN	Guy Landry Hazoume			
E. M. Rowell	BOLIVIA	M. Baptista Gumucio	Thomas A. Nassif	MOROCCO	Maati Jorio
Natale H. Bellocchi	BOTSWANA	Serara T. Ketlogetswe	Peter Jon de Vos	MOZAMBIQUE	Valeriano Ferrao
Diego C. Asencio	BRAZIL	Sergio Correa DaCosta	L. W. Lane, Jr.	NAURU	T. W. Star
Barrington King	BRUNEI DARUSSALAM	Pengiran Haji Idriss	Leon J. Weil	NEPAL	Bhekh Bahadur Thapa
			L. Paul Bremer III	NETHERLANDS	Richard H. Fein
Melvyn Levitsky	BULGARIA	Stoyan I. Zhulev	Paul M. Cleveland	NEW ZEALAND	Wallace E. Rowling
Leonardo Neher	BURKINA FASO	Traore Melegue [2]	Harry E. Bergold, Jr.	NICARAGUA	Carlos Tunnermann
D. A. O'Donohue	BURMA	U Maung Maung Gyi	Richard W. Bogosian	NIGER	Joseph Diatta
James R. Bullington	BURUNDI	Edouard Kadigiri	Thomas W. M. Smith	NIGERIA	Ignatius C. Olisemeka
M. R. R. Frechette	CAMEROON	Paul Pondi	Robert D. Stuart	NORWAY	Kjell Eliassen
T. M. T. Niles	CANADA	Allan E. Gotlieb	G. C. Montgomery	OMAN	Ali Salim Bader Al-Hinai
John Melvin Yates	CAPE VERDE	J. Fernandes Lopes	Deane R. Hinton	PAKISTAN	Ejaz Azim
Edmund DeJarnette	CENTRAL AFR. REP.	C. Lingama-Toleque	Everett E. Briggs	PANAMA	Gabriel de la Guardia
John Blane	CHAD	Mahamat Ali Adoum	Paul F. Gardner	PAPUA NEW GUINEA	Renagi Renagi Lohia
H. G. Barnes, Jr.	CHILE	Hernan Felipe Errazuriz			
Winston Lord	CHINA	Han Xu	Clyde D. Taylor	PARAGUAY	M. Martinez Mendieta
Charles A. Gillespie, Jr.	COLOMBIA	Rodrigo Lloreda	David C. Jordan	PERU	Luis Marchand
Robert B. Keating	COMOROS	Ali Mlahaili	Stephen W. Bosworth	PHILIPPINES	Benjamin T. Romualdez
Alan Wood Lukens	CONGO	Stanislas Batchi	(vacant)	POLAND	Zdzislaw Ludwiczak
Lewis Arthur Tambs	COSTA RICA	Federico Vargas Peralta	Frank Shakespeare	PORTUGAL	Leonardo Mathias
Richard W. Boehm	CYPRUS	Andrew J. Jacovides	Joseph Ghougassian	QATAR	A. B. Al-Ameri
William H. Luers	CZECHOSLOVAKIA	Stanislav Suja	Roger Kirk	ROMANIA	Nicolae Gavrilescu
Terence A. Todman	DENMARK	Eigil Jorgensen	J. E. Upston	RWANDA	Simon Insonere
John P. Ferriter	DJIBOUTI	Saleh Hadji Farah Dirir	Thomas H. Anderson, Jr.	ST CHRISTOPHER AND NEVIS	William Herbert
T. H. Anderson, Jr.	DOMINICA	Franklin Baron			
Lowell C. Kilday	DOMINICAN REP.	Eulogio Santaella	T. H. Anderson, Jr.	ST. LUCIA	Joseph Edsel Edmunds
Fernando E. Rondon	ECUADOR	Mario Ribadeneira	Thomas H. Anderson, Jr.	ST. VINCENT AND THE GRENADINES	(vacant)
(vacant)	EGYPT	El Sayed A. R. El Reedy			
Edwin G. Corr	EL SALVADOR	Pablo Mauricio Alvergue	Larry C. Williamson	SÃO TOME AND PRINCIPE	Joaquim Rafael Branco
Francis S. Ruddy	EQUATORIAL GUINEA	Florencio Maye Ela			
			Walter Leon Cutler	SAUDI ARABIA	Bandar Bin Sultan
(vacant)	ETHIOPIA	Girma Amare [2]	Lannon Walker	SENEGAL	Falilou Kane
Carl E. Dillery	FIJI	R. J. F. Radrodro	Irvin Hicks	SEYCHELLES	Giovinella Gonthier
Keith Foote Nyborg	FINLAND	Richard Muller	Arthur W. Lewis	SIERRA LEONE	Dauda S. Kamara
Joe M. Rodgers	FRANCE	Emmanuel de Margerie	J. Stapleton Roy	SINGAPORE	Tommy T. B. Koh
Larry C. Williamson	GABON	Mocktar Abdoulaye-Mbingt	Paul F. Gardner	SOLOMON ISLANDS	Francis Saemala
			Peter S. Bridges	SOMALIA	Mohamud Haji Nur
R. T. Hennemeyer	GAMBIA	Lamin A. Mbye	Herman W. Nickel	SOUTH AFRICA	J. A. H. Beukes
Francis J. Meehan	GERMANY (E)	Gerhard Herder	Thomas O. Enders	SPAIN	Gabriel Manueco
Richard R. Burt	GERMANY (W)	Guenther van Well	James W. Spain	SRI LANKA	Ernest Corea
Robert E. Fritts	GHANA	Eric K. Otoo	Hume A. Horan	SUDAN	Salah Ahmed
Charles H. Price II	GREAT BRITAIN	Oliver Wright	Robert E. Barbour	SURINAM	Donald A. McLeod
Robert V. Keeley	GREECE	George D. Papoulias	Harvey F. Nelson, Jr.	SWAZILAND	Peter H. Mtetwa
Roy T. Haverkamp	GRENADA	A.D. Xavier	Gregory J. Newell	SWEDEN	Count Wilhelm Wachtmeister
A. Martinez Piedra	GUATEMALA	Eduardo Palomo			
James D. Rosenthal	GUINEA	Tolo Beavogui	Faith Ryan Whittlesey	SWITZERLAND	Klaus Jacobi
(vacant)	GUINEA- BISSAU	Inacio Semedo, Jr.	William L. Eagleton, Jr.	SYRIA	Rafic Jouejati
Clint A. Lauderdale	GUYANA	Cedric Hilburn Grant	John W. Shirley	TANZANIA	Asterius M. Hyera
C. E. McManaway, Jr.	HAITI	Adrien L. Raymond	William A. Brown	THAILAND	Kasem S. Kasemsri
William A. Wilson	HOLY SEE	The Most Rev. Piolaghi	Owen W. Roberts	TOGO	Ellom-Kodjo Schuppius
John Arthur Ferch	HONDURAS	Juan Agurcia Ewing	Carl E. Dillery	TONGA	S. T. Taumoepeau
Nicolas M. Salgo	HUNGARY	Vencel Hazi	Sheldon J. Krys	TRINIDAD AND TOBAGO	James O'Neil-Lewis
Nicholas Ruwe	ICELAND	Hans G. Andersen			
John Gunther Dean	INDIA	K. Shankar Bajpai	Peter Sebastian	TUNISIA	Habib Ben Yahia
John H. Holdridge	INDONESIA	A. Hasnan Habib	Robert Strausz-Hupé	TURKEY	Sukru Elekdag
David G. Newton	IRAQ	Nizar Hamdoon	Carl E. Dillery	TUVALU	Ionatana Ionatana
Margaret M. Heckler	IRELAND	Padraic N. MacKernan	Robert G. Houdek	UGANDA	John W. Lwamafa
Thomas R. Pickering	ISRAEL	Meir Rosenne	Arthur A. Hartman	USSR	A. F. Dobrynin
Maxwell M. Rabb	ITALY	Rinaldo Petrignani	George Q. Lumsden, Jr.	UNITED ARAB EMIRATES	Ahmed S. Al-Mokarrab
Robert H. Miller	IVORY COAST	Rene Amany			
Michael Sotirhos	JAMAICA	Keith Johnson	Malcolm R. Wilkey	URUGUAY	Hector Luisi
Michael J. Mansfield	JAPAN	Nobuo Matsunaga	(vacant)	VENEZUELA	Valentin Hernandez
Paul H. Boeker	JORDAN	Mohamed Kamal	H. Monroe Browne	WESTERN SAMOA	Maiava I. Toma
Gerald E. Thomas	KENYA	Wafula Wabuge	William A. Rugh	YEMEN	Mohsin A. Alaini
Carl E. Dillery	KIRIBATI	Atanraoi Baiteke	John D. Scanlan	YUGOSLAVIA	Mico Rakic
Richard L. Walker	KOREA (S)	Byong Hion Lew	Brandon H. Grove, Jr.	ZAIRE	Kasongo Mutuale
A. C. E. Quainton	KUWAIT	S. S. N. Al- Sabah	Paul J. Hare	ZAMBIA	Nalumino Mundia
(vacant)	LAOS	Bounkeut Sangsomsak [2]	David C. Miller, Jr.	ZIMBABWE	E. R. M. Garwe

[1] As of December 1985. [2] Chargé d'affaires. [3] Nominated but not confirmed.

UNITED STATES: Major Legislation Enacted During the First Session of the 99th Congress

SUBJECT	PURPOSE
Salmon Treaty	Ratifies the treaty between the United States and Canada concerning Pacific salmon. Signed March 15, 1985. Public Law 99-5.
African Famine Relief	Appropriates $784 million for food, seeds, clothing, and shelter for victims of the African famine. Signed April 2. Public Law 99-8.
Weather Satellites	Commemorates the 25th anniversary of U.S. weather satellites. Signed April 4. Public Law 99-12.
Unemployment	Phases out special assistance for the long-term unemployed. Signed April 4. Public Law 99-15.
Cocopah Indians	Declares that the United States holds in trust for the Cocopah Indian Tribes of Arizona certain lands in Yuma County, AZ. Signed April 15. Public Law 99-23.
Tax Records	Repeals a 1984 law requiring taxpayers to maintain daily accounts when claiming tax breaks for business use of automobiles, home computers, or other equipment. Signed May 24. Public Law 99-44.
Saccharin	Amends the Saccharin Study and Labeling Act to extend the period during which the secretary of health and human services may not take certain actions to restrict the continued use of saccharin or of any food, drug, or cosmetic containing saccharin. Signed May 24. Public Law 99-45.
Israel	Approves and implements the Free Trade Agreement between the United States and Israel. Signed June 11. Public Law 99-47.
Boy Scouts	Marks the 75th anniversary of the Boy Scouts of America. Signed July 3. Public Law 99-60.
Trade	Extends the Export Administration Act through fiscal 1989. Eases several licensing and procedural restrictions on the sale of products to other countries and limits presidential authority to impose trade embargoes. Tightens controls to prevent advanced equipment from falling into the hands of unfriendly nations and increases the penalties for companies that evade export controls. Signed July 12. Public Law 99-64.
Soviet Jewry	Appeals for the release of Soviet Jewry. Signed August 6. Public Law 99-81.
Foreign Aid	Establishes overall policy guidelines for foreign aid, and authorizes $12.8 billion for military, economic, and development aid for fiscal years 1986 and 1987. Signed August 8. Public Law 99-83.
U.S.-USSR Communication	Authorizes the secretary of defense to provide to the USSR, on a reimbursable basis, equipment and services necessary to improve the U.S.-USSR Direct Communication Link for crisis control. Signed August 8. Public Law 99-85.
George and Ira Gershwin	Provides that special gold medals be presented to honor George and Ira Gershwin. Signed August 9. Public Law 99-86.
Peace Corps	Recognizes both Peace Corps volunteers and the Peace Corps itself on the agency's 25th anniversary, 1985–86. Signed October 1. Public Law 99-111.
Taxation	Revises a provision of the 1984 Deficit Reduction Act to reduce the amount of interest the Internal Revenue Service would "impute" for tax purposes on low-rate, seller-financed real-estate transactions. Signed October 11. Public Law 99-121.
Liberty	Designates the 12-month period ending on Oct. 28, 1986, as the "Centennial Year of Liberty in the United States." Signed October 28. Public Law 99-136.
Defense	As part of the defense authorization bill, allocates $2.6 billion for the MX missile program. Limits to 50 the number of MX missiles that could be deployed in existing missile silos. Signed November 8. Public Law 99-145.
National Institutes of Health	Provides a three-year, $7.7 billion reauthorization for biomedical research at the National Institutes of Health. Creates a new institute for research on arthritis. House and Senate override presidential veto on November 12 and November 20, respectively. Public Law 99-158.
Budget Deficit	Establishes binding deficit targets over the next five years and requires a balanced federal budget by Oct. 1, 1990 (fiscal year 1991). Increases the debt ceiling to $2.079 trillion from $1.824 trillion. Signed December 12. Public Law 99-177.
China Nuclear Accord	Approves a 30-year agreement providing for the sale of nuclear equipment and supplies to China. Signed December 16. Public Law 99-183.
Spending	Appropriates $368.2 billion to keep the government in operation until Sept. 30, 1986, the end of fiscal 1986. Shuts down the five-year-old Synthetic Fuels Corporation and funds a "clean coal" technology program instead. Allows U.S. senators to accept an extra $7,500 in honoraria for speeches and articles (a total of $30,000 or 40% of their salaries). Continues funding for mass transit and Amtrak at close to 1985 levels. Approves $2.75 billion for the Strategic Defense Initiative ("Star Wars"). Signed December 19. Public Law 99-190.
Farming	Reauthorizes federal farm programs for fiscal 1986–90. Signed December 23. Public Law 99-198.
Farm Credit System	Creates a new Farm Credit Capital Corporation to restructure bad loans from the network of 37 banks and 800-plus farmer-owned lending corporations and redistributes surplus funds among them. Restructures the Farm Credit Administration with oversight and management responsibility. Signed December 23. Public Law 99-205.
Micronesia	The Compact of Free Association with Micronesia bestows limited autonomy on Micronesia, the last remaining U.S. trust territory in the Pacific. Signed January 14. Public Law 99-239.
Radioactive Waste	Imposes strict deadlines for states to establish their own disposal systems for low-level radioactive waste. Signed January 15. Public Law 99-240.

SOCIETIES AND ORGANIZATIONS

This listing includes some of the most noteworthy associations, societies, foundations, and trusts of the United States and Canada. The information was verified by the organization concerned.

Academy of Motion Picture Arts & Sciences. Membership: 5,000. Executive director, James M. Roberts. Headquarters: 8949 Wilshire Blvd., Beverly Hills, CA 90211.

Alcoholics Anonymous (The General Service Board of A.A., Inc.). Membership: more than 1,000,000 in more than 62,800 groups worldwide in 114 countries. Chairman, Gordon Patrick. Headquarters: 468 Park Ave. S., New York, NY. Mailing address: Box 459, Grand Central Station, New York, NY 10163.

American Academy and Institute of Arts and Letters. Membership: 250. Executive director, Margaret M. Mills. Headquarters: 633 W. 155th St., New York, NY 10032.

American Academy of Political and Social Science. Membership: 10,500, including 5,500 libraries. President, Marvin E. Wolfgang. Headquarters: 3937 Chestnut St., Philadelphia, PA 19104.

American Anthropological Association. Membership: 10,268. Executive director, Edward J. Lehman. Headquarters: 1703 New Hampshire Ave. NW, Washington, DC 20009.

American Association for the Advancement of Science. Membership: 140,000 and 285 affiliated groups. Meeting: Philadelphia, May 22–27, 1986. President, Gerard Piel; executive officer, William D. Carey. Headquarters: 1330 H Street NW, Washington, DC 20005.

American Association of Museums. Membership: 9,000. Meeting: New York City, 1986. Director: Lawrence L. Reger. Headquarters: 1055 Thomas Jefferson St. NW, Suite 428, Washington, DC 20007.

American Association of Retired Persons. Membership: 19,000,000. Biennial convention: May 27–30, 1986, Anaheim, CA. Executive director, Cyril F. Brickfield. Headquarters: 1909 K St. NW, Washington, DC 20049.

American Association of University Professors. Membership: 62,000. President, Paul H. L. Walter. Headquarters: 1012 14th St. NW, Washington, DC 20005.

American Association of University Women. Membership: 193,000. President, Sarah Harder. Headquarters: 2401 Virginia Ave. NW, Washington, DC 20037.

American Astronomical Society. Membership: 4,100. Meetings: Houston, TX, Jan. 5–9, 1986; Ames, Iowa, June 22–26, 1986. Executive officer, Peter B. Boyce. Headquarters: 1816 Jefferson Place NW, Washington, DC 20036.

American Automobile Association. Membership: 25,500,000 in 167 affiliated clubs. President, James B. Creal. Headquarters: 8111 Gatehouse Rd., Falls Church, VA 22047.

American Bankers Association (ABA). Membership: nearly 13,000. President, James G. Cairns, Jr. Annual convention: San Francisco, CA, Oct. 25–29, 1986. Headquarters: 1120 Connecticut Ave. NW, Washington, DC 20036.

American Bar Association. Membership: 316,400. Annual meeting: New York City, Aug. 7–14, 1986; Midyear meeting: Baltimore, MD, Feb. 5–12, 1986. President, William W. Falsgraf; president-elect, Eugene C. Thomas; executive director and chief operating officer, Thomas H. Gonser. Headquarters: 750 N. Lake Shore Drive, Chicago, IL 60611.

American Bible Society. Distribution: 114,458,279 copies. Annual meeting: New York City, May 8, 1986. President, Edmund F. Wagner; general officers, Charles W. Baas, Alice E. Ball, John D. Erickson. Headquarters: 1865 Broadway, New York, NY 10023.

American Booksellers Association, Inc. Membership: 4,792. Convention: New Orleans, May 24–27, 1986. President, Gail See; executive director, Bernard Rath. Headquarters: 122 E. 42nd St., New York, NY 10168.

American Cancer Society, Inc. Membership: 200 voting members; 58 chartered divisions. Executive vice-president, Lane W. Adams. Headquarters: 90 Park Avenue, New York, NY 10016.

American Chemical Society. Membership: 134,000. National meetings, 1986: New York City, April 13–18; Anaheim, CA, Sept. 8–12. President, Ellis K. Fields. Headquarters: 1155 16th St. NW, Washington, DC 20035.

American Civil Liberties Union. Membership: 250,000. President, Norman Dorsen; executive director, Ira Glasser. Headquarters: 132 W. 43rd St., New York, NY 10036.

American Correctional Association. Membership: 17,000. Executive director, Anthony P. Travisono. Headquarters: 4321 Hartwick Rd., College Park, MD 20740.

American Council on Education. Membership: 1,271 institutional members, 109 associated organizations, 56 constituent organizations, 62 affiliates, and 22 international affiliates. Annual meeting: San Francisco, CA, Oct. 6–8, 1986. President, Robert H. Atwell. Headquarters: One Dupont Circle NW, Washington, DC 20036.

American Council of Learned Societies. Membership: 45 professional societies concerned with the humanities and the humanistic aspects of the social sciences. President, John William Ward. Headquarters: 228 East 45th St., New York, NY 10017.

American Dental Association. Membership: 140,000. Annual session: Miami Beach, FL, Oct. 18–23, 1986. President, Abraham Kobren, D.D.S.; executive director, John M. Coady, D.D.S. Headquarters: 211 East Chicago Ave., Chicago, IL 60611.

American Economic Association. Membership: 20,000 and 6,000 subscribers. President, Charles Kindleberger. Headquarters: 1313 21st Avenue South, Nashville, TN 37212.

American Farm Bureau Federation. Membership: 3,350,882 families. Annual meeting: Atlanta, GA, Jan. 1986. President, Robert B. Delano. Headquarters: 225 Touhy Ave., Park Ridge, IL 60068.

American Geographical Society. Fellows and subscribers: 5,500. President, John E. Gould; director, Mary Lynne Bird. Headquarters: 156 Fifth Ave., Suite 600, New York, NY 10010.

American Geophysical Union. Membership: about 17,000 individuals. Meetings: spring—Baltimore, MD, May 19–23, 1986; fall—San Francisco, CA, Dec 8–12, 1986. President, Charles L. Drake. Headquarters: 2000 Florida Ave. NW, Washington, DC 20009.

American Heart Association. Membership: 140,000 in 55 affiliates, 70 chapters, and approximately 1,500 local subdivisions. President, Thomas J. Ryan, M.D. Headquarters: 7320 Greenville Ave., Dallas, TX 75231.

American Historical Association. Membership: 13,000. Annual meeting: Chicago, IL, Dec 27–30, 1986. President, Carl N. Degler; executive director, Samuel Gammon. Headquarters: 400 A St. SE, Washington, DC 20003.

American Horticultural Society. Membership: 40,000. Annual meeting: San Francisco, CA, August 1986. President, Edward N. Dane. Headquarters: River Farm, Box 0105, Mount Vernon, VA 22121.

American Hospital Association. Membership: 38,521 persons; 6,217 institutions. Annual meeting: Washington, DC, Feb. 2–5, 1986. Convention: Toronto, Ont., Aug. 4–6, 1986. Chairman of the board, Scott Parker. Headquarters: 840 North Lake Shore Drive, Chicago, IL 60611.

American Hotel & Motel Association. Membership: 8,700. Annual convention: Las Vegas, NV, May 11–16, 1986. Executive vice-president, Kenneth F. Hine. Headquarters: 888 Seventh Ave., New York, NY 10106.

American Institute of Aeronautics and Astronautics. Membership: 31,030 plus 7,595 student members. Annual meeting: Crystal City, VA, April 29–May 1,, 1986. Executive director, James J. Harford. Headquarters: 1633 Broadway, New York, NY 10019.

American Institute of Architects. Membership: 45,000. Convention, 1986: San Antonio, TX, June 8–11. President, R. Bruce Patty, FAIA. Headquarters: 1735 New York Avenue NW, Washington, DC 20006.

American Institute of Biological Sciences. Membership: 8,000 with 40 societies and 7 affiliate organizations. Annual meeting: University of Massachusetts, Amherst, Aug. 10–14, 1986. President, C. Herb Ward. Headquarters: 730 11th St. NW, Washington, DC 20001.

American Institute of Certified Public Accountants. Membership: 235,000. Annual meeting: Kansas City, MO, Oct. 19–21, 1986. Chairman, Herman J. Lowe. Headquarters: 1211 Avenue of the Americas, New York, NY 10036–8775.

American Institute of Chemical Engineers. Membership: 60,000. President, J. P. Sachs. Headquarters: 345 E. 47th Street, New York, NY 10017.

American Institute of Graphic Arts. Membership: 3,500. President, Colin Forbes; executive director, Caroline Hightower. Headquarters: 1059 Third Ave., New York, NY 10021.

American Institute of Mining, Metallurgical and Petroleum Engineers, Inc. Membership: 90,000. Annual meeting: New Orleans, LA, Feb. 2–6, 1986. President, Norman T. Mills. Headquarters: 345 E. 47th Street, New York, NY 10017.

American Institute of Nutrition. Membership: 2,250. Annual meeting: St. Louis, April 13–18, 1986. Executive officer, R. G. Allison, Ph.D. Headquarters: 9650 Rockville Pike, Bethesda, MD 20814.

American Legion, The. Membership: 2,650,000. National Executive Committee is chief administrative body between national conventions. National convention: Cincinnati, OH, Aug. 29–Sept. 4, 1986. Headquarters: 700 N. Pennsylvania St., Indianapolis, IN 46204.

American Library Association. Membership: 40,000. Meetings, 1986: Midwinter—Chicago, IL, Jan. 18–23; annual conference—New York City, June 28–July 3. Executive director, Thomas J. Galvin. Headquarters: 50 E. Huron, Chicago, IL 60611.

American Lung Association. Membership: 140 affiliated groups. Annual meeting: Kansas City, MO, May 11–14, 1986. President, Walter Hatcher. Headquarters: 1740 Broadway, New York, NY 10019.

American Management Association. Membership: 80,000. Chairman of the board, James R. Martin; president, Thomas R. Horton. Headquarters: 135 W. 50th St., New York, NY 10020.

American Mathematical Society. Membership: 21,516. President, Irving Kaplaxsky; secretary, Everett Pitcher. Headquarters: P. O. Box 6248, Providence, RI 02940.

American Medical Association. Membership: 258,000. President, Harrison L. Rogers, Jr., M.D.; president-elect, John J. Coury, Jr., M.D. Headquarters: 555 N. Dearborn St., Chicago, IL 60610.

American Meteorological Society. Membership: 10,000 including 128 corporate members. President, Dr. Clifford J. Murino. Headquarters: 45 Beacon St., Boston, MA 02108.

American Newspaper Publishers Association. Membership: 1,390. Annual convention: San Francisco, CA, April 21–23, 1986. Chairman and president, Richard J. V. Johnson. Executive offices: The Newspaper Center, 11600 Sunrise Valley Dr., Reston, VA 22091. Mailing address: The Newspaper Center, Box 17407, Dulles International Airport, Washington, DC 20041.

American Nurses' Association. Membership: 188,000 in 53 state and territorial associations. National convention: Anaheim, CA, June 13–19, 1986. President, Eunice Cole. Headquarters: 2420 Pershing Road, Kansas City, MO 64108.

American Physical Society. Membership: 36,454 American and foreign. Annual meeting: Atlanta, GA, Jan. 27–30, 1986. President, Robert R. Wilson; executive secretary, W. W. Havens, Jr. Headquarters: 335 E. 45th St., New York, NY 10017.

American Psychiatric Association. Membership: 31,258; 76 district branches. Annual meeting: Washington, DC, May 10–16, 1986. President, Carol C. Nadelson, M.D. Headquarters: 1400 K Street NW, Washington, DC 20005.

American Psychological Association. Membership: 60,000. Annual meeting: Washington, DC, Aug. 22–26, 1986. President, Robert Perloff. Headquarters: 1200 17th St. NW, Washington, DC 20036.

American Red Cross. Chapters: 2,910. National convention: Indianapolis, IN, June 1–4, 1986. Chairman, George F. Moody; president, Richard F. Schubert. Headquarters: 17th and D Sts. NW, Washington, DC 20006.

American Society of Civil Engineers. Membership: 100,000. Executive director, Edward O. Pfrang. Headquarters: 345 E. 47th St., New York, NY 10017–2398.

American Society of Composers, Authors, and Publishers. Membership: 26,188 composer members; 2,150 associate members; 9,751 publisher members. President, Hal David; secretary, Morton Gould. One Lincoln Plaza, New York, NY 10023.

American Society of Mechanical Engineers. Membership: 112,000. President, L. S. Fletcher. Headquarters: 345 E. 47th St., New York, NY 10017.

American Sociological Association. Membership: 14,000. Meeting: New York City, Aug. 30–Sept. 3, 1986. President, Matilda White Riley, Executive office: 1722 N St. NW, Washington, DC 20036.

American Statistical Association. Membership: 15,000. President, Donald W. Marquardt. Meeting: Chicago, IL, Aug. 18–21, 1986. Headquarters: 806 15th St. NW, Suite 640, Washington, DC 20005.

American Youth Hostels, Inc. Membership: 100,000; 31 councils in the United States. Executive director, Robert Johnson. Headquarters: 1332 I St. NW, Suite 800, Washington, DC 20005.

Archaeological Institute of America. Membership: 9,700; subscription to *Archaeology*: 75,000; subscription to *American Journal of Archaeology*: 4,500. President: James R. Wiseman; executive director, Raymond A. Liddell. Annual meeting: San Antonio, TX, Dec. 27–30, 1986. Headquarters: P. O. Box 1901, Kenmore Station, Boston, MA 02215.

Arthritis Foundation. Membership: 71 chapters. Annual scientific meeting: New Orleans, LA, June 2–7, 1986. Chairman, Stanley K. Rubin III; president, Clifford M. Clarke. Headquarters: 1314 Spring St. NW, Atlanta, GA 30309.

Association of American Publishers. Membership: approximately 350. Annual meeting, Palm Beach, FL, March 2–5, 1986. Chairman of the board, Jeremiah Kaplan; president, Townsend W. Hoopes; vice-presidents, Thomas McKee and Richard Kleeman. Addresses: 220 E. 23rd St., New York, NY 10010; and 2005 Massachusetts Ave. NW, Washington, DC 20036.

Association of Junior Leagues, Inc. Membership: 262 member leagues in U.S., Canada, Mexico, and the United Kingdom. Annual conference: San Diego, CA, May 3–7, 1986. President, Carole P. Hart. Headquarters: 825 Third Ave., New York, NY 10022.

Association of Operating Room Nurses, Inc. Membership: 33,177 with 335 local chapters. Convention: March 9–14, 1986. President, Ruth E. Vaiden; executive director, Clifford H. Jordan. Headquarters: 10170 E. Mississippi Ave., Denver, CO 80231.

Benevolent and Protective Order of Elks. Membership: 1,621,356 in 2,280 lodges. Convention: Denver, CO, July 13–18, 1986. Grand

exalted ruler, Frank O. Garland; grand secretary, S. F. Kocur. Headquarters: 2750 Lake View Ave., Chicago, IL 60614.

Bide-A-Wee Home Association. Executive director, Ursula Goetz. Headquarters: 410 E. 38th St., New York, NY 10016.

Big Brothers/Big Sisters of America. Membership: 400+ local affiliated agencies. National conference: Clearwater, FL, June 17–21, 1986. Interim president, Benjamin Sprafkin. Headquarters: 230 North 13th Street, Philadelphia, PA 19107.

B'nai B'rith International. Membership: 500,000 in approximately 3,000 men's, women's, and youth lodges, chapters, and units. President, Gerald Kraft; executive vice-president, Daniel Thursz. Headquarters: 1640 Rhode Island Ave. NW, Washington, DC 20036.

Boat Owners Association of the United States. Membership: 167,000. President, Richard Schwartz. Headquarters: 880 S. Pickett St., Alexandria, VA 22304.

Boy Scouts of America. Membership: total youth members and leaders, 4,754,479 in 413 local councils. Biennial meeting: Louisville, KY, May 23, 1986. President, Sanford N. McDonnell; chief scout executive, Ben H. Love. National office: 1325 Walnut Hill Lane, Irving, TX 75038–3096.

Boys Clubs of America. Youth served: 1,275,000 in 1,100 affiliated clubs. National conference: Phoenix, AZ, May 16–20, 1986. Chairman, John L. Burns; national director, William R. Bricker. Headquarters: 771 First Ave., New York, NY 10017.

Camp Fire, Inc. Membership: 500,000 boys and girls in more than 35,000 communities. President, Phyllis Schoedel. Headquarters: 4601 Madison Ave., Kansas City, MO 64112.

Canadian Library Association. Membership: 4,050 personal, 1,000 institutional, 5,050 total. 1986 annual conference: Quebec City. Executive director, Paul Kitchen. Headquarters: 151 Sparks St., Ottawa, Ont. K1P 5E3.

Canadian Medical Association. Membership: 38,000. Annual meeting: Winnipeg, Manitoba, Aug. 10–15, 1986. Secretary general, B. E. Freamo. Address: 1867 Alta Vista Drive, Ottawa, Ontario K1G 3Y6.

Chamber of Commerce, U.S. Membership: approximately 4,200 associations and state and local chambers, approximately 182,000 business members. Annual meeting: Washington, DC, April 27–29, 1986. President, Richard L. Lesher; chairman of the board, Frank Morsani. Headquarters: 1615 H Street NW, Washington, DC 20062.

Common Cause. Membership: 250,000. Chairman, Archibald Cox. Headquarters: 2030 M St. NW, Washington, DC 20036.

Consumers Union of United States, Inc. Executive director, Rhoda H. Karpatkin. Headquarters: 256 Washington St., Mount Vernon, NY 10553.

Council of Better Business Bureaus. Membership: 1,000. Headquarters: 1515 Wilson Blvd., Suite 300, Arlington, VA 22209.

Council on Foreign Relations, Inc. Membership: 2,310. Annual meeting: New York City, fall 1986. President, Winston Lord. Headquarters: 58 E. 68th St., New York, NY 10021.

Daughters of the American Revolution (National Society). Membership: 212,000 in 3,150 chapters. Continental congress: Washington, DC, April 14–18, 1986. President general, Mrs. Walter Hughey King. Headquarters: 1776 D St. NW, Washington, DC 20006.

Esperanto League for North America, Inc. Membership: 750. President, Dr. Duncan Charters. Headquarters: P. O. Box 1129, El Cerrito, CA 94530.

Foreign Policy Association. President, Archie E. Albright. Headquarters: 205 Lexington Ave., New York, NY 10016.

Freemasonry, Ancient Accepted Scottish Rite of (Northern Masonic Jurisdiction): Supreme Council, 33°. Membership: 472,438 in 113 valleys. Sovereign grand commander, Stanley F. Maxwell. Headquarters: 33 Marrett Rd., Lexington, MA 02173.

Freemasonry, Ancient and Accepted Scottish Rite of (Southern Jurisdiction): Supreme Council, 33°. Membership: 641,785 in 221 affiliated groups. Sovereign grand commander, Henry C. Clausen. Headquarters: 1733 16th St. NW, Washington, DC 20009.

Future Farmers of America. Membership: 452,665 in 50 state associations. National FFA convention: Kansas City, MO, Nov. 13–15, 1986. Executive secretary, Coleman Harris. Headquarters: Box 15160, Alexandria, VA 22309.

Gamblers Anonymous. Membership: 12,000. National executive secretary, James J. Zeysing. Headquarters: 1543 W. Olympic Blvd., Suite 533, Los Angeles, CA 90015.

Garden Club of America, The. Membership: 15,000 in 186 clubs. Annual meeting: Pittsburgh, PA, May 19–21, 1986. President, Mrs. Frank M. Donahue. Headquarters: 598 Madison Ave., New York, NY 10022.

General Federation of Women's Clubs. Membership: 500,000 in 11,000 U.S. clubs and 10,000,000 worldwide. International president, Jeri Winger. Headquarters: 1734 N St. NW, Washington, DC 20036.

Geological Society of America. Membership: 16,000. President, Brian J. Skinner; executive director, F. Michael Wahl. Headquarters: 3300 Penrose Place, P. O. Box 9140, Boulder, CO 80301.

Girl Scouts of the U.S.A. Membership: 2,871,000. National president, Betty F. Pilsbury; national executive director, Frances R. Hesselbein. Headquarters: 830 Third Avenue, New York, NY 10022.

Humane Society of the United States. Membership: approximately 300,000. Annual convention: Miami Beach, FL, October 1986. President, John A. Hoyt. Headquarters: 2100 L St. NW, Washington, DC 20037.

Institute of Electrical and Electronics Engineers, Inc. Membership: 262,000. President, Charles A. Eldon. Headquarters: 345 E. 47th Street, New York, NY 10017.

Jewish War Veterans of the U.S.A. Membership: 100,000 in 450 units. 91st annual national convention: Hawaii, Sept. 2–9, 1986. National commander, Samuel Greenberg; national executive director, Harris B. Stone. Headquarters: 1811 R St. NW, Washington, DC 20009.

Kiwanis International. Membership: 315,000 in 8,200 clubs in U.S. and abroad. President, Raymond W. Lansford. Headquarters: 3636 Woodview Trace, Indianapolis, IN 46268.

Knights of Columbus. Membership: 1,412,581. Supreme knight, Virgil C. Dechant. Headquarters: Columbus Plaza, New Haven, CT 06507.

Knights of Pythias, Supreme Lodge. Membership: 106,965 in 1,043 subordinate lodges. Supreme chancellor, Jack R. Klai. Office: 35 East Rose Street, Stockton, CA 95202.

League of Women Voters of the U.S. Membership: 110,000. President, Dorothy S. Ridings. Headquarters: 1730 M St. NW, Washington, DC 20036.

Lions Clubs International. Membership: 1,360,000 in 36,900 clubs in 158 countries and areas. Annual convention: New Orleans, LA, July 9–12, 1986. President, Joseph L. Wroblewski. Headquarters: 300 22nd St., Oak Brook, IL 60570.

March of Dimes Birth Defects Foundation. Membership: 410 chapters. President, Charles L. Massey. Headquarters: 1275 Mamaroneck Ave., White Plains, NY 10605.

Mental Health Association. Membership: 650 state and local organizations. Headquarters: 1021 Prince St., Alexandria, VA 22314–2971.

Modern Language Association of America. Membership: 26,000. Annual convention: New York City, Dec. 27–30, 1986. President, Theodore J. Ziolkowski. Headquarters: 62 Fifth Ave., New York, NY 10011.

National Academy of Sciences. Membership: approximately 1,344. Annual meeting: Washington, DC, Apr. 26–30, 1986. President, Frank Press. Headquarters: 2101 Constitution Ave. NW, Washington, DC 20418.

National Association for the Advancement of Colored People. Membership: 450,000 in 1,700 branches and 500 youth and college chapters. National convention: Baltimore, MD, June 29–July 3, 1986. President, Enolia McMillan; board chairman, William S. Gibson; executive director, Benjamin Hooks. Headquarters: 186 Remsen St., Brooklyn Heights, NY 11201.

National Association of Manufacturers. Membership: 13,200. President, Alexander B. Trowbridge. Headquarters: 1776 F St. NW, Washington, DC 20006.

National Audubon Society. Membership: 550,000 in 490 local groups. President, Peter A. A. Berle. Headquarters: 950 Third Ave., New York, NY 10022.

National Committee for Prevention of Child Abuse. Executive director, Anne H. Cohn. Headquarters: 332 S. Michigan Ave., Suite 950, Chicago, IL 60604.

National Conference of Christians and Jews, Inc. Membership: 75 regional offices. President, Jacqueline G. Wexler. Headquarters: 71 Fifth Ave., Suite 1100, New York, NY 10003.

National Council on the Aging, Inc. Membership: 5,000. Executive director, Jack Ossofsky. Annual conference: Washington, DC, April 9–12, 1986. Headquarters: 600 Maryland Ave. SW, West Wing 100, Washington, DC 20024.

National Council of the Churches of Christ in the U.S.A. Membership: 31 Protestant, Anglican, and Orthodox denominations. General secretary, Arie R. Brouwer. Headquarters: 475 Riverside Dr., New York, NY 10115.

National Easter Seal Society. Annual conference: Mobile, AL, mid-November 1986. President, R. B. Coats. Headquarters: 2023 West Ogden Ave., Chicago, IL 60612.

National Education Association of the U.S. Membership: 1,700,000, with units in every state, and 12,000 local affiliates. Annual convention: Louisville, KY, July 1–6, 1986. President, Mary Hatwood Futrell. Headquarters: 1201 16th St. NW, Washington, DC 20036.

National Federation of Business and Professional Women's Clubs, Inc. Membership: 160,000 in 3,700 clubs. President, Anne Steinbeck. Headquarters: 2012 Massachusetts Ave. NW, Washington, DC 20036.

National Federation of Independent Business, Inc. Membership: 560,000. President, John Sloan, Jr. Administrative office: 150 W. 20th Ave., San Mateo, CA 94403. Legislative and research office: 600 Maryland Ave. SW, Suite 700, Washington, DC 20024.

National Federation of Music Clubs. Membership: 500,000 in 4,300 clubs and 12 national affiliates. President, Mrs. Dwight D. Robinson. Headquarters: 1336 North Delaware St., Indianapolis, IN 46202.

National Fire Protection Association. Membership: 32,500. Annual meeting: Atlanta, GA, May 19–22, 1986; fall meeting: Denver, CO, Nov. 17–19, 1986. President, Robert W. Grant. Headquarters: Batterymarch Park, Quincy, MA 02269.

National Organization for Women. Membership: 250,000 in 800 local groups. President, Eleanor Smeal. Headquarters: 1401 New York Ave. NW, Suite 800, Washington, DC 20005.

National PTA (National Parent-Teacher Association). Membership: 5,600,000 in 25,000 local units. National convention: Little Rock, AR, June 20–23, 1986. President, Ann P. Kahn. Headquarters: 700 N. Rush St., Chicago, IL 60611.

National Safety Council. Membership: 12,500. President, T. C. Gilchrest. Headquarters: 444 N. Michigan Ave., Chicago, IL 60611.

National Urban League, Inc. President, John E. Jacob. Annual convention: San Francisco, CA, July 20–23, 1986. Headquarters: 500 E. 62nd St., New York, NY 10021.

National Women's Christian Temperance Union. Membership: approximately 200,000 in 5,000 local unions. National convention: Knoxville, TN, August 1986. President, Mrs. Kermit S. Edgar. Headquarters: 1730 Chicago Ave., Evanston, IL 60201.

Parents Without Partners, Inc. International membership: 250,000. International convention: Washington, DC, July 1–6, 1986. Executive director: Maurine McKinley. International office: 7910 Woodmont Ave., Suite 1008, Bethesda, MD 20814.

Phi Beta Kappa. Membership: 424,000. Secretary, Kenneth M. Greene. Headquarters: 1811 Q St. NW, Washington, DC 20009.

Photographic Society of America. Membership: 16,200. President, Harold D. Lorimor. Headquarters: 2005 Walnut St., Philadelphia, PA 19103.

Planned Parenthood Federation of America, Inc. (Planned Parenthood–World Population). Membership: 188 U.S. affiliates. President, Faye Wattleton; chairperson of the Federation, Allan Rosenfield, M.D. Headquarters: 810 Seventh Ave., New York, NY 10019

Rotary International. Membership: 975,800 in 21,386 clubs functioning in 159 countries and geographical regions. International convention: Las Vegas, NV, June 1–4, 1986. General secretary, Herbert A. Pigman. Headquarters: 1600 Ridge Ave., Evanston, IL 60201.

Salvation Army, The. Membership: 428,046. National commander, Norman Marshall. National headquarters: 799 Bloomfield Ave., Verona, NJ 07044.

Special Libraries Association. Membership: 11,300. Annual conference: Boston, MA, 1986. President, H. Robert Malinowsky. Headquarters: 1700 18th St. NW, Washington, DC 20009.

United Dairy Industry Association (including American Dairy Association, Dairy Research Inc., National Dairy Council). Annual convention: Columbus, OH, March 26–27, 1986. Acting chief executive officer, Edward A. Peterson. Headquarters: Dairy Center, 6300 N. River Rd., Rosemont, IL 60018.

United States Jaycees. Membership: 270,000 in 7,000 affiliated chapters. Annual meeting: Milwaukee, WI, June 15–20, 1986. President, Ken Zimmerman. Headquarters: P.O. Box 7, Tulsa, OK 74121–0007.

U.S. Metric Association. Membership: 3,500. President, Valerie Antoine. Headquarters: 10245 Andasol Ave., Northridge, CA 91325

United Way of America. Service organization for more than 2,200 autonomous local United Way organizations. 1986 volunteer leaders conference: Cincinnati Convention Center, Cincinnati, OH, May 3–6, 1986. Chairman of the board of governors, James D. Robinson III, chairman and chief executive officer, American Express Co. Headquarters: 701 N. Fairfax St., Alexandria, VA 22314.

Veterans of Foreign Wars of the United States. Membership: VFW and Auxiliary 2,710,000. Commander-in-chief, John S. Staum. Headquarters: VFW Building, Broadway at 34th St., Kansas City, MO 64111.

World Council of Churches (U.S. Conference). Membership: 31 churches or denominations in U.S. Moderator, Dr. Sylvia Talbot. Headquarters: 150 route de Ferney, 1211 Geneva 20, Switzerland. New York office: 475 Riverside Dr., Room 1062, New York, NY 10115.

YMCA of the USA. Membership: 13,000,000 in 2,200 associations. Board chairman, James W. Ashley. Headquarters: 101 North Wacker Dr., Chicago, IL 60606.

YWCA of the USA. Members and participants: approximately 2,000,000. President, Glendora M. Putnam. Headquarters: 726 Broadway, New York, NY 10003.

Zionist Organization of America. Membership: 130,000 in 600 districts. President, Alleck A. Resnick; executive vice-president, Paul Flacks. 85th national convention: Baltimore, MD, Sept. 25–28, 1986. Headquarters: ZOA House, 4 East 34th St., New York, NY 10016.

Contributors

591

CULLEN, ROBERT B., General Editor, Former Moscow Bureau Chief, *Newsweek:* USSR—*Life Today*

CUNNIFF, JOHN, Business News Analyst, The Associated Press; Author, *How to Stretch Your Dollar:* BUSINESS AND CORPORATE AFFAIRS—*Takeovers;* UNITED STATES—*The Economy*

CUNNINGHAM, PEGGY, Reporter, *Baltimore News American:* MARYLAND

CURRIER, CHET, Financial Writer, The Associated Press; Author, *The Investor's Encyclopedia:* STOCKS AND BONDS

CURTIS, L. PERRY, JR., Professor of History, Brown University: IRELAND

DANIELS, ROBERT V., Professor of History, University of Vermont: VERMONT

DARBY, JOSEPH W., III, Reporter, *The Times-Picayune/States-Item:* LOUISIANA

DEEB, MARIUS, Professor, Center for Contemporary Arab Studies, Georgetown University; Author, *The Lebanese Civil War:* JORDAN; LEBANON; SYRIA

De GREGORIO, GEORGE, Sports Department, *The New York Times;* Author, *Joe DiMaggio, An Informal Biography:* BIOGRAPHY—*Mary Decker Slaney;* SPORTS—*Boxing, Skiing, Swimming, Track and Field*

DELZELL, CHARLES F., Professor of History, Vanderbilt University; Author, *Italy in the Twentieth Century:* ITALY

DENNIS, LARRY, Senior Editor, *Golf Digest;* Coauthor, *How to Become a Complete Golfer:* SPORTS—*Golf*

DIETERICH, H. R., Professor, History/American Studies, University of Wyoming: WYOMING

DRIGGS, DON W., Chairman, Department of Political Science, University of Nevada; Coauthor, *The Nevada Constitution: Origin and Growth:* NEVADA

DUBIN, REGGI ANN, Transportation Consultant, Reggi Ann Dubin Associates Ltd.: TRANSPORTATION

DUFF, ERNEST A., Professor of Politics, Randolph-Macon Woman's College; Author, *Agrarian Reform in Colombia, Violence and Repression in Latin America, Leader and Party in Latin America:* COLOMBIA

DUNN, CHRISTOPHER, Professor of Political Science, University of Saskatchewan: SASKATCHEWAN

DURRENCE, J. LARRY, Department of History and Political Science, Florida Southern College; Mayor, Lakeland, FL: FLORIDA

ELKINS, ANN M., Fashion Director, *Good Housekeeping Magazine:* FASHION

ELVING, PHYLLIS, Free-lance Travel Writer; Editor, *Pacific Travel News* magazine: TRAVEL

ENSTAD, ROBERT H., Writer, *Chicago Tribune:* CHICAGO; ILLINOIS

EWEGEN, BOB, Editorial Writer, *The Denver Post:* COLORADO

FAGEN, MORTON D., AT&T Bell Laboratories (retired); Editor, *A History of Engineering and Science in the Bell System,* Vols. I and II: COMMUNICATION TECHNOLOGY

FERNANDEZ, GENEVIEVE, Home Building/Decorating Editor, *Good Housekeeping Magazine;* Author, *American Traditional, ABCs of Decorating:* INTERIOR DESIGN

FRANCIS, DAVID R., Economic Columnist, *The Christian Science Monitor:* INTERNATIONAL TRADE AND FINANCE; JAPAN—*Japanese-U.S. Trade*

FRAZIER, SHERVERT H., Director, National Institute of Mental Health: MEDICINE AND HEALTH—*Mental Health*

FREDERICK, WILLIAM H., Professor of History, Ohio University: INDONESIA

FRIEDMAN, ROBERT, Reporter, *The San Juan Star:* PUERTO RICO

FRIIS, ERIK J., Editor and Publisher, *The Scandinavian-American Bulletin;* Coeditor, *Nordic Democracy;* Editor, *The Scandinavian Presence in North America:* DENMARK; FINLAND; SWEDEN

GAILEY, HARRY A., Professor of History, San Jose State University: NIGERIA; ZAIRE

GARFIELD, ROBERT, Associate Professor of History, Director of Common Studies, DePaul University; Editor, *Readings in World Civilizations:* KENYA; TANZANIA; UGANDA

GEIS, GILBERT, Professor, Program in Social Ecology, University of California, Irvine; Author, *On White Collar Crime:* CRIME; CRIME—*White-Collar Crime*

GIBSON, ROBERT C., Assistant Regional Editor, *The Billings Gazette:* MONTANA

GJESTER, THØR, Editor, *Økonomisk Revy,* Oslo: NORWAY

GOODMAN, DONALD, Associate Professor of Sociology, John Jay College of Criminal Justice, City University of New York: PRISONS

GORDON, MAYNARD M., Editor, *Motor News Analysis:* AUTOMOBILES

GRAYSON, GEORGE W., John Marshall Professor of Government and Citizenship, College of William and Mary; Author, *The Politics of Mexican Oil, The United States and Mexico: Patterns of Influence:* BIOGRAPHY—*José Sarney;* BRAZIL; PORTUGAL; SPAIN; SPAIN—*Gibraltar;* THIRD WORLD

GREEN, MAUREEN, Author-Journalist: GREAT BRITAIN—*The Arts;* LITERATURE—*English;* LONDON

GROTH, ALEXANDER J., Professor of Political Science, University of California, Davis; Author, *People's Poland, Government and Politics;* Coauthor, *Contemporary Politics: Europe, Public Policy Across Nations:* POLAND

HADWIGER, DON F., Professor, Department of Political Science, Iowa State University; Author, *Politics of Agricultural Research;* Coauthor, *Policy Process in American Agriculture:* AGRICULTURE

HAKKARINEN, IDA, Research Meteorologist, General Software Corporation, Landover, MD: METEOROLOGY—*The Weather Year*

HALL, KENNETH N., Professor, Department of Nutritional Sciences, University of Connecticut; Advisor, "Nutrition Research News Letter": FOOD

HAND, SAMUEL B., Professor of History, University of Vermont: VERMONT

HARVEY, ROSS M., Assistant Deputy Minister, Department of Culture and Communications, Government of the Northwest Territories: NORTHWEST TERRITORIES

HATHORN, RAMON, Professor of French Studies, University of Guelph: LITERATURE—*Canadian in French*

HELMREICH, ERNST C., Professor of History, Emeritus, Bowdoin College; Author, *The German Churches under Hitler: Background, Struggle, and Epilogue:* AUSTRIA

HELMREICH, J. E., Professor of History, Allegheny College; Author, *Belgium and Europe: A Study in Small Power Diplomacy:* BELGIUM

HELMREICH, PAUL C., Professor of History, Wheaton College; Author, *From Paris to Sèvres: The Partition of the Ottoman Empire at the Peace Conference of 1919–1920:* GENEVA; SWITZERLAND

HENBERG, MARVIN, Department of Philosophy, University of Idaho: IDAHO

HENDERSON, GREGORY, Professor, Korea Institute, Fairbank Center, Harvard University; Author, *Korea: The Politics of the Vortex:* KOREA

HENDERSON, JIM, Former National Team Administrator, United States Soccer Federation; Former Publisher, *Annual Soccer Guide:* SPORTS—*Soccer*

HIRSCHOFF, PAULA M., Assistant Editor, *Africa Report:* ALGERIA; MOROCCO; SUDAN; TUNISIA

HOLLIE, PAMELA, Reporter, *The New York Times:* TOYS OF THE 1980s

HOOVER, HERBERT T., Professor of History, University of South Dakota; Author, *To Be an Indian, The Chitimacha People, The Sioux, The Practice of Oral History:* SOUTH DAKOTA

HOPKO, THE REV. THOMAS, Assistant Professor, St. Vladimir's Orthodox Theological Seminary: RELIGION—*Orthodox Eastern*

HOYT, CHARLES K., Associate Editor, *Architectural Record;* Author, *More Places for People* and *Interior Spaces Designed by Architects:* ARCHITECTURE

HULBERT, DAN, *The Dallas Times Herald:* TELEVISION AND RADIO

HUTH, JOHN F., JR., Free-lance Writer, Reporter (retired), *The Plain Dealer,* Cleveland: OHIO

JAFFE, HERMAN J., Professor, Department of Anthropology and Archeology, Brooklyn College, City University of New York: ANTHROPOLOGY

JENNINGS, PETER, Anchor and Senior Editor, ABC's "World News Tonight": THE YEAR IN REVIEW

JEWELL, MALCOLM E., Professor of Political Science, University of Kentucky; Coauthor, *American State Political Parties and Elections, Kentucky Politics:* KENTUCKY

JOHNSTON, ROBERT L., Editor/Associate Publisher, *The Chicago Catholic:* RELIGION—*Roman Catholicism*

JONES, H. G., Curator, North Carolina Collection, University of North Carolina at Chapel Hill: NORTH CAROLINA; OBITUARIES—*Sam J. Ervin, Jr.*

JOSEPH, LOU, Senior Medical Writer, Hill and Knowlton: MEDICINE AND HEALTH—*Dentistry*

KARNES, THOMAS L., Professor of History Emeritus, Arizona State University; Author, *Latin American Policy of the United States, Failure of Union: Central America 1824–1960;* BIOGRAPHY—*Daniel Ortega;* CENTRAL AMERICA

KASH, DON E., George Lynn Cross Research Professor of Political Science, University of Oklahoma; Coauthor, *Our Energy Future, Energy Under the Oceans;* Author, *U.S. Energy Policy: Crisis and Complacency:* ENERGY

KEHR, ERNEST A., Director, Stamp News Bureau; Author, *The Romance of Stamp Collecting:* STAMPS AND STAMP COLLECTING

KIMBALL, LORENZO D., Professor of Political Science, University of Utah: UTAH

KIMBELL, CHARLES L., Senior Foreign Mineral Specialist, U.S. Bureau of Mines: STATISTICAL AND TABULAR DATA—*Mineral and Metal Production Tables*

KING, PETER J., Associate Professor of History, Carleton University, Ottawa: ONTARIO; OTTAWA

KING, RESA W., Senior Correspondent, *Business Week:* MEDICINE AND HEALTH—*Malpractice*

KINNEAR, MICHAEL, Professor of History, University of Manitoba: MANITOBA

KISSELGOFF, ANNA, Chief Dance Critic, *The New York Times:* DANCE

KNAPP, ELAINE STUART, Editor, *State Government News:* UNITED STATES—*State Lotteries*

KOVALIC, JOAN M., Project Director and General Counsel, WESTON, Inc; Former Executive Director and General Counsel, Interstate Conference on Water Problems: ENVIRONMENT —*U.S. Water Resources*

KRAUSE, AXEL, Economic Correspondent, *International Herald Tribune,* Paris: FRANCE

LAI, CHUEN-YAN DAVID, Associate Professor of Geography, University of Victoria, British Columbia: HONG KONG

LAWRENCE, ROBERT M., Professor of Political Science, Colorado State University; Coeditor, *Arms Control and Disarmament: Practice and Promise, Nuclear Proliferation: Phase II:* ARMS CONTROL; MILITARY AFFAIRS; MILITARY AFFAIRS—*Defense Contracting—Waste and Abuse*

LEE, STEWART M., Chairman, Department of Economics and Business Administration, Geneva College; Coauthor, *Economics for Consumers:* BUSINESS AND CORPORATE AFFAIRS; CONSUMER AFFAIRS

LEVINE, LOUIS, Professor, Department of Biology, City College of New York; Author, *Biology of the Gene, Biology for a Modern Society:* GENETICS; MICROBIOLOGY

LEVITT, MORRIS J., Professor, Department of Political Science, Howard University; Coauthor, *Of, By, and For the People: State & Local Government and Politics:* WASHINGTON, DC

LEWIS, JEROME R., Director for Public Administration, College of Urban Affairs and Public Policy, University of Delaware: DELAWARE

LOBRON, BARBARA L., Writer, Editor, Photographer; Associate Editor, *America: Photographic Statements, Personal Pictures:* PHOTOGRAPHY

LYLES, JEAN CAFFEY, Associate Editor, Religious News Service; Author, *A Practical Vision of Christian Unity:* RELIGION— *Protestantism*

MABRY, DONALD J., Professor of History, Mississippi State University; Author, *Mexico's Accional Nacional, The Mexican University and the State;* Coauthor, *Neighbors—Mexico and the United States:* MEXICO

MARCOPOULOS, GEORGE J., Associate Professor of History, Tufts University: BIOGRAPHY—*Andreas Papandreou;* CYPRUS; GREECE

MASOTTI, LOUIS H., Professor of Political Science, Urban Affairs and Policy Research, Northwestern University; Author, *The New Urban Politics, The City in Comparative Perspective:* CITIES AND URBAN AFFAIRS

MATHESON, JIM, Sports Writer, *Edmonton Journal:* SPORTS— *Ice Hockey*

MATTHEWS, WILLIAM H., III, Professor of Geology, Lamar University: GEOLOGY

McCORQUODALE, SUSAN, Political Science Department, Memorial University of Newfoundland: NEWFOUNDLAND

McFADDEN, ROBERT D., Reporter, *The New York Times;* Coauthor, *No Hiding Place:* NEW YORK CITY

McGILL, DAVID A., Professor of Marine Science, U.S. Coast Guard Academy: OCEANOGRAPHY

MICHAELIS, PATRICIA A., Curator of Manuscripts, Kansas State Historical Society: KANSAS

MILLER, LUTHER, Editor, *Railway Age:* TRANSPORTATION—*The U.S. Passenger Railroad*

MIRE, JOSEPH, George Meany Center for Labor Studies:LABOR

MITCHELL, GARY, Professor of Physics, North Carolina State University: PHYSICS

MORTON, DESMOND, Professor of History, Enndale College, University of Toronto; Author, *A Short History of Canada, Bloody Victory: Canadians and the D-Day Campaign, Working People: An Illustrated History of the Canadian Labour Movement, A Military History of Canada:* CANADA

MORTON, GERALD W., Professor, School of Liberal Arts, Auburn University; Coauthor, *Wrestling to Rasslin: Ancient*

Sport to American Spectacle: SPORTS—*Pro Wrestling's New Hold*

MULLINER, K., Assistant to Director of Libraries, Ohio University; Coeditor, *Southeast Asia: An Emerging Center of World Influence?, Malaysia Studies II:* MALAYSIA; SINGAPORE

MURPHY, ROBERT F., *The Hartford Courant:* CONNECTICUT

NADLER, PAUL S., Professor of Finance, Rutgers University; Author, *Commercial Banking in the Economy, Paul Nadler Writes About Banking:* BANKING

NAFTALIN, ARTHUR, Professor of Public Affairs, University of Minnesota: MINNESOTA

NEUMANN, JIM, *The Forum,* Fargo, ND: NORTH DAKOTA

NEWLAND, ED, Assistant State Editor, *Richmond Times-Dispatch:* VIRGINIA

NOLAN, WILLIAM C., Professor of Political Science, Southern Arkansas University: ARKANSAS

NYREN, KARL, Senior Editor, *Library Journal:* LIBRARIES

OCHSENWALD, WILLIAM, Associate Professor of History, Virginia Polytechnic Institute; Author, *The Hijaz Railroad, Religion, Society, and the State in Arabia;* Coeditor, *Nationalism in a Non-National State: The Dissolution of the Ottoman Empire:* SAUDI ARABIA

O'CONNOR, ROBERT E., Associate Professor of Political Science, The Pennsylvania State University; Author, *Politics and Structure: Essentials of American National Government:* PENNSYLVANIA; PHILADELPHIA

O'MEARA, PATRICK, Director, African Studies Program, Indiana University; Coeditor, *Africa, International Politics in Southern Africa, Southern Africa, The Continuing Crisis:* SOUTH AFRICA 1985; AFRICA; ZIMBABWE

PALMER, NORMAN D., Professor Emeritus of Political Science and South Asian Studies, University of Pennsylvania; Author, *The United States and India: The Dimensions of Influence, Elections and Political Development: The South Asian Experience:* INDIA; SRI LANKA

PARKER, FRANKLIN, Benedum Professor of Education, West Virginia University; Author, *Battle of the Books, British Schools and Ours, U.S. Higher Education: A Guide to Education Sources;* Coauthor, *Crucial Issues in Education:* BIOGRAPHY—*William J. Bennett;* EDUCATION

PASCOE, ELAINE, Free-lance Writer and Editor; Author, *Racial Prejudice:* BIOGRAPHY—*Bill Cosby, Grace Bumbry;* CHILDREN; WOMEN; STATISTICAL AND TABULAR DATA—*Nations of the World*

PAWEL, MIRIAM, Albany Bureau Chief, *Newsday:* NEW YORK STATE

PEARSON, NEALE J., Professor of Political Science, Texas Tech University: CHILE; PERU; VENEZUELA

PERETZ, DON, Professor of Political Science, State University of New York at Binghamton; Author, *The West Bank—History, Politics, Society & Economy, Government and Politics of Israel, The Middle East Today:* EGYPT; ISRAEL

PERKINS, KENNETH J., Assistant Professor of History, University of South Carolina: LIBYA; RELIGION—*Islam*

PETERSON, RUSSELL W., President (1979–85), National Audubon Society: THE LEGACY OF JOHN JAMES AUDUBON

PIOTROWSKI, WILLIAM L., National Aeronautics and Space Administration: SPACE EXPLORATION (article written independent of NASA)

PIPPIN, LARRY L., Professor of Political Science, University of the Pacific; Author, *The Rémon Era:* ARGENTINA; PARAGUAY

PLATT, HERMANN K., Professor of History, Saint Peter's College: NEW JERSEY

POOLE, PETER A., Author, *The Vietnamese in Thailand, Eight Presidents and Indochina:* CAMBODIA; THAILAND; VIETNAM; VIETNAM—*The Ten Years Since Saigon's Fall*

POULLADA, LEON B., Professor of Political Science, Center for Afghanistan Studies, University of Nebraska; Author, *Reform and Rebellion in Afghanistan:* AFGHANISTAN

QUIRK, WILLIAM H., Construction Consultant; Former North American Editor, *Construction Industry International:* ENGINEERING, CIVIL

RAGUSA, ISA, Research Art Historian, Department of Art and Archaeology, Princeton University: ART

REUNING, WINIFRED, Writer, Polar Programs, National Science Foundation: POLAR RESEARCH

RICCIUTI, EDWARD R., Free-lance Writer; Author, *Audubon Society Book of Wild Animals, The Beachwalker's Guide:* ENVIRONMENT; ZOOS AND ZOOLOGY

RICHARDSON, RON, Deputy Business Editor, *Far Eastern Economic Review,* Hong Kong: EAST ASIA—*From World War to Economic Emergence*

RICHTER, WILLIAM L., Professor and Head, Department of Political Science, Kansas State University: BANGLADESH; PAKISTAN

RIGGAN, WILLIAM, Associate Editor, *World Literature Today,* University of Oklahoma; Author, *Picaros, Madmen, Naïfs, and Clowns, Comparative Literature and Literary Theory:* LITERATURE—*World*

ROBINSON, LEIF J., Editor, *Sky and Telescope:* ASTRONOMY

ROBOCK, ALAN, Professor, Department of Meteorology, University of Maryland: METEOROLOGY

ROSS, RUSSELL M., Professor of Political Science, University of Iowa; Author, *Government and Administration of Iowa:* IOWA

ROTHSTEIN, MORTON, Professor, Department of History, University of California, Davis: SOCIAL WELFARE

ROWEN, HERBERT H., Professor, Rutgers University, New Brunswick; Author, *John de Witt: Grand Pensionary of Holland, 1625–1672;* Editor, *The Low Countries in Early Modern Times: A Documentary History:* NETHERLANDS

ROWLETT, RALPH M., Professor of Anthropology, University of Missouri; Coauthor, *Neolithic Levels on the Titelberg;* Editor, *Personal Ornament in the Ancient World:* ARCHAEOLOGY

RUBIN, JIM, Supreme Court Correspondent, The Associated Press: LAW

RUFF, NORMAN J., Assistant Professor, University of Victoria; Coauthor, *Reins of Power: Governing British Columbia:* BRITISH COLUMBIA

SALSINI, PAUL, *The Milwaukee Journal:* WISCONSIN

SAVAGE, DAVID, Professor of English (retired), Simon Fraser University: CANADA—*The Arts;* LITERATURE—*Canadian in English*

SAWATSKY, DON, Free-lance Writer, Whitehorse, Yukon: YUKON

SCHLOSSBERG, DAN, Author, *The Baseball Book of Why, The Baseball Catalog, Baseballaffs, Barons of the Bullpen, Hammerin' Hank: The Henry Aaron Story:* BIOGRAPHY—*George Thomas Seaver;* SPORTS—*Baseball*

SCHROEDER, RICHARD C., Washington Bureau Chief, *Vision;* Syndicated Writer, U.S. Newspapers: CARIBBEAN; DRUGS AND ALCOHOL; GUYANA; LATIN AMERICA; REFUGEES AND IMMIGRATION; REFUGEES AND IMMIGRATION—*The Sanctuary Movement*

SCHULZINGER, ROBERT D., Professor of History, University of Colorado; Author, *American Diplomacy in the Twentieth Century, The Wise Men of Foreign Affairs: The History of the Council on Foreign Relations:* UNITED STATES—*Foreign Affairs,* UNITED STATES—*U.S.-Soviet Summitry*

SCHWAB, PETER, Professor of Political Science, State University of New York at Purchase; Author, *Decision Making in Ethiopia, Haile Selassie I, Ethiopia: Politics, Economics, and Society:* ETHIOPIA

SETH, R. P., Professor of Economics, Mount Saint Vincent University, Halifax: CANADA—*The Economy;* NOVA SCOTIA

SEYBOLD, PAUL G., Professor, Department of Chemistry, Wright State University: CHEMISTRY

SHEPRO, CARL E., Professor of Political Science, University of Alaska at Fairbanks: ALASKA

SHERATON, MIMI, Food Critic, *Time;* Author, *Visions of Sugarplums, From My Mother's Kitchen, The German Cookbook, The Seducer's Cookbook;* Coauthor, *Is Salami & Eggs Better Than Sex?:* THE AMERICAN MENU

SHOGAN, ROBERT, National Political Correspondent, Washington Bureau, *Los Angeles Times;* Author, *A Question of Judgment, Promises to Keep:* BIOGRAPHY—*Robert Dole;* UNITED STATES—*Domestic Affairs*

SIEGEL, STANLEY E., Professor of History, University of Houston; Author, *A Political History of the Texas Republic, 1836–1845, Houston: Portrait of the Supercity on Buffalo Bayou:* TEXAS

SIMMONS, MARC, Author, *Albuquerque: A Narrative History, New Mexico: A Bicentennial History:* NEW MEXICO

SIMON, JEFFREY D., The Rand Corporation, Santa Monica, CA: TERRORISM

SNODSMITH, RALPH L., Ornamental Horticulturist; Author, *Ralph Snodsmith's Tips from the Garden Hotline:* GARDENING AND HORTICULTURE

SPERA, DOMINIC, Professor of Music, Indiana University; Author, *The Prestige Series—16 Original Compositions for Jazz Band:* MUSIC—*Jazz*

STARR, JOHN BRYAN, Lecturer, Department of Political Science, Yale University; Executive Director, Yale-China Association; Author, *Continuing the Revolution: The Political Thought of Mao;* Editor, *The Future of U.S.-China Relations:* CHINA; TAIWAN

STERN, JEROME, Associate Professor of English, Florida State University; Editor, *Studies in Popular Culture:* BIOGRAPHY—*William Kennedy;* LITERATURE—*American*

STEWART, WILLIAM H., Associate Professor of Political Science, the University of Alabama; Author, *The Alabama Constitutional Commission, Alabama and the Energy Crisis:* ALABAMA

STOUDEMIRE, ROBERT H., Distinguished Professor Emeritus, University of South Carolina: SOUTH CAROLINA

SULLIVAN, JEREMIAH J., Associate Professor of Business Communications, University of Washington; Author, *Pacific Basin Enterprise and the Changing Law of the Sea, Foreign Investment in the U.S. Fishing Industry:* WASHINGTON

SUNDERLIN, LISA A., Assistant Editor, *The Numismatist:* COINS AND COIN COLLECTING

SUNY, RONALD GRIGOR, Alex Manoogian Professor of Modern Armenian History, University of Michigan; Author, *The Baku Commune, 1917–1918: Class and Nationality in the Russian Revolution, Armenia in the Twentieth Century:* BIOGRAPHY—*Mikhail Gorbachev;* OBITUARIES—*Konstantin Chernenko;* USSR

SYLVESTER, LORNA LUTES, Associate Editor, *Indiana Magazine of History,* Indiana University; Editor, *No Cheap Padding: Seventy-Five Years of the "Indiana Magazine of History":* INDIANA

TABORSKY, EDWARD, Professor of Government, University of Texas, Austin; Author, *Communism in Czechoslovakia, 1948–1960, Communist Penetration of the Third World:* CZECHOSLOVAKIA

TAYLOR, WILLIAM L., Professor of History, Plymouth State College: NEW HAMPSHIRE

TESAR, JENNY, Medicine and Science Writer: COMPUTERS; MEDICINE AND HEALTH; MEDICINE AND HEALTH—*Walk-in Medical Clinics*

THEISEN, CHARLES W., Assistant News Editor, *The Detroit News:* MICHIGAN

TOWNE, RUTH W., Professor of History, Northeast Missouri State University: MISSOURI

TURNER, ARTHUR CAMPBELL, Professor of Political Science, University of California, Riverside; Author, *Tension Areas in World Affairs;* Coauthor, *Control of Foreign Relations:* IRAN; IRAQ; MIDDLE EAST

TURNER, CHARLES H., Free-lance Writer: HAWAII

VAN RIPER, PAUL P., Professor Emeritus and Head, Department of Political Science, Texas A&M University: POSTAL SERVICE

VOLSKY, GEORGE, Center for Advanced International Studies, University of Miami: CUBA

WATTERS, ELSIE M., Vice President—Research, Tax Foundation, Inc.: TAXATION

WEIKER, WALTER F., Professor of Political Science, Rutgers University: TURKEY

WEISS, PAULETTE, Free-lance Writer and Consultant to the Music Industry; Author, *The Rock Video Book:* MUSIC—*Popular;* MUSIC—*Music Videos:* RECORDINGS

WENTZ, RICHARD E., Professor of Religious Studies, Arizona State University; Author, *The Contemplation of Otherness: The Critical Vision of Religion, Saga of the American Soul:* RELIGION—*Far Eastern*

WHITE, AUGUSTUS A., III, Doctor of Medicine, Department of Orthopedic Surgery, Beth Israel Hospital, Boston, MA: BACK PAIN

WILLIAMS, DENNIS A., Education Editor, *Newsweek:* EDUCATION—*The U.S. Illiteracy Problem*

WILLIAMS, HUBERT, President, Police Foundation: CRIME—*The Victim's Response*

WILLIS, F. ROY, Professor of History, University of California, Davis; Author, *France, Germany and the New Europe, 1945–1968, Italy Chooses Europe,* and *The French Paradox:* EUROPE

WILMS, DENISE MURCKO, Assistant Editor, *Booklist;* Editor, *Science Books for Children;* Coauthor, *A Guide to Non-Sexist Children's Books,* Vol. 2: LITERATURE—*Children's*

WINCHESTER, N. BRIAN, Associate Director, African Studies Program, Indiana University: SOUTH AFRICA 1985; AFRICA

WOLF, WILLIAM, Film Critic, Gannett News Service; Author, *The Marx Brothers, The Landmark Films, The Cinema and Our Century:* MOTION PICTURES; OBITUARIES—*Orson Welles*

WOOD, JOHN, Professor of Political Science, University of Oklahoma: OKLAHOMA

YAMASHITA, ELIZABETH S., Professor, School of Journalism and Mass Communication, University of Oklahoma: PUBLISHING

YOUNGER, R. M., Author, *Australia and the Australians, Australia's Great River, Australia! Australia! March to Nationhood:* AUSTRALIA

ZACEK, JOSEPH FREDERICK, Professor of History, State University of New York, Albany; Author, *Palacký: The Historian as Scholar and Nationalist:* ALBANIA; BULGARIA; HUNGARY; ROMANIA; YUGOSLAVIA

Index

Main article headings appear in this index as bold-faced capitals; subjects within articles appear as lower-case entries. Both the general references and the subentries should be consulted for maximum usefulness of this index. Illustrations are indexed herein. Cross references are to the entries in this index.